An Essential Shakespeare

NINE PLAYS AND THE SONNETS

An Essential Shakespeare

NINE PLAYS *and the* SONNETS

Russell Fraser
THE UNIVERSITY OF MICHIGAN

THE MACMILLAN COMPANY
NEW YORK
Collier-Macmillan Limited · LONDON

For
ALEXANDER

And when through all the town there ran
The servants of Your enemy,
A woman and a man,
Unless the Holy Writings lie,
Hurried through the smooth and rough
And through the fertile and waste,
Protecting, till the danger past,
With human love.

W. B. Yeats

The Macmillan Company
866 Third Avenue, New York, New York 10022

Collier-Macmillan Canada, Ltd., Toronto, Ontario

Library of Congress catalog card number: 73-144146

First Printing

PREFACE

Shakespeare's surviving achievement is comprised in thirty-eight plays, one hundred and fifty-four sonnets, two long narrative poems, *Venus and Adonis* and *The Rape of Lucrece*, and two shorter poems, the first an elegy known as *The Phoenix and the Turtle*, the second a doleful *Lover's Complaint*, attributed to Shakespeare but not certainly written by him. Of this considerable body of dramatic and nondramatic poetry, nine plays and all the sonnets are reprinted here. The text was prepared initially by the eminent Shakespearean scholar, O. J. Campbell.

The introductory essay focuses on Shakespeare's continuing vitality and importance. Each of the ten selections is followed by a brief critical discussion. Readers should turn to these discussions not first but last, after they have read the plays and poems. The great desideratum in the study of Shakespeare is the collision of the student's intelligence with the work itself. Criticism is valuable in helping to illuminate the work, but it ought not to be permitted, or not at first, to come between the reader and his primary business. In the first instance, the reader should conceive of this business as essentially personal, the interacting of his mind and Shakespeare's.

A factual account dealing with dates of composition, printing, and ascertainable sources precedes each play. In this account Shakespeare's plays and poems are described as appearing in quarto (abbreviated as Q), in octavo, or in the so-called First Folio of 1623 (F). These terms are still current in modern printing. The term *folio* denotes a book in which large sheets of similar size, folded once to produce two pages on each side, are sewn together. If these single sheets are folded twice, to make four pages on either side of the sheet, the resulting book is called a *quarto*. In an octavo, the sheet is folded three times, yielding eight pages per side. Most of Shakespeare's work was printed first in quarto.

A selection of books for further reading accompanies each work. The purpose of this suggested reading list, which is not exhaustive but representative, is to direct the student to useful commentary on the particular play or on the sonnets. The same principle obtains here as with the critical discussions: first the play, and after that the commentators.

A more comprehensive collection of readings is given at the back of the book. This collection is divided into three parts: criticism, background and biography, and reference works. The first category is mostly restricted to well-known interpretations of Shakespeare which go beyond the treatment of a single play. Some famous critics appearing in the general reading list—for example, A. C. Bradley on Shakespearean tragedy—are cited again in the suggested reading list for individual plays. In paperback editions of recommended reading, the name of the publisher follows the title.

The general bibliography concludes with a listing of film versions of the plays reprinted in this volume and recordings of these plays and the sonnets.

R. F.

CONTENTS

Introduction
Shakespeare for Our Time

Who is Shakespeare that we should be mindful of him? Simple economy requires that we raise the question in preface to a reading of Shakespeare's plays and poems. Life is short. Art, if long, is also various. Shakespeare does not hold the stage alone. Prophets without number compete for our attention, are forever seizing us by the lapels. Each has got hold of the key to the mystery. Each is confident that the tale he tells will put us in possession of the secrets of health and wealth. This tale is more persuasive as it looks to a practical end. The modern prophet who grounds his claim to a hearing in the relevance or usefulness of what he has to say is reflecting faithfully the temper of the time. We ourselves are very likely to invoke the same criterion in estimating the different voices that assault us, on television, in the columns of the daily paper, in books, the making of which there is evidently no end. What profit can we pick from their counsels? That is the governing question. Others abide this question. Why not Shakespeare?

No doubt the appeal to relevance is often naïve, as it is couched in material terms. One ought first of all to see that what relates or bears does not necessarily ring like a coin or even lay up treasures in Heaven. Nonetheless, it is a mistake to sneer at relevance as a touchstone of value. Any writer worth reading, whether he is as new as today or, like Shakespeare, dead three and a half centuries, is valuable to us exactly and only as he meets us where we live, as he relates to our daily and most vital concerns. In this constant figuring in our thought we recognize our contemporary, whatever the lapse of years between his time and ours.

The honor one pays to Shakespeare, as it is felt to be obligatory, dictated by unthinking custom, is merely a cultural reflex. Shakespeare, we say, is a classic. But what does that signify? Maybe it signifies no more than what Shakespeare himself calls "mouth honor"—voluble praise that is at bottom insincere. This easy praise is more pernicious as it denies the canonized writer a place in the present and refers him to a waxworks or historical museum. We honor Shakespeare for his noble sentiment and his pithiness of speech. Only we do not read him very often, and we never think to bring him to bear. He is, in Romeo's phrase, "Beauty too rich for use." Really to pay honor is to scrutinize the plays and poems, not simply to applaud but to assay them, to ask: does Shakespeare address himself in meaningful ways to those grievous problems which confront us in the here and now?

This, taken almost at random from the news of the day, is one such problem.

The subject is the short and simple annals of the poor, as recorded in Cokeville, Tennessee:

> Four small children, one of them crippled, burned to death in their home early this morning while neighbors, including their grandfather, stood by helplessly outside the blazing house.
>
> The fire broke out about 6:30 A.M., half an hour after the father had left for work at a stone company.
>
> The grandfather arrived about half an hour after the fire began and found the house engulfed in flames with the porch falling in.
>
> "It was so old and it went up so fast there was no chance to get anyone out," he said.

Does Shakespeare, in his tragedies, grapple with this problem of apparently fortuitous and inexplicable suffering? If not, the less Shakespeare he.

Among the many vices associated with academic life, perhaps pedantry is the worst. What pedantry means, in a nutshell, is the giving out by the professor and the taking in by the student of inert information: facts that accumulate, only to gather dust; facts that, as we inspect them, engender only a shrug of the shoulders. "Knowledge is power." That is perhaps the most reverberant truth formulated in the Age of Shakespeare. The pedant has no commerce with truth as a quickening agent. Between knowledge and the uses of knowledge, he runs up a barricade. The pedant is the enemy to education, rightly read, as he believes in his heart that knowledge is sterile. "Beware of the merely learned man," wrote Bernard Shaw. "He is an idler who kills time with study." Proper study is dynamic. It does not while away the time but transforms it.

The implication for us, as we are students, is clear. We are not, or should not be, mindless antiquarians. We do not read Shakespeare—or Stendhal or Dante—because they are part of our heritage, which means, customarily, fossils embedded in a petrified culture. Ideally or properly, we read these older writers because they are alive, because as vital writers they are able to transcend their own long-vanished time—whether the nineteenth century or the thirteenth or the Elizabethan Age—and to bear on our present business. They are, in a phrase, for our time, in that they communicate to us in fruitful ways as we seek to negotiate the difficulties of our vexed and prosaic existence.

For clarity's sake, one should pause, just here, to define the terms at issue. There is in this proposition no thought of imputing to Shakespeare the coarser kind of utility or value. Some things are certain: among them is the fact that one will never be a penny richer for the study of Shakespeare's plays and poems. One cannot use them to help in consummating a business deal. They do not serve as protection against disease or the manifold ills our flesh is heir to. They are no stay against fire in the night. Many of us suppose that literature is an adjunct to morality, that it offers in more vivid or more palatable ways a guide to judicious or responsible behavior. But that is not a tenable supposition. There is really no point in looking to Shakespeare for assistance in becoming a better man, in the sense of making the right choices, as one marries and begets children, and gives and takes affection, and endures the absence of affection. Still, it is fair to assert that Shakespeare is good for us or relevant to us, though not in the conventional acceptance of the words.

Shakespeare is good—one should try to be very modest and tentative in making claims on his behalf—because he puts us in touch with the deepest recesses of our being. He is good because he helps us to understand the nature of man and the world he inhabits and the experience that is his daily portion. We cannot translate this understanding, in material terms. It has no price current; it does not sell, it does not buy. But as one fulfills the definition of a man, he will covet beyond everything else the understanding which accrues from a reading of the poems and plays.

Critical to this assertion or proposition is a judgment of human nature which is at least as old as Aristotle. Man is *homo sapiens*, the thinking animal. Simply by virtue of what he is, man desires to know. The knowledge he is after may be exciting or depressing, it may be ugly and vicious, or comely, attractive, and suggestive of good. The kind of knowledge one gathers does not matter. What matters is the verity of things, the way things actually are.

The identifying of man as primarily a detector of truth is fraught with implication. What is implied and even required is uncommon boldness and honesty in the prosecuting of truth. This implication or requirement is distasteful to the censor, from the Spanish Inquisitor in the time of Shakespeare to the Communist bullies in our own time, whose vocation is to harry free spirits like Pasternak or Alexander Solzhenitsyn. Shakespeare himself finds the implication congenial. Shakespeare, unlike these self-appointed guardians of our morals and manners, refuses to tinker with truth. He is, among writers, the great connoisseur of reality. He tells it, not as it should be, but as it is.

The sentimentalist denies that a little child, afflicted with bone disease, perishes in the fire, apparently without cause. The authoritarian rulers of the sixteenth and seventeenth centuries—in Italy as the Counter Reformation takes hold, in Protestant England, in Calvin's Geneva—force the poet to submit to censorship and correction, partly because he reports in his poems such fearsome events. The modern book burner, Soviet style, is more imaginative in his dealings with unpalatable fact. His response to the artist who trades in this fact is to shut him away in a lunatic asylum.

Shakespeare, as his observation is total and his reporting of it unreservedly honest, is a prime candidate for censorship or the asylum. He draws no fictitious correspondence between the unthinkable event that overtakes the unfortunate victim and a supposed lack in the victim of moral or prudential behavior. He does not appease us by pretending that we get our just deserts (the sense of "poetic justice"). Why does Mercutio die? Is he guilty? Or sinful? Do Romeo and Juliet deserve what happens to them? How does one rationalize the strangling of Desdemona, or the slaughter of Lady Macduff and her children, or the spectacle of Cordelia dead in the arms of King Lear?

Cordelia is hanged because Lear grows old before he grows wise, and because the villainous Edmund, like other wicked characters in Shakespeare's plays, is indifferent to human life. " 'Tis but a man gone." That is how the villain is apt to respond, when matters of life and death are in the cards. In this sense, we can rationalize—which means that we can find out some sequence or pattern or reasonable explanation in the tragic death or fact of evil. But that is cold comfort to Cordelia, as to the child who burns in his bed.

It is of course endlessly possible to assign reasons for the existence of evil. That is what Milton is doing—assigning or seeking reasons—in his attempt to justify the ways of God to man. Shakespeare, in the writing of the tragedies, is committed in part to the same exercise. But none of the reasons one posits is ultimately sufficient. "The words of heaven," says Claudio, in *Measure for Measure*—he is remembering St. Paul's Epistle to the Romans (9:15–18)—are apposite, as they are finally mysterious:

> on whom it will, it will;
> on whom it will not, so.

Evil is; Shakespeare, without flinching, registers its existence in his plays. That is one reason why we trust him, and find him still valuable, after three hundred and fifty years. He is, in the premier sense, our teacher. He bequeathes to us the gift of understanding.

Now to enter an important qualification. Certainly Shakespeare is involved with consequential business. In the comedies not less than the tragedies, he is the presenter of something more substantial than lighthearted entertainment, what is called in *Twelfth Night* "matter for a May morning." On the other hand, to cast him in the role of philosopher is to misconceive his genius and falsify the nature of his art. Very likely the author of the plays would himself have been convulsed at the notion or proposal that he is dealing with Truth as a capital-letter abstraction. Shakespeare is not so solemn as this, he is not so portentous. To write him off as "playhouse poetry," delightful but insubstantial, is no more gross an error than to put him forward as an intellectual vacuum cleaner, intent on sweeping up fact and seeking earnestly to lesson or instruct us. A foutre for this vacuum cleaner! Whatever the identity of the man who was Shakespeare, he is not a precursor of modern science, on its rationalizing or abstracting side. He is not Sir Francis Bacon. His intelligence and bias are at a remove from that of the lawgiver or scientific or moral preceptor. The truths (not Truth) which he turns up in the course of his "studies" in human nature do not always tend toward conclusions, or not in a sense which the legislators of conduct would approve and understand. Mostly, Shakespeare is satisfied to contemplate these truths. The more purposive man will squeeze them for their kernel of profit. Shakespeare is not especially purposive.

This is not to suggest that the contemplative activity one associates with him is self-indulgent or gratuitous. The entail of this activity is real, although impalpable; in fact, it is dynamic. This entail or ultimate end is a rejoicing in the truths one encounters as they mirror the visible world. We do not read Shakespeare, or not consciously, to glean information. We read Shakespeare because he is exhilarating. In *The Tempest,* he makes us happy. Who will dispute the assertion? What is more to the point: he makes us happy in *King Lear.*

Agony is the essence of *King Lear,* and so remorseless is it that Samuel Johnson, who was not a shrinking kind of man, could not bear to read the play through. Ernest Hemingway, by contrast, made a habit of returning often to this terrible story because, as he said, it cheered him up. That seems a heartless and frivolous paradox. The man who enunciates it is not, however, to be characterized as hard of heart. The reverse is true. W. B. Yeats, in one of the great poems in English, resolves the paradox for us. Yeats's poem—it is called "Lapis Lazuli"—begins with an account of the bombing of London by the Germans in the First World War, and the response of "hysterical women" to this tragic event. The women, who refuse to be budged from their melancholy posture, insist that something "drastic" be done. They are sick of "poets that are always gay." They want us to dispense with poetry, as no longer relevant. The right response to impending tragedy is strident expostulation. Tragedy requires putting on a long face.

But the poet in his fictions is wiser. All of us, he knows, perform our tragic play. That is the nature of the human condition. But Hamlet and Lear, Ophelia, Cordelia, even in the final exigent "Do not break up their lines to weep." Everything to which men aspire, all the work of human hands, though it achieve a momentary realization, goes down. Still, "Hamlet and Lear are gay." The tragic record of the past, in which the future is certainly predicted, is transfigured by this gaiety. Hand wringing is not appropriate, and not only because it is unseemly or self-pitying. Stoicism is not appropriate either. It is a passive or merely negative philosophy; it is insufficiently engaged. And engagement, an affirmative act, is what Yeats is requiring of us, and Shakespeare in his tragedies.

The content of the tragedies is harrowing, but it is real; in Johnson's phrase, it is a just representation. And the reality pleases. It is not entirely the justness or the accuracy to which we respond, though that is a part of our pleasure. It is the ardor and the quickness, as of "quick bright things," and even though they "come to confusion." Life is full of "strange mutations." That is what Edgar learns, in *King Lear*—as also, that "The worst returns to laughter." Life is endlessly inspiriting, healing and renewing even as it wounds. It is the ultimate value and does not willingly yield to age.

In the conclusion of Yeats's poem, two old men, who know all there is to know of human misery and disappointment, look down from a mountain top on "all the tragic scene." With them is a serving-man, who plays a musical instrument. This office he fulfills is incongruous, it is even offensive to the criers-up of doom, whom we have always with us. But the serving-man, who is the poet, though doom is of the air he breathes, is not inclined to be lugubrious. The melodies he plays are mournful; the burden of the melodies is gay.

"I speak of Africa and golden joys." The voice is that of Ancient Pistol, a humorous character in the second part of *Henry IV*. But in this assertion Shakespeare's voice is also resounding, and his intention and commitment—though the words are too suggestive of meditated purposes—are implicitly communicated to us. This more basic commitment is, out of love, to render reality, which is not always drossy but sometimes is converted to gold—the milieu in which we live or might live, the particular stuff or quality of which we are made and which is not always naked to inspection. The result of the commitment is, precisely, delight. As we love and honor ourselves, as we estimate ourselves with a deeper and more sensible gauge, we derive fierce pleasure and great excitement from this rendering—that is, if we are healthy. The world is good, and nowhere is it delineated with more loving exactitude—in terms of what is actual, in terms of what is possible—than in Shakepeare's poems and plays.

Shakespeare as artist is like his heroine Marina, in the late romance called *Pericles.* With his pen, as she with her needle, he composes "Nature's own shape of bud, bird, branch, or berry." So tangible is this composing or depicting, so real is it, that Shakepeare's art may be said to "sister" or to match natural roses. He opens to us our environing world as, in our nearsightedness or in our fatigue, we rarely perceive it. Like Hamlet, he tents us to the quick: he stabs us with an acute and piercing pleasure that is almost kindred to pain. He gives us back our senses:

> daffodils,
> That come before the swallow dares, and take
> The winds of March with beauty.

These lines from *The Winter's Tale* epitomize the artist whose allegiance is to sensuous and natural beauty. The showing forth of this beauty is never scanted or grudged. Every rift, to cite a phrase of the poet John Keats, is loaded with ore. Shakespeare, whose eye is unwinking and unwearied, is prodigal of similar passages. One thinks of Oberon, in *A Midsummer-Night's Dream:* "I know a bank where the wild thyme blows"; or of the glimpsing of the floor of heaven, in *The Merchant of Venice,* "thick inlaid with patines of bright gold"; or of the lines from the sonnets, almost without number: "Rough winds do shake the darling buds of May," "Bare ruined choirs where late the sweet birds sang," "first-born flowers, and all things rare That heaven's air in this huge rondure hems."

But "beautiful" lines of poetry, however taking, are not really to the purpose here. This purpose is not to commend the Shakespeare whom most of us remember, a little vaguely, on appropriate occasions, as a storehouse of Elegant Extracts. The purpose is rather to present and praise that Shakespeare whose devotion to and delight in the natural world are manifest, as he forces the concrete into the heart of things.

The best way to interpret or elucidate this saying is to look at the plays themselves—Shakespeare is always the most appropriate gloss on Shakespeare. For example, the literal delineating of the storm at sea with which *The Tempest* begins: a real ship driving on the rocks (not compounded, as in opera, of papier maché), and manned by real seamen who know whereof they speak and understand what they are doing, and who persuade us, accordingly, of the integrity of their language and labor. An illustration even more graphic and more palpable is the extraordinary opening scene of the second act of *Henry IV*, Part I: carriers, readying their pack horses for the journey to London and talking laconically and with absolute fidelity to fact of mouldy peas and beans, and the "bots" or worms that afflict the horses, and the price of oats, and the lack of a chamber pot, and the breeding of fleas out of urine. That is beauty, but not as a neurasthenic poetaster or conventional appreciator of beauty conceives it.

In *A Midsummer-Night's Dream*, a disastrous change in nature accompanies and also signalizes or defines the breaking of concord between Oberon, the King of the Faeries, and Titania, his Queen. Titania laments this change. The foulness of the weather is disagreeable to her. But she is not satisfied to say just that. What she says is not more "beautiful," in our too exclusive or too narrow sense, but more solid, more circumstantial, and so more nearly true. Oberon with his brawls has disturbed their sport:

> Therefore the winds, piping to us in vain,
> As in revenge, have suck'd up from the sea
> Contagious fogs: which falling in the land
> Have every pelting river made so proud
> That they have overborne their continents:
> The ox hath therefore stretch'd his yoke in vain,
> The ploughman lost his sweat, and the green corn
> Hath rotted ere his youth attain'd a beard;
> The fold stands empty in the drownèd field,
> And crows are fatted with the murrion [diseased] flock.

If this is beauty—and it is—the word and all it denotes are badly in need of redefining. For the new and more ample definition we require, it is open to us to consult the plays and poems.

But the exuberance of Ancient Pistol, who sings delightedly of Africa and golden joys, is not yet exhausted in its implication. It is true that Shakespeare is the chief naturalist among poets. Always, he begins with physical fact: this time, this place. Always, his absorption in the fact is enraptured—and the assertion will hold whether the material he is scrutinizing or passing through his fingers lifts our hearts—like the paeon to Spring in the fourth act of *The Winter's Tale;* or is acutely distasteful—like the metaphors of disease with which *Hamlet* abounds; or revolting—the scurrilous discourse of Thersites in *Troilus and Cressida;* or coarsely amusing—the lewd sexual reference of Lucio and Pompey in *Measure for Measure*. Always, and whatever the business in hand, Shakespeare is himself as he revels in that business. But this delighting and self-delighting Shakespeare is not simply a naturalistic writer or a mindless painter or recorder of phenomenal fact. After all he is to be distinguished from the makers of the naturalistic novel, like Zola or Theodore Dreiser, or from the imagist poets, like W. C. Williams. He is not satisfied, finally, with the art of *trompe l'oeil*—the putting on canvas of physical phenomena with such marvelous precision that these phenomena deceive the eye and are mistaken for the thing itself. Shakespeare, though he venerates reality, does not rest content with the presentation of reality. He sisters or matches Nature, but—given the intensity of his depicting—he transcends Nature, he overgoes it.

Transcendence, an almost magical change, is the essence of Shakespeare's achievement. In his work, a striking metamorphosis is effected. He confronts a world of iron or bronze, and like the alchemist he turns it to gold. This alchemic Shakespeare possesses, more than any other poet, that uncanny ability of which Shelley writes in *Prometheus Unbound*. He creates for us, as we give him our suffrage, "Forms more real than living man, Nurslings of immortality!" Or, to quote Shakespeare on Shakespeare, his dramatic and poetic accomplishment, all that he touches and transforms, is

> like a thing
> Made by some other deity than nature,
> That shapes man better.

The quotation is from the tragedy of *Coriolanus*. It is intended to get at and to convey the peculiar quality of the hero from whom the play takes its title. This hero, a Roman soldier of extraordinary prowess, is perceived and bodied forth as larger than life. But that is not because Shakespeare is taking liberties with life, or distorting or falsifying what really is. On the contrary, what Shakespeare is doing when writing at the top of his bent—in *Hamlet*, in *King Lear*, in *Antony and Cleopatra*—is presenting man as he might be, at full stretch.

> What a piece of work is a man! how noble in reason! how infinite in faculty! in form and moving how express and admirable! in action how like an angel! in apprehensions how like a god! the beauty of the world! the paragon of animals!

That is Hamlet, on the demigod man, to whom we approximate as all our powers are dilated or fulfilled. But Hamlet's vision, and Shakespeare's, comprehends the entire spectrum. And so man is rendered also in terms of the littleness potential in him. He is "like a god"— and "this quintessence of dust."

Most of us, in what we see and estimate and understand, do not traverse the entire spectrum. In our reading of human beings, we entertain only a limited number of possibilities. Man, as we envisage him, is an amalgam of specific combinations, drawn from but not exhausting the whole range of the possible. Here, we seem to take our warrant from Nature itself, which embodies these limited possibilities or specific combinations in this man or that, and offers him to our view as total or fully formed. Shakespeare's eye is more penetrating. He is more catholic, more truly encyclopedic—but that is not it exactly: what we are adjudicating here is not breadth but depth of knowledge, and perhaps not depth either, but quality and kind. Aristotle is the type of the encyclopedic man, and is supposed to know it all: whatever is classifiable in the light of day. Shakespeare is not so circumambient, his lore not so amenable to classification; but like the Witches in *Macbeth*, unlike the scientist or Stagyrite, he looks into the seeds of things. In his ken, everything latent or embryonic or potential is included, though it may bulk no larger—to take a line from *King John*—than the "baby figure of the mass of things to come." These latencies, this baby figure, he actualizes in the persons of his greatest heroes. This is the sense, and verification, of the paradox, that Shakespeare is more nearly true than Nature. The forms his imagination casts up and bodies forth are more real than living man. The golden world he fabricates is not a more attractive copy but, in embryo, a more faithful and more accurate copy of reality than the brazen world in which we think we dwell. The spacious mirror he sets before us has got to be spacious, as what the mirror reflects is not partial but plenary.

In the colossal hero of *Antony and Cleopatra*, the much less considerable Octavius, who hunts the hero to death, discerns a magnified copy of his own fortunes, his character as it might be, and finally, his own demise. We, as auditors of the play, are like Octavius. In the spacious mirror which is the tragic protagonist, we see ourselves.

The winding up of Antony's story offers the clearest and most luminous example in all Shakespeare of this magnitude of vision which is more to the point than a naturalistic vision, as it is more nearly comprehensive. The hero is dead, fallen on his sword, the suicide of the heroine impends; and now, at the farthest verge of her life, Cleopatra looks back over the tragic and exhilarating journey she has gone. Her auditor is the well-disposed but prosaic and essentially unimaginative Roman soldier, Dolabella, who is perhaps a version of us all before we have been exalted and instructed by the play. To this man, Cleopatra offers her vision, and Shakespeare's vision, of possibilities.

> I dream'd there was an Emperor Antony:
> O, such another sleep, that I might see
> But such another man! . . .
> His face was as the heavens; and therein stuck
> A sun and moon, which kept their course, and lighted
> The little O, the earth. . . .
> His legs bestrid the ocean: his rear'd arm
> Crested the world: his voice was propertied
> As all the tunèd spheres, and that to friends;
> But when he meant to quail and shake the orb,
> He was as rattling thunder. For his bounty,
> There was no winter in 't; an autumn 'twas
> That grew the more by reaping: his delights
> Were dolphin-like; they show'd his back above
> The element they lived in: in his livery
> Walk'd crowns and crownets; realms and islands were
> As plates dropp'd from his pocket.

Then, abruptly, we are brought back to the banal exigencies of the present. Cleopatra inquires:

> Think you there was, or might be, such a man
> As this I dream'd of?

And Dolabella, whose vision is so much more circumscribed than that of Shakespeare's serpent of old Nile, and whose imagination is so much less richly stored, answers, as he must: "Gentle madam, no." But we, to whom this iridescent language is also addressed, as we have taken the play to heart, dispute the negative rejoinder. At the end, our suffrage goes, not to the petty realist, whose ability to apprehend and to estimate reality is impoverished, but to the Egyptian queen, whose more piercing eye encompasses forms more real than living man. Like Ophelia, remembering the Hamlet that was, we also have seen what we have seen. This seeing, this benison even, is afforded to us by Shakespeare, and that is what it means to describe his dramatic poetry as a means of grace.

To claim so much for Shakespeare's art is sufficiently audacious, and certainly the claim ought not to go unchallenged. One will want, properly, to query and to test it, to see if he can prove it on his pulses. Honesty enjoins this kind of proving or personal validating. The perfunctionary acceptance of Shakespeare the classic is the bane of academic study. Like an unthinking genuflection in church, it is to be described, in the pejorative sense, as mere piety. Better to be honest than pious, better to ask, as one turns to Shakespeare or to any other "classic": What of import does he have to say to me now? If the answer is nothing, the right response is to close up the book.

But not cursorily, and not in haste! Considerable effort is mandatory, if the answer to this governing question is to be a meaningful answer. The language of Shakespeare is not always our language. The conventions on which his plays and poems depend—the existence of fairies like Titania and her retinue, and monstrous creatures like Caliban and Sycorax his dam, witchcraft that can really work wonders, as in *Macbeth,* the sanctity of kingship, love at first sight—these conventions are as dead as the long-dead Elizabethans who gave them substance and vitality, four centuries ago. To come to terms with Shakespeare, as with all older writers, one must make himself familiar with much that has been swallowed up forever "in the dark backward and abysm of time." One must practice philology. One must cultivate and exercise an historical imagination.

A good deal of troublesome business is got over at once as we are able to locate the writer securely in his workshop, which means in the vanished context in which his art was forged. It is useful to realize that Shakespeare is not often an original writer, that apparently it challenged him to take his stories from the work of journeymen playwrights and poets whose more elementary purpose was only to titillate or, in a witless sense, to amuse. Shakespeare's habit and pleasure —in *Twelfth Night,* in *Othello,* in *Measure for Measure*—is to make a silk purse of a sow's ear. The sensational stories that are his basic data often were equipped with supernatural baggage as they came to his hand. That is true, for instance, of *Hamlet.* This baggage did not presumably make for embarrassment, in Shakespeare or in his audience either. No doubt most of Shakespeare's patrons in the theatre believed in the existence of goblins and ghosts, or were willing for the moment—for what Shakespeare calls "the two hours' traffic of our stage"—to suspend their disbelief. The same willingness marks the reception of art in any age, not excluding our own. We do not suppose that Washington Irving believed in little men, or Swift in *Gulliver's Travels,* or Shakespeare in *A Midsummer-Night's Dream.* But whether or not the writer gives assent to the specific (or superficial) truth of the material he is deploying is unimportant to us. We are satisfied to take his fictions on faith. Who believes in Dante's fictions as set forth in the *Commedia,* and who is vexed as belief eludes him? What concerns us is not so much the stuff of the plot but, more basically, the theme, which the plot discovers and conveys.

The hostile critic who rejects poetry because he finds it essentially fabulous is not, of course, to be answered so summarily as this. Flights of fancy (as he would say), like Ariel or Puck or the mythological persons who entertain us in the fourth act of *The Tempest*—these do not especially perturb him. Only he would argue that Shakespeare is occasionally just as suspect or as patient of error in his presentation of real human beings. Lies or vulgar errors, a legacy to the playwright of the age for which he wrote, are of the warp and woof of Shakespeare's writing. As that is so, he is necessarily obsolete.

This case against Shakespeare appears to take strength from the plays. In the early tragedy *Richard III,* the villain is confronted by the ghosts of all his victims—the brother he has murdered, the wife, the little princes, his former accomplices in crime. We see these unearthly apparitions rise before us, presumably from a trapdoor in the floor of the stage. But we know that there are no ghosts. Is Shakespeare to be charged with superstition? As the charge is established, his reading of character and consequence will surely be felt as impaired.

But the charge is not established. The distressful ghosts of *Richard III* function "metaphorically." This means that they serve to objectify, to present in concrete ways, Richard's troubled state of mind. The villain cries, as he wakes from his terrible nightmare: "O coward conscience, how dost thou afflict me!" It is the idea of conscience on which we want to fix. The villain is disturbed, even physiologically, by the crimes he has committed. The ghosts that rise to haunt him are intended to dramatize or to embody that disturbance. It is the same in *Julius Caesar,* as when Brutus, on the eve of the final battle, is menaced by the spirit of the friend he has slain. It is the same in *Macbeth.*

What is the meaning of the blood-boltered Banquo, who materializes abruptly as the hero-villain prepares to dine with his thanes? The answer is implicit in the plot of the play. Macbeth and Lady Macbeth are unable to sleep. They cannot "stomach" their wickedness, and so they undergo what is called "a great perturbation in nature." After all, the effect follows from its cause. Only the sequence is rendered metaphorically. "Unnatural deeds," says the Doctor who ministers to Lady Macbeth, "Do breed unnatural troubles." Macbeth is troubled—he hallucinates, as we might put it—because he feels his secret murders sticking on his hands. His pestered senses recoil and start, "When all that is within him does condemn Itself for being there."

In Shakespeare, as opposed to the conventional horror story, spirits from another world—which have no reality—intrude on the action of the play, not to horrify, not to attest to the outmoded belief of the playwright, but to tell us something about the character who perceives them. What is important is not the ghost, but the affliction of the bedeviled man and the cause of his affliction. It is not the sensational fact with which we are to concern ourselves; it is the significance of the fact.

In *Hamlet*, graves stand tenantless and the "sheeted dead" walk forth. That is what Horatio tells us, and our senses corroborate the truth of his account. Beyond the confines of the play, this particular truth may be open to question. Here, it functions as an indispensable cog in the dramatic machinery; as an element of plot. Like the radically implausible Love Test which initiates the action of *King Lear*, it is the lever or prise which gets the play going. Our business, and Shakespeare's, is at a remove from the grisly phenomenon itself. Focus belongs properly to what issues or results.

A similar comment holds for the Witches in *Macbeth*. Are there really such creatures? That is very doubtful. What is their function, then, in the play? This function is to present to the hero evil under the aspect of good. When Bernard Shaw in *Man and Superman* brings the Devil on stage, we do not suppose that Shaw wants us to believe in his literal existence—except for this: that the evil symbolized by or objectified in the idea of the Devil (or the unnatural hags of *Macbeth*) does certainly exist. We encounter this evil, this beguiling summons to meanness or dishonorable conduct, every day of our lives. Our role as human beings is to reject it. Macbeth, as he hearkens to the Witches, is disloyal to his nature. His destruction follows: "And damn'd all those that trust them!"

The shrewd and sensitive reader of Shakespeare's plays will decline to be put off or distracted by the obsolete details or notations which mark the surface of the plays. He will ask himself, rather, What do they signify? One may take as illustrative the white magic of Prospero, the love potions of *A Midsummer-Night's Dream*, the bizarre and ostensibly foolish business of young women dressed up as young men (*Twelfth Night*, *As You Like It*), a daughter's refusal to affirm her love for a parent (*King Lear*). Do we really believe that comets foretell the deaths of princes? or that wicked behavior on earth is accompanied—as in *Hamlet*, *Julius Caesar*, *Macbeth*, *King Lear*—by convulsions in nature: storms and earthquakes and other eccentricities? Surely we do not believe; neither, perhaps, did Shakespeare accept these notations, these metaphors, as fact. Shakespeare has, however, an end in view that is independent of the superficial details on which he levies in telling his story. When, for example, he associates evil in the microcosm (the man himself) with commotion in the heavens or the macrocosm (the greater world that contains the man) what he is trying to get at, and to dramatize, is the profoundly aberrant or eccentric character of evil. Evil behavior is hostile to the ends and purposes of our being. That is the root proposition. Evil tears us apart; it destroys our harmony, our equilibrium, as when (and now the metaphor follows) a star shoots madly from its sphere, or the bay tree withers, or the ocean makes head against the kingdom of the shore. Evil is a kind of suicide. That is why *The Tempest,* which has to do with the perfidy of Alonso and Antonio and their hangers-on, begins with a storm at sea; and why the heavens in *King Lear* pour down stinking pitch, in concert with the unkind behavior of Goneril and Regan and Edmund; and why, on the murder of King Hamlet, the moon is sick almost to doomsday with eclipse.

In the age of Shakespeare, the homilist or preacher does not question that prayer can move mountains. Some of us, perhaps, are skeptical. What is Shakespeare's position? Does he wish us to assume that King Henry wins at Agincourt because he is prayerful? or the virtuous Richmond at the battle of Bosworth Field? Again, in making answer, we will want to ask ourselves what it signifies to get down on one's knees. Conceivably, this humble posture signifies a lack of arrogance, a measure of equability or inner peace, which is far different from the fevered boasting of the French in *Henry V* or the hysteria of the villain in *Richard III.* Humility, equability, these are qualities which help to sustain a man, and whether God's in His Heaven or not. Piety and prayerfulness denote the man who is at harmony with himself. They denote also a more harmonious relation between man and the environment from which he takes his being and to which, in the end, this being is resigned. It is possible, as Robert Frost suggests in one of his poems, that man keeps the universe alone. It does not follow that man is formed as by spontaneous generation, or that he is, in the wretched phrase we parrot without understanding, "self made." Iago, Shakespeare's most notorious villain, declines to pray because he believes that the individual ego exists in a vacuum. " 'Tis in ourselves that we are thus or thus." In consequence, Iago is destroyed—but not by "God." The effective agent is his own misreading of human nature. The psychology of the villain, his grasp of the total milieu, are defective. He is oblivious of that myriad of fine but perdurable connections by which all men are yoked together, and sustained. It is one thing to say, with the preacher: The villain is not a good man. It is more important and more interesting to observe that the villain is not sufficiently realistic.

One hears much in Shakespeare's plays about the sanctity of kingship. The king is presented as God's deputy. He is a sacrosanct figure, anointed by the Lord. Few of us are likely to endorse this proposition. Unless we are more than ordinarily ingenuous, we see our own leaders as fallible men. Does Shakespeare, in giving precedence to the king, assert that he is favored of Heaven? The question answers itself. King Lear, when the rain comes to wet him and the wind to make him chatter, discovers the limitations of kingship, as also his pathetic fraternity with the rest of human kind. "They told me I was everything. 'Tis a lie, I am not ague proof." The king, as Henry V confesses, "is but a man." The violet smells to him as to us all, the sky on which he gazes is our common sky. "All his senses have but human conditions. His ceremonies laid by, in his nakedness he appears but a man."

Still, the king as Shakespeare presents him is an exalted figure. But that is not as he differs or is eccentric in his human condition. It is as he summarizes this condition. He is the cynosure of all eyes, "the observed of all observers," but what we are observing in his spectacular progress is a giant emblem of ourselves. In the violent death of a great political leader, as the history of our own times reminds us, every man is violated. The point of the quotation from *Hamlet:* "Never alone Did the King sigh but with a general groan," is not to the uniqueness of the king but to his catholicity. He is in his suffering the avatar or incarnation of his subjects, who are grieving for themselves.

"Every emancipation," says Karl Marx, "is a restoration of the human world." Every man is enfranchised a little as one single man is freed. By the same token, every man is enfeebled as the titan is dragged to his death. That is the sense of John Donne's saying: "Any man's death diminishes me, because I am involved in mankind." The titan is set apart from the rest of mankind, not because he is singular in first and last things, but that his role as representative may be felt more acutely and be more clearly perceived. The assassination of the statesman differs from the murder of the common man in that it is transacted on a loftier stage. It fires the imagination and touches the heart of the multitude, as the multitude is compelled to bear witness. It shatters the false security and evasion by which we are customarily buffered. It instructs us in the chaos and terror that are forever lapping at the shores of the world.

In the preeminence which Shakespeare reserves to the king, social considerations have also their important place. These considerations are often misconstrued, and especially as one is angrily (myopically) partisan, on the radical or the conservative side. The king, as Shakespeare imagines him, is not a deific figure who moves at will among his hinds or lowly subjects. In fact his movements are circumscribed. To him, as to these subjects, particular functions are allotted. The encroaching of each on each is forbidden, and even viewed with holy horror—as when in *Hamlet* rebellion is likened to the ocean "overpeering of his list," rising above the borders that ought to confine it, and eating at the flats or shores. In this usurpation earth and water alike are confounded. It is as if

> the world were now but to begin,
> Antiquity forgot, custom not known,
> The ratifiers and props of every word.

Is Shakespeare, in his incessant commending of due form and custom and propriety, committed also to a belief in the necessary governance of the king? We will never know, and we should not greatly care. For what matters is a vision of society, of man relating to man in a precisely reticulated structure, that is as pertinent in this second half of the twentieth century as when Shakespeare conceived and enunciated his vision in the England of Queen Elizabeth and King James. Society, as Shakespeare sees it, is not an abstraction but an organism that lives. Like a tree, like the human body, this organism is made up of nicely cohering parts. Break this coherence and anarchy, which is the annuling of life, follows irresistibly.

In our own time, the kings have mostly departed. But the organic reading of society, and man in society, does not rely for its continuing vitality on the pompous title that runs before a king. Shakespeare as sociologist or political thinker is lucky. His hope for survival is not tied to the eroded content of the Elizabethan World Picture, the cosmology of an antique age. That is another way of saying that he is not so much a spokesman for the prepossessions of his time, neither is he much concerned to explode them. What engages him at bottom is the nature of *kind* in the Elizabethan and more comprehensive sense—the human condition to which all social and political commentary must ultimately refer.

And now it is apparent how Shakespeare, whose remoteness is incontestable, can speak across the centuries to Marx or J. M. Keynes, can come to terms with Social Democracy or the corporate state or the angry utopians of our own time who, like Brutus in the play, make a fetish of discord to exorcise some sick offense within their minds. Already Shakespeare knows them all. Like the scrupulous recorder of fact in any age, he founds his sociology and politics, not on the outworn formulations of old books and old creeds—which means, paradoxically, on the up-to-date shibboleths of the time—but on an inspection of the constant which is human behavior in its varying manifestations. As that is so, he is involved in a perpetual altercation or dialog with every social or economic theorist who has lived and written since his day. Shakespeare anticipates the prescriptive theorists of the right and left ("prescriptive," as they are drawing blueprints for social change), and engages them in debate by sensing and denying their first premise. This premise is that contractual change—all that has to do with forms and modes of government, and with the political and economic arrangement of the state—is the decisive change. Shakespeare, on the evidence of his plays, is at bottom mistrustful of contractual expedients, as constituting any ultimate *vade mecum.* He appears to believe, with Robert Frost, that the only revolution that's coming is a one-man revolution.

That is a point of view one may find depressing or exasperating; it continues, however, to claim our respectful attention. Dr. Johnson, almost two centuries after Shakespeare, expresses this point of view in a remarkable couplet:

> How little, of all the ills that human hearts endure,
> That part, which laws, or kings, can cause or cure.

Shakespeare himself might have written these lines, in token of the skepticism pervasive in his work, except that Shakespeare in his maturity is not partial to sententious couplets, rarely speaks *in propria persona,* and never speaks his meaning, in so many words.

Shakespeare living now would doubtless conform (one suspects, without much ado) to the politics, as also to the manners and mores, of the greatest number of his contemporaries. He is *par excellence* the equable man and disinclined to quarrel for an eggshell. This equability or easiness has, however, its limits. One does not imagine Shakespeare adhering with real conviction to political parties or putting his faith in political or social panaceas. His good will and his compassion are endless, and are matched only by his disbelief in the kingdom of God on earth.

In the second part of *Henry IV*, a wise ecclesiastic, who is not Shakespeare but is perhaps close to Shakespeare, encapsulates this disbelief:

> An habitation giddy and unsure
> Hath he that buildeth on the vulgar heart.

This pessimistic reading of our prospects in all sublunary business describes Shakespeare in his role as behavioral scientist. That is, hypothetically, a difficult role for him to play. As he seeks to anatomize the wellsprings of conduct, as he generalizes thereon, he courts comparison with the masters of modern psychology. In the light of this comparison, how persuasive are the tentative judgments at which he arrives in the plays? Not less than Shakespeare, and perhaps with more assurance, Sigmund Freud and his colleagues and successors are endeavoring to say what it means actually and potentially to be human. As we decide that their endeavors have radically changed our understanding of personality, it will follow that Shakespeare, at least in this particular, is to be written off as obsolete.

Reflection suggests, however, that Freud's revolution (as opposed to his fascination and continuing appeal as moralist and critic and culture hero) has to do, not so much with his reading of human nature, as with his treatment of specific maladies associated with the human condition. Freud in his sphere resembles Marx in his. Each is a prescriptive thinker. Each is laying down the law, prescribing for us what we ought to do in response to a condition which already exists (and for which neither is deific enough, really to account)—alienation of personality, the inequitable distribution of wealth. In diagnosing or describing this condition—which, in Freud's case, is the nature of man—there is no perceptible advance over Shakespeare. There is no progress, in the sense of displacing. There is rather confirmation, corroboration, albeit in an alien tongue.

So much Freud himself is eager to concede. He is not, he insists, the "discoverer of the unconscious"—the title fastened on him by admiring disciples on the occasion of his seventieth birthday. Credit for the discovery goes to the "poets and philosophers." Freud's contribution is to put the insight of his predecessors to work. "What I discovered," he says, "was the scientific method by which the unconscious can be studied."

This study, as the professional psychologist pursues it, has an end in view more specific and more immediately kinetic than the investigations of the playwright and poet. The distinction between the two kinds or orders of intelligence ought not, however, to obscure the more basic affinity that ties them together and discovers their kinship across centuries of time. Freud and Shakespeare are each of the empirical or analytic party. Each comes to his particular truth as he involves himself in brute fact up to the elbows. The truth each discerns may ramify, it may be open to generalization. But it is always in its elaborating *ad hoc* or *ad hominem*, always rooted in a provincial or indigenous context. Like the mythological figure Antaeus, it keeps its vitality forever unimpaired, as it is always in touch with the earth from which it springs.

This enduring connection informs and makes credible the analysis of behavior in the psychological treatises of Freud as in the plays of Shakespeare, and appears to dictate the strong and sometimes startling resemblance in the emergent "thought" of either writer. Shakespeare is not a systematic thinker, nor do the casual judgments he utters by the way lend themselves to codification. Freud, reduced to his scientific content, is not so memorable as Freud the tragic visionary, to whom man seems enfettered as by a primal curse—what Shakespeare calls "the imposition hereditary ours"—but whose dour view of behavior is also a compassionate and greatly generous view, one insistent, paradoxically, on human dignity and human value. Nonetheless, and having entered these important reservations, it is possible and appropriate to take the play and the treatise as expressive in similar ways of a formal psychology, or *gestalt*.

The kernel of Freud's psychology is a positing in man of unceasing and irreconcilable conflict between the forces of darkness and destruction—Freud calls these forces the id—and those of civilization and order—emblematized in the ego. "In popular language," Freud tells us in his *New Introductory Lectures on Psychoanalysis*, "we may say that the ego stands for reason and circumspection, while the id stands for the untamed passions." To mull over this formulation is to see that it is basically a pouring of old wine in new bottles, and as such is reminiscent of the psychology Shakespeare develops and dramatizes three hundred years before.

> Two such opposèd kings encamp them still
> In man as well as herbs, grace and rude will;
> And where the worser is predominant,
> Full soon the canker death eats up that plant.

The speaker is Friar Laurence in *Romeo and Juliet*. The burden of his speech is a divining in man of mortal warfare between powerful and endlessly antagonistic forces—here, the forces of grace (on which Freud, in the pessimism of his old age, is driven back) and ebullient and ungovernable will. Shakespeare's early history *Richard II* offers a more explicit statement of this contentious reading of human psychology. An old counselor is deeply disturbed at the irrational behavior of the king. He is, however, not especially hopeful of coercing this behavior. As he says:

> Then all too late comes counsel to be heard,
> Where will doth mutiny with wit's regard.

"Will" in this speech is identical with Freud's "untamed passions." It is another way of describing the id. "Wit" means, conversely, "reason and circumspection" —what Freud calls the ego.

The goal, in Shakespeare as in Freud, is to extend and confirm the hegemony of the ego. The prosecuting of this goal Freud likens to "reclamation work, like the draining of the Zuyder Zee." Happiness ensues, as the dark and turbid world beneath the waters is reclaimed. "Where id was," writes Freud, in his role as comic dramatist, "there shall ego be." Compare Prospero in *The Tempest,* on the reasserting of intelligence and self-control in the villains of that play:

> as the morning steals upon the night,
> Melting the darkness, so their rising senses
> Begin to chase the ignorant fumes that mantle
> Their clearer reason.

The point is to the quelling of ignorance and barbarism, "the offending Adam" in us all. Shakespeare, like Freud, enforces the point as he imagines the contention between the waters and the land. In *The Tempest,* however, sanity is figured, not as the sea is vanquished but as the sea reclaims its own:

> Their understanding
> Begins to swell, and the approaching tide
> Will shortly fill the reasonable shore
> That now lies foul and muddy.

Reclamation is not always in prospect. Tragedy ensues when, in Shakespeare's plays, rude will, which is the id, triumphs over the reason or ego. Mark Antony is destroyed because he makes his will lord of his reason. Othello is destroyed because he lets his blood (the id, ungoverned passion) rule his safer guides; passion, having collied or blackened his best judgment, assays—attempts, and successfully—to lead the way. That is Freud's understanding, precisely. It is also the conventional Judaeo-Christian reading of behavior.

Neither Shakespeare nor Freud nor the writers of Scripture venture to tell us why this internecine war should be predicable of the human condition. "Yea, the heart is desperately wicked," says the Hebrew prophet Jeremiah. Freud, in a hundred places, is one with him there. But perhaps this dyspeptic observation does not take us very far. King Cymbeline—to levy on Shakespeare—is simply incredulous when confronted with the iniquitous behavior of his queen. "Who is't can read a woman?" The question is rhetorical and begs the deeper question that lies behind. Whence comes evil? Let it be said what must be said: our approach to the heart of the mystery is abortive. But the nature of the conflict between reason and passion, and the issue of the conflict: these admit of rationalization.

In his study entitled *The Ego and the Id,* Freud identifies the ego with "reason and sanity, in contrast to the id which contains the passions." Again, a metaphor is utilized, to explain how these two are related. "In its relation to the id [the ego] is like a man on horseback, who has to hold in check the superior strength of the horse." This same metaphor occurs to Shakespeare. King Lear, in his madness, which is also perception, is describing the nature of woman—and, inferentially, of all human creatures. "Down from the waist they are Centaurs," he says, lustful beings, half human, half horse,

Though women all above:
But to the girdle do the gods inherit,
Beneath is all the fiends'.

That is an unpromising description of our nature. In part, we are bestial and capable of infinite ill. The sentimentalist denies this awful capability. Shakespeare is the antithesis of the sentimental man. Like Freud, he does not blink the evil potential in us. In the tragedies he looks fully at the Lake of Darkness each human being encloses. Among moderns, it is perhaps the man who averts his eyes who will describe this steadfast Shakespeare as obsolete.

When in *King Lear* Edgar, the good man, reads the letter which Goneril has addressed to the maleficent Edmund—a letter proposing the murder of her husband—he says, "O undistinguished space of woman's will!" In this will, in our will, all evil is latent. When in *Macbeth* Banquo is told that his line will one day reign in Scotland, he is obviously tempted to anticipate that prophecy, perhaps to hurry it on by committing murder. He says:

merciful powers,
Restrain in me the cursèd thoughts that nature
Gives way to in repose!

He sees what Shakespeare sees, that our nature is not to be left unrestrained or ungoverned; that there is, in the words of Prospero, a fire in our blood; that reason, like the man on horseback, has constantly to reign in the superior strength of the horse.

Shakespeare, in *The Tempest,* makes incarnate the idea of the Centaur, or beast in man, in his depicting of the relation between Prospero and Caliban. What is this Caliban? It is a

most lying slave,
Whom stripes may move, not kindness!

Or it is an

Abhorrèd slave,
Which any print of goodness wilt not take,
Being capable of all ill!

But what possible connection has this monstrous creature to a benevolent man like Prospero? The hero himself, in the last scene of the play, answers for us:

this thing of darkness I
Acknowledge mine.

Even the best and best-willing of men, as he is wise, knows himself "capable of all ill!"

The history of our own times, replete with mass murder and acts of violence against the human person on a scale hardly thinkable to previous generations, glosses or exemplifies this daunting proposition. We are apt, however, to derive a specious comfort from the record of history. Very scale and remoteness engender the fallacious belief that we ourselves are not participants but only observers, that what we are observing in "the march of events" is not human, not personal, but the abstract chronicle of contending economic or political forces, or warring factions or nations. As we are lessoned by Shakespeare's plays, this crooked comfort is denied us. The horror dramatized in the tragedy of *King Lear* does not differ qualitatively from the horrors enacted on the historical stage. "Out, vile jelly, where is thy lustre now!" Shakespeare, as he reduces history to apprehensible size, assimilates history. He demands that we confront it in personal terms. He wills us to understand that atrocities are not committed by nations. They are committed by men against other men.

But Shakespeare is less ruthful, even than this. Indifferent to the tender image we conceive of ourselves, he forbids us to externalize. As the perpetrator of genocide, the slaughter of an entire race, prosecutes his evil purpose at a remove, we are tempted to see him as a shadowy creature, an aberration, whose kinship with the rest of humanity is open to doubt. But after all he is not to be distinguished—so much we are forced to surmise—from the villainous protagonists of *King Lear*, from Cornwall, for instance, who is the more personal instrument of the sufferings of old Gloucester. In terms of what is possible—the "baby figure of the mass of things to come"—he is not to be distinguished from ourselves.

In every case, the root of immoral behavior is the same. The engineer of this behavior plumes or exalts the will. "Our power," says Cornwall, "Shall do a courtesy to our wrath." This is to say: wickedness is not out there on the fringes of things, independent of human contriving. Lunacy, what Othello calls the "error of the moon," does not govern in making for the tragic denouement. No "demi-devil" compels us. Of such melodramatic constraints, we are free. Wickedness—and here one wants to differentiate between the grossly human act and that merely gratuitous and arbitrary disaster which is perhaps heaven sent!—wickedness ensues as what is meet and decorous gives place to what I desire.

Shakespeare is implacable in holding up the mirror, and allows us to make no mistake. Othello, on the other hand, is certainly mistaken. He thinks himself a "fool," ensnared, ineluctably, by the vile insinuations of Iago. Perhaps the Devil does literally walk up and down in the earth? In the final scene of the play, too late except for pity, the villain is apprehended. "I look down towards his feet," Othello cries, expecting to see there the disfiguring mark by which our ancient enemy is recognized. And then he adds, ruefully, "but that's a fable." Our enemy is not detectable, as by the cloven hoof. He does not proclaim openly his menace and contempt, and so it is not easy to fend against him. Neither is he exterior to us. The enemy is within.

> This thing of darkness I
> Acknowledge mine.

Romeo and Juliet

A NOTE ON THE TEXT

Romeo and Juliet was written probably in 1594 or 1595. The style, marked and sometimes marred by youthful exuberance, playing on words, and a delight in language for its own sake, suggests an early and self-indulgent Shakespeare. It is, however, appropriate to the subject of the play.

A first edition, in quarto, appeared in 1597. It is much shorter than the second quarto of 1599, leading scholars to suppose that Q1 is a pirated copy, purloined by an unscrupulous printer, published without intelligent supervision or correction, and hence subject to many errors and omissions. Q2 was perhaps printed from the manuscript used in the playhouse. It was followed by a third quarto in 1609, which is the basis of the Folio version of 1623.

The story of Romeo and Juliet exists in several European literatures. Shakespeare came to it by way of Arthur Brooke's narrative poem, first printed in 1562, entitled *The Tragical History of Romeus and Juliet*. Since Brooke records in his preface a recent performance of the story on stage, it is apparent that even before Shakespeare's birth playwrights had detected in it an appeal inherently dramatic.

ROMEO AND JULIET

DRAMATIS PERSONÆ

ESCALUS, *prince of Verona.*
PARIS, *a young nobleman, kinsman to the prince.*
MONTAGUE, } *heads of two houses at variance with each other.*
CAPULET, }
An old man, cousin to Capulet.
ROMEO, *son to Montague.*
MERCUTIO, *kinsman to the prince, and friend to Romeo.*
BENVOLIO, *nephew to Montague, and friend to Romeo.*
TYBALT, *nephew to Lady Capulet.*
FRIAR LAURENCE, } *Franciscans.*
FRIAR JOHN, }
BALTHASAR, *servant to Romeo.*
SAMPSON, } *servants to Capulet.*
GREGORY, }
PETER, *servant to Juliet's nurse.*
ABRAHAM, *servant to Montague.*
An APOTHECARY.
Three MUSICIANS.
PAGE *to Paris; another* PAGE; *an* OFFICER.

LADY MONTAGUE, *wife to Montague.*
LADY CAPULET, *wife to Capulet.*
JULIET, *daughter to Capulet.*
NURSE *to Juliet.*

CITIZENS *of Verona; several Men and Women, relations to both houses;* MASKERS, GUARDS, WATCHMEN, *and* ATTENDANTS.

CHORUS.

SCENE: *Verona; Mantua.*

PROLOGUE

Two households, both alike in dignity,
In fair Verona, where we lay our scene,
From ancient grudge break to new mutiny,
Where civil blood makes civil hands unclean.
From forth the fatal loins of these two foes 5
A pair of star-cross'd lovers take their life;
Whose misadventured piteous overthrows
Do with their death bury their parents' strife.
The fearful passage of their death-mark'd love,
And the continuance of their parents' rage,
Which, but their children's end, nought could remove, 11
Is now the two hours' traffic of our stage;
The which if you with patient ears attend,
What here shall miss, our toil shall strive to mend.

Prologue: 3. **mutiny,** strife. 6. **star-cross'd,** thwarted by unfavorable positions of the stars, so doomed by Fate. 9. **passage,** progress. 12. **two hours' traffic of our stage,** since a play of Shakespeare was normally acted in two hours, the printed text must have either been cut or very rapidly recited. 14. **miss,** be lacking. **Act I, Scene i:** 1. **carry coals,** i.e., take insults. 3. **choler,** the one of the four humors which produces anger.

ACT I

SCENE I. *Verona. A public place.*

[*Enter* SAMPSON *and* GREGORY, *of the house of Capulet, armed with swords and bucklers.*]

SAM. Gregory, o' my word, we'll not carry coals.

GRE. No, for then we should be colliers.

SAM. I mean, an' we be in choler, we'll draw.

GRE. Ay, while you live, draw your neck out o' the collar.

SAM. I strike quickly, being moved.

GRE. But thou art not quickly moved to strike.

SAM. A dog of the house of Montague moves me. 10

GRE. To move is to stir; and to be valiant is to stand: therefore, if thou art moved, thou runn'st away.

SAM. A dog of that house shall move me to stand: I will take the wall of any man or maid of Montague's. 16

GRE. That shows thee a weak slave; for the weakest goes to the wall.

SAM. True; and therefore women, being the weaker vessels, are ever thrust to the wall: therefore I will push Montague's men from the wall, and thrust his maids to the wall. 22

GRE. The quarrel is between our masters and us their men.

SAM. 'Tis all one, I will show myself a tyrant: when I have fought with the men, I will be cruel with the maids, and cut off their heads.

GRE. The heads of the maids? 29

SAM. Ay, the heads of the maids, or their maidenheads; take it in what sense thou wilt.

GRE. They must take it in sense that feel it.

SAM. Me they shall feel while I am able to stand: and 'tis known I am a pretty piece of flesh. 35

GRE. 'Tis well thou art not fish; if thou hadst, thou hadst been poor John. Draw thy tool; here comes two of the house of the Montagues.

SAM. My naked weapon is out: quarrel, I will back thee. 40

GRE. How! turn thy back and run?

SAM. Fear me not.

GRE. No, marry; I fear thee!

SAM. Let us take the law of our sides; let them begin.

GRE. I will frown as I pass by, and let them take it as they list.

SAM. Nay, as they dare. I will bite my thumb at them; which is a disgrace to them, if they bear it. 50

[*Enter* ABRAHAM *and* BALTHASAR.]

ABR. Do you bite your thumb at us, sir?

SAM. I do bite my thumb, sir.

ABR. Do you bite your thumb at us, sir?

SAM. [*Aside to Gre.*] Is the law of our side, if I say ay? 55

GRE. No.

SAM. No, sir, I do not bite my thumb at you sir, but I bite my thumb, sir.

GRE. Do you quarrel, sir?

ABR. Quarrel, sir! no, sir. 60

SAM. If you do, sir, I am for you: I serve as good a man as you.

ABR. No better.

SAM. Well, sir.

GRE. Say 'better:' here comes one of my master's kinsmen.

SAM. Yes, better, sir.

ABR. You lie.

SAM. Draw, if you be men. Gregory, remember thy swashing blow. [*They fight.* 70

[*Enter* BENVOLIO.]

BEN. Part, fools!
Put up your swords; you know not what you do. [*Beats down their swords.*

[*Enter* TYBALT.]

TYB. What, art thou drawn among these heartless hinds?
Turn thee, Benvolio, look upon thy death.

BEN. I do but keep the peace: put up thy sword, 75
Or manage it to part these men with me.

TYB. What, drawn, and talk of peace! I hate the word,
As I hate hell, all Montagues, and thee:
Have at thee, coward! [*They fight.*

[*Enter several of both houses, who join the fray; then enter* CITIZENS, *with clubs.*]

FIRST CIT. Clubs, bills, and partisans! strike! beat them down! 80
Down with the Capulets! down with the Montagues!

[*Enter* CAPULET *in his gown, and* LADY CAPULET.]

CAP. What noise is this? Give me my long sword, ho!

LA. CAP. A crutch, a crutch! why call you for a sword?

15. **take the wall**, it was an act of intentional rudeness to take the side of a road nearest the wall from a stranger, because that part of the road was freest from mud and filth. 37. **poor John**, salt hake, a poor kind of fish. 48-9. **bite my thumb**, this was an insulting gesture.

65-6. **one of . . . kinsmen**, i.e., Tybalt. 70. **swashing**, smashing. 80. **bills**, long-handled pikes; **partisans**, long-handled spears with sharp blades on the ends. The three words formed the rallying cry of London apprentices when bent on mischief.

CAP. My sword, I say! Old Montague is come,
And flourishes his blade in spite of me. 85

[*Enter* MONTAGUE *and* LADY MONTAGUE.]

MON. Thou villain Capulet,—Hold me not, let me go.
LA. MON. Thou shalt not stir a foot to seek a foe.

[*Enter* PRINCE, *with* Attendants.]

PRIN. Rebellious subjects, enemies to peace,
Profaners of this neighbour-stainèd steel,—
Will they not hear? What, ho! you men, you beasts, 90
That quench the fire of your pernicious rage
With purple fountains issuing from your veins,
On pain of torture, from those bloody hands
Throw your mistemper'd weapons to the ground,
And hear the sentence of your movèd prince.
Three civil brawls, bred of an airy word, 95
By thee, old Capulet, and Montague,
Have thrice disturb'd the quiet of our streets,
And made Verona's ancient citizens
Cast by their grave beseeming ornaments, 100
To wield old partisans, in hands as old,
Canker'd with peace, to part your canker'd hate:
If ever you disturb our streets again,
Your lives shall pay the forfeit of the peace.
For this time, all the rest depart away: 105
You, Capulet, shall go along with me:
And, Montague, come you this afternoon,
To know our further pleasure in this case,
To old Free-town, our common judgement-place.
Once more, on pain of death, all men depart.
[*Exeunt all but* MONTAGUE, LADY MONTAGUE, *and* BENVOLIO.

MON. Who set this ancient quarrel new abroach? 111
Speak, nephew, were you by when it began?
BEN. Here were the servants of your adversary,
And yours, close fighting ere I did approach:
I drew to part them: in the instant came 115
The fiery Tybalt, with his sword prepared,
Which, as he breathed defiance to my ears,
He swung about his head and cut the winds,
Who nothing hurt withal hiss'd him in scorn:
While we were interchanging thrusts and blows, 120
Came more and more and fought on part and part,
Till the prince came, who parted either part.
LA. MON. O, where is Romeo? saw you him to-day?
Right glad I am he was not at this fray.
BEN. Madam, an hour before the worshipp'd sun 125
Peer'd forth the golden window of the east,
A troubled mind drave me to walk abroad;
Where, underneath the grove of sycamore
That westward rooteth from the city's side,
So early walking did I see your son: 130
Towards him I made, but he was ware of me
And stole into the covert of the wood:
I, measuring his affections by my own,
That most are busied when they're most alone,
Pursued my humour not pursuing his, 135
And gladly shunn'd who gladly fled from me.
MON. Many a morning hath he there been seen,
With tears augmenting the fresh morning's dew,
Adding to clouds more clouds with his deep sighs;
But all so soon as the all-cheering sun 140
Should in the furthest east begin to draw
The shady curtains from Aurora's bed,
Away from light steals home my heavy son,
And private in his chamber pens himself,
Shuts up his windows, locks fair daylight out
And makes himself an artificial night: 146
Black and portentous must this humour prove,
Unless good counsel may the cause remove.
BEN. My noble uncle, do you know the cause?
MON. I neither know it nor can learn of him.
BEN. Have you importuned him by any means? 151
MON. Both by myself and many other friends:
But he, his own affections' counsellor,
Is to himself—I will not say how true—

85. in spite of, to defy. 89. Profaners, disgracers; neighbour-stained, stained with the blood of your neighbors. 94. mistemper'd, tempered for an evil purpose. 95. moved, aroused to wrath. 100. grave . . . ornaments, the equipment befitting their dignity. 102. canker'd . . . canker'd, corroded . . . malignant. 109. Free-town, translation of Villa Franca in Brooke's poem. 111. set . . . abroach, renewed. 121. part and part, either side. 131. ware, aware. 133. affections, inclinations. 143. heavy, sad.

But to himself so secret and so close, 155
So far from sounding and discovery,
As is the bud bit with an envious worm,
Ere he can spread his sweet leaves to the air,
Or dedicate his beauty to the sun.
Could we but learn from whence his sorrows grow, 160
We would as willingly give cure as know.

[*Enter* ROMEO.]

BEN. See, where he comes: so please you, step aside;
I'll know his grievance, or be much denied.
MON. I would thou wert so happy by thy stay,
To hear true shrift. Come, madam, let's away.
[*Exeunt* MONTAGUE *and* LADY. 165
BEN. Good morrow, cousin.
ROM. Is the day so young?
BEN. But new struck nine.
ROM. Ay me! sad hours seem long.
Was that my father that went hence so fast?
BEN. It was. What sadness lengthens Romeo's hours?
ROM. Not having that, which, having, makes them short. 170
BEN. In love?
ROM. Out—
BEN. Of love?
ROM. Out of her favour, where I am in love.
BEN. Alas, that love, so gentle in his view, 175
Should be so tyrannous and rough in proof!
ROM. Alas, that love, whose view is muffled still,
Should, without eyes, see pathways to his will!
Where shall we dine? O me! What fray was here?
Yet tell me not, for I have heard it all. 180
Here's much to do with hate, but more with love.
Why, then, O brawling love! O loving hate!
O any thing, of nothing first create!
O heavy lightness! serious vanity!
Mis-shapen chaos of well-seeming forms! 185
Feather of lead, bright smoke, cold fire, sick health!
Still-waking sleep, that is not what it is!
This love feel I, that feel no love in this.
Dost thou not laugh?
BEN. No, coz, I rather weep. 189
ROM. Good heart, at what?
BEN. At thy good heart's oppression.
ROM. Why, such is love's transgression.
Griefs of mine own lie heavy in my breast,
Which thou wilt propagate, to have it prest
With more of thine: this love that thou hast shown
Doth add more grief to too much of mine own. 195
Love is a smoke raised with the fume of sighs;
Being purged, a fire sparkling in lovers' eyes;
Being vex'd, a sea nourish'd with lovers' tears:
What is it else? a madness most discreet,
A choking gall and a preserving sweet. 200
Farewell, my coz.
BEN. Soft! I will go along;
An if you leave me so, you do me wrong.
ROM. Tut, I have lost myself; I am not here;
This is not Romeo, he's some other where.
BEN. Tell me in sadness, who is that you love. 205
ROM. What, shall I groan and tell thee?
BEN. Groan! why, no:
But sadly tell me who.
ROM. Bid a sick man in sadness make his will:
Ah, word ill urged to one that is so ill!
In sadness, cousin, I do love a woman. 210
BEN. I aim'd so near, when I supposed you loved.
ROM. A right good mark-man! And she's fair I love.
BEN. A right fair mark, fair coz, is soonest hit.
ROM. Well, in that hit you miss: she'll not be hit
With Cupid's arrow; she hath Dian's wit; 215
And, in strong proof of chastity well arm'd,
From love's weak childish bow she lives unharm'd.
She will not stay the siege of loving terms,
Nor bide the encounter of assailing eyes,
Nor ope her lap to saint-seducing gold: 220
O, she is rich in beauty, only poor,
That when she dies with beauty dies her store.
BEN. Then she hath sworn that she will still live chaste?

155. close, reticent. 156. sounding, i.e., being probed. 157. envious, malicious. 163. denied, refused. 164. happy, fortunate. 165. shrift, confession. 175. view, appearance. 176. in proof, when experienced. 177. whose . . . still, whose eyes are always blindfolded. 193. propagate, increase; to have it, by having it. 196. fume, mist. 197. purged, cleaned (of smoke). 200. gall, bitterness. 201. Soft, i.e., wait a minute. 205. sadness, seriousness. 216. proof, tested armor. 218. stay, endure; loving terms, professions of love. 222. store, riches, i.e., if she dies childless, her beauty will perish with her. Romeo develops the idea in 225-6.

ROM. She hath, and in that sparing makes huge waste,
For beauty starved with her severity 225
Cuts beauty off from all posterity.
She is too fair, too wise, wisely too fair,
To merit bliss by making me despair:
She hath forsworn to love, and in that vow
Do I live dead that live to tell it now. 230

BEN. Be ruled by me, forget to think of her.

ROM. O, teach me how I should forget to think.

BEN. By giving liberty unto thine eyes;
Examine other beauties.

ROM. 'Tis the way
To call hers exquisite, in question more: 235
These happy masks that kiss fair ladies' brows
Being black put us in mind they hide the fair;
He that is strucken blind cannot forget
The precious treasure of his eyesight lost:
Show me a mistress that is passing fair, 240
What doth her beauty serve, but as a note
Where I may read who pass'd that passing fair?
Farewell: thou canst not teach me to forget.

BEN. I'll pay that doctrine, or else die in debt. [*Exeunt.*

SCENE II. *A street.*

[*Enter* CAPULET, PARIS, *and* SERVANT.]

CAP. But Montague is bound as well as I,
In penalty alike; and 'tis not hard, I think,
For men so old as we to keep the peace.

PAR. Of honourable reckoning are you both;
And pity 'tis you lived at odds so long. 5
But now, my lord, what say you to my suit?

CAP. But saying o'er what I have said before:
My child is yet a stranger in the world;
She hath not seen the change of fourteen years;
Let two more summers wither in their pride,
Ere we think her ripe to be a bride. 11

PAR. Younger than she are happy mothers made.

CAP. And too soon marr'd are those so early made.
The earth hath swallow'd all my hopes but she,
She is the hopeful lady of my earth: 15
But woo her, gentle Paris, get her heart,
My will to her consent is but a part;
An she agree, within her scope of choice
Lies my consent and fair according voice.
This night I hold an old accustom'd feast, 20
Whereto I have invited many a guest,
Such as I love; and you, among the store,
One more, most welcome, makes my number more.
At my poor house look to behold this night
Earth-treading stars that make dark heaven light: 25
Such comfort as do lusty young men feel
When well-apparell'd April on the heel
Of limping winter treads, even such delight
Among fresh female buds shall you this night
Inherit at my house; hear all, all see, 30
And like her most whose merit most shall be:
Which on more view, of many mine being one
May stand in number, though in reckoning none.
Come, go with me. [*To* SERV., *giving a paper.*] Go, sirrah, trudge about
Through fair Verona; find those persons out
Whose names are written there, and to them say, 36
My house and welcome on their pleasure stay.
[*Exeunt* CAPULET *and* PARIS.

SERV. Find them out whose names are written here! It is written, that the shoemaker should meddle with his yard, and the tailor with 40 his last, the fisher with his pencil, and the painter with his nets; but I am sent to find those persons whose names are here writ, and can never find what names the writing person hath here writ. I must to the learned—In good time. 45

[*Enter* BENVOLIO *and* ROMEO.]

BEN. Tut, man, one fire burns out another's burning,
One pain is lessen'd by another's anguish;
Turn giddy, and be holp by backward turning;
One desperate grief cures with another's languish:
Take thou some new infection to thy eye, 50
And the rank poison of the old will die.

224. sparing, abstinence. 225. starved, i.e., starved to death. 235. in question more, considered more thoroughly. 240. passing, surpassingly. 244. pay that doctrine, give that instruction. Scene ii: 4. reckoning, reputation. 8. stranger in the world, inexperienced in social life, the ways of the world. 15. earth, body. 18. an, if; scope, range.

19. fair . . . voice, approval entirely agreeing (with hers). 22. store, mass, crowd. 32-3. which . . . none, my daughter, being one of these many ladies, on further view of the group, may count as one of their company, though worth more than any of them; reckoning, estimation. 34. sirrah, a term of address implying inferiority. 48. holp, helped.

ROM. Your plaintain-leaf is excellent for that.
BEN. For what, I pray thee?
ROM. For your broken shin.
BEN. Why, Romeo, art thou mad?
ROM. Not mad, but bound more than a madman is; 55
Shut up in prison, kept without my food,
Whipp'd and tormented and—God-den, good fellow.
SERV. God gi' god-den. I pray, sir, can you read? 59
ROM. Ay, mine own fortune in my misery.
SERV. Perhaps you have learned it without book: but, I pray, can you read any thing you see?
ROM. Ay, if I know the letters and the language.
SERV. Ye say honestly: rest you merry! 65
ROM. Stay, fellow; I can read. [*Reads.*]
"Signior Martino and his wife and daughters; County Anselme and his beauteous sisters; the lady widow of Vitruvio; Signior Placentio and his lovely nieces; Mercutio and his brother Valentine; mine uncle Capulet, his wife, and daughters; my fair niece Rosaline; Livia; Signior Valentio and his cousin Tybalt; Lucio and the lively Helena."
A fair assembly: whither should they come?
SERV. Up.
ROM. Whither?
SERV. To supper; to our house.
ROM. Whose house?
SERV. My master's. 80
ROM. Indeed, I should have asked you that before.
SERV. Now I'll tell you without asking: my master is the great rich Capulet; and if you be not of the house of Montagues, I pray, come and crush a cup of wine. Rest you merry! 86
[*Exit.*
BEN. At this same ancient feast of Capulet's
Sups the fair Rosaline whom thou so lovest,
With all the admired beauties of Verona:
Go thither; and, with unattainted eye, 90
Compare her face with some that I shall show,
And I will make thee think thy swan a crow.
ROM. When the devout religion of mine eye
Maintains such falsehood, then turn tears to fires;
And these, who often drown'd could never die, 95
Transparent heretics, be burnt for liars!
One fairer than my love! the all-seeing sun
Ne'er saw her match since first the world begun.
BEN. Tut, you saw her fair, none else being by,
Herself poised with herself in either eye: 100
But in that crystal scales let there be weigh'd
Your lady's love against some other maid
That I will show you shining at this feast,
And she shall scant show well that now shows best.
ROM. I'll go along, no such sight to be shown, 105
But to rejoice in splendour of mine own.
[*Exeunt.*

SCENE III. *A room in Capulet's house.*

[*Enter* LADY CAPULET *and* NURSE.]

LA. CAP. Nurse, where's my daughter? call her forth to me.
NURSE. Now, by my maidenhead, at twelve year old,
I bade her come. What, lamb! what, ladybird!
God forbid! Where's this girl? What, Juliet!

[*Enter* JULIET.]

JUL. How now! who calls?
NURSE. Your mother. 5
JUL. Madam, I am here.
What is your will?
LA. CAP. This is the matter:—Nurse, give leave awhile,
We must talk in secret:—nurse, come back again;
I have remember'd me, thou's hear our counsel.
Thou know'st my daughter's of a pretty age. 10
NURSE. Faith, I can tell her age unto an hour.
LA. CAP. She's not fourteen.
NURSE. I'll lay fourteen of my teeth,—
And yet, to my teen be it spoken, I have but four,—
She is not fourteen. How long is it now
To Lammas-tide?

65. rest you merry, stay happy. A colloquial expression of farewell. 86. crush a cup, drink a bottle. 90. unattained, sound, hence unprejudiced. 95. these, i.e., my eyes.

100. poised, weighed. 104. scant, barely. Scene iii: 7. give leave, leave us. 9. thou's, thou shalt. 13. teen, sorrow. 15. Lammas-tide, August 1.

LA. CAP. A fortnight and odd days. 15
NURSE. Even or odd, of all days in the year,
Come Lammas-eve at night shall she be fourteen.
Susan and she—God rest all Christian souls!—
Were of an age: well, Susan is with God;
She was too good for me: but, as I said, 20
On Lammas-eve at night shall she be fourteen;
That shall she, marry; I remember it well.
'Tis since the earthquake now eleven years;
And she was wean'd,—I never shall forget it,—
Of all the days of the year, upon that day: 25
For I had then laid wormwood to my dug,
Sitting in the sun under the dove-house wall;
My lord and you were then at Mantua:—
Nay, I do bear a brain:—but, as I said,
When it did taste the wormwood on the nipple 30
Of my dug and felt it bitter, pretty fool,
To see it tetchy and fall out with the dug!
"Shake" quoth the dove-house: 'twas no need, I trow,
To bid me trudge:
And since that time it is eleven years; 35
For then she could stand alone; nay, by the rood,
She could have run and waddled all about;
For even the day before, she broke her brow:
And then my husband—God be with his soul!
A' was a merry man—took up the child: 40
"Yea," quoth he, "dost thou fall upon thy face?
Thou wilt fall backward when thou hast more wit;
Wilt thou not, Jule?" and, by my holidame,
The pretty wretch left crying and said "Ay."
To see, now, how a jest shall come about! 45
I warrant, an I should live a thousand years,
I never should forget it: "Wilt thou not, Jule?" quoth he;
And, pretty fool, it stinted and said "Ay."
LA. CAP. Enough of this; I pray thee, hold thy peace.
NURSE. Yes, madam: yet I cannot choose but laugh, 50
To think it should leave crying and say "Ay."
And yet, I warrant, it had upon its brow
A bump as big as a young cockerel's stone;
A parlous knock; and it cried bitterly:
"Yea," quoth my husband, "fall'st upon thy face? 55
Thou wilt fall backward when thou comest to age;
Wilt thou not, Jule?" it stinted and said "Ay."
JUL. And stint thou too, I pray thee, nurse, say I.
NURSE. Peace, I have done. God mark thee to his grace!
Thou wast the prettiest babe that e'er I nursed:
An I might live to see thee married once, 61
I have my wish.
LA. CAP. Marry, that "marry" is the very theme
I came to talk of. Tell me, daughter Juliet,
How stands your disposition to be married? 65
JUL. It is an honour that I dream not of.
NURSE. An honour! were not I thine only nurse,
I would say thou hadst suck'd wisdom from thy teat.
LA. CAP. Well, think of marriage now; younger than you,
Here in Verona, ladies of esteem, 70
Are made already mothers: by my count,
I was your mother much upon these years
That you are now a maid. Thus then in brief:
The valiant Paris seeks you for his love.
NURSE. A man, young lady! lady, such a man 75
As all the world—why, he's a man of wax.
LA. CAP. Verona's summer hath not such a flower.
NURSE. Nay, he's a flower; in faith, a very flower.
LA. CAP. What say you? can you love the gentleman?
This night you shall behold him at our feast;
Read o'er the volume of young Paris' face 81
And find delight writ there with beauty's pen;
Examine every married lineament
And see how one another lends content,
And what obscured in this fair volume lies 85
Find written in the margent of his eyes.
This precious book of love, this unbound lover,
To beautify him, only lacks a cover:
The fish lives in the sea, and 'tis much pride

29. **bear a brain**, have a mind; the Nurse is proud of her stupidly accurate memory. 32. **tetchy**, fretful. 36. **rood**, holy cross. 40. **A'**, he. 43. **holidame**, sacred relic. 48. **stinted**, stopped. 49. **hold thy peace**, stop talking. 53. **stone**, testicle. 54. **parlous**, grievous = "awful." 59. **mark**, choose. 65. **How . . . married?**, How are you inclined toward marriage? 76. **man of wax**, beautiful as a wax figure of a man, i.e., perfect. 83. **married**, harmonious. 86. **margent**, margin. 89. **fish lives in the sea**, the fish from which the fishskin binding of the book is to be made, i.e., the lover is not yet caught.

For fair without the fair within to hide: 90
That book in many's eyes doth share the glory,
That in gold clasps locks in the golden story;
So shall you share all that he doth possess,
By having him, making yourself no less.

NURSE. No less! nay, bigger; women grow by men. 95

LA. CAP. Speak briefly, can you like of Paris' love?

JUL. I'll look to like, if looking liking move:
But no more deep will I endart mine eye
Than your consent gives strength to make it fly. 99

[*Enter a* SERVANT.]

SERV. Madam, the guests are come, supper served up, you called, my young lady asked for, the nurse cursed in the pantry, and every thing in extremity. I must hence to wait; I beseech you, follow straight.

LA. CAP. We follow thee. [*Exit* SERVANT.]
Juliet, the county stays. 105

NURSE. Go, girl, seek happy nights to happy days. [*Exeunt.*

SCENE IV. *A street.*

[*Enter* ROMEO, MERCUTIO, BENVOLIO, *with five or six* MASKERS, TORCH-BEARERS, *and others.*]

ROM. What, shall this speech be spoke for our excuse?
Or shall we on without apology?

BEN. The date is out of such prolixity:
We'll have no Cupid hood wink'd with a scarf,
Bearing a Tartar's painted bow of lath, 5
Scaring the ladies like a crow-keeper;
Nor no without-book prologue, faintly spoke
After the prompter, for our entrance:
But let them measure us by what they will;
We'll measure them a measure, and be gone. 10

ROM. Give me a torch: I am not for this ambling;
Being but heavy, I will bear the light.

MER. Nay, gentle Romeo, we must have you dance.

ROM. Not I, believe me: you have dancing shoes
With nimble soles: I have a soul of lead 15
So stakes me to the ground I cannot move.

MER. You are a lover; borrow Cupid's wings,
And soar with them above a common bound.

ROM. I am too sore enpierced with his shaft
To soar with his light feathers, and so bound,
I cannot bound a pitch above dull woe: 21
Under love's heavy burden do I sink.

MER. And, to sink in it, should you burden love;
Too great oppression for a tender thing.

ROM. Is love a tender thing? it is too rough,
Too rude, too boisterous, and it pricks like thorn. 26

MER. If love be rough with you, be rough with love;
Prick love for pricking, and you beat love down.
Give me a case to put my visage in:
A visor for a visor! what care I 30
What curious eye doth quote deformities?
Here are the beetle brows shall blush for me.

BEN. Come, knock and enter; and no sooner in,
But every man betake him to his legs.

ROM. A torch for me: let wantons light of heart 35
Tickle the senseless rushes with their heels,
For I am proverb'd with a grandsire phrase;
I'll be a candle-holder, and look on.
The game was ne'er so fair, and I am done.

MER. Tut, dun's the mouse, the constable's own word: 40
If thou art dun, we'll draw thee from the mire
Of this sir-reverence love, wherein thou stick'st
Up to the ears. Come, we burn daylight, ho!

ROM. Nay, that's not so.

MER. I mean, sir, in delay

97. **look to like,** look forward to liking. 105. **county,** count, Italian "conte"; **stays,** waits. Scene iv: 1. **speech,** Maskers formerly were preceded by a messenger in costume introducing them with a set speech. That "prolixity" has become out-of-date. 4. **hood wink'd,** blindfolded. 5. **Tartar's . . . bow.** Bows of the Tartars resembled the Roman bows with which Cupid was habitually painted. 6. **crow-keeper,** boy hired to scare off crows. 10. **measure them a measure,** dance a stately dance for them. 11. **ambling,** affected walking. 21. **pitch,** height to which a hawk soars to strike at its prey. 29. **case,** i.e., mask. 30. **visor for a visor,** mask for a face ugly as a mask. 31. **quote,** note. 36. **rushes,** used as a floor-covering. 37. **grandsire phrase,** ancient saying; **candle-holder,** the proverb is "A good candle-holder, i.e., a spectator, is a good gamester." 39. **the game . . . done,** reference here to the proverb, "He does well who gives over [stops playing] when the game is fairest." 40. **dun's the mouse,** an obscure phrase meaning "keep still as a mouse." 41. **dun,** like "Dobbin," a proverbial name for a horse. Reference is to a Christmas game called "Dun is on the mire" in which a heavy log was dragged out of the mud by the players. 42. **sir-reverence,** corruption of "save-reverence," a phrase begging pardon for something to follow. Mercutio suggests that love is filthy as mud.

We waste our lights in vain, like lamps by day. 45
Take our good meaning, for our judgement sits
Five times in that ere once in our five wits.

ROM. And we mean well in going to this mask;
But 'tis no wit to go.

MER. Why, may one ask?

ROM. I dream'd a dream to-night.

MER. And so did I. 50

ROM. Well, what was yours?

MER. That dreamers often lie.

ROM. In bed asleep, while they do dream things true.

MER. O, then, I see Queen Mab hath been with you.
She is the fairies' midwife, and she comes
In shape no bigger than an agate-stone 55
On the fore-finger of an alderman,
Drawn with a team of little atomies
Athwart men's noses as they lie asleep;
Her waggon-spokes made of long spinners' legs,
The cover of the wings of grasshoppers, 60
The traces of the smallest spider's web,
The collars of the moonshine's watery beams,
Her whip of cricket's bone, the lash of film,
Her waggoner a small grey-coated gnat,
Not half so big as a round little worm 65
Prick'd from the lazy finger of a maid;
Her chariot is an empty hazel-nut
Made by the joiner squirrel or old grub,
Time out o' mind the fairies' coachmakers.
And in this state she gallops night by night 70
Through lovers' brains, and then they dream of love;
O'er courtiers' knees, that dream on court'sies straight,
O'er lawyers' fingers, who straight dream on fees,
O'er ladies' lips, who straight on kisses dream,
Which oft the angry Mab with blisters plagues, 75
Because their breaths with sweetmeats tainted are:
Sometime she gallops o'er a courtier's nose,
And then dreams he of smelling out a suit;
And sometime comes she with a tithe-pig's tail
Tickling a parson's nose as a' lies asleep, 80
Then dreams he of another benefice:
Sometime she driveth o'er a soldier's neck,
And then dreams he of cutting foreign throats,
Of breaches, ambuscadoes, Spanish blades,
Of healths five-fathom deep; and then anon 85
Drums in his ear, at which he starts and wakes,
And being thus frighted swears a prayer or two
And sleeps again. This is that very Mab
That plats the manes of horses in the night,
And bakes the elf-locks in foul sluttish hairs, 90
Which once untangled much misfortune bodes:
This is the hag, when maids lie on their backs,
That presses them and learns them first to bear,
Making them women of good carriage:
This is she—

ROM. Peace, peace, Mercutio, peace! 95
Thou talk'st of nothing.

MER. True, I talk of dreams,
Which are the children of an idle brain,
Begot of nothing but vain fantasy,
Which is as thin of substance as the air
And more inconstant than the wind, who wooes 100
Even now the frozen bosom of the north,
And, being anger'd, puffs away from thence,
Turning his face to the dew-dropping south.

BEN. This wind, you talk of, blows us from ourselves;
Supper is done, and we shall come too late.

ROM. I fear, too early: for my mind misgives 106
Some consequence yet hanging in the stars
Shall bitterly begin his fearful date
With this night's revels, and expire the term
Of a despisèd life clos'd in my breast 110
By some vile forfeit of untimely death.
But He that hath the steerage of my course
Direct my sail! On, lusty gentlemen!

BEN. Strike, drum.

[*Exeunt.*

47. **five wits,** five faculties of the mind: common sense, imagination, fantasy, judgment, and reason. 53. **Mab,** a Celtic name for the Queen of the Fairies. 55. **agate-stone,** large seal ring. 57. **atomies,** mites, tiny animals. 59. **spinners,** spiders. 61. **traces,** harness. 63. **film,** gossamer. 64. **waggoner,** coachman. 65-66. **worm . . . maid,** alludes to superstition that "worms breed in the fingers of the idle."

78. **suit,** (1) petition for favor (2) fine clothes. 79. **tithe-pig,** every tenth pig paid to the parson as his due. 89. **plats,** plaits. 90. **elf-locks,** tangled hair. Allusion to the superstition that tangles in a horse's mane were "witches' stirrups." 98. **vain,** foolish. 108. **date,** time. 109-110. **expire . . . life,** cause the lease of my despised life to end.

SCENE V. *A hall in Capulet's house.*

[MUSICIANS *waiting. Enter* SERVINGMEN, *with napkins.*]

FIRST SERV. Where's Potpan, that he helps not to take away? He shift a trencher? he scrape a trencher!

SEC. SERV. When good manners shall lie all in one or two men's hands and they unwashed too, 'tis a foul thing. 6

FIRST SERV. Away with the joint-stools, remove the court-cupboard, look to the plate. Good thou, save me a piece of marchpane; and, as thou lovest me, let the porter let in Susan Grindstone and Nell, Antony, and Potpan! 11

SEC. SERV. Ay, boy, ready.

FIRST SERV. You are looked for and called for, asked for and sought for, in the great chamber.

SEC. SERV. We cannot be here and there too. 15
Cheerly, boys; be brisk awhile, and the longer liver take all.

[*Enter* CAPULET, *with* JULIET *and others of his house, meeting the* GUESTS *and* MASKERS.]

CAP. Welcome, gentlemen! ladies that have their toes
Unplagued with corns will have a bout with you.
Ah ha, my mistresses! which of you all 20
Will now deny to dance? she that makes dainty,
She, I'll swear, hath corns; am I come near ye now?
Welcome, gentlemen! I have seen the day
That I have worn a visor and could tell
A whispering tale in a fair lady's ear, 25
Such as would please: 'tis gone, 'tis gone, 'tis gone:
You are welcome, gentlemen! Come, musicians, play.
A hall, a hall! give room! and foot it, girls.
[*Music plays, and they dance.*]
More light, you knaves; and turn the tables up,
And quench the fire, the room is grown too hot. 30
Ah, sirrah, this unlook'd-for sport comes well.
Nay, sit, nay, sit, good cousin Capulet;
For you and I are past our dancing days:
How long is 't now since last yourself and I
Were in a mask?

SEC. CAP. By 'r lady, thirty years. 35

CAP. What, man! 'tis not so much, 'tis not so much:
'Tis since the nuptial of Lucentio,
Come pentecost as quickly as it will,
Some five and twenty years; and then we mask'd.

SEC. CAP. 'Tis more, 'tis more: his son is elder, sir; 40
His son is thirty.

CAP. Will you tell me that?
His son was but a ward two years ago.

ROM. [*To a* SERVINGMAN] What lady is that, which doth enrich the hand
Of yonder knight?

SERV. I know not, sir. 45

ROM. O, she doth teach the torches to burn bright!
It seems she hangs upon the cheek of night
Like a rich jewel in an Ethiope's ear;
Beauty too rich for use, for earth too dear!
So shows a snowy dove trooping with crows,
As yonder lady o'er her fellows shows. 51
The measure done, I'll watch her place of stand,
And, touching hers, make blessèd my rude hand.
Did my heart love till now? forswear it, sight!
For I ne'er saw true beauty till this night. 55

TYB. This, by his voice, should be a Montague.
Fetch me my rapier, boy. What dares the slave
Come hither, cover'd with an antic face,
To fleer and scorn at our solemnity?
Now, by the stock and honour of my kin, 60
To strike him dead I hold it not a sin.

CAP. Why, how now, kinsman! wherefore storm you so?

TYB. Uncle, this is a Montague, our foe,
A villain that is hither come in spite,
To scorn at our solemnity this night. 65

CAP. Young Romeo is it?

TYB. 'Tis he, that villain Romeo.

CAP. Content thee, gentle coz, let him alone;

Scene v: 3. **trencher**, wooden plate. 7. **joint-stools**, stools made by a joiner. 8. **court-cupboard**, sideboard. 9. **marchpane**, a confection made of sugar and almonds. 16. **longer liver**, last survivor. 19. **have a bout**, dance a figure. 21. **makes dainty**, hesitates from shyness. 28. **a hall**, clear the floor (of the hall) for dancing. 29. **turn the tables up**, take the tables off the trestles and fold them up. 38. **pentecost**, seventh Sunday after Advent, i.e., Whitsunday. 58. **antic face**, fantastic mask. 59. **fleer**, sneer; **solemnity**, celebration, party.

He bears him like a portly gentleman;
And, to say truth, Verona brags of him
To be a virtuous and well govern'd youth: 70
I would not for the wealth of all the town
Here in my house do him disparagement:
Therefore be patient, take no note of him:
It is my will, the which if thou respect,
Show a fair presence and put off these frowns,
An ill-beseeming semblance for a feast. 76

TYB. It fits, when such a villain is a guest:
I'll not endure him.

CAP. He shall be endured:
What, goodman boy! I say, he shall: go to;
Am I the master here, or you? go to. 80
You'll not endure him! God shall mend my soul!
You'll make a mutiny among my guests!
You will set cock-a-hoop! you'll be the man!

TYB. Why, uncle, 'tis a shame.

CAP. Go to, go to;
You are a saucy boy: is 't so, indeed? 85
This trick may chance to scathe you, I know what:
You must contrary me! marry, 'tis time.
Well said, my hearts! You are a princox; go:
Be quiet, or—More light, more light! For shame!
I'll make you quiet. What, cheerly, my hearts!

TYB. Patience perforce with wilful choler meeting 91
Makes my flesh tremble in their different greeting.
I will withdraw: but this intrusion shall
Now seeming sweet convert to bitter gall.
[*Exit.*

ROM. [*To* JULIET] If I profane with my unworthiest hand 95
This holy shrine, the gentle fine is this:
My lips, two blushing pilgrims, ready stand
To smooth that rough touch with a tender kiss.

JUL. Good pilgrim, you do wrong your hand too much,
Which mannerly devotion shows in this;
For saints have hands that pilgrims' hands do touch, 101
And palm to palm is holy palmers' kiss.

ROM. Have not saints lips, and holy palmers too?

JUL. Ay, pilgrim, lips that they must use in prayer.

ROM. O, then, dear saint, let lips do what hands do; 105
They pray, grant thou, lest faith turn to despair.

JUL. Saints do not move, though grant for prayers' sake.

ROM. Then move not, while my prayer's effect I take.
Thus from my lips, by yours, my sin is purged.

JUL. Then have my lips the sin that they have took. 110

ROM. Sin from my lips? O trespass sweetly urged!
Give me my sin again.

JUL. You kiss by the book.

NURSE. Madam, your mother craves a word with you.

ROM. What is her mother?

NURSE. Marry, bachelor,
Her mother is the lady of the house, 115
And a good lady, and a wise and virtuous:
I nursed her daughter, that you talk'd withal;
I tell you, he that can lay hold of her
Shall have the chinks.

ROM. Is she a Capulet?
O dear account! my life is my foe's debt. 120

BEN. Away, be gone; the sport is at the best.

ROM. Ay, so I fear; the more is my unrest.

CAP. Nay, gentlemen, prepare not to be gone;
We have a trifling foolish banquet towards.
Is it e'en so? why, then, I thank you all; 125
I thank you, honest gentlemen; good night.
More torches here! Come on then, let's to bed.
Ah, sirrah, by my fay, it waxes late:
I'll to my rest.
[*Exeunt all but* JULIET *and* NURSE.

JUL. Come hither, nurse. What is yond gentleman? 130

NURSE. The son and heir of old Tiberio.

JUL. What's he that now is going out of door?

68. **portly**, dignified. 72. **do . . . disparagement**, disgrace him. 79. **goodman boy**, a doubly insulting phrase. Goodman was a term applied to a person below the rank of gentleman; boy = youngster. 83. **cock-a-hoop**, everything in disorder. 88. **princox**, impertinent boy. 91. **patience perforce**, patience forced upon me. 94. **convert**, change to. 95-108. **If I profane . . . effect I take**, these lines form a Shakespearean sonnet. 99. **pilgrim**. Romeo was disguised as a pilgrim or palmer. 107. **move**, take the initiative. 112. **by the book**, according to rule. 119. **chinks**, money. 120. **my foe's debt**, due to my foe, i.e., because he loves Juliet he is at the mercy of his foe Capulet. 124. **foolish**, trivial; **banquet**, refreshments of fruit, wine, and candy; **towards**, ready to be served. 125. **Is it e'en so?** Do you insist on leaving? 128. **fay**, faith. 132. **What's**, who is.

NURSE. Marry, that, I think, be young Petrucio.

JUL. What's he that follows there, that would not dance?

NURSE. I know not. 135

JUL. Go, ask his name: if he be married,
My grave is like to be my wedding bed.

NURSE. His name is Romeo, and a Montague;
The only son of your great enemy.

JUL. My only love sprung from my only hate! 140
Too early seen unknown, and known too late!
Prodigious birth of love it is to me,
That I must love a loathèd enemy.

NURSE. What's this? what's this?

JUL. A rhyme I learn'd even now
Of one I danced withal. [*One calls within "Juliet."*

NURSE. Anon, anon! 145
Come, let's away; the strangers all are gone. [*Exeunt.*

ACT II

PROLOGUE

[*Enter* CHORUS.]

CHOR. Now old desire doth in his deathbed lie,
And young affection gapes to be his heir;
That fair for which love groan'd for and would die,
With tender Juliet match'd, is now not fair.
Now Romeo is beloved and loves again, 5
Alike bewitchèd by the charm of looks,
But to his foe supposed he must complain,
And she steal love's sweet bait from fearful hooks:
Being held a foe, he may not have access
To breathe such vows as lovers use to swear; 10
And she as much in love, her means much less
To meet her new-beloved any where:
But passion lends them power, time means, to meet,
Tempering extremities with extreme sweet. [*Exit.*

SCENE I. *A lane by the wall of Capulet's orchard.*

[*Enter* ROMEO.]

ROM. Can I go forward when my heart is here?
Turn back, dull earth, and find thy centre out.
[*He climbs the wall, and leaps down within it.*

[*Enter* BENVOLIO *and* MERCUTIO.]

BEN. Romeo! my cousin Romeo!

MER. He is wise;
And, on my life, hath stol'n him home to bed.

BEN. He ran this way, and leap'd this orchard wall: 5
Call, good Mercutio.

MER. Nay, I'll conjure too.
Romeo! humours! madman! passion! lover!
Appear thou in the likeness of a sigh:
Speak but one rhyme, and I am satisfied;
Cry but "Ay me!" pronounce but "love" and "dove;" 10
Speak to my gossip Venus one fair word,
One nick-name for her purblind son and heir,
Young Adam Cupid, he that shot so trim,
When King Cophetua loved the beggar-maid!
He heareth not, he stirreth not, he moveth not;
The ape is dead, and I must conjure him. 16
I conjure thee by Rosaline's bright eyes,
By her high forehead and her scarlet lip,
By her fine foot, straight leg and quivering thigh
And the demesnes that there adjacent lie, 20
That in thy likeness thou appear to us!

BEN. An if he hear thee, thou wilt anger him.

MER. This cannot anger him: 'twould anger him

142. prodigious, portentous, ominous. 145. Anon, right away. Act II, Prologue: 1. old desire, Romeo's love for Rosaline. 10. use to, are accustomed to. Scene i: s.d. orchard, garden. 2. dull earth, Romeo's body; centre, i.e., Juliet. 6. conjure, call up a spirit. 11. gossip, intimate friend. 12. purblind, very blind. 13. Adam, probably a reference to Adam Bell, the famous archer of the ballads; trim, strongly. 14. Cophetua, a reference to the following lines in the ballad King Cophetua and the Beggar Maid:

> The blinded boy that shoots so trim
> From heaven down did hie,
> He drew a dart and shot at him
> In place where he did lie.

20. demesnes, regions.

To raise a spirit in his mistress' circle
Of some strange nature, letting it there stand
Till she had laid it and conjured it down; 26
That were some spite: my invocation
Is fair and honest, and in his mistress' name
I conjure only but to raise up him.

BEN. Come, he hath hid himself among these trees, 30
To be consorted with the humorous night:
Blind is his love and best befits the dark.

MER. If love be blind, love cannot hit the mark.
Now will he sit under a medlar tree, 34
And wish his mistress were that kind of fruit
As maids call medlars, when they laugh alone.
O, Romeo, that she were, O, that she were
An open et cætera, thou a poperin pear!
Romeo, good night: I'll to my truckle-bed;
This field-bed is too cold for me to sleep: 40
Come, shall we go?

BEN. Go, then; for 'tis in vain
To seek him here that means not to be found.
[*Exeunt.*

SCENE II. *Capulet's orchard.*

[*Enter* ROMEO.]

ROM. He jests at scars that never felt a wound.

[JULIET *appears above at a window.*]

But, soft! what light through yonder window breaks?
It is the east, and Juliet is the sun.
Arise, fair sun, and kill the envious moon,
Who is already sick and pale with grief, 5
That thou her maid art far more fair than she:
Be not her maid, since she is envious;
Her vestal livery is but sick and green
And none but fools do wear it; cast it off.
It is my lady, O, it is my love! 10
O, that she knew she were!
She speaks, yet she says nothing: what of that?
Her eye discourses; I will answer it.
I am too bold, 'tis not to me she speaks:
Two of the fairest stars in all the heaven, 15
Having some business, do entreat her eyes
To twinkle in their spheres till they return.
What if her eyes were there, they in her head?
The brightness of her cheek would shame those stars,
As daylight doth a lamp; her eyes in heaven 20
Would through the airy region stream so bright
That birds would sing and think it were not night.
See, how she leans her cheek upon her hand!
O, that I were a glove upon that hand,
That I might touch that cheek!

JUL. Ay me!

ROM. She speaks: 25
O, speak again, bright angel! for thou art
As glorious to this night, being o'er my head,
As is a wingèd messenger of heaven
Unto the white-upturnèd wondering eyes
Of mortals that fall back to gaze on him 30
When he bestrides the lazy-pacing clouds
And sails upon the bosom of the air.

JUL. O Romeo, Romeo! wherefore art thou Romeo?
Deny thy father and refuse thy name;
Or, if thou wilt not, be but sworn my love, 35
And I'll no longer be a Capulet.

ROM. [*Aside*] Shall I hear more, or shall I speak at this?

JUL. 'Tis but thy name that is my enemy;
Thou art thyself, though not a Montague.
What's Montague? it is nor hand, nor foot, 40
Nor arm, nor face, nor any other part
Belonging to a man. O, be some other name!
What's in a name? that which we call a rose
By any other name would smell as sweet;
So Romeo would, were he not Romeo call'd, 45
Retain that dear perfection which he owes
Without that title. Romeo, doff thy name,
And for that name which is no part of thee
Take all myself.

ROM. I take thee at thy word:
Call me but love, and I'll be new baptized; 50
Henceforth I never will be Romeo.

JUL. What man art thou that thus bescreen'd in night
So stumblest on my counsel?

ROM. By a name
I know not how to tell thee who I am:
My name, dear saint, is hateful to myself, 55
Because it is an enemy to thee;
Had I it written, I would tear the word.

27. spite, vexation, annoyance. 28. honest, chaste. 31. consorted with, an associate of; humorous, damp. 38. poperin pear, a cant term for male genitals. 39. truckle-bed, a small low bed shoved under an ordinary bed. 40. field-bed, large bed, i.e., the ground. Scene ii: 5. sick, of sickly color. 8. vestal livery, virgin's costume. 46. owes, owns. 53. counsel, intimate thoughts.

JUL. My ears have not yet drunk a hundred words
Of that tongue's utterance, yet I know the sound:
Art thou not Romeo and a Montague? 60
ROM. Neither, fair saint, if either thee dislike.
JUL. How camest thou hither, tell me, and wherefore?
The orchard walls are high and hard to climb,
And the place death, considering who thou art,
If any of my kinsmen find thee here. 65
ROM. With love's light wings did I o'er-perch these walls;
For stony limits cannot hold love out,
And what love can do that dares love attempt;
Therefore thy kinsmen are no let to me.
JUL. If they do see thee, they will murder thee. 70
ROM. Alack, there lies more peril in thine eye
Than twenty of their swords: look thou but sweet,
And I am proof against their enmity.
JUL. I would not for the world they saw thee here.
ROM. I have night's cloak to hide me from their sight; 75
And but thou love me, let them find me here:
My life were better ended by their hate,
Than death proroguèd, wanting of thy love.
JUL. By whose direction found'st thou out this place?
ROM. By love, who first did prompt me to inquire; 80
He lent me counsel and I lent him eyes.
I am no pilot; yet, wert thou as far
As that vast shore wash'd with the farthest sea,
I would adventure for such merchandise.
JUL. Thou know'st the mask of night is on my face, 85
Else would a maiden blush bepaint my cheek
For that which thou hast heard me speak to-night.
Fain would I dwell on form, fain, fain deny
What I have spoke: but farewell compliment!
Dost thou love me? I know thou wilt say "Ay." 90
And I will take thy word: yet, if thou swear'st,
Thou mayst prove false; at lovers' perjuries,
They say, Jove laughs. O gentle Romeo,
If thou dost love, pronounce it faithfully:
Or if thou think'st I am too quickly won, 95
I'll frown and be perverse and say thee nay,
So thou wilt woo; but else, not for the world.
In truth, fair Montague, I am too fond,
And therefore thou mayst think my 'haviour light:
But trust me, gentleman, I'll prove more true
Than those that have more cunning to be strange. 101
I should have been more strange, I must confess,
But that thou overheard'st, ere I was ware,
My true love's passion; therefore pardon me,
And not impute this yielding to light love, 105
Which the dark night hath so discovered.
ROM. Lady, by yonder blessed moon I swear
That tips with silver all these fruit-tree tops—
JUL. O, swear not by the moon, the inconstant moon,
That monthly changes in her circled orb, 110
Lest that thy love prove likewise variable.
ROM. What shall I swear by?
JUL. Do not swear at all;
Or, if thou wilt, swear by thy gracious self,
Which is the god of my idolatry,
And I'll believe thee.
ROM. If my heart's dear love—
JUL. Well, do not swear: although I joy in thee, 116
I have no joy of this contract to-night:
It is too rash, too unadvised, too sudden;
Too like the lightning, which doth cease to be
Ere one can say "It lightens." Sweet, good night! 120
This bud of love, by summer's ripening breath,
May prove a beauteous flower when next we meet.
Good night, good night! as sweet repose and rest
Come to thy heart as that within my breast!
ROM. O, wilt thou leave me so unsatisfied?
JUL. What satisfaction canst thou have to-night? 126
ROM. The exchange of thy love's faithful vow for mine.

61. dislike, displease. 66. o'er-perch, fly over and perch beyond. 73. proof, protected by armor. 76. And but, if only. 78. prorogued, postponed; wanting of, lacking.

89. compliment, ceremony. 94. pronounce it, say so. 101. strange, reserved. 110. orb, sphere. 117. contract, betrothal.

JUL. I gave thee mine before thou didst request it:
And yet I would it were to give again.
ROM. Wouldst thou withdraw it? for what purpose, love? 130
JUL. But to be frank, and give it thee again.
And yet I wish but for the thing I have:
My bounty is as boundless as the sea,
My love as deep; the more I give to thee,
The more I have, for both are infinite. 135
[NURSE *calls within.*]
I hear some noise within; dear love, adieu!
Anon, good nurse! Sweet Montague, be true.
Stay but a little, I will come again.
[*Exit, above.*
ROM. O blessèd, blessèd night! I am afeard,
Being in night, all this is but a dream, 140
Too flattering-sweet to be substantial.

[*Re-enter* JULIET, *above.*]

JUL. Three words, dear Romeo, and good night indeed.
If that thy bent of love be honourable,
Thy purpose marriage, send me word to-morrow, 144
By one that I'll procure to come to thee,
Where and what time thou wilt perform the rite;
And all my fortunes at thy foot I'll lay
And follow thee my lord throughout the world.
NURSE. [*Within*] Madam!
JUL. I come, anon.—But if thou mean'st not well, 150
I do beseech thee—
NURSE [*Within*] Madam!
JUL. By and by, I come:—
To cease thy suit, and leave me to my grief:
To-morrow will I send.
ROM. So thrive my soul—
JUL. A thousand times good night! 155
[*Exit, above.*
ROM. A thousand times the worse, to want thy light.
Love goes toward love, as schoolboys from their books,
But love from love, toward school with heavy looks. [*Retiring.*

[*Re-enter* JULIET, *above.*]

JUL. Hist! Romeo, hist! O, for a falconer's voice,
To lure this tassel-gentle back again! 160
Bondage is hoarse, and may not speak aloud;
Else would I tear the cave where Echo lies,
And make her airy tongue more hoarse than mine,
With repetition of my Romeo's name.
ROM. It is my soul that calls upon my name:
How silver-sweet sound lovers' tongues by night, 166
Like softest music to attending ears!
JUL. Romeo!
ROM. My dear?
JUL. At what o'clock to-morrow
Shall I send to thee?
ROM. At the hour of nine.
JUL. I will not fail: 'tis twenty years till then. 170
I have forgot why I did call thee back.
ROM. Let me stand here till thou remember it.
JUL. I shall forget, to have thee still stand there,
Remembering how I love thy company.
ROM. And I'll still stay, to have thee still forget, 175
Forgetting any other home but this.
JUL. 'Tis almost morning; I would have thee gone:
And yet no further than a wanton's bird;
Who lets it hop a little from her hand,
Like a poor prisoner in his twisted gyves, 180
And with a silk thread plucks it back again,
So loving-jealous of his liberty.
ROM. I would I were thy bird.
JUL. Sweet, so would I:
Yet I should kill thee with much cherishing.
Good night, good night! parting is such sweet sorrow, 185
That I shall say good night till it be morrow.
[*Exit, above.*
ROM. Sleep dwell upon thine eyes, peace in thy breast!
Would I were sleep and peace, so sweet to rest!
Hence will I to my ghostly father's cell,
His help to crave, and my dear hap to tell. 190
[*Exit.*

131. frank, generous. **143. bent of love,** purpose of your love. **152. by and by,** at once. **160. tassel-gentle,** male hawk. **161. bondage is hoarse,** i.e., because of being imprisoned by my parents I must whisper. **175. still stay,** continues to stay. **178. wanton's,** spoiled child's. **180. gyves,** shackles. **189. ghostly,** spiritual. **190. dear hap,** good fortune.

SCENE III. FRIAR LAURENCE'S *cell.*

[*Enter* FRIAR LAURENCE, *with a basket.*]

FRI. L. The grey-eyed morn smiles on the frowning night,
Chequering the eastern clouds with streaks of light,
And flecked darkness like a drunkard reels
From forth day's path and Titan's fiery wheels:
Now, ere the sun advance his burning eye, 5
The day to cheer and night's dank dew to dry,
I must up-fill this osier cage of ours
With baleful weeds and precious-juiced flowers.
The earth that's nature's mother is her tomb;
What is her burying grave that is her womb, 10
And from her womb children of divers kind
We sucking on her natural bosom find,
Many for many virtues excellent,
None but for some and yet all different.
O, mickle is the powerful grace that lies 15
In herbs, plants, stones, and their true qualities:
For nought so vile that on the earth doth live
But to the earth some special good doth give,
Nor aught so good but strain'd from that fair use
Revolts from true birth, stumbling on abuse:
Virtue itself turns vice, being misapplied; 21
And vice sometimes by action dignified.
Within the infant rind of this small flower
Poison hath residence and medicine power:
For this, being smelt, with that part cheers each part; 25
Being tasted, slays all senses with the heart.
Two such opposed kings encamp them still
In man as well as herbs, grace and rude will;
And where the worser is predominant,
Full soon the canker death eats up that plant. 30

[*Enter* ROMEO.]

ROM. Good morrow, father.
FRI. L. Benedicite!
What early tongue so sweet saluteth me?
Young son, it argues a distemper'd head
So soon to bid good morrow to thy bed:
Care keeps his watch in every old man's eye,
And where care lodges, sleep will never lie; 36
But where unbruised youth with unstuff'd brain
Doth couch his limbs, there golden sleep doth reign:
Therefore thy earliness doth me assure
Thou art up-roused by some distemperature;
Or if not so, then here I hit it right, 41
Our Romeo hath not been in bed to-night.
ROM. That last is true; the sweeter rest was mine.
FRI. L. God pardon sin! wast thou with Rosaline? 44
ROM. With Rosaline, my ghostly father? no;
I have forgot that name, and that name's woe.
FRI. L. That's my good son: but where hast thou been, then?
ROM. I'll tell thee, ere thou ask it me again.
I have been feasting with mine enemy,
Where on a sudden one hath wounded me, 50
That's by me wounded: both our remedies
Within thy help and holy physic lies:
I bear no hatred, blessed man, for, lo,
My intercession likewise steads my foe.
FRI. L. Be plain, good son, and homely in thy drift; 55
Riddling confession finds but riddling shrift.
ROM. Then plainly know my heart's dear love is set
On the fair daughter of rich Capulet:
As mine on hers, so hers is set on mine;
And all combined, save what thou must combine 60
By holy marriage: when and where and how
We met, we woo'd and made exchange of vow,
I'll tell thee as we pass; but this I pray,
That thou consent to marry us to-day.
FRI. L. Holy Saint Francis, what a change is here! 65
Is Rosaline, whom thou didst love so dear,
So soon forsaken? young men's love then lies
Not truly in their hearts, but in their eyes.
Jesu Maria, what a deal of brine 69
Hath wash'd thy sallow cheeks for Rosaline!
How much salt water thrown away in waste,
To season love, that of it doth not taste!
The sun not yet thy sighs from heaven clears
Thy old groans ring yet in my ancient ears;
Lo, here upon thy cheek the stain doth sit 75

Scene iii: 2. chequering, variegating. 3. flecked, dappled. 7. osier cage, wicker basket. 15. mickle, much. 25. that part, i.e., the smell. 28. grace, i.e., divine grace. 30. canker, canker-worm. 33. distemper'd, diseased. 37. unstuff'd, not overloaded (with humors). 52. physic, art of healing. 54. steads, aids. 55. homely . . . drift, i.e., say what you mean simply. 56. shrift, absolution. 72. season, keep fresh as by salting.

Of an old tear that is not wash'd off yet:
If e'er thou wast thyself and these woes thine,
Thou and these woes were all for Rosaline:
And art thou changed? pronounce this sentence then,
Women may fall, when there's no strength in men. 80

ROM. Thou chid'st me oft for loving Rosaline.

FRI. L. For doting, not for loving, pupil mine.

ROM. And bad'st me bury love.

FRI. L. Not in a grave,
To lay one in, another out to have.

ROM. I pray thee, chide not: she whom I love now 85
Doth grace for grace and love for love allow;
The other did not so.

FRI. L. O, she knew well
Thy love did read by rote and could not spell.
But come, young waverer, come, go with me,
In one respect I'll thy assistant be; 90
For this alliance may so happy prove,
To turn your household's rancour to pure love.

ROM. O, let us hence; I stand on sudden haste.

FRI. L. Wisely and slow; they stumble that run fast. [*Exeunt.*

SCENE IV. *A street.*

[*Enter* BENVOLIO *and* MERCUTIO.]

MER. Where the devil should this Romeo be?
Came he not home to-night?

BEN. Not to his father's; I spoke with his man.

MER. Ah, that same pale hard-hearted wench, that Rosaline,
Torments him so, that he will sure run mad. 5

BEN. Tybalt, the kinsman of old Capulet,
Hath sent a letter to his father's house.

MER. A challenge, on my life.

BEN. Romeo will answer it.

MER. Any man that can write may answer a letter. 10

BEN. Nay, he will answer the letter's master, how he dares, being dared.

MER. Alas, poor Romeo! he is already dead; stabbed with a white wench's black eye; shot thorough the ear with a love-song; the very pin of his heart cleft with the blind bow-boy's butt-shaft: and is he a man to encounter Tybalt? 17

BEN. Why, what is Tybalt?

MER. More than prince of cats, I can tell you. O, he is the courageous captain of compliments. He fights as you sing prick-song, keeps time, distance, and proportion; rests me his minim rest, one, two, and the third in your bosom: the very butcher of a silk button, a duellist, a duellist; a gentleman of the very first house, of the first and second cause: ah, the immortal passado! the punto reverso! the hai! 27

BEN. The what?

MER. The pox of such antic, lisping, affecting fantasticoes; these new tuners of accents! "By Jesu, a very good blade! a very tall man! a very good whore!" Why, is not this a lamentable thing, grandsire, that we should be thus afflicted with these strange flies, these fashion-mongers, these perdonami's, who stand so much on the new form, that they cannot sit at ease on the old bench? O, their bones, their bones! 37

[*Enter* ROMEO.]

BEN. Here comes Romeo, here comes Romeo. 38

MER. Without his roe, like a dried herring: O flesh, flesh, how art thou fishified! Now is he for the numbers that Petrarch flowed in: Laura to his lady was but a kitchen-wench; marry, she had a better love to be-rhyme her; Dido a dowdy; Cleopatra a gipsy; Helen and Hero hildings and harlots; Thisbe a grey 45 eye or so, but not to the purpose. Signior

88. **by rote,** by repeating of conventional expressions. 79. **sentence,** maxim. 93. **stand on,** insist upon. Scene iv: 12. **dared,** challenged. 16. **pin,** center of the target. 17. **butt-shaft,** blunt arrow used for shooting at a target. 19. **prince of cats,** the name of the cat in the beast epic of Reynard the Fox was Tibert or Tybalt. 20. **captain of compliments,** master of ceremony or ritual. 21. **prick-song,** music sung from notes. 22. **proportion,** rhythm. 23. **minim,** half rest. 26. **first house,** best school; **first and second cause,** recognized justifications for quarreling according to the code of dueling. 27. **passado,** forward thrust; **punto reverso,** backhanded stroke; **hai,** home thrust. 30. **fantasticoes,** affected fellows. 35. **perdonami's,** affected users of foreign terms. 36. **form,** (1) fashion, (2) bench. 37. **bones,** pun on (1) French "bon" and (2) English "bone." 39. **without his roe,** i.e., without the "Ro" of Romeo, so leaving "meo," an exclamation of woe. 41. **Petrarch,** an Italian poet of the fourteenth century, the founder of the sonnet vogue. 42. **Laura,** the woman to whom he addressed his poems. 45. **hildings,** good for nothings.

Romeo, bon jour! there's a French salutation to your French slop. You gave us the counterfeit fairly last night.

ROM. Good morrow to you both. What counterfeit did I give you? 50

MER. The slip, sir, the slip; can you not conceive?

ROM. Pardon, good Mercutio, my business was great; and in such a case as mine a man may strain courtesy. 55

MER. That's as much as to say, such a case as yours constrains a man to bow in the hams.

ROM. Meaning, to court'sy.

MER. Thou hast most kindly hit it.

ROM. A most courteous exposition. 60

MER. Nay, I am the very pink of courtesy.

ROM. Pink for flower.

MER. Right.

ROM. Why, then is my pump well flowered. 64

MER. Well said: follow me this jest now till thou hast worn out thy pump, that when the single sole of it is worn, the jest may remain after the wearing sole singular.

ROM. O single-soled jest, solely singular for the singleness! 70

MER. Come between us, good Benvolio; my wits faint.

ROM. Switch and spurs, switch and spurs; or I'll cry a match.

MER. Nay, if thy wits run the wild-goose 75 chase, I have done, for thou hast more of the wild-goose in one of thy wits than, I am sure, I have in my whole five: was I with you there for the goose?

ROM. Thou wast never with me for any thing when thou wast not there for the goose. 80

MER. I will bite thee by the ear for that jest.

ROM. Nay, good goose, bite not.

MER. Thy wit is a very bitter sweeting; it is a most sharp sauce.

ROM. And is it not well served in to a sweet goose? 86

MER. O, here's a wit of cheveril, that stretches from an inch narrow to an ell broad!

ROM. I stretch it out for that word "broad;" which added to the goose, proves thee far and wide a broad goose. 91

MER. Why, is not this better now than groaning for love? now art thou sociable, now art thou Romeo; now art thou what thou art, by art as well as by nature; for this drivelling love is like a great natural, that runs lolling up and down to hide his bauble in a hole.

BEN. Stop there, stop there.

MER. Thou desirest me stop in my tale against the hair. 100

BEN. Thou wouldst else have made thy tale large.

MER. O, thou art deceived; I would have made it short: for I was come to the whole depth of my tale; and meant, indeed, to occupy the argument no longer. 106

ROM. Here's goodly gear!

[*Enter* NURSE *and* PETER.]

MER. A sail, a sail!

BEN. Two, two; a shirt and a smock.

NURSE. Peter! 110

PETER. Anon!

NURSE. My fan, Peter.

MER. Good Peter, to hide her face; for her fan's the fairer face.

NURSE. God ye good morrow, gentlemen.

MER. God ye good den, fair gentlewoman.

NURSE. Is it good den? 117

MER. 'Tis no less, I tell you, for the bawdy hand of the dial is now upon the prick of noon.

NURSE. Out upon you! what a man are you!

ROM. One, gentlewoman, that God hath made for himself to mar.

NURSE. By my troth, it is well said; "for himself to mar," quoth a'? Gentlemen, can any of you tell me where I may find the young Romeo? 125

ROM. I can tell you; but young Romeo will be older when you have found him than he was when you sought him: I am the youngest of that name, for fault of a worse.

48. **slop,** large loose trousers. 51. **Slip,** counterfeit coins were called slips. 56. **case,** mask. 59. **kindly,** naturally, appropriately. 64. **pump well flowered,** the pump is pinked or perforated with ornamental design. 69. **single-soled,** contemptible, with a quibble on "soul." 70. **singleness,** silliness. 74. **cry a match,** claim to have won my bet. 75. **wild goose chase,** a horse race in which all must follow the leader wherever he goes. 81. **bite thee by the ear,** i.e., as a sign of affection (as horses do). 83. **sweeting,** pun on a kind of apple called a sweeting. 87. **cheveril,** leather of a kid. 88. **ell,** 45 inches. 91. **broad,** obvious. 96. **natural,** idiot. 97. **bauble,** fool's stick, ornamented with a fool's head or puppet, sometimes with an inflated bladder. 100. **against the hair,** against the grain. 102. **large,** licentious. 106. **occupy the argument,** treat the theme. 107. **gear,** matter, stuff. 119. **prick,** point of the dial on a clock.

NURSE. You say well. 130

MER. Yea, is the worst well? very well took, i' faith; wisely, wisely.

NURSE. If you be he, sir, I desire some confidence with you.

BEN. She will indite him to some supper.

MER. A bawd, a bawd, a bawd! So ho! 136

ROM. What hast thou found?

MER. No hare, sir; unless a hare, sir, in a lenten pie, that is something stale and hoar ere it be spent. [*Sings.*]

An old hare hoar, 141
And an old hare hoar,
Is very good meat in lent:
But a hare that is hoar
Is too much for a score, 145
When it hoars ere it be spent.

Romeo, will you come to your father's? we'll to dinner, thither.

ROM. I will follow you.

MER. Farewell, ancient lady; farewell, [*singing*] "lady, lady, lady." 151

[*Exeunt* MERCUTIO *and* BENVOLIO.

NURSE. Marry, farewell! I pray you, sir, what saucy merchant was this, that was so full of his ropery?

ROM. A gentleman, nurse, that loves to hear himself talk, and will speak more in a minute than he will stand to in a month. 157

NURSE. An a' speak any thing against me, I'll take him down, an a' were lustier than he is, and twenty such Jacks; and if I cannot, I'll find those that shall. Scurvy knave! I am none of his flirt-gills; I am none of his skains-mates. And thou must stand by too, and suffer every knave to use me at his pleasure? 164

PETER. I saw no man use you at his pleasure; if I had, my weapon should quickly have been out, I warrant you: I dare draw as soon as another man, if I see occasion in a good quarrel, and the law on my side. 169

NURSE. Now, afore God, I am so vexed, that every part about me quivers. Scurvy knave! Pray you, sir, a word: and as I told you, my young lady bade me inquire you out; what she bade me say, I will keep to myself: but first let me tell ye, if ye should lead 175 her into a fool's paradise, as they say, it were a very gross kind of behaviour, as they say: for the gentlewoman is young; and, therefore, if you should deal double with her, truly it were an ill thing to be offered to any gentlewoman, and very weak dealing. 181

ROM. Nurse, commend me to thy lady and mistress. I protest unto thee—

NURSE. Good heart, and, i' faith, I will tell her as much: Lord, Lord, she will be a joyful woman. 186

ROM. What wilt thou tell her, nurse? thou dost not mark me.

NURSE. I will tell her, sir, that you do protest; which, as I take it, is a gentlemanlike offer.

ROM. Bid her devise 191
Some means to come to shrift this afternoon;
And there she shall at Friar Laurence' cell
Be shrived and married. Here is for thy pains.

NURSE. No, truly, sir; not a penny.

ROM. Go to; I say you shall.

NURSE. This afternoon, sir? well, she shall be there.

ROM. And stay, good nurse, behind the abbey wall: 199
Within this hour my man shall be with thee,
And bring thee cords made like a tackled stair;
Which to the high top-gallant of my joy
Must be my convoy in the secret night.
Farewell; be trusty, and I'll quit thy pains:
Farewell; commend me to thy mistress. 205

NURSE. Now God in heaven bless thee! Hark you sir.

ROM. What say'st thou, my dear nurse?

NURSE. Is your man secret? Did you ne'er hear say,
Two may keep counsel, putting one away?

ROM. I warrant thee, my man's as true as steel. 210

NURSE. Well, sir; my mistress is the sweetest lady—Lord, Lord! when 'twas a little prating thing:—O, there is a nobleman in town, one Paris, that would fain lay knife

134. **confidence**, her mistake for "conference." 135. **indite**, his intentional mistake for "invite." 136. **So ho**, a hunter's cry when he sights a hare. 138. **hare**, slang for harlot. 139. **lenten**, i.e., meatless. 144. **hoar**, moldy, punning all the way through on "whore." 151. **lady, lady, lady**, from the ballad of Chaste Susanna. 153. **saucy merchant**, impudent fellow. 154. **ropery**, her mistake for "roguery." 160. **Jacks**, contemptuous for "fellows." 162. **flirt-gills**, loose women. 163. **skains-mates**, skains suggest sempstresses who had bad reputations. 181. **weak**, shifty.

183. **protest**, vow. 188. **mark**, pay attention to. 201. **tackled stair**, rope ladder; **stair**, series of steps. 202. **top-gallant**, i.e., the summit. A top gallant mast is the small mast attached to the fore and main masts. 203. **convoy**, conveyance. 204. **quit thy pains**, reward your trouble.

aboard; but she, good soul, had as lief see 215
a toad, a very toad, as see him. I anger her sometimes and tell her that Paris is the properer man; but, I'll warrant you, when I say so, she looks as pale as any clout in the versal world. Doth not rosemary and Romeo begin both with a letter? 220

ROM. Ay, nurse; what of that? both with an R.

NURSE. Ah, mocker! that's the dog's name; R is for the— No; I know it begins with some other letter:—and she hath the prettiest sententious of it, of you and rosemary, that it would do you good to hear it. 227

ROM. Commend me to thy lady.

NURSE. Ay, a thousand times.

[*Exit* ROMEO.]

Peter!

PET. Anon!

NURSE. Peter, take my fan, and go before, and apace. [*Exeunt.*

SCENE V. *Capulet's orchard.*

[*Enter* JULIET.]

JUL. The clock struck nine when I did send the nurse;
In half an hour she promised to return.
Perchance she cannot meet him: that's not so.
O, she is lame! love's heralds should be thoughts,
Which ten times faster glide than the sun's beams, 5
Driving back shadows over louring hills:
Therefore do nimble-pinion'd doves draw love,
And therefore hath the wind-swift Cupid wings.
Now is the sun upon the highmost hill
Of this day's journey, and from nine till twelve 10
Is three long hours, yet she is not come.
Had she affections and warm youthful blood,
She would be as swift in motion as a ball;
My words would bandy her to my sweet love,
And his to me: 15
But old folks, many feign as they were dead;
Unwieldy, slow, heavy and pale as lead.
O God, she comes!

[*Enter* NURSE *and* PETER.]

O honey nurse, what news?
Hast thou met with him? Send thy man away.

NURSE. Peter, stay at the gate. [*Exit* PETER.

JUL. Now, good sweet nurse,—O Lord, why look'st thou sad? 21
Though news be sad, yet tell them merrily;
If good, thou shamest the music of sweet news
By playing it to me with so sour a face.

NURSE. I am a-weary, give me leave awhile: 25
Fie, how my bones ache! what a jaunt have I had!

JUL. I would thou hadst my bones, and I thy news.
Nay, come, I pray thee, speak; good, good nurse, speak.

NURSE. Jesu, what haste? can you not stay awhile?
Do you not see that I am out of breath? 30

JUL. How art thou out of breath, when thou hast breath
To say to me that thou art out of breath?
The excuse that thou dost make in this delay
Is longer than the tale thou dost excuse.
Is thy news good, or bad? answer to that;
Say either, and I'll stay the circumstance:
Let me be satisfied, is't good or bad? 37

NURSE. Well, you have made a simple choice; you know not how to choose a man: Romeo! no, not he; though his face be better than any man's, yet his leg excels all men's; and for a hand, and a foot, and a body, though they be not to be talked on, yet they are past compare: he is not the flower of courtesy, but, I'll warrant him, as gentle as a lamb. Go thy ways, wench; serve God. What, have you dined at home? 46

JUL. No, no: but all this did I know before.
What says he of our marriage? what of that?

NURSE. Lord, how my head aches! what a head have I!
It beats as it would fall in twenty pieces. 50
My back o' t' other side,—O my back, my back!

217. properer, handsomer. 219. clout, rag; versal, universal. 220. rosemary, symbolizing remembrance; a, the same. 223. the dog's name; R, sounding like a growl, "R" was known as the dog's letter. 226. sententious, her mistake for "sentences," maxims. Scene v: 7. love, i.e., Venus, whose chariot was drawn by doves. 14. bandy, strike back and forth like a tennis ball. 21. sad, serious. 25. give me leave, let me alone. 36. stay the circumstance, wait for details. 38. simple, silly.

Beshrew your heart for sending me about,
To catch my death with jaunting up and down!

JUL. I' faith, I am sorry that thou art not well.
Sweet, sweet, sweet nurse, tell me, what says my love? 55

NURSE. Your love says, like an honest gentleman, and a courteous, and a kind, and a handsome, and, I warrant, a virtuous,— Where is your mother?

JUL. Where is my mother! why, she is within; 60
Where should she be? How oddly thou repliest!
"Your love says, like an honest gentleman,
Where is your mother?"

NURSE. O God's lady dear!
Are you so hot? marry, come up, I trow;
Is this the poultice for my aching bones? 65
Henceforward do your messages yourself.

JUL. Here's such a coil! come, what says Romeo?

NURSE. Have you got leave to go to shrift to-day?

JUL. I have.

NURSE. Then hie you hence to Friar Laurence' cell; 70
There stays a husband to make you a wife:
Now comes the wanton blood up in your cheeks,
They'll be in scarlet straight at any news.
Hie you to church; I must another way,
To fetch a ladder, by the which your love 75
Must climb a bird's nest soon when it is dark:
I am the drudge and toil in your delight,
But you shall bear the burden soon at night.
Go; I'll to dinner; hie you to the cell. 79

JUL. Hie to high fortune! Honest nurse, farewell. [*Exeunt.*

SCENE VI. FRIAR LAURENCE'S *cell.*

[*Enter* FRIAR LAURENCE *and* ROMEO.]

FRI. L. So smile the heavens upon this holy act,
That after hours with sorrow chide us not!

ROM. Amen, amen! but come what sorrow can,
It cannot countervail the exchange of joy
That one short minute gives me in her sight: 5
Do thou but close our hands with holy words,
Then love-devouring death do what he dare;
It is enough I may but call her mine.

FRI. L. These violent delights have violent ends
And in their triumph die, like fire and powder, 10
Which as they kiss consume: the sweetest honey
Is loathsome in his own deliciousness
And in the taste confounds the appetite:
Therefore love moderately; long love doth so;
Too swift arrives as tardy as too slow. 15

[*Enter* JULIET.]

Here comes the lady: O, so light a foot
Will ne'er wear out the everlasting flint:
A lover may bestride the gossamer
That idles in the wanton summer air,
And yet not fall; so light is vanity. 20

JUL. Good even to my ghostly confessor.

FRI. L. Romeo shall thank thee, daughter, for us both.

JUL. As much to him, else is his thanks too much.

ROM. Ah, Juliet, if the measure of thy joy
Be heap'ed like mine and that thy skill be more 25
To blazon it, then sweeten with thy breath
This neighbour air, and let rich music's tongue
Unfold the imagined happiness that both
Receive in either by this dear encounter.

JUL. Conceit, more rich in matter than in words, 30
Brags of his substance, not of ornament:
They are but beggars that can count their worth;
But my true love is grown to such excess
I cannot sum up sum of half my wealth.

FRI. L. Come, come with me, and we will make short work; 35
For, by your leaves, you shall not stay alone
Till holy church incorporate two in one.
[*Exeunt.*

52. beshrew, plague take or bad luck to. 53. jaunting, trudging wearily. 64. come up, an expression of impatience. 67. coil, fuss. 70. hie, hurry. 73. They'll . . . news, i.e., she blushes easily. Scene vi: 4. countervail, equal. 12. his, its. 13. confounds, destroys. 18. gossamer, floating threads of spiders' webs. 26. blazon, proclaim. 30. conceit, imagination, i.e., the imagination that is more rich, etc. 32. worth, wealth.

ACT III

SCENE I. *A public place.*

[*Enter* MERCUTIO, BENVOLIO, PAGE, *and* SERVANTS.]

BEN. I pray thee, good Mercutio, let's retire:
The day is hot, the Capulets abroad,
And, if we meet, we shall not scape a brawl;
For now, these hot days, is the mad blood stirring. 4

MER. Thou art like one of those fellows that when he enters the confines of a tavern claps me his sword upon the table and says "God send me no need of thee!" and by the operation of the second cup draws it on the drawer, when indeed there is no need. 10

BEN. Am I like such a fellow?

MER. Come, come, thou art as hot a Jack in thy mood as any in Italy, and as soon moved to be moody, and as soon moody to be moved.

BEN. And what to? 15

MER. Nay, an there were two such, we should have none shortly, for one would kill the other. Thou! why, thou wilt quarrel with a man that hath a hair more, or a hair less, in his beard, than thou hast: thou wilt quarrel with a man for cracking nuts, having no other reason but because thou hast hazel eyes: what eye but such an eye would spy out such a quarrel? Thy head is as full of quarrels as an egg is full of meat, and yet thy head hath been beaten as addle as an egg for quarrelling: thou hast quarrelled with a man for coughing in the street, because he hath wakened thy dog that hath lain asleep in the sun: didst thou not fall out with a tailor for wearing his new doublet before Easter? with another, for tying his new shoes with old riband? and yet thou wilt tutor me from quarrelling! 33

BEN. An I were so apt to quarrel as thou art, any man should buy the fee-simple of my life for an hour and a quarter.

MER. The fee simple! O simple!

BEN. By my head, here come the Capulets.

MER. By my heel, I care not.

[*Enter* TYBALT *and others.*]

TYB. Follow me close, for I will speak to them. 40
Gentlemen, good den: a word with one of you.

MER. And but one word with one of us? couple it with something; make it a word and a blow.

TYB. You shall find me apt enough to that, sir, an you will give me occasion.

MER. Could you not take some occasion without giving?

TYB. Mercutio, thou consort'st with Romeo,— 47

MER. Consort! what, dost thou make us minstrels? an thou make minstrels of us, look to hear nothing but discords: here's my fiddlestick; here's that shall make you dance. 'Zounds, consort! 52

BEN. We talk here in the public haunt of men:
Either withdraw unto some private place,
And reason coldly of your grievances, 55
Or else depart; here all eyes gaze on us.

MER. Men's eyes were made to look, and let them gaze;
I will not budge for no man's pleasure, I.

[*Enter* ROMEO.]

TYB. Well, peace be with you, sir: here comes my man.

MER. But I'll be hang'd, sir, if he wear your livery: 60
Marry, go before to field, he'll be your follower;
Your worship in that sense may call him "man."

TYB. Romeo, the hate I bear thee can afford
No better term than this,—thou art a villain.

ROM. Tybalt, the reason that I have to love thee 65
Doth much excuse the appertaining rage
To such a greeting: villain am I none;
Therefore farewell; I see thou know'st me not.

Act III, Scene i: 10. drawer, quibble on (1) one who first draws (2) waiter or pot-boy in a tavern. **14. moody,** angry. **15. what to,** moved to what. **35. fee-simple,** absolute ownership. **41. den,** i.e., evening. **47. consort'st,** (1) keep company with (2) consort—combine to make musical harmony. **52. 'Zounds,** by God's wounds. **56. depart,** separate. **59. my man,** i.e., the man I was looking for. **61. field,** i.e., place for a duel. **66. appertaining rage,** rage appertaining to.

TYB. Boy, this shall not excuse the injuries
That thou hast done me; therefore turn and draw. 70

ROM. I do protest, I never injured thee,
But love thee better than thou canst devise,
Till thou shalt know the reason of my love:
And so, good Capulet,—which name I tender
As dearly as my own,—be satisfied.

MER. O calm, dishonourable, vile submission!
Alla stoccata carries it away. [*Draws.*]
Tybalt, you rat-catcher, will you walk?

TYB. What wouldst thou have with me? 79

MER. Good king of cats, nothing but one of your nine lives; that I mean to make bold withal, and, as you shall use me hereafter, dry-beat the rest of the eight. Will you pluck your sword out of his pilcher by the ears? make haste, lest mine be about your ears ere it be out. 85

TYB. I am for you. [*Drawing.*

ROM. Gentle Mercutio, put thy rapier up.

MER. Come, sir, your passado. [*They fight.*

ROM. Draw, Benvolio; beat down their weapons. 89
Gentlemen, for shame, forbear this outrage!
Tybalt, Mercutio, the prince expressly hath
Forbidden bandying in Verona streets:
Hold, Tybalt! good Mercutio!

[TYBALT *under* ROMEO'S *arm stabs* MERCUTIO, *and flies with his followers.*

MER. I am hurt. 93
A plague o' both your houses! I am sped.
Is he gone, and hath nothing?

BEN. What, art thou hurt?

MER. Ay, ay, a scratch, a scratch; marry, 'tis enough.
Where is my page? Go, villain, fetch a surgeon. [*Exit* PAGE.

ROM. Courage, man; the hurt cannot be much. 98

MER. No, 'tis not so deep as a well, nor so wide as a church-door; but 'tis enough, 'twill serve: ask for me to-morrow, and you shall find me a grave man. I am peppered, I warrant, for this world. A plague o' both your houses! 'Zounds, a dog, a rat, a mouse, a cat, to scratch a man to death! a braggart, a 105 rogue, a villain, that fights by the book of arithmetic! Why the devil came you between us? I was hurt under your arm.

ROM. I thought all for the best. 109

MER. Help me into some house, Benvolio,
Or I shall faint. A plague o' both your houses!
They have made worms' meat of me: I have it,
And soundly too: your houses!

[*Exeunt* MERCUTIO *and* BENVOLIO.

ROM. This gentleman, the prince's near ally, 114
My very friend, hath got his mortal hurt
In my behalf; my reputation stain'd
With Tybalt's slander,—Tybalt, that an hour
Hath been my kinsman! O sweet Juliet,
Thy beauty hath made me effeminate
And in my temper soften'd valour's steel! 120

[*Re-enter* BENVOLIO.]

BEN. O Romeo, Romeo, brave Mercutio's dead!
That gallant spirit hath aspired the clouds,
Which too untimely here did scorn the earth.

ROM. This day's black fate on more days doth depend;
This but begins the woe others must end. 125

BEN. Here comes the furious Tybalt back again.

ROM. Alive, in triumph! and Mercutio slain!
Away to heaven, respective lenity,
And fire-eyed fury be my conduct now!

[*Re-enter* TYBALT.]

Now, Tybalt, take the villain back again, 130
That late thou gavest me; for Mercutio's soul
Is but a little way above our heads,
Staying for thine to keep him company:
Either thou, or I, or both, must go with him.

TYB. Thou, wretched boy, that didst consort him here, 135
Shalt with him hence.

ROM. This shall determine that.

[*They fight;* TYBALT *falls.*

BEN. Romeo, away, be gone!
The citizens are up, and Tybalt slain.
Stand not amazed: the prince will doom thee death,
If thou art taken: hence, be gone, away! 140

69. **boy**, a term of contempt. 74. **tender**, hold. 77. **alla stoccata**, a thrust; **carries it away**, carries the day. 78. **rat-catcher**, because the king of cats. 83. **dry-beat**, beat without drawing blood. 84. **pilcher**, scabbard. 92. **bandying**, contending, dueling. 94. **sped**, done for. 106-7. **book of arithmetic**, i.e., by the rules of fencing teachers.

114. **ally**, relative. 122. **aspired**, soared to. 124. **depend**, impend. 128. **respective lenity**, considerate gentleness. 129. **conduct**, conductor. 135. **consort**, attend. 139. **amazed**, stupified.

ROM. O, I am fortune's fool!
BEN. Why dost thou stay?
[*Exit* ROMEO.

[*Enter* CITIZENS, &c.]

FIRST CIT. Which way ran he that kill'd Mercutio?
Tybalt, that murderer, which way ran he?
BEN. There lies that Tybalt.
FIRST CIT. Up, sir, go with me;
I charge thee in the prince's name, obey. 145

[*Enter* PRINCE, *attended;* MONTAGUE, CAPULET, *their* WIVES, *and others.*]

PRIN. Where are the vile beginners of this fray?
BEN. O noble prince, I can discover all
The unlucky manage of this fatal brawl:
There lies the man, slain by young Romeo,
That slew thy kinsman, brave Mercutio. 150
LA. CAP. Tybalt, my cousin! O my brother's child!
O prince! O cousin! husband! O, the blood is spilt
Of my dear kinsman! Prince, as thou art true,
For blood of ours, shed blood of Montague.
O cousin, cousin! 155
PRIN. Benvolio, who began this bloody fray?
BEN. Tybalt, here slain, whom Romeo's hand did slay;
Romeo that spoke him fair, bade him bethink
How nice the quarrel was, and urged withal
Your high displeasure: all this uttered 160
With gentle breath, calm look, knees humbly bow'd,
Could not take truce with the unruly spleen
Of Tybalt deaf to peace, but that he tilts
With piercing steel at bold Mercutio's breast,
Who, all as hot, turns deadly point to point,
And, with a martial scorn, with one hand beats 166
Cold death aside, and with the other sends
It back to Tybalt, whose dexterity
Retorts it: Romeo he cries aloud,
"Hold, friends! friends, part!" and, swifter than his tongue, 170
His agile arm beats down their fatal points,
And 'twixt them rushes; underneath whose arm
An envious thrust from Tybalt hit the life
Of stout Mercutio, and then Tybalt fled;
But by and by comes back to Romeo, 175
Who had but newly entertain'd revenge,
And to 't they go like lightning, for, ere I
Could draw to part them, was stout Tybalt slain,
And, as he fell, did Romeo turn and fly.
This is the truth, or let Benvolio die. 180
LA. CAP. He is a kinsman to the Montague;
Affection makes him false; he speaks not true:
Some twenty of them fought in this black strife,
And all those twenty could but kill one life.
I beg for justice, which thou, prince, must give; 185
Romeo slew Tybalt, Romeo must not live.
PRIN. Romeo slew him, he slew Mercutio;
Who now the price of his dear blood doth owe?
MON. Not Romeo, prince, he was Mercutio's friend;
His fault concludes but what the law should end. 190
The life of Tybalt.
PRIN. And for that offence
Immediately we do exile him hence:
I have an interest in your hate's proceeding,
My blood for your rude brawls doth lie a-bleeding;
But I'll amerce you with so strong a fine 195
That you shall all repent the loss of mine:
I will be deaf to pleading and excuses;
Nor tears nor prayers shall purchase out abuses:
Therefore use none: let Romeo hence in haste,
Else, when he's found, that hour is his last.
Bear hence this body and attend our will: 201
Mercy but murders, pardoning those that kill.
[*Exeunt.*

SCENE II. *Capulet's orchard.*

[*Enter* JULIET.]

JUL. Gallop apace, you fiery-footed steeds,
Towards Phœbus' lodging: such a waggoner
As Phaethon would whip you to the west,
And bring in cloudy night immediately.

141. fortune's fool, the mock of Fortune. 147. discover, reveal. 148. manage, conduct. 158. spoke him fair, addressed him politely. 159. nice, trivial. 162. take truce, make peace; unruly spleen, uncontrollable anger. 163. tilts, strikes. 169. retorts it, hurls it back. 173. envious, malicious. 175. by and by, immediately. 182. affection, partiality. 194. my blood, because Mercutio was his kinsman. 195. amerce, punish by a fine.

Spread thy close curtain, love-performing night, 5
That runaways' eyes may wink, and Romeo
Leap to these arms, untalk'd of and unseen.
Lovers can see to do their amorous rites
By their own beauties; or, if love be blind,
It best agrees with night. Come, civil night, 10
Thou sober-suited matron, all in black,
And learn me how to lose a winning match,
Play'd for a pair of stainless maidenhoods:
Hood my unmann'd blood, bating in my cheeks,
With thy black mantle; till strange love, grown bold, 15
Think true love acted simple modesty.
Come, night; come, Romeo; come, thou day in night;
For thou wilt lie upon the wings of night
Whiter than new snow on a raven's back.
Come, gentle night, come, loving, blackbrow'd night, 20
Give me my Romeo; and, when he shall die,
Take him and cut him out in little stars,
And he will make the face of heaven so fine
That all the world will be in love with night
And pay no worship to the garish sun. 25
O, I have bought the mansion of a love,
But not possess'd it, and, though I am sold,
Not yet enjoy'd: so tedious is this day
As is the night before some festival
To an impatient child that hath new robes 30
And may not wear them. O, here comes my nurse,
And she brings news; and every tongue that speaks
But Romeo's name speaks heavenly eloquence.

[*Enter* NURSE, *with cords.*]

Now, nurse, what news? What hast thou there? the cords
That Romeo bid thee fetch?

NURSE. Ay, ay, the cords. 35
[*Throws them down.*

JUL. Ay me! what news? why dost thou wring thy hands?

NURSE. Ay, well-a-day! he's dead, he's dead, he's dead!
We are undone, lady, we are undone!
Alack the day! he's gone, he's kill'd, he's dead!

JUL. Can heaven be so envious?

NURSE. Romeo can, 40
Though heaven cannot: O Romeo, Romeo!
Who ever would have thought it? Romeo!

JUL. What devil art thou, that dost torment me thus?
This torture should be roar'd in dismal hell.
Hath Romeo slain himself? say thou but "I," 45
And that bare vowel "I" shall poison more
Than the death-darting eye of cockatrice:
I am not I, if there be such an I;
Or those eyes shut, that make thee answer "I."
If he be slain, say "I"; or if not, no: 50
Brief sounds determine of my weal or woe.

NURSE. I saw the wound, I saw it with mine eyes,—
God save the mark!—here on his manly breast:
A piteous corse, a bloody piteous corse;
Pale, pale as ashes, all bedaub'd in blood, 55
All in gore-blood; I swounded at the sight.

JUL. O, break, my heart! poor bankrupt, break at once!
To prison, eyes, ne'er look on liberty!
Vile earth, to earth resign; end motion here;
And thou and Romeo press one heavy bier! 60

NURSE. O Tybalt, Tybalt, the best friend I had!
O courteous Tybalt! honest gentleman!
That ever I should live to see thee dead!

JUL. What storm is this that blows so contrary?
Is Romeo slaughter'd, and is Tybalt dead? 65
My dear-loved cousin, and my dearer lord?
Then, dreadful trumpet, sound the general doom!
For who is living, if those two are gone?

NURSE. Tybalt is gone, and Romeo banished;
Romeo that kill'd him, he is banished. 70

JUL. O God! did Romeo's hand shed Tybalt's blood?

Scene ii: 6. **runaways'**, i.e., the sun is called runaway because Phaeton, the son of Helios, who drove the horses of the sun for a day, was not able to control them and they ran away. To save the universe from burning up, Jupiter killed him by a thunderbolt. **wink**, close. When the sun closes his eyes, night comes. 10. **civil**, sober. 12. **learn**, teach. 14. **hood**, cover; **unmann'd**, untamed; **bating**, fluttering—all terms in falconry. 15. **strange**, reserved. 25. **garish**, glaring. 40. **envious**, malicious. 45. **"I,"** i.e., aye. 47. **cockatrice**, fabulous serpent supposed to slay with its glance. 49. **those eyes**, i.e., Romeo's. 51. **determine of**, decide. 53. **God save the mark**, an oath designed to avert an ill omen. 56. **gore-blood**, clotted blood. 59. **vile earth**, wretched body. 67. **dreadful trumpet**, i.e., that announces doomsday.

NURSE. It did, it did; alas the day, it did!
JUL. O serpent heart, hid with a flowering face!
Did ever dragon keep so fair a cave?
Beautiful tyrant! fiend angelical! 75
Dove-feather'd raven! wolvish-ravening lamb!
Despisèd substance of divinest show!
Just opposite to what thou justly seem'st,
A damned saint, an honourable villain!
O nature, what hadst thou to do in hell, 80
When thou didst bower the spirit of a fiend
In mortal paradise of such sweet flesh?
Was ever book containing such vile matter
So fairly bound? O, that deceit should dwell
In such a gorgeous palace!
NURSE. There's no trust, 85
No faith, no honesty in men; all perjured,
All forsworn, all naught, all dissemblers.
Ah, where's my man? give me some aqua vitæ:
These griefs, these woes, these sorrows make me old.
Shame come to Romeo!
JUL. Blister'd be thy tongue 90
For such a wish! he was not born to shame:
Upon his brow shame is ashamed to sit;
For 'tis a throne where honour may be crown'd
Sole monarch of the universal earth.
O, what a beast was I to chide at him! 95
NURSE. Will you speak well of him that kill'd your cousin?
JUL. Shall I speak ill of him that is my husband?
Ah, poor my lord, what tongue shall smooth thy name,
When I, thy three-hours wife, have mangled it?
But, wherefore, villain, didst thou kill my cousin? 100
That villain cousin would have kill'd my husband:
Back, foolish tears, back to your native spring;
Your tributary drops belong to woe,
Which you, mistaking, offer up to joy.
My husband lives, that Tybalt would have slain; 105
And Tybalt's dead, that would have slain my husband:
All this is comfort; wherefore weep I then?
Some word there was, worser than Tybalt's death,
That murder'd me: I would forget it fain;
But, O, it presses to my memory, 110
Like damnèd guilty deeds to sinners' minds:
"Tybalt is dead, and Romeo—banishèd,"
That "banishèd," that one word "banishèd,"
Hath slain ten thousand Tybalts. Tybalt's death
Was woe enough, if it had ended there: 115
Or, if sour woe delights in fellowship
And needly will be rank'd with other griefs,
Why follow'd not, when she said "Tybalt's dead,"
Thy father, or thy mother, nay, or both,
Which modern lamentation might have moved? 120
But with a rearward following Tybalt's death,
"Romeo is banishèd," to speak that word,
Is father, mother, Tybalt, Romeo, Juliet,
All slain, all dead. "Romeo is banishèd!"
There is no end, no limit, measure, bound, 125
In that word's death; no words can that woe sound.
Where is my father, and my mother, nurse?
NURSE. Weeping and wailing over Tybalt's corse:
Will you go to them? I will bring you thither.
JUL. Wash they his wounds with tears: mine shall be spent, 130
When theirs are dry, for Romeo's banishment.
Take up those cords: poor ropes, you are beguiled,
Both you and I; for Romeo is exiled:
He made you for a highway to my bed;
But I, a maid, die maiden-widowèd. 135
Come, cords, come, nurse; I'll to my wedding-bed;
And death, not Romeo, take my maidenhead!
NURSE. Hie to your chamber: I'll find Romeo
To comfort you: I wot well where he is.
Hark ye, your Romeo will be here at night: 140
I'll to him; he is hid at Laurence' cell.
JUL. O, find him! give this ring to my true knight,
And bid him come to take his last farewell.
[*Exeunt.*

78. just . . . justly, exact . . . exactly. 81. bower, lodge. 87. naught, worthless. 98. smooth, (1) literal meaning to contrast with "mangle" and (2) flatter. 117. needly, of necessity. 120. modern, ordinary. 121. rearward, rear guard—pun on rear word. 126. sound, make audible.

SCENE III. FRIAR LAURENCE'S *cell.*

[*Enter* FRIAR LAURENCE.]

FR. L. Romeo, come forth; come forth, thou fearful man:
Affliction is enamour'd of thy parts,
And thou art wedded to calamity.

[*Enter* ROMEO.]

ROM. Father, what news? what is the prince's doom?
What sorrow craves acquaintance at my hand, 5
That I yet know not?
FRI. L. Too familiar
Is my dear son with such sour company:
I bring thee tidings of the prince's doom.
ROM. What less than dooms-day is the prince's doom?
FRI. L. A gentler judgement vanish'd from his lips, 10
Not body's death, but body's banishment.
ROM. Ha, banishment! be merciful, say "death;"
For exile hath more terror in his look,
Much more than death: do not say "banishment."
FRI. L. Hence from Verona art thou banishèd: 15
Be patient, for the world is broad and wide.
ROM. There is no world without Verona walls,
But purgatory, torture, hell itself.
Hence-banishèd is banish'd from the world,
And world's exile is death: then banishèd, 20
Is death mis-term'd; calling death banishment,
Thou cutt'st my head off with a golden axe,
And smilest upon the stroke that murders me.
FRI. L. O deadly sin! O rude unthankfulness!
Thy fault our law calls death; but the kind prince, 25
Taking thy part, hath rush'd aside the law,
And turn'd that black word death to banishment
This is dear mercy, and thou seest it not.
ROM. 'Tis torture, and not mercy: heaven is here,
Where Juliet lives; and every cat and dog 30
And little mouse, every unworthy thing,
Live here in heaven and may look on her;
But Romeo may not: more validity,
More honourable state, more courtship lives
In carrion-flies than Romeo: they may seize 35
On the white wonder of dear Juliet's hand
And steal immortal blessing from her lips,
Who, even in pure and vestal modesty,
Still blush, as thinking their own kisses sin;
But Romeo may not; he is banishèd: 40
Flies may do this, but I from this must fly:
They are free men, but I am banishèd.
And say'st thou yet that exile is not death?
Hadst thou no poison mix'd, no sharp-ground knife,
No sudden mean of death, though ne'er so mean, 45
But "banishèd" to kill me?—"banishèd"?
O friar, the damnèd use that word in hell;
Howlings attend it: how hast thou the heart,
Being a divine, a ghostly confessor,
A sin-absolver, and my friend profess'd, 50
To mangle me with that word "banishèd"?
FRI. L. Thou fond mad man, hear me but speak a word.
ROM. O, thou wilt speak again of banishment.
FRI. L. I'll give thee armour to keep off that word;
Adversity's sweet milk, philosophy, 55
To comfort thee, though thou art banishèd.
ROM. Yet "banishèd"? Hang up philosophy!
Unless philosophy can make a Juliet,
Displant a town, reverse a prince's doom,
It helps not, it prevails not: talk no more. 60
FRI. L. O, then I see that madmen have no ears.
ROM. How should they, when that wise men have no eyes?
FRI. L. Let me dispute with thee of thy estate.
ROM. Thou canst not speak of that thou dost not feel:
Wert thou as young as I, Juliet thy love, 65
An hour but married, Tybalt murderèd,
Doting like me and like me banishèd,
Then mightst thou speak, then mightst thou tear thy hair.
And fall upon the ground, as I do now,

Scene iii: 1. fearful, full of fear. 4. doom, decree. 7. sour, painful. 10. vanish'd, issued, i.e., breath vanishing from the lips like smoke. 26. rush'd, brushed. 33. validity, value. 45. mean, means; mean, base. 52. fond, foolish. 59. displant, move. 63. dispute . . . estate, discuss with you the condition of your affairs.

Taking the measure of an unmade grave. 70
[*Knocking within.*

FRI. L. Arise; one knocks; good Romeo, hide thyself.

ROM. Not I; unless the breath of heart-sick groans,
Mist-like, infold me from the search of eyes.
[*Knocking.*

FRI. L. Hark, how they knock! Who's there? Romeo, arise;
Thou wilt be taken. Stay awhile! Stand up; 75
[*Knocking.*]
Run to my study. By and by! God's will,
What simpleness is this! I come, I come!
[*Knocking.*]
Who knocks so hard? whence come you? what's your will?

NURSE. [*Within*] Let me come in, and you shall know my errand;
I come from Lady Juliet.

FR. L. Welcome, then. 80

[*Enter* NURSE.]

NURSE. O holy friar, O, tell me, holy friar,
Where is my lady's lord, where's Romeo?

FRI. L. There on the ground, with his own tears made drunk.

NURSE. O, he is even in my mistress' case,
Just in her case! O woful sympathy! 85
Piteous predicament! Even so lies she,
Blubbering and weeping, weeping and blubbering.
Stand up, stand up; stand, an you be a man:
For Juliet's sake, for her sake, rise and stand;
Why should you fall into so deep an O? 90

ROM. Nurse!

NURSE. Ah sir! ah sir! Well, death's the end of all.

ROM. Spakest thou of Juliet? how is it with her?
Doth she not think me an old murderer, 94
Now I have stain'd the childhood of our joy
With blood removed but little from her own?
Where is she? and how doth she? and what says
My conceal'd lady to our cancell'd love?

NURSE. O, she says nothing, sir, but weeps and weeps;
And now falls on her bed; and then starts up, 100
And Tybalt calls; and then on Romeo cries,
And then down falls again.

ROM. As if that name,
Shot from the dead level of a gun,
Did murder her; as that name's cursèd hand
Murder'd her kinsman. O, tell me, friar, tell me, 105
In what vile part of this anatomy
Doth my name lodge? tell me that I may sack
The hateful mansion. [*Drawing his sword.*

FRI. L. Hold thy desperate hand:
Art thou a man? thy form cries out thou art:
Thy tears are womanish; thy wild acts denote
The unreasonable fury of a beast: 111
Unseemly woman in a seeming man!
Or ill-beseeming beast in seeming both!
Thou hast amazed me: by my holy order,
I thought thy disposition better temper'd. 115
Hast thou slain Tybalt? wilt thou slay thyself?
And slay thy lady too that lives in thee,
By doing damnèd hate upon thyself?
Why rail'st thou on thy birth, the heaven, and earth?
Since birth, and heaven, and earth, all three do meet 120
In thee at once; which thou at once wouldst lose.
Fie, fie, thou shamest thy shape, thy love, thy wit;
Which, like a usurer, abound'st in all,
And usest none in that true use indeed
Which should bedeck thy shape, thy love, thy wit: 125
Thy noble shape is but a form of wax,
Digressing from the valour of a man;
Thy dear love sworn but hollow perjury,
Killing that love which thou hast vow'd to cherish;
Thy wit, that ornament to shape and love, 130
Mis-shapen in the conduct of them both,
Like powder in a skilless soldier's flask,
Is set a-fire by thine own ignorance,
And thou dismember'd with thine own defence.
What, rouse thee, man! thy Juliet is alive, 135
For whose dear sake thou wast but lately dead;

76. **By and by,** wait a moment. 90. **O,** i.e., an exclamation of grief. 94. **old,** confirmed. 98. **conceal'd lady,** i.e., my wife, though the fact is concealed from the world.

103. **level,** aim. 106. **anatomy,** body. 107. **sack,** destroy. 125. **wit,** understanding. 127. **digressing,** deviating. 134. **And thou,** etc., and you blown to pieces by the powder which should have served as your means of defence.

There art thou happy: Tybalt would kill thee,
But thou slew'st Tybalt; there art thou happy too:
The law that threaten'd death becomes thy friend
And turns it to exile; there art thou happy: 140
A pack of blessings lights upon thy back;
Happiness courts thee in her best array;
But, like a misbehaved and sullen wench,
Thou pout'st upon thy fortune and thy love:
Take heed, take heed, for such die miserable. 145
Go, get thee to thy love, as was decreed,
Ascend her chamber, hence and comfort her:
But look thou stay not till the watch be set,
For then thou canst not pass to Mantua;
Where thou shalt live, till we can find a time 150
To blaze your marriage, reconcile your friends,
Beg pardon of the prince, and call thee back
With twenty hundred thousand times more joy
Than thou went'st forth in lamentation.
Go before, nurse: commend me to thy lady;
And bid her hasten all the house to bed, 156
Which heavy sorrow makes them apt unto:
Romeo is coming.

NURSE. O Lord, I could have stay'd here all the night
To hear good counsel: O, what learning is! 160
My lord, I'll tell my lady you will come.

ROM. Do so, and bid my sweet prepare to chide.

NURSE. Here, sir, a ring she bid me give you, sir:
Hie you, make haste, for it grows very late. [*Exit.*

ROM. How well my comfort is revived by this! 165

FRI. L. Go hence; good night; and here stands all your state:
Either be gone before the watch be set,
Or by the break of day disguised from hence:
Sojourn in Mantua; I'll find out your man,
And he shall signify from time to time 170
Every good hap to you that chances here:
Give me thy hand; 'tis late: farewell; good night.

ROM. But that a joy past joy calls out on me,
It were a grief, so brief to part with thee:
Farewell. [*Exeunt.* 175

SCENE IV. *A room in Capulet's house.*

[*Enter* CAPULET, LADY CAPULET, *and* PARIS.]

CAP. Things have fall'n out, sir, so unluckily,
That we have had no time to move our daughter:
Look you, she loved her kinsman Tybalt dearly,
And so did I:—Well, we were born to die.
'Tis very late, she'll not come down to-night:
I promise you, but for your company, 6
I would have been a-bed an hour ago.

PAR. These times of woe afford no time to woo.
Madam, good night: commend me to your daughter.

LA. CAP. I will, and know her mind early to-morrow; 10
To-night she is mew'd up to her heaviness.

CAP. Sir Paris, I will make a desperate tender
Of my child's love: I think she will be ruled
In all respects by me; nay, more, I doubt it not.
Wife, go you to her ere you go to bed; 15
Acquaint her here of my son Paris' love;
And bid her, mark you me, on Wednesday next—
But, soft! what day is this?

PAR. Monday, my lord.

CAP. Monday! ha, ha! Well, Wednesday is too soon,
O' Thursday let it be: o' Thursday, tell her, 20
She shall be married to this noble earl.
Will you be ready? do you like this haste?
We'll keep no great ado,—a friend or two;
For, hark you, Tybalt being slain so late,
It may be thought we held him carelessly, 25
Being our kinsman, if we revel much:
Therefore we'll have some half a dozen friends,

137. There . . . happy, in that you are fortunate. 148. watch, guard. 151. blaze, make public. 157. apt, inclined. 166. here . . . state, your fortune depends on doing what follows. 174. brief, briefly. Scene iv: 2. move, urge.

11. mew'd up, cooped up. 12. desperate tender, bold offer. 23. keep . . . ado, make no great fuss. 25. held him carelessly, had little regard for him.

And there an end. But what say you to Thursday?
PAR. My lord, I would that Thursday were to-morrow.
CAP. Well, get you gone: o' Thursday be it, then. 30
Go you to Juliet ere you go to bed,
Prepare her, wife, against this wedding-day.
Farewell, my lord. Light to my chamber, ho!
Afore me! it is so very very late,
That we may call it early by and by. 35
Good night. [*Exeunt.*

SCENE V. *Capulet's orchard.*

[*Enter* ROMEO *and* JULIET *above, at the window.*]

JUL. Wilt thou be gone? it is not yet near day:
It was the nightingale, and not the lark,
That pierced the fearful hollow of thine ear;
Nightly she sings on yond pomegranate-tree:
Believe me, love, it was the nightingale. 5
ROM. It was the lark, the herald of the morn,
No nightingale: look, love, what envious streaks
Do lace the severing clouds in yonder east:
Night's candles are burnt out, and jocund day
Stands tiptoe on the misty mountain tops. 10
I must be gone and live, or stay and die.
JUL. Yond light is not day-light, I know it, I:
It is some meteor that the sun exhales,
To be to thee this night a torch-bearer,
And light thee on thy way to Mantua: 15
Therefore stay yet; thou need'st not to be gone.
ROM. Let me be ta'en, let me be put to death;
I am content, so thou wilt have it so.
I'll say yon grey is not the morning's eye,
'Tis but the pale reflex of Cynthia's brow; 20
Nor that is not the lark, whose notes do beat
The vaulty heaven so high above our heads:
I have more care to stay than will to go:
Come, death, and welcome! Juliet wills it so.
How is 't, my soul? let's talk; it is not day. 25
JUL. It is, it is: hie hence, be gone, away!
It is the lark that sings so out of tune,
Straining harsh discords and unpleasing sharps.
Some say the lark makes sweet division;
This doth not so, for she divideth us: 30
Some say the lark and loathèd toad change eyes;
O, now I would they had changed voices too!
Since arm from arm that voice doth us affray,
Hunting thee hence with hunt's-up to the day.
O, now be gone; more light and light it grows. 35
ROM. More light and light; more dark and dark our woes!

[*Enter* NURSE, *to the chamber.*]

NURSE. Madam!
JUL. Nurse?
NURSE. Your lady mother is coming to your chamber:
The day is broke; be wary, look about. 40
[*Exit.*
JUL. Then, window, let day in, and let life out. 41
ROM. Farewell, farewell! one kiss, and I'll descend. [*He goeth down.*
JUL. Art thou gone so? love, lord, ay, husband, friend!
I must hear from thee every day in the hour,
For in a minute there are many days: 45
O, by this count I shall be much in years
Ere I again behold my Romeo!
ROM. Farewell!
I will omit no opportunity
That may convey my greetings, love, to thee.
JUL. O, think'st thou we shall ever meet again? 51
ROM. I doubt it not; and all these woes shall serve
For sweet discourses in our time to come.
JUL. O God, I have an ill-divining soul!
Methinks I see thee, now thou art below, 55
As one dead in the bottom of a tomb:
Either my eyesight fails, or thou look'st pale.
ROM. And trust me, love, in my eyes so do you:

32. **against,** in expectation of. 34. **Afore me,** about equivalent to "God knows," or the phrase may be a command to either the torch bearer or Paris to precede him. 35. **by and by,** immediately. Scene v: 8. **lace,** light up with stripes of color. 13. **exhales,** meteors were supposed to be formed of vapors sucked up by the sun. 20. **reflex,** reflection; **Cynthia,** the moon. 23. **care,** desire. 28. **sharps,** shrill sounds. 29. **division,** melody. 33. **affray,** frighten. 34. **hunt's up,** song to awaken huntsmen; so an early morning song.

Dry sorrow drinks our blood. Adieu, adieu!
[*Exit.*

JUL. O fortune, fortune! all men call thee fickle: 60
If thou art fickle, what dost thou with him
That is renown'd for faith? Be fickle, fortune;
For then, I hope, thou wilt not keep him long,
But send him back.

LA. CAP. [*Within*] Ho, daughter! are you up? 65

JUL. Who is 't that calls? is it my lady mother?
Is she not down so late, or up so early?
What unaccustom'd cause procures her hither?

[*Enter* LADY CAPULET.]

LA. CAP. Why, how now, Juliet!

JUL. Madam, I am not well.

LA. CAP. Evermore weeping for your cousin's death? 70
What, wilt thou wash him from his grave with tears?
An if thou couldst, thou couldst not make him live;
Therefore, have done: some grief shows much of love;
But much of grief shows still some want of wit.

JUL. Yet let me weep for such a feeling loss. 75

LA. CAP. So shall you feel the loss, but not the friend
Which you weep for.

JUL. Feeling so the loss,
I cannot choose but ever weep the friend.

LA. CAP. Well, girl, thou weep'st not so much for his death,
As that the villain lives which slaughter'd him. 80

JUL. What villain, madam?

LA. CAP. That same villain, Romeo.

JUL. [*Aside*] Villain and he be many miles asunder.—
God pardon him! I do, with all my heart;
And yet no man like he doth grieve my heart.

LA. CAP. That is, because the traitor murderer lives. 85

JUL. Ay, madam, from the reach of these my hands:
Would none but I might venge my cousin's death!

LA. CAP. We will have vengeance for it, fear thou not:
Then weep no more. I'll send to one in Mantua,
Where that same banish'd runagate doth live, 90
Shall give him such an unaccustom'd dram,
That he shall soon keep Tybalt company:
And then, I hope, thou wilt be satisfied.

JUL. Indeed, I never shall be satisfied
With Romeo, till I behold him—dead— 95
Is my poor heart so for a kinsman vex'd:
Madam, if you could find out but a man
To bear a poison, I would temper it;
That Romeo should, upon receipt thereof,
Soon sleep in quiet. O, how my heart abhors 100
To hear him named, and cannot come to him,
To wreak the love I bore my cousin
Upon his body that hath slaughter'd him!

LA. CAP. Find thou the means, and I'll find such a man.
But now I'll tell thee joyful tidings, girl. 105

JUL. And joy comes well in such a needy time:
What are they, I beseech your ladyship?

LA. CAP. Well, well, thou hast a careful father, child;
One who, to put thee from thy heaviness,
Hath sorted out a sudden day of joy, 110
That thou expect'st not nor I look'd not for.

JUL. Madam, in happy time, what day is that?

LA. CAP. Marry, my child, early next Thursday morn,
The gallant, young and noble gentleman,
The County Paris, at Saint Peter's Church, 115
Shall happily make thee there a joyful bride.

JUL. Now, by Saint Peter's Church and Peter too,
He shall not make me there a joyful bride.
I wonder at this haste; that I must wed
Ere he, that should be husband, comes to woo. 120

59. **dry sorrow,** sorrow was supposed to consume the blood and leave the victim pale. 67. **down,** abed. 68. **procures her,** induces her to come. 75. **feeling,** heart felt.

84. **like,** as much as. 86. **from,** beyond. 90. **runagate,** fugitive. 91. **unaccustomed,** strange. 98. **temper,** used equivocally (1) mix, (2) qualify. 99. **That,** so that. 106. **needy,** poverty-stricken. 110. **sorted out,** chosen. 112. **in happy time,** that's good.

I pray you, tell my lord and father, madam,
I will not marry yet; and, when I do, I swear,
It shall be Romeo, whom you know I hate,
Rather than Paris. These are news indeed!

LA. CAP. Here comes your father; tell him so yourself, 125
And see how he will take it at your hands.

[*Enter* CAPULET *and* NURSE.]

CAP. When the sun sets, the air doth drizzle dew;
But for the sunset of my brother's son
It rains downright.
How now! a conduit, girl? what, still in tears?
Evermore showering? In one little body 131
Thou counterfeit'st a bark, a sea, a wind;
For still thy eyes, which I may call the sea,
Do ebb and flow with tears; the bark thy body is,
Sailing in this salt flood; the winds, thy sighs; 135
Who, raging with thy tears, and they with them,
Without a sudden calm, will overset
Thy tempest-tossèd body. How now, wife!
Have you deliver'd to her our decree?

LA. CAP. Ay, sir; but she will none, she gives you thanks. 140
I would the fool were married to her grave!

CAP. Soft! take me with you, take me with you, wife.
How! will she none? doth she not give us thanks?
Is she not proud? doth she not count her blest,
Unworthy as she is, that we have wrought
So worthy a gentleman to be her bridegroom? 146

JUL. Not proud, you have; but thankful, that you have:
Proud can I never be of what I hate;
But thankful even for hate, that is meant love.

CAP. How now, how now, chop-logic! What is this? 150
"Proud," and "I thank you," and "I thank you not;"
And yet "not proud:" mistress minion, you,
Thank me no thankings, nor proud me no prouds,
But fettle your fine joints 'gainst Thursday next,
To go with Paris to Saint Peter's Church, 155
Or I will drag thee on a hurdle thither.
Out, you green-sickness carrion! out, you baggage!
You tallow-face!

LA. CAP. Fie, fie! what, are you mad?

JUL. Good father, I beseech you on my knees,
Hear me with patience but to speak a word. 160

CAP. Hang thee, young baggage! disobedient wretch!
I tell thee what: get thee to church o' Thursday,
Or never after look me in the face:
Speak not, reply not, do not answer me;
My fingers itch. Wife, we scarce thought us blest 165
That God had lent us but this only child;
But now I see this one is one too much,
And that we have a curse in having her:
Out on her, hilding!

NURSE. God in heaven bless her!
You are to blame, my lord, to rate her so. 170

CAP. And why, my lady wisdom? hold your tongue,
Good prudence; smatter with your gossips, go.

NURSE. I speak no treason.

CAP. O, God ye god-den.

NURSE. May not one speak?

CAP. Peace, you mumbling fool!
Utter your gravity o'er a gossip's bowl; 175
For here we need it not.

LA. CAP. You are too hot.

CAP. God's bread! it makes me mad:
Day, night, hour, tide, time, work, play,
Alone, in company, still my care hath been
To have her match'd: and having now provided 180
A gentleman of noble parentage,
Of fair demesnes, youthful, and nobly train'd,
Stuff'd, as they say, with honourable parts,
Proportion'd as one's thought would wish a man;
And then to have a wretched puling fool, 185

130. **a conduit**, fountain. 140. **will none**, refuses to obey it. 142. **Soft**, wait a minute; **take me with you**, let me understand you. 145. **wrought**, procured. 150. **chop-logic**, sophistical arguer. 152. **minion**, spoilt child. 154. **fettle**, get ready. 156. **hurdle**, a sledge on which criminals were dragged to execution. 157. **green-sickness**, a form of anaemia, refers to Juliet's pallor. 169. **hilding**, good for nothing. 170. **rate**, berate, scold. 172. **smatter**, chatter. 173. **God ye god-den**, God give you good evening. 175. **gravity**, grave remarks, used contemptuously. 177. **God's bread**, i.e., by the holy sacrament. 182. **demesnes**, estates.

A whining mammet, in her fortune's tender,
To answer "I'll not wed; I cannot love,
I am too young; I pray you, pardon me."
But, an you will not wed, I'll pardon you:
Graze where you will, you shall not house with me: 190
Look to 't, think on 't, I do not use to jest.
Thursday is near; lay hand on heart, advise:
An you be mine, I'll give you to my friend;
An you be not, hang, beg, starve, die in the streets, 194
For, by my soul, I'll ne'er acknowledge thee,
Nor what is mine shall never do thee good:
Trust to 't, bethink you; I'll not be forsworn. [*Exit.*

JUL. Is there no pity sitting in the clouds,
That sees into the bottom of my grief?
O, sweet my mother, cast me not away! 200
Delay this marriage for a month, a week;
Or, if you do not, make the bridal bed
In that dim monument where Tybalt lies.

LA. CAP. Talk not to me, for I'll not speak a word:
Do as thou wilt, for I have done with thee. 205 [*Exit.*

JUL. O God!—O nurse, how shall this be prevented?
My husband is on earth, my faith in heaven;
How shall that faith return again to earth,
Unless that husband send it me from heaven
By leaving earth? comfort me, counsel me.
Alack, alack, that heaven should practise stratagems 211
Upon so soft a subject as myself!
What say'st thou? hast thou not a word of joy?
Some comfort, nurse.

NURSE. Faith, here it is.
Romeo is banish'd; and all the world to nothing, 215
That he dares ne'er come back to challenge you;
Or, if he do, it needs must be by stealth.
Then, since the case so stands as now it doth,
I think it best you married with the county.
O, he's a lovely gentleman! 220
Romeo's a dishclout to him: an eagle, madam,
Hath not so green, so quick, so fair an eye
As Paris hath. Beshrew my very heart,
I think you are happy in this second match,
For it excels your first: or if it did not, 225
Your first is dead; or 'twere as good he were,
As living here and you no use of him.

JUL. Speakest thou from thy heart?

NURSE. And from my soul too;
Or else beshrew them both.

JUL. Amen!

NURSE. What?

JUL. Well, thou has comforted me marvellous much. 230
Go in; and tell my lady I am gone,
Having displeased my father, to Laurence' cell,
To make confession and to be absolved.

NURSE. Marry, I will; and this is wisely done. [*Exit.*

JUL. Ancient damnation! O most wicked fiend! 235
Is it more sin to wish me thus forsworn,
Or to dispraise my lord with that same tongue
Which she hath praised him with above compare
So many thousand times? Go, counsellor;
Thou and my bosom henceforth shall be twain. 240
I'll to the friar, to know his remedy:
If all else fail, myself have power to die. [*Exit.*

ACT IV

SCENE I. FRIAR LAURENCE'S *cell.*

[*Enter* FRIAR LAURENCE *and* PARIS.]

FRI. L. On Thursday, sir? the time is very short.

PAR. My father Capulet will have it so;
And I am nothing slow to slack his haste.

FRI. L. You say you do not know the lady's mind:
Uneven is the course, I like it not. 5

PAR. Immoderately she weeps for Tybalt's death,
And therefore have I little talk'd of love;
For Venus smiles not in a house of tears.

186. **mammet**, doll; **in her fortune's tender**, on the offer of good fortune. 192. **advise**, think it over. 207. **my faith**, my marriage vow. 211. **stratagems**, dreadful deeds.

216. **challenge**, claim. 235. **Ancient damnation**, you damned old woman. **Act IV, Scene i**: 2. **father**, i.e., intended father-in-law. 3. **I . . . haste**, i.e., I am not so reluctant as to check his desire for haste. 5. **uneven**, rough.

Now, sir, her father counts it dangerous
That she doth give her sorrow so much sway,
And in his wisdom hastes our marriage, 11
To stop the inundation of her tears;
Which, too much minded by herself alone,
May be put from her by society:
Now do you know the reason of this haste. 15

FRI. L. [*Aside*] I would I knew not why it should be slow'd.
Look, sir, here comes the lady towards my cell.

[*Enter* JULIET.]

PAR. Happily met, my lady and my wife!

JUL. That may be, sir, when I may be a wife.

PAR. That may be must be, love, on Thursday next. 20

JUL. What must be shall be.

FRI. L. That's a certain text.

PAR. Come you to make confession to this father?

JUL. To answer that, I should confess to you.

PAR. Do not deny to him that you love me.

JUL. I will confess to you that I love him. 25

PAR. So will ye, I am sure, that you love me.

JUL. If I do so, it will be of more price,
Being spoke behind your back, than to your face.

PAR. Poor soul, thy face is much abused with tears.

JUL. The tears have got small victory by that; 30
For it was bad enough before their spite.

PAR. Thou wrong'st it, more than tears, with that report.

JUL. That is no slander, sir, which is a truth;
And what I spake, I spake it to my face.

PAR. Thy face is mine, and thou hast slander'd it. 35

JUL. It may be so, for it is not mine own.
Are you at leisure, holy father, now;
Or shall I come to you at evening mass?

FRI. L. My leisure serves me, pensive daughter, now.
My lord, we must entreat the time alone. 40

PAR. God shield I should disturb devotion!
Juliet, on Thursday early will I rouse ye:
Till then, adieu; and keep this holy kiss. [*Exit.*

JUL. O, shut the door! and when thou hast done so,
Come weep with me; past hope, past cure, past help! 45

FRI. L. Ah, Juliet, I already know thy grief;
It strains me past the compass of my wits:
I hear thou must, and nothing may prorogue it,
On Thursday next be married to this county.

JUL. Tell me not, friar, that thou hear'st of this, 50
Unless thou tell me how I may prevent it:
If, in thy wisdom, thou canst give no help,
Do thou but call my resolution wise,
And with this knife I'll help it presently.
God join'd my heart and Romeo's, thou our hands; 55
And ere this hand, by thee to Romeo seal'd,
Shall be the label to another deed,
Or my true heart with treacherous revolt
Turn to another, this shall slay them both:
Therefore, out of thy long-experienced time,
Give me some present counsel, or, behold, 61
'Twixt my extremes and me this bloody knife
Shall play the umpire, arbitrating that
Which the commission of thy years and art
Could to no issue of true honour bring. 65
Be not so long to speak; I long to die,
If what thou speak'st speak not of remedy.

FRI. L. Hold, daughter: I do spy a kind of hope,
Which craves as desperate an execution
As that is desperate which we would prevent.
If, rather than to marry County Paris, 71
Thou hast the strength of will to slay thyself,
Then it is likely thou wilt undertake
A thing like death to chide away this shame,
That copest with death himself to scape from it; 75
And, if thou darest, I'll give thee remedy.

JUL. O, bid me leap, rather than marry Paris,
From off the battlements of yonder tower,
Or walk in thievish ways; or bid me lurk
Where serpents are; chain me with roaring bears; 80
Or shut me nightly in a charnel-house,
O'er-cover'd quite with dead men's rattling bones,

31. spite, vexation. 40. entreat the time alone, beg to be left alone. 41. shield, forbid (that). 48. prorogue, postpone. 57. label, a slip affixed to a deed to carry the seal. 60. time, i.e., of life. 62. extremes, extremities, straits.

64. commission, authority. 74. chide, drive. 75. copest, contends. 79. thievish ways, roads infested by robbers. 81. charnel-house, vault where bones of the dead are stored.

With reeky shanks and yellow chapless skulls;
Or bid me go into a new-made grave
And hide me with a dead man in his shroud;
Things that, to hear them told, have made me tremble; 86
And I will do it without fear or doubt,
To live an unstain'd wife to my sweet love.

FRI. L. Hold, then; go home, be merry, give consent
To marry Paris: Wednesday is to-morrow: 90
To-morrow night look that thou lie alone;
Let not thy nurse lie with thee in thy chamber:
Take thou this vial, being then in bed,
And this distillèd liquor drink thou off;
When presently through all thy veins shall run
A cold and drowsy humour, for no pulse 96
Shall keep his native progress, but surcease:
No warmth, no breath, shall testify thou livest;
The roses in thy lips and cheeks shall fade
To paly ashes, thy eyes' windows fall, 100
Like death, when he shuts up the day of life;
Each part, deprived of supple government,
Shall, stiff and stark and cold, appear like death:
And in this borrow'd likeness of shrunk death
Thou shalt continue two and forty hours, 105
And then awake as from a pleasant sleep.
Now, when the bridegroom in the morning comes
To rouse thee from thy bed, there art thou dead:
Then, as the manner of our country is,
In thy best robes uncover'd on the bier 110
Thou shalt be borne to that same ancient vault
Where all the kindred of the Capulets lie.
In the mean time, against thou shalt awake,
Shall Romeo by my letters know our drift,
And hither shall he come: and he and I 115
Will watch thy waking, and that very night
Shall Romeo bear thee hence to Mantua.
And this shall free thee from this present shame;
If no inconstant toy, nor womanish fear,
Abate thy valour in the acting it. 120

JUL. Give me, give me! O, tell not me of fear!

FRI. L. Hold; get you gone, be strong and prosperous
In this resolve: I'll send a friar with speed
To Mantua, with my letters to thy lord.

JUL. Love give me strength! and strength shall help afford. 125
Farewell, dear father! [*Exeunt.*

SCENE II. *Hall in Capulet's house.*

[*Enter* CAPULET, LADY CAPULET, NURSE, *and two* SERVINGMEN.]

CAP. So many guests invite as here are writ.
[*Exit* FIRST SERVANT.]
Sirrah, go hire me twenty cunning cooks.

SEC. SERV. You shall have none ill, sir; for I'll try if they can lick their fingers.

CAP. How canst thou try them so? 5

SEC. SERV. Marry, sir, 'tis an ill cook that cannot lick his own fingers: therefore he that cannot lick his fingers goes not with me.

CAP. Go, be gone. [*Exit* SEC. SERVANT.]
We shall be much unfurnish'd for this time. 10
What, is my daughter gone to Friar Laurence?

NURSE. Ay, forsooth.

CAP. Well, he may chance to do some good on her:
A peevish self-will'd harlotry it is.

NURSE. See where she comes from shrift with merry look. 15

[*Enter* JULIET.]

CAP. How now, my headstrong! where have you been gadding?

JUL. Where I have learn'd me to repent the sin
Of disobedient opposition
To you and your behests, and am enjoin'd
By holy Laurence to fall prostrate here, 20
And beg your pardon: pardon, I beseech you!
Henceforward I am ever ruled by you.

CAP. Send for the county; go tell him of this:
I'll have this knot knit up to-morrow morning.

JUL. I met the youthful lord at Laurence' cell; 25
And gave him what becomèd love I might,
Not stepping o'er the bounds of modesty.

CAP. Why, I am glad on 't; this is well: stand up:
This is as 't should be. Let me see the county;
Ay, marry, go, I say, and fetch him hither. 30

83. **reeky**, smoky, hence malodorous; **chapless**, jawless. 96. **humour**, fluid. 97. **surcease**, cease. 102. **supple government**, the power to make the body supple. 113. **against**, by the time that. 114. **drift**, intention. 119. **inconstant toy**, fickle whim. Scene ii: 14. **peevish**, silly; **harlotry**, hussy. 26. **becomed**, fitting.

Now, afore God! this reverend holy friar,
All our whole city is much bound to him.

JUL. Nurse, will you go with me into my closet,
To help me sort such needful ornaments
As you think fit to furnish me to-morrow? 35

LA. CAP. No, not till Thursday; there is time enough.

CAP. Go, nurse, go with her; we'll to church to-morrow. [*Exeunt* JULIET *and* NURSE.

LA. CAP. We shall be short in our provision:
'Tis now near night.

CAP. Tush, I will stir about,
And all things shall be well, I warrant thee, wife: 40
Go thou to Juliet, help to deck up her;
I'll not to bed to-night; let me alone;
I'll play the housewife for this once. What, ho!
They are all forth. Well, I will walk myself
To County Paris, to prepare him up 45
Against to-morrow: my heart is wondrous light,
Since this same wayward girl is so reclaim'd.
[*Exeunt.*

SCENE III. JULIET's *chamber*

[*Enter* JULIET *and* NURSE.]

JUL. Ay, those attires are best: but, gentle nurse,
I pray thee, leave me to myself to-night;
For I have need of many orisons
To move the heavens to smile upon my state,
Which, well thou know'st, is cross and full of sin. 5

[*Enter* LADY CAPULET.]

LA. CAP. What, are you busy, ho? need you my help?

JUL. No, madam; we have cull'd such necessaries
As are behoveful for our state to-morrow:
So please you, let me now be left alone,
And let the nurse this night sit up with you; 10
For, I am sure, you have your hands full all,
In this so sudden business.

LA. CAP. Good night:
Get thee to bed, and rest; for thou hast need.
[*Exeunt* LADY CAPULET *and* NURSE.

JUL. Farewell! God knows when we shall meet again.
I have a faint cold fear thrills through my veins, 15
That almost freezes up the heat of life:
I'll call them back again to comfort me:
Nurse! what should she do here?
My dismal scene I needs must act alone.
Come, vial. 20
What if this mixture do not work at all?
Shall I be married then to-morrow morning?
No, no: this shall forbid it: lie thou there.
[*Laying down her dagger.*]
What if it be a poison, which the friar
Subtly hath minister'd to have me dead, 25
Lest in this marriage he should be dishonour'd,
Because he married me before to Romeo?
I fear it is: and yet, methinks, it should not,
For he hath still been tried a holy man.
How if, when I am laid into the tomb, 30
I wake before the time that Romeo
Come to redeem me? there's a fearful point!
Shall I not, then, be stifled in the vault,
To whose foul mouth no healthsome air breathes in,
And there die strangled ere my Romeo comes?
Or, if I live, is it not very like, 36
The horrible conceit of death and night,
Together with the terror of the place,—
As in a vault, an ancient receptacle,
Where, for these many hundred years, the bones 40
Of all my buried ancestors are pack'd;
Where bloody Tybalt, yet but green in earth,
Lies festering in his shroud; where, as they say,
At some hours in the night spirits resort;—
Alack, alack, is it not like that I, 45
So early waking, what with loathsome smells,
And shrieks like mandrakes' torn out of the earth,
That living mortals, hearing them, run mad:—
O, if I wake, shall I not be distraught,
Environèd with all these hideous fears? 50
And madly play with my forefathers' joints?
And pluck the mangled Tybalt from his shroud?

33. closet, private chamber. 45. up, completely. Scene iii: 3. orisons, prayers. 5. cross, contrary. 8. behoveful, useful; state, celebration. 15. faint, causing faintness. 25. minister'd, administered. 29. tried, proved. 37. conceit, idea. 47. shrieks like mandrakes', the root of the mandrake resembles a human figure. It was supposed to utter a shriek when uprooted.

And, in this rage, with some great kinsman's bone,
As with a club, dash out my desperate brains?
O, look! methinks I see my cousin's ghost 55
Seeking out Romeo, that did spit his body
Upon a rapier's point: stay, Tybalt, stay!
Romeo, I come! this do I drink to thee.
[*She falls upon her bed, within the curtains.*

SCENE IV. *Hall in Capulet's house.*

[*Enter* LADY CAPULET *and* NURSE.]

LA. CAP. Hold, take these keys, and fetch more spices, nurse.
NURSE. They call for dates and quinces in the pastry.

[*Enter* CAPULET.]

CAP. Come, stir, stir, stir! the second cock hath crow'd,
The curfew-bell hath rung, 'tis three o'clock:
Look to the baked meats, good Angelica: 5
Spare not for cost.
NURSE. Go, you cot-quean, go,
Get you to bed; faith, you'll be sick to-morrow
For this night's watching.
CAP. No, not a whit: what! I have watch'd ere now
All night for lesser cause, and ne'er been sick.
LA. CAP. Ay, you have been a mouse-hunt in your time; 11
But I will watch you from such watching now.
[*Exeunt* LADY CAPULET *and* NURSE.
CAP. A jealous-hood, a jealous-hood!

[*Enter three or four* SERVINGMEN, *with spits, logs, and baskets.*]

Now, fellow,
What's there?
FIRST SERV. Things for the cook, sir; but I know not what.
CAP. Make haste, make haste. [*Exit* FIRST SERV.] Sirrah, fetch drier logs: 15
Call Peter, he will show thee where they are.
SEC. SERV. I have a head, sir, that will find out logs,
And never trouble Peter for the matter. [*Exit.*
CAP. Mass, and well said; a merry whoreson, ha!
Thou shalt be logger-head. Good faith, 'tis day: 20
The county will be here with music straight,
For so he said he would: I hear him near.
[*Music within.*]
Nurse! Wife! What, ho! What, nurse, I say!

[*Re-enter* NURSE.]

Go waken Juliet, go and trim her up;
I'll go and chat with Paris: hie, make haste,
Make haste; the bridegroom he is come already: 26
Make haste, I say. [*Exeunt.*

SCENE V. JULIET'S *chamber.*

[*Enter* NURSE.]

NURSE. Mistress! what, mistress! Juliet! fast, I warrant her, she:
Why, lamb! why, lady! fie, you slug-a-bed!
Why, love, I say! madam! sweet-heart! why, bride!
What, not a word? you take your pennyworths now;
Sleep for a week; for the next night, I warrant, 5
The County Paris hath set up his rest,
That you shall rest but little. God forgive me,
Marry, and amen, how sound is she asleep!
I must needs wake her. Madam, madam, madam!
Ay, let the county take you in your bed; 10
He'll fright you up, i' faith. Will it not be?
[*Undraws the curtains.*]
What, dress'd! and in your clothes! and down again!
I must needs wake you: Lady! lady! lady!
Alas, alas! Help, help! my lady's dead!
O, well-a-day, that ever I was born! 15
Some aqua vitæ, ho! My lord! my lady!

[*Enter* LADY CAPULET.]

LA. CAP. What noise is here?
NURSE. O lamentable day!
LA. CAP. What is the matter?
NURSE. Look, look! O heavy day!

Scene iv: 2. **pastry**, pantry. 4. **curfew**, originally an evening bell. The word came to be applied to other ringings. 5. **baked meats**, pies. 6. **cot-quean**, contemptuous for a man who acts as housewife. 8. **night's watching**, staying awake all night. 11. **mouse-hunt**, pursuer of women.

13. **jealous-hood**, jealous person, as often in Shakespeare, the abstract for the concrete. 20. **logger-head**, blockhead. 24. **trim her up**, get her dressed. Scene v: 1. **fast**, fast asleep. 2. **slug-a-bed**, sleepy head. 4. **pennyworths**, little bits. 6. **set up his rest**, staked his all, i.e., resolved.

LA. CAP. O me, O me! My child, my only life,
Revive, look up, or I will die with thee! 20
Help, help! Call help.

[*Enter* CAPULET.]

CAP. For shame, bring Juliet forth; her lord is come.
NURSE. She's dead, deceased, she's dead; alack the day!
LA. CAP. Alack the day, she's dead, she's dead, she's dead!
CAP. Ha! let me see her: out, alas! she's cold; 25
Her blood is settled, and her joints are stiff;
Life and these lips have long been separated:
Death lies on her like an untimely frost
Upon the sweetest flower of all the field.
NURSE. O lamentable day!
LA. CAP. O woful time! 30
CAP. Death, that hath ta'en her hence to make me wail,
Ties up my tongue, and will not let me speak.

[*Enter* FRIAR LAURENCE *and* PARIS, *with* MUSICIANS.]

FRI. L. Come, is the bride ready to go to church?
CAP. Ready to go, but never to return.
O son! the night before thy wedding-day 35
Hath Death lain with thy wife. There she lies,
Flower as she was, deflowerèd by him.
Death is my son-in-law, Death is my heir;
My daughter he hath wedded: I will die,
And leave him all; life, living, all is Death's.
PAR. Have I thought long to see this morning's face, 41
And doth it give me such a sight as this?
LA. CAP. Accursed, unhappy, wretched, hateful day!
Most miserable hour that e'er time saw
In lasting labour of his pilgrimage! 45
But one, poor one, one poor and loving child,
But one thing to rejoice and solace in,
And cruel death hath catch'd it from my sight!
NURSE. O woe! woful, woful, woful day!
Most lamentable day, most woful day, 50
That ever, ever, I did yet behold!
O day! O day! O day! O hateful day!
Never was seen so black a day as this:
O woful day, O woful day!
PAR. Beguiled, divorced, wronged, spited, slain! 55
Most detestable death, by thee beguiled,
By cruel cruel thee quite overthrown!
O love! O life! not life, but love in death!
CAP. Despised, distressed, hated, martyr'd, kill'd!
Uncomfortable time, why camest thou now
To murder, murder our solemnity? 61
O child! O child! my soul, and not my child!
Dead art thou! Alack! my child is dead;
And with my child my joys are burièd.
FRI. L. Peace, ho, for shame! confusion's cure lives not 65
In these confusions. Heaven and yourself
Had part in this fair maid; now heaven hath all,
And all the better is it for the maid:
Your part in her you could not keep from death,
But heaven keeps his part in eternal life. 70
The most you sought was her promotion;
For 'twas your heaven she should be advanced:
And weep ye now, seeing she is advanced
Above the clouds, as high as heaven itself?
O, in this love, you love your child so ill, 75
That you run mad, seeing that she is well:
She's not well married that lives married long;
But she's best married that dies married young.
Dry up your tears, and stick your rosemary
On this fair corse; and, as the custom is, 80
In all her best array bear her to church:
For though fond nature bids us all lament,
Yet nature's tears are reason's merriment.
CAP. All things that we ordainèd festival,
Turn from their office to black funeral; 85
Our instruments to melancholy bells,
Our wedding cheer to a sad burial feast,
Our solemn hymns to sullen dirges change,
Our bridal flowers serve for a buried corse,
And all things change them to the contrary. 90
FRI. L. Sir, go you in; and, madam, go with him;
And go, Sir Paris; every one prepare

26. settled, congealed. 37. deflowered, ravished. 41. thought long, longed. 61. solemnity, festivity. 65. confusion's, destruction's. 72. advanced, advanced in rank. 73. advanced, exalted. 79. rosemary, the evergreen, emblem of both remembrance and immortality, was used at both weddings and funerals. 82. fond, foolish. 83. yet . . . merriment, yet Reason laughs at the tears which natural affection makes us shed.

To follow this fair corse unto her grave:
The heavens do lour upon you for some ill;
Move them no more by crossing their high will. 95

[*Exeunt* CAPULET, LADY CAPULET, PARIS, *and* FRIAR.

FIRST MUS. Faith, we may put up our pipes, and be gone.

NURSE. Honest good fellows, ah, put up, put up;
For, well you know, this is a pitiful case. [*Exit.*

FIRST MUS. Ay, by my troth, the case may be amended. 101

[*Enter* PETER.]

PET. Musicians, O, musicians, "Heart's ease, Heart's ease:" O, an you will have me live, play "Heart's ease."

FIRST MUS. Why "Heart's ease"?

PET. O, musicians, because my heart itself plays "My heart is full of woe:" O, play me some merry dump, to comfort me. 108

FIRST MUS. Not a dump we; 'tis no time to play now.

PET. You will not, then?

FIRST MUS. No.

PET. I will then give it you soundly.

FIRST MUS. What will you give us?

PET. No money, on my faith, but the gleek; I will give you the minstrel. 116

FIRST MUS. Then will I give you the serving-creature.

PET. Then will I lay the serving-creature's dagger on your pate. I will carry no crotchets: I'll re you, I'll fa you; do you note me? 121

FIRST MUS. An you re us and fa us, you note us.

SEC. MUS. Pray you, put up your dagger, and put out your wit.

PET. Then have at you with my wit! I will dry-beat you with an iron wit, and put up my iron dagger. Answer me like men:
"When griping grief the heart doth wound,
And doleful dumps the mind oppress,
Then music with her silver sound" 130
why "silver sound"? why "music with her silver sound"? What say you, Simon Catling?

FIRST MUS. Marry, sir, because silver hath a sweet sound.

PET. Pretty! What say you, Hugh Rebeck?

SEC. MUS. I say "silver sound," because musicians sound for silver.

PET. Pretty too! What say you, James Soundpost? 139

THIRD MUS. Faith, I know not what to say.

PET. O, I cry you mercy; you are the singer: I will say for you. It is "music with her silver sound," because musicians have no gold for sounding: 143
"Then music with her silver sound
With speedy help doth lend redress."

[*Exit.*

FIRST MUS. What a pestilent knave is this same!

SEC. MUS. Hang him, Jack! Come, we'll in here; tarry for the mourners, and stay dinner. [*Exeunt.*

ACT V

SCENE I. *Mantua. A street.*

[*Enter* ROMEO.]

ROM. If I may trust the flattering truth of sleep,
My dreams presage some joyful news at hand:
My bosom's lord sits lightly in his throne;
And all this day an unaccustom'd spirit
Lifts me above the ground with cheerful thoughts. 5
I dreamt my lady came and found me dead—
Strange dream, that gives a dead man leave to think!—
And breathed such life with kisses in my lips,
That I revived, and was an emperor.
Ah me! how sweet is love itself possess'd, 10
When but love's shadows are so rich in joy!

101. **case**, the musician quibbles on the meaning "cover"; **may be amended**, could be a better one. 108. **dump**, mournful air. 115. **gleek**, gibe. 120-1. **carry**, endure; **crotchets**, (1) quarter notes, (2) caprices. 124. **put out**, extinguish. Peter takes it as the opposite of put up (your dagger), i.e., unsheath. 128-130. **When . . . silver sound**, part of a song by Richard Edwards published in **The Paradise of Dainty Devises** (1576). 132. **Catling**, a small lute string made of catgut. 135. **Rebeck**, the name of a three-stringed violin. 139. **Soundpost**, the peg on the inside of a stringed instrument directly under the bridge. 143. **sounding**, playing. 146. **pestilent**, vexatious. **Act V, Scene i**: 3. **bosom's lord**, i.e., the heart. 11. **shadows**, phantoms.

[*Enter* BALTHASAR, *booted*.]

News from Verona!—How now, Balthasar!
Dost thou not bring me letters from the friar?
How doth my lady? Is my father well?
How fares my Juliet? that I ask again, 15
For nothing can be ill, if she be well.
BAL. Then she is well, and nothing can be ill:
Her body sleeps in Capels' monument,
And her immortal part with angels lives.
I saw her laid low in her kindred's vault, 20
And presently took post to tell it you:
O, pardon me for bringing these ill news,
Since you did leave it for my office, sir.
ROM. Is it even so? then I defy you, stars!
Thou know'st my lodging: get me ink and paper, 25
And hire post-horses; I will hence to-night.
BAL. I do beseech you, sir, have patience:
Your looks are pale and wild, and do import
Some misadventure.
ROM. Tush, thou art deceived:
Leave me, and do the thing I bid thee do. 30
Hast thou no letters to me from the friar?
BAL. No, my good lord.
ROM. No matter: get thee gone,
And hire those horses; I'll be with thee straight. [*Exit* BALTHASAR.]
Well, Juliet, I will lie with thee to-night.
Let's see for means: O mischief, thou art swift 35
To enter in the thoughts of desperate men!
I do remember an apothecary,—
And hereabouts he dwells,—which late I noted
In tatter'd weeds, with overwhelming brows,
Culling of simples; meagre were his looks, 40
Sharp misery had worn him to the bones:
And in his needy shop a tortoise hung,
An alligator stuff'd, and other skins
Of ill-shaped fishes; and about his shelves
A beggarly account of empty boxes, 45
Green earthen pots, bladders and musty seeds,
Remnants of packthread and old cakes of roses,
Were thinly scatter'd, to make up a show.
Noting this penury, to myself I said
"An if a man did need a poison now, 50
Whose sale is present death in Mantua,
Here lives a caitiff wretch would sell it him."
O, this same thought did but forerun my need;
And this same needy man must sell it me.
As I remember, this should be the house. 55
Being holiday, the beggar's shop is shut.
What, ho! apothecary!

[*Enter* APOTHECARY.]

AP. Who calls so loud?
ROM. Come hither, man. I see that thou art poor:
Hold, there is forty ducats: let me have
A dram of poison, such soon-speeding gear 60
As will disperse itself through all the veins
That the life-weary taker may fall dead
And that the trunk may be discharged of breath
As violently as hasty powder fired
Doth hurry from the fatal cannon's womb. 65
AP. Such mortal drugs I have; but Mantua's law
Is death to any he that utters them.
ROM. Art thou so bare and full of wretchedness,
And fear'st to die? famine is in thy cheeks,
Need and oppression starveth in thine eyes, 70
Contempt and beggary hangs upon thy back;
The world is not thy friend nor the world's law;
The world affords no law to make thee rich;
Then be not poor, but break it, and take this.
AP. My poverty, but not my will, consents. 75
ROM. I pay thy poverty, and not thy will.
AP. Put this in any liquid thing you will,
And drink it off; and, if you had the strength
Of twenty men, it would dispatch you straight.
ROM. There is thy gold, worse poison to men's souls, 80
Doing more murders in this loathsome world,
Than these poor compounds that thou mayst not sell.
I sell thee poison; thou hast sold me none.
Farewell: buy food, and get thyself in flesh.
Come, cordial and not poison, go with me 85
To Juliet's grave; for there must I use thee.
[*Exeunt*.

s.d. booted, wearing riding boots. 18. monument, burial vault. 21. took post, started with post horses. 24. defy, disown, repudiate. 27. patience, courage. 39. weeds, clothes; overwhelming, overhanging. 40. simples, medicinal herbs. 45. beggarly account, meagre collection. 47. cakes of roses, petals of roses pressed into cakes. 51. present, immediate. 52. catiff, miserable creature. 59. ducats, gold coins of varying value. 60. gear, stuff. 63. trunk, body. 67. utters, issues, sells. 73. affords, provides. 85. cordial, stimulant.

SCENE II. FRIAR LAURENCE'S *cell.*

[*Enter* FRIAR JOHN.]

FRI. J. Holy Franciscan friar! brother, ho!

[*Enter* FRIAR LAURENCE.]

FRI. L. This same should be the voice of Friar John.
Welcome from Mantua: what says Romeo?
Or, if his mind be writ, give me his letter.

FRI. J. Going to find a bare-foot brother out, 5
One of our order, to associate me,
Here in this city visiting the sick,
And finding him, the searchers of the town,
Suspecting that we both were in a house
Where the infectious pestilence did reign, 10
Seal'd up the doors, and would not let us forth;
So that my speed to Mantua there was stay'd.

FRI. L. Who bare my letter, then, to Romeo?

FRI. J. I could not send it,—here it is again,—
Nor get a messenger to bring it thee, 15
So fearful were they of infection.

FRI. L. Unhappy fortune! by my brotherhood,
The letter was not nice but full of charge
Of dear import, and the neglecting it
May do much danger. Friar John, go hence;
Get me an iron crow, and bring it straight 21
Unto my cell.

FRI. J. Brother, I'll go and bring it thee.
[*Exit.*

FRI. L. Now must I go to the monument alone;
Within this three hours will fair Juliet wake:
She will beshrew me much that Romeo 26
Hath had no notice of these accidents;
But I will write again to Mantua,
And keep her at my cell till Romeo come;
Poor living corse, closed in a dead man's tomb! [*Exit.* 30

SCENE III. *A churchyard; in it a tomb belonging to the Capulets.*

[*Enter* PARIS, *and his* PAGE *bearing flowers and a torch.*]

PAR. Give me thy torch, boy: hence, and stand aloof:
Yet put it out, for I would not be seen.
Under yond yew-trees lay thee all along,
Holding thine ear close to the hollow ground;
So shall no foot upon the churchyard tread, 5
Being loose, unfirm, with digging up of graves,
But thou shalt hear it: whistle then to me,
As signal that thou hear'st something approach.
Give me those flowers. Do as I bid thee, go.

PAGE. [*Aside*] I am almost afraid to stand alone 10
Here in the churchyard; yet I will adventure.
[*Retires.*

PAR. Sweet flower, with flowers thy bridal bed I strew,—
O woe! thy canopy is dust and stones;—
Which with sweet water nightly I will dew,
Or, wanting that, with tears distill'd by moans: 15
The obsequies that I for thee will keep
Nightly shall be to strew thy grave and weep. [*The* PAGE *whistles.*]
The boy gives warning something doth approach.
What cursèd foot wanders this way to-night,
To cross my obsequies and true love's rite? 20
What, with a torch! muffle me, night, awhile.
[*Retires.*

[*Enter* ROMEO *and* BALTHASAR, *with a torch, mattock, &c.*]

ROM. Give me that mattock and the wrenching iron.
Hold, take this letter; early in the morning
See thou deliver it to my lord and father.
Give me the light: upon thy life, I charge thee, 25
Whate'er thou hear'st or seest, stand all aloof,
And do not interrupt me in my course.
Why I descend into this bed of death,
Is partly to behold my lady's face;
But chiefly to take thence from her dead finger 30
A precious ring, a ring that I must use
In dear employment: therefore hence, be gone:
But if thou, jealous, dost return to pry
In what I further shall intend to do,
By heaven, I will tear thee joint by joint 35

Scene ii: 6. associate, accompany. **8. searchers,** sanitary police. **12. stay'd,** stopped. **18. nice,** trivial; **charge,** importance. **19. dear import,** important significance. **21. crow,** crowbar. **26. beshrew,** blame severely. **Scene iii: 3. all along,** at full length. **13. canopy,** covering. **14. sweet water,** perfume. **20. cross,** thwart. **21. muffle,** conceal. **22. wrenching iron,** i.e., crowbar. **33. jealous,** suspicious.

And strew this hungry churchyard with thy limbs:
The time and my intents are savage-wild,
More fierce and more inexorable far
Than empty tigers or the roaring sea.

BAL. I will be gone, sir, and not trouble you. 40

ROM. So shalt thou show me friendship. Take thou that:
Live, and be prosperous: and farewell, good fellow.

BAL. [*Aside*] For all this same, I'll hide me hereabout:
His looks I fear, and his intents I doubt. [*Retires.*

ROM. Thou detestable maw, thou womb of death, 45
Gorged with the dearest morsel of the earth,
Thus I enforce thy rotten jaws to open,
And, in despite, I'll cram thee with more food! [*Opens the tomb.*

PAR. This is that banish'd haughty Montague,
That murder'd my love's cousin, with which grief, 50
It is supposed, the fair creature died;
And here is come to do some villainous shame
To the dead bodies: I will apprehend him. [*Comes forward.*]
Stop thy unhallow'd toil, vile Montague!
Can vengeance be pursued further than death?
Condemnèd villain, I do apprehend thee: 56
Obey, and go with me; for thou must die.

ROM. I must indeed; and therefore came I hither.
Good gentle youth, tempt not a desperate man;
Fly hence, and leave me: think upon these gone; 60
Let them affright thee. I beseech thee, youth,
Put not another sin upon my head,
By urging me to fury: O, be gone!
By heaven, I love thee better than myself;
For I come hither arm'd against myself: 65
Stay not, be gone; live, and hereafter say,
A madman's mercy bade thee run away.

PAR. I do defy thy conjurations,
And apprehend thee for a felon here. 69

ROM. Wilt thou provoke me? then have at thee, boy! [*They fight.*

PAGE. O Lord, they fight! I will go call the watch. [*Exit.*

PAR. O, I am slain! [*Falls.*] If thou be merciful,
Open the tomb, lay me with Juliet. [*Dies.*

ROM. In faith I will. Let me peruse this face.
Mercutio's kinsman, noble County Paris! 75
What said my man, when my betossèd soul
Did not attend him as we rode? I think
He told me Paris should have married Juliet:
Said he not so? or did I dream it so?
Or am I mad, hearing him talk of Juliet, 80
To think it was so? O, give me thy hand,
One writ with me in sour misfortune's book!
I'll bury thee in a triumphant grave;
A grave? O, no! a lantern, slaughter'd youth,
For here lies Juliet, and her beauty makes 85
This vault a feasting presence full of light.
Death, lie thou there, by a dead man interr'd. [*Laying* PARIS *in the tomb.*]
How oft when men are at the point of death
Have they been merry! which their keepers call
A lightning before death: O, how may I 90
Call this a lightning? O my love! my wife!
Death, that hath suck'd the honey of thy breath,
Hath had no power yet upon thy beauty:
Thou art not conquer'd; beauty's ensign yet
Is crimson in thy lips and in thy cheeks, 95
And death's pale flag is not advanced there.
Tybalt, liest thou there in thy bloody sheet?
O, what more favour can I do to thee,
Than with that hand that cut thy youth in twain
To sunder his that was thine enemy? 100
Forgive me, cousin! Ah, dear Juliet,
Why art thou yet so fair? shall I believe
That unsubstantial death is amorous,
And that the lean abhorrèd monster keeps
Thee here in dark to be his paramour? 105
For fear of that, I still will stay with thee;
And never from this palace of dim night
Depart again: here, here will I remain
With worms that are thy chamber-maids; O, here
Will I set up my everlasting rest, 110
And shake the yoke of inauspicious stars

44. **doubt**, am suspicious of. 45. **maw**, stomach. 48. **despite**, scorn. 53. **apprehend**, seize. 68. **conjurations**, entreaties. 74. **peruse**, examine. 76. **betossed**, tossed about. 77. **attend him**, pay attention to him. 82. **writ**, inscribed.

84. **lantern**, lighthouse. Lantern was a small windowed dome set in the roof of a hall. 86. **feasting presence**, festive presence chamber. 89. **keepers**, nurses. 90. **lightning**, i.e., a shedding of light by spirits. 110. **set . . . rest**, see IV, v. 6: make my final resolution; rest also = repose.

From this world-wearied flesh. Eyes, look your last!
Arms, take your last embrace! and, lips, O you
The doors of breath, seal with a righteous kiss
A dateless bargain to engrossing death! 115
Come, bitter conduct, come, unsavoury guide!
Thou desperate pilot, now at once run on
The dashing rocks thy sea-sick weary bark!
Here's to my love! [*Drinks*] O true apothecary!
Thy drugs are quick. Thus with a kiss I die.
[*Dies.* 120

[*Enter, at the other end of the churchyard,* FRIAR LAURENCE, *with a lantern, crow, and spade.*]

FRI. L. Saint Francis be my speed! how oft to-night
Have my old feet stumbled at graves! Who's there?

BAL. Here's one, a friend, and one that knows you well.

FRI. L. Bliss be upon you! Tell me, good my friend,
What torch is yond, that vainly lends his light
To grubs and eyeless skulls? as I discern, 126
It burneth in the Capels' monument.

BAL. It doth so, holy sir; and there's my master,
One that you love.

FRI. L. Who is it?

BAL. Romeo.

FRI. L. How long hath he been there?

BAL. Full half an hour. 130

FRI. L. Go with me to the vault.

BAL. I dare not, sir:
My master knows not but I am gone hence;
And fearfully did menace me with death,
If I did stay to look on his intents.

FRI. L. Stay, then; I'll go alone. Fear comes upon me: 135
O, much I fear some ill unlucky thing.

BAL. As I did sleep under this yew-tree here,
I dreamt my master and another fought,
And that my master slew him.

FRI. L. Romeo! [*Advances.*]
Alack, alack, what blood is this, which stains
The stony entrance of this sepulchre? 141
What mean these masterless and gory swords
To lie discolour'd by this place of peace?
[*Enters the tomb.*]
Romeo! O, pale! Who else? what, Paris, too?
And steep'd in blood? Ah, what an unkind hour 145
Is guilty of this lamentable chance!
The lady stirs. [JULIET *wakes.*

JUL. O comfortable friar! where is my lord?
I do remember well where I should be,
And there I am. Where is my Romeo? 150
[*Noise within.*

FRI. L. I hear some noise, Lady, come from that nest
Of death, contagion, and unnatural sleep:
A greater power than we can contradict
Hath thwarted our intents. Come, come away.
Thy husband in thy bosom there lies dead;
And Paris too. Come, I'll dispose of thee 156
Among a sisterhood of holy nuns:
Stay not to question, for the watch is coming;
Come, go, good Juliet [*Noise again*], I dare no longer stay.

JUL. Go, get thee hence, for I will not away.
[*Exit* FRI. L.]
What's here? a cup, closed in my true love's hand? 161
Poison, I see, hath been his timeless end:
O churl! drunk all, and left no friendly drop
To help me after? I will kiss thy lips;
Haply some poison yet doth hang on them,
To make me die with a restorative. 166
[*Kisses him.*]
Thy lips are warm.

FIRST WATCH. [*Within*] Lead, boy: which way?

JUL. Yea, noise? then I'll be brief. O happy dagger! [*Snatching* ROMEO's *dagger.*]
This is thy sheath [*Stabs herself*]; there rust, and let me die. 170
[*Falls on* ROMEO's *body, and dies.*

[*Enter* WATCH, *with the* PAGE *of* PARIS.]

PAGE. This is the place; there, where the torch doth burn.

FIRST WATCH. The ground is bloody; search about the churchyard:
Go, some of you, whoe'er you find attach.
Pitiful sight! here lies the county slain;
And Juliet bleeding, warm, and newly dead,
Who here hath lain these two days burièd. 176
Go, tell the prince: run to the Capulets:

115. dateless, eternal; engrossing, monopolizing. 116. conduct, escort. 121. speed, protector. 122. stumbled at graves, supposed to be a bad omen. 127. monument, tomb. 134. look . . . intents, observe his efforts. 148. comfortable, comforting. 162. timeless, untimely. 173. attach, arrest.

Raise up the Montagues: some others search:
We see the ground whereon these woes do lie;
But the true ground of all these piteous woes
We cannot without circumstance descry. 181

[*Re-enter some of the* WATCH, *with* BALTHASAR.]

SEC. WATCH. Here's Romeo's man; we found him in the churchyard.

FIRST WATCH. Hold him in safety, till the prince come hither.

[*Re-enter others of the* WATCH, *with* FRIAR LAURENCE.]

THIRD WATCH. Here is a friar, that trembles, sighs, and weeps:
We took this mattock and this spade from him, 185
As he was coming from this churchyard side.

FIRST WATCH. A great suspicion: stay the friar too.

[*Enter the* PRINCE *and* ATTENDANTS.]

PRINCE. What misadventure is so early up,
That calls our person from our morning's rest?

[*Enter* CAPULET, LADY CAPULET, *and others.*]

CAP. What should it be, that they so shriek abroad? 190

LA. CAP. The people in the street cry Romeo,
Some Juliet, and some Paris; and all run,
With open outcry, toward our monument.

PRINCE. What fear is this which startles in our ears?

FIRST WATCH. Sovereign, here lies the County Paris slain; 195
And Romeo dead; and Juliet, dead before,
Warm and new kill'd.

PRINCE. Search, seek, and know how this foul murder comes.

FIRST WATCH. Here is a friar, and slaughter'd Romeo's man;
With instruments upon them. fit to open 200
These dead men's tombs.

CAP. O heavens! O wife, look how our daughter bleeds!
This dagger hath mista'en,—for, lo, his house
Is empty on the back of Montague,—
And it mis-sheathed in my daughter's bosom!

LA. CAP. O me! this sight of death is as a bell, 206
That warns my old age to a sepulchre.

[*Enter* MONTAGUE *and others.*]

PRINCE. Come, Montague; for thou art early up,
To see thy son and heir more early down.

MON. Alas, my liege, my wife is dead to-night; 210
Grief of my son's exile hath stopp'd her breath:
What further woe conspires against mine age?

PRINCE. Look, and thou shalt see.

MON. O thou untaught! what manners is in this,
To press before thy father to a grave? 215

PRINCE. Seal up the mouth of outrage for a while,
Till we can clear these ambiguities,
And know their spring, their head, their true descent;
And then will I be general of your woes,
And lead you even to death: meantime forbear, 220
And let mischance be slave to patience.
Bring forth the parties of suspicion.

FRI. L. I am the greatest, able to do least,
Yet most suspected, as the time and place
Doth make against me, of this direful murder:
And here I stand, both to impeach and purge
Myself condemned and myself excused. 227

PRINCE. Then say at once what thou dost know in this.

FRI. L. I will be brief, for my short date of breath
Is not so long as is a tedious tale. 230
Romeo, there dead, was husband to that Juliet;
And she, there dead, that Romeo's faithful wife:
I married them; and their stol'n marriage-day
Was Tybalt's dooms-day, whose untimely death
Banish'd the new-made bridegroom from this city, 235
For whom, and not for Tybalt, Juliet pined.
You, to remove that siege of grief from her,
Betroth'd and would have married her perforce
To County Paris: then comes she to me,

181. circumstance, particulars. 187. stay, detain. 203. house, i.e., scabbard. 204. back, the dagger was carried on the back below the waist. 206. bell, i.e., the bell rung to announce the passing of a sick person. 207. warns, summons. 216. outrage, fury. 222. parties of, persons under. 226. purge, clear (from suspicion). 229. my . . . breath, the little time I have to live.

And, with wild looks, bid me devise some mean 240
To rid her from this second marriage,
Or in my cell there would she kill herself.
Then gave I her, so tutor'd by my art,
A sleeping potion; which so took effect
As I intended, for it wrought on her 245
The form of death: meantime I writ to Romeo,
That he should hither come as this dire night,
To help to take her from her borrow'd grave,
Being the time the potion's force should cease.
But he which bore my letter, Friar John, 250
Was stay'd by accident, and yesternight
Return'd my letter back. Then all alone
At the prefixèd hour of her waking,
Came I to take her from her kindred's vault;
Meaning to keep her closely at my cell, 255
Till I conveniently could send to Romeo:
But when I came, some minute ere the time
Of her awaking, here untimely lay
The noble Paris and true Romeo dead.
She wakes; and I entreated her come forth, 260
And bear this work of heaven with patience:
But then a noise did scare me from the tomb;
And she, too desperate, would not go with me,
But, as it seems, did violence on herself.
All this I know; and to the marriage 265
Her nurse is privy; and, if aught in this
Miscarried by my fault, let my old life
Be sacrificed, some hour before his time,
Unto the rigour of severest law.

PRINCE. We still have known thee for a holy man. 270
Where's Romeo's man? what can he say in this?

BAL. I brought my master news of Juliet's death;
And then in post he came from Mantua
To this same place, to this same monument.
This letter he early bid me give his father,
And threaten'd me with death, going in the vault, 276
If I departed not and left him there.

PRINCE. Give me the letter; I will look on it.
Where is the county's page, that raised the watch?
Sirrah, what made your master in this place?

PAGE. He came with flowers to strew his lady's grave; 281
And bid me stand aloof, and so I did:
Anon comes one with light to ope the tomb;
And by and by my master drew on him;
And then I ran away to call the watch. 285

PRINCE. This letter doth make good the friar's words,
Their course of love, the tidings of her death:
And here he writes that he did buy a poison
Of a poor 'pothecary, and therewithal 289
Came to this vault to die, and lie with Juliet.
Where be these enemies? Capulet! Montague!
See, what a scourge is laid upon your hate,
That heaven finds means to kill your joys with love.
And I for winking at your discords too
Have lost a brace of kinsmen: all are punish'd.

CAP. O brother Montague, give me thy hand: 296
This is my daughter's jointure, for no more
Can I demand.

MON. But I can give thee more:
For I will raise her statue in pure gold;
That while Verona by that name is known, 300
There shall no figure at such rate be set
As that of true and faithful Juliet.

CAP. As rich shall Romeo's by his lady's lie;
Poor sacrifices of our enmity!

PRINCE. A glooming peace this morning with it brings; 305
The sun, for sorrow, will not show his head:
Go hence, to have more talk of these sad things;
Some shall be pardon'd, and some punishèd:
For never was a story of more woe
Than this of Juliet and her Romeo. 310

[*Exeunt.*

247. as this, this very. 253. prefixed, agreed upon previously. 255. closely, secretly. 273. post, haste. 280. made, was doing. 284. by and by, immediately. 297. jointure, dowry. 301. rate, value.

AFTERWORD

Productions of *Romeo and Juliet* in our time often insist on modern dress and modern idiom and manners. The producer, as he seeks to foster and to emphasize a superficial modernity in Shakespeare's tale of a pair of star-crossed lovers, is apparently unwilling to accept the play, as written. One senses, in his nervous attempt to "make it new," an uneasy belief that the play is not really universal, not "for all time." If he were to speak to us frankly, he might acknowledge that for him, *Romeo and Juliet* reflects in damaging ways the dead ideas of the time which brought it to birth, a time which has been swallowed up forever in history. The conventions which Shakespeare inherits, and with which he works in constructing his plot, are obsolete conventions. For that reason the plot of the play no longer carries conviction. Apologies are in order, as when we say that Shakespeare was after all the child of his age.

The merely defensive reader will counter these objections by asserting that Shakespeare, being Shakespeare, can do no wrong. The right kind of reader is a critic, not an acolyte paying homage. He will want to meet head-on the implicit suggestion that *Romeo and Juliet* is a play for its own time, rather than for ours. Here are a number of consequential details the reader will have to consider as he seeks to exercise his critical intelligence.

The young lovers are characterized as "star-crossed lovers." But though astrology, in the Age of Aquarius, is once again a vastly popular preoccupation—perhaps as we realize that forces beyond our ken are powerfully influential for the course of human destiny—most of us do not believe in the domination of the stars. Shakespeare, apparently, allows the stars a determining role in his story. That is one count against Shakespeare's credibility. It is not the only count.

For the winding up of the play, Shakespeare depends on the operation of chance or fate. A crucial letter miscarries. Friar John, who is supposed to inform Romeo of Juliet's trance-like sleep, is prevented by plague (an accidental detail) from reaching his destination. Friar Laurence, hurrying to open the tomb, stumbles over gravestones and is fatally delayed. The death of Juliet, like that of Romeo, is brought about by accident. It is what the Chorus describes as a "misadventured" overthrow. Juliet awakens, not before the suicide of Romeo, but just after. Evidently the playwright, like a puppet master, has his hands on all the ropes.

Shakespeare when he has got into his stride is said to manage these things much better. The governing presence of an old-fashioned deity, whether embodied in astrological influence or heredity or chance, is not nearly so obvious in his later work. In the mature Shakespeare—for example, in *King Lear*—it is convenient to say that the hero is the immediate cause of his own downfall. He grows old before he grows wise. To recite another critical commonplace: in the later tragedies, character is fate. This commonplace does not hold up, when applied to the action of *Romeo and Juliet*. Neither the hero nor heroine is master of his fate but the product of "fatal loins." Does the continuing and decisive impact of the past, like the important role of chance or fate, make the play less impressive?

At this point, if one is really to come to terms with Shakespeare's tragedy—which means, first of all, to discover what is vital and pertinent about it—he will want to stop short and consult his own reaction. He will want to look at the play with fresh eyes, his own eyes. If *Romeo and Juliet* is deeply moving and lastingly popular, why is that? Dr. Johnson, who is the best of Shakespeare's critics, suggests an answer. "Nothing," says Johnson, "can please many or please long but just representations of general nature." *Romeo and Juliet* is such an accurate or just representation. It is not shipwrecked in time—the definition of a literary monument—nor does it dramatize in its essentials a discredited or outmoded reading of human beings and the painful business with which they are involved. The disquieting truth which Shakespeare enforces in *Romeo and Juliet* is reaffirmed in *King Lear*, in *Othello*, in *Hamlet*, and remains current today. This truth is that all men and women, simply by virtue of their kind, are endlessly vulnerable to the slings and arrows of fortune. To put it another way: freedom, in first and last things, is an illusion.

Othello is free, to murder or to hold his hand; and Mark Antony, to obey the strong imperatives of the time: the summons to honor and duty, or else to lose himself in "dotage." But no man, to quote from one of Shakespeare's sonnets, has power "to tell of good or evil luck," or to accomplish or withhold the coming on of either. None of us is privy to what succeeds in unknown fate. None of us is capable of giving direction to the unpredictable and yet unshunnable event. That is the point of the nautical imagery which Shakespeare employs in *Romeo and Juliet*. Romeo is characterized as a "desperate pilot." The "steerage" of his course is decreed. The bark he endeavors to sail answers only imperfectly to his commands.

An insistence on this tragic limitation is the burden of Shakespeare's last plays. Pericles, who is dogged by misfortune, is lessoned by it. Man, he perceives, is not the master of his fate:

> Time's the King of men:
> He's both their parent, and he is their grave,
> And gives them what he will, not what they crave.

The same perception is implicit already, in the melancholy chronicle of *Romeo and Juliet*. The high resolve of the lovers is in fee to mortality, not less than the foolish crotchets of old Capulet, or the spasmodic irascibility of Tybalt, or the ill-fated love of the County Paris. "Time's the King of men." The cycle of death and birth, in which human beings are inextricably involved, is indifferent to their importunate direction. This much, at least, Friar Laurence understands:

> The earth that's Nature's mother is her tomb,
> What is her burying grave, that is her womb.

Shakespeare's heroine bears witness to the illusory nature of self-sufficiency or self-determination. She is a pawn, required to participate in the senseless and enduring quarrel between the families of Montague and Capulet, a quarrel with which she has no concern and for which she is in no way responsible. On learning that Romeo is a Montague, she cries, "My only love sprung from my only hate!" A mere name is nothing, and yet it is able to hunt the lovers to death. Romeo, whenever he attempts to steer his own course, is sure to come to grief. His praiseworthy intention is to interrupt the duel between Mercutio and Tybalt. The unlooked-for result is the death of Mercutio and Tybalt. Romeo is apparently what he calls himself, in despair: "fortune's fool!"—the plaything of forces he can neither control nor comprehend. The entire action of the play conforms to the saying of Friar Laurence, another man whose good intentions are consistently baffled, in the final scene:

> A greater power than we can contradict
> Hath thwarted our intents.

The absence of ultimate freedom, like the ultimate defeat that is our common portion, is illustrated in Shakespeare's play by an ancient and familiar doctrine, known to the Elizabethans as "judicial astrology." This doctrine is to be read as an exemplum or cautionary tale, not necessarily true in itself but suggestive of truth. Shakespeare's more sophisticated contemporaries were inclined, with increasing skepticism, to call it in question, but not the point it communicates. To miss this point is to see the play as a cultural document, than which no mistake is more damaging to the vitality of a work of art. Cultural documents belong in rare book rooms and are intended for the perusal of the few. *Romeo and Juliet* belongs on the stage, and is the continuing inheritance of the multitude. It does not live as it illustrates an archaic cosmology known sometimes as the Elizabethan World Picture. It lives because it comments on the here and now. We accept the tragic plight of star-crossed lovers, not as we are willing to suspend our disbelief, but as we perceive that their plight, even in its particulars, is verifiable out of our own experience.

The business of scholarship, as transacted in footnotes and historical introductions, is to make the past apprehensible to the present. But scholarship does not illuminate, it darkens—or to vary the metaphor, it is like a red herring, which puts us off the scent, as it assumes that a play or poem is the sum of the ideas which compose it and is to be equated with its intellectual content. Shakespeare's ideas or suppositions, which may be false in point of fact, are not stated abstractly but in terms of the imagination, and it is the imaginative content that redeems them. W. B. Yeats, in his dubious character of philosopher or thinking man, was preoccupied with the phases of the moon; Conan Doyle, the creator of Sherlock Holmes, conversed with ectoplasm. One can say that they were crazy. Perhaps it is more fruitful to see and say what is implied, what is emblematized in the private eccentricities of the poet, the novelist, and the playwright.

When Romeo hears that Juliet is dead, he decides to take the course of things into his hands. Bravely, he announces: "Then I defy you, stars!" He proclaims his own sovereignty—and is in that moment absolutely the sport of chance. In the supposed domination of the heavens, this sovereign chance is figured by the playwright. The figure itself does not matter, even though the playwright may accept it as literal truth. For us it functions metaphorically, saying or showing forth one thing in terms of another.

The nature and use of metaphor in Shakespeare's plays is worth considering. In *Richard II*, another of the early tragedies, trees are said to wither and meteors to fall from the heavens and the pale moon to turn blood-red, as the hero-king is pushed from his throne. These ominous signs, according to one of the characters, "forerun the death or fall of kings." That is, on the face of it, not very plausible. Only a grossly superstitious man will suppose that disasters in the cosmos are the result of violent or immoral activity among men. Shakespeare stresses the connection of the two, not because he is superstitious, but because he wants to emphasize, as vividly as possible, the profoundly unnatural dislocation which has occurred, in the failure of the king to manage his kingdom and in the rebellion of loyal subjects against him. Commotion in the physical universe is a means of defining and lighting up moral and social commotion. Shakespeare is employing a metaphor to clarify the extent and also the character of unnatural behavior.

No one knows whether Shakespeare assigned to the stars occult or overmastering power. The question is not worth canvassing. Astrology is a concave mirror, in which we behold a distorted image of the truth. Like the continuing influence of the past—the fatal loins from which the lovers derive their life—or like the misadventures which collaborate in their death, astrology signifies our fettered condition. All of us are like Romeo, in his role of pilot or captain. However valiant we are, however shrewdly we plot our course, at last we run our weary bark on the rocks. That is the nature of the tragic vision.

Shakespeare remains faithful to this vision throughout his career as a playwright. *Romeo and Juliet* is, however, unlike any other of Shakespeare's plays in one important respect. It records the overthrow, not of maturity, as in *Othello*, not of old age, as in *King Lear*, but of youth. That is one way of explaining its perennial appeal. *Romeo and Juliet* is unique and infinitely poignant in that it tells of quick bright things come to confusion. The lovers are not permitted to grow old in their love, but die as they achieve a brief moment of triumph. They are "like fire and powder Which as they kiss consume." The peculiar pain of the play lies in the emphasis on youthful aspiration unfulfilled. The tragic conclusion, which is forever, is counterbalanced by an "exchange of joy," lasting but "one short minute." *Romeo and Juliet* is a race against time, whose victory is foreordained. So light a foot as Juliet's "Will ne'er wear out the everlasting flint." The tedious narrative poem from which Shakespeare drew the plot of his play shows no especial awareness of time's hostility or the swiftness of its progress. Nine months go by, and still the lovers meet, and renew their vows, and are able to rejoice in the consciousness of great expectations. Shakespeare is not so compassionate. Five days is all the span he allows to Romeo and Juliet. In this fiery period, they meet, and declare and consummate their love and, in the process, put their adolescence behind them. Now they are ready to die.

Romeo, on his first entrance in the play, is a moonstruck youth, in love with the idea of love. His infatuation with the girl called Rosaline is intended to convey his romantic foolishness and callowness. Juliet, initially, is not mature enough, even to entertain the thought of loving. "But no more deep will I endart mine eye," she says to her domineering father, "Than your consent gives strength to make it fly." Juliet is the type of the dutiful maiden, whose heart and mind are, to this point, untouched. So far, the right husband for her is Paris, the choice of her parents and, predictably, a mannequin like herself.

Neither the sentimental Romeo nor the complaisant Juliet is particularly interesting. Each is just such a figure as one meets in the slick-paper magazines. But the sudden onset of love, as dramatized in the great and touching scene at the end of Act I, works an irreversible change in them both, and so sets them apart forever from their prosaic and recognizable contemporaries. Mercutio, for all his charm, is a familiar figure. Love and lust, in his cynical and humorous understanding, are the same. What is Romeo's business in the orchard? It is—necessarily! Mercutio would say—to appease his ruttish desires,

To raise a spirit in his mistress' circle
Of some strange nature, letting it there stand
Till she had laid it and conjured it down.

The language of Benvolio is more seemly than this; and also, like Mercutio's, free of sentimental cant. But Benvolio, in the advice he proffers, does not ascend beyond common sense, which is mostly more common than sensible. Tybalt is an angry young man, whose personality is exhausted in the point of his sword. Paris is a man of wax.

It is, however, the comparison with their elders that establishes, conclusively, the singularity of the lovers, and in this comparison the tragic fate of Romeo and Juliet is augured. Friar Laurence, who personifies the wisdom of age, is satisfied with the uttering of bromides, saws and sayings which sound like the truth but deny it as they make it excessively simple. Juliet's Nurse is amusing in her coarseness, and defined and delimited by it. Old Capulet and Montague are headstrong parents out of melodrama (which is more like life than art), not so much wicked as determined to have their own way.

This callous and unthinking determination makes inevitable the ending of the play, which can be described as a contest between youth and age, a contest whose issue is never in doubt. Youth is impatient, and rightly.

But old folks, many feign as they were dead,
Unwieldy, slow, heavy and pale as lead.

The parents and their bigoted and self-satisfied milieu are, collectively, "old desire." Against them is pitted "young affection," which looks to a new and less selfish existence, and finds it only for an incandescent moment. Friar Laurence, in whom youthful ardor has died a long time ago, talks easily of "Adversity's sweet milk, philosophy." Romeo's answer is appropriate and telling: "Thou canst not speak of that thou dost not feel." Everything is on the side of the lovers but one thing, and that is power, which is the possession of age. As the power to direct their own destiny is wanting, the lovers are destroyed.

Late in the play, just before he enters the "womb of death," Romeo sums up in one memorable line this story of the blighting of young hopes: "The time and my intents are savage-wild." An unbridgeable gulf is fixed between his own purpose and the society in which he lives, necessarily as a subject. One can say that the play moves towards harmony at the end, in that the death of the lovers puts period to the embittered feud of Montague and Capulet. "A glooming peace this morning with it brings." But that is no help to Romeo and Juliet.

Suggested Reading

Boas, F. S., *Shakspere and His Predecessors* (1896; rev. ed., 1940).

Charlton, H. B., *Romeo and Juliet as an Experimental Tragedy* (1940).

Dickey, Franklin, *Not Wisely But Too Well* (1957).

Dowden, Edward, *Transcripts and Studies* (1888).

Granville-Barker, Harley, *Prefaces to Shakespeare*, ed. M. St. Clare Byrne, 4 vols. (1948). Princeton.

Lawler, John, *Early Shakespeare* (1961).

Mahood, M. M., *Shakespeare's Wordplay* (1957). Barnes and Noble.

Moore, Olin H., *The Legend of Romeo and Juliet* (1950).

Stoll, Elmer Edgar, *Shakespeare's Young Lovers* (1937).

Talbert, Ernest, *Elizabethan Drama and Shakespeare's Early Plays* (1963).

Tannenbaum, Samuel A., *Shakespeare's Romeo and Juliet: A Concise Bibliography* (1950).

Van Doren, Mark, *Shakespeare* (1939). Anchor.

Vyvyan, John, *Shakespeare and the Rose of Love* (1960).

Williams, Charles, *The English Poetic Mind* (1932).

Wilson, Harold S., *On the Design of Shakespearian Tragedy* (1957). Toronto.

A Midsummer-Night's Dream

A NOTE ON THE TEXT

A Midsummer-Night's Dream was written in 1594 or 1595. Probably it is to be dated just a little later than *Romeo and Juliet,* which it resembles in subject and style. A first quarto, advertising the play as having been "sundry times publickely acted," appeared in 1600; a second, reprinting the first, and ascribed incorrectly to the same year, in 1619. This second quarto, revised, supplied the text for the Folio of 1623.

It has often been conjectured—plausibly, in view of the pairings-off at the end —that Shakespeare wrote his comedy to celebrate a contemporary wedding. Hints for the plot are strewn throughout his wide and random reading. The tale of Pyramus and Thisbe derives from Ovid's *Metamorphoses,* as translated by the poetaster Arthur Golding and published in 1567. (Shakespeare, though he knew Latin, was mostly inclined to lean on an English version.) In an earlier comedy, *Love's Labour's Lost,* he had incorporated a crudely amateurish play-within-the-play, for the entertainment of royal persons. He had also experimented previously, in *The Two Gentlemen of Verona,* with the story of inconstant lovers. From a reading of Chaucer, the English writer to whom he is closest in spirit, he would have gathered something of the marriage of Theseus and Hippolyta. (Chaucer touches briefly on this marriage in the *Knight's Tale,* the first of *The Canterbury Tales.*) The career of Theseus is described more fully by the Greek biographer Plutarch in his *Lives of the Noble Grecians and Romans,* a source to which Shakespeare often returned.

Puck and the faeries come straight from English folklore, as available to Shakespeare from his boyhood in the Midlands. One can see his imagination beginning to work on this popular material in the long account of Queen Mab, delivered by Mercutio in the first act of *Romeo and Juliet.* Essentially, it is the latter play, turned inside out, that is the primary source for the plot of *A Midsummer-Night's Dream.*

A MIDSUMMER-NIGHT'S DREAM

DRAMATIS PERSONÆ

THESEUS, *Duke of Athens.*
EGEUS, *father to Hermia.*
LYSANDER, }
DEMETRIUS, } *in love with Hermia.*
PHILOSTRATE, *master of the revels to Theseus.*
QUINCE, *a carpenter.*
SNUG, *a joiner.*
BOTTOM, *a weaver.*
FLUTE, *a bellows-mender.*
SNOUT, *a tinker.*
STARVELING, *a tailor.*
HIPPOLYTA, *queen of the Amazons, betrothed to Theseus.*
HERMIA, *daughter to Egeus, in love with Lysander.*
HELENA, *in love with Demetrius.*
OBERON, *king of the fairies.*
TITANIA, *queen of the fairies.*
PUCK, or ROBIN GOODFELLOW.
PEASEBLOSSOM, }
COBWEB, }
MOTH, }
MUSTARDSEED, } *fairies.*
Other FAIRIES *attending their King and Queen.*
ATTENDANTS *on Theseus and Hippolyta.*
SCENE: *Athens, and a wood near it.*

ACT I

SCENE I. *Athens. The palace of* THESEUS.

[*Enter* THESEUS, HIPPOLYTA, PHILOSTRATE, *and* ATTENDANTS.]

THE. Now, fair Hippolyta, our nuptial hour
Draws on apace; four happy days bring in
Another moon: but, O, methinks, how slow
This old moon wanes! she lingers my desires
Like to a step-dame or a dowager 5
Long withering out a young man's revenue.
HIP. Four days will quickly steep themselves in night;
Four nights will quickly dream away the time;
And then the moon, like to a silver bow
New-bent in heaven, shall behold the night
Of our solemnities.
THE. Go, Philostrate, 11
Stir up the Athenian youth to merriments;
Awake the pert and nimble spirit of mirth:
Turn melancholy forth to funerals;
The pale companion is not for our pomp. 15
[*Exit* PHILOSTRATE.]
Hippolyta, I woo'd thee with my sword,
And won thy love, doing thee injuries;
But I will wed thee in another key,
With pomp, with triumph and with revelling.

[*Enter* EGEUS, HERMIA, LYSANDER, *and* DEMETRIUS.]

EGE. Happy be Theseus, our renownèd duke!
THE. Thanks, good Egeus: what's the news with thee? 21
EGE. Full of vexation come I, with complaint
Against my child, my daughter Hermia.
Stand forth, Demetrius. My noble lord,
This man hath my consent to marry her. 25
Stand forth, Lysander: and, my gracious duke,
This man hath bewitch'd the bosom of my child:

Dramatis Personae: The name of each artisan suggests his craft: **Quince,** or quoins, wedges of wood; **Snug,** tight-fitting; **Bottom,** core of a ball of yarn and the ball itself; **Flute,** the mender of the pipes or flutes of an organ. **Act I, Scene i: 4. lingers,** delays the fulfillment of. **5. dowager,** a widow with property inherited from her husband. **6. withering out,** making dwindle. **13. pert,** lively. **19. triumph,** public show. **27. bosom,** i.e., the seat of the emotions.

Thou, thou, Lysander, thou hast given her rhymes
And interchanged love-tokens with my child:
Thou hast by moonlight at her window sung
With feigning voice verses of feigning love, 31
And stolen the impression of her fantasy
With bracelets of thy hair, rings, gawds, conceits,
Knacks, trifles, nosegays, sweetmeats, messengers
Of strong prevailment in unharden'd youth:
With cunning hast thou filch'd my daughter's heart, 36
Turn'd her obedience, which is due to me,
To stubborn harshness: and, my gracious duke,
Be it so she will not here before your grace
Consent to marry with Demetrius, 40
I beg the ancient privilege of Athens,
As she is mine, I may dispose of her:
Which shall be either to this gentleman
Or to her death, according to our law
Immediately provided in that case. 45

THE. What say you, Hermia? be advised, fair maid;
To you your father should be as a god;
One that composed your beauties, yea, and one
To whom you are but as a form in wax
By him imprinted and within his power 50
To leave the figure or disfigure it.
Demetrius is a worthy gentleman.

HER. So is Lysander.

THE. In himself he is;
But in this kind, wanting your father's voice,
The other must be held the worthier. 55

HER. I would my father look'd but with my eyes.

THE. Rather your eyes must with his judgement look.

HER. I do entreat your grace to pardon me.
I know not by what power I am made bold,
Nor how it may concern my modesty, 60
In such a presence here to plead my thoughts;
But I beseech your grace that I may know
The worst that may befall me in this case,
If I refuse to wed Demetrius.

THE. Either to die the death or to abjure
For ever the society of men. 66
Therefore, fair Hermia, question your desires;
Know of your youth, examine well your blood,
Whether, if you yield not to your father's choice,
You can endure the livery of a nun, 70
For aye to be in shady cloister mew'd,
To live a barren sister all your life,
Chanting faint hymns to the cold fruitless moon.
Thrice-blessèd they that master so their blood,
To undergo such maiden pilgrimage; 75
But earthlier happy is the rose distill'd,
Than that which withering on the virgin thorn
Grows, lives and dies in single blessedness.

HER. So will I grow, so live, so die, my lord,
Ere I will yield my virgin patent up 80
Unto his lordship, whose unwishèd yoke
My soul consents not to give sovereignty.

THE. Take time to pause; and, by the next new moon—
The sealing-day betwixt my love and me,
For everlasting bond of fellowship— 85
Upon that day either prepare to die
For disobedience to your father's will,
Or else to wed Demetrius, as he would;
Or on Diana's altar to protest
For aye austerity and single life. 90

DEM. Relent, sweet Hermia: and, Lysander, yield
Thy crazèd title to my certain right.

LYS. You have her father's love, Demetrius;
Let me have Hermia's: do you marry him.

EGE. Scornful Lysander! true, he hath my love, 95
And what is mine my love shall render him.
And she is mine, and all my right of her
I do estate unto Demetrius.

LYS. I am, my lord, as well derived as he,
As well possess'd; my love is more than his;
My fortunes every way as fairly rank'd, 101
If not with vantage, as Demetrius';
And, which is more than all these boasts can be,
I am beloved of beauteous Hermia: 104
Why should not I then prosecute my right?

31. feigning, deceptive; feigning, feigned. 32. and . . . fantasy, captured her imagination by impressing your image upon it. 33. gawds, pieces of jewelry; conceits, showy trinkets. 34. knacks, knick-knacks; sweetmeats, candy. 35. strong prevailment, great influence. 45. immediately, expressly. 51. disfigure, obliterate. 54. kind, instance; wanting, lacking; voice, approval. 60. concern, befit. 71. mew'd, shut up. 74. blood, passion. 76. earthlier happy, happier on earth. 80. patent, phrase formed on the analogy of "letters patent," here, identification mark, i.e., maidenhead. 89. protest, vow. 92. crazed, unsound. 98. estate unto, settle upon. 99. well-derived, of as good birth. 100. as well possess'd, as well off.

Demetrius, I'll avouch it to his head,
Made love to Nedar's daughter, Helena,
And won her soul; and she, sweet lady, dotes,
Devoutly dotes, dotes in idolatry,
Upon this spotted and inconstant man. 110

THE. I must confess that I have heard so much,
And with Demetrius thought to have spoke thereof;
But, being over-full of self-affairs,
My mind did lose it. But, Demetrius, come;
And come, Egeus; you shall go with me, 115
I have some private schooling for you both.
For you, fair Hermia, look you arm yourself
To fit your fancies to your father's will;
Or else the law of Athens yields you up—
Which by no means we may extenuate— 120
To death, or to a vow of single life.
Come, my Hippolyta: what cheer, my love?
Demetrius and Egeus, go along:
I must employ you in some business
Against our nuptial and confer with you 125
Of something nearly that concerns yourselves.

EGE. With duty and desire we follow you.

[*Exeunt all but* LYSANDER *and* HERMIA.

LYS. How now, my love! why is your cheek so pale?
How chance the roses there do fade so fast?

HER. Belike for want of rain, which I could well 130
Beteem them from the tempest of my eyes.

LYS. Ay me! for aught that I could ever read,
Could ever hear by tale or history,
The course of true love never did run smooth;
But, either it was different in blood,— 135

HER. O cross! too high to be enthrall'd to low.

LYS. Or else misgraffèd in respect of years,—

HER. O spite! too old to be engaged to young.

LYS. Or else it stood upon the choice of friends,—

HER. O hell! to choose love by another's eyes. 140

LYS. Or, if there were a sympathy in choice,
War, death, or sickness did lay siege to it,
Making it momentany as a sound,
Swift as a shadow, short as any dream;
Brief as the lightning in the collied night, 145
That, in a spleen, unfolds both heaven and earth,
And ere a man hath power to say "Behold!"
The jaws of darkness do devour it up:
So quick bright things come to confusion.

HER. If then true lovers have been ever cross'd, 150
It stands as an edict in destiny:
Then let us teach our trial patience,
Because it is a customary cross,
As due to love as thoughts and dreams and sighs,
Wishes and tears, poor fancy's followers. 155

LYS. A good persuasion: therefore, hear me, Hermia.
I have a widow aunt, a dowager
Of great revénue, and she hath no child:
From Athens is her house remote seven leagues;
And she respects me as her only son. 160
There, gentle Hermia, may I marry thee;
And to that place the sharp Athenian law
Cannot pursue us. If thou lovest me then,
Steal forth thy father's house to-morrow night;
And in the wood, a league without the town,
Where I did meet thee once with Helena, 166
To do observance to a morn of May,
There will I stay for thee.

HER. My good Lysander!
I swear to thee, by Cupid's strongest bow,
By his best arrow with the golden head, 170
By the simplicity of Venus' doves,
By that which knitteth souls and prospers loves,
And by that fire which burn'd the Carthage queen,
When the false Troyan under sail was seen,
By all the vows that ever men have broke, 175
In number more than ever women spoke,
In that same place thou hast appointed me,
To-morrow truly will I meet with thee.

LYS. Keep promise, love. Look, here comes Helena. 179

[*Enter* HELENA.]

HER. God speed fair Helena! whither away?

HEL. Call you me fair? that fair again unsay.

106. **avouch . . . head,** affirm it to his face. 120. **extenuate,** mitigate, alleviate. 125. **against,** in anticipation of. 126. **nearly that,** that intimately. 130. **belike,** probably. 131. **Beteem them,** bring forth for them. 136. **cross,** perversity; **enthrall'd to low,** made servant to one of low birth. 137. **misgraffed,** badly matched. 139. **stood upon,** concerned. 143. **momentany,** momentary. 145. **collied,** coal-black. 146. **spleen,** fit of anger. 149. **confusion,** ruin. 152. **teach . . . patience,** teach ourselves patience to endure the trial. 155. **fancy's,** love's. 160. **respects,** regards. 167. **do . . . May,** celebrate May Day. 172. **that . . . loves,** i.e., the girdle of Venus. 173. **And . . . Queen,** according to Vergil's **Aeneid** [Book IV], Dido, deserted by Aeneas, burned herself to death on a funeral pyre.

Demetrius loves your fair: O happy fair!
Your eyes are lode-stars; and your tongue's sweet air
More tuneable than lark to shepherd's ear,
When wheat is green, when hawthorn buds appear. 185
Sickness is catching: O, were favour so,
Yours would I catch, fair Hermia, ere I go;
My ear should catch your voice, my eye your eye,
My tongue should catch your tongue's sweet melody.
Were the world mine, Demetrius being bated,
The rest I'ld give to be to you translated. 191
O, teach me how you look, and with what art
You sway the motion of Demetrius' heart.

HER. I frown upon him, yet he loves me still.

HEL. O that your frowns would teach my smiles such skill! 195

HER. I give him curses, yet he gives me love.

HEL. O that my prayers could such affection move!

HER. The more I hate, the more he follows me.

HEL. The more I love, the more he hateth me.

HER. His folly, Helena, is no fault of mine.

HEL. None, but your beauty: would that fault were mine! 201

HER. Take comfort: he no more shall see my face;
Lysander and myself will fly this place.
Before the time I did Lysander see,
Seem'd Athens as a paradise to me: 205
O, then, what graces in my love do dwell,
That he hath turn'd a heaven unto a hell!

LYS. Helen, to you our minds we will unfold:
To-morrow night, when Phœbe doth behold
Her silvery visage in the watery glass, 210
Decking with liquid pearl the bladed grass,
A time that lovers' flights doth still conceal,
Through Athens' gates have we devised to steal.

HER. And in the wood, where often you and I
Upon faint primrose beds were wont to lie, 215
Emptying our bosoms of their counsel sweet,
There my Lysander and myself shall meet;
And thence from Athens turn away our eyes,
To seek new friends and stranger companies.
Farewell, sweet playfellow: pray thou for us;
And good luck grant thee thy Demetrius! 221
Keep word, Lysander: we must starve our sight
From lovers' food till morrow deep midnight.

LYS. I will, my Hermia. [*Exit* HERM.
Helena, adieu:
As you on him, Demetrius dote on you! [*Exit.*

HEL. How happy some o'er other some can be! 226
Through Athens I am thought as fair as she.
But what of that? Demetrius thinks not so;
He will not know what all but he do know:
And as he errs, doting on Hermia's eyes, 230
So I, admiring of his qualities:
Things base and vile, holding no quantity,
Love can transpose to form and dignity:
Love looks not with the eyes, but with the mind;
And therefore is wing'd Cupid painted blind:
Nor hath Love's mind of any judgement taste;
Wings and no eyes figure unheedy haste: 237
And therefore is Love said to be a child,
Because in choice he is so oft beguiled.
As waggish boys in game themselves forswear,
So the boy Love is perjured every where: 241
For ere Demetrius look'd on Hermia's eyne,
He hail'd down oaths that he was only mine;
And when this hail some heat from Hermia felt,
So he dissolved, and showers of oaths did melt.
I will go tell him of fair Hermia's flight: 246
Then to the wood will he to-morrow night
Pursue her; and for this intelligence
If I have thanks, it is a dear expense:
But herein mean I to enrich my pain, 250
To have his sight thither and back again.
[*Exit.*

SCENE II. *Athens.* QUINCE'S *house.*

[*Enter* QUINCE, SNUG, BOTTOM, FLUTE, SNOUT, *and* STARVELING.]

QUIN. Is all our company here?

BOT. You were best to call them generally, man by man, according to the scrip.

182. your fair, your beauty. 183. lode-stars, guiding stars. 184. tuneable, musical. 186. favour, (1) physical appearance, (2) affection. 190. bated, excepted. 191. translated, transformed. 193. notion, inclination. 209. Phœbe, Diana, the moon. 215. faint, pale. 237. figure, are a symbol of. 240. waggish, playful. 242. eyne, eyes. 248. intelligence, news. 249. dear expense, a thing that will cost me dear. Scene ii: 2. generally, severally, the first of Bottom's many malapropisms. 3. scrip, written list.

QUIN. Here is the scroll of every man's name, which is thought fit, through all Athens, to play in our interlude before the duke and the duchess, on his wedding-day at night. 7

BOT. First, good Peter Quince, say what the play treats on, then read the names of the actors, and so grow to a point. 10

QUIN. Marry, our play is, The most lamentable comedy, and most cruel death of Pyramus and Thisby.

BOT. A very good piece of work, I assure you, and a merry. Now, good Peter Quince, call forth your actors by the scroll. Masters, spread yourselves. 17

QUIN. Answer as I call you. Nick Bottom, the weaver.

BOT. Ready. Name what part I am for, and proceed. 21

QUIN. You, Nick Bottom, are set down for Pyramus.

BOT. What is Pyramus? a lover, or a tyrant?

QUIN. A lover, that kills himself most gallant for love.

BOT. That will ask some tears in the true performing of it: if I do it, let the audience look to their eyes; I will move storms, I will condole in some measure. To the rest: 29 yet my chief humour is for a tyrant: I could play Ercles rarely, or a part to tear a cat in, to make all split.

> The raging rocks
> And shivering shocks
> Shall break the locks
> Of prison gates;
> And Phibbus' car
> Shall shine from far
> And make and mar
> The foolish Fates. 40

This was lofty! Now name the rest of the players. This is Ercles' vein, a tyrant's vein; a lover is more condoling.

QUIN. Francis Flute, the bellows-mender.

FLU. Here, Peter Quince. 45

QUIN. Flute, you must take Thisby on you.

FLU. What is Thisby? a wandering knight?

QUIN. It is the lady that Pyramus must love.

FLU. Nay, faith, let not me play a woman; I have a beard coming. 50

QUIN. That's all one: you shall play it in a mask, and you may speak as small as you will.

BOT. An I may hide my face, let me play Thisby too, I'll speak in a monstrous little voice, "Thisne, Thisne;" "Ah Pyramus, my lover dear! thy Thisby dear, and lady dear!" 56

QUIN. No, no; you must play Pyramus: and, Flute, you Thisby.

BOT. Well, proceed.

QUIN. Robin Starveling, the tailor. 60

STAR. Here, Peter Quince.

QUIN. Robin Starveling, you must play Thisby's mother. Tom Snout, the tinker.

SNOUT. Here, Peter Quince. 64

QUIN. You, Pyramus' father: myself, Thisby's father. Snug, the joiner; you, the lion's part: and, I hope, here is a play fitted.

SNUG. Have you the lion's part written? pray you, if it be, give it to me, for I am slow of study. 70

QUIN. You may do it extempore, for it is nothing but roaring.

BOT. Let me play the lion too: I will roar, that I will do any man's heart good to hear me; I will roar, and that I will make the duke say "Let him roar again, let him roar again."

QUIN. An you should do it too terribly, you would fright the duchess and the ladies, that they would shriek; and that were enough to hang us all.

ALL. That would hang us, every mother's son. 80

BOT. I grant you, friends, if that you should fright the ladies out of their wits, they would have no more discretion but to hang us: but I will aggravate my voice so that I will roar you as gently as any sucking dove; I will roar you as 'twere any nightingale. 86

QUIN. You can play no part but Pyramus; for Pyramus is a sweet-faced man; a proper man, as one shall see in a summer's day; a most lovely gentleman-like man: therefore you must needs play Pyramus. 91

BOT. Well, I will undertake it. What beard were I best to play it in?

QUIN. Why, what you will.

BOT. I will discharge it in either your straw-colour beard, your orange-tawny beard, your

10. **grow to**, come to. 29. **condole**, lament. 31. **Ercles**, Hercules was a ranting character in the earlier drama; **tear a cat**, proverbial for "rant." 32. **make all split**, proverbial for "cause an uproar." 37. **Phibbus'**, Phoebus'. 47. **wandering knight**, knight errant. 53. **small**, shrilly. 54. **an**, if. 67. **fitted**, i.e., cast. 84. **aggravate**, he means "moderate." 85. **sucking**, i.e., not full-fledged. 88. **proper**. handsome. 95. **discharge**, perform.

purple-in-grain beard, or your French-crown-colour beard, your perfect yellow. 98

QUIN. Some of your French crowns have no hair at all, and then you will play barefaced. But, masters, here are your parts: and I am to entreat you, request you and desire you, to con them by to-morrow night; and meet me in the palace wood, a mile without the town, by moonlight; there will we rehearse, for if we meet in the city, we shall be dogged with company, and our devices known. In the meantime I will draw a bill of properties, such as our play wants. I pray you, fail me not. 110

BOT. We will meet; and there we may rehearse most obscenely and courageously. Take pains; be perfect: adieu.

QUIN. At the duke's oak we meet.

BOT. Enough; hold or cut bow-strings.

[*Exeunt.*

ACT II

SCENE I. *A wood near Athens.*

[*Enter, from opposite sides, a* FAIRY, *and* PUCK.]

PUCK. How now, spirit! whither wander you?

FAI. Over hill, over dale,
Thorough bush, thorough brier,
Over park, over pale,
Thorough flood, thorough fire, 5
I do wander every where,
Swifter than the moon's sphere;
And I serve the fairy queen,
To dew her orbs upon the green.
The cowslips tall her pensioners be: 10
In their gold coats spots you see;
Those be rubies, fairy favours,
In those freckles live their savours:
I must go seek some dewdrops here
And hang a pearl in every cowslip's ear. 15
Farewell, thou lob of spirits; I'll be gone:
Our queen and all her elves come here anon.

PUCK. The king doth keep his revels here to-night:
Take heed the queen come not within his sight;
For Oberon is passing fell and wrath, 20
Because that she as her attendant hath
A lovely boy, stolen from an Indian king;
She never had so sweet a changeling;
And jealous Oberon would have the child
Knight of his train, to trace the forests wild;
But she perforce withholds the lovèd boy, 26
Crowns him with flowers and makes him all her joy:
And now they never meet in grove or green,
By fountain clear, or spangled starlight sheen,
But they do square, that all their elves for fear 30
Creep into acorn-cups and hide them there.

FAI. Either I mistake your shape and making quite,
Or else you are that shrewd and knavish sprite
Call'd Robin Goodfellow: are not you he
That frights the maidens of the villagery; 35
Skim milk, and sometimes labour in the quern
And bootless make the breathless housewife churn;
And sometime make the drink to bear no barm;
Mislead night-wanderers, laughing at their harm?
Those that Hobgoblin call you and sweet Puck, 40
You do their work, and they shall have good luck:
Are not you he?

PUCK. Thou speak'st aright;
I am that merry wanderer of the night.
I jest to Oberon and make him smile
When I a fat and bean-fed horse beguile, 45
Neighing in likeness of a filly foal:
And sometime lurk I in a gossip's bowl,
In very likeness of a roasted crab,
And when she drinks, against her lips I bob
And on her wither'd dewlap pour the ale. 50
The wisest aunt, telling the saddest tale,

97. **purple-in-grain**, deep red. 97-8. **French-crown-colour**, i.e., golden. 103. **con**, learn by heart. 107. **devices**, i.e., dramatic plans. 112. **obscenely**, mistake for "obscurely," i.e., privately. 115. **hold . . . strings**, i.e., be on hand or give up the play. Act II, Scene i: 4. **pale**, fence. 9. **orbs**, fairy rings. 10. **pensioners**, royal bodyguard. 16. **lob**, lout. 20. **passing fell**, extremely angry. 23. **changeling**, a child left by the fairies in the place of one they have stolen. Here merely "stolen child." 30. **square**, quarrel; that, so that. 33. **shrewd**, mischievous, vexatious. 36. **quern**, hand mill for grinding wheat. 37. **bootless**, vainly. 38. **barm**, yeast formed on brewing liquors. 47. **bowl**, i.e., of liquor. 48. **crab**, crabapple, often put in drink. 50. **dewlap**, loose skin about the throat. 51. **aunt**, old woman.

Sometime for three-foot stool mistaketh me;
Then slip I from her bum, down topples she,
And "tailor" cries, and falls into a cough;
And then the whole quire hold their hips and laugh, 55
And waxen in their mirth and neeze and swear
A merrier hour was never wasted there.
But, room, fairy! here comes Oberon.

FAI. And here my mistress. Would that he were gone!

[*Enter, from one side,* OBERON, *with his train; from the other,* TITANIA, *with hers.*]

OBE. Ill met by moonlight, proud Titania. 60

TITA. What, jealous Oberon! Fairies, skip hence:
I have forsworn his bed and company.

OBE. Tarry, rash wanton: am not I thy lord?

TITA. Then I must be thy lady: but I know
When thou hast stolen away from fairy land,
And in the shape of Corin sat all day, 66
Playing on pipes of corn and versing love
To amorous Phillida. Why art thou here,
Come from the farthest steppe of India?
But that, forsooth, the bouncing Amazon,
Your buskin'd mistress and your warrior love,
To Theseus must be wedded, and you come 72
To give their bed joy and prosperity.

OBE. How canst thou thus for shame, Titania,
Glance at my credit with Hippolyta, 75
Knowing I know thy love to Theseus?
Didst thou not lead him through the glimmering night
From Perigenia, whom he ravished?
And make him with fair Ægle break his faith,
With Ariadne and Antiopa? 80

TITA. These are the forgeries of jealousy:
And never, since the middle summer's spring,
Met we on hill, in dale, forest or mead,
By pavèd fountain or by rushy brook,
Or in the beached margent of the sea, 85
To dance our ringlets to the whistling wind,
But with thy brawls thou hast disturb'd our sport.
Therefore the winds, piping to us in vain,
As in revenge, have suck'd up from the sea
Contagious fogs; which falling in the land 90
Have every pelting river made so proud
That they have overborne their continents:
The ox hath therefore stretch'd his yoke in vain,
The ploughman lost his sweat, and the green corn
Hath rotted ere his youth attain'd a beard; 95
The fold stands empty in the drownèd field,
And crows are fatted with the murrion flock;
The nine men's morris is fill'd up with mud,
And the quaint mazes in the wanton green
For lack of tread are undistinguishable: 100
The human mortals want their winter here;
No night is now with hymn or carol blest:
Therefore the moon, the governess of floods,
Pale in her anger, washes all the air,
That rheumatic diseases do abound: 105
And thorough this distemperature we see
The seasons alter: hoary-headed frosts
Fall in the fresh lap of the crimson rose,
And on old Hiems' thin and icy crown
An odorous chaplet of sweet summer buds 110
Is, as in mockery, set: the spring, the summer,
The childing autumn, angry winter, change
Their wonted liveries, and the mazed world,
By their increase, now knows not which is which:
And this same progeny of evils comes 115
From our debate, from our dissension;
We are their parents and original.

OBE. Do you amend it then; it lies in you:
Why should Titania cross her Oberon?
I do but beg a little changeling boy, 120
To be my henchman.

TITA. Set your heart at rest:
The fairy land buys not the child of me.
His mother was a votaress of my order:
And, in the spicèd Indian air, by night,
Full often hath she gossip'd by my side, 125
And sat with me on Neptune's yellow sands,
Marking the embarkèd traders on the flood,

54. **"tailor,"** allusion obscure, probably a play on the word "tail." 55. **quire,** company. 56. **neeze,** sneeze. 66-8. **corin . . . Phillida,** conventional names of shepherds in pastoral literature. See Introduction. 67. **pipes of corn,** pipes made out of oaten straws. 69. **steppe,** mountain range. 70. **bouncing,** big and lusty; **Amazon,** Hippolyta, Queen of the Amazons. 71. **buskin'd,** wearing half-boots. 75. **glance at,** allude to contemptuously; **credit,** reputation. 78-80. **Perigenia . . . Antiopa,** these are the women whom, according to Plutarch (**Life of Theseus**), Theseus had loved. 82. **middle summer's spring,** the beginning of midsummer. 85. **in,** on. 86. **ringlets,** round dances. 91. **pelting,** paltry. 92. **continents,** banks. 97. **murrion,** diseased. 98. **nine men's morris,** squares on the village green, marked out by nine stones, on which a kind of bowling game was played. 99. **quaint mazes,** intricate figures marked out on the green; **wanton green,** luxuriant grass. 101. **want,** lack. 106. **thorough,** through; **distemperature,** bad weather. 109. **Hiems',** God of Winter. 112. **childing,** fruitful. 113. **mazed,** bewildered. 117. **original,** source. 121. **henchman,** attendant page. 127. **embarked traders,** merchant ships.

When we have laugh'd to see the sails conceive
And grow big-bellied with the wanton wind;
Which she, with pretty and with swimming gait 130
Following,—her womb then rich with my young squire,—
Would imitate, and sail upon the land,
To fetch me trifles, and return again,
As from a voyage, rich with merchandise.
But she, being mortal, of that boy did die; 135
And for her sake do I rear up her boy,
And for her sake I will not part with him.

OBE. How long within this wood intend you stay?

TITA. Perchance till after Theseus' wedding-day.
If you will patiently dance in our round 140
And see our moonlight revels, go with us;
If not, shun me, and I will spare your haunts.

OBE. Give me that boy, and I will go with thee.

TITA. Not for thy fairy kingdom. Fairies, away!
We shall chide downright, if I longer stay. 145

[*Exit* TITANIA *with her train.*

OBE. Well, go thy way: thou shalt not from this grove
Till I torment thee for this injury.
My gentle Puck, come hither. Thou rememberest
Since once I sat upon a promontory,
And heard a mermaid on a dolphin's back 150
Uttering such dulcet and harmonious breath
That the rude sea grew civil at her song
And certain stars shot madly from their spheres,
To hear the sea-maid's music.

PUCK. I remember.

OBE. That very time I saw, but thou couldst not, 155
Flying between the cold moon and the earth,
Cupid all arm'd: a certain aim he took
At a fair vestal thronèd by the west,
And loosed his love-shaft smartly from his bow,
As it should pierce a hundred thousand hearts;
But I might see young Cupid's fiery shaft 161
Quench'd in the chaste beams of the watery moon,
And the imperial votaress passèd on,
In maiden meditation, fancy-free.
Yet mark'd I where the bolt of Cupid fell: 165
It fell upon a little western flower,
Before milk-white, now purple with love's wound,
And maidens call it love-in-idleness.
Fetch me that flower; the herb I shew'd thee once:
The juice of it on sleeping eye-lids laid 170
Will make or man or woman madly dote
Upon the next live creature that it sees.
Fetch me this herb; and be thou here again
Ere the leviathan can swim a league.

PUCK. I'll put a girdle round about the earth 175
In forty minutes. [*Exit.*

OBE. Having once this juice,
I'll watch Titania when she is asleep,
And drop the liquor of it in her eyes.
The next thing then she waking looks upon,
Be it on lion, bear, or wolf, or bull, 180
On meddling monkey, or on busy ape,
She shall pursue it with the soul of love:
And ere I take this charm from off her sight,
As I can take it with another herb,
I'll make her render up her page to me. 185
But who comes here? I am invisible;
And I will overhear their conference.

[*Enter* DEMETRIUS, HELENA *following him.*]

DEM. I love thee not, therefore pursue me not.
Where is Lysander and fair Hermia?
The one I'll slay, the other slayeth me. 190
Thou told'st me they were stolen unto this wood;
And here am I, and wode within this wood,
Because I cannot meet my Hermia.
Hence, get thee gone, and follow me no more.

HEL. You draw me, you hard-hearted adamant; 195
But yet you draw not iron, for my heart
Is true as steel: leave you your power to draw,
And I shall have no power to follow you.

DEM. Do I entice you? do I speak you fair?
Or, rather, do I not in plainest truth 200

140. round, i.e., round dance. 142. spare, avoid. 149. since, when. 148-168. Thou . . . love-in-idleness, for the occasion to which this probably refers, see the Introduction. 151. breath, voice. 153. And . . . spheres, i.e., skyrockets and other forms of fireworks. 158. vestal, vestal virgin, hence virgin. 163. imperial votaress, i.e., Queen Elizabeth. 164. fancy-free, untouched by love. 165. bolt, arrow. 168. love-in-idleness, pansy. 174. leviathan, whale. 175. I'll . . . earth, I fly around the earth. 192. wode, mad. 195. adamant, loadstone. 197. leave, give up. 199. speak you fair, speak to you in a friendly manner.

Tell you, I do not, nor I cannot love you?
HEL. And even for that do I love you the more.
I am your spaniel; and, Demetrius,
The more you beat me, I will fawn on you:
Use me but as your spaniel, spurn me, strike me, 205
Neglect me, lose me; only give me leave,
Unworthy as I am, to follow you.
What worser place can I beg in your love,—
And yet a place of high respect with me,—
Than to be usèd as you use your dog? 210
DEM. Tempt not too much the hatred of my spirit,
For I am sick when I do look on thee.
HEL. And I am sick when I look not on you.
DEM. You do impeach your modesty too much,
To leave the city and commit yourself 215
Into the hands of one that loves you not;
To trust the opportunity of night
And the ill counsel of a desert place
With the rich worth of your virginity.
HEL. Your virtue is my privilege: for that
It is not night when I do see your face, 221
Therefore I think I am not in the night;
Nor doth this wood lack worlds of company,
For you in my respect are all the world:
Then how can it be said I am alone, 225
When all the world is here to look on me?
DEM. I'll run from thee and hide me in the brakes,
And leave thee to the mercy of wild beasts.
HEL. The wildest hath not such a heart as you.
Run when you will, the story shall be changed:
Apollo flies, and Daphne holds the chase; 231
The dove pursues the griffin; the mild hind
Makes speed to catch the tiger; bootless speed,
When cowardice pursues and valour flies.
DEM. I will not stay thy questions; let me go: 235
Or, if thou follow me, do not believe
But I shall do thee mischief in the wood.
HEL. Ay, in the temple, in the town, the field,
You do me mischief. Fie, Demetrius!
Your wrongs do set a scandal on my sex: 240
We cannot fight for love, as men may do;
We should be woo'd and were not made to woo. [*Exit* DEM.]
I'll follow thee and make a heaven of hell,
To die upon the hand I love so well. [*Exit.*
OBE. Fare thee well, nymph: ere he do leave this grove, 245
Thou shalt fly him and he shall seek thy love.

[*Re-enter* PUCK.]

Hast thou the flower there? Welcome, wanderer.
PUCK. Ay, there it is.
OBE. I pray thee, give it me.
I know a bank where the wild thyme blows,
Where oxlips and the nodding violet grows, 250
Quite over-canopied with luscious woodbine,
With sweet musk-roses and with eglantine:
There sleeps Titania sometime of the night,
Lull'd in these flowers with dances and delight;
And there the snake throws her enamell'd skin, 255
Weed wide enough to wrap a fairy in:
And with the juice of this I'll streak her eyes,
And make her full of hateful fantasies.
Take thou some of it, and seek through this grove:
A sweet Athenian lady is in love 260
With a disdainful youth: anoint his eyes;
But do it when the next thing he espies
May be the lady: thou shalt know the man
By the Athenian garments he hath on. 264
Effect it with some care that he may prove
More fond on her than she upon her love:
And look thou meet me ere the first cock crow.
PUCK. Fear not, my lord, your servant shall do so. [*Exeunt.*

SCENE II. *Another part of the wood.*

[*Enter* TITANIA, *with her train.*]

TITA. Come, now a roundel and a fairy song;
Then, for the third part of a minute, hence;
Some to kill cankers in the musk-rose buds,
Some war with rere-mice for their leathern wings,

214. **impeach**, discredit. 220. **privilege**, protection. 224. **in my respect**, as far as I am concerned. 227. **brakes**, thickets. 231. **holds the chase**, in Ovid, Apollo pursues Daphne; here the rôles are reversed. 232. **griffin**, fabulous beast with an eagle's head attached to a lion's body; **hind**, doe. 235. **stay thy questions**, listen to your talk. 244. **upon**, by. 249. **blows**, blossoms. 250. **oxlips**, hybrid primroses. 251. **woodbine**, honeysuckle, Virginia creeper. 252. **eglantine**, the sweetbrier. 256. **weed**, garment. 257. **streak her eyes**, rub her eyelids. 266. **fond**, doting. **Scene ii**: 1. **roundel**, dance in a ring. 3. **cankers**, cankerworms. 4. **rere-mice**, bats.

To make my small elves coats, and some keep back 5
The clamorous owl that nightly hoots and wonders
At our quaint spirits. Sing me now asleep;
Then to your offices and let me rest.

THE FAIRIES SING.

You spotted snakes with double tongue,
Thorny hedgehogs, be not seen; 10
Newts and blind-worms, do no wrong,
Come not near our fairy queen.
Philomel, with melody
Sing in our sweet lullaby;
Lulla, lulla, lullaby, lulla, lulla, lullaby: 15
Never harm,
Nor spell nor charm,
Come our lovely lady nigh;
So, good night, with lullaby.

Weaving spiders, come not here; 20
Hence, you long-legg'd spinners, hence!
Beetles black, approach not near;
Worm nor snail, do no offence.
Philomel, with melody, &c.

A FAIRY. Hence, away! now all is well: 25
One aloof stand sentinel.
[*Exeunt* FAIRIES. TITANIA *sleeps.*

[*Enter* OBERON, *and squeezes the flower on* TITANIA'S *eyelids.*]

OBE. What thou seest when thou dost wake,
Do it for thy true-love take,
Love and languish for his sake:
Be it ounce, or cat, or bear, 30
Pard, or boar with bristled hair,
In thy eye that shall appear
When thou wakest, it is thy dear:
Wake when some vile thing is near.
[*Exit.*

[*Enter* LYSANDER *and* HERMIA.]

LYS. Fair love, you faint with wandering in the wood; 35
And to speak troth, I have forgot our way:
We'll rest us, Hermia, if you think it good,
And tarry for the comfort of the day.

HER. Be it so, Lysander: find you out a bed;
For I upon this bank will rest my head. 40

LYS. One turf shall serve as pillow for us both;
One heart, one bed, two bosoms and one troth.

HER. Nay, good Lysander; for my sake, my dear,
Lie further off yet, do not lie so near.

LYS. O, take the sense, sweet, of my innocence! 45
Love takes the meaning in love's conference.
I mean, that my heart unto yours is knit
So that but one heart we can make of it;
Two bosoms interchainèd with an oath;
So then two bosoms and a single troth. 50
Then by your side no bed-room me deny;
For lying so, Hermia, I do not lie.

HER. Lysander riddles very prettily:
Now much beshrew my manners and my pride,
If Hermia meant to say Lysander lied. 55
But, gentle friend, for love and courtesy
Lie further off; in human modesty,
Such separation as may well be said
Becomes a virtuous bachelor and a maid,
So far be distant; and, good night, sweet friend:
Thy love ne'er alter till thy sweet life end! 61

LYS. Amen, amen, to that fair prayer, say I;
And then end life when I end loyalty!
Here is my bed: sleep give thee all his rest!

HER. With half that wish the wisher's eyes be press'd! [*They sleep.* 65

[*Enter* PUCK.]

PUCK. Through the forest have I gone,
But Athenian found I none,
On whose eyes I might approve
This flower's force in stirring love.
Night and silence.—Who is here? 70
Weeds of Athens he doth wear:
This is he, my master said,
Despisèd the Athenian maid;
And here the maiden, sleeping sound,
On the dank and dirty ground. 75
Pretty soul! she durst not lie
Near this lack-love, this kill-courtesy.
Churl, upon thy eyes I throw
All the power this charm doth owe.
When thou wakest, let love forbid
Sleep his seat on thy eyelid: 81

7. quaint, dainty. 8. offices, duties. 11. blind worms, legless lizards, small snakelike animals. 13. Philomel, i.e., the nightingale. 30. ounce, lynx; cat, wildcat. 31. Pard, leopard. 36. troth, truth. 50. troth, troth-plight. 54. beshrew, curse (a mild oath). 57. human, courteous. 68. approve, test. 79. owe, possess.

So awake when I am gone;
For I must now to Oberon. [*Exit.*

[*Enter* DEMETRIUS *and* HELENA, *running.*]

HEL. Stay, though thou kill me, sweet Demetrius.
DEM. I charge thee, hence, and do not haunt me thus. 85
HEL. O, wilt thou darkling leave me? do not so.
DEM. Stay, on thy peril: I alone will go. [*Exit.*
HEL. O, I am out of breath in this fond chase!
The more my prayer, the lesser is my grace.
Happy is Hermia, wheresoe'er she lies; 90
For she hath blessèd and attractive eyes.
How came her eyes so bright? Not with salt tears:
If so, my eyes are oftener wash'd than hers.
No, no, I am as ugly as a bear;
For beasts that meet me run away for fear:
Therefore no marvel though Demetrius 96
Do, as a monster, fly my presence thus.
What wicked and dissembling glass of mine
Made me compare with Hermia's sphery eyne?
But who is here? Lysander! on the ground!
Dead? or asleep? I see no blood, no wound.
Lysander, if you live, good sir, awake. 102
LYS. [*Awaking*] And run through fire I will for thy sweet sake.
Transparent Helena! Nature shows art,
That through thy bosom makes me see thy heart. 105
Where is Demetrius? O, how fit a word
Is that vile name to perish on my sword!
HEL. Do not say so, Lysander; say not so.
What though he love your Hermia? Lord, what though? 109
Yet Hermia still loves you: then be content.
LYS. Content with Hermia! No; I do repent
The tedious minutes I with her have spent.
Not Hermia but Helena I love:
Who will not change a raven for a dove?
The will of man is by his reason sway'd; 115
And reason says you are the worthier maid.
Things growing are not ripe until their season:
So I, being young, till now ripe not to reason;
And touching now the point of human skill,
Reason becomes the marshal to my will 120
And leads me to your eyes, where I o'erlook
Love's stories written in love's richest book.
HEL. Wherefore was I to this keen mockery born?
When at your hands did I deserve this scorn?
Is't not enough, is't not enough, young man,
That I did never, no, nor never can, 126
Deserve a sweet look from Demetrius' eye,
But you must flout my insufficiency?
Good troth, you do me wrong, good sooth, you do,
In such disdainful manner me to woo. 130
But fare you well: perforce I must confess
I thought you lord of more true gentleness.
O, that a lady, of one man refused,
Should of another therefore be abused! [*Exit.*
LYS. She sees not Hermia. Hermia, sleep thou there: 135
And never mayst thou come Lysander near!
For as a surfeit of the sweetest things
The deepest loathing to the stomach brings,
Or as the heresies that men do leave
Are hated most of those they did deceive, 140
So thou, my surfeit and my heresy,
Of all be hated, but the most of me!
And, all my powers, address your love and might
To honour Helen and to be her knight! [*Exit.*
HER. [*Awaking*] Help me, Lysander, help me! do thy best
To pluck this crawling serpent from my breast!
Ay me, for pity! what a dream was here!
Lysander, look how I do quake with fear:
Methought a serpent eat my heart away,
And you sat smiling at his cruel prey. 150
Lysander! what, removed? Lysander! lord!
What, out of hearing? gone? no sound, no word?
Alack, where are you? speak, an if you hear;
Speak, of all loves! I swoon almost with fear.
No? then I well perceive you are not nigh: 155
Either death or you I'll find immediately. [*Exit.*

86. darkling, in the dark. 88. fond, foolish. 89. grace, good fortune. 98. dissembling, deceiving. 99. sphery eyne, starry eyes. 118. ripe, grown ripe. 119. point, apex. 120. will, passion. 128. flout, make fun of, insult. 150. prey, preying [on me]. 154. of all loves, for the sake of all love.

ACT III

SCENE I. *The wood.* TITANIA *lying asleep.*

[*Enter* QUINCE, SNUG, BOTTOM, FLUTE, SNOUT, *and* STARVELING.]

BOT. Are we all met?

QUIN. Pat, pat; and here's a marvellous convenient place for our rehearsal. This green plot shall be our stage, this hawthorn-brake our tiring-house; and we will do it in action as we will do it before the duke. 6

BOT. Peter Quince,—

QUIN. What sayest thou, bully Bottom?

BOT. There are things in this comedy of Pyramus and Thisby that will never please. First, Pyramus must draw a sword to kill himself; which the ladies cannot abide. How answer you that? 13

SNOUT. By'r lakin, a parlous fear.

STAR. I believe we must leave the killing out, when all is done.

BOT. Not a whit: I have a device to make all well. Write me a prologue; and let the prologue seem to say, we will do no harm with our swords and that Pyramus is not killed indeed; and, for the more better assurance, tell them that I Pyramus am not Pyramus, but Bottom the weaver: this will put them out of fear.

QUIN. Well, we will have such a prologue; and it shall be written in eight and six. 25

BOT. No, make it two more; let it be written in eight and eight.

SNOUT. Will not the ladies be afeard of the lion?

STAR. I fear it, I promise you. 29

BOT. Masters, you ought to consider with yourselves: to bring in—God shield us!—a lion among ladies, is a most dreadful thing; for there is not a more fearful wild-fowl than your lion living; and we ought to look to't.

SNOUT. Therefore another prologue must tell he is not a lion. 36

BOT. Nay, you must name his name, and half his face must be seen through the lion's neck: and he himself must speak through, saying thus, or to the same defect,—"Ladies,"—or "Fair ladies,—I would wish you,"—or "I would request you,"—or "I would entreat you,—not to fear, not to tremble: my life for yours. If you think I come hither as a lion, it were pity of my life: no, I am no such thing; I am a man as other men are;" and there indeed let him name his name, and tell them plainly he is Snug the joiner.

QUIN. Well, it shall be so. But there is two hard things; that is, to bring the moonlight into a chamber; for, you know, Pyramus and Thisby meet by moonlight. 51

SNOUT. Doth the moon shine that night we play our play?

BOT. A calendar, a calendar! look in the almanac; find out moonshine, find out moonshine.

QUIN. Yes, it doth shine that night.

BOT. Why, then may you leave a casement of the great chamber window, where we play, open, and the moon may shine in at the casement. 59

QUIN. Ay; or else one must come in with a bush of thorns and a lanthorn, and say he comes to disfigure, or to present, the person of Moonshine. Then, there is another thing: we must have a wall in the great chamber; for Pyramus and Thisby, says the story, did talk through the chink of a wall.

SNOUT. You can never bring in a wall. What say you, Bottom? 68

BOT. Some man or other must present Wall: and let him have some plaster, or some loam, or some rough-cast about him, to signify 71 wall; and let him hold his fingers thus, and through that cranny shall Pyramus and Thisby whisper.

QUIN. If that may be, then all is well. Come, sit down, every mother's son, and rehearse your parts. Pyramus, you begin: when you have spoken your speech, enter into that brake: and so every one according to his cue.

[*Enter* PUCK *behind.*]

Act III, Scene i: 5. **tiring-house,** dressing room. 8. **bully Bottom,** "good old" Bottom. 14. **By'r lakin,** by our ladykin, i.e., Virgin Mary; **parlous,** dangerous, risky.

25. **eight and six,** alternate lines of eight and six syllables. 40. **defect,** mistake for "effect." 45. **pity of my life,** sad thing for me. 58. **great chamber,** hall of a great house. 62. **disfigure,** mistake for "prefigure." 71. **rough-cast,** coarse plaster.

PUCK. What hempen home-spuns have we swaggering here,
So near the cradle of the fairy queen? 80
What, a play toward! I'll be an auditor;
An actor too perhaps, if I see cause.

QUIN. Speak, Pyramus. Thisby, stand forth.

BOT. Thisby, the flowers of odious savours sweet,—

QUIN. Odours, odours. 85

BOT. —— odours savours sweet:
So hath thy breath, my dearest Thisby dear.
But hark, a voice! stay thou but here awhile,
And by and by I will to thee appear. [*Exit.*

PUCK. A stranger Pyramus than e'er played here. [*Exit.* 90

FLU. Must I speak now?

QUIN. Ay, marry, must you; for you must understand he goes but to see a noise that he heard, and is to come again.

FLU. Most radiant Pyramus, most lily-white of hue, 95
Of colour like the red rose on triumphant brier,
Most brisky juvenal and eke most lovely Jew,
As true as truest horse that yet would never tire
I'll meet thee, Pyramus, at Ninny's tomb.

QUIN. "Ninus' tomb," man: why, you 100 must not speak that yet; that you answer to Pyramus: you speak all your part at once, cues and all. Pyramus enter: your cue is past; it is, "never tire."

FLU. O,—As true as truest horse, that yet would never tire.

[*Re-enter* PUCK, *and* BOTTOM *with an ass's head.*]

BOT. If I were fair, Thisby, I were only thine.

QUIN. O monstrous! O strange! we are haunted. Pray, masters! fly, masters! Help!
[*Exeunt* QUINCE, SNUG, FLUTE, SNOUT, *and* STARVELING.

PUCK. I'll follow you, I'll lead you about a round,
Through bog, through bush, through brake, through brier: 110
Sometime a horse I'll be, sometime a hound,
A hog, a headless bear, sometime a fire;
And neigh, and bark, and grunt, and roar, and burn,
Like horse, hound, hog, bear, fire, at every turn. [*Exit.*

BOT. Why do they run away? this is a knavery of them to make me afeard. 116

[*Re-enter* SNOUT.]

SNOUT. O Bottom, thou art changed! what do I see on thee?

BOT. What do you see? you see an ass-head of your own, do you? [*Exit* SNOUT.

[*Re-enter* QUINCE.]

QUIN. Bless thee, Bottom! bless thee! thou art translated. [*Exit.* 122

BOT. I see their knavery: this is to make an ass of me; to fright me, if they could. But I will not stir from this place, do what they can: I will walk up and down here, and I will sing, that they shall hear I am not afraid. [*Sings.*

The ousel cock so black of hue,
With orange-tawny bill,
The throstle with his note so true, 130
The wren with little quill,—

TITA. [*Awakening*] What angel wakes me from my flowery bed?

BOT. [*Sings.*]
The finch, the sparrow and the lark,
The plain-song cuckoo gray,
Whose note full many a man doth mark,
And dares not answer nay;— 136
for, indeed, who would set his wit to so foolish a bird? who would give a bird the lie, though he cry "cuckoo" never so?

TITA. I pray thee, gentle mortal, sing again:
Mine ear is much enamour'd of thy note; 141
So is mine eye enthrallèd to thy shape;
And thy fair virtue's force perforce doth move me
On the first view to say, to swear, I love thee. 144

BOT. Methinks, mistress, you should have little reason for that: and yet, to say the truth, reason and love keep little company together now-a-days; the more the pity that some honest neighbours will not make them friends.

81. **toward**, about to begin. 97. **brisky juvenal**, brisk youth; **Jew**, nonsensical repetition of the first syllable of juvenal. 100. **Ninus**, founder of Babylon, at whose tomb in Ovid's story the lovers used to meet. 109. **about a round**, round about. 122. **translated**, transformed. 128. **ousel**, blackbird. 130. **throstle**, thrush. 131. **quill**, pipe.

134. **plain song**, singing a simple air. 139. **"cuckoo,"** the word sounded like "cuckold," which meant a deceived husband. What married man dare contradict the bird's accusation? 143. **fair virtue's force**, the power of your beauty.

Nay, I can gleek upon occasion. 150

TITA. Thou art as wise as thou art beautiful.

BOT. Not so, neither: but if I had wit enough to get out of this wood, I have enough to serve mine own turn.

TITA. Out of this wood do not desire to go:
Thou shalt remain here, whether thou wilt or no. 156
I am a spirit of no common rate:
The summer still doth tend upon my state;
And I do love thee: therefore, go with me;
I'll give thee fairies to attend on thee, 160
And they shall fetch thee jewels from the deep,
And sing while thou on pressèd flowers dost sleep:
And I will purge thy mortal grossness so
That thou shalt like an airy spirit go.
Peaseblossom! Cobweb! Moth! and Mustardseed! 165

[*Enter* PEASEBLOSSOM, COBWEB, MOTH, *and* MUSTARDSEED.]

PEAS. Ready.

COB. And I.

MOTH. And I.

MUS. And I.

ALL. Where shall we go?

TITA. Be kind and courteous to this gentleman;
Hop in his walks and gambol in his eyes;
Feed him with apricocks and dewberries,
With purple grapes, green figs, and mulberries; 170
The honey-bags steal from the humble-bees,
And for night-tapers crop their waxen thighs
And light them at the fiery glow-worm's eyes,
To have my love to bed and to arise;
And pluck the wings from painted butterflies
To fan the moonbeams from his sleeping eyes:
Nod to him, elves, and do him courtesies.

PEAS. Hail, mortal!

COB. Hail!

MOTH. Hail! 180

MUS. Hail!

BOT. I cry your worships mercy, heartily: I beseech your worship's name.

COB. Cobweb.

BOT. I shall desire you of more acquaintance, good Master Cobweb: if I cut my finger, I shall make bold with you. Your name, honest gentleman?

PEAS. Peaseblossom. 189

BOT. I pray you, commend me to Mistress Squash, your mother, and to Master Peascod, your father. Good Master Peaseblossom, I shall desire you of more acquaintance too. Your name, I beseech you, sir?

MUS. Mustardseed. 195

BOT. Good Master Mustardseed, I know your patience well: that same cowardly, giant-like ox-beef hath devoured many a gentleman of your house: I promise you your kindred hath made my eyes water ere now. I desire your more acquaintance, good Master Mustardseed. 201

TITA. Come, wait upon him; lead him to my bower.
The moon methinks looks with a watery eye;
And when she weeps, weeps every little flower,
Lamenting some enforcèd chastity. 205
Tie up my love's tongue, bring him silently.
[*Exeunt.*

SCENE II. *Another part of the wood.*

[*Enter* OBERON.]

OBE. I wonder if Titania be awaked;
Then, what it was that next came in her eye,
Which she must dote on in extremity.

[*Enter* PUCK.]

Here comes my messenger.
How now, mad spirit!
What night-rule now about this haunted grove? 5

PUCK. My mistress with a monster is in love.
Near to her close and consecrated bower,
While she was in her dull and sleeping hour,
A crew of patches, rude mechanicals,
That work for bread upon Athenian stalls, 10
Were met together to rehearse a play
Intended for great Theseus' nuptial-day.
The shallowest thick-skin of that barren sort,

150. **gleek,** scoff. 157. **rate,** value, estimation. 158. **still,** always; **tend upon,** serve as an attendant. 168. **gambol,** caper. 172. **crop,** snip off. 182. **I . . . mercy,** I beg your worship's pardon. 191. **squash,** unripe peaspod. 197. **patience,** sufferings. 205. **enforced,** violated. **Scene ii:** 2. **next,** first. 3. **in extremity,** extremely. 5. **night-rule,** mischief. 9. **patches,** clowns, dolts; **mechanicals,** laborers. 10. **upon Athenian stalls,** in Athenian shops. 13. **barren sort,** stupid crowd.

Who Pyramus presented, in their sport
Forsook his scene and enter'd in a brake: 15
When I did him at this advantage take,
An ass's nole I fixèd on his head:
Anon his Thisbe must be answerèd,
And forth my mimic comes. When they him spy,
As wild geese that the creeping fowler eye, 20
Or russet-pated choughs, many in sort,
Rising and cawing at the gun's report,
Sever themselves and madly sweep the sky,
So, at his sight, away his fellows fly;
And, at our stamp, here o'er and o'er one falls; 25
He murder cries and help from Athens calls.
Their sense thus weak, lost with their fears thus strong,
Made senseless things begin to do them wrong;
For briers and thorns at their apparel snatch;
Some sleeves, some hats, from yielders all things catch. 30
I led them on in this distracted fear,
And left sweet Pyramus translated there:
When in that moment, so it came to pass,
Titania waked and straightway loved an ass.

OBE. This falls out better than I could devise. 35
But hast thou yet latch'd the Athenian's eyes
With the love-juice, as I did bid thee do?

PUCK. I took him sleeping,—that is finish'd too,—
And the Athenian woman by his side;
That, when he waked, of force she must be eyed. 40

[*Enter* HERMIA *and* DEMETRIUS.]

OBE. Stand close: this is the same Athenian.

PUCK. This is the woman, but not this the man.

DEM. O, why rebuke you him that loves you so?
Lay breath so bitter on your bitter foe.

HER. Now I but chide; but I should use thee worse, 45
For thou, I fear, hast given me cause to curse.
If thou hast slain Lysander in his sleep,
Being o'er shoes in blood, plunge in the deep,
And kill me too.
The sun was not so true unto the day 50
As he to me: would he have stolen away
From sleeping Hermia? I'll believe as soon
The whole earth may be bored and that the moon
May through the centre creep and so displease
Her brother's noontide with the Antipodes. 55
It cannot be but thou hast murder'd him;
So should a murderer look, so dead, so grim.

DEM. So should the murder'd look, and so should I,
Pierced through the heart with your stern cruelty: 59
Yet you, the murderer, look as bright, as clear,
As yonder Venus in her glimmering sphere.

HER. What's this to my Lysander? where is he?
Ah, good Demetrius, wilt thou give him me?

DEM. I had rather give his carcass to my hounds.

HER. Out, dog! out, cur! thou drivest me past the bounds 65
Of maiden's patience. Hast thou slain him, then?
Henceforth be never number'd among men!
O, once tell true, tell true, even for my sake!
Durst thou have look'd upon him being awake,
And hast thou kill'd him sleeping? O brave touch 70
Could not a worm, an adder, do so much?
An adder did it; for with doubler tongue
Than thine, thou serpent, never adder stung.

DEM. You spend your passion on a misprised mood:
I am not guilty of Lysander's blood; 75
Nor is he dead, for aught that I can tell.

HER. I pray thee, tell me then that he is well.

DEM. An if I could, what should I get therefore?

HER. A privilege never to see me more.
And from thy hated presence part I so: 80
See me no more, whether he be dead or no.
[*Exit.*

DEM. There is no following her in this fierce vein:
Here therefore for a while I will remain.
So sorrow's heaviness doth heavier grow
For debt that bankrupt sleep doth sorrow owe;
Which now in some slight measure it will pay,
If for his tender here I make some stay. 87
[*Lies down and sleeps.*

15. **brake**, thicket. 17. **nole**, head. 19. **mimic**, buffoon. 21. **russet-pated choughs**, gray-headed grackles; **in sort**, together. 36. **latch'd**, charmed. 40. **of force**, of necessity.

41. **close**, hidden. 54. **center**, i.e., of the earth. 57. **dead**, deadly. 70. **brave touch**, splendid exploit. 71. **worm**, snake. 74. **on a misprised mood**, in mistaken anger. 82. **in . . . vein**, while she is in this fierce mood. 87. **If . . . stay**, if I wait for sleep's offer [of himself].

OBE. What hast thou done? thou hast mistaken quite
And laid the love-juice on some true-love's sight:
Of thy misprision must perforce ensue 90
Some true love turn'd and not a false turn'd true.

PUCK. Then fate o'er-rules, that, one man holding troth,
A million fail, confounding oath on oath.

OBE. About the wood go swifter than the wind,
And Helena of Athens look thou find: 95
All fancy-sick she is and pale of cheer,
With sighs of love, that costs the fresh blood dear:
By some illusion see thou bring her here:
I'll charm his eyes against she do appear.

PUCK. I go, I go; look how I go, 100
Swifter than arrow from the Tartar's bow. [*Exit.*

OBE. Flower of this purple dye,
Hit with Cupid's archery,
Sink in apple of his eye.
When his love he doth espy, 105
Let her shine as gloriously
As the Venus of the sky.
When thou wakest, if she be by,
Beg of her for remedy.

[*Re-enter* PUCK.]

PUCK. Captain of our fairy band, 110
Helena is here at hand;
And the youth, mistook by me,
Pleading for a lover's fee.
Shall we their fond pageant see?
Lord, what fools these mortals be! 115

OBE. Stand aside: the noise they make
Will cause Demetrius to awake.

PUCK. Then will two at once woo one;
That must needs be sport alone;
And those things do best please me
That befall preposterously. 121

[*Enter* LYSANDER *and* HELENA.]

LYS. Why should you think that I should woo in scorn?
Scorn and derision never come in tears:
Look, when I vow, I weep; and vows so born,
In their nativity all truth appears. 125
How can these things in me seem scorn to you,
Bearing the badge of faith, to prove them true?

HEL. You do advance your cunning more and more.
When truth kills truth, O devilish-holy fray!
These vows are Hermia's: will you give her o'er? 130
Weigh oath with oath, and you will nothing weigh:
Your vows to her and me, put in two scales,
Will even weigh, and both as light as tales.

LYS. I had no judgement when to her I swore.

HEL. Nor none, in my mind, now you give her o'er. 135

LYS. Demetrius loves her, and he loves not you.

DEM. [*Awaking*] O Helen, goddess, nymph, perfect, divine!
To what, my love, shall I compare thine eyne?
Crystal is muddy. O, how ripe in show
Thy lips, those kissing cherries, tempting grow! 140
That pure congealèd white, high Taurus' snow,
Fann'd with the eastern wind, turns to a crow
When thou hold'st up thy hand: O, let me kiss
This princess of pure white, this seal of bliss!

HEL. O spite! O hell! I see you all are bent
To set against me for your merriment: 146
If you were civil and knew courtesy,
You would not do me thus much injury.
Can you not hate me, as I know you do,
But you must join in souls to mock me too?
If you were men, as men you are in show, 151
You would not use a gentle lady so;
To vow, and swear, and superpraise my parts,
When I am sure you hate me with your hearts.
You both are rivals, and love Hermia; 155

90. **misprision**, mistake. 96. **fancy-sick**, love-sick; **cheer**, face. 97. **sighs of love**, allusion to the belief that each sigh costs the heart a drop of blood. 98. **illusion**, deception. 99. **against**, by the time that. 114. **fond pageant**, silly spectacle. 121. **preposterously**, contrary to reason.

124-5. **vows . . . appears**, i.e., vows born in tears seem at their birth to be wholly true. 141. **Taurus**, a mountain range in Asia Minor. 144. **seal**, pledge, ratification. 153. **superpraise**, overpraise.

And now both rivals, to mock Helena:
A trim exploit, a manly enterprise,
To conjure tears up in a poor maid's eyes
With your derision! none of noble sort
Would so offend a virgin and extort 160
A poor soul's patience, all to make you sport.

LYS. You are unkind, Demetrius; be not so;
For you love Hermia; this you know I know:
And here, with all good will, with all my heart,
In Hermia's love I yield you up my part; 165
And yours of Helena to me bequeath,
Whom I do love and will do till my death.

HEL. Never did mockers waste more idle breath.

DEM. Lysander, keep thy Hermia; I will none:
If e'er I loved her, all that love is gone. 170
My heart to her but as guest-wise sojourn'd,
And now to Helen is it home return'd,
There to remain.

LYS. Helen, it is not so.

DEM. Disparage not the faith thou dost not know,
Lest, to thy peril, thou aby it dear. 175
Look, where thy love comes; yonder is thy dear.

[*Re-enter* HERMIA.]

HER. Dark night, that from the eye his function takes,
The ear more quick of apprehension makes;
Wherein it doth impair the seeing sense,
It pays the hearing double recompense. 180
Thou art not by mine eye, Lysander, found;
Mine ear, I thank it, brought me to thy sound
But why unkindly didst thou leave me so?

LYS. Why should he stay, whom love doth press to go?

HER. What love could press Lysander from my side? 185

LYS. Lysander's love, that would not let him bide,
Fair Helena, who more engilds the night
Than all yon fiery oes and eyes of light.
Why seek'st thou me? could not this make thee know,
The hate I bear thee made me leave thee so?

HER. You speak not as you think: it cannot be. 191

HEL. Lo, she is one of this confederacy!
Now I perceive they have conjoin'd all three
To fashion this false sport, in spite of me.
Injurious Hermia! most ungrateful maid! 195
Have you conspired, have you with these contrived
To bait me with this foul derision?
Is all the counsel that we two have shared,
The sisters' vows, the hours that we have spent,
When we have chid the hasty-footed time 200
For parting us,—O, is it all forgot?
All school-days' friendship, childhood innocence?
We, Hermia, like two artificial gods,
Have with our needles created both one flower,
Both on one sampler, sitting on one cushion, 205
Both warbling of one song, both in one key,
As if our hands, our sides, voices and minds,
Had been incorporate. So we grew together,
Like to a double cherry, seeming parted,
But yet an union in partition; 210
Two lovely berries moulded on one stem;
So, with two seeming bodies, but one heart;
Two of the first, like coats in heraldry,
Due but to one and crownèd with one crest.
And will you rent our ancient love asunder,
To join with men in scorning your poor friend? 216
It is not friendly, 'tis not maidenly:
Our sex, as well as I, may chide you for it,
Though I alone do feel the injury.

HER. I am amazèd at your passionate words. 220
I scorn you not: it seems that you scorn me.

HEL. Have you not set Lysander, as in scorn,
To follow me and praise my eyes and face?
And made your other love, Demetrius,
Who even but now did spurn me with his foot, 225
To call me goddess, nymph, divine and rare,
Precious, celestial? Wherefore speaks he this
To her he hates? and wherefore doth Lysander
Deny your love, so rich within his soul,
And tender me, forsooth, affection, 230

157. trim, fine (used ironically). 160. extort, torture. 169. will none, i.e., none of her. 171. as guest-sojourned, has made a short stay. 175. aby, atone for. 177. his, its.

188. oes, circles, i.e., stars. 195. injurious, insulting. 203. artificial, skilled in art. 205. sampler, a piece of embroidery. 208. incorporate, parts of the same body. 213-4. Two . . . one crest, i.e., the two bodies are like the double coats of arms which belong to husband and wife, yet have but one crest, as we have but one heart.

But by your setting on, by your consent?
What though I be not so in grace as you,
So hung upon with love, so fortunate,
But miserable most, to love unloved?
This you should pity rather than despise. 235

HER. I understand not what you mean by this.

HEL. Ay, do, persévər, counterfeit sad looks,
Make mouths upon me when I turn my back;
Wink each at other; hold the sweet jest up:
This sport, well carried, shall be chronicled.
If you have any pity, grace, or manners, 241
You would not make me such an argument.
But fare ye well: 'tis partly my own fault;
Which death or absence soon shall remedy.

LYS. Stay, gentle Helena; hear my excuse:
My love, my life, my soul, fair Helena! 246

HEL. O excellent!

HER. Sweet, do not scorn her so.

DEM. If she cannot entreat, I can compel.

LYS. Thou canst compel no more than she entreat:
Thy threats have no more strength than her weak prayers. 250
Helen, I love thee; by my life, I do:
I swear by that which I will lose for thee,
To prove him false that says I love thee not.

DEM. I say I love thee more than he can do.

LYS. If thou say so, withdraw, and prove it too. 255

DEM. Quick, come!

HER. Lysander, whereto tends all this?

LYS. Away, you Ethiope!

DEM. No, no; he'll . . .
Seem to break loose; take on as you would follow,
But yet come not: you are a tame man, go!

LYS. Hang off, thou cat, thou burr! vile thing, let loose, 260
Or I will shake thee from me like a serpent!

HER. Why are you grown so rude? what change is this?
Sweet love,—

LYS. Thy love! out, tawny Tartar, out!
Out, loathèd medicine! hated potion, hence!

HER. Do you not jest?

HEL. Yes, sooth; and so do you.

LYS. Demetrius, I will keep my word with thee.

DEM. I would I had your bond, for I perceive 267
A weak bond holds you: I'll not trust your word.

LYS. What, should I hurt her, strike her, kill her dead?
Although I hate her, I'll not harm her so. 270

HER. What, can you do me greater harm than hate?
Hate me! wherefore? O me! what news, my love!
Am not I Hermia? are not you Lysander?
I am as fair now as I was erewhile.
Since night you loved me; yet since night you left me: 275
Why, then you left me—O, the gods forbid!—
In earnest, shall I say?

LYS. Ay, by my life;
And never did desire to see thee more.
Therefore be out of hope, of question, of doubt;
Be certain, nothing truer; 'tis no jest 280
That I do hate thee and love Helena.

HER. O me! you juggler! you canker-blossom!
You thief of love! what, have you come by night
And stolen my love's heart from him?

HEL. Fine, i' faith!
Have you no modesty, no maiden shame,
No touch of bashfulness? What, will you tear 286
Impatient answers from my gentle tongue?
Fie, fie! you counterfeit, you puppet, you!

HER. Puppet? why so? ay, that way goes the game.
Now I perceive that she hath made compare
Between our statures; she hath urged her height; 291
And with her personage, her tall personage,
Her height, forsooth, she hath prevail'd with him.
And are you grown so high in his esteem,
Because I am so dwarfish and so low? 295
How low am I, thou painted maypole? speak;
How low am I? I am not yet so low
But that my nails can reach unto thine eyes.

237. **persévər**, persevere; **sad**, serious. 238. **make mouths upon**, make faces at. 242. **argument**, plot for a story. 260. **hang off**, let go. 267. **bond**, written agreement. 272. **what news**, i.e., what's the matter. 274. **erewhile**, a little while ago. 282. **juggler**, deceiver; **canker-blossom**, canker worm. 288. **puppet**, doll-like person; the epithet suggests that she was very small. Cf. **dwarfish**, line 295.

HEL. I pray you, though you mock me, gentlemen,
Let her not hurt me: I was never curst; 300
I have no gift at all in shrewishness;
I am a right maid for my cowardice:
Let her not strike me. You perhaps may think,
Because she is something lower than myself,
That I can match her.
HER. Lower! hark, again. 305
HEL. Good Hermia, do not be so bitter with me.
I evermore did love you, Hermia,
Did ever keep your counsels, never wrong'd you;
Save that, in love unto Demetrius,
I told him of your stealth unto this wood. 310
He follow'd you; for love I follow'd him;
But he hath chid me hence and threaten'd me
To strike me, spurn me, nay, to kill me too:
And now, so you will let me quiet go,
To Athens will I bear my folly back 315
And follow you no further: let me go:
You see how simple and how fond I am.
HER. Why, get you gone: who is't that hinders you?
HEL. A foolish heart, that I leave here behind.
HER. What, with Lysander?
HEL. With Demetrius. 320
LYS. Be not afraid; she shall not harm thee, Helena.
DEM. No, sir, she shall not, though you take her part.
HEL. O, when she's angry, she is keen and shrewd!
She was a vixen when she went to school;
And though she be but little, she is fierce. 325
HER. "Little" again! nothing but "low" and "little"!
Why will you suffer her to flout me thus?
Let me come to her.
LYS. Get you gone, you dwarf;
You minimus, of hindering knot-grass made;
You bead, you acorn.
DEM. You are too officious 330
In her behalf that scorns your services.
Let her alone: speak not of Helena;
Take not her part; for, if thou dost intend
Never so little show of love to her,
Thou shalt aby it.
LYS. Now she holds me not; 335
Now follow, if thou darest, to try whose right,
Of thine or mine, is most in Helena.
DEM. Follow! nay, I'll go with thee, cheek by jole. [*Exeunt* LYSANDER *and* DEMETRIUS.
HER. You, mistress, all this coil is 'long of you:
Nay, go not back.
HEL. I will not trust you, I, 340
Nor longer stay in your curst company.
Your hands than mine are quicker for a fray,
My legs are longer though, to run away. [*Exit.*
HER. I am amazed, and know not what to say. [*Exit.*
OBE. This is thy negligence: still thou mistakest, 345
Or else committ'st thy knaveries wilfully.
PUCK. Believe me, king of shadows, I mistook.
Did not you tell me I should know the man
By the Athenian garments he had on?
And so far blameless proves my enterprise,
That I have 'nointed an Athenian's eyes; 351
And so far am I glad it so did sort
As this their jangling I esteem a sport.
OBE. Thou see'st these lovers seek a place to fight:
Hie therefore, Robin, overcast the night; 355
The starry welkin cover thou anon
With drooping fog as black as Acheron,
And lead these testy rivals so astray
As one come not within another's way.
Like to Lysander sometime frame thy tongue, 360
Then stir Demetrius up with bitter wrong;
And sometime rail thou like Demetrius;
And from each other look thou lead them thus,
Till o'er their brows death-counterfeiting sleep
With leaden legs and batty wings doth creep:
Then crush this herb into Lysander's eye; 366
Whose liquor hath this virtuous property,

300. curst, shrewish. 302. I . . . cowardice, in my lack of courage I am a true woman. 310. stealth, stealing away. 313. spurn, kick. 323. shrewd, sharp-tongued. 329. minimus, tiny creature; knot-grass, a weed, the infusion of which was supposed to stunt growth. 333. intend, extend. 335. aby, pay for it. 338. jole, jowl, chin. 339. coil, turmoil; 'long of, because of. 345. negligence, carelessness. 352. sort, turn out. 353. jangling, wrangling. 357. Acheron, a river in Hades. 359. As, so that. 361. wrong, insults. 367. virtuous, potent.

To take from thence all error with his might,
And make his eyeballs roll with wonted sight.
When they next wake, all this derision 370
Shall seem a dream and fruitless vision,
And back to Athens shall the lovers wend,
With league whose date till death shall never end.
Whiles I in this affair do thee employ,
I'll to my queen and beg her Indian boy: 375
And then I will her charmèd eye release
From monster's view, and all things shall be peace.

PUCK. My fairy lord, this must be done with haste,
For night's swift dragons cut the clouds full fast,
And yonder shines Aurora's harbinger; 380
At whose approach, ghosts, wandering here and there,
Troop home to churchyards: damnèd spirits all,
That in crossways and floods have burial,
Already to their wormy beds are gone;
For fear lest day should look their shames upon, 385
They wilfully themselves exile from light
And must for aye consort with black-brow'd night.

OBE. But we are spirits of another sort:
I with the morning's love have oft made sport,
And, like a forester, the groves may tread, 390
Even till the eastern gate, all fiery-red,
Opening on Neptune with fair blessèd beams,
Turns into yellow gold his salt green streams.
But, notwithstanding, haste; make no delay:
We may effect this business yet ere day. 395
[*Exit.*

PUCK. Up and down, up and down,
I will lead them up and down:
I am fear'd in field and town:
Goblin, lead them up and down.
Here comes one. 400

[*Re-enter* LYSANDER.]

LYS. Where art thou, proud Demetrius? speak thou now.

PUCK. Here, villain; drawn and ready. Where art thou?

LYS. I will be with thee straight.

PUCK. Follow me, then,
To plainer ground.
[*Exit* LYSANDER, *as following the voice.*

[*Re-enter* DEMETRIUS.]

DEM. Lysander! speak again:
Thou runaway, thou coward, art thou fled?
Speak! In some bush? Where dost thou hide thy head? 406

PUCK. Thou coward, art thou bragging to the stars,
Telling the bushes that thou look'st for wars,
And wilt not come? Come, recreant; come, thou child,
I'll whip thee with a rod: he is defiled 410
That draws a sword on thee.

DEM. Yea, art thou there?

PUCK. Follow my voice: we'll try no manhood here. [*Exeunt.*

[*Re-enter* LYSANDER.]

LYS. He goes before me and still dares me on:
When I come where he calls, then he is gone.
The villain is much lighter-heel'd than I: 415
I follow'd fast, but faster he did fly;
That fallen am I in dark uneven way,
And here will rest me. [*Lies down.*] Come, thou gentle day!
For if but once thou show me thy grey light,
I'll find Demetrius and revenge this spite. 420
[*Sleeps.*

[*Re-enter* PUCK *and* DEMETRIUS.]

PUCK. Ho, ho, ho! Coward, why comest thou not?

DEM. Abide me, if thou darest; for well I wot
Thou runn'st before me, shifting every place,
And darest not stand, nor look me in the face.
Where art thou now?

PUCK. Come hither: I am here.

368. **with his might**, by his power. 379. **night's swift dragons**, Shakespeare conceived the dragons as being yoked to Night's chariot. 380. **Aurora's harbinger**, forerunner of the dawn, i.e., the morning star. 383. **in crossways**, suicides were buried at the crossroads; **floods**, drowned persons having had no burial rites, would be unable to enter purgatory or heaven. 388. **of another sort**, i.e., not infernal and so able to endure daylight. 389. **morning's love**, either Cephalus, a youth loved of Aurora, or the goddess herself. 402. **drawn**, with sword drawn. 404. **plainer**, more level. 409. **recreant**, coward. 422. **wot**, know. 432. **abate**, shorten.

DEM. Nay, then, thou mock'st me. Thou shalt buy this dear, 426
If ever I thy face by daylight see:
Now, go thy way. Faintness constraineth me
To measure out my length on this cold bed.
By day's approach look to be visited. 430
[*Lies down and sleeps.*

[*Re-enter* HELENA.]

HEL. O weary night, O long and tedious night,
Abate thy hours! Shine comforts from the east,
That I may back to Athens by daylight,
From these that my poor company detest:
And sleep, that sometimes shuts up sorrow's eye, 435
Steal me awhile from mine own company.
[*Lies down and sleeps.*

PUCK. Yet but three? Come one more;
Two of both kinds makes up four.
Here she comes, curst and sad:
Cupid is a knavish lad, 440
Thus to make poor females mad.

[*Re-enter* HERMIA.]

HER. Never so weary, never so in woe,
Bedabbled with the dew and torn with briers,
I can no further crawl, no further go;
My legs can keep no pace with my desires.
Here will I rest me till the break of day. 446
Heavens shield Lysander, if they mean a fray!
[*Lies down and sleeps.*

PUCK. On the ground
Sleep sound:
I'll apply 450
To your eye,
Gentle lover, remedy.
[*Squeezing the juice on* LYSANDER'S *eyes.*]
When thou wakest,
Thou takest
True delight 455
In the sight
Of thy former lady's eye:
And the country proverb known,
That every man should take his own,
In your waking shall be shown: 460
Jack shall have Jill;
Nought shall go ill;
The man shall have his mare again, and all shall be well. [*Exit.*

ACT IV

SCENE I. *The same.* LYSANDER, DEMETRIUS, HELENA, *and* HERMIA *lying asleep.*

[*Enter* TITANIA *and* BOTTOM; PEASEBLOSSOM, COBWEB, MOTH, MUSTARDSEED, *and other* FAIRIES *attending;* OBERON *behind unseen.*]

TITA. Come, sit thee down upon this flowery bed,
While I thy amiable cheeks do coy,
And stick musk-roses in thy sleek smooth head,
And kiss thy fair large ears, my gentle joy.

BOT. Where's Peaseblossom? 5

PEAS. Ready.

BOT. Scratch my head, Peaseblossom. Where's Mounsieur Cobweb?

COB. Ready. 9

BOT. Mounsieur Cobweb, good mounsieur, get you your weapons in your hand, and kill me a red-hipped humble-bee on the top of a thistle; and, good mounsieur, bring me the honey-bag. Do not fret yourself too much in the action, mounsieur; and, good mounsieur, have a care the honey-bag break not; I would be loath to have you overflown with a honey-bag, signior. Where's Mounsieur Mustardseed?

MUS. Ready. 19

BOT. Give me your neaf, Mounsieur Mustardseed. Pray you, leave your courtesy, good mounsieur.

MUS. What's your will?

BOT. Nothing, good mounsieur, but to help Cavalery Cobweb to scratch. I must 25 to the barber's, mounsieur; for methinks I am marvellous hairy about the face; and I am such a tender ass, if my hair do but tickle me, I must scratch.

TITA. What, wilt thou hear some music, my sweet love? 30

BOT. I have a reasonable good ear in music. Let's have the tongs and the bones.

439. curst, shrewish. Act IV, Scene i: 2. coy, stroke, caress. 20. neaf, fist. 21. leave your courtesy, i.e., put on your hat. 25. Cavalery, cavaliero, i.e., gentleman. 32. tongs and bones, crude musical instruments; tongs—a kind of triangle; bones—clappers.

TITA. Or say, sweet love, what thou desirest to eat.

BOT. Truly, a peck of provender: I could munch your good dry oats. Methinks I have a great desire to a bottle of hay: good hay, sweet hay, hath no fellow. 36

TITA. I have a venturous fairy that shall seek
The squirrel's hoard, and fetch thee new nuts.

BOT. I had rather have a handful or two of dried peas. But, I pray you, let none of your people stir me: I have an exposition of sleep come upon me. 42

TITA. Sleep thou, and I will wind thee in my arms.
Fairies, be gone, and be all ways away.
[*Exeunt* FAIRIES.]
So doth the woodbine the sweet honeysuckle
Gentle entwist; the female ivy so
Enrings the barky fingers of the elm.
O, how I love thee! how I dote on thee!
[*They sleep.*

[*Enter* PUCK.]

OBE. [*Advancing*] Welcome, good Robin. See'st thou this sweet sight?
Her dotage now I do begin to pity: 50
For, meeting her of late behind the wood,
Seeking sweet favours for this hateful fool,
I did upbraid her and fall out with her;
For she his hairy temples then had rounded
With coronet of fresh and fragrant flowers;
And that same dew, which sometime on the buds 56
Was wont to swell like round and orient pearls,
Stood now within the pretty flowerets' eyes
Like tears that did their own disgrace bewail.
When I had at my pleasure taunted her 60
And she in mild terms begg'd my patience,
I then did ask of her changeling child;
Which straight she gave me, and her fairy sent
To bear him to my bower in fairy land.
And now I have the boy, I will undo 65
This hateful imperfection of her eyes:
And, gentle Puck, take this transformèd scalp
From off the head of this Athenian swain;
That, he awaking when the other do,
May all to Athens back again repair 70
And think no more of this night's accidents
But as the fierce vexation of a dream.
But first I will release the fairy queen.
Be as thou wast wont to be;
See as thou wast wont to see: 75
Dian's bud o'er Cupid's flower
Hath such force and blessèd power.
Now, my Titania; wake you, my sweet queen.

TITA. My Oberon! what visions have I seen!
Methought I was enamour'd of an ass. 80

OBE. There lies your love.

TITA. How came these things to pass?
O, how mine eyes do loathe his visage now!

OBE. Silence awhile. Robin, take off this head.
Titania, music call; and strike more dead
Than common sleep of all these five the sense. 85

TITA. Music, ho! music, such as charmeth sleep! [*Music, still.*

PUCK. Now, when thou wakest, with thine own fool's eyes peep.

OBE. Sound, music! Come, my queen, take hands with me,
And rock the ground whereon these sleepers be. 90
Now thou and I are new in amity
And will to-morrow midnight solemnly
Dance in Duke Theseus' house triumphantly
And bless it to all fair prosperity:
There shall the pair of faithful lovers be 95
Wedded, with Theseus, all in jollity.

PUCK. Fairy king, attend, and mark:
I do hear the morning lark.

OBE. Then, my queen, in silence sad,
Trip we after night's shade: 100
We the globe can compass soon,
Swifter than the wandering moon.

TITA. Come, my lord, and in our flight
Tell me how it came this night
That I sleeping here was found 105
With these mortals on the ground.
[*Exeunt.*
[*Horns winded within.*

35. bottle, bundle (of hay). 41. exposition of, Bottom means "disposition to." 44. all ways, in every direction. 52. favours, nosegays. 57. orient, lustrous, because the most beautiful pearls were supposed to come from the Orient. 69. other, others. 72. fierce, violent. 76. Dian's bud, a plant, agnus castus, which was supposed to preserve chastity. 84-5. strike . . . sleep, make them sleep more soundly than normal. 85. these five, Bottom and the two pair of lovers. 86. s.d. Music, still, continuous music. 87. peep, take a look. 99. sad, serious.

[*Enter* THESEUS, HIPPOLYTA, EGEUS, *and train.*]

THE. Go, one of you, find out the forester;
For now our observation is perform'd;
And since we have the vaward of the day, 109
My love shall hear the music of my hounds.
Uncouple in the western valley; let them go:
Dispatch, I say, and find the forester.
[*Exit an* ATTENDANT.]
We will, fair queen, up to the mountain's top
And mark the musical confusion
Of hounds and echo in conjunction. 115

HIP. I was with Hercules and Cadmus once,
When in a wood of Crete they bay'd the bear
With hounds of Sparta: never did I hear
Such gallant chiding; for, besides the groves,
The skies, the fountains, every region near
Seem'd all one mutual cry: I never heard 121
So musical a discord, such sweet thunder.

THE. My hounds are bred out of the Spartan kind,
So flew'd, so sanded, and their heads are hung
With ears that sweep away the morning dew;
Crook-knee'd, and dew-lapp'd like Thessalian bulls; 126
Slow in pursuit, but match'd in mouth like bells,
Each under each. A cry more tuneable
Was never holla'd to, nor cheer'd with horn,
In Crete, in Sparta, nor in Thessaly: 130
Judge when you hear. But, soft! what nymphs are these?

EGE. My lord, this is my daughter here asleep;
And this, Lysander; this Demetrius is;
This Helena, old Nedar's Helena:
I wonder of their being here together. 135

THE. No doubt they rose up early to observe
The rite of May, and, hearing our intent,
Came here in grace of our solemnity.
But speak, Egeus; is not this the day
That Hermia should give answer of her choice? 140

EGE. It is, my lord.

THE. Go, bid the huntsmen wake them with their horns. [*Horns and shout within.* LYS., DEM., HEL., *and* HER., *wake and start up.*]
Good morrow, friends. Saint Valentine is past:
Begin these wood-birds but to couple now?

LYS. Pardon, my lord.

THE. I pray you all, stand up. 145
I know you two are rival enemies:
How comes this gentle concord in the world,
That hatred is so far from jealousy,
To sleep by hate, and fear no enmity?

LYS. My lord, I shall reply amazedly, 150
Half sleep, half waking: but as yet, I swear,
I cannot truly say how I came here;
But, as I think,—for truly would I speak,
And now I do bethink me, so it is,—
I came with Hermia hither: our intent 155
Was to be gone from Athens, where we might,
Without the peril of the Athenian law.

EGE. Enough, enough, my lord; you have enough:
I beg the law, the law, upon his head.
They would have stolen away; they would, Demetrius, 160
Thereby to have defeated you and me,
You of your wife and me of my consent,
Of my consent that she should be your wife.

DEM. My lord, fair Helen told me of their stealth,
Of this their purpose hither to this wood; 165
And I in fury hither follow'd them,
Fair Helena in fancy following me.
But, my good lord, I wot not by what power,—
But by some power it is,—my love to Hermia,
Melted as the snow, seems to me now 170
As the remembrance of an idle gawd
Which in my childhood I did dote upon;
And all the faith, the virtue of my heart,
The object and the pleasure of mine eye,
Is only Helena. To her, my lord, 175
Was I betroth'd ere I saw Hermia:
But, like in sickness, did I loathe this food;
But, as in health, come to my natural taste,
Now I do wish it, love it, long for it,
And will for evermore be true to it. 180

THE. Fair lovers, you are fortunately met:
Of this discourse we more will hear anon.
Egeus, I will overbear your will;

108. observation, May Day rites. **109. vaward,** vanguard, i.e., early part. 112. Dispatch, hurry. **119. chiding,** clamor. 124. flew'd, with large hanging chaps; **sanded,** of a sandy color. 127. mouth, voice. Elizabethan huntsmen chose hounds whose baying would make harmony. **128. Each under each,** each harmonious with the rest; cry, pack of hounds. 138. **in grace of our solemnity,** to do honor to our wedding ceremony. **s.d. within,** offstage. 144. **Begin . . . couple now,** birds were supposed to choose their mates on St. Valentine's Day. **156. where,** wherever. **157. without,** beyond the reach of. **158. enough,** i.e., enough to convict him. **167. in fancy,** out of love. **171. idle gawd,** worthless trifle.

For in the temple, by and by, with us
These couples shall eternally be knit: 185
And, for the morning now is something worn,
Our purposed hunting shall be set aside.
Away with us to Athens; three and three,
We'll hold a feast in great solemnity.
Come, Hippolyta. 190

[*Exeunt* THESEUS, HIPPOLYTA, EGEUS, *and train.*

DEM. These things seem small and undistinguishable,
Like far-off mountains turned into clouds.

HER. Methinks I see these things with parted eye,
When every thing seems double.

HEL. So methinks:
And I have found Demetrius like a jewel, 195
Mine own, and not mine own.

DEM. Are you sure
That we are awake? It seems to me
That yet we sleep, we dream. Do not you think
The duke was here, and bid us follow him?

HER. Yea; and my father.

HEL. And Hippolyta. 200

LYS. And he did bid us follow to the temple.

DEM. Why, then, we are awake: let's follow him;
And by the way let us recount our dreams.

[*Exeunt.*

BOT. [*Awaking*] When my cue comes, call me, and I will answer: my next is, "Most 205 fair Pyramus." Heigh-ho! Peter Quince! Flute, the bellows-mender! Snout, the tinker! Starveling! God's my life, stolen hence, and left me asleep! I have had a most rare vision. I have had a dream, past the wit of 210 man to say what dream it was: man is but an ass, if he go about to expound this dream. Methought I was—there is no man can tell what. Methought I was,—and methought I had,—but man is but a 215 patched fool, if he will offer to say what methought I had. The eye of man hath not heard, the ear of man hath not seen, man's hand is not able to taste, his tongue to conceive, nor his heart to report, what my 220 dream was. I will get Peter Quince to write a ballad of this dream: it shall be called Bottom's Dream, because it hath no bottom; and I will sing it in the latter end of a play, before the duke: peradventure, to 225 make it the more gracious, I shall sing it at her death. [*Exit.*

SCENE II. *Athens.* QUINCE'S *house.*

[*Enter* QUINCE, FLUTE, SNOUT, *and* STARVELING.]

QUIN. Have you sent to Bottom's house? is he come home yet?

STAR. He cannot be heard of. Out of doubt he is transported. 4

FLU. If he come not, then the play is marred: it goes not forward, doth it?

QUIN. It is not possible: you have not a man in all Athens able to discharge Pyramus but he.

FLU. No, he hath simply the best wit of any handicraft man in Athens. 10

QUIN. Yea, and the best person too; and he is a very paramour for a sweet voice.

FLU. You must say 'paragon:' a paramour is, God bless us, a thing of naught.

[*Enter* SNUG.]

SNUG. Masters, the duke is coming from 15 the temple, and there is two or three lords and ladies more married: if our sport had gone forward, we had all been made men.

FLU. O sweet bully Bottom! Thus hath he lost sixpence a day during his life; he 20 could not have 'scaped sixpence a day: an the duke had not given him sixpence a day for playing Pyramus, I'll be hanged; he would have deserved it: sixpence a day in Pyramus, or nothing. 25

[*Enter* BOTTOM.]

BOT. Where are these lads? where are these hearts?

QUIN. Bottom! O most courageous day! O most happy hour!

BOT. Masters, I am to discourse wonders: but ask me not what; for if I tell you, I am no true Athenian. I will tell you every thing, right as it fell out.

QUIN. Let us hear, sweet Bottom. 33

BOT. Not a word of me. All that I will tell you is, that the duke hath dined. Get

184. by and by, immediately. 193. parted eye, unfocused eyes. 212. go about, attempt. 216. patched, dressed in motley. Scene ii: 4. transported, carried off. 14. a thing of naught, a wicked thing. 21. sixpence a day, i.e., as a royal pension. 26. hearts, good fellows.

your apparel together, good strings to your beards, new ribbons to your pumps; meet presently at the palace; every man look o'er his part; for the short and the long is, our play is preferred. In any case, let 40
Thisby have clean linen; and let not him that plays the lion pare his nails, for they shall hang out for the lion's claws. And, most dear actors, eat no onions nor garlic, for we are to utter sweet breath; and I do not doubt but to hear them say, it is a sweet comedy. No more words: away! go, away! [*Exeunt.*

ACT V

SCENE I. *Athens. The palace of* THESEUS.

[*Enter* THESEUS, HIPPOLYTA, PHILOSTRATE, LORDS, *and* ATTENDANTS.]

HIP. 'Tis strange, my Theseus, that these lovers speak of.
THE. More strange than true: I never may believe
These antique fables, nor these fairy toys.
Lovers and madmen have such seething brains,
Such shaping fantasies, that apprehend 5
More than cool reason ever comprehends.
The lunatic, the lover and the poet
Are of imagination all compact:
One sees more devils than vast hell can hold,
That is, the madman: the lover, all as frantic, 10
Sees Helen's beauty in a brow of Egypt:
The poet's eye, in a fine frenzy rolling,
Doth glance from heaven to earth, from earth to heaven;
And as imagination bodies forth
The forms of things unknown, the poet's pen 15
Turns them to shapes and gives to airy nothing
A local habitation and a name.
Such tricks hath strong imagination,
That, if it would but apprehend some joy,
It comprehends some bringer of that joy; 20
Or in the night, imagining some fear,
How easy is a bush supposed a bear!
HIP. But all the story of the night told over,
And all their minds transfigured so together,
More witnesseth than fancy's images 25
And grows to something of great constancy;
But, howsoever, strange and admirable.
THE. Here come the lovers, full of joy and mirth.

[*Enter* LYSANDER, DEMETRIUS, HERMIA, *and* HELENA.]

Joy, gentle friends! joy and fresh days of love
Accompany your hearts!
LYS. More than to us 30
Wait in your royal walks, your board, your bed!
THE. Come now; what masques, what dances shall we have,
To wear away this long age of three hours
Between our after-supper and bed-time?
Where is our usual manager of mirth? 35
What revels are in hand? Is there no play,
To ease the anguish of a torturing hour?
Call Philostrate.
PHIL. Here, mighty Theseus.
THE. Say, what abridgement have you for this evening?
What masque? what music? How shall we beguile 40
The lazy time, if not with some delight?
PHIL. There is a brief how many sports are ripe:
Make choice of which your highness will see first. [*Giving a paper.*
THE. [*Reads*] "The battle with the Centaurs, to be sung
By an Athenian eunuch to the harp." 45
We'll none of that: that have I told my love,
In glory of my kinsman Hercules.
[*Reads*] "The riot of the tipsy Bacchanals,
Tearing the Thracian singer in their rage."
That is an old device; and it was play'd 50
When I from Thebes came last a conqueror.

38. **presently**, at once. 40. **preferred**, chosen over its rivals for presentation. Act V, Scene i: 2. **may**, can. 3. **antique**, strange; **toys**, trifles. 8. **Are . . . compact**, are wholly composed of the power of seeing things. 11. **Sees Helen's . . . Egypt**, sees in the face of a dusky gypsy the beauty of Helen of Troy. 25. **More . . . images**, is evidence of more than just imagination. 26. **constancy**, certainty. 39. **abridgement**, pastime. 42. **brief**, list. 44. **The battle . . . Centaurs**, Ovid tells of a battle between the Centaurs and Lapithae. 48-9. **The riot . . . . rage**, Orpheus was torn limb from limb by the maenads, female priests of Bacchus.

[*Reads*] "The thrice three Muses mourning for the death
Of Learning, late deceased in beggary."
That is some satire, keen and critical,
Not sorting with a nuptial ceremony. 55
[*Reads*] "A tedious brief scene of young Pyramus
And his love Thisbe; very tragical mirth."
Merry and tragical! tedious and brief!
That is, hot ice and wondrous strange snow.
How shall we find the concord of this discord? 60

PHIL. A play there is, my lord, some ten words long,
Which is as brief as I have known a play;
But by ten words, my lord, it is too long,
Which makes it tedious; for in all the play
There is not one word apt, one player fitted:
And tragical, my noble lord, it is; 66
For Pyramus therein doth kill himself.
Which, when I saw rehearsed, I must confess,
Made mine eyes water; but more merry tears
The passion of loud laughter never shed. 70

THE. What are they that do play it?

PHIL. Hard-handed men that work in Athens here,
Which never labour'd in their minds till now,
And now have toil'd their unbreathed memories
With this same play, against your nuptial. 75

THE. And we will hear it.

PHIL. No, my noble lord;
It is not for you: I have heard it over,
And it is nothing, nothing in the world;
Unless you can find sport in their intents,
Extremely stretch'd and conn'd with cruel pain, 80
To do you service.

THE. I will hear that play;
For never anything can be amiss,
When simpleness and duty tender it.
Go, bring them in: and take your places, ladies. [*Exit* PHILOSTRATE.

HIP. I love not to see wretchedness o'ercharged 85
And duty in his service perishing.

THE. Why, gentle sweet, you shall see no such thing.

HIP. He says they can do nothing in this kind.

THE. The kinder we, to give them thanks for nothing. 89
Our sport shall be to take what they mistake:
And what poor duty cannot do, noble respect
Takes it in might, not merit.
Where I have come, great clerks have purposed
To greet me with premeditated welcomes;
Where I have seen them shiver and look pale, 95
Make periods in the midst of sentences,
Throttle their practised accent in their fears
And in conclusion dumbly have broke off,
Not paying me a welcome. Trust me, sweet,
Out of this silence yet I pick'd a welcome; 100
And in the modesty of fearful duty
I read as much as from the rattling tongue
Of saucy and audacious eloquence.
Love, therefore, and tongue-tied simplicity
In least speak most, to my capacity. 105

[*Re-enter* PHILOSTRATE.]

PHIL. So please your grace, the Prologue is address'd.

THE. Let him approach.
[*Flourish of trumpets*.

[*Enter* QUINCE *for the* PROLOGUE.]

PRO. If we offend, it is with our good will
That you should think, we come not to offend,
But with good will. To show our simple skill, 110
That is the true beginning of our end.
Consider then we come but in despite.
We do not come as minding to content you,
Our true intent is. All for your delight
We are not here. That you should here repent you, 115
The actors are at hand and by their show
You shall know all that you are like to know.

THE. This fellow doth not stand upon points. 118

LYS. He hath rid his prologue like a rough colt; he knows not the stop. A good moral,

55. not sorting with, not fitting for. 74. unbreathed, unexercised. 75. against, in preparation for. 80. stretch'd, strained; conn'd, learned by heart. 85. o'ercharged, oppressed. 86. perishing, ruining itself. 92. Takes . . . merit, i.e., takes the will for the deed. 93. clerks, learned men. 96. periods, long stops. 105. capacity, sympathetic comprehension. 106. Prologue is address'd, the speaker of the prologue is ready. 108ff. Quince perverts the sense of his speech by blundering punctuation. 118. stand upon points, "pays no attention to punctuation," also "does not care about trifles." 120. the stop, quibble on (1) period or end of a sentence, (2) signal to halt, e.g., "whoa."

my lord: it is not enough to speak, but to speak true.

HIP. Indeed he hath played on his prologue like a child on a recorder; a sound, but not in government. 124

THE. His speech was like a tangled chain; nothing impaired, but all disordered. Who is next?

[*Enter* PYRAMUS *and* THISBE, WALL, MOONSHINE, *and* LION.]

PRO. Gentles, perchance you wonder at this show;
But wonder on, till truth make all things plain.
This man is Pyramus, if you would know;
This beauteous lady Thisby is certain. 131
This man, with lime and rough-cast, doth present
Wall, that vile Wall which did these lovers sunder;
And through Wall's chink, poor souls, they are content
To whisper. At the which let no man wonder. 135
This man, with lanthorn, dog, and bush of thorn,
Presenteth Moonshine; for, if you will know,
By moonshine did these lovers think no scorn
To meet at Ninus' tomb, there, there to woo. 139
This grisly beast, which Lion hight by name,
The trusty Thisby, coming first by night,
Did scare away, or rather did affright;
And, as she fled, her mantle she did fall,
Which Lion vile with bloody mouth did stain.
Anon comes Pyramus, sweet youth and tall, 145
And finds his trusty Thisby's mantle slain:
Whereat, with blade, with bloody blameful blade,
He bravely broach'd his boiling bloody breast;
And Thisby, tarrying in mulberry shade,
His dagger drew, and died. For all the rest, 150
Let Lion, Moonshine, Wall, and lovers twain
At large discourse, while here they do remain.
[*Exeunt* PROLOGUE, PYRAMUS, THISBE, LION, *and* MOONSHINE.

THE. I wonder if the lion be to speak.

DEM. No wonder, my lord: one lion may, when many asses do. 155

WALL. In this same interlude it doth befall
That I, one Snout by name, present a wall;
And such a wall, as I would have you think,
That had in it a crannied hole or chink,
Through which the lovers, Pyramus and Thisby, 160
Did whisper often very secretly.
This loam, this rough-cast and this stone doth show
That I am that same wall; the truth is so:
And this the cranny is, right and sinister,
Through which the fearful lovers are to whisper. 165

THE. Would you desire lime and hair to speak better?

DEM. It is the wittiest partition that ever I heard discourse, my lord.

[*Re-enter* PYRAMUS.]

THE. Pyramus draws near the wall: silence! 170

PYR. O grim-look'd night! O night with hue so black!
O night, which ever art when day is not!
O night, O night! alack, alack, alack,
I fear my Thisby's promise is forgot!
And thou, O wall, O sweet, O lovely wall, 175
That stand'st between her father's ground and mine!
Thou wall, O wall, O sweet and lovely wall,
Show me thy chink, to blink through with mine eyne! [*Wall holds up his fingers.*]
Thanks, courteous wall: Jove shield thee well for this!
But what see I? No Thisby do I see. 180
O wicked wall, through whom I see no bliss!
Cursed be thy stones for thus deceiving me!

THE. The wall, methinks, being sensible, should curse again.

PYR. No, in truth, sir, he should not. "Deceiving me" is Thisby's cue: she is to enter now, and I am to spy her through the wall.

123. recorder, a wind instrument something like a flute. 124. in government, under control. 140. hight, is called. 143. fall, let fall. 145. tall, brave. 148. broach'd, opened, i.e., stabbed. 153. be to speak, is going to speak.

164. cranny, chink; sinister, left. 168. partition, quibble on (1) wall, (2) a section of a book. 171. grim-look'd, grim-faced. 183. sensible, capable of feeling.

You shall see, it will fall pat as I told you. Yonder she comes.

[*Re-enter* THISBE.]

THIS. O wall, full often hast thou heard my moans, 190
For parting my fair Pyramus and me!
My cherry lips have often kiss'd thy stones,
Thy stones with lime and hair knit up in thee.

PYR. I see a voice: now will I to the chink,
To spy an I can hear my Thisby's face.
Thisby! 195

THIS. My love thou art, my love I think.

PYR. Think what thou wilt, I am thy lover's grace;
And, like Limander, am I trusty still.

THIS. And I like Helen, till the Fates me kill. 200

PYR. Not Shafalus to Procrus was so true.

THIS. As Shafalus to Procrus, I to you.

PYR. O, kiss me through the hole of this vile wall!

THIS. I kiss the wall's hole, not your lips at all.

PYR. Wilt thou at Ninny's tomb meet me straightway? 205

THIS. 'Tide life, 'tide death, I come without delay. [*Exeunt* PYRAMUS *and* THISBE.

WALL. Thus have I, Wall, my part discharged so;
And, being done, thus Wall away doth go. [*Exit.*

THE. Now is the mural down between the two neighbours.

DEM. No remedy, my lord, when walls are so wilful to hear without warning. 212

HIP. This is the silliest stuff that ever I heard.

THE. The best in this kind are but shadows; and the worst are no worse, if imagination amend them.

HIP. It must be your imagination then, and not theirs.

THE. If we imagine no worse of them than they of themselves, they may pass for excellent men. Here come two noble beasts in, a man and a lion. 221

[*Re-enter* LION *and* MOONSHINE.]

LION. You, ladies, you, whose gentle hearts do fear
The smallest monstrous mouse that creeps on floor,
May now perchance both quake and tremble here,
When lion rough in wildest rage doth roar 225
Then know that I, one Snug the joiner, am
A lion-fell, nor else no lion's dam;
For, if I should as lion come in strife
Into this place, 'twere pity on my life.

THE. A very gentle beast, and of a good conscience. 231

DEM. The very best at a beast, my lord, that e'er I saw.

LYS. This lion is a very fox for his valour.

THE. True; and a goose for his discretion. 235

DEM. Not so, my lord; for his valour cannot carry his discretion; and the fox carries the goose.

THE. His discretion, I am sure, cannot carry his valour; for the goose carries not the fox. It is well: leave it to his discretion, and let us listen to the moon. 242

MOON. This lanthorn doth the hornèd moon present;—

DEM. He should have worn the horns on his head.

THE. He is no crescent, and his horns are invisible within the circumference.

MOON. This lanthorn doth the horned moon present;
Myself the man i' the moon do seem to be.

THE. This is the greatest error of all the rest: the man should be put into the lanthorn. How is it else the man i' the moon? 252

DEM. He dares not come there for the candle; for, you see, it is already in snuff.

HIP. I am aweary of this moon: would he would change!

THE. It appears, by his small light of discretion, that he is in the wane; but yet, in courtesy, in all reason, we must stay the time.

LYS. Proceed, Moon. 260

MOON. All that I have to say, is, to tell you

198. **Limander**, blunder for Leander. 199. **Helen**, he means Hero. 200. **Shafalus to Procrus**, blunder for "Cephalus to Procris." 206. **'Tide . . . death**, whether life or death betide [happens]. 209. **mural**, wall. 227. **lion-fell**, lion skin, i.e., he is a lion only in that he is cased in a lion skin. 229. **'twere . . . life**, i.e., I should be in danger of hanging. 245-6. **He . . . head**, the ancient joke about the horns of a cuckold. 253. **for**, because of. 254. **in snuff**, quibble (1) in need of snuffing, (2) offended. 259. **stay . . . time**, see it through.

that the lanthorn is the moon; I, the man in the moon; this thorn-bush, my thorn-bush; and this dog, my dog.

DEM. Why, all these should be in the lanthorn; for all these are in the moon. But, silence! here comes Thisbe.

[*Re-enter* THISBE.]

THIS. This is old Ninny's tomb. Where is my love?

LION. [*Roaring*] *Oh*— [THISBE *runs off*.

DEM. Well roared, Lion. 270

THE. Well run, Thisbe.

HIP. Well shone, Moon. Truly, the moon shines with a good grace.

[*The* LION *shakes* THISBE'S *mantle, and exit*.

THE. Well moused, Lion.

LYS. And so the lion vanished. 275

DEM. And then came Pyramus.

[*Re-enter* PYRAMUS.]

PYR. Sweet Moon, I thank thee for thy sunny beams;
I thank thee, Moon, for shining now so bright;
For, by thy gracious, golden, glittering gleams,
I trust to take of truest Thisby sight. 280
But stay, O spite!
But mark, poor knight,
What dreadful dole is here!
Eyes, do you see?
How can it be? 285
O dainty duck! O dear!
Thy mantle good,
What, stain'd with blood!
Approach, ye Furies fell!
O Fates, come, come, 290
Cut thread and thrum;
Quail, crush, conclude, and quell!

THE. This passion, and the death of a dear friend, would go near to make a man look sad.

HIP. Beshrew my heart, but I pity the man. 295

PYR. O wherefore, Nature, didst thou lions frame?
Since lion vile hath here deflower'd my dear:
Which is—no, no—which was the fairest dame
That lived, that loved, that liked, that look'd with cheer.
Come, tears, confound; 300
Out, sword, and wound
The pap of Pyramus;
Ay, that left pap,
Where heart doth hop: [*Stabs himself*.
Thus die I, thus, thus, thus. 305
Now am I dead,
Now am I fled;
My soul is in the sky:
Tongue, lose thy light;
Moon, take thy flight: 310
[*Exit* MOONSHINE.]
Now die, die, die, die, die. [*Dies*.

DEM. No die, but an ace, for him; for he is but one.

LYS. Less than an ace, man; for he is dead; he is nothing.

THE. With the help of a surgeon he might yet recover, and prove an ass.

HIP. How chance Moonshine is gone before Thisbe comes back and finds her lover?

THE. She will find him by starlight. Here she comes; and her passion ends the play. 321

[*Re-enter* THISBE.]

HIP. Methinks she should not use a long one for such a Pyramus: I hope she will be brief.

DEM. A mote will turn the balance, which Pyramus, which Thisbe, is the better; he for a man, God warrant us; she for a woman, God bless us.

LYS. She hath spied him already with those sweet eyes.

DEM. And thus she means, videlicet:—

THIS. Asleep, my love? 331
What, dead, my dove?
O Pyramus, arise!
Speak, speak. Quite dumb?
Dead, dead? A tomb 335
Must cover thy sweet eyes.
These lily lips,
This cherry nose,
These yellow cowslip cheeks,
Are gone, are gone: 340
Lovers, make moan:
His eyes were green as leeks.
O Sisters Three,
Come, come to me,

274. **moused**, shaken (as a cat shakes a mouse). 283. **dole**, grief. 289. **fell**, fierce. 291. **thread and thrum**, the warp of a piece of cloth and the fringe-like threads at the end. 292. **quail**, subdue; **quell**, kill. 299. **with cheer**, with a face.

312. **No . . . ace**, pun (1) die = perish, (2) die = the singular of dice. 330. **means**, moans. 343. **Sisters Three**, the Fates.

With hands as pale as milk; 345
Lay them in gore,
Since you have shore
With shears his thread of silk.
Tongue, not a word:
Come, trusty sword; 350
Come, blade, my breast imbrue:
[*Stabs herself.*]
And, farewell, friends;
Thus Thisby ends:
Adieu, adieu, adieu. [*Dies.*

THE. Moonshine and Lion are left to bury the dead.

DEM. Ay, and Wall too.

BOT. [*Starting up*] No, I assure you; the wall is down that parted their fathers. Will it please you to see the epilogue, or to hear a Bergomask dance between two of our company? 360

THE. No epilogue, I pray you; for your play needs no excuse. Never excuse; for when the players are all dead, there need none to be blamed. Marry, if he that writ it had played Pyramus and hanged himself in Thisbe's garter, it would have been a fine tragedy: and so it is, truly; and very notably discharged. But, come, your Bergomask; let your epilogue alone. [*A dance.*]
The iron tongue of midnight hath told twelve: 370
Lovers, to bed; 'tis almost fairy time.
I fear we shall out-sleep the coming morn
As much as we this night have overwatch'd.
This palpable-gross play hath well beguiled
The heavy gait of night. Sweet friends, to bed. 375
A fortnight hold we this solemnity,
In nightly revels and new jollity. [*Exeunt.*

[*Enter* PUCK.]

PUCK. Now the hungry lion roars,
And the wolf behowls the moon;
Whilst the heavy ploughman snores, 380
All with weary task fordone.
Now the wasted brands do glow,
Whilst the screech-owl, screeching loud,
Puts the wretch that lies in woe
In remembrance of a shroud. 385
Now it is the time of night
That the graves all gaping wide,
Every one lets forth his sprite,
In the church-way paths to glide:
And we fairies, that do run 390
By the triple Hecate's team,
From the presence of the sun,
Following darkness like a dream,
Now are frolic: not a mouse
Shall disturb this hallow'd house: 395
I am sent with broom before,
To sweep the dust behind the door.

[*Enter* OBERON *and* TITANIA *with their train.*]

OBE. Through the house give glimmering light,
By the dead and drowsy fire:
Every elf and fairy sprite 400
Hop as light as bird from brier;
And this ditty, after me,
Sing, and dance it trippingly.

TITA. First, rehearse your song by rote,
To each word a warbling note: 405
Hand in hand, with fairy grace,
Will we sing, and bless this place.
[*Song and dance.*

OBE. Now, until the break of day,
Through this house each fairy stray.
To the best bride-bed will we, 410
Which by us shall blessèd be;
And the issue there create
Ever shall be fortunate.
So shall all the couples three
Ever true in loving be; 415
And the blots of Nature's hand
Shall not in their issue stand;
Never mole, hare lip, nor scar,
Nor mark prodigious, such as are
Despisèd in nativity, 420
Shall upon their children be.
With this field-dew consecrate,
Every fairy take his gait;
And each several chamber bless,
Through this palace, with sweet peace;
And the owner of it blest 426
Ever shall in safety rest.
Trip away; make no stay;
Meet me all by break of day.
[*Exeunt* OBERON, TITANIA, *and train.*

351. imbrue, wet with gore. 360. Bergomask dance, a grotesque rustic dance (named from the Italian town Bergamo). 374. palpable-gross, palpably crude. 381. fordone, worn out. 391. triple Hecate, Diana was three-formed; she was called Cynthia in heaven, Diana on earth, Hecate in hell. 394. frolic, gay. 397. To . . . door, Robin Goodfellow was a domestic sprite, who could be induced to do the housework by night. 412. create, created. 419. prodigious, unnatural. 422. consecrate, consecrated. 424. several, separate.

PUCK. If we shadows have offended, 430
Think but this, and all is mended,
That you have but slumber'd here
While these visions did appear.
And this weak and idle theme,
No more yielding but a dream, 435
Gentles, do not reprehend:
If you pardon, we will mend:
And, as I am an honest Puck,
If we have unearnèd luck
Now to 'scape the serpent's tongue, 440
We will make amends ere long;
Else the Puck a liar call:
So, good night unto you all.
Give me your hands, if we be friends,
And Robin shall restore amends. 445
[*Exit.*

440. serpent's tongue, i.e., hissing. 444. Give . . . hands, applaud.

AFTERWORD

Already, in his early days as a writer for the stage, Shakespeare opens to us a delight in appearing to contradict himself that is both attractive and immensely disconcerting. This enduring aspect of his mind and temperament is very conspicuous in *A Midsummer-Night's Dream.* The play is a comedy, verging frequently on farce. *Romeo and Juliet*, which was presumably written about the same time, is deeply and earnestly tragic. But to read the two plays in tandem is to discover unmistakeably that one is the mirror image of the other.

That is an extraordinary fact, and hard to assimilate. Most writers—most men—strike in the beginning a characteristic stance from which they depart only rarely thereafter. A modern playwright, like Arthur Miller or Tennessee Williams, seems to change with the writing of each new play. This apparent change is, however, mostly technical. The writer is increasingly in command of his craft. He is more efficient, more practiced. Increasingly, he knows what to do in the theatre. But he is likely to remain constant to the dramatic themes which concern him in the beginning. What is more important, his treatment of those themes is unlikely to vary. He is the dramatic spokesman for a single point of view. Shakespeare, like the chameleon that changes its color at will, is the most various and inconstant of playwrights. Emerson's saying, that a foolish consistency is the hobgoblin of little minds, is apparently the rubric under which his plays are written. He expresses in one play, and with complete sincerity, a point of view which he is willing to abandon in the next play. For Shakespeare, nothing is sacred. Or, to put the case more precisely, for Shakespeare everything is sacred, the affirmative position and also the negation of it. Believing in the importance or integrity of either, Shakespeare speaks for them both.

Romeo and Juliet demonstrates, to our lasting sorrow, that "the course of true love never did run smooth." The same demonstration preoccupies Shakespeare in *A Midsummer-Night's Dream*, except that he finds it now a theme for ironic speculation. The passion of his tragic lovers, which transcends even the grave, is recapitulated in that of Helena, who "dotes, Devoutly dotes, dotes in idolatry" upon her Demetrius. But these lovers, as the language instructs us, are comic in their passion. Romeo, when he falls in love with Juliet—as everyone remembers, at first sight—is provided with one of the most memorable and affecting speeches in the play:

> What lady's that which doth enrich the hand
> Of yonder knight? . . .
> Oh, she doth teach the torches to burn bright!
> It seems she hangs upon the cheek of night
> Like a rich jewel in an Ethiop's ear—
> Beauty too rich for use, for earth too dear!

Writing only a little later, Shakespeare reverses the coin. Titania, the Queen of the Faeries, is smitten. Bottom, transformed into an ass, is the angel that wakes her. The braying of this ass is delightful to her ear, his monstrous shape enthralling to her eye. And so she is moved. "On the first view to say, to swear, I love thee." So much, in this play, for love at first sight.

Demetrius, who has rejected the advances of Helena, a woman who excites in him a sour contempt, is made abruptly to reverse himself, as if by witchcraft. Now, in his fevered imagination, the white snow on the mountains turns to a crow, when Helena holds up her white hand. We remember the simile Romeo applies to Juliet:

> So shows a snowy dove trooping with crows
> As yonder lady o'er her fellows shows—

and we wonder that Shakespeare, shifting easily from the portrayal of heartfelt emotion to a parody of it, could employ, in cold blood, exactly the same comparative terms.

The business of the playwright is like that of the psychologist. It is to look hard at the emotions which shake us, as we are human, and to lay bare their nature and cause. Love is such an emotion. In *Romeo and Juliet,* love is heaven-sent, like the lightning; and also, says Juliet, boundless and infinite, like the sea. We are persuaded that the description is just. In *A Midsummer-Night's Dream,* Lysander, who protests to Hermia the undying nature of his love, is able to assert, only minutes later, "Not Hermia but Helena I love." He adds, as if attempting to explain what is clearly inexplicable: "Who will not change a raven for a dove?" Again we recall, ironically, the exalted language of *Romeo and Juliet.*

But Lysander has more to say. He has shown us, unconsciously, how impermanent is love, and how easily it moves, guest-wise, from one woman to another. Now he takes on himself the role of philosopher. He is going to instruct us in the origin of love. Friar Laurence, who anticipates him here, supposes that love is nothing more than physical attraction:

> Young men's love then lies
> Not truly in their hearts, but in their eyes.

We know, or think we know, that Friar Laurence is wrong. Lysander also thinks he knows. Love, in his view, is a matter of careful and reasonable choosing. Intellectual affinity is the origin of love.

> The will of man is by his reason swayed,
> And reason says you are the worthier maid.

As reason directs or marshals his passion, Lysander transfers his affection to Helena.

This account of the origin and nature of love is, however, radically imperfect. That much we learn from the magic potion with which the eyes of the lovers are anointed. Meditated choice is not to the purpose. There is no rationalizing the onset of love, and not much point in seeking to dignify it either. "Reason and love keep little company together," says Bottom, who is for once an accurate reporter. Cupid is painted blind to suggest to us the irrational and comic nature of that activity we persist in honoring with the romantic name of love. Throughout Athens Helena is thought as fair as Hermia. "But what of that? Demetrius thinks not so." As he errs, doting on Hermia, Helena errs also, doting on him.

> Things base and vile, holding no quantity,
> Love can transpose to form and dignity.

Case in point: the infatuation of Titania, who "waked, and straightway loved an ass." One can say of her that "Love looks not with the eyes, but with the mind." What this means, however, is that we conceive within us a violent and senseless attraction, unrelated to the real merit of the object. Love, viewed from a particular point of vantage, is a matter of animal magnetism, like that of the horse for the mare. It operates like adamant, or lode-stars. Or else it is a sickness, unfortunately catching.

The function of the rude mechanicals is to point up the comic nature of this sickness. The unselfconscious or involuntary man, who "catches" what ails him, who does what he does willy nilly, is always, if sufficiently distanced from us, a comic figure. So with Bottom and his retinue. As these lovers *manqué* enact what is called "the most lamentable comedy, and most cruel death of Pyramus and Thisby," the pretensions of romantic and tragic love, which the analogous or complementary tale is meant to caricature, are necessarily called in question. Obscene and ribald speech is, in the little playlet, the language of passion, though the actors are sublimely ignorant of the congruity of what they are saying. The love-death, on their vulgar representation, is not august and sacrificial. It is absurd. When Bottom, "starting up" from the dead (as the stage direction takes pains to inform us) announces that "the wall is down that parted their fathers," we are confronted with a grotesque and farcical version of the reconciliation of Capulet and Montague.

Here, the complacent ironist or cynical man concludes his assessment of the play. In his exclusive or parochial view, there is no question but what this bathetic reminiscence of *Romeo and Juliet* strips from romantic tragedy the last vestige of dignity and meaning. The whole intention, he thinks, is merely to denigrate or explode. What passes for love, as Iago, the type of the cynic, instructs us, is only a "sect or scion" of "our unbitted lusts." Romantic amorists, like Lysander, like Othello himself, as they attribute to love a character more exalted than this, are proper targets for the splenetic laughter of the playwright.

That is one reading of *A Midsummer-Night's Dream*, and it is tenable: there is much in the play to support it. But this reading is not catholic enough. It leaves out of account the endless equivocations or transformations to which Shakespeare is prone. For not only does Shakespeare change color from one play to the next. He manages this startling transformation (or shift or modifying in his point of view) within the confines of a single play. If *A Midsummer-Night's*

Dream is altogether a parody of romantic love, what can the burlesque playlet of Pyramus and Thisbe be intended to parody?

The answer is complex, and the straightforward intelligence, which detests ambiguity and qualification, and which has dominated the centuries since Shakespeare's time almost to the present, does not come to it readily. This answer, in a nutshell (except that Shakespeare does not lend himself to close confinement), is that skepticism and approval coexist in *A Midsummer-Night's Dream.* Bottom is the ass he is made to resemble; and also a poet whose richly complicated dream "hath no bottom." The "rare vision" he experiences transcends the wit of the commonsensical man, like Duke Theseus. The lover is a lunatic; and he too is like the poet who works on his imagination until, from "airy nothing," he fabricates an image more real than substantial fact. He misconceives and, simultaneously, he perceives more truly. He beholds "Helen's beauty in a brow of Egypt": the commonplace features of a gypsy become, as he gazes on them with his uncanny eye, the features of Helen of Troy. The lover, like the poet, endows and reinvests. It is easy to say that he errs in this activity, and that is partly what Shakespeare is saying. But the adverb is decisive. A more comprehensive view of Shakespeare's play will emphasize, even as it disputes, the integrity of "fancy." It will recognize that "the story of the night told over" makes a compelling whole that is more and less than rational.

The interchangeable lovers, Helena and Demetrius, Lysander and Hermia, take themselves very seriously. So do Romeo and Juliet. The "tedious brief scene" of their mythological counterparts, a scene in which lewdness mingles with "very tragical mirth," presents that seriousness to us under an aspect more risible than sympathetic. Parody for the moment is uppermost. Even the real or high romantic thing—so Shakespeare is bidding us consider—may be fruitful of amusement. That is the nature of parody, when it works—to disengage us emotionally, and hence to let us see from a different point of view.

But Shakespeare in this play is not simply a parodist. What he is making is an emulsion, in which the irreverent analogue, the parodic or skeptical version, merges easily with the thing itself. Neither, to the dismay of the rationalizing intelligence, is precipitated out. Each, as we acknowledge, to our perplexity but also to our enlightenment, possesses its own validity. This acknowledgment is the peculiar yield, or accruing of profit, in Shakespeare's exploration of opposites. He sees, and makes us see, that every important and interesting situation can be understood in more than one way. The love of Romeo and Juliet is, in its tragic intensity, absolutely believable. But look at it in a different mood tomorrow. Then it will be obvious that eternal vows are made to be broken and are faintly pompous in the uttering, and that the mortals who utter them with such assurance and self-delusion are fools.

This wry perception does not deny the possibility of romance, nor endorse the partial wisdom of the cynic, who believes that the ludicrous image is what romantic tragedy comes down to. *A Midsummer-Night's Dream* is a valid account of love, which means that it mixes together attitudes and ideas a foolish consistency supposes immiscible. The cynicism of Puck, like the hard sense of

Duke Theseus, is appropriate; and also the claim, as entered in this play, to "the simplicity of Venus' doves" and the noble pathos of romantic love, as it must "come to confusion." Love is devoid of judgment, hasty, and often beguiled, and so it forfeits our serious consideration. Conversely, love must win us, as we rue its fragility, as we perceive that war, death, and sickness assail it,

> Making it momentany as a sound,
> Swift as a shadow, short as any dream;
> Brief as the lightning in the collied night,
> That, in a spleen, unfolds both heaven and earth,
> And ere a man hath power to say "Behold!"
> The jaws of darkness do devour it up.

The vexed and contradictory story of the night, though it is "strange and admirable," productive of incredulous wonder, grows nonetheless "to something of great constancy." *A Midsummer-Night's Dream* is of a piece. Shakespeare, who manages to hold in suspension the antithetical truths of which the play is made, without losing his mind or his capacity to judge, is like the Roman god Janus, who can look both ways at once. This talent or habit is not finally to be described as inconsistency, but as the ability to see life in the round.

Suggested Reading

Barber, C. L., *Shakespere's Festive Comedy* (1959). Meridian.
Briggs, Katharine M., *The Anatomy of Puck* (1959).
Brown, John R., *Shakespeare and His Comedies* (1957). Barnes and Noble.
Chambers, E. K., *A Book of Homage to Shakespeare* (1916).
Charlton, H. B., *Shakespearian Comedy* (1938). Barnes and Noble.
Chesterton, G. K., *G. K. Chesterton: An Anthology* (1957).
Craig, Hardin, *An Interpretation of Shakespeare* (1948).
Evans, Bertrand, *Shakespeare's Comedies* (1960). Oxford.
Gestetner, J. M., *Shakespeare's "Midsummer-Night's Dream"* (1958).
Gordon, George, *Shakespearian Comedy* (1944).
Kermode, Frank, *Early Shakespeare* (1961).
Knight, G. Wilson, *The Shakespearian Tempest* (1932).
Latham, Minor W., *The Elizabethan Fairies* (1930)
Merchant, William M., *Early Shakespeare* (1961).
Palmer, John, *Comic Characters of Shakespeare* (1946). Papermac.
Parrott, Thomas More, *Shakespearean Comedy* (1949).
Priestly, J. B., *The English Comic Character* (1925).
Sidgwick, Frank, *Sources and Analogues of "A Midsummer-Night's Dream"* (1908).
Wilson, J. Dover, *Shakespeare's Happy Comedies* (1962).
Young, David P., *Something of Great Constancy: The Art of "A Midsummer-Night's Dream"* (1966).

King Henry IV, Part I

A NOTE ON THE TEXT

Shakespeare, having achieved a popular success with his history of *Richard II*, carried forward the story in *King Henry IV: Part I.* His sequel was written probably in 1597, the year in which the earlier play was first published. *King Henry IV: Part I*, like *Richard II*, depends for its basic historical materials on the *Chronicle Historie of England* by Raphael Holinshed (first edition 1577; revised and enlarged 1587). For the madcap adventures of Prince Hal, however, Shakespeare draws on an additional source, an anonymous play dating from the time of the Spanish Armada (1588) and entitled *The Famous Victories of Henry V*.

The source play may be described as Christmas cake drama. It mingles comedy and martial business, without point or feeling for sequence, and is intended only, in an elementary sense, to entertain. Shakespeare himself is not indifferent to entertainment, which he supplies abundantly by inventing and dramatizing the exploits of Falstaff and his retinue. This departure from history is, however, more than pleasing, in that it serves to enforce and clarify the major themes of the play. Finally, Shakespeare, who is often an extremely topical writer, introduces in the mock-speeches of Falstaff (II.iv) a parody of the hyperbolic or inflated style associated with the tragic actor Edward Alleyn, the star of a company rivalling Shakespeare's and known as the Admiral's Men.

The first quarto of the first part of *King Henry IV*, published in 1598, emphasizes on its title page Shakespeare's inventiveness, in calling attention to "the humorous conceits of Sir John Falstaffe," the most popular of all Shakespeare's characters. A second quarto, in 1599, essentially duplicates the first. Subsequent editions, attesting to the applause with which the play was greeted, followed in 1604, 1608, 1613, and 1622. From one of these editions comes the text on which the First Folio version is based.

THE FIRST PART OF KING HENRY THE FOURTH

DRAMATIS PERSONÆ

KING HENRY *the Fourth.*
HENRY, *Prince of Wales,* } *sons to the King.*
JOHN OF LANCASTER, }
EARL OF WESTMORELAND.
SIR WALTER BLUNT.
THOMAS PERCY, *Earl of Worcester.*
HENRY PERCY, *Earl of Northumberland.*
HENRY PERCY, *surnamed* HOTSPUR, *his son.*
EDMUND MORTIMER, *Earl of March.*
RICHARD SCROOP, *Archbishop of York.*
ARCHIBALD, *Earl of Douglas.*
OWEN GLENDOWER.
SIR RICHARD VERNON.
SIR JOHN FALSTAFF.
SIR MICHAEL, *a friend to the Archbishop of York.*
POINS.
GADSHILL.
PETO.
BARDOLPH.

LADY PERCY, *wife to Hotspur, and sister to Mortimer.*
LADY MORTIMER, *daughter to Glendower, and wife to Mortimer.*
MISTRESS QUICKLY, *hostess of a tavern in Eastcheap.*

LORD, OFFICERS, SHERIFF, VINTNER, CHAMBERLAIN, DRAWERS, *two* CARRIERS, TRAVELLERS, *and* ATTENDANTS.

SCENE: *England.*

ACT I

SCENE I. *London. The palace.*

[*Enter* KING HENRY, LORD JOHN OF LANCASTER, *the* EARL OF WESTMORELAND, SIR WALTER BLUNT, *and others.*]

KING. So shaken as we are, so wan with care,
Find we a time for frighted peace to pant,
And breathe short-winded accents of new broils
To be commenced in strands afar remote.
No more the thirsty entrance of this soil 5
Shall daub her lips with her own children's blood;
No more shall trenching war channel her fields,
Nor bruise her flowerets with the armèd hoofs
Of hostile paces: those opposèd eyes,
Which, like the meteors of a troubled heaven,
All of one nature, of one substance bred, 11
Did lately meet in the intestine shock
And furious close of civil butchery
Shall now, in mutual well-beseeming ranks,
March all one way and be no more opposed 15
Against acquaintance, kindred and allies:
The edge of war, like an ill-sheathèd knife,
No more shall cut his master. Therefore, friends,
As far as to the sepulchre of Christ,
Whose soldier now, under whose blessèd cross 20
We are impressèd and engaged to fight,
Forthwith a power of English shall we levy;
Whose arms were moulded in their mothers' womb

Act I, Scene i: 2. Find we, Let us find. 5. thirsty entrance, parched mouth. 7. trenching war, trench warfare. 10. meteors, comets or shooting stars, both regarded as evil omens. 12. intestine shock, clash of civil war. 13. close, encounter. 14. mutual, united; well-beseeming, seemly. 21. impressèd, enlisted. 22. power, armed force.

To chase these pagans in those holy fields
Over whose acres walk'd those blessed feet 25
Which fourteen hundred years ago were nail'd
For our advantage on the bitter cross.
But this our purpose now is twelve month old,
And bootless 'tis to tell you we will go:
Therefore we meet not now. Then let me hear 30
Of you, my gentle cousin Westmoreland,
What yesternight our council did decree
In forwarding this dear expedience.

WEST. My liege, this haste was hot in question,
And many limits of the charge set down 35
But yesternight: when all athwart there came
A post from Wales loaden with heavy news;
Whose worst was, that the noble Mortimer,
Leading the men of Herefordshire to fight
Against the irregular and wild Glendower, 40
Was by the rude hands of that Welshman taken,
A thousand of his people butchered;
Upon whose dead corpse there was such misuse,
Such beastly shameless transformation,
By those Welshwomen done as may not be
Without much shame retold or spoken of. 46

KING. It seems then that the tidings of this broil
Brake off our business for the Holy Land.

WEST. This match'd with other did, my gracious lord;
For more uneven and unwelcome news 50
Came from the north and thus it did import:
On Holy-rood day, the gallant Hotspur there,
Young Harry Percy and brave Archibald,
That ever-valiant and approvèd Scot,
At Holmedon met, 55
Where they did spend a sad and bloody hour;
As by discharge of their artillery,
And shape of likelihood, the news was told;
For he that brought them, in the very heat
And pride of their contention did take horse,
Uncertain of the issue any way. 61

KING. Here is a dear, a true industrious friend,
Sir Walter Blunt, new lighted from his horse,
Stain'd with the variation of each soil
Betwixt that Holmedon and this seat of ours; 65
And he hath brought us smooth and welcome news.
The Earl of Douglas is discomfited:
Ten thousand bold Scots, two and twenty knights,
Balk'd in their own blood did Sir Walter see
On Holmedon's plains. Of prisoners, Hotspur took 70
Mordake the Earl of Fife, and eldest son
To beaten Douglas; and the Earl of Athol,
Of Murray, Angus, and Menteith:
And is not this an honourable spoil?
A gallant prize? ha, cousin, is it not? 75

WEST. In faith,
It is a conquest for a prince to boast of.

KING. Yea, there thou makest me sad and makest me sin
In envy that my Lord Northumberland
Should be the father to so blest a son, 80
A son who is the theme of honour's tongue;
Amongst a grove, the very straightest plant;
Who is sweet Fortune's minion and her pride:
Whilst I, by looking on the praise of him,
See riot and dishonour stain the brow 85
Of my young Harry. O that it could be proved
That some night-tripping fairy had exchanged
In cradle-clothes our children where there lay,
And call'd mine Percy, his Plantagenet!
Then would I have his Harry, and he mine. 90
But let him from my thoughts. What think you, coz,
Of this young Percy's pride? the prisoners,
Which he in this adventure hath surprised,
To his own use he keeps; and sends me word,
I shall have none but Mordake Earl of Fife.

WEST. This is his uncle's teaching: this is Worcester, 96
Malevolent to you in all aspects;
Which makes him prune himself, and bristle up

29. **bootless . . . you**, it is needless for me to tell you we will go. 30. **Therefore**, for this. 33. **dear expedience**, expedition close to our heart. 34. **hot in question**, hotly debated. 35. **limits of the charge**, estimates of the expense. 36. **athwart**, perversely. 38. **worst**, i.e., worst news. 40. **irregular**, lawless. 44. **transformation**, mutilation. 49. **This . . . other**, this piece of news matched with another. 50. **uneven**, disagreeable. 52. **Holy-rood day**, September 14. 55. **Holmedon**, Humbleton, a town in Northumberland. 57. **by**, judging from. 58. **shape of likelihood**, probable evidence. 60. **pride**, height. 64. **variation of each**, every kind of. 66. **smooth**, pleasant. 67. **discomfited**, defeated. 69. **Balk'd**, heaped up in ridges. 71-2. **Mordake . . . beaten Douglas**, not correct. Mordake Stewart was the son of Robert, Duke of Albany and so grandson of King Robert II of Scotland. 83. **minion**, favorite. 98. **prune**, preen, i.e., ruffle up his feathers in pride.

The crest of youth against your dignity.

KING. But I have sent for him to answer this; 100
And for this cause awhile we must neglect
Our holy purpose to Jerusalem.
Cousin, on Wednesday next our council we
Will hold at Windsor; so inform the lords:
But come yourself with speed to us again; 105
For more is to be said and to be done
Than out of anger can be uttered.

WEST. I will, my liege. [*Exeunt.*

SCENE II. *London. An apartment of the* PRINCE'S.

[*Enter the* PRINCE OF WALES *and* FALSTAFF.]

FAL. Now, Hal, what time of day is it, lad?

PRINCE. Thou art so fat-witted, with drinking of old sack and unbuttoning thee after supper and sleeping upon benches after noon, that thou hast forgotten to demand that 5 truly which thou wouldst truly know. What a devil hast thou to do with the time of the day? Unless hours were cups of sack and minutes capons and clocks the tongues of bawds and dials the signs of leaping-houses and the blessed sun himself a fair hot wench in flame-coloured taffeta, I see no reason why thou shouldst be so superfluous to demand the time of the day. 13

FAL. Indeed, you come near me now, Hal; for we that take purses go by the moon and the seven stars, and not by Phœbus, he, "that wandering knight so fair." And, I prithee, sweet wag, when thou art king, as, God save thy grace,—majesty I should say, for grace thou wilt have none,— 20

PRINCE. What, none?

FAL. No, by my troth, not so much as will serve to be prologue to an egg and butter.

PRINCE. Well, how then? come, roundly, roundly. 25

FAL. Marry, then, sweet wag, when thou art king, let not us that are squires of the night's body be called thieves of the day's beauty; let us be Diana's foresters, gentlemen of the shade, minions of the moon, and let men say we be men of good government, being governed, as the sea is, by our noble and chaste mistress the moon, under whose countenance we steal. 33

PRINCE. Thou sayest well, and it holds well too; for the fortune of us that are the moon's men doth ebb and flow like the sea, being governed, as the sea is, by the moon. As, for proof, now: a purse of gold most resolutely snatched on Monday night and most dissolutely spent on Tuesday morning; got with swearing "Lay by" and spent with crying "Bring in;" now in as low an ebb as the foot of the ladder and by and by in as high a flow as the ridge of the gallows. 43

FAL. By the Lord, thou sayest true, lad. And is not my hostess of the tavern a most sweet wench?

PRINCE. As the honey of Hybla, my old lad of the castle. And is not a buff jerkin a most sweet robe of durance? 49

FAL. How now, how now, mad wag! what, in thy quips and thy quiddities? what a plague have I to do with a buff jerkin?

PRINCE. Why, what a pox have I to do with my hostess of the tavern? 54

FAL. Well, thou hast called her to a reckoning many a time and oft.

PRINCE. Did I ever call for thee to pay thy part?

FAL. No; I'll give thee thy due, thou hast paid all there. 60

PRINCE. Yea, and elsewhere, so far as my coin would stretch; and where it would not, I have used my credit. 63

FAL. Yea, and so used it that, were it not here apparent that thou art heir apparent— But, I prithee, sweet wag, shall there be gallows standing in England when thou art king? and resolution thus fobbed as it is with the rusty curb of old father antic the law? Do not thou, when thou art king, hang a 70 thief.

PRINCE. No; thou shalt.

FAL. Shall I? O rare! By the Lord, I'll be a brave judge.

PRINCE. Thou judgest false already: I mean, thou shalt have the hanging of the thieves and so become a rare hangman. 76

Scene ii: 3. **sack**, sherry. 4. **upon benches**, in privies. 10. **leaping-houses**, brothels. 14. **you come near me**, talk to the point. 16. **seven stars**, the Pleiades. 25. **roundly**, speak plainly. 33. **countenance**, (1) face, (2) authority. 34. **holds well**, is consistent. 40. **"Lay by,"** highwayman's cry like "Hands up." 47. **Hybla**, town in Sicily famous for its honey. 48. **lad of the castle**, pun on Oldcastle, Falstaff's name in the first version of Henry IV. 48. **buff jerkin**, leather coat (worn by Sheriff's men). 49. **durance**, pun on two meanings—"durability" and "imprisonment." 51. **quips**, gibes; **quiddities**, quibbles. 68. **fobbed**, cheated. 69. **antic**, buffoon. 73. **brave**, excellent.

FAL. Well, Hal, well; and in some sort it jumps with my humour as well as waiting in the court, I can tell you.

PRINCE. For obtaining of suits? 80

FAL. Yea, for obtaining of suits, whereof the hangman hath no lean wardrobe. 'Sblood, I am as melancholy as a gib cat or a lugged bear.

PRINCE. Or an old lion, or a lover's lute.

FAL. Yea, or the drone of a Lincolnshire bagpipe.

PRINCE. What sayest thou to a hare, or the melancholy of Moor-ditch? 88

FAL. Thou hast the most unsavoury similes and art indeed the most comparative, rascalliest, sweet young prince. But, Hal, I prithee, trouble me no more with vanity. I would to God thou and I knew where a commodity of good names were to be bought. An old lord of the council rated me the other day in the street about you, sir, but I marked him not; and yet he talked very wisely, but I regarded him not; and yet he talked wisely, and in the street too.

PRINCE. Thou didst well; for wisdom cries out in the streets, and no man regards 100 it.

FAL. O, thou hast damnable iteration and art indeed able to corrupt a saint. Thou hast done much harm upon me, Hal; God forgive thee for it! Before I knew thee, Hal, I knew nothing; and now am I, if a man should speak truly, little better than one of the wicked. I must give over this life, and I will give it over: by the Lord, an I do not, I am a villain: I'll be damned for never a king's son in Christendom. 109

PRINCE. Where shall we take a purse to-morrow, Jack?

FAL. 'Zounds, where thou wilt, lad; I'll make one; an I do not, call me villain and baffle me.

PRINCE. I see a good amendment of life in thee; from praying to purse-taking. 115

FAL. Why, Hal, 'tis my vocation, Hal; 'tis no sin for a man to labour in his vocation. 117

[*Enter* POINS.]

Poins! Now shall we know if Gadshill have set a match. O, if men were to be saved by merit, what hole in hell were hot enough for him? This is the most omnipotent villain that ever cried 'Stand' to a true man.

PRINCE. Good morrow, Ned. 123

POINS. Good morrow, sweet Hal. What says Monsieur Remorse? what says Sir John Sack and Sugar? Jack! how agrees the devil and thee about thy soul, that thou soldest him on Good-Friday last for a cup of Madeira and a cold capon's leg? 129

PRINCE. Sir John stands to his word, the devil shall have his bargain; for he was never yet a breaker of proverbs: he will give the devil his due.

POINS. Then art thou damned for keeping thy word with the devil.

PRINCE. Else he had been damned for cozening the devil. 137

POINS. But, my lads, my lads, to-morrow morning, by four o'clock, early at Gadshill! there are pilgrims going to Canterbury with rich offerings, and traders riding to London with fat purses: I have vizards for you all; you have horses for yourselves: Gadshill lies to-night in Rochester: I have bespoke supper to-morrow night in Eastcheap: we may 145 do it as secure as sleep. If you will go, I will stuff your purses full of crowns; if you will not, tarry at home and be hanged.

FAL. Hear ye, Yedward; if I tarry at home and go not, I'll hang you for going. 150

POINS. You will, chops?

FAL. Hal, wilt thou make one?

PRINCE. Who, I rob? I a thief? not I, by my faith.

FAL. There's neither honesty, manhood, 155 nor good fellowship in thee, nor thou camest not of the blood royal, if thou darest not stand for ten shillings.

PRINCE. Well then, once in my days I'll be a madcap. 160

FAL. Why, that's well said.

78. **jumps,** agrees; **waiting in the court,** i.e., either as a courtier or as a judge. 82. **lean wardrobe,** the hangman obtained the clothes of his victim. 83. **gib cat,** tomcat; **lugged,** dragged along (by a rope). 88. **Moor-ditch,** an ill-smelling ditch which drained Moorfields in the suburbs. 90. **comparative,** given to comparisons, hence witty. 93. **commodity,** supply. 94. **rated,** scolded. 99-100. **for . . . it,** a reference to Proverbs I, 20-24. 101. **damnable iteration,** habit of quoting Scripture for an evil end.

113. **baffle,** disgrace, originally a punishment for an unworthy knight, part of which was to hang him up by the heels. 117. **vocation,** cant Puritan term for the station of life to which God has called one. 119. **set a match,** arranged a hold-up. 132. **breaker of proverbs,** i.e., one to prove proverbs false. 137. **cozening,** cheating. 142. **vizards,** masks. 144. **bespoke,** ordered. 145. **Eastcheap,** a part of London's east side. 149. **Yedward,** i.e., Edward. 151. **chops,** fat jaws. 157. **royal,** pun on "royal," a coin worth 10s.

PRINCE. Well, come what will, I'll tarry at home.

FAL. By the Lord, I'll be a traitor then, when thou art king.

PRINCE. I care not.

POINS. Sir John, I prithee, leave the prince and me alone: I will lay him down such reasons for this adventure that he shall go. 169

FAL. Well, God give thee the spirit of persuasion and him the ears of profiting, that what thou speakest may move and what he hears may be believed, that the true prince may, for recreation sake, prove a false thief; for the poor abuses of the time want countenance. Farewell: you shall find me in Eastcheap.

PRINCE. Farewell, thou latter spring! farewell, All-hallown summer! 178

[*Exit* FALSTAFF.

POINS. Now, my good sweet honey lord, ride with us to-morrow: I have a jest to execute that I cannot manage alone. Falstaff, Bardolph, Peto and Gadshill shall rob those men that we have already waylaid; yourself and I will not be there; and when they have the booty, if you and I do not rob them, cut this head off from my shoulders.

PRINCE. How shall we part with them in setting forth? 188

POINS. Why, we will set forth before or after them, and appoint them a place of meeting, wherein it is at our pleasure to fail, and then will they adventure upon the exploit themselves; which they shall have no sooner achieved, but we'll set upon them. 194

PRINCE. Yea, but 'tis like that they will know us by our horses, by our habits and by every other appointment, to be ourselves.

POINS. Tut! our horses they shall not see; I'll tie them in the wood; our vizards we will change after we leave them: and, sirrah, I have cases of buckram for the nonce, to immask our noted outward garments. 202

PRINCE. Yea, but I doubt they will be too hard for us.

POINS. Well, for two of them, I know them to be as true-bred cowards as ever turned back; and for the third, if he fight longer than he sees reason, I'll forswear arms. The virtue of this jest will be, the incomprehensible lies that this same fat rogue will tell us when we meet at supper: how thirty, at least, he fought with; what wards, what blows, what extremities he endured; and in the reproof of this lies the jest. 213

PRINCE. Well, I'll go with thee: provide us all things necessary and meet me to-morrow night in Eastcheap; there I'll sup. Farewell.

POINS. Farewell, my lord. [*Exit.*

PRINCE. I know you all, and will awhile uphold
The unyoked humour of your idleness:
Yet herein will I imitate the sun, 220
Who doth permit the base contagious clouds
To smother up his beauty from the world,
That, when he please again to be himself,
Being wanted, he may be more wonder'd at,
By breaking through the foul and ugly mists
Of vapours that did seem to strangle him. 226
If all the year were playing holidays,
To sport would be as tedious as to work;
But when they seldom come, they wish'd for come,
And nothing pleaseth but rare accidents. 230
So, when this loose behaviour I throw off
And pay the debt I never promisèd,
By how much better than my word I am,
By so much shall I falsify men's hopes;
And like bright metal on a sullen ground, 235
My reformation, glittering o'er my fault,
Shall show more goodly and attract more eyes
Than that which hath no foil to set it off.
I'll so offend, to make offence a skill; 239
Redeeming time when men think least I will.
[*Exit.*

SCENE III. *London. The palace.*

[*Enter the* KING, NORTHUMBERLAND, WORCESTER, HOTSPUR, SIR WALTER BLUNT, *with others.*]

KING. My blood hath been too cold and temperate,

170-1. **spirit . . . profiting**, one of the cant phrases of Puritan preachers. 175. **time**, age; **want countenance**, need encouragement. 178. **All-hallown summer**, Falstaff has artificially prolonged his summer (i.e., his youth) till November 1 (i.e., into old age). 196. **habits**, clothes. 197. **appointment**, piece of equipment. 201. **cases of buckram for the nonce**, suits of stiffened linen for the occasion. 202. **noted**, known. 203. **doubt**, fear. 211. **wards**, defensive motions in fencing. 212. **extremities**, perils. 213. **reproof**, refutation. 219. **unyoked . . . idleness**, free indulgence in folly. 221. **contagious**, noxious, conveying contagion. 224. **wanted**, needed. 230. **accidents**, events. 235. **sullen ground**, dark background. 240. **Redeeming time**, making amends for the time I have lost.

Unapt to stir at these indignities,
And you have found me; for accordingly
You tread upon my patience: but be sure
I will from henceforth rather be myself, 5
Mighty and to be fear'd, than my condition;
Which hath been smooth as oil, soft as young down,
And therefore lost that title of respect
Which the proud soul ne'er pays but to the proud.

WOR. Our house, my sovereign liege, little deserves 10
The scourge of greatness to be used on it;
And that same greatness too which our own hands
Have holp to make so portly.

NORTH. My lord,—

KING. Worcester, get thee gone; for I do see 15
Danger and disobedience in thine eye:
O, sir, your presence is too bold and peremptory,
And majesty might never yet endure
The moody frontier of a servant brow.
You have good leave to leave us: when we need 20
Your use and counsel, we shall send for you.
[*Exit.* WOR.]
You were about to speak. [*To* NORTH.

NORTH. Yea, my good lord.
Those prisoners in your highness' name demanded,
Which Harry Percy here at Holmedon took,
Were, as he says, not with such strength denied 25
As is deliver'd to your majesty:
Either envy, therefore, or misprision
Is guilty of this fault and not my son.

HOT. My liege, I did deny no prisoners.
But I remember, when the fight was done, 30
When I was dry with rage and extreme toil,
Breathless and faint, leaning upon my sword,
Came there a certain lord, neat, and trimly dress'd,
Fresh as a bridegroom; and his chin new reap'd
Show'd like a stubble-land at harvest-home; 35
He was perfumèd like a milliner;
And 'twixt his finger and his thumb he held
A pouncet-box, which ever and anon
He gave his nose and took 't away again;
Who therewith angry, when it next came there, 40
Took it in snuff; and still he smiled and talk'd,
And as the soldiers bore dead bodies by,
He call'd them untaught knaves, unmannerly,
To bring a slovenly unhandsome corse
Betwixt the wind and his nobility. 45
With many holiday and lady terms
He question'd me; amongst the rest, demanded
My prisoners in your majesty's behalf.
I then, all smarting with my wounds being cold,
To be so pester'd with a popinjay, 50
Out of my grief and my impatience,
Answer'd neglectingly I know not what,
He should, or he should not; for he made me mad
To see him shine so brisk and smell so sweet
And talk so like a waiting-gentlewoman 55
Of guns and drums and wounds,—God save the mark!—
And telling me the sovereign'st thing on earth
Was parmaceti for an inward bruise;
And that it was great pity, so it was,
This villanous salt-petre should be digg'd 60
Out of the bowels of the harmless earth,
Which many a good tall fellow had destroy'd
So cowardly; and but for these vile guns,
He would himself have been a soldier.
This bald unjointed chat of his, my lord, 65
I answer'd indirectly, as I said;
And I beseech you, let not his report
Come current for an accusation
Betwixt my love and your high majesty.

BLUNT. The circumstance consider'd, good my lord, 70
Whate'er Lord Harry Percy then had said
To such a person and in such a place,
At such a time, with all the rest retold,
May reasonably die and never rise
To do him wrong or any way impeach 75
What then he said, so he unsay it now.

Scene iii: 3. found me, i.e., found me so. **6. condition,** natural disposition. **8. title of respect,** claim to be respected. **13. portly,** imposing. **19. moody,** angry; **frontier,** forehead; also, military outwork. **27. misprision,** misunderstanding. **29. deny,** refuse (to hand over). **35. harvest-home,** i.e., time of harvest when the fields are bare. **36. milliner,** a vendor of fancy articles. **38. pouncet-box,** box containing perfume. **40. who,** which, i.e., the nose. **41. took it in snuff,** became offended. **46. holiday,** elegant; **lady,** effeminate. **50. popinjay,** parrot. **51. grief,** pain. **52. neglectingly,** absent-mindedly. **56. God save the mark,** avert the omen from my mention of the word "wounds." **58. parmaceti,** the sperm of a whale. **62. tall,** brave. **65. bald . . . chat,** paltry, disconnected chatter. **66. indirectly,** vaguely. **68. come current,** be accepted (as valid coin). **75. impeach,** call in question.

KING. Why, yet he doth deny his prisoners,
But with proviso and exception,
That we at our own charge shall ransom straight
His brother-in-law, the foolish Mortimer; 80
Who, on my soul, hath wilfully betray'd
The lives of those that he did lead to fight
Against that great magician, damn'd Glendower,
Whose daughter, as we hear, the Earl of March 84
Hath lately married. Shall our coffers, then,
Be emptied to redeem a traitor home?
Shall we buy treason? and indent with fears,
When they have lost and forfeited themselves?
No, on the barren mountains let him starve;
For I shall never hold that man my friend 90
Whose tongue shall ask me for one penny cost
To ransom home revolted Mortimer.

HOT. Revolted Mortimer!
He never did fall off, my sovereign liege,
But by the chance of war: to prove that true 95
Needs no more but one tongue for all those wounds,
Those mouthèd wounds, which valiantly he took,
When on the gentle Severn's sedgy bank,
In single opposition, hand to hand,
He did confound the best part of an hour 100
In changing hardiment with great Glendower:
Three times they breathed and three times did they drink,
Upon agreement, of swift Severn's flood;
Who then, affrighted with their bloody looks,
Ran fearfully among the trembling reeds, 105
And hid his crisp head in the hollow bank
Bloodstainèd with these valiant combatants.
Never did base and rotten policy
Colour her working with such deadly wounds;
Nor never could the noble Mortimer 110
Receive so many, and all willingly:
Then let not him be slander'd with revolt.

KING. Thou dost belie him, Percy, thou dost belie him;
He never did encounter with Glendower:
I tell thee, 115
He durst as well have met the devil alone
As Owen Glendower for an enemy.
Art thou not ashamed? But, sirrah, henceforth
Let me not hear you speak of Mortimer:
Send me your prisoners with the speediest means 120
Or you shall hear in such a kind from me
As will displease you. My Lord Northumberland,
We license your departure with your son.
Send us your prisoners, or you will hear of it.

[*Exeunt* KING HENRY, BLUNT, *and train.*

HOT. An if the devil come and roar for them, 125
I will not send them: I will after straight
And tell him so; for I will ease my heart,
Albeit I make a hazard of my head.

NORTH. What, drunk with choler? stay and pause awhile:
Here comes your uncle.

[*Re-enter* WORCESTER.]

HOT. Speak of Mortimer! 130
'Zounds, I will speak of him; and let my soul
Want mercy, if I do not join with him:
Yea, on his part I'll empty all these veins,
And shed my dear blood drop by drop in the dust,
But I will lift the down-trod Mortimer 135
As high in the air as this unthankful king,
As this ingrate and canker'd Bolingbroke.

NORTH. Brother, the king hath made your nephew mad.

WOR. Who struck this heat up after I was gone?

HOT. He will, forsooth, have all my prisoners; 140
And when I urged the ransom once again
Of my wife's brother, then his cheek look'd pale,
And on my face he turn'd an eye of death,
Trembling even at the name of Mortimer.

WOR. I cannot blame him: was not he proclaim'd 145
By Richard that dead is the next of blood?

NORTH. He was; I heard the proclamation:
And then it was when the unhappy king,—
Whose wrongs in us God pardon!—did set forth
Upon his Irish expedition; 150
From whence he intercepted did return

78. But . . . proviso, except on condition. 87. indent, make a contract. 91. cost, expenditure. 94 fall off, revolt. 100. confound, consume. 101. changing hardiment, exchanging valiant blows. 106. crisp, rippling. 108. policy, cunning. 109. Colour, disguise. 121. kind, manner. 128. make a hazard, risk. 137. canker'd, malignant.

To be deposed and shortly murderèd.
WOR. And for whose death we in the world's wide mouth
Live scandalized and foully spoken of.
HOT. But, soft, I pray you; did King Richard then 155
Proclaim my brother Edmund Mortimer
Heir to the crown?
NORTH. He did; myself did hear it.
HOT. Nay, then I cannot blame his cousin king,
That wish'd him on the barren mountains starve.
But shall it be, that you, that set the crown
Upon the head of this forgetful man 161
And for his sake wear the detested blot
Of murderous subornation, shall it be,
That you a world of curses undergo,
Being the agents, or base second means, 165
The cords, the ladder, or the hangman rather?
O, pardon me that I descend so low,
To show the line and the predicament
Wherein you range under this subtle king;
Shall it for shame be spoken in these days, 170
Or fill up chronicles in time to come,
That men of your nobility and power
Did gage them both in an unjust behalf,
As both of you—God pardon it!—have done,
To put down Richard, that sweet lovely rose, 175
And plant this thorn, this canker, Bolingbroke?
And shall it in more shame be further spoken,
That you are fool'd, discarded and shook off
By him for whom these shames ye underwent? 179
No; yet time serves wherein you may redeem
Your banish'd honours and restore yourselves
Into the good thoughts of the world again,
Revenge the jeering and disdain'd contempt
Of this proud king, who studies day and night
To answer all the debt he owes to you 185
Even with the bloody payment of your deaths:
Therefore, I say,—
WOR. Peace, cousin, say no more:
And now I will unclasp a secret book,
And to your quick-conceiving discontents
I'll read you matter deep and dangerous, 190
As full of peril and adventurous spirit
As to o'er-walk a current roaring loud
On the unsteadfast footing of a spear.
HOT. If he fall in, good night! or sink or swim:
Send danger from the east unto the west, 195
So honour cross it from the north to south,
And let them grapple: O, the blood more stirs
To rouse a lion than to start a hare!
NORTH. Imagination of some great exploit
Drives him beyond the bounds of patience.
HOT. By heaven, methinks it were an easy leap, 201
To pluck bright honour from the pale-faced moon,
Or dive into the bottom of the deep,
Where fathom-line could never touch the ground,
And pluck up drownèd honour by the locks;
So he that doth redeem her thence might wear 206
Without corrival all her dignities:
But out upon this half-faced fellowship!
WOR. He apprehends a world of figures here,
But not the form of what he should attend. 210
Good cousin, give me audience for a while.
HOT. I cry you mercy.
WOR. Those same noble Scots
That are your prisoners,—
HOT. I'll keep them all;
By God, he shall not have a Scot of them;
No, if a Scot would save his soul, he shall not: 215
I'll keep them, by this hand.
WOR. You start away
And lend no ear unto my purposes.
Those prisoners you shall keep.
HOT. Nay, I will; that's flat:
He said he would not ransom Mortimer;
Forbade my tongue to speak of Mortimer; 220
But I will find him when he lies asleep,
And in his ear I'll holla "Mortimer!"
Nay,
I'll have a starling shall be taught to speak
Nothing but "Mortimer," and give it him, 225
To keep his anger still in motion.
WOR. Hear you, cousin; a word.

156. brother, i.e., brother-in-law. 163. murderous subornation, of inciting someone to commit murder. 165. second means, assistants. 168. line, class; predicament, category. 173. gage, engage. 176. canker, wild-rose. 183. disdain'd, disdainful. 185. answer, render account of. 200. patience, self-control. 207. corrival, competitor. 208. half-faced fellowship, i.e., partnership in something in which there is not enough for two. 226. still, always.

HOT. All studies here I solemnly defy,
Save how to gall and pinch this Bolingbroke:
And that same sword-and-buckler Prince of Wales, 230
But that I think his father loves him not
And would be glad he met with some mischance,
I would have him poison'd with a pot of ale.
WOR. Farewell, kinsman: I'll talk to you
When you are better temper'd to attend. 235
NORTH. Why, what a wasp-stung and impatient fool
Art thou to break into this woman's mood,
Tying thine ear to no tongue but thine own!
HOT. Why, look you, I am whipp'd and scourged with rods,
Nettled and stung with pismires, when I hear
Of this vile politician, Bolingbroke. 241
In Richard's time,—what do you call the place?—
A plague upon it, it is in Gloucestershire;
'Twas where the madcap duke his uncle kept,
His uncle York; where I first bow'd my knee 245
Unto this king of smiles, this Bolingbroke,—
'Sblood!—
When you and he came back from Ravenspurgh.
NORTH. At Berkley castle.
HOT. You say true: 250
Why, what a candy deal of courtesy
This fawning greyhound then did proffer me!
Look, "when his infant fortune came to age,"
And "gentle Harry Percy," and "kind cousin";
O, the devil take such cozeners! God forgive me! 255
Good uncle, tell your tale; I have done.
WOR. Nay, if you have not, to it again;
We will stay your leisure.
HOT. I have done, i' faith.
WOR. Then once more to your Scottish prisoners.
Deliver them up without their ransom straight, 260
And make the Douglas' son your only mean
For powers in Scotland; which, for divers reasons
Which I shall send you written, be assured,
Will easily be granted. You, my lord,
[*To* NORTHUMBERLAND.]
Your son in Scotland being thus employ'd, 265
Shall secretly into the bosom creep
Of that same noble prelate, well beloved,
The archbishop.
HOT. Of York, is it not?
WOR. True; who bears hard 270
His brother's death at Bristol, the Lord Scroop.
I speak not this in estimation,
As what I think might be, but what I know
Is ruminated, plotted and set down,
And only stays but to behold the face 275
Of that occasion that shall bring it on.
HOT. I smell it: upon my life, it will do well.
NORTH. Before the game is afoot, thou still let'st slip.
HOT. Why, it cannot choose but be a noble plot:
And then the power of Scotland and of York,
To join with Mortimer, ha?
WOR. And so they shall. 281
HOT. In faith, it is exceedingly well aim'd.
WOR. And 'tis no little reason bids us speed,
To save our heads by raising of a head;
For, bear ourselves as even as we can, 285
The king will always think him in our debt,
And think we think ourselves unsatisfied,
Till he hath found a time to pay us home:
And see already how he doth begin
To make us strangers to his looks of love. 290
HOT. He does, he does: we'll be revenged on him.
WOR. Cousin, farewell: no further go in this
Than I by letters shall direct your course.
When time is ripe, which will be suddenly,
I'll steal to Glendower and Lord Mortimer;
Where you and Douglas and our powers at once, 296
As I will fashion it, shall happily meet,
To bear our fortunes in our own strong arms,
Which now we hold at much uncertainty.
NORTH. Farewell, good brother: we shall thrive, I trust. 300
HOT. Uncle, adieu: O, let the hours be short
Till fields and blows and groans applaud our sport! [*Exeunt.*

228. defy, renounce. 240. pismires, ants. 244. kept, lived. 251. candy, flattering, i.e., hypocritical. 255. cozeners, cheaters. 261. only means, sole agent. 262. powers, armed forces. 272. in estimation, as conjecture. 278. let'st slip, let the hounds loose. 284. head, armed force. 285. bear . . . can, however discreetly we may act.

ACT II

SCENE I. *Rochester. An inn yard.*

[*Enter a* CARRIER *with a lantern in his hand.*]

FIRST CAR. Heigh-ho! an it be not four by the day, I'll be hanged: Charles' wain is over the new chimney, and yet our horse not packed. What, ostler!

OST. [*Within*] Anon, anon. 5

FIRST CAR. I prithee, Tom, beat Cut's saddle, put a few flocks in the point; poor jade, is wrung in the withers out of all cess.

[*Enter another* CARRIER.]

SEC. CAR. Peas and beans are as dank here as a dog, and that is the next way to give poor jades the bots: this house is turned upside down since Robin Ostler died. 12

FIRST CAR. Poor fellow, never joyed since the price of oats rose; it was the death of him.

SEC. CAR. I think this be the most villanous house in all London road for fleas: I am stung like a tench.

FIRST CAR. Like a tench! by the mass, there is ne'er a king christen could be better bit than I have been since the first cock. 20

SEC. CAR. Why, they will allow us ne'er a jordan, and then we leak in your chimney; and your chamber-lye breeds fleas like a loach.

FIRST CAR. What, ostler! come away and be hanged! come away.

SEC. CAR. I have a gammon of bacon and two razes of ginger, to be delivered as far as Charing-cross. 28

FIRST CAR. God's body! the turkeys in my pannier are quite starved. What, ostler! A plague on thee! hast thou never an eye in thy head? canst not hear? An 'twere not as good deed as drink, to break the pate on thee, I am a very villain. Come, and be hanged! hast no faith in thee? 35

[*Enter* GADSHILL.]

GADS. Good morrow, carriers. What's o'clock?

FIRST CAR. I think it be two o'clock.

GADS. I prithee, lend me thy lantern, to see my gelding in the stable.

FIRST CAR. Nay, by God, soft; I know a trick worth two of that, i' faith. 41

GADS. I pray thee, lend me thine.

SEC. CAR. Ay, when? canst tell? Lend me thy lantern, quoth he? marry, I'll see thee hanged first.

GADS. Sirrah carrier, what time do you mean to come to London?

SEC. CAR. Time enough to go to bed with a candle, I warrant thee. Come, neighbour Mugs, we'll call up the gentlemen: they will along with company, for they have great charge. [*Exeunt* CARRIERS.

GADS. What, ho! chamberlain! 52

CHAM. [*Within*] At hand, quoth pick-purse.

GADS. That's even as fair as—at hand, quoth the chamberlain; for thou variest no more from picking of purses than giving direction doth from labouring; thou layest the plot how. 58

[*Enter* CHAMBERLAIN.]

CHAM. Good morrow, Master Gadshill. It holds current that I told you yesternight: there's a franklin in the wild of Kent hath brought three hundred marks with him in gold: I heard him tell it to one of his company last night at supper; a kind of auditor; one that hath abundance of charge too, God knows what. They are up already, and call for eggs and butter: they will away presently.

GADS. Sirrah, if they meet not with Saint Nicholas' clerks, I'll give thee this neck. 69

CHAM. No, I'll none of it: I pray thee, keep that for the hangman; for I know thou worshippest Saint Nicholas as truly as a man of falsehood may. 72

GADS. What talkest thou to me of the hangman? if I hang, I'll make a fat pair of gallows; for if I hang, old Sir John hangs with me, and thou knowest he is no starveling.

Act II, Scene i: 2. Charles' wain, the great bear or big dipper. 5. Anon, right away. 7. flocks, tufts of wool; point, pummel; wrung, galled. 8. cess, measure. 11. bots, worms. 17. stung like a tench, an allusion to the belief that the spots on this sort of fish were caused by bites of lice. 19. christen, in Christendom. 22. jordan, chamber-pot. 23. chamber-lye, urine; loach, prolific fish. 26. gammon, side. 27. razes of ginger, bundles of ginger roots. 30. pannier, large wicker basket. 40. soft, wait a minute. 51. great charge, a lot of (money). 52. chamberlain, servant in charge of the bed chambers at an inn. 60. holds current, is still true. 61. franklin, farm owner; wild, i.e., weald or hilly country in Kent. 68-9. St. Nicholas' clerks, highwaymen.

Tut! there are other Trojans that thou dreamest not of, the which for sport sake are content to do the profession some grace; that would, if matters should be looked into, for their own credit sake, make all whole. I am joined with no foot land-rakers, no long-staff sixpenny strikers, none of these mad mustachio purple-hued malt-worms; 83 but with nobility and tranquillity, burgomasters and great oneyers, such as can hold in, such as will strike sooner than speak, and speak sooner than drink, and drink sooner than pray: and yet, 'zounds, I lie; for they pray continually to their saint, the commonwealth; or rather, not pray to her, but prey on her, for they ride up and down on her and make her their boots. 91

CHAM. What, the commonwealth their boots? will she hold out water in foul way?

GADS. She will, she will; justice hath liquored her. We steal as in a castle, cocksure; we have the receipt of fern-seed, we walk invisible.

CHAM. Nay, by my faith, I think you are more beholding to the night than to fern-seed for your walking invisible.

GADS. Give me thy hand: thou shalt have a share in our purchase, as I am a true man.

CHAM. Nay, rather let me have it, as you are a false thief. 103

GADS. Go to; "homo" is a common name to all men. Bid the ostler bring my gelding out of the stable. Farewell, you muddy knave.

[*Exeunt.*

SCENE II. *The highway, near Gadshill.*

[*Enter* PRINCE HENRY *and* POINS.]

POINS. Come, shelter, shelter: I have removed Falstaff's horse, and he frets like a gummed velvet.

PRINCE. Stand close.

[*Enter* FALSTAFF.]

FAL. Poins! Poins, and be hanged! Poins!

PRINCE. Peace, ye fat-kidneyed rascal! what a brawling dost thou keep!

FAL. Where's Poins, Hal?

PRINCE. He is walked up to the top of the hill: I'll go seek him. 9

FAL. I am accursed to rob in that thief's company: the rascal hath removed my horse, and tied him I know not where. If I travel but four foot by the squier further afoot, I shall break my wind. Well, I doubt not but to die a fair death for all this, if I 'scape hanging for killing that rogue. I have forsworn 16 his company hourly any time this two and twenty years, and yet I am bewitched with the rogue's company. If the rascal have not given me medicines to make me love him, I'll be hanged; it could not be else; I have drunk medicines. Poins! Hal! a plague upon 22 you both! Bardolph! Peto! I'll starve ere I'll rob a foot further. An 'twere not as good a deed as drink, to turn true man and to leave these rogues, I am the veriest varlet that ever chewed with a tooth. Eight yards 27 of uneven ground is threescore and ten miles afoot with me; and the stony-hearted villains know it well enough: a plague upon it when thieves cannot be true one to another! [*They whistle.*] Whew! A plague upon you all! Give me my horse, you rogues; give me my horse, and be hanged!

PRINCE. Peace, ye fat-guts! lie down; lay thine ear close to the ground and list if thou canst hear the tread of travellers. 35

FAL. Have you any levers to lift me up again, being down? 'Sblood, I'll not bear mine own flesh so far afoot again for all the coin in thy father's exchequer. What a plague mean ye to colt me thus? 40

PRINCE. Thou liest; thou art not colted, thou art uncolted.

FAL. I prithee, good Prince Hal, help me to my horse, good king's son.

PRINCE. Out, ye rogue! shall I be your ostler? 45

FAL. Go hang thyself in thine own heir-apparent garters! If I be ta'en, I'll peach for this. An I have not ballads made on you all and sung to filthy tunes, let a cup of sack be

77. **Trojans,** disreputable fellows. 81. **foot land-rakers,** footpads. 82. **long-staff . . . strikers,** robbers armed with long staves who will knock out their victims for a sixpence. 83. **mustachio . . . worms,** drunkards whose beards are stained with ale. 85. **oneyers,** high sounding equivalent of "ones." 91. **boots,** with a pun on "booty."

93. **in foul way,** on a muddy road. 94. **liquored,** greased. 95. **liquored,** (1) water-proofed, (2) intoxicated. 96. **of fern-seed,** fern-seed was supposed to make its possessor invisible. 101. **purchase,** plunder. **Scene ii: 3. gummed velvet,** velvet stiffened with gum was likely to chafe (fret). 13. **squier,** square, foot rule. 16. **forsworn,** sworn off. 20. **medicines,** i.e., love-potions. 25. **true man,** honest man, perhaps = informer. 40. **colt,** fool. 48. **An,** if.

my poison: when a jest is so forward, and afoot too! I hate it. 50

[*Enter* GADSHILL, BARDOLPH *and* PETO *with him.*]

GADS. Stand.

FAL. So I do, against my will.

POINS. O, 'tis our setter: I know his voice. Bardolph, what news? 54

BARD. Case ye, case ye; on with your vizards: there's money of the king's coming down the hill; 'tis going to the king's exchequer.

FAL. You lie, ye rogue; 'tis going to the king's tavern.

GADS. There's enough to make us all. 60

FAL. To be hanged.

PRINCE. Sirs, you four shall front them in the narrow lane; Ned Poins and I will walk lower: if they 'scape from your encounter, then they light on us. 65

PETO. How many be there of them?

GADS. Some eight or ten.

FAL. 'Zounds, will they not rob us?

PRINCE. What, a coward, Sir John Paunch?

FAL. Indeed, I am not John of Gaunt, your grandfather; but yet no coward, Hal. 71

PRINCE. Well, we leave that to the proof.

POINS. Sirrah Jack, thy horse stands behind the hedge: when thou needest him, there thou shalt find him. Farewell, and stand fast. 75

FAL. Now cannot I strike him, if I should be hanged.

PRINCE. Ned, where are our disguises?

POINS. Here, hard by: stand close.

[*Exeunt* PRINCE *and* POINS.

FAL. Now, my masters, happy man be his dole, say I: every man to his business. 81

[*Enter the* TRAVELLERS.]

FIRST TRAV. Come, neighbour: the boy shall lead our horses down the hill; we'll walk afoot awhile, and ease our legs.

THIEVES. Stand!

TRAVELLERS. Jesus bless us! 86

FAL. Strike; down with them; cut the villains' throats: ah! whoreson caterpillars! bacon-fed knaves! they hate us youth: down with them: fleece them. 90

TRAVELLERS. O, we are undone, both we and ours for ever!

FAL. Hang ye, gorbellied knaves, are ye undone? No, ye fat chuffs; I would your store were here! On, bacons, on! What, ye knaves! young men must live. You are grandjurors, are ye? we'll jure ye, 'faith. 97

[*Here they rob them and bind them. Exeunt.*

[*Re-enter* PRINCE HENRY *and* POINS.]

PRINCE. The thieves have bound the true men. Now could thou and I rob the thieves and go merrily to London, it would be argument for a week, laughter for a month and a good jest for ever. 102

POINS. Stand close; I hear them coming.

[*Enter the* THIEVES *again.*]

FAL. Come, my masters, let us share, and then to horse before day. An the Prince and Poins be not two arrant cowards, there's no equity stirring: there's no more valour in that Poins than in a wild-duck.

PRINCE. Your money!

POINS. Villains! 110

[*As they are sharing, the* PRINCE *and* POINS *set upon them; they all run away; and* FALSTAFF, *after a blow or two, runs away too, leaving the booty behind them.*]

PRINCE. Got with much ease. Now merrily to horse:
The thieves are all scatter'd and possess'd with fear
So strongly that they dare not meet each other; 113
Each takes his fellow for an officer.
Away, good Ned. Falstaff sweats to death,
And lards the lean earth as he walks along:
Were't not for laughing, I should pity him.

POINS. How the rogue roar'd! [*Exeunt.*

SCENE III. *Warkworth castle.*

[*Enter* HOTSPUR, *solus, reading a letter.*]

HOT. "But, for mine own part, my lord, I could be well contented to be there, in respect

50. forward, advanced. 53. setter, arranger [of the robbery], i.e., Gadshill. 55. case ye, put on your masks.

80-1. happy . . . dole, may happiness be his reward. 88. whoreson, bastard. 93. gorbellied, fat-bellied. 94. chuffs, miserly churls. 95. store, all that you own; bacons, swine. 97. grand-jurors, i.e., men of substance and dignity. 107. equity stirring, justice abroad. 116. lards, sweat was thought to be melted fat.

of the love I bear your house." He could be contented: why is he not, then? In respect of the love he bears our house: he shows in 5 this, he loves his own barn better than he loves our house. Let me see some more. "The purpose you undertake is dangerous;"—why, that's certain: 'tis dangerous to take a cold, to sleep, to drink; but I tell you, my lord fool, out of this nettle, danger, we pluck this flower, safety. "The purpose you undertake is 10 dangerous; the friends you have named uncertain; the time itself unsorted; and your whole plot too light for the counterpoise of so great an opposition." Say you so, say you so? I say unto you again, you are a shallow 15 cowardly hind, and you lie. What a lack-brain is this! By the Lord, our plot is a good plot as ever was laid; our friends true and constant: a good plot, good friends, and full of expectation; an excellent plot, very good friends. What a frosty-spirited rogue is 20 this! Why, my lord of York commends the plot and the general course of the action. 'Zounds, an I were now by this rascal, I could brain him with his lady's fan. Is there not my father, my uncle and myself? lord Edmund Mortimer, my lord of York and Owen Glendower? is there not besides the Douglas? have I not all their letters to meet me in arms by the ninth of the next month? and are they not some of them set forward already? What a pagan rascal is this! an infidel! Ha! you shall see now in very sincerity of fear and cold heart, will he to the king and lay open all our proceedings. O, I could divide myself and go to buffets, for moving such a dish of skim milk with so honourable an action! Hang him! let him tell the king: we are prepared. I will set forward to-night.

[*Enter* LADY PERCY.]

How now, Kate! I must leave you within these two hours.

LADY. O, my good lord, why are you thus alone? 40
For what offence have I this fortnight been
A banish'd woman from my Harry's bed?
Tell me, sweet lord, what is't that takes from thee
Thy stomach, pleasure and thy golden sleep?
Why dost thou bend thine eyes upon the earth, 45
And start so often when thou sit'st alone?
Why hast thou lost the fresh blood in thy cheeks;
And given my treasures and my rights of thee
To thick-eyed musing and cursed melancholy?
In thy faint slumbers I by thee have watch'd,
And heard thee murmur tales of iron wars; 51
Speak terms of manage to thy bounding steed;
Cry "Courage! to the field!" And thou hast talk'd
Of sallies and retires, of trenches, tents,
Of palisadoes, frontiers, parapets, 55
Of basilisks, of cannon, culverin,
Of prisoners' ransom and of soldiers slain,
And all the currents of a heady fight.
The spirit within thee hath been so at war
And thus hath so bestirr'd thee in thy sleep, 60
That beads of sweat have stood upon thy brow,
Like bubbles in a late-disturbed stream;
And in thy face strange motions have appear'd,
Such as we see when men restrain their breath
On some great sudden hest. O, what portents are these? 65
Some heavy business hath my lord in hand,
And I must know it, else he loves me not.

HOT. What, ho!

[*Enter* SERVANT.]

Is Gilliams with the packet gone?

SERV. He is, my lord, an hour ago.

HOT. Hath Butler brought those horses from the sheriff? 70

SERV. One horse, my lord, he brought even now.

HOT. What horse? a roan, a crop-ear, is it not?

SERV. It is, my lord.

HOT. That roan shall be my throne.
Well, I will back him straight: O esperance!
Bid Butler lead him forth into the park. 75
[*Exit* SERVANT.

LADY. But hear you, my lord.

HOT. What say'st thou, my lady?

LADY. What is it carries you away?

Scene iii: 12. unsorted, ill-chosen. 13. light, frivolous. 19. expectation, promise. 44. stomach, appetite. 49. thick-eyed, dull-eyed. 52. of manage, used in training horses. 55. palisadoes, fences made of stakes; frontiers, barriers (for defense). 56. basilisks, large brass cannon; culverin, long cannon. 58. currents, events; heady, rash. 62. late, recently. 65. hest, command. 74. esperance, hope—the motto of the Percies.

HOT. Why, my horse, my love, my horse.
LADY. Out, you mad-headed ape! 80
A weasel hath not such a deal of spleen
As you are toss'd with. In faith,
I'll know your business, Harry, that I will.
I fear my brother Mortimer doth stir
About his title, and hath sent for you 85
To line his enterprize: but if you go,—
HOT. So far afoot, I shall be weary, love.
LADY. Come, come, you paraquito, answer me
Directly unto this question that I ask:
In faith, I'll break thy little finger, Harry, 90
An if thou wilt not tell me all things true.
HOT. Away,
Away, you trifler! Love! I love thee not,
I care not for thee, Kate: this is no world
To play with mammets and to tilt with lips: 95
We must have bloody noses and crack'd crowns,
And pass them current too. God's me, my horse!
What say'st thou, Kate? what would'st thou have with me?
LADY. Do you not love me? do you not, indeed? 99
Well, do not then; for since you love me not,
I will not love myself. Do you not love me?
Nay, tell me if you speak in jest or no.
HOT. Come, wilt thou see me ride?
And when I am o' horseback, I will swear
I love thee infinitely. But hark you, Kate; 105
I must not have you henceforth question me
Whither I go, nor reason whereabout:
Whither I must, I must; and, to conclude,
This evening must I leave you, gentle Kate.
I know you wise, but yet no farther wise 110
Than Harry Percy's wife: constant you are,
But yet a woman: and for secrecy,
No lady closer; for I well believe
Thou wilt not utter what thou dost not know;
And so far will I trust thee, gentle Kate. 115
LADY. How! so far?
HOT. Not an inch further. But hark you, Kate:
Whither I go, thither shall you go too;
To-day will I set forth, to-morrow you.
Will this content you, Kate?
LADY. It must of force. 120
[*Exeunt.*

SCENE IV. *The Boar's-Head Tavern, Eastcheap.*

[*Enter the* PRINCE, *and* POINS.]

PRINCE. Ned, prithee, come out of that fat room, and lend me thy hand to laugh a little.

POINS. Where hast been, Hal?

PRINCE. With three or four loggerheads amongst three or four score hogsheads. I 5 have sounded the very base-string of humility. Sirrah, I am sworn brother to a leash of drawers; and can call them all by their christen names, as Tom, Dick, and Francis. They take it already upon their salvation, that though 10 I be but Prince of Wales, yet I am the king of courtesy; and tell me flatly I am no proud Jack, like Falstaff, but a Corinthian, a lad of mettle, a good boy, by the Lord, so they call me, and when I am king of England, I shall command all the good lads in Eastcheap. 15 They call drinking deep, dyeing scarlet; and when you breathe in your watering, they cry "hem," and bid you play it off. To conclude, I am so good a proficient in one quarter of an hour, that I can drink with any tinker in 20 his own language during my life. I tell thee, Ned, thou hast lost much honour, that thou wert not with me in this action. But, sweet Ned,—to sweeten which name of Ned, I give thee this pennyworth of sugar, clapped 25 even now into my hand by an under-skinker, one that never spake other English in his life than "Eight shillings and sixpence," and "You are welcome," with this shrill addition, "Anon, anon, sir! Score a pint of bastard in the Half-moon," or so. But, Ned, to drive away the 30 time till Falstaff come, I prithee, do thou stand in some by-room, while I question my puny drawer to what end he gave me the sugar; and do thou never leave calling "Francis," that his tale to me may be nothing but "Anon." Step aside, and I'll show thee a precedent.

POINS. Francis!

81. **spleen**, impetuosity. 86. **line**, support. 88. **paraquito**, little parrot. 95. **mammets**, dolls. 97. **crack'd crowns**, broken heads, with a pun on cracked crowns (the coins) which would not pass current. 107. **whereabout**, about what. Scene iv: 1. **fat**, vat. 4. **loggerheads**, blockheads. 12. **Corinthian**, gay blade. 17. **watering**, drinking. 18. **play it off**, drink it down. 20-1. **tinker . . . language**, (1) tinkers were heavy drinkers, (2) they talked a jargon of their own. 26. **under-skinker**, tapster's assistant. 28. **Anon**, right away. 29. **bastard**, sweet Spanish wine; **Half-Moon**, name of a room in the tavern. 33. **puny**, pun on puisné—younger son, so the second drawer. 37. **precedent**, example.

PRINCE. Thou art perfect. 39

POINS. Francis!

[*Exit* POINS.

[*Enter* FRANCIS.]

FRAN. Anon, anon, sir. Look down into the Pomgarnet, Ralph.

PRINCE. Come hither, Francis.

FRAN. My lord?

PRINCE. How long hast thou to serve, Francis? 45

FRAN. Forsooth, five years, and as much as to—

POINS. [*Within*] Francis!

FRAN. Anon, anon, sir. 49

PRINCE. Five year! by'r lady, a long lease for the clinking of pewter. But, Francis, darest thou be so valiant as to play the coward with thy indenture and show it a fair pair of heels and run from it? 54

FRAN. O Lord, sir, I'll be sworn upon all the books in England, I could find in my heart.

POINS. [*Within*] Francis!

FRAN. Anon, sir.

PRINCE. How old art thou, Francis?

FRAN. Let me see—about Michaelmas next I shall be— 61

POINS. [*Within*] Francis!

FRAN. Anon, sir. Pray stay a little, my lord.

PRINCE. Nay, but hark you, Francis: for the sugar thou gavest me, 'twas a pennyworth, was't not? 66

FRAN. O Lord, I would it had been two!

PRINCE. I will give thee for it a thousand pound: ask me when thou wilt, and thou shalt have it. 70

POINS. [*Within*] Francis!

FRAN. Anon, anon.

PRINCE. Anon, Francis? No, Francis; but to-morrow, Francis; or Francis, o' Thursday; or indeed, Francis, when thou wilt. But, Francis! 75

FRAN. My lord?

PRINCE. Wilt thou rob this leathern jerkin, crystal-button, not-pated, agate-ring, puke-stocking, caddis-garter, smooth-tongue, Spanish-pouch,— 80

FRAN. O Lord, sir, who do you mean?

PRINCE. Why, then, your brown bastard is your only drink; for look you, Francis, your white canvas doublet will sully: in Barbary, sir, it cannot come to so much. 85

FRAN. What, sir?

POINS. [*Within*] Francis!

PRINCE. Away, you rogue! dost thou not hear them call? 89

[*Here they both call him; the drawer stands amazed, not knowing which way to go.*

[*Enter* VINTNER.]

VINT. What, standest thou still, and hearest such a calling? Look to the guests within. [*Exit* FRANCIS.] My lord, old Sir John, with half-a-dozen more, are at the door: shall I let them in? 94

PRINCE. Let them alone awhile, and then open the door. [*Exit* VINTNER.] Poins!

[*Re-enter* POINS.]

POINS. Anon, anon, sir.

PRINCE. Sirrah, Falstaff and the rest of the thieves are at the door: shall we be merry? 99

POINS. As merry as crickets, my lad. But hark ye; what cunning match have you made with this jest of the drawer? come, what's the issue? 103

PRINCE. I am now of all humours that have showed themselves humours since the old days of goodman Adam to the pupil age of this present twelve o'clock at midnight.

[*Re-enter* FRANCIS.]

What's o'clock, Francis?

FRAN. Anon, anon, sir. [*Exit.* 109

PRINCE. That ever this fellow should have fewer words than a parrot, and yet the son of a woman! His industry is up-stairs and downstairs; his eloquence the parcel of a reckoning. I am not yet of Percy's mind, the Hotspur of the north; he that kills me some six or seven 115 dozen of Scots at a breakfast, washes his hands, and says to his wife "Fie upon this quiet life! I want work." "O my sweet Harry," says she, "how many hast thou killed to-day?" "Give my roan horse a drench," says he; and an- 120

42. **Pomgarnet,** Pomegranate, the name of another room in the tavern. 53. **indenture,** contract binding an apprentice to his master. 77-80. **Wilt . . . -pouch,** list enumerates the outward characteristics of an inn-keeper. 78. **not-pated,** crop-haired; **puke-stocking,** dark woolen stocking. 79. **caddis-garter,** worsted-garter; **Spanish,** of Spanish leather.

82-5. **Why . . . so much,** Prince talks nonsense to confuse and delay the waiter. 84. **sully,** get soiled; **Barbary,** North Africa. 95. **let them alone,** let them wait. 101. **match,** game. 104. **humours,** whims. 106. **pupil age,** youth. 113. **parcel,** item. 120. **drench,** purge.

swers "Some fourteen," an hour after; "a trifle, a trifle." I prithee, call in Falstaff: I'll play Percy, and that damned brawn shall play Dame Mortimer his wife. "Rivo!" says the drunkard. Call in ribs, call in tallow. 125

[*Enter* FALSTAFF, GADSHILL, BARDOLPH, *and* PETO; FRANCIS *following with wine*.]

POINS. Welcome, Jack: where hast thou been?

FAL. A plague of all cowards, I say, and a vengeance too! marry, and amen! Give me a cup of sack, boy. Ere I lead this life long, I'll sew nether stocks and mend them and foot them too. A plague of all cowards! Give me a cup of sack, rogue. Is there no virtue extant? 132 [*He drinks.*

PRINCE. Didst thou never see Titan kiss a dish of butter? pitiful-hearted Titan, that melted at the sweet tale of the sun's! if thou didst, then behold that compound. 136

FAL. You rogue, here's lime in this sack too: there is nothing but roguery to be found in villanous man: yet a coward is worse than a cup of sack with lime in it. A villanous coward! Go thy ways, old Jack; die when thou wilt, if manhood, good manhood, be not forgot upon the face of the earth, then am I a shotten herring. There live not three good men unhanged in England; and one of them is fat and grows old: God help the while! a bad world, I say. I would I were a weaver; I could sing psalms or any thing. A plague of all cowards, I say still.

PRINCE. How now, wool-sack! what mutter you? 149

FAL. A king's son! If I do not beat thee out of thy kingdom with a dagger of lath, and drive all thy subjects afore thee like a flock of wild-geese, I'll never wear hair on my face more. You Prince of Wales! 154

PRINCE. Why, you whoreson round man, what's the matter?

FAL. Are not you a coward? answer me to that: and Poins there?

POINS. 'Zounds, ye fat paunch, and ye call me coward, by the Lord, I'll stab thee. 160

FAL. I call thee coward! I'll see thee damned ere I call thee coward: but I would give a thousand pound I could run as fast as thou canst. You are straight enough in the shoulders, you care not who sees your back: call you that backing of your friends? A plague upon such backing! give me them that will face me. Give me a cup of sack: I am a rogue, if I drunk to-day. 169

PRINCE. O villain! thy lips are scarce wiped since thou drunkest last.

FAL. All's one for that. [*He drinks.*] A plague of all cowards, still say I.

PRINCE. What's the matter? 174

FAL. What's the matter! there be four of us here have ta'en a thousand pound this day morning.

PRINCE. Where is it, Jack? where is it?

FAL. Where is it! taken from us it is: a hundred upon poor four of us. 180

PRINCE. What, a hundred, man?

FAL. I am a rogue, if I were not at half-sword with a dozen of them two hours together. I have 'scaped by miracle. I am eight times thrust through the doublet, four through the hose; my buckler cut through and through; my sword hacked like a hand-saw—ecce signum! I never dealt better since I was a man: all would not do. A plague of all cowards! Let them speak: if they speak more or less than truth, they are villains and the sons of darkness. 191

PRINCE. Speak, sirs; how was it?

GADS. We four set upon some dozen—

FAL. Sixteen at least, my lord.

GADS. And bound them. 195

PETO. No, no, they were not bound.

FAL. You rogue, they were bound, every man of them; or I am a Jew else, an Ebrew Jew.

GADS. As we were sharing, some six or seven fresh men set upon us— 200

FAL. And unbound the rest, and then come in the other.

PRINCE. What, fought you with them all?

FAL. All! I know not what you call all; 204 but if I fought not with fifty of them, I am a bunch of radish: if there were not two or

123. **brawn**, mass of flesh. 124. **"Rivo,"** exclamation used in drinking bouts. 130. **nether stocks**, stockings. 133. **Titan**, i.e., Hyperion, the sun. 134. **that**, antecedent is "butter." 137. **lime**, used to adulterate wine and to stimulate thirst. 143. **shotten herring**, a herring that has just spawned and so is very thin. 146. **the while**, the present age.

147. **weaver**, a pious Protestant from the Low Countries. 151. **dagger of lath**, the conventional weapon of the Vice in the Interludes. 174. **matter**, subject, i.e., What are you talking about? 182. **half-sword**, close quarters. 185. **doublet**, coat. 186. **hose**, breeches; **buckler**, small shield. 187. **ecce signum**, behold the proof.

three and fifty upon poor old Jack, then am I no two-legged creature.

PRINCE. Pray God you have not murdered some of them. 210

FAL. Nay, that's past praying for: I have peppered two of them; two I am sure I have paid, two rogues in buckram suits. I tell thee what, Hal, if I tell thee a lie, spit in my face, call me horse. Thou knowest my old ward; here I lay, and thus I bore my point. Four rogues in buckram let drive at me— 217

PRINCE. What, four? thou saidst but two even now.

FAL. Four, Hal; I told thee four. 220

POINS. Ay, ay, he said four.

FAL. These four came all a-front, and mainly thrust at me. I made me no more ado but took all their seven points in my target, thus. 225

PRINCE. Seven? why, there were but four even now.

FAL. In buckram?

POINS. Ay, four, in buckram suits.

FAL. Seven, by these hilts, or I am a villain else. 230

PRINCE. Prithee, let him alone; we shall have more anon.

FAL. Dost thou hear me, Hal?

PRINCE. Ay, and mark thee too, Jack. 234

FAL. Do so, for it is worth the listening to. These nine in buckram that I told thee of—

PRINCE. So, two more already.

FAL. Their points being broken,—

POINS. Down fell their hose. 239

FAL. Began to give me ground: but I followed me close, came in foot and hand; and with a thought seven of the eleven I paid.

PRINCE. O monstrous! eleven buckram men grown out of two! 244

FAL. But, as the devil would have it, three misbegotten knaves in Kendal green came at my back and let drive at me; for it was so dark, Hal, that thou couldst not see thy hand. 248

PRINCE. These lies are like their father that begets them; gross as a mountain, open, palpable. Why, thou clay-brained guts, thou knotty-pated fool, thou whoreson, obscene, greasy tallow-catch,— 253

FAL. What, art thou mad? art thou mad? is not the truth the truth?

PRINCE. Why, how couldst thou know these men in Kendal green, when it was so dark thou couldst not see thy hand? come, tell us your reason: what sayest thou to this? 259

POINS. Come, your reason, Jack, your reason.

FAL. What, upon compulsion? 'Zounds, an I were at the strappado, or all the racks in the world, I would not tell you on compulsion. Give you a reason on compulsion! if reasons were as plentiful as blackberries, I would give no man a reason upon compulsion, I. 266

PRINCE. I'll be no longer guilty of this sin; this sanguine coward, this bed-presser, this horseback-breaker, this huge hill of flesh,— 269

FAL. 'Sblood, you starveling, you elf-skin, you dried neat's tongue, you bull's pizzle, you stock-fish! O for breath to utter what is like thee! you tailor's-yard, you sheath, you bow-case, you vile standing-tuck,— 274

PRINCE. Well, breathe awhile, and then to it again: and when thou hast tired thyself in base comparisons, hear me speak but this.

POINS. Mark, Jack. 278

PRINCE. We two saw you four set on four and bound them, and were masters of their wealth. Mark now, how a plain tale shall put you down. Then did we two set on you four; and, with a word, out-faced you from your prize, and have it; yea, and can show it you here in the house; and, Falstaff, you carried your guts away as nimbly, with as quick dexterity, and roared for mercy and still run and roared, as ever I heard bull-calf. What a slave art thou, to hack thy sword as thou hast done, and then say it was in fight! What trick, what device, what starting-hole, canst thou now find out to hide thee from this open and apparent shame? 292

POINS. Come, let's hear, Jack; what trick hast thou now?

FAL. By the Lord, I knew ye as well as he that made ye. Why, hear you, my masters: was it for me to kill the heir-apparent? should I turn upon the true prince? why, thou knowest I am as valiant as Hercules: but beware

213. paid, killed. 215. ward, posture of defense. 223. mainly, violently. 224. target, round shield. 238. points, (1) swords' points; (2) laces to which hose were fastened to the doublet. 253. tallow-catch, a tub or roll of fat taken by the butcher to the tallow chandler. 262. strappado, a machine used for the infliction of a form of torture. 264. reasons, pun on "raisins." 270. elf-skin, probably snake skin, a traditional cloak for fairies. 271. neat's, ox's. 272. stock-fish, dried fish, usually cod. 283. out-faced, brow-beat. 291. starting-hole, a hole into which a rabbit goes to elude pursuers.

instinct; the lion will not touch the true prince. Instinct is a great matter; I was now a 300 coward on instinct. I shall think the better of myself and thee during my life; I for a valiant lion, and thou for a true prince. But, by the Lord, lads, I am glad you have the money. Hostess, clap to the doors: watch 305 to-night, pray to-morrow. Gallants, lads, boys, hearts of gold, all the titles of good fellowship come to you! What, shall we be merry? shall we have a play extempore?

PRINCE. Content; and the argument shall be thy running away. 311

FAL. Ah, no more of that, Hal, an thou lovest me!

[*Enter* HOSTESS.]

HOST. O Jesu, my lord the prince!

PRINCE. How now, my lady the hostess! what sayest thou to me?

HOST. Marry, my lord, there is a nobleman of the court at door would speak with you: he says he comes from your father. 319

PRINCE. Give him as much as will make him a royal man, and send him back again to my mother.

FAL. What manner of man is he?

HOST. An old man.

FAL. What doth gravity out of his bed at midnight? Shall I give him his answer? 326

PRINCE. Prithee, do, Jack.

FAL. 'Faith, and I'll send him packing. [*Exit.*

PRINCE. Now, sirs: by'r lady, you fought fair; so did you, Peto; so did you, Bardolph: you are lions too, you ran away upon instinct, you will not touch the true prince; no, fie! 332

BARD. 'Faith, I ran when I saw others run.

PRINCE. 'Faith, tell me now in earnest, how came Falstaff's sword so hacked?

PETO. Why, he hacked it with his dagger, and said he would swear truth out of England but he would make you believe it was done in fight, and persuaded us to do the like. 339

BARD. Yea, and to tickle our noses with spear-glass to make them bleed, and then to beslubber our garments with it and swear it was the blood of true men. I did that I did not this seven year before, I blushed to hear his monstrous devices. 344

PRINCE. O villain, thou stolest a cup of sack eighteen years ago, and wert taken with the manner, and ever since thou hast blushed extempore. Thou hadst fire and sword on thy side, and yet thou rannest away: what instinct hadst thou for it? 350

BARD. My lord, do you see these meteors? do you behold these exhalations?

PRINCE. I do.

BARD. What think you they portend?

PRINCE. Hot livers and cold purses. 355

BARD. Choler, my lord, if rightly taken.

PRINCE. No, if rightly taken, halter.

[*Re-enter* FALSTAFF.]

Here comes lean Jack, here comes bare-bone. How now, my sweet creature of bombast! How long is't ago, Jack, since thou sawest thine own knee? 361

FAL. My own knee! when I was about thy years, Hal, I was not an eagle's talon in the waist; I could have crept into any alderman's thumb-ring: a plague of sighing and grief! it blows a man up like a bladder. There's villanous news abroad: here was Sir John 366 Bracy from your father; you must to the court in the morning. That same mad fellow of the north, Percy, and he of Wales, that gave Amamon the bastinado and made Lucifer cuckold and swore the devil his true liegeman upon the cross of a Welsh hook—what a plague call you him? 373

POINS. O, Glendower.

FAL. Owen, Owen, the same; and his son-in-law Mortimer, and old Northumberland, and that sprightly Scot of Scots, Douglas, that runs o' horseback up a hill perpendicular,—

PRINCE. He that rides at high speed and with his pistol kills a sparrow flying. 380

FAL. You have hit it.

PRINCE. So did he never the sparrow.

FAL. Well, that rascal hath good mettle in him; he will not run. 384

PRINCE. Why, what a rascal art thou then, to praise him so for running!

305. **watch**, keep awake. 312. **an**, if. 321. **royal**, puns on names of coins; a noble = 6s. 3d; a royal = 10s. 341. **beslubber**, smear. 346-7. **taken with the manner**, caught in the act. 348. **blushed extempore**, Bardolph's drinking has given him a perpetual red nose. 355. **hot . . . purses**, pun on choler: "anger" and "collar." 359. **bombast**, cotton wadding. 370. **Amamon**, name of a devil; **bastinado**, a beating. 371. **liegeman**, subject. 372. **Welsh hook**, a pike with a curved blade.

FAL. O' horseback, ye cuckoo; but afoot he will not budge a foot.

PRINCE. Yes, Jack, upon instinct. 389

FAL. I grant ye, upon instinct. Well, he is there too, and one Mordake, and a thousand blue-caps more: Worcester is stolen away tonight; thy father's beard is turned white with the news: you may buy land now as cheap as stinking mackerel. 395

PRINCE. Why, then, it is like, if there come a hot June and this civil buffeting hold, we shall buy maidenheads as they buy hobnails, by the hundreds. 399

FAL. By the mass, lad, thou sayest true; it is like we shall have good trading that way. But tell me, Hal, art not thou horrible afeard? thou being heir-apparent, could the world pick thee out three such enemies again as that fiend Douglas, that spirit Percy, and that devil Glendower? Art thou not horribly afraid? doth not thy blood thrill at it? 407

PRINCE. Not a whit, i' faith; I lack some of thy instinct.

FAL. Well, thou wilt be horribly chid tomorrow when thou comest to thy father: if thou love me, practise an answer. 412

PRINCE. Do thou stand for my father, and examine me upon the particulars of my life.

FAL. Shall I? content: this chair shall be my state, this dagger my sceptre, and this cushion my crown. 417

PRINCE. Thy state is taken for a joined-stool, thy golden sceptre for a leaden dagger, and thy precious rich crown for a pitiful bald crown! 420

FAL. Well, an the fire of grace be not quite out of thee, now shalt thou be moved. Give me a cup of sack to make my eyes look red, that it may be thought I have wept; for I must speak in passion, and I will do it in King Cambyses' vein. 426

PRINCE. Well, here is my leg.

FAL. And here is my speech. Stand aside, nobility.

HOST. O Jesu, this is excellent sport, i' faith!

FAL. Weep not, sweet queen; for trickling
tears are vain.

HOST. O, the father, how he holds his countenance! 433

FAL. For God's sake, lords, convey my tristful queen;
For tears do stop the flood-gates of her eyes.

HOST. O Jesu, he doth it as like one of these harlotry players as ever I see! 437

FAL. Peace, good pint-pot; peace, good tickle-brain. Harry, I do not only marvel where thou spendest thy time, but also how thou art accompanied: for though the camomile, the more it is trodden on the faster it grows, yet youth, the more it is wasted the sooner it wears. That thou art my son, I have partly thy mother's word, partly my own opinion, but chiefly a villanous trick of thine eye and a foolish hanging of thy nether lip, that doth warrant me. If then thou be son to me, here lies the point; why, being son to me, art thou so pointed at? Shall the 449 blessed sun of heaven prove a micher and eat blackberries? a question not to be asked. Shall the son of England prove a thief and take purses? a question to be asked. There is a thing, Harry, which thou hast often heard of and it is known to many in our land by the name of pitch: this pitch, as ancient writers do report, doth defile; so doth the company thou keepest: for, Harry, now I do not speak to thee in drink but in tears, not in pleasure but in passion, not in words only, but in woes also: and yet there is a virtuous man whom I have often noted in thy company, but I know not his name. 461

PRINCE. What manner of man, an it like your majesty?

FAL. A goodly portly man, i' faith, and a corpulent; of a cheerful look, a pleasing eye and a most noble carriage; and, as I think, his age some fifty, or, by'r lady, inclining to three score; and now I remember me, his name is Falstaff: if that man should be lewdly given, he deceiveth me; for, Harry, I see virtue in his looks. If then the tree may be known 470 by the fruit, as the fruit by the tree, then, peremptorily I speak it, there is virtue in that Falstaff: him keep with, the rest banish. And

392. **blue-caps**, blue bonnets, i.e., Scotchmen. 416. **state**, throne. 418. **joined-stool**, stool made by a joiner. 426. **King Cambyses' vein**, i.e., bombast. **Cambises** (1572) **A Lamentable Tragedie** by Thomas Preston had become proverbial for its bombastic, high-flown style. Falstaff imitates it in lines 431, 434-5. 427. **leg**, obeisance. 434. **tristful**, sad. 437. **harlotry**, worthless. 439. **tickle-brain**, a kind of strong liquor. 441-75. **for though the camomile**, etc. In these speeches Falstaff parodies the exaggerated balance, antithesis, alliteration, and other features of the style of Lyly's **Euphues** (1578); **camomile**, an aromatic creeping plant. 447. **nether**, lower. 448. **warrant me**, give me proof. 450. **micher**, sneak-thief. 463. **portly**, dignified. 468. **lewdly given**, viciously inclined.

tell me now, thou naughty varlet, tell me, where hast thou been this month? 475

PRINCE. Dost thou speak like a king? Do thou stand for me, and I'll play my father.

FAL. Depose me? if thou dost it half so gravely, so majestically, both in word and matter, hang me up by the heels for a rabbit-sucker or a poulter's hare. 481

PRINCE. Well, here I am set.

FAL. And here I stand: judge, my masters.

PRINCE. Now, Harry, whence come you?

FAL. My noble lord, from Eastcheap. 485

PRINCE. The complaints I hear of thee are grievous.

FAL. 'Sblood, my lord, they are false: nay, I'll tickle ye for a young prince, i' faith. 489

PRINCE. Swearest thou, ungracious boy? henceforth ne'er look on me. Thou are violently carried away from grace: there is a devil haunts thee in the likeness of an old fat man, a tun of man is thy companion. Why dost thou converse with that trunk of humours, that bolting-hutch of beastliness, 495 that swollen parcel of dropsies, that huge bombard of sack, that stuffed cloak-bag of guts, that roasted Manningtree ox with the pudding in his belly, that reverend vice, that grey iniquity, that father ruffian, that vanity 500 in years? Wherein is he good, but to taste sack and drink it? wherein neat and cleanly, but to carve a capon and eat it? wherein cunning, but in craft? wherein crafty, but in villany? wherein villanous, but in all things? wherein worthy, but in nothing? 505

FAL. I would your grace would take me with you: whom means your grace?

PRINCE. That villanous abominable misleader of youth, Falstaff, that old white-bearded Satan.

FAL. My lord, the man I know. 510

PRINCE. I know thou dost.

FAL. But to say I know more harm in him than in myself, were to say more than I know. That he is old, the more the pity, his white hairs do witness it; but that he is, saving your reverence, a whoremaster, that I utterly 515 deny. If sack and sugar be a fault, God help the wicked! if to be old and merry be a sin, then many an old host that I know is damned: if to be fat be to be hated, then Pharaoh's lean kine are to be loved. No, my good 520 lord; banish Peto, banish Bardolph, banish Poins: but for sweet Jack Falstaff, kind Jack Falstaff, true Jack Falstaff, valiant Jack Falstaff, and therefore more valiant, being, as he is, old Jack Falstaff, banish not him thy Harry's company, banish not him thy Harry's company: banish plum Jack, and banish all the world. 527

PRINCE. I do, I will. [*A knocking heard.*

[*Exeunt* HOSTESS, FRANCIS, *and* BARDOLPH.

[*Re-enter* BARDOLPH, *running*.]

BARD. O, my lord, my lord! the sheriff with a most monstrous watch is at the door.

FAL. Out, ye rogue! Play out the play: I have much to say in the behalf of that Falstaff. 532

[*Re-enter the* HOSTESS.]

HOST. O Jesu, my lord, my lord!

PRINCE. Heigh, heigh! the devil rides upon a fiddlestick: what's the matter? 535

HOST. The sheriff and all the watch are at the door: they are come to search the house. Shall I let them in?

FAL. Dost thou hear, Hal? never call a true piece of gold a counterfeit: thou art essentially mad, without seeming so. 541

PRINCE. And thou a natural coward, without instinct.

FAL. I deny your major: if you will deny the sheriff, so; if not, let him enter: if I become not a cart as well as another man, a plague on my bringing up! I hope I shall as soon be strangled with a halter as another.

PRINCE. Go, hide thee behind the arras: the rest walk up above. Now, my masters, for a true face and good conscience. 551

FAL. Both which I have had: but their date is out, and therefore I'll hide me.

474. **varlet**, knave. 480. **rabbit-sucker**, a suckling rabbit. 481. **poulter's**, poulterer's. 489. **I'll . . . prince**, I'll annoy you in my impersonation of the Prince. 490. **Ungracious**, graceless. 493. **tun**, large barrel. 495. **bolting-hutch**, bin for bolted (sifted) meal or flour. 497. **bombard**, leathern drinking vessel. 498. **Manningtree ox**, Manningtree, a town in Essex, famous for its fairs, at which oxen were roasted whole. 499. **vice**, i.e., the character in the morality plays. 503. **cunning**, skillful. 505. **take . . . you**, make me understand you. 530. **monstrous watch**, a very large guard. 534-5. **devil . . . fiddlestick**, a proverb, here a contemptuous exclamation. 540-1. **thou . . . mad**, you are really demented, i.e., if you don't realize that the sheriff is actually at the door. 542. **natural coward**, i.e., in being frightened at the sheriff's appearance. 543. **your major**, i.e., major premise. 546. **a cart**, hangman's cart, tumbrel. 549. **arras**, tapestry curtain hung before a wall. 552-3. **their date is out**, they are out of date with me.

PRINCE. Call in the sheriff.
[*Exeunt all except the* PRINCE *and* PETO.]

[*Enter* SHERIFF *and the* CARRIER.]

Now, master sheriff, what is your will with me? 555

SHER. First, pardon me, my lord. A hue and cry
Hath follow'd certain men unto this house.

PRINCE. What men?

SHER. One of them is well known, my gracious lord,
A gross fat man.

CAR. As fat as butter. 560

PRINCE. The man, I do assure you, is not here:
For I myself at this time have employ'd him.
And, sheriff, I will engage my word to thee
That I will, by to-morrow dinner-time,
Send him to answer thee, or any man, 565
For any thing he shall be charged withal:
And so let me entreat you leave the house.

SHER. I will, my lord. There are two gentlemen
Have in this robbery lost three hundred marks.

PRINCE. It may be so: if he have robb'd these men, 570
He shall be answerable; and so farewell.

SHER. Good night, my noble lord.

PRINCE. I think it is good morrow, is it not?

SHER. Indeed, my lord, I think it be two o'clock. [*Exeunt* SHERIFF *and* CARRIER.

PRINCE. This oily rascal is know as well as Paul's. Go, call him forth. 576

PETO. Falstaff!—Fast asleep behind the arras, and snorting like a horse.

PRINCE. Hark, how hard he fetches breath. Search his pockets. [*He searcheth his pockets, and findeth certain papers.*] What hast thou found? 582

PETO. Nothing but papers, my lord.

PRINCE. Let's see what they be: read them.

PETO. [*Reads*]

Item, A capon, ...	2s. 2d.
Item, Sauce, ...	4d.
Item, Sack, two gallons, .	5s. 8d.
Item, Anchovies and sack after supper, . . .	2s. 6d.
Item, Bread, . . .	ob. 590

556. hue and cry, a technical term meaning the pursuit of criminals, originally with shouting and the belling of hounds as in a chase. 576. Paul's, St. Paul's Cathedral.

PRINCE. On monstrous! but one half-pennyworth of bread to this intolerable deal of sack! What there is else, keep close; we'll read it at more advantage: there let him sleep till day. I'll to the court in the morning. We must all to the wars, and thy place shall be 596 honourable. I'll procure this fat rogue a charge of foot; and I know his death will be a march of twelve-score. The money shall be paid back again with advantage. Be with me betimes in the morning; and so, good morrow, Peto. 601

PETO. Good morrow, good my lord.
[*Exeunt.*

ACT III

SCENE I. *Bangor. The* ARCHDEACON'S *house.*

[*Enter* HOTSPUR, WORCESTER, MORTIMER, *and* GLENDOWER.]

MORT. These promises are fair, the parties sure,
And our induction full of prosperous hope.

HOT. Lord Mortimer, and cousin Glendower,
Will you sit down?
And uncle Worcester: a plague upon it! 5
I have forgot the map.

GLEND. No, here it is.
Sit, cousin Percy; sit, good cousin Hotspur,
For by that name as oft as Lancaster
Doth speak of you, his cheek looks pale and with
A rising sigh he wisheth you in heaven. 10

HOT. And you in hell, as oft as he hears
Owen Glendower spoke of.

GLEND. I cannot blame him: at my nativity
The front of heaven was full of fiery shapes,
Of burning cressets; and at my birth 15
The frame and huge foundation of the earth
Shaked like a coward.

HOT. Why, so it would have done at the same season, if your mother's cat had but

590. ob., obolus, a Greek coin, here a halfpenny. 597. a charge of foot, command of infantry. 598-9. death . . . twelve score, a march of twelve score (240) yards will be the death of him. 599. advantage, interest. Act III, Scene i: 2. induction, beginning. 14. front, forehead. 15. cressets, iron vessels for holding burning oil. He means meteors.

kittened, though yourself had never been born. 20

GLEND. I say the earth did shake when I was born.

HOT. And I say the earth was not of my mind,
If you suppose as fearing you it shook.

GLEND. The heavens were all on fire, the earth did tremble.

HOT. O, then the earth shook to see the heavens on fire, 25
And not in fear of your nativity.
Diseased nature oftentimes breaks forth
In strange eruptions; oft the teeming earth
Is with a kind of colic pinch'd and vex'd
By the imprisoning of unruly wind 30
Within her womb which, for enlargement striving,
Shakes the old beldam earth and topples down
Steeples and moss-grown towers. At your birth
Our grandam earth, having this distemperature,
In passion shook.

GLEND. Cousin, of many men 35
I do not bear these crossings. Give me leave
To tell you once again that at my birth
The front of heaven was full of fiery shapes,
The goats ran from the mountains, and the herds
Were strangely clamorous to the frighted fields. 40
These signs have mark'd me extraordinary;
And all the courses of my life do show
I am not in the roll of common men.
Where is he living, clipp'd in with the sea
That chides the banks, of England, Scotland, Wales, 45
Which calls me pupil, or hath read to me?
And bring him out that is but woman's son
Can trace me in the tedious ways of art
And hold me pace in deep experiments.

HOT. I think there's no man speaks better
Welsh. I'll to dinner. 51

MORT. Peace, cousin Percy; you will make him mad.

GLEND. I can call spirits from the vasty deep.

HOT. Why, so can I, or so can any man;
But will they come when you do call for them? 55

GLEND. Why, I can teach you, cousin, to command
The devil.

HOT. And I can teach thee, coz, to shame the devil
By telling truth: tell truth and shame the devil.
If thou have power to raise him, bring him hither, 60
And I'll be sworn I have power to shame him hence.
O, while you live, tell truth and shame the devil!

MORT. Come, come, no more of this unprofitable chat.

GLEND. Three times hath Henry Bolingbroke made head
Against my power; thrice from the banks of Wye 65
And sandy-bottom'd Severn have I sent him
Bootless home and weather-beaten back.

HOT. Home without boots, and in foul weather too!
How 'scapes he agues, in the devil's name?

GLEND. Come, here's the map: shall we divide our right 70
According to our threefold order ta'en?

MORT. The archdeacon hath divided it
Into three limits very equally:
England, from Trent and Severn hitherto,
By south and east is to my part assign'd: 75
All westward, Wales beyond the Severn shore,
And all the fertile land within that bound,
To Owen Glendower: and, dear coz, to you
The remnant northward, lying off from Trent.
And our indentures tripartite are drawn; 80
Which being sealed interchangeably,
A business that this night may execute,
To-morrow, cousin Percy, you and I
And my good Lord of Worcester will set forth
To meet your father and the Scottish power,
As is appointed us, at Shrewsbury. 86
My father Glendower is not ready yet,
Nor shall we need his help these fourteen days.

27-33. **Diseased . . . towers,** earthquakes were supposed to be caused by wind in the belly of the earth. 32. **beldam,** grandmother. 34. **distemperature,** disorder. 35. **passion,** agitation. 36. **crossings,** contradictions. 43. **roll,** register. 44. **clipp'd in,** encircled. 46. **read to,** taught. 48. **trace,** follow; **art,** magic. 64-5. **made . . . power,** attacked my forces. 67. **bootless,** having gained no advantage. 73. **limits,** divisions. 74. **hitherto,** to this point. 80. **indentures tripartite,** agreement signed in triplicate. 81. **interchangeably,** i.e., by each party to the agreement.

Within that space you may have drawn together
Your tenants, friends and neighbouring gentlemen. 90

GLEND. A shorter time shall send me to you, lords:
And in my conduct shall your ladies come;
From whom you now must steal and take no leave,
For there will be a world of water shed
Upon the parting of your wives and you. 95

HOT. Methinks my moiety, north from Burton here,
In quantity equals not one of yours:
See how this river comes me cranking in,
And cuts me from the best of all my land
A huge half-moon, a monstrous cantle out. 100
I'll have the current in this place damm'd up;
And here the smug and silver Trent shall run
In a new channel, fair and evenly;
It shall not wind with such a deep indent,
To rob me of so rich a bottom here. 105

GLEND. Not wind? it shall, it must; you see it doth.

MORT. Yea, but
Mark how he bears his course, and runs me up
With like advantage on the other side;
Gelding the opposed continent as much 110
As on the other side it takes from you.

WOR. Yea, but a little charge will trench him here
And on this north side win this cape of land;
And then he runs straight and even.

HOT. I'll have it so: a little charge will do it.

GLEND. I'll not have it alter'd. 116

HOT. Will not you?

GLEND. No, nor you shall not.

HOT. Who shall say me nay?

GLEND. Why, that will I.

HOT. Let me not understand you, then; speak it in Welsh. 120

GLEND. I can speak English, lord, as well as you;
For I was train'd up in the English court;
Where, being but young, I framèd to the harp
Many an English ditty lovely well
And gave the tongue a helpful ornament, 125
A virtue that was never seen in you.

HOT. Marry,
And I am glad of it with all my heart:
I had rather be a kitten and cry mew
Than one of these same metre ballad-mongers;
I had rather hear a brazen canstick turn'd, 131
Or a dry wheel grate on the axle-tree;
And that would set my teeth nothing on edge,
Nothing so much as mincing poetry:
'Tis like the forced gait of a shuffling nag. 135

GLEND. Come, you shall have Trent turn'd.

HOT. I do not care: I'll give thrice so much land
To any well-deserving friend;
But in the way of bargain, mark ye me,
I'll cavil on the ninth part of a hair. 140
Are the indentures drawn? shall we be gone?

GLEND. The moon shines fair; you may away by night:
I'll haste the writer, and withal
Break with your wives of your departure hence.
I am afraid my daughter will run mad, 145
So much she doteth on her Mortimer.
[*Exit.*

MORT. Fie, cousin Percy! how you cross my father!

HOT. I cannot choose: sometime he angers me
With telling me of the moldwarp and the ant,
Of the dreamer Merlin and his prophecies, 150
And of a dragon and a finless fish,
A clip-wing'd griffin and a moulten raven,
A couching lion and a ramping cat,
And such a deal of skimble-skamble stuff
As puts me from my faith. I tell you what:
He held me last night at least nine hours 156
In reckoning up the several devils' names
That were his lackeys: I cried "hum," and "well, go to,"
But mark'd him not a word. O, he is as tedious
As a tired horse, a railing wife; 160
Worse than a smoky house. I had rather live
With cheese and garlic in a windmill, far,
Than feed on cates and have him talk to me

96. **moiety**, share, usually one-half. 98. **comes me cranking in**, comes bending in on my portion. 100 **cantle**, slice, segment. 102. **smug**, tidy, well-kept. 104. **indent**, indentation. 105. **bottom**, valley. 110. **gelding**, cutting from; **opposed continent**, land on the opposite side. 112. **charge**, expense; **trench**, divert into a new channel. 123. **framed to the harp**, set to music for the harp. 131. **canstick**, brass candlestick being cut out on a lathe. 134. **mincing**, affectedly elegant. 143. **writer**, i.e., the scrivener who is to draw up the argument; **withal**, at the same time. 144. **Break with**, inform. 145. **run mad**, become crazy. 149. **moldwarp**, mole. 150. **Merlin**, the famous prophet, magician of Welsh fable. 152. **griffin**, a mythical monster, half lion and half eagle; **moulten**, moulting. 153. **couching**, couchant, a heraldic term, i.e., lying down with hand raised; **ramping**, rampant, also heraldic term, meaning rearing on his hind legs with paws extended. 154. **deal . . skamble**, lot of rambling. 155. **faith**, i.e., belief (in anything he says). 163. **cates**, delicacies.

In any summer-house in Christendom.
MORT. In faith, he is a worthy gentleman,
Exceedingly well read, and profited 166
In strange concealments, valiant as a lion
And wondrous affable and as bountiful
As mines of India. Shall I tell you, cousin?
He holds your temper in a high respect 170
And curbs himself even of his natural scope
When you come 'cross his humour; faith, he does:
I warrant you, that man is not alive
Might so have tempted him as you have done,
Without the taste of danger and reproof: 175
But do not use it oft, let me entreat you.
WOR. In faith, my lord, you are too wilful-blame;
And since your coming hither have done enough
To put him quite beside his patience.
You must needs learn, lord, to amend this fault: 180
Though sometimes it show greatness, courage, blood,—
And that's the dearest grace it renders you,—
Yet oftentimes it doth present harsh rage,
Defect of manners, want of government,
Pride, haughtiness, opinion and disdain: 185
The least of which haunting a nobleman
Loseth men's hearts and leaves behind a stain
Upon the beauty of all parts besides,
Beguiling them of commendation.
HOT. Well, I am school'd: good manners be your speed! 190
Here come our wives, and let us take our leave.

[*Re-enter* GLENDOWER *with the* LADIES.]

MORT. This is the deadly spite that angers me;
My wife can speak no English, I no Welsh.
GLEND. My daughter weeps: she will not part with you;
She'll be a soldier too, she'll to the wars. 195
MORT. Good father, tell her that she and my aunt Percy
Shall follow in your conduct speedily.
[GLENDOWER *speaks to her in Welsh, and she answers him in the same.*
GLEND. She is desperate here; a peevish self-will'd harlotry, one that no persuasion can do good upon. [*The* LADY *speaks in Welsh.*
MORT. I understand thy looks: that pretty Welsh 201
Which thou pour'st down from these swelling heavens
I am too perfect in; and, but for shame,
In such a parley should I answer thee.
[*The* LADY *speaks again in Welsh.*]
I understand thy kisses and thou mine, 205
And that's a feeling disputation:
But I will never be a truant, love,
Till I have learn'd thy language; for thy tongue
Makes Welsh as sweet as ditties highly penn'd,
Sung by a fair queen in a summer's bower, 210
With ravishing division, to her lute.
GLEND. Nay, if you melt, then will she run mad. [*The* LADY *speaks again in Welsh.*
MORT. O, I am ignorance itself in this!
GLEND. She bids you on the wanton rushes lay you down
And rest your gentle head upon her lap, 215
And she will sing the song that pleaseth you
And on your eyelids crown the god of sleep,
Charming your blood with pleasing heaviness,
Making such difference 'twixt wake and sleep
As is the difference betwixt day and night 220
The hour before the heavenly-harness'd team
Begins his golden progress in the east.
MORT. With all my heart I'll sit and hear her sing:
By that time will our book, I think, be drawn.
GLEND. Do so; 225
And those musicians that shall play to you
Hang in the air a thousand leagues from hence,
And straight they shall be here: sit, and attend.
HOT. Come, Kate, thou art perfect in lying down: come, quick, quick, that I may lay my head in thy lap. 231
LADY P. Go, ye giddy goose. [*Music plays.*
HOT. Now I perceive the devil understands Welsh;
And 'tis no marvel he is so humorous.
By'r lady, he is a good musician. 235
LADY P. Then should you be nothing but

166. profited, proficient. 167. concealments, occult arts. 171. curbs . . . scope, restrains even his natural expansiveness. 176. use it oft, often tempt his nature (as you just have). 177. wilful-blame, willfully blameworthy. 181. blood, spirit. 182. dearest, most valuable. 183. present, represent. 184. government, self-control. 185. opinion, obstinacy. 189. Beguiling, depriving. 192. spite, vexation. 197. in your conduct, under your escort. 199. harlotry, hussy. 206. disputation, conversation. 209. highly penn'd, extremely well composed. 211. division, a florid phrase in a melody. 214. wanton, luxurious, soft. 224. book, agreement. 234. humorous, capricious.

musical, for you are altogether governed by humours. Lie still, ye thief, and hear the lady sing in Welsh.

HOT. I had rather hear Lady, my brach, howl in Irish. 241

LADY P. Wouldst thou have thy head broken?

HOT. No.

LADY P. Then be still.

HOT. Neither; 'tis a woman's fault. 245

LADY P. Now God help thee!

HOT. To the Welsh lady's bed.

LADY P. What's that?

HOT. Peace! she sings.

[*Here the* LADY *sings a Welsh song.*

HOT. Come, Kate, I'll have your song too.

LADY P. Not mine, in good sooth. 251

HOT. Not yours, in good sooth! Heart! you swear like a comfit-maker's wife. "Not you, in good sooth," and "as true as I live," and "as God shall mend me," and "as sure as day,"
And givest such sarcenet surety for thy oaths,
As if thou never walk'st further than Finsbury.
Swear me, Kate, like a lady as thou art,
A good mouth-filling oath, and leave "in sooth,"
And such protest of pepper-gingerbread, 260
To velvet-guards and Sunday-citizens.
Come, sing.

LADY P. I will not sing.

HOT. 'Tis the next way to turn tailor, or be red-breast teacher. An the indentures be drawn, I'll away within these two hours; and so, come in when ye will. [*Exit.* 267

GLEND. Come, come, Lord Mortimer; you are as slow
As hot Lord Percy is on fire to go.
By this our book is drawn; we'll but seal, 270
And then to horse immediately.

MORT. With all my heart. [*Exeunt.*

SCENE II. *London. The palace.*

[*Enter the* KING, PRINCE OF WALES, *and others.*]

KING. Lords, give us leave; the Prince of Wales and I
Must have some private conference: but be near at hand,
For we shall presently have need of you.
[*Exeunt* LORDS.]
I know not whether God will have it so,
For some displeasing service I have done, 5
That, in his secret doom, out of my blood
He'll breed revengement and a scourge for me;
But thou dost in thy passages of life
Make me believe that thou art only mark'd
For the hot vengeance and the rod of heaven
To punish my mistreadings. Tell me else, 11
Could such inordinate and low desires,
Such poor, such bare, such lewd, such mean attempts,
Such barren pleasures, rude society,
As thou art match'd withal and grafted to, 15
Accompany the greatness of thy blood
And hold their level with thy princely heart?

PRINCE. So please your majesty, I would I could
Quit all offences with as clear excuse
As well as I am doubtless I can purge 20
Myself of many I am charged withal:
Yet such extenuation let me beg,
As, in reproof of many tales devised,
Which oft the ear of greatness needs must hear,
By smiling pick-thanks and base newsmongers, 25
I may, for some things true, wherein my youth
Hath faulty wander'd and irregular,
Find pardon on my true submission.

KING. God pardon thee! yet let me wonder, Harry,
At thy affections, which do hold a wing 30
Quite from the flight of all thy ancestors.
Thy place in council thou hast rudely lost,
Which by thy younger brother is supplied,
And art almost an alien to the hearts
Of all the court and princes of my blood: 35
The hope and expectation of thy time
Is ruin'd, and the soul of every man
Prophetically doth forethink thy fall.
Had I so lavish of my presence been,
So common-hackney'd in the eyes of men, 40
So stale and cheap to vulgar company,
Opinion, that did help me to the crown,

240. brach, bitch. 253. comfit-maker's, confectioner's. 256. sarcenet, silky, flimsy. 257. Finsbury, recreation and athletic ground outside the city, beyond Moorgate. 261. velvet-guards, velvet trimmings, then the citizens' wives who wore them. 264. turn tailor, tailors usually sang at their work. 265. red-breast teacher, trainer of song birds. 270. book is drawn, agreement is drawn up. Scene ii: 6. doom, judgment. 8. passages, courses. 19. quit, clear myself of. 20. as I am doubtless, I have no doubt. 23. reproof, disproof. 25. pick-thanks, flatterers. 30. affections, impulses. 36. time, reign. 42. opinion, i.e., public opinion.

Had still kept loyal to possession
And left me in reputeless banishment,
A fellow of no mark nor likelihood. 45
By being seldom seen, I could not stir
But like a comet I was wonder'd at;
That men would tell their children "This is he;"
Others would say "Where, which is Bolingbroke?"
And then I stole all courtesy from heaven, 50
And dress'd myself in such humility
That I did pluck allegiance from men's hearts,
Loud shouts and salutations from their mouths,
Even in the presence of the crowned king.
Thus did I keep my person fresh and new;
My presence, like a robe pontifical, 56
Ne'er seen but wonder'd at: and so my state,
Seldom but sumptuous, showed like a feast
And won by rareness such solemnity.
The skipping king, he ambled up and down 60
With shallow jesters and rash bavin wits,
Soon kindled and soon burnt; carded his state,
Mingled his royalty with capering fools,
Had his great name profanèd with their scorns
And gave his countenance, against his name,
To laugh at gibing boys and stand the push 66
Of every beardless vain comparative,
Grew a companion to the common streets,
Enfeoff'd himself to popularity;
That, being daily swallow'd by men's eyes, 70
They surfeited with honey and began
To loathe the taste of sweetness, whereof a little
More than a little is by much too much.
So when he had occasion to be seen,
He was but as the cuckoo is in June, 75
Heard, not regarded; seen, but with such eyes
As, sick and blunted with community,
Afford no extraordinary gaze,
Such as is bent on sun-like majesty
When it shines seldom in admiring eyes; 80
But rather drowsed and hung their eyelids down,
Slept in his face and render'd such aspect
As cloudy men use to their adversaries,
Being with his presence glutted, gorged and full. 84
And in that very line, Harry, standest thou;
For thou hast lost thy princely privilege
With vile participation: not an eye
But is a-weary of thy common sight,
Save mine, which hath desired to see thee more;
Which now doth that I would not have it do,
Make blind itself with foolish tenderness. 91

PRINCE. I shall hereafter, my thrice gracious lord,
Be more myself.

KING. For all the world
As thou art to this hour was Richard then
When I from France set foot at Ravenspurgh, 95
And even as I was then is Percy now.
Now, by my sceptre and my soul to boot,
He hath more worthy interest to the state
Than thou the shadow of succession;
For of no right, nor colour like to right, 100
He doth fill fields with harness in the realm,
Turns head against the lion's armèd jaws,
And, being no more in debt to years than thou,
Leads ancient lords and reverend bishops on
To bloody battles and to bruising arms. 105
What never-dying honour hath he got
Against renownèd Douglas! whose high deeds,
Whose hot incursions and great name in arms
Holds from all soldiers chief majority
And military title capital 110
Through all the kingdoms that acknowledge Christ:
Thrice hath this Hotspur, Mars in swathling clothes,
This infant warrior, in his enterprizes
Discomfited great Douglas, ta'en him once,
Enlargèd him and made a friend of him, 115
To fill the mouth of deep defiance up
And shake the peace and safety of our throne.
And what say you to this? Percy, Northumberland,
The Archbishop's grace of York, Douglas, Mortimer,
Capitulate against us and are up. 120
But wherefore do I tell these news to thee?
Why, Harry, do I tell thee of my foes,
Which art my near'st and dearest enemy?

43. possession, i.e., the sovereignty of Richard II. 45. likelihood, promise. 56. robe pontifical, a bishop's robe. 57. state, presence, bearing. 60. skipping, flighty. 61. bavin, brushwood, hence "easily kindled." 62. carded, diluted, debased. 66. stand the push, resist the attack. 67. comparative, rival (in strained wit). 69. Enfeoff'd . . . popularity, became a slave to low company. 77. community, familiarity. 82. face, presence. 87. vile participation, base association. 98. interest, claim. 99. shadow of succession, i.e., Hal's claim to the succession, compared to Percy's, is a mere shadow. 100. colour like, semblance. 101. harness, armor. 109. majority, pre-eminence. 110. capital, supreme. 115. enlarged him, set him free. 120. capitulate, make an agreement, i.e., combine; are up, are in rebellion.

Thou that art like enough, through vassal fear,
Base inclination and the start of spleen, 125
To fight against me under Percy's pay,
To dog his heels and curtsy at his frowns,
To show how much thou art degenerate.

PRINCE. Do not think so; you shall not find it so:
And God forgive them that so much have sway'd 130
Your majesty's good thoughts away from me!
I will redeem all this on Percy's head
And in the closing of some glorious day
Be bold to tell you that I am your son;
When I will wear a garment all of blood 135
And stain my favours in a bloody mask,
Which, wash'd away, shall scour my shame with it:
And that shall be the day, whene'er it lights,
That this same child of honour and renown,
This gallant Hotspur, this all-praisèd knight,
And your unthought-of Harry chance to meet.
For every honour sitting on his helm, 142
Would they were multitudes, and on my head
My shames redoubled! for the time will come,
That I shall make this northern youth exchange 145
His glorious deeds for my indignities.
Percy is but my factor, good my lord,
To engross up glorious deeds on my behalf;
And I will call him to so strict account,
That he shall render every glory up, 150
Yea, even the slightest worship of his time,
Or I will tear the reckoning from his heart.
This, in the name of God, I promise here:
The which if He be pleased I shall perform,
I do beseech your majesty may salve 155
The long-grown wounds of my intemperance:
If not, the end of life cancels all bands;
And I will die a hundred thousand deaths
Ere break the smallest parcel of this vow.

KING. A hundred thousand rebels die in this:
Thou shalt have charge and sovereign trust herein. 161

[*Enter* BLUNT.]

How now, good Blunt? thy looks are full of speed.

BLUNT. So hath the business that I come to speak of.
Lord Mortimer of Scotland hath sent word
That Douglas and the English rebels met 165
The eleventh of this month at Shrewsbury:
A mighty and a fearful head they are,
If promises be kept on every hand,
As ever offer'd foul play in a state.

KING. The Earl of Westmoreland set forth to-day; 170
With him my son, Lord John of Lancaster;
For this advertisement is five days old:
On Wednesday next, Harry, you shall set forward;
On Thursday we ourselves will march: our meeting 174
Is Bridgenorth: and, Harry, you shall march
Through Gloucestershire; by which account,
Our business valuèd, some twelve days hence
Our general forces at Bridgenorth shall meet.
Our hands are full of business: let's away;
Advantage feeds him fat, while men delay. 180

[*Exeunt.*

SCENE III. *Eastcheap. The Boar's-Head Tavern.*

[*Enter* FALSTAFF *and* BARDOLPH.]

FAL. Bardolph, am I not fallen away vilely since this last action? do I not bate? do I not dwindle? Why, my skin hangs about me like an old lady's loose gown; I am withered like an old apple-john. Well, I'll repent, and that suddenly, while I am in some liking; I shall 6 be out of heart shortly, and then I shall have no strength to repent. An I have not forgotten what the inside of a church is made of, I am a peppercorn, a brewer's horse: the inside of a church! Company, villanous company, hath been the spoil of me.

BARD. Sir John, you are so fretful, you cannot live long. 14

FAL. Why, there is it: come sing me a bawdy song; make me merry. I was as virtuously given as a gentleman need to be; virtuous

124. vassal, slavish. 125. start of spleen, burst of anger. 136. favours, features. 147. factor, agent. 148. engross up, amass; on my behalf, for my account. 157. bands, bonds. 161. charge and sovereign trust herein, command and supreme responsibility in this coming battle. 164. Lord . . . Scotland, Lord March of Scotland, whom Shakespeare evidently confused with the English Earl of March, properly called Mortimer. 167. head, armed force. 172. advertisement, news. 177. Our . . . valued, the time necessary for our business being estimated. 180. advantage . . . fat, opportunity fattens himself. Scene iii: 2. bate, waste away. 5. apple-john, a kind of apple whose flavor is improved by shriveling. 6. liking, good health. 10. peppercorn, dried berry of the pepper plant; brewer's horse, i.e., a heavy, stupid horse. 17. given, inclined.

enough; swore little; diced not above seven times a week; went to a bawdy-house not above once in a quarter—of an hour; paid money that I borrowed, three or four times; lived well and in good compass: and now I live out of all order, out of all compass. 23

BARD. Why, you are so fat, Sir John, that you must needs be out of all compass, out of all reasonable compass, Sir John.

FAL. Do thou amend thy face, and I'll amend my life: thou art our admiral, thou bearest the lantern in the poop, but 'tis in the nose of thee; thou art the Knight of the Burning Lamp. 30

BARD. Why, Sir John, my face does you no harm.

FAL. No, I'll be sworn; I make as good use of it as many a man doth of a Death's-head or a memento mori: I never see thy face but I think upon hell-fire and Dives that lived in 35 purple; for there he is in his robes, burning, burning. If thou wert any way given to virtue, I would swear by thy face; my oath should be "By this fire, that's God's angel:" but thou art altogether given over; and wert in- 40 deed, but for the light in thy face, the son of utter darkness. When thou rannest up Gadshill in the night to catch my horse, if I did not think thou hadst been an ignis fatuus or a ball of wildfire, there's no purchase 45 in money. O, thou art a perpetual triumph, an everlasting bonfire-light! Thou hast saved me a thousand marks in links and torches, walking with thee in the night betwixt tavern and tavern: but the sack that thou hast 50 drunk me would have bought me lights as good cheap at the dearest chandler's in Europe. I have maintained that salamander of yours with fire any time this two and thirty years; God reward me for it! 55

BARD. 'Sblood, I would my face were in your belly!

FAL. God-a-mercy! so should I be sure to be heart-burned.

[*Enter* HOSTESS.]

How now, Dame Partlet the hen! have you inquired yet who picked my pocket? 61

HOST. Why, Sir John, what do you think, Sir John? do you think I keep thieves in my house? I have searched, I have inquired, so has my husband, man by man, boy by boy, servant by servant: the tithe of a hair was never lost in my house before.

FAL. Ye lie, hostess: Bardolph was shaved and lost many a hair; and I'll be sworn my pocket was picked. Go to, you are a woman, go. 70

HOST. Who, I? no; I defy thee: God's light, I was never called so in mine own house before.

FAL. Go to, I know you well enough.

HOST. No, Sir John; you do not know me, Sir John. I know you, Sir John: you owe me money, Sir John; and now you pick a quarrel to beguile me of it: I bought you a dozen of shirts to your back.

FAL. Dowlas, filthy dowlas: I have given them away to bakers' wives, and they have made bolters of them. 81

HOST. Now, as I am a true woman, holland of eight shillings an ell. You owe money here besides, Sir John, for your diet and by-drinkings, and money lent you, four and twenty pound.

FAL. He had his part of it; let him pay.

HOST. He? alas, he is poor; he hath nothing. 88

FAL. How! poor? look upon his face; what call you rich? let them coin his nose, let them coin his cheeks: I'll not pay a denier. What, will you make a younker of me? shall I not take mine ease in mine inn but I shall have my pocket picked? I have lost a seal-ring of my grandfather's worth forty mark. 95

HOST. O Jesu, I have heard the prince tell him, I know not how oft, that that ring was copper!

FAL. How! the prince is a Jack, a sneak-cup: 'sblood, an he were here, I would cudgel him like a dog, if he would say so. 101

22. **good compass,** reasonable limits. 25. **compass,** girth. 28. **admiral,** flag ship. 29. **poop,** stern. 34. **memento mori,** reminder of death, usually a skull and crossbones. 35. **Dives,** the rich man in the parable told by Luke 16: 19-31. 39. **God's angel,** an illusion to Psalms 104: 4. 44. **ignis fatuus,** will-o-the-wisp. 45. **wild-fire,** also will-o-the-wisp. 46. **triumph,** pageant. 48. **links,** torches. 53. **salamander,** a lizard supposed to live in fire. 60. **Partlet,** a traditional name for a hen. 66. **tithe,** literally a tenth part, then any very small part. 68. **shaved,** infected with syphilis. 79. **dowlas,** coarse linen cloth. 81. **bolters,** cloths for sifting meal. 82. **holland,** fine linen. 83. **ell,** 45 inches. 84-5. **by-drinkings,** drinks between meals. 91. **denier,** very small coin worth about 1/10 of a penny. 92. **younker,** greenhorn. 99. **Jack,** knave; **sneak-cup,** one who shirks in drinking.

[*Enter the* PRINCE *and* PETO, *marching, and* FALSTAFF *meets them playing on his truncheon like a fife.*]

How now, lad! is the wind in that door, i' faith? must we all march?

BARD. Yea, two and two, Newgate fashion.

HOST. My lord, I pray you, hear me. 105

PRINCE. What sayest thou, Mistress Quickly? How doth thy husband? I love him well; he is an honest man.

HOST. Good my lord, hear me.

FAL. Prithee, let her alone, and list to me.

PRINCE. What sayest thou, Jack? 111

FAL. The other night I fell asleep here behind the arras and had my pocket picked: this house is turned bawdy-house; they pick pockets.

PRINCE. What didst thou lose, Jack? 115

FAL. Wilt thou believe me, Hal? three or four bonds of forty pound a-piece, and a seal-ring of my grandfather's.

PRINCE. A trifle, some eight-penny matter. 119

HOST. So I told him, my lord; and I said I heard your grace say so: and, my lord, he speaks most vilely of you, like a foul-mouthed man as he is; and said he would cudgel you.

PRINCE. What! he did not?

HOST. There's neither faith, truth, nor womanhood in me else. 126

FAL. There's no more faith in thee than in a stewed prune; nor no more truth in thee than in a drawn fox; and for womanhood, Maid Marian may be the deputy's wife of the ward to thee. Go, you thing, go. 131

HOST. Say, what thing! what thing?

FAL. What thing? why, a thing to thank God on.

HOST. I am no thing to thank God on, I would thou shouldst know it; I am an honest man's wife: and, setting thy knighthood aside, thou art a knave to call me so.

FAL. Setting thy womanhood aside, thou art a beast to say otherwise. 140

HOST. Say, what beast, thou knave, thou?

FAL. What beast! why, an otter.

PRINCE. An otter, Sir John! why an otter?

FAL. Why, she's neither fish nor flesh; a man knows not where to have her. 145

HOST. Thou art an unjust man in saying so: thou or any man knows where to have me, thou knave, thou!

PRINCE. Thou sayest true, hostess; and he slanders thee most grossly. 150

HOST. So he doth you, my lord; and said this other day you ought him a thousand pound.

PRINCE. Sirrah, do I owe you a thousand pound? 155

FAL. A thousand pound, Hal! a million: thy love is worth a million: thou owest me thy love.

HOST. Nay, my lord, he called you Jack, and said he would cudgel you.

FAL. Did I, Bardolph? 160

BARD. Indeed, Sir John, you said so.

FAL. Yea, if he said my ring was copper.

PRINCE. I say 'tis copper: darest thou be as good as thy word now? 164

FAL. Why, Hal, thou knowest, as thou art but man, I dare: but as thou art prince, I fear thee as I fear the roaring of the lion's whelp.

PRINCE. And why not as the lion?

FAL. The king himself is to be feared as the lion: dost thou think I'll fear thee as I fear thy father? nay, an I do, I pray God my girdle break. 171

PRINCE. O, if it should, how would thy guts fall about thy knees! But, sirrah, there's no room for faith, truth, nor honesty in this bosom of thine; it is all filled up with guts and midriff. Charge an honest woman with 175 picking thy pocket! why, thou whoreson, impudent, embossed rascal, if there were anything in thy pocket but tavern-reckonings, memorandums of bawdy-houses, and one poor penny-worth of sugar-candy to make thee long-winded, if thy pocket were enriched with any other injuries but these, I am a villain: and yet you will stand to it; you will not pocket up wrong: art thou not 184 ashamed?

FAL. Dost thou hear, Hal? thou knowest in the state of innocency Adam fell; and what should poor Jack Falstaff do in the days of villany? Thou seest I have more

104. **Newgate**, a London prison; **fashion**, chained together, two and two. 129. **drawn fox**, drawn away from his hole and so full of tricks to get back. 130. **Maid Marian**, an awkward character in the Morris dance; **deputy**, the Deputy of the Ward acted as magistrate in the absence of the Alderman. His wife was, of course, a stately creature. 145. **have**, classify. 152. **ought**, owed. 177. **embossed**, swollen, i.e., with fat. 182. **injuries**, "to pocket injuries" was a common phrase. Here "injuries" = contemptible objects. 188. **days of villainy**, i.e., these wicked times.

flesh than another man, and therefore more frailty. You confess then, you picked my pocket? 190

PRINCE. It appears so by the story.

FAL. Hostess, I forgive thee: go, make ready breakfast; love thy husband, look to thy servants, cherish thy guests: thou shalt find me tractable to any honest reason: thou seest I am pacified still. Nay, prithee, be gone. [*Exit* HOSTESS.] Now, Hal, to the news at 196 court: for the robbery, lad, how is that answered?

PRINCE. O, my sweet beef, I must still be good angel to thee: the money is paid back again. 200

FAL. O, I do not like that paying back; 'tis a double labour.

PRINCE. I am good friends with my father and may do any thing.

FAL. Rob me the exchequer the first thing thou doest, and do it with unwashed hands too.

BARD. Do, my lord.

PRINCE. I have procured thee, Jack, a charge of foot. 209

FAL. I would it had been of horse. Where shall I find one that can steal well? O for a fine thief, of the age of two and twenty or thereabouts! I am heinously unprovided. Well, God be thanked for these rebels, they offend none but the virtuous: I laud them, I praise them.

PRINCE. Bardolph! 216

BARD. My lord?

PRINCE. Go bear this letter to Lord John of Lancaster, to my brother John; this to my Lord of Westmoreland. [*Exit* BARDOLPH.] Go, Peto, to horse, to horse; for thou and I have thirty miles to ride yet ere dinner time. [*Exit* PETO.] Jack, meet me to-morrow in the Temple hall at two o'clock in the afternoon.
There shalt thou know thy charge; and there receive 225
Money and order for their furniture.
The land is burning; Percy stands on high;
And either we or they must lower lie. [*Exit.*

FAL. Rare words! brave world! Hostess, my breakfast, come! 229
O, I could wish this tavern were my drum! [*Exit.*

194. tractable, amenable. 198. still, always. 205. with unwashed hands, i.e., in haste, at once. 213. heinously

ACT IV

SCENE I. *The rebel camp near Shrewsbury.*

[*Enter* HOTSPUR, WORCESTER, *and* DOUGLAS.]

HOT. Well said, my noble Scot: if speaking truth
In this fine age were not thought flattery,
Such attribution should the Douglas have,
As not a soldier of this season's stamp
Should go so general current through the world. 5
By God, I cannot flatter; I do defy
The tongues of soothers; but a braver place
In my heart's love hath no man than yourself:
Nay, task me to my word; approve me, lord.

DOUG. Thou art the king of honour: 10
No man so potent breathes upon the ground
But I will beard him.

HOT. Do so, and 'tis well.

[*Enter a* MESSENGER *with letters.*]

What letters hast thou there?—I can but thank you.

MESS. These letters come from your father.

HOT. Letters from him! why comes he not himself? 15

MESS. He cannot come, my lord; he is grievous sick.

HOT. 'Zounds! how has he the leisure to be sick
In such a justling time? Who leads his power?
Under whose government come they along?

MESS. His letters bear his mind, not I, my lord. 20

WOR. I prithee, tell me, doth he keep his bed?

MESS. He did, my lord, four days ere I set forth;
And at the time of my departure thence

unprovided, disgracefully badly equipped. 224. Temple Hall, Hall of the Inner Temple, one of the residences of law students. 226. furniture, equipment. 230. drum, drummer. The captain was always accompanied by a drummer. Falstaff wishes the tavern were always with him. Act IV, Scene i: 3. attribution, citation of honors. 4. season's stamp, minted in this year. 7. soothers, flatterers; braver, superior. 9. task . . . word, put my promise to proof. 18. justling, jostling, busy.

He was much fear'd by his physicians.
WOR. I would the state of time had first been whole 25
Ere he by sickness had been visited:
His health was never better worth than now.
HOT. Sick now! droop now! this sickness doth infect
The very life-blood of our enterprise;
'Tis catching hither, even to our camp. 30
He writes me here, that inward sickness—
And that his friends by deputation could not
So soon be drawn, nor did he think it meet
To lay so dangerous and dear a trust
On any soul removed but on his own. 35
Yet doth he give us bold advertisement,
That with our small conjunction we should on,
To see how fortune is disposed to us;
For, as he writes, there is no quailing now,
Because the king is certainly possess'd 40
Of all our purposes. What say you to it?
WOR. Your father's sickness is a maim to us.
HOT. A perilous gash, a very limb lopp'd off:
And yet, in faith, it is not; his present want
Seems more than we shall find it: were it good
To set the exact wealth of all our states 46
All at one cast? to set so rich a main
On the nice hazard of one doubtful hour?
It were not good; for therein should we read
The very bottom and the soul of hope, 50
The very list, the very utmost bound
Of all our fortunes.
DOUG. 'Faith, and so we should;
Where now remains a sweet reversion:
We may boldly spend upon the hope of what
Is to come in: 55
A comfort of retirement lives in this.
HOT. A rendezvous, a home to fly unto,
If that the devil and mischange look big
Upon the maidenhead of our affairs.
WOR. But yet I would your father had been here. 60
The quality and hair of our attempt
Brooks no division: it will be thought
By some, that know not why he is away,
That wisdom, loyalty and mere dislike
Of our proceedings kept the earl from hence:
And think how such an apprehension 66
May turn the tide of fearful faction
And breed a kind of question in our cause;
For well you know we of the offering side
Must keep aloof from strict arbitrement, 70
And stop all sight-holes, every loop from whence
The eye of reason may pry in upon us:
This absence of your father's draws a curtain,
That shows the ignorant a kind of fear
Before not dreamt of.
HOT. You strain too far. 75
I rather of his absence make this use:
It lends a lustre and more great opinion,
A larger dare to our great enterprise,
Than if the earl were here; for men must think,
If we without his help can make a head 80
To push against a kingdom, with his help
We shall o'erturn it topsy-turvy down.
Yet all goes well, yet all our joints are whole.
DOUG. As heart can think: there is not such a word
Spoke of in Scotland as this term of fear. 85

[*Enter* SIR RICHARD VERNON.]

HOT. My cousin Vernon! welcome, by my soul.
VER. Pray God my news be worth a welcome, lord.
The Earl of Westmoreland, seven thousand strong,
Is marching hitherwards; with him Prince John.
HOT. No harm: what more?
VER. And further, I have learn'd, 90
The king himself in person is set forth,
Or hitherwards intended speedily,
With strong and mighty preparation.
HOT. He shall be welcome too. Where is his son, 94
The nimble-footed madcap Prince of Wales,
And his comrades, that daff'd the world aside,
And bid it pass?
VER. All furnish'd, all in arms;
All plumed like estridges that with the wind

24. **fear'd**, feared for. 32. **by deputation**, by means of agents. 35. **soul removed**, person remotely concerned. 36. **advertisement**, advice. 37. **conjunction**, joint forces. 44. **want**, absence. 46. **set**, risk. 47. **cast**, throw of the dice; main, stake. 48. **nice hazard**, delicately balanced (i.e., precarious) risk. 51. **list**, limit. 53. **where**, whereas; reversion, hope of future inheritance or profit. 56. **comfort of retirement**, support to which we may turn.

58. **look big**, i.e., threaten. 61. **hair**, fabric, i.e., nature. 67. **fearful faction**, timid conspirators. 69. **offering**, attacking. 70. **arbitrement**, judicial inquiry. 74. **fear**, i.e., on our side. 77. **opinion**, credit. 80. **make a head**, raise a force. 96. **daff'd**, thrust. 98. **estridges**, goshawks, a reference to the plumes on the birds' crest.

Baited like eagles having lately bathed;
Glittering in golden coats, like images; 100
As full of spirit as the month of May,
And gorgeous as the sun at midsummer;
Wanton as youthful goats, wild as young bulls.
I saw young Harry, with his beaver on,
His cuisses on his thighs, gallantly arm'd, 105
Rise from the ground like feather'd Mercury,
And vaulted with such ease into his seat,
As if an angel dropp'd down from the clouds,
To turn and wind a fiery Pegasus
And witch the world with noble horsemanship. 110

HOT. No more, no more: worse than the sun in March,
This praise doth nourish agues. Let them come;
They come like sacrifices in their trim,
And to the fire-eyed maid of smoky war
All hot and bleeding will we offer them: 115
The mailèd Mars shall on his altar sit
Up to the ears in blood. I am on fire
To hear this rich reprisal is so nigh
And yet not ours. Come, let me taste my horse,
Who is to bear me like a thunderbolt 120
Against the bosom of the Prince of Wales:
Harry to Harry shall, hot horse to horse,
Meet and ne'er part till one drop down a corse.
O that Glendower were come!

VER. There is more news:
I learn'd in Worcester, as I rode along, 125
He cannot draw his power this fourteen days.

DOUG. That's the worst tidings that I hear of yet.

WOR. Ay, by my faith, that bears a frosty sound.

HOT. What may the king's whole battle reach unto?

VER. To thirty thousand.

HOT. Forty let it be: 130
My father and Glendower being both away,
The powers of us may serve so great a day.
Come, let us take a muster speedily:
Doomsday is near; die all, die merrily.

DOUG. Talk not of dying: I am out of fear
Of death or death's hand for this one-half year. [*Exeunt.* 136

SCENE II. *A public road near Coventry.*

[*Enter* FALSTAFF *and* BARDOLPH.]

FAL. Bardolph, get thee before to Coventry; fill me a bottle of sack: our soldiers shall march through; we'll to Sutton Co'fil' to-night.

BARD. Will you give me money, captain?

FAL. Lay out, lay out. 5

BARD. This bottle makes an angel.

FAL. An if it do, take it for thy labour; and if it make twenty, take them all; I'll answer the coinage. Bid my lieutenant Peto meet me at town's end. 10

BARD. I will, captain: farewell. [*Exit.*

FAL. If I be not ashamed of my soldiers, I am a soused gurnet. I have misused the 13 king's press damnably. I have got, in exchange of a hundred and fifty soldiers, three hundred and odd pounds. I press me none but good householders, yeomen's sons; inquire me out contracted bachelors, such as had been asked twice on the banns; such a commodity of warm slaves, as had as lieve hear the devil as a drum; such as fear the report of a caliver worse than a struck fowl or a hurt wild-duck. 20 I pressed me none but such toasts-and-butter, with hearts in their bellies no bigger than pins' heads, and they have bought out their services; and now my whole charge consists of ancients, corporals, lieutenants, 25 gentlemen of companies, slaves as ragged as Lazarus in the painted cloth, where the glutton's dogs licked his sores; and such as indeed were never soldiers, but discarded unjust serving-men, younger sons to younger 30 brothers, revolted tapsters and ostlers trade-fallen, the cankers of a calm world and a long peace, ten times more dishonourable ragged than an old faced ancient: and such have I, to fill up the rooms of them that have 35 bought out their services, that you would think

99. **bathed**, "bated," meaning "beating their wings," is a better reading. 100. **images**, i.e., images of saints. 104. **beaver**, visor, here used for the entire helmet. 105. **cuisses**, thigh armor. 109. **wind**, wheel. 110. **witch**, bewitch. 113. **sacrifices in their trim**, decked out like sacrificial animals. 118. **reprisal**, prize. 129. **battle**, army. **Scene ii**: 3. **Sutton Co'fil'**, Sutton Coldfield, near Coventry in Warwickshire. 5. **lay out**, spend freely, cf. modern "shell out." 6. **makes an angel**, i.e., makes 10s. I have spent.

8. **answer**, take the responsibility for. 13. **soused gurnet**, pickled gurnard (a fish we call searobbin). 14. **king's press**, royal warrant for conscription of troops. 17. **yeomen**, small land owner. 17. **contracted**, engaged to be married. 18. **commodity**, assortment. 20. **caliver**, musket. 25. **ancients**, flag bearers. 27. **painted cloth**, hangings, a cheap substitute for tapestry. 32. **trade-fallen**, out of a job; **cankers**, canker worms. 34. **faced**, better reading feaz'd = frayed; **ancient**, flag.

that I had a hundred and fifty tattered prodigals lately come from swine-keeping, from eating draff and husks. A mad fellow met me on the way and told me I had unloaded all the gibbets and pressed the dead bodies. No 40 eye hath seen such scarecrows. I'll not march through Coventry with them, that's flat: nay, and the villains march wide betwixt the legs, as if they had gyves on; for indeed I had the most of them out of prison. There's but 45 a shirt and a half in all my company; and the half shirt is two napkins tacked together and thrown over the shoulders like a herald's coat without sleeves; and the shirt, to say the truth, stolen from my host at Saint Alban's, or the red-nose inkeeper of Daventry. But that's 50 all one; they'll find linen enough on every hedge.

[*Enter the* PRINCE *and* WESTMORELAND.]

PRINCE. How now, blown Jack! how now, quilt.

FAL. What, Hal! how now, mad wag! what a devil dost thou in Warwickshire? My good Lord of Westmoreland, I cry you mercy: I thought your honour had already been at Shrewsbury. 59

WEST. Faith, Sir John, 'tis more than time that I were there, and you too; but my powers are there already. The king, I can tell you, looks for us all: we must away all night.

FAL. Tut, never fear me: I am as vigilant as a cat to steal cream. 65

PRINCE. I think, to steal cream indeed, for thy theft hath already made thee butter. But tell me, Jack, whose fellows are these that come after?

FAL. Mine, Hal, mine.

PRINCE. I did never see such pitiful rascals. 70

FAL. Tut, tut; good enough to toss; food for powder, food for powder; they'll fill a pit as well as better: tush, man, mortal men, mortal men.

WEST. Ay, but Sir John, methinks they are exceeding poor and bare, too beggarly. 75

FAL. 'Faith, for their poverty, I know not where they had that; and for their bareness, I am sure they never learned that of me.

PRINCE. No, I'll be sworn; unless you call three fingers on the ribs bare. But, sirrah, make haste: Percy is already in the field. 81

FAL. What, is the king encamped?

WEST. He is, Sir John: I fear we shall stay too long.

FAL. Well.
To the latter end of a fray and the beginning of a feast
Fits a dull fighter and a keen guest. [*Exeunt.*

SCENE III. *The rebel camp near Shrewsbury.*

[*Enter* HOTSPUR, WORCESTER, DOUGLAS, *and* VERNON.]

HOT. We'll fight with him to-night.
WOR. It may not be.
DOUG. You give him then advantage.
VER. Not a whit.
HOT. Why say you so? looks he not for supply?
VER. So do we.
HOT. His is certain, ours is doubtful.
WOR. Good cousin, be advised; stir not to-night. 5
VER. Do not, my lord.
DOUG. You do not counsel well:
You speak it out of fear and cold heart.
VER. Do me no slander, Douglas: by my life,
And I dare well maintain it with my life,
If well-respected honour bid me on, 10
I hold as little counsel with weak fear
As you, my lord, or any Scot that this day lives:
Let it be seen to-morrow in the battle
Which of us fears.
DOUG. Yea, or to-night.
VER. Content.
HOT. To-night, say I. 15
VER. Come, come, it may not be. I wonder much,
Being men of such great leading as you are,
That you foresee not what impediments
Drag back our expedition: certain horse
Of my cousin Vernon's are not yet come up:
Your uncle Worcester's horse came but to-day; 21
And now their pride and mettle is asleep,

38. **draff,** hog wash. 45. **gyves,** shackles. 57. **cry you mercy,** beg your pardon. 63. **must away,** keep marching. 71. **toss,** i.e., on a pike. 75. **bare,** threadbare. 76. **for,** as for. 80. **three fingers,** i.e., the breadth of three fingers.

Scene iii: 3. **supply,** reinforcements. 10. **well-respected,** well-considered. 17. **leading,** leadership. 19. **expedition,** haste. 22. **mettle,** vigor.

Their courage with hard labour tame and dull,
That not a horse is half the half of himself.
HOT. So are the horses of the enemy 25
In general, journey-bated and brought low:
The better part of ours are full of rest.
WOR. The number of the king exceedeth ours:
For God's sake, cousin, stay till all come in.
[*The trumpet sounds a parley.*

[*Enter* SIR WALTER BLUNT.]

BLUNT. I come with gracious offers from the king, 30
If you vouchsafe me hearing and respect.
HOT. Welcome, Sir Walter Blunt; and would to God
You were of our determination!
Some of us love you well; and even those some
Envy your great deservings and good name, 35
Because you are not of our quality,
But stand against us like an enemy.
BLUNT. And God defend but still I should stand so,
So long as out of limit and true rule
You stand against anointed majesty. 40
But to my charge. The king hath sent to know
The nature of your griefs, and whereupon
You conjure from the breast of civil peace
Such bold hostility, teaching his duteous land
Audacious cruelty. If that the king 45
Have any way your good deserts forgot,
Which he confesseth to be manifold,
He bids you name your griefs; and with all speed
You shall have your desires with interest
And pardon absolute for yourself and these 50
Herein misled by your suggestion.
HOT. The king is kind; and well we know the king
Knows at what time to promise, when to pay.
My father and my uncle and myself
Did give him that same royalty he wears; 55
And when he was not six and twenty strong,
Sick in the world's regard, wretched and low,
A poor unminded outlaw sneaking home,
My father gave him welcome to the shore;
And when he heard him swear and vow to God 60
He came but to be Duke of Lancaster,
To sue his livery and beg his peace,
With tears of innocency and terms of zeal,
My father, in kind heart and pity moved,
Swore him assistance and perform'd it too. 65
Now when the lords and barons of the realm
Perceived Northumberland did lean to him,
The more and less came in with cap and knee;
Met him in boroughs, cities, villages,
Attended him on bridges, stood in lanes, 70
Laid gifts before him, proffer'd him their oaths,
Gave him their heirs, as pages follow'd him
Even at the heels in golden multitudes.
He presently, as greatness knows itself,
Steps me a little higher than his vow 75
Made to my father, while his blood was poor,
Upon the naked shore at Ravenspurgh;
And now, forsooth, takes on him to reform
Some certain edicts and some strait decrees
That lie too heavy on the commonwealth, 80
Cries out upon abuses, seems to weep
Over his country's wrongs; and by this face,
This seeming brow of justice, did he win
The hearts of all that he did angle for;
Proceeded further; cut me off the heads 85
Of all the favourites that the absent king
In deputation left behind him here,
When he was personal in the Irish war.
BLUNT. Tut, I came not to hear this.
HOT. Then to the point.
In short time after, he deposed the king; 90
Soon after that, deprived him of his life;
And in the neck of that, task'd the whole state;
To make that worse, suffer'd his kinsman March,
Who is, if every owner were well placed,
Indeed his king, to be engaged in Wales, 95
There without ransom to lie forfeited;
Disgraced me in my happy victories,
Sought to entrap me by intelligence;
Rated mine uncle from the council-board;

26. **journey-bated**, tired from travel. s.d. **trumpet**, trumpeter, i.e., of the theatre. 33. **determination**, resoluteness. 36. **quality**, fellowship. 38. **defend**, forbid. 39. **out of limit**, beyond the jurisdiction; **rule**, government. 42. **whereupon**, for that reason. 51. **suggestion**, instigation. 62. **sue his livery**, claim the lands his by right of inheritance. 68. **the more and less**, those of both high and low estate; **with . . . knee**, i.e., kneeling with cap in hand. 73. **golden**, richly attired. 76. **blood was poor**, in low spirits. 88. **personal**, in person. 92. **in the neck of**, following that immediately; **task'd**, taxed. 95. **engaged**, held as a hostage. 98. **intelligence**, information derived from spies. 99. **rated**, drove by scolding.

In rage dismiss'd my father from the court;
Broke oath on oath, committed wrong on wrong, 101
And in conclusion drove us to seek out
This head of safety; and withal to pry
Into his title, the which we find
Too indirect for long continuance. 105

BLUNT. Shall I return this answer to the king?

HOT. Not so, Sir Walter: we'll withdraw awhile.
Go to the king; and let there be impawn'd
Some surety for a safe return again,
And in the morning early shall my uncle 110
Bring him our purposes: and so farewell.

BLUNT. I would you would accept of grace and love.

HOT. And may be so we shall.

BLUNT. Pray God you do.
[*Exeunt.*

SCENE IV. *York. The* ARCHBISHOP'S *palace.*

[*Enter the* ARCHBISHOP OF YORK *and* SIR MICHAEL.]

ARCH. Hie, good Sir Michael; bear this sealed brief
With wingèd haste to the lord marshal;
This to my cousin Scroop, and all the rest
To whom they are directed. If you knew
How much they do import, you would make haste. 5

SIR. M. My good lord,
I guess their tenour.

ARCH. Like enough you do.
To-morrow, good Sir Michael, is a day
Wherein the fortune of ten thousand men
Must bide the touch; for, sir, at Shrewsbury,
As I am truly given to understand, 11
The king with mighty and quick-raisèd power
Meets with Lord Harry: and, I fear, Sir Michael,
What with the sickness of Northumberland,
Whose power was in the first proportion, 15
And what with Owen Glendower's absence thence,
Who with them was a rated sinew too
And comes not in, o'er-ruled by prophecies,
I fear the power of Percy is too weak
To wage an instant trial with the king. 20

SIR M. Why, my good lord, you need not fear;
There is Douglas and Lord Mortimer.

ARCH. No, Mortimer is not there.

SIR M. But there is Mordake, Vernon, Lord Harry Percy,
And there is my Lord of Worcester and a head 25
Of gallant warriors, noble gentlemen.

ARCH. And so there is: but yet the king hath drawn
The special head of all the land together:
The Prince of Wales, Lord John of Lancaster,
The noble Westmoreland and warlike Blunt;
And many moe corrivals and dear men 31
Of estimation and command in arms.

SIR M. Doubt not, my lord, they shall be well opposed.

ARCH. I hope no less, yet needful 'tis to fear;
And, to prevent the worst, Sir Michael, speed: 35
For if Lord Percy thrive not, ere the king
Dismiss his power, he means to visit us,
For he hath heard of our confederacy,
And 'tis but wisdom to make strong against him: 39
Therefore make haste. I must go write again
To other friends; and so farewell, Sir Michael.
[*Exeunt.*

ACT V

SCENE I. *The* KING'S *camp near Shrewsbury.*

[*Enter the* KING, PRINCE OF WALES, LORD JOHN OF LANCASTER, EARL OF WESTMORELAND, SIR WALTER BLUNT, *and* FALSTAFF.]

KING. How bloodily the sun begins to peer
Above yon busky hill! the day looks pale
At his distemperature.

PRINCE. The southern wind

103. **head of safety,** protecting army. 105. **Too indirect,** in too indirect a line. Scene iv: 1. **brief,** dispatch. 2. **lord marshal,** Earl of Norfolk. 10. **bide the touch,** be put to the test. 15. **proportion,** magnitude. 17. **rated sinew,** highly regarded force. 31. **moe corrivals,** more confederates; **dear,** worthy. 32. **estimation,** reputation. Act V, Scene i: 2. **busky,** wooded. 3. **his,** i.e., the sun's; **distemperature,** unusual appearance.

Doth play the trumpet to his purposes,
And by his hollow whistling in the leaves 5
Foretells a tempest and a blustering day.

KING. Then with the losers let it sympathise,
For nothing can seem foul to those that win.
[*The trumpet sounds.*]

[*Enter* WORCESTER *and* VERNON.]

How now, my Lord of Worcester! 'tis not well 9
That you and I should meet upon such terms
As now we meet. You have deceived our trust,
And made us doff our easy robes of peace,
To crush our old limbs in ungentle steel:
This is not well, my lord, this is not well.
What say you to it? will you again unknit 15
This churlish knot of all-abhorrèd war?
And move in that obedient orb again
Where you did give a fair and natural light,
And be no more an exhaled meteor,
A prodigy of fear and a portent 20
Of broachèd mischief to the unborn times?

WOR. Hear me, my liege:
For mine own part, I could be well content
To entertain the lag-end of my life
With quiet hours; for I do protest, 25
I have not sought the day of this dislike.

KING. You have not sought it! how comes it, then?

FAL. Rebellion lay in his way, and he found it.

PRINCE. Peace, chewet, peace!

WOR. It pleased your majesty to turn your looks 30
Of favour from myself and all our house;
And yet I must remember you, my lord,
We were the first and dearest of your friends.
For you my staff of office did I break
In Richard's time; and posted day and night
To meet you on the way, and kiss your hand, 36
When yet you were in place and in account
Nothing so strong and fortunate as I.
It was myself, my brother and his son,
That brought you home and boldly did outdare 40
The dangers of the time. You swore to us,
And you did swear that oath at Doncaster,
That you did nothing purpose 'gainst the state;
Nor claim no further than your new-fall'n right,
The seat of Gaunt, dukedom of Lancaster: 45
To this we swore our aid. But in short space
It rain'd down fortune showering on your head;
And such a flood of greatness fell on you,
What with our help, what with the absent king,
What with the injuries of a wanton time, 50
The seeming sufferances that you had borne,
And the contrarious winds that held the king
So long in his unlucky Irish wars
That all in England did repute him dead:
And from this swarm of fair advantages 55
You took occasion to be quickly woo'd
To gripe the general sway into your hand;
Forgot your oath to us at Doncaster;
And being fed by us you used us so
As that ungentle gull, the cuckoo's bird, 60
Useth the sparrow; did oppress our nest;
Grew by our feeding to so great a bulk
That even our love durst not come near your sight
For fear of swallowing; but with nimble wing
We were enforced, for safety sake, to fly 65
Out of your sight and raise this present head;
Whereby we stand opposèd by such means
As you yourself have forged against yourself
By unkind usage, dangerous countenance,
And violation of all faith and troth 70
Sworn to us in your younger enterprise.

KING. These things indeed you have articulate,
Proclaim'd at market-crosses, read in churches,
To face the garment of rebellion
With some fine colour that may please the eye 75
Of fickle changelings and poor discontents,
Which gape and rub the elbow at the news
Of hurlyburly innovation:

4. **trumpet**, trumpeter. 17. **orb**, sphere of action. 19. **exhaled**, i.e., drawn up from the earth by the heat of the sun. 21. **broached**, already tapped, i.e., loosed. 29. **chewet**, jackdaw, hence "witless chatterer." 32. **remember you**, call to your mind. 45. **seat**, estate. 50. **injuries**, evils; **wanton**, unruly, rebellious. 51. **sufferances**, suffering. 60. **gull**, nestling; the cuckoo lays its eggs in the sparrow's nest and the larger fledgling crowds out the sparrow's young. 64. **swallowing**, being swallowed. 69. **dangerous countenance**, threatening looks. 72. **articulate**, specified in articles. 74. **face**, adorn. 78. **innovation**, change producing civil confusion, hence revolution.

And never yet did insurrection want
Such water-colours to impaint his cause; 80
Nor moody beggars, starving for a time
Of pellmell havoc and confusion.

PRINCE. In both your armies there is many a soul
Shall pay full dearly for this encounter,
If once they join in trial. Tell your nephew,
The Prince of Wales doth join with all the world 86
In praise of Henry Percy: by my hopes,
This present enterprise set off his head,
I do not think a braver gentleman,
More active-valiant or more valiant-young, 90
More daring or more bold, is now alive
To grace this latter age with noble deeds.
For my part, I may speak it to my shame,
I have a truant been to chivalry;
And so I hear he doth account me too; 95
Yet this before my father's majesty—
I am content that he shall take the odds
Of his great name and estimation,
And will, to save the blood on either side,
Try fortune with him in a single fight. 100

KING. And, Prince of Wales, so dare we venture thee,
Albeit considerations infinite
Do make against it. No, good Worcester, no,
We love our people well; even those we love
That are misled upon your cousin's part; 105
And, will they take the offer of our grace,
Both he and they and you, yea, every man
Shall be my friend again and I'll be his:
So tell your cousin, and bring me word
What he will do: but if he will not yield, 110
Rebuke and dread correction wait on us
And they shall do their office. So, be gone;
We will not now be troubled with reply:
We offer fair; take it advisedly.

[*Exeunt* WORCESTER *and* VERNON.

PRINCE. It will not be accepted, on my life: 115
The Douglas and the Hotspur both together
Are confident against the world in arms.

KING. Hence, therefore, every leader to his charge;
For, on their answer, will we set on them:
And God befriend us, as our cause is just! 120

[*Exeunt all but the* PRINCE OF WALES *and* FALSTAFF.

FAL. Hal, if thou see me down in the battle and bestride me, so; 'tis a point of friendship.

PRINCE. Nothing but a colossus can do thee that friendship. Say thy prayers, and farewell.

FAL. I would 'twere bed-time, Hal, and all well. 126

PRINCE. Why, thou owest God a death. [*Exit.*

FAL. 'Tis not due yet; I would be loath to pay him before his day. What need I be so forward with him that calls not on me? Well, 'tis no matter; honour pricks me on. Yea, 130 but how if honour prick me off when I come on? how then? Can honour set to a leg? no: or an arm? no: or take away the grief of a wound? no. Honour hath no skill in surgery, then? no. What is honour? a word. What 135 is in that word honour? what is that honour? air. A trim reckoning! Who hath it? he that died o' Wednesday. Doth he feel it? no. Doth he hear it? no. 'Tis insensible, then? Yea, to the dead. But will it not live with the living? no. Why? detraction will not suffer it. Therefore I'll none of it. Honour is a mere scutcheon: and so ends my catechism. [*Exit.* 144

SCENE II. *The rebel camp.*

[*Enter* WORCESTER *and* VERNON.]

WOR. O, no, my nephew must not know, Sir Richard,
The liberal and kind offer of the king.

VER. 'Twere best he did.

WOR. Then are we all undone.
It is not possible, it cannot be,
The king should keep his word in loving us; 5
He will suspect us still and find a time
To punish this offence in other faults:
Suspicion all our lives shall be stuck full of eyes;
For treason is but trusted like the fox,

79. **want**, lack. 80. **water-colours**, unsubstantial pretexts. 81. **moody**, discontented. 87. **hopes**, i.e., of salvation. 88. **set . . . head**, subtracted from his account. 98. **estimation**, reputation. 102. **Albeit**, were it not that. 111. **wait on us**, are our attendants. 114. **take it advisedly**, i.e., you will accept it if you are wise. 129. **forward**, prematurely eager; **call . . . me**, does not demand payment of me. 131. **prick me off**, mark me off as a dead man. 137. **trim reckoning**, a fine balance sheet! 143. **scutcheon**, a hatchment or panel on which the arms of a deceased person are temporarily displayed, usually at his funeral. Scene ii: 8. **stuck full of eyes**, an allusion to Argus who had a hundred eyes. When he died Hera transplanted them to the tail of a peacock.

Who, ne'er so tame, so cherish'd and lock'd up, 10
Will have a wild trick of his ancestors.
Look how we can, or sad or merrily,
Interpretation will misquote our looks,
And we shall feed like oxen at a stall,
The better cherish'd, still the nearer death. 15
My nephew's trespass may be well forgot;
It hath the excuse of youth and heat of blood,
And an adopted name of privilege,
A hare-brain'd Hotspur, govern'd by a spleen:
All his offences live upon my head 20
And on his father's; we did train him on,
And, his corruption being ta'en from us,
We, as the spring of all, shall pay for all.
Therefore, good cousin, let not Harry know,
In any case, the offer of the king. 25

VER. Deliver what you will; I'll say 'tis so.
Here comes your cousin.

[*Enter* HOTSPUR *and* DOUGLAS.]

HOT. My uncle is return'd:
Deliver up my Lord of Westmoreland.
Uncle, what news? 30

WOR. The king will bid you battle presently.

DOUG. Defy him by the Lord of Westmoreland.

HOT. Lord Douglas, go you and tell him so.

DOUG. Marry, and shall, and very willingly. [*Exit.*

WOR. There is no seeming mercy in the king. 35

HOT. Did you beg any? God forbid!

WOR. I told him gently of our grievances,
Of his oath-breaking; which he mended thus,
By now forswearing that he is forsworn:
He calls us rebels, traitors; and will scourge 40
With haughty arms this hateful name in us.

[*Re-enter* DOUGLAS.]

DOUG. Arm, gentlemen; to arms! for I have thrown
A brave defiance in King Henry's teeth,
And Westmoreland, that was engaged, did bear it;
Which cannot choose but bring him quickly on. 45

WOR. The Prince of Wales stepp'd forth before the king,
And, nephew, challenged you to single fight.

HOT. O, would the quarrel lay upon our heads,
And that no man might draw short breath to-day
But I and Harry Monmouth! Tell me, tell me, 50
How show'd his tasking? seem'd it in contempt?

VER. No, by my soul; I never in my life
Did hear a challenge urged more modestly,
Unless a brother should a brother dare
To gentle exercise and proof of arms. 55
He gave you all the duties of a man;
Trimm'd up your praises with a princely tongue,
Spoke your deservings like a chronicle,
Making you ever better than his praise
By still dispraising praise valued with you; 60
And, which became him like a prince indeed,
He made a blushing cital of himself;
And chid his truant youth with such a grace
As if he master'd there a double spirit
Of teaching and of learning instantly. 65
There did he pause: but let me tell the world,
If he outlive the envy of this day,
England did never owe so sweet a hope,
So much miscónstrued in his wantonness.

HOT. Cousin, I think thou art enamourèd 70
On his follies: never did I hear
Of any prince so wild a libertine.
But be he as he will, yet once ere night
I will embrace him with a soldier's arm,
That he shall shrink under my courtesy. 75
Arm, arm with speed: and, fellows, soldiers, friends,
Better consider what you have to do
Than I, that have not well the gift of tongue,
Can lift your blood up with persuasion.

[*Enter a* MESSENGER.]

MESS. My lord, here are letters for you. 80

HOT. I cannot read them now.
O gentlemen, the time of life is short!

12. **sad**, seriously. 13. **misquote**, misread. 18. **adopted name of privilege**, a nickname (Hotspur) which excuses his headlong conduct. 19. **spleen**, i.e., an impetuous temperament. 21. **train**, lure. 31. **bid**, offer. 35. **no seeming mercy**, no pretense of mercy. 44. **engaged**, held as a hostage. 51. **tasking**, challenge. 56. **duties of**, respect due. 57. **Trimm'd up**, decked out. 59. **Making . . . praise**, continuing to say that you deserved better words of praise than he could command. 60. **valued**, compared. 62. **cital**, mention. 67. **envy**, ill will. 68. **owe**, own. 69. **So . . . wantonness**, whose wildness has been so much misinterpreted. 75. **shrink**, shudder. 79. **lift . . . up**, stir your emotions (to action).

To spend that shortness basely were too long,
If life did ride upon a dial's point,
Still ending at the arrival of an hour. 85
An if we live, we live to tread on kings;
If die, brave death, when princes die with us!
Now, for our consciences, the arms are fair,
When the intent of bearing them is just.

[*Enter another* MESSENGER.]

MESS. My lord, prepare; the king comes on apace. 90

HOT. I thank him, that he cuts me from my tale,
For I profess not talking; only this—
Let each man do his best: and here draw I
A sword, whose temper I intend to stain
With the best blood that I can meet withal 95
In the adventure of this perilous day.
Now, Esperance! Percy! and set on.
Sound all the lofty instruments of war,
And by that music let us all embrace;
For, heaven to earth, some of us never shall
A second time do such a courtesy. 101

[*The trumpets sound. They embrace, and exeunt.*

SCENE III. *Plain between the camps.*

[*The* KING *enters with his power. Alarum to the battle. Then enter* DOUGLAS *and* SIR WALTER BLUNT.]

BLUNT. What is thy name, that in the battle thus
Thou crossest me? what honour dost thou seek
Upon my head?

DOUG. Know then, my name is Douglas;
And I do haunt thee in the battle thus
Because some tell me that thou art a king. 5

BLUNT. They tell thee true.

DOUG. The Lord of Stafford dear to-day hath bought
Thy likeness, for instead of thee, King Harry,
This sword hath ended him: so shall it thee,
Unless thou yield thee as my prisoner. 10

BLUNT. I was not born a yielder, thou proud Scot;
And thou shalt find a king that will revenge
Lord Stafford's death. [*They fight.* DOUGLAS *kills* BLUNT.

[*Enter* HOTSPUR.]

HOT. O Douglas, hadst thou fought at Holmedon thus,
I never had triumph'd upon a Scot. 15

DOUG. All's done, all's won; here breathless lies the king.

HOT. Where?

DOUG. Here.

HOT. This, Douglas? no: I know this face full well:
A gallant knight he was, his name was Blunt;
Semblably furnish'd like the king himself. 21

DOUG. A fool go with thy soul, whither it goes!
A borrow'd title hast thou bought too dear:
Why didst thou tell me that thou wert a king?

HOT. The king hath many marching in his coats. 25

DOUG. Now, by my sword, I will kill all his coats;
I'll murder all his wardrobe, piece by piece,
Until I meet the king.

HOT. Up, and away!
Our soldiers stand full fairly for the day. 29

[*Exeunt.*

[*Alarum. Enter* FALSTAFF, *solus.*]

FAL. Though I could 'scape shot-free at London, I fear the shot here; here's no scoring but upon the pate. Soft! who are you? Sir Walter Blunt: there's honour for you! here's no vanity! I am as hot as molten lead, and as heavy too: God keep lead out of 35 me! I need no more weight than mine own bowels. I have led my ragamuffins where they are peppered: there's not three of my hundred and fifty left alive; and they are for the town's end, to beg during life. But who comes here? 40

[*Enter the* PRINCE.]

PRINCE. What, stand'st thou idle here? lend me thy sword:
Many a nobleman lies stark and stiff
Under the hoofs of vaunting enemies,
Whose deaths are yet unrevenged: I prithee, lend me thy sword. 44

84. a dial's point, hand of a clock. 88. for, as for. 89. intent, cause. 100. heaven to earth, i.e., I'll wager heaven against earth. Scene iii: 21. Semblably furnish'd, similarly accoutered. 29. stand . . . day, look as though they would do well today. 30. shot-free, i.e., without paying. 31. scoring, (1) marking up of charges, (2) hacking. 39. town's end, outskirts of a town, where beggars congregated.

FAL. O Hal, I prithee, give me leave to breathe awhile. Turk Gregory never did such deeds in arms as I have done this day. I have paid Percy, I have made him sure.

PRINCE. He is, indeed; and living to kill thee. I prithee, lend me thy sword. 50

FAL. Nay, before God, Hal, if Percy be alive, thou get'st not my sword; but take my pistol, if thou wilt.

PRINCE. Give it me: what, is it in the case?

FAL. Ay, Hal; 'tis hot, 'tis hot; there's that will sack a city. [*The* PRINCE *draws it out, and finds it to be a bottle of sack.*

PRINCE. What, is it a time to jest and dally now? [*He throws the bottle at him. Exit.* 58

FAL. Well, if Percy be alive, I'll pierce him. If he do come in my way, so: if he do not, if I come in his willingly, let him make a 61 carbonado of me. I like not such grinning honour as Sir Walter hath: give me life: which if I can save, so; if not, honour comes unlooked for, and there's an end. [*Exit.* 65

SCENE IV. *Another part of the field.*

[*Alarum. Excursions. Enter the* KING, *the* PRINCE, LORD JOHN OF LANCASTER, *and* EARL OF WESTMORELAND.]

KING. I prithee,
Harry, withdraw thyself; thou bleed'st too much.
Lord John of Lancaster, go you with him.

LAN. Not I, my lord, unless I did bleed too.

PRINCE. I beseech your majesty, make up, 5
Lest your retirement do amaze your friends.

KING. I will do so.
My Lord of Westmoreland, lead him to his tent.

WEST. Come, my lord, I'll lead you to your tent.

PRINCE. Lead me, my lord? I do not need your help: 10
And God forbid a shallow scratch should drive
The Prince of Wales from such a field as this,
Where stain'd nobility lies trodden on,
And rebels' arms triumph in massacres!

LAN. We breathe too long: come, cousin Westmoreland, 15
Our duty this way lies; for God's sake, come.
[*Exeunt* PRINCE JOHN *and* WESTMORELAND.

PRINCE. By God, thou hast deceived me, Lancaster;
I did not think thee lord of such a spirit:
Before, I loved thee as a brother, John;
But now, I do respect thee as my soul. 20

KING. I saw him hold Lord Percy at the point
With lustier maintenance than I did look for
Of such an ungrown warrior.

PRINCE. O, this boy
Lends mettle to us all! [*Exit.*

[*Enter* DOUGLAS.]

DOUG. Another king! they grow like Hydra's heads: 25
I am the Douglas, fatal to all those
That wear those colours on them: what art thou,
That counterfeit'st the person of a king?

KING. The king himself; who, Douglas, grieves at heart
So many of his shadows thou hast met 30
And not the very king. I have two boys
Seek Percy and thyself about the field:
But, seeing thou fall'st on me so luckily,
I will assay thee: so, defend thyself.

DOUG. I fear thou art another counterfeit;
And yet, in faith, thou bear'st thee like a king: 36
But mine I am sure thou art, whoe'er thou be,
And thus I win thee. [*They fight; the* KING *being in danger, re-enter* PRINCE OF WALES

PRINCE. Hold up thy head, vile Scot, or thou art like
Never to hold it up again! the spirits 40
Of valiant Shirley, Stafford, Blunt, are in my arms:
It is the Prince of Wales that threatens thee;
Who never promiseth but he means to pay.
[*They fight:* DOUGLAS *flies.*]
Cheerly, my lord: how fares your grace?
Sir Nicholas Gawsey hath for succour sent, 45
And so hath Clifton: I'll to Clifton straight.

KING. Stay, and breathe awhile:
Thou hast redeem'd thy lost opinion,

46. **Turk Gregory,** Pope Gregory VII, reported to be as cruel as a Turk. 48. **paid,** i.e., killed; **sure,** safe, harmless. 62. **carbonado,** meat slashed across for broiling. 65. **end,** (1) of my speech, (2) of my life. **Scene iv: 5. make up,** advance. 6. **amaze,** alarm. 15. **breathe,** pause. 21. **at the point,** at the spear's length. 22. **lustier maintenance,** more valiant behavior. 25. **Hydra,** a mythical serpent any one of whose nine heads when cut off at once grew again. 48. **opinion,** reputation. 49. **makest some tender of,** have some regard for.

And show'd thou makest some tender of my life,
In this fair rescue thou hast brought to me. 50

PRINCE. O God! they did me too much injury
That ever said I hearken'd for your death.
If it were so, I might have let alone
The insulting hand of Douglas over you,
Which would have been as speedy in your end 55
As all the poisonous potions in the world
And saved the treacherous labour of your son.

KING. Make up to Clifton: I'll to Sir Nicholas Gawsey. [*Exit.*

[*Enter* HOTSPUR.]

HOT. If I mistake not, thou art Harry Monmouth.

PRINCE. Thou speak'st as if I would deny my name. 60

HOT. My name is Harry Percy.

PRINCE. Why, then I see
A very valiant rebel of the name.
I am the Prince of Wales; and think not, Percy,
To share with me in glory any more:
Two stars keep not their motion in one sphere; 65
Nor can one England brook a double reign,
Of Harry Percy and the Prince of Wales.

HOT. Nor shall it, Harry; for the hour is come
To end the one of us; and would to God
Thy name in arms were now as great as mine!

PRINCE. I'll make it greater ere I part from thee; 71
And all the budding honours on thy crest
I'll crop, to make a garland for my head.

HOT. I can no longer brook thy vanities. [*They fight.*

[*Enter* FALSTAFF.]

FAL. Well said, Hal! to it, Hal! Nay, you shall find no boy's play here, I can tell you. 76

[*Re-enter* DOUGLAS; *he fights with* FALSTAFF, *who falls down as if he were dead, and exit* DOUGLAS. HOTSPUR *is wounded, and falls.*]

HOT. O, Harry, thou hast robb'd me of my youth!
I better brook the loss of brittle life
Than those proud titles thou hast won of me;
They wound my thoughts worse than thy sword my flesh: 80
But thought's the slave of life, and life time's fool;
And time, that takes survey of all the world,
Must have a stop. O, I could prophesy,
But that the earthy and cold hand of death
Lies on my tongue: no, Percy, thou art dust, 85
And food for— [*Dies.*

PRINCE. For worms, brave Percy: fare thee well, great heart!
Ill-weaved ambition, how much art thou shrunk!
When that this body did contain a spirit,
A kingdom for it was too small a bound; 90
But now two paces of the vilest earth
Is room enough; this earth that bears thee dead
Bears not alive so stout a gentleman.
If thou wert sensible of courtesy,
I should not make so dear a show of zeal: 95
But let my favours hide thy mangled face;
And, even in thy behalf, I'll thank myself
For doing these fair rites of tenderness.
Adieu, and take thy praise with thee to heaven!
Thy ignominy sleep with thee in the grave, 100
But not remember'd in thy epitaph!

[*He spieth* FALSTAFF *on the ground.*]

What, old acquaintance! could not all this flesh
Keep in a little life? Poor Jack, farewell!
I could have better spared a better man:
O, I should have a heavy miss of thee, 105
If I were much in love with vanity!
Death hath not struck so fat a deer to-day,
Though many dearer, in this bloody fray.
Embowell'd will I see thee by and by:
Till then in blood by noble Percy lie. 110
[*Exit.*

52. hearken'd for, waited eagerly for the news of. **54. insulting,** exulting. **55. in your end,** in accomplishing your death. **65. Two . . . sphere,** allusion to the fact that each sphere that revolved around the sun was supposed to contain one planet. **74. brook . . . vanities,** endure your hollow boasting. **81. But . . . fool,** thought ends with life, and Time is the lord of life. **82-3. And time . . . stop,** and Time, which measures everything in life, must itself stop some day. **90. bound,** enclosure. **95. dear,** heartfelt; **zeal,** admiration. **96. favours,** he covers his face with the plumes of his helmet. A favour is any kind of badge worn in the helmet. **109. embowell'd,** disembowelled, i.e., for embalming.

FAL. [*Rising up*] Embowelled! if thou embowel me to-day, I'll give you leave to powder me and eat me too to-morrow. 'Sblood, 'twas time to counterfeit, or that hot termagant Scot had paid me scot and lot too. 115 Counterfeit? I lie, I am no counterfeit: to die, is to be a counterfeit; for he is but the counterfeit of a man who hath not the life of a man: but to counterfeit dying, when a man thereby liveth, is to be no counterfeit, but the true and perfect image of life indeed. 120 The better part of valour is discretion; in the which better part I have saved my life. 'Zounds, I am afraid of this gunpowder Percy, though he be dead: how, if he should counterfeit too and rise? by my faith, I am afraid he would prove the better counter- 126 feit. Therefore I'll make him sure; yea, and I'll swear I killed him. Why may not he rise as well as I? Nothing confutes me but eyes, and nobody sees me. Therefore, sirrah [*stabbing him*], with a new wound in your thigh, come you along with me. 132

[*Takes up* HOTSPUR *on his back.*

[*Re-enter the* PRINCE OF WALES *and* LORD JOHN OF LANCASTER.]

PRINCE. Come, brother John; full bravely hast thou flesh'd
Thy maiden sword.

LAN. But, soft! whom have we here?
Did you not tell me this fat man was dead?

PRINCE. I did; I saw him dead, 136
Breathless and bleeding on the ground. Art thou alive?
Or is it fantasy that plays upon our eyesight?
I prithee, speak; we will not trust our eyes
Without our ears: thou art not what thou seem'st. 140

FAL. No, that's certain; I am not a double man: but if I be not Jack Falstaff, then am I a Jack. There is Percy [*throwing the body down*]: if your father will do me any honour, so; if not, let him kill the next Percy himself. I look to be either earl or duke, I can assure you. 146

PRINCE. Why, Percy I killed myself and saw thee dead.

FAL. Didst thou? Lord, Lord, how this world is given to lying! I grant you I was down and out of breath; and so was he: but we rose both at an instant and fought a long 150 hour by Shrewsbury clock. If I may be believed, so; if not, let them that should reward valour bear the sin upon their own heads. I'll take it upon my death, I gave him this wound in the thigh: if the man were 155 alive and would deny it, 'zounds, I would make him eat a piece of my sword.

LAN. This is the strangest tale that ever I heard.

PRINCE. This is the strangest fellow, brother John.
Come, bring your luggage nobly on your back:
For my part, if a lie may do thee grace, 161
I'll gild it with the happiest terms I have.

[*A retreat is sounded.*]

The trumpet sounds retreat; the day is ours.
Come, brother, let us to the highest of the field, 164
To see what friends are living, who are dead.

[*Exeunt* PRINCE OF WALES *and* LANCASTER.

FAL. I'll follow, as they say, for reward. He that rewards me, God reward him! If I do grow great, I'll grow less; for I'll purge, and leave sack, and live cleanly as a nobleman should do. [*Exit.*

SCENE V. *Another part of the field.*

[*The trumpets sound. Enter the* KING, PRINCE OF WALES, LORD JOHN OF LANCASTER, EARL OF WESTMORELAND, *with* WORCESTER *and* VERNON *prisoners.*]

KING. Thus ever did rebellion find rebuke.
Ill-spirited Worcester! did not we send grace,
Pardon and terms of love to all of you?
And wouldst thou turn our offers contrary?
Misuse the tenour of thy kinsman's trust? 5
Three knights upon our party slain to-day,
A noble earl and many a creature else
Had been alive this hour,
If like a Christian thou hadst truly borne
Betwixt our armies true intelligence. 10

112. powder, salt, i.e., pickle. 114. termagant, supposed by the Crusaders to be a god of the Saracens. 115. scot and lot, completely. 121. part, quality. 134. flesh'd, covered with blood, hence initiated. 138. fantasy, illusion. 141-2. double man, wraith; Jack, knave. 150. at an instant, at the same moment. 154. take . . . death, stake my life on it. 161. lie, i.e., of yours; do thee grace, win you favor. 162. gild . . . have, furbish it up with the most favorable expressions I can command. Scene v: 1. rebuke, check. 2. Ill-spirited, malicious. 4. turn . . . contrary, misrepresent. 5. tenour, purport; kinsman's trust, i.e., trust put in you as Percy's kinsman.

WOR. What I have done my safety urged me to;
And I embrace this fortune patiently,
Since not to be avoided it falls on me.

KING. Bear Worcester to the death and Vernon too:
Other offenders we will pause upon. 15

[*Exeunt* WORCESTER *and* VERNON, *guarded.*]

How goes the field?

PRINCE. The noble Scot, Lord Douglas, when he saw
The fortune of the day quite turn'd from him,
The noble Percy slain, and all his men
Upon the foot of fear, fled with the rest; 20
And falling from a hill, he was so bruised
That the pursuers took him. At my tent
The Douglas is; and I beseech your grace
I may dispose of him.

KING. With all my heart.

PRINCE. Then, brother John of Lancaster, to you 25
This honourable bounty shall belong.
Go to the Douglas, and deliver him
Up to his pleasure, ransomless and free:
His valour shown upon our crests to-day
Hath taught us how to cherish such high deeds 30
Even in the bosom of our adversaries.

LAN. I thank your grace for this high courtesy,
Which I shall give away immediately.

KING. Then this remains, that we divide our power.
You, son John, and my cousin Westmoreland 35
Towards York shall bend you with your dearest speed,
To meet Northumberland and the prelate Scroop,
Who, as we hear, are busily in arms:
Myself and you, son Harry, will towards Wales,
To fight with Glendower and the Earl of March. 40
Rebellion in this land shall lose his sway,
Meeting the check of such another day:
And since this business so fair is done,
Let us not leave till all our own be won.

[*Exeunt*

20. Upon . . . fear, fleeing in fear. 33. give away, announce. 36. dearest, best. 44. leave, cease from acting.

AFTERWORD

History seeks to tell the truth about the past. Literature, when it turns to the past for its subject matter—as in the chronicle history plays of Shakespeare—is often careless of the facts at its disposal. In dealing with the record, things as they actually happened, literature is not so accurate or so scrupulous as history. And yet it is more nearly true. Shakespeare's most famous history play, the first part of *King Henry IV*, illustrates this paradox very well.

Shakespeare's subject is the troubled reign of the usurper-king, from whom the play takes its title. This is Henry Bolingbroke, a young nobleman of the House of Lancaster, who initiates a rebellion against King Richard II and seizes the throne for himself. Henceforward, Bolingbroke is known to history as King Henry IV. For thirteen years he governs the kingdom, beating back incessant challenges to his authority. On his death, the kingship passes to his son, Prince Hal, who rules in turn as Henry V. Shakespeare devotes four plays to this historical sequence, beginning with the unhappy story of Richard II. Already, at the outset of his career, he had written another tetralogy on the life and death of Henry VI, the son of Prince Hal, and on the brief triumph of his antagonist, the villainous Richard III. At last, in 1485 at the battle of Bosworth Field, Richard III, who had overthrown the House of Lancaster, is himself defeated, and Shakespeare's Lancastrian cycle, eight plays in all, is brought to a close.

The historical background summarized here covers roughly a century. There is in this complicated story no apparent thread or consistent pattern. Kings and would-be kings struggle for power, gain it and lose it. Across the vast stage, one following another, they move like clamorous ghosts. If the record of the past, as the historian presents it, suggests a coherent pattern, it is only that of waves breaking eternally and to no purpose against the shore, and then receding and then advancing again. That is a possible description of history. It is sound and fury, signifying nothing. Shakespeare is dissatisfied with this description, as being insufficiently true. Shakespeare is intent on discovering motivation or design in the events he is dramatizing. He is concerned with the roots of things, with the whys and wherefores. Events, as he perceives them, do not follow each other in merely chronological sequence; they follow each other for cause. One event begets directly the event which succeeds it. It is interesting to observe the working out of this more acute perception in the action of *King Henry IV: Part I.*

The prime fact of the story is a tragic fact and has already been entered before the play proper begins. It is the deposing of King Richard II, the lawful ruler, and his murder at Pomfret Castle, at the hands of Bolingbroke's men. From this fact, all subsequent action derives. After all, there is meaning in history. Human behavior determines the course of events.

A different and essentially unhuman reading of events, first elevated to dogma in the early years of the seventeenth century, proposes that the king is divine and invested from on high with the right to rule his subjects as he pleases. This mystical idea receives its quietus in the history plays of Shakespeare. King John, the insufficient hero of one of these plays, is supported partly, he thinks, by the divinity that hedges a king. "Our strong possession and our right for us." That is how he responds to the claims of an ambitious rival. But his mother, Queen Elinor, whose more realistic assessment tallies evidently with Shakespeare's, looks, not to the symbol, but to the man and his capacity. She answers:

> Your strong possession much more than your right,
> Or else it must go wrong with you and me.

King Richard is a feckless sovereign, not strong in possession, so that whatever his right, he is ultimately forced to relinquish the throne. What happens—the historical record—is the consequence and emanation of personality.

Henry Bolingbroke, the usurper, illustrates this contingent relation not less vividly than the ruler he displaces. Bolingbroke as ruler is more forthputting than King Richard, and more adroit in the exercise of power. And he engages our sympathies as he has been victimized, stripped of lands and title by his rapacious sovereign. But the claim to rule, which this energetic victim prosecutes successfully, as it takes strength from personal considerations is also vitiated by them. Bolingbroke, like Macbeth, dares do more than may become a man. He is mistaken in judgment, he is defective in character, as he endeavors to "find out right with wrong." What follows, for the man as also for the kingdom, is Shakespeare's concern in his Lancastrian plays.

Concern with sequence or causality informs the opening line of the first part of *King Henry IV*. "So shaken as we are, so wan with care." Bolingbroke, who utters these words, holds power uneasily, as a mandatory consequence of the crime he has committed. This crime continues to haunt him, as the action unfolds. The rebellion of Harry Hotspur and the Northern lords recapitulates faithfully his own rebellion, in earlier days. Though, at the end of the play, Hotspur is defeated and killed at the decisive battle of Shrewsbury, this battle is felt as decisive only for the moment. Fresh troubles are brewing. Northumberland still lives; Owen Glendower is mustering his forces; the Archbishop of York is up in arms. That is how it must continue, until the curse on the House of Lancaster, a curse inspired by the murder of Richard II, is expiated finally in the equivalent murder of the last of the Lancastrian kings. Always, the blood falls back upon men.

That is Shakespeare's point of view, or his reading of history. Unlike the historian or the preacher, however, he does not enunciate this point of view in so many words. The plot of the play is his vehicle or vessel, and partly its function is to embody such ideas as he has gathered from his perusal of the facts. Among the ideas Shakespeare gathers is the supposition, or rather the discovery that the survival of political man, like that of any other organism, or like that of the universe which contains us all, depends on obedience to certain governing imperatives. Shakespeare is not prescriptive, like God on Mount Sinai. He does not hand down a table of commandments. He has found out, from conducting the investigation which is the play, that the kingdom is analogous to the human body. Disease is injurious to the body. It has its counterpart in civil strife, which is —not simply wicked: that it what the preacher would tell us—but subversive of health and life. For that reason, Shakespeare presents it, in his opening scene, as an "intestine shock."

The operation of the heavens supplies another analogy. For the continuing of this operation, harmony is imperative. A vagrant or wandering star, which shoots madly from its orbit, violates harmony and hence the condition of its being. In the rebel Worcester, this process of self-destruction is enacted. Worcester is an "exhaled meteor." He is aberrant and therefore a portent of mischief, but the greatest mischief he does—as the analogy is followed through—is to himself. His nephew Hotspur, another and more glamorous breaker of concord, suffers the same fate and for the same necessary reasons.

> Two stars keep not their motion in one sphere,
> Nor can one England brook a double reign
> Of Harry Percy and the Prince of Wales.

The interacting of cause and effect is embodied in analogy or metaphor. It is embodied also in the collison of character. From the beginning of *King Henry IV: Part I*, Hal and Hotspur are presented as natural antagonists. Here Shakespeare is taking liberties with history, which does not record the opposition of these two, the better to illuminate the nature and consequence of different modes of political behavior. Hotspur is the theme of honor's tongue, but also an anarch, drunk with his own choler, who apprehends, not reality, but a world of figures or fantastic shapes. He is a "harebrained Hotspur, governed by a spleen." The contrast Hal offers is, at first, not especially hopeful. He is said to be stained with riot and dishonor. That is the exaggerated opinion of his agitated parent. Still, there is evidence to support this opinion. Hal is demeaned by his association with the low company that frequents the Boar's Head Tavern in Eastcheap. He participates, like a common highwayman, in the robbery at Gadshill. So far, he has sounded the base string of humility or degradation. On the other hand, he has his wits about him from the beginning. Unlike Hotspur, he is not deceived by the company he keeps. "I know you all," he declares in a famous soliloquy, early in the play. When time is ripe, he will redeem himself on Percy's head.

The ultimate redemption of Prince Hal, in victorious combat against Hotspur, is the apex of the play. But interest, even at this pivotal moment, is not centered exclusively in the two antagonists. Falstaff also demands attention. Always with him it is a time to jest and dally, as when at Shrewsbury he draws from his case not a pistol but a bottle of sack. Shakespeare follows the fortunes of Falstaff from scene to scene in juxtaposition with the fortunes of Prince Hal and King Henry and Hotspur. This method of proceeding by comparison and contrast is Shakespeare's way of getting at the truth—inferentially. The inference we draw from the complementary ordering of scenes is that Falstaff is another anarch or lord of misrule, a comic version of the rebels, a counterfeit copy of the King. And so, in propriety, Falstaff, like Hotspur, like Worcester, is destroyed. That is the right culmination of Shakespeare's play. Prince Hal, whose education is completed, emerges at the end his own man. At his feet are the bodies of the rebel and the fat knight, each of whom represents a disastrous mode of behavior Hal has learned, in his maturing, to renounce.

This account of the play is true in essentials, but it is not true enough, not sufficiently comprehensive, and the more perceptive the reader, the more will he feel the need to eke it out. He might ask himself, for instance, to what degree he is really persuaded of growth and change in Prince Hal. If, already in Act I, Hal "knows" his vulgar companions, reads them aright in their folly and their iniquity, what is left for him to learn? The contrary case of Huck Finn, whose significant adventures are the possession of every school boy, gives point to the question. Huck is the protagonist of a genuine *Bildungsroman*—a type of tale which records the education of the hero. At first this hero supposes easily, taking his cue from the age and society in which he is born, that black men are chattel. At last he discovers that Nigger Jim, his companion on the long journey down river—a journey to enlightenment—is like himself. With this discovery, the education of the hero, who does literally grow and change, is complete.

One is tempted to say that the education of Prince Hal, potentially the suspenseful matter of five acts, is complete from the beginning. Critical opinion seeks to evade this awkward possibility. The Prince is said to soliloquize and to profess understanding, that the audience may anticipate the happy ending it craves. Shakespeare is announcing that, whatever the temporary "declension" of Prince Hal, he will enter at last on his kingdom.

The trouble with this rationalization is that the tipping of the hand it attributes to the playwright is not simply clumsy but gratuitous. The tradition of the madcap Prince of Wales, who sloughs off his ignominious youth, was greatly popular dramatic fare in Shakespeare's time. No overtures to the audience were required. As that is so, it is more plausible to see Shakespeare, in his version, as modifying the traditional account. The hero in *King Henry IV: Part I*, and also in the two plays that chronicle his further adventures, is an equivocal hero, notably phlegmatic in his treatment of friends, feline by temper, devious when he has to be, featuring perhaps a touch of the hypocrite, sometimes enacting Samuel Johnson's proposition that patriotism is the last refuge of a scoundrel. And yet the qualifying of heroic stature in Prince Hal, made necessary by the unattractive characteristics which certainly describe him on one side, does not —so magnanimous is Shakespeare—preclude for Hal the role of hero. Only he is a particolored hero, not this and that by turns but this and that concurrently— like the web of our life, which mingles "good and ill together."

It is the same, on a scale far more imposing, with Falstaff. He is, on one side, that "reverend vice" or "gray iniquity" hypothesized and reprehended by Prince Hal. And therefore it is right that Hal put him away. But the role Shakespeare is fashioning is more inclusive than this, and hence not so clear as the moralist requires, or so crisply definable. Falstaff is vice incarnate, but as he is incarnate he is more than the sum of his characteristics. He functions as a comic antidote to the official humbug that conceals and describes the political intriguing of the makers and shakers with whom the historian is concerned. This Falstaff presents the truth about history, and embodies the truth in his person. He is, concurrently, the obverse of truth, mendacious in reporting, villainous in all things. To Hal's assumption of an autonomous role, Falstaff's death at Shrewsbury is the necessary prelude.

Except, of course, for this: that Falstaff rises from the dead, to exert his disreputable attractions another day. Shakespeare is not willing, like the moralist, to put Q.E.D. to the narrative as he brings it to a close. He is the playwright thinking, whose business is to explicate the workings of politics and history. But these workings are conceived in terms of flesh and blood, which is not amenable to easy generalizations. Hal is a scapegrace, whose robust antics we are eager to condone; and a prig, whose fishiness repels us; and an ardent and faithful spirit who pays what he promises. Falstaff is a liar, a coward, an old fat man; and simultaneously the most memorable character of the play, in whose mistreadings we rejoice, even as we deplore them. So with Hotspur, the king of honor, the beloved of his wife, the mark and glass of all the age—and dust and food for worms.

Shakespeare, like an executioner, condemns his characters impartially. Their faults are gross, open, and palpable. Judgment follows. But this pitiless Shakespeare is also greatly generous. Moral judgment is transcended, in the continuing life with which his characters are endowed.

Suggested Reading

Bennett, H. S., "Sir John Fastolf," in *Six Medieval Men and Women* (1955). Atheneum.

Bradley, A. C., "The Rejection of Falstaff," *Oxford Lectures* (1909).

Campbell, Lily B., *Shakespeare's Histories* (1947).

Charlton, H. B., *Falstaff* (1935).

———, *Shakespearian Comedy* (1938). Barnes and Noble.

Crane, Milton, *Shakespeare's Prose* (1951). Phoenix.

Danby, John F., *Shakespeare's Doctrine of Nature* (1949). Humanities.

Divine, Hugh W., *A Study of Some of the Problems in the Falstaff Plays* (1942).

Empson, William, *Some Versions of Pastoral* (1935). New Directions.

Fiehler, Rudolf, *Sir John Oldcastle, the Original of Falstaff* (1950).

Fletcher, B. J., *Shakespeare's Use of Holinshed's Chronicles in "Richard III," and "Macbeth"* (1937).

Hunter, E. K., *Shakespeare and Common Sense* (1954).

Jenkins, Harold, *The Structural Problem in Shakespeare's Henry the Fourth* (1956).

Knight, G. Wilson, *The Shakespearian Tempest* (1932).

Knights, L. C., *Determinations* (1934).

———, *Some Shakespearian Themes* (1959). Stanford.

Langbaum, Robert, *The Poetry of Experience* (1957). Norton.

Marriott, John A. R., *English History in Shakespeare* (1918).

Masefield, John, *William Shakespeare* (1911). Premier.

MORGANN, MAURICE, *Essay on the Dramatic Character of Sir John Falstaff* (1777; ed. William Arthur Gill, 1912).

MURRY, JOHN MIDDLETON, *Shakespeare* (1936). Hillary.

NICOLL, A. and J., *Holinshed's Chronicle As Used in Shakespeare's Plays* (1927).

PALMER, JOHN, *Political Characters of Shakespeare* (1945). Papermac.

REESE, M. M., *The Cease of Majesty* (1961).

RIBNER, IRVING, *The English History Play in the Age of Shakespeare* (rev. ed., 1965).

SCHELLING, FELIX E., *The English Chronicle Play* (1902).

SEN GUPTA, S. C., *Shakespearian Comedy* (1950).

SEWELL, ARTHUR, *Character and Society in Shakespeare* (1951).

SOMERSET, R. (Lord Raglan), *The Hero: A Study in Tradition, Myth, and Drama* (1936; reprinted 1949).

STEWART, J. I . M., *Character and Motive in Shakespeare* (1949).

TILLYARD, E. M. W., *Shakespeare's History Plays* (1944). Macmillan.

TRAVERSI, DEREK A., *An Approach to Shakespeare* (enlarged ed., 2 vols., 1968). Anchor.

———, *Shakespeare from "Richard II" to "Henry V"* (1957).

UNGER, LEONARD, "Deception and Self-Deception in Shakespeare's *Henry IV*," in *The Man in the Name* (1956).

WILSON, J. DOVER, *The Fortunes of Falstaff* (1943).

Twelfth Night

A NOTE ON THE TEXT

On the twelfth day after Christmas falls the feast of the Epiphany, which celebrates the coming of the Magi to the newly born Christ. For a holiday performance on this joyous occasion, *Twelfth Night* was presumably written. Its subtitle, *What You Will,* suggests a mindless entertainment. This suggestion is corroborated by the plot of the play; and belied altogether by the theme.

The plot in its essentials probably came to Shakespeare from the second story in a popular collection by the Elizabethan soldier and romancer Barnabe Rich, whose *Farewell to Militarie Profession* was printed in 1581. Rich's tale of cross-wooing and "barful strife" is entitled "Apolonius and Silla." It is not an original tale. Elements of it are encountered frequently in European literature, for example in Italian comedy of the sixteenth century. An archetypal source is the *Menaechmi* of the Roman comic dramatist Plautus, whose account of the confusion inspired by the resemblance of twins had already provided Shakespeare with a model in *The Comedy of Errors.* John Manningham, a barrister associated with the Middle Temple, one of the London law schools, records in his diary the similarity of these two plays to *Twelfth Night.* Manningham's entry is dated February 2, 1602, and is our earliest notice of a performance of the play.

Twelfth Night was first printed in the Folio of 1623. Composition is assigned generally to 1600 or 1601, on the evidence of topical references to events occurring in that period. But perhaps students of the play will be persuaded at least as readily in assigning a date by a felt connection in style or theme to *Hamlet*, which was written ascertainably in these opening years of the seventeenth century.

TWELFTH NIGHT; OR, WHAT YOU WILL

DRAMATIS PERSONÆ

ORSINO, *Duke of Illyria.*
SEBASTIAN, *brother to Viola.*
ANTONIO, *a sea captain, friend to Sebastian.*
A Sea Captain, friend to Viola.
VALENTINE, } *gentlemen attending on the Duke.*
CURIO, }
SIR TOBY BELCH, *uncle to Olivia.*
SIR ANDREW AGUECHEEK.
MALVOLIO, *steward to Olivia.*
FABIAN, } *servants to Olivia.*
FESTE, *a Clown,* }
OLIVIA.
VIOLA.
MARIA, *Olivia's woman.*
LORDS, PRIESTS, SAILORS, OFFICERS, MUSICIANS, *and other* ATTENDANTS.

SCENE: *A city in Illyria, and the sea-coast near it.*

ACT I

SCENE I. *The* DUKE's *palace.*

[*Enter* DUKE, CURIO, *and other* LORDS; MUSICIANS *attending.*]

DUKE. If music be the food of love, play on;
Give me excess of it, that, surfeiting,
The appetite may sicken, and so die.
That strain again! it had a dying fall:
O, it came o'er my ear like the sweet sound, 5
That breathes upon a bank of violets,
Stealing and giving odour! Enough; no more:
'Tis not so sweet now as it was before.
O spirit of love! how quick and fresh art thou,
That, notwithstanding thy capacity 10
Receiveth as the sea, nought enters there,
Of what validity and pitch soe'er,
But falls into abatement and low price,
Even in a minute: so full of shapes is fancy
That it alone is high fantastical. 15
CUR. Will you go hunt, my lord?
DUKE. What, Curio?
CUR. The hart.
DUKE. Why, so I do, the noblest that I have:
O, when mine eyes did see Olivia first,
Methought she purged the air of pestilence!
That instant was I turn'd into a hart; 21
And my desires, like fell and cruel hounds,
E'er since pursue me.

[*Enter* VALENTINE.]

How now! what news from her?
VAL. So please my lord, I might not be admitted;
But from her handmaid do return this answer:
The element itself, till seven years' heat, 26
Shall not behold her face at ample view;
But, like a cloistress, she will veiled walk
And water once a day her chamber round
With eye-offending brine: all this to season 30
A brother's dead love, which she would keep fresh
And lasting in her sad remembrance.
DUKE. O, she that hath a heart of that fine frame
To pay this debt of love but to a brother,
How will she love, when the rich golden shaft

Act I, Scene i: 3. appetite, i.e., for music. **4. dying fall,** cadence played more and more softly. **5. sound,** i.e., of the wind. **9. quick,** living, vigorous. **10. That,** seeing that. **12. validity,** value; **pitch,** height, hence excellence. **14. so . . . fancy,** love is so full of imagination. **15. high fantastical,** i.e., is replete with fantasies. **18. the noblest . . . have,** i.e., Olivia's heart. **20. Methought . . . pestilence,** but I was wrong; she did not purge it of the pestilence of love. **21-3. That instant . . . pursue me,** a reference to the myth of Actaeon, who, because he saw Diana bathing, was transformed into a hart and torn to pieces by his own hounds. **26. element,** sky; **till . . . heat,** till seven summers have passed. **27. ample,** full. **28. cloistress,** nun. **30. season,** i.e., preserve in the brine of her tears. **31. a brother's . . . love,** i.e., memory of a dead brother's love for her. **35. golden shaft,** i.e., the shaft by which Cupid aroused love.

Hath kill'd the flock of all affections else 36
That live in her; when liver, brain and heart,
These sovereign thrones, are all supplied, and fill'd
Her sweet perfections with one self king!
Away before me to sweet beds of flowers: 40
Love-thoughts lie rich when canopied with bowers. [*Exeunt.*

SCENE II. *The sea-coast.*

[*Enter* VIOLA, *a* CAPTAIN, *and* SAILORS.]

VIO. What country, friends, is this?
CAP. This is Illyria, lady.
VIO. And what should I do in Illyria?
My brother he is in Elysium.
Perchance he is not drown'd: what think you, sailors? 5
CAP. It is perchance that you yourself were saved.
VIO. O my poor brother! and so perchance may he be.
CAP. True, madam: and, to comfort you with chance,
Assure yourself, after our ship did split,
When you and those poor number saved with you 10
Hung on our driving boat, I saw your brother,
Most provident in peril, bind himself,
Courage and hope both teaching him the practice,
To a strong mast that lived upon the sea;
Where, like Arion on the dolphin's back, 15
I saw him hold acquaintance with the waves
So long as I could see.
VIO. For saying so, there's gold:
Mine own escape unfoldeth to my hope,
Whereto thy speech serves for authority, 20
The like of him. Know'st thou this country?
CAP. Ay, madam, well; for I was bred and born
Not three hours' travel from this very place.
VIO. Who governs here?
CAP. A noble duke, in nature as in name.
VIO. What is his name? 26
CAP. Orsino.
VIO. Orsino! I have heard my father name him:
He was a bachelor then.
CAP. And so is now, or was so very late; 30
For but a month ago I went from hence,
And then 'twas fresh in murmur,—as, you know,
What great ones do the less will prattle of,—
That he did seek the love of fair Olivia.
VIO. What's she? 35
CAP. A virtuous maid, the daughter of a count
That died some twelvemonth since, then leaving her
In the protection of his son, her brother,
Who shortly also died: for whose dear love,
They say, she hath abjured the company 40
And sight of men.
VIO. O that I served that lady
And might not be delivered to the world,
Till I had made mine own occasion mellow,
What my estate is!
CAP. That were hard to compass;
Because she will admit no kind of suit, 45
No, not the duke's.
VIO. There is a fair behaviour in thee, captain;
And though that nature with a beauteous wall
Doth oft close in pollution, yet of thee
I will believe thou hast a mind that suits 50
With this thy fair and outward character.
I prithee, and I'll pay thee bounteously,
Conceal me what I am, and be my aid
For such disguise as haply shall become 54
The form of my intent. I'll serve this duke:
Thou shalt present me as an eunuch to him:
It may be worth thy pains; for I can sing
And speak to him in many sorts of music
That will allow me very worth his service.
What else may hap to time I will commit; 60
Only shape thou thy silence to my wit.
CAP. Be you his eunuch, and your mute I'll be:

36. **affections else,** other affections. 37. **liver, brain and heart,** liver was thought to be the seat of the passions, the brain of the judgment, the heart of the affections. 39. **self,** single, i.e., the man she might love. **Scene ii:** 4. **Elysium,** Greek equivalent of Heaven. 7. **perchance,** (1) perhaps, (2) by chance. 10. **poor number,** wretched few. 11. **driving,** driven before the wind. 14. **lived,** kept afloat. 15. **Arion,** a mythical Greek musician who leapt into the sea to escape the murderous plot of sailors and then so charmed a dolphin with his music that it bore him to safety on its back. 16. **acquaintance,** i.e., his own. 21. **The like of him,** i.e., that he too has survived. 30. **late,** lately. 32. **fresh in murmur,** was beginning to be whispered about. 42. **delivered,** made known. 43-4. **Till . . . estate is,** until I thought the time suitable for disclosing my identity. 44. **were . . . compass,** would be hard to accomplish. 46. **fair behaviour,** attractive manner. 51. **outward character,** appearance. 54-5. **shall . . . intent,** will suit the nature of my purpose. 59. **allow . . . service,** approve me as worth employing. 61. **Only . . . wit,** only co-operate with my plan by keeping silent.

When my tongue blabs, then let mine eyes not see.

VIO. I thank thee: lead me on. [*Exeunt.*

SCENE III. OLIVIA'S *house.*

[*Enter* SIR TOBY BELCH *and* MARIA.]

SIR TO. What a plague means my niece, to take the death of her brother thus? I am sure care's an enemy to life.

MAR. By my troth, Sir Toby, you must come in earlier o' nights: your cousin, my lady, takes great exceptions to your ill hours. 6

SIR TO. Why, let her except, before excepted.

MAR. Ay, but you must confine yourself within the modest limits of order. 9

SIR TO. Confine! I'll confine myself no finer than I am: these clothes are good enough to drink in; and so be these boots too: an they be not, let them hang themselves in their own straps. 13

MAR. That quaffing and drinking will undo you: I heard my lady talk of it yesterday; and of a foolish knight that you brought in one night here to be her wooer. 17

SIR. TO. Who, Sir Andrew Aguecheek?

MAR. Ay, he.

SIR TO. He's as tall a man as any 's in Illyria.

MAR. What's that to the purpose? 21

SIR TO. Why, he has three thousand ducats a year.

MAR. Ay, but he'll have but a year in all these ducats: he's a very fool and a prodigal.

SIR TO. Fie, that you'll say so! he plays o' the viol-de-gamboys, and speaks three or four languages word for word without book, and hath all the good gifts of nature. 29

MAR. He hath indeed, almost natural: for besides that he's a fool, he's a great quarreller; and but that he hath the gift of a coward to allay the gust he hath in quarrelling, 'tis thought among the prudent he would quickly have the gift of a grave. 35

SIR TO. By this hand, they are scoundrels and substractors that say so of him. Who are they?

MAR. They that add, moreover, he's drunk nightly in your company. 39

SIR TO. With drinking healths to my niece: I'll drink to her as long as there is a passage in my throat and drink in Illyria: he's a coward and a coystrill that will not drink to my niece till his brains turn o' the toe like a parish-top. What, wench! Castiliano vulgo! for here comes Sir Andrew Agueface. 46

[*Enter* SIR ANDREW AGUECHEEK.]

SIR AND. Sir Toby Belch! how now, Sir Toby Belch!

SIR TO. Sweet Sir Andrew!

SIR AND. Bless you, fair shrew. 50

MAR. And you too, sir.

SIR TO. Accost, Sir Andrew, accost.

SIR AND. What's that?

SIR TO. My niece's chambermaid.

SIR AND. Good Mistress Accost, I desire better acquaintance. 56

MAR. My name is Mary, sir.

SIR AND. Good Mistress Mary Accost,—

SIR TO. You mistake, knight: "accost" is front her, board her, woo her, assail her. 60

SIR AND. By my troth, I would not undertake her in this company. Is that the meaning of "accost"?

MAR. Fare you well, gentlemen. 64

SIR TO. An thou let part so, Sir Andrew, would thou mightst never draw sword again.

SIR AND. An you part so, mistress, I would I might never draw sword again. Fair lady, do you think you have fools in hand?

MAR. Sir, I have not you by the hand. 70

SIR AND. Marry, but you shall have; and here's my hand.

MAR. Now, sir, "thought is free:" I pray you, bring your hand to the buttery-bar and let it drink.

Scene iii: 3. **care,** low spirits. 5. **cousin,** was used to designate any relationship more distant than brother or sister; here, niece. 7. **except, before excepted,** a legal phrase meaning, "with the exceptions before named." In Sir Toby's tipsy mouth it has little precise signification. His vague meaning is, "Let her make her usual objections." 8-9. **confine . . . order,** i.e., exercise that restraint which a respectable life demands. 10. **confine,** dress. 20. **tall,** sturdy, with a pun on the usual meaning. 22. **ducats,** gold coins of substantial, but fluctuating, value. 27. **viol-de-gamboys,** a small precursor of the violincello. 28. **without book,** by heart. 30. **natural,** (1) naturally, (2) like a born idiot. 33. **gust,** taste. 43. **coystrill,** base fellow. 45. **parish top,** a large whip-top kept in English villages which the unemployed were made to whip to keep them warm and out of mischief; **Castiliano vulgo,** probably high-sounding nonsense. If he intended "volto," he means, "look as grave as a Spaniard." 50. **fair shrew,** handsome scoundrel. 51. **And you too,** i.e., and you're another. 52. **accost,** greet her politely, make up to her. 54. **chambermaid,** lady-in-waiting, companion, not a servant 60. **front,** attack. 65. **An,** if. 74. **buttery-bar,** a small bar in the provision room from which ale was served. The phrase "in a barmaid's mouth" meant, "Kiss me and give me a tip."

SIR AND. Wherefore, sweet-heart? what's your metaphor? 76

MAR. It's dry, sir.

SIR AND. Why, I think so: I am not such an ass but I can keep my hand dry. But what's your jest? 80

MAR. A dry jest, sir.

SIR AND. Are you full of them?

MAR. Ay, sir, I have them at my fingers' ends: marry, now I let go your hand, I am barren. [*Exit.* 84

SIR TO. O knight, thou lackest a cup of canary: when did I see thee so put down?

SIR AND. Never in your life, I think; unless you see canary put me down. Methinks sometimes I have no more wit than a Christian or an ordinary man has: but I am a great eater of beef and I believe that does harm to my wit. 91

SIR TO. No question.

SIR AND. An I thought that, I 'ld forswear it. I'll ride home to-morrow, Sir Toby.

SIR TO. Pourquoi, my dear knight? 95

SIR AND. What is "pourquoi"? do or not do? I would I had bestowed that time in the tongues that I have in fencing, dancing and bear-baiting: O, had I but followed the arts!

SIR TO. Then hadst thou had an excellent head of hair. 101

SIR AND. Why, would that have mended my hair?

SIR TO. Past question; for thou sees it will not curl by nature. 105

SIR AND. But it becomes me well enough, does 't not?

SIR TO. Excellent; it hangs like flax on a distaff; and I hope to see a housewife take thee between her legs and spin it off. 110

SIR AND. Faith, I'll home to-morrow, Sir Toby: your niece will not be seen; or if she be, it's four to one she'll none of me: the count himself here hard by woos her. 114

SIR TO. She'll none o' the count: she'll not match above her degree, neither in estate, years, nor wit; I have heard her swear 't. Tut, there 's life in 't, man.

SIR AND. I'll stay a month longer. I am a fellow o' the strangest mind i' the world; I delight in masques and revels sometimes altogether. 121

SIR TO. Art thou good at these kickshawses, knight?

SIR AND. As any man in Illyria, whatsoever he be, under the degree of my betters; and yet I will not compare with an old man. 126

SIR TO. What is thy excellence in a galliard, knight?

SIR AND. Faith, I can cut a caper.

SIR TO. And I can cut the mutton to 't. 130

SIR AND. And I think I have the back-trick simply as strong as any man in Illyria.

SIR TO. Wherefore are these things hid? wherefore have these gifts a curtain before 'em? are they like to take dust, like Mistress Mall's picture? why dost thou not go to church in a galliard and come home in a coranto? My very walk should be a jig; I would not so much as make water but in a sink-a-pace. What dost thou mean? Is it a world to hide virtues in? I did think, by the excellent constitution of thy leg, it was formed under the star of a galliard. 142

SIR AND. Ay, 'tis strong, and it does indifferent well in a flame-coloured stock. Shall we set about some revels?

SIR TO. What shall we do else? were we not born under Taurus? 147

SIR AND. Taurus! That's sides and heart.

SIR TO. No, sir; it is legs and thighs. Let me see thee caper: ha! higher: ha, ha! excellent! [*Exeunt.*

SCENE IV. *The* DUKE'S *palace.*

[*Enter* VALENTINE, *and* VIOLA *in man's attire.*]

VAL. If the duke continue these favours towards you, Cesario, you are like to be much advanced: he hath known you but three days, and already you are no stranger. 4

VIO. You either fear his humour or my neg-

79. **dry**, a dry hand was a sign of meanness and impotence. 81. **dry**, stupid, with a pun on the usual meaning. 84. **barren**, i.e., barren of wit. 86. **canary**, sweet wine from the Canary Islands; **put down**, floored. 98. **tongues**, (1) curling-tongs (2) languages. 104. **past question**, beyond all doubt. 116. **degree**, rank. 122. **kickshawses**, delicacies, trifles. 125. **under . . . betters**, just so he is not any better at them than I am. 126. **old**, probably "experienced." 127. **galliard**, a lively dance ending with a caper (leap). 130. **mutton**, caper sauce was and is often served with mutton. 131-2. **back-trick**, a series of backward steps in the galliard. 134. **curtain**, oil paintings were covered with curtains, except when exhibited on special occasions. 135. **Mistress Mall**, probably some notorious woman. 137. **coranto**, a dance characterized by swift running steps. 139. **sink-a-pace**, cinque-pace, a five-step dance. 142. **under . . . galliard**, that is, a star favorable to a galliard. 147. **Taurus**, a constellation which was supposed to govern legs, not sides and heart, as Andrew mistakenly supposes. **Scene iv**: 2. **like**, likely.

ligence, that you call in question the continuance of his love: is he inconstant, sir, in his favours?

VAL. No, believe me.

VIO. I thank you. Here comes the count.

[*Enter* DUKE, CURIO, *and* ATTENDANTS.]

DUKE. Who saw Cesario, ho? 10

VIO. On your attendance, my lord; here.

DUKE. Stand you a while aloof. Cesario,
Thou know'st no less but all; I have unclasp'd
To thee the book even of my secret soul:
Therefore, good youth, address thy gait unto her; 15
Be not denied access, stand at her doors,
And tell them, there thy fixèd foot shall grow
Till thou have audience.

VIO. Sure, my noble lord,
If she be so abandon'd to her sorrow
As it is spoke, she never will admit me. 20

DUKE. Be clamorous and leap all civil bounds
Rather than make unprofited return.

VIO. Say I do speak with her, my lord, what then?

DUKE. O, then unfold the passion of my love,
Surprise her with discourse of my dear faith:
It shall become thee well to act my woes; 26
She will attend it better in thy youth
Than in a nuncio's of more grave aspect.

VIO. I think not so, my lord.

DUKE. Dear lad, believe it;
For they shall yet belie thy happy years, 30
That say thou art a man: Diana's lip
Is not more smooth and rubious; thy small pipe
Is as the maiden's organ, shrill and sound,
And all is semblative a woman's part.
I know thy constellation is right apt 35
For this affair. Some four or five attend him;
All, if you will; for I myself am best
When least in company. Prosper well in this,
And thou shalt live as freely as thy lord,
To call his fortunes thine.

VIO. I'll do my best 40
To woo your lady: [*Aside*] yet, a barful strife!
Whoe'er I woo, myself would be his wife.
[*Exeunt.*

11. **On your attendance,** at your service. 20. **spoke,** reported. 21. **leap . . . bounds,** ignore all restraints of politeness. 22. **make . . . return,** come back from a fruitless errand. 26. **act,** portray. 27. **attend . . . youth,** pay more attention to it because of your youth. 28. **nuncio's,** messenger's. 32. **rubious,** rosy. 33. **organ,** voice; **sound,** i.e., not cracked as a boy's voice would be. 34. **semblative . . . part,** resembles a boy who acts a woman's part in a play. 35. **constellation . . . apt,** i.e., your nature determined by the stars is well fitted. 41. **barful strife,** conflict, full of difficulties. **Scene v: s.d. Clown,** the term applied to the low comedy actor in a company. The domestic jester was usually called "the fool." 3. **in way . . . excuse,** to make an excuse for you. 6. **fear no colours,** fear no enemy; pun on (1) "collar" = hangman's noose, (2) "choler" = anger. 7. **Make that good,** explain that. 9. **lenten,** scanty, like food in Lent. Maria means this joke is poor. 12-3. **may . . . foolery,** I dare you to say that when you are fooling. 18. **turned away,** dismissed. 21. **for,** as for. 21-2. **let . . . out,** i.e., let us wait until the end of summer to see whether it happens. 25. **points,** pun on laces which held up the gaskins or breeches. 28-9. **go thy way,** i.e., good luck to you. 29-31. **if . . . Illyria,** i.e., if Sir Toby ever sobers up, he will see that you are the wittiest girl in Illyria. 34. **were best,** had better.

SCENE V. OLIVIA'S *house.*

[*Enter* MARIA *and* CLOWN.]

MAR. Nay, either tell me where thou hast been, or I will not open my lips so wide as a bristle may enter in way of thy excuse: my lady will hang thee for thy absence.

CLO. Let her hang me: he that is well hanged in this world needs to fear no colours. 5

MAR. Make that good.

CLO. He shall see none to fear.

MAR. A good lenten answer: I can tell thee where that saying was born, of "I fear no colours." 10

CLO. Where, good Mistress Mary?

MAR. In the wars; and that may you be bold to say in your foolery.

CLO. Well, God give them wisdom that have it; and those that are fools, let them use their talents. 16

MAR. Yet you will be hanged for being so long absent; or to be turned away, is not that as good as a hanging to you? 19

CLO. Many a good hanging prevents a bad marriage; and, for turning away, let summer bear it out.

MAR. You are resolute, then?

CLO. No so, neither; but I am resolved on two points. 25

MAR. That if one break, the other will hold; or, if both break, your gaskins fall.

CLO. Apt, in good faith; very apt. Well, go thy way; if Sir Toby would leave drinking, thou wert as witty a piece of Eve's flesh as any in Illyria. 31

MAR. Peace, you rogue, no more o' that. Here comes my lady: make your excuse wisely, you were best. [*Exit.* 34

CLO. Wit, an 't be thy will, put me into good fooling! Those wits, that think they have thee, do very oft prove fools; and I, that am sure I lack thee, may pass for a wise man: for what says Quinapalus? "Better a witty fool than a foolish wit." 40

[*Enter* LADY OLIVIA *with* MALVOLIO.]

God bless thee, lady!

OLI. Take the fool away.

CLO. Do you not hear, fellows? Take away the lady.

OLI. Go to, you're a dry fool; I'll no more of you: besides, you grow dishonest. 46

CLO. Two faults, madonna, that drink and good counsel will amend: for give the dry fool drink, then is the fool not dry: bid the dishonest man mend himself; if he mend, he is no longer dishonest; if he cannot let the botcher mend him. Any thing that's mended is but patched: virtue that transgresses is but patched with sin; and sin that amends is but patched with virtue. If that this simple syl- 55 logism will serve, so; if it will not, what remedy? As there is no true cuckold but calamity, so beauty's a flower. The lady bade take away the fool; therefore, I say again, take her away.

OLI. Sir, I bade them take away you. 60

CLO. Misprision in the highest degree! Lady, cucullus non facit monachum; that's as much to say as I wear not motley in my brain. Good madonna, give me leave to prove you a fool.

OLI. Can you do it? 65

CLO. Dexteriously, good madonna.

OLI. Make your proof.

CLO. I must catechize you for it, madonna: good my mouse of virtue, answer me.

OLI. Well, sir, for want of other idleness, I'll bide your proof. 71

CLO. Good madonna, why mournest thou?

OLI. Good fool, for my brother's death.

CLO. I think his soul is in hell, madonna.

OLI. I know his soul is in heaven, fool. 75

CLO. The more fool, madonna, to mourn for your brother's soul being in heaven. Take away the fool, gentlemen.

OLI. What think you of this fool, Malvolio? doth he not mend? 80

MAL. Yes, and shall do till the pangs of death shake him: infirmity, that decays the wise, doth ever make the better fool.

CLO. God send you, sir, a speedy infirmity, for the better increasing your folly! Sir Toby will be sworn that I am no fox; but he will not pass his word for two pence that you are no fool.

OLI. How say you to that, Malvolio? 88

MAL. I marvel your ladyship takes delight in such a barren rascal: I saw him put down the other day with an ordinary fool that has no more brain than a stone. Look you now, he's out of his guard already; unless you laugh and minister occasion to him, he is gagged. I protest, I take these wise men, that crow so at these set kind of fools, no better than the fools' zanies. 96

OLI. O, you are sick of self-love, Malvolio, and taste with a distempered appetite. To be generous, guiltless and of free disposition, is to take those things for bird-bolts that 100 you deem cannon-bullets: there is no slander in an allowed fool, though he do nothing but rail; nor no railing in a known discreet man, though he do nothing but reprove.

CLO. Now Mercury endue thee with leasing, for thou speakest well of fools! 106

[*Re-enter* MARIA.]

MAR. Madam, there is at the gate a young gentleman much desires to speak with you.

OLI. From the Count Orsino, is it?

MAR. I know not, madam: 'tis a fair young man, and well attended. 111

OLI. Who of my people hold him in delay?

MAR. Sir Toby, madam, your kinsman.

OLI. Fetch him off, I pray you; he speaks nothing but madman: fie on him! [*Exit* MARIA.] Go you, Malvolio: if it be a suit from the count, I am sick, or not at home; what

36-7. that . . . thee, that think they have the better of you in an exchange of wit. 39. **Quinapalus**, a learned sounding authority invented by Feste; **witty**, wise. 45. **dry**, dull. 46. **dishonest**, unreliable. 52. **botcher**, mender of old clothes. 53. **patched**, an allusion to fool's parti-colored costume. 61. **Misprison**, misapprehension. 62. **cucullus . . . monachum**, the cowl doesn't make the monk. 69. **mouse**, a term of endearment. 70. **idleness**, trifling pastime. 80. **mend**, improve in wit. 83. **make the better fool**, make a fool sillier. 90. **barren**, without ideas; **put down**, beaten in a wit combat. 91. **ordinary fool**, a mere half-wit. 93. **minister occasion**, provide him with a topic. 95. **set**, professional, artificial. 96. **zanies**, buffoons who awkwardly imitated the tricks of the professional jesters. 98. **distempered**, disordered. 99. **free**, open. 100. **bird-bolts**, blunt arrows. 102. **allowed**, licensed. 103. **railing**, scolding; **known discreet**, with a reputation for wisdom. 105. **Mercury**, god of thievery and falsehood; **leasing**, lying devoid of malice. 112. **hold . . . delay**, are keeping him out. 114. **Fetch**, call. 114-5. **he . . . madman**, he always talks like a crazy man.

you will, to dismiss it. [*Exit* MALVOLIO.] Now you see, sir, how your fooling grows old, and people dislike it. 119

CLO. Thou hast spoke for us, madonna, as if thy eldest son should be a fool; whose skull Jove cram with brains! for,—here he comes—one of thy kin has a most weak pia mater.

[*Enter* SIR TOBY.]

OLI. By mine honour, half drunk. What is he at the gate, cousin? 125

SIR TO. A gentleman.

OLI. A gentleman! what gentleman?

SIR TO. 'Tis a gentleman here—a plague o' these pickle-herring! How now, sot!

CLO. Good Sir Toby! 130

OLI. Cousin, cousin, how have you come so early by this lethargy?

SIR TO. Lechery! I defy lechery. There's one at the gate.

OLI. Ay, marry, what is he? 135

SIR TO. Let him be the devil, an he will, I care not: give me faith, say I. Well, it's all one. [*Exit.*

OLI. What's a drunken man like, fool?

CLO. Like a drowned man, a fool and a mad man: one draught above heat makes him a fool; the second mads him; and a third drowns him. 141

OLI. Go thou and seek the crowner, and let him sit o' my coz; for he's in the third degree of drink, he's drowned: go, look after him.

CLO. He is but mad yet, madonna; and the fool shall look to the madman. [*Exit.* 146

[*Re-enter* MALVOLIO.]

MAL. Madam, yond young fellow swears he will speak with you. I told him you were sick; he takes on him to understand so much, and therefore comes to speak with you. I told him you were asleep; he seems to have a foreknowledge of that too, and therefore comes to speak with you. What is to be said to him, lady? he's fortified against any denial.

OLI. Tell him he shall not speak with me. 155

MAL. Has been told so; and he says, he'll stand at your door like a sheriff's post, and be the supporter to a bench, but he'll speak with you.

OLI. What kind o' man is he?

MAL. Why, of mankind. 160

OLI. What manner of man?

MAL. Of very ill manner; he'll speak with you, will you or no.

OLI. Of what personage and years is he?

MAL. Not yet old enough for a man, 165 nor young enough for a boy; as a squash is before 'tis a peascod, or a codling when 'tis almost an apple: 'tis with him in standing water, between boy and man. He is very well-favoured and he speaks very shrewishly; one would think his mother's milk were scarce out of him. 171

OLI. Let him approach: call in my gentlewoman.

MAL. Gentlewoman, my lady calls. [*Exit.*

[*Re-enter* MARIA.]

OLI. Give me my veil: come, throw it o'er
my face. 175
We'll once more hear Orsino's embassy.

[*Enter* VIOLA, *and* ATTENDANTS.]

VIO. The honourable lady of the house, which is she?

OLI. Speak to me; I shall answer for her. Your will? 180

VIO. Most radiant, exquisite and unmatchable beauty,—I pray you, tell me if this be the lady of the house, for I never saw her: I would be loath to cast away my speech, for besides that it is excellently well penned, I have taken great pains to con it. Good beauties, let me sustain no scorn; I am very comptible, even to the least sinister usage.

OLI. Whence came you, sir? 189

VIO. I can say little more than I have studied, and that question's out of my part. Good

118. **old,** stale. 123. **pia mater,** inner lining of the brain. The speech means, "May Jove cram your son's skull with brains, for idiocy runs in your family (and here comes the proof of it)." 128. **here—,** at this point Sir Toby hiccoughs. 132. **lethargy,** stupor, i.e., drunkenness. 137. **give me faith,** i.e., I hope to escape the Devil not by good works but by faith. 140. **one . . . heat,** one drink more than enough to warm him. 142. **crowner,** coroner. 143. **sit o',** hold an inquest on. 146. **look to,** look after. 149. **takes on him,** pretends. 157. **sheriff's post,** a post set up to mark the office of a magistrate. 160. **of mankind,** like any man. 164. **personage,** appearance. 166. **squash,** an unripe peascod. 167. **codling,** unripe apple. 168. **in standing water,** i.e., the instant at the turn of the tide when the water is still. 169-70. **well-favoured,** handsome. 170. **shrewishly,** i.e., shrilly (for a man). 184. **cast away,** waste. 186. **con,** learn by heart. 188. **comptible . . . usage,** susceptible to the least discourtesy. 191. **out of my part,** not in the lines written for me.

gentle one, give me a modest assurance if you be the lady of the house, that I may proceed in my speech.

OLI. Are you a comedian? 194

VIO. No, my profound heart: and yet, by the very fangs of malice I swear, I am not that I play. Are you the lady of the house?

OLI. If I do not usurp myself, I am. 198

VIO. Most certain, if you are she, you do usurp yourself; for what is yours to bestow is not yours to reserve. But this is from my commission: I will on with my speech in your praise, and then show you the heart of my message.

OLI. Come to what is important in 't: I forgive you the praise. 205

VIO. Alas, I took great pains to study it, and 'tis poetical.

OLI. It is the more like to be feigned: I pray you, keep it in. I heard you were saucy at my gates, and allowed your approach rather to wonder at you than to hear you. If you be not mad, be gone; if you have reason, be brief: 'tis not that time of moon with me to make one in so skipping a dialogue.

MAR. Will you hoist sail, sir? here lies your way. 216

VIO. No, good swabber; I am to hull here a little longer. Some mollification for your giant, sweet lady. Tell me your mind: I am a messenger. 220

OLI. Sure, you have some hideous matter to deliver, when the courtesy of it is so fearful. Speak your office.

VIO. It alone concerns your ear. I bring no overture of war, no taxation of homage: I hold the olive in my hand; my words are as full of peace as matter. 226

OLI. Yet you began rudely. What are you? what would you? 229

VIO. The rudeness that hath appeared in me have I learned from my entertainment. What I am, and what I would, are as secret as maidenhead; to your ears, divinity, to any other's, profanation. 234

OLI. Give us the place alone; we will hear this divinity. [*Exeunt* MARIA *and* ATTENDANTS.
Now, sir, what is your text?

VIO. Most sweet lady,—

OLI. A comfortable doctrine, and much may be said of it. Where lies your text? 240

VIO. In Orsino's bosom.

OLI. In his bosom! In what chapter of his bosom?

VIO. To answer by the method, in the first of his heart. 245

OLI. O, I have read it: it is heresy. Have you no more to say?

VIO. Good madam, let me see your face.

OLI. Have you any commission from your lord to negotiate with my face? You are 250 now out of your text: but we will draw the curtain and show you the picture. Look you, sir, such a one I was this present: is 't not well done? [*Unveiling.*

VIO. Excellently done, if God did all.

OLI. 'Tis in grain, sir; 'twill endure wind and weather. 256

VIO. 'Tis beauty truly blent, whose red and white
Nature's own sweet and cunning hand laid on:
Lady, you are the cruell'st she alive,
If you will lead these graces to the grave 260
And leave the world no copy.

OLI. O, sir, I will not be so hard-hearted; I will give out divers schedules of my beauty: it shall be inventoried, and every particle and utensil labelled to my will: as, item, two lips, indifferent red; item, two grey eyes, with lids to them; item, one neck, one chin, and so forth. Were you sent hither to praise me?

VIO. I see you what you are, you are too proud; 269
But, if you were the devil, you are fair. 270
My lord and master loves you: O, such love
Could be but recompensed, though you were crown'd
The nonpareil of beauty!

OLI. How does he love me?

VIO. With adorations, fertile tears,
With groans that thunder love, with sighs of fire. 275

192-3. **modest . . . be**, enough assurance to convince me that you are. 194. **comedian**, actor. 198. **usurp myself**, act as an impostor. 201-2. **from my commission**, outside my instructions. 212. **not mad**, i.e., completely mad. 213. **that time of moon with me**, i.e., I am not lunatic enough. 214. **skipping**, flighty. 217. **swabber**, a deck washer, i.e., a common sailor; **hull**, float. 219. **giant**, ladies of romance were often guarded by a giant. Here an ironic reference to the size of the boy playing Maria. 222. **courtesy**, ceremonious preliminaries. 225. **taxation of**, demand for. 231. **entertainment**, reception. 239. **comfortable**, comforting. 244. **by the method**, i.e., to keep up the figure of a sermon. 253. **such . . . present**, this is the way I looked —right now. 255. **in grain**, fast dyed. 265. **labelled . . . will**, attached to my will like an inventory. 268. **praise**, appraise, with a quibble on the usual meaning. 273. **nonpareil**, something without equal. 274. **fertile**, i.e., copious.

OLI. Your lord does know my mind; I cannot love him:
Yet I suppose him virtuous, know him noble,
Of great estate, of fresh and stainless youth;
In voices well divulged, free, learn'd and valiant;
And in dimension and the shape of nature 280
A gracious person: but yet I cannot love him;
He might have took his answer long ago.

VIO. If I did love you in my master's flame,
With such a suffering, such a deadly life,
In your denial I would find no sense; 285
I would not understand it.

OLI. Why, what would you?

VIO. Make me a willow cabin at your gate,
And call upon my soul within the house;
Write loyal cantons of contemned love 289
And sing them loud even in the dead of night;
Halloo your name to the reverberate hills
And make the babbling gossip of the air
Cry out "Olivia!" O, you should not rest
Between the elements of air and earth,
But you should pity me!

OLI. You might do much.
What is your parentage? 296

VIO. Above my fortunes, yet my state is well:
I am a gentleman.

OLI. Get you to your lord;
I cannot love him: let him send no more;
Unless, perchance, you come to me again, 300
To tell me how he takes it. Fare you well:
I thank you for your pains: spend this for me.

VIO. I am no fee'd post, lady; keep your purse:
My master, not myself, lacks recompense.
Love make his heart of flint that you shall love; 305
And let your fervour, like my master's, be
Placed in contempt! Farewell, fair cruelty. [*Exit.*

OLI. "What is your parentage?"
"Above my fortunes, yet my state is well:
I am a gentleman." I'll be sworn thou art; 310
Thy tongue, thy face, thy limbs, actions and spirit,
Do give thee five-fold blazon: not too fast: soft, soft!
Unless the master were the man. How now!
Even so quickly may one catch the plague?
Methinks I feel this youth's perfections 315
With an invisible and subtle stealth
To creep in at mine eyes. Well, let it be.
What ho, Malvolio!

[*Re-enter* MALVOLIO.]

MAL. Here, madam, at your service.

OLI. Run after that same peevish messenger,
The county's man: he left this ring behind him, 320
Would I or not: tell him I'll none of it.
Desire him not to flatter with his lord,
Nor hold him up with hopes; I am not for him:
If that the youth will come this way to-morrow, 324
I'll give him reasons for 't: hie thee, Malvolio.

MAL. Madam, I will. [*Exit.*

OLI. I do I know not what, and fear to find
Mine eye too great a flatterer for my mind.
Fate, show thy force: ourselves we do not owe;
What is decreed must be, and be this so. [*Exit.*

ACT II

SCENE I. *The sea-coast.*

[*Enter* ANTONIO *and* SEBASTIAN.]

ANT. Will you stay no longer? nor will you not that I go with you?

SEB. By your patience, no. My stars shine darkly over me: the malignancy of my fate might perhaps distemper yours; therefore I 5 shall crave of you your leave that I may bear my evils alone: it were a bad recompense for your love, to lay any of them on you.

279. **well divulged,** well spoken of; **free,** generous. 280. **dimension,** bodily proportions. 283. **flame,** passion. 284. **deadly,** doomed to death (if his love is unrequited). 287. **willow,** a symbol of unrequited love. 288. **my soul,** i.e., Olivia. 289. **cantons,** songs. 292. **babbling . . . air,** echo. 295. **but,** unless. 297. **state is well,** present position is good. 303. **fee'd post,** hired messenger. 307. **placed in,** treated with. 312. **five-fold blazon,** coat of arms composed of the five features just listed; **soft,** be careful. 319. **peevish,** silly little. 320. **county's,** count's. 322. **flatter with,** deceive with false hopes. 329. **owe,** own. **Act II, Scene i:** 3. **By your patience,** i.e., be patient enough to understand my refusal. 4. **malignancy,** malevolence. 5. **distemper,** injure.

ANT. Let me yet know of you whither you are bound. 10

SEB. No, sooth, sir: my determinate voyage is mere extravagancy. But I perceive in you so excellent a touch of modesty, that you will not extort from me what I am willing to keep in; therefore it charges me in manners the rather to express myself. You must know of me then, Antonio, my name is Sebastian, which I called Roderigo. My father was that Sebastian of Messaline, whom I know you have heard of. He left behind him myself and a sister, both born in an hour: if the 20 heavens had been pleased would we had so ended! but you, sir, altered that; for some hour before you took me from the breach of the sea was my sister drowned.

ANT. Alas the day! 25

SEB. A lady, sir, though it was said she much resembled me, was yet of many accounted beautiful: but, though I could not with such estimable wonder overfar believe that, yet thus far I will boldly publish her; she bore a mind that envy could not but call fair. She is drowned already, sir, with salt water, though I seem to drown her remembrance again with more. 33

ANT. Pardon me, sir, your bad entertainment.

SEB. O good Antonio, forgive me your trouble.

ANT. If you will not murder me for my love, let me be your servant. 37

SEB. If you will not undo what you have done, that is, kill him whom you have recovered, desire it not. Fare ye well at once: my bosom is full of kindness, and I am yet 41 so near the manners of my mother, that upon the least occasion more mine eyes will tell tales of me. I am bound to the Count Orsino's court: farewell. [*Exit.*

ANT. The gentleness of all the gods go with thee! 45

I have many enemies in Orsino's court,
Else would I very shortly see thee there.
But, come what may, I do adore thee so,
That danger shall seem sport, and I will go. [*Exit.*

SCENE II. *A street.*

[*Enter* VIOLA, MALVOLIO *following.*]

MAL. Were not you even now with the Countess Olivia?

VIO. Even now, sir; on a moderate pace I have since arrived but hither.

MAL. She returns this ring to you, sir: 5 you might have saved me my pains, to have taken it away yourself. She adds, moreover, that you should put your lord into a desperate assurance she will none of him: and one thing more, that you be never so hardy to come again in his affairs, unless it be to report your lord's taking of this. Receive it so. 12

VIO. She took the ring of me: I'll none of it.

MAL. Come, sir, you peevishly threw it to her; and her will is, it should be so returned: if it be worth stooping for, there it lies in your eye; if not, be it his that finds it. [*Exit.*

VIO. I left no ring with her: what means this lady?
Fortune forbid my outside have not charm'd her!
She made good view of me; indeed, so much,
That sure methought her eyes had lost her tongue, 21
For she did speak in starts distractedly.
She loves me, sure; the cunning of her passion
Invites me in this churlish messenger.
None of my lord's ring! why, he sent her none. 25
I am the man: if it be so, as 'tis,
Poor lady, she were better love a dream.
Disguise, I see, thou art a wickedness,
Wherein the pregnant enemy does much.
How easy is it for the proper-false 30
In women's waxen hearts to set their forms!
Alas, our frailty is the cause, not we!
For such as we are made of, such we be.
How will this fadge? my master loves her dearly;

11. **determinate voyage**, fixed plans for travel. 12. **extravagancy**, aimless wandering. 13. **modesty**, restraint. 15. **it . . . manners**, courtesy demands. 16. **express**, reveal. 17. **Messaline**, purely fictitious place. 23. **breach of the sea**, i.e., breakers. 29. **such estimable wonder**, with such esteem and admiration; **overfar believe that**, believe that too completely. 30. **publish her**, speak frankly about her. 34. **entertainment**, reception. 36. **If . . . servant**, i.e., I love you so much that your refusal to let me be your servant would kill me. 39. **recovered**, rescued. 42. **manners of my mother**, i.e., a woman's tendency to weep.

43. **least occasion**, slightest provocation. **Scene ii:** 4. **arrived but hither**, got only as far as this. 8. **desperate assurance**, certainty that there is no hope. 12. **so**, i.e., with this understanding. 14. **peevishly**, in a fit of temper. 24. **Invites me**, leads me on. 29. **pregnant enemy**, resourceful devil (who could assume any shape to tempt man). 30. **proper-false**, handsome deceiver. 34. **fadge**, turn out.

And I, poor monster, fond as much on him; 35
And she, mistaken, seems to dote on me.
What will become of this? As I am man,
My state is desperate for my master's love;
As I am woman,—now alas the day!—
What thriftless sighs shall poor Olivia breathe! 40
O time! thou must untangle this, not I;
It is too hard a knot for me to untie! [*Exit.*

SCENE III. OLIVIA's *house*.

[*Enter* SIR TOBY *and* SIR ANDREW.]

SIR TO. Approach, Sir Andrew: not to be abed after midnight is to be up betimes; and "diluculo surgere," thou know'st,—

SIR AND. Nay, by my troth, I know not: but I know, to be up late is to be up late. 5

SIR TO. A false conclusion: I hate it as an unfilled can. To be up after midnight and to go to bed then, is early: so that to go to bed after midnight is to go to bed betimes. Does not our life consist of the four elements? 10

SIR AND. Faith, so they say; but I think it rather consists of eating and drinking.

SIR TO. Thou'rt a scholar; let us therefore eat and drink. Marian, I say! a stoup of wine!

[*Enter* CLOWN.]

SIR AND. Here comes the fool, i' faith. 15

CLO. How now, my hearts! did you never see the picture of "we three"?

SIR TO. Welcome, ass. Now let's have a catch. 18

SIR AND. By my troth, the fool has an excellent breast. I had rather than forty shillings I had such a leg, and so sweet a breath to sing, as the fool has. In sooth, thou wast in very gracious fooling last night, when thou spokest of Pigrogromitus, of the Vapians passing the equinoctial of Queubus: 'twas very good, i' faith. I sent thee sixpence for thy leman: hadst it? 26

CLO. I did impeticos thy gratillity; for Malvolio's nose is no whipstock: my lady has a white hand, and the Myrmidons are no bottle-ale houses.

SIR AND. Excellent! why, this is the best fooling, when all is done. Now, a song. 31

SIR TO. Come on; there is sixpence for you: let's have a song.

SIR AND. There's a testril of me too: if one knight give a— 35

CLO. Would you have a love-song, or a song of good life?

SIR TO. A love-song, a love-song.

SIR AND. Ay, ay: I care not for good life.

CLO. [*Sings*]

O mistress mine, where are you roaming? 40
O, stay and hear; your true love's coming,
That can sing both high and low:
Trip no further, pretty sweeting;
Journeys end in lovers meeting,
Every wise man's son doth know. 45

SIR AND. Excellent good, i' faith.

SIR TO. Good, good.

CLO. [*Sings*]

What is love? 'tis not hereafter;
Present mirth hath present laughter;
What 's to come is still unsure: 50
In delay there lies no plenty;
Then come kiss me, sweet and twenty,
Youth's a stuff will not endure.

SIR AND. A mellifluous voice, as I am true knight.

SIR TO. A contagious breath.

SIR AND. Very sweet and contagious, i' faith. 57

SIR TO. To hear by the nose, it is dulcet in contagion. But shall we make the welkin dance indeed? shall we rouse the night-owl in a catch that will draw three souls out of one weaver? shall we do that? 62

35. **monster**, i.e., both man and woman; **fond**, dote. 40. **thriftless**, wasted. **Scene iii: 2. betimes**, early. 3. **"diluculo sugere,"** part of proverb **"diliculo sugere saluberrimum est"**—"it is most healthful to get up early," a saying out of Lilly's Grammar, studied in all the grammar-schools. 4. **by my troth**, on my word; **I know not**, i.e., I don't know anything about that. 7. **can**, tankard. 10. **four elements**, earth, air, fire, and water. 14. **stoup**, cup. 17. **of "we three,"** of two fools or two asses with the inscription "we three." 18. **catch**, a round. 20. **breast**, singing voice. 21. **breath**, voice. 24. **Pigrogromitus, Vapians, Queubus**, all nonsense, pretended erudition. 26. **leman**, sweetheart. 27-9. **I did impeticos . . . bottle-ale houses**, Though seemingly nonsensical, the passage means: "I did pocket your gratuity, because though Malvolio is nosy enough to discover my truancy, he can't use his long nose as a whip-handle. My sweetheart is a lady [has a white hand] and the tavern we frequent [the Myrmidons] is not the cheap kind of place that sells ale in small bottles [that your miserable sixpence could buy]." 34. **testril**, he means "tester," a sixpence. 55. **contagious breath**, catchy tune. 58-9. **To hear . . . contagion**, if we could hear by the nose (the channel of contagion), we should call the song a sweet contagion (as opposed to the ill-smelling breath of disease). 59. **makes the welkin dance**, drink until the sky seems to reel. 62. **weaver**, many weavers were Psalm-singing Protestant refugees from Belgium.

SIR AND. An you love me, let 's do 't: I am dog at a catch.

CLO. By'r lady, sir, and some dogs will catch well. 65

SIR AND. Most certain. Let our catch be, "Thou knave."

CLO. "Hold thy peace, thou knave," knight? I shall be constrained in 't to call thee knave, knight. 70

SIR AND. 'Tis not the first time I have constrained one to call me knave. Begin, fool: it begins "Hold thy peace."

CLO. I shall never begin if I hold my peace.

SIR AND. Good, i' faith. Come, begin. 75 [*Catch sung.*

[*Enter* MARIA.]

MAR. What a caterwauling do you keep here! If my lady have not called up her steward Malvolio and bid him turn you out of doors, never trust me. 79

SIR TO. My lady's a Cataian, we are politicians, Malvolio's a Peg-a-Ramsey, and "Three merry men be we." Am not I consanguineous? am I not of her blood? Tillyvally. Lady! [*Sings*] "There dwelt a man in Babylon, lady, lady!" 84

CLO. Beshrew me, the knight's in admirable fooling.

SIR AND. Ay, he does well enough if he be disposed, and so do I too: he does it with a better grace, but I do it more natural.

SIR TO. [*Sings*] "O, the twelfth day of December,"— 91

MAR. For the love o' God, peace!

[*Enter* MALVOLIO.]

MAL. My masters, are you mad? or what are you? Have you no wit, manners, nor honesty, but to gabble like tinkers at this time of night? Do ye make an alehouse of my lady's house, that ye squeak out your coziers' catches without any mitigation or remorse of voice? Is there no respect of place, persons, nor time in you? 99

SIR TO. We did keep time, sir, in our catches. Sneck up!

MAL. Sir Toby, I must be round with you. My lady bade me tell you, that, though she harbours you as her kinsman, she's nothing allied to your disorders. If you can separate yourself and your misdemeanours, you are welcome to the house; if not, an it would please you to take leave of her, she is very willing to bid you farewell.

SIR TO. "Farewell, dear heart, since I must needs be gone." 110

MAR. Nay, good Sir Toby.

CLO. "His eyes do show his days are almost done."

MAL. Is 't even so?

SIR TO. "But I will never die." 115

CLO. Sir Toby, there you lie.

MAL. This is much credit to you.

SIR TO. "Shall I bid him go?"

CLO. "What an if you do?"

SIR TO. "Shall I bid him go, and spare not?" 120

CLO. "O no, no, no, no, you dare not."

SIR TO. Out o' tune, sir: ye lie. Art any more than a steward? Dost thou think, because thou art virtuous, there shall be no more cakes and ale? 125

CLO. Yes, by Saint Anne, and ginger shall be hot i' the mouth too.

SIR TO. Thou'rt i' the right. Go, sir, rub your chain with crums. A stoup of wine, Maria! 129

MAL. Mistress Mary, if you prized my lady's favour at any thing more than contempt, you would not give means for this uncivil rule: she shall know of it, by this hand. [*Exit.*

MAR. Go shake your ears.

SIR AND. 'Twere as good a deed as to drink when a man's a-hungry, to challenge him the field, and then to break promise with him and make a fool of him.

SIR TO. Do 't, knight: I'll write thee a challenge; or I'll deliver thy indignation to him by word of mouth. 141

MAR. Sweet Sir Toby, be patient for tonight: since the youth of the count's was

76. **keep**, carry on. 80. **Cataian**, Chinaman, hence, a cheat; **politicians**, conspirators. 81. **Peg-a-Ramsey**, scare-crow. 83. **Tillyvally**, about = nonsense. 85. **Beshrew**, about = plague take me. 89. **natural**, pun on meaning of "idiot." 94. **wit**, sense. 95. **honesty**, sense of decency; **tinkers**, were proverbial drunkards and their trade was noisy. 97. **coziers'**, cobblers'. 98. **remorse of voice**, i.e., pity on our ears. 101. **Sneck up**, hang yourself. 102. **round**, frank. 104. **nothing**, in no way. 105. **disorders**, misconduct. 117. **This . . . you**, i.e., this is a fine way for you to act. 123. **steward**, manager of the household or estate. 125. **cakes and ale**, proverbial for "social gaiety." 128. **chain**, steward's badge of office; **with crums**, used for polishing silver. 132. **means**, i.e., wine. 133. **rule**, conduct. 137. **the field**, i.e., to a duel; **break promise**, i.e., not show up.

to-day with my lady, she is much out of quiet. For Monsieur Malvolio, let me alone 145 with him: if I do not gull him into a nayword, and make him a common recreation, do not think I have wit enough to lie straight in my bed: I know I can do it.

SIR TO. Possess us, possess us; tell us something of him. 150

MAR. Marry, sir, sometimes he is a kind of puritan.

SIR AND. O, if I thought that, I 'ld beat him like a dog!

SIR TO. What, for being a puritan? thy exquisite reason, dear knight? 156

SIR AND. I have no exquisite reason for 't, but I have reason good enough.

MAR. The devil a puritan that he is, or any thing constantly, but a time-pleaser; an affectioned ass, that cons state without book and utters it by great swarths: the best persuaded of himself, so crammed, as he thinks, with excellencies, that it is his grounds of faith that all that look on him love him; and on that vice in him will my revenge find notable cause to work. 166

SIR TO. What wilt thou do?

MAR. I will drop in his way some obscure epistles of love; wherein, by the colour of his beard, the shape of his leg, the manner of his gait, the expressure of his eye, forehead, and complexion, he shall find himself most feelingly personated. I can write very like my lady your niece: on a forgotten matter we can hardly make distinction of our hands. 175

SIR TO. Excellent! I smell a device.

SIR AND. I have 't in my nose too.

SIR TO. He shall think, by the letters that thou wilt drop, that they come from my niece, and that she's in love with him. 180

MAR. My purpose is, indeed, a horse of that colour.

SIR AND. And your horse now would make him an ass.

MAR. Ass, I doubt not. 185

SIR AND. O, 'twill be admirable!

MAR. Sport royal, I warrant you: I know my physic will work with him. I will plant you two, and let the fool make a third, where he shall find the letter: observe his construction of it. For this night, to bed, and dream on the event. Farewell. [*Exit.* 192

SIR TO. Good night, Penthesilea.

SIR AND. Before me, she's a good wench.

SIR TO. She's a beagle, true-bred, and one that adores me: what o' that? 196

SIR AND. I was adored once too.

SIR TO. Let's to bed, knight. Thou hadst need send for more money.

SIR AND. If I cannot recover your niece, I am a foul way out. 201

SIR TO. Send for money, knight: if thou hast her not i' the end, call me cut.

SIR AND. If I do not, never trust me, take it how you will. 205

SIR TO. Come, come, I'll go burn some sack; 'tis too late to go to bed now: come, knight; come, knight. [*Exeunt.*

SCENE IV. *The* DUKE'S *Palace*

[*Enter* DUKE, VIOLA, CURIO, *and others.*]

DUKE. Give me some music. Now, good morrow, friends.
Now, good Cesario, but that piece of song,
That old and antic song we heard last night:
Methought it did relieve my passion much,
More than light airs and recollected terms 5
Of these most brisk and giddy-paced times:
Come, but one verse.

CUR. He is not here, so please your lordship, that should sing it.

DUKE. Who was it? 10

CUR. Feste, the jester, my lord; a fool that the lady Olivia's father took much delight in. He is about the house.

DUKE. Seek him out, and play the tune the while. [*Exit* CURIO. *Music plays.*]
Come hither, boy: if ever thou shalt love, 15
In the sweet pangs of it remember me;
For such as I am all true lovers are,

145-6. **out of quiet,** disquieted, uneasy; **For,** as for. 147-8. **nayword,** byword, an object of scorn. 148. **recreation,** laughing stock. 149. **possess,** i.e., "put us wise." 156. **exquisite,** subtle. 160. **time-pleaser,** time-server; **affectioned,** affected. 161. **cons . . . book,** memorizes rules of polite deportment. 162. **swarths,** swaths. 162-3. **best persuaded of himself,** having the best opinion of himself. 164. **his . . . of faith,** the foundation of his belief. 165. **notable cause,** excellent material on which. 168. **obscure,** i.e., in their phrasing. 171. **expressure,** form. 172. **complexion,** outward appearance. 173. **personated,** depicted. 174. **forgotten matter,** i.e., a piece of writing we have forgotten about. 181-2. **horse . . . colour,** trick of that sort. 193. **Penthesilea,** queen of the Amazons, another ironical allusion to Maria's small size. 200. **recover,** win. 201. **foul way out,** badly out of pocket. 203. **cut,** horse with docked tail. 206. **burn,** heat and spice. **Scene iv:** 2. **but,** only. 3. **antic,** quaint. 5. **recollected terms,** intricate musical phrases. 14. **the while,** in the meantime.

Unstaid and skittish in all motions else,
Save in the constant image of the creature
That is beloved. How dost thou like this tune?

VIO. It gives a very echo to the seat 21
Where Love is throned.

DUKE. Thou dost speak masterly:
My life upon 't, young though thou art, thine eye
Hath stay'd upon some favour that it loves: 25
Hath it not, boy?

VIO. A little, by your favour.

DUKE. What kind of woman is 't?

VIO. Of your complexion.

DUKE. She is not worth thee, then. What years, i' faith?

VIO. About your years, my lord.

DUKE. Too old, by heaven: let still the woman take 30
An elder than herself; so wears she to him,
So sways she level in her husband's heart:
For, boy, however we do praise ourselves,
Our fancies are more giddy and unfirm,
More longing, wavering, sooner lost and worn, 35
Than women's are.

VIO. I think it well, my lord.

DUKE. Then let thy love be younger than thyself,
Or thy affection cannot hold the bent;
For women are as roses, whose fair flower
Being once display'd, doth fall that very hour. 40

VIO. And so they are: alas, that they are so;
To die, even when they to perfection grow!

[*Re-enter* CURIO *and* CLOWN.]

DUKE. O, fellow, come, the song we had last night.
Mark it, Cesario, it is old and plain;
The spinsters and the knitters in the sun 45
And the free maids that weave their thread with bones
Do use to chant it: it is silly sooth,
And dallies with the innocence of love,
Like the old age.

CLO. Are you ready, sir? 50

DUKE. Ay; prithee, sing. [*Music.*

SONG.

CLO. Come away, come away, death,
And in sad cypress let me be laid;
Fly away, fly away, breath;
I am slain by a fair cruel maid. 55
My shroud of white, stuck all with yew,
O, prepare it!
My part of death, no one so true
Did share it.

Not a flower, not a flower sweet, 60
On my black coffin let there be strown;
Not a friend, not a friend greet
My poor corpse, where my bones shall be thrown:
A thousand thousand sighs to save,
Lay me, O, where 65
Sad true lover never find my grave,
To weep there!

DUKE. There's for thy pains.

CLO. No pains, sir; I take pleasure in singing, sir. 70

DUKE. I'll pay thy pleasure then.

CLO. Truly, sir, and pleasure will be paid, one time or another.

DUKE. Give me now leave to leave thee. 74

CLO. Now, the melancholy god protect thee; and the tailor make thy doublet of changeable taffeta, for thy mind is a very opal. I would have men of such constancy put to sea, that their business might be every thing and their intent every where; for that's it that always makes a good voyage of nothing. Farewell. [*Exit.* 81

DUKE. Let all the rest give place.

[CURIO *and* ATTENDANTS *retire.*]

Once more, Cesario,
Get thee to yond same sovereign cruelty:
Tell her, my love, more noble than the world,
Prizes not quantity of dirty lands; 85

18. **Unstaid . . . else,** fickle and changeable in all other emotions. 23. **masterly,** as an experienced person. 25. **stay'd,** lingered; **favour,** face. 27. **complexion,** appearance. 31. **wears she,** adapts herself. 32. **sways she level,** settles to a perfect balance (like a scale). 33. **praise,** appraise. 34. **fancies,** impulses toward love. 35. **worn,** worn out. 38. **the bent,** i.e., firm (like a drawn bow). 42. **even,** just. 44. **plain,** simple. 45. **spinsters,** women who spin. 46. **free,** carefree; **bones,** bone bobbins. 47. **silly sooth,** simple truth.

48. **dallies,** trifles. 49. **age,** times. 53. **cypress,** coffin made of cypress wood. 58-9. **My part . . . share it,** i.e., no more faithful lover ever died; **My part of death,** i.e., death, my lot. 72. **paid,** paid for. 77. **changeable,** shot, i.e., changeable in color according to the way it is struck by the light. 78. **opal,** which also varies in color with changing light. 80. **intent every where,** can do business anywhere. 81. **of nothing,** with no preconceived plan.

The parts that fortune hath bestow'd upon her,
Tell her, I hold as giddily as fortune;
But 'tis that miracle and queen of gems
That nature pranks her in attracts my soul.
VIO. But if she cannot love you, sir? 90
DUKE. I cannot be so answer'd.
VIO. Sooth, but you must.
Say that some lady, as perhaps there is,
Hath for your love as great a pang of heart
As you have for Olivia: you cannot love her;
You tell her so; must she not then be answer'd? 95
DUKE. There is no woman's sides
Can bide the beating of so strong a passion
As love doth give my heart; no woman's heart
So big, to hold so much; they lack retention.
Alas, their love may be call'd appetite, 100
No motion of the liver, but the palate,
That suffer surfeit, cloyment and revolt;
But mine is all as hungry as the sea,
And can digest as much: make no compare
Between that love a woman can bear me 105
And that I owe Olivia.
VIO. Ay, but I know—
DUKE. What dost thou know?
VIO. Too well what love women to men may owe:
In faith, they are as true of heart as we.
My father had a daughter loved a man, 110
As it might be, perhaps, were I a woman,
I should your lordship.
DUKE. And what's her history?
VIO. A blank, my lord. She never told her love,
But let concealment, like a worm i' the bud,
Feed on her damask cheek: she pined in thought, 115
And with a green and yellow melancholy
She sat like patience on a monument,
Smiling at grief. Was not this love indeed?
We men may say more, swear more: but indeed
Our shows are more than will; for still we prove 120
Much in our vows, but little in our love.
DUKE. But died thy sister of her love, my boy?
VIO. I am all the daughters of my father's house,
And all the brothers too: and yet I know not.
Sir, shall I to this lady?
DUKE. Ay, that's the theme.
To her in haste; give her this jewel; say, 126
My love can give no place, bide no denay.
[*Exeunt.*

SCENE V. OLIVIA'S *garden.*

[*Enter* SIR TOBY, SIR ANDREW, *and* FABIAN.]

SIR TO. Come thy ways, Signior Fabian.

FAB. Nay, I'll come: if I lose a scruple of this sport, let me be boiled to death with melancholy.

SIR TO. Wouldst thou not be glad to have the niggardly rascally sheep-biter come by some notable shame?

FAB. I would exult, man: you know, he brought me out o' favour with my lady about a bear-baiting here. 10

SIR TO. To anger him we'll have the bear again; and we will fool him black and blue: shall we not, Sir Andrew?

SIR AND. An we do not, it is pity of our lives.

SIR TO. Here comes the little villain.

[*Enter* MARIA.]

How now, my metal of India! 17

MAR. Get ye all three into the box-tree: Malvolio's coming down this walk: he has been yonder i' the sun practising behaviour to his own shadow this half hour: observe him, for the love of mockery; for I know this letter will make a contemplative idiot of him. Close, in the name of jesting! Lie thou there [*throws down a letter*]; for here comes the trout that must be caught with tickling. 26
[*Exit.*

86. **parts**, gifts. 87. **I . . . fortune**, i.e., am no more interested in her wealth than is Fortune. 88. **miracle . . . gems**, i.e., beauty. 89. **pranks her in**, adorns her with. 97. **bide**, endure. 99. **retention**, constancy. 101. **liver**, the supposed seat of the passions; **palate**, seat of sensations. 102. **cloyment**, sickness resulting from overeating. 115. **damask**, like a damask rose. 116. **green**, signified hope; **yellow**, signified jealousy. 117. **monument**, tomb. 120. **Our shows . . . will**, our protestations of love are greater than our desire [to love]. 127. **give no place**, yield precedence to nothing else; **bide no denay**, take no denial. **Scene v**: 1. **Come thy ways**, come on. 2. **scruple**, the tiniest part. 6. **sheep-biter**, i.e., sneaking cur. 14. **pity . . . lives**, "just too bad." 17. **metal of India**, i.e., gold. 18. **box-tree**, box-hedge. 23. **contemplative**, with a fixed stare. 24. **Close**, lie low. 26. **tickling**, trout can be caught by stroking them about the gills. Trout also = an "easy mark"; tickling also = flattery.

[*Enter* MALVOLIO.]

MAL. 'Tis but fortune; all is fortune. Maria once told me she did affect me: and I have heard herself come thus near, that, should she fancy, it should be one of my complexion. Besides, she uses me with a more exalted respect than any one else that follows her. What should I think on 't? 33

SIR TO. Here's an overweening rogue!

FAB. O, peace! Contemplation makes a rare turkey-cock of him: how he jets under his advanced plumes!

SIR AND. 'Slight, I could so beat the rogue!

SIR TO. Peace, I say.

MAL. To be Count Malvolio! 40

SIR TO. Ah, rogue!

SIR AND. Pistol him, pistol him.

SIR TO. Peace, peace!

MAL. There is example for 't; the lady of the Strachy married the yeoman of the wardrobe. 45

SIR AND. Fie on him, Jezebel!

FAB. O, peace! now he's deeply in: look how imagination blows him.

MAL. Having been three months married to her, sitting in my state,— 50

SIR TO. O, for a stone-bow, to hit him in the eye!

MAL. Calling my officers about me, in my branched velvet gown; having come from a daybed, where I have left Olivia sleeping,—

SIR TO. Fire and brimstone!

FAB. O, peace, peace! 57

MAL. And then to have the humour of state; and after a demure travel of regard, telling them I know my place as I would they should do theirs, to ask for my kinsman Toby,— 61

SIR TO. Bolts and shackles!

FAB. O peace, peace, peace! now, now.

MAL. Seven of my people, with an obedient start, make out for him: I frown the while; and perchance wind up my watch, 66 or play with my—some rich jewel. Toby approaches; courtesies there to me—

SIR TO. Shall this fellow live?

FAB. Though our silence be drawn from us with cars, yet peace. 71

MAL. I extend my hand to him thus, quenching my familiar smile with an austere regard of control,— 74

SIR TO. And does not Toby take you a blow o' the lips then?

MAL. Saying, "Cousin Toby, my fortunes having cast me on your niece give me this prerogative of speech,"—

SIR TO. What, what? 80

MAL. "You must amend your drunkenness."

SIR TO. Out, scab!

FAB. Nay, patience, or we break the sinews of our plot.

MAL. "Besides, you waste the treasure of your time with a foolish knight,"—

SIR AND. That's me, I warrant you.

MAL. "One Sir Andrew,"—

SIR AND. I knew 'twas I; for many do call me fool. 90

MAL. What employment have we here? [*Taking up the letter.*

FAB. Now is the woodcock near the gin.

SIR TO. O, peace! and the spirit of humours intimate reading aloud to him!

MAL. By my life, this is my lady's hand: these be her very C's, her U's and her T's; and thus makes she her great P's. It is, in contempt of question, her hand.

SIR AND. Her C's, her U's and her T's: why that? 100

MAL. [*Reads*] "To the unknown beloved, this, and my good wishes:" her very phrases! By your leave, wax. Soft! and the impressure her Lucrece, with which she uses to seal: 'tis my lady. To whom should this be? 105

FAB. This wins him, liver and all.

MAL. [*Reads*]

Jove knows I love:
 But who?
Lips, do not move;
No man must know. 110

28. did affect me, was attracted to me. 29. thus near, as near as this to saying. 32. follows, serves. 35. Contemplation, thinking about himself. 36. jets, struts. 37. advanced, raised. 38. 'Slight, by God's light. 44. for't, i.e., for a lady's marrying a social inferior. 46. Jezebel, Sir Andrew is confused; Jezebel was an impudent woman of the Old Testament. 48. blows him, puffs him up. 50. state, chair covered with a canopy. 51. stone-bow, crossbow which shot stones. 54. branched, flowered. 58-9. humour of state, airs of a person of authority. 59. demure . . . regard, grave sweep of my eyes. 64. people, servants. 65. make out for him, go to fetch him. 68. courtesies, makes a formal bow. 71. cars, cart-horses. 74. regard of control, glance of authority. 92. woodcock, a proverbially stupid bird; gin, snare. 98. in . . . question, to question it would be absurd. 103. wax, i.e., wax with which the letter was sealed; Soft, wait a moment. 103-4. impressure her Lucrece, i.e., the seal engraved with a likeness of the chaste Lucrece. 106. liver, i.e., the seat of the emotions.

"No man must know." What follows? the numbers altered! "No man must know:" if this should be thee, Malvolio?

SIR TO. Marry, hang thee, brock!

MAL. [*Reads*]

I may command where I adore;
But silence, like a Lucrece knife,
With bloodless stroke my heart doth gore:
M, O, A, I, doth sway my life.

FAB. A fustian riddle!

SIR TO. Excellent wench, say I. 120

MAL. "M, O, A, I, doth sway my life." Nay, but first, let me see, let me see, let me see.

FAB. What dish o' poison has she dressed him!

SIR TO. And with what wing the staniel checks at it! 125

MAL. "I may command where I adore." Why, she may command me: I serve her; she is my lady. Why, this is evident to any formal capacity; there is no obstruction in this: and the end,—what should that alphabetical position portend? If I could make that resemble something in me,—Softly! M, O, A, I,—

SIR TO. O, ay, make up that: he is now at a cold scent. 134

FAB. Sowter will cry upon't for all this, though it be as rank as a fox. 136

MAL. M,—Malvolio; M,—why, that begins my name.

FAB. Did not I say he would work it out? the cur is excellent at faults. 140

MAL. M,—but then there is no consonancy in the sequel; that suffers under probation: A should follow, but O does.

FAB. And O shall end, I hope.

SIR TO. Ay, or I'll cudgel him, and make him cry O! 146

MAL. And then I comes behind.

FAB. Ay, an you had any eye behind you, you might see more detraction at your heels than fortunes before you. 150

MAL. M, O, A, I; this simulation is not as the former: and yet, to crush this a little, it would bow to me, for every one of these letters are in my name. Soft! here follows prose. 154

[*Reads*] "If this fall into thy hand, revolve. In my stars I am above thee; but be not afraid of greatness: some are born great, some achieve greatness and some have greatness thrust upon 'em. Thy Fates open their hands; let thy blood and spirit embrace them; and, to inure thyself to what thou art 160 like to be, cast thy humble slough and appear fresh. Be opposite with a kinsman, surly with servants; let thy tongue tang arguments of state; put thyself into the trick of singularity: she thus advises thee that sighs 165 for thee. Remember who commended thy yellow stockings, and wished to see thee ever cross-gartered: I say, remember. Go to, thou art made, if thou desirest to be so; if not, let me see thee a steward still, the fellow of servants, and not worthy to touch Fortune's fingers. Farewell. She that would alter services with thee, 172

"THE FORTUNATE-UNHAPPY."

Daylight and champain discovers not more: this is open. I will be proud, I will read politic authors, I will baffle Sir Toby, I will 175 wash off gross acquaintance, I will be point-devise the very man. I do not now fool myself, to let imagination jade me; for every reason excites to this, that my lady loves me. She did commend my yellow stockings 180 of late, she did praise my leg being cross-gartered; and in this she manifests herself to my love, and with a kind of injunction drives me to these habits of her liking. I thank my

112. **numbers**, metre. 114. **brock**, badger, a term of contempt. 119. **fustian**, high-sounding nonsensical. 123. **dressed**, cooked up. 124. **staniel**, an untrained hawk. 125. **checks**, i.e., swerves from its quarry to pounce upon an inferior bird. 129. **formal capacity**, normally sane intelligence. 133. **make up that**, put that together. 134. **cold scent**, i.e., wrong track. 135-6. **Sowter . . . rank as a fox**, even a stupid hound (sowter = bungler) will follow the scent, though, as a matter of fact, it is as strong as a fox. 140. **at faults**, at following breaks in the scent. 141. **consonancy**, consistency. 142. **suffers under probation**, cannot stand examination. 144. **O shall end**, i.e., our trick will end in a cry of distress. 151-2. **this . . . former**, this part of the disguised meaning is not so easy to get as what went before. 152. **crush**, force (the meaning). 153. **bow to me**, be made to apply to me. 155. **revolve**, ponder. 159. **blood**, passion. 161. **slough**, snake's skin. 162. **opposite with**, antagonistic to. 163. **tang . . . state**, ring the changes on their social rank. 164-5, **trick of singularity**, affectation of eccentricity. 168. **cross-gartered**, garters worn both above and below the knee and crossed at the back were out of fashion and worn only by menials. 172. **alter services**, i.e., become your servant. 173. **champain discovers**, open country reveals. 175. **politic**, dealing with affairs of state; **baffle**, treat with contempt. 176-7. **point-devise**, to the last detail. 178. **jade me**, wear me out; so, "deceive."

stars I am happy. I will be strange, stout, 185
in yellow stockings, and cross-gartered, even
with the swiftness of putting on. Jove and
my stars be praised! Here is yet a postscript.
[*Reads*] "Thou canst not choose but know
who I am. If thou entertainest my love, let it
appear in thy smiling; thy smiles become thee
well; therefore in my presence still smile, dear
my sweet, I prithee." 193

Jove, I thank thee: I will smile; I will do
everything that thou wilt have me. [*Exit.*

FAB. I will not give my part of this sport
for a pension of thousands to be paid from
the Sophy.

SIR TO. I could marry this wench for this
device. 200

SIR AND. So could I too.

SIR TO. And ask no other dowry with her
but such another jest.

SIR AND. Nor I neither.

FAB. Here comes my noble gull-catcher. 205

[*Re-enter* MARIA.]

SIR TO. Wilt thou set thy foot o' my neck?

SIR AND. Or o'mine either?

SIR TO. Shall I play my freedom at tray-trip, and become thy bond-slave?

SIR AND. I' faith, or I either? 210

SIR TO. Why, thou hast put him in such a
dream, that when the image of it leaves him
he must run mad.

MAR. Nay, but say true; does it work upon
him? 215

SIR TO. Like aqua-vitæ with a midwife.

MAR. If you will then see the fruits of the
sport, mark his first approach before my
lady: he will come to her in yellow stockings,
and 'tis a colour she abhors, and cross- 220
gartered, a fashion she detests; and he will
smile upon her, which will now be so unsuitable to her disposition, being addicted to a
melancholy as she is, that it cannot but turn
him into a notable contempt. If you will see
it, follow me. 225

SIR TO. To the gates of Tartar, thou most
excellent devil of wit!

SIR AND. I'll make one too. [*Exeunt.*

185. **happy**, lucky; **strange**, distant; **stout**, overbearing. 186-7. **even . . . putting on**, the very moment I put them on. 190. **entertainest**, accept. 198. **Sophy**, Shah of Persia, whose wealth was fabulous. 200. **device**, trick. 208-9. **play . . . tray-trip**, Shall we shake dice to see whether I shall be your slave? 216. **aqua-vitae**, whisky or brandy. 223. **disposition**, mood. 224. **notable contempt**, object of great contempt. 226. **Tartar**, Tartarus, the lowest part of Hell. 228. **one**, one of the party. Act III, Scene i: 2. **tabor**, small drum. Probably a reference to a tavern called the Tabor where Tarleton, a famous clown, had lived. 3. **live by**, (1) get my living by, (2) live near. 8. **lies by**, sleeps beside. 10. **stands by**, gets its money from. 13-4. **sentence . . . good wit**, any statement may be stretched like a kid (cheveril) glove in the interest of wit. 16-7, **dally nicely**, trifle over ingeniously. 17-8. **make them wanton**, give them a double meaning. 25. **since . . . them**, probably a reference to an order of June, 1599, which prohibited the writing of satire.

ACT III

SCENE I. OLIVIA'S *garden.*

[*Enter* VIOLA, *and* CLOWN *with a tabor.*]

VIO. Save thee, friend, and thy music: dost
thou live by thy tabor?

CLO. No, sir, I live by the church.

VIO. Art thou a churchman?

CLO. No such matter, sir: I do live by the
church; for I do live at my house, and my
house doth stand by the church.

VIO. So thou mayst say, the king lies by a
beggar, if a beggar dwell near him; or, the
church stands by thy tabor, if thy tabor
stand by the church. 11

CLO. You have said, sir. To see this age!
A sentence is but a cheveril glove to a good
wit: how quickly the wrong side may be
turned outward! 15

VIO. Nay, that's certain; they that dally
nicely with words may quickly make them
wanton.

CLO. I would, therefore, my sister had had
no name, sir. 20

VIO. Why, man?

CLO. Why, sir, her name's a word; and to
dally with that word might make my sister
wanton. But indeed words are very rascals
since bonds disgraced them. 25

VIO. Thy reason, man?

CLO. Troth, sir, I can yield you none without words; and words are grown so false, I
am loath to prove reason with them.

VIO. I warrant thou art a merry fellow and
carest for nothing. 31

CLO. Not so, sir, I do care for something;
but in my conscience, sir, I do not care for
you: if that be to care for nothing, sir, I
would it would make you invisible. 35

VIO. Art not thou the Lady Olivia's fool?

CLO. No, indeed, sir; the Lady Olivia has no folly: she will keep no fool, sir, till she be married; and fools are as like husbands as pilchards are to herrings; the husband 's the bigger: I am indeed not her fool, but her corrupter of words. 41

VIO. I saw thee late at the Count Orsino's.

CLO. Foolery, sir, does walk about the orb like the sun, it shines every where. I would be sorry, sir, but the fool should be as oft with your master as with my mistress: I think I saw your wisdom there. 47

VIO. Nay, an thou pass upon me, I'll no more with thee. Hold, there's expenses for thee.

CLO. Now Jove, in his next commodity of hair, send thee a beard! 51

VIO. By my troth, I'll tell thee, I am almost sick for one; [*Aside*] though I would not have it grow on my chin. Is thy lady within?

CLO. Would not a pair of these have bred, sir? 55

VIO. Yes, being kept together and put to use. 57

CLO. I would play Lord Pandarus of Phrygia, sir, to bring a Cressida to this Troilus.

VIO. I understand you, sir; 'tis well begged. 60

CLO. The matter, I hope, is not great, sir, begging but a beggar: Cressida was a beggar. My lady is within, sir. I will construe to them whence you come; who you are and what you would are out of my welkin, I might say "element," but the word is overworn.

[*Exit.* 66

VIO. This fellow is wise enough to play the fool;
And to do that well craves a kind of wit:
He must observe their mood on whom he jests,
The quality of persons, and the time, 70
And, like the haggard, check at every feather
That comes before his eye. This is a practice
As full of labour as a wise man's art:
For folly that he wisely shows is fit;
But wise men, folly-fall'n, quite taint their wit. 75

[*Enter* SIR TOBY *and* SIR ANDREW.]

SIR TO. Save you, gentleman.

VIO. And you, sir.

SIR AND. Dieu vous garde, monsieur.

VIO. Et vous aussi; votre serviteur.

SIR AND. I hope, sir, you are; and I am yours. 81

SIR TO. Will you encounter the house? my niece is desirous you should enter, if your trade be to her.

VIO. I am bound to your niece, sir; I mean, she is the list of my voyage. 86

SIR TO. Taste your legs, sir; put them to motion.

VIO. My legs do better understand me, sir, than I understand what you mean by bidding me taste my legs. 91

SIR TO. I mean, to go, sir, to enter.

VIO. I will answer you with gait and entrance. But we are prevented.

[*Enter* OLIVIA *and* MARIA.]

Most excellent accomplished lady, the heavens rain odours on you! 96

SIR AND. That youth's a rare courtier: "Rain odours," well.

VIO. My matter hath no voice, lady, but to your own most pregnant and vouchsafed ear. 100

SIR AND. "Odours," "pregnant" and "vouchsafed:" I'll get 'em all three all ready.

OLI. Let the garden door be shut, and leave me to my hearing. [*Exeunt* SIR TOBY, SIR ANDREW, *and* MARIA.] Give me your hand, sir. 105

VIO. My duty, madam, and most humble service.

OLI. What is your name?

VIO. Cesario is your servant's name, fair princess.

OLI. My servant, sir! 'Twas never merry world 109

40. **pilchards**, fish resembling herring. 42. **late**, recently. 43. **orb**, earth. 45. **but . . . should be**, if the fool were not. 48. **pass upon**, make a (verbal) thrust at. 49. **expenses**, a tip. 50. **commodity**, consignment. 57. **to use**, out at interest. 58. **Pandarus**, Cressida's uncle who arranged an assignation between her and Troilus. In one version of the story she became a leper and beggar (cf. I. 62). 63. **construe**, explain. 65. **welkin**, the sky. 66. **element**, the sky. 68. **craves**, demands. 70. **quality**, social position. 71. **haggard**, badly trained falcon. 73. **art**, profession. 75. **folly-fall'n**, acting like a fool. 75. **taint their wit**, corrupt their intelligence. 78. **Dieu . . . monsieur**, God keep you, sir. 79. **Et . . . serviteur**, And you too, sir—(I am) at your service. 82. **encounter**, go towards. 86. **list**, end, goal. 87. **taste**, test. 94. **prevented**, forestalled. 98. **well**, excellent. 99. **matter . . . voice**, i.e., I cannot deliver my message. 100. **pregnant**, alert; **vouchsafed**, yielded condescendingly.

Since lowly feigning was call'd compliment:
You're servant to the Count Orsino, youth.
VIO. And he is yours, and his must needs be yours:
Your servant's servant is your servant, madam.
OLI. For him, I think not on him: for his thoughts,
Would they were blanks, rather than fill'd with me! 115
VIO. Madam, I come to whet your gentle thoughts
On his behalf.
OLI. O, by your leave, I pray you,
I bade you never speak again of him:
But, would you undertake another suit,
I had rather hear you to solicit that 120
Than music from the spheres.
VIO. Dear lady,—
OLI. Give me leave, beseech you. I did send,
After the last enchantment you did here,
A ring in chase of you: so did I abuse
Myself, my servant and, I fear, you: 125
Under your hard construction must I sit,
To force that on you, in a shameful cunning,
Which you knew none of yours: what might you think? 128
Have you not set mine honour at the stake
And baited it with all the unmuzzled thoughts
That tyrannous heart can think? To one of your receiving 131
Enough is shown: a cypress, not a bosom,
Hideth my heart. So, let me hear you speak.
VIO. I pity you.
OLI. That's a degree to love.
VIO. No, not a grize; for 'tis a vulgar proof, 135
That very oft we pity enemies.
OLI. Why, then, methinks 'tis time to smile again.
O world, how apt the poor are to be proud!
If one should be a prey, how much the better
To fall before the lion than the wolf! 140
[*Clock strikes.*]
The clock upbraids me with the waste of time.
Be not afraid, good youth, I will not have you:
And yet, when wit and youth is come to harvest,
Your wife is like to reap a proper man:
There lies your way, due west. 145
VIO. Then westward-ho! Grace and good disposition
Attend your ladyship!
You'll nothing, madam, to my lord by me?
OLI. Stay:
I prithee, tell me what thou think'st of me.
VIO. That you do think you are not what you are. 151
OLI. If I think so, I think the same of you.
VIO. Then think you right: I am not what I am.
OLI. I would you were as I would have you be!
VIO. Would it be better, madam, than I am? 155
I wish it might, for now I am your fool.
OLI. O, what a deal of scorn looks beautiful
In the contempt and anger of his lip!
A murderous guilt shows not itself more soon
Than love that would seem hid: love's night is noon. 160
Cesario, by the roses of the spring,
By maidhood, honour, truth and every thing,
I love thee so, that, maugre all thy pride,
Nor wit nor reason can my passion hide.
Do not extort thy reasons from this clause, 165
For that I woo, thou therefore hast no cause;
But rather reason thus with reason fetter,
Love sought is good, but given unsought is better.
VIO. By innocence I swear, and by my youth,
I have one heart, one bosom and one truth,
And that no woman has; nor never none 171
Shall mistress be of it, save I alone.

110. **lowly feigning,** pretended humility; **compliment,** courtesy. 112. **his,** i.e., servant. 122. **Give me leave,** i.e., to speak on. 123. **enchantment you did,** charm you worked. 124. **abuse,** act unjustly toward. 126. **hard construction,** unfavorable judgment. 128. **might you think,** must you have thought. 129-131. **Have . . . can think?** the figure in these lines is taken from the sport of bear-baiting, in which a bear was tied to a stake and set upon by large dogs. 131. **receiving,** understanding. 132. **cypress,** black, gauze-like material. 134. **degree to,** step toward. 135. **grize,** step; **vulgar proof,** common experience. 137. **to smile,** i.e., to show courage. 144. **proper,** handsome. 145. **due west,** i.e., at your departure my sun sets.

146. **westward-ho,** the cry of boatmen on the Thames, bound for the western part of London, the seat of the royal palace; **Grace,** the grace of God. 151. **that . . . you are,** i.e., in love with a woman. 154. **as,** what. 156. **fool,** i.e., you are sharpening your wit on me. 160. **love's . . . noon,** i.e., love, when one attempts to conceal it, it is as obvious as ordinary objects at noonday. 163. **maugre,** in spite of. 165. **extort,** wrest; **this,** i.e., the following. 166. **For . . . cause,** because I am doing the wooing you have no reason to return my love. 167. **with reason fetter,** controlled by reason. 170. **bosom,** passion; **truth,** loyalty.

And so adieu, good madam: never more
Will I my master's tears to you deplore.

OLI. Yet come again; for thou perhaps mayst move 175
That heart, which now abhors, to like his love. [*Exeunt.*

SCENE II. OLIVIA'S *house.*

[*Enter* SIR TOBY, SIR ANDREW, *and* FABIAN.]

SIR AND. No, faith, I'll not stay a jot longer.

SIR TO. Thy reason, dear venom, give thy reason.

FAB. You must needs yield your reason, Sir Andrew. 5

SIR AND. Marry, I saw your niece do more favours to the count's serving-man than ever she bestowed upon me; I saw't i' the orchard.

SIR TO. Did she see thee the while, old boy? tell me that. 10

SIR AND. As plain as I see you now.

FAB. This was a great argument of love in her toward you.

SIR AND. 'Slight, will you make an ass o' me?

FAB. I will prove it legitimate, sir, upon the oaths of judgement and reason. 16

SIR TO. And they have been grand-jury-men since before Noah was a sailor.

FAB. She did show favour to the youth in your sight only to exasperate you, to 20 awake your dormouse valour, to put fire in your heart, and brimstone in your liver. You should then have accosted her; and with some excellent jests, fire-new from the mint, you should have banged the youth into 25 dumbness. This was looked for at your hand, and this was balked: the double gilt of this opportunity you let time wash off, and you are now sailed into the north of my lady's opinion; where you will hang like an icicle on a Dutchman's beard, unless you do redeem it by some laudable attempt either of valour or policy. 31

SIR AND. An 't be any way, it must be with valour; for policy I hate: I had as lief be a Brownist as a politician.

SIR TO. Why, then, build me thy fortunes upon the basis of valour. Challenge me the count's youth to fight with him; hurt him in eleven places: my niece shall take note of it; and assure thyself, there is no love-broker in the world can more prevail in man's commendation with woman than report of valour. 41

FAB. There is no way but this, Sir Andrew.

SIR AND. Will either of you bear me a challenge to him? 44

SIR TO. Go, write it in a martial hand; be curst and brief; it is no matter how witty, so it be eloquent and full of invention: taunt him with the license of ink: if thou thou'st him some thrice, it shall not be amiss; and as many lies as will lie in thy sheet of paper, 50 although the sheet were big enough for the bed of Ware in England, set 'em down: go, about it. Let there be gall enough in thy ink, though thou write with a goose-pen, no matter: about it. 54

SIR AND. Where shall I find you?

SIR TO. We'll call thee at the cubiculo: go. [*Exit* SIR ANDREW.

FAB. This is a dear manakin to you, Sir Toby.

SIR TO. I have been dear to him, lad, some two thousand strong, or so.

FAB. We shall have a rare letter from him: but you'll not deliver 't? 61

SIR TO. Never trust me, then; and by all means stir on the youth to an answer. I think oxen and wainropes cannot hale them together. For Andrew, if he were opened, and you find so much blood in his liver as will clog the foot of a flea, I'll eat the rest of the anatomy. 67

FAB. And his opposite, the youth, bears in his visage no great presage of cruelty.

[*Enter* MARIA.]

Scene ii: 1. **jot**, a small particle (of time). 12. **argument**, proof. 14. **'Slight**, by God's light. 21. **dormouse**, a tiny mouse-like creature that hibernates; so, torpid and timid. 24. **fire-new**, i.e., red hot. 27. **balked**, neglected; **double gilt**, twice gold-plated. 28. **north**, i.e., cold (with disdain). 31. **policy**, shrewdness. 34. **Brownist**, a strict Puritan sect, founded by Robert Brown; **politician**, schemer. 39. **love-broker**, professional matchmaker. 40. **man's . . . woman**, in commending a man to a woman 46. **curst**, savage. 48. **license of ink**, the freedom pen and ink permits; **thou'st**, "thou" was a familiar form of address; when used to equals who were not intimates, it was a mild insult. 49. **some thrice**, three times or so. 52. **bed of Ware**, a famous bed at an inn in Ware. It was nearly twelve feet square and able to accommodate eight to twelve persons. 53. **gall**, bitterness. 56. **cubiculo**, bedroom. 57. **manakin to you**, puppet of yours. 58. **I . . . him**, I have cost him. 64. **wainropes**, ropes fastening oxen to a cart. 66. **liver**, the supposed seat of courage. 67. **anatomy**, body, here = corpse 68. **opposite**, opponent.

SIR TO. Look, where the youngest wren of nine comes. 71

MAR. If you desire the spleen, and will laugh yourselves into stitches, follow me. Yond gull Malvolio is turned heathen, a very renegado; for there is no Christian, that means to be saved by believing rightly, can ever believe such impossible passages of grossness. He's in yellow stockings.

SIR TO. And cross-gartered? 79

MAR. Most villanously; like a pedant that keeps a school i' the church. I have dogged him, like his murderer. He does obey every point of the letter that I dropped to betray him: he does smile his face into more lines than is in the new map with the augment- 85 ation of the Indies: you have not seen such a thing as 'tis. I can hardly forbear hurling things at him. I know my lady will strike him: if she do, he'll smile and take't for a great favour.

SIR TO. Come, bring us, bring us where he is. [*Exeunt.*

SCENE III. *A street.*

[*Enter* SEBASTIAN *and* ANTONIO.]

SEB. I would not by my will have troubled you;
But, since you make your pleasure of your pains,
I will no further chide you.

ANT. I could not stay behind you: my desire,
More sharp than filèd steel, did spur me forth; 5
And not all love to see you, though so much
As might have drawn one to a longer voyage,
But jealousy what might befall your travel,
Being skilless in these parts; which to a stranger,
Unguided and unfriended, often prove 10
Rough and unhospitable: my willing love,
The rather by these arguments of fear,
Set forth in your pursuit.

SEB. My kind Antonio,
I can no other answer make but thanks,
And thanks; and ever thanks; and oft good turns 15
Are shuffled off with such uncurrent pay:
But, were my worth as is my conscience firm,
You should find better dealing. What's to do?
Shall we go see the reliques of this town?

ANT. To-morrow, sir: best first go see your lodging. 20

SEB. I am not weary, and 'tis long to night:
I pray you, let us satisfy our eyes
With the memorials and the things of fame
That do renown this city.

ANT. Would you'ld pardon me;
I do not without danger walk these streets: 25
Once, in a sea-fight, 'gainst the count his galleys
I did some service; of such note indeed,
That were I ta'en here it would scarce be answer'd.

SEB. Belike you slew great number of his people.

ANT. The offence is not of such a bloody nature; 30
Albeit the quality of the time and quarrel
Might well have given us bloody argument.
It might have since been answer'd in repaying
What we took from them; which, for traffic's sake, 34
Most of our city did: only myself stood out;
For which, if I be lapsed in this place,
I shall pay dear.

SEB. Do not then walk too open.

ANT. It doth not fit me. Hold, sir, here's my purse.
In the south suburbs, at the Elephant,
Is best to lodge: I will bespeak our diet, 40
Whiles you beguile the time and feed your knowledge
With viewing of the town: there shall you have me.

SEB. Why I your purse?

ANT. Haply your eye shall light upon some toy

70. **youngest . . . nine**, the last hatched of a brood is often the smallest. 72. **spleen**, i.e., a fit of violent laughter. 75. **renegado**, Christian turned heathen. 77-8. **such . . . grossness**, such stupid acts. 80. **pedant**, schoolmaster. 85-6. **new . . . Indies**, a map which had appeared in 1599 showing the East Indies in greater detail than previous maps. **Scene iii: 1. by my will**, willingly. 2. **your pains**, i.e., putting yourself out. 6. **not . . . you**, i.e., my desire was not. 8. **jealousy what**, apprehension of what. 9. **skilless**, ignorant of. 12. **The rather . . . fear**, the readier because of these promptings of fear (for your safety). 16. **uncurrent**, money not legal tender; hence worthless. 17. **worth**, wealth; **conscience**, consciousness (of what I owe you). 19. **reliques**, antiquities, "sights." 28. **answer'd**, atoned for. 31. **quality of the time**, nature of the circumstances. 33. **answer'd in**, made up for by. 36. **be lapsed**, be arrested. 40. **bespeak our diet**, engage our food and lodgings. 44. **toy**, trifle.

You have desire to purchase; and your store,
I think, is not for idle markets, sir. 46

SEB. I'll be your purse-bearer and leave you
For an hour.

ANT. To the Elephant.

SEB. I do remember. [*Exeunt.*

SCENE IV. OLIVIA'S *garden.*

[*Enter* OLIVIA *and* MARIA.]

OLI. I have sent after him: he says he'll come;
How shall I feast him? what bestow of him?
For youth is bought more oft than begg'd or borrow'd.
I speak too loud.
Where is Malvolio? he is sad and civil, 5
And suits well for a servant with my fortunes:
Where is Malvolio?

MAR. He's coming, madam; but in very strange manner. He is, sure, possessed, madam.

OLI. Why, what's the matter? does he rave? 10

MAR. No, madam, he does nothing but smile: your ladyship were best to have some guard about you, if he come; for, sure, the man is tainted in 's wits.

OLI. Go call him hither. [*Exit* MARIA.] I am as mad as he, 15
If sad and merry madness equal be

[*Re-enter* MARIA, *with* MALVOLIO.]

How now, Malvolio!

MAL. Sweet lady, ho, ho.

OLI. Smilest thou?
I sent for thee upon a sad occasion. 20

MAL. Sad, lady! I could be sad: this does make some obstruction in the blood, this cross-gartering; but what of that? if it please the eye of one, it is with me as the very true sonnet is, "Please one, and please all." 25

OLI. Why, how dost thou, man? what is the matter with thee?

MAL. Not black in my mind, though yellow in my legs. It did come to his hands, and commands shall be executed: I think we do know the sweet Roman hand. 31

OLI. Wilt thou go to bed, Malvolio?

MAL. To bed! ay, sweet-heart, and I'll come to thee.

OLI. God comfort thee! Why dost thou smile so and kiss thy hand so oft? 36

MAR. How do you, Malvolio?

MAL. At your request! yes; nightingales answer daws.

MAR. Why appear you with this ridiculous boldness before my lady? 41

MAL. "Be not afraid of greatness:" 'twas well writ.

OLI. What meanest thou by that, Malvolio?

MAL. "Some are born great,"—

OLI. Ha!

MAL. "Some achieve greatness,"—

OLI. What sayest thou?

MAL. "And some have greatness thrust upon them." 50

OLI. Heaven restore thee!

MAL. "Remember who commended thy yellow stockings,"—

OLI. Thy yellow stockings!

MAL. "And wished to see thee cross-gartered."

OLI. Cross-gartered! 56

MAL. "Go to, thou are made, if thou desirest to be so;"—

OLI. Am I made? 59

MAL. "If not, let me see thee a servant still."

OLI. Why, this is very midsummer madness.

[*Enter* SERVANT.]

SER. Madam, the young gentleman of the Count Orsino's is returned: I could hardly entreat him back: he attends your ladyship's pleasure. 65

OLI. I'll come to him. [*Exit* SERVANT.] Good Maria, let this fellow be looked to. Where's my cousin Toby? Let some of my people have a special care of him: I would not have him miscarry for the half of my dowry. 70

[*Exeunt* OLIVIA *and* MARIA.

MAL. O, ho! do you come near me now? no worse man than Sir Toby to look to me! This concurs directly with the letter: she sends

45. **your store,** your resources. 46. **idle markets,** foolish purchases. Scene iv: 2. **of,** on. 5. **sad and civil,** grave and polite. 9. **possessed,** of an evil spirit, i.e., crazy. 20. **sad occasion,** serious business. 25. **sonnet,** poem, reference is to a vulgar ballad. 31. **Roman hand,** Italian style of handwriting, then beginning to supersede the more German-English style. 38. **At your request,** Must I answer questions from so lowly a creature as you? 39. **daws,** crows. 61. **midsummer madness,** refers to a wild way of celebrating midsummer eve. 67. **to,** after. 70. **miscarry,** come to harm; **dowry,** fortune. 71. **come near me,** i.e., begin to catch my meaning. 73. **concurs directly,** agrees exactly.

him on purpose, that I may appear stubborn to him; for she incites me to that in the letter. "Cast thy humble slough," says she; "be opposite with a kinsman, surly with servants; let thy tongue tang with arguments of state; put thyself into the trick of singularity," and consequently sets down the manner how; as, a sad face, a reverend carriage, a slow 80 tongue, in the habit of some sir of note, and so forth. I have limed her; but it is Jove's doing, and Jove make me thankful! And when she went away now, "Let this fellow be looked to:" fellow! not Malvolio, nor after my 85 degree, but fellow. Why, every thing adheres together, that no dram of a scruple, no scruple of a scruple, no obstacle, no incredulous or unsafe circumstance—What can be said? Nothing that can be can come between me and the full prospect of my hopes. Well, Jove, not I, is the doer of this, and he is to be thanked. 92

[*Re-enter* MARIA, *with* SIR TOBY *and* FABIAN.]

SIR TO. Which way is he, in the name of sanctity? If all the devils of hell be drawn in little, and Legion himself possessed him, yet I'll speak to him. 96

FAB. Here he is, here he is. How is 't with you, sir? how is 't with you, man?

MAL. Go off; I discard you: let me enjoy my private: go off. 100

MAR. Lo, how hollow the fiend speaks within him! did not I tell you? Sir Toby, my lady prays you to have a care of him.

MAL. Ah, ha! does she so? 104

SIR TO. Go to, go to; peace, peace; we must deal gently with him: let me alone. How do you, Malvolio? how is 't with you? What, man! defy the devil: consider, he's an enemy to mankind.

MAL. Do you know what you say? 110

MAR. La you, an you speak ill of the devil, how he takes it at heart! Pray God, he be not bewitched! 113

FAB. Carry his water to the wise woman.

MAR. Marry, and it shall be done to-morrow morning, if I live. My lady would not lose him for more than I'll say.

MAL. How now, mistress!

MAR. O Lord! 119

SIR TO. Prithee, hold thy peace; this is not the way: do you not see you move him? let me alone with him.

FAB. No way but gentleness; gently, gently: the fiend is rough, and will not be roughly used. 124

SIR TO. Why, how now, my bawcock! how dost thou, chuck?

MAL. Sir!

SIR TO. Ay, Biddy, come with me. What, man! 'tis not for gravity to play at cherry-pit with Satan: hang him, foul collier! 130

MAR. Get him to say his prayers, good Sir Toby, get him to pray.

MAL. My prayers, minx!

MAR. No, I warrant you, he will not hear of godliness. 135

MAL. Go, hang yourselves all! you are idle shallow things: I am not of your element: you shall know more hereafter. [*Exit.*

SIR TO. Is 't possible? 139

FAB. If this were played upon a stage now, I could condemn it as an improbable fiction.

SIR TO. His very genius hath taken the infection of the device, man.

MAR. Nay, pursue him now, lest the device take air and taint.

FAB. Why, we shall make him mad indeed.

MAR. The house will be the quieter. 147

SIR TO. Come, we'll have him in a dark room and bound. My niece is already in the belief that he's mad: we may carry it thus, for our pleasure and his penance, till our very pastime, tired out of breath, prompt us to have mercy on him: at which time we will bring the device to the bar and crown thee for a finder of madmen. But see, but see. 155

[*Enter* SIR ANDREW.]

74. **stubborn**, rude. 79. **consequently**, in what follows. 80. **as**, namely. 81. **habit**, dress. 82. **limed**, snared (as with the sticky substance called bird-lime, by which birds were caught). 86. **degree**, rank. 88. **scruple**, (1) 1/3 of a dram, (2) doubt. 89. **incredulous**, incredible. 93. **Which way**, where. 94-5. **drawn in little**, contracted into a small space. 95. **Legion**, the Devil. 106. **let me alone**, leave it to me. 111. **La you**, i.e., just see. 114. **Carry . . . wise woman**, analysis of urine was practiced by quacks as well as physicians. 121. **the way**, i.e., to handle an insane man. 124. **rough**, violent. 125. **bawcock**, fine fellow ("beau-coq"). 126. **chuck**, chick. 129. **cherry-pit**, a children's game in which cherry pits were pitched into a small hole; the phrase means "to be on intimate terms with." 130. **foul**, dirty. 137. **your element**, made of the same stuff as you. 142. **genius**, soul. 145. **device . . . taint**, the plot become exposed and spoil. 150. **carry it thus**, manage it in this way. 154. **bring . . . bar**, put the plot on trial. 155. **finder of madmen**, i.e., a person appointed by the court to examine a man for insanity.

FAB. More matter for a May morning.

SIR AND. Here's the challenge, read it: I warrant there's vinegar and pepper in 't.

FAB. Is 't so saucy? 159

SIR AND. Ay, is 't, I warrant him: do but read.

SIR TO. Give me. [*Reads*] "Youth, whatsoever thou art, thou art but a scurvy fellow."

FAB. Good, and valiant. 164

SIR TO. [*Reads*] "Wonder not, nor admire not in thy mind, why I do call thee so, for I will show thee no reason for 't".

FAB. A good note; that keeps you from the blow of the law. 169

SIR TO. [*Reads*] "Thou comest to the lady Olivia, and in my sight she uses thee kindly: but thou liest in thy throat; that is not the matter I challenge thee for."

FAB. Very brief, and to exceeding good sense–less. 175

SIR TO. [*Reads*] "I will waylay thee going home; where if it be thy chance to kill me,"–

FAB. Good.

SIR TO. [*Reads*] "Thou killest me like a rogue and a villain." 180

FAB. Still you keep o' the windy side of the law: good.

SIR TO. [*Reads*] "Fare thee well; and God have mercy upon one of our souls! He may have mercy upon mine; but my hope is 185 better, and so look to thyself. Thy friend, as thou usest him, and thy sworn enemy,

ANDREW AGUECHEEK."

If this letter move him not, his legs cannot: I'll give 't him. 189

MAR. You may have very fit occasion for 't: he is now in some commerce with my lady, and will by and by depart.

SIR TO. Go, Sir Andrew; scout me for him at the corner of the orchard like a bum-baily: so soon as ever thou seest him, draw; and, as thou drawest, swear horrible; for it comes to pass off that a terrible oath, with a swaggering accent sharply twanged off, gives manhood more approbation than ever proof itself would have earned him. Away! 200

SIR AND. Nay, let me alone for swearing. [*Exit.*

SIR TO. Now will not I deliver his letter: for the behaviour of the young gentleman gives him out to be of good capacity and breeding; his employment between his lord and my niece confirms no less: therefore this let- 205 ter, being so excellently ignorant, will breed no terror in the youth: he will find it comes from a clodpole. But, sir, I will deliver his challenge by word of mouth; set upon Aguecheek a notable report of valour; and drive the 210 gentleman, as I know his youth will aptly receive it, into a most hideous opinion of his rage, skill, fury and impetuosity. This will so fright them both that they will kill one another by the look, like cockatrices. 215

[*Re-enter* OLIVIA, *with* VIOLA.]

FAB. Here he comes with your niece: give them way till he take leave, and presently after him.

SIR TO. I will meditate the while upon some horrid message for a challenge. 220

[*Exeunt* SIR TOBY, FABIAN, *and* MARIA.

OLI. I have said too much unto a heart of stone
And laid mine honour too unchary on 't:
There's something in me that reproves my fault;
But such a headstrong potent fault it is,
That it but mocks reproof. 225

VIO. With the same 'haviour that your passion bears
Goes on my master's grief.

OLI. Here, wear this jewel for me, 'tis my picture;
Refuse it not; it hath no tongue to vex you;
And I beseech you come again to-morrow. 230
What shall you ask of me that I'll deny,
That honour saved may upon asking give?

VIO. Nothing but this; your true love for my master.

OLI. How with mine honour may I give him that
Which I have given to you?

VIO. I will acquit you. 235

156. **May morning,** May Day was celebrated with great merriment. 160. **I warrant him,** I'll give surety that he [Cesario] is. 165-6. **admire not,** be not surprised. 168. **note,** observation. 181. **windy,** safe. 191. **commerce,** conversation. 192. **by and by,** immediately. 193. **scout,** be on the lookout. 194. **bum-baily,** a sheriff's officer who arrested for debt. 199. **approbation,** convincing evidence (of manhood). 201. **let . . . swearing,** just leave the swearing to me. 208. **clodpole,** blockhead. 209. **set upon,** bestow upon. 211. **aptly,** readily. 215. **cockatrices,** fabulous creatures hatched from roosters' eggs and able to kill by a glance. 217-8. **give them way,** avoid them. 218. **presently,** at once. 222. **laid . . . unchary,** have too heedlessly risked my honor. 227. **goes on,** marks the course of. 231. **shall,** i.e., can. 232. **honour saved may,** honor may safely. 235. **acquit,** release.

OLI. Well, come again to-morrow: fare thee well:
A fiend like thee might bear my soul to hell.
[*Exit.*

[*Re-enter* SIR TOBY *and* FABIAN.]

SIR TO. Gentleman, God save thee.

VIO. And you, sir. 239

SIR TO. That defence thou hast, betake thee to 't: of what nature the wrongs are thou hast done him, I know not; but thy intercepter, full of despite, bloody as the hunter, attends thee at the orchard-end: dismount thy tuck, be yare in thy preparation, for thy assailant is quick, skilful and deadly. 246

VIO. You mistake, sir; I am sure no man hath any quarrel to me: my remembrance is very free and clear from any image of offence done to any man. 250

SIR TO. You'll find it otherwise, I assure you: therefore, if you hold your life at any price, betake you to your guard; for your opposite hath in him what youth, strength, skill and wrath can furnish man withal.

VIO. I pray you, sir, what is he? 256

SIR TO. He is knight, dubbed with unhatched rapier and on carpet consideration; but he is a devil in private brawl: souls and bodies hath he divorced three; and his incensement at this moment is so implacable, that satisfaction can be none but by pangs of death and sepulchre. Hob, nob, is his word; give 't or take 't. 263

VIO. I will return again into the house and desire some conduct of the lady. I am no fighter. I have heard of some kind of men that put quarrels purposely on others, to taste their valour: belike this is a man of that quirk. 268

SIR TO. Sir, no, his indignation derives itself out of a very competent injury: therefore, get you on and give him his desire. Back you shall not to the house, unless you undertake that with me which with as much safety you might answer him: therefore, on, or strip your sword stark naked; for meddle you must, that's certain, or forswear to wear iron about 276 you.

VIO. This is as uncivil as strange. I beseech you, do me this courteous office, as to know of the knight what my offence to him is: it is something of my negligence, nothing of my purpose. 280

SIR TO. I will do so. Signior Fabian, stay you by this gentleman till my return. [*Exit.*

VIO. Pray you, sir, do you know of this matter?

FAB. I know the knight is incensed against you, even to a mortal arbitrement; but nothing of the circumstance more.

VIO. I beseech you, what manner of man is he? 289

FAB. Nothing of that wonderful promise, to read him by his form, as you are like to find him in the proof of his valour. He is, indeed, sir, the most skilful, bloody and fatal opposite that you could possibly have found in any part of Illyria. Will you walk towards him? I will make your peace with him if I can. 296

VIO. I shall be much bound to you for 't: I am one that had rather go with sir priest than sir knight: I care not who knows so much of my mettle. [*Exeunt.* 300

[*Re-enter* SIR TOBY, *with* SIR ANDREW.]

SIR TO. Why, man, he's a very devil; I have not seen such a firago. I had a pass with him, rapier, scabbard and all, and he gives me the stuck in with such a mortal motion, that it is inevitable; and on the answer, he pays you as surely as your feet hit the ground they step on. They say he has been fencer to the Sophy. 307

SIR AND. Pox on 't, I'll not meddle with him.

SIR TO. Ay, but he will not now be pacified: Fabian can scarce hold him yonder. 310

SIR AND. Plague on 't, an I thought he had been valiant and so cunning in fence, I'ld have seen him damned ere I'ld have challenged him. Let him let the matter slip, and I'll give him my horse, grey Capilet. 315

240. That, whatever. 242-3. intercepter, opponent. 243. despite, malice; bloody as the hunter, bloodthirsty as a hound. 244-5. dismount thy tuck, draw your sword. 245. yare, speedy. 254. opposite, opponent. 255. withal, with. 257-8. unhatched, unhacked. 258. on carpet consideration, knighted, not for military prowess, but on a carpet at court often for money paid the king. 263. Hob, nob, hit or miss. 265. conduct, escort. 268. taste, test. 270. competent, sufficient (according to the laws of duelling).

273. that, i.e., a duel. 275. meddle, mix (in this affair) i.e., by fighting. 276. forswear to wear, swear not to wear. 286. arbitrement, combat. 291. form, appearance. 294. opposite, opponent. 297. bound, obliged. 302. firago, Toby combines fire and virago (a violent woman). 304. stuck in, Toby's name for the fencing term "stoccata" = a thrust. 306. answer, counter-thrust. 307. Sophy, the Shah of Persia. 312. cunning in fence, skillful at fencing.

SIR. TO. I'll make the motion: stand here, make a good show on 't: this shall end without the perdition of souls. [*Aside*] Marry, I'll ride your horse as well as I ride you. 319

[*Re-enter* FABIAN *and* VIOLA.]

[*To* FAB.] I have his horse to take up the quarrel: I have persuaded him the youth's a devil.

FAB. He is as horribly conceited of him; and pants and looks pale, as if a bear were at his heels. 324

SIR TO. [*To* VIO.] There's no remedy, sir; he will fight with you for 's oath sake: marry, he hath better bethought him of his quarrel, and he finds that now scarce to be worth talking of: therefore draw, for the supportance of his vow; he protests he will not hurt you. 330

VIO. [*Aside*] Pray God defend me! A little thing would make me tell them how much I lack of a man.

FAB. Give ground, if you see him furious. 334

SIR TO. Come, Sir Andrew, there's no remedy; the gentleman will, for his honour's sake, have one bout with you; he cannot by the duello avoid it: but he has promised me, as he is a gentleman and a soldier, he will not hurt you. Come on; to 't.

SIR AND. Pray God, he keep his oath!

VIO. I do assure you, 'tis against my will. [*They draw.*

[*Enter* ANTONIO.]

ANT. Put up your sword. If this young gentleman
Have done offence, I take the fault on me:
If you offend him, I for him defy you. 345

SIR TO. You, sir! why, what are you?

ANT. One, sir, that for his love dares yet do more
Than you have heard him brag to you he will.

SIR TO. Nay, if you be an undertaker, I am for you. [*They draw.* 350

[*Enter* OFFICERS.]

FAB. O good Sir Toby, hold! here come the officers.

SIR TO. I'll be with you anon.

VIO. Pray, sir, put your sword up, if you please. 355

SIR AND. Marry, will I, sir; and, for that I promised you, I'll be as good as my word: he will bear you easily and reins well.

FIRST OFF. This is the man; do thy office.

SEC. OFF. Antonio, I arrest thee at the suit of Count Orsino. 361

ANT. You do mistake me, sir.

FIRST OFF. No, sir, no jot; I know your favour well,
Though now you have no sea-cap on your head.
Take him away: he knows I know him well.

ANT. I must obey. [*To* VIO.] This comes with seeking you: 366
But there's no remedy; I shall answer it.
What will you do, now my necessity
Makes me to ask you for my purse? It grieves me
Much more for what I cannot do for you 370
Than what befalls myself. You stand amazed;
But be of comfort.

SEC. OFF. Come, sir, away.

ANT. I must entreat of you some of that money.

VIO. What money, sir? 375
For the fair kindness you have show'd me here,
And, part, being prompted by your present trouble,
Out of my lean and low ability
I'll lend you something: my having is not much;
I'll make division of my present with you: 380
Hold, there's half my coffer.

ANT. Will you deny me now?
Is 't possible that my deserts to you
Can lack persuasion? Do not tempt my misery,
Lest that it make me so unsound a man
As to upbraid you with those kindnesses 385
That I have done for you.

VIO. I know of none;
Nor know I you by voice or any feature:
I hate ingratitude more in a man
Than lying, vainness, babbling, drunkenness,

316. **motion,** proposition. 320. **take up,** settle. 322. **He is . . . conceited,** he has just as terrifying an idea. 327. **better bethought him,** thought better of, i.e., changed his mind about. 329-30. **supportance of,** for the sake of keeping. 337-8. **by the duello,** according to the duelling code. 349. **undertaker,** meddler. 354. **with you anon,** back with you immediately. 360. **at the suit,** upon the complaint. 362. **me,** i.e., my identity. 363. **favour,** face. 367. **answer,** be answerable for. 377. **part,** partly. 378. **ability,** means. 379. **my having,** what I have. 380. **present,** i.e., present resources. 381. **coffer,** funds. 382. **my deserts to you,** my claims on you. 384. **unsound,** mean-spirited. 389. **vainness,** boastfulness.

Or any taint of vice whose strong corruption
Inhabits our frail blood. 391

ANT. O heavens themselves!

SEC. OFF. Come, sir, I pray you, go.

ANT. Let me speak a little. This youth that you see here
I snatch'd one half out of the jaws of death,
Relieved him with such sanctity of love, 395
And to his image, which methought did promise
Most venerable worth, did I devotion.

FIRST OFF. What's that to us? The time goes by: away!

ANT. But O how vile an idol proves this god!
Thou hast, Sebastian, done good feature shame. 400
In nature there's no blemish but the mind;
None can be call'd deform'd but the unkind:
Virtue is beauty, but the beauteous evil
Are empty trunks o'erflourish'd by the devil.

FIRST OFF. The man grows mad: away with him! Come, come, sir. 405

ANT. Lead me on. [*Exit with* OFFICERS.

VIO. Methinks his words do from such passion fly,
That he believes himself: so do not I.
Prove true, imagination, O, prove true, 409
That I, dear brother, be now ta'en for you!

SIR TO. Come hither, knight; come hither, Fabian: we'll whisper o'er a couplet or two of most sage saws.

VIO. He named Sebastian: I my brother know
Yet living in my glass; even such and so 415
In favour was my brother, and he went
Still in this fashion, colour, ornament,
For him I imitate: O, if it prove,
Tempests are kind and salt waves fresh in love. [*Exit.* 419

SIR TO. A very dishonest paltry boy, and more a coward than a hare: his dishonesty appears in leaving his friend here in necessity and denying him; and for his cowardship, ask Fabian.

FAB. A coward, a most devout coward, religious in it. 426

SIR AND. 'Slid, I'll after him again and beat him.

SIR TO. Do; cuff him soundly, but never draw thy sword.

SIR AND. An I do not,— [*Exit.*

FAB. Come, let's see the event. 431

SIR TO. I dare lay any money 'twill be nothing yet. [*Exeunt.*

ACT IV

SCENE I. *Before* OLIVIA'S *house.*

[*Enter* SEBASTIAN *and* CLOWN.]

CLO. Will you make me believe that I am not sent for you?

SEB. Go to, go to, thou art a foolish fellow: Let me be clear of thee.

CLO. Well held out, i' faith! No, I do not 5 know you; nor I am not sent to you by my lady, to bid you come speak with her; nor your name is not Master Cesario; nor this is not my nose neither. Nothing that is so is so.

SEB. I prithee, vent thy folly somewhere else: Thou know'st not me. 11

CLO. Vent my folly! he has heard that word of some great man and now applies it to a fool. Vent my folly! I am afraid this great lubber, the world, will prove a cockney. I prithee now, ungird thy strangeness and tell me what I shall vent to my lady: shall I vent to her that thou art coming? 18

SEB. I prithee, foolish Greek, depart from me: There's money for thee: if you tarry longer, I shall give worse payment.

CLO. By my troth, thou hast an open hand. These wise men that give fools money get

394. **one half**, i.e., when he was half dead. 395. **with . . . love**, with the same holy charity (that prompted me to save his life). 396. **image**, i.e., the idea that I had formed of him. 397. **venerable worth**, worthy of honor. 400. **done . . . shame**, shamed your handsome appearance. 401. **nature**, i.e., man's fundamental nature. 402. **unkind**, unnatural, depraved. 403-4. **beauteous . . . devil**, handsome evil persons are like empty chests, ornamented by the devil. 413. **sage saws**, wise proverbs. 414-5. **I my brother . . . glass**, I am the living image of my brother. 416-7. **he went Still**, he was always dressed. 418. **prove**, i.e., prove true. 420. **dishonest**, dishonorable; **paltry**, contemptible. 422. **necessity**, need. 425-6. **religious in it**, i.e., cowardice is his religion. 427. **'Slid**, by God's eyelid. 432. **lay any money**, bet anything. 432-3. **'twill . . . yet**, that in any case it will come to nothing. Act IV, Scene i: 1. **Will you**, Do you wish? 5. **Well held out**, you stick to it well. 14-5. **I am . . . a cockney**, i.e., (if we catch the habit of talking in this highfalutin' way) I fear that even the simplest of us will seem to be affected fops. 19. **Greek**, jester. 22. **open**, generous.

themselves a good report—after fourteen years' purchase. 25

[*Enter* SIR ANDREW, SIR TOBY, *and* FABIAN.]

SIR AND. Now, sir, have I met you again? there's for you.

SEB. Why, there's for thee, and there, and there.
Are all the people mad?

SIR TO. Hold, sir, or I'll throw your dagger o'er the house. 31

CLO. This will I tell my lady straight: I would not be in some of your coats for two pence. [*Exit.*

SIR TO. Come on, sir; hold.

SIR AND. Nay, let him alone: I'll go another way to work with him: I'll have an action of battery against him, if there be any law in Illyria: though I struck him first, yet it's no matter for that. 35

SEB. Let go thy hand. 40

SIR TO. Come, sir, I will not let you go. Come, my young soldier, put up your iron: you are well fleshed; come on.

SEB. I will be free from thee. What wouldst thou now?
If thou darest tempt me further, draw thy sword. 45

SIR TO. What, what? Nay, then I must have an ounce or two of this malapert blood from you.

[*Enter* OLIVIA.]

OLI. Hold, Toby; on thy life I charge thee, hold!

SIR TO. Madam! 50

OLI. Will it be ever thus? Ungracious wretch,
Fit for the mountains and the barbarous caves,
Where manners ne'er were preach'd! out of my sight!
Be not offended, dear Cesario.
Rudesby, be gone!

[*Exeunt* SIR TOBY, SIR ANDREW, *and* FABIAN.]

I prithee, gentle friend, 55
Let thy fair wisdom, not thy passion, sway
In this uncivil and unjust extent
Against thy peace. Go with me to my house,
And hear thou there how many fruitless pranks
This ruffian hath botch'd up, that thou thereby
Mayst smile at this: thou shalt not choose but go: 61
Do not deny. Beshrew his soul for me,
He started one poor heart of mine in thee.

SEB. What relish is in this? how runs the stream?
Or I am mad, or else this is a dream: 65
Let fancy still my sense in Lethe steep;
If it be thus to dream, still let me sleep!

OLI. Nay, come, I prithee; would thou'ldst be ruled by me!

SEB. Madam, I will.

OLI. O, say so, and so be!

[*Exeunt.*

SCENE II. OLIVIA'S *house.*

[*Enter* MARIA *and* CLOWN.]

MAR. Nay, I prithee, put on this gown and this beard; make him believe thou art Sir Topas the curate: do it quickly; I'll call Sir Toby the whilst. [*Exit.* 4

CLO. Well, I'll put it on, and I will dissemble myself in 't; and I would I were the first that ever dissembled in such a gown. I am not tall enough to become the function well, nor lean enough to be thought a good student; but to be said an honest man and a good housekeeper goes as fairly as to say a careful man and a great scholar. The competitors enter. 12

[*Enter* SIR TOBY *and* MARIA.]

SIR TO. Jove bless thee, master Parson.

CLO. Bonos dies, Sir Toby: for, as the old

24. report, i.e., of a legal verdict. 24-5. after . . . purchase, at an exhorbitant price, for the sales price of a piece of land was computed as equivalent to twelve, not fourteen years' rent. 35-6. I'll go . . . with him, I'll get at him in another way. 36-7. I'll . . . battery, I'll bring suit for assault and battery. 42. iron, sword. 43. well fleshed, tasted enough blood. 47. malapert, saucy. 55. Rudesby, ruffian. 57. extent, assault. 60. botch'd up, clumsily perpetrated; that, so that. 63. started, startled, roused; heart, pun on hart. 64. relish, flavor, meaning. 66. fancy, love; Lethe, a river in Hades which brought forgetfulness to those who drank its waters. 69. so be, so let it be. Scene ii: 2. Sir, a title given to parish priests. 4. the whilst, in the meantime. 5-6. dissemble, disguise. 7. dissembled, played the hypocrite. 8. tall, imposing; become the function, fit the rôle. 11. good housekeeper, one who lives well; goes . . . say, meets the requirements as well. 12. careful, lean with want; competitors, confederates. 14. Bonos dies, mistake for "bonus dies." The Clown begins to rehearse his part of the priest by talking in what he thinks is Latin.

hermit of Prague, that never saw pen and ink, very wittily said to a niece of King 16 Gorboduc, "That that is is;" so I, being master Parson, am master Parson; for, what is "that" but "that," and "is" but "is"?

SIR TO. To him, Sir Topas. 20

CLO. What, ho, I say! peace in this prison!

SIR TO. The knave counterfeits well; a good knave.

MAL. [*Within*] Who calls there?

CLO. Sir Topas the curate, who comes to visit Malvolio the lunatic. 26

MAL. Sir Topas, Sir Topas, good Sir Topas, go to my lady.

CLO. Out, hyperbolical fiend! how vexest thou this man! talkest thou nothing but of ladies? 30

SIR TO. Well said, master Parson.

MAL. Sir Topas, never was man thus wronged: good Sir Topas, do not think I am mad: they have laid me here in hideous darkness. 34

CLO. Fie, thou dishonest Satan! I call thee by the most modest terms; for I am one of those gentle ones that will use the devil himself with courtesy: sayest thou that house is dark?

MAL. As hell, Sir Topas. 39

CLO. Why, it hath bay windows transparent as barricadoes, and the clearstories toward the south north are as lustrous as ebony; and yet complainest thou of obstruction?

MAL. I am not mad, Sir Topas: I say to you, this house is dark. 45

CLO. Madman, thou errest: I say, there is no darkness but ignorance; in which thou art more puzzled than the Egyptians in their fog.

MAL. I say, this house is as dark as ignorance, though ignorance were as dark as 50 hell; and I say, there was never man thus abused. I am no more mad than you are: make the trial of it in any constant question.

CLO. What is the opinion of Pythagoras concerning wild fowl? 55

MAL. That the soul of our grandam might haply inhabit a bird.

CLO. What thinkest thou of his opinion?

MAL. I think nobly of the soul, and no way approve his opinion. 60

CLO. Fare thee well. Remain thou still in darkness: thou shalt hold the opinion of Pythagoras ere I will allow of thy wits, and fear to kill a woodcock, lest thou dispossess the soul of thy grandam. Fare thee well. 65

MAL. Sir Topas, Sir Topas!

SIR TO. My most exquisite Sir Topas!

CLO. Nay, I am for all waters.

MAR. Thou mightst have done this without thy beard and gown: he sees thee not. 70

SIR TO. To him in thine own voice, and bring me word how thou findest him: I would we were well rid of this knavery. If he may be conveniently delivered, I would he were, for I am now so far in offence with my 75 niece that I cannot pursue with any safety this sport to the upshot. Come by and by to my chamber. [*Exeunt* SIR TOBY *and* MARIA.

CLO. [*Singing*] "Hey, Robin, jolly Robin,
Tell me how thy lady does."

MAL. Fool! 80

CLO. "My lady is unkind, perdy."

MAL. Fool!

CLO. "Alas, why is she so?"

MAL. Fool, I say!

CLO. "She loves another"—Who calls, ha?

MAL. Good fool, as ever thou wilt deserve well at my hand, help me to a candle, and pen, ink and paper: as I am a gentleman, I will live to be thankful to thee for 't.

CLO. Master Malvolio? 90

MAL. Ay, good fool.

CLO. Alas, sir, how fell you besides your five wits?

MAL. Fool, there was never man so notoriously abused: I am as well in my wits, fool, as thou art. 96

CLO. But as well? then you are mad indeed, if you be no better in your wits than a fool.

MAL. They have here propertied me; keep me in darkness, send ministers to me, asses,

15-7. **hermit of Prague . . . niece of King Gorboduc,** Feste invents these persons. His allusions are pointless, designed to make an impression of learning. The entire speech is nonsense. 22. **counterfeits,** impersonates. 28. **hyperbolical,** extravagant. Feste thinks he is saying "superdiabolical." 34. **darkness,** insane people were often imprisoned in dark chambers. 36. **modest,** moderate. 41. **barricadoes,** barricades made of casks filled with earth; **clearstories,** rows of windows high up in the walls of a church or a great hall. 42. **lustrous,** luminous. 48. **Egyptians . . . fog,** the darkness Moses called down upon Egypt. See Exodus I, 21. 53. **constant question,** logical discussion. 54. **Pythagoras,** a Greek philosopher who believed in the transmigration of souls. 63. **allow of thy wits,** admit the soundness of your mind. 64. **dispossess the soul,** drive the soul out of the body it inhabits. 68. **for all waters,** can fish in all waters, i.e., turn my hand to anything. 74. **delivered,** freed. 75. **offence,** displeasure. 77. **upshot,** conclusion. 81. **perdy,** in truth. 92. **fell you besides,** did you fall out of?; **five wits,** i.e., common wit (intellect), imagination, fantasy, estimation, memory. 94-5. **notoriously,** outrageously. 99. **propertied,** stowed me away like a stage "property."

and do all they can to face me out of my wits. 101

CLO. Advise you what you say; the minister is here. Malvolio, Malvolio, thy wits the heavens restore! endeavour thyself to sleep, and leave thy vain bibble babble. 105

MAL. Sir Topas!

CLO. Maintain no words with him, good fellow. Who, I, sir? not I, sir. God be wi' you, good Sir Topas. Marry, amen. I will, sir, I will.

MAL. Fool, fool, fool, I say! 110

CLO. Alas, sir, be patient. What say you, sir? I am shent for speaking to you.

MAL. Good fool, help me to some light and some paper: I tell thee, I am as well in my wits as any man in Illyria. 115

CLO. Well-a-day that you were, sir!

MAL. By this hand, I am. Good fool, some ink, paper and light; and convey what I will set down to my lady: it shall advantage thee more than ever the bearing of letter did.

CLO. I will help you to 't. But tell me true, are you not mad indeed? or do you but counterfeit? 123

MAL. Believe me, I am not; I tell thee true.

CLO. Nay, I'll ne'er believe a madman till I see his brains. I will fetch you light and paper and ink.

MAL. Fool, I'll requite it in the highest degree: I prithee, be gone.

CLO. [*Singing*] I am gone, sir, 130
And anon, sir,
I'll be with you again,
In a trice,
Like to the old Vice,
Your need to sustain; 135

Who, with dagger of lath,
In his rage and his wrath,
Cries, ah, ha! to the devil:
Like a mad lad,
Pare thy nails, dad; 140
Adieu, good man devil. [*Exit.*

101. **face**, bully. 102. **Advise you**, be careful. 107-8. **God be wi' you**, good-bye. 112. **shent**, scolded. 134. **Vice**, the Devil's foolish servant in the morality plays. He commonly bore a sham dagger of lath with which he used to try to pare the Devil's nails. 141. **good man**, about = "old boy." **Scene iii**: 6. **was**, had been; **credit**, report. 9. **disputes well with**, is justified in doubting the report of. 12. **instance**, example; **discourse**, reason. 15. **trust**, belief. 17. **sway her house**, control her household; **followers**, retainers. 18. **Take . . . dispatch**, understand affairs and give orders for their administration. 21. **deceivable**, deceptive. 24. **chantry**, private chapel, endowed for saying masses for her brother's soul; **by**, near-by.

SCENE III. OLIVIA'S *garden.*

[*Enter* SEBASTIAN.]

SEB. This is the air; that is the glorious sun;
This pearl she gave me, I do feel 't and see 't;
And though 'tis wonder that enwraps me thus,
Yet 'tis not madness. Where's Antonio, then?
I could not find him at the Elephant: 5
Yet there he was; and there I found this credit,
That he did range the town to seek me out.
His counsel now might do me golden service;
For though my soul disputes well with my sense,
That this may be some error, but no madness, 10
Yet doth this accident and flood of fortune
So far exceed all instance, all discourse,
That I am ready to distrust mine eyes
And wrangle with my reason that persuades me
To any other trust but that I am mad 15
Or else the lady's mad; yet, if 'twere so,
She could not sway her house, command her followers,
Take and give back affairs and their dispatch
With such a smooth, discreet and stable bearing
As I perceive she does: there's something in 't 20
That is deceiveable. But here the lady comes.

[*Enter* OLIVIA *and* PRIEST.]

OLI. Blame not this haste of mine. If you mean well,
Now go with me and with this holy man
Into the chantry by: there, before him,
And underneath that consecrated roof, 25
Plight me the full assurance of your faith;
That my most jealous and too doubtful soul
May live at peace. He shall conceal it
Whiles you are willing it shall come to note,
What time we will our celebration keep 30
According to my birth. What do you say?

SEB. I'll follow this good man, and go with you;
And, having sworn truth, ever will be true.

OLI. Then lead the way, good father; and heavens so shine, 34
That they may fairly note this act of mine!
[*Exeunt.*

29. **Whiles**, until; **come to note**, be made known. 30. **What**, at which; **our celebration keep**, hold the marriage ceremony. 35. **fairly note**, regard with favor.

ACT V

SCENE I. *Before* OLIVIA'S *house.*

[*Enter* CLOWN *and* FABIAN.]

FAB. Now, as thou lovest me, let me see his letter.

CLO. Good Master Fabian, grant me another request.

FAB. Any thing. 5

CLO. Do not desire to see this letter.

FAB. This is, to give a dog, and in recompense desire my dog again.

[*Enter* DUKE, VIOLA, CURIO, *and* LORDS.]

DUKE. Belong you to the Lady Olivia, friends? 9

CLO. Ay, sir; we are some of her trappings.

DUKE. I know thee well: how dost thou, my good fellow?

CLO. Truly, sir, the better for my foes and the worse for my friends.

DUKE. Just the contrary; the better for thy friends.

CLO. No, sir, the worse.

DUKE. How can that be? 19

CLO. Marry, sir, they praise me and make an ass of me; now my foes tell me plainly I am an ass: so that by my foes, sir, I profit in the knowledge of myself, and by my friends I am abused: so that, conclusions to be as kisses, if your four negatives make your two affirmatives, why then, the worse for my friends and the better for my foes. 26

DUKE. Why, this is excellent.

CLO. By my troth, sir, no; though it please you to be one of my friends.

DUKE. Thou shalt not be the worse for me: there's gold. 31

CLO. But that it would be double-dealing, sir, I would you could make it another.

DUKE. O, you give me ill counsel.

CLO. Put your grace in your pocket, sir, for this once, and let your flesh and blood obey it.

DUKE. Well, I will be so much a sinner, to be a double-dealer: there's another. 38

CLO. Primo, secundo, tertio, is a good play; and the old saying is, the third pays for all: the triplex, sir, is a good tripping measure; or the bells of Saint Bennet, sir, may put you in mind; one, two, three. 43

DUKE. You can fool no more money out of me at this throw: if you will let your lady know I am here to speak with her, and bring her along with you, it may awake my bounty further. 47

CLO. Marry, sir, lullaby to your bounty till I come again. I go, sir; but I would not have you to think that my desire of having 50 is the sin of covetousness: but, as you say, sir, let your bounty take a nap, I will awake it anon. [*Exit.*

VIO. Here comes the man, sir, that did rescue me.

[*Enter* ANTONIO *and* OFFICERS.]

DUKE. That face of his I do remember well;
Yet, when I saw it last, it was besmear'd
As black as Vulcan in the smoke of war: 56
A bawbling vessel was he captain of,
For shallow draught and bulk unprizable;
With which such scathful grapple did he make
With the most noble bottom of our fleet, 60
That very envy and the tongue of loss
Cried fame and honour on him. What's the matter?

FIRST OFF. Orsino, this is that Antonio
That took the Phœnix and her fraught from Candy;
And this is he that did the Tiger board, 65
When your young nephew Titus lost his leg:
Here in the streets, desperate of shame and state,

Act V, Scene i: 3-4. **another request**, request instead. 10. **trappings**, ornaments. 11. **how dost thou**, (1) How is your health? (2) How are you behaving? 24. **abused**, deceived. 24-5. **conclusions . . . kisses**, i.e., the conclusion follows the reasoning as closely as lips in kissing. 25. **four negatives, etc.**, Feste's reasoning, as usual, is nonsense. 35. **grace**, a triple pun: (1) spiritual health, (2) favor, (3) the customary way of addressing a Duke; **in your pocket**, the phrase has two meanings: (1) the literal one, (2) disregard. 36. **flesh and blood**, used in three senses: (1) your hand, (2) human instinct, (3) man's lower nature; **it**, i.e., bad advice. 37-8. **to be**, as to be. 39. **Primo . . . tertio**, reference to a game played by schoolboys. 40. **third . . . for all**, about equal to "three times and out." 41. **triplex**, three-quarter or waltz time. 42. **Saint Bennet**, Church of St. Benedict in London, famous for its bells. 45. **throw**, i.e., of the dice. 48. **lullaby to your bounty**, let your generosity go to sleep. 56. **Vulcan**, god of metal-working and the forge. 57. **bawbling**, insignificant. 58. **for**, because of; **unprizable**, valueless. 59. **scathful grapple**, destructive fight at close quarters. 60. **bottom**, vessel. 61. **tongue of loss**, voice of the losers. 62. **matter**, business in question. 64. **fraught from Candy**, freight from Candia (the modern Crete). 67. **desperate . . . state**, reckless of his disgrace and plight.

In private brabble did we apprehend him.
VIO. He did me kindness, sir, drew on my side;
But in conclusion put strange speech upon me: 70
I know not what 'twas but distraction.
DUKE. Notable pirate! thou salt-water thief!
What foolish boldness brought thee to their mercies,
Whom thou, in terms so bloody and so dear,
Hast made thine enemies?
ANT. Orsino, noble sir,
Be pleased that I shake off these names you give me: 76
Antonio never yet was thief or pirate,
Though I confess, on base and ground enough,
Orsino's enemy. A witchcraft drew me hither:
That most ingrateful boy there by your side,
From the rude sea's enraged and foamy mouth 81
Did I redeem; a wreck past hope he was:
His life I gave him and did thereto add
My love, without retention or restraint,
All his in dedication; for his sake 85
Did I expose myself, pure for his love,
Into the danger of this adverse town;
Drew to defend him when he was beset:
Where being apprehended, his false cunning,
Not meaning to partake with me in danger, 90
Taught him to face me out of his acquaintance,
And grew a twenty years removèd thing
While one would wink; denied me mine own purse,
Which I had recommended to his use
Not half an hour before.
VIO. How can this be? 95
DUKE. When came he to this town?
ANT. To-day, my lord; and for three months before,
No interim, not a minute's vacancy,
Both day and night did we keep company.

[*Enter* OLIVIA *and* ATTENDANTS.]

DUKE. Here comes the countess: now heaven walks on earth. 100
But for thee, fellow; fellow, thy words are madness:
Three months this youth hath tended upon me;
But more of that anon. Take him aside.
OLI. What would my lord, but that he may not have,
Wherein Olivia may seem serviceable? 105
Cesario, you do not keep promise with me.
VIO. Madam!
DUKE. Gracious Olivia,—
OLI. What do you say, Cesario? Good my lord,—
VIO. My lord would speak; my duty hushes me. 110
OLI. If it be aught to the old tune, my lord,
It is as fat and fulsome to mine ear
As howling after music.
DUKE. Still so cruel?
OLI. Still so constant, lord.
DUKE. What, to perverseness? you uncivil lady, 115
To whose ingrate and unauspicious altars
My soul the faithfull'st offerings hath breathed out
That e'er devotion tender'd! What shall I do?
OLI. Even what it please my lord, that shall become him.
DUKE. Why should I not, had I the heart to do it, 120
Like to the Egyptian thief at point of death,
Kill what I love?—a savage jealousy
That sometime savours nobly. But hear me this:
Since you to non-regardance cast my faith,
And that I partly know the instrument 125
That screws me from my true place in your favour,
Live you the marble-breasted tyrant still;
But this your minion, whom I know you love,
And whom, by heaven I swear, I tender dearly,
Him will I tear out of that cruel eye, 130
Where he sits crowned in his master's spite.
Come, boy, with me; my thoughts are ripe in mischief:

68. **brabble**, brawl. 70. **put . . . upon me**, talked to me in a strange way. 71. **but distraction**, unless madness. 73. **brought . . . mercies**, put you at the mercy of those. 74. **in terms**, under circumstances; **dear**, dire. 78. **confess**, admit; **on . . . enough**, for sound enough reasons. 82. **wreck**, a shipwrecked person. 86. **pure**, entirely. 87. **adverse**, hostile. 89. **where . . . apprehended**, when I was arrested there. 91. **to face me out of**, impudently to deny.

94. **recommended**, consigned. 98. **vacancy**, separation. 112. **fat and fulsome**, gross and nauseous. 115, **uncivil**, impolite. 119. **that**, provided that. 121. **Egyptian thief**, Thyamis, a character in the Ethiopica, a Greek romance by Heliodorus, who, when in danger of death, tries to kill his mistress so that he may not be separated from her. 123. **savours nobly**, seems noble. 125. **the instrument**, i.e., Cesario. 126. **screws**, twists. 128. **minion**, favorite. 129. **tender dearly**, hold dear. 131. **in . . . spite**, to the ruin of his master. 132. **in**, for.

I'll sacrifice the lamb that I do love,
To spite a raven's heart within a dove.
VIO. And I, most jocund, apt and willingly,
To do you rest, a thousand deaths would die. 136
OLI. Where goes Cesario?
VIO. After him I love
More than I love these eyes, more than my life,
More, by all mores, than e'er I shall love wife.
If I do feign, you witnesses above 140
Punish my life for tainting of my love!
OLI. Ay me, detested! how am I beguiled!
VIO. Who does beguile you? who does do you wrong?
OLI. Hast thou forgot thyself? is it so long?
Call forth the holy father.
DUKE. Come, away! 145
OLI. Whither, my lord? Cesario, husband, stay.
DUKE. Husband!
OLI. Ay, husband: can he that deny?
DUKE. Her husband, sirrah!
VIO. No, my lord, not I.
OLI. Alas, it is the baseness of thy fear
That makes thee strangle thy propriety: 150
Fear not, Cesario; take thy fortunes up;
Be that thou know'st thou art, and then thou art
As great as that thou fear'st.

[*Enter* PRIEST.]

O, welcome, father!
Father, I charge thee, by thy reverence,
Here to unfold, though lately we intended 155
To keep in darkness what occasion now
Reveals before 'tis ripe, what thou dost know
Hath newly pass'd between this youth and me.
PRIEST. A contract of eternal bond of love,
Confirm'd by mutual joinder of your hands,
Attested by the holy close of lips, 161
Strengthen'd by interchangement of your rings;
And all the ceremony of this compact
Seal'd in my function, by my testimony:
Since when, my watch hath told me, toward my grave 165
I have travell'd but two hours.
DUKE. O thou dissembling cub! what wilt thou be
When time hath sow'd a grizzle on thy case?
Or will not else thy craft so quickly grow,
That thine own trip shall be thine overthrow? 170
Farewell, and take her; but direct thy feet
Where thou and I henceforth may never meet.
VIO. My Lord, I do protest—
OLI. O, do not swear!
Hold little faith, though thou hast too much fear.

[*Enter* SIR ANDREW.]

SIR AND. For the love of God, a surgeon!
Send one presently to Sir Toby. 176
OLI. What's the matter?
SIR AND. He has broke my head across and given Sir Toby a bloody coxcomb too: for the love of God, your help! I had rather than forty pound I were at home. 181
OLI. Who has done this, Sir Andrew?
SIR AND. The count's gentleman, one Cesario: we took him for a coward, but he's the very devil incardinate. 185
DUKE. My gentleman, Cesario?
SIR AND. 'Od's lifelings, here he is! You broke my head for nothing; and that that I did, I was set on to do 't by Sir Toby.
VIO. Why do you speak to me? I never hurt you: 190
You drew your sword upon me without cause;
But I bespake you fair, and hurt you not.
SIR AND. If a bloody coxcomb be a hurt, you have hurt me: I think you set nothing by a bloody coxcomb. 195

[*Enter* SIR TOBY *and* CLOWN.]

Here comes Sir Toby halting: you shall hear more: but if he had not been in drink, he would have tickled you othergates than he did.
DUKE. How now, gentleman! how is 't with you? 200
SIR TO. That's all one: has hurt me, and

135. apt, ready. 136. do you rest, give you peace. 141. tainting of, defiling. 142. detested, renounced; beguiled, deceived. 144. holy father, i.e., Olivia's private chaplain. 150. strangle thy propriety, deny your identity. 151. take . . . up, take advantage of your good fortune. 152. that . . . art, i.e., my husband. 153. that . . . fear'st, i.e., the Duke. 156. occasion, circumstances. 160. joinder, clasping. 164. seal'd in my function, ratified by me in my official capacity (of priest). 168. grizzle, crop of grey hair; case, skin. 174. hold little faith, show at least a little sense of honor. 176. presently, at once. 185. incardinate, Sir Andrew means "incarnate." 192. bespake you fair, spoke politely to you. 194. set nothing by, think nothing of. 196. halting, limping. 198. othergates, in another way. 201. That's all one, It doesn't matter.

there's the end on 't. Sot, didst see Dick surgeon, sot?

CLO. O, he's drunk, Sir Toby, an hour agone; his eyes were set at eight i' the morning. 205

SIR TO. Then he's a rogue, and a passy measures pavin: I hate a drunken rogue.

OLI. Away with him! Who hath made this havoc with them?

SIR AND. I'll help you, Sir Toby, because we'll be dressed together. 211

SIR TO. Will you help? an ass-head and a coxcomb and a knave, a thin-faced knave, a gull!

OLI. Get him to bed, and let his hurt be look'd to. 215

[*Exeunt* CLOWN, FABIAN, SIR TOBY, *and* SIR ANDREW.

[*Enter* SEBASTIAN.]

SEB. I am sorry, madam, I have hurt your kinsman;
But, had it been the brother of my blood,
I must have done no less with wit and safety.
You throw a strange regard upon me, and by that
I do perceive it hath offended you: 220
Pardon me, sweet one, even for the vows
We made each other but so late ago.

DUKE. One face, one voice, one habit, and two persons,
A natural perspective, that is and is not!

SEB. Antonio, O my dear Antonio! 225
How have the hours rack'd and tortured me,
Since I have lost thee!

ANT. Sebastian are you?

SEB. Fear'st thou that, Antonio?

ANT. How have you made division of yourself?
An apple, cleft in two, is not more twin 230
Than these two creatures. Which is Sebastian?

OLI. Most wonderful!

SEB. Do I stand there? I never had a brother;
Nor can there be that deity in my nature,
Of here and every where. I had a sister, 235
Whom the blind waves and surges have devour'd.
Of charity, what kin are you to me?
What countryman? what name? what parentage?

VIO. Of Messaline: Sebastian was my father;
Such a Sebastian was my brother too, 240
So went he suited to his watery tomb:
If spirits can assume both form and suit
You come to fright us.

SEB. A spirit I am indeed;
But am in that dimension grossly clad
Which from the womb I did participate. 245
Were you a woman, as the rest goes even,
I should my tears let fall upon your cheek,
And say "Thrice-welcome, drownèd Viola!"

VIO. My father had a mole upon his brow.

SEB. And so had mine. 250

VIO. And died that day when Viola from her birth
Had number'd thirteen years.

SEB. O, that record is lively in my soul!
He finishèd indeed his mortal act
That day that made my sister thirteen years. 255

VIO. If nothing lets to make us happy both
But this my masculine usurp'd attire,
Do not embrace me till each circumstance
Of place, time, fortune, do cohere and jump
That I am Viola: which to confirm, 260
I'll bring you to a captain in this town,
Where lie my maiden weeds; by whose gentle help
I was preserved to serve this noble count.
All the occurrence of my fortune since
Hath been between this lady and this lord. 265

SEB. [*To* OLIVIA] So comes it, lady, you have been mistook:
But nature to her bias drew in that.
You would have been contracted to a maid;
Nor are you therein, by my life, deceived,
You are betroth'd both to a maid and man. 270

DUKE. Be not amazed; right noble is his blood.

205. **set**, glazed with drunkenness. 206-7. **passy . . . pavin**, English of Italian "Passamezzo pavana," a slow and stately dance, the strains of which are eight measures each. He is calling the surgeon a "slow poke." 217. **brother of my blood**, i.e., own brother. 218. **safety**, i.e., with regard to my own safety. 219. **strange regard**, distant look. 221. **for**, for the sake of. 223. **one habit**, the same costume. 224. **natural perspective**, a deception practised by Nature, usually brought about by a contrivance which by mirrors multiplied a single object.

234-5. **deity . . . every where**, i.e., I cannot, like a God, be in several places at once. 237. **Of**, in the name of. 241. **suited**, dressed. 242. **suit**, clothing, i.e., of living persons. 244. **dimension . . . clad**, shape consisting of flesh and blood. 245. **participate**, receive a share in. 246. **rest**, i.e., of the evidence; **goes even**, confirms. 256. **lets to make us**, keep us from being. 259. **jump**, fit together to prove. 264. **occurrence**, course of events. 267. **bias**, tendency of a bowling ball to curve. The phrase means, "Nature followed her bias (natural tendency) in that (in making you love someone who resembled me)." 271. **amazed**, dumbfounded.

If this be so, as yet the glass seems true,
I shall have share in this most happy wreck.
[*To* VIOLA] Boy, thou hast said to me a thousand times 274
Thou never shouldst love woman like to me.

VIO. And all those sayings will I overswear;
And all those swearings keep as true in soul
As doth that orbèd continent the fire
That severs day from night.

DUKE. Give me thy hand;
And let me see thee in thy woman's weeds. 280

VIO. The captain that did bring me first on shore
Hath my maid's garments: he upon some action
Is now in durance, at Malvolio's suit,
A gentleman, and follower of my lady's.

OLI. He shall enlarge him: fetch Malvolio hither: 285
And yet, alas, now I remember me,
They say, poor gentleman, he's much distract.

[*Re-enter* CLOWN *with a letter, and* FABIAN.]

A most extracting frenzy of mine own
From my remembrance clearly banish'd his.
How does he, sirrah? 290

CLO. Truly, madam, he holds Belzebub at the stave's end as well as a man in his case may do: has here writ a letter to you; I should have given 't you to-day morning, but as a madman's epistles are no gospels, so it skills not much when they are delivered. 296

OLI. Open 't, and read it.

CLO. Look then to be well edified when the fool delivers the madman. [*Reads*] "By the Lord, madam,"— 300

OLI. How now! art thou mad?

CLO. No, madam, I do but read madness: an your ladyship will have it as it ought to be, you must allow Vox.

OLI. Prithee, read i' thy right wits. 305

CLO. So I do, madonna; but to read his right wits is to read thus: therefore perpend, my princess, and give ear.

OLI. Read it you, sirrah. [*To* FABIAN.

FAB. [*Reads*] "By the Lord, madam, you 310 wrong me, and the world shall know it: though you have put me into darkness and given your drunken cousin rule over me, yet have I the benefit of my senses as well as your ladyship. I have your own letter that induced me to the semblance I put on; with the which I doubt not but to do myself much right, or you much shame. Think of me as you please. I leave my duty a little unthought of and speak out of my injury.

"THE MADLY-USED MALVOLIO."

OLI. Did he write this? 320

CLO. Ay, madam.

DUKE. This savours not much of distraction.

OLI. See him deliver'd, Fabian; bring him hither. [*Exit* FABIAN.]
My lord, so please you, these things further thought on,
To think me as well a sister as a wife, 325
One day shall crown the alliance on 't, so please you,
Here at my house and at my proper cost.

DUKE. Madam, I am most apt to embrace your offer.
[*To* VIOLA] Your master quits you; and for your service done him,
So much against the mettle of your sex, 330
So far beneath your soft and tender breeding,
And since you call'd me master for so long,
Here is my hand: you shall from this time be
Your master's mistress.

OLI. A sister! you are she.

[*Re-enter* FABIAN, *with* MALVOLIO.]

DUKE. Is this the madman?

OLI. Ay, my lord, this same. 335
How now, Malvolio!

MAL. Madam, you have done me wrong,
Notorious wrong.

272. **glass**, the "perspective" of line 224. 276. **overswear**, swear to again. 278. **orbed continent**, the sphere thought to contain the sun; **fire**, sun. 280. **weeds**, clothes. 282. **upon some action**, as the result of some legal action. 283. **in durance**, under arrest. 285. **enlarge**, release. 287. **distract**, crazed. 288. **extracting frenzy**, absorbing obsession. 291. **Belzebub**, Beelzebub was the Jewish prince of demons. 292. **at the stave's end**, at arm's length. The figure is taken from the old-fashioned cudgel (short heavy stick) play; **case**, situation. 296. **skills not much**, does not make much difference. 299. **delivers**, expresses (the thoughts of). 304. **Vox**, the appropriate (loud, for a madman) tone of voice. 306-7. **his right wits**, his wits aright. 307. **perpend**, pay attention. 315. **induced . . . put on**, persuaded me to appear as I did. 316-7. **do myself much right**, set myself emphatically right. 319. **madly-used**, treated as a madman. 323. **deliver'd**, released. 326. **crown the alliance**, i.e., by a double wedding. 327. **proper cost**, own expense. 328. **apt**, ready. 329. **quits**, releases. 330. **mettle**, natural disposition. 333. **Here is my hand**, this taking of hands was part of the formal betrothal ceremony.

OLI. Have I, Malvolio? no.

MAL. Lady, you have. Pray you, peruse that letter.
You must not now deny it is your hand: 339
Write from it, if you can, in hand or phrase;
Or say 'tis not your seal, not your invention:
You can say none of this: well, grant it then
And tell me, in the modesty of honour,
Why you have given me such clear lights of favour,
Bade me come smiling and cross-garter'd to you, 345
To put on yellow stockings and to frown
Upon Sir Toby and the lighter people;
And, acting this in an obedient hope,
Why have you suffer'd me to be imprison'd,
Kept in a dark house, visited by the priest, 350
And made the most notorious geck and gull
That e'er invention play'd on? tell me why.

OLI. Alas, Malvolio, this is not my writing,
Though, I confess, much like the character:
But out of question 'tis Maria's hand. 355
And now I do bethink me, it was she
First told me thou wast mad; then camest in smiling,
And in such forms which here were presupposed
Upon thee in the letter. Prithee, be content:
This practice hath most shrewdly pass'd upon thee; 360
But when we know the grounds and authors of it,
Thou shalt be both the plaintiff and the judge
Of thine own cause.

FAB. Good madam, hear me speak,
And let no quarrel nor no brawl to come
Taint the condition of this present hour, 365
Which I have wonder'd at. In hope it shall not,
Most freely I confess, myself and Toby
Set this device against Malvolio here,
Upon some stubborn and uncourteous parts
We had conceived against him: Maria writ
The letter at Sir Toby's great importance; 371
In recompense whereof he hath married her.
How with a sportful malice it was follow'd,
May rather pluck on laughter than revenge;
If that the injuries be justly weigh'd 375
That have on both sides pass'd.

OLI. Alas, poor fool, how have they baffled thee!

CLO. Why, "some are born great, some achieve greatness, and some have greatness thrown upon them." I was one, sir, in this interlude; one Sir Topas, sir; but that's all one. "By the Lord, fool, I am not mad." But do you remember? "Madam, why laugh you at such a barren rascal? an you smile not, he's gagged:" and thus the whirligig of time brings in his revenges. 385

MAL. I'll be revenged on the whole pack of you. [*Exit.*

OLI. He hath been most notoriously abused.

DUKE. Pursue him, and entreat him to a peace:
He hath not told us of the captain yet: 390
When that is known and golden time convents,
A solemn combination shall be made
Of our dear souls. Meantime, sweet sister,
We will not part from hence. Cesario, come;
For so you shall be, while you are a man;
But when in other habits you are seen,
Orsino's mistress and his fancy's queen.

[*Exeunt all, except* CLOWN.

CLO. [*Sings*]
When that I was and a little tiny boy,
With hey, ho, the wind and the rain,
A foolish thing was but a toy, 400
For the rain it raineth every day.

But when I came to man's estate,
With hey, ho, &c.
'Gainst knaves and thieves men shut their gate,
For the rain, &c. 405

But when I came, alas! to wive,
With hey, ho, &c.
By swaggering could I never thrive,
For the rain, &c.

340. write, i.e., write differently. 343. in . . . of honour, with the restraint which honor demands. 344. clear . . . favour, revelations of your regard. 347. lighter, of inferior rank. 351. geck, dupe. 352. invention play'd on, a trick imposed on. 354. character, handwriting. 358. forms, behavior; presupposed Upon thee, suggested to you beforehand. 359. be content, do not be downhearted. 360. practice, plot; shrewdly pass'd, maliciously imposed. 361. grounds, motives. 365. Taint the condition, spoil the (happy) circumstances. 371. importance, insistence. 373. How, the manner in which; it, i.e., the letter. 374. pluck on, excite. 376. on . . . pass'd, inflicted on either side. 377. baffled, disgraced. 380. was one, i.e., played a part. 381. interlude, i.e., little comedy. 385. whirligig of time, the ceaselessly revolving wheel of the Goddess Fortune. 391. convents, calls (us) together. 400. A foolish . . . toy, i.e., the foolish things I did were not taken seriously. 404. 'Gainst . . . their gate, i.e., men shut their gates against me, as though I were a thief and a knave. 408. swaggering, bullying, i.e., I could not bully anyone into marrying me.

But when I came unto my beds, 410
With hey, ho, &c.
With toss-pots still had drunken heads,
For the rain, &c.

412. tosspots, topers, i.e,, the only women who would pass the night with me were drunken sots.

A great while ago the world begun,
With hey, ho, &c.
But that's all one, our play is done,
And we'll strive to please you every day. [*Exit.*

AFTERWORD

Shakespeare's comedies act on us with an appeal less immediate than Shakespeare's tragedies. We respond at once to Hamlet's dilemma, though his situation and behavior are vastly complex. The problems of Viola, Orsino, and Olivia are or seem to be more elusive. The dress in which the tragic character is clothed—Hamlet's sable suits of woe—may be remote from our own experience, like the accents in which he speaks and the time and place he inhabits. But very obviously this character is grappling with the ultimate reality, which is death, and so we honor his claim to our respectful attention. Shakespeare's comedies, on the other hand, are not realistic but romantic. The stories they dramatize do not encourage belief. For that reason, we are apt to dispute their pertinence. What have they to say to us? *Twelfth Night,* which is the greatest of Shakespeare's comedies, has much to say. Its purport or meaning—not its message!—is, however, obscured by the romantic nonsense that is the plot. As that is so, it is important to scrutinize the elements of which the plot is made. This is the indicated question to put: is the story Shakespeare tells simple nonsense after all, or is it fruitful of meaning beneath the skin?

In *Twelfth Night,* as often in Shakespearean comedy, the improbable business of mistaken identity is decisive for the working out of the plot. The playwright introduces identical twins, who are not especially conspicuous in everyday life. The confusion that results occupies an impressive part of the action. This confusion is compounded by an outrageous resort to disguise. Women pretend to be men, and in their pretended role are made love to by other women. "I am not what I am," says Viola. She is speaking to Olivia, who thinks herself in love as she is "beguiled" by a "most exacting frenzy" or madness. Olivia has relinquished the power of true perception. (Possibly it has never been hers.) She is charmed by the outside of things, which is said to impose without difficulty on women's waxen hearts. Feste the Clown, who, despite his appointed function, is no fool in the grain, remarks on the untrustworthy nature of the outside or surface, and the gulf that opens between appearance and reality. The cowl, says Feste, does not make the monk. *Cucullus non facit monachum.* Men are not what they seem —except that Olivia, because of the imperfection of her faculties, is prone to take them at face value.

Now we want to ask: is the myopia which afflicts this foolish woman peculiar to her or does it disable other persons in the play? If blind or foolish behavior is pervasive in the enclosed world of *Twelfth Night,* perhaps it holds in the greater world as well. Perhaps, under the aspect of metaphor, we are being asked to consider so many versions of ourselves. Shakespeare, elaborating the metaphor that is the plot, is piling one improbability on another to suggest to us that nothing is too gross or ridiculous for human beings to swallow, given the strong corruption which inhabits "our frail blood." That is the point and use of disguise and mistaken identity. The object we suppose ourselves to apprehend for what it really is resembles a "natural perspective," which reveals one image or face when looked at straight on and another and perhaps a contradictory image when our point of vantage has shifted.

In *Twelfth Night*, confusion is the norm because it describes the human condition. Olivia, as she is blind to the truth in others, is a familiar figure—and also in her blindness to the truth about herself. In her exaggerated mourning, she usurps herself, and so denies her proper role as a woman. What is hers to bestow is not hers to reserve. Malvolio, the arrogant steward, is sick of self-love, the prisoner of a diseased imagination. It is right to confine him as a madman, for he is more puzzled in the darkness of his ignorance than the Egyptians in their fog. But our laughter is not wholly at Malvolio's expense. His ignorance, we begin to surmise, is a caricature, in which our own follies are heightened.

Folly, whether harmless and therefore comic, as in the fatuous behavior of Malvolio, or destructive and therefore tragic—Othello's case—takes its rise from faulty perception, what the Clown calls "misprision" or mistaking. The death of Christ is the archetypal folly, and tragedy, but the perpetrators of this tragic folly are to be forgiven "for they know not what they do." None of us, apparently, is acute enough, really to know. The eye, as Olivia discovers—but the discovery is bootless—flatters and cozens the mind with false reporting. To Hamlet, in a graver context, evil is explicable as reason panders or truckles to the will. But explaining is not redressing. We know that we err, and know what follows therefrom; and we continue, says Mark Antony, to "adore our errors." What then?

We are not to be censured—this is the corollary—simply as we misconceive. "Who cannot be crushed with a plot?" Parolles, the comic villain in *All's Well That Ends Well,* raises the question, which might be raised by Malvolio. We are censurable as, like Malvolio, we withhold from other men the suffrage we bestow on ourselves. "Dost thou think because thou art virtuous, there shall be no more cakes and ale?"

Whether Malvolio is "a kind of Puritan"—an absorbing question to those critics whose eye is always roving from the business at hand—does not signify. The intellectual error, the endemic misprision to which all of us are prone, in our politics, in our social or religious prepossessions, is not at issue, and perhaps it is not especially reprehensible. "Our frailty is the cause, not we!" Malvolio is the butt of laughter and scorn as he is "the best persuaded of himself, so crammed, as he thinks, with excellencies, that it is his grounds of faith that all that look on him love him."

But who, in this context, is deserving of praise? Not the man of capacious intellect, or not for his intellectuality, but the man who is generous and of a free or innocent disposition: Sebastian, whose "bosom is full of kindness"; Viola, who is said to bear a mind devoid of malice, "that envy could not but call fair."

The characters of *Twelfth Night* dance to the tune of a "greater power than we can contradict." This is to say: No man is truly free in what he does. But some men, beneath the skin, are "of free disposition." That is the only important distinction between man and man. Antonio, the sea captain, is set apart from Malvolio, as he manifests an excellent "touch of modesty." Otherwise, and like

Malvolio, he seems, not a man endowed with free will, but a pawn or mechanical figure. Antonio is moved by no rational purpose in befriending Sebastian, the brother of Viola. What is called "witchcraft" impels him. Is there a better way of explicating human attachment? The conduct of Sebastian is equally irrational. The journey on which he has embarked—in company with us all—is only wandering without point, like that of a meteor or vagrant star. Duke Orsino, who rules in this muddled principality, is, on his own description, unstaid and skittish, at least as giddy and infirm as his subjects. Though man is customarily defined as a thinking creature, who has pinned his faith to judgment and reason "since before Noah was a sailor," judgment and reason are no help to him here. Those to whom wisdom is imputed, like Sir Andrew, when we hear of him first, are fools. Those to whom it is by convention denied, like Feste the Clown, are wise. In the unlikely world of Shakespearean comedy, which distorts to make us see, "Nothing that is so is so."

How is this disastrous confusion resolved? It is resolved, so the chastened Antonio instructs us, as we reject the vile idol or image which is the look of the thing and seek the truth which lies hid below the surface. That is useful instruction to follow in approaching the bizarre surface or plot of the play.

> In nature there's no blemish but the mind;
> None can be call'd deform'd but the unkind:
> Virtue is beauty, but the beauteous evil
> Are empty trunks, o'erflourished by the devil.

As we are truly wise, we will become fools and babes, ready, like Sebastian, to distrust our eyes and wrangle with our reason: to discredit what it tells us. For how, in our insufficiency, should we know? "Virtue that transgresses is but patched with sin; and sin that amends is but patched with virtue." Human beings, on this skeptical reading of their nature and capacity, which is also a greatly tolerant reading, cannot do better than commit their fortunes to time or fate. Viola is wise in acknowledging that we do not really possess ourselves. And therefore she bows her head, not to God but to the lack of essential power that is characteristic of human kind. "What is decreed must be."

Comedy requires a happy ending. Shakespeare in *Twelfth Night* fulfills the requirement. What is decreed is the marriage of Orsino and Viola, Sebastian and Olivia, who are united at last in spite of themselves. "Journeys end in lovers meeting." It is understood that the lovers, if left to their own slender resources, would perhaps have found out a different fate, not so happy, perhaps a tragic fate. For all the ingredients of tragedy are here, and not the least of these ingredients is the want of stature in the protagonists of the play. "What fools these mortals be!" The saying of Puck, in *A Midsummer Night's Dream,* is attested once again.

But Shakespeare, in *Twelfth Night* as in the earlier comedy, is benevolent. He saves the life of Sebastian, who is the boy on the dolphin. He decrees that no blood will be shed in the mock-combat between Sir Andrew and Viola in her role as Cesario, the pretended page. As "golden time convents" or determines, he apportions happiness to his protagonists. Only he makes painfully and comically apparent that these feeble protagonists are not so much deserving as lucky.

That is a sobering analysis of human psychology, and it is borne out generally in Shakespearean comedy. Tragedy, as it emphasizes responsibility and meditated choice, is more hopeful. But Shakespeare, in presenting his pessimistic analysis, is not dour or filled with gloom. Gaiety is the word for *Twelfth Night.* We are all frail and foolish, as the plot of the play discovers, fellow passengers in a voyage which is "mere extravagancy." But we are not in our unheroic progress to pine in thought, or sit like Patience on a monument. It is not so good to invoke in song the melancholy god as to partake of cakes and ale.

What is love? 'Tis not hereafter;
Present mirth hath present laughter;
What's to come is still unsure.

But what's to come, as Feste sings in the mysterious and deeply moving conclusion to the play, is also fixed and known from the beginning. "For the rain it raineth every day." *Twelfth Night* is a perfect harmony, never achieved before or since, in which the sanctity of present laughter is joined to an awareness of the ending of all things.

Suggested Reading

BARBER, C. L., *Shakespeare's Festive Comedy* (1959). Meridian.
BROWN, JOHN R., *Shakespeare and His Comedies* (1957). Barnes and Noble.
BUSH, GEOFFREY, *Shakespeare and the Natural Condition* (1956).
CHARLTON, H. B., *Shakespearian Comedy* (1938). Barnes and Noble.
DRAPER, JOHN W., *The "Twelfth Night" of Shakespeare's Audience* (1950).
EVANS, BERTRAND, *Shakespeare's Comedies* (1960). Oxford.
GOLDSMITH, ROBERT H., *Wise Fools in Shakespeare* (1955).
GORDON, GEORGE, *Shakespearian Comedy* (1944).
HARDY, B., *Twelfth Night* (1962).
HOTSON, LESLIE, *The First Night of Twelfth Night* (1954).
LEECH, CLIFFORD, *Twelfth Night and Shakespearian Comedy* (1957).
PARROTT, THOMAS MARC, *Shakespearean Comedy* (1949).
PETTET, E. C., *Shakespeare and the Romance Tradition* (1949).
SUMMERS, JOSEPH H., "The Masks of 'Twelfth Night'," *The University Review,* XXII (1955), 25–32; reprinted in *Shakespeare, Modern Essays in Criticism,* ed. Leonard F. Dean (1967).
WELSFORD, ENID, *The Fool* (1935).

Hamlet

A NOTE ON THE TEXT

Shakespeare's *Hamlet,* written sometime in the years 1600–1602, is the culminating and most famous version of a story that has held the interest of writers and their public for more than seven hundred years. As contemporary references attest, a play dealing with the fortunes of Prince Hamlet had been presented in England not later than 1589 and was still being acted in the following decade. This early dramatic effort is ascribed commonly to the Elizabethan playwright, Thomas Kyd. The ascription is plausible, for *The Spanish Tragedy* (1587), an immensely successful play which is certainly the work of Kyd, resembles Shakespeare's *Hamlet* at many points. Each play is an example of the lurid and very popular genre known as "revenge tragedy."

Behind Kyd, if he is the author of the original or so-called *Ur-Hamlet,* lies a narrative "Hystorie of Hamblet," included in the fifth volume of the *Histoires tragiques* (1576) by François de Belleforest. The ultimate source of the story is the *Historia Danica* of Saxo Grammaticus, a medieval chronicle dating from the twelfth century.

Shakespeare's play was registered for publication in 1602. A pirated edition, marred by omissions and distortions, appeared in quarto in 1603. A second quarto, published a year later, offers a more nearly comprehensive text. Q2, which is also prone to inaccuracy, was reprinted in 1607 and 1611. Copy for the Folio edition of 1623 is supposed by many scholars to have been a manuscript, used in the playhouse. The making of an acceptable text of the play requires the collating or comparing of these various editions, and is an uncommonly difficult task. In the editing of *Hamlet,* not less than in matters of interpretation, complexity is the rule.

HAMLET, PRINCE OF DENMARK

DRAMATIS PERSONÆ

CLAUDIUS, *king of Denmark.*
HAMLET, *son to the late, and nephew to the present king.*
POLONIUS, *lord chamberlain.*
HORATIO, *friend to Hamlet.*
LAERTES, *son to Polonius.*
VOLTIMAND, CORNELIUS, ROSENCRANTZ, GUILDENSTERN, OSRIC, A GENTLEMAN, } *courtiers.*
A PRIEST.
MARCELLUS, BERNARDO, } *officers.*
FRANCISCO, *a soldier.*
REYNALDO, *servant to Polonius.*
PLAYERS.
Two CLOWNS, *grave-diggers.*
FORTINBRAS, *prince of Norway.*
A CAPTAIN.
ENGLISH AMBASSADORS.
GERTRUDE, *queen of Denmark, and mother to Hamlet.*
OPHELIA, *daughter to Polonius.*
LORDS, LADIES, OFFICERS, SOLDIERS, SAILORS, MESSENGERS, *and other* ATTENDANTS. GHOST *of Hamlet's father.*

SCENE: *Denmark.*

ACT I

SCENE I. *Elsinore. A platform before the castle.*

[FRANCISCO *at his post. Enter to him* BERNARDO.]

BER. Who's there?
FRAN. Nay, answer me: stand, and unfold yourself.
BER. Long live the king!
FRAN. Bernardo?
BER. He. 5
FRAN. You come most carefully upon your hour.
BER. 'Tis now struck twelve; get thee to bed, Francisco.
FRAN. For this relief much thanks: 'tis bitter cold,
And I am sick at heart.
BER. Have you had quiet guard?
FRAN. Not a mouse stirring. 10
BER. Well, good night.
If you do meet Horatio and Marcellus,
The rivals of my watch, bid them make haste.
FRAN. I think I hear them. Stand, ho! Who's there?

[*Enter* HORATIO *and* MARCELLUS.]

HOR. Friends to this ground.
MAR. And liegemen to the Dane. 15
FRAN. Give you good night.
MAR. O, farewell, honest soldier:
Who hath relieved you?
FRAN. Bernardo has my place.
Give you good night. [*Exit.*
MAR. Holla! Bernardo!
BER. Say,
What, is Horatio there?
HOR. A piece of him.
BER. Welcome, Horatio: welcome, good Marcellus. 20
MAR. What, has this thing appear'd again to-night?
BER. I have seen nothing.

Act I, Scene i: 2. answer me, i.e., give the countersign; **unfold yourself,** tell who you are and what you want. **3. long . . . king,** the pass word, or countersign. **6. carefully . . . hour,** i.e., on the dot. **13. rivals,** companions.
15. liegemen . . . Dane, loyal subjects of the Danish King. **16. Give you,** may God give you. **18. Say,** say on. **19. What,** i.e., tell me.

MAR. Horatio says 'tis but our fantasy,
And will not let belief take hold of him
Touching this dreaded sight, twice seen of us: 25
Therefore I have entreated him along
With us to watch the minutes of this night;
That if again this apparition come,
He may approve our eyes and speak to it.

HOR. Tush, tush, 'twill not appear.

BER. Sit down awhile; 30
And let us once again assail your ears,
That are so fortified against our story
What we have two nights seen.

HOR. Well, sit we down,
And let us hear Bernardo speak of this.

BER. Last night of all, 35
When yond same star that's westward from the pole
Had made his course to illume that part of heaven
Where now it burns, Marcellus and myself,
The bell then beating one,—

[*Enter* GHOST.]

MAR. Peace, break thee off; look, where it comes again! 40

BER. In the same figure, like the king that's dead.

MAR. Thou art a scholar; speak to it, Horatio.

BER. Looks it not like the king? mark it, Horatio.

HOR. Most like: it harrows me with fear and wonder.

BER. It would be spoke to.

MAR. Question it, Horatio.

HOR. What art thou that usurp'st this time of night, 46
Together with that fair and warlike form
In which the majesty of buried Denmark
Did sometimes march? by heaven I charge thee, speak!

MAR. It is offended.

BER. See, it stalks away! 50

HOR. Stay! speak, speak! I charge thee, speak! [*Exit* GHOST.

MAR. 'Tis gone, and will not answer.

BER. How now, Horatio! you tremble and look pale:
Is not this something more than fantasy?
What think you on 't? 55

HOR. Before my God, I might not this believe
Without the sensible and true avouch
Of mine own eyes.

MAR. Is it not like the king?

HOR. As thou art to thyself:
Such was the very armour he had on 60
When he the ambitious Norway combated;
So frown'd he once, when, in an angry parle,
He smote the sledded Polacks on the ice.
'Tis strange.

MAR. Thus twice before, and jump at this dead hour, 65
With martial stalk hath he gone by our watch.

HOR. In what particular thought to work I know not;
But in the gross and scope of my opinion,
This bodes some strange eruption to our state.

MAR. Good now, sit down, and tell me, he that knows, 70
Why this same strict and most observant watch
So nightly toils the subject of the land,
And why such daily cast of brazen cannon,
And foreign mart for implements of war;
Why such impress of shipwrights, whose sore task 75
Does not divide the Sunday from the week;
What might be toward, that this sweaty haste
Doth make the night joint-labourer with the day:
Who is 't that can inform me?

HOR. That can I;
At least, the whisper goes so. Our last king, 80
Whose image even but now appear'd to us,
Was, as you know, by Fortinbras of Norway,
Thereto prick'd on by a most emulate pride,
Dared to the combat; in which our valiant Hamlet—

23. **fantasy,** imagination. 29. **approve our eyes,** verify what we have seen. 35. **Last . . . all,** only last night. 36. **pole,** north star. 40. **Peace . . . off,** keep still, stop talking. 42. **scholar,** i.e., you know Latin. The set phrases which exorcised an evil spirit were in Latin. 44. **harrows,** plows up, torments. 46. **usurp'st,** wrongfully take possession of. 47. **Together with,** i.e., wrongfully assume; **warlike form,** i.e., the King as he looked in battle array. 49. **sometimes,** formerly. 57. **sensible . . . avouch,** true testimony of the senses. 61. **Norway,** King of Norway. 62. **parle,** encounter. 63. **sledded,** who ride in sledges. 65. **jump,** exactly. 67. **In . . . not,** i.e., I do not know just what to think about it. 68. **gross and scope,** main drift. 69. **bodes,** forebodes; **eruption,** i.e., calamity. 70. **Good now,** come then. 72. **toils the subject,** makes the subjects toil. 73. **cast,** casting. 74. **mart for,** trade in. 75. **impress,** drafting; **sore,** difficult. 77. **toward,** in preparation. 81. **of Norway,** King of Norway, father of young Fortinbras. 83. **emulate,** jealous. 84. **Hamlet,** i.e., "our last king," of line 80.

For so this side of our known world esteem'd
him— 85
Did slay this Fortinbras; who, by a seal'd
compact,
Well ratified by law and heraldry,
Did forfeit, with his life, all those his lands
Which he stood seized of, to the conqueror:
Against the which, a moiety competent 90
Was gagèd by our king; which had return'd
To the inheritance of Fortinbras,
Had he been vanquisher; as, by the same
covenant,
And carriage of the article design'd,
His fell to Hamlet. Now, sir, young Fortin-
bras, 95
Of unimprovèd mettle hot and full,
Hath in the skirts of Norway here and there
Shark'd up a list of lawless resolutes,
For food and diet, to some enterprise
That hath a stomach in 't; which is no other—
As it doth well appear unto our state— 101
But to recover of us, by strong hand
And terms compulsatory, those foresaid lands
So by his father lost: and this, I take it,
Is the main motive of our preparations, 105
The source of this our watch and the chief
head
Of this post-haste and romage in the land.
BER. I think it be no other but e'en so:
Well may it sort that this portentous figure
Comes armed through our watch; so like the
king 110
That was and is the question of these wars.
HOR. A mote it is to trouble the mind's eye.
In the most high and palmy state of Rome,
A little ere the mightiest Julius fell,
The graves stood tenantless and the sheeted
dead 115
Did squeak and gibber in the Roman streets:
As stars with trains of fire and dews of blood,
Disasters in the sun; and the moist star
Upon whose influence Neptune's empire
stands
Was sick almost to doomsday with eclipse: 120
And even the like precurse of fierce events,
As harbingers preceding still the fates
And prologue to the omen coming on,
Have heaven and earth together demonstrated
Unto our climatures and countrymen.— 125
But soft, behold! lo, where it comes again!

[*Re-enter* GHOST.]

I'll cross it, though it blast me. Stay, illusion!
If thou hast any sound, or use of voice,
Speak to me:
If there be any good thing to be done, 130
That may to thee do ease and grace to me,
Speak to me: [*Cock crows.*]
If thou art privy to thy country's fate,
Which, happily, foreknowing may avoid,
O, speak! 135
Or if thou has uphoarded in thy life
Extorted treasure in the womb of earth,
For which, they say, you spirits oft walk in
death,
Speak of it: stay, and speak! Stop it, Marcel-
lus.
MAR. Shall I strike at it with my parti-
san? 140
HOR. Do, if it will not stand.
BER. 'Tis here!
HOR. 'Tis here!
MAR. 'Tis gone! [*Exit* GHOST.]
We do it wrong, being so majestical,
To offer it the show of violence;
For it is, as the air, invulnerable, 145
And our vain blows malicious mockery.
BER. It was about to speak, when the cock
crew.
HOR. And then it started like a guilty thing
Upon a fearful summons. I have heard,
The cock, that is the trumpet to the morn,

85. **so**, i.e., as valiant. 86. **sealed compact**, formal agreement. 87. **Well . . . heraldry**, i.e., in accordance with both law and the usages of chivalry. 89. **stood . . . of**, had in his possession. 90. **moiety competent**, an equal portion (of land). 91 **gaged**, pledged; **had return'd**, would have reverted to. 94. **carriage . . . design'd**, terms of the agreement as drawn up. 96. **unimproved mettle**, untried courage. 97. **skirts**, remote districts. 98. **Shark'd up**, collected through trickery; **resolutes**, reckless men. 100. **hath . . . in 't**, requires courage; **which**, i.e., the purpose of the enterprise. 103. **compulsatory**, dictated by force. 106. **head**, origin. 107. **post-haste and romage**, great haste and bustle. 109. **Well . . . sort**, i.e., this may well be the reason. 111. **question**, cause. 113. **palmy**, flourishing. 115. **sheeted**, in their shrouds. 116, a line seems to have dropped out between ll. 116 and 117. 116. **gibber**, make inarticulate sounds. 117. **As . . . fire**, meteors. 118. **Disasters**, unlucky omens; **moist star**, the moon, because it influences the tides. 120. **sick . . . doomsday**, turned almost completely dark. In Matthew XIV, 29, it is prophesied that on doomsday the sun "shall be darkened and the moon not give her light." 121. **precurse**, warning. 122. **harbingers**, advance agents; **still**, always. 123. **omen**, fatal event. 125. **climatures**, regions. 127. **cross**, i.e., cross his path, supposed to be an invitation to misfortune; **blast me**, cause me to wither away. 131. **grace**, blessedness. 133. **art privy to**, know the secret of. 134. **happily**, by good fortune. 136. **uphoarded**, stored up. 137. **Extorted treasure**, wealth wrung by force (from its rightful owner). 140. **partisan**, long-shafted spear. 146. **vain**, ineffective; **malicious mockery**, futile gestures of hatred.

Doth with his lofty and shrill-sounding throat 151
Awake the god of day; and, at his warning,
Whether in sea or fire, in earth or air,
The extravagant and erring spirit hies
To his confine: and of the truth herein 155
This present object made probation.

MAR. It faded on the crowing of the cock.
Some say that ever 'gainst that season comes
Wherein our Saviour's birth is celebrated, 159
The bird of dawning singeth all night long:
And then, they say, no spirit dare stir abroad;
The nights are wholesome; then no planets strike,
No fairy takes, nor witch hath power to charm,
So hallow'd and so gracious is the time.

HOR. So have I heard and do in part believe it. 165
But, look, the morn, in russet mantle clad,
Walks o'er the dew of yon high eastward hill:
Break we our watch up; and by my advice,
Let us impart what we have seen to-night
Unto young Hamlet; for, upon my life, 170
This spirit, dumb to us, will speak to him.
Do you consent we shall acquaint him with it,
As needful in our loves, fitting our duty?

MAR. Let's do 't, I pray; and I this morning know 174
Where we shall find him most conveniently.
[*Exeunt.*

SCENE II. *A room of state in the castle.*

[*Enter the* KING, QUEEN, HAMLET, POLONIUS, LAERTES, VOLTIMAND, CORNELIUS, LORDS, *and* ATTENDANTS.]

KING. Though yet of Hamlet our dear brother's death
The memory be green, and that it us befitted
To bear our hearts in grief and our whole kingdom
To be contracted in one brow of woe,
Yet so far hath discretion fought with nature
That we with wisest sorrow think on him, 6
Together with remembrance of ourselves.
Therefore our sometime sister, now our queen,
The imperial jointress to this warlike state,
Have we, as 'twere with a defeated joy,— 10
With an auspicious and a dropping eye,
With mirth in funeral and with dirge in marriage,
In equal scale weighing delight and dole,—
Taken to wife: nor have we herein barr'd
Your better wisdoms, which have freely gone
With this affair along. For all, our thanks. 16
Now follows, that you know, young Fortinbras,
Holding a weak supposal of our worth,
Or thinking by our late dear brother's death
Our state to be disjoint and out of frame, 20
Colleagued with the dream of his advantage,
He hath not fail'd to pester us with message,
Importing the surrender of those lands
Lost by his father, with all bonds of law,
To our most valiant brother. So much for him. 25
Now for ourself and for this time of meeting:
Thus much the business is: we have here writ
To Norway, uncle of young Fortinbras,—
Who, impotent and bed-rid, scarcely hears
Of this his nephew's purpose,—to suppress 30
His further gait herein; in that the levies,
The lists and full proportions, are all made
Out of his subject: and we here dispatch
You, good Cornelius, and you, Voltimand,
For bearers of this greeting to old Norway; 35
Giving to you no further personal power
To business with the king, more than the scope
Of these delated articles allow.
Farewell, and let your haste commend your duty.

COR., VOL. In that and all things will we show our duty. 40

151. **lofty**, high-pitched. 154. **extravagant**, straying; **erring**, wandering. 155. **confine**, habitation. 156. **made probation**, give proof. 158. **'gainst . . . comes**, at the approach of that season. 160. **bird of dawning**, the cock. 162. **strike**, exert a baleful influence. 163. **takes**, bewitches. 164. **gracious**, blessed. 173. **As . . . loves**, as something our love dictates. **Scene ii**: 2. **that**, though. 5. **discretion**, common sense; **nature**, natural impulse (to excessive grief). 7. **remembrance of ourselves**, consideration of our duties (as living men). 8. **our sometime**, my former. 9. **imperial jointress to**, royal inheritor of. 10. **defeated**, impaired. 11. **auspicious**, joyful; **dropping**, weeping. 13. **dole**, grief. 14-5. **barr'd . . . wisdoms**, ignored your wiser opinions (as to my proper course of action). 17. **that**, that which. 18. **weak supposal**, disparaging opinion. 20. **out of frame**, in disorder. 21. **Colleagued with**, supported by; **advantage**, good chance. 23. **Importing**, urging. 24. **with . . . law**, together with all legal claim to them. 27. **business**, present state of affairs. 31. **gait**, action. 32. **proportions**, quotas. 33. **Out . . . subject**, i.e., from the King of Norway's subjects. 37. **To business**, to transact business. 38. **delated articles**, detailed instructions. 39. **let . . . duty**, let prompt action take the place of a ceremonious farewell.

KING. We doubt it nothing: heartily farewell. [*Exeunt* VOLTIMAND *and* CORNELIUS.]
And now, Laertes, what's the news with you?
You told us of some suit, what is 't, Laertes?
You cannot speak of reason to the Dane,
And lose your voice: what wouldst thou beg, Laertes, 45
That shall not be my offer, not thy asking?
The head is not more native to the heart,
The hand more instrumental to the mouth,
Than is the throne of Denmark to thy father.
What wouldst thou have, Laertes?

LAER. My dread lord, 50
Your leave and favour to return to France;
From whence though willingly I came to Denmark,
To show my duty in your coronation,
Yet now, I must confess, that duty done,
My thoughts and wishes bend again toward France 55
And bow them to your gracious leave and pardon.

KING. Have you your father's leave? What says Polonius?

POL. He hath, my lord, wrung from me my slow leave
By laboursome petition, and at last
Upon his will I seal'd my hard consent: 60
I do beseech you, give him leave to go.

KING. Take thy fair hour, Laertes; time be thine,
And thy best graces spend it at thy will!
But now, my cousin Hamlet, and my son,—

HAM. [*Aside*] A little more than kin, and less than kind. 65

KING. How is it that the clouds still hang on you?

HAM. Not so, my lord; I am too much i' the sun.

QUEEN. Good Hamlet, cast thy nighted colour off,
And let thine eye look like a friend on Denmark.
Do not forever with thy vailèd lids 70
Seek for thy noble father in the dust:
Thou know'st 'tis common; all that lives must die,
Passing through nature to eternity.

HAM. Ay, madam, it is common.

QUEEN. If it be,
Why seems it so particular with thee? 75

HAM. Seems, madam! nay, it is; I know not "seems."
'Tis not alone my inky cloak, good mother,
Nor customary suits of solemn black,
Nor windy suspiration of forced breath,
No, nor the fruitful river in the eye, 80
Nor the dejected 'haviour of the visage,
Together with all forms, moods, shapes of grief,
That can denote me truly: these indeed seem,
For they are actions that a man might play:
But I have that within which passeth show; 85
These but the trappings and the suits of woe.

KING. 'Tis sweet and commendable in your nature, Hamlet,
To give these mourning duties to your father:
But, you must know, your father lost a father;
That father lost, lost his, and the survivor bound 90
In filial obligation for some term
To do obsequious sorrow: but to perséver
In obstinate condolement is a course
Of impious stubbornness; 'tis unmanly grief;
It shows a will most incorrect to heaven, 95
A heart unfortified, a mind impatient,
An understanding simple and unschool'd:
For what we know must be and is as common
As any the most vulgar thing to sense,
Why should we in our peevish opposition 100
Take it to heart? Fie! 'tis a fault to heaven,
A fault against the dead, a fault to nature,
To reason most absurd; whose common theme
Is death of fathers, and who still hath cried,
From the first corse till he that died to-day,
"This must be so." We pray you, throw to earth 106

45. lose your voice, fail to have your wish granted. **46. shall . . . offer,** that I shall not freely offer. **47. native,** related by nature. **48. instrumental,** serviceable. **50. dread,** respected. **51. leave and favour,** kind permission. **53. show my duty,** pay my respects. **56 bow them to,** beg; **leave and pardon,** permission to go. **58. slow leave,** grudging consent. **60. will,** desire; **sealed . . . consent,** given with reluctance. **62. Take . . . hour,** enjoy the happiness of youth; **time be thine,** pass the time as you wish. **63. thy . . . will,** may you wish to spend it as your best qualities dictate. **64. cousin,** used for any relationship outside the immediate family. **65. less than kind,** lower in moral nature than our family (kind). **67. i' the sun,** (1) glory of the court, (2) of a son. **70. vailed,** lowered. **79. windy . . . breath,** forced sighs. **80. fruitful,** full. **81. 'haviour,** expression. **85. passeth show,** is too strong to be expressed by outward manifestations (of grief). **86. trappings,** outward signs. **92. obsequious sorrow,** sorrow suitable for a funeral. **93. condolement,** mourning. **95. incorrect,** unsubmissive. **96. unfortified,** i.e., by religion. **99. As any . . . sense,** as any of the most ordinary sense impressions. **103. whose,** antecedent is "nature."

This unprevailing woe, and think of us
As of a father: for let the world take note,
You are the most immediate to our throne;
And with no less nobility of love 110
Than that which dearest father bears his son,
Do I impart toward you. For your intent
In going back to school in Wittenberg,
It is most retrograde to our desire:
And we beseech you, bend you to remain 115
Here, in the cheer and comfort of our eye,
Our chiefest courtier, cousin, and our son.

QUEEN. Let not thy mother lose her prayers, Hamlet:
I pray thee, stay with us; go not to Wittenberg.

HAM. I shall in all my best obey you, madam. 120

KING. Why, 'tis a loving and a fair reply:
Be as ourself in Denmark. Madam, come;
This gentle and unforced accord of Hamlet
Sits smiling to my heart: in grace whereof,
No jocund health that Denmark drinks today, 125
But the great cannon to the clouds shall tell,
And the king's rouse the heavens shall bruit again,
Re-speaking earthly thunder. Come away.

[*Exeunt all but* HAMLET.

HAM. O, that this too too solid flesh would melt,
Thaw and resolve itself into a dew! 130
Or that the Everlasting had not fix'd
His canon 'gainst self-slaughter! O God! God!
How weary, stale, flat and unprofitable,
Seem to me all the uses of this world!
Fie on 't! ah fie! 'tis an unweeded garden, 135
That grows to seed; things rank and gross in nature
Possess it merely. That it should come to this!
But two months dead: nay, not so much, not two:
So excellent a king; that was, to this,
Hyperion to a satyr; so loving to my mother
That he might not beteem the winds of heaven 141
Visit her face too roughly. Heaven and earth!
Must I remember? why, she would hang on him,
As if increase of appetite had grown
By what it fed on: and yet, within a month—
Let me not think on 't—Frailty, thy name is woman!— 146
A little month, or ere those shoes were old
With which she follow'd my poor father's body,
Like Niobe, all tears:—why she, even she—
O God! a beast, that wants discourse of reason, 150
Would have mourn'd longer—married with my uncle,
My father's brother, but no more like my father
Than I to Hercules: within a month:
Ere yet the salt of most unrighteous tears
Had left the flushing in her gallèd eyes, 155
She married. O, most wicked speed, to post
With such dexterity to incestuous sheets!
It is not nor it cannot come to good:
But break, my heart; for I must hold my tongue.

[*Enter* HORATIO, MARCELLUS, *and* BERNARDO.]

HOR. Hail to your lordship!

HAM. I am glad to see you well: 160
Horatio,—or I do forget myself.

HOR. The same, my lord, and your poor servant ever.

HAM. Sir, my good friend; I'll change that name with you:
And what make you from Wittenberg, Horatio?
Marcellus? 165

MAR. My good lord—

HAM. I am very glad to see you. Good even, sir.
But what, in faith, make you from Wittenberg?

HOR. A truant disposition, good my lord.

HAM. I would not hear your enemy say so, 170

107. unprevailing, useless. 109. most immediate, closest, i.e., next heir. 112. Do . . . you, do I express myself to you. 114. retrograde, contrary. 115. bend you, show an inclination. 120. in . . . best, to the best of my ability. 123. accord, consent. 124. in grace whereof, in thanksgiving for which. 127. rouse, deep draught, here, a toast; bruit again, re-echo. 132. canon, law. 134. uses . . . world, human experience. 137. merely, completely. 140. Hyperion, the Greek sun god, the most beautiful of all gods; Satyr, an ugly, lascivious beast, half goat and half man. 141. beteem, allow. 149. Niobe, a character in Greek mythology. The gods, angered at her boasting of her children, slew them all and turned Niobe into a mass of rock from which her tears flowed in a never-ending stream. 150. discourse, faculty. 154. unrighteous, i.e., because insincere. 155. left . . . eyes, ceased to flow in her reddened eyes. 156. post, hurry. 157. dexterity, speed. 163. change, exchange. 164. what . . . from? what are you doing away from? 169. truant disposition, a whim to play the truant.

Nor shall you do mine ear that violence,
To make it truster of your own report
Against yourself: I know you are no truant.
But what is your affair in Elsinore?
We'll teach you to drink deep ere you depart. 175

HOR. My lord, I came to see your father's funeral.

HAM. I pray thee, do not mock me, fellow-student;
I think it was to see my mother's wedding.

HOR. Indeed, my lord, it follow'd hard upon.

HAM. Thrift, thrift, Horatio! the funeral baked meats 180
Did coldly furnish forth the marriage tables.
Would I had met my dearest foe in heaven
Or ever I had seen that day, Horatio!
My father!—methinks I see my father.

HOR. Where, my lord?

HAM. In my mind's eye, Horatio. 185

HOR. I saw him once; he was a goodly king.

HAM. He was a man, take him for all in all,
I shall not look upon his like again.

HOR. My lord, I think I saw him yester-night.

HAM. Saw? who? 190

HOR. My lord, the king your father.

HAM. The king my father!

HOR. Season your admiration for a while
With an attent ear, till I may deliver,
Upon the witness of these gentlemen,
This marvel to you.

HAM. For God's love, let me hear.

HOR. Two nights together had these gentlemen, 196
Marcellus and Bernardo, on their watch,
In the dead vast and middle of the night,
Been thus encounter'd. A figure like your father,
Armed at point exactly, cap-a-pe, 200
Appears before them, and with solemn march
Goes slow and stately by them: thrice he walk'd
By their oppress'd and fear-surprised eyes,
Within his truncheon's length; whilst they, distill'd
Almost to jelly with the act of fear, 205
Stand dumb and speak not to him. This to me
In dreadful secrecy impart they did;
And I with them the third night kept the watch:
Where, as they had deliver'd, both in time,
Form of the thing, each word made true and good, 210
The apparition comes: I knew your father;
These hands are not more like.

HAM. But where was this?

MAR. My lord, upon the platform where we watch'd.

HAM. Did you not speak to it?

HOR. My lord, I did;
But answer made it none: yet once methought 215
It lifted up it head and did address
Itself to motion, like as it would speak;
But even then the morning cock crew loud,
And at the sound it shrunk in haste away,
And vanish'd from our sight.

HAM. 'Tis very strange. 220

HOR. As I do live, my honour'd lord, 'tis true;
And we did think it writ down in our duty
To let you know of it.

HAM. Indeed, indeed, sirs, but this troubles me.
Hold you the watch to-night?

MAR., BER. We do, my lord. 225

HAM. Arm'd, say you?

MAR., BER. Arm'd, my lord.

HAM. From top to toe?

MAR., BER. My lord, from head to foot.

HAM. Then saw you not his face?

HOR. O, yes, my lord; he wore his beaver up. 230

HAM. What, look'd he frowningly?

HOR. A countenance more in sorrow than in anger.

HAM. Pale or red?

HOR. Nay, very pale.

HAM. And fix'd his eyes upon you?

HOR. Most constantly.

172. **truster**, believer. 174. **affair**, actual business. 179. **hard upon**, close after. 180. **baked meats**, meat pies, 181. **Did coldly furnish forth**, were served up cold at. 182. **dearest**, worst-hated. 186. **goodly**, handsome and regal. 192. **Season your admiration**, restrain your astonishment. 193. **attent**, attentive; **deliver**, report. 198. **vast**, great emptiness. 200. **at point**, completely; **cap-a-pe**, from head to foot. 203. **oppress'd**, overwhelmed (by dread). 204. **truncheon**, an officer's short staff; **distill'd**, dissolved, i.e., quaking with fear like jelly. 205. **with the act**, through the action. 207. **In . . . secrecy**, as a terrifying secret. 213. **platform**, i.e., level walk along the ramparts. 216-7. **address . . . motion**, began to make movements. 230. **beaver**, visor (of a helmet).

HAM. I would I had been there. 235
HOR. It would have much amazèd you.
HAM. Very like, very like. Stay'd it long?
HOR. While one with moderate haste might tell a hundred.
MAR.
BER. } Longer, longer.
HOR. Not when I saw 't.
HAM. His beard was grizzled,—no? 240
HOR. It was, as I have seen it in his life,
A sable silver'd.
HAM. I will watch to-night;
Perchance 'twill walk again.
HOR. I warrant it will.
HAM. If it assume my noble father's person, 244
I'll speak to it, though hell itself should gape
And bid me hold my peace. I pray you all,
If you have hitherto conceal'd this sight,
Let it be tenable in your silence still;
And whatsoever else shall hap to-night,
Give it an understanding, but no tongue: 250
I will requite your loves. So, fare you well:
Upon the platform, 'twixt eleven and twelve,
I'll visit you.
ALL. Our duty to your honour.
HAM. Your loves, as mine to you: farewell.
[*Exeunt all but* HAMLET.]
My father's spirit in arms! all is not well;
I doubt some foul play: would the night were come! 256
Till then sit still, my soul: foul deeds will rise,
Though all the earth o'erwhelm them, to men's eyes. [*Exit.*

SCENE III. *A room in* POLONIUS' *house.*

[*Enter* LAERTES *and* OPHELIA.]

LAER. My necessaries are embark'd: farewell:
And, sister, as the winds give benefit
And convoy is assistant, do not sleep,
But let me hear from you.
OPH. Do you doubt that?
LAER. For Hamlet and the trifling of his favour, 5
Hold it a fashion and a toy in blood,
A violet in the youth of primy nature,
Forward, not permanent, sweet, not lasting,
The perfume and suppliance of a minute;
No more.
OPH. No more but so?
LAER. Think it no more: 10
For nature, crescent, does not grow alone
In thews and bulk, but, as this temple waxes,
The inward service of the mind and soul
Grows wide withal. Perhaps he loves you now,
And now no soil nor cautel doth besmirch 15
The virtue of his will: but you must fear,
His greatness weigh'd, his will is not his own;
For he himself is subject to his birth:
He may not, as unvalued persons do,
Carve for himself; for on his choice depends 20
The safety and health of this whole state;
And therefore must his choice be circumscribed
Unto the voice and yielding of that body
Whereof he is the head. Then if he says he loves you,
It fits your wisdom so far to believe it 25
As he in his particular act and place
May give his saying deed; which is no further
Than the main voice of Denmark goes withal.
Then weigh what loss your honour may sustain,
If with too credent ear you list his songs, 30
Or lose your heart, or your chaste treasure open
To his unmaster'd importunity.
Fear it, Ophelia, fear it, my dear sister,
And keep you in the rear of your affection,
Out of the shot and danger of desire. 35
The chariest maid is prodigal enough,
If she unmask her beauty to the moon:

236. amazed, utterly bewildered. 238. tell, count. 240. grizzled, gray. 242. Sable silver'd, i.e., black flecked with white. 247. conceal'd, kept secret. 248. tenable, held fast. 251. requite your loves, repay your kindness. 254. Your loves . . . you, i.e., offer me the affection of a friend and I will do the same. 256. doubt, suspect. Scene iii: 1. necessaries, baggage. 2. as, according as. 3. convoy is assistant, means of conveyance is at hand. 5. For, as for. 6. fashion, whim; toy in blood, an idle fancy of passion. 7. primy nature, i.e., spring. 8. Forward, premature. 9. suppliance of, diversion to fill. 11. nature, crescent, the nature of a human being, as it grows. 12. thews, sinews, i.e., strength; temple, i.e., body. 13. inward service of, service conducted inside by. 14. Grows wide withal, expands at the same time. 15. cautel, deceit. 16. virtue of his will, his virtuous intentions. 17. His . . . weigh'd, when you consider his high rank. 19. unvalued persons, i.e., commoners. 20. Carve, choose. 23. voice and yielding, approval and assent. 26-7. in his . . . saying deed, acting as his peculiar circumstances and rank allow, may keep his promises. 28. main voice, public approval; goes withal, permits. 30. credent, credulous. 32. unmaster'd importunity, unrestrained persistence. 34. keep . . . affection, i.e., keep your love out of danger of being wounded. 36. chariest, most scrupulous; prodigal enough, generous enough with her favors.

Virtue itself 'scapes not calumnious strokes:
The canker galls the infants of the spring,
Too oft before their buttons be disclosed, 40
And in the morn and liquid dew of youth
Contagious blastments are most imminent.
Be wary then; best safety lies in fear:
Youth to itself rebels, though none else near.
OPH. I shall the effect of this good lesson keep, 45
As watchman to my heart. But, good my brother,
Do not, as some ungracious pastors do,
Show me the steep and thorny way to heaven;
Whiles, like a puff'd and reckless libertine,
Himself the primrose path of dalliance treads,
And recks not his own rede. 51
LAER. O, fear me not.
I stay too long: but here my father comes.

[*Enter* POLONIUS.]

A double blessing is a double grace;
Occasion smiles upon a second leave.
POL. Yet here, Laertes! aboard, aboard, for shame! 55
The wind sits in the shoulder of your sail,
And you are stay'd for. There; my blessing with thee!
And these few precepts in thy memory
See thou character. Give thy thoughts no tongue,
Nor any unproportion'd thought his act. 60
Be thou familiar, but by no means vulgar.
Those friends thou hast, and their adoption tried,
Grapple them to thy soul with hoops of steel;
But do not dull thy palm with entertainment
Of each new-hatch'd, unfledged comrade. Beware 65
Of entrance to a quarrel, but being in,
Bear 't that the opposèd may beware of thee.
Give every man thy ear, but few thy voice;
Take each man's censure, but reserve thy judgement.
Costly thy habit as thy purse can buy, 70
But not express'd in fancy; rich, not gaudy;
For the apparel oft proclaims the man,
And they in France of the best rank and station
Are of a most select and generous chief in that.
Neither a borrower nor a lender be; 75
For loan oft loses both itself and friend,
And borrowing dulls the edge of husbandry.
This above all: to thine own self be true,
And it must follow, as the night the day,
Thou canst not then be false to any man. 80
Farewell: my blessing season this in thee!
LAER. Most humbly do I take my leave, my lord.
POL. The time invites you; go; your servants tend.
LAER. Farewell, Ophelia; and remember well
What I have said to you.
OPH. 'Tis in my memory lock'd, 85
And you yourself shall keep the key of it.
LAER. Farewell. [*Exit.*
POL. What is 't, Ophelia, he hath said to you?
OPH. So please you, something touching the Lord Hamlet.
POL. Marry, well bethought: 90
'Tis told me, he hath very oft of late
Given private time to you; and you yourself
Have of your audience been most free and bounteous:
If it be so, as so 't is put on me,
And that in way of caution, I must tell you, 95
You do not understand yourself so clearly
As it behooves my daughter and your honour.
What is between you? give me up the truth.
OPH. He hath, my lord, of late made many tenders
Of his affection to me. 100
POL. Affection! pooh! you speak like a green girl,
Unsifted in such perilous circumstance.

38. **calumnious,** slanderous. 39. **canker,** cankerworm. 40. **buttons,** buds. 42. **blastments,** blights. 44. **Youth . . . else near,** youth of its very nature is rebellious, even though subject to no outward temptation. 45. **effect,** purport. 47. **ungracious,** worldly. 49. **puff'd,** bloated. 50. **dalliance,** self-indulgence. 51. **recks,** heeds; **rede,** advice; **fear me not,** don't worry about me. 54. **Occasion . . . leave,** i.e., it is good luck to say farewell twice. 56. **The . . . sail,** i.e., you have a favorable wind. 59. **character,** write down. 60. **unproportion'd,** unbalanced, ill-considered. 61. **familiar,** approachable; **vulgar,** too familiar. 62. **adoption tried,** loyalty tested. 64. **dull . . . entertainment,** callous your palm by giving a welcome to everyone. 67. **Bear't,** act in such a way. 69. **Take . . . censure,** listen to everyone's opinion. 70. **habit,** clothing, 71. **express'd in fancy,** bizarre in design. 74. **Are . . . chief in that,** show their best aristocratic and discriminating taste in (the choice of clothes). 77. **husbandry,** thrift. 81. **season this,** make this (advice) bear fruit. 83. **invites,** summons; **tend,** wait for you. 90. **Marry, well bethought,** by the Virgin Mary, well remembered. 92. **Given . . . you,** seen you alone. 93. **audience,** company. 94. **'t is . . . me,** I have been informed. 99. **tenders,** offers of pay. 102. **Unsifted,** untried.

Do you believe his tenders, as you call them?
OPH. I do not know, my lord, what I should think.
POL. Marry, I'll teach you: think yourself a baby; 105
That you have ta'en these tenders for true pay,
Which are not sterling. Tender yourself more dearly;
Or—not to crack the wind of the poor phrase,
Running it thus—you'll tender me a fool.
OPH. My lord, he hath impórtuned me with love 110
In honourable fashion.
POL. Ay, fashion you may call it; go to, go to.
OPH. And hath given countenance to his speech, my lord,
With almost all the holy vows of heaven.
POL. Ay, springes to catch woodcocks. I do know, 115
When the blood burns, how prodigal the soul
Lends the tongue vows: these blazes, daughter,
Giving more light than heat, extinct in both,
Even in their promise, as it is a-making, 119
You must not take for fire. From this time
Be somewhat scanter of your maiden presence;
Set your entreatments at a higher rate
Than a command to parley. For Lord Hamlet,
Believe so much in him, that he is young,
And with a larger tether may he walk 125
Than may be given you: in few, Ophelia,
Do not believe his vows; for they are brokers,
Not of that dye which their investments show,
But mere implorators of unholy suits,
Breathing like sanctified and pious bawds, 130
The better to beguile. This is for all:
I would not, in plain terms, from this time forth,
Have you so slander any moment leisure,
As to give words or talk with the Lord Hamlet.
Look to 't, I charge you: come your ways. 135
OPH. I shall obey, my lord. [*Exeunt.*

SCENE IV. *The platform.*

[*Enter* HAMLET, HORATIO, *and* MARCELLUS.]

HAM. The air bites shrewdly; it is very cold.
HOR. It is a nipping and an eager air.
HAM. What hour now?
HOR. I think it lacks of twelve.
MAR. No, it is struck.
HOR. Indeed? I heard it not: then it draws near the season 5
Wherein the spirit held his wont to walk.
[*A flourish of trumpets, and ordnance shot off, within.*]
What does this mean, my lord?
HAM. The king doth wake to-night and takes his rouse,
Keeps wassail, and the swaggering up-spring reels;
And, as he drains his draughts of Rhenish down, 10
The kettle-drum and trumpet thus bray out
The triumph of his pledge.
HOR. Is it a custom?
HAM. Ay, marry, is 't:
But to my mind, though I am native here
And to the manner born, it is a custom 15
More honour'd in the breach than the observance.
This heavy-headed revel east and west
Makes us traduced and tax'd of other nations:
They clepe us drunkards, and with swinish phrase
Soil our addition; and indeed it takes 20
From our achievements, though perform'd at height,

107. **sterling**, real money; **Tender**, regard; **more dearly**, of higher value. 108. **crack the wind**, i.e., make the phrase pant (as though it were a wounded horse). 109. **tender me**, present me with (i.e., a fool for a daughter). 112. **fashion**, mere form; **go to**, nonsense! 113. **given countenance to**, confirmed. 115. **springes**, traps; **woodcocks**, stupid birds, hence simpletons. 116. **blood**, passion; **prodigal**, lavishly. 118. **extinct in both**, i.e., both show and substance of this love. 119. **Even . . . promise**, even while the lover is promising. 122. **entreatments**, favors entreated. 123. **command to parley**, request for conference (to discuss terms of surrender). 124. **so much in him**, only so much about him as. 126. **few**, brief. 127. **brokers**, procurers; **investments**, garments. 129. **implorators . . . suits**, i.e., tempters to vice. 130. **Breathing**, soliciting in whispers; **sanctified**, hypocritical. 131. **This . . . all**, the sum of my advice is this. 133. **slander**, disgrace. 135. **your ways**, along. **Scene iv**: 1. **shrewdly**, keenly. 2. **eager**, sharp. 6. **held his wont**, was accustomed. 8. **wake**, revel; **takes his rouse**, is drinking heavily. 9. **Keeps wassail**, holds a drinking bout; **up-spring**, upstart. 10. **Rhenish**, Rhine wine. 12. **pledge**, toast. 13. **marry**, i.e., by the Virgin Mary, a mild oath. 15. **to . . . born**, used to the custom from birth. 17. **east and west**, far and wide. 18. **traduced and tax'd**, censured and reproached. 19. **clepe**, call. 19-20. **with . . . addition**, smirch our good name by calling us swine. 21. **perform'd at height**, the best of which we are capable.

The pith and marrow of our attribute.
So, oft it chances in particular men,
That for some vicious mole of nature in them,
As, in their birth—wherein they are not guilty, 25
Since nature cannot choose his origin—
By the o'ergrowth of some complexion,
Oft breaking down the pales and forts of reason,
Or by some habit that too much o'er-leavens
The form of plausive manners, that these men, 30
Carrying, I say, the stamp of one defect,
Being nature's livery, or fortune's star,—
Their virtues else—be they as pure as grace,
As infinite as man may undergo— 34
Shall in the general censure take corruption
From that particular fault: the dram of eale
Doth all the noble substance often dout
To his own scandal.

HOR. Look, my lord, it comes!

[*Enter* GHOST.]

HAM. Angels and ministers of grace defend us!
Be thou a spirit of health or goblin damn'd, 40
Bring with thee airs from heaven or blasts from hell,
Be thy intents wicked or charitable,
Thou comest in such a questionable shape
That I will speak to thee: I'll call thee Hamlet,
King, father, royal Dane: O, answer me! 45
Let me not burst in ignorance; but tell
Why thy canónized bones, hearsèd in death,
Have burst their cerements; why the sepulchre,
Wherein we saw thee quietly interr'd,
Hath oped his ponderous and marble jaws, 50
To cast thee up again. What may this mean,
That thou, dead corse, again in cómplete steel
Revisit'st thus the glimpses of the moon,
Making night hideous; and we fools of nature
So horridly to shake our disposition 55
With thoughts beyond the reaches of our souls?
Say, why is this? wherefore? what should we do? [GHOST *beckons* HAMLET.

HOR. It beckons you to go away with it,
As if it some impartment did desire
To you alone.

MAR. Look, with what courteous action 60
It waves you to a more removèd ground:
But do not go with it.

HOR. No, by no means.

HAM. It will not speak; then I will follow it.

HOR. Do not, my lord.

HAM. Why, what should be the fear?
I do not set my life at a pin's fee; 65
And for my soul, what can it do to that,
Being a thing immortal as itself?
It waves me forth again: I'll follow it.

HOR. What if it tempt you toward the flood, my lord,
Or to the dreadful summit of the cliff 70
That beetles o'er his base into the sea,
And there assume some other horrible form,
Which might deprive your sovereignty of reason
And draw you into madness? think of it:
The very place puts toys of desperation, 75
Without more motive, into every brain
That looks so many fathoms to the sea
And hears it roar beneath.

HAM. It waves me still.
Go on; I'll follow thee.

MAR. You shall not go, my lord.

HAM. Hold off your hands. 80

HOR. Be ruled; you shall not go.

HAM. My fate cries out,
And makes each petty artery in this body
As hardy as the Nemean lion's nerve.
Still am I call'd. Unhand me, gentleman.
By heaven, I'll make a ghost of him that lets me! 85
I say, away! Go on; I'll follow thee.
[*Exeunt* GHOST *and* HAMLET.

HOR. He waxes desperate with imagination.

22. **attribute,** reputation. 24. **mole of nature,** natural blemish. 27. **complexion,** natural quality. 28. **pales,** defenses. 29. **o'er-leavens,** spoils (by overdevelopment of some quality, good in itself). 30. **plausive,** pleasing. 32. **nature's livery,** mark of nature, i.e., inborn; **fortune's star,** i.e., the result of chance. 34. **As . . . undergo,** as boundless as a man is capable of. 35. **general censure,** popular opinion. 36. **eale,** evil. 37. **dout,** do out, banish. 38. **scandal,** disgrace. 40. **spirit of health,** blessed spirit; **goblin damn'd,** devil from Hell. 43. **questionable,** inviting question. 47. **canonized,** consecrated, i.e., buried with all the rites of the church. 48. **cerements,** winding sheet. 54. **fools,** weak children. 55. **shake . . . disposition,** upset our mental equilibrium. 59. **impartment,** communication. 61. **removed,** distant. 65. **fee,** value. 69. **flood,** i.e., the sea (which washed the castle's walls). 71. **beetles,** juts out. 73. **deprive . . . of,** i.e., dethrone. 75. **toys of desperation,** desperate notions. 78. **waves me still,** keeps beckoning to me. 81. **cries out,** i.e., commands me. 83. **Nemean lion,** a monster slain by Hercules; **nerve,** sinews. 85. **lets,** prevents. 87. **imagination,** false conception, illusion.

MAR. Let's follow; 'tis not fit thus to obey him.
HOR. Have after. To what issue will this come?
MAR. Something is rotten in the state of Denmark. 90
HOR. Heaven will direct it.
MAR. Nay, let's follow him. [Exeunt.

SCENE V. *Another part of the platform.*

[*Enter* GHOST *and* HAMLET.]

HAM. Where wilt thou lead me? speak; I'll go no further.
GHOST. Mark me.
HAM. I will.
GHOST. My hour is almost come,
When I to sulphurous and tormenting flames
Must render up myself.
HAM. Alas, poor ghost!
GHOST. Pity me not, but lend thy serious hearing 5
To what I shall unfold.
HAM. Speak; I am bound to hear.
GHOST. So art thou to revenge, when thou shalt hear.
HAM. What?
GHOST. I am thy father's spirit,
Doom'd for a certain term to walk the night,
And for the day confined to fast in fires, 11
Till the foul crimes done in my days of nature
Are burnt and purged away. But that I am forbid
To tell the secrets of my prison-house,
I could a tale unfold whose lightest word 15
Would harrow up thy soul, freeze thy young blood,
Make thy two eyes, like stars, start from their spheres,
Thy knotted and combinèd locks to part
And each particular hair to stand an end,
Like quills upon the fretful porpentine: 20
But this eternal blazon must not be
To ears of flesh and blood. List, list, O, list!
If thou didst ever thy dear father love—
HAM. O God!
GHOST. Revenge his foul and most unnatural murder. 25
HAM. Murder!
GHOST. Murder most foul, as in the best it is;
But this most foul, strange and unnatural.
HAM. Haste me to know't, that I, with wings as swift
As meditation or the thoughts of love, 30
May sweep to my revenge.
GHOST. I find thee apt;
And duller shouldst thou be than the fat weed
That roots itself in ease on Lethe wharf,
Wouldst thou not stir in this. Now, Hamlet, hear:
'Tis given out that, sleeping in my orchard, 35
A serpent stung me; so the whole ear of Denmark
Is by a forgèd process of my death
Rankly abused: but know, thou noble youth,
The serpent that did sting thy father's life
Now wears his crown.
HAM. O my prophetic soul! 40
My uncle!
GHOST. Ay, that incestuous, that adulterate beast,
With witchcraft of his wit, with traitorous gifts,—
O wicked wit and gifts, that have the power
So to seduce!—won to his shameful lust 45
The will of my most seeming-virtuous queen.
O Hamlet, what a falling-off was there
From me, whose love was of that dignity
That it went hand in hand even with the vow
I made to her in marriage, and to decline 50
Upon a wretch whose natural gifts were poor
To those of mine!
But virtue, as it never will be moved,
Though lewdness court it in a shape of heaven,
So lust, though to a radiant angel link'd, 55
Will sate itself in a celestial bed,
And prey on garbage.
But, soft! methinks I scent the morning air;
Brief let me be. Sleeping within my orchard,
My custom always of the afternoon, 60
Upon my secure hour thy uncle stole,
With juice of cursèd hebenon in a vial,

89. Have after, follow him; **issue,** result. **91. it,** i.e., the result. **Scene v: 2. hour,** i.e., the dawn. **6. bound,** duty bound. **11. fast,** do penance. **12. foul crimes,** ugly sins (those which every mortal man commits); **days of nature,** mortal life. **17. spheres,** orbits. **19. an end,** on end. **20. porpentine,** porcupine. **21. eternal blazon,** disclosure of matters concerning eternal life. **27. in the best,** at best, i.e., when committed for a good reason. **31. apt,** responsive. **32. fat,** slimy. **33. wharf,** bank. **35. orchard,** garden. **37. process,** official account. **38. abused,** deceived. **42. adulterate,** adulterous. **54. shape of heaven,** i.e., angel's form. **61. secure,** unsuspecting. **62. hebenon,** henbane.

And in the porches of my ears did pour
The leperous distillment; whose effect
Holds such an enmity with blood of man 65
That swift as quicksilver it courses through
The natural gates and alleys of the body,
And with a sudden vigour it doth posset
And curd, like eager droppings into milk,
The thin and wholesome blood: so did it mine; 70
And a most instant tetter bark'd about,
Most lazar-like, with vile and loathsome crust,
All my smooth body.
Thus was I, sleeping, by a brother's hand
Of life, of crown, of queen, at once dispatch'd: 75
Cut off even in the blossoms of my sin,
Unhousel'd, disappointed, unaneled,
No reckoning made, but sent to my account
With all my imperfections on my head:
O, horrible! O, horrible! most horrible! 80
If thou hast nature in thee, bear it not;
Let not the royal bed of Denmark be
A couch for luxury and damned incest.
But, howsoever thou pursuest this act,
Taint not thy mind, nor let thy soul contrive
Against thy mother aught: leave her to heaven 86
And to those thorns that in her bosom lodge,
To prick and sting her. Fare thee well at once!
The glow-worm shows the matin to be near,
And 'gins to pale his uneffectual fire: 90
Adieu, adieu! Hamlet, remember me. [*Exit.*

HAM. O all you host of heaven! O earth! what else?
And shall I couple hell? O, fie! Hold, hold, my heart;
And you, my sinews, grow not instant old,
But bear me stiffly up. Remember thee! 95
Ay, thou poor ghost, while memory holds a seat
In this distracted globe. Remember thee!
Yea, from the table of my memory
I'll wipe away all trivial fond records,
All saws of books, all forms, all pressures past, 100
That youth and observation copied there;
And thy commandment all alone shall live
Within the book and volume of my brain,
Unmix'd with baser matter: yes, by heaven!
O most pernicious woman! 105
O villain, villain, smiling, damned villain!
My tables,—meet it is I set it down,
That one may smile, and smile, and be a villain;
At least I'm sure it may be so in Denmark: [*Writing.*]
So, uncle, there you are. Now to my word;
It is "Adieu, adieu! remember me." 111
I have sworn 't.

MAR. } HOR. } [*Within*] My lord, my lord,—

MAR. [*Within*] Lord Hamlet,—

HOR. [*Within*] Heaven secure him!

HAM. So be it!

HOR. [*Within*] Hillo, ho, ho, my lord! 115

HAM. Hillo, ho, ho, boy! come, bird, come.

[*Enter* HORATIO *and* MARCELLUS.]

MAR. How is 't, my noble lord?

HOR. What news, my lord?

HAM. O, wonderful!

HOR. Good my lord, tell it.

HAM. No; you'll reveal it.

HOR. Not I, my lord, by heaven.

MAR. Nor I, my lord. 120

HAM. How say you, then; would heart of man once think it?
But you'll be secret?

HOR. } MAR. } Ay, by heaven, my lord.

HAM. There's ne'er a villain dwelling in all Denmark
But he's an arrant knave.

HOR. There needs no ghost, my lord, come from the grave 125
To tell us this.

HAM. Why, right; you are i' the right;
And so, without more circumstance at all,
I hold it fit that we shake hands and part:

63. **porches**, entrances. 64. **leperous distillment**, liquid causing leprosy. 68. **posset**, curdle. 69. **curd**, thicken; **eager**, sour. 71. **tetter . . . about**, eruption broke out. 72. **lazar-like**, like leprosy. 75. **at once dispatch'd**, suddenly deprived of all together. 77. **Unhousel'd . . . unaneled**, without having received the sacrament, unprepared (through confession), without final ceremony of anointing with holy oil. 78. **reckoning**, i.e., of his sins through confession; **account**, i.e., payment for my sins. 81. **thou . . . thee**, you have a son's natural feeling. 83. **luxury**, lust. 84. **pursuest**, seek to avenge. 85. **Taint not**, i.e., with suspicions of your mother. 89. **matin**, dawn. 90. **uneffectual**, i.e., ineffectual because of daylight. 97. **globe**, head of mine. 98. **table**, notebook. 99. **fond**, foolish. 100. **saws**, wise sayings; **forms**, ideas; **pressures past**, impressions from the past. 110. **word**, cue. 113. **secure**, protect. 116. **Hillo . . . come**, call used by falconer to call back his hawk. 121. **How say you?** What do you think about this?; **once think**, ever believe. 124. **arrant**, out and out. 127. **circumstance**, ceremony.

You, as your business and desire shall point you;
For every man has business and desire, 130
Such as it is; and for mine own poor part,
Look you, I'll go pray.

HOR. These are but wild and whirling words, my lord.

HAM. I'm sorry they offend you, heartily;
Yes 'faith, heartily.

HOR. There's no offence, my lord.

HAM. Yes, by Saint Patrick, but there is, Horatio, 136
And much offence too. Touching this vision here,
It is an honest ghost, that let me tell you:
For your desire to know what is between us,
O'ermaster 't as you may. And now, good friends, 140
As you are friends, scholars and soldiers,
Give me one poor request.

HOR. What is 't, my lord? we will.

HAM. Never make known what you have seen to-night.

HOR. } MAR. } My lord, we will not.

HAM. Nay, but swear't.

HOR. In faith,
My lord, not I.

MAR. Nor I, my lord, in faith. 146

HAM. Upon my sword.

MAR. We have sworn, my lord, already.

HAM. Indeed, upon my sword, indeed.

GHOST. [*Beneath*] Swear.

HAM. Ah, ha, boy! say'st thou so? art thou there, truepenny? 150
Come on—you hear this fellow in the cellarage—
Consent to swear.

HOR. Propose the oath, my lord.

HAM. Never to speak of this that you have seen,
Swear by my sword.

GHOST. [*Beneath*] Swear. 155

HAM. Hic et ubique? then we'll shift our ground.
Come hither, gentlemen,
And lay your hands again upon my sword:
Never to speak of this that you have heard,
Swear by my sword. 160

GHOST. [*Beneath*] Swear.

HAM. Well said, old mole! canst work i' the earth so fast?
A worthy pioner! Once more remove, good friends.

HOR. O day and night, but this is wondrous strange!

HAM. And therefore as a stranger give it welcome. 165
There are more things in heaven and earth, Horatio,
Than are dreamt of in your philosophy.
But come;
Here, as before, never, so help you mercy,
How strange or odd soe'er I bear myself, 170
As I perchance hereafter shall think meet
To put an antic disposition on,
That you, at such times seeing me, never shall,
With arms encumber'd thus, or this headshake,
Or by pronouncing of some doubtful phrase, 175
As "Well, well, we know," or "We could, an if we would,"
Or "If we list to speak," or "There be, an if they might,"
Or such ambiguous giving out, to note
That you know aught of me: this not to do,
So grace and mercy at your most need help you, 180
Swear.

GHOST. [*Beneath*] Swear.

HAM. Rest, rest, perturbèd spirit! [*They swear.*] So, gentlemen,
With all my love I do commend me to you:
And what so poor a man as Hamlet is 185
May do, to express his love and friending to you,
God willing, shall not lack. Let us go in together;
And still your fingers on your lips, I pray.
The time is out of joint: O cursèd spite,
That ever I was born to set it right! 190
Nay, come, let's go together. [*Exeunt.*

129. **point**, direct. 131. **whirling**, incoherent. 136. **Saint Patrick**, possibly because he was supposed to be the keeper of Purgatory. 138. **honest**, real (and not a demon). 140. **O'ermaster't**, control it. 147. **Upon my sword**, because the hilt of the sword formed a cross. 150. **truepenny**, trusty old fellow. 156. **Hic et ubique?** Here and everywhere? 163. **pioner**, sapper, military engineer (who used to dig tunnels); **remove**, shift your position. 167. **philosophy**, science. 170. **How**, however. 171. **As**, whenever. 172. **put . . . on**, adopt grotesque behavior. 174. **encumber'd**, folded. 177. **list to speak**, cared to talk. 178. **giving out**, pronouncement. 184. **commend . . . you**, put myself in your hands. 186. **friending**, good will. 187. **lack**, be lacking; **together**, i.e., as equals. 189. **time . . . joint**, the world is in a state of confusion; **spite**, affliction.

ACT II

SCENE I. *A room in* POLONIUS' *house.*

[*Enter* POLONIUS *and* REYNALDO.]

POL. Give him this money and these notes, Reynaldo.
REY. I will, my lord.
POL. You shall do marvellous wisely, good Reynaldo,
Before you visit him, to make inquire
Of his behaviour.
REY. My lord, I did intend it. 5
POL. Marry, well said; very well said. Look you, sir,
Inquire me first what Danskers are in Paris;
And how, and who, what means, and where they keep,
What company, at what expense; and finding
By this encompassment and drift of question 10
That they do know my son, come you more nearer
Than your particular demands will touch it:
Take you, as 'twere, some distant knowledge of him;
As thus, "I know his father and his friends,
And in part him:" do you mark this, Reynaldo? 15
REY. Ay, very well, my lord.
POL. "And in part him; but" you may say "not well:
But, if 't be he I mean, he's very wild;
Addicted so and so:" and there put on him
What forgeries you please; marry, none so rank 20
As may dishonour him; take heed of that;
But, sir, such wanton, wild and usual slips
As are companions noted and most known
To youth and liberty.
REY. As gaming, my lord.
POL. Ay, or drinking, fencing, swearing, quarrelling, 25
Drabbing: you may go so far.
REY. My lord, that would dishonour him.
POL. 'Faith, no; as you may season it in the charge.
You must not put another scandal on him,
That he is open to incontinency; 30
That's not my meaning: but breathe his faults so quaintly
That they may seem the taints of liberty,
The flash and outbreak of a fiery mind,
A savageness in unreclaimèd blood,
Of general assault.
REY. But, my good lord,— 35
POL. Wherefore should you do this?
REY. Ay, my lord,
I would know that.
POL. Marry, sir, here's my drift;
And, I believe, it is a fetch of warrant:
You laying these slight sullies on my son,
As 'twere a thing a little soil'd i' the working,
Mark you, 41
Your party in converse, him you would sound,
Having ever seen in the prenominate crimes
The youth you breathe of guilty, be assured
He closes with you in this consequence; 45
"Good sir," or so, or "friend," or "gentleman,"
According to the phrase or the addition
Of man and country.
REY. Very good, my lord.
POL. And then, sir, does he this—he does —what was I about to say? By the mass, I was about to say something: where did I leave? 51
REY. At "closes in the consequence," at "friend or so," and "gentleman."
POL. At "closes in the consequence," ay, marry;
He closes thus: "I know the gentleman; 55
I saw him yesterday, or t'other day,
Or then, or then; with such, or such; and, as you say,
There was a' gaming; there o'ertook in 's rouse;

Act II, Scene i: 7. **Inquire me**, ask for me.; **Danskers**, Danes. 8. **means**, money [they have]; **keep**, live. 9. **What company**, i.e., they keep. 10. **encompassment**, roundabout approach; **drift**, gradual approach. 12. **particular demands**, specific questions. 13. **Take you**, pretend. 19. **put on**, ascribe to. 20. **forgeries**, invented stories; **rank**, gross. 22. **wanton**, gay. 23. **companions noted**, observed to be companions. 28. **season . . . charge**, tone down the accusation even while you are making it. 26. **Drabbing**, whoring. 30. **That**, namely that; **open to incontinency**, given to habitual licentiousness. 31. **quaintly**, artfully. 32. **liberty**, lack of self-control. 34. **unreclaimèd blood**, untamed passion. 35. **general assault**, common to all [young men]. 37. **drift**, scheme. 38. **fetch of warrant**, device that is sure to work. 39. **You laying**, when you lay; **sullies**, aspersions. 40. **'twere**, i.e., he were; **working**, making. 43. **prenominate**, already mentioned. 45. **closes**, agrees; **in this consequence**, as follows. 47. **addition**, mode of address. 51. **leave**, leave off. 58. **o'ertook in 's rouse**, overcome by drink.

There falling out at tennis:" or perchance,
"I saw him enter such a house of sale," 60
Videlicet, a brothel, or so forth.
See you now;
Your bait of falsehood takes this carp of truth:
And thus do we of wisdom and of reach,
With windlasses and with assays of bias, 65
By indirections find directions out:
So by my former lecture and advice,
Shall you my son. You have me, have you not?

REY. My lord, I have.

POL. God be wi' you; fare you well.

REY. Good my lord! 70

POL. Observe his inclination in yourself.

REY. I shall, my lord.

POL. And let him ply his music.

REY. Well, my lord.

POL. Farewell!

[*Exit* REYNALDO.]

[*Enter* OPHELIA.]

How now, Ophelia! what's the matter?

OPH. O, my lord, my lord, I have been so affrighted! 75

POL. With what, i' the name of God?

OPH. My lord, as I was sewing in my closet,
Lord Hamlet, with his doublet all unbraced,
No hat upon his head; his stockings foul'd,
Ungarter'd, and down-gyvèd to his ancle; 80
Pale as his shirt; his knees knocking each other;
And with a look so piteous in purport
As if he had been loosèd out of hell
To speak of horrors—he comes before me.

POL. Mad for thy love?

OPH. My lord, I do not know;
But truly, I do fear it.

POL. What said he? 86

OPH. He took me by the wrist and held me hard;
Then goes he to the length of all his arm;
And, with his other hand thus o'er his brow,
He falls to such perusal of my face 90
As he would draw it. Long stay'd he so;
At last, a little shaking of mine arm
And thrice his head thus waving up and down,
He raised a sigh so piteous and profound
As it did seem to shatter all his bulk 95
And end his being: that done, he lets me go:
And, with his head over his shoulder turn'd,
He seem'd to find his way without his eyes;
For out o' doors he went without their helps,
And, to the last, bended their light on me. 100

POL. Come, go with me: I will go seek the king.
This is the very ecstasy of love,
Whose violent property fordoes itself
And leads the will to desperate undertakings
As oft as any passion under heaven 105
That does afflict our natures. I am sorry.
What, have you given him any hard words of late?

OPH. No, my good lord, but, as you did command,
I did repel his letters and denied
His access to me.

POL. That hath made him mad. 110
I am sorry that with better heed and judgement
I had not quoted him: I fear'd he did but trifle,
And meant to wreck thee; but, beshrew my jealousy!
By heaven, it is as proper to our age
To cast beyond ourselves in our opinions 115
As it is common for the younger sort
To lack discretion. Come, go we to the king:
This must be known; which, being kept close, might move
More grief to hide than hate to utter love. 119

[*Exeunt.*

SCENE II. *A room in the castle.*

[*Enter* KING, QUEEN, ROSENCRANTZ, GUILDENSTERN, *and* ATTENDANTS.]

KING. Welcome, dear Rosencrantz and Guildenstern!

61. **Videlicet,** that is to say. 64. **of reach,** of vision. 65. **windlasses,** round-about approaches; **assays of bias,** indirect ways. Bias was the curve a bowler put on his ball. 66. **find directions out,** i.e., discover the truth. 68. **you my son,** i.e., find out the truth about my son; **have,** understand. 71. **in yourself,** by your own inclinations. 73. **Well,** very well. 77. **closet,** private sitting room. 78. **doublet,** sleeveless jacket; **unbraced,** unfastened. 79. **foul'd,** muddy. 80. **down-gyved,** hanging down like fetters. 85. **for thy love,** because of his love for you. 88. **goes . . . arm,** i.e., he holds me at arm's length. 102. **ecstasy,** insanity. 103. **property,** nature; **fordoes itself,** destroys the person afflicted. 112. **quoted,** observed. 113. **jealousy,** suspicion. 114. **proper,** natural; **our age,** i.e., old age. 115. **cast beyond,** overshoot. 118. **being kept close,** if it were concealed. 118-9. **might move . . . utter love,** might cause more grief through its concealment than it would arouse hatred (on the part of Hamlet and/or his parents) through telling it.

Moreover that we much did long to see you,
The need we have to use you did provoke
Our hasty sending. Something have you heard
Of Hamlet's transformation; so call it, 5
Sith nor the exterior nor the inward man
Resembles that it was. What it should be,
More than his father's death, that thus hath put him
So much from the understanding of himself,
I cannot dream of: I entreat you both, 10
That, being of so young days brought up with him,
And sith so neighbour'd to his youth and haviour,
That you vouchsafe your rest here in our court
Some little time: so by your companies
To draw him on to pleasures, and to gather, 15
So much as from occasion you may glean,
Whether aught, to us unknown, afflicts him thus,
That, open'd, lies within our remedy.

QUEEN. Good gentlemen, he hath much talk'd of you;
And sure I am two men there are not living 20
To whom he more adheres. If it will please you
To show us so much gentry and good will
As to expend your time with us awhile,
For the supply and profit of our hope,
Your visitation shall receive such thanks 25
As fits a king's remembrance.

ROS. Both your majesties
Might, by the sovereign power you have of us,
Put your dread pleasures more into command
Than to entreaty.

GUIL. But we both obey,
And here give up ourselves, in the full bent 30
To lay our service freely at your feet,
To be commanded.

KING. Thanks, Rosencrantz and gentle Guildenstern.

QUEEN. Thanks, Guildenstern and gentle Rosencrantz:
And I beseech you instantly to visit 35
My too much changèd son. Go, some of you,
And bring these gentlemen where Hamlet is.

GUIL. Heavens make our presence and our practices
Pleasant and helpful to him!

QUEEN. Ay, amen!

[*Exeunt* ROSENCRANTZ, GUILDENSTERN, *and some* ATTENDANTS.

[*Enter* POLONIUS.]

POL. The ambassadors from Norway, my good lord, 40
Are joyfully return'd.

KING. Thou still hast been the father of good news.

POL. Have I, my lord? I assure my good liege,
I hold my duty, as I hold my soul,
Both to my God and to my gracious king: 45
And I do think, or else this brain of mine
Hunts not the trail of policy so sure
As it hath used to do, that I have found
The very cause of Hamlet's lunacy.

KING. O, speak of that; that do I long to hear. 50

POL. Give first admittance to the ambassadors;
My news shall be the fruit to that great feast.

KING. Thyself do grace to them, and bring them in. [*Exit* POLONIUS.]
He tells me, my dear Gertrude, he hath found
The head and source of all your son's distemper. 55

QUEEN. I doubt it is no other but the main;
His father's death, and our o'erhasty marriage.

KING. Well, we shall sift him.

[*Re-enter* POLONIUS, *with* VOLTIMAND *and* CORNELIUS.]

Welcome, my good friends!
Say, Voltimand, what from our brother Norway?

VOLT. Most fair return of greetings and desires. 60
Upon our first, he sent out to suppress

Scene ii: 2. **Moreover that**, besides the fact that. 7. **that**, what. 8-9. **put him . . . from**, robbed him of. 9. **the . . . of himself**, i.e., of his self-control. 11. **of so . . . days**, from such an early age. 13. **vouchsafe your rest**, agree to stay. 14. **so**, so as. 16. **from occasion**, i.e., when opportunity offers. 18. **open'd**, disclosed. 21. **more adheres**, is more attached. 22. **gentry**, courtesy. 24. **supply and profit**, advancement and fulfillment. 26. **fits**, befits. 27. **of**, over. 28. **dread pleasures**, revered wishes. 30. **in . . . bent**, as much as we can—a figure from archery, i.e., stretched to the uttermost. 38. **practices**, actions. 42. **still**, always. 44-5. **I hold . . . king**, i.e., I regard my duty to my gracious King [as sacred] as my soul's duty to my God. 47. **policy**, statecraft. 52. **fruit**, dessert. 53. **do . . . them**, welcome them. 55. **distemper**, illness, i.e., melancholy. 56. **main**, chief cause. 61. **first**, i.e., representations.

His nephew's levies; which to him appear'd
To be a preparation 'gainst the Polack;
But, better look'd into, he truly found
It was against your highness: whereat grieved, 65
That so his sickness, age and impotence
Was falsely borne in hand, sends out arrests
On Fortinbras; which he, in brief, obeys;
Receives rebuke from Norway, and in fine
Makes vow before his uncle never more 70
To give the assay of arms against your majesty.
Whereon old Norway, overcome with joy,
Gives him three thousand crowns in annual fee,
And his commission to employ those soldiers,
So levied as before, against the Polack: 75
With an entreaty, herein further shown,
[*Giving a paper.*]
That it might please you to give quiet pass
Through your dominions for this enterprise,
On such regards of safety and allowance
As therein are set down.

KING. It likes us well; 80
And at our more consider'd time we'll read,
Answer, and think upon this business.
Meantime we thank you for your well-took labour:
Go to your rest; at night we'll feast together:
Most welcome home!
[*Exeunt* VOLTIMAND *and* CORNELIUS.

POL. This business is well ended.
My liege, and madam, to expostulate 86
What majesty should be, what duty is,
Why day is day, night night, and time is time,
Were nothing but to waste night, day and time.
Therefore, since brevity is the soul of wit, 90
And tediousness the limbs and outward flourishes,
I will be brief: your noble son is mad:
Mad call I it; for, to define true madness,
What is 't but to be nothing else but mad?
But let that go.

QUEEN. More matter, with less art. 95

POL. Madam, I swear I use no art at all.
That he is mad, 'tis true: 'tis true 'tis pity;
And pity 'tis 'tis true: a foolish figure;
But farewell it, for I will use no art.
Mad let us grant him, then: and now remains 100
That we find out the cause of this effect,
Or rather say, the cause of this defect,
For this effect defective comes by cause:
Thus it remains, and the remainder thus.
Perpend. 105
I have a daughter—have while she is mine—
Who, in her duty and obedience, mark,
Hath given me this: now gather, and surmise.
[*Reads*]
"To the celestial and my soul's idol, the most beautified Ophelia," 110
That's an ill phrase, a vile phrase; "beautified" is a vile phrase: but you shall hear. Thus:
[*Reads*]
"In her excellent white bosom, these, &c."

QUEEN. Came this from Hamlet to her?

POL. Good madam, stay awhile; I will be faithful. 115
[*Reads*]
"Doubt thou the stars are fire;
Doubt that the sun doth move;
Doubt truth to be a liar;
But never doubt I love. 119
"O dear Ophelia, I am ill at these numbers; I have not art to reckon my groans: but that I love thee best, O most best, believe it. Adieu.
"Thine evermore, most dear lady, whilst this machine is to him,
HAMLET."
This, in obedience, hath my daughter shown me, 125
And more above, hath his solicitings,
As they fell out by time, by means and place,
All given to mine ear.

KING. But how hath she
Received his love?

67. **falsely . . . hand,** dishonestly taken advantage of; **arrests,** a royal summons. 69. **in fine,** finally. 71. **give . . . arms,** i.e., attack. 73. **three . . . fee,** yielding an annual income of three thousand crowns. A crown was worth five shillings. 77. **quiet pass,** peaceful passage. 79. **On . . . allowance,** i.e., on such pledges to permit and to safeguard the passage (of the troops). 80. **It likes us well,** it meets our approval. 81. **at . . . time,** at a time more suitable for deliberation. 86. **expostulate,** his grandiloquent way of saying "expound." 90. **wit,** good sense. 91. **outward flourishes,** rhetorical ornaments. 95. **matter,** substance; **art,** elaboration. 98. **figure,** figure of speech. 99. **farewell it,** good-bye to my foolish figure. 105. **Perpend,** consider. 110. **beautified,** an emphatic but not uncommon synonym for beautiful. Polonius thinks it affected, suggesting the use of make-up. 113. **these,** these lines, a conventional beginning of an Elizabethan letter. 115. **stay awhile,** i.e., don't interrupt; **be faithful,** to the text of the letter. 120. **ill,** unskillful; **these numbers,** this verse-making. 121. **reckon,** i.e., put into verse. 124. **machine,** body. 126. **above,** besides; **solicitings,** wooing.

POL. What do you think of me?

KING. As of a man faithful and honourable. 130

POL. I would fain prove so. But what might you think,
When I had seen this hot love on the wing—
As I perceived it, I must tell you that,
Before my daughter told me—what might you,
Or my dear majesty your queen here, think, 135
If I had play'd the desk or table-book,
Or given my heart a winking, mute and dumb,
Or look'd upon this love with idle sight;
What might you think? No, I went round to work,
And my young mistress thus I did bespeak:
"Lord Hamlet is a prince, out of thy star; 141
This must not be:" and then I prescripts gave her,
That she should lock herself from his resort,
Admit no messengers, receive no tokens.
Which done, she took the fruits of my advice; 145
And he, repulsed—a short tale to make—
Fell into a sadness, then into a fast,
Thence to a watch, thence into a weakness,
Thence to a lightness, and, by this declension,
Into the madness wherein now he raves, 150
And all we mourn for.

KING. Do you think 'tis this?

QUEEN. It may be, very likely.

POL. Hath there been such a time—I'd fain know that—
That I have positively said " 'Tis so,"
When it proved otherwise?

KING. Not that I know. 155

POL. [*Pointing to his head and shoulder*] Take this from this, if this be otherwise:
If circumstances lead me, I will find
Where truth is hid, though it were hid indeed
Within the centre.

KING. How may we try it further?

POL. You know, sometimes he walks four hours together 160
Here in the lobby.

QUEEN. So he does indeed.

POL. At such a time I'll loose my daughter to him:
Be you and I behind an arras then;
Mark the encounter: if he love her not
And be not from his reason fall'n thereon, 165
Let me be no assistant for a state,
But keep a farm and carters.

KING. We will try it.

QUEEN. But, look, where sadly the poor wretch comes reading.

POL. Away, I do beseech you, both away:
I'll board him presently.

[*Exeunt* KING, QUEEN, *and* ATTENDANTS.]

[*Enter* HAMLET, *reading.*]

O, give me leave: 170
How does my good Lord Hamlet?

HAM. Well, God-a-mercy.

POL. Do you know me, my lord?

HAM. Excellent well; you are a fishmonger.

POL. Not I, my lord. 175

HAM. Then I would you were so honest a man.

POL. Honest, my lord!

HAM. Ay, sir; to be honest, as this world goes, is to be one man picked out of ten thousand.

POL. That's very true, my lord. 180

HAM. For if the sun breed maggots in a dead dog, being a god kissing carrion,—Have you a daughter?

POL. I have, my lord.

HAM. Let her not walk i' the sun: conception is a blessing: but not as your daughter may conceive. Friend, look to 't. 187

POL. [*Aside*] How say you by that? Still harping on my daughter: yet he knew me not at first; he said I was a fishmonger: he is far gone, far gone: and truly in my youth I suffered much extremity for love; very near

131. **prove so,** show that I am. 136. **play'd . . . table-book,** i.e., shut the knowledge up as in a desk or notebook. 137. **given . . . a winking,** made my heart shut its eyes (on what was happening). 138. **idle sight,** unseeing eyes. 139. **round,** directly. 140. **bespeak,** address. 141. **star,** i.e., in a sphere above yours. 142. **prescripts,** instructions. 143. **resort,** company. 148. **watch,** state of insomnia. 149. **lightness,** mental instability; **declension,** i.e., progress from bad to worse. 156. **this be otherwise,** i.e., if I be wrong. 159. **centre,** center of the earth; **try,** test. 160. **four,** cant for "several." 161. **lobby,** porch or cloister. 163. **arras,** tapestry hanging loose against the wall. 164. **encounter,** behavior.

166. **assistant . . . state,** public official. 170. **board him presently,** accost him at once; **give me leave,** I beg your pardon (for the interruption). 172. **God-a-mercy,** I thank you. 174. **fishmonger,** probably a peddler of fish, whose trade was humble and foul-smelling. It was also a cant term for "bawd." 182. **god kissing carrion,** the sun god by touching a dead dog with its rays breeds maggots in the rotting flesh. 185. **i' the sun,** i.e., out of doors where temptation lurks. 185-6. **conception,** (1) understanding, (2) state of pregnancy. 188. **How . . . that?** What do you think of that?

this. I'll speak to him again. What do you read, my lord?

HAM. Words, words, words.

POL. What is the matter, my lord? 195

HAM. Between who?

POL. I mean, the matter that you read, my lord. 197

HAM. Slanders, sir: for the satirical rogue says here that old men have grey beards, that their faces are wrinkled, their eyes purging thick amber and plum-tree gum and that they have a plentiful lack of wit, together with most weak hams: all which, sir, though I most powerfully and potently believe, yet I hold it not honesty to have it thus set down, for yourself, sir, should be old as I am, if like a crab you could go backward. 206

POL. [*Aside*] Though this be madness, yet there is method in 't. Will you walk out of the air, my lord?

HAM. Into my grave. 210

POL. Indeed, that is out o' the air. [*Aside*] How pregnant sometimes his replies are! a happiness that often madness hits on, which reason and sanity could not so prosperously be delivered of. I will leave him, and suddenly contrive the means of meeting between him and my daughter.—My honourable lord, I will most humbly take my leave of you. 218

HAM. You cannot, sir, take from me any thing that I will more willingly part withal: except my life, except my life, except my life.

POL. Fare you well, my lord.

HAM. These tedious old fools!

[*Enter* ROSENCRANTZ *and* GUILDENSTERN.]

POL. You go to seek the Lord Hamlet; there he is.

ROS. [*To* POLONIUS] God save you, sir! 225

[*Exit* POLONIUS.

GUIL. My honoured lord!

ROS. My most dear lord!

HAM. My excellent good friends! How dost thou, Guildenstern? Ah, Rosencrantz! Good lads, how do ye both? 230

ROS. As the indifferent children of the earth.

GUIL. Happy, in that we are not over-happy;
On fortune's cap we are not the very button.

HAM. Nor the soles of her shoe?

ROS. Neither, my lord. 235

HAM. Then you live about her waist, or in the middle of her favours?

GUIL. 'Faith, her privates we.

HAM. In the secret parts of fortune? O, most true; she is a strumpet. What's the news? 240

ROS. None, my lord, but that the world's grown honest.

HAM. Then is doomsday near: but your news is not true. Let me question more in particular: what have you, my good friends, deserved at the hands of fortune, that she sends you to prison hither? 247

GUIL. Prison, my lord!

HAM. Denmark's a prison.

ROS. Then is the world one. 250

HAM. A goodly one; in which there are many confines, wards and dungeons, Denmark being one o' the worst.

ROS. We think not so, my lord.

HAM. Why, then, 'tis none to you; for there is nothing either good or bad, but thinking makes it so: to me it is a prison.

ROS. Why then, your ambition makes it one; 'tis too narrow for your mind. 259

HAM. O God, I could be bounded in a nutshell and count myself a king of infinite space, were it not that I have bad dreams.

GUIL. Which dreams indeed are ambition, for the very substance of the ambitious is merely the shadow of a dream. 265

HAM. A dream itself is but a shadow.

ROS. Truly, and I hold ambition of so airy and light a quality that it is but a shadow's shadow.

HAM. Then are our beggars bodies, and our monarchs and outstretched heroes the beggars' shadows. Shall we to the court? for, by my fay, I cannot reason. 272

ROS. }
GUIL. } We'll wait upon you.

HAM. No such matter: I will not sort you with the rest of my servants, for, to speak to

195. matter, (1) subject matter, (2) cause of a dispute. 204. honesty, decency. 213. happiness, pointedness. 214. prosperously, successfully. 215. suddenly, immediately. 231. indifferent, ordinary. 235. Neither, not that either. 251. goodly, extensive. 252. confines, places of confinement; wards, prison cells. 270. outstretched, elongated (like a shadow). The passage means: Beggars who lack ambition are the only substantial beings. Hence monarchs and heroes who become puffed up with ambition must be mere elongated shadows of the beggars. 272. fay, faith; reason, argue. 273. wait upon, accompany. 274. sort, classify.

you like an honest man, I am most dreadfully attended. But, in the beaten way of friendship, what make you at Elsinore?

ROS. To visit you, my lord; no other occasion. 279

HAM. Beggar that I am, I am even poor in thanks; but I thank you: and sure, dear friends, my thanks are too dear a halfpenny. Were you not sent for? Is it your own inclining? Is it a free visitation? Come, deal justly with me: come, come; nay, speak.

GUIL. What should we say, my lord? 286

HAM. Why, any thing, but to the purpose. You were sent for; and there is a kind of confession in your looks which your modesties have not craft enough to colour: I know the good king and queen have sent for you.

ROS. To what end, my lord? 292

HAM. That you must teach me. But let me conjure you, by the rights of our fellowship, by the consonancy of our youth, by the obligation of our ever-preserved love, and by what more dear a better proposer could charge you withal, be even and direct with me, whether you were sent for, or no?

ROS. [*Aside to* GUIL.] What say you? 300

HAM. [*Aside*] Nay, then, I have an eye of you.—If you love me, hold not off.

GUIL. My lord, we were sent for.

HAM. I will tell you why; so shall my anticipation prevent your discovery, and 305 your secrecy to the king and queen moult no feather. I have of late—but wherefore I know not—lost all my mirth, forgone all custom of exercises; and indeed it goes so heavily with my disposition that this goodly frame, the earth, seems to me a sterile promon- 310 tory, this most excellent canopy, the air, look you, this brave o'erhanging firmament, this majestical roof fretted with golden fire, why, it appears no other thing to me than a foul and pestilent congregation of vapours. What a piece of work is a man! how noble in 315 reason! how infinite in faculty! in form and moving how express and admirable! in action how like an angel! in apprehension how like a god! the beauty of the world! the paragon of animals! And yet, to me, what is this quintessence of dust? man delights not me: no, nor woman neither, though by your smiling you seem to say so. 323

ROS. My lord, there was no such stuff in my thoughts.

HAM. Why did you laugh then, when I said "man delights not me"? 327

ROS. To think, my lord, if you delight not in man, what lenten entertainment the players shall receive from you: we coted them on the way; and hither are they coming, to offer you service. 331

HAM. He that plays the king shall be welcome; his majesty shall have tribute of me; the adventurous knight shall use his foil and target; the lover shall not sigh gratis; the humorous man shall end his part in peace; the clown shall make those laugh whose lungs are tickle o' the sere; and the lady shall say her mind freely, or the blank verse shall halt for 't. What players are they? 340

ROS. Even those you were wont to take delight in, the tragedians of the city.

HAM. How chances it they travel? their residence, both in reputation and profit, was better both ways. 345

ROS. I think their inhibition comes by the means of the late innovation.

HAM. Do they hold the same estimation they did when I was in the city? are they so followed? 350

ROS. No, indeed, are they not.

HAM. How comes it? do they grow rusty?

ROS. Nay, their endeavour keeps in the wonted pace: but there is, sir, an aery of chil-

276-7. **dreadfully attended,** i.e., I have companions who fill me with dread. 277. **beaten way,** the traveled road. 278. **make you,** are you doing. 282. **a,** by a. 284. **free visitation,** voluntary visit. 289. **modesties,** sense of decency. 290. **colour,** disguise. 294. **conjure,** solemnly urge. 295. **consonancy,** congeniality. 297. **what,** whatever else; **proposer,** speaker. 298. **charge you withal,** urge upon you; **even,** straightforward. 301-2. **have . . . you,** see through you. 305. **prevent your discovery,** anticipate your disclosure. 306. **moult no feather,** i.e., remain intact. 307. **forgone,** given up. 309. **frame,** structure. 312. **brave,** beautiful. 313. **fretted,** adorned; **golden fire,** the stars. 316. **piece of work,** masterpiece. 317. **faculty,** capacity. 318. **express,** well adapted to its purpose. 321. **quintessence,** the fifth or purest essence of which the heavenly bodies were supposed to be composed. 329. **lenten entertainment,** meagre (i.e., inhospitable) reception. 330. **coted,** overtook and passed. 333-4. **foil and target,** rapier and shield. 335. **humorous man,** the actor playing the humor character, i.e., the one ruled by a single folly; **in peace,** i.e., without interruption from the audience. 337. **tickle o' the sere,** quick on the trigger. 339. **or . . . for't,** even though the blank verse has to limp to permit her to do it. 344. **residence,** i.e., in one of the London theatres. 345. **both ways,** i.e., both for their reputation and for their profit. 346. **inhibition,** formal prohibition from acting. 347. **late innovation,** recent novelty, probably the acting of the Children of the Revels in the Blackfriars' Theatre. 349-50. **so followed,** i.e., as popular as they were. 354. **aery,** nest (of a hawk or eagle).

dren, little eyases, that cry out on the top 355
of question, and are most tyrannically clapped
for 't: these are now the fashion, and so
berattle the common stages—so they call
them—that many wearing rapiers are afraid
of goose-quills and dare scarce come
thither. 360

HAM. What, are they children? who maintains 'em? how are they escoted? Will they pursue the quality no longer than they can sing? will they not say afterwards, if they should grow themselves to common play- 365 ers—as it is most like, if their means are no better—their writers do them wrong, to make them exclaim against their own succession? 368

ROS. 'Faith, there has been much to do on both sides; and the nation holds it no sin to tarre them to controversy: there was, for a while, no money bid for argument, unless the poet and the player went to cuffs in the question. 373

HAM. Is 't possible?

GUIL. O, there has been much throwing about of brains.

HAM. Do the boys carry it away?

ROS. Ay, that they do, my lord; Hercules and his load too. 379

HAM. It is not very strange; for mine uncle is king of Denmark, and those that would make mows at him while my father lived, give twenty, forty, fifty, an hundred ducats a-piece for his picture in little. 'Sblood, there is something in this more than natural, if philosophy could find it out. 385

[*Flourish of trumpets within.*

GUIL. There are the players.

HAM. Gentlemen, you are welcome to Elsinore. Your hands, come then: the appurtenance of welcome is fashion and ceremony: let me comply with you in this garb, lest my extent to the players, which, I tell 390 you, must show fairly outward, should more appear like entertainment than yours. You are welcome: but my uncle-father and aunt-mother are deceived.

GUIL. In what, my dear lord? 395

HAM. I am but mad north-north-west: when the wind is southerly I know a hawk from a handsaw.

[*Re-enter* POLONIUS.]

POL. Well be with you, gentlemen!

HAM. Hark you, Guildenstern; and you too: at each ear a hearer: that great baby you see there is not yet out of his swaddling-clouts. 401

ROS. Happily he's the second time come to them; for they say an old man is twice a child.

HAM. I will prophesy he comes to tell me of the players; mark it. You say right, sir: o' Monday morning; 'twas so indeed. 407

POL. My lord, I have news to tell you.

HAM. My lord, I have news to tell you. When Roscius was an actor in Rome,—

POL. The actors are come hither, my lord.

HAM. Buz, buz!

POL. Upon mine honour,— 413

HAM. Then came each actor on his ass,—

POL. The best actors in the world, either for tragedy, comedy, history, pastoral, pastoral-comical, historical-pastoral, tragical-historical, tragical-comical-historical-pastoral, scene individable, or poem unlimited: Seneca cannot be too heavy, nor Plautus too light. For the law of writ and the liberty, these are the only men. 421

355. **eyases,** young hawks. 355-6. **on . . . question,** at a pitch higher and shriller than that of ordinary conversation. 356. **tyrannically,** violently. 358. **berattle,** run down. 359. **wearing rapiers,** i.e., gentlemen of fashion. 360. **goose-quills,** pens and so dramatists who satirize them. 362. **escoted,** supported. 363. **pursue the quality,** continue in their profession. 363-4. **than . . . sing,** i.e., until their voices change. 365. **common,** regular (i.e., professional). 366. **like,** likely; **means are no better,** if no better opportunity offers. 368. **exclaim against,** run down; **succession,** future profession. 369. **to do,** commotion. 370. **both sides,** i.e., the children and the adult companies. 371. **tarre,** egg on. 372. **argument,** plot for a play. 373. **went to cuffs,** came to blows; **question,** controversy. 377. **carry it away,** win out. 378-9. **Hercules . . . load,** the Globe Theatre; its sign was Hercules carrying a globe on his shoulders. 382. **mows,** faces. 384. **picture in little,** miniature; **'Sblood,** God's blood, a violent oath. 385. **philosophy,** human knowledge. 388. **appurtenance,** proper accompaniment; **fashion and ceremony,** fashionable ceremony. 389. **comply,** show formal courtesy; **garb,** fashion. 390. **extent,** expression of welcome. 391. **show . . . outward,** be clearly manifested. 391-2. **more . . . yours,** seems more cordial than that which I have shown you. 396. **north-north-west,** only when the wind comes from a little west of north. 397-8. **hawk . . . handsaw,** i.e., I can distinguish between two objects having no resemblance to each other. 401. **swaddling-clouts,** linen bandages wrapped around newborn babies. 402. **Happily,** perhaps. 410. **Roscius,** a famous Roman actor, also nickname of Alleyn, the principal actor in the rival Admiral's Men. 412. **Buz, buz,** contemptuous exclamation meaning his news was stale. 419. **scene individable,** play observing unity of place; **poem unlimited,** a play failing to observe the foregoing unity. 421. **law . . . liberty,** written or extemporal plays.

HAM. O Jephthah, judge of Israel, what a treasure hadst thou!

POL. What a treasure had he, my lord?

HAM. Why,

"One fair daughter, and no more,
The which he loved passing well."

POL. [*Aside*] Still on my daughter.

HAM. Am I not i' the right, old Jephthah?

POL. If you call me Jephthah, my lord, I have a daughter that I love passing well. 431

HAM. Nay, that follows not.

POL. What follows, then, my lord?

HAM. Why,

"As by lot, God wot,"

and then, you know,

"It came to pass, as most like it was,"—

the first row of the pious chanson will show you more; for look, where my abridgement comes. 439

[*Enter four or five* PLAYERS.]

You are welcome, masters; welcome, all. I am glad to see thee well. Welcome, good friends. O, my old friend! thy face is valanced since I saw thee last: comest thou to beard me in Denmark? What, my young lady and mistress! By'r lady, your ladyship is nearer to heaven than when I saw you last, by the altitude of a chopine. Pray God, your voice, like a piece of uncurrent gold, be not cracked within the ring. Masters, you are all welcome. We'll e'en to 't like French falconers, fly at any thing we see: we'll have a speech straight: come, give us a taste of your quality; come, a passionate speech. 452

FIRST PLAY. What speech, my lord?

HAM. I heard thee speak me a speech once, but it was never acted; or, if it was, not above once; for the play, I remember, 455 pleased not the million; 'twas caviare to the general: but it was—as I received it, and others, whose judgements in such matters cried in the top of mine—an excellent play, well digested in the scenes, set down with as much modesty as cunning. I remember, 461 one said there were no sallets in the lines to make the matter savoury, nor no matter in the phrase that might indict the author of affectation; but called it an honest method, 465 as wholesome as sweet, and by very much more handsome than fine. One speech in it I chiefly loved: 'twas Æneas' tale to Dido; and thereabout of it especially, where he speaks of Priam's slaughter: if it live in your memory, begin at this line: let me see, let me see— 471

"The rugged Pyrrhus, like the Hyrcanian beast,"—

it is not so:—it begins with Pyrrhus:—

"The rugged Pyrrhus, he whose sable arms,
Black as his purpose, did the night resemble 475
When he lay couched in the ominous horse,
Hath now this dread and black complexion smear'd
With heraldry more dismal; head to foot
Now is he total gules; horridly trick'd
With blood of fathers, mothers, daughters, sons, 480
Baked and impasted with the parching streets,
That lend a tyrannous and damned light
To their lord's murder: roasted in wrath and fire,
And thus o'er-sized with coagulate gore,
With eyes like carbuncles, the hellish Pyrrhus 485
Old grandsire Priam seeks."

So, proceed you.

POL. 'Fore God, my lord, well spoken, with good accent and good discretion.

FIRST PLAY. "Anon he finds him 490
Striking too short at Greeks; his antique sword,

422. **Jephthah . . . Israel,** title of a popular ballad on the subject of Jephthah and his daughter. The story of his sacrifice of his daughter is in Judges, II:30-40. 431. **passing,** surpassingly. 438. **row,** stanza; **pious chanson,** sacred ballad. 439. **more,** i.e., of the story; **abridgement,** i.e., the person who will force me to curtail my quotation from the ballad. 442-3. **valanced,** fringed (with a beard). 447. **chopine,** thick-soled shoe. 449. **cracked . . . ring,** a crack in a gold coin within a ring enclosing the sovereign's head in the center of the coin made it unfit for legal tender. 451. **straight,** at once. 452. **quality,** professional skill. 456-7. **caviare to the general,** like caviar, not relished by the crowd. 459. **cried . . . mine,** were of stronger (more authoritative) voice than mine. 461. **modesty as cunning,** restraint as skill. 462. **sallets,** tasty bits, i.e., spicy jests. 464. **indict,** convict. 465. **honest,** in good taste. 466-7. **handsome than fine,** well proportioned than ornate. 472. **Pyrrhus,** the son of Achilles and one of the best of the Greek heroes in the Trojan War; **Hyrcanian beast,** the tiger of Hyrcania, a wild district north of the Caspian Sea. 474. **sable arms,** i.e., with a black design on his shield. 476. **ominous horse,** the hollow wooden horse at the siege of Troy. 478. **heraldry,** i.e., the symbolic decoration on a coat of arms. 479. **gules,** heraldic term for red; **tricked,** heraldic term for "decorated." 481. **impasted,** made into a paste, i.e., clotted; **parching,** because of the fire raging in the city. 482. **tyrannous,** fierce. 484. **o'er-sized,** smeared over; **size,** glue. 487. **So . . . you,** go on from this point. 488. **discretion,** interpretation. 490. **"Anon,** immediately after. 491. **antique,** used long before.

Rebellious to his arm, lies where it falls,
Repugnant to command: unequal match'd,
Pyrrhus at Priam drives; in rage strikes wide;
But with the whiff and wind of his fell sword 495
The unnerved father falls. Then senseless Ilium,
Seeming to feel this blow, with flaming top
Stoops to his base, and with a hideous crash
Takes prisoner Pyrrhus' ear: for, lo! his sword,
Which was declining on the milky head 500
Of reverend Priam, seem'd i' the air to stick:
So, as a painted tyrant, Pyrrhus stood,
And like a neutral to his will and matter,
Did nothing.
But, as we often see, against some storm, 505
A silence in the heavens, the rack stand still,
The bold winds speechless and the orb below
As hush as death, anon the dreadful thunder
Doth rend the region, so, after Pyrrhus' pause,
Arousèd vengeance sets him new a-work; 510
And never did the Cyclops' hammers fall
On Mars's armour forged for proof eterne
With less remorse than Pyrrhus' bleeding sword
Now falls on Priam.
Out, out, thou strumpet, Fortune! All you gods, 515
In general synod, take away her power;
Break all the spokes and fellies from her wheel,
And bowl the round nave down the hill of heaven,
As low as to the fiends!"

POL. This is too long. 520

HAM. It shall to the barber's, with your beard. Prithee, say on: he's for a jig or a tale of bawdry, or he sleeps: say on: come to Hecuba.

FIRST PLAY. "But who, O, who had seen the mobled queen—" 525

HAM. "The mobled queen?"

POL. That's good; "mobled queen" is good.

FIRST PLAY. "Run barefoot up and down, threatening the flames
With bisson rheum; a clout upon that head
Where late the diadem stood, and for a robe, 530
About her lank and all o'er-teemèd loins,
A blanket, in the alarm of fear caught up;
Who this had seen, with tongue in venom steep'd,
'Gainst Fortune's state would treason have pronounced:
But if the gods themselves did see her then
When she saw Pyrrhus make malicious sport 536
In mincing with his sword her husband's limbs,
The instant burst of clamour that she made,
Unless things mortal move them not at all,
Would have made milch the burning eyes of heaven, 540
And passion in the gods."

POL. Look, whether he has not turned his colour and has tears in 's eyes. Pray you, no more.

HAM. 'Tis well; I'll have thee speak out the rest soon. Good my lord, will you see the players well bestowed? Do you hear, let them be well used; for they are the abstract and brief chronicles of the time: after your death you were better have a bad epitaph than their ill report while you live. 551

POL. My lord, I will use them according to their desert.

493. **Repugnant to**, resisting. 496. **unnerved**, weak in his sinews; **senseless Ilium**, the citadel of Troy, incapable of feeling. 498. **his**, its. 499. **Takes prisoner**, that is, deafens. 502. **painted tyrant**, a tyrant as depicted on the painted cloths which adorned the walls of great halls, usually with uplifted arm. 503. **neutral**, person indifferent; **will and matter**, purpose and its fulfilment. 505. **against**, just before. 506. **rack**, mass of cloud. 507. **orb below**, the round earth. 509. **region**, upper air. 512. **for proof eterne**, i.e., to wear forever. 515. **strumpet**, harlot. 516. **general synod**, full assembly. 517. **fellies**, rims. 518. **nave**, hub. 522. **jig**, a musical farce usually presented as an afterpiece to the main drama. 525. **mobled**, muffled, i.e., with a scarf wrapped round her head; the unusual and homely word prompts Hamlet's interruption. 529. **bisson rheum**, blinding tears. 531. **o'er-teemed**, worn out from childbearing. 534. **state**, governance of the world. 540. **milch**, milky or moist; **eyes of heaven**, the stars. 542. **turned**, changed. 545. **'Tis well**, i.e., that will do. 547. **bestowed**, lodged. 548. **abstract**, summary. 549. **time**, i.e., events.

HAM. God's bodykins, man, much better: use every man after his desert, and who should 'scape whipping? Use them after your own honour and dignity: the less they deserve, the more merit is in your bounty. Take them in.

POL. Come, sirs. 559

HAM. Follow him, friends: we'll hear a play to-morrow. [*Exit* POLONIUS *with all the* PLAYERS *but the* FIRST.] Dost thou hear me, old friend; can you play the Murder of Gonzago?

FIRST PLAY. Ay, my lord.

HAM. We'll ha't to-morrow night. You could, for a need, study a speech of some dozen or sixteen lines, which I would set down and insert in 't, could you not?

FIRST PLAY. Ay, my lord. 569

HAM. Very well. Follow that lord; and look you mock him not. [*Exit* FIRST PLAYER.] My good friends, I'll leave you till night: you are welcome to Elsinore.

ROS. Good my lord!

HAM. Ay, so, God be wi' ye; [*Exeunt* ROSENCRANTZ *and* GUILDENSTERN.] Now I am alone. 575
O, what a rogue and peasant slave am I!
Is it not monstrous that this player here,
But in a fiction, in a dream of passion,
Could force his soul so to his own conceit
That from her working all his visage wann'd, 580
Tears in his eyes, distraction in 's aspect,
A broken voice, and his whole function suiting
With forms to his conceit? and all for nothing!
For Hecuba!
What's Hecuba to him, or he to Hecuba, 585
That he should weep for her? What would he do,
Had he the motive and the cue for passion
That I have? He would drown the stage with tears
And cleave the general ear with horrid speech,
Make mad the guilty and appal the free, 590
Confound the ignorant, and amaze indeed
The very faculties of eyes and ears.
Yet I,
A dull and muddy-mettled rascal, peak,
Like John-a-dreams, unpregnant of my cause, 595
And can say nothing; no, not for a king,
Upon whose property and most dear life
A damn'd defeat was made. Am I a coward?
Who calls me villain? breaks my pate across?
Plucks off my beard, and blows it in my face?
Tweaks me by the nose? gives me the lie i' the throat, 601
As deep as to the lungs? who does me this?
Ha!
'Swounds, I should take it: for it cannot be
But I am pigeon-liver'd and lack gall 605
To make oppression bitter, or ere this
I should have fatted all the region kites
With this slave's offal: bloody, bawdy villain!
Remorseless, treacherous, lecherous, kindless villain!
O, vengeance! 610
Why, what an ass am I! This is most brave,
That I, the son of a dear father murder'd,
Prompted to my revenge by heaven and hell,
Must, like a whore, unpack my heart with words,
And fall a-cursing, like a very drab, 615
A scullion!
Fie upon 't! foh! About, my brain! I have heard
That guilty creatures sitting at a play
Have by the very cunning of the scene
Been struck so to the soul that presently 620
They have proclaim'd their malefactions;
For murder, though it have no tongue, will speak
With most miraculous organ. I'll have these players
Play something like the murder of my father
Before mine uncle: I'll observe his looks; 625
I'll tent him to the quick: if he but blench,

554. **God's bodykins,** a vulgar and outlandish oath. Bodykins = little body and refers to the bread or holy wafer in the Communion service. 556. **after,** according to. 566. **for a need,** if there were need. 576. **peasant,** base. 578. **dream of passion,** imaginary emotion. 579. **to his own conceit,** i.e., should so accept the conception (of the part he acts). 580. **wann'd,** grew pale. 582-3. **whole function . . . conceit,** all his physical powers acting in harmony with his conception. 589. **cleave . . . ear,** penetrate the ears of everyone (in the audience). 590. **free,** innocent. 591. **amaze,** stun. 594. **muddy-mettled,** dull-spirited. 594-5. **peak . . . dreams,** mope like day-dreamer. 595. **unpregnant of,** i.e., barren of plans for revenge. 597. **property,** personality. 598. **defeat,** destruction. 599. **breaks . . . across,** strikes me over the head. 605. **pigeon-liver'd,** the pigeon's liver was supposed to secrete no gall, the source of bitterness. 607. **region,** of the upper air. 608. **offal,** rotting flesh. 609. **kindless,** unnatural. 611. **most brave,** makes a fine display. 615. **drab,** prostitute. 616. **scullion,** a menial kitchen servant. 617. **About,** get to work. 620. **presently,** immediately. 626. **tent,** probe; **blench,** flinch.

I know my course. The spirit that I have seen
May be the devil: and the devil hath power
To assume a pleasing shape; yea, and perhaps
Out of my weakness and my melancholy, 630
As he is very potent with such spirits,
Abuses me to damn me: I'll have grounds
More relative than this: the play's the thing
Wherein I'll catch the conscience of the king.
[*Exit.*

ACT III

SCENE I. *A room in the castle.*

[*Enter* KING, QUEEN, POLONIUS, OPHELIA, ROSENCRANTZ, *and* GUILDENSTERN.]

KING. And can you, by no drift of circumstance,
Get from him why he puts on this confusion,
Grating so harshly all his days of quiet
With turbulent and dangerous lunacy?

ROS. He does confess he feels himself distracted; 5
But from what cause he will by no means speak.

GUIL. Nor do we find him forward to be sounded,
But, with a crafty madness, keeps aloof,
When we would bring him on to some confession
Of his true state.

QUEEN. Did he receive you well? 10

ROS. Most like a gentleman.

GUIL. But with much forcing of his disposition.

ROS. Niggard of question; but, of our demands,
Most free in his reply.

QUEEN. Did you assay him
To any pastime? 15

ROS. Madam, it so fell out, that certain players
We o'er-raught on the way: of these we told him;
And there did seem in him a kind of joy
To hear of it: they are about the court,
And, as I think, they have already order 20
This night to play before him.

POL. 'Tis most true:
And he beseech'd me to entreat your majesties
To hear and see the matter.

KING. With all my heart; and it doth much content me
To hear him so inclined. 25
Good gentlemen, give him a further edge,
And drive his purpose on to these delights.

ROS. We shall, my lord.
[*Exeunt* ROSENCRANTZ *and* GUILDENSTERN.

KING. Sweet Gertrude, leave us too;
For we have closely sent for Hamlet hither,
That he, as 'twere by accident, may here 30
Affront Ophelia:
Her father and myself, lawful espials,
Will so bestow ourselves that, seeing, unseen,
We may of their encounter frankly judge,
And gather by him, as he is behaved, 35
If 't be the affliction of his love or no
That thus he suffers for.

QUEEN. I shall obey you.
And for your part, Ophelia, I do wish
That your good beauties be the happy cause
Of Hamlet's wildness: so shall I hope your virtues 40
Will bring him to his wonted way again,
To both your honours.

OPH. Madam, I wish it may.
[*Exit* QUEEN.

POL. Ophelia, walk you here. Gracious, so please you,
We will bestow ourselves. [*To* OPHELIA] Read on this book;
That show of such an exercise may colour 45
Your loneliness. We are oft to blame in this,—
'Tis too much proved—that with devotion's visage

631. **spirits,** humors (of melancholy). 632. **abuses,** deceives. 633. **relative,** i.e., more related (to the facts); **this,** i.e., the ghost's testimony. 634. **catch . . . king,** make the king betray the consciousness of his guilt. Act III, Scene i: 1. **drift of circumstance,** manipulation of the conversation. 2. **puts on . . . confusion,** shows this distraction. 3. **Grating,** vexing. 7. **forward,** willing; **sounded,** questioned. 12. **forcing . . . disposition,** against his will. 13. **Niggard of question,** unwilling to open conversation. 14-5. **assay . . . pastime,** try to interest him in any sort of amusement? 17. **o'er-raught,** overtook and passed. 23. **matter,** i.e., performance. 26. **edge,** incitement (to this interest). 29. **closely,** secretly. 31. **Affront,** meet face to face. 32. **lawful espials,** legitimate spies. 33. **bestow,** station. 34. **frankly,** easily. 40. **wildness,** madness. 41. **way,** frame of mind. 45. **exercise,** religious devotion; **colour,** seem to explain. 47. **'Tis . . . proved** i.e., as experience has made only too evident; **devotion's visage,** the appearance of devoutness.

And pious action we do sugar o'er
The devil himself.

KING. [*Aside*] O, 'tis too true!
How smart a lash that speech doth give my conscience! 50
The harlot's cheek, beautied with plastering art,
Is not more ugly to the thing that helps it
Than is my deed to my most painted word:
O heavy burthen!

POL. I hear him coming: let's withdraw, my lord. [*Exeunt* KING *and* POLONIUS. 55

[*Enter* HAMLET.]

HAM. To be, or not to be: that is the question:
Whether 'tis nobler in the mind to suffer
The slings and arrows of outrageous fortune,
Or to take arms against a sea of troubles,
And by opposing end them? To die: to sleep;
No more; and by a sleep to say we end 61
The heart-ache and the thousand natural shocks
That flesh is heir to, 'tis a consummation
Devoutly to be wish'd. To die, to sleep;
To sleep: perchance to dream: ay, there's the rub; 65
For in that sleep of death what dreams may come
When we have shuffled off this mortal coil,
Must give us pause: there's the respect
That makes calamity of so long life;
For who would bear the whips and scorns of time, 70
The oppressor's wrong, the proud man's contumely,
The pangs of déspised love, the law's delay,
The insolence of office and the spurns
That patient merit of the unworthy takes,
When he himself might his quietus make 75
With a bare bodkin? who would fardels bear,
To grunt and sweat under a weary life,
But that the dread of something after death,
The undiscover'd country from whose bourn
No traveller returns, puzzles the will 80
And makes us rather bear those ills we have
Than fly to others that we know not of?
Thus conscience does make cowards of us all;
And thus the native hue of resolution 84
Is sicklied o'er with the pale cast of thought,
And enterprises of great pitch and moment
With this regard their currents turn awry,
And lose the name of action.—Soft you now!
The fair Ophelia! Nymph, in thy orisons
Be all my sins remember'd.

OPH. Good my lord, 90
How does your honour for this many a day?

HAM. I humbly thank you; well, well, well.

OPH. My lord, I have remembrances of yours,
That I have longed long to re-deliver;
I pray you, now receive them.

HAM. No, not I; 95
I never gave you aught.

OPH. My honour'd lord, you know right well you did;
And, with them, words of so sweet breath composed
As made the things more rich: their perfume lost,
Take these again; for to the noble mind 100
Rich gifts wax poor when givers prove unkind.
There, my lord.

HAM. Ha, ha! are you honest?

OPH. My lord?

HAM. Are you fair? 105

OPH. What means your lordship?

HAM. That if you be honest and fair, your honesty should admit no discourse to your beauty.

OPH. Could beauty, my lord, have better commerce than with honesty? 110

HAM. Ay, truly; for the power of beauty will sooner transform honesty from what it is to a bawd than the force of honesty can translate beauty into his likeness: this was sometime a paradox, but now the time gives it proof. I did love you once. 116

52. **to,** compared to; **the thing,** i.e., the paint. 58. **slings,** the missiles sent from a sling. 61. **to say,** let us say. 65. **rub,** hindrance (an unevenness of the ground in the game of bowls). 67. **shuffled,** cast; **coil,** (1) turmoil, (2) a ring of rope wound round an object (as the flesh encircles the soul). 68. **respect,** consideration. 70. **time,** the world. 72. **despised,** rejected. 73. **office,** officials. 74. **of,** from. 75. **quietus,** full discharge (of a debt), here = death. 76. **bare bodkin,** mere stiletto; **fardels,** burdens. 79. **undiscover'd,** unexplored; **bourn,** boundary. 80. **puzzles,** renders helpless, paralyzes. 83. **conscience,** reflection. 84. **native hue,** natural healthy color. 85. **sicklied o'er,** given a sickly tinge; **cast of thought,** shade which thought gives it. 86. **pitch,** height, a term in falconry. 87. **With this regard,** because of this consideration. 88. **Soft you now,** But wait! 89. **Nymph,** (1) fair maiden, (2) in Elizabethan times = harlot; **orisons,** prayers. 98. **breath,** i.e., meaning. 103. **honest,** chaste. 108. **admit . . . to,** allow no communication with. 110. **commerce,** intercourse. 113. **bawd,** procurer. 115. **the time,** present age.

OPH. Indeed, my lord, you made me believe so.

HAM. You should not have believed me; for virtue cannot so inoculate our old stock but we shall relish of it: I loved you not. 120

OPH. I was the more deceived.

HAM. Get thee to a nunnery: why wouldst thou be a breeder of sinners? I am myself indifferent honest; but yet I could accuse me of such things that it were better 125 my mother had not borne me: I am very proud, revengeful, ambitious, with more offences at my beck than I have thoughts to put them in, imagination to give them shape, or time to act them in. What should such fellows as I do crawling between earth and heaven? We are arrant knaves, all; believe none of us. Go thy ways to a nunnery. Where's your father? 133

OPH. At home, my lord.

HAM. Let the doors be shut upon him, that he may play the fool no where but in's own house. Farewell. 137

OPH. O, help him, you sweet heavens!

HAM. If thou dost marry, I'll give thee this plague for thy dowry: be thou as chaste as ice, as pure as snow, thou shalt not escape calumny. Get thee to a nunnery, go: farewell. Or, if thou wilt needs marry, marry a fool; for wise men know well enough what monsters you make of them. To a nunnery, go, and quickly too. Farewell. 146

OPH. O heavenly powers, restore him!

HAM. I have heard of your paintings too, well enough; God has given you one face, and you make yourselves another: you jig, 150 you amble, and you lisp, and nick-name God's creatures, and make your wantonness your ignorance. Go to, I'll no more on 't; it hath made me mad. I say, we will have no more marriages: those that are married already, all but one, shall live; the rest shall keep as they are. To a nunnery, go. [*Exit.* 157

OPH. O, what a noble mind is here o'erthrown!
The courtier's, soldier's, scholar's, eye, tongue, sword;
The expectancy and rose of the fair state, 160
The glass of fashion and the mould of form,
The observed of all observers, quite, quite down!
And I, of ladies most deject and wretched,
That suck'd the honey of his music vows,
Now see that noble and most sovereign reason, 165
Like sweet bells jangled, out of tune and harsh;
That unmatch'd form and feature of blown youth
Blasted with ecstasy: O, woe is me,
To have seen what I have seen, see what I see!

[*Re-enter* KING *and* POLONIUS.]

KING. Love! his affections do not that way tend; 170
Nor what he spake, though it lack'd form a little,
Was not like madness. There's something in his soul,
O'er which his melancholy sits on brood;
And I do doubt the hatch and the disclose
Will be some danger: which for to prevent,
I have in quick determination 176
Thus set it down: he shall with speed to England,
For the demand of our neglected tribute:
Haply the seas and countries different
With variable objects shall expel 180
This something-settled matter in his heart,
Whereon his brains still beating puts him thus
From fashion of himself. What think you on 't?

POL. It shall do well: but yet do I believe
The origin and commencement of his grief
Sprung from neglected love. How now, Ophelia! 186
You need not tell us what Lord Hamlet said;
We heard it all. My lord, do as you please;
But, if you hold it fit, after the play
Let his queen mother all alone entreat him 190

119. **inoculate**, graft. 120. **relish of**, taste. 124. **indifferent honest**, fairly virtuous. 128. **beck**, bidding. 131. **arrant**, downright. 145. **monsters**, cuckolds (husbands with faithless wives) were said to wear horns; **nunnery**, besides the usual meaning, in Elizabethan days = house of prostitution. 150. **jig**, walk with affected provocative movements. 151. **lisp**, talk affectedly. 151-2. **nick-name . . . creatures**, give indecent names to. 152-3. **make . . . ignorance**, pretend you are too innocent to understand what you are saying. 159. **The . . . sword**, i.e., the courtier's eye, the scholar's tongue, the soldier's sword. 160. **fair**, because he adorned it. 161. **glass**, mirror; **mould of form**, model of polite behavior. 167. **feature of blown**, bodily shape of fully matured. 168. **ecstasy**, madness. 173. **sits on brood**, broods. 174. **disclose**, disclosure. 180. **variable objects**, unfamiliar sights. 181. **something-settled matter**, i.e., obsession. 182. **still beating**, constantly going over and over again. 183. **From . . . himself**, i.e., makes him unlike himself. 184. **It . . . well**, i.e., your plan is good. 186. **neglected**, unreturned.

To show his grief: let her be round with him;
And I'll be placed, so please you, in the ear
Of all their conference. If she find him not,
To England send him, or confine him where
Your wisdom best shall think.

KING. It shall be so: 195
Madness in great ones must not unwatch'd go.
[*Exeunt.*

SCENE II. *A hall in the castle.*

[*Enter* HAMLET *and* PLAYERS.]

HAM. Speak the speech, I pray you, as I pronounced it to you, trippingly on the tongue: but if you mouth it, as many of your players do, I had as lief the town-crier spoke my lines. Nor do not saw the air too much with your hand, thus, but use all gently; for in the very torrent, tempest, and, as I may say, the whirlwind of passion, you must acquire and beget a temperance that may give it smoothness. O, it offends me 9 to the soul to hear a robustious periwig-pated fellow tear a passion to tatters, to very rags, to split the ears of the groundlings, who for the most part are capable of nothing but inexplicable dumb-shows and noise: I would have such a fellow whipped for o'er-doing Termagant; it out-herods Herod: pray you, avoid it.

FIRST PLAY. I warrant your honour. 17

HAM. Be not too tame neither, but let your own discretion be your tutor: suit the action to the word, the word to the action; with this special observance, that you o'er-step not the modesty of nature: for any thing so overdone is from the purpose of playing, whose end, both at the first and now, was and is, to hold, as 't were, the mirror up to nature; to show virtue her own feature, scorn 25 her own image, and the very age and body of the time his form and pressure. Now this overdone, or come tardy off, though it 28 make the unskillful laugh, cannot but make the judicious grieve; the censure of the which one must in your allowance o'erweigh a whole theatre of others. O, there be players that I have seen play, and heard others praise, and that highly, not to speak it profanely, that, neither having the accent of Christians nor the gait of Christian, pagan, nor man, have so strutted and bellowed that I have thought some of nature's journeymen had made men and not made them well, they imitated humanity so abominably.

FIRST PLAY. I hope we have reformed that indifferently with us, sir. 41

HAM. O, reform it altogether. And let those that play your clowns speak no more than is set down for them; for there be of them that will themselves laugh, to set on some quantity of barren spectators to laugh too; though, in the mean time, some necessary question of the play be then to be considered: that's villanous, and shows a most pitiful ambition in the fool that uses it. Go, make you ready. [*Exeunt players.* 50

[*Enter* POLONIUS, ROSENCRANTZ, *and* GUILDENSTERN.]

How now, my lord! will the king hear this piece of work?

POL. And the queen too, and that presently.

HAM. Bid the players make haste. [*Exit* POLONIUS.] Will you two help to hasten them?

ROS. }
GUIL. } We will, my lord.

[*Exeunt* ROSENCRANTZ *and* GUILDENSTERN.

HAM. What ho! Horatio!

[*Enter* HORATIO.]

HOR. Here, sweet lord, at your service.

HAM. Horatio, thou art e'en as just a man

191. **show his grief,** reveal the cause of his grief; **round,** plain and direct. 193. **find him,** i.e., find him out, get at his secret. **Scene ii:** 2. **trippingly,** without exaggerated emphasis. 4. **your players,** actors in general. 8. **temperance,** moderation. 10. **robustious,** boisterous; **periwig-pated,** wearing a wig. 12. **groundlings,** those who stood on the ground in an Elizabethan theatre and so the least intelligent part of the audience. 13. **capable of,** can appreciate. 14. **inexplicable,** meaningless; **dumb-shows,** scenes acted in pantomime. 15 **Termagant,** a violent and noisy character in the mystery plays, supposed to be a god of the Saracens. 16. **Herod,** the Jewish King who ordered the slaughter of the children. In the mystery plays he was a ranting tyrant. 17. **I warrant your honour,** your lordship is quite right. 19. **discretion,** judgment. 21. **modesty,** moderation. 22. **from,** contrary to; **playing,** acting. 23. **at the first,** in earliest times. 25. **feature,** form. 26. **age and body of the time,** accurate picture of the age; **form and pressure,** their appearance in general and in detail. 28. **come tardy off,** done half-heartedly. 29. **unskilful,** uncritical. 30. **the which one,** i.e., a single judicious person. 31. **allowance,** estimation. 38. **journeymen,** those not yet become masters of their trade. 41. **indifferently,** fairly well. 44. **there . . . them,** there are some clowns. 46. **barren,** i.e., of intelligence. 47-8. **necessary question,** essential subject matter. 49. **villainous,** cheap. 49. **pitiful,** contemptible. 51. **piece of work,** masterpiece. 53. **presently,** at once. 59. **just,** well balanced.

As e'er my conversation coped withal. 60
HOR. O, my dear lord,—
HAM. Nay, do not think I flatter;
For what advancement may I hope from thee
That no revénue hast but thy good spirits,
To feed and clothe thee? Why should the poor be flatter'd?
No, let the candied tongue lick absurd pomp,
And crook the pregnant hinges of the knee 66
Where thrift may follow fawning. Dost thou hear?
Since my dear soul was mistress of her choice
And could of men distinguish, her election
Hath seal'd thee for herself; for thou hast been 70
As one, in suffering all, that suffers nothing,
A man that fortune's buffets and rewards
Hast ta'en with equal thanks: and blest are those
Whose blood and judgement are so well commingled,
That they are not a pipe for fortune's finger
To sound what stop she please. Give me that man 76
That is not passion's slave, and I will wear him
In my heart's core, ay, in my heart of heart,
As I do thee.—Something too much of this.—
There is a play to-night before the king; 80
One scene of it comes near the circumstance
Which I have told thee of my father's death.
I prithee, when thou seest that act afoot,
Even with the very comment of thy soul
Observe mine uncle: if his occulted guilt 85
Do not itself unkennel in one speech,
It is a damnèd ghost that we have seen,
And my imaginations are as foul
As Vulcan's stithy. Give him heedful note;
For I mine eyes will rivet to his face, 90
And after we will both our judgements join
In censure of his seeming.
HOR. Well, my lord:
If he steal aught the whilst this play is playing,
And 'scape detecting, I will pay the theft.

HAM. They are coming to the play; I must be idle:
Get you a place.

[*Danish march. A flourish. Enter* KING, QUEEN, POLONIUS, OPHELIA, ROSENCRANTZ, GUILDENSTERN, *and others.*]

KING. How fares our cousin Hamlet?

HAM. Excellent, i' faith; of the chameleon's dish: I eat the air, promise-crammed: you cannot feed capons so. 100

KING. I have nothing with this answer, Hamlet; these words are not mine.

HAM. No, nor mine now. [*To* POLONIUS] My lord, you played once i' the university, you say?

POL. That did I, my lord; and was accounted a good actor. 106

HAM. What did you enact?

POL. I did enact Julius Cæsar: I was killed i' the Capitol; Brutus killed me.

HAM. It was a brute part of him to kill so capital a calf there. Be the players ready? 111

ROS. Ay, my lord; they stay upon your patience.

QUEEN. Come hither, my dear Hamlet, sit by me. 115

HAM. No, good mother, here's metal more attractive.

POL. [*To the* KING] O, ho! do you mark that?

HAM. Lady, shall I lie in your lap?
[*Lying down at* OPHELIA'S *feet.*

OPH. No, my lord. 120

HAM. I mean, my head upon your lap?

OPH. Ay, my lord.

HAM. Do you think I meant country matters?

OPH. I think nothing, my lord.

HAM. That's a fair thought to lie between maids' legs. 126

OPH. What is, my lord?

HAM. Nothing.

OPH. You are merry, my lord.

HAM. Who, I? 130

OPH. Ay, my lord.

60. **conversation coped withal**, my experience has had to do with. 65. **candied**, sugared, hence flattering; **lick absurd pomp**, fawn upon absurdly pompous persons. 66. **pregnant hinges**, ready-to-act (supple) joints. 67. **thrift**, worldly advantage. The phrase means, "where flattery pays." 69. **of men**, among men; **election**, choice. 74. **blood and judgement**, emotion and reason. 83. **afoot**, being enacted. 84. **comment . . . soul**, concentration of your entire attention. 85. **occulted**, concealed. 87. **damned ghost**, a devil. 88. **imaginations**, suspicions. 89. **stithy**, blacksmith's forge. 89. **Give . . . note**, pay close attention to him. 92. **censure . . . seeming**, judgment of his behavior. 95. **be idle**, seem crazy. 98-9. **chameleon's dish**, the air, so the Elizabethans believed. 101. **I . . . with**, I can make nothing of. 102. **not mine**, no answer to my question. 110. **part**, act. 112. **stay . . . patience**, wait until you are ready.

HAM. O God, your only jig-maker. What should a man do but be merry? for, look you, how cheerfully my mother looks, and my father died within these two hours.

OPH. Nay, 'tis twice two months, my lord. 136

HAM. So long? Nay then, let the devil wear black, for I'll have a suit of sables. O heavens! died two months ago, and not forgotten yet? Then there's hope a great man's memory may outlive his life half a year: but by'r lady, he must build churches, then; or else shall he suffer not thinking on, with the hobby-horse, whose epitaph is "For, O, for, O, the hobby-horse is forgot." 145

Hautboys play. The dumb-show enters.

[*Enter a* KING *and a* QUEEN *very lovingly; the* QUEEN *embracing him, and he her. She kneels, and makes show of protestation unto him. He takes her up, and declines his head upon her neck: lays him down upon a bank of flowers: she, seeing him asleep, leaves him. Anon comes in a fellow, takes off his crown, kisses it, and pours poison in the* KING's *ears, and exit. The* QUEEN *returns; finds the* KING *dead, and makes passionate action. The* POISONER, *with some two or three* MUTES, *comes in again, seeming to lament with her. The dead body is carried away. The* POISONER *wooes the* QUEEN *with gifts: she seems loath and unwilling awhile, but in the end accepts his love.*] [*Exeunt.*

OPH. What means this, my lord?

HAM. Marry, this is miching mallecho; it means mischief.

OPH. Belike this show imports the argument of the play. 150

[*Enter* PROLOGUE.]

HAM. We shall know by this fellow: the players cannot keep counsel; they'll tell all.

OPH. Will he tell us what this show meant?

HAM. Ay, or any show that you'll show him: be not you ashamed to show, he'll not shame to tell you what it means.

OPH. You are naught, you are naught: I'll mark the play.

PRO. For us, and for our tragedy,
Here stooping to your clemency, 160
We beg your hearing patiently. [*Exit.*

HAM. Is this a prologue, or the posy of a ring?

OPH. 'Tis brief, my lord.

HAM. As woman's love.

[*Enter two* PLAYERS, KING *and* QUEEN.]

P. KING. Full thirty times hath Phœbus' cart gone round 165
Neptune's salt wash and Tellus' orbèd ground,
And thirty dozen moons with borrow'd sheen
About the world have times twelve thirties been,
Since love our hearts and Hymen did our hands
Unite commutual in most sacred bands. 170

P. QUEEN. So many journeys may the sun and moon
Make us again count o'er ere love be done!
But, woe is me, you are so sick of late,
So far from cheer and from your former state,
That I distrust you. Yet, though I distrust, 175
Discomfort you, my lord, it nothing must:
For women's fear and love holds quantity;
In neither aught, or in extremity.
Now, what my love is, proof hath made you know;
And as my love is sized, my fear is so: 180
Where love is great, the littlest doubts are fear;
Where little fears grow great, great love grows there.

P. KING. 'Faith, I must leave thee, love, and shortly too;
My operant powers their functions leave to do:

132. **jig-maker,** man to write a jig, a song and dance afterpiece. 138. **sables,** black fur, i.e., mourning. The phrase means I'll wear mourning even if the Devil does, too. 143. **suffer . . . with,** endure not being remembered along with. 145. **hobby-horse is forgot,** the hobby-horse had been a popular figure in the May Day celebrations. It had gone out of style in Shakespeare's day, partly because the Puritans thought it a relic of heathen rites. The word was also a cant term for harlot. **s.d. dumb-show,** a play presented in pantomime; **makes . . . protestation,** acts out a formal declaration (of affection); **Anon,** presently. 147. **miching mallecho,** a sneaking (cowardly) crime. 149. **Belike,** perhaps; **imports the argument,** reveals the plot. 152. **counsel,** a secret. 157. **naught,** indecent. 162. **posy of a ring,** a short rime (usually sentimental) engraved on the inside of a ring. 166. **Tellus' . . . ground,** the round earth. Shakespeare made the verse of this play bombastic. 170. **commutual,** in mutual love. 175. **distrust,** am worried about you. 176. **Discomfort,** worry. 177-8. **For . . . extremity,** In women anxiety for a person's welfare is proportionate to the love. They feel neither love nor fear, or a great deal of both. 179. **proof,** experience. 181. **the littlest . . . fear,** the slightest cause for anxiety produces fear. 184. **My . . . do,** My physical powers cease to function.

And thou shalt live in this fair world behind, 185
Honour'd, beloved; and haply one as kind
For husband shalt thou—

P. QUEEN. O, confound the rest!
Such love must needs be treason in my breast:
In second husband let me be accurst! 189
None wed the second but who kill'd the first.

HAM. [*Aside*] Wormwood, wormwood.

P. QUEEN. The instances that second marriage move
Are base respects of thrift, but none of love:
A second time I kill my husband dead,
When second husband kisses me in bed. 195

P. KING. I do believe you think what now you speak;
But what we do determine oft we break.
Purpose is but the slave to memory,
Of violent birth, but poor validity:
Which now, like fruit unripe, sticks on the tree; 200
But fall, unshaken, when they mellow be.
Most necessary 'tis that we forget
To pay ourselves what to ourselves is debt:
What to ourselves in passion we propose,
The passion ending, doth the purpose lose.
The violence of either grief or joy 206
Their own enactures with themselves destroy:
Where joy most revels, grief doth most lament;
Grief joys, joy grieves, on slender accident.
This world is not for aye, nor 'tis not strange
That even our loves should with our fortunes change; 211
For 'tis a question left us yet to prove,
Whether love lead fortune, or else fortune love.
The great man down, you mark his favourite flies;
The poor advanced makes friends of enemies.
And hitherto doth love on fortune tend; 216
For who not needs shall never lack a friend,
And who in want a hollow friend doth try,
Directly seasons him his enemy.
But, orderly to end where I begun, 220
Our wills and fates do so contrary run
That our devices still are overthrown;
Our thoughts are ours, their ends none of our own:
So think thou wilt no second husband wed;
But die thy thoughts when thy first lord is dead. 225

P. QUEEN. Nor earth to me give food, nor heaven light!
Sport and repose lock from me day and night!
To desperation turn my trust and hope!
An anchor's cheer in prison be my scope! 229
Each opposite that blanks the face of joy
Meet what I would have well and it destroy!
Both here and hence pursue me lasting strife,
If, once a widow, ever I be wife!

HAM. If she should break it now!

P. KING. 'Tis deeply sworn. Sweet, leave me here awhile; 235
My spirits grow dull, and fain I would beguile
The tedious day with sleep. [*Sleeps.*

P. QUEEN. Sleep rock thy brain;
And never come mischance between us twain!
[*Exit.*

HAM. Madam, how like you this play?

QUEEN. The lady doth protest too much, methinks. 240

HAM. O, but she'll keep her word.

KING. Have you heard the argument? Is there no offence in 't?

HAM. No, no, they do but jest, poison in jest; no offence i' the world.

KING. What do you call the play? 246

HAM. The Mouse-trap. Marry, how? Tropically. This play is the image of a murder done in Vienna: Gonzago is the duke's name; his wife, Baptista: you shall see anon; 't is a knavish piece of work: but what o' 250 that? your majesty and we that have free souls, it touches us not: let the galled jade wince, our withers are unwrung.

185. **behind**, i.e., after my death. 187. **confound the rest**, strike dumb the rest [that you were going to say]. 192. **instances**, motives; **move**, induce. 193. **respects**, considerations. 199. **validity**, strength. 202-3. **Most necessary . . . debt**, i.e., it is inevitable that we should find it easy to break a promise (pay a debt) made to ourselves. 207. **enactures**, impulses to action. 208. **Where**, in persons in whom. 209. **on slender accident**, because of trifling incidents. 211. **our loves**, love others have for us. 213. **Whether . . . love**, whether the regard of our fellows brings worldly success or vice versa. 216. **hitherto**, up to now. 219. **seasons . . . enemy**, ripens him into an enemy.

220. **orderly**, properly; **where**, with the point with which. 222. **devices still**, our plans always. 224. **think thou**, though you think. 225. **die thy thoughts**, your resolution will die. 226. **Nor . . . food**, may earth give me no food. 229. **anchor's**, anchorite's, hermit's; **cheer**, fare. 230. **opposite that blanks**, adverse event that blots out. 231. **would have well**, should like. 232. **here and hence**, this world and the next. 234. **If**, what if. 236. **beguile**, while away. 242. **argument**, plot. 248. **Tropically**, figuratively. 248. **image**, representation. 250. **anon**, presently. 252. **free**, i.e., from guilt. 253. **galled jade**, old broken down horse covered with sores from saddle or harness; **withers**, shoulder bones of a horse; **unwrung**, unchafed.

[*Enter* LUCIANUS.]

This is one Lucianus, nephew to the king.

OPH. You are as good as a chorus, my lord. 255

HAM. I could interpret between you and your love, if I could see the puppets dallying.

OPH. You are keen, my lord, you are keen.

HAM. It would cost you a groaning to take off my edge. 260

OPH. Still better, and worse.

HAM. So you must take your husbands. Begin, murderer; pox, leave thy damnable faces, and begin. Come: "the croaking raven doth bellow for revenge." 265

LUC. Thoughts black, hands apt, drugs fit, and time agreeing;
Confederate season, else no creature seeing;
Thou mixture rank, of midnight weeds collected,
With Hecate's ban thrice blasted, thrice infected,
Thy natural magic and dire property, 270
On wholesome life usurp immediately.

[*Pours the poison into the sleeper's ears.*

HAM. He poisons him i' the garden for 's estate. His name's Gonzago: the story is extant, and writ in choice Italian: you shall see anon how the murderer gets the love of Gonzago's wife. 275

OPH. The king rises.

HAM. What, frighted with false fire!

QUEEN. How fares my lord?

POL. Give o'er the play.

KING. Give me some light: away! 280

ALL. Lights, lights, lights!

[*Exeunt all but* HAMLET *and* HORATIO.

HAM. Why, let the stricken deer go weep,
The hart ungallèd play;
For some must watch, while some must sleep:
So runs the world away. 285
Would not this, sir, and a forest of feathers—if the rest of my fortunes turn Turk with me—with two Provincial roses on my razed shoes, get me a fellowship in a cry of players, sir?

HOR. Half a share. 290

HAM. A whole one, I.
For thou dost know, O Damon dear,
This realm dismantled was
Of Jove himself; and now reigns here
A very, very—pajock. 295

HOR. You might have rhymed.

HAM. O good Horatio, I'll take the ghost's word for a thousand pound. Didst perceive?

HOR. Very well, my lord.

HAM. Upon the talk of the poisoning? 300

HOR. I did very well note him.

HAM. Ah, ha! Come, some music! come, the recorders!
For if the king like not the comedy, 304
Why then, belike, he likes it not, perdy.
Come, some music!

[*Re-enter* ROSENCRANTZ *and* GUILDENSTERN.]

GUIL. Good my lord, vouchsafe me a word with you.

HAM. Sir, a whole history.

GUIL. The king, sir,— 310

HAM. Ay, sir, what of him?

GUIL. Is in his retirement marvellous distempered.

HAM. With drink, sir?

GUIL. No, my lord, rather with choler. 315

HAM. Your wisdom should show itself more richer to signify this to his doctor; for, for me to put him to his purgation would perhaps plunge him into far more choler. 319

GUIL. Good my lord, put your discourse into some frame and start not so wildly from my affair.

HAM. I am tame, sir: pronounce.

GUIL. The queen, your mother, in most great affliction of spirit, hath sent me to you.

HAM. You are welcome. 325

256. **interpret,** like an actor who explained the action of puppets. 258. **keen,** bitter, also "sexually aroused." 263. **pox,** plague take it. 267. **Confederate season,** the time co-operating (with the murderer); **else no creature,** i.e., except time. 269. **Hecate,** goddess of witchcraft; **ban,** curse. 270. **dire property,** harmful quality. 271. **usurp,** take harmful effect. 273. **His,** i.e., the murdered man's. 277. **false fire,** discharge of a blank cartridge. 279. **Give o'er,** stop. 282. **stricken . . . weep,** an allusion to the notion that a wounded deer goes off to weep and die alone. 284. **watch,** stay awake, i.e., those whose sense of guilt keeps them awake. 286. **this,** i.e., manner of declamation; **feathers,** i.e., that often decorated an actor's hat. 287. **turn Turk,** prove false, like a Christian who turns Mohammedan. 288. **Provincial roses,** i.e., a variety of large rose, here the rosettes on an actor's shoes; **razed,** ornamented by open work. 289. **cry,** pack (of hounds). 290. **Half a share,** Shakespeare's company divided the ownership among the actors, the less important receiving only half a share. 292. **Damon,** the Greeks Damon and Pythias were ideally faithful friends. 293. **dismantled,** shorn of adornment. 294. **Jove,** i.e., his father. 295. **pajock,** peacock, thought to be cruel and lustful. 303. **recorders,** musical instruments resembling clarinets. 305. **belike,** evidently; **perdy,** corruption of "per dieu," a mild oath about = in truth. 312. **distempered,** ill. 315. **choler,** a bilious attack with a play on the meaning "anger." 316. **should,** would. 317. **to signify,** by reporting. 321. **frame,** logical form.

GUIL. Nay, good my lord, this courtesy is not of the right breed. If it shall please you to make me a wholesome answer, I will do your mother's commandment: if not, your pardon and my return shall be the end of my business.

HAM. Sir, I cannot. 331

GUIL. What, my lord?

HAM. Make you a wholesome answer; my wit's diseased: but, sir, such answer as I can make, you shall command; or, rather, as you say, my mother: therefore no more, but to the matter: my mother, you say,—

ROS. Then thus she says; your behaviour hath struck her into amazement and admiration. 339

HAM. O wonderful son, that can so astonish a mother! But is there no sequel at the heels of this mother's admiration? Impart.

ROS. She desires to speak with you in her closet, ere you go to bed.

HAM. We shall obey, were she ten times our mother. Have you any further trade with us?

ROS. My lord, you once did love me.

HAM. So do I still, by these pickers and stealers. 349

ROS. Good my lord, what is your cause of distemper? you do, surely, bar the door upon your own liberty, if you deny your griefs to your friend.

HAM. Sir, I lack advancement.

ROS. How can that be, when you have the voice of the king himself for your succession in Denmark?

HAM. Ay, sir, but "While the grass grows,"—the proverb is something musty. 359

[*Re-enter* PLAYERS *with recorders.*]

O, the recorders! let me see one. To withdraw with you:—why do you go about to recover the wind of me, as if you would drive me into a toil?

GUIL. O, my lord, if my duty be too bold, my love is too unmannerly. 364

HAM. I do not well understand that. Will you play upon this pipe?

GUIL. My lord, I cannot.

HAM. I pray you.

GUIL. Believe me, I cannot.

HAM. I do beseech you. 370

GUIL. I know no touch of it, my lord.

HAM. 'Tis as easy as lying: govern these ventages with your fingers and thumb, give it breath with your mouth, and it will discourse most eloquent music. Look you, these are the stops.

GUIL. But these cannot I command to any utterance of harmony; I have not the skill. 378

HAM. Why, look you now, how unworthy a thing you make of me! You would play upon me; you would seem to know my stops; you would pluck out the heart of my mystery; you would sound me from my lowest note to the top of my compass: and there is much music, excellent voice, in this little organ; yet cannot you make it speak. 'Sblood, do you think I am easier to be played on than a pipe? Call me what instrument you will, though you can fret me, yet you cannot play upon me.

[*Enter* POLONIUS.]

God bless you, sir! 390

POL. My lord, the queen would speak with you, and presently.

HAM. Do you see yonder cloud that's almost in shape of a camel?

POL. By the mass, and 'tis like a camel, indeed.

HAM. Methinks it is like a weasel.

POL. It is backed like a weasel.

HAM. Or like a whale?

POL. Very like a whale. 399

HAM. Then I will come to my mother by and by. They fool me to the top of my bent. I will come by and by.

POL. I will say so.

HAM. By and by is easily said.

[*Exit* POLONIUS.]

328. **wholesome,** sensible. 334. **wit,** intelligence. 339. **admiration,** astonishment. 343. **closet,** private sitting room. 349. **pickers and stealers,** hands, referring to the phrase in the catechism of the English Church, "To keep my hands from picking and stealing." 352. **deny,** refuse to impart. 356. **voice,** vote, promise. 358. **"While . . . grows,"** the last part of this proverb is, "the silly horse starves." 360-1. **withdraw,** speak in private. 362. **recover . . . me,** get me to windward, a hunting phrase meaning to get the prey between the hunter and the wind, and so avoid giving it the scent of the pursuer. 363. **toil,** net. 363-4. **if . . . unmannerly,** if I have been officious in doing my duty by you it is my love for you that is to blame. 371. **touch,** any act of the hands in playing an instrument. 373. **ventages,** stops on the recorder. 384. **compass,** the range of a voice. 384. **organ,** musical instrument, here the recorder. 388. **fret,** pun (1) irritate, (2) finger the frets on a stringed instrument. 392. **presently,** at once. 401. **fool,** treat me as though I were a fool (madman); **top of my bent,** limit of my endurance, i.e., extent to which a bow can be bent.

Leave me, friends.

[*Exeunt all but* HAMLET.]

'Tis now the very witching time of night,
When churchyards yawn and hell itself breathes out
Contagion to this world: now could I drink hot blood,
And do such bitter business as the day
Would quake to look on. Soft! now to my mother. 410
O heart, lose not thy nature; let not ever
The soul of Nero enter this firm bosom:
Let me be cruel, not unnatural:
I will speak daggers to her, but use none; 414
My tongue and soul in this be hypocrites;
How in my words soever she be shent,
To give them seals never, my soul, consent!

[*Exit.*

SCENE III. *A room in the castle.*

[*Enter* KING, ROSENCRANTZ, *and* GUILDENSTERN.]

KING. I like him not, nor stands it safe with us
To let his madness range. Therefore prepare you;
I your commission will forthwith dispatch,
And he to England shall along with you:
The terms of our estate may not endure 5
Hazard so near us as doth hourly grow
Out of his lunacies.

GUIL. We will ourselves provide:
Most holy and religious fear it is
To keep those many many bodies safe
That live and feed upon your majesty. 10

ROS. The single and peculiar life is bound,
With all the strength and armour of the mind,
To keep itself from noyance; but much more
That spirit upon whose weal depend and rest
The lives of many. The cease of majesty 15
Dies not alone; but, like a gulf, doth draw
What's near it with it: it is a massy wheel,
Fix'd on the summit of the highest mount,
To whose huge spokes ten thousand lesser things
Are mortised and adjoin'd; which, when it falls, 20
Each small annexment, petty consequence,
Attends the boisterous ruin. Never alone
Did the king sigh, but with a general groan.

KING. Arm you, I pray you, to this speedy voyage;
For we will fetters put upon this fear, 25
Which now goes too free-footed.

ROS. / GUIL. We will haste us.

[*Exeunt* ROSENCRANTZ *and* GUILDENSTERN.

[*Enter* POLONIUS.]

POL. My lord, he's going to his mother's closet:
Behind the arras I'll convey myself,
To hear the process; I'll warrant she'll tax him home:
And, as you said, and wisely was it said, 30
'Tis meet that some more audience than a mother,
Since nature make them partial, should o'er-hear
The speech, of vantage. Fare you well, my liege:
I'll call upon you ere you go to bed,
And tell you what I know.

KING. Thanks, dear my lord. 35

[*Exit* POLONIUS.]

O, my offence is rank, it smells to heaven;
It hath the primal eldest curse upon 't,
A brother's murder. Pray can I not,
Though inclination be as sharp as will:
My stronger guilt defeats my strong intent; 40
And, like a man to double business bound,
I stand in pause where I shall first begin,
And both neglect. What if this cursèd hand
Were thicker than itself with brother's blood,
Is there not rain enough in the sweet heavens
To wash it white as snow? Whereto serves mercy 46
But to confront the visage of offence?

406. **witching time**, time when witches are most about, i.e., midnight. 412. **Nero**, the Roman Emperor who murdered his mother. 415. **be hypocrites**, give a false impression (of my real feelings. 416. **shent**, rebuked. 417. **To . . . seals**, i.e., confirm them with action. Scene iii: 1. **him**, i.e., his actions. 2. **range**, be at large. 3. **dispatch**, draw up. 5. **terms . . . estate**, circumstances surrounding my office [of King]. 7. **provide**, make ready. 11. **single and peculiar**, individual and private. 13. **noyance**, harm. 15. **cease**, death; **majesty**, a king. 16. **gulf**, whirlpool. 20. **mortised**, firmly attached. 22. **boisterous ruin**, thunderous downfall.

23. **general**, i.e., of all society. 24. **Arm**, prepare. 28. **convey**, place secretly. 29. **process**, course of events, what is going on; **tax him home**, censure him severely. 31. **meet**, fitting. 33. **of vantage**, besides. 37. **primal . . . curse**, the curse put upon Cain, the first fratricide. 39. **inclination . . . will**, desire [to pray] be as strong as my determination [to do so]. 41. **double . . . bound**; under obligation to do two things at the same time. 42. **stand . . . where**, pause to consider which. 47. **confront**, **oppose** face to face.

And what's in prayer but this two-fold force,
To be forestallèd ere we come to fall,
Or pardon'd being down? Then I'll look up;
My fault is past. But, O, what form of prayer
Can serve my turn? "Forgive me my foul murder"? 52
That cannot be: since I am still possess'd
Of those effects for which I did the murder,
My crown, mine own ambition and my queen. 55
May one be pardon'd and retain the offence?
In the corrupted currents of this world
Offence's gilded hand may shove by justice,
And oft 'tis seen the wicked prize itself
Buys out the law: but 'tis not so above; 60
There is no shuffling, there the action lies
In his true nature; and we ourselves compell'd,
Even to the teeth and forehead of our faults,
To give in evidence. What then? what rests?
Try what repentance can: what can it not? 65
Yet what can it when one can not repent?
O wretched state! O bosom black as death!
O limèd soul, that, struggling to be free,
Art more engaged! Help, angels! Make assay!
Bow, stubborn knees; and, heart with strings of steel, 70
Be soft as sinews of the new-born babe!
All may be well. [*Retires and kneels.*]

[*Enter* HAMLET.]

HAM. Now might I do it pat, now he is praying;
And now I'll do 't. And so he goes to heaven;
And so am I revenged. That would be scann'd: 75
A villain kills my father; and for that,
I, his sole son, do this same villain send
To heaven.
O, this is hire and salary, not revenge.
He took my father grossly, full of bread; 80
With all his crimes broad blown, as flush as May;
And how his audit stands who knows save heaven?
But in our circumstance and course of thought,
'Tis heavy with him: and am I then revenged,
To take him in the purging of his soul, 85
When he is fit and season'd for his passage?
No!
Up, sword; and know thou a more horrid hent:
When he is drunk asleep, or in his rage,
Or in the incestuous pleasure of his bed; 90
At gaming, swearing, or about some act
That has no relish of salvation in 't;
Then trip him, that his heels may kick at heaven,
And that his soul may be as damn'd and black
As hell, whereto it goes. My mother stays: 95
This physic but prolongs thy sickly days.
[*Exit.*]

KING. [*Rising*] My words fly up, my thoughts remain below:
Words without thoughts never to heaven go.
[*Exit.*]

SCENE IV. *The* QUEEN'S *closet.*

[*Enter* QUEEN *and* POLONIUS.]

POL. He will come straight. Look you lay home to him:
Tell him his pranks have been too broad to bear with,
And that your grace hath screen'd and stood between
Much heat and him. I'll sconce me even here.
Pray you, be round with him. 5

HAM. [*Within*] Mother, mother, mother!

QUEEN. I'll warrant you,
Fear me not: withdraw, I hear him coming.
[POLONIUS *hides behind the arras.*

[*Enter* HAMLET.]

HAM. Now, mother, what's the matter?

QUEEN. Hamlet, thou hast thy father much offended.

49. **forestalled,** prevented. 54. **effects,** intended results. 58. **gilded,** i.e., lined with gold; **shove by,** push aside. 59-60. **wicked . . . the law,** the money gained through crime may be used to corrupt the judge. 61. **shuffling,** trickery; **action lies,** a plea is made in accordance with. 62. his, its. 63. **teeth . . . faults,** i.e., face to face with our sins (which will appear in court against us). 64. **rests,** remains [for me to do]. 68. **limed,** caught as a bird with birdlime. 69. **Make assay,** i.e., I will make the attempt. 75. **would be scann'd,** should be looked into. 79. **hire and salary,** i.e., like paying him for the deed. 80. **grossly,** unpurified by repentance; **full of bread.** cf. Ezekiel XVI, 49: "This was the iniquity . . . of Sodom, pride, fullness of bread." 81. **crimes broad blown,** sins in full flower; **flush,** lusty. 82. **audit,** i.e., official appraisal of his account. 83. **in our . . . thought,** i.e., according to our earthly ideas. 84. **'Tis . . . him,** things go hard with him. 85. **take,** i.e., kill. 86. **season'd,** prepared (by having sought forgiveness for his sins). 88. **hent,** seizure, i.e., occasion for seizure. 89. **rage,** sexual passion. 92. **relish,** trace. 93. **heels . . . heaven,** i.e., fall headfirst to Hell. 95. **stays,** waits (for me). 96. **physic,** i.e., purgation (through prayer); **sickly,** evil. **Scene iv:** 1. **straight,** right away; **lay home,** speak plain truth. 2. **broad,** unrestrained. 4. **heat,** anger of the King; **sconce,** screen, conceal. 5. **round,** downright. 6. **I'll warrant you,** rest assured that I will.

HAM. Mother, you have my father much offended. 10

QUEEN. Come, come, you answer with an idle tongue.

HAM. Go, go, you question with a wicked tongue.

QUEEN. Why, how now, Hamlet!

HAM. What's the matter now?

QUEEN. Have you forgot me?

HAM. No, by the rood, not so:
You are the queen, your husband's brother's wife; 15
And—would it were not so!—you are my mother.

QUEEN. Nay, then, I'll set those to you that can speak.

HAM. Come, come, and sit you down; you shall not budge;
You go not till I set you up a glass
Where you may see the inmost part of you. 20

QUEEN. What wilt thou do? thou wilt not murder me?
Help, help, ho!

POL. [*Behind*] What, ho! help, help, help!

HAM. [*Drawing*] How now! a rat? Dead, for a ducat, dead!

[*Makes a pass through the arras.*

POL. [*Behind*] O, I am slain!

[*Falls and dies.*

QUEEN. O me, what hast thou done?

HAM. Nay, I know not:
Is it the king? 26

QUEEN. O, what a rash and bloody deed is this!

HAM. A bloody deed! almost as bad, good mother,
As kill a king, and marry with his brother.

QUEEN. As kill a king!

HAM. Ay, lady, 'twas my word. 30
[*Lifts up the arras and discovers* POLONIUS.]
Thou wretched, rash, intruding fool, farewell!
I took thee for thy better: take thy fortune;
Thou find'st to be too busy is some danger.
Leave wringing of your hands: peace! sit you down,
And let me wring your heart; for so I shall,
If it be made of penetrable stuff, 36
If damnèd custom have not brass'd it so
That it be proof and bulwark against sense.

QUEEN. What have I done, that thou darest wag thy tongue
In noise so rude against me?

HAM. Such an act 40
That blurs the grace and blush of modesty,
Calls virtue hypocrite, takes off the rose
From the fair forehead of an innocent love
And sets a blister there, makes marriage-vows
As false as dicers' oaths: O, such a deed 45
As from the body of contraction plucks
The very soul, and sweet religion makes
A rhapsody of words: heaven's face doth glow;
Yea, this solidity and compound mass,
With tristful visage, as against the doom, 50
Is thought-sick at the act.

QUEEN. Ay me, what act,
That roars so loud, and thunders in the index?

HAM. Look here, upon this picture, and on this.
The counterfeit presentment of two brothers.
See, what a grace was seated on this brow; 55
Hyperion's curls; the front of Jove himself;
An eye like Mars, to threaten and command;
A station like the herald Mercury
New-lighted on a heaven-kissing hill;
A combination and a form indeed, 60
Where every god did seem to set his seal,
To give the world assurance of a man:
This was your husband. Look you now, what follows:
Here is your husband; like a mildew'd ear,
Blasting his wholesome brother. Have you eyes? 65
Could you on this fair mountain leave to feed,
And batten on this moor? Ha! have you eyes?
You cannot call it love; for at your age
The hey-day in the blood is tame, it's humble,

11. **idle**, silly. 14. **me**, who I am; **rood**, holy cross. 17. **that can speak**, i.e., as you need to be spoken to. 23. **Dead, for a ducat**, I'll wager a ducat that he is dead. 33. **busy**, prying. 37. **brass'd**, covered with brass, i.e., impenetrable. 38. **proof**, armor; **sense**, both reason and feeling. 42. **rose**, i.e., the adornment, beauty. 44. **blister**, women guilty of adultery were branded on the forehead. 46. **body of contraction**, the contents of the marriage contract. 48. **rhapsody**, jumble; **glow**, blush (with shame). 49. **solidity . . . mass**, i.e., this solid earth compounded of various elements. 50. **tristful**, sorrowful; **against the doom**, ready for doomsday. 52. **index**, table of contents. 54. **counterfeit presentment**, painted portrait. 56. **Hyperion**, a Greek sun god; **front**, forehead. 58. **station**, standing position, i.e., carriage. 59. **New-lighted**, just alighted. 62. **assurance of a man**, guarantee that this is a man. 65. **Blasting . . . brother**, blighting the healthy ear next it. 66. **leave to feed**, stop feeding. 67. **batten**, stuff yourself gluttonously. 69. **hey-day . . . blood**, youthful passion; **tame**, under control.

And waits upon the judgement: and what judgement 70
Would step from this to this? Sense, sure, you have,
Else could you not have motion; but sure, that sense
Is apoplex'd; for madness would not err,
Nor sense to ecstasy was ne'er so thrall'd
But it reserved some quantity of choice, 75
To serve in such a difference. What devil was 't
That thus hath cozen'd you at hoodman-blind?
Eyes without feeling, feeling without sight,
Ears without hands or eyes, smelling sans all,
Or but a sickly part of one true sense 80
Could not so mope.
O shame! where is thy blush? Rebellious hell,
If thou canst mutine in a matron's bones,
To flaming youth let virtue be as wax,
And melt in her own fire: proclaim no shame
When the compulsive ardour gives the charge, 86
Since frost itself as actively doth burn
And reason pandars will.

QUEEN. O Hamlet, speak no more:
Thou turn'st mine eyes into my very soul;
And there I see such black and grainèd spots
As will not leave their tinct.

HAM. Nay, but to live 91
In the rank sweat of an enseamèd bed,
Stew'd in corruption, honeying and making love
Over the nasty sty,—

QUEEN. O, speak to me no more;
These words, like daggers, enter in mine ears; 95
No more, sweet Hamlet!

HAM. A murderer and a villain;
A slave that is not twentieth part the tithe
Of your precedent lord; a vice of kings;
A cutpurse of the empire and the rule,
That from a shelf the precious diadem stole, 100
And put it in his pocket!

QUEEN. No more!

HAM. A king of shreds and patches,—

[*Enter* GHOST.]

Save me, and hover o'er me with your wings,
You heavenly guards! What would your gracious figure?

QUEEN. Alas, he's mad! 105

HAM. Do you not come your tardy son to chide,
That, lapsed in time and passion, lets go by
The important acting of your dread command?
O, say!

GHOST. Do not forget: this visitation 110
Is but to whet thy almost blunted purpose.
But, look, amazement on thy mother sits:
O, step between her and her fighting soul:
Conceit in weakest bodies strongest works:
Speak to her, Hamlet.

HAM. How is it with you, lady? 115

QUEEN. Alas, how is 't with you,
That you do bend your eye on vacancy
And with the incorporal air do hold discourse?
Forth at your eyes your spirits wildly peep;
And, as the sleeping soldiers in the alarm, 120
Your bedded hairs, like life in excrements,
Start up, and stand an end. O gentle son,
Upon the heat and flame of thy distemper
Sprinkle cool patience. Whereon do you look?

HAM. On him, on him! Look you, how pale he glares! 125
His form and cause conjoin'd, preaching to stones,
Would make them capable. Do not look upon me;
Lest with this piteous action you convert
My stern effects: then what I have to do
Will want true colour; tears perchance for blood. 130

QUEEN. To whom do you speak this?

70. **waits upon**, is subject to. 71. **Sense**, the five senses. 72. **motion**, impulse. 73. **apoplex'd**, paralyzed; **err**, lead you to make this mistake. 74. **ecstasy**, insanity; **thrall'd**, enslaved. 75. **quantity of choice**, ability to choose. 77. **cozen'd**, cheated; **hoodman-blind**, blindman's buff. 79. **sans all**, without any of the other senses. 81. **so mope**, be so dull. 83. **mutine**, rebel. 85. **her**, i.e., youth's. 86. **compulsive**, compelling; **gives the charge**, makes the attack. 88. **will**, desire. 90. **grained**, dyed in unfailing colors. 91. **leave their tinct**, lose their color. 92. **enseamed**, covered with grease. 97. **is not**, i.e., is not worth; **tithe**, tenth. 98. **precedent lord**, i.e., former husband; **vice of**, clown among. The Vice was the clown of the morality plays. 99. **cutpurse**, thief. 102. **shreds and patches**, the conventional costume of the Vice. 107. **lapsed . . . passion**, having let time and the strength of his resolution slip away. 112. **amazement**, distraction. 113. **fighting soul**, i.e., the conflict in her soul. 114. **Conceit**, imagination. 120. **in the alarm**, i.e., when called to arms. 121. **bedded**, laid smooth and flat; **excrements**, outgrowths. 123. **distemper**, perturbation. 127. **capable**, i.e., of emotion. 128-9. **convert . . . effects**, turn me from my stern course of action. 130. **want true colour**, lose its proper character.

HAM. Do you see nothing there?
QUEEN. Nothing at all; yet all that is I see.
HAM. Nor did you nothing hear?
QUEEN. No, nothing but ourselves.
HAM. Why, look you there! look, how it steals away!
My father, in his habit as he lived! 135
Look, where he goes, even now, out at the portal! [*Exit* GHOST.
QUEEN. This is the very coinage of your brain:
This bodiless creation ecstasy
Is very cunning in.
HAM. Ecstasy!
My pulse, as yours, doth temperately keep time, 140
And makes as healthful music: it is not madness
That I have utter'd: bring me to the test,
And I the matter will re-word, which madness
Would gambol from. Mother, for love of grace,
Lay not that flattering unction to your soul,
That not your trespass, but my madness speaks: 146
It will but skin and film the ulcerous place,
Whiles rank corruption, mining all within,
Infects unseen. Confess yourself to heaven;
Repent what's past; avoid what is to come; 150
And do not spread the compost on the weeds,
To make them ranker. Forgive me this my virtue;
For in the fatness of these pursy times
Virtue itself of vice must pardon beg,
Yea, curb and woo for leave to do him good.
QUEEN. O Hamlet, thou hast cleft my heart in twain. 156
HAM. O, throw away the worser part of it,
And live the purer with the other half.
Good night: but go not to mine uncle's bed;
Assume a virtue, if you have it not. 160
That monster, custom, who all sense doth eat,
Of habits devil, is angel yet in this,
That to the use of actions fair and good
He likewise gives a frock or livery,
That aptly is put on. Refrain to-night, 165
And that shall lend a kind of easiness
To the next abstinence: the next more easy;
For use almost can change the stamp of nature,
And either curb the devil, or throw him out
With wondrous potency. Once more, good night: 170
And when you are desirous to be bless'd,
I'll blessing beg of you. For this same lord,
[*Pointing to* POLONIUS.]
I do repent: but heaven hath pleased it so,
To punish me with this and this with me,
That I must be their scourge and minister.
I will bestow him, and will answer well 176
The death I gave him. So, again, good night.
I must be cruel, only to be kind:
Thus bad begins and worse remains behind.
One word more, good lady.
QUEEN. What shall I do? 180
HAM. Not this, by no means, that I bid you do:
Let the bloat king tempt you again to bed;
Pinch wanton on your cheek; call you his mouse;
And let him, for a pair of reechy kisses,
Or paddling in your neck with his damn'd fingers, 185
Make you to ravel all this matter out,
That I essentially am not in madness,
But mad in craft. 'Twere good you let him know;
For who, that's but a queen, fair, sober, wise,
Would from a paddock, from a bat, a gib, 190
Such dear concernings hide? who would do so?
No, in despite of sense and secrecy,
Unpeg the basket on the house's top,
Let the birds fly, and, like the famous ape
To try conclusions, in the basket creep, 195
And break your own neck down.

135. **in . . . lived**, in the clothes he wore when alive. 138-9. **bodiless . . . cunning in**, the cunning which characterizes madness is very skilful in creating something out of nothing. 140. **temperately keep time**, beat calmly. 145. **flattering unction**, soothing salve. 150. **avoid . . . come**, avoid doing wrong in the future. 153. **fatness**, grossness; **pursy**, disgustingly corpulent. 155. **curb**, bow the knee. 161. **all sense doth eat**, destroys all sense of right and wrong. 162. **Of habits devil**, the wicked attendant on habits. 165. **aptly is put on**, is easily donned. 166. **shall**, is certain to. 168. **use**, habit. 171. **bless'd**, i.e., by Heaven, repentant. 174. **this**, the dead man, i.e., the murder. 175. **their**, i. e., Heaven's. 176. **bestow**, dispose of; **answer well**, willingly be held responsible for. 181. **Not . . . do**, i.e., at least avoid doing the things I bid you not to do, namely. 182. **bloat**, bloated (with debauchery). 184. **reechy**, filthy. 186. **ravel . . . out**, unravel, give away. 187. **essentially**, in my real nature. 189. **that's but**, except. 190. **paddock**, toad; **gib**, tomcat. 191. **dear concernings**, matters of such deep importance. 193-4. **Unpeg . . . ape**, the reference is to the story of an ape who opened a basket of birds on the house top and, after watching them fly away one by one, tried to imitate them and jumped to his death. 195. **try conclusions**, repeat the experiment.

QUEEN. Be thou assured, if words be made of breath,
And breath of life, I have no life to breathe
What thou hast said to me.

HAM. I must to England; you know that?

QUEEN. Alack, 200
I had forgot: 'tis so concluded on.

HAM. There's letters seal'd: and my two schoolfellows,
Whom I will trust as I will adders fang'd,
They bear the mandate; they must sweep my way,
And marshal me to knavery. Let it work, 205
For 'tis the sport to have the enginer
Hoist with his own petar: and 't shall go hard
But I will delve one yard below their mines,
And blow them at the moon: O, 'tis most sweet,
When in one line two crafts directly meet. 210
This man shall set me packing:
I'll lug the guts into the neighbour room.
Mother, good night. Indeed this counsellor
Is now most still, most secret and most grave,
Who was in life a foolish prating knave. 215
Come, sir, to draw toward an end with you.
Good night, mother.

[*Exeunt severally;* HAMLET *dragging in Polonius.*

ACT IV

SCENE I. *A room in the castle.*

[*Enter* KING, QUEEN, ROSENCRANTZ, *and* GUILDENSTERN.]

KING. There's matter in these sighs, these profound heaves:
You must translate: 'tis fit we understand them.
Where is your son?

QUEEN. Bestow this place on us a little while.

[*Exeunt* ROSENCRANTZ *and* GUILDENSTERN.]

Ah, mine own lord, what have I seen to-night! 5

KING. What, Gertrude? How does Hamlet?

QUEEN. Mad as the sea and wind, when both contend
Which is the mightier: in his lawless fit,
Behind the arras hearing something stir,
Whips out his rapier, cries, "A rat, a rat!" 10
And, in this brainish apprehension, kills
The unseen good old man.

KING. O heavy deed!
It had been so with us, had we been there:
His liberty is full of threats to all;
To you yourself, to us, to every one. 15
Alas, how shall this bloody deed be answer'd?
It will be laid to us, whose providence
Should have kept short, restrain'd and out of haunt,
This mad young man: but so much was our love,
We would not understand what was most fit;
But, like the owner of a foul disease, 21
To keep it from divulging, let it feed
Even on the pith of life. Where is he gone?

QUEEN. To draw apart the body he hath kill'd:
O'er whom his very madness, like some ore
Among a mineral of metals base, 26
Shows itself pure; he weeps for what is done.

KING. O Gertrude, come away!
The sun no sooner shall the mountains touch,
But we will ship him hence: and this vile deed
We must, with all our majesty and skill, 31
Both countenance and excuse. Ho, Guildenstern!

[*Re-enter* ROSENCRANTZ *and* GUILDENSTERN.]

Friends both, go join you with some further aid:
Hamlet in madness hath Polonius slain,
And from his mother's closet hath he dragg'd him: 35

201. **concluded on,** decided. 204. **bear the mandate,** have the instructions; **sweep my way,** clear my path. 205. **knavery,** the evil to be done to Hamlet. 206. **'tis the sport,** it will be my game; **enginer,** inventor. 207. **Hoist,** blown up; **petar,** bomb. 207-8. **'t shall go hard But,** about = I miss my guess if I do not. 210. **crafts,** crafty schemes. 211. **packing,** a quibble on three meanings: (1) loading, (2) plotting, (3) hurrying off. 212. **neighbour,** next. Act IV, Scene i: 1. **matter,** serious meaning. 2. **translate,** explain. 4. **Bestow . . . us,** i.e., leave us. 11. **brainish apprehension,** brainsick delusion. 12. **heavy,** hard to bear. 13. **us,** i.e., me, the King. 14. **His liberty,** his being at liberty. 16. **answer'd,** explained away. 17. **providence,** foresight. 18. **short,** on short tether; **haunt,** contact with other people. 22. **divulging,** coming to light. 24. **draw apart,** take away. 26. **mineral,** mine. 33. **join you with,** procure.

Go seek him out; speak fair, and bring the body
Into the chapel. I pray you, haste in this.
[*Exeunt* ROSENCRANTZ *and* GUILDENSTERN.
Come, Gertrude, we'll call up our wisest friends;
And let them know, both what we mean to do,
And what's untimely done so, haply, slander 40
Whose whisper o'er the world's diameter,
As level as the cannon to his blank,
Transports his poison'd shot, may miss our name,
And hit the woundless air. O, come away!
My soul is full of discord and dismay.
[*Exeunt.*

SCENE II. *Another room in the castle.*

[*Enter* HAMLET.]

HAM. Safely stowed.

ROS. / GUIL. [*Within*] Hamlet! Lord Hamlet!

HAM. But soft, what noise? who calls on Hamlet? O, here they come.

[*Enter* ROSENCRANTZ *and* GUILDENSTERN.]

ROS. What have you done, my lord, with the dead body? 5

HAM. Compounded it with dust, whereto 'tis kin.

ROS. Tell us where 'tis, that we may take it thence
And bear it to the chapel.

HAM. Do not believe it.

ROS. Believe what? 10

HAM. That I can keep your counsel and not mine own. Besides, to be demanded of a sponge! what replication should be made by the son of a king? 14

ROS. Take you me for a sponge, my lord?

HAM. Ay, sir, that soaks up the king's countenance, his rewards, his authorities. But such officers do the king best service in the end: he keeps them, like an ape, in the corner of his jaw; first mouthed, to be last swallowed: when he needs what you have gleaned, it is but squeezing you, and, sponge, you shall be dry again. 23

ROS. I understand you not, my lord.

HAM. I am glad of it: a knavish speech sleeps in a foolish ear.

ROS. My lord, you must tell us where the body is, and go with us to the king. 28

HAM. The body is with the king, but the king is not with the body. The king is a thing—

GUIL. A thing, my lord! 31

HAM. Of nothing: bring me to him. Hide fox, and all after. [*Exeunt.*

SCENE III. *Another room in the castle.*

[*Enter* KING, *attended.*]

KING. I have sent to seek him, and to find the body.
How dangerous is it that this man goes loose!
Yet must not we put the strong law on him:
He's loved of the distracted multitude,
Who like not in their judgement, but their eyes; 5
And where 'tis so, the offender's scourge is weigh'd,
But never the offence. To bear all smooth and even,
This sudden sending him away must seem
Deliberate pause: diseases desperate grown
By desperate appliance are relieved, 10
Or not at all.

[*Enter* ROSENCRANTZ.]

How now! what hath befall'n?

ROS. Where the dead body is bestow'd, my lord,
We cannot get from him.

KING. But where is he?

ROS. Without, my lord; guarded, to know your pleasure.

KING. Bring him before us. 15

ROS. Ho, Guildenstern! bring in my lord.

[*Enter* HAMLET *and* GUILDENSTERN.]

36. **fair,** civilly, tactfully. 42. **level,** straight; **blank,** the center of the target. 44. **woundless,** invulnerable. **Scene ii:** 1. **stowed,** disposed of. 6. **Compounded,** mixed. 11. **counsel,** secrets, i.e., that you are spying on me. 12. **demanded of,** questioned by. 13. **replication,** formal reply. 17. **countenance,** favor. 20. **mouthed,** rolled about in the mouth.

25. **knavish,** sinister. 32-3. **Hide fox,** the cry used in hide and seek. **Scene iii:** 4. **distracted,** confused. 5. **in,** in accordance with. 6. **scourge,** punishment; **weigh'd,** taken into consideration. 7. **bear all,** keep everything running. 9. **Deliberate pause,** a carefully planned rest (or vacation). 10. **appliance,** remedy 14. **Without,** outside.

KING. Now, Hamlet, where's Polonius?
HAM. At supper.
KING. At supper! where? 19
HAM. Not where he eats, but where he is eaten: a certain convocation of politic worms are e'en at him. Your worm is your only emperor for diet: we fat all creatures else to fat us, and we fat ourselves for maggots: your fat king and your lean beggar is but variable service, two dishes, but to one table: that's the end. 26
KING. Alas, alas!
HAM. A man may fish with the worm that hath eat of a king, and eat of the fish that hath fed of that worm. 30
KING. What dost thou mean by this?
HAM. Nothing but to show you how a king may go a progress through the guts of a beggar.
KING. Where is Polonius?
HAM. In heaven; send thither to see: if your messenger find him not there, seek him i' the other place yourself. But indeed, if you find him not within this month, you shall nose him as you go up the stairs into the lobby.
KING. Go seek him there. 40
[*To some* ATTENDANTS.
HAM. He will stay till you come.
[*Exeunt* ATTENDANTS.
KING. Hamlet, this deed, for thine especial safety,—
Which we do tender, as we dearly grieve
For that which thou hast done,—must send thee hence
With fiery quickness: therefore prepare thyself; 45
The bark is ready, and the wind at help,
The associates tend, and everything is bent
For England.
HAM. For England!
KING. Ay, Hamlet.
HAM. Good.
KING. So is it, if thou knew'st our purposes.
HAM. I see a cherub that sees them. But, come; for England! Farewell, dear mother.
KING. Thy loving father, Hamlet. 52
HAM. My mother: father and mother is man and wife; man and wife is one flesh; and so, my mother. Come, for England!
[*Exit.*
KING. Follow him at foot; tempt him with speed aboard;
Delay it not; I'll have him hence to-night:
Away! for every thing is seal'd and done
That else leans on the affair: pray you, make haste.
[*Exeunt* ROSENCRANTZ *and* GUILDENSTERN.]
And, England, if my love thou hold'st at aught— 60
As my great power thereof may give thee sense,
Since yet thy cicatrice looks raw and red
After the Danish sword, and thy free awe
Pays homage to us—thou mayst not coldly set
Our sovereign process; which imports at full,
By letters congruing to that effect, 66
The present death of Hamlet. Do it, England;
For like the hectic in my blood he rages,
And thou must cure me: till I know 'tis done,
Howe'er my haps, my joys were ne'er begun. [*Exit.* 70

SCENE IV. *A plain in Denmark.*

[*Enter* FORTINBRAS, *a* CAPTAIN, *and* SOLDIERS, *marching.*]

FOR. Go, captain, from me greet the Danish king;
Tell him that, by his license, Fortinbras
Craves the conveyance of a promised march
Over his kingdom. You know the rendezvous.
If that his majesty would aught with us, 5
We shall express our duty in his eye;
And let him know so.
CAP. I will do 't, my lord.
FOR. Go softly on.
[*Exeunt* FORTINBRAS *and* SOLDIERS.

21. **politic**, statesman-like. 22. **e'en**, right now. 25. **variable service**, choice of alternatives. 33. **go a progress**, make a royal journey. 39. **lobby**, anteroom. 43. **Which . . . grieve**, which we hold as dearly as we grieve. 46. **at help**, favorable. 47. **associates**, companions; **tend**, wait for you; **bent**, ready. 50. **cherub**, one of the angels, hence one who sees everything. 56. **at foot**, at his heels; **tempt**, coax.

59. **else . . . affair**, has anything else to do with the business. 60. **England**, the King of England. 61. **As . . . sense**, in accordance with the sense of it (my value) which my great power may give you. 62. **yet**, still; **cicatrice**, scar. 63. **free**, i.e., not now compelled by Danish rule. 64. **coldly set**, estimate lightly the importance of. 65. **process**, behest; **imports at full**, fully implies. 68. **hectic**, fever. 70. **Howe'er my haps**, whatever my lot; **my joys . . . begun**, I shall never begin to enjoy it. **Scene iv:** 3. **conveyance**, official escort. 6. **in his eye**, i.e., by appearing before him. 8. **softly**, slowly.

[*Enter* HAMLET, ROSENCRANTZ, GUILDENSTERN, *and others.*]

HAM. Good sir, whose powers are these?
CAP. They are of Norway, sir. 10
HAM. How purposed, sir, I pray you?
CAP. Against some part of Poland.
HAM. Who commands them, sir?
CAP. The nephew to old Norway, Fortinbras.
HAM. Goes it against the main of Poland, sir, 15
Or for some frontier?
CAP. Truly to speak, and with no addition,
We go to gain a little patch of ground
That hath in it no profit but the name.
To pay five ducats, five, I would not farm it; 20
Nor will it yield to Norway or the pole
A ranker rate, should it be sold in fee.
HAM. Why, then the Polack never will defend it.
CAP. Yes, it is already garrison'd.
HAM. Two thousand souls and twenty thousand ducats 25
Will not debate the question of this straw:
This is the imposthume of much wealth and peace,
That inward breaks, and shows no cause without
Why the man dies. I humbly thank you, sir.
CAP. God be wi' you, sir. [*Exit.*
ROS. Will 't please you go, my lord? 30
HAM. I'll be with you straight. Go a little before. [*Exeunt all except* HAMLET.]
How all occasions do inform against me,
And spur my dull revenge! What is a man,
If his chief good and market of his time
Be but to sleep and feed? a beast, no more.
Sure, he that made us with such large discourse, 36
Looking before and after, gave us not
That capability and god-like reason
To fust in us unused. Now, whether it be
Bestial oblivion, or some craven scruple 40
Of thinking too precisely on the event,
A thought which, quarter'd, hath but one part wisdom
And ever three parts coward, I do not know
Why yet I live to say "This thing's to do;"
Sith I have cause and will and strength and means 45
To do 't. Examples gross as earth exhort me:
Witness this army of such mass and charge
Led by a delicate and tender prince,
Whose spirit with divine ambition puff'd
Makes mouths at the invisible event, 50
Exposing what is mortal and unsure
To all that fortune, death and danger dare,
Even for an egg-shell. Rightly to be great
Is not to stir without great argument,
But greatly to find quarrel in a straw 55
When honour's at the stake. How stand I then,
That have a father kill'd, a mother stain'd,
Excitements of my reason and my blood,
And let all sleep? while, to my shame, I see
The imminent death of twenty thousand men, 60
That, for a fantasy and trick of fame,
Go to their graves like beds, fight for a plot
Whereon the numbers cannot try the cause,
Which is not tomb enough and continent
To hide the slain? O, from this time forth, 65
My thoughts be bloody, or be nothing worth!
[*Exit.*

SCENE V. *Elsinore. A room in the castle.*

[*Enter* QUEEN, HORATIO, *and a* GENTLEMAN.]

QUEEN. I will not speak with her.
GENT. She is importunate, indeed distract:
Her mood will needs be pitied.
QUEEN. What would she have?
GENT. She speaks much of her father; says she hears
There's tricks i' the world; and hems, and beats her heart; 5

11. **How purposed?** what is their business? 15. **the main,** the whole. 19. **the name,** i.e., its name as one of Norway's possessions. 20. **five ducats,** i.e., as an annual rental. 22. **ranker,** larger; **sold in fee,** sold outright (and the proceeds invested). 26. **debate,** settle; **straw,** trifling matter. 27. **imposthume,** hidden abscess. 28. **without,** outwardly. 32. **inform,** bear witness. 34. **market . . . time,** that for which he markets (uses) his time. 36. **discourse,** power of reasoning. 38. **and,** of. 39. **fust,** grow moldy. 40. **Bestial oblivion,** the forgetfulness of an animal. 41. **event,** outcome. 46. **gross,** obvious. 47. **such . . . charge,** so large and so expensive. 48. **delicate and tender,** gentle and refined. 50. **invisible event,** unknown outcome. 54. **argument,** cause. 58. **Excitements,** incitements; **blood,** passion. 61. **fantasy and trick,** illusion and whim. 61. **try the cause,** i.e., fight the battle (for possession of it). 64. **continent,** receptacle. Scene v: 3. **will needs,** should be. 5. **tricks,** deceptions; **heart,** breast.

Spurns enviously at straws; speaks things in doubt,
That carry but half sense: her speech is nothing,
Yet the unshaped use of it doth move
The hearers to collection; they aim at it,
And botch the words up fit to their own thoughts; 10
Which, as her winks, and nods, and gestures yield them,
Indeed would make one think there might be thought,
Though nothing sure, yet much unhappily.

HOR. 'Twere good she were spoken with: for she may strew
Dangerous conjectures in ill-breeding minds.

QUEEN. Let her come in. [*Exit* HORATIO.] 16
To my sick soul, as sin's true nature is,
Each toy seems prologue to some great amiss:
So full of artless jealousy is guilt,
It spills itself in fearing to be spilt. 20

[*Re-enter* HORATIO, *with* OPHELIA.]

OPH. Where is the beauteous majesty of Denmark?

QUEEN. How now, Ophelia!

OPH. [*Sings*] How should I your true love know
From another one?
By his cockle hat and staff, 25
And his sandal shoon.

QUEEN. Alas, sweet lady, what imports this song?

OPH. Say you? nay, pray you, mark.
[*Sings*] He is dead and gone, lady,
He is dead and gone; 30
At his head a grass-green turf,
At his heels a stone.

QUEEN. Nay, but, Ophelia,—

OPH. Pray you, mark
[*Sings*] White his shroud as the mountain snow,— 35

[*Enter* KING.]

QUEEN. Alas, look here, my lord.

OPH. [*Sings*] Larded with sweet flowers;
Which bewept to the grave did go
With true-love showers.

KING. How do you, pretty lady? 40

OPH. Well, God 'ild you! They say the owl was a baker's daughter. Lord, we know what we are, but know not what we may be. God be at your table!

KING. Conceit upon her father. 45

OPH. Pray you, let's have no words of this; but when they ask you what it means, say you this:
[*Sings*] To-morrow is Saint Valentine's day,
All in the morning betime,
And I a maid at your window, 50
To be your Valentine.
Then up he rose, and donn'd his clothes,
And dupp'd the chamber-door;
Let in the maid, that out a maid
Never departed more. 55

KING. Pretty Ophelia!

OPH. Indeed, la, without an oath, I'll make an end on 't:
[*Sings*] By Gis and by Saint Charity,
Alack, and fie for shame! 60
Young men will do 't, if they come to 't;
By cock, they are to blame.
Quoth she, before you tumbled me,
You promised me to wed.
So would I ha' done, by yonder sun, 65
An thou hadst not come to my bed.

KING. How long hath she been thus?

OPH. I hope all will be well. We must be patient: but I cannot choose but weep, to think they should lay him i' the cold ground. My brother shall know of it: and so I thank you for your good counsel. Come, my coach! Good night, ladies; good night, sweet ladies; good night, good night. [*Exit.*

6. **Spurns . . . straws**, kicks angrily at trifles; **speaks . . . doubt**, talks incoherently. 7. **is nothing**, makes no sense. 8. **unshaped use of it**, i.e., disconnected utterances. 9. **collection**, inference; **aim**, guess. 10. **botch**, patch; **fit . . . thoughts**, harmonize with their own suspicions. 11. **yield**, accompany. 12. **thought**, sense (behind them). 13. **unhappily**, suggesting mischief. 15. **ill-breeding**, that breed evil. 17. **as . . . is**, i.e., as must always be the case when one has a feeling of guilt. 18. **amiss**, disaster. 19. **jealousy**, suspicion. 20. **spills itself**, gives itself away. 25. **cockle hat**, a hat with a cockle shell stuck in it as a sign its owner has been on a pilgrimage to a remote shrine. A lover was often referred to as a pilgrim and his lady as the saint whose shrine he visited. 28. **Say you?** Is that what you want to know? 37. **Larded**, decorated. 41. **'ild**, yield or reward. 42. **owl . . . daughter**, reference to a folk tale that a baker's daughter was turned into an owl for trying to skimp the bread her mother baked for Christ. 45. **Conceit upon**, thinking about. 46. **let's . . . this**, don't mention this to anyone. 49. **in the morning**, because it was believed that the first girl a man saw on Valentine's day would be his true love; **betime**, early. 53. **dupp'd**, opened. 59. **Gis**, Jesus. 62. **cock**, distortion of "God."

KING. Follow her close; give her good watch,
I pray you. 75
[*Exit* HORATIO.]
O, this is the poison of deep grief; it springs
All from her father's death. O Gertrude, Gertrude,
When sorrows come, they come not single spies,
But in battalions. First, her father slain:
Next, your son gone; and he most violent author 80
Of his own just remove: the people muddied,
Thick and unwholesome in their thoughts and whispers,
For good Polonius' death; and we have done but greenly,
In hugger-mugger to inter him: poor Ophelia
Divided from herself and her fair judgement, 85
Without the which we are pictures, or mere beasts:
Last, and as much containing as all these,
Her brother is in secret come from France;
Feeds on his wonder, keeps himself in clouds,
And wants not buzzers to infect his ear 90
With pestilent speeches of his father's death;
Wherein necessity, of matter beggar'd,
Will nothing stick our person to arraign
In ear and ear. O my dear Gertrude, this,
Like to a murdering-piece, in many places 95
Gives me superfluous death. [*A noise within.*
QUEEN. Alack, what noise is this?
KING. Where are my Switzers? Let them guard the door.

[*Enter another* GENTLEMAN.]

What is the matter?
GENT. Save yourself, my lord:
The ocean, overpeering of his list,
Eats not the flats with more impetuous haste 100
Than young Laertes, in a riotous head,
O'erbears your officers. The rabble call him lord;
And, as the world were now but to begin,
Antiquity forgot, custom not known,
The ratifiers and props of every word, 105
They cry "Choose we: Laertes shall be king:"
Caps, hands, and tongues, applaud it to the clouds:
"Laertes shall be king, Laertes king!"
QUEEN. How cheerfully on the false trail they cry!
O, this is counter, you false Danish dogs! 110
KING. The doors are broke.
[*Noise within.*

[*Enter* LAERTES, *armed;* DANES *following.*]

LAER. Where is this king? Sirs, stand you all without.
DANES. No, let 's come in.
LAER. I pray you, give me leave.
DANES. We will, we will.
[*They retire without the door.*
LAER. I thank you: keep the door. O thou vile king, 115
Give me my father!
QUEEN. Calmly, good Laertes.
LAER. That drop of blood that's calm proclaims me bastard,
Cries cuckold to my father, brands the harlot
Even here, between the chaste unsmirchèd brows
Of my true mother.
KING. What is the cause, Laertes,
That thy rebellion looks so giant-like? 121
Let him go, Gertrude; do not fear our person:
There's such divinity doth hedge a king,
That treason can but peep to what it would,
Acts little of his will. Tell me, Laertes, 125
Why thou art thus incensed. Let him go, Gertrude.
Speak, man.
LAER. Where is my father?
KING. Dead.
QUEEN. But not by him.
KING. Let him demand his fill.
LAER. How came he dead? I'll not be juggled with: 130

78. **come not**, come not like. 81. **remove**, removal; **muddied**, stirred up (like a muddy pool). 83. **greenly**, foolishly. 84. **hugger-mugger**, hastily and secretly. 86. **pictures**, i.e., imitations of men. 87. **containing**, i.e., causes for sorrow. 89. **wonder**, i.e., at his father's death; **in clouds**, befogged. 90. **wants not buzzers**, does not lack scandal-mongers. 92. **Wherein . . . beggar'd**, the necessity (of inventing a story), lacking facts. 93. **nothing stick**, not hesitate at all. 94. **In ear and ear**, from person to person. 95. **murdering-piece**, a mortar which scatters its shots. 96. **superfluous death**, many wounds any one of which would be fatal. 97. **Switzers**, bodyguard of Swiss mercenaries. 99. **overpeering of his list**, rising above its boundary (i.e., customary level). 100. **flats**, lowlands. 101. **head**, armed force. 102. **O'erbears**, overcomes. 105. **word**, suggestion, insinuation. 106. **Choose we**, let us choose. 110. **counter**, following the scent in the wrong direction. 113. **leave**, i.e.,, to go in alone. 122. **fear**, fear for. 123. **divinity**, divine protection; **hedge**, enclose. 124. **peep to**, look furtively at. 125. **his**, i.e., **treasons**.

To hell, allegiance! vows, to the blackest devil!
Conscience and grace, to the profoundest pit!
I dare damnation. To this point I stand,
That both the worlds I give to negligence,
Let come what comes; only I'll be revenged
Most throughly for my father.

KING. Who shall stay you? 136

LAER. My will, not all the world:
And for my means, I'll husband them so well,
They shall go far with little.

KING. Good Laertes,
If you desire to know the certainty 140
Of your dear father's death, is 't writ in your revenge,
That, swoopstake, you will draw both friend and foe,
Winner and loser?

LAER. None but his enemies.

KING. Will you know them then?

LAER. To his good friends thus wide I'll ope my arms; 145
And like the kind life-rendering pelican,
Repast them with my blood.

KING. Why, now you speak
Like a good child and a true gentleman.
That I am guiltless of your father's death,
And am most sensibly in grief for it, 150
It shall as level to your judgement pierce
As day does to your eye.

DANES. [*Within*] Let her come in.

LAER. How now! what noise is that?

[*Re-enter* OPHELIA.]

O heat, dry up my brains! tears seven times salt,
Burn out the sense and virtue of mine eye. 155
By heaven, thy madness shall be paid with weight,
Till our scale turn the beam. O rose of May!
Dear maid, kind sister, sweet Ophelia!
O heavens! is't possible, a young maid's wits
Should be as mortal as an old man's life? 160
Nature is fine in love, and where 'tis fine,
It sends some precious instance of itself
After the thing it loves.

OPH. [*Sings*]
They bore him barefaced on the bier;
Hey non nonny, nonny, hey nonny; 165
And in his grave rain'd many a tear:—
Fare you well, my dove!

LAER. Hadst thou thy wits, and didst persuade revenge,
It could not move thus.

OPH. [*Sings*]
You must sing a-down a-down,
An you call him a-down-a. 171
O, how the wheel becomes it! It is the false steward, that stole his master's daughter.

LAER. This nothing 's more than matter.

OPH. There's rosemary, that's for remembrance; pray, love, remember: and there is pansies, that 's for thoughts.

LAER. A document in madness, thoughts and remembrance fitted. 179

OPH. There's fennel for you, and columbines: there's rue for you; and here's some for me: we may call it herb-grace o' Sundays: O, you must wear your rue with a difference. There's a daisy: I would give you some violets, but they withered all when my father died: they say he made a good end,— 186
[*Sings*] For bonny sweet Robin is all my joy.

LAER. Thought and affliction, passion, hell itself,
She turns to favour and to prettiness.

OPH. [*Sings*]
And will he not come again? 190
And will he not come again?
No, no, he is dead:
Go to thy death-bed:
He never will come again.

131. **vows,** i.e., of allegiance to you. 132. **grace,** spiritual well-being or salvation. 133. **To . . . stand,** I am resolved on this point. 134. **both . . . negligence,** i.e., I disregard both heaven and hell. 137. **My . . . world,** not the whole world unless I wish it. 138. **for my means,** as for my means (of achieving revenge). 142. **swoopstake,** i.e., like a gambler who sweeps up all the stakes on the table. 146. **life-rendering pelican,** the female pelican was supposed to feed her young with her own blood. 147. **repast,** feed. 150. **most . . . grief,** grieve most deeply. 151. **level,** with as straight an aim. 152. **day,** the rising run. 154. **heat,** i.e., generated by anger. 155. **sense and virtue,** sensation and power. 156. **with weight,** according to an even balance. 157. **scale . . . beam,** with vengeance outweigh the offense. 161. **fine in love,** refined by love. 162. **instance,** sample; in this case, her wits. 168. **persuade,** urge me to. 172. **O . . . becomes it,** how well the refrain suits the title of the song. 174. **This . . . matter,** this nonsense is more revealing than sensible talk. 177. **pansies,** pensées for "thoughts." 178. **document in,** lessons conveyed through. 180. **fennel for you,** emblem of flattery for the Queen; **columbines,** emblem of ingratitude. 182. **herb-grace,** rue when mixed with holy water. 183. **rue,** emblem of sorrow and repentance; **difference,** a heraldic term describing the distinction between two coats of arms belonging to different members of the same family. 184. **daisy,** for faithlessness. 188. **Thought,** sorrow. 189. **favor,** charm.

His beard was as white as snow, 195
All flaxen was his poll:
He is gone, he is gone,
And we cast away moan:
God ha' mercy on his soul!
And of all Christian souls, I pray God. God be wi' ye. [*Exit.*

LAER. Do you see this, O God? 201

KING. Laertes, I must commune with your grief,
Or you deny me right. Go but apart,
Make choice of whom your wisest friends you will,
And they shall hear and judge 'twixt you and me: 205
If by direct or by collateral hand
They find us touch'd, we will our kingdom give,
Our crown, our life, and all that we call ours,
To you in satisfaction; but if not, 209
Be you content to lend your patience to us,
And we shall jointly labour with your soul
To give it due content.

LAER. Let this be so;
His means of death, his obscure funeral—
No trophy, sword, nor hatchment o'er his bones,
No noble rite nor formal ostentation— 215
Cry to be heard, as 'twere from heaven to earth,
That I must call 't in question.

KING. So you shall;
And where the offence is let the great axe fall.
I pray you, go with me. [*Exeunt.*

SCENE VI. *Another room in the castle.*

[*Enter* HORATIO *and a* SERVANT.]

HOR. What are they that would speak with me?

SERV. Sailors, sir: they say they have letters for you.

HOR. Let them come in. [*Exit* SERVANT.]
I do not know from what part of the world
I should be greeted, if not from lord Hamlet.

[*Enter* SAILORS.]

FIRST SAIL. God bless you, sir. 6

HOR. Let him bless thee too.

FIRST SAIL. He shall, sir, an 't please him. There's a letter for you, sir; it comes from the ambassador that was bound for England; if your name be Horatio, as I am let to know it is. 11

HOR. [*Reads*] "Horatio, when thou shalt have overlooked this, give these fellows some means to the king: they have letters for him. Ere we were two days old at sea, a pirate of very warlike appointment gave us chase. Finding ourselves too slow of sail, we put on a compelled valour, and in the grapple I boarded them: on the instant they got clear of our ship; so I alone became their prisoner. They have dealt with me like thieves of 21 mercy: but they knew what they did; I am to do a good turn for them. Let the king have the letters I have sent; and repair thou to me with as much speed as thou wouldst fly death. I have words to speak in thine ear will make thee dumb; yet are they much too light for the bore of the matter. These good fellows will bring thee where I am. Rozencrantz and Guildenstern hold their course for England: of them I have much to tell thee. Farewell.

"He that thou knowest thine, HAMLET."

Come, I will make you way for these your letters;
And do 't the speedier, that you may direct me
To him from whom you brought them. 34
[*Exeunt.*

SCENE VII. *Another room in the castle.*

[*Enter* KING *and* LAERTES.]

KING. Now must your conscience my acquittance seal,
And you must put me in your heart for friend,

196. **poll**, head. 198. **cast away**, who are forsaken. 200. **of**, on. 202. **commune with**, share. 203. **apart**, away. 206. **collateral**, indirect. 207. **touch'd**, i.e., with guilt. 212. **give . . . content**, convince you of the truth (i.e., of my allegation). 213. **obscure**, secret. 214. **trophy**, memorial; **hatchment**, tablet, bearing the coat of arms of the deceased. 215. **ostentation**, ceremony. 217. **call't in question**, look into it. Scene vi: 8. **an't**, if it. 11. **let to know**, informed. 13. **overlooked**, looked over. 14. **means**, means of access. 16. **appointment**, equipment. 17-8. **put . . . valour**, perforce acted bravely. 18. **in the grapple**, when the ships were grappled together. 21-2. **thieves of mercy**, merciful thieves. 24. **repair**, return. 27. **bore**, calibre, importance. 29. **hold . . . for**, continue on their way to. 32. **make . . . for**, gain you access to. Scene vii: 1. **conscience . . . seal**, your knowledge of the facts must acquit me of any guilt.

Sith you have heard, and with a knowing ear,
That he which hath your noble father slain
Pursued my life.

LAER. It well appears: but tell me 5
Why you proceeded not against these feats,
So crimeful and so capital in nature,
As by your safety, wisdom, all things else,
You mainly were stirr'd up.

KING. O, for two special reasons;
Which may to you, perhaps, seem much unsinew'd, 10
But yet to me they are strong. The queen his mother
Lives almost by his looks; and for myself—
My virtue or my plague, be it either which—
She's so conjunctive to my life and soul,
That, as the star moves not but in his sphere,
I could not but by her. The other motive, 16
Why to a public count I might not go,
Is the great love the general gender bear him;
Who, dipping all his faults in their affection,
Would, like the spring that turneth wood to stone, 20
Convert his gyves to graces; so that my arrows,
Too slightly timber'd for so loud a wind,
Would have reverted to my bow again,
And not where I had aim'd them.

LAER. And so have I a noble father lost; 25
A sister driven into desperate terms,
Whose worth, if praises may go back again,
Stood challenger on mount of all the age
For her perfections: but my revenge will come.

KING. Break not your sleeps for that: you must not think 30
That we are made of stuff so flat and dull
That we can let our beard be shook with danger
And think it pastime. You shortly shall hear more:
I loved your father, and we love ourself;
And that, I hope, will teach you to imagine— 35

[*Enter a* MESSENGER.]

How now! what news?

MESS. Letters, my lord, from Hamlet:
This to your majesty; this to the queen.

KING. From Hamlet! who brought them?

MESS. Sailors, my lord, they say; I saw them not:
They were given me by Claudio; he received them 40
Of him that brought them.

KING. Laertes, you shall hear them.
Leave us. [*Exit* MESSENGER.]

[*Reads*] "High and mighty, You shall know I am set naked on your kingdom. To-morrow shall I beg leave to see your kingly eyes: when I shall, first asking your pardon thereunto, recount the occasion of my sudden and more strange return.

"HAMLET."

What should this mean? Are all the rest come back?
Or is it some abuse, and no such thing? 50

LAER. Know you the hand?

KING. 'Tis Hamlet's character. "Naked!"
And in a postscript here, he says "alone."
Can you advise me?

LAER. I'm lost in it, my lord. But let him come; 55
It warms the very sickness in my heart,
That I shall live and tell him to his teeth,
"Thus didst thou."

KING. If it be so, Laertes—
As how should it be so? how otherwise?—
Will you be ruled by me?

LAER. Ay, my lord; 60
So you will not o'errule me to a peace.

KING. To thine own peace. If he be now return'd,
As checking at his voyage, and that he means
No more to undertake it, I will work him
To an exploit, now ripe in my device, 65
Under the which he shall not choose but fall:
And for his death no wind of blame shall breathe,

5. **Pursued**, sought. 6. **proceeded not**, took no legal action; **feats**, deeds. 7. **capital**, punishable by death. 8-9. **As . . . stirr'd up**, as anxiety for your safety, wisdom, and every other consideration strongly urged you. 10. **unsinew'd**, weak. 12. **Lives . . . looks**, acts as though her life depended on his mere glance. 13. **be . . . which**, whichever you choose to call it. 14. **conjunctive**, closely joined. 15. **sphere**, orbit. 16. **motive**, reason. 17. **count**, reckoning. 18. **general gender**, common people. 20. **the spring**, reference to a famous spring in Yorkshire. 21. **gyves**, fetters, turns his limitations to virtues. 22. **slightly timber'd**, i.e., light-shafted; **loud**, violent. 26. **terms**, conditions. 27. **if praises . . . again**, if I may praise her for what she was before she became mad. 28-9. **Stood . . . perfections**, challenged from horseback the age to dispute the claim that she surpassed all others in perfection. 32. **our . . . danger**, let danger threaten us to our face. 44. **naked**, destitute. 50. **abuse**, deception. 52. **character**, handwriting. 55. **lost in it**, at a loss to explain it. 59. **otherwise**, than true. 63. **checking**, balking. A falcon "checked" when she stopped her flight to dart at some unsuitable object. 65. **ripe in my device**, i.e., completely planned.

But even his mother shall uncharge the practice
And call it accident.

LAER. My lord, I will be ruled;
The rather, if you could devise it so 70
That I might be the organ.

KING. It falls right.
You have been talk'd of since your travel much,
And that in Hamlet's hearing, for a quality
Wherein, they say, you shine: your sum of parts
Did not together pluck such envy from him
As did that one, and that, in my regard, 76
Of the unworthiest siege.

LAER. What part is that, my lord?

KING. A very riband in the cap of youth,
Yet needful too; for youth no less becomes
The light and careless livery that it wears 80
Than settled age his sables and his weeds,
Importing health and graveness. Two months since,
Here was a gentleman of Normandy:—
I've seen myself, and served against, the French,
And they can well on horseback: but this gallant 85
Had witchcraft in 't; he grew unto his seat;
And to such wondrous doing brought his horse,
As had he been incorpsed and demi-natured
With the brave beast: so far he topp'd my thought,
That I, in forgery of shapes and tricks, 90
Come short of what he did.

LAER. A Norman was 't?

KING. A Norman.

LAER. Upon my life, Lamond.

KING. The very same.

LAER. I know him well: he is the brooch indeed
And gem of all the nation. 95

KING. He made confession of you,
And gave you such a masterly report
For art and exercise in your defence
And for your rapier most especial,
That he cried out, 'twould be a sight indeed,
If one could match you: the scrimers of their nation, 101
He swore, had neither motion, guard, nor eye,
If you opposed them. Sir, this report of his
Did Hamlet so envenom with his envy
That he could nothing do but wish and beg 105
Your sudden coming o'er, to play with him.
Now, out of this,—

LAER. What out of this, my lord?

KING. Laertes, was your father dear to you?
Or are you like the painting of a sorrow,
A face without a heart?

LAER. Why ask you this? 110

KING. Not that I think you did not love your father;
But that I know love is begun by time;
And that I see, in passages of proof,
Time qualifies the spark and fire of it.
There lives within the very flame of love 115
A kind of wick or snuff that will abate it;
And nothing is at a like goodness still;
For goodness, growing to a plurisy,
Dies in his own too much: that we would do,
We should do when we would; for this "would" changes 120
And hath abatements and delays as many
As there are tongues, are hands, are accidents;
And then this "should" is like a spendthrift sigh,
That hurts by easing. But, to the quick o' the ulcer:—
Hamlet comes back: what would you undertake, 125
To show yourself your father's son in deed
More than in words?

LAER. To cut his throat i' the church.

KING. No place, indeed, should murder sanctuarize;

68. **uncharge the practice**, acquit the plan of treachery. 71. **organ**, instrument, agent (of his death). 74. **your . . . parts**, all your talents. 77. **siege**, rank. 78. **very riband**, mere ornament. 81. **sables**, rich furs; **weeds**, garments. 82. **Importing . . . graveness**, suiting the gravity (of settled age) and protecting its health (because of their warmth). 85. **can well**, are skillful. 88. **incorpsed and demi-natured**, made one body with and half shared the nature of. 89. **topp'd**, surpassed; **thought**, expectations. 90. **in forgery**, in imagining. 93. **Lamond**, perhaps Pietro Monte (La Mont) a famous French horseman. 96. **confession**, full report. 97. **you . . . report**, reported you to be such a master. 98. **For art and exercise**, in the theory and practice. 101. **scrimers**, fencers. 106. **sudden coming o'er**, your immediate return; **play**, fence. 113. **passages of proof**, well-authenticated examples. 114. **qualifies**, diminishes. 116. **wick or snuff**, a charred wick (of a candle). 117. **at**, of; **still**, always. 118. **plurisy**, excess. 119. **that**, what. 120. **"would,"** i.e., impulse to action. 123-4. **like . . . easing**, i.e., evaporates like a sigh (which was supposed by drawing blood from the heart to weaken it even while relieving it). 124. **quick**, most sensitive part; so the heart of the difficulty. 128. **sanctuarize**, afford sanctuary and so offer protection to a man from being murdered.

Revenge should have no bounds. But, good Laertes,
Will you do this, keep close within your chamber. 130
Hamlet return'd shall know you are come home:
We'll put on those shall praise your excellence
And set a double varnish on the fame
The Frenchman gave you, bring you in fine together 134
And wager on your heads: he, being remiss,
Most generous and free from all contriving,
Will not peruse the foils; so that, with ease,
Or with a little shuffling, you may choose
A sword unbated, and in a pass of practice
Requite him for your father.

LAER. I will do 't: 140
And, for that purpose, I'll anoint my sword.
I bought an unction of a mountebank,
So mortal that, but dip a knife in it,
Where it draws blood no cataplasm so rare,
Collected from all simples that have virtue 145
Under the moon, can save the thing from death
That is but scratch'd withal: I'll touch my point
With this contagion, that, if I gall him slightly,
It may be death.

KING. Let's further think of this;
Weigh what convenience both of time and means 150
May fit us to our shape: if this should fail,
And that our drift look through our bad performance,
'Twere better not assay'd: therefore this project
Should have a back or second, that might hold,
If this should blast in proof. Soft! let me see:
We'll make a solemn wager on your cunnings: 156
I ha 't:
When in your motion you are hot and dry—
As make your bouts more violent to that end—
And that he calls for drink, I'll have prepared him 160
A chalice for the nonce, whereon but sipping,
If he by chance escape your venom'd stuck,
Our purpose may hold there.

[*Enter* QUEEN.]

How now, sweet queen!

QUEEN. One woe doth tread upon another's heel,
So fast they follow: your sister's drown'd, Laertes. 165

LAER. Drown'd! O, where?

QUEEN. There is a willow grows aslant a brook,
That shows his hoar leaves in the glassy stream;
There with fantastic garlands did she come
Of crow-flowers, nettles, daisies, and long purples 170
That liberal shepherds give a grosser name,
But our cold maids do dead men's fingers call them:
There, on the pendent boughs her coronet weeds
Clambering to hang, an envious sliver broke;
When down her weedy trophies and herself
Fell in the weeping brook. Her clothes spread wide; 176
And, mermaid-like, awhile they bore her up:
Which time she chanted snatches of old tunes;
As one incapable of her own distress,
Or like a creature native and indued 180
Unto that element: but long it could not be
Till that her garments, heavy with their drink,
Pull'd the poor wretch from her melodious lay
To muddy death.

LAER. Alas, then, she is drown'd?

QUEEN. Drown'd, drown'd. 185

LAER. Too much of water hast thou, poor Ophelia,

132. **put on those,** incite persons who. 134. **in fine,** finally. 135. **remiss,** gentle, i.e., gentlemanly. 136. **generous,** free from suspicion; **contriving,** plotting. 137. **peruse,** examine carefully. 139. **unbated,** unblunted; **pass of practice,** a lunge with a treacherously prepared sword. 142. **unction,** salve; **mountebank,** quack doctor. 144. **cataplasm,** poultice. 145. **simples,** herbs; **virtue,** medicinal property. 148. **gall,** scratch. 151. **fit . . . shape,** adapt us to our plan. 152. **drift . . . performance,** intention were disclosed by bungling. 156. **solemn,** formal; **cunnings,** skills. 158. **motion,** exercise. 159. **As,** i.e., as you must make. 160. **that,** when. 161. **nonce,** special occasion. 162. **stuck,** thrust. 163. **hold there,** be accomplished in that way. 168. **hoar,** gray, refers to the color of the under surface. 170. **crow-flowers,** buttercups; **long purples,** a kind of orchid, "orchis mascula," a popular phallic symbol. 171. **liberal,** licentious. 173. **coronet weeds,** garland made of wild flowers. 174. **envious sliver,** spiteful branch. 175. **weedy trophies,** memorials (to put on her father's grave) made of wild flowers. 180. **indued,** adapted by nature.

And therefore I forbid my tears: but yet
It is our trick; nature her custom holds,
Let shame say what it will: when these are
gone,
The woman will be out. Adieu, my lord: 190
I have a speech of fire, that fain would blaze,
But that this folly douts it. [*Exit.*

KING. Let's follow, Gertrude:
How much I had to do to calm his rage!
Now fear I this will give it start again;
Therefore let's follow. [*Exeunt.*

ACT V

SCENE I. *A churchyard.*

[*Enter two* CLOWNS, *with spades, &c.*]

FIRST CLO. Is she to be buried in Christian burial that willfully seeks her own salvation?

SEC. CLO. I tell thee she is; and therefore make her grave straight: the crowner hath sat on her, and finds it Christian burial.

FIRST CLO. How can that be, unless she drowned herself in her own defence?

SEC. CLO. Why, 'tis found so. 8

FIRST CLO. It must be "se offendendo," it cannot be else. For here lies the point: if I drown myself wittingly, it argues an act: and an act hath three branches; it is, to act, to do, and to perform: argal, she drowned herself wittingly. 14

SEC. CLO. Nay, but hear you, goodman delver,—

FIRST CLO. Give me leave. Here lies the water; good: here stands the man; good: if the man go to this water, and drown himself, it is, will he, nill he, he goes,—mark you that; but if the water come to him and drown him, he drowns not himself: argal, he that is not guilty of his own death shortens not his own life.

SEC. CLO. But is this law? 23

FIRST CLO. Ay, marry, is 't; crowner's quest law.

SEC. CLO. Will you ha' the truth on 't? If this had not been a gentlewoman, she should have been buried out o' Christian burial. 28

FIRST CLO. Why, there thou say'st: and the more pity that great folk should have countenance in this world to drown or hang themselves, more than their even Christian. Come, my spade. There is no ancient gentlemen but gardeners, ditchers, and grave-makers: they hold up Adam's profession. 35

SEC. CLO. Was he a gentleman?

FIRST CLO. A' was the first that ever bore arms.

SEC. CLO. Why, he had none. 39

FIRST CLO. What, art a heathen? How dost thou understand the Scripture? The Scripture says "Adam digged:" could he dig without arms? I'll put another question to thee: if thou answerest me not to the purpose, confess thyself— 44

SEC. CLO. Go to.

FIRST CLO. What is he that builds stronger than either the mason, the shipwright, or the carpenter?

SEC. CLO. The gallows-maker; for that frame outlives a thousand tenants. 50

FIRST CLO. I like thy wit well, in good faith: the gallows does well; but how does it well? it does well to those that do ill: now thou dost ill to say the gallows is built stronger than the church: argal, the gallows may do well to thee. To 't again, come.

SEC. CLO. "Who builds stronger than a mason, a shipwright, or a carpenter?"

FIRST CLO. Ay, tell me that, and unyoke.

SEC. CLO. Marry, now I can tell. 60

FIRST CLO. To 't.

SEC. CLO. Mass, I cannot tell.

[*Enter* HAMLET *and* HORATIO, *at a distance.*]

FIRST CLO. Cudgel thy brains no more about it, for your dull ass will not mend his pace with beating; and, when you are asked 65

188. **trick,** way. 189. **these,** i.e., tears. 190. **The . . . out,** i.e., all my gentler impulses will be gone. 192. **this . . . douts it,** i.e., this weakness (the tears) puts it out (i.e., the speech of fire). **Act V, Scene i: s.d., Clowns,** country louts. 1-2. **Christian burial,** i.e., within the churchyard; suicides were not allowed to be buried in consecrated ground. 4. **straight,** at once. 4-5. **crowner . . . her,** the coroner has rendered his decision about her. 9. **"se offendendo,"** he means "se defendendo," i.e., in self-defense. 13. **argal,** ergo, therefore. 14. **wittingly,** on purpose. 15. **delver,** digger. 16. **Give me leave,** listen to me. 24. **quest,** inquest. 28. **out . . . burial,** outside the churchyard. 29. **there . . . say'st,** now you are talking. 31. **countenance,** permission. 32. **even,** fellow. 44. **confess thyself,** "and be hanged" is the rest of the proverb. 45. **Go to,** come, come. 53. **does well,** is a good enough answer. 59. **unyoke,** i.e., your team—your job is done.

this question next, say "a grave-maker:" the houses that he makes last till doomsday. Go, get thee to Yaughan: fetch me a stoup of liquor. [*Exit* SEC. CLOWN.]

[*He digs, and sings.*]

In youth, when I did love, did love,
Methought it was very sweet, 70
To contract, Oh, the time, for, ah, my behoove,
Oh, methought, there was nothing meet.

HAM Has this fellow no feeling of his business, that he sings at grave-making?

HOR. Custom hath made it in him a property of easiness. 76

HAM. 'Tis e'en so: the hand of little employment hath the daintier sense.

FIRST CLO. [*Sings*]

But age, with his stealing steps,
Hath claw'd me in his clutch, 80
And hath shipped me intil the land,
As if I had never been such.

[*Throws up a skull.*

HAM. That skull had a tongue in it, and could sing once: how the knave jowls it to the ground, as if it were Cain's jaw-bone, that did the first murder! It might be the pate of a politician, which this ass now o'erreaches; one that would circumvent God, might it not?

HOR. It might, my lord. 89

HAM. Or of a courtier; which could say "Good morrow, sweet lord! How dost thou, good lord?" This might be my lord such-a-one, that praised my lord such-a-one's horse, when he meant to beg it; might it not?

HOR. Ay, my lord. 95

HAM. Why, e'en so: and now my Lady Worm's; chapless, and knocked about the mazzard with a sexton's spade: here's fine revolution, an we had the trick to see 't. Did these bones cost no more the breeding, but to play at loggats with 'em? mine ache to think on 't. 101

FIRST CLO. [*Sings*]

A pick-axe, and a spade, a spade,
For and a shrouding sheet:
O, a pit of clay for to be made
For such a guest is meet. 105

[*Throws up another skull.*

HAM. There's another: why may not that be the skull of a lawyer? Where be his quiddities now, his quillets, his cases, his tenures, and his tricks? why does he suffer this rude knave now to knock him about the sconce with a dirty shovel, and will not tell him of his action of battery? Hum! This fellow 112 might be in 's time a great buyer of land, with his statutes, his recognizances, his fines, his double vouchers, his recoveries: is this the fine of his fines, and the recovery of his recoveries, to have his fine pate full of fine dirt? will his vouchers vouch him no more of his purchases, and double ones too, than the length and breadth of a pair of indentures? The very conveyances of his lands will hardly lie in this box; and must the inheritor himself have no more, ha? 121

HOR. Not a jot more, my lord.

HAM. Is not parchment made of sheepskins?

HOR. Ay, my lord, and of calf-skins too. 124

HAM. They are sheep and calves which seek out assurance in that. I will speak to this fellow. Whose grave's this, sirrah?

FIRST. CLO. Mine sir.

[*Sings*] O, a pit of clay for to be made
For such a guest is meet. 130

HAM. I think it be thine, indeed; for thou liest in 't.

FIRST CLO. You lie out on 't, sir, and therefor it is not yours: for my part, I do not lie in 't, and yet it is mine.

HAM. Thou dost lie in 't, to be in 't and say it is thine: 'tis for the dead, not for the quick; therefore thou liest.

68. **Yaughan,** probably the name of an alehouse keeper well-known to Shakespeare's audience; **stoup,** a large mug. 71. **contract . . . the time,** make the time pass quickly; **ah,** he grunts as he wields his pick-axe; **behoove,** advantage. 76. **property of uneasiness,** an untroubled peculiarity or occupation. 77-8. **hand . . . sense,** the hand unused to work is more sensitive (i.e., not calloused). 81. **intil the land,** ashore. 84. **jowls,** hurls. 85. **jaw-bone,** the tradition was that Cain killed Abel with the jawbone of an ass. 87. **politician,** plotter; **o'erreaches,** (1) gets the better of, (2) reaches over. 97. **chapless,** jawless. 98. **mazzard,** head. 99. **trick,** knack. 101. **play at loggats,** game in which skull-shaped pieces of wood (loggats) were thrown at stakes fixed in the ground, like quoits.

107. **quiddities,** quibbles. 98. **quillets,** evasions of the real issue by hair-splitting distinctions in the meaning of words; **tenures,** leases. 110. **sconce,** head. 112. **battery,** assault and battery. 114. **statutes,** mortgages; **recognizances,** promissory notes. 114-5. **fines, recoveries,** terms formerly used in transfer of real estate. 117. **fine,** play on the meaning "end." 119. **pair of indentures,** contracts issued in duplicate. 120. **conveyances,** deeds. 121. **inheritor,** owner, with a pun on the more usual meaning. 126. **assurance in that,** safety in legal documents. 127. **sirrah,** form of address used to a social inferior. 137. **quick,** living.

FIRST CLO. 'Tis a quick lie, sir; 'twill away again, from me to you. 140

HAM. What man dost thou dig it for?

FIRST CLO. For no man, sir.

HAM. What woman, then?

FIRST CLO. For none, neither.

HAM. Who is to be buried in 't?

FIRST CLO. One that was a woman, sir; but, rest her soul, she's dead. 147

HAM. How absolute the knave is! we must speak by the card, or equivocation will undo us. By the Lord, Horatio, these three years I have taken note of it; the age is grown so picked that the toe of the peasant comes so near the heel of the courtier, he galls his kibe. How long hast thou been a grave-maker?

FIRST CLO. Of all the days i' the year, I came to 't that day that our last king Hamlet overcame Fortinbras. 157

HAM. How long is that since?

FIRST CLO. Cannot you tell that? every fool can tell that: it was the very day that young Hamlet was born; he that is mad, and sent into England.

HAM. Ay, marry, why was he sent into England?

FIRST CLO. Why, because he was mad: he shall recover his wits there; or, if he do not, it 's no great matter there.

HAM. Why?

FIRST CLO. 'Twill not be seen in him there; there the men are as mad as he. 170

HAM. How came he mad?

FIRST CLO. Very strangely, they say.

HAM. How strangely?

FIRST CLO. Faith, e'en with losing his wits.

HAM. Upon what ground?

FIRST CLO. Why, here in Denmark: I have been sexton here, man and boy, thirty years.

HAM. How long will a man lie i' the earth ere he rot? 179

FIRST CLO. I' faith, if he be not rotten before he die—as we have many pocky corses now-a-days, that will scarce hold the laying in—he will last you some eight year or nine year: a tanner will last you nine year. 184

HAM. Why he more than another?

FIRST CLO. Why, sir, his hide is so tanned with his trade, that he will keep out water a great while; and your water is a sore decayer of your whoreson dead body. Here's a skull now; this skull has lain in the earth three and twenty years. 191

HAM. Whose was it?

FIRST CLO. A whoreson mad fellow's it was: whose do you think it was?

HAM. Nay, I know not.

FIRST CLO. A pestilence on him for a mad rogue! a' poured a flagon of Rhenish on my head once. This same skull, sir, was Yorick's skull, the king's jester.

HAM. This?

FIRST CLO. E'en that.

HAM. Let me see. [*Takes the skull.*] Alas, poor Yorick! I knew him, Horatio: a fellow of infinite jest, of most excellent fancy: he hath borne me on his back a thousand 205 times; and now, how abhorred in my imagination it is! my gorge rises at it. Here hung those lips that I have kissed I know not how oft. Where be your gibes now? your gambols? your songs? your flashes of merri- 210 ment, that were wont to set the table on a roar? Not one now, to mock your own grinning? quite chap-fallen? Now get you to my lady's chamber, and tell her, let her paint an inch thick, to this favour she must come; make her laugh at that. Prithee, Horatio, tell me one thing.

HOR. What's that, my lord?

HAM. Dost thou think Alexander looked o' this fashion i' the earth?

HOR. E'en so. 220

HAM. And smelt so? pah!

[*Puts down the skull.*

HOR. E'en so, my lord.

HAM. To what base uses we may return, Horatio! Why may not imagination trace the noble dust of Alexander, till he find it stopping a bung-hole? 226

HOR. 'Twere to consider too curiously, to consider so.

HAM. No, faith, not a jot; but to follow him thither with modesty enough, and likeli- 230

139. **quick**, swift because the joke is tossed swiftly back and forth. 148. **absolute**, meticulously accurate. 149. **card**, compass, so considering every point; **equivocation**, ambiguity. 152. **picked**, refined, fastidious. 153. **galls his kibe**, chafes his chilblain. 167. **no great matter**, doesn't make much difference. 181. **pocky**, rotten with venereal disease. 188. **sore**, grievous. 189. **whoreson**, bastardly.

197. **Rhenish**, Rhine wine. 204. **of infinite jest**, with an endless number of jokes. 211. **on a roar**, roaring with laughter. 212. **chap-fallen**, a pun (1) down in the mouth, (2) having no lower jaw. 215. **favour**, appearance. 222. **E'en so**, just like that. 223. **base**, vile. 227. **consider too curiously**, think about it too minutely. 230. **with modesty**, without exaggeration.

hood to lead it: as thus: Alexander died, Alexander was buried, Alexander returneth into dust; the dust is earth; of earth we make loam; and why of that loam, whereto he was converted, might they not stop a beer-barrel? 235

Imperious Cæsar, dead and turn'd to clay,
Might stop a hole to keep the wind away:
O, that that earth, which kept the world in awe,
Should patch a wall to expel the winter's flaw!

But soft! but soft! aside: here comes the king, 240

[*Enter* PRIESTS, *&c. in procession; the Corpse of* OPHELIA; LAERTES *and* MOURNERS, *following;* KING, QUEEN, *their trains, &c.*]

The queen, the courtiers: who is this they follow?
And with such maimèd rites? This doth betoken
The corse they follow did with desperate hand
Fordo it own life: 'twas of some estate.
Couch we awhile, and mark. 245

[*Retiring with* HORATIO.

LAER. What ceremony else?

HAM. That is Laertes,
A very noble youth: mark.

LAER. What ceremony else?

FIRST PRIEST. Her obsequies have been as far enlarged
As we have warranty: her death was doubtful; 250
And, but that great command o'ersways the order,
She should in ground unsanctified have lodged
Till the last trumpet; for charitable prayers,
Shards, flints and pebbles should be thrown on her:
Yet here she is allow'd her virgin crants, 255
Her maiden strewments and the bringing home
Of bell and burial.

LAER. Must there no more be done?

FIRST PRIEST. No more be done:
We should profane the service of the dead
To sing a requiem and such rest to her 260
As to peace-parted souls.

LAER. Lay her i' the earth:
And from her fair and unpolluted flesh
May violets spring! I tell thee, churlish priest,
A ministering angel shall my sister be,
When thou liest howling.

HAM. What, the fair Ophelia!

QUEEN. Sweets to the sweet: farewell! 266

[*Scattering flowers.*]

I hoped thou shouldst have been my Hamlet's wife;
I thought thy bride-bed to have deck'd, sweet maid,
And not have strew'd thy grave.

LAER. O, treble woe
Fall ten times treble on that cursèd head, 270
Whose wicked deed thy most ingenious sense
Deprived thee of! Hold off the earth awhile,
Till I have caught her once more in mine arms: [*Leaps into the grave.*]
Now pile your dust upon the quick and dead,
Till of this flat a mountain you have made,
To o'ertop old Pelion, or the skyish head 276
Of blue Olympus.

HAM. [*Advancing*] What is he whose grief
Bears such an emphasis? whose phrase of sorrow
Conjures the wandering stars, and makes them stand
Like wonder-wounded hearers? This is I, 280
Hamlet the Dane. [*Leaps into the grave.*

LAER. The devil take thy soul!

[*Grappling with him.*

HAM. Thou pray'st not well.
I prithee, take thy fingers from my throat;
For, though I am not splenitive and rash,
Yet have I something in me dangerous, 285
Which let thy wiseness fear: hold off thy hand.

KING. Pluck them asunder.

QUEEN. Hamlet, Hamlet!

234. **loam,** clay; **whereto,** into which. 236. **Imperious,** imperial. 239. **flaw,** gust of wind. 240. **aside,** stand aside. 242. **maimed,** incomplete. 244. **Fordo it,** destroy its; **estate,** high rank. 245. **Couch,** hide. 246. **What ceremony else?** Are there to be no further ceremonies? 250. **warranty,** permission; **doubtful,** suspicious. 254. **Shards,** pieces of broken pottery. 255. **crants,** garland. 256. **strewments,** the strewing of flowers; **bringing home,** (1) bringing home a bride after a wedding, (2) bringing Ophelia to her eternal home. 260. **requiem,** i.e., mass for the dead. 261. **peace-parted souls,** souls that died in peace. 269. **treble,** triple. 271. **most ingenious sense,** i.e., reason. 274. **quick,** living. 276. **o'ertop,** rise higher than; **Pelion,** the mountain that the giants, in their war with the gods, piled up on Mt. Ossa, so as to reach Olympus. 279. **wandering stars,** planets. 284. **splenitive,** hot-tempered.

ALL. Gentlemen,—

HOR. Good my lord, be quiet.

[*The* ATTENDANTS *part them, and they come out of the grave.*

HAM. Why, I will fight with him upon this theme
Until my eyelids will no longer wag. 290

QUEEN. O my son, what theme?

HAM. I loved Ophelia: forty thousand brothers
Could not, with all their quantity of love,
Make up my sum. What wilt thou do for her?

KING. O, he is mad, Laertes. 295

QUEEN. For love of God, forbear him.

HAM. 'Swounds, show me what thou'lt do:
Woo 't weep? woo 't fight? woo 't fast? woo 't tear thyself?
Woo 't drink up eisel? eat a crocodile?
I'll do 't. Dost thou come here to whine? 300
To outface me with leaping in her grave?
Be buried quick with her, and so will I:
And, if thou prate of mountains, let them throw
Millions of acres on us, till our ground
Singeing his pate against the burning zone,
Make Ossa like a wart! Nay, an thou'lt mouth,
I'll rant as well as thou. 307

QUEEN. This is mere madness:
And thus awhile the fit will work on him;
Anon, as patient as the female dove,
When that her golden couplets are disclosed,
His silence will sit drooping.

HAM. Hear you, sir; 311
What is the reason that you use me thus?
I loved you ever: but it is no matter;
Let Hercules himself do what he may, 314
The cat will mew and dog will have his day.

[*Exit.*

KING. I pray you, good Horatio, wait upon him. [*Exit* HORATIO.]
[*To* LAERTES] Strengthen your patience in our last night's speech;
We'll put the matter to the present push.
Good Gertrude, set some watch over your son.
This grave shall have a living monument: 320
An hour of quiet shortly shall we see;
Till then, in patience our proceeding be.

[*Exeunt.*

SCENE II. *A hall in the castle.*

[*Enter* HAMLET *and* HORATIO.]

HAM. So much for this, sir: now shall you see the other;
You do remember all the circumstance?

HOR. Remember it, my lord!

HAM. Sir, in my heart there was a kind of fighting,
That would not let me sleep: methought I lay 5
Worse than the mutines in the bilboes. Rashly,
And praised be rashness for it, let us know,
Our indiscretion sometimes serves us well,
When our deep plots do pall: and that should teach us
There's a divinity that shapes our ends, 10
Rough-hew them how we will,—

HOR. That is most certain.

HAM. Up from my cabin,
My sea-gown scarf'd about me, in the dark
Groped I to find out them; had my desire, 14
Finger'd their packet, and in fine withdrew
To mine own room again; making so bold,
My fears forgetting manners, to unseal
Their grand commission; where I found, Horatio,—
O royal knavery!—an exact command, 19
Larded with many several sorts of reasons
Importing Denmark's health and England's too,
With, ho! such bugs and goblins in my life,
That, on the supervise, no leisure bated,
No, not to stay the grinding of the axe, 24
My head should be struck off.

HOR. Is 't possible?

HAM. Here's the commission: read it at more leisure.
But wilt thou hear me how I did proceed?

290. **wag**, move (with no ludicrous connotation). 296. **forbear**, have patience with. 298. **Woo't**, wilt, a form used only by illiterates and so insulting. 299. **eisel**, vinegar, a supposed antidote to anger. 305. **burning zone**, the sun's orbit. 306. **mouth**, i.e., use extravagant language. 307. **mere**, complete. 310. **golden couplets**, the two newly hatched young of a dove are covered with golden down. 317. **in**, by remembering; **last night's speech**, i.e., what we said last night. 318. **present push**, immediate test. 320. **living**, lasting. Scene ii: 1. **this**, this part of the story. 2. **circumstances**, details. 6. **mutines**, mutineers; **bilboes**, fetters. 9. **pall**, fail. 11. **Rough . . . will**, shape them as roughly as we please. 13. **sea-gown**, short-sleeved gown reaching to the knee; **scarf'd**, thrown like a scarf. 14. **find out**, discover. 15. **Finger'd**, stole; **in fine**, finally. 20. **Larded**, dressed up. 21. **Importing**, bearing upon; **health**, welfare. 22. **such . . . life**, i.e., with exclamations about the evils I had done; **bugs**, bugbears. 23. **on the supervise**, upon looking it over; **leisure bated**, delay allowed. 24. **stay**, wait for.

HOR. I beseech you.

HAM. Being thus be-netted round with villanies,—
Ere I could make a prologue to my brains, 30
They had begun the play—I sat me down,
Devised a new commission, wrote it fair:
I once did hold it, as our statists do,
A baseness to write fair and labour'd much
How to forget that learning, but, sir, now
It did me yeoman's service: wilt thou know
The effect of what I wrote? 37

HOR. Ay, good my lord.

HAM. An earnest conjuration from the king,
As England was his faithful tributary,
As love between them like the palm might flourish, 40
As peace should still her wheaten garland wear
And stand a comma 'tween their amities,
And many such-like "As"es of great charge,
That, on the view and knowing of these contents, 44
Without debatement further, more or less,
He should the bearers put to sudden death,
Not shriving-time allow'd.

HOR. How was this seal'd?

HAM. Why, even in that was heaven ordinant.
I had my father's signet in my purse,
Which was the model of that Danish seal; 50
Folded the writ up in form of the other,
Subscribed it, gave 't the impression, placed it safely,
The changeling never known. Now, the next day
Was our sea-fight; and what to this was sequent
Thou know'st already. 55

HOR. So Guildenstern and Rosencrantz go to 't.

HAM. Why, man, they did make love to this employment;
They are not near my conscience; their defeat
Does by their own insinuation grow: 59
'Tis dangerous when the baser nature comes
Between the pass and fell incensèd points
Of mighty opposites.

HOR. Why, what a king is this!

HAM. Does it not, thinks't thee, stand me now upon—
He that hath kill'd my king and whored my mother,
Popp'd in between the election and my hopes, 65
Thrown out his angle for my proper life,
And with such cozenage—is't not perfect conscience,
To quit him with this arm? and is 't not to be damn'd,
To let this canker of our nature come
In further evil? 70

HOR. It must be shortly known to him from England
What is the issue of the business there.

HAM. It will be short: the interim is mine;
And a man's life's no more than to say "One."
But I am very sorry, good Horatio, 75
That to Laertes I forgot myself;
For, by the image of my cause, I see
The portraiture of his: I'll court his favours:
But, sure, the bravery of his grief did put me
Into a towering passion.

HOR. Peace! who comes here? 80

[*Enter* OSRIC.]

OSR. Your lordship is right welcome back to Denmark.

HAM. I humbly thank you, sir. Dost know this water-fly?

HOR. No, my good lord. 85

HAM. Thy state is the more gracious; for 'tis a vice to know him. He hath much land, and fertile: let a beast be lord of beasts, and his crib shall stand at the king's mess: 'tis a chough; but, as I say, spacious in the possession of dirt. 90

OSR. Sweet lord, if your lordship were at

30. **make . . . brains**, begin to think (how to act). 32. **fair**, legibly. 33. **statists**, statesmen. 34. **baseness**, mark of low social position. 36. **yeoman's**, substantial. 37. **effect**, gist. 38. **conjuration**, entreaty. 42. **comma**, here = connecting link. 43. **"As"es**, pun on "asses"; **charge**, weight. 45. **debatement**, discussion. 46. **sudden**, immediate. 47. **shriving-time**, time for confession and absolution. 48. **ordinant**, ordering events. 52. **Subscribed**, signed; **gave . . . impression**, i.e., stamped it with the King's seal. 53. **changeling . . . known**, substitution never detected. 54. **sequent**, subsequent. 56. **to 't**, i.e., to their doom. 57. **make . . . employment**, fairly begged to be treated in this way. 58. **near**, on; **defeat**, destruction.

59. **insinuation**, meddling. 60. **baser**, lower in rank. 61. **pass**, thrust; **fell**, cruel. 62. **opposites**, opponents. 63. **stand . . . upon**, become my duty. 65. **election**, the Danish monarch was elective. 66. **Thrown . . . angle**, angled for; **proper**, very. 67. **cozenage**, deceit. 68. **quit**, get even with. 69. **canker of our nature**, ulcer of humanity. 69-70. **come In**, wreak. 74. **to say "One,"** i.e., to get one good hit (in fencing). 77. **image . . . cause**, reflection of my situation. 79. **bravery**, ostentation. 86. **state**, situation; **gracious**, favorable. 88-9. **let . . . mess**, let a man be rich enough and he can get into courtly society. 90. **chough**, a crow, i.e., a chatterer.

leisure, I should impart a thing to you from his majesty.

HAM. I will receive it, sir, with all diligence of spirit. Put your bonnet to his right use; 95 'tis for the head.

OSR. I thank your lordship, it is very hot.

HAM. No, believe me, 'tis very cold; the wind is northerly.

OSR. It is indifferent cold, my lord, indeed. 100

HAM. But yet methinks it is very sultry and hot for my complexion.

OSR. Exceedingly, my lord; it is very sultry, —as 'twere,—I cannot tell how. But, my lord, his majesty bade me signify to you that he has laid a great wager on your head: sir, this is the matter,—

HAM. I beseech you, remember— 108

[HAMLET *moves him to put on his hat.*

OSR. Nay, good my lord; for mine ease, in good faith. Sir, here is newly come to court Laertes; believe me, an absolute gentleman, full of most excellent differences, of very soft society and great showing: indeed, to speak feelingly of him, he is the card or calendar of gentry, for you shall find in him the continent of what part a gentleman would see. 116

HAM. Sir, his definement suffers no perdition in you; though, I know, to divide him inventorially would dizzy the arithmetic of memory, and yet but yaw neither, in re- 120 spect of his quick sail. But, in the verity of extolment, I take him to be a soul of great article; and his infusion of such dearth and rareness, as, to make true diction of him, his semblable in his mirror; and who else would trace him, his umbrage, nothing more. 126

OSR. Your lordship speaks most infallibly of him.

HAM. The concernancy, sir? why do we wrap the gentleman in our more rawer breath?

OSR. Sir? 130

HOR. Is 't not possible to understand in another tongue? You will do't, sir, really.

HAM. What imports the nomination of this gentleman?

OSR. Of Laertes? 135

HOR. His purse is empty already; all's golden words are spent.

HAM. Of him, sir.

ORS. I know you are not ignorant— 139

HAM. I would you did, sir; yet, in faith, if you did, it would not much approve me. Well, sir?

OSR. You are not ignorant of what excellence Laertes is— 144

HAM. I dare not confess that, lest I should compare with him in excellence; but, to know a man well, were to know himself.

OSR. I mean, sir, for his weapon; but in the imputation laid on him by them, in his meed he's unfellowed. 150

HAM. What's his weapon?

OSR. Rapier and dagger.

HAM. That's two of his weapons: but, well.

OSR. The king, sir, hath wagered with him six Barbary horses: against the which he 155 has imponed, as I take it, six French rapiers and poniards, with their assigns, as girdle, hangers, and so: three of the carriages, in faith, are very dear to fancy, very responsive to the hilts, most delicate carriages, and 160 of very liberal conceit.

HAM. What call you the carriages?

HOR. I knew you must be edified by the margent ere you had done.

OSR. The carriages, sir, are the hangers.

HAM. The phrase would be more german to the matter, if we could carry cannon by our sides: I would it might be hangers till then. But, on: six Barbary horses against six French swords, their assigns, and three liberal-conceited carriages; that's the French bet

95. **bonnet**, cap. 100. **indifferent**, rather. 102. **complexion**, temperament. 111. **absolute**, perfect. 112. **differences**, distinguishing qualities, accomplishments; **soft**, refined. 113. **great showing**, fine appearance. 114. **feelingly**, justly; **card**, compass. 115. **continent**, summary. 115-16. **the . . . see**, all the qualities of a perfect gentleman. 117. **his definement**, the description of him. 119-20. **arithmetic of memory**, the power of reckoning. 120-1. **yaw . . . sail**, i.e., the enumeration of Laertes' virtues is but a zig-zag-moving boat in trying to overtake the quick sailing of his attainments; **yaw**, move zigzag. 122. **article**, importance. 123. **of such dearth**, so exceptional; **rareness**, rarity. 124. **semblable**, image, i.e., no one is like him but his image in the mirrors. 125. **trace**, follow, imitate. 126. **umbrage**, shadow. 128. **The concernancy?** i.e., What has that to do with the matter? 131-2. **Is't . . . tongue?** i.e., Can't you understand your own jargon in another man's mouth? 133. **nomination**, naming. 141. **approve**, command. 147. **know himself**, i.e., a man can really know no one well but himself. 148. **for his weapon**, in the use of his weapon (in dueling). 149. **imputation**, reputation. 150. **meed**, merits; **unfellowed**, without equal. 156. **imponed**, wagered. 157. **poniards**, daggers; **assigns**, appendages. 158. **hangers**, straps attaching the sword to a belt. 159. **very responsive**, corresponding exactly. 160. **delicate carriages**, i.e., hangers of delicate workmanship; **liberal conceit**, elaborate design. 163. **margent**, marginal comment. 165. **german**, germane, appropriate.

against the Danish. Why is this "imponed," as you call it? 171

OSR. The king, sir, hath laid, that in a dozen passes between yourself and him, 173 he shall not exceed you three hits: he hath laid on twelve for nine; and it would come to immediate trial, if your lordship would vouchsafe the answer.

HAM. How if I answer "no"?

OSR. I mean, my lord, the opposition of your person in trial. 179

HAM. Sir, I will walk here in the hall: if it please his majesty, 't is the breathing time of day with me; let the foils be brought, the gentleman willing, and the king hold his purpose, I will win for him an I can; if not, I will gain nothing but my shame and the odd hits. 185

OSR. Shall I re-deliver you e'en so?

HAM. To this effect, sir; after what flourish your nature will.

OSR. I commend my duty to your lordship.

HAM. Yours, yours. [*Exit* OSRIC.] He does well to commend it himself; there are no tongues else for's turn.

HOR. This lapwing runs away with the shell on his head. 194

HAM. He did comply with his dug, before he sucked it. Thus has he—and many more of the same breed that I know the drossy age dotes on—only got the tune of the time and outward habit of encounter; a kind of yesty collection, which carries them through and through the most fond and winnowed opinions; and do but blow them to their trial, the bubbles are out. 202

[*Enter a* LORD.]

LORD. My lord, his majesty commended him to you by young Osric, who brings back to him, that you attend him in the hall: 205 he sends to know if your pleasure hold to play with Laertes, or that you will take longer time.

HAM. I am constant to my purposes; they follow the king's pleasure: if his fitness speaks, mine is ready; now or whensoever, provided I be so able as now. 211

LORD. The king and queen and all are coming down.

HAM. In happy time.

LORD. The queen desires you to use some gentle entertainment to Laertes before you fall to play.

HAM. She well instructs me. [*Exit* LORD.

HOR. You will lose this wager, my lord. 219

HAM. I do not think so; since he went into France, I have been in continual practice; I shall win at the odds. But thou wouldst not think how ill all's here about my heart: but it is no matter.

HOR. Nay, good my lord,— 224

HAM. It is but foolery; but it is such a kind of gain-giving, as would perhaps trouble a woman.

HOR. If your mind dislike any thing, obey it: I will forestall their repair hither, and say you are not fit. 229

HAM. Not a whit, we defy augury: there's a special providence in the fall of a sparrow. If it be now, 'tis not to come; if it be not to come, it will be now; if it be not now, yet it will come: the readiness is all: since no man has aught of what he leaves, what is't to leave betimes? Let be. 235

[*Enter* KING, QUEEN, LAERTES, LORDS, OSRIC, *and* ATTENDANTS *with foils, &c.*]

KING. Come, Hamlet, come, and take this hand from me.

[*The* KING *puts* LAERTES' *hand into* HAMLET'S.

HAM. Give me your pardon, sir: I've done you wrong;
But pardon 't, as you are a gentleman.
This presence knows,
And you must needs have heard, how I am punish'd 240
With sore distraction. What I have done,

172. laid, bet. 173-5. he . . . twelve for nine, i.e., that in a dozen bouts Laertes cannot beat Hamlet by more than three up (to use a golf term). 176. vouchsafe the answer, accept the challenge. 181. breathing time, time for exercise. 186. re-deliver you, take back your message. 193-4. lapwing . . . head, the lapwing (a kind of English sandpiper) was supposed to be so precocious that it ran away from its nest before completely hatched. 195. comply . . . dug, bowed to his mother's breast. 197. drossy, worthless. 199. outward . . . encounter, superficial social manners; yesty collection, frothy anthology (of phrases). 200-1. which . . . opinions, which permeates (and contaminates) the most trivial and the most refined judgments (of social manners). 202. blow . . . trial, test them by blowing on them; are out, disappear. 205. that . . . him, the news that you are to await him. 209-10. his fitness speaks, it meets his convenience. 214. In happy time, that's good. 215-6. use . . . entertainment, give a friendly welcome. 225. foolery, an absurd thing. 226. gain-giving, misgiving. 228. repair, coming. 230. defy augury, despise the superstitious belief in omens. 235. Let be, i.e., cease trying to dissuade me. 239. presence, royal assembly. 241. sore distraction, grievous mental confusion (madness).

That might your nature, honour and exception
Roughly awake, I here proclaim was madness.
Was 't Hamlet wrong'd Laertes? Never Hamlet:
If Hamlet from himself be ta'en away, 245
And when he's not himself does wrong Laertes,
Then Hamlet does it not, Hamlet denies it.
Who does it, then? His madness: if 't be so,
Hamlet is of the faction that is wrong'd;
His madness is poor Hamlet's enemy. 250
Sir, in this audience,
Let my disclaiming from a purposed evil
Free me so far in your most generous thoughts,
That I have shot mine arrow o'er the house,
And hurt my brother.

LAER. I am satisfied in nature,
Whose motive, in this case, should stir me most 256
To my revenge: but in my terms of honour
I stand aloof; and will no reconcilement,
Till by some elder masters, of known honour,
I have a voice and precedent of peace, 260
To keep my name ungored. But till that time,
I do receive your offer'd love like love,
And will not wrong it.

HAM. I embrace it freely;
And will this brother's wager frankly play.
Give us the foils. Come on.

LAER. Come, one for me.

HAM. I'll be your foil, Laertes: in mine ignorance 266
Your skill shall, like a star i' the darkest night,
Stick fiery off indeed.

LAER. You mock me, sir.

HAM. No, by this hand.

KING. Give them the foils, young Osric. Cousin Hamlet, 270
You know the wager?

HAM. Very well, my lord;
Your grace hath laid the odds o' the weaker side.

KING. I do not fear it; I have seen you both:
But since he is better'd, we have therefore odds.

LAER. This is too heavy, let me see another. 275

HAM. This likes me well. These foils have all a length? [*They prepare to play.*

OSR. Ay, my good lord.

KING. Set me the stoups of wine upon that table.
If Hamlet give the first or second hit,
Or quit in answer of the third exchange, 280
Let all the battlements their ordnance fire;
The king shall drink to Hamlet's better breath;
And in the cup an union shall he throw,
Richer than that which four successive kings
In Denmark's crown have worn. Give me the cups; 285
And let the kettle to the trumpet speak,
The trumpet to the cannoneer without,
The cannons to the heavens, the heavens to earth,
"Now the king drinks to Hamlet." Come, begin:
And you, the judges, bear a wary eye. 290

HAM. Come on, sir.

LAER. Come, my lord. [*They play.*

HAM. One.

LAER. No.

HAM. Judgement.

OSR. A hit, a very palpable hit.

LAER. Well; again.

KING. Stay; give me drink. Hamlet, this pearl is thine;
Here's to thy health.

[*Trumpets sound, and cannon shot off within.*]

Give him the cup.

HAM. I'll play this bout first; set it by awhile. 295
Come. [*They play.*] Another hit; what say you?

LAER. A touch, a touch, I do confess.

KING. Our son shall win.

242. **exception,** disapproval. 243. **Roughly awake,** arouse by my rough (crude) conduct. 251. **audience,** royal presence. 255. **nature,** my natural feelings. 256. **Whose motive,** the promptings of which. 257. **in . . . honour,** as I understand the code of honor. 258. **will no,** will agree to no. 259. **masters,** experts. 260. **voice and precedent,** decision based on precedent; **of peace,** for making up the quarrel. 261. **name ungored,** reputation unsullied. 264. **frankly play,** fence without bitterness. 266. **foil,** (1) a blunted sword, (2) a background to set off the brilliance of a jewel. 268. **Stick fiery off,** shine in brilliant contrast. 274. **is better'd,** considered you superior. 276. **likes,** suits. 278. **stoups,** goblets. 280. **quit . . . of,** scores a draw in. 283. **union,** large pearl. 286. **kettle,** kettle drum. 290. **bear . . . eye,** watch very carefully. 298. **shall,** will surely; **fat,** sweaty.

QUEEN. He's fat, and scant of breath.
Here, Hamlet, take my napkin, rub thy brows: 299
The queen carouses to thy fortune, Hamlet.

HAM. Good madam!

KING. Gertrude, do not drink.

QUEEN. I will, my lord; I pray you, pardon me.

KING. [*Aside*] It is the poison'd cup: it is too late.

HAM. I dare not drink yet, madam; by and by.

QUEEN. Come, let me wipe thy face. 305

LAER. My lord, I'll hit him now.

KING. I do not think 't.

LAER. [*Aside*] And yet 'tis almost 'gainst my conscience.

HAM. Come, for the third, Laertes: you but dally,
I pray you, pass with your best violence;
I am afeard you make a wanton of me. 310

LAER. Say you so? come on. [*They play.*

OSR. Nothing, neither way.

LAER. Have at you now!

[LAERTES *wounds* HAMLET; *then, in scuffling, they change rapiers, and* HAMLET *wounds* LAERTES.

KING. Part them; they are incensed.

HAM. Nay, come, again. [*The* QUEEN *falls.*

OSR. Look to the queen there, ho!

HOR. They bleed on both sides. How is it, my lord? 315

OSR. How is 't, Laertes?

LAER. Why, as a woodcock to mine own springe, Osric;
I am justly kill'd with mine own treachery.

HAM. How does the queen?

KING. She swounds to see them bleed.

QUEEN. No, no, the drink, the drink,—O my dear Hamlet,— 320
The drink, the drink! I am poison'd. [*Dies.*

HAM. O villany! Ho! let the door be lock'd:
Treachery! Seek it out.

LAER. It is here, Hamlet: Hamlet, thou art slain;
No medicine in the world can do thee good;
In thee there is not half an hour of life; 326
The treacherous instrument is in thy hand,
Unbated and envenom'd: the foul practice
Hath turn'd itself on me; lo, here I lie, 329
Never to rise again: thy mother's poison'd:
I can no more: the king, the king's to blame.

HAM. The point envenom'd too!
Then, venom, to thy work. [*Stabs the* KING.

ALL. Treason! treason!

KING. O, yet defend me, friends; I am but hurt. 335

HAM. Here, thou incestuous, murderous, damnèd Dane,
Drink off this potion. Is thy union here?
Follow my mother. [*King dies.*

LAER. He is justly served;
It is a poison temper'd by himself.
Exchange forgiveness with me, noble Hamlet: 340
Mine and my father's death come not upon thee,
Nor thine on me! [*Dies.*

HAM. Heaven make thee free of it! I follow thee.
I am dead, Horatio. Wretched queen, adieu!
You that look pale and tremble at this chance, 345
That are but mutes or audience to this act,
Had I but time—as this fell sergeant, death,
Is strict in his arrest—O, I could tell you—
But let it be. Horatio, I am dead;
Thou livest; report me and my cause aright
To the unsatisfied.

HOR. Never believe it: 351
I am more an antique Roman than a Dane:
Here's yet some liquor left.

HAM. As thou'rt a man,
Give me the cup: let go; by heaven, I'll have't.
O good Horatio, what a wounded name, 355
Things standing thus unknown, shall live behind me!
If thou didst ever hold me in thy heart,
Absent thee from felicity awhile,
And in this harsh world draw thy breath in pain,
To tell my story. [*March afar off, and shot within.*]
What warlike noise is this?

299. napkin, handkerchief. **300. carouses,** drinks a full goblet. **309. pass,** thrust. **310. make . . . me,** treat me as though I were a child. **312. Nothing, neither way,** i.e., neither has scored a hit. **314. Look to,** take care of. **317. springe,** trap, i.e., a foolish victim of my own plot. **324. It is here,** i.e., I am the inventor of the treachery. **328. Unbated.** not blunted; **practice,** plot. **331. can,** can say. **335. hurt,** slightly wounded. **338. served,** treated. **339. temper'd,** concocted. **341. come . . . thee,** are not to be laid at your door. **346. mutes,** actors without speaking parts—"supers." **347. fell sergeant,** cruel police officer. **351. unsatisfied,** uninformed.

OSR. Young Fortinbras, with conquest come from Poland, 361
To the ambassadors of England gives
This warlike volley.

HAM. O, I die, Horatio;
The potent poison quite o'er-crows my spirit:
I cannot live to hear the news from England;
But I do prophesy the election lights 366
On Fortinbras: he has my dying voice;
So tell him, with the occurrents, more and less,
Which have solicited. The rest is silence.
[*Dies.*

HOR. Now cracks a noble heart. Good night, sweet prince; 370
And flights of angels sing thee to thy rest!
Why does the drum come hither?
[*March within.*

[*Enter* FORTINBRAS, *the* ENGLISH AMBASSADORS, *and others.*]

FORT. Where is this sight?

HOR. What is it ye would see?
If aught of woe or wonder, cease your search.

FORT. This quarry cries on havoc. O proud death, 375
What feast is toward in thine eternal cell,
That thou so many princes at a shot
So bloodily hast struck?

FIRST AMB. The sight is dismal;
And our affairs from England come too late:
The ears are senseless that should give us hearing, 380
To tell him his commandment is fulfill'd,
That Rosencrantz and Guildenstern are dead:
Where should we have our thanks?

HOR. Not from his mouth,
Had it the ability of life to thank you:
He never gave commandment for their death. 385
But since, so jump upon this bloody question,
You from the Polack wars, and you from England,
Are here arrived, give order that these bodies
High on a stage be placed to the view;
And let me speak to the yet unknowing world 390
How these things came about: so shall you hear
Of carnal, bloody, and unnatural acts,
Of accidental judgements, casual slaughters,
Of deaths put on by cunning and forced cause,
And, in this upshot, purposes mistook 395
Fall'n on the inventors' heads: all this can I
Truly deliver.

FORT. Let us haste to hear it,
And call the noblest to the audience.
For me, with sorrow I embrace my fortune:
I have some rights of memory in this kingdom, 400
Which now to claim my vantage doth invite me.

HOR. Of that I shall have also cause to speak,
And from his mouth whose voice will draw on more:
But let this same be presently perform'd,
Even while men's minds are wild; lest more mischance, 405
On plots and errors, happen.

FORT. Let four captains
Bear Hamlet, like a soldier, to the stage;
For he was likely, had he been put on,
To have proved most royally: and, for his passage,
The soldiers' music and the rites of war 410
Speak loudly for him.
Take up the bodies: such a sight as this
Becomes the field, but here shows much amiss.
Go, bid the soldiers shoot.
[*A dead march. Exeunt, bearing off the dead bodies; after which a peal of ordnance is shot off.*

364. **o'er-crows my spirit**, triumphs over my vital energy. 367. **voice**, vote. 368. **occurrents**, events. 369. **solicited**, brought about. 375. **quarry**, heap of dead bodies; **cries on havoc**, proclaims there has been a general slaughter here. 376. **toward**, in preparation. 379. **affairs**, reports of affairs. 380. **senseless**, deaf. 383. **his**, i.e., the King's. 384. **ability of life**, power of a living person. 386. **so jump upon**, following so close upon; **question**, quarrel. 389. **stage**, platform. 392. **carnal**, sensual. 393. **accidental judgements**, punishments inflicted by accident; **casual**, accidental. 394. **put on**, brought about; **forced cause**, i.e., necessitated by self-defense. 395. **upshot**, conclusion (of the tragedy); **purposes mistook**, intentions miscarried. 400. **rights of memory**, remembered claims. 401. **my vantage . . . invite me**, my rights invite me (to seize). 403. **voice . . . more**, vote will influence more [votes]. 404. **this same**, i.e., arrangements for telling the story; **presently perform'd**, done at once. 405. **wild**, greatly excited. 406. **On**, as a result of. 408. **put on**, promoted (to the throne). 409. **for his passage**, to mark his passing. 411. **Speak**, let speak. 413. **field**, battlefield; **shows much amiss**, is very inappropriate.

AFTERWORD

Shakespeare's plays are often described as universal or timeless. That is an accurate description. Shakespeare is nonetheless a provincial writer, who refers constantly in these plays to the foibles and preoccupations of the time in which he lived. The wealth of contemporary detail which he delights in commending to our attention ought to mystify or fatigue us, as it applies only to the England of Queen Elizabeth and King James. Its effect is, however, quite different. Paradoxically, we identify with Shakespeare's heroes and heroines, not as they are universal but as they are peculiar and concrete.

The tragedy of *Hamlet* exemplifies this paradox. Topical references are of the warp and woof of the play. Through Rosencrantz and Guildenstern, we hear of the painted signboard—Hercules, carrying the world on his shoulders—which hung before the Globe Playhouse in Shakespeare's London. Information is thrust at us—we may think it at first gratuitous—regarding the stage war between the adult actors, like those assembled in Shakespeare's company, the Lord Chamberlain's Men, and the very popular companies of boy actors, whose competition was increasingly formidable in the early years of the seventeenth century. Hamlet himself, putting aside his tragic role temporarily, speaks for Shakespeare in offering advice to the players on the right technique to adopt in the theatre. The pompous style of Christopher Marlowe, the greatest of Shakespeare's predecessors in the drama, is parodied in the long speech which Hamlet and the First Player share between them. Evidently, the taste of the age seems to Shakespeare so inadequate as to require special comment. An excellent play, he makes Hamlet observe, is likely to displease the million. It is caviar to the general. What the drossy age dotes on is superficiality, as epitomized in the courtier Osric. Hamlet in the Graveyard Scene finds occasion to reminisce on the breaking down of social barriers and norms of conduct. The disintegration of which he has taken note "this three years" is most conspicuous in England. There, the men are all as mad as he is.

This fascinated attention to contemporary business, which characterizes *Hamlet* and is manifest in all of Shakespeare's work, discloses to us a side of the playwright we might not otherwise have suspected. Shakespeare on this side is to be described as a social annalist or historian, whose concern is not simply to depict the sufferings of an isolated ego—Prince Hamlet, the melancholy Dane—but to delineate a context, a full and circumstantial world to which the individual ego is critically related. We trust him, and not least in this most popular and enduring of all his plays, because of his insistence, like that of an archaeologist, on filling out the background, on estimating and establishing the soil from which his protagonist springs. Hamlet, the abstract symbol of unease and dislocation, is nothing. Shakespeare's Hamlet is a man in his habit as he lived. From him, the social critic and commentator on the stage, we learn that the way to universal significance and an appeal that transcends time is, first of all, through absorption in parochial things. *Hamlet* the play speaks meaningfully to our own time, even after the lapse of centuries, as it is committed to rendering a particular moment in history. The topicality with which the play abounds constitutes the indispensable point from which one departs, in his quest for the general truth. First the array of particulars, after that the summarizing law.

But these topical references function also as a comment on the action and purport of the play, and even though their pertinence is not immediately apparent. Hercules, who calls to mind Shakespeare's playhouse, is a greatly active and vigorous figure, who destroys with his own hands the Nemean lion, and shoulders without complaining the weight of the world. When Hamlet, grappling with Laertes over the corpse of Ophelia, invokes the name of this mythological hero, we are made conscious instinctively of the want, in Hamlet himself, of the vigorous activity appropriate to a prince and leader of men.

Hamlet is not a private but a public person, and therefore it is important that Shakespeare record the character and felt pressure of the greater world or "general gender" beyond the court. The tragedy of *Hamlet* is enacted in the eyes of the multitude, whose fortunes are bound up inextricably with those of the Prince. He is the expectancy and rose of the state: the heir apparent to the throne of Denmark. His conduct is crucial for the "safety and health of this whole state." The majesty to which he is expected to succeed is like a massive wheel, to whose huge spokes "ten thousand lesser things" are connected. We are not allowed to forget the consequential presence of these lesser things. Claudius is unable to deal directly with Hamlet, because he is "loved of the distracted multitude." But this love is untrustworthy, for it is founded not on judgment but appearance. The people in their thoughts are muddied and unwholesome, as quick to follow Laertes as Hamlet. If, as we are made irresistibly to feel, the people is a rabble and the time disjointed and debased, perhaps we will estimate with more charity or more caution Hamlet's notorious reluctance to act and his unwillingness to shoulder responsibility.

The constant glancing at theatrical business is, like the contemptuous portrayal of the age, intended to sharpen our awareness of the ambiguity of Hamlet's position. Exaggerated modes of acting, hollow displays of affection, as in the Dumb Show and the play-within-the-play, ranting language that is a counterfeit of the real thing—these remind us obliquely that Shakespeare's tragedy is an essay in discrimination. As we seek to understand the hysteria, perhaps the madness, with which the Prince is afflicted, we will wish concurrently to distinguish between true and spurious emotion. Hamlet, the man who knows not "seems," who wears his heart on his sleeve, is the antithesis of the play actor. But the milieu in which he lives, presided over by a player-king and his seeming-virtuous queen, is false to the core. In Hamlet's world, hypocrisy is regnant. Perhaps the hero, who disdains to play the hypocrite and, as he is truthful, unpacks his heart with bitter words, is peculiar only by contrast.

Hamlet is man in society; and also himself alone. Each description is tenable of him, and each is important for a total reading of the play. "Two truths are told," like the contradictory tidings the Witches address to Macbeth. The modern producer, as his instinct is to find and seize the governing thread, is inclined to attend exclusively to one aspect of Hamlet's story. The role of Fortinbras—as single-mindedness overbears the myriadmindedness of Shakespeare—is understood to be dispensable. Omit to present this ostensibly minor figure, whose public ardors contrast powerfully with the private and interior struggle which characterizes the Prince, and the bias of the play shifts radically from political and social tragedy to a domestic and more nearly personal imbroglio. Omit to focus on Hamlet's sexual nausea, his preoccupation with suicide, his loathing of the world as "an unweeded garden" possessed by "things rank and gross in nature," and the play tends to become what it was to Shakespeare's predecessors—the exterior and hence melodramatic chronicle of a public revenger who seeks the life of the king, not least because the king is a usurper who has "popped in" between the election and his hopes. Here are two Hamlets: one of them the producer is likely to choose, depending on his proclivities and hence his reading of the play.

But choice is malapropos. One wants to amalgamate, to claim the whole man. Each Hamlet is of Shakespeare's devising: the deeply troubled protagonist who is innocent of dynastic ambitions, whose important life is endured in the isolation of the heart; and the prime mover on the public stage, who is subject to his royal birth, who walks "with a larger tether" than the generality of men. The play confesses, not the unity of exclusiveness and narrow estimation, but a more comprehensive unity, like that of life itself, which associates diverse and even contradictory elements to make a "mingled yarn." This yarn or combining of disparate things is more persuasive and more nearly true as it is mingled. Focus in *Hamlet* is not reserved to the inner problems of the hero, nor to the social and political problems which beset him. Focus, as in a kaleidoscope, which is the appropriate image for the play, is continually shifting.

In the opening scene, we are asked to attend, not on the Prince, but on the "warlike form" of Hamlet's father. The dead king is represented as a military hero, who vanquishes in single combat King Fortinbras of Norway. A readiness to take action "when honor's at the stake" characterizes the older generation. Young Fortinbras, the son of the defeated king, is marked by the same alacrity, as witness the revenge he is preparing against Denmark. The officers of the Watch, reflecting on the appearance of the Ghost and the imminent outbreak of war, are full of apprehension. Their talk is of "some strange eruption to our state," and of "post-haste and romage" (agitated activity) throughout the land. They recall the frightening omens which preceded the death of Julius Caesar, another mighty figure from the past. So far, they have nothing to say of young Hamlet or of the personal troubles that afflict him.

But the information Shakespeare is putting before us speaks inferentially, by comparison and contrast, to the character of the Prince. Always, we are asked to judge Hamlet in terms of his context. Against his incapacity to act is the background of unhesitating action. Young Fortinbras, who comes nearer and nearer as the play progresses, is not given to thinking too precisely on the event. Radically unlike Hamlet, he is willing to fight "for an eggshell." That is true of Laertes, who sweeps to his revenge without delay and evidently without scruple or thought. The fiercely energetic behavior of these persons, each of whom is committed to requiting a father's death, is partly to be admired, partly to be defined as recklessness and folly. How does the definition illuminate Hamlet's dilemma?

Shakespeare, who declines to pass judgment on his hero, supplies us abundantly with the grounds of judgment. Horatio, the confidant on whom Hamlet relies, functions as part of this judgmental process. Horatio seems to embody the norm or standard by which we measure the aberration of the hero. In this, he is apparently like Banquo in *Macbeth* or like Edgar in *King Lear*. But appearances, as often in Hamlet's world, are deceiving. The man who declines to "let belief take hold of him," who attributes to "fantasy" the apparition on the battlements, is not the man against whom we must measure Prince Hamlet. Horatio is approved as he is not "passion's slave," as he accepts with equanimity "fortune's buffets and rewards," and in this description Hamlet himself, in his morbidity and hysteria, is partly indicted. The qualifying word is, however, decisive. Horatio, in proof, is not so equable as stolid, not so much constant in the teeth of mental suffering as insensible of it. "There are more things in Heaven and earth" than are dreamed of in his philosophy. After all, he is not the *punctum indifferens* or point of rest we are seeking. Where, in *Hamlet,* is this point of rest? Perhaps Shakespeare, for once, locates it in the person of his hero.

The technique of proceeding by comparison and contrast is a familiar part of Shakespeare's dramatic equipment. In this play, he employs it with notable success. He lays bare to our inspection the corrupt and time-serving character of the Danish court, whose ruler is a cutpurse. The typical chamberlain or court official is Polonius, a tedious old fool who manipulates his willing daughter like a piece of goods. Fellowship is presented by Rosencrantz and Guildenstern, whom Hamlet is wise to trust as he would "adders fanged." Detail by detail, character by character, Shakespeare builds the picture of a world as rotten as the pocky corpse with which we become acquainted in the Graveyard Scene.

In the ending of the play, interest centers on the death of the hero. But the world and its business are not permitted to recede. The inestimable thing, which is the man himself, has its necessary complement in the context or environing foil. The dark presence of the slaughtered Prince works vividly on our senses. But Hamlet, though he dominates, is not the sole inhabitant of this tragic milieu. Young Fortinbras with conquest comes from Poland to prosecute his claim to the throne. We recall that, in an earlier time, King Hamlet "smote the sledded Polacks on the ice." Now, history repeats itself, but with a poignant difference. The past impinges on the present. The particular event—which, as it is particular, idiosyncratic, is finally mysterious—is invested with public significance.

As that is so, it is not tenable, finally, to read Shakespeare's play as the ego-centered chronicle of an anguished young man, motivated by personal disorder. That is what Claudius thinks, and partly, of course, he is right. *Hamlet* is open to a multitude of different and even conflicting interpretations, and that is one reason why it is the most popular play ever written. The Hamlet whom Claudius sees and fears is the unpredictable and hence dangerous neurotic, who proclaims to his treacherous school-fellows, "O God, I could be bounded in a nutshell and count myself a king of infinite space were it not that I have bad dreams."

There is, however, another and more considerable Hamlet, whom we remember as he interacts profoundly with the life of his times. This Hamlet is the public figure, the courtier, soldier, and scholar, "The observed of all observers." In him is documented the unrelenting attention of his creator to the claims of a world beyond the self. This is to say that Shakespeare, in his abiding concern with the total context, is a greatly political writer. His subject is not man in a vacuum, but man in society. *Hamlet,* as it pursues the connection, is politics, writ large.

Suggested Reading

Alexander, Peter, *Hamlet: Father and Son* (1955). Penguin.

Bevington, David M., ed., *Twentieth Century Interpretations of "Hamlet"* (1968). Prentice-Hall.

Bowers, Fredson T., *Elizabethan Revenge Tragedy* (1940). Penguin.

Bradley, A. C., *Shakespearean Tragedy* (1904). Premier. Papermac.

Brown, John R., and Bernard Harris, eds., *Hamlet* (1964).

Campbell, Lily B., *Shakespeare's Tragic Heroes: Slaves of Passion* (1930). Barnes and Noble.

Charney, Maurice, *Style in "Hamlet"* (1969).

Conklin, Paul S., *A History of Hamlet Criticism: 1601–1821* (1957).

Cooperman, Stanley, *Hamlet's Wounded Name* (1965).

Cross, Brenda, *The Film Hamlet: A Record of Its Production* (1948).

Dent, Alan, ed., *Hamlet: The Film and the Play* (1948).

Derlin, Christopher, *Hamlet's Divinity and Other Essays* (1964).

Draper, John W., *The "Hamlet" of Shakespeare's Audience* (1939).

Eliot, T. S., "Hamlet and His Problems," in *The Sacred Wood* (1920).

Elliott, G. R., *Scourge and Minister* (1951). Penguin.

Fergusson, Francis, *The Idea of a Theater* (1949). Penguin.

Granville-Barker, H., *Prefaces to Shakespeare,* ed. M. St. Clare Byrne, 4 vols. (1948). Princeton.

Hankins, John E., *The Character of Hamlet and Other Essays* (1951). Penguin.

Holmes, Martin, *The Guns of Elsinore* (1965).

Jones, Ernest, *Hamlet and Oedipus* (1910; rev. ed., 1949). Penguin. Anchor.

Knight, G. Wilson, *The Imperial Theme* (1931). Barnes and Noble.

———, *The Wheel of Fire* (enlarged ed. 1954). Barnes and Noble.

Knights, L. C., *An Approach to Hamlet* (1960). Penguin.

Levin, Harry, *The Question of Hamlet* (1959). Penguin.

Lewis, C. S., *Hamlet: The Prince or the Poem?* (1942).

de Madariaga, Salvador, *On Hamlet* (1948, reprinted with new preface, 1964). Penguin.

Prosser, Eleanor, *Hamlet and Revenge* (1967).

Raven, Anton, *A Hamlet Bibliography and Reference Guide: 1877–1935* (1936).

Rosen, William, *Shakespeare and the Craft of Tragedy* (1960).

SACKS, CLAIRE, and EDGAR WHAN, eds., *Hamlet, Enter Critic* (1960). Appleton-Century Crofts.

SANTAYANA, GEORGE, *Life and Letters* (1928).

Shakespeare Survey, IX (1956), ed. Allardyce Nicoll (volume devoted to *Hamlet*).

STOLL, ELMER EDGAR, *Hamlet: An Historical and Comparative Study* (1919).

WALDOCK, A. J., *Hamlet: A Study in Critical Method* (1931).

WALKER, ROY, *The Time Is Out of Joint* (1948). Penguin.

WELLEK, RENE, *A History of Modern Criticism: 1750–1950* (1955).

WILLIAMSON, CLAUDE C. H., *Readings on the Character of Hamlet, 1661–1947* (1950).

WILSON, J. DOVER, *What Happens in Hamlet* (3rd ed., 1951). Penguin. Cambridge.

Othello

A NOTE ON THE TEXT

The ultimate source of *Othello*, an Italian romance of the sixteenth century, is an unusually rewarding study. This source is the *Hecatommithi* or *Hundred Tales* of Giraldi Cinthio, published in 1566 and presumably adapted at a later date for English readers. It records exactly the conventional view of the black man as barbarian, and in fact may be described as a tragedy of miscegenation. Shakespeare takes the outlines of his plot from Cinthio's story but transforms completely its meaning and elementary point of view.

A likely date for the composition of *Othello* is the period 1602–1604. The play was written probably in the same years as *Hamlet* and *Twelfth Night*, each of which it resembles in charting the disparity between what is and what seems to be. *Othello* was played at Court before King James I on November 1, 1604. A first quarto appeared in 1622, a second in 1630. In the interval, the play was published in the Folio of 1623. The three versions are dissimilar in many respects. Modern editors generally assign priority to the Folio version.

OTHELLO, THE MOOR OF VENICE

DRAMATIS PERSONÆ

DUKE OF VENICE.
BRABANTIO, *a senator.*
Other senators.
GRATIANO, *brother to Brabantio.*
LODOVICO, *kinsman to Brabantio.*
OTHELLO, *a noble Moor in the service of the Venetian state.*
CASSIO, *his lieutenant.*
IAGO, *his ancient.*
RODERIGO, *a Venetian gentleman.*
MONTANO, *Othello's predecessor in the government of Cyprus.*
CLOWN, *servant to Othello.*
DESDEMONA, *daughter to Brabantio and wife to Othello.*
EMILIA, *wife to Iago.*
BIANCA, *mistress to Cassio.*
SAILOR, MESSENGER, HERALD, OFFICERS, GENTLEMEN, MUSICIANS, *and* ATTENDANTS.
SCENE: *Venice: a Sea-port in Cyprus.*

ACT I

SCENE I. *Venice. A street.*

[*Enter* RODERIGO *and* IAGO.]

ROD. Tush! never tell me; I take it much unkindly
That thou, Iago, who hast had my purse
As if the strings were thine, shouldst know of this.
IAGO. 'Sblood, but you will not hear me:
If ever I did dream of such a matter, 5
Abhor me.
ROD. Thou told'st me thou didst hold him in thy hate.
IAGO. Despise me, if I do not. Three great ones of the city,
In personal suit to make me his lieutenant,
Off-capp'd to him: and, by the faith of man, 10
I know my price, I am worth no worse a place:
But he, as loving his own pride and purposes,
Evades them, with a bombast circumstance
Horribly stuff'd with epithets of war;
And, in conclusion, 15
Nonsuits my mediators; for, "Certes," says he,
"I have already chose my officer."
And what was he?
Forsooth, a great arithmetician,
One Michael Cassio, a Florentine, 20
A fellow almost damn'd in a fair wife;
That never set a squadron in the field,
Nor the division of a battle knows
More than a spinster; unless the bookish theoric,
Wherein the togèd consuls can propose 25
As masterly as he: mere prattle, without practice,
Is all his soldiership. But he, sir, had the election:
And I, of whom his eyes had seen the proof
At Rhodes, at Cyprus and on other grounds
Christian and heathen, must be be-lee'd and calm'd 30
By debitor and creditor: this counter-caster.
He, in good time, must his lieutenant be,

Act I, Scene i: 3. **this,** i.e., Desdemona's elopement. 4. **'Sblood,** by God's blood. 10. **Off-capp'd,** stood with cap in hand (like suppliants). 13. **bombast circumstance,** high-sounding circumlocution. Bombast is cotton padding. 14. **epithets of war,** military terms. 16. **Nonsuits,** rejects the petition of. 19. **arithmetician,** a man whose knowledge of military tactics is derived only from books. 20. **Florentine,** i.e., a fellow fit only for commerce. Cassio was not a Florentine. 21. **wife,** woman. Cassio is not married. 23. **division,** disposition of troops. 24. **Spinster,** a man whose occupation is spinning; **theoric,** theory. 25. **toged,** wearing the toga, the gown of a civilian officer; **consuls,** here = senators; **propose,** speak. 29. **Rhodes . . . Cyprus,** outposts of Venice in her war with the Turks. 30. **be-lee'd,** placed in the lee of, i.e., where Cassio keeps the wind from his sails. 31. **counter-caster,** bookkeeper. 32. **in good time,** forsooth.

And I—God bless the mark!—his Moorship's ancient.
ROD. By heaven, I rather would have been his hangman.
IAGO. Why, there's no remedy; 'tis the curse of service, 35
Preferment goes by letter and affection,
And not by old gradation, where each second
Stood heir to the first. Now, sir, be judge yourself,
Whether I in any just term am affined
To love the Moor.
ROD. I would not follow him then. 40
IAGO. O, sir, content you;
I follow him to serve my turn upon him:
We cannot all be masters, nor all masters
Cannot be truly follow'd. You shall mark
Many a duteous and knee-crooking knave, 45
That, doting on his own obsequious bondage,
Wears out his time, much like his master's ass,
For nought but provender, and when he's old, cashier'd:
Whip me such honest knaves. Others there are
Who, trimm'd in forms and visages of duty,
Keep yet their hearts attending on themselves, 51
And, throwing but shows of service on their lords,
Do well thrive by them and when they have lined their coats
Do themselves homage: these fellows have some soul;
And such a one do I profess myself. For, sir,
It is as sure as you are Roderigo, 56
Were I the Moor, I would not be Iago:
In following him, I follow but myself;
Heaven is my judge, not I for love and duty,
But seeming so, for my peculiar end: 60
For when my outward action doth demonstrate
The native act and figure of my heart
In compliment extern, 'tis not long after
But I will wear my heart upon my sleeve
For daws to peck at: I am not what I am. 65
ROD. What a full fortune does the thicklips owe,
If he can carry 't thus!
IAGO. Call up her father,
Rouse him: make after him, poison his delight,
Proclaim him in the streets; incense her kinsmen,
And, though he in a fertile climate dwell, 70
Plague him with flies: though that his joy be joy,
Yet throw such changes of vexation on 't,
As it may lose some colour.
ROD. Here is her father's house; I'll call aloud.
IAGO. Do, with like timorous accent and dire yell 75
As when, by night and negligence, the fire
Is spied in populous cities.
ROD. What, ho, Brabantio! Signior Brabantio, ho!
IAGO. Awake! what, ho, Brabantio! thieves! thieves! thieves!
Look to your house, your daughter and your bags! 80
Thieves! thieves!

[BRABANTIO *appears above, at a window.*]

BRA. What is the reason of this terrible summons?
What is the matter there?
ROD. Signior, is all your family within?
IAGO. Are your doors lock'd?
BRA. Why, wherefore ask you this? 85
IAGO. 'Zounds, sir, you're robb'd; for shame, put on your gown;
Your heart is burst, you have lost half your soul;
Even now, now, very now, an old black ram
Is tupping your white ewe. Arise, arise;
Awake the snorting citizens with the bell, 90
Or else the Devil will make a grandsire of you:
Arise, I say.

33. **God . . . mark**, originally a person's appeal to avert an evil omen. Here an ironical apology for mentioning so low a thing as himself; **ancient**, ensign, standard bearer. 36. **letter**, i.e., of recommendation; **affection**, personal regard, i.e., favoritism. 37. **old gradation**, the established system of promotion, i.e., seniority. 39. **in . . . term**, justly in any respect; **affined**, bound. 41. **content you**, don't worry. 46. **obsequious**, submissive. 47. **time**, i.e., time of life. 48. **cashier'd**, dismissed. 49. **knaves**, servants. 52. **throwing**, bestowing, used contemptuously. 60. **peculiar**, personal. 62. **Native . . . figure**, genuine operation and handwriting. 63. **compliment extern**, external form.

65. **daws**, jackdaws or grackles. 66. **full fortune**, great good luck; **owe**, own. 67. **carry 't thus**, about = "get away with this." 69. **proclaim him**, i.e., have the town-crier advertise him. 72. **changes**, variety. 73. **colour**, excuse (for its existence). 75. **timorous**, terrifying. 76. **by . . . negligence**, "at" night and "through" negligence. 80. **bags**, money bags. 83. **matter**, source of the trouble. 88. **very now**, just now. 89. **tupping**, covering like a ram; **tup** = ram. 90. **snorting**, snoring. 91. **Devil**, the Devil in old pictures was represented as black.

BRA. What, have you lost your wits?
ROD. Most reverend signior, do you know my voice?
BRA. Not I: what are you?
ROD. My name is Roderigo.
BRA. The worser welcome:
I have charged thee not to haunt about my doors: 96
In honest plainness thou hast heard me say
My daughter is not for thee; and now, in madness,
Being full of supper and distempering draughts,
Upon malicious bravery, dost thou come 100
To start my quiet.
ROD. Sir, sir, sir,—
BRA. But thou must needs be sure
My spirit and my place have in them power
To make this bitter to thee.
ROD. Patience, good sir.
BRA. What tell'st thou me of robbing? this is Venice; 105
My house is not a grange.
ROD. Most grave Brabantio,
In simple and pure soul I come to you.
IAGO. 'Zounds, sir, you are one of those that will not serve God, if the devil bid you. Because we come to do you service and 110 you think we are ruffians, you'll have your daughter covered with a Barbary horse; you'll have your nephews neigh to you; you'll have coursers for cousins and gennets for germans.
BRA. What profane wretch art thou? 115
IAGO. I am one, sir, that comes to tell you your daughter and the Moor are now making the beast with two backs.
BRA. Thou art a villain.
IAGO. You are—a senator.
BRA. This thou shalt answer; I know thee, Roderigo. 120
ROD. Sir, I will answer any thing. But, I beseech you,
If't be your pleasure and most wise consent,
As partly I find it is, that your fair daughter,
At this odd-even and dull watch o' the night,
Transported, with no worse nor better guard
But with a knave of common hire, a gondolier, 126
To the gross clasps of a lascivious Moor,—
If this be known to you and your allowance,
We then have done you bold and saucy wrongs; 129
But if you know not this, my manners tell me
We have your wrong rebuke. Do not believe
That, from the sense of all civility,
I thus would play and trifle with your reverence:
Your daughter, if you have not given her leave,
I say again, hath made a gross revolt; 135
Tying her duty, beauty, wit and fortunes
In an extravagant and wheeling stranger
Of here and every where. Straight satisfy yourself:
If she be in her chamber or your house,
Let loose on me the justice of the state 140
For thus deluding you.
BRA. Strike on the tinder, ho!
Give me a taper! call up all my people!
This accident is not unlike my dream:
Belief of it oppresses me already.
Light, I say! light! [*Exit above.*
IAGO. Farewell; for I must leave you:
It seems not meet, nor wholesome to my place, 146
To be produced—as, if I stay, I shall—
Against the Moor: for, I do know, the state,
However this may gall him with some check,
Cannot with safety cast him, for he's embark'd 150
With such loud reason to the Cyprus wars,
Which even now stand in act, that, for their souls,
Another of his fathom they have none,
To lead their business: in which regard,
Though I do hate him as I do hell-pains, 155
Yet, for necessity of present life,
I must show out a flag and sign of love,
Which is indeed but sign. That you shall surely find him,

99. **distempering**, intoxicating. 100. **bravery**, bravado. 101. **start**, disturb. 106. **grange**, lonely farmhouse (where it would be easy to commit a robbery). 113. **nephews**, grandsons. 114. **gennets**, Moorish horses; **germans**, relatives. 120. **answer**, i.e., reply to a challenge. 124. **odd-even**, interval between midnight and 1:00 A.M. 125. **Transported**, gone off. 126. **knave**, menial. 128. **allowance**, by your permission. 129. **saucy**, outrageous. 132. **from**, contrary to. 135. **gross revolt**, indecent departure (from duty). 137. **extravagant**, vagabond; **wheeling**, wandering. 138. **Straight**, straightway. 141. **tinder**, inflammable material kept in a metal box, used for kindling fire. 143. **accident**, event. 147. **produced**, i.e., as a witness. 149. **check**, rebuke. 150. **cast**, dismiss. 151. **loud**, impressive, emphatic. 152. **stand in act**, are going on. 153. **fathom**, capacity. 154. **regard**, respect.

Lead to the Sagittary the raisèd search; 159
And there will I be with him. So, farewell.
[*Exit.*

[*Enter, below,* BRABANTIO, *and* SERVANTS *with torches.*]

BRA. It is too true an evil: gone she is;
And what's to come of my despisèd time
Is nought but bitterness. Now, Roderigo,
Where didst thou see her? O unhappy girl!
With the Moor, say'st thou? Who would be a father! 165
How didst thou know 'twas she? O, she deceives me
Past thought! What said she to you? Get more tapers:
Raise all my kindred. Are they married, think you?

ROD. Truly, I think they are.

BRA. O heaven! How got she out? O treason of the blood! 170
Fathers, from hence trust not your daughters' minds
By what you see them act. Is there not charms
By which the property of youth and maidhood
May be abused? Have you not read, Roderigo,
Of some such thing?

ROD. Yes, sir, I have indeed. 175

BRA. Call up my brother. O, would you had had her!
Some one way, some another. Do you know
Where we may apprehend her and the Moor?

ROD. I think I can discover him, if you please
To get good guard and go along with me. 180

BRA. Pray you, lead on. At every house I'll call;
I may command at most. Get weapons, ho!
And raise some special officers of night.
On, good Roderigo: I'll deserve your pains.
[*Exeunt.*

SCENE II. *Another street.*

[*Enter* OTHELLO, IAGO, *and* ATTENDANTS *with torches.*]

IAGO. Though in the trade of war I have slain men,
Yet do I hold it very stuff o' the conscience
To do no contrived murder: I lack iniquity
Sometimes to do me service: nine or ten times
I had thought to have yerk'd him here under the ribs. 5

OTH. 'Tis better as it is.

IAGO. Nay, but he prated,
And spoke such scurvy and provoking terms
Against your honour
That, with the little godliness I have,
I did full hard forbear him. But, I pray you, sir, 10
Are you fast married? Be assured of this,
That the magnifico is much beloved,
And hath in his effect a voice potential
As double as the duke's: he will divorce you;
Or put upon you what restraint and grievance 15
The law, with all his might to enforce it on.
Will give him cable.

OTH. Let him do his spite;
My services which I have done the signiory
Shall out-tongue his complaints. 'Tis yet to know,—
Which, when I know that boasting is an honour, 20
I shall promulgate—I fetch my life and being
From men of royal siege, and my demerits
May speak unbonneted to as proud a fortune
As this that I have reach'd: for know, Iago,
But that I love the gentle Desdemona, 25
I would not my unhousèd free condition
Put into circumscription and confine
For the sea's worth. But, look! what lights come yond?

IAGO. Those are the raisèd father and his friends:
You were best go in.

OTH. Not I; I must be found: 30
My parts, my title and my perfect soul

159. **The Sagittary,** either an inn or the commanding officer's residence at the Arsenal. 162. **time,** i.e., time of life. 170. **treason . . . blood,** treachery of my own child. 173. **property,** distinctive quality. 174. **abused,** deceived. 182. **command,** find helpers. 183. **officers of night,** police. **Scene ii:** 2. **stuff,** matter. 3. **contrived,** deliberate. 5. **yerk'd,** stabbed. 10. **full . . . forbear,** with great difficulty spared. 11. **fast.** firmly. 12. **magnifico,** Venetian senator. 13. **effect,** influence; **potential,** powerful. 14. **As double,** twice as effective. 15. **grievance,** punishment. 17. **cable,** rope (for acting). 18. **signiory,** Venetian senate. 22. **siege,** rank; **demerits,** deserts. 23. **unbonneted,** with hat off, i.e., courteously. 26. **unhoused,** undomesticated. 27. **circumscription,** restraint. 28. **sea's worth,** treasures of gold and precious stones were thought to lie buried in the bottom of the sea. 31. **parts,** abilities; **title,** reputation; **perfect soul,** unsmirched honor.

Shall manifest me rightly. Is it they?

IAGO. By Janus, I think no.

[*Enter* CASSIO, *and certain* OFFICERS *with torches.*]

OTH. The servants of the duke, and my lieutenant.
The goodness of the night upon you, friends! 35
What is the news?

CAS. The duke does greet you, general,
And he requires your haste-post-haste appearance,
Even on the instant.

OTH. What is the matter, think you?

CAS. Something from Cyprus, as I may divine:
It is a business of some heat: the galleys 40
Have sent a dozen sequent messengers
This very night at one another's heels,
And many of the consuls, raised and met,
Are at the duke's already: you have been hotly call'd for;
When, being not at your lodging to be found, 45
The senate hath sent about three several quests
To search you out.

OTH. 'Tis well I am found by you.
I will but spend a word here in the house,
And go with you. [*Exit.*

CAS. Ancient, what makes he here?

IAGO. 'Faith, he to-night hath boarded a land carack: 50
If it prove lawful prize, he's made for ever.

CAS. I do not understand.

IAGO. He's married.

CAS. To who?

[*Re-enter* OTHELLO.]

IAGO. Marry, to—Come, captain, will you go?

OTH. Have with you.

CAS. Here comes another troop to seek for you.

IAGO. It is Brabantio. General, be advised; 55
He comes to bad intent.

[*Enter* BRABANTIO, RODERIGO, *and* OFFICERS *with torches and weapons.*]

OTH. Holla! stand there!

ROD. Signior, it is the Moor.

BRA. Down with him, thief!

[*They draw on both sides.*

IAGO. You, Roderigo! come, sir, I am for you.

OTH. Keep up your bright swords, for the dew will rust them.
Good signior, you shall more command with years 60
Than with your weapons.

BRA. O thou foul thief, where hast thou stow'd my daughter?
Damn'd as thou art, thou hast enchanted her;
For I'll refer me to all things of sense,
If she in chains of magic were not bound, 65
Whether a maid so tender, fair and happy,
So opposite to marriage that she shunn'd
The wealthy curlèd darlings of our nation,
Would ever have, to incur a general mock, 69
Run from her guardage to the sooty bosom
Of such a thing as thou, to fear, not to delight.
Judge me the world, if 'tis not gross in sense
That thou hast practised on her with foul charms,
Abused her delicate youth with drugs or minerals
That weaken motion: I'll have't disputed on; 75
'Tis probable and palpable to thinking.
I therefore apprehend and do attach thee
For an abuser of the world, a practiser
Of arts inhibited and out of warrant.
Lay hold upon him: if he do resist, 80
Subdue him at his peril.

OTH. Hold your hands,
Both you of my inclining, and the rest:
Were it my cue to fight, I should have known it

32. **manifest**, reveal. 37. **haste . . . haste**, immediate. 40. **heat**, urgency; **galleys**, naval officers. 41. **sequent**, successive. 43. **consuls**, councilors, senators; **raised**, awakened. 49. **makes**, does. 50. **carack**, large merchantman. 53. **Have . . . you**, I will accompany you. 55. **advised**, cautious. 56. **to . . . intent**, with evil intention. 64. **refer me**, appeal. 67. **opposite**, averse. 68. **curled**, foppish, elegant.

69. **general mock**, universal derision. 70. **guardage**, guardianship. 71. **fear**, frighten. 72. **gross in sense**, obvious to perception. 73. **practised on**, plotted against. 74. **abused**, corrupted; **minerals**, medicines, potions. 75. **weaken motion**, impairs the mental faculties; **disputed on**, debated (in court). 77. **apprehend**, arrest; **attach**, indict. 78. **abuser**, corrupter; **world**, community. 79. **inhibited**, prohibited; **out of warrant**, forbidden. 82. **inclining**, following.

Without a prompter. Where will you that I go
To answer this your charge?

BRA. To prison, till fit time
Of law and course of direct session 86
Call thee to answer.

OTH. What if I do obey?
How may the duke be therewith satisfied,
Whose messengers are here about my side,
Upon some present business of the state 90
To bring me to him?

FIRST OFF. 'Tis true, most worthy signior;
The duke's in council, and your noble self,
I am sure, is sent for.

BRA. How! the duke in council!
In this time of the night! Bring him away: 95
Mine's not an idle cause: the duke himself,
Or any of my brothers of the state,
Cannot but feel this wrong as 'twere their own;
For if such actions may have passage free,
Bond-slaves and pagans shall our statesmen be. [*Exeunt.*

SCENE III. *A council-chamber.*

[*The* DUKE *and* SENATORS *sitting at a table;* OFFICERS *attending.*]

DUKE. There is no composition in these news
That gives them credit.

FIRST SEN. Indeed, they are disproportion'd;
My letters say a hundred and seven galleys.

DUKE. And mine, a hundred and forty.

SEC. SEN. And mine, two hundred:
But though they jump not on a just account,— 5
As in these cases, where the aim reports,
'Tis oft with difference—yet do they all confirm
A Turkish fleet, and bearing up to Cyprus.

DUKE. Nay, it is possible enough to judgement:
I do not so secure me in the error, 10
But the main article I do approve
In fearful sense.

SAILOR. [*Within*] What, ho! what, ho! what, ho!

FIRST OFF. A messenger from the galleys.

[*Enter a* SAILOR.]

DUKE. Now, what's the business?

SAIL. The Turkish preparation makes for Rhodes;
So was I bid report here to the state 15
By Signior Angelo.

DUKE. How say you by this change?

FIRST SEN. This cannot be,
By no assay of reason: 'tis a pageant,
To keep us in false gaze. When we consider
The importancy of Cyprus to the Turk, 20
And let ourselves again but understand,
That as it more concerns the Turk than Rhodes,
So may he with more facile question bear it,
For that it stands not in such warlike brace,
But altogether lacks the abilities 25
That Rhodes is dress'd in: if we make thought of this,
We must not think the Turk is so unskilful
To leave that latest which concerns him first,
Neglecting an attempt of ease and gain,
To wake and wage a danger profitless. 30

DUKE. Nay, in all confidence, he's not for Rhodes.

FIRST OFF. Here is more news.

[*Enter a* MESSENGER.]

MESS. The Ottomites, reverend and gracious,
Steering with due course towards the isle of Rhodes,
Have there injointed them with an after fleet. 35

FIRST SEN. Ay, so I thought. How many, as you guess?

MESS. Of thirty sail: and now they do restem
Their backward course, bearing with frank appearance

86. **course . . . session,** trial in the ordinary courts, i.e., he was not to be tried by a special commission of his peers. 95. **away,** along. 96. **idle,** trivial. Scene iii: 1. **composition,** consistency. 2. **gives . . . credit,** makes them credible. 2. **disproportion'd,** contradictory. 5. **jump,** agree; **just,** exact. 6. **aim reports,** report is founded on conjecture. 8. **bearing up to,** heading for. 10-2. **I do not . . . sense,** I do not feel myself so secure because of the discrepancy (in these accounts) as not to believe and dread the essential fact. 17. **How say you by,** What do you say to? 18. **no . . . reason,** by any reasonable test; **pageant,** show, pretense. 19. **in . . . gaze,** looking in the wrong direction. 23. **more . . . bear it,** more easily compel a decision by force of arms. 24. **brace,** state of defense. 30. **wage,** hazard. 33. **Ottomites,** Turks. 35. **injointed,** joined; **after,** sent after [them]. 37. **restem,** steer again. 38. **with . . . appearance,** openly.

Their purposes toward Cyprus. Signior Montano,
Your trusty and most valiant servitor, 40
With his free duty recommends you thus,
And prays you to believe him.

DUKE. 'Tis certain, then, for Cyprus.
Marcus Luccicos, is not he in town?

FIRST SEN. He's now in Florence. 45

DUKE. Write from us to him; post-post-haste dispatch.

FIRST SEN. Here comes Brabantio and the valiant Moor.

[*Enter* BRABANTIO, OTHELLO, IAGO, RODERIGO, *and* OFFICERS.]

DUKE. Valiant Othello, we must straight employ you
Against the general enemy Ottoman.
[*To* BRABANTIO] I did not see you; welcome, gentle signior; 50
We lack'd your counsel and your help tonight.

BRA. So did I yours. Good your grace, pardon me;
Neither my place nor aught I heard of business
Hath raised me from my bed, nor doth the general care
Take hold on me, for my particular grief 55
Is of so flood-gate and o'erbearing nature
That it engluts and swallows other sorrows
And it is still itself.

DUKE. Why, what's the matter?

BRA. My daughter! O, my daughter!

DUKE AND SEN. Dead?

BRA. Ay, to me;
She is abused, stol'n from me, and corrupted
By spells and medicines bought of mountebanks; 61
For nature so preposterously to err,
Being not deficient, blind, or lame of sense,
Sans witchcraft could not.

DUKE. Who'er he be that in this foul proceeding 65
Hath thus beguiled your daughter of herself
And you of her, the bloody book of law
You shall yourself read in the bitter letter
After your own sense, yea, though our proper son
Stood in your action.

BRA. Humbly I thank your grace. 70
Here is the man, this Moor, whom now, it seems,
Your special mandate for the state-affairs
Hath hither brought.

DUKE AND SEN. We are very sorry for 't.

DUKE [*To* OTHELLO] What, in your own part, can you say to this?

BRA. Nothing, but this is so. 75

OTH. Most potent, grave, and reverend signiors,
My very noble and approved good masters,
That I have ta'en away this old man's daughter,
It is most true; true, I have married her:
The very head and front of my offending 80
Hath this extent, no more. Rude am I in my speech,
And little bless'd with the soft phrase of peace;
For since these arms of mine had seven years' pith,
Till now some nine moons wasted, they have used
Their dearest action in the tented field, 85
And little of this great world can I speak,
More than pertains to feats of broil and battle,
And therefore little shall I grace my cause
In speaking for myself. Yet, by your gracious patience,
I will a round unvarnish'd tale deliver 90
Of my whole course of love; what drugs, what charms,
What conjuration and what mighty magic,
For such proceeding I am charged withal,
I won his daughter.

BRA. A maiden never bold;
Of spirit so still and quiet, that her motion 95
Blush'd at herself; and she, in spite of nature,
Of years, of country, credit, every thing,
To fall in love with what she fear'd to look on!
It is a judgement maim'd and most imperfect
That will confess perfection so could err 100

41. **free duty**, willing deference; **recommends**, advises, informs. 46. **post . . . dispatch**, superlative haste. 56. **flood-gate**, headlong, like water rushing through a sluice. 57. **engluts**, engulfs. 60. **abused**, deceived. 61. **mountebanks**, quacks. 62. **preposterously to err**, so ridiculously to go astray. 64. **Sans**, without. 69. **proper**, own. 70. **stood . . . action**, were the subject of your accusations.

76. **signiors**, senators. 80. **front**, forehead. 83. **pith**, strength. 85. **dearest**, most important. 88. **grace**, favor, advance. 89. **patience**, sufferance, consent. 90. **round**, straightforward. 95. **motion**, emotional impulses. 96. **herself**, i.e., themselves. 97. **credit**, i.e., her good name.

Against all rules of nature, and must be driven
To find out practices of cunning hell,
Why this should be. I therefore vouch again
That with some mixtures powerful o'er the blood,
Or with some dram conjured to this effect, 105
He wrought upon her.

DUKE. To vouch this, is no proof,
Without more wider and more overt test
Than these thin habits and poor likelihoods
Of modern seeming do prefer against him.

FIRST SEN. But, Othello, speak: 110
Did you by indirect and forcèd courses
Subdue and poison this young maid's affections?
Or came it by request and such fair question
As soul to soul affordeth?

OTH. I do beseech you,
Send for the lady to the Sagittary, 115
And let her speak of me before her father:
If you do find me foul in her report,
The trust, the office I do hold of you,
Not only take away, but let your sentence
Even fall upon my life.

DUKE. Fetch Desdemona hither. 120

OTH. Ancient, conduct them; you best know the place.

[*Exeunt* IAGO *and* ATTENDANTS.]

And, till she come, as truly as to heaven
I do confess the vices of my blood,
So justly to your grave ears I'll present
How I did thrive in this fair lady's love, 125
And she in mine.

DUKE. Say it, Othello.

OTH. Her father loved me; oft invited me;
Still question'd me the story of my life,
From year to year, the battles, sieges, fortunes, 130
That I have pass'd.
I ran it through, even from my boyish days,
To the very moment that he bade me tell it;
Wherein I spake of most disastrous chances,
Of moving accidents by flood and field, 135
Of hair-breadth scapes i' the imminent deadly breach,
Of being taken by the insolent foe
And sold to slavery, of my redemption thence
And portance in my travels' history:
Wherein of antres vast and deserts idle, 140
Rough quarries, rocks and hills whose heads touch heaven,
It was my hint to speak,—such was the process;
And of the Cannibals that each other eat,
The Anthropophagi and men whose heads
Do grow beneath their shoulders. This to hear 145
Would Desdemona seriously incline:
But still the house-affairs would draw her thence:
Which ever as she could with haste dispatch,
She'ld come again, and with a greedy ear
Devour up my discourse: which I observing,
Took once a pliant hour, and found good means 151
To draw from her a prayer of earnest heart
That I would all my pilgrimage dilate,
Whereof by parcels she had something heard,
But not intentively: I did consent, 155
And often did beguile her of her tears,
When I did speak of some distressful stroke
That my youth suffer'd. My story being done,
She gave me for my pains a world of sighs:
She swore, in faith, 'twas strange, 'twas passing strange, 160
'Twas pitiful, 'twas wondrous pitiful:
She wish'd she had not heard it, yet she wish'd
That heaven had made her such a man: she thank'd me,
And bade me, if I had a friend that loved her,
I should but teach him how to tell my story, 165
And that would woo her. Upon this hint I spake:
She loved me for the dangers I had pass'd,
And I loved her that she did pity them.
This only is the witchcraft I have used:
Here comes the lady; let her witness it. 170

[*Enter* DESDEMONA, IAGO, *and* ATTENDANTS.]

DUKE. I think this tale would win my daughter too.

102. **practices**, stratagems. 103. **vouch**, assert. 104. **blood**, passion. 105. **conjured**, charmed by incantations. 107. **more wider**, more obvious. 108. **thin habits**, superficial appearances; **poor likelihoods**, improbable charges. 109. **modern seeming**, slight suspicion. 111. **indirect**, devious. 113. **question**, conversation. 124. **justly**, truthfully. 125. **thrive**, prosper, succeed. 129. **still**, continually. 130. **fortunes**, adventures. 134. **chanees**, accidents. 136. **imminent deadly breach**, the terribly dangerous overhanging sides of a gap made in the enemy's fortifications. 139. **portance**, behavior. 140. **antres**, caves; **idle**, barren. 141. **hint**, opportunity; **process**, proceeding. 144. **Anthropophagi**, man-eaters. 147. **still**, constantly. 153. **dilate**, tell in detail. 154. **by parcels**, in part. 155. **intentively**, attentively. 160. **passing**, exceedingly. 163. **her**, for her.

Good Brabantio,
Take up this mangled matter at the best:
Men do their broken weapons rather use
Than their bare hands.

BRA. I pray you, hear her speak:
If she confess that she was half the wooer, 176
Destruction on my head, if my bad blame
Light on the man! Come hither, gentle mistress:
Do you perceive in all this noble company
Where most you owe obedience?

DES. My noble father, 180
I do perceive here a divided duty:
To you I am bound for life and education;
My life and education both do learn me
How to respect you; you are the lord of duty;
I am hitherto your daughter: but here's my husband, 185
And so much duty as my mother show'd
To you, preferring you before her father,
So much I challenge that I may profess
Due to the Moor my lord.

BRA. God be wi' you! I have done.
Please it your grace, on to the state-affairs:
I had rather to adopt a child than get it. 191
Come hither, Moor:
I here do give thee that with all my heart
Which, but thou hast already, with all my heart
I would keep from thee. For your sake, jewel,
I am glad at soul I have no other child; 196
For thy escape would teach me tyranny,
To hang clogs on them. I have done, my lord.

DUKE. Let me speak like yourself, and lay a sentence,
Which, as a grise or step, may help these lovers 200
Into your favour.
When remedies are past, the griefs are ended
By seeing the worst, which late on hopes depended.
To mourn a mischief that is past and gone
Is the next way to draw new mischief on. 205
What cannot be preserved when fortune takes,
Patience her injury a mockery makes.
The robb'd that smiles steals something from the thief;
He robs himself that spends a bootless grief.

BRA. So let the Turk of Cyprus us beguile;
We lost it not, so long as we can smile. 211
He bears the sentence well that nothing bears
But the free comfort which from thence he hears,
But he bears both the sentence and the sorrow
That, to pay grief, must of poor patience borrow. 215
These sentences, to sugar, or to gall,
Being strong on both sides, are equivocal:
But words are words; I never yet did hear
That the bruised heart was piercèd through the ear.
I humbly beseech you, proceed to the affairs of state. 220

DUKE. The Turk with a most mighty preparation makes for Cyprus. Othello, the fortitude of the place is best known to you; and though we have there a substitute of most allowed sufficiency, yet opinion, a sovereign mistress of effects, throws a more safer voice on you: you must therefore be content to slubber the gloss of your new fortunes with this more stubborn and boisterous expedition. 229

OTH. The tyrant custom, most grave senators,
Hath made the flinty and steel couch of war
My thrice-driven bed of down: I do agnize
A natural and prompt alacrity
I find in hardness, and do undertake
These present wars against the Ottomites. 235
Most humbly therefore bending to your state,
I crave fit disposition for my wife,
Due reference of place and exhibition,
With such accommodation and besort
As levels with her breeding.

DUKE. If you please, 240
Be 't at her father's.

BRA. I'll not have it so.

OTH. Nor I.

DES. Nor I; I would not there reside,
To put my father in impatient thoughts

173. **Take up . . . best**, make the best of. 183. **learn**, teach. 184. **lord of duty**, man to whom I owe duty. 185. **hitherto**, to that extent. 188. **challenge**, claim. 191. **get**, beget. 199. **like yourself**, i.e., as you ought. 200. **grise**, a step (in a flight of steps). 205. **next**, nearest, surest. 207. **Patience**, endurance. 209. **bootless**, useless. 212-3. **He . . . comfort**, He can easily take sententious consolation who only has to listen to the freely given consolation. 214-5. **But . . . borrow**, But the man who has to endure both that sort of consolation and the sorrow, must be very patient. 216. **sentences**, aphorisms; **gall**, vex.

217. **equivocal**, equivalent. 223. **fortitude**, strength. 225. **allowed**, acknowledged; **opinion**, i.e., public opinion. 228. **slubber**, soil. 232. **thrice-driven**, i.e., the feathers thrice driven by a fan which separates the light from the heavy; **agnize**, acknowledge. 234. **hardness**, hardship. 236. **state**, ruling body. 238. **exhibition**, allowance. 239. **besort**, retinue. 240. **levels with**, suits.

By being in his eye. Most gracious duke,
To my unfolding lend your prosperous ear;
And let me find a charter in your voice, 246
To assist my simpleness.

DUKE. What would you, Desdemona?

DES. That I did love the Moor to live with him,
My downright violence and storm of fortunes
May trumpet to the world: my heart's subdued 251
Even to the very quality of my lord:
I saw Othello's visage in his mind,
And to his honours and his valiant parts
Did I my soul and fortunes consecrate. 255
So that, dear lords, if I be left behind,
A moth of peace, and he go to the war,
The rites for which I love him are bereft me,
And I a heavy interim shall support
By his dear absence. Let me go with him. 260

OTH. Let her have your voices.
Vouch with me, heaven, I therefore beg it not,
To please the palate of my appetite,
Nor to comply with heat—the young affects
In me defunct—and proper satisfaction, 265
But to be free and bounteous to her mind:
And heaven defend your good souls, that you think
I will your serious and great business scant
For she is with me: no, when light-wing'd toys
Of feather'd Cupid seel with wanton dullness
My speculative and officed instruments, 271
That my disports corrupt and taint my business,
Let housewives make a skillet of my helm,
And all indign and base adversities
Make head against my estimation! 275

DUKE. Be it as you shall privately determine,
Either for her stay or going: the affair cries haste,
And speed must answer it.

FIRST SEN. You must away to-night.

OTH. With all my heart.

DUKE. At nine i' the morning here we'll meet again. 280
Othello, leave some officer behind,
And he shall our commission bring to you;
With such things else of quality and respect
As doth import you.

OTH. So please your grace, my ancient;
A man he is of honesty and trust: 285
To his conveyance I assign my wife,
With what else needful your good grace shall think
To be sent after me.

DUKE. Let it be so.
Good night to every one. [*To* BRAB.] And, noble signior,
If virtue no delighted beauty lack, 290
Your son-in-law is far more fair than black.

FIRST SEN. Adieu, brave Moor; use Desdemona well.

BRA. Look to her, Moor, if thou hast eyes to see:
She has deceived her father, and may thee.

[*Exeunt* DUKE, SENATORS, OFFICERS, *&c.*

OTH. My life upon her faith! Honest Iago,
My Desdemona must I leave to thee: 296
I prithee, let thy wife attend on her;
And bring them after in the best advantage.
Come, Desdemona; I have but an hour
Of love, of worldly matters and direction, 300
To spend with thee: we must obey the time.

[*Exeunt* OTHELLO *and* DESDEMONA.

ROD. Iago,—

IAGO. What say'st thou, noble heart?

ROD. What will I do, thinkest thou?

IAGO. Why, go to bed, and sleep. 305

ROD. I will incontinently drown myself.

IAGO. If thou dost, I shall never love thee after. Why, thou silly gentleman!

ROD. It is silliness to live when to live is torment; and then have we a prescription to die when death is our physician. 311

IAGO. O villanous! I have looked upon the world for four times seven years; and since I could distinguish betwixt a benefit and an injury, I never found man that knew how to

245. **unfolding**, i.e., what I am going to reveal; **prosperous**, propitious. 246. **charter**, guaranty. 247. **simpleness**, simplicity. 250. **My . . . fortunes**, the unrestrained impetuosity of taking my fortunes, as it were, by storm. 252. **quality**, distinctive characteristic, i.e., his color. 260. **dear**, deeply felt. 261. **voices**, votes, i.e., approval. 264. **heat**, passion; **young affects**, youthful desires. 266. **mind**, i.e., her wish to accompany him. 267. **defend**, forbid. 268. **scant**, neglect. 270. **seel**, sew up the eyes (as of a falcon). 271. **speculative . . . instruments**, visual and active powers. 272. **that**, so that; **disports**, pastimes. 273. **skillet . . . helm**, a saucepan of my head. 274. **indign**, unworthy, disgraceful. 275. **make head**, constitute an armed force; **estimation**, reputation. 283. **of quality and respect**, pertaining to your honored rank. 284. **import**, concern. 287. **needful . . . think**, your grace shall think needful. 290-1. **If . . . black**, If worth is in itself beautiful, your son-in-law, though black, is indeed fair. 295. **faith**, fidelity, loyalty. 298. **in . . . advantage**, at the most favorable opportunity. 300. **of . . . direction**, for the management of private affairs. 306. **incontinently**, immediately.

love himself. Ere I would say, I would drown myself for the love of a guinea-hen, I would change my humanity with a baboon.

ROD. What should I do? I confess it is my shame to be so fond; but it is not in my virtue to amend it. 321

IAGO. Virtue! a fig! 'tis in ourselves that we are thus or thus. Our bodies are our gardens, to the which our wills are gardeners; so that if we will plant nettles, or sow lettuce, set hyssop and weed up thyme, supply it with one gender of herbs, or distract it with many, either to have it sterile with idleness, or manured with industry, why, the power and corrigible authority of this lies in our wills. If the balance of our lives had not one 330 scale of reason to poise another of sensuality, the blood and baseness of our natures would conduct us to most preposterous conclusions: but we have reason to cool our raging motions, our carnal stings, our unbitted lusts, whereof I take this that you call love 336 to be a sect or scion.

ROD. It cannot be.

IAGO. It is merely a lust of the blood and a permission of the will. Come, be a man. Drown thyself! drown cats and blind puppies. I have professed me thy friend and I confess me knit to thy deserving with cables of perdurable toughness; I could never better stead thee than now. Put money in thy purse; follow thou the wars; defeat thy favour with an usurped beard; I say, put money 345 in thy purse. It cannot be that Desdemona should long continue her love to the Moor,—put money in thy purse,—nor he his to her: it was a violent commencement, and 350 thou shalt see an answerable sequestration:—put but money in thy purse. These Moors are changeable in their wills:—fill thy purse with money:—the food that to him now is as luscious as locusts, shall be to him shortly as bitter as coloquintida. She must 355 change for youth: when she is sated with his body, she will find the error of her choice: she must have change, she must: therefore put money in thy purse. If thou wilt needs damn thyself, do it a more delicate way than drowning. Make all the money thou canst: if sanctimony and a frail vow betwixt an erring barbarian and a super-subtle Venetian be not too hard for my wits and all the tribe of hell, thou shalt enjoy her; therefore make money. A pox of drowning thyself! it is clean out of the way: seek thou rather to be hanged in compassing thy joy than to be drowned and go without her.

ROD. Wilt thou be fast to my hopes, if I depend on the issue? 370

IAGO. Thou art sure of me:—go, make money:—I have told thee often, and I re-tell thee again and again, I hate the Moor: my cause is hearted; thine hath no less reason. Let us be conjunctive in our revenge against him; if thou canst cuckold him, thou dost thyself a pleasure, me a sport. There are many events in the womb of time which will be delivered. Traverse! go, provide thy money. We will have more of this to-morrow. Adieu. 380

ROD. Where shall we meet i' the morning?

IAGO. At my lodging.

ROD. I'll be with thee betimes.

IAGO. Go to, farewell. Do you hear, Roderigo?

ROD. What say you?

IAGO. No more of drowning, do you hear?

ROD. I am changed: I'll go sell all my land. [*Exit.*

IAGO. Thus do I ever make my fool my purse;
For I mine own gain'd knowledge should profane, 390
If I would time expend with such a snipe,
But for my sport and profit. I hate the Moor;
And it is thought abroad, that 'twixt my sheets
He has done my office: I know not if 't be true;
But I, for mere suspicion in that kind, 395
Will do as if for surety. He holds me well;

317. **guinea-hen**, cant name for harlot. 321. **virtue**, manhood. 326. **gender**, kind; **distract . . . many**, scatter many on it. 328. **idleness**, lying fallow. 329. **corrigible authority**, corrective control. 331. **poise**, balance. 332. **blood and baseness**, base passions. 333. **conclusions**, results. 334-5. **motions**, sexual appetites. 335. **unbitted**, unbridled. 337. **sect**, cutting; **scion**, shoot. 339. **permission . . . will**, sexual license. 343. **perdurable**, very hard. 344. **stead**, help. 345. **defeat . . . favor**, disguise your face. 346. **usurped**, assumed, i.e., grown for the purpose. 351. **answerable sequestration**, corresponding rupture. 354. **locusts**, fruit of the carob tree, an evergreen tree of the Mediterranean region. 355. **coloquintida**, colocynth, or bitter apple. 362. **erring**, vagabond. 367. **compassing**, obtaining. 370. **depend . . . issue**, trust [you] for the result. 374. **hearted**, fixed in my heart. 375. **conjunctive**, united. 379. **Traverse**, a military term, "Forward march." 384. **betimes**, soon. 391. **snipe**, a proverbially silly bird. 395. **kind**, direction. 396. **for surety**, upon a certainty.

The better shall my purpose work on him.
Cassio's a proper man: let me see now:
To get his place and to plume up my will
In double knavery—How, how?—Let's see:—
After some time, to abuse Othello's ear 401
That he is too familiar with his wife.
He hath a person and a smooth dispose
To be suspected, framed to make women false.
The Moor is of a free and open nature, 405
That thinks men honest that but seem to be so,
And will as tenderly be led by the nose
As asses are.
I have 't. It is engender'd. Hell and night
Must bring this monstrous birth to the world's light. [*Exit.*

ACT II

SCENE I. *A Seaport in Cyprus. An open place near the quay.*

[*Enter* MONTANO *and two* GENTLEMEN.]

MON. What from the cape can you discern at sea?
FIRST GENT. Nothing at all: it is a high-wrought flood;
I cannot, 'twixt the heaven and the main,
Descry a sail.
MON. Methinks the wind hath spoke aloud at land; 5
A fuller blast ne'er shook our battlements:
If it hath ruffian'd so upon the sea,
What ribs of oak, when mountains melt on them,
Can hold the mortise? What shall we hear of this?
SEC. GENT. A segregation of the Turkish fleet: 10
For do but stand upon the foaming shore,
The chidden billow seems to pelt the clouds;
The wind-shaked surge, with high and monstrous mane,
Seems to cast water on the burning bear,
And quench the guards of the ever-fixèd pole:
I never did like molestation view 16
On the enchafèd flood.
MON. If that the Turkish fleet
Be not enshelter'd and embay'd, they are drown'd;
It is impossible they bear it out.

[*Enter a third* GENTLEMAN.]

THIRD GENT. News, lads! our wars are done.
The desperate tempest hath so bang'd the Turks, 21
That their designment halts: a noble ship of Venice
Hath seen a grievous wreck and sufferance
On most part of their fleet.
MON. How! is this true?
THIRD GENT. The ship is here put in,
A Veronesa; Michael Cassio, 26
Lieutenant to the warlike Moor Othello,
Is come on shore: the Moor himself at sea,
And is in full commission here for Cyprus.
MON. I am glad on 't; 'tis a worthy governor. 30
THIRD GENT. But this same Cassio, though he speak of comfort
Touching the Turkish loss, yet he looks sadly,
And prays the Moor be safe; for they were parted
With foul and violent tempest.
MON. Pray heavens he be;
For I have served him, and the man commands 35
Like a full soldier. Let's to the seaside, ho!
As well to see the vessel that's come in
As to throw out our eyes for brave Othello,
Even till we make the main and the aerial blue
An indistinct regard.
THIRD GENT. Come, let's do so; 40
For every minute is expectancy
Of more arrivance.

398. **proper**, handsome. 399. **plume up**, i.e., put a feather in the cap of, glorify. 401. **abuse**, deceive. 402. **he**, i.e., Cassio. 403-4. **He . . . suspected**, he has a personality and an ingratiating manner of a sort to make him suspected. 405. **free**, i.e., from guile. Act II, Scene i: 2. **high . . . flood**, heavy sea. 7. **ruffian'd**, played the ruffian, i.e., been boisterous. 9. **hold the mortise**, remain jointed. 10. **segregation**, dispersion. 14. **burning bear**, constellation of Ursa Major or the Big Dipper. 15. **guards**, two stars called pointers in the constellation now known as **Boötes**, originally called Arcturus; **pole**, polestar or North Star. 16. **molestation**, disturbance. 17. **enchafed**, chafed, angry. 18. **embay'd**, anchored in some bay. 22. **designment**, enterprise; **halts**, limps. 23. **sufferance**, disaster. 26. **Veronesa**, a ship fitted out by Verona, then subject to Venice. 36. **full**, thorough. 40. **regard**, view, i.e., till the line between the sea and the sky becomes indistinct. 42. **arrivance**, arrival.

[*Enter* CASSIO.]

CAS. Thanks, you the valiant of this warlike isle,
That so approve the Moor! O, let the heavens
Give him defence against the elements, 45
For I have lost him on a dangerous sea.

MON. Is he well shipp'd?

CAS. His bark is stoutly timber'd, and his pilot
Of very expert and approved allowance;
Therefore my hopes, not surfeited to death, 50
Stand in bold cure.

[*A cry within:* "A sail, a sail a sail!"

[*Enter a fourth* GENTLEMAN.]

CAS. What noise?

FOURTH GENT. The town is empty; on the brow o' the sea
Stand ranks of people, and they cry "A sail!"

CAS. My hopes do shape him for the governor. [*Guns heard.* 55

SEC. GENT. They do discharge their shot of courtesy:
Our friends at least.

CAS. I pray you, sir, go forth,
And give us truth who 'tis that is arrived.

SEC. GENT. I shall. [*Exit.*

MON. But, good lieutenant, is your general wived? 60

CAS. Most fortunately: he hath achieved a maid
That paragons description and wild fame;
One that excels the quirks of blazoning pens,
And in the essential vesture of creation
Does tire the ingener.

[*Re-enter second* GENTLEMAN.]

How now! who has put in?

SEC. GENT. 'Tis one Iago, ancient to the general. 66

CAS. Has had most favourable and happy speed:
Tempests themselves, high seas and howling winds,
The gutter'd rocks and congregated sands,—
Traitors ensteep'd to clog the guiltless keel,—
As having sense of beauty, do omit 71
Their mortal natures, letting go safely by
The divine Desdemona.

MON. What is she?

CAS. She that I spake of, our great captain's captain,
Left in the conduct of the bold Iago, 75
Whose footing here anticipates our thoughts
A se'nnight's speed. Great Jove, Othello guard,
And swell his sail with thine own powerful breath,
That he may bless this bay with his tall ship,
Make love's quick pants in Desdemona's arms,
Give renew'd fire to our extincted spirits, 80
And bring all Cyprus comfort!

[*Enter* DESDEMONA, EMILIA, IAGO, RODERIGO, *and* ATTENDANTS.]

O, behold,
The riches of the ship is come on shore!
Ye men of Cyprus, let her have your knees.
Hail to thee, lady! and the grace of heaven,
Before, behind thee and on every hand, 86
Enwheel thee round!

DES. I thank you, valiant Cassio.
What tidings can you tell me of my lord?

CAS. He is not yet arrived: nor know I aught
But that he's well and will be shortly here.

DES. O, but I fear—How lost you company?

CAS. The great contention of the sea and skies 92
Parted our fellowship—but, hark! a sail.

[*Within:* "A sail, a sail!" *Guns heard.*

SEC. GENT. They give their greeting to the citadel:
This likewise is a friend. 95

CAS. See for the news.

[*Exit* GENTLEMAN.]

Good ancient, you are welcome. [*To* EMILIA] Welcome, mistress:
Let it not gall your patience, good Iago,
That I extend my manners; 'tis my breeding
That gives me this bold show of courtesy. 100

[*Kissing her.*

IAGO. Sir, would she give you so much of her lips

49. approved allowance, established competence. 50-1. not . . . bold cure, not utterly destroyed, remain confident of being fulfilled. 55. shape him for, imagine him to be. 61. achieved, won. 62. paragons, surpasses; wild fame, unrestrained reports. 63. quirks, extravagant fancies; blazoning, extolling. 64. essential . . . creation, native endowments. 65. ingener, inventor (of eulogies). 69. gutter'd, jagged. 70. ensteep'd, submerged. 71. omit, throw off. 72. mortal, deadly, destructive. 76. footing, landing. 77. se'nnight's, week's. 81. extincted, extinguished. 87. enwheel, encircle. 98. gall your patience, wound your composure. 99. extend, show; breeding, bringing up, i.e., as a gentleman which makes it proper to me to kiss the wife of a social inferior.

As of her tongue she oft bestows on me,
You'ld have enough.

DES. Alas, she has no speech.

IAGO. In faith, too much;
I find it still, when I have list to sleep: 105
Marry, before your ladyship, I grant,
She puts her tongue a little in her heart,
And chides with thinking.

EMIL. You have little cause to say so.

IAGO. Come on, come on; you are pictures out of doors, 110
Bells in your parlours, wild-cats in your kitchens,
Saints in your injuries, devils being offended,
Players in your housewifery, and housewives in your beds.

DES. O, fie upon thee, slanderer!

IAGO. Nay, it is true, or else I am a Turk:
You rise to play and go to bed to work. 116

EMIL. You shall not write my praise.

IAGO. No, let me not.

DES. What wouldst thou write of me, if thou shouldst praise me?

IAGO. O gentle lady, do not put me to 't;
For I am nothing, if not critical. 120

DES. Come on, assay. There's one gone to the harbour?

IAGO. Ay, madam.

DES. I am not merry; but I do beguile
The thing I am, by seeming otherwise.
Come, how wouldst thou praise me? 125

IAGO. I am about it; but indeed my invention
Comes from my pate as birdlime does from frize;
It plucks out brains and all: but my Muse labours,
And thus she is deliver'd.
If she be fair and wise, fairness and wit, 130
The one's for use, the other useth it.

DES. Well praised! How if she be black and witty?

IAGO. If she be black, and thereto have a wit,
She'll find a white that shall her blackness fit.

DES. Worse and worse. 135

EMIL. How if fair and foolish?

IAGO. She never yet was foolish that was fair;
For even her folly help'd her to an heir.

DES. These are old fond paradoxes to make fools laugh i' the alehouse. What miserable praise hast thou for her that's foul and foolish? 141

IAGO. There's none so foul and foolish thereunto,
But does foul pranks which fair and wise ones do. 143

DES. O heavy ignorance! thou praisest the worst best. But what praise couldst thou bestow on a deserving woman indeed, one that, in the authority of her merit, did justly put on the vouch of very malice itself?

IAGO. She that was ever fair and never proud, 149
Had tongue at will and yet was never loud,
Never lack'd gold and yet went never gay,
Fled from her wish and yet said "Now I may,"
She that being anger'd, her revenge being nigh,
Bade her wrong stay and her displeasure fly,
She that in wisdom never was so frail 155
To change the cod's head for the salmon's tail,
She that could think and ne'er disclose her mind,
See suitors following and not look behind,
She was a wight, if ever such wight were,—

DES. To do what? 160

IAGO. To suckle fools and chronicle small beer.

DES. O most lame and impotent conclusion! Do not learn of him, Emilia, though he be thy husband. How say you, Cassio? is he not a most profane and liberal counsellor? 165

CAS. He speaks home, madam: you may relish him more in the soldier than in the scholar.

IAGO. [*Aside*] He takes her by the palm: ay, well said, whisper: with as little a web as this will I ensnare as great a fly as Cassio. Ay, smile upon her, do; I will gyve thee in thine own courtship. You say true; 'tis so, indeed: if such tricks as these strip you out

105. **still,** always; **list,** inclination. 110. **pictures,** i.e., painted and speechless. 112. **Saints . . . injuries,** say insulting things with a sanctimonious air. 113. **players,** triflers; **housewives,** hussies, wanton creatures. 120. **critical,** censorious. 124. **thing I am,** i.e., anxiety. 127. **birdlime,** sticky substance spread on twigs for catching birds; **frize,** coarse woolen cloth. 133. **black,** a brunette and hence ugly. 134. **white,** (1) a fair person, (2) a wight (i.e., a person. 139. **fond,** silly. 141. **foul,** ugly. 148. **put . . . vouch,** challenge the testimony. 151. **gay,** showy, gaudy. 156. **To . . . tail,** i.e., to exchange a delicacy for refuse. 161. **chronicle . . . beer,** keep petty household accounts. 165. **profane,** coarse; **liberal,** licentious. 166. **home,** with utter frankness. 169. **well said,** well done. 171. **gyve,** fetter. 172. **courtship,** courtesy.

of your lieutenantry, it had been better you had not kissed your three fingers so oft, which now again you are most apt to play the sir in. Very good; well kissed! an excellent courtesy! 'tis so, indeed. Yet again your fingers to your lips? would they were clyster-pipes for your sake! [*Trumpet within.*] The Moor! I know his trumpet. 180

CAS. 'Tis truly so.

DES. Let's meet him and receive him.

CAS. Lo, where he comes!

[*Enter* OTHELLO *and* ATTENDANTS.]

OTH. O my fair warrior!

DES. My dear Othello!

OTH. It gives me wonder great as my content 185
To see you here before me. O my soul's joy!
If after every tempest come such calms,
May the winds blow till they have waken'd death!
And let the labouring bark climb hills of seas
Olympus-high and duck again as low 190
As hell's from heaven! If it were now to die,
'Twere now to be most happy; for, I fear,
My soul hath her content so absolute
That not another comfort like to this
Succeeds in unknown fate.

DES. The heavens forbid 195
But that our loves and comforts should increase,
Even as our days do grow!

OTH. Amen to that, sweet powers!
I cannot speak enough of this content;
It stops me here; it is too much of joy: 199
And this, and this, the greatest discords be [*Kissing her.*]
That e'er our hearts shall make!

IAGO. [*Aside*] O, you are well tuned now!
But I'll set down the pegs that make this music,
As honest as I am.

OTH. Come, let us to the castle.
News, friends; our wars are done, the Turks are drown'd. 204
How does my old acquaintance of this isle?
Honey, you shall be well desired in Cyprus;
I have found great love amongst them. O my sweet,
I prattle out of fashion, and I dote
In mine own comforts. I prithee, good Iago,
Go to the bay and disembark my coffers: 210
Bring thou the master to the citadel;
He is a good one, and his worthiness
Does challenge much respect. Come, Desdemona,
Once more, well met at Cyprus.

[*Exeunt* OTHELLO, DESDEMONA, *and* ATTENDANTS.

IAGO. Do thou meet me presently at the harbour. Come hither. If thou be'st valiant,—as, they say, base men being in love have then a nobility in their natures more than is native to them,—list me. The lieutenant tonight watches on the court of guard:—first, I must tell thee this—Desdemona is directly in love with him. 221

ROD. With him! why, 'tis not possible.

IAGO. Lay thy finger thus, and let thy soul be instructed. Mark me with what violence she first loved the Moor, but for bragging and telling her fantastical lies: and will she love him still for prating? let not thy discreet heart think it. Her eye must be fed; and what delight shall she have to look on the devil? When the blood is made dull with the act of sport, there should be, again to inflame 230 it and to give satiety a fresh appetite, loveliness in favour, sympathy in years, manners and beauties; all which the Moor is defective in: now, for want of these required conveniences, her delicate tenderness will find itself abused, begin to heave the gorge, disrelish and abhor the Moor; very nature will instruct her in it and compel her to some second choice. Now, sir, this granted,—as it is a most pregnant and unforced position—who stands so eminent in the degree of this fortune as Cassio does? a knave very voluble; no 241 further conscionable than in putting on the mere form of civil and humane seeming, for the better compassing of his salt and most hidden loose affection? why, none; why, none: a slipper and subtle knave, a finder of 246

175. **kissed . . . fingers,** as a piece of gallantry to Desdemona. 177. **sir,** gallant. 179. **clyster-pipes,** tubes used for enemas. 185. **content,** joy. 199. **here,** i.e., in the heart. 202. **set . . . pegs,** loosen the pegs and so untune the instrument. 206. **well-desired,** well-loved. 208. **out of fashion,** unconventionally. 211. **master,** ship's master, i.e., captain. 213. **challenge,** demand. 215. **presently,** immediately. 219. **court of guard,** guardhouse. 223. **thus,** i.e., on your lips (while in silence you listen to me). 229. **blood,** passion. 232. **favour,** countenance. 234. **conveniences,** attractions. 235. **abused,** deceived; **heave the gorge,** be nauseated. 238. **pregnant . . . position,** a significant and convincing argument. 241. **voluble,** unstable. 242. **conscionable,** conscientious. 243. **humane seeming,** the appearance of morality. 244. **salt,** licentious. 246. **slipper,** slippery.

occasions, that has an eye can stamp and counterfeit advantages, though true advantage never present itself; a devilish knave. Besides, the knave is handsome, young, and hath all those requisites in him that folly and green minds look after: a pestilent complete knave: and the woman hath found him already.

ROD. I cannot believe that in her; she's full of most blessed condition. 255

IAGO. Blessed fig's-end! the wine she drinks is made of grapes: if she had been blessed, she would never have loved the Moor. Blessed pudding! Didst thou not see her paddle with the palm of his hand? didst not mark that? 260

ROD. Yes, that I did; but that was but courtesy.

IAGO. Lechery, by this hand; an index and obscure prologue to the history of lust and foul thoughts. They met so near with their lips that their breaths embraced together. Villanous thoughts, Roderigo! when these mutualities so marshal the way, hard at hand comes the master and main exercise, the incorporate conclusion, Pish! But, sir, be you ruled by me: I have brought you from 270 Venice. Watch you to-night; for the command, I'll lay 't upon you. Cassio knows you not, I'll not be far from you: do you find some occasion to anger Cassio, either by speaking too loud, or tainting his discipline; or from what other course you please, which the time shall more favourably minister. 277

ROD. Well.

IAGO. Sir, he is rash and very sudden in choler, and haply may strike at you: provoke him, that he may; for even out of that will I cause these of Cyprus to mutiny; whose qualification shall come into no true taste again but by the displanting of Cassio. So shall you have a shorter journey to your de- 285 sires by the means I shall then have to prefer them; and the impediment most profitably removed, without the which there were no expectation of our prosperity.

ROD. I will do this, if I can bring it to any opportunity. 290

IAGO. I warrant thee. Meet me by and by at the citadel: I must fetch his necessaries ashore. Farewell.

ROD. Adieu. [*Exit.*

IAGO. That Cassio loves her, I do well believe it; 295
That she loves him, 'tis apt and of great credit:
The Moor, howbeit that I endure him not,
Is of a constant, loving, noble nature,
And I dare think he'll prove to Desdemona
A most dear husband. Now, I do love her too; 300
Not out of absolute lust, though peradventure
I stand accountant for as great a sin,
But partly led to diet my revenge,
For that I do suspect the lusty Moor
Hath leap'd into my seat; the thought whereof
Doth, like a poisonous mineral, gnaw my inwards; 306
And nothing can or shall content my soul
Till I am even'd with him, wife for wife,
Or failing so, yet that I put the Moor
At least into a jealousy so strong 310
That judgement cannot cure. Which thing to do,
If this poor trash of Venice, whom I trash
For his quick hunting, stand the putting on,
I'll have our Michael Cassio on the hip,
Abuse him to the Moor in the rank garb— 315
For I fear Cassio with my night-cap too—
Make the Moor thank me, love me and reward me,
For making him egregiously an ass
And practising upon his peace and quiet
Even to madness. 'Tis here, but yet confused: 320
Knavery's plain face is never seen till used.
[*Exit.*

SCENE II. *A street.*

[*Enter a* HERALD *with a proclamation;* PEOPLE *following.*]

HER. It is Othello's pleasure, our noble and valiant general, that, upon certain tidings now

247. stamp . . . advantages, create and fashion favorable occasions. 252. green, inexperienced. 255. condition, qualities. 259. paddle, caress. 263. index, then placed at the front of a book. 267. marshal, lead. 269. incorporate, intimately united. 275. tainting, disparaging. 277. minister, furnish. 283. qualification, appeasement; come . . . taste, not be made palatable. 286. prefer, promote. 289. prosperity, success. 291. I warrant thee, I'll guaranty you will; by and by, at once. 292. his, i.e., Othello's. 296. apt . . . credit, natural and very credible. 310. jealousy, suspicion. 312. trash, rubbish, worthless fellow; trash, check, hold back (a hunting term). 315. rank garb, coarse fashion. 319. practicing upon, plotting against.

arrived, importing the mere perdition of the Turkish fleet, every man put himself into triumph; some to dance, some to make 5 bonfires, each man to what sport and revels his addiction leads him: for, besides these beneficial news, it is the celebration of his nuptial. So much was his pleasure should be proclaimed. All offices are open, and there 10 is full liberty of feasting from this present hour of five till the bell have told eleven. Heaven bless the isle of Cyprus and our noble general Othello! [*Exeunt.*

SCENE III. *A hall in the castle.*

[*Enter* OTHELLO, DESDEMONA, CASSIO, *and* ATTENDANTS.]

OTH. Good Michael, look you to the guard to-night:
Let's teach ourselves that honourable stop,
Not to outsport discretion.

CAS. Iago hath direction what to do;
But, notwithstanding, with my personal eye 5
Will I look to 't.

OTH. Iago is most honest.
Michael, good night: to-morrow with your earliest
Let me have speech with you. [*To* DESDEMONA] Come, my dear love,
The purchase made, the fruits are to ensue;
That profit's yet to come 'tween me and you. 10
Good night.

[*Exeunt* OTHELLO, DESDEMONA, *and* ATTENDANTS.

[*Enter* IAGO.]

CAS. Welcome, Iago; we must to the watch.

IAGO. Not this hour, lieutenant; 'tis not yet ten o' the clock. Our general cast us thus early for the love of his Desdemona; who let us not therefore blame: he hath not yet made wanton the night with her; and she is sport for Jove. 17

CAS. She's a most exquisite lady.

IAGO. And, I'll warrant her, full of game.

CAS. Indeed, she's a most fresh and delicate creature. 21

IAGO. What an eye she has! methinks it sounds a parley of provocation.

CAS. An inviting eye; and yet methinks right modest.

IAGO. And when she speaks, is it not an alarum to love? 27

CAS. She is indeed perfection.

IAGO. Well, happiness to their sheets! Come, lieutenant, I have a stoup of wine; and here without are a brace of Cyprus gallants that would fain have a measure to the health of black Othello. 33

CAS. Not to-night, good Iago: I have very poor and unhappy brains for drinking: I could well wish courtesy would invent some other custom of entertainment.

IAGO. O, they are our friends; but one cup: I'll drink for you. 39

CAS. I have drunk but one cup to-night, and that was craftily qualified too, and, behold, what innovation it makes here: I am unfortunate in the infirmity, and dare not task my weakness with any more. 44

IAGO. What, man! 'tis a night of revels: the gallants desire it.

CAS. Where are they?

IAGO. Here at the door; I pray you, call them in.

CAS. I'll do 't; but it dislikes me. [*Exit.*

IAGO. If I can fasten but one cup upon him, 50
With that which he hath drunk to-night already,
He'll be as full of quarrel and offence
As my young mistress' dog. Now, my sick fool Roderigo,
Whom love hath turn'd almost the wrong side out,
To Desdemona hath to-night caroused 55
Potations pottle-deep; and he's to watch:
Three lads of Cyprus, noble swelling spirits,
That hold their honours in a wary distance,
The very elements of this warlike isle,
Have I to-night fluster'd with flowing cups, 60
And they watch too. Now, 'mongst this flock of drunkards,
Am I to put our Cassio in some action

Scene ii: 3. **mere perdition,** complete loss. 7. **addiction,** inclination. 10. **offices,** rooms in which food and drink were prepared and served. Scene iii: 2. **stop,** restraint. 7. **with your earliest,** as early as possible. 14. **cast,** dismissed. 19. **game,** sport. 30. **stoup,** a large flagon.

41. **craftily qualified,** slyly diluted (by Cassio). 42. **innovation,** disturbance; **here,** i.e., in his head. 44. **task,** impose upon. 56. **pottle . . . deep,** i.e., to the bottom of the pottle or tankard, i.e., "bottoms up." 57. **swelling,** swaggering. 58. **hold . . . distance,** are very sensitive about their honor. 59. **very elements,** perfect specimens. 61. **watch,** are on guard duty.

That may offend the isle.—But here they come:
If consequence do but approve my dream,
My boat sails freely, both with wind and stream. 65

[*Re-enter* CASSIO; *with him* MONTANO *and* GENTLEMEN; SERVANTS *following with wine.*]

CAS. 'Fore God, they have given me a rouse already.

MON. Good faith, a little one; not past a pint, as I am a soldier.

IAGO. Some wine, ho! 70
[*Sings*] And let me the canakin clink, clink;
And let me the canakin clink:
A soldier's a man;
A life's but a span;
Why, then, let a soldier drink. 75
Some wine, boys!

CAS. 'Fore God, an excellent song.

IAGO. I learned it in England, where, indeed, they are most potent in potting: your Dane, your German, and your swag-bellied Hollander—Drink, ho!—are nothing to your English. 81

CAS. Is your Englishman so expert in his drinking?

IAGO. Why, he drinks you, with facility, your Dane dead drunk; he sweats not to overthrow your Almain; he gives your Hollander a vomit, ere the next pottle can be filled. 87

CAS. To the health of our general!

MON. I am for it, lieutenant; and I'll do you justice. 90

IAGO. O sweet England!
King Stephen was a worthy peer,
His breeches cost him but a crown;
He held them sixpence all too dear,
With that he call'd the tailor lown. 95
He was a wight of high renown,
And thou art but of low degree:
'Tis pride that pulls the country down;
Then take thine auld cloak about thee.
Some wine, ho! 100

CAS. Why, this is a more exquisite song than the other.

IAGO. Will you hear 't again?

CAS. No; for I hold him to be unworthy of his place that does those things. Well, God's above all; and there be souls must be saved, and there be souls must not be saved.

IAGO. It's true, good lieutenant.

CAS. For mine own part,—no offence to the general, nor any man of quality,—I hope to be saved. 111

IAGO. And so do I too, lieutenant.

CAS. Ay, but, by your leave, not before me; the lieutenant is to be saved before the ancient. Let's have no more of this; let's to our affairs.— Forgive us our sins!—Gentlemen, let's look to our business. Do not think, gentlemen, I am drunk: this is my ancient; this is my right hand, and this is my left: I am not drunk now; I can stand well enough, and speak well enough. 120

ALL. Excellent well.

CAS. Why, very well then; you must not think then that I am drunk. [*Exit.*

MON. To the platform, masters; come, let's set the watch. 125

IAGO. You see this fellow that is gone before;
He is a soldier fit to stand by Cæsar
And give direction: and do but see his vice;
'Tis to his virtue a just equinox,
The one as long as the other: 'tis pity of him.
I fear the trust Othello puts him in, 131
On some odd time of his infirmity,
Will shake this island.

MON. But is he often thus?

IAGO. 'Tis evermore the prologue to his sleep:
He'll watch the horologe a double set, 135
If drink rock not his cradle.

MON. It were well
The general were put in mind of it.
Perhaps he sees it not; or his good nature
Prizes the virtue that appears in Cassio,
And looks not on his evils: is not this true? 140

[*Enter* RODERIGO.]

IAGO. [*Aside to him*] How now, Roderigo!
I pray you, after the lieutenant; go.
[*Exit* RODERIGO.

MON. And 'tis great pity that the noble Moor
Should hazard such a place as his own second

64. consequence, the result; approve my dream, confirm my expectation. 66. rouse, a full bumper. 71. canakin, small drinking vessel. 74. span, the distance between the little finger and thumb of an outstretched hand; hence, "small space" or "brief time." 79. swag-bellied, bulging-bellied, i.e., pot-bellied. 86. Almain, German; pottle, tankard. 89-90. I'll . . . justice, i.e., I'll drink as much as you. 95. lown, lout. 110. quality, rank. 129. just equinox, exact counterpart. 130. some odd time, some time or other. 135. watch, keep awake; horologue . . . set, twice around the clock.

With one of an ingraft infirmity: 145
It were an honest action to say
So to the Moor.

IAGO. Not I, for this fair island:
I do love Cassio well; and would do much
To cure him of this evil—But, hark! what noise? [*Cry within:* "Help! help!"

[*Re-enter* CASSIO, *driving in* RODERIGO.]

CAS. You rogue! you rascal!

MON. What's the matter, lieutenant?

CAS. A knave teach me my duty! 151
I'll beat the knave into a twiggen bottle.

ROD. Beat me!

CAS. Dost thou prate, rogue? [*Striking* RODERIGO.

MON. Nay, good lieutenant; [*Staying him.*]
I pray you, sir, hold your hand.

CAS. Let me go, sir,
Or I'll knock you o'er the mazzard.

MON. Come, come, you're drunk. 155

CAS. Drunk! [*They fight.*

IAGO. [*Aside to* RODERIGO] Away, I say; go out, and cry a mutiny. [*Exit* RODERIGO.]
Nay, good lieutenant,—alas, gentlemen;—
Help, ho!—Lieutenant,—sir,—Montano,—sir;—
Help, masters!—Here's a goodly watch indeed! [*Bell rings.*] 160
Who's that which rings the bell?—Diablo, ho!
The town will rise: God's will, lieutenant, hold!
You will be shamed for ever.

[*Re-enter* OTHELLO *and* ATTENDANTS.]

OTH. What is the matter here?

MON. 'Zounds, I bleed still; I am hurt to the death. [*Faints.*

OTH. Hold, for your lives! 165

IAGO. Hold, ho! Lieutenant,—sir,—Montano,—gentlemen,—
Have you forgot all sense of place and duty?
Hold! the general speaks to you; hold, hold, for shame!

OTH. Why, how now, ho! from whence ariseth this?
Are we turn'd Turks, and to ourselves do that 170
Which heaven hath forbid the Ottomites?
For Christian shame, put by this barbarous brawl:
He that stirs next to carve for his own rage
Holds his soul light; he dies upon his motion.
Silence that dreadful bell: it frights the isle
From her propriety. What is the matter, masters? 176
Honest Iago, that look'st dead with grieving,
Speak, who began this? on thy love, I charge thee.

IAGO. I do not know: friends all but now, even now,
In quarter, and in terms like bride and groom 180
Devesting them for bed; and then, but now—
As if some planet had unwitted men—
Swords out, and tilting one at other's breast,
In opposition bloody. I cannot speak
Any beginning to this peevish odds; 185
And would in action glorious I had lost
Those legs that brought me to a part of it!

OTH. How comes it, Michael, you are thus forgot?

CAS. I pray you, pardon me; I cannot speak.

OTH. Worthy Montano, you were wont be civil; 190
The gravity and stillness of your youth
The world hath noted, and your name is great
In mouths of wisest censure: what's the matter,
That you unlace your reputation thus 194
And spend your rich opinion for the name
Of a night-brawler? give me answer to it.

MON. Worthy Othello, I am hurt to danger:
Your officer, Iago, can inform you,—
While I spare speech, which something now offends me,—
Of all that I do know: nor know I aught 200
By me that's said or done amiss this night;
Unless self-charity be sometimes a vice,
And to defend ourselves it be a sin
When violence assails us.

OTH. Now, by heaven,
My blood begins my safer guides to rule; 205

145. **ingraft**, deeply rooted. 146. **honest**, honorable. 152. **twiggen bottle**, bottle covered with a network of interwoven twigs. 155. **mazzard**, head. 157. **cry a mutiny**, i.e., raise an uproar. 161. **Diablo**, Spanish for "Devil." 167. **place**, your position. 170. **turn'd Turks**, proverbial for "radically changed for the worse." 173. **carve . . . rage**, indulge his appetite for rage. 174. **upon his motion**, the moment he moves. 176. **From her propriety**, out of herself. 180. **In quarter**, on good terms. 181. **Devesting them**, undressing themselves. 185. **peevish odds**, childish quarrel. 188. **you . . . forgot**, have thus forgotten yourself. 190. **civil**, well behaved. 191. **stillness**, calmness. 193. **censure**, judgment. 194. **unlace**, loosen, disgrace. 195. **rich opinion**, valuable reputation. 199. **offends**, pains. 205. **blood**, passion.

And passion, having my best judgement collied,
Assays to lead the way: if I once stir,
Or do but lift this arm, the best of you
Shall sink in my rebuke. Give me to know
How this foul rout began, who set it on; 210
And he that is approved in this offence,
Though he had twinn'd with me, both at a birth,
Shall lose me. What! in a town of war,
Yet wild, the people's hearts brimful of fear,
To manage private and domestic quarrel, 215
In night, and on the court and guard of safety!
'Tis monstrous. Iago, who began 't?

MON. If partially affined, or leagued in office,
Thou dost deliver more or less than truth,
Thou art no soldier.

IAGO. Touch me not so near: 220
I had rather have this tongue cut from my mouth
Than it should do offence to Michael Cassio;
Yet, I persuade myself, to speak the truth
Shall nothing wrong him. Thus it is, general.
Montano and myself being in speech, 225
There comes a fellow crying out for help;
And Cassio following him with determined sword,
To execute upon him. Sir, this gentleman
Steps in to Cassio, and entreats his pause:
Myself the crying fellow did pursue, 230
Lest by his clamour—as it so fell out—
The town might fall in fright: he, swift of foot,
Outran my purpose; and I return'd the rather
For that I heard the clink and fall of swords,
And Cassio high in oath; which till to-night
I ne'er might say before. When I came back— 236
For this was brief—I found them close together,
At blow and thrust; even as again they were
When you yourself did part them.
More of this matter cannot I report: 240
But men are men; the best sometimes forget:
Though Cassio did some little wrong to him,
As men in rage strike those that wish them best,
Yet surely Cassio, I believe, received 244
From him that fled some strange indignity,
Which patience could not pass.

OTH. I know, Iago,
Thy honesty and love doth mince this matter,
Making it light to Cassio. Cassio, I love thee;
But never more be officer of mine.

[*Re-enter* DESDEMONA, *attended.*]

Look, if my gentle love be not raised up! 250
I'll make thee an example.

DES. What's the matter?

OTH. All's well now, sweeting; come away to bed.
Sir, for your hurts, myself will be your surgeon:
Lead him off. [*To* MONTANO, *who is led off.*]
Iago, look with care about the town,
And silence those whom this vile brawl distracted.
Come, Desdemona: 'tis the soldiers' life
To have their balmy slumbers waked with strife. [*Exeunt all but* IAGO *and* CASSIO.

IAGO. What, art you hurt, lieutenant?

CAS. Ay, past all surgery. 260

IAGO. Marry, heaven forbid!

CAS. Reputation, reputation, reputation! O, I have lost my reputation! I have lost the immortal part of myself, and what remains is bestial. My reputation, Iago, my reputation! 265

IAGO. As I am an honest man, I thought you had received some bodily wound; there is more sense in that than in reputation. Reputation is an idle and most false imposition; oft got without merit, and lost without 270 deserving: you have lost no reputation at all, unless you repute yourself such a loser. What, man! there are ways to recover the general again: you are but now cast in his mood, a punishment more in policy than in malice; even so as one would beat his offenceless dog to affright an imperious lion: sue to him again, and he's yours. 277

CAS. I will rather sue to be despised than to deceive so good a commander with so

206. collied, blackened, i.e., obscured. 211. approved in, proved guilty of. 214. wild, lacking order. 216. court and guard, the guarding place, i.e., the guardhouse. 218. partially affined, made partial by nearness of relationship; leagued in office, because a fellow officer. 219. deliver, speak. 228. execute, wreak his anger. 229. entreats his pause, begs him to stop. 246. patience . . . pass, i.e., was more than he could endure. 268. sense, feeling. 269. idle, empty, useless; imposition, delusion. 273. recover, reconcile. 274. cast, dismissed. 275. mood, anger.

slight, so drunken, and so indiscreet an officer. Drunk? and speak parrot? and squabble? swagger? swear? and discourse fustian with one's own shadow? O thou invisible spirit of wine, if thou hast no name to be known by, let us call thee devil!

IAGO. What was he that you followed with your sword? What had he done to you?

CAS. I know not.

IAGO. Is 't possible? 288

CAS. I remember a mass of things, but nothing distinctly; a quarrel, but nothing wherefore. O God, that men should put an enemy in their mouths to steal away their brains! that we should, with joy, pleasance, revel and applause, transform ourselves into beasts! 294

IAGO. Why, but you are now well enough: how came you thus recovered?

CAS. It hath pleased the devil drunkenness to give place to the devil wrath: one unperfectness shows me another, to make me frankly despise myself. 300

IAGO. Come, you are too severe a moraler: as the time, the place, and the condition of this country stands, I could heartily wish this had not befallen; but, since it is as it is, mend it for your own good. 305

CAS. I will ask him for my place again; he shall tell me I am a drunkard! Had I as many mouths as Hydra, such an answer would stop them all. To be now a sensible man, by and by a fool, and presently a beast! O strange! Every inordinate cup is unblessed and the ingredient is a devil. 312

IAGO. Come, come, good wine is a good familiar creature, if it be well used: exclaim no more against it. And, good lieutenant, I think you think I love you.

CAS. I have well approved it, sir. I drunk! 317

IAGO. You or any man living may be drunk at a time, man. I'll tell you what you shall do. Our general's wife is now the general: I may say so in this respect, for that he hath devoted and given up himself to the contemplation, mark, and denotement of her parts and graces: confess yourself freely to her; importune her help to put you in your place again: she is of so free, so kind, so apt, 325 so blessed a disposition, she holds it a vice in her goodness not to do more than she is requested: this broken joint between you and her husband entreat her to splinter; and, my fortunes against any lay worth naming, this crack of your love shall grow stronger than it was before. 331

CAS. You advise me well.

IAGO. I protest, in the sincerity of love and honest kindness. 334

CAS. I think it freely; and betimes in the morning I will beseech the virtuous Desdemona to undertake for me: I am desperate of my fortunes if they check me here.

IAGO. You are in the right. Good night, lieutenant; I must to the watch. 340

CAS. Good night, honest Iago. [*Exit.*

IAGO. And what's he then that says I play the villain?
When this advice is free I give and honest,
Probal to thinking and indeed the course
To win the Moor again? For 'tis most easy
The inclining Desdemona to subdue 346
In any honest suit: she's framed as fruitful
As the free elements. And then for her
To win the Moor—were 't to renounce his baptism,
All seals and symbols of redeemèd sin, 350
His soul is so enfetter'd to her love,
That she may make, unmake, do what she list,
Even as her appetite shall play the god
With his weak function. How am I then a villain
To counsel Cassio to this parallel course, 355
Directly to his good? Divinity of hell!
When devils will the blackest sins put on,
They do suggest at first with heavenly shows,
As I do now: for whiles this honest fool
Plies Desdemona to repair his fortunes 360
And she for him pleads strongly to the Moor,
I'll pour this pestilence into his ear,

281. **speak parrot**, talk nonsense. 282. **fustian**, high-sounding bombast. 293. **pleasance**, pleasure. 301. **moraler**, moralizer. 308. **Hydra**, a fabulous monster with nine heads, slain by Hercules. 314. **familiar**, affable. 317. **approved**, proved. 320. **for that**, because. 322. **denotement**, indication. 323. **parts**, qualities. 325. **free**, innocent; **apt**, kindly disposed. 329. **splinter**, bind with splints. 330. **lay**, wager. 331. **crack**, breach. 335. **betimes**, early. 337. **undertake**, accept responsibility. 337-8. **desperate . . . here**, I despair of my career if it is stopped short at this point. 344. **Probal**, probable. 346. **inclining**, favorably disposed; **subdue**, overcome by persuasion. 347. **fruitful**, bountiful. 348. **free elements**, elements out of which all things are produced. 354. **function**, operation of his mind. 355. **parallel**, i.e., parallel to his wishes. 357. **put on**, instigate. 358. **suggest**, tempt. 362. **pestilence**, poison.

That she repeals him for her body's lust;
And by how much she strives to do him good,
She shall undo her credit with the Moor. 365
So will I turn her virtue into pitch,
And out of her own goodness make the net
That shall enmesh them all.

[*Re-enter* RODERIGO.]

How now, Roderigo! 368

ROD. I do follow here in the chase, not like a hound that hunts, but one that fills up the cry. My money is almost spent; I have been to-night exceedingly well cudgelled; and I think the issue will be, I shall have so much experience for my pains, and so, with no money at all and a little more wit, return again to Venice.

IAGO. How poor are they that have not patience!
What wound did ever heal but by degrees?
Thou know'st we work by wit, and not by witchcraft;
And wit depends on dilatory time.
Does 't not go well? Cassio hath beaten thee, 380
And thou, by that small hurt, hast cashier'd Cassio:
Though other things grow fair against the sun,
Yet fruits that blossom first will first be ripe:
Content thyself awhile. By the mass, 'tis morning;
Pleasure and action make the hours seem short.
Retire thee; go where thou art billeted:
Away, I say; thou shalt know more hereafter:
Nay, get thee gone. [*Exit* RODERIGO.] Two things are to be done:
My wife must move for Cassio to her mistress;
I'll set her on; 390
Myself the while to draw the Moor apart,
And bring him jump when he may Cassio find
Soliciting his wife: ay, that's the way:
Dull not device by coldness and delay. [*Exit.*

ACT III

SCENE I. *Before the castle.*

[*Enter* CASSIO *and some* MUSICIANS.]

CAS. Masters, play here; I will content your pains;
Something that's brief; and bid "Good morrow, general." [*Music.*

[*Enter* CLOWN.]

CLO. Why, masters, have your instruments been in Naples, that they speak i' the nose thus?

FIRST MUS. How, sir, how! 5

CLO. Are these, I pray you, wind-instruments?

FIRST MUS. Ay, marry, are they, sir.

CLO. O, thereby hangs a tail.

FIRST MUS. Whereby hangs a tale, sir? 9

CLO. Marry, sir, by many a wind-instrument that I know. But, masters, here's money for you: and the general so likes your music, that he desires you, for love's sake, to make no more noise with it.

FIRST MUS. Well, sir, we will not.

CLO. If you have any music that may not be heard, to 't again: but, as they say, to hear music the general does not greatly care.

FIRST MUS. We have none such, sir.

CLO. Then put up your pipes in your bag, for I'll away: go, vanish into air; away! 21
[*Exeunt* MUSICIANS.

CAS. Dost thou hear, my honest friend?

CLO. No, I hear not your honest friend; I hear you.

CAS. Prithee, keep up thy quillets. There's a poor piece of gold for thee: if the gentlewoman that attends the general's wife be stirring, tell her there's one Cassio entreats her a little favour of speech: wilt thou do this?

CLO. She is stirring, sir: if she will stir hither, I shall seem to notify unto her. 31

CAS. Do, good my friend. [*Exit* CLOWN.]

[*Enter* IAGO.]

363. repeals, tries to have him restored (to his place). 365. undo her credit, destroy her reputation. 370. cry, pack. 373. issue, outcome. 378. wit . . . time, ingenuity must wait for sluggish time. 391. apart, aside. 392. jump, exactly. Act III, Scene i: 1. content, reward. 2. bid . . . general, i.e., the customary serenade of a newly-married couple on the morning after their wedding night. 4. in Naples, i.e., Neapolitans spoke with a nasal drawl. 24. keep . . . quillets, put your wise-cracks away.

In happy time, Iago.
IAGO. You have not been a-bed, then?
CAS. Why, no; the day had broke
Before we parted. I have made bold, Iago, 35
To send in to your wife: my suit to her
Is, that she will to virtuous Desdemona
Procure me some access.
IAGO. I'll send her to you presently;
And I'll devise a mean to draw the Moor
Out of the way, that your converse and business 40
May be more free.
CAS. I humbly thank you for 't. [*Exit* IAGO.] I never knew
A Florentine more kind and honest.

[*Enter* EMILIA.]

EMIL. Good morrow, good lieutenant: I am sorry
For your displeasure; but all will sure be well.
The general and his wife are talking of it; 46
And she speaks for you stoutly: the Moor replies,
That he you hurt is of great fame in Cyprus
And great affinity and that in wholesome wisdom
He might not but refuse you, but he protests he loves you 50
And needs no other suitor but his likings
To take the safest occasion by the front
To bring you in again.
CAS. Yet, I beseech you,
If you think fit, or that it may be done,
Give me advantage of some brief discourse
With Desdemona alone.
EMIL. Pray you, come in: 56
I will bestow you where you shall have time
To speak your bosom freely.
CAS. I am much bound to you. [*Exeunt.*

SCENE II. *A room in the castle.*

[*Enter* OTHELLO, IAGO, *and* GENTLEMEN.]

OTH. These letters give, Iago, to the pilot;
And by him do my duties to the senate:
That done, I will be walking on the works;
Repair there to me.
IAGO. Well, my good lord, I'll do 't.
OTH. This fortification, gentlemen, shall we see 't?
GENT. We'll wait upon your lordship.
[*Exeunt.*

SCENE III. *The garden of the castle.*

[*Enter* DESDEMONA, CASSIO, *and* EMILIA.]

DES. Be thou assured, good Cassio, I will do
All my abilities in thy behalf.
EMIL. Good madam, do: I warrant it grieves my husband,
As if the case were his.
DES. O, that's an honest fellow. Do not doubt, Cassio,
But I will have my lord and you again
As friendly as you were.
CAS. Bounteous madam,
Whatever shall become of Michael Cassio,
He's never any thing but your true servant.
DES. I know 't; I thank you. You do love my lord: 10
You have known him long; and be you well assured
He shall in strangeness stand no further off
Than in a politic distance.
CAS. Ay, but, lady,
That policy may either last so long,
Or feed upon such nice and waterish diet, 15
Or breed itself so out of circumstance,
That, I being absent and my place supplied,
My general will forget my love and service.
DES. Do not doubt that; before Emilia here
I give thee warrant of thy place: assure thee, 20
If I do vow a friendship, I'll perform it
To the last article: my lord shall never rest;
I'll watch him tame and talk him out of patience;
His bed shall seem a school, his board a shrift;
I'll intermingle every thing he does 25
With Cassio's suit: therefore be merry, Cassio;
For thy solicitor shall rather die
Than give thy cause away.

32. **In happy time,** i.e., I am glad to see you. 38. **presently,** at once. 40. **converse,** conversation. 45. **displeasure,** i.e., Othello's displeasure with you. 49. **affinity,** family connections; **wholesome,** sound. 52. **occasion,** opportunity; **front,** forelock. 57. **bestow,** put you in a place. 58. **speak . . . freely,** say whatever you wish. Scene ii: 2. **do my duties,** pay my respects. 3. **works,** fortifications. Scene iii: 2. **All my abilities,** to the best of my ability. 12. **strangeness,** aloofness. 13. **politic,** expedient. 15. **nice,** reluctantly given. 16. **breed . . . circumstance,** increase itself so much from mere accidents. 19. **doubt,** suspect. 20. **warrant,** assurance. 23. **watch him tame,** tame him by keeping him awake (a method of training falcons). 24. **shrift,** confessional. 28. **away,** up.

EMIL. Madam, here comes my lord.
CAS. Madam, I'll take my leave. 30
DES. Why, stay, and hear me speak.
CAS. Madam, not now: I am very ill at ease,
Unfit for mine own purposes.
DES. Well, do your discretion.
[*Exit* CASSIO.

[*Enter* OTHELLO *and* IAGO.]

IAGO. Ha! I like not that.
OTH. What dost thou say?
IAGO. Nothing, my lord: or if—I know not what. 36
OTH. Was not that Cassio parted from my wife?
IAGO. Cassio, my lord! No, sure, I cannot think it,
That he would steal away so guilty-like,
Seeing you coming.
OTH. I do believe 'twas he. 40
DES. How now, my lord!
I have been talking with a suitor here,
A man that languishes in your displeasure.
OTH. Who is 't you mean?
DES. Why, your lieutenant, Cassio. Good my lord, 45
If I have any grace or power to move you,
His present reconciliation take;
For if he be not one that truly loves you,
That errs in ignorance and not in cunning,
I have no judgement in an honest face: 50
I prithee, call him back.
OTH. Went he hence now?
DES. Ay, sooth; so humbled
That he hath left part of his grief with me,
To suffer with him. Good love, call him back.
OTH. Not now, sweet Desdemona; some other time. 55
DES. But shall 't be shortly?
OTH. The sooner, sweet, for you.
DES. Shall 't be to-night at supper?
OTH. No, not to-night.
DES. To-morrow dinner, then?
OTH. I shall not dine at home;
I meet the captains at the citadel.
DES. Why, then, to-morrow night; or Tuesday morn; 60
On Tuesday noon, or night; on Wednesday morn:
I prithee, name the time, but let it not
Exceed three days: in faith, he's penitent;
And yet his trespass, in our common reason—
Save that, they say, the wars must make examples 65
Out of their best—is not almost a fault
To incur a private check. When shall he come?
Tell me, Othello: I wonder in my soul,
What you would ask me, that I should deny,
Or stand so mammering on. What! Michael Cassio, 70
That came a-wooing with you, and so many a time,
When I have spoke of you dispraisingly,
Hath ta'en your part; to have so much to do
To bring him in! Trust me, I could do much,—
OTH. Prithee, no more: let him come when he will; 75
I will deny thee nothing.
DES. Why, this is not a boon;
'Tis as I should entreat you wear your gloves,
Or feed on nourishing dishes, or keep you warm,
Or sue to you to do a peculiar profit
To your own person: nay, when I have a suit 80
Wherein I mean to touch your love indeed,
It shall be full of poise and difficult weight
And fearful to be granted.
OTH. I will deny thee nothing:
Whereon, I do beseech thee, grant me this,
To leave me but a little to myself. 85
DES. Shall I deny you? no: farewell, my lord.
OTH. Farewell, my Desdemona: I'll come to thee straight.
DES. Emilia, come. Be as your fancies teach you:
Whate'er you be, I am obedient.
[*Exeunt* DESDEMONA *and* EMILIA.
OTH. Excellent wretch! Perdition catch my soul, 90
But I do love thee! and when I love thee not,
Chaos is come again.
IAGO. My noble lord,—

33. mine own purposes, i.e., to plead my cause. 47. His . . . take, accept at once his plea for reconciliation. 49. in cunning, knowingly, intentionally. 52. sooth, truly. 64. common reason, common sense. 66. not almost, hardly. 67. check, rebuke. 70. mammering, hesitating, originally "stammering." 73. have . . . do, to make such a fuss. 79. peculiar, private. 82. poise, weight, importance. 83. fearful . . . granted, granted only with apprehension; deny, refuse. 88. Be . . . you, i.e., Be what you like, i.e., please yourself. 90. wretch, term of mingled tenderness and pity.

OTH. What dost thou say, Iago?
IAGO. Did Michael Cassio, when you woo'd my lady,
Know of your love? 95
OTH. He did, from first to last: why dost thou ask?
IAGO. But for a satisfaction of my thought;
No further harm.
OTH. Why of thy thought, Iago?
IAGO. I did not think he had been acquainted with her.
OTH. O, yes; and went between us very oft.
IAGO. Indeed! 101
OTH. Indeed! ay, indeed: discern'st thou aught in that?
Is he not honest?
IAGO. Honest, my lord!
OTH. Honest! ay, honest.
IAGO. My lord, for aught I know.
OTH. What dost thou think?
IAGO. Think, my lord!
OTH. Think, my lord!
By heaven, he echoes me, 106
As if there were some monster in his thought
Too hideous to be shown. Thou dost mean something:
I heard thee say even now, thou likedst not that,
When Cassio left my wife: what didst not like? 110
And when I told thee he was of my counsel
In my whole course of wooing, thou criedst "Indeed!"
And didst contract and purse thy brow together,
As if thou then hadst shut up in thy brain
Some horrible conceit: if thou dost love me,
Show me thy thought. 116
IAGO. My lord, you know I love you.
OTH. I think thou dost;
And, for I know thou'rt full of love and honesty,
And weigh'st thy words before thou givest them breath,
Therefore these stops of thine fright me the more: 120
For such things in a false disloyal knave
Are tricks of custom, but in a man that's just
They are close delations, working from the heart
That passion cannot rule.
IAGO. For Michael Cassio,
I dare be sworn I think that he is honest. 125
OTH. I think so too.
IAGO. Men should be what they seem;
Or those that be not, would they might seem none!
OTH. Certain, men should be what they seem.
IAGO. Why, then, I think Cassio's an honest man.
OTH. Nay, there's more in this: 130
I prithee, speak to me as to thy thinkings,
As thou dost ruminate, and give thy worst of thoughts
The worst of words.
IAGO. Good my lord, pardon me:
Though I am bound to every act of duty,
I am not bound to that all slaves are free to.
Utter my thoughts? Why, say they are vile and false; 136
As where's that palace whereinto foul things
Sometimes intrude not? who has a breast so pure,
But some uncleanly apprehensions
Keep leets and law-days and in session sit 140
With meditations lawful?
OTH. Thou dost conspire against thy friend, Iago,
If thou but think'st him wrong'd and makest his ear
A stranger to thy thoughts.
IAGO. I do beseech you—
Though I perchance am vicious in my guess,
As, I confess, it is my nature's plague 146
To spy into abuses, and oft my jealousy
Shapes faults that are not—that your wisdom yet,
From one that so imperfectly conceits,
Would take no notice, nor build yourself a trouble 150
Out of his scattering and unsure observance.
It were not for your quiet nor your good,
Nor for my manhood, honesty, or wisdom,
To let you know my thoughts.

103. **honest**, honorable. 111. **of my counsel**, in my confidence. 115. **conceit**, conception. 120. **stops**, interruptions. 123. **close delations**, secret accusations. 124. **passion . . . rule**, i.e., that cannot control its indignation; **For**, As for. 127. **seem none**, i.e., not seem to be honorable men.

130. **yet . . . more**, there's yet more. 131. **As . . . thinkings**, i.e., as frankly as to your own thoughts. 135. **free to**, i.e., to do or not to do. 139. **apprehensions**, suspicions. 140. **leets**, days on which courts are in session. 145. **vicious**, wrong. 147. **jealousy**, suspicion. 149. **imperfectly conceits**, has such imperfect ideas. 151. **scattering . . . observance**, random and uncertain observation.

OTH. What dost thou mean?
IAGO. Good name in man and woman, dear my lord, 155
Is the immediate jewel of their souls:
Who steals my purse steals trash; 'tis something, nothing;
'Twas mine, 'tis his, and has been slave to thousands;
But he that filches from me my good name
Robs me of that which not enriches him 160
And makes me poor indeed.
OTH. By heaven, I'll know thy thoughts.
IAGO. You cannot, if my heart were in your hand;
Nor shall not, whilst 'tis in my custody. 164
OTH. Ha!
IAGO. O, beware, my lord, of jealousy;
It is the green-eyed monster which doth mock
The meat it feeds on: that cuckold lives in bliss
Who, certain of his fate, loves not his wronger;
But, O, what damnèd minutes tells he o'er
Who dotes, yet doubts, suspects, yet strongly loves! 170
OTH. O misery!
IAGO. Poor and content is rich and rich enough,
But riches fineless is as poor as winter
To him that ever fears he shall be poor.
Good heaven, the souls of all my tribe defend
From jealousy!
OTH. Why, why is this? 176
Think'st thou I'ld make a life of jealousy,
To follow still the changes of the moon
With fresh suspicions? No; to be once in doubt
Is once to be resolved: exchange me for a goat, 180
When I shall turn the business of my soul
To such exsufflicate and blown surmises,
Matching thy inference. 'Tis not to make me jealous
To say my wife is fair, feeds well, loves company,
Is free of speech, sings, plays and dances well;
Where virtue is, these are more virtuous: 186
Nor from mine own weak merits will I draw
The smallest fear or doubt of her revolt;
For she had eyes, and chose me. No, Iago;
I'll see before I doubt; when I doubt, prove;
And on the proof, there is no more but this,—
Away at once with love or jealousy! 192
IAGO. I am glad of it; for now I shall have reason
To show the love and duty that I bear you
With franker spirit: therefore, as I am bound,
Receive it from me. I speak not yet of proof.
Look to your wife; observe her well with Cassio;
Wear your eye thus, not jealous nor secure:
I would not have your free and noble nature,
Out of self-bounty, be abused; look to 't: 200
I know our country disposition well;
In Venice they do let heaven see the pranks
They dare not show their husbands; their best conscience
Is not to leave 't undone, but keep 't unknown.
OTH. Dost thou say so? 205
IAGO. She did deceive her father, marrying you;
And when she seem'd to shake and fear your looks,
She loved them most.
OTH. And so she did.
IAGO. Why, go to then;
She that, so young, could give out such a seeming,
To seel her father's eyes up close as oak— 210
He thought 'twas witchcraft—but I am much to blame;
I humbly do beseech you of your pardon
For too much loving you.
OTH. I am bound to thee for ever.
IAGO. I see this hath a little dash'd your spirits.
OTH. Not a jot, not a jot.
IAGO. I' faith, I fear it has.
I hope you will consider what is spoke 216
Comes from my love. But I do see you're moved:
I am to pray you not to strain my speech
To grosser issues nor to larger reach
Than to suspicion. 220
OTH. I will not.

156. immediate, most precious. 166. doth mock, makes a mockery of. 169. tells . . . o'er, counts. 173. fineless, boundless. 182. exsufflicate and blown, unsubstantial and blown up (like a bubble). 188. doubt, suspicion; revolt, inconstancy. 190. prove, test. 198. secure, free from suspicion.

200. self-bounty, natural generosity. 201. our . . . disposition, prevailing spirit of our country. 209. give . . . seeming, present such a false appearance. 210. seel, sew up (as the eyes of a falcon); oak, i.e., the grain of an oak. 219. grosser issues, more obvious conclusions.

IAGO. Should you do so, my lord,
My speech should fall into such vile success
As my thoughts aim not at. Cassio's my worthy friend—
My lord, I see you're moved.

OTH. No, not much moved:
I do not think but Desdemona's honest. 225

IAGO. Long live she so! and long live you to think so!

OTH. And yet, how nature erring from itself,—

IAGO. Ay, there's the point: as—to be bold with you—
Not to affect many proposed matches
Of her own clime, complexion, and degree, 230
Whereto we see in all things nature tends—
Foh! one may smell in such a will most rank,
Foul disproportion, thoughts unnatural.
But pardon me; I do not in position
Distinctly speak of her; though I may fear 235
Her will, recoiling to her better judgement,
May fall to match you with her country forms
And happily repent.

OTH. Farewell, farewell:
If more thou dost perceive, let me know more;
Set on thy wife to observe: leave me, Iago. 240

IAGO. [*Going*] My lord, I take my leave.

OTH. Why did I marry? This honest creature doubtless
Sees and knows more, much more, than he unfolds.

IAGO. [*Returning*] My Lord, I would I might entreat your honour
To scan this thing no further; leave it to time: 245
Though it be fit that Cassio have his place,
For, sure, he fills it up with great ability,
Yet, if you please to hold him off awhile,
You shall by that perceive him and his means: 249
Note, if your lady strain his entertainment
With any strong or vehement importunity;
Much will be seen in that. In the mean time,
Let me be thought too busy in my fears—
As worthy cause I have to fear I am—
And hold her free, I do beseech your honour.

OTH. Fear not my government. 256

IAGO. I once more take my leave. [*Exit.*

OTH. This fellow's of exceeding honesty,
And knows all qualities, with a learned spirit,
Of human dealings. If I do prove her haggard, 260
Though that her jesses were my dear heartstrings,
I'ld whistle her off and let her down the wind,
To prey at fortune. Haply, for I am black
And have not those soft parts of conversation
That chamberers have, or for I am declined
Into the vale of years,—yet that's not much— 266
She's gone. I am abused; and my relief
Must be to loathe her. O curse of marriage,
That we can call these delicate creatures ours,
And not their appetites! I had rather be a toad, 270
And live upon the vapour of a dungeon,
Than keep a corner in the thing I love
For others' uses. Yet, 'tis the plague of great ones;
Prerogatived are they less than the base;
'Tis destiny unshunnable, like death: 275
Even then this forkèd plague is fated to us
When we do quicken. Desdemona comes:

[*Re-enter* DESDEMONA *and* EMILIA.]

If she be false, O, then heaven mocks itself!
I'll not believe 't.

DES. How now, my dear Othello!
Your dinner, and the generous islanders 280
By you invited, do attend your presence.

OTH. I am to blame.

DES. Why do you speak so faintly?
Are you not well?

222. **success**, consequences. 225. **honest**, chaste. 227. **erring**, straying. 229. **affect**, like. 230. **complexion**, temperament, perhaps also a reference to her fair skin in contrast to the dark Moorish Othello; **degree**, rank. 232. **will**, sexual desire; **rank**, disgusting. 234. **position**, formal assertion. 236. **recoiling**, reverting. 237. **fall to match**, begin to compare; **country forms**, the appearance of her fellow countrymen, who are white. 238. **happily**, haply, perhaps. 249. **his means**, i.e., the means he adopts to regain your favor. 250. **strain his entertainment**, over-urge his reinstatement. 255. **free**, innocent. 256. **government**, self-control. 259. **learned**, experienced. 260. **haggard**, wild, untamed hawk. 261. **jesses**, strap attached to the foot of the hawk by which the falconer held her. 262. **down the wind**, i.e., go free; trained hawks always flew against the wind. 263. **at fortune**, at random; **for**, because; **black**, of dark complexion, in Elizabethan speech used as the opposite of fair. 264. **parts of conversation**, gifts for social intercourse. 265. **chamberers**, gallants. 267. **abused**, deceived. 274. **prerogatived**, privileged. 276. **forked plague**, the horns of a cuckold. 277. **quicken**, begin to show signs of life, i.e., in our mother's womb. 280. **generous**, noble.

OTH. I have a pain upon my forehead here.
DES. 'Faith, that's with watching; 'twill away again: 285
Let me but bind it hard, within this hour
It will be well.
OTH. Your napkin is too little:
[*He puts the handkerchief from him; and it drops.*]
Let it alone. Come, I'll go in with you.
DES. I am very sorry that you are not well.
[*Exeunt* OTHELLO *and* DESDEMONA.
EMIL. I am glad I have found this napkin:
This was her first remembrance from the Moor: 291
My wayward husband hath a hundred times
Woo'd me to steal it; but she so loves the token,
For he conjured her she should ever keep it,
That she reserves it evermore about her 295
To kiss and talk to. I'll have the work ta'en out,
And give 't Iago: what he will do with it
Heaven knows, not I;
I nothing but to please his fantasy.

[*Re-enter* IAGO.]

IAGO. How now! what do you here alone?
EMIL. Do not you chide; I have a thing for you. 301
IAGO. A thing for me? it is a common thing—
EMIL. Ha!
IAGO. To have a foolish wife.
EMIL. O, is that all? What will you give me now 305
For that same handkerchief?
IAGO. What handkerchief?
EMIL. What handkerchief!
Why, that the Moor first gave to Desdemona;
That which so often you did bid me steal.
IAGO. Hast stol'n it from her? 310
EMIL. No, 'faith; she let it drop by negligence,
And, to the advantage, I, being here, took 't up.
Look, here it is.
IAGO. A good wench; give it me.
EMIL. What will you do with 't, that you have been so earnest
To have me filch it?
IAGO. [*Snatching it*] Why, what's that to you? 315
EMIL. If it be not for some purpose of import,
Give 't me again: poor lady, she'll run mad
When she shall lack it
IAGO. Be not acknown on 't; I have use for it.
Go, leave me. [*Exit* EMILIA.] 320
I will in Cassio's lodging lose this napkin,
And let him find it. Trifles light as air
Are to the jealous confirmations strong
As proofs of holy writ: this may do something.
The Moor already changes with my poison:
Dangerous conceits are, in their natures, poisons, 326
Which at the first are scarce found to distaste,
But with a little act upon the blood,
Burn like the mines of sulphur. I did say so:
Look, where he comes!

[*Re-enter* OTHELLO.]

Not poppy, nor mandragora, 330
Nor all the drowsy syrups of the world,
Shall ever medicine thee to that sweet sleep
Which thou owedst yesterday.
OTH. Ha! ha! false to me?
IAGO. Why, how now, general! no more of that.
OTH. Avaunt! be gone! thou hast set me on the rack: 335
I swear 'tis better to be much abused
Than but to know 't a little.
IAGO. How now, my lord!
OTH. What sense had I of her stol'n hours of lust?
I saw't not, thought it not, it harm'd not me:
I slept the next night well, was free and merry; 340
I found not Cassio's kisses on her lips:
He that is robb'd, not wanting what is stol'n,
Let him not know 't, and he's not robb'd at all.

285. watching, lying awake. 287. napkin, handkerchief. 292. wayward, willful, insistent. 294. conjured her, make her swear with an oath. 295. reserves, keeps. 296. work ta'en out, embroidery copied. 299. fantasy, whim. 312. to the advantage, thus giving me the opportunity. 318. lack, miss. 319. Be . . . it, do not admit any knowledge of it. 326. conceits, conceptions. 327. to distaste, to be distasteful. 328. act, action. 330. mandragora, mandrake root, a sleeping drug. 333. owedst, owned, had. 342. wanting, missing.

IAGO. I am sorry to hear this.
OTH. I had been happy, if the general camp, 345
Pioners and all, had tasted her sweet body,
So I had nothing known. O, now, for ever
Farewell the tranquil mind! farewell content!
Farewell the plumèd troop, and the big wars,
That make ambition virtue! O, farewell! 350
Farewell the neighing steed, and the shrill trump,
The spirit-stirring drum, the ear-piercing fife,
The royal banner, and all quality,
Pride, pomp and circumstance of glorious war!
And, O you mortal engines, whose rude throats 355
The immortal Jove's dread clamours counterfeit,
Farewell! Othello's occupation's gone!
IAGO. Is 't possible, my lord?
OTH. Villain, be sure thou prove my love a whore,
Be sure of it; give me the ocular proof; 360
Or, by the worth of man's eternal soul,
Thou hadst been better have been born a dog
Than answer my waked wrath!
IAGO. Is 't come to this?
OTH. Make me to see 't; or, at the least, so prove it,
That the probation bear no hinge nor loop 365
To hang a doubt on; or woe upon thy life!
IAGO. My noble lord,—
OTH. If thou dost slander her and torture me,
Never pray more; abandon all remorse;
On horror's head horrors accumulate; 370
Do deeds to make heaven weep, all earth amazed;
For nothing canst thou to damnation add
Greater than that.
IAGO. O grace! O heaven forgive me!
Are you a man? have you a soul or sense?
God be wi' you; take mine office. O wretched fool, 375
That livest to make thine honesty a vice!
O monstrous world! Take note, take note, O world,
To be direct and honest is not safe.
I thank you for this profit; and from hence
I'll love no friend, sith love breeds such offence. 380
OTH. Nay, stay: thou shouldst be honest.
IAGO. I should be wise, for honesty's a fool
And loses that it works for.
OTH. By the world,
I think my wife be honest and think she is not;
I think that thou art just and think thou art not. 385
I'll have some proof. Her name, that was as fresh
As Dian's visage, is now begrimed and black
As mine own face. If there be cords, or knives,
Poison, or fire, or suffocating streams,
I'll not endure it. Would I were satisfied! 390
IAGO. I see, sir, you are eaten up with passion:
I do repent me that I put it to you.
You would be satisfied?
OTH. Would! nay, I will.
IAG. And may: but, how? how satisfied, my lord? 394
Would you, the supervisor, grossly gape on—
Behold her topp'd?
OTH. Death and damnation! O!
IAGO. It were a tedious difficulty, I think,
To bring them to that prospect: damn them then,
If ever mortal eyes do see them bolster
More than their own! What then? how then? 400
What shall I say? Where's satisfaction?
It is impossible you should see this,
Were they as prime as goats, as hot as monkeys,
As salt as wolves in pride, and fools as gross
As ignorance made drunk. But yet, I say, 405
If imputation and strong circumstances,
Which lead directly to the door of truth,
Will give you satisfaction, you may have 't.
OTH. Give me a living reason she's disloyal.
IAGO. I do not like the office: 410

345. **the general camp**, the camp in general. 346. **pioners**, sappers, i.e., the vilest men in the army. Soldiers were assigned to this dangerous duty as punishment. 347. **So**, provided that. 349. **plumed**, wearing plumes in their helmets. 354. **circumstance**, ceremony. 355. **mortal engines**, deadly cannon. 356. **counterfeit**, imitate. 365. **probation**, proof. 369. **remorse**, hope for pity. 375. **God . . . you**, good-bye. 379. **profit**, profitable lesson. 380. **sith**, since. 384. **honest**, chaste. 387. **Dian**, Diana, goddess of chastity. 390. **satisfied**, convinced. 398. **prospect**, exposure. 399. **bolster**, i.e., sleep together. 403. **prime**, licentious. 404. **salt**, sensual; **in pride**, in heat. 406. **imputation**, opinion based on circumstantial evidence. 409. **living**, i.e., one not founded on surmise.

But, sith I am enter'd in this cause so far,
Prick'd to 't by foolish honesty and love,
I will go on. I lay with Cassio lately;
And, being troubled with a raging tooth,
I could not sleep. 415
There are a kind of men so loose of soul,
That in their sleeps will mutter their affairs:
One of this kind is Cassio:
In sleep I heard him say "Sweet Desdemona,
Let us be wary, let us hide our loves;" 420
And then, sir, would he gripe and wring my hand,
Cry "O sweet creature!" and then kiss me hard,
As if he pluck'd up kisses by the roots
That grew upon my lips: then laid his leg
Over my thigh, and sigh'd, and kiss'd; and then 425
Cried "Cursed fate that gave thee to the Moor!"

OTH. O monstrous! monstrous!

IAGO. Nay, this was but his dream.

OTH. But this denoted a foregone conclusion:
'Tis a shrewd doubt, though it be but a dream.

IAGO. And this may help to thicken other proofs 430
That do demonstrate thinly.

OTH. I'll tear her all to pieces.

IAGO. Nay, but be wise: yet we see nothing done;
She may be honest yet. Tell me but this,
Have you not sometimes seen a handkerchief
Spotted with strawberries in your wife's hand? 435

OTH. I gave her such a one; 'twas my first gift.

IAGO. I know not that: but such a handkerchief—
I am sure it was your wife's—did I to-day
See Cassio wipe his beard with.

OTH. If it be that,—

IAGO. If it be that, or any that was hers, 440
It speaks against her with the other proofs.

OTH. O, that the slave had forty thousand lives!
One is too poor, too weak for my revenge.
Now do I see 'tis true. Look here, Iago;
All my fond love thus do I blow to heaven.
'Tis gone. 446
Arise, black vengeance, from thy hollow cell!
Yield up, O love, thy crown and hearted throne
To tyrannous hate! Swell, bosom, with thy fraught,
For 'tis of aspics' tongues!

IAGO. Yet be content. 450

OTH. O, blood, blood, blood!

IAGO. Patience, I say; your mind perhaps may change.

OTH. Never, Iago. Like to the Pontic sea,
Whose icy current and compulsive course
Ne'er feels retiring ebb, but keeps due on 455
To the Propontic and the Hellespont,
Even so my bloody thoughts, with violent pace,
Shall ne'er look back, ne'er ebb to humble love,
Till that a capable and wide revenge
Swallow them up. Now, by yond marble heaven, 460
[*Kneels*] In the due reverence of a sacred vow
I here engage my words.

IAGO. Do not rise yet.
[*Kneels*] Witness, you ever-burning lights above,
You elements that clip us round about,
Witness that here Iago doth give up 465
The execution of his wit, hands, heart,
To wrong'd Othello's service! Let him command,
And to obey shall be in me remorse,
What bloody business ever. [*They rise.*

OTH. I greet thy love,
Not with vain thanks, but with acceptance bounteous, 470
And will upon the instant put thee to 't:
Within these three days let me hear thee say
That Cassio's not alive.

IAGO. My friend is dead; 'tis done at your request:
But let her live.

412. **prick'd**, spurred on. 428. **foregone conclusion**, previous experience. 429. **shrewd doubt**, strong ground for suspecting evil. 430. **thicken**, strengthen. 433. **yet**, as yet. 435. **strawberries**, pattern of strawberries. 445. **fond**, foolish. 448. **hearted**, fixed in the heart. 449. **fraught**, freight. 450. **aspics'**, asps', poisonous snakes'. 452. **Patience**, self-control. 453. **Pontic sea**, Black Sea. 456. **Propontic**, Sea of Marmora; **Hellespont**, the Dardanelles. 459. **capable**, comprehensive. 460. **marble**, i.e., gleaming like marble. 462. **engage**, pledge. 464. **clip**, embrace, surround. 465. **give up**, dedicate. 466. **execution . . . wit**, exercise of his intelligence. 468. **remorse**, pity, i.e., obedience will be an act of pity (not of cruelty). 471. **put thee to't**, give you something to do.

OTH. Damn her, lewd minx! O, damn her! 475
Come, go with me apart; I will withdraw,
To furnish me with some swift means of death
For the fair devil. Now art thou my lieutenant.

IAGO. I am your own for ever. [*Exeunt.*

SCENE IV. *Before the castle.*

[*Enter* DESDEMONA, EMILIA, *and* CLOWN.]

DES. Do you know, sirrah, where Lieutenant Cassio lies?

CLO. I dare not say he lies any where.

DES. Why, man?

CLO. He's a soldier, and for one to say a soldier lies, is stabbing. 6

DES. Go to: where lodges he?

CLO. To tell you where he lodges, is to tell you where I lie.

DES. Can any thing be made of this? 10

CLO. I know not where he lodges, and for me to devise a lodging and say he lies here or he lies there, were to lie in mine own throat.

DES. Can you inquire him out, and be edified by report? 15

CLO. I will catechize the world for him; that is, make questions, and by them answer.

DES. Seek him, bid him come hither: tell him I have moved my lord on his behalf, and hope all will be well. 20

CLO. To do this is within the compass of man's wit; and therefore I will attempt the doing it. [*Exit.*

DES. Where should I lose that handkerchief, Emilia?

EMIL. I know not, madam.

DES. Believe me, I had rather have lost my purse 25
Full of crusadoes: and, but my noble Moor
Is true of mind and made of no such baseness
As jealous creatures are, it were enough
To put him to ill thinking.

EMIL. Is he not jealous?

DES. Who, he? I think the sun where he was born 30
Drew all such humours from him.

EMIL. Look, where he comes.

DES. I will not leave him now till Cassio
Be call'd to him.

[*Enter* OTHELLO.]

How is 't with you, my lord?

OTH. Well, my good lady. [*Aside*] O, hardness to dissemble!—
How do you, Desdemona?

DES. Well, my good lord.

OTH. Give me your hand: this hand is moist, my lady. 36

DES. It yet hath felt no age nor known no sorrow.

OTH. This argues fruitfulness and liberal heart:
Hot, hot, and moist: this hand of yours requires 39
A sequester from liberty, fasting and prayer,
Much castigation, exercise devout;
For here's a young and sweating devil here,
That commonly rebels. 'Tis a good hand,
A frank one.

DES. You may, indeed, say so;
For 'twas that hand that gave away my heart. 45

OTH. A liberal hand: the hearts of old gave hands;
But our new heraldry is hands, not hearts.

DES. I cannot speak of this. Come now, your promise.

OTH. What promise, chuck?

DES. I have sent to bid Cassio come speak with you. 50

OTH. I have a salt and sorry rheum offends me;
Lend me thy handkerchief.

DES. Here, my lord.

OTH. That which I gave you.

DES. I have it not about me.

OTH. Not?

DES. No, indeed, my lord.

OTH. That is a fault.
That handkerchief 55
Did an Egyptian to my mother give;
She was a charmer, and could almost read

476. **apart**, aside. **Scene iv**: 1. **lies**, dwells. 15. **inquire him out**, seek information about him; **edified**, enlightened. 17. **answer**, be enabled to answer. 23. **should**, could.

26. **crusadoes**, Portuguese gold coins stamped with a cross, current in England; but, except that. 36. **moist**, a moist hand was supposed to be a sign of desire. 38. **liberal**, too generous, yielding. 40. **sequester**, separation. 41. **exercise**, performance of religious duties. 47. **hands not hearts**, i.e., loveless marriages. 51. **salt**, here = watery; **sorry rheum**, painful cold in the head. 56. **Egyptian**, gypsy. 57. **charmer**, enchantress.

The thoughts of people: she told her, while she kept it,
'Twould make her amiable and subdue my father
Entirely to her love, but if she lost it 60
Or made a gift of it, my father's eye
Should hold her loathed and his spirits should hunt
After new fancies: she, dying, gave it me;
And bid me, when my fate would have me wive,
To give it her. I did so: and take heed on 't;
Make it a darling like your precious eye; 66
To lose 't or give 't away were such perdition
As nothing else could match.

DES. Is 't possible?

OTH. 'Tis true: there's magic in the web of it:
A sibyl, that had number'd in the world 70
The sun to course two hundred compasses,
In her prophetic fury sew'd the work;
The worms were hallow'd that did breed the silk;
And it was dyed in mummy which the skilful
Conserved of maidens' hearts.

DES. Indeed! is 't true? 75

OTH. Most veritable; therefore look to 't well.

DES. Then would to God that I had never seen 't!

OTH. Ha! wherefore?

DES. Why do you speak so startingly and rash?

OTH. Is 't lost? is 't gone? speak, is it out o' the way? 80

DES. Heaven bless us!

OTH. Say you?

DES. It is not lost; but what an if it were?

OTH. How!

DES. I say, it is not lost.

OTH. Fetch 't, let me see 't. 85

DES. Why, so I can, sir, but I will not now.
This is a trick to put me from my suit:
Pray you, let Cassio be received again.

OTH. Fetch me the handkerchief: my mind misgives.

DES. Come, come; 90
You'll never meet a more sufficient man.

OTH. The handkerchief!

DES. I pray, talk me of Cassio.

OTH. The handkerchief!

DES A man that all his time
Hath founded his good fortunes on your love,
Shared dangers with you,— 95

OTH. The handkerchief!

DES. In sooth, you are to blame.

OTH. Away! [*Exit.*

EMIL. Is not this man jealous?

DES. I ne'er saw this before. 100
Sure, there's some wonder in this handkerchief:
I am most unhappy in the loss of it.

EMIL. 'Tis not a year or two shows us a man:
They are all but stomachs, and we all but food;
They eat us hungerly, and when they are full,
They belch us. Look you, Cassio and my husband! 106

[*Enter* CASSIO *and* IAGO.]

IAGO. There is no other way; 'tis she must do 't:
And, lo, the happiness! go, and importune her.

DES. How now, good Cassio! what's the news with you?

CAS. Madam, my former suit: I do beseech you 110
That by your virtuous means I may again
Exist, and be a member of his love
Whom I with all the office of my heart
Entirely honour: I would not be delay'd.
If my offence be of such mortal kind 115
That nor my service past, nor present sorrows,
Nor purposed merit in futurity,
Can ransom me into his love again,
But to know so must be my benefit;
So shall I clothe me in a forced content, 120
And shut myself up in some other course,
To fortune's alms.

DES. Alas, thrice-gentle Cassio!

59. **amiable,** lovable. 67. **such perdition,** such a loss. 70. **sibyl,** prophetess of the ancient world, here = sorceress. 71. **course . . . compasses,** two hundred annual circuits. 72. **prophetic fury,** divinely inspired madness. 74. **mummy,** the embalming fluid that oozed from mummies was supposed to be medicinal. 75. **conserved of,** prepared as a preservative out of. 79. **startingly and rash,** abruptly and violently. 89. **misgives,** is apprehensive. 91. **sufficient,** competent. 93. **time,** lifetime. 108. **happiness,** good luck. 111. **virtuous,** strong, effective. 113. **office,** services. 115. **mortal,** deadly. 119. **my benefit,** an act of kindness to me. 121. **shut . . . in,** confine myself to. 122. **to fortune's alms,** to whatever fortune is willing to bestow upon me.

My advocation is not now in tune;
My lord is not my lord; nor should I know him,
Were he in favour as in humour alter'd. 125
So help me every spirit sanctified,
As I have spoken for you all my best
And stood within the blank of his displeasure
For my free speech! you must awhile be patient:
What I can do I will; and more I will 130
Than for myself I dare: let that suffice you.

IAGO. Is my lord angry?

EMIL. He went hence but now,
And certainly in strange unquietness.

IAGO. Can he be angry? I have seen the cannon,
When it hath blown his ranks into the air, 135
And, like the devil, from his very arm
Puff'd his own brother:—and can he be angry?
Something of moment then: I will go meet him:
There's matter in't indeed, if he be angry. 139

DES. I prithee, do so. [*Exit* IAGO.]
Something, sure, of state,
Either from Venice, or some unhatch'd practice
Made demonstrable here in Cyprus to him,
Hath puddled his clear spirit; and in such cases
Men's natures wrangle with inferior things,
Though great ones are their object. 'Tis even so; 145
For let our finger ache, and it indues
Our other healthful members even to that sense
Of pain: nay, we must think men are not gods,
Nor of them look for such observances
As fit the bridal. Beshrew me much, Emilia,
I was, unhandsome warrior as I am, 151
Arraigning his unkindness with my soul;
But now I find I had suborn'd the witness,
And he's indicted falsely.

EMIL. Pray heaven it be state-matters, as you think, 155
And no conception nor no jealous toy
Concerning you.

DES. Alas the day! I never gave him cause

EMIL. But jealous souls will not be answer'd so;
They are not ever jealous for the cause, 160
But jealous for they are jealous: 'tis a monster
Begot upon itself, born on itself.

DES. Heaven keep that monster from Othello's mind!

EMIL. Lady, amen.

DES. I will go seek him. Cassio, walk here about: 165
If I do find him fit, I'll move your suit
And seek to effect it to my uttermost.

CAS. I humbly thank your ladyship.

[*Exeunt* DESDEMONA *and* EMILIA.

[*Enter* BIANCA.]

BIAN. Save you, friend Cassio!

CAS. What make you from home?
How is it with you, my most fair Bianca? 170
I' faith, sweet love, I was coming to your house.

BIAN. And I was going to your lodging, Cassio.
What, keep a week away? seven days and nights?
Eight score eight hours? and lovers' absent hours,
More tedious than the dial eight score times? 175
O weary reckoning!

CAS. Pardon me, Bianca:
I have this while with leaden thoughts been press'd;
But I shall, in a more continuate time,
Strike off this score of absence. Sweet Bianca,

[*Giving her* DESDEMONA'*s handkerchief*.]

Take me this work out.

BIAN. O Cassio, whence came this? 180
This is some token from a newer friend:
To the felt absence now I feel a cause:
Is 't come to this? Well, well.

CAS. Go to, woman!
Throw your vile guesses in the devil's teeth,
From whence you have them. You are jealous now 185

123. **advocation**, advocacy. 125. **favour**, face; **as**, as much as. 128. **blank**, range, literally: the white spot at the center of a target. 137. **Puff'd**, blown to pieces. 141. **unhatch'd practice**, unrevealed plot. 143. **puddled**, muddied. 146. **indues**, endows. 151. **unhandsome**, unfair.

153. **suborn'd**, procured to commit perjury. 156. **conception**, mere fancy; **jealous toy**, whim of suspicion. 169. **What . . . home?** What are you doing away from home? 175. **dial . . . times**, one hundred and sixty hours by the clock. 178. **continuate**, uninterrupted (by other affairs). 179. **strike . . . score**, erase this record. 180. **Take . . . out**, copy this embroidery for me.

That this is from some mistress, some remembrance:
No, in good troth, Bianca.
BIAN. Why, whose is it?
CAS. I know not, sweet: I found it in my chamber.
I like the work well: ere it be demanded—
As like enough it will—I'ld have it copied: 190
Take it, and do 't; and leave me for this time.
BIAN. Leave you! wherefore?
CAS. I do attend here on the general;
And think it no addition, nor my wish,
To have him see me woman'd.
BIAN. Why, I pray you? 195
CAS. Not that I love you not.
BIAN. But that you do not love me.
I pray you, bring me on the way a little,
And say if I shall see you soon at night.
CAS. 'Tis but a little way that I can bring you;
For I attend here: but I'll see you soon. 200
BIAN. 'Tis very good; I must be circumstanced. [*Exeunt.*

ACT IV

SCENE I. *Cyprus. Before the castle.*

[*Enter* OTHELLO *and* IAGO.]

IAGO. Will you think so?
OTH. Think so, Iago!
IAGO. What,
To kiss in private?
OTH. An unauthorized kiss.
IAGO. Or to be naked with her friend in bed
An hour or more, not meaning any harm?
OTH. Naked in bed, Iago, and not mean harm! 5
It is hypocrisy against the Devil:
They that mean virtuously, and yet do so,
The Devil their virtue tempts, and they tempt heaven.
IAGO. So they do nothing, 'tis a venial slip:
But if I give my wife a handkerchief,— 10
OTH. What then?
IAGO. Why, then, 'tis hers, my lord; and, being hers,
She may, I think, bestow 't on any man.
OTH. She is protectress of her honour too:
May she give that? 15
IAGO. Her honour is an essence that's not seen:
They have it very oft that have it not:
But, for the handkerchief,—
OTH. By heaven, I would most gladly have forgot it.
Thou said'st—O, it comes o'er my memory,
As doth the raven o'er the infected house, 21
Boding to all—he had my handkerchief.
IAGO. Ay, what of that?
OTH. That's not so good now.
IAGO. What,
If I had said I had seen him do you wrong?
Or heard him say,—as knaves be such abroad, 25
Who having, by their own importunate suit,
Or voluntary dotage of some mistress,
Convinced or supplied them, cannot choose
But they must blab—
OTH. Hath he said any thing?
IAGO. He hath, my lord; but be you well assured, 30
No more than he'll unswear.
OTH. What hath he said?
IAGO. 'Faith, that he did—I know not what he did.
OTH. What? what?
IAGO. Lie—
OTH. With her?
IAGO. With her, on her; what you will.
OTH. Lie with her! lie on her! We say lie 35 on her, when they belie her. Lie with her! that's fulsome. — Handkerchief — confessions — handkerchief!—To confess, and be hanged for his labour;—first, to be hanged, and then to confess.—I tremble at it. Nature would not invest herself in such shadowing passion without some instruction. It is not words that

193. attend, wait for. 194. addition, honor, credit. 197. bring, accompany. 198. soon at night, this very night. 201. circumstanced, yield to circumstances. Act IV, Scene i: 6. hypocrisy, i.e., seeming to sin without sinning; against the Devil, i.e., in the Devil's presence. 8. tempt heaven, by putting themselves in a situation in which it is difficult to avoid sinning. 21. raven, the raven was thought to hover over a house in which there was sickness or infection. 22. boding, foreboding evil. 27. dotage of, doting upon. 28. convinced or supplied, won by importunity or gratified the desires of. 37. fulsome, disgusting. 38. To confess . . . hanged, a proverb. 40-1. Nature . . . instruction, natural imagination would not arouse such darkening (blinding) passion in me unless it were based on fact.

shake me thus. Pish! Noses, ears, and lips.—
Is 't possible? — Confess — handkerchief! — O
devil! [*Falls in a trance.*

IAGO. Work on, 45
My medicine, work! Thus credulous fools are
caught;
And many worthy and chaste dames even
thus,
All guiltless, meet reproach. What, ho! my
lord!
My lord, I say! Othello!

[*Enter* CASSIO.]

How now, Cassio!

CAS. What's the matter? 50

IAGO. My lord is fall'n into an epilepsy:
This is his second fit; he had one yesterday.

CAS. Rub him about the temples.

IAGO. No, forbear;
The lethargy must have his quiet course:
If not, he foams at mouth and by and by 55
Breaks out to savage madness. Look, he stirs:
Do you withdraw yourself a little while,
He will recover straight: when he is gone,
I would on great occasion speak with you.
[*Exit* CASSIO.]
How is it, general? have you not hurt your
head? 60

OTH. Dost thou mock me?

IAGO. I mock you! no, by heaven.
Would you would bear your fortune like a
man!

OTH. A horned man's a monster and a beast.

IAGO. There's many a beast then in a populous city,
And many a civil monster. 65

OTH. Did he confess it?

IAGO. Good sir, be a man;
Think every bearded fellow that's but yoked
May draw with you: there's millions now
alive
That nightly lie in those unproper beds
Which they dare swear peculiar: your case is
better. 70
O, 'tis the spite of hell, the fiend's arch-mock,
To lip a wanton in a secure couch,
And to suppose her chaste! No, let me know;
And knowing what I am, I know what she
shall be.

OTH. O, thou art wise; 'tis certain.

IAGO. Stand you awhile apart; 75
Confine yourself but in a patient list.
Whilst you were here o'erwhelmed with your
grief—
A passion most unsuiting such a man—
Cassio came hither: I shifted him away,
And laid good 'scuse upon your ecstasy, 80
Bade him anon return and here speak with
me;
The which he promised. Do but encave yourself,
And mark the fleers, the gibes, and notable
scorns,
That dwell in every region of his face;
For I will make him tell the tale anew, 85
Where, how, how oft, how long ago, and
when
He hath, and is again to cope your wife:
I say, but mark his gesture. Marry, patience;
Or I shall say you are all in all in spleen,
And nothing of a man.

OTH. Dost thou hear, Iago? 90
I will be found most cunning in my patience;
But—dost thou hear?—most bloody.

IAGO. That's not amiss;
But yet keep time in all. Will you withdraw?
[OTHELLO *retires.*]
Now will I question Cassio of Bianca,
A housewife that by selling her desires 95
Buys herself bread and clothes: it is a creature
That dotes on Cassio; as 'tis the strumpet's
plague
To beguile many and be beguiled by one:
He, when he hears of her, cannot refrain
From the excess of laughter. Here he
comes: 100

[*Re-enter* CASSIO.]

As he shall smile, Othello shall go mad;
And his unbookish jealousy must construe
Poor Cassio's smiles, gestures and light behaviour,

54. **lethargy,** epileptic attack. 55. **by and by,** at once. 59. **on . . . occasion,** about a very urgent matter. 63. **horned man,** i.e., cuckold. 65. **civil,** in civilized life. 68. **yoked,** shares your fate. 69. **unproper,** not their own. 70. **peculiar,** private. 71. **spite,** malice. 72. **lip,** kiss; **secure,** free from suspicion. 76. **in . . . list,** within the bounds of patience; list = enclosure. 79. **shifted him away,** managed to get rid of him. 80. **ecstasy,** swoon. 82. **encave,** conceal. 83. **fleers,** sneers. 84. **region,** part. 87. **cope,** do business with. 88. **patience,** self-control. 89. **All . . . spleen,** completely the victim of anger. 91. **cunning,** crafty; **patience,** self-control. 93. **keep time,** observe judgment. 95. **housewife,** hussy. 102. **unbookish,** ignorant. 103. **light,** wanton.

Quite in the wrong. How do you now, lieutenant?

CAS. The worser that you give me the addition 105
Whose want even kills me.

IAGO. Ply Desdemona well, and you are sure on 't.
[*Speaking lower*] Now, if this suit lay in Bianca's power,
How quickly should you speed!

CAS. Alas, poor caitiff!

OTH. Look, how he laughs already! 110

IAGO. I never knew a woman love man so.

CAS. Alas, poor rogue! I think, i' faith, she loves me.

OTH. Now he denies it faintly, and laughs it out.

IAGO. Do you hear, Cassio? 115

OTH. Now he importunes him
To tell it o'er: go to; well said, well said.

IAGO. She gives it out that you shall marry her:
Do you intend it?

CAS. Ha, ha, ha! 120

OTH. Do you triumph, Roman? do you triumph?

CAS. I marry her! what? a customer! Prithee, bear some charity to my wit; do not think it so unwholesome. Ha, ha, ha! 125

OTH. So, so, so, so: they laugh that win.

IAGO. 'Faith, the cry goes that you shall marry her.

CAS. Prithee, say true.

IAGO. I am a very villain else.

OTH. Have you scored me? Well. 130

CAS. This is the monkey's own giving out: she is persuaded I will marry her, out of her own love and flattery, not out of my promise.

OTH. Iago beckons me; now he begins the story. 135

CAS. She was here even now; she haunts me in every place. I was the other day talking on the sea-bank with certain Venetians; and thither comes the bauble, and, by this hand, she falls me thus about my neck— 140

OTH. Crying, "O dear Cassio!" as it were: his gesture imports it.

CAS. So hangs, and lolls, and weeps upon me; so hales, and pulls me: ha, ha, ha!

OTH. Now he tells how she plucked him to my chamber. O, I see that nose of yours, but not that dog I shall throw it to. 147

CAS. Well, I must leave her company.

IAGO. Before me! look, where she comes.

CAS. 'Tis such another fitchew! marry, a perfumed one. 151

[*Enter* BIANCA.]

What do you mean by this haunting of me?

BIAN. Let the devil and his dam haunt you! What did you mean by that same handkerchief you gave me even now? I was a fine fool to take it. I must take out the work?—A likely piece of work, that you should find it in your chamber, and not know who left it there! This is some minx's token, and I must take out the work? There; give it your hobby-horse: wheresoever you had it, I'll take out no work on 't. 161

CAS. How now, my sweet Bianca! how now! how now!

OTH. By heaven, that should be my handkerchief! 165

BIAN. An you'll come to supper to-night, you may; an you will not, come when you are next prepared for. [*Exit.*

IAGO. After her, after her.

CAS. 'Faith, I must; she'll rail in the street else. 171

IAGO. Will you sup there?

CAS. 'Faith, I intend so.

IAGO. Well, I may chance to see you; for I would very fain speak with you. 175

CAS. Prithee, come; will you?

IAGO. Go to; say no more. [*Exit* CASSIO.

OTH. [*Advancing*] How shall I murder him, Iago?

IAGO. Did you perceive how he laughed at his vice? 181

OTH. O Iago!

IAGO. And did you see the handkerchief?

OTH. Was that mine?

IAGO. Yours, by this hand: and to see how he prizes the foolish woman your wife! she gave it him, and he hath given it his whore.

105. addition, title. 109. caitiff, wretch. 117. well said, well done. 121. Roman, suggested by triumph. 122. customer, harlot. 124. bear . . . wit, have some respect for my intelligence. 125. unwholesome, sick. 127. cry goes, common report is; shall, are surely going to. 130. scored, made up my reckoning, settled my fate. 133. flattery, i.e., self-flattery. 135. beckons, signals. 139. bauble, plaything. 144. hales, harasses. 145. plucked, dragged. 149. before me, on my life. 151. such . . . fitchew, one of these polecats, who are eager when in heat. 160. hobby horse, whore. 162. How now? What's the matter? 164. should be, must be. 166. An, if. 174-5. I . . . fain, I am very anxious to.

OTH. I would have him nine years a-killing. A fine woman! a fair woman! a sweet woman!

IAGO. Nay, you must forget that. 190

OTH. Ay, let her rot, and perish, and be damned to-night; for she shall not live: no, my heart is turned to stone; I strike it, and it hurts my hand. O, the world hath not a sweeter creature: she might lie by an emperor's side and command him tasks.

IAGO. Nay, that's not your way. 197

OTH. Hang her! I do but say what she is: so delicate with her needle: an admirable musician: O! she will sing the savageness out of a bear: of so high and plenteous wit and invention:— 201

IAGO. She's the worse for all this.

OTH. O, a thousand thousand times: and then, of so gentle a condition!

IAGO. Ay, too gentle. 205

OTH. Nay, that's certain: but yet the pity of it, Iago! O Iago, the pity of it, Iago!

IAGO. If you are so fond over her iniquity, give her patent to offend; for, if it touch not you, it comes near nobody. 210

OTH. I will chop her into messes: cuckold me!

IAGO. O, 'tis foul in her.

OTH. With mine officer!

IAGO. That's fouler.

OTH. Get me some poison, Iago; this night: I'll not expostulate with her, lest her body and beauty unprovide my mind again: this night, Iago. 219

IAGO. Do it not with poison, strangle her in her bed, even the bed she hath contaminated.

OTH. Good, good: the justice of it pleases: very good.

IAGO. And for Cassio, let me be his undertaker: you shall hear more by midnight. 225

OTH. Excellent good. [*A trumpet within.*]
What trumpet is that same?

IAGO. Something from Venice, sure, 'tis Lodovico
Come from the duke: and, see, your wife is with him.

[*Enter* LODOVICO, DESDEMONA, *and* ATTENDANTS.]

LOD. Save you, worthy general!

OTH. With all my heart, sir.

LOD. The duke and senators of Venice greet you. [*Gives him a letter.* 230

OTH. I kiss the instrument of their pleasures. [*Opens the letter, and reads.*

DES. And what's the news, good cousin Lodovico?

IAGO. I am very glad to see you, signior;
Welcome to Cyprus.

LOD. I thank you. How does Lieutenant Cassio? 235

IAGO. Lives, sir.

DES. Cousin, there's fall'n between him and my lord
An unkind breach: but you shall make all well.

OTH. Are you sure of that?

DES. My lord?

OTH. [*Reads*] "This fail you not to do, as you will—" 240

LOD. He did not call; he's busy in the paper.
Is there division 'twixt my lord and Cassio?

DES. A most unhappy one: I would do much
To atone them, for the love I bear to Cassio.

OTH. Fire and brimstone!

DES. My lord?

OTH. Are you wise? 245

DES. What, is he angry?

LOD. May be the letter moved him;
For, as I think, they do command him home,
Deputing Cassio in his government.

DES. Trust me, I am glad on 't.

OTH. Indeed!

DES. My lord?

OTH. I am glad to see you mad.

DES. Why, sweet Othello,—

OTH. [*Striking her*] Devil! 251

DES. I have not deserved this.

LOD. My lord, this would not be believed in Venice,
Though I should swear I saw 't: 'tis very much:
Make her amends; she weeps.

OTH. O devil, devil! 255
If that the earth could teem with woman's tears,

197. **your way,** the way you should be thinking about her. 201. **invention,** mental activity in general. 204. **condition,** disposition. 208. **fond over,** foolish about. 209. **patent,** formal license. 211. **messes,** small pieces of food. 218. **unprovide,** unfit, weaken. 224. **let . . . undertaker,** let me take care of him. 229. **with . . . heart,** (1) a reply to Lodovico's salutation, (2) a salutation, i.e., "I greet you with all my heart." 238. **unkind breach,** unnatural rupture.

244. **atone them,** bring them together, reconcile them. 248. **Deputing,** substituting. 256. **if . . . tears,** if women's tears could impregnate the earth.

Each drop she falls would prove a crocodile.
Out of my sight!

DES. I will not stay to offend you. [*Going.*

LOD. Truly, an obedient lady:
I do beseech your lordship, call her back. 260

OTH. Mistress!

DES. My lord?

OTH. What would you with her, sir?

LOD. Who, I, my lord?

OTH. Ay; you did wish that I would make her turn:
Sir, she can turn, and turn, and yet go on,
And turn again; and she can weep, sir, weep;
And she's obedient, as you say, obedient, 266
Very obedient. Proceed you in your tears.
Concerning this, sir,—O well-painted passion!—
I am commanded home. Get you away;
I'll send for you anon. Sir, I obey the mandate, 270
And will return to Venice. Hence, avaunt!
[*Exit* DESDEMONA.]
Cassio shall have my place. And, sir, to-night,
I do entreat that we may sup together:
You are welcome, sir, to Cyprus.—Goats and monkeys! [*Exit.*

LOD. Is this the noble Moor whom our full senate 275
Call all in all sufficient? Is this the nature
Whom passion could not shake? whose solid virtue
The shot of accident, nor dart of chance,
Could neither graze nor pierce?

IAGO. He is much changed.

LOD. Are his wits safe? is he not light of brain? 280

IAGO. He's that he is: I may not breathe my censure
What he might be: if what he might he is not,
I would to heaven he were!

LOD. What, strike his wife!

IAGO. 'Faith, that was not so well; yet would I knew
That stroke would prove the worst!

LOD. Is it his use?
Or did the letters work upon his blood, 286
And new-create this fault?

IAGO. Alas, alas!
It is not honesty in me to speak
What I have seen and known. You shall observe him,
And his own courses will denote him so 290
That I may save my speech: do but go after,
And mark how he continues.

LOD. I am sorry that I am deceived in him.
[*Exeunt.*

SCENE II. *A room in the castle.*

[*Enter* OTHELLO *and* EMILIA.]

OTH. You have seen nothing then?

EMIL. Nor ever heard, nor ever did suspect.

OTH. Yes, you have seen Cassio and she together.

EMIL. But then I saw no harm, and then I heard
Each syllable that breath made up between them. 5

OTH. What, did they never whisper?

EMIL. Never, my lord.

OTH. Nor send you out o' the way?

EMIL. Never.

OTH. To fetch her fan, her gloves, her mask, nor nothing?

EMIL. Never, my lord. 10

OTH. That's strange.

EMIL. I durst, my lord, to wager she is honest,
Lay down my soul at stake: if you think other,
Remove your thought; it doth abuse your bosom.
If any wretch have put this in your head, 15
Let heaven requite it with the serpent's curse!
For, if she be not honest, chaste, and true,
There's no man happy; the purest of their wives
Is foul as slander.

OTH. Bid her come hither: go.
[*Exit* EMILIA.]
She says enough; yet she's a simple bawd 20
That cannot say as much. This is a subtle whore,
A closet lock and key of villanous secrets:

257. **falls**, lets fall; **crocodile**, who was supposed to shed tears over the man he devours. 268. **well-painted passion**, well-feigned emotion. 274. **Goats and monkeys**, both very licentious animals. 276. **sufficient**, competent. 280. **safe**, sound. 281. **censure**, opinion. 285. **use**, habit.

286. **blood**, passion. 288. **honesty in me**, proper for me. 290. **courses**, conduct; **denote**, describe. Scene ii: 12. **honest**, chaste. 13. **at stake**, as the stake. 14. **remove**, put away, banish; **abuse**, pervert; **bosom**, i.e., the source of your passion. 16. **serpent's curse**, God's curse on the serpent in the Garden of Eden, cf. Genesis III, 14. 22. **closet . . . key**, secret storehouse.

And yet she'll kneel and pray; I have seen her do 't.

[*Enter* DESDEMONA *with* EMILIA.]

DES. My lord, what is your will?
OTH. Pray, chuck, come hither.
DES. What is your pleasure?
OTH. Let me see your eyes; 25
Look in my face.
DES. What horrible fancy 's this?
OTH. [*To* EMILIA] Some of your function, mistress;
Leave procreants alone and shut the door;
Cough, or cry "hem", if any body come:
Your mystery, your mystery: nay, dispatch.
[*Exit* EMILIA.
DES. Upon my knees, what doth your speech import? 31
I understand a fury in your words,
But not the words.
OTH. Why, what art thou?
DES. Your wife, my lord; your true
And loyal wife.
OTH. Come, swear it, damn thyself;
Lest, being like one of heaven, the devils themselves 36
Should fear to seize thee: therefore be double damn'd:
Swear thou art honest.
DES. Heaven doth truly know it.
OTH. Heaven truly knows that thou art false as hell.
DES. To whom, my lord? with whom? how am I false? 40
OTH. O Desdemona! away! away! away!
DES. Alas the heavy day! Why do you weep?
Am I the motive of these tears, my lord?
If haply you my father do suspect
An instrument of this your calling back, 45
Lay not your blame on me: if you have lost him,
Why, I have lost him too.
OTH. Had it pleased heaven
To try me with affliction; had they rain'd
All kinds of sores and shames on my bare head,
Steep'd me in poverty to the very lips, 50
Given to captivity me and my utmost hopes,
I should have found in some place of my soul
A drop of patience: but, alas, to make me
A fixèd figure for the time of scorn
To point his slow unmoving finger at! 55
Yet could I bear that too; well, very well:
But there, where I have garner'd up my heart,
Where either I must live, or bear no life;
The fountain from the which my current runs,
Or else dries up; to be discarded thence! 60
Or keep it as a cistern for foul toads
To knot and gender in! Turn thy complexion there,
Patience, thou young and rose-lipp'd cherubin,—
Ay, there, look grim as hell!
DES. I hope my noble lord esteems me honest. 65
OTH. O, ay; as summer flies are in the shambles,
That quicken even with blowing. O thou weed,
Who art so lovely fair and smell'st so sweet
That the sense aches at thee, would thou hadst ne'er been born!
DES. Alas, what ignorant sin have I committed? 70
OTH. Was this fair paper, this most goodly book,
Made to write "whore" upon? What committed!
Committed! O thou public commoner!
I should make very forges of my cheeks,
That would to cinders burn up modesty, 75
Did I but speak thy deeds. What committed!
Heaven stops the nose at it and the moon winks,
The bawdy wind that kisses all it meets
Is hush'd within the hollow mine of earth,
And will not hear it. What committed! 80
Impudent strumpet!
DES. By heaven, you do me wrong.
OTH. Are not you a strumpet?
DES. No, as I am a Christian:
If to preserve this vessel for my lord
From any other foul unlawful touch

27. **some . . . function,** perform your duties (of bawd). 30. **mystery,** trade; **dispatch,** hurry up. 43. **motive,** cause. 48. **they,** i.e., the heavenly powers. 54. **fixed figure,** Othello apparently imagines himself set in a pillory; **time of scorn,** scornful world. 55. **slow,** i.e., to change its direction; **unmoving,** seeming not to move. 59. **my current,** i.e., the current of my life. 62. **knot,** entangle; **gender,** engender; **turn . . . complexion,** i.e., turn pale. 66. **shambles,** slaughter-house. 67. **quicken . . . blowing,** that are impregnated again as soon as they lay their eggs. 70. **ignorant sin,** sin committed in ignorance. 73. **commoner,** harlot. 77. **winks,** closes its eyes. 83. **vessel,** body of mine.

Be not to be a strumpet, I am none. 85
OTH. What, not a whore?
DES. No, as I shall be saved.
OTH. Is 't possible?
DES. O, heaven forgive us!
OTH. I cry you mercy, then:
I took you for that cunning whore of Venice
That married with Othello. [*Raising his voice*]
You, mistress, 90
That have the office opposite to Saint Peter,
And keep the gate of hell!

[*Re-enter* EMILIA.]

You, you, ay, you!
We have done our course; there's money for your pains:
I pray you, turn the key and keep our counsel.
[*Exit.*
EMIL. Alas, what does this gentleman conceive? 95
How do you, madam? how do you, my good lady?
DES. 'Faith, half asleep.
EMIL. Good madam, what's the matter with my lord?
DES. With who?
EMIL. Why, with my lord, madam. 100
DES. Who is thy lord?
EMIL. He that is yours, sweet lady.
DES. I have none: do not talk to me, Emilia;
I cannot weep; nor answer have I none,
But what should go by water. Prithee, to-night
Lay on my bed my wedding sheets: remember; 105
And call thy husband hither.
EMIL. Here's a change indeed! [*Exit.*
DES. 'Tis meet I should be used so, very meet.
How have I been behaved, that he might stick
The small'st opinion on my least misuse?

[*Re-enter* EMILIA *with* IAGO.]

IAGO. What is your pleasure, madam? How is 't with you? 110
DES. I cannot tell. Those that do teach young babes
Do it with gentle means and easy tasks:
He might have chid me so; for, in good faith,
I am a child to chiding.
IAGO. What's the matter, lady?
EMIL. Alas, Iago, my lord hath so bewhored her, 115
Thrown such despite and heavy terms upon her,
As true hearts cannot bear.
DES. Am I that name, Iago?
IAGO. What name, fair lady?
DES. Such as she says my lord did say I was.
EMIL. He call'd her whore: a beggar in his drink 120
Could not have laid such terms upon his callet.
IAGO. Why did he so?
DES. I do not know; I am sure I am none such.
IAGO. Do not weep, do not weep. Alas the day!
EMIL. Hath she forsook so many noble matches, 125
Her father and her country and her friends,
To be call'd whore? would it not make one weep?
DES. It is my wretched fortune.
IAGO. Beshrew him for 't!
How comes this trick upon him?
DES. Nay, heaven doth know.
EMIL. I will be hang'd, if some eternal villain, 130
Some busy and insinuating rogue,
Some cogging, cozening slave, to get some office,
Have not devised this slander; I'll be hanged else.
IAGO. Fie, there is no such man; it is impossible.
DES. If any such there be, heaven pardon him! 135
EMIL. A halter pardon him! and hell gnaw his bones!
Why should he call her whore? who keeps her company?
What place? what time? what form? what likelihood?
The Moor's abused by some most villanous knave,
Some base notorious knave, some scurvy fellow. 140

88. **cry . . . mercy**, beg your pardon. 91. **office**, occupation; **Saint Peter**, i.e., that of St. Peter, who held the Keys of Heaven. 104. **go by water**, be expressed by tears. 108. **been behaved**, conducted myself; **stick**, attach. 109. **small'st . . . misuse**, the least bit of censure on my slightest misconduct. 116. **despite**, contempt; **heavy terms**, grievous expressions. 121. **laid . . . callet**, called his whore such names. 128. **Beshrew**, curse. 130. **eternal**, infernal. 131. **busy**, meddling. 132. **cogging**, deceiving; **cozening**, cheating. 139. **abused**, deceived. 140. **notorious**, egregious, flagrant.

O heaven, that such companions thou'ldst unfold,
And put in every honest hand a whip
To lash the rascals naked through the world
Even from the east to the west!

IAGO. Speak within door.

EMIL. O, fie upon them! Some such squire he was 145
That turn'd your wit the seamy side without,
And made you to suspect me with the Moor.

IAGO. You are a fool; go to.

DES. O good Iago,
What shall I do to win my lord again?
Good friend, go to him; for, by this light of heaven, 150
I know not how I lost him. Here I kneel:
If e'er my will did trespass 'gainst his love,
Either in discourse of thought or actual deed,
Or that mine eyes, mine ears, or any sense,
Delighted them in any other form; 155
Or that I do not yet, and ever did,
And ever will—though he do shake me off
To beggarly divorcement—love him dearly,
Comfort forswear me! Unkindness may do much;
And his unkindness may defeat my life, 160
But never taint my love. I cannot say "whore."
It doth abhor me now I speak the word;
To do the act that might the addition earn
Not the world's mass of vanity could make me.

IAGO. I pray you, be content; 'tis but his humour: 165
The business of the state does him offence,
And he does chide with you.

DES. If 'twere no other,—

IAGO. 'Tis but so, I warrant.
[*Trumpets within.*]
Hark, how these instruments summon to supper!
The messengers of Venice stay the meat: 170
Go in, and weep not; all things shall be well.
[*Exeunt* DESDEMONA *and* EMILIA.]

[*Enter* RODERIGO.]

How now, Roderigo!

ROD. I do not find that thou dealest justly with me.

IAGO. What in the contrary? 175

ROD. Every day thou daffest me with some device, Iago; and rather, as it seems to me now, keepest from me all conveniency than suppliest me with the least advantage of hope. I will indeed no longer endure it, nor am I yet persuaded to put up in peace what already I have foolishly suffered. 182

IAGO. Will you hear me, Roderigo?

ROD. 'Faith, I have heard too much, for your words and performances are no kin together.

IAGO. You charge me most unjustly. 186

ROD. With nought but truth. I have wasted myself out of my means. The jewels you have had from me to deliver to Desdemona would half have corrupted a votarist: you have told me she hath received them and returned me expectations and comforts of sudden respect and acquaintance, but I find none. 192

IAGO. Well; go to; very well.

ROD. Very well! go to! I cannot go to, man; nor 'tis not very well: nay, I think it is scurvy, and begin to find myself fopped in it.

IAGO. Very well. 198

ROD. I tell you 'tis not very well. I will make myself known to Desdemona: if she will return me my jewels, I will give over my suit and repent my unlawful solicitation; if not, assure yourself I will seek satisfaction of you.

IAGO. You have said now. 204

ROD. Ay, and said nothing but what I protest intendment of doing.

IAGO. Why, now I see there's mettle in thee, and even from this instant do build on thee a better opinion than ever before. Give me thy hand, Roderigo: thou hast taken against me a most just exception; but yet, I protest, I have dealt most directly in thy affair.

ROD. It hath not appeared. 213

IAGO. I grant indeed it hath not appeared, and your suspicion is not without wit and judgement. But, Roderigo, if thou hast that in thee indeed, which I have greater reason

141. **companions**, contemptuous for "fellows"; **unfold**, uncover. 144. **speak . . . door**, don't talk so loud. 145. **squire**, contemptuous for a "person." 146. **wit**, intelligence. 153. **discourse**, range. 159. **comfort forswear me**, may consolation abandon me. 160. **defeat**, destroy. 162. **it . . . me**, it fills me with horror. 163. **addition**, term. 164. **vanity**, finery. 165. **be content**, don't worry. 170. **stay the meat**, are waiting for supper. 173. **dealest justly**, are acting in a straightforward manner. 176. **daffest me**, put me off. 177. **device**, deception. 178. **conveniency**, opportunity. 181. **put . . . peace**, submit silently to. 188. **wasted . . . means**, squandered my money. 190. **votarist**, nun. 192. **sudden respect**, immediate attention. 194. **go to**, here is a remonstrance. 197. **fopped**, duped. 204. **you have said**, Really! 206. **intendment**, intention. 212. **directly**, straightforwardly.

to believe now than ever, I mean purpose, courage and valour, this night show it: if thou the next night following enjoy not Desdemona, take me from this world with treachery and devise engines for my life. 221

ROD. Well, what is it? is it within reason and compass?

IAGO. Sir, there is especial commission come from Venice to depute Cassio in Othello's place.

ROD. Is that true? why, then Othello and Desdemona return again to Venice. 228

IAGO. O, no; he goes into Mauritania and takes away with him the fair Desdemona, unless his abode be lingered here by some accident: wherein none can be so determinate as the removing of Cassio. 233

ROD. How do you mean, removing of him?

IAGO. Why, by making him uncapable of Othello's place; knocking out his brains.

ROD. And that you would have me to do? 237

IAGO. Ay, if you dare do yourself a profit and a right. He sups to-night with a harlotry, and thither will I go to him: he knows not yet of his honourable fortune. If you will watch his going thence, which I will fashion to fall out between twelve and one, you may take him at your pleasure: I will be near to second your attempt, and he shall fall between us. Come, stand not amazed at it, but go along with me; I will show you such a necessity in his death that you shall think yourself bound to put it on him. It is now high supper-time, and the night grows to waste: about it. 250

ROD. I will hear further reason for this.

IAGO. And you shall be satisfied.

[*Exeunt.*

SCENE III. *Another room in the castle.*

[*Enter* OTHELLO, LODOVICO, DESDEMONA, EMILIA, *and* ATTENDANTS.]

LOD. I do beseech you, sir, trouble yourself no further.

OTH. O, pardon me; 'twill do me good to walk.

LOD. Madam, good night; I humbly thank your ladyship.

DES. Your honour is most welcome.

OTH. Will you walk, sir?

O,—Desdemona,— 5

DES. My lord?

OTH. Get you to bed on the instant; I will be returned forthwith: dismiss your attendant there: look it be done.

DES. I will, my lord. 10

[*Exeunt* OTHELLO, LODOVICO, *and* ATTENDANTS.

EMIL. How goes it now? he looks gentler than he did.

DES. He says he will return incontinent:
He hath commanded me to go to bed,
And bade me to dismiss you.

EMIL. Dismiss me!

DES. It was his bidding; therefore, good Emilia, 15
Give me my nightly wearing, and adieu:
We must not now displease him.

EMIL. I would you had never seen him!

DES. So would not I: my love doth so approve him,
That even his stubbornness, his checks, his frowns,— 20
Prithee, unpin me,—have grace and favour in them.

EMIL. I have laid those sheets you bade me on the bed.

DES. All's one. Good faith, how foolish are our minds!
If I do die before thee, prithee, shroud me
In one of those same sheets. 25

EMIL. Come, come, you talk.

DES. My mother had a maid call'd Barbara:
She was in love, and he she loved proved mad
And did forsake her: she had a song of "willow;"
An old thing 'twas, but it express'd her fortune,
And she died singing it: that song to-night 30
Will not go from my mind; I have much to do,
But to go hang my head all at one side,
And sing it like poor Barbara. Prithee, dispatch.

221. **engines,** instruments of torture. 223. **compass,** the bounds of moderation. 225. **depute,** substitute. 229. **Mauritania,** Roman name for the region now Morocco and western Algeria. 230. **abode be lingered,** stay be protracted. 232. **determinate,** decisive. 239. **harlotry,** courtesan. 246. **amazed,** in a daze. 249. **high supper-time,** high time for supper. 12. **incontinent,** immediately. 16. **nightly wearing,** night clothes. 20. **stubbornness,** harshness; **checks,** rebukes. 23. **All's one,** that's of no importance. 25. **talk,** i.e., talk nonsense. 27. **proved mad,** turned out to be wild, i.e., inconstant. 31. **much to do,** i.e., to make a great effort. 32. **But,** not to. 33. **dispatch,** hurry.

EMIL. Shall I go fetch your night-gown?
DES. No, unpin me here.
This Lodovico is a proper man. 35
EMIL. A very handsome man.
DES. He speaks well.
EMIL. I know a lady in Venice would have walked barefoot to Palestine for a touch of his nether lip. 40
DES. [*Singing*] The poor soul sat sighing by a sycamore tree,
Sing all a green willow;
Her hand on her bosom, her head on her knee,
Sing willow, willow, willow:
The fresh streams ran by her, and murmur'd her moans; 45
Sing willow, willow, willow;
Her salt tears fell from her, and soften'd the stones;—
Lay by these:—
[*Singing*] Sing willow, willow, willow;
Prithee, hie thee; he'll come anon:— 50
[*Singing*] Sing all a green willow must be my garland.
Let nobody blame him; his scorn I approve,—
Nay, that's not next.—Hark! who is 't that knocks?
EMIL. It's the wind.
DES. [*Singing*] I call'd my love false love; but what said he then? 55
Sing willow, willow, willow:
If I court moe women, you'll couch with moe men.—
So, get thee gone; good night. Mine eyes do itch;
Doth that bode weeping?
EMIL. 'Tis neither here nor there.
DES. I have heard it said so. O, these men, these men! 60
Dost thou in conscience think,—tell me, Emilia,—
That there be women do abuse their husbands
In such gross kind?
EMIL. There be some such, no question.
DES. Wouldst thou do such a deed for all the world? 64
EMIL. Why, would not you?
DES. No, by this heavenly light!
EMIL. Nor I neither by this heavenly light;
I might do 't as well i' the dark.
DES. Wouldst thou do such a deed for all the world?
EMIL. The world's a huge thing: it is a great price
For a small vice. 69
DES. In troth, I think thou wouldst not.
EMIL. In troth, I think I should; and undo 't when I had done. Marry, I would not do such a thing for a joint-ring, nor for measures of lawn, nor for gowns, petticoats, nor caps, nor any petty exhibition; but, for the whole world,—why, who would not make her husband a cuckold to make him a monarch? I should venture purgatory for 't.
DES. Beshrew me, if I would do such a wrong
For the whole world. 79
EMIL. Why, the wrong is but a wrong i' the world; and having the world for your labour, 'tis a wrong in your own world, and you might quickly make it right.
DES. I do not think there is any such woman. 84
EMIL. Yes, a dozen; and as many to the vantage as would store the world they played for.
But I do think it is their husbands' faults
If wives do fall: say that they slack their duties,
And pour our treasures into foreign laps,
Or else break out in peevish jealousies, 90
Throwing restraint upon us; or say they strike us,
Or scant our former having in despite;
Why, we have galls, and though we have some grace,
Yet have we some revenge. Let husbands know
Their wives have sense like them: they see and smell 95
And have their palates both for sweet and sour,
As husbands have. What is it that they do

35. **proper**, handsome. 41. The song is Shakespeare's adaptation of a ballad, one form of which is to be found in Percy's Reliques. 49. **Lay by these**, put these things away. 50. **anon**, soon. 57. **moe**, more. 61. **in conscience**, in your inmost thought. 62. **abuse**, deceive. 63. **gross kind**, an impure way. 73. **joint-ring**, a ring made in interlocking halves, a common lover's token. 74. **measures**, i.e., yards. 75. **exhibition**, allowance of money. 78. **venture**, risk. 85-6. **to the vantage**, to boot. 90. **peevish jealousies**, foolish suspicions. 92. **scant**, cut down; **having**, allowance; **in despite**, out of malice. 93. **galls**, feelings of resentment; **grace**, disposition to forgive. 95. **sense**, feeling.

When they change us for others? Is it sport?
I think it is: and doth affection breed it?
I think it doth: is 't frailty that thus errs? 100
It is so too: and have not we affections,
Desires for sport, and frailty, as men have?
Then let them use us well: else let them know,
The ills we do, their ills instruct us so.

DES. Good night, good night: heaven me such uses send, 105
Not to pick bad from bad, but by bad mend!
[*Exeunt.*

ACT V

SCENE I. *Cyprus. A street.*

[*Enter* IAGO *and* RODERIGO.]

IAGO. Here, stand behind this bulk; straight will he come:
Wear thy good rapier bare, and put it home:
Quick, quick; fear nothing; I'll be at thy elbow:
It makes us, or it mars us; think on that,
And fix most firm thy resolution. 5

ROD. Be near at hand; I may miscarry in 't.

IAGO. Here, at thy hand: be bold, and take thy stand. [*Retires.*

ROD. I have no great devotion to the deed;
And yet he hath given me satisfying reasons:
'Tis but a man gone. Forth, my sword: he dies. 10

IAGO. I have rubb'd this young quat almost to the sense,
And he grows angry. Now, whether he kill Cassio,
Or Cassio him, or each do kill the other,
Every way makes my gain: live Roderigo,
He calls me to a restitution large 15
Of gold and jewels that I bobb'd from him,
As gifts to Desdemona;
It must not be: if Cassio do remain,
He hath a daily beauty in his life
That makes me ugly; and, besides, the Moor
May unfold me to him; there stand I in much peril: 21
No, he must die. But so: I hear him coming.

[*Enter* CASSIO.]

ROD. I know his gait, 'tis he.—Villain, thou diest! [*Makes a pass at* CASSIO.

CAS. That thrust had been mine enemy indeed,
But that my coat is better than thou know'st:
I will make proof of thine. 26
[*Draws, and wounds* RODERIGO.

ROD. O, I am slain!
[IAGO *from behind wounds* CASSIO *in the leg, and exit.*

CAS. I am maim'd for ever. Help, ho! murder! murder! [*Falls.*

[*Enter* OTHELLO.]

OTH. The voice of Cassio: Iago keeps his word.

ROD. O, villain that I am!

OTH. It is even so.

CAS. O, help, ho! light! a surgeon! 30

OTH. 'Tis he:—O brave Iago, honest and just,
That hast such noble sense of thy friend's wrong!
Thou teachest me. Minion, your dear lies dead,
And your unblest fate hies: strumpet, I come.
Forth of my heart those charms, thine eyes, are blotted; 35
Thy bed, lust-stain'd, shall with lust's blood be spotted. [*Exit.*

[*Enter* LODOVICO *and* GRATIANO.]

CAS. What, ho! no watch? no passage? murder! murder!

GRA. 'Tis some mischance; the cry is very direful.

CAS. O, help!

LOD. Hark! 40

ROD. O wretched villain!

LOD. Two or three groan: it is a heavy night:
These may be counterfeits: let's think 't unsafe

99. affection, inclination. 105. uses, practices. 106. pick, gather. Act V, Scene i: 1. bulk, projecting part of a building. 2. put it home, thrust it in to the hilt. 6. miscarry, fail. 11. quat, pimple; sense, quick. 16. bobb'd . . . him, cheated him. 21. unfold, betray. 25. coat, coat or shirt of mail. 26. proof, trial. 33. Minion, lady-love (used contemptuously). 34. unblest, accursed; hies, hurries (toward you). 37. watch, sentry; passage, passers-by. 42. heavy, thick, cloudy.

To come in to the cry without more help.

RODERIGO. Nobody come? then shall I bleed to death. 45

LODOVICO. Hark!

[*Re-enter* IAGO, *with a light.*]

GRATIANO. Here's one comes in his shirt, with light and weapons.

IAGO. Who's there? whose noise is this that cries on murder?

LODOVICO. We do not know.

IAGO. Did not you hear a cry?

CASSIO. Here, here! for heaven's sake, help me!

IAGO. What's the matter? 50

GRATIANO. This is Othello's ancient, as I take it.

LODOVICO. The same indeed; a very valiant fellow.

IAGO. What are you here that cry so grievously?

CASSIO. Iago? O, I am spoil'd, undone by villains!
Give me some help.

IAGO. O me, lieutenant! what villains have done this?

CASSIO. I think that one of them is hereabout,
And cannot make away.

IAGO. O treacherous villains!
What are you there? come in, and give some help. [*To* LODOVICO *and* GRATIANO.

RODERIGO. O, help me here! 60

CASSIO. That's one of them.

IAGO. O murderous slave! O villain!
[*Stabs* RODERIGO.

RODERIGO. O damn'd Iago! O inhuman dog!

IAGO. Kill men i' the dark!—Where be these bloody thieves?—
How silent is this town!—Ho! murder! murder!—
What may you be? are you of good or evil?

LODOVICO. As you shall prove us, praise us. 66

IAGO. Signior Lodovico?

LODOVICO. He, sir.

IAGO. I cry you mercy. Here's Cassio hurt by villains.

GRATIANO. Cassio! 70

IAGO. How is 't, brother!

CASSIO. My leg is cut in two.

IAGO. Marry, heaven forbid!
Light, gentlemen: I'll bind it with my shirt.

[*Enter* BIANCA.]

BIANCA. What is the matter, ho? who is 't that cried?

IAGO. Who is 't that cried? 75

BIANCA. O my dear Cassio! my sweet Cassio!
O Cassio, Cassio, Cassio!

IAGO. O notable strumpet! Cassio, may you suspect
Who they should be that have thus mangled you?

CASSIO. No. 80

GRATIANO. I am sorry to find you thus: I have been to seek you.

IAGO. Lend me a garter. So. O, for a chair,
To bear him easily hence!

BIANCA. Alas, he faints! O Cassio, Cassio, Cassio!

IAGO. Gentlemen all, I do suspect this trash
To be a party in this injury. 86
Patience awhile, good Cassio. Come, come;
Lend me a light. Know we this face or no?
Alas, my friend and my dear countryman
Roderigo! no:—yes, sure:—O heaven! Roderigo. 90

GRATIANO. What, of Venice?

IAGO. Even he, sir: did you know him?

GRATIANO. Know him! ay.

IAGO. Signior Gratiano? I cry you gentle pardon;
These bloody accidents must excuse my manners,
That so neglected you.

GRATIANO. I am glad to see you. 95

IAGO. How do you, Cassio? O, a chair, a chair!

GRATIANO. Roderigo!

IAGO. He, he, 'tis he. [*A chair brought in.*]
O, that's well said; the chair.
Some good man bear him carefully from hence;
I'll fetch the general's surgeon. [*To* BIANCA]
For you, mistress, 100
Save you your labour. He that lies slain here, Cassio,
Was my dear friend: what malice was between you?

CASSIO. None in the world; nor do I know the man.

IAGO. [*To* BIAN.] What, look you pale? O, bear him out o' the air.

[CASSIO *and* RODERIGO *are borne off.*]

44. **come . . . cry**, answer the appeal. 47. **cries on**, cries out. 65. **what**, who. 66. **prove**, test. 69. **I . . . mercy**, I beg your pardon. 71. **brother**, i.e., brother officer.

82. **chair**, i.e., sedan chair. 85. **trash**, worthless creature, i.e., Bianca. 98. **well said**, well done. 101. **save . . . labour**, you need do nothing further.

Stay you, good gentlemen. Look you pale, mistress? 105
Do you perceive the gastness of her eye?
Nay, if you stare, we shall hear more anon.
Behold her well; I pray you, look upon her:
Do you see, gentlemen? nay, guiltiness will speak,
Though tongues were out of use. 110

[*Enter* EMILIA.]

EMIL. 'Las, what's the matter? what's the matter, husband?

IAGO. Cassio hath here been set on in the dark
By Roderigo and fellows that are scaped:
He's almost slain, and Roderigo dead.

EMIL. Alas, good gentleman! alas, good Cassio!

IAGO. This is the fruit of whoring. Prithee, Emilia,
Go know of Cassio where he supp'd to-night.
[*To* BIANCA] What, do you shake at that?

BIAN. He supp'd at my house; but I therefore shake not.

IAGO. O, did he so? I charge you, go with me. 120

EMIL. Fie, fie upon thee, strumpet!

BIAN. I am no strumpet; but of life as honest
As you that thus abuse me.

EMIL. As I! foh! fie upon thee!

IAGO. Kind gentlemen, let's go see poor Cassio dress'd. 124
Come, mistress, you must tell 's another tale.
Emilia, run you to the citadel,
And tell my lord and lady what hath happ'd.
Will you go on? I pray. [*Aside*] This is the night
That either makes me or fordoes me quite.
[*Exeunt.*

SCENE II. *A bedchamber in the castle:* DESDEMONA *in bed asleep; a light burning.*

[*Enter* OTHELLO.]

OTH. It is the cause, it is the cause, my soul,—
Let me not name it to you, you chaste stars!—
It is the cause. Yet I'll not shed her blood;
Nor scar that whiter skin of hers than snow,
And smooth as monumental alabaster. 5
Yet she must die, else she'll betray more men.
Put out the light, and then put out the light:
If I quench thee, thou flaming minister,
I can again thy former light restore,
Should I repent me: but once put out thy light, 10
Thou cunning'st pattern of excelling nature,
I know not where is that Promethean heat
That can thy light relume. When I have pluck'd the rose,
I cannot give it vital growth again,
It must needs wither: I'll smell it on the tree. 15
[*Kissing her.*]
Ah, balmy breath, that dost almost persuade
Justice to break her sword! One more, one more.
Be thus when thou art dead, and I will kill thee,
And love thee after. One more, and this the last:
So sweet was ne'er so fatal. I must weep, 20
But they are cruel tears: this sorrow's heavenly;
It strikes where it doth love. She wakes.

DES. Who's there? Othello?

OTH. Ay, Desdemona.

DES. Will you come to bed, my lord?

OTH. Have you pray'd to-night, Desdemona?

DES. Ay, my lord. 25

OTH. If you bethink yourself of any crime
Unreconciled as yet to heaven and grace,
Solicit for it straight.

DES. Alas, my lord, what do you mean by that?

OTH. Well, do it, and be brief; I will walk by: 30
I would not kill thy unpreparèd spirit;
No; heaven forfend! I would not kill thy soul.

DES. Talk you of killing?

OTH. Ay, I do.

106. **gastness**, ghastliness. 124. **dress'd**, i.e., his wounds dressed. 129. **fordoes**, undoes, destroys. Scene ii: 1. **cause**, i.e., the great provocation, perhaps with some suggestion of "ground for legal action," a meaning which makes Othello regard his deed as an act of justice.

2. **chaste**, the stars in classical poetry were the virgin attendants of the moon, Diana, the goddess of chastity. 5. **monumental alabaster**, alabaster figures on Elizabethan tombs. 8. **minister**, servant. 11. **cunning'st**, most ingenuously contrived. 12. **Promethean heat**, the divine creative fire stolen by Prometheus from heaven. 13. **relume**, rekindle. 21. **sorrow's heavenly**, i.e., because it is grief for doing an act of divine justice. 27. **heaven and grace**, heaven's mercy. 30. **by**, aside. 32. **forfend**, forbid.

DES. Then heaven
Have mercy on me!
OTH. Amen, with all my heart!
DES. If you say so, I hope you will not kill me. 35
OTH. Hum!
DES. And yet I fear you; for you are fatal then
When your eyes roll so: why I should fear I know not,
Since guiltiness I know not; but yet I feel I fear.
OTH. Think on thy sins.
DES. They are loves I bear to you. 40
OTH. Ay, and for that thou diest.
DES. That death's unnatural that kills for loving.
Alas, why gnaw you so your nether lip?
Some bloody passion shakes your very frame:
These are portents; but yet I hope, I hope, 45
They do not point on me.
OTH. Peace, and be still!
DES. I will so. What's the matter?
OTH. That handkerchief which I so loved and gave thee
Thou gavest to Cassio.
DES. No, by my life and soul!
Send for the man, and ask him.
OTH. Sweet soul, take heed, 50
Take heed of perjury; thou art on thy death-bed.
DES. Ay, but not yet to die.
OTH. Yes, presently:
Therefore confess thee freely of thy sin;
For to deny each article with oath
Cannot remove nor choke the strong conception 55
That I do groan withal. Thou art to die.
DES. Then Lord have mercy on me!
OTH. I say, amen.
DES. And have you mercy too! I never did
Offend you in my life; never loved Cassio
But with such general warranty of heaven 60
As I might love; I never gave him token.
OTH. By heaven, I saw my handkerchief in 's hand.
O perjured woman! thou dost stone my heart,
And makest me call what I intend to do
A murder, which I thought a sacrifice: 65
I saw the handkerchief.
DES. He found it then;
I never gave it him: send for him hither;
Let him confess a truth.
OTH. He hath confess'd.
DES. What, my lord?
OTH. That he hath used thee.
DES. How? unlawfully?
OTH. Ay. 70
DES. He will not say so.
OTH. No, his mouth is stopp'd;
Honest Iago hath ta'en order for 't.
DES. O! my fear interprets: what, is he dead?
OTH. Had all his hairs been lives, my great revenge
Had stomach for them all. 75
DES. Alas! he is betray'd and I undone.
OTH. Out, strumpet! weep'st thou for him to my face?
DES. O, banish me, my lord, but kill me not!
OTH. Down, strumpet!
DES. Kill me to-morrow: let me live to-night! 80
OTH. Nay, if you strive,—
DES. But half an hour!
OTH. Being done, there is no pause.
DES. But while I say one prayer!
OTH. It is too late. [*He stifles her.*
EMIL. [*Within*] My lord, my lord! what, ho! my lord, my lord!
OTH. What noise is this? Not dead? not yet quite dead? 85
I that am cruel am yet merciful;
I would not have thee linger in thy pain:
So, so.
EMIL. [*Within*] What, ho! my lord, my lord!
OTH. Who's there?
EMIL. [*Within*] O, good my lord, I would speak a word with you! 90
OTH. Yes: 'tis Emilia. By and by. She's dead.
'Tis like she comes to speak of Cassio's death.—
The noise was here. Ha! no more moving?
Still as the grave. Shall she come in? were 't good?—
I think she stirs again:—no. What's best to do? 95
If she come in, she'll sure speak to my wife:

37. fatal, ominous. 45. portents, signs presaging disaster. 52. presently, at once. 55. conception, intention, plan. 56. withal, with. 60. warranty, sanction. 63. stone, turn to stone. 72. ta'en order, taken measure. 75. stomach, appetite. 82. Being . . . pause, i.e., now that the execution of the retribution has begun, there can be no delay. 91. By and by, at once.

My wife! my wife! what wife? I have no wife.
O, insupportable! O heavy hour!
Methinks it should be now a huge eclipse
Of sun and moon, and that the affrighted globe 100
Should yawn at alteration.
EMIL. [*Within*] I do beseech you
That I may speak with you, O, good my lord!
OTH. I had forgot thee: O, come in, Emilia:
Soft; by and by. Let me the curtains draw.
Where art thou? [*Unlocks the door.*]

[*Enter* EMILIA.]

What's the matter with thee now?
EMIL. O, my good lord, yonder's foul murders done!
OTH. What, now?
EMIL. But now, my lord.
OTH. It is the very error of the moon;
She comes more nearer earth than she was wont, 110
And makes men mad.
EMIL. Cassio, my lord, hath kill'd a young Venetian
Call'd Roderigo.
OTH. Roderigo kill'd!
And Cassio kill'd!
EMIL. No, Cassio is not kill'd.
OTH. Not Cassio kill'd! then murder's out of tune,
And sweet revenge grows harsh.
DES. O, falsely, falsely murder'd!
EMIL. Alas, what cry is that?
OTH. That! what?
EMIL. Out, and alas! that was my lady's voice. 119
Help! help, ho! help! O lady, speak again!
Sweet Desdemona! O sweet mistress, speak!
DES. A guiltless death I die.
EMIL. O, who hath done this deed?
DES. Nobody; I myself. Farewell:
Commend me to my kind lord: O, farewell! [*Dies.* 125
OTH. Why, how should she be murder'd?
EMIL. Alas, who knows?
OTH. You heard her say herself, it was not I.
EMIL. She said so: I must needs report the truth.
OTH. She's like a liar, gone to burning hell:
'Twas I that kill'd her.
EMIL. O, the more angel she, 130
And you the blacker devil!
OTH. She turn'd to folly, and she was a whore.
EMIL. Thou dost belie her, and thou art a devil.
OTH. She was false as water.
EMIL. Thou art rash as fire, to say
That she was false: O, she was heavenly true!
OTH. Cassio did top her; ask thy husband else. 136
O, I were damn'd beneath all depth in hell,
But that I did proceed upon just grounds
To this extremity. Thy husband knew it all.
EMIL. My husband! 140
OTH. Thy husband.
EMIL. That she was false to wedlock?
OTH. Ay, with Cassio. Nay, had she been true,
If heaven would make me such another world
Of one entire and perfect chrysolite, 145
I'ld not have sold her for it.
EMIL. My husband!
OTH. Ay, 'twas he that told me first:
An honest man he is, and hates the slime
That sticks on filthy deeds.
EMIL. My husband!
OTH. What needs this iteration, woman? I say thy husband. 150
EMIL. O mistress, villany hath made mocks with love!
My husband say that she was false!
OTH. He, woman;
I say thy husband: dost understand the word?
My friend, thy husband, honest, honest Iago.
EMIL. If he say so, may his pernicious soul 155
Rot half a grain a day! he lies to the heart:
She was too fond of her most filthy bargain.
OTH. Ha!
EMIL. Do thy worst:
This deed of thine is no more worthy heaven 160
Than thou wast worthy her.
OTH. Peace, you were best.

101. **yawn at alteration,** gape in astonishment at the change, i.e., earthquakes were believed to accompany eclipses of the sun. 109. **error,** aberration, i.e., departure of the moon from its normal course. 126. **should she,** can she have been. 132. **folly,** lewdness. 139. **extremity,** extremely severe act. 145. **chrysolite,** supposed to be one of the largest and most precious of stones. 151. **made . . . of,** made sport of. 156. **gain,** any small particle. 161. **Peace . . . best,** you had better keep still.

EMIL. Thou hast not half that power to do me harm
As I have to be hurt. O gull! O dolt!
As ignorant as dirt! thou has done a deed—
I care not for thy sword; I'll make thee known, 165
Though I lost twenty lives.—Help! help, ho! help!
The Moor hath kill'd my mistress! Murder! murder!

[*Enter* MONTANO, GRATIANO, IAGO, *and others.*]

MON. What is the matter? How now, general!
EMIL. O, are you come, Iago? you have done well,
That men must lay their murders on your neck. 170
GRA. What is the matter?
EMIL. Disprove this villain, if thou be'st a man:
He says thou told'st him that his wife was false:
I know thou didst not, thou'rt not such a villain:
Speak, for my heart is full. 175
IAGO. I told him what I thought, and told no more
Than what he found himself was apt and true.
EMIL. But did you ever tell him she was false?
IAGO. I did.
EMIL. You told a lie; an odious, damnèd lie; 180
Upon my soul, a lie, a wicked lie.
She false with Cassio!—did you say with Cassio?
IAGO. With Cassio, mistress. Go to, charm your tongue.
EMIL. I will not charm my tongue; I am bound to speak:
My mistress here lies murder'd in her bed,—
ALL. O heavens forfend! 186
EMIL. And your reports have set the murder on.
OTH. Nay, stare not, masters: it is true, indeed.
GRA. 'Tis a strange truth.
MON. O monstrous act!
EMIL. Villany, villany, villany! 190
I think upon 't, I think: I smell 't: O villany!—
I thought so then:—I'll kill myself for grief:—
O villany, villany!
IAGO. What, are you mad? I charge you, get you home.
EMIL. Good gentlemen, let me have leave to speak: 195
'Tis proper I obey him, but not now.
Perchance, Iago, I will ne'er go home.
OTH. O! O! O! [*He falls on the bed.*
EMIL. Nay, lay thee down and roar;
For thou hast kill'd the sweetest innocent
That e'er did lift up eye.
OTH. [*Rising*] O, she was foul! 200
I scarce did know you, uncle: there lies your niece,
Whose breath, indeed, these hands have newly stopp'd:
I know this act shows horrible and grim.
GRA. Poor Desdemona! I am glad thy father's dead: 204
Thy match was mortal to him, and pure grief
Shore his old thread in twain: did he live now,
This sight would make him do a desperate turn,
Yea, curse his better angel from his side,
And fall to reprobation.
OTH. 'Tis pitiful; but yet Iago knows 210
That she with Cassio hath the act of shame
A thousand times committed; Cassio confess'd it:
And she did gratify his amorous works
With that recognizance and pledge of love
Which I first gave her; I saw it in his hand:
It was a handkerchief, an antique token 216
My father gave my mother.
EMIL. O heaven! O heavenly powers!
IAGO. Come, hold your peace.
EMIL. 'Twill out, 'twill out: I peace!
No, I will speak as liberal as the north: 220
Let heaven and men and devils, let them all,
All, all, cry shame against me, yet I'll speak.
IAGO. Be wise, and get you home.
EMIL. I will not.
[IAGO *offers to stab* EMILIA.

163. to be hurt, to endure being hurt. 172. **Disprove,** refute. 177. **apt,** likely. 183. **charm,** check with a charm or spell. 186. **forfend,** forbid. 187. **set . . . on,** instigated. 192. **then,** i.e., when she believed some cozening slave had slandered Desdemona (cf. IV. ii, 130 ff.). 205. **mortal,** fatal; **pure,** unmitigated. 206. **shore,** sheared, cut. 209. **reprobation,** damnation. 214. **recognizance,** token. 220. **liberal . . . north,** freely as the north wind.

GRA. Fie!
Your sword upon a woman?

EMIL. O thou dull Moor! that handkerchief thou speak'st of 225
I found by fortune and did give my husband;
For often, with a solemn earnestness,
More than indeed belong'd to such a trifle,
He begg'd of me to steal it.

IAGO. Villanous whore!

EMIL. She give it Cassio! no, alas! I found it, 230
And I did give 't my husband.

IAGO. Filth, thou liest!

EMIL. By heaven, I do not, I do not, gentlemen.
O murderous coxcomb! what should such a fool
Do with so good a woman?

OTH. Are there no stones in heaven
But what serve for the thunder?—Precious villain! 235

[*He runs at* IAGO: IAGO, *from behind, stabs* EMILIA, *and exit.*

GRA. The woman falls; sure, he hath kill'd his wife.

EMIL. Ay, ay: O, lay me by my mistress' side.

GRA. He's gone, but his wife's kill'd.

MON. 'Tis a notorious villain. Take you this weapon,
Which I have here recover'd from the Moor:
Come, guard the door without; let him not pass, 241
But kill him rather. I'll after that same villain,
For 'tis a damned slave.

[*Exeunt* MONTANO *and* GRATIANO.

OTH. I am not valiant neither.
But every puny whipster gets my sword:
But why should honour outlive honesty? 245
Let it go all.

EMIL. What did thy song bode, lady?
Hark, canst thou hear me? I will play the swan,
And die in music. [*Singing*] Willow, willow, willow.—
Moor, she was chaste; she loved thee, cruel Moor;
So come my soul to bliss, as I speak true; 250
So speaking as I think, I die, I die. [*Dies.*

OTH. I have another weapon in this chamber;
It is a sword of Spain, the ice-brook's temper:—
O, here it is. Uncle, I must come forth.

GRA. [*Within*] If thou attempt it, it will cost thee dear: 255
Thou hast no weapon, and perforce must suffer.

OTH. Look in upon me then and speak with me,
Or, naked as I am, I will assault thee.

[*Re-enter* GRATIANO.]

GRA. What is the matter?

OTH. Behold, I have a weapon;
A better never did itself sustain 260
Upon a soldier's thigh: I have seen the day,
That, with this little arm and this good sword,
I have made my way through more impediments
Than twenty times your stop: but, O vain boast!
Who can control his fate? 'tis not so now. 265
Be not afraid, though you do see me weapon'd;
Here is my journey's end, here is my butt,
And very sea-mark of my utmost sail.
Do you go back dismay'd? 'tis a lost fear;
Man but a rush against Othello's breast, 270
And he retires. Where should Othello go?
Now, how dost thou look now? O ill-starr'd wench!
Pale as thy smock! when we shall meet at compt,
This look of thine will hurl my soul from heaven,
And fiends will snatch at it. Cold, cold, my girl! 275
Even like thy chastity. O cursèd slave!
Whip me, ye devils,
From the possession of this heavenly sight!
Blow me about in winds! roast me in sulphur!

226. fortune, chance. 233. coxcomb, fool. 234. stones, thunderbolts. It was thought that real stones fell whenever it thundered. 244. whipster, whippersnapper, i.e., a boy who whips a top. 245. honour . . . honesty, reputation for courage outlive honor. 246. bode, portend. 253. ice-brook's temper, tempered in ice-cold water. 258. naked, unarmed. 264. stop, i.e., power to stop me. 267. butt, goal. 268. sea-mark, beacon, limit; utmost sail, last voyage. 270. man . . . rush, do but attack. 273. smock, undergarment, chemise; compt, the last reckoning on judgment day.

Wash me in steep-down gulfs of liquid fire! 280
O Desdemona! Desdemona! dead!
Oh! Oh! Oh!

[*Enter* LODOVICO, MONTANO, CASSIO *carried in a chair, and* OFFICERS *with* IAGO, *prisoner.*]

LOD. Where is this rash and most unfortunate man?
OTH. That's he that was Othello: here I am.
LOD. Where is that viper? bring the villain forth. 285
OTH. I look down towards his feet; but that's a fable.
If that thou be'st a devil, I cannot kill thee.
[*Wounds* IAGO.
LOD. Wrench his sword from him.
IAGO. I bleed, sir; but not kill'd.
OTH. I am not sorry neither: I'ld have thee live;
For, in my sense, 'tis happiness to die. 290
LOD. O thou Othello, that wert once so good,
Fall'n in the practice of a damnèd slave,
What shall be said to thee?
OTH. Why, any thing:
An honourable murderer, if you will; 294
For nought I did in hate, but all in honour.
LOD. This wretch hath part confess'd his villany:
Did you and he consent in Cassio's death?
OTH. Ay.
CAS. Dear general, I never gave you cause.
OTH. I do believe it, and I ask you pardon.
Will you, I pray, demand that demi-devil 301
Why he hath thus ensnared my soul and body?
IAGO. Demand me nothing: what you know, you know:
From this time forth I never will speak word.
LOD. What, not to pray?
GRA. Torments will ope your lips.
OTH. Well, thou dost best. 306
LOD. Sir, you shall understand what hath befall'n,
Which, as I think, you know not. Here is a letter
Found in the pocket of the slain Roderigo;
And here another: the one of them imports 310
The death of Cassio to be undertook
By Roderigo.
OTH. O villain!
CAS. Most heathenish and most gross!
LOD. Now here's another discontented paper,
Found in his pocket too; and this, it seems,
Roderigo meant to have sent this damnèd villain; 316
But that belike Iago in the interim
Came in and satisfied him.
OTH. O the pernicious caitiff!
How came you, Cassio, by that handkerchief
That was my wife's?
CAS. I found it in my chamber: 320
And he himself confess'd but even now
That there he dropp'd it for a special purpose
Which wrought to his desire.
OTH. O fool! fool! fool!
CAS. There is besides in Roderigo's letter,
How he upbraids Iago, that he made him 325
Brave me upon the watch; whereon it came
That I was cast: and even but now he spake,
After long seeming dead, Iago hurt him,
Iago set him on.
LOD. You must forsake this room, and go with us: 330
Your power and your command is taken off,
And Cassio rules in Cyprus. For this slave,
If there be any cunning cruelty
That can torment him much and hold him long,
It shall be his. You shall close prisoner rest,
Till that the nature of your fault be known 336
To the Venetian state. Come, bring him away.
OTH. Soft you; a word or two before you go.
I have done the state some service, and they know 't. 339
No more of that. I pray you, in your letters,
When you shall these unlucky deeds relate,
Speak of me as I am; nothing extenuate,
Nor set down aught in malice: then must you speak

286. **feet**, i.e., to see if they are cloven, like the Devil's. 290. **in my sense**, my feeling is. 292. **practice**, plot, snare. 295. **in honour**, i.e., in defense of my honor. 297. **consent in**, conspire together. 301. **demand**, ask. 310. **imports**, conveys as its purport. 314. **discontented**, expressing dissatisfaction. 317. **belike**, probably. 318. **caitiff**, wretch. 323. **wrought . . . desire**, had the effect he desired. 326. **brave**, bully; **upon the watch**, i.e., when I was on sentry duty. 327. **cast**, dismissed. 331. **off**, away. 332. **For**, as for. 333. **cunning**, ingeniously contrived. 335. **close prisoner rest**, remain in close confinement. 338. **Soft you**, wait a minute.

Of one that loved not wisely but too well;
Of one not easily jealous, but being wrought
Perplex'd in the extreme; of one whose hand, 346
Like the base Indian, threw a pearl away
Richer than all his tribe; of one whose subdued eyes,
Albeit unusèd to the melting mood,
Drop tears as fast as the Arabian trees 350
Their medicinal gum. Set you down this;
And say besides, that in Aleppo once,
Where a malignant and a turban'd Turk
Beat a Venetian and traduced the state,
I took by the throat the circumcised dog, 355
And smote him, thus. [*Stabs himself.*

LOD. O bloody period!

GRA. All that's spoke is marr'd.

OTH. I kiss'd thee ere I kill'd thee: no way but this;
Killing myself, to die upon a kiss.
[*Falls on the bed, and dies.*

CAS. This did I fear, but thought he had no weapon; 360
For he was great of heart.

LOD. [*To* IAGO] O Spartan dog,
More fell than anguish, hunger, or the sea!
Look on the tragic loading of this bed;
This is thy work: the object poisons sight;
Let it be hid. Gratiano, keep the house, 365
And seize upon the fortunes of the Moor,
For they succeed on you. To you, lord governor,
Remains the censure of this hellish villain;
The time, the place, the torture: O, enforce it!
Myself will straight aboard; and to the state
This heavy act with heavy heart relate. 371
[*Exeunt.*

345. **wrought**, worked upon. 346. **Perplex'd**, distracted. 347. **base Indian**, rude American Indian, i.e., any savage (who is ignorant of the value of jewels). 348. **subdued**, conquered (by grief). 352. **Aleppo**, a Syrian town in which the Venetians had special trading privileges. In Aleppo it was death for a Christian to strike a Turk. 357. **period**, end; **All . . . marr'd**, all that we have said has proved useless. 361. **Spartan dog**, Spartan dogs were noted for their ferocity. 362. **fell**, cruel. 363. **loading**, burden. 368. **censure**, condemnation.

AFTERWORD

In the imagination of Shakespeare's England, the black man looms powerfully. His origins are mysterious and touched with superstitious awe. Like Othello, telling over his "travels' history," he has held acquaintance with

> The Anthropophagi and men whose heads
> Do grow beneath their shoulders.

Shakespeare bears witness to the fascinated interest of his contemporaries in this romantic and improbable figure. His account of Othello, the Moor of Venice, is indebted deeply, and with a conscious awareness of the debt he is incurring, to the lurid imagery by which the black man is recognized. Insistence on color, and the moral attitudes and associations color evokes, is everywhere in the play. Blackness, by long custom, denotes the wicked man. It is the badge of Othello, who might so easily have been depicted as a tawny-colored Moor. So far, we might say, Shakespeare the racist.

But Shakespeare, in focusing attention on the color of his hero's skin and the sinister expectations it arouses, is erecting a straw man, which he anticipates that we will topple. He is willing us to look intently at the surface of things. Then, having elicited from us the expected reaction, he wheels on us abruptly; he makes us see that the superficial truth, as conveyed by physiognomy or the pigmentation of the skin, is a lie. In *Othello,* color drenches the play—and is understood at last to be irrelevant.

Many readers of Shakespeare, black men not less than white men, fail to grasp this critical point. Like the deluded or myopic characters of the typical Shakespearean comedy—like Malvolio, for instance, in *Twelfth Night*—they are inclined to take everything at face value. Convention, which identifies blackness with badness, affirms also that whiteness is good. Such readers as are conventional themselves do not think to query the stereotype. Instead, they fall in with it easily, and assume that Shakespeare is doing the same. Really, they are like the villain Iago, a small-minded man whose responses are always stock responses—predictable, limited, and hence open to error. If Shakespeare's plays instruct us at all, it is in the untrustworthy nature of appearance. Even Iago is not always blind to the disjunction or opposition between appearance and reality. Reputation, as he argues very cogently, is often "an idle and most false imposition," which bears no sure relation to the truth. His own character supports the description. He is reputed an honest Florentine. But as he observes to Roderigo, the instrument of his villainous purpose: "I am not what I am."

The perceptive reader of the play will want to be aware from the beginning that Shakespeare is trading deliberately in this important opposition, between the face or visage and the character it frequently belies.

> In Nature there's no blemish but the mind,
> None can be call'd deform'd but the unkind.

From the dramatizing of this theme in *Twelfth Night,* Shakespeare derives a comic situation. In *Othello,* he turns the coin. He discloses to us the springs of tragedy, in the confusing of real substance with show.

The confusion is very ancient that defines a man's substance in terms of the color of his skin. Shakespeare himself, in his early days as a playwright, is briefly a party to it. *Titus Andronicus,* a grisly melodrama he concocts in imitation of the once-popular tragedies of blood, offers as its principal villain a "barbarous Moor" named Aaron, whose swarthy hue and "fleece of wooly hair" argue his villainous spirit. Aaron embodies precisely the vulgar conception of negritude, as familiar in art and literature from the Middle Ages almost to the present time. In medieval and Renaissance paintings, Satan, the Prince of Darkness, is invariably a black man. That is why Iago, informing Brabantio of the marriage of Desdemona and Othello, says derisively that "the Devil will make a grandsire of you." Iago, who is the type of the myopic man, accepts the equation of darkness and wickedness. Today, this equation is only beginning to give ground. The conventional hero of innumerable westerns is recognized as his hair is blond and his complexion is fair. Customarily, he enters riding a white horse. Put against this description the color which convention assigns to the villain.

Shakespeare, in *Othello,* appears to embrace the convention. Here, from the First Act, are descriptions of the Moor. He is "the thick lips," a thing of "sooty bosom," a Barbary horse, "an old black ram." We want to inquire, however, whence these descriptions come. They come from Iago, about whom the great truth is that he is a man of very ordinary penetration, and from Roderigo, the foolish and frustrated lover, whom love has turned the wrong side out, and from Brabantio, the outraged parent. These are the voices of unthinking convention. No doubt they are echoed by many persons attending Shakespeare's play, and not only in Shakespeare's time. Othello's features are "begrimed"; he is therefore, to the man who cannot see beyond his nose, necessarily disgusting or wicked. But as the action progresses, we are compelled to acknowledge that the equation is a false equation, or *non sequitur.*

The plot of the play is our means of asserting what is true. How, for example, is it possible that Desdemona should love Othello? Brabantio has an answer. He supposes her to be "enchanted" with "foul charms" or "drugs or minerals." Desdemona proposes a different explanation, and we are wise as we listen attentively, for what she says is very close to the heart of the play. To the implicit question, What has subdued her affection, she replies: "I saw Othello's visage in his mind." But Othello's visage, on the surface, is black, Iago's is white. What follows? In fact what follows is our sudden and startled awareness that the customary association, on which we have been building all this while, is inadequate, superficial.

"There's no art to find the mind's construction in the face." That is to quote from *Macbeth,* which explores, like *Othello,* the opposition between fair words and features, and the foul thoughts and intentions that harbor within. This black man, who is the Moor, is virtuous; and therefore he is comely. Essential comeliness, as we remember from *Twelfth Night,* turns not on appearance but on a "mind that envy could not but call fair." The Duke of Venice, attempting to placate Brabantio, speaks to this dependency. Brabantio, objecting to the marriage, is blind:

> If virtue no delighted beauty lack,
> Your son-in-law is far more fair than black.

Is blackness the mark of the Devil? As we reflect on the words of the Duke and Desdemona, each of whom is concerned to dispute the common wisdom, we will want to be conscious of the fair-appearing Iago, whose presence on stage is indispensable to the total effect. Iago is the white Devil. The terrible anguish the play occasions, as also its purport or meaning, is in this: that as we attend only on appearance, we are involved, perhaps fatally, in the spiritual darkness which is ignorance. Othello is so involved, as he discovers at the end, and to his infinite cost. He has been, what Emilia calls him, a gull, a dolt, a fool, "As ignorant as dirt!" Now his eyes are opened. But revelation comes too late.

Credulity brings about the destruction of Othello. The Moor is

> of a free and open nature,
> That thinks men honest that but seem to be so.

But all men are credulous, weak in their "function" or intellect, and hence likely, as Desdemona implies, to err in ignorance. In this sense, Othello's despairing resignation is approved: "Who can control his fate?" But the fall of valor in the soul: that is another and far more anguishing story, and aloof from the machinations of the villain or the hero's naivete.

Spiritual destruction is the core of the tragedy of *Othello*. For the accomplishing of this destruction or metamorphosis, volition is felt as decisive. Othello, in Hamlet's phrase, makes love to his employment. He builds his damnation on the "scattering and unsure observance" of Iago. He connives at the rule of blood or passion over his "safer guides." On his willful activity, the forfeiting of manhood and the assumption of bestiality depend.

> Exchange me for a goat,
> When I shall turn the business of my soul
> To such exsufflicate and blown surmises,
> Matching thy inference.

The source of the tragic denouement is located, not in plots and stratagems, but in the hero himself. This hero, who was "once so good," whose "solid virtue" has been proof against accident or the "dart of chance," is brought low as he gives entertainment to the "uncleanly apprehensions" which harbor within his own breast.

As the good man is defiled and his virtue turned into pitch, the hatred of the villainous man is assuaged. This hatred, if terrifying, is familiar. It is the instinctive animus of the little man for the greater. The boundary lines which really divide are not between nations or races, "but between the Gullivers of all countries and the Lilliputians." That is the Soviet poet Yevtushenko, memorializing the death of Robert Kennedy. Brightness, not of physiognomy but talent, distinguishes the man of heroic stature. But brightness is also the weakness or vulnerability of stature, and the mark at which grayness takes aim. "On the brow of the favored" this distinguishing mark is set, "like the cross of murder on the doors of the Huguenots."

Othello is favored and so he is marked. He is supremely the poet, whose music testifies to his largeness of soul. The accents in which he speaks are unmistakable.

> I fetch my life and being
> From men of royal siege.

> Keep up your bright swords, for the dew will rust them.

> O, now forever
> Farewell the tranquil mind! farewell content!
> Farewell the plumèd troop, and the big wars,
> That make ambition virtue!

> I have another weapon in this chamber.
> It is a sword of Spain, the ice-brook's temper.

Iago is incapable of this amplitude of manner and speech. He is essentially a prosaic figure, a man of narrow and impoverished spirit, who must, as his own resources are scanty, identify goodness with hypocrisy and eloquence with fustian or rodomontade. The Othello music is nauseating to him. He cannot comprehend it, he himself is indicted by it, and therefore it is only, as he says in the savage outburst with which the play begins,

> a bombast circumstance
> Horribly stuff'd with epithets of war.

Othello, whose parts or qualities are manifest to the world, is a ranting braggart. Desdemona, the paragon of virtue, is a supersubtle Venetian whose nature must instruct her in adultery. Cassio, the constant friend and capable lieutenant, is a devious friend, "framed to make women false." Neither is he a soldier, but only a pedant and prattler.

Cassio, like his master, is prone to the sweeping gesture and grandiloquent phrase. See, by way of illustration, the flourish with which he describes and salutes Desdemona, on her arrival in Cyprus. Courtesy is his habitual garment. For that reason, Cassio also incurs the hatred of Iago. Courtesy, as the little man construes it, is lechery. In one of the most fearful lines in all Shakespeare, Iago reveals the source of the hatred that consumes him.

> He hath a daily beauty in his life
> That makes me ugly.

This profound opposition, not of black man and white man but of beauty and ugliness, requires the deaths of Cassio and Desdemona and the Moor.

The malignant behavior of Iago, which seems in its intensity difficult to explain, is after all sufficiently motivated. Iago is, in spirit, a pigmy, whose littleness is a festering sore. Othello, who is, in all ways, his superior, is nonetheless destroyed. The outcome of this struggle between littleness and greatness is unexpected, and correspondingly painful. *Othello* is the most harrowing of Shakespeare's tragedies as it records the bringing low of grandeur and the triumph of dwarfish size.

Suggested Reading

Bradley, A. C., *Shakespearean Tragedy* (1904). Papermac. Premier.

Brock, J. H. E., *Iago and Some Shakespearean Villains* (1937).

Charlton, H. B., *Shakespearian Tragedy* (1948).

Coe, Charles N., *Shakespeare's Villains* (1957).

Dean, Leonard F., ed., *A Casebook on Othello* (1961). Crowell.

Dickey, Franklin, *Not Wisely But Too Well* (1957).

Draper, John W., *The "Othello" of Shakespeare's Audience* (1952).

Eliot, T. S., "Shakespeare and the Stoicism of Seneca" (1927), in *Selected Essays 1917–1932* (1932).

Elliott, George R., *Flaming Minister* (1953). Penguin.

Flatter, Richard, *The Moor of Venice* (1950).

Granville-Barker, Harley, "Othello," in *Prefaces to Shakespeare*, ed. M. St. Clare Byrne, 4 vols. (1948). Princeton.

Hayden, Hiram, *The Counter-Renaissance* (1950). Harbinger.

Heilman, Robert B., *Magic in the Web* (1956). Penguin. University of Kentucky.

Knight, G. Wilson, "The 'Othello' Music," in *The Wheel of Fire* (enlarged ed., 1954). Barnes and Noble.

Langbaum, Robert, *The Poetry of Experience* (1957). Norton.

Leavis, F. R., "Diabolic Intellect and the Noble Hero," in *The Common Pursuit* (1952). Penguin.

Leech, Clifford, *Shakespeare's Tragedies* (1950). Phoenix.

Moulton, R. G., *Shakespeare As a Dramatic Artist* (1893; reprinted 1966). Dover.

Rosenberg, Marvin, *The Masks of Othello* (1961) Penguin.

Rymer, Thomas, *A Short View of Tragedy* (1693).

Spivack, Bernard, *Shakespeare and the Allegory of Evil* (1958). Penguin.

Stirling, Brents, *Unity in Shakespearian Tragedy* (1956).

Stoll, Elmer Edgar, *Othello* (1915).

———, *Shakespeare and Other Masters* (1940).

Swinburne, Algernon Charles, *Three Plays of Shakespeare* (1909).

Tannenbaum, Samuel A., *Shakespeare's "Othello": A Concise Bibliography* (1943).

Wilson, Harold S., *On the Design of Shakespearian Tragedy* (1957). Toronto.

Measure for Measure

A NOTE ON THE TEXT

Measure for Measure was first printed in the Folio of 1623. The text of this single version, which is occasionally muddled, is thought to have been copied from Shakespeare's manuscript. Composition is assigned generally to 1604. The Revels Accounts, which detail expenditures for entertainment at Court, record a performance of the play before King James I on December 26, 1604.

The closest parallel to the story Shakespeare tells in *Measure for Measure*, and therefore the most likely source, is a melodramatic narrative by the Elizabethan poet and dramatist, George Whetstone. In a collection of prose tales, entitled *The Heptameron of Civil Discourses*, Whetstone explores, but only superficially, the unequal contest between Lord Promos, a lascivious Hungarian, and the beautiful Cassandra, who submits to his lust as the price of her brother's freedom. Four years earlier, in 1578, Whetstone had attempted a dramatic treatment of this story, published as *Promos and Cassandra*.

Shakespeare's version is, in outline form, very similar. Shakespeare incorporates, however, the disgusting activity of Lucio and Pompey, and so affords a clue to his more serious intention. Whetstone's romance is sensational. Shakespeare, as he provides a background conformable to the sordid business of the central story, gives to that story an interest more than sensational or peculiar. In *Measure for Measure*, Shakespeare is not simply diverting his auditors, but holding up the mirror, that they may see themselves.

MEASURE FOR MEASURE

DRAMATIS PERSONÆ

VINCENTIO, *the Duke.*
ANGELO, *the Deputy.*
ESCALUS, *an ancient Lord.*
CLAUDIO, *a young gentleman.*
LUCIO, *a fantastic.*
Two other like gentlemen.
PROVOST.
THOMAS, PETER, } *two friars.*
A JUSTICE.
VARRIUS.
ELBOW, *a simple constable.*
FROTH, *a foolish gentleman.*
POMPEY, *clown, servant to Mistress Overdone.*
ABHORSON, *an executioner.*
BARNARDINE, *a dissolute prisoner.*
ISABELLA, *sister to Claudio.*
MARIANA, *betrothed to Angelo.*
JULIET, *beloved of Claudio.*
FRANCISCA, *a nun.*
MISTRESS OVERDONE, *a bawd.*
LORDS, OFFICERS, CITIZENS, BOY, *and* ATTENDANTS.

SCENE: *Vienna.*

ACT I

SCENE I. *An Apartment in the* DUKE'S *Palace.*

[*Enter* DUKE, ESCALUS, LORDS, *and* ATTENDANTS.]

DUKE. Escalus.
ESCAL. My lord?
DUKE. Of government the properties to unfold,
Would seem in me to affect speech and discourse,
Since I am put to know that your own science
Exceeds, in that, the lists of all advice 6
My strength can give you: then no more remains,
But that, to your sufficiency, as your worth is able,
And let them work. The nature of our people, 10
Our city's institutions, and the terms
For common justice, you're as pregnant in,
As art and practice hath enriched any
That we remember. There is our commission, [*Giving it.*]
From which we would not have you warp. Call hither, 15
I say, bid come before us Angelo. [*Exit an* ATTENDANT.]
What figure of us think you he will bear?
For you must know, we have with special soul
Elected him our absence to supply,
Lent him our terror, drest him with our love, 20
And given his deputation all the organs
Of our own power: what think you of it?
ESCAL. If any in Vienna be of worth
To undergo such ample grace and honour,
It is Lord Angelo.
DUKE. Look where he comes. 25

[*Enter* ANGELO.]

ANG. Always obedient to your Grace's will
I come to know your pleasure.
DUKE. Angelo,
There is a kind of character in thy life,

Act I, Scene i: 3. **properties**, principles. 4. **would . . . discourse**, would seem as if I wished to show off my ability to make a speech. 5. **put to know**, in a position to know. 6. **lists**, limits. 9. **sufficiency**, competence; **as . . . able**, as your authority is appropriate. The text at this point is corrupt. Perhaps a line has dropped out. 11-12. **terms . . . justice**, conditions on which common justice is meted out. 12. **pregnant**, expert. 13. **art**, theory. 15. **warp**, deviate. 17. **figure**, image, i.e., what kind of representative. 18. **with special soul**, as an act of special confidence. 19. **Elected . . . supply**, chosen him to fill our place in our absence. 21. **deputation**, position as deputy; **organs**, instruments. 24. **undergo**, sustain. 28. **character**, hand-writing, hence, stamp.

That, to th' observer doth thy history
Fully unfold. Thy self and thy belongings 30
Are not thine own so proper, as to waste
Thyself upon thy virtues, they on thee.
Heaven doth with us as we with torches do,
Not light them for themselves; for if our virtues
Did not go forth of us, 'twere all alike 35
As if we had them not. Spirits are not finely touch'd
But to fine issues, nor Nature never lends
The smallest scruple of her excellence,
But, like a thrifty goddess, she determines
Herself the glory of a creditor, 40
Both thanks and use. But I do bend my speech
To one that can my part in him advertise;
Hold, therefore, Angelo.
[*Tendering his commission.*]
In our remove be thou at full ourself;
Mortality and mercy in Vienna 45
Live in thy tongue and heart. Old Escalus,
Though first in question, is thy secondary.
Take thy commission. [*Giving it.*

ANG. Now, good my lord,
Let there be some more test made of my metal,
Before so noble and so great a figure 50
Be stamp'd upon it.

DUKE. No more evasion:
We have with a leaven'd and preparèd choice
Proceeded to you; therefore take your honours.
Our haste from hence is of so quick condition
That it prefers itself, and leaves unquestion'd 55
Matters of needful value. We shall write to you,
As time and our concernings shall importune,
How it goes with us: and do look to know
What doth befall you here. So, fare you well:
To the hopeful execution do I leave you 60
Of your commissions.

ANG. Yet, give leave, my lord,
That we may bring you something on the way.

DUKE. My haste may not admit it;
Nor need you, on mine honour, have to do
With any scruple: your scope is as mine own, 65
So to enforce or qualify the laws
As to your soul seems good. Give me your hand;
I'll privily away: I love the people,
But do not like to stage me to their eyes.
Though it do well, I do not relish well 70
Their loud applause and Aves vehement,
Nor do I think the man of safe discretion
That does affect it. Once more, fare you well.

ANG. The heavens give safety to your purposes!

ESCAL. Lead forth and bring you back in happiness! 75

DUKE. I thank you. Fare you well. [*Exit.*

ESCAL. I shall desire you, sir, to give me leave
To have free speech with you; and it concerns me
To look into the bottom of my place:
A power I have, but of what strength and nature 80
I am not yet instructed.

ANG. 'Tis so with me. Let us withdraw together,
And we may soon our satisfaction have
Touching that point.

ESCAL. I'll wait upon your honour. [*Exeunt.*

SCENE II. *A Street.*

[*Enter* LUCIO *and two* GENTLEMEN.]

LUC. If the Duke with the other dukes comes not to composition with the King of Hungary, why then, all the dukes fall upon the king.

30-2. thy belongings . . . on thee, your good qualities are not so exclusively your own private property as to permit you to waste them on a self-contained moral life. **33-4. Heaven . . . for themselves,** an imaginative paraphrase of Matthew V, 15-16. "Neither do men light a candle and put it under a bushel," etc. **36-7. Spirits . . . fine issues,** Spirits are not accurately tested except by fine deeds. **38. scruple,** third part of a dram, hence, any minute quantity. **39-41. She determines . . . use,** with just pride she makes the usual demands of a creditor (1) thanks for the benefits received and (2) interest on the loan (in the form of creditable actions). **42. That . . . advertise,** that can teach me my business of governing, which I now turn over to him. **43. Hold,** i.e., take the commission. **44. remove,** absence. **45. Mortality,** Power over life and death. **47. first . . . secondary,** first to be summoned is your subordinate. **52. With . . . choice,** As the result of a deliberate and considered choice. **55. prefers itself,** takes precedence; **unquestioned,** unexamined. **56. needful value,** urgent importance. **57. concernings,** concerns. **60. hopeful,** hoped-for, i.e., successful. **62. bring you something,** accompany you somewhat. **64. have . . . scruple,** have any scruples about using your power to the full. **65. scope,** i.e., the scope of your power. **66. qualify,** moderate. **69. stage me,** exhibit myself. **70. do well,** is fitting. **71. Aves,** salutations, "Hails." **73. does affect it,** likes it. This passage (II: 68-72) flatters a weakness of King James, who disliked and feared crowds. **79. To look into . . . place,** To examine thoroughly the extent of my authority (the duties of my official position). **82. satisfaction,** full information. **84. wait upon,** accompany. **Scene ii: 2. composition,** an agreement, a vague reference to some war which seems to be imminent.

FIR. GENT. Heaven grant us its peace, but not the King of Hungary's! 5

SEC. GENT. Amen.

LUC. Thou concludest like the sanctimonious pirate, that went to sea with the Ten Commandments, but scraped one out of the table.

SEC. GENT. "Thou shalt not steal"? 10

LUC. Ay, that he razed.

FIR. GENT. Why, 'twas a commandment to command the captain and all the rest from their functions: they put forth to steal. There's not a soldier of us all, that, in the thanksgiving before meat, doth relish the petition well that prays for peace. 17

SEC. GENT. I never heard any soldier dislike it.

LUC. I believe thee, for I think thou never wast where grace was said. 20

SEC. GENT. No? a dozen times at least.

FIR. GENT. What, in metre?

LUC. In any proportion or in any language.

FIR. GENT. I think, or in any religion. 24

LUC. Ay; why not? Grace is grace, despite of all controversy: as, for example, thou thyself art a wicked villain, despite of all grace.

FIR. GENT. Well, there went but a pair of shears between us.

LUC. I grant; as there may between the lists and the velvet: thou art the list. 31

FIR. GENT. And thou the velvet: thou art good velvet; thou art a three-piled piece, I warrant thee. I had as lief be a list of an English kersey as be piled, as thou art piled, for a French velvet. Do I speak feelingly now? 36

LUC. I think thou dost; and, indeed, with most painful feeling of thy speech: I will, out of thine own confession, learn to begin thy health; but, whilst I live, forget to drink after thee. 40

FIR. GENT. I think I have done myself wrong, have I not?

SEC. GENT. Yes, that thou hast, whether thou art tainted or free.

LUC. Behold, behold, where Madam Mitigation comes! I have purchased as many diseases under her roof as come to— 45

SEC. GENT. To what, I pray?

LUC. Judge.

SEC. GENT. To three thousand dolours a year. 51

FIR. GENT. Ay, and more.

LUC. A French crown more.

FIR. GENT. Thou art always figuring diseases in me; but thou art full of error: I am sound.

LUC. Nay, not as one would say, healthy; but so sound as things that are hollow: thy bones are hollow; impiety has made a feast of thee. 57

[*Enter* MISTRESS OVERDONE.]

FIR. GENT. How now! which of your hips has the most profound sciatica?

MRS. OV. Well, well; there 's one yonder arrested and carried to prison was worth five thousand of you all. 60

SEC. GENT. Who 's that, I pray thee?

MRS. OV. Marry, sir, that 's Claudio, Signior Claudio. 65

FIR. GENT. Claudio to prison! 'Tis not so.

MRS. OV. Nay, but I know 'tis so. I saw him arrested; saw him carried away; and, which is more, within these three days his head to be chopped off. 70

LUC. But, after all this fooling, I would not have it so. Art thou sure of this?

MRS. OV. I am too sure of it; and it is for getting Madam Julietta with child. 74

LUC. Believe me, this may be: he promised to meet me two hours since, and he was ever precise in promise-keeping.

SEC. GENT. Besides, you know, it draws something near to the speech we had to such a purpose. 80

FIR. GENT. But most of all, agreeing with the proclamation.

LUC. Away! let 's go learn the truth of it.

[*Exeunt* LUCIO *and* GENTLEMEN.

MRS. OV. Thus, what with the war, what

12. **from . . . functions,** to perform their proper tasks. 17. **the petition,** the authorized grace concluded as follows: "God save our King and Realm, and send us peace in Christ." 23. **proportion,** metre. 25. **controversy,** religious difference. 28-9. **there . . . between us,** i.e., we were both cut from the same piece of cloth. 30. **lists,** outer edge of any piece of cloth, which is made of plain material. 33. **three-piled,** i.e., richest and finest. 35. **kersey,** coarse woolen cloth. 36. **piled,** here a pun on "peeled," meaning bald, one of the results of syphilis, called "the French disease"; **feelingly,** (1) to the purpose, (2) to make you feel pain. 38. **painful feeling,** i.e., because he has syphilitic sores in his mouth. 39-40. **forget . . . after thee,** i.e., he will be careful not to drink out of the same cup with him for fear of contracting his disease. 41. **done myself wrong,** given myself away. 44. **free,** i.e., free of syphilis. 51. **dolours,** (1) griefs, (2) dollars. 53. **French crown,** (a) a coin, (b) head bald from the ravages of syphilis, called the French disease. 54. **figuring,** imagining. 56. **sound,** (1) in good health, (2) the sound given by hollow things when struck. 79-80. **it draws . . . purpose,** it somewhat confirms the conversation we had about some such an eventuality.

with the sweat, what with the gallows and what with poverty, I am custom-shrunk. 85

[*Enter* POMPEY.]

How now! what 's the news with you.

POM. Yonder man is carried to prison.

MRS. OV. Well: what has he done?

POM. A woman.

MRS. OV. But what 's his offence? 90

POM. Groping for trouts in a peculiar river.

MRS. OV. What, is there a maid with child by him?

POM. No; but there 's a woman with maid by him. You have not heard of the proclamation, have you? 96

MRS. OV. What proclamation, man?

POM. All houses of resort in the suburbs of Vienna must be plucked down.

MRS. OV. And what shall become of those in the city? 101

POM. They shall stand for seed: they had gone down too, but that a wise burgher put in for them.

MRS. OV. But shall all our houses of resort in the suburbs be pulled down? 105

POM. To the ground, mistress.

MRS. OV. Why, here's a change indeed in the commonwealth! What shall become of me?

POM. Come; fear not you: good counsellors lack no clients: though you change your place, you need not change your trade; I 'll be your tapster still. Courage! there will be pity taken on you; you that have worn your eyes almost out in the service, you will be considered.

MRS. OV. What 's to do here, Thomas tapster? Let's withdraw. 116

POM. Here comes Signior Claudio, led by the provost to prison; and there's Madam Juliet. [*Exeunt.*

[*Enter* PROVOST, CLAUDIO, JULIET, *and* OFFICERS.]

CLAUD. Fellow, why dost thou show me thus to the world? 120
Bear me to prison were I am committed.

PROV. I do it not in evil disposition,
But from Lord Angelo by special charge.

CLAUD. Thus can the demi-god Authority
Make us pay down for our offence by weight. 125
The words of heaven; on whom it will, it will;
On whom it will not, so: yet still 'tis just.

[*Re-enter* LUCIO *and two* GENTLEMEN.]

LUC. Why, how now, Claudio! whence comes this restraint?

CLAUD. From too much liberty, my Lucio, liberty:
As surfeit is the father of much fast, 130
So every scope by the immoderate use
Turns to restraint. Our natures do pursue—
Like rats that ravin down their proper bane,—
A thirsty evil, and when we drink we die.

LUC. If I could speak so wisely under 135 an arrest, I would send for certain of my creditors. And yet, to say the truth, I had as lief have the foppery of freedom as the morality of imprisonment. What 's thy offence, Claudio?

CLAUD. What but to speak of would offend again. 140

LUC. What, is 't murder?

CLAUD. No.

LUC. Lechery?

CLAUD. Call it so.

PROV. Away, sir! you must go. 145

CLAUD. One word, good friend. Lucio, a word with you. [*Takes him aside.*

LUC. A hundred, if they 'll do you any good.
Is lechery so looked after?

CLAUD. Thus stands it with me: upon a true contract
I got possession of Julietta's bed: 150
You know the lady; she is fast my wife,
Save that we do the denunciation lack
Of outward order: this we came not to,
Only for propagation of a dower
Remaining in the coffer of her friends, 155
From whom we thought it meet to hide our love
Till time had made them for us. But it chances
The stealth of our most mutual entertainment

84. **sweat**, the plague. 85. **I . . . custom shrunk**, My business is shrinking. 91. **peculiar**, private. 94. **maid**, a name given to the young of certain kinds of fish. 97. **suburbs**, the London brothels were situated outside the city limits. 103. **put . . . them**, put in a bid for them. 105. **houses of resort**, brothels. 112. **tapster**, the waiter in a tavern who was often also a pimp. 117. **provost**, jailer. 125. **by weight**, heavily. 126-7. **The words . . . just**, a corrupt passage. Probably a reference to Romans, IX: 15, 18. "I will have mercy on whom I will have mercy . . . therefore hath He mercy on whom He will have mercy and whom He will He hardenth." 130. **surfeit**, over-eating. 132. **scope**, license. 133. **ravin**, gulp down; **proper bane**, own poison. 134. **thirsty evil**, an evil causing thirst. 137. **foppery**, folly. 148. **looked after**, taken care of. 149. **true contract**, formal betrothal, considered valid and binding without religious ceremony. 151. **fast my wife**, my wife by "handfast," i.e., betrothed. 152. **denunciation**, formal declaration. 154. **propagation**, increase. 155. **coffer**, strongbox, i.e., secure-keeping. 156. **meet**, proper. 157. **them**, i.e., her friends.

With character too gross is writ on Juliet.
LUC. With child, perhaps?
CLAUD. Unhappily, even so. 160
And the new deputy now for the duke,—
Whether it be the fault and glimpse of newness,
Or whether that the body public be
A horse whereon the governor doth ride,
Who, newly in the seat, that it may know 165
He can command, lets it straight feel the spur;
Whether the tyranny be in his place,
Or in his eminence that fills it up,
I stagger in:—but this new governor
Awakes me all the enrollèd penalties 170
Which have, like unscour'd armour, hung by the wall
So long that nineteen zodiacs have gone round,
And none of them been worn; and, for a name,
Now puts the drowsy and neglected act
Freshly on me: 'tis surely for a name. 175
LUC. I warrant it is: and thy head stands so tickle on thy shoulders that a milkmaid, if she be in love, may sigh it off. Send after the duke and appeal to him.
CLAUD. I have done so, but he's not to be found. 180
I prithee, Lucio, do me this kind service.
This day my sister should the cloister enter,
And there receive her approbation.
Acquaint her with the danger of my state;
Implore her, in my voice, that she make friends 185
To the strict deputy; bid herself assay him.
I have great hope in that; for in her youth
There is a prone and speechless dialect,
Such as move men; beside, she hath prosperous art
When she will play with reason and discourse, 190
And well she can persuade.
LUC. I pray she may; as well for the encouragement of the like, which else would stand under grievous imposition, as for the enjoying of thy life, who I would be sorry should be thus foolishly lost at a game of 195 tick-tack. I'll to her.
CLAUD. I thank you, good friend Lucio.
LUC. Within two hours.
CLAUD. Come, officer, away!
[*Exeunt.*

SCENE III. *A Monastery.*

[*Enter* DUKE *and* FRIAR THOMAS.]

DUKE. No, holy father; throw away that thought:
Believe not that the dribbling dart of love
Can pierce a complete bosom. Why I desire thee
To give me secret harbour, hath a purpose
More grave and wrinkled than the aims and ends 5
Of burning youth.
FRIAR T. May your Grace speak of it?
DUKE. My holy sir, none better knows than you
How I have ever lov'd the life remov'd,
And held in idle price to haunt assemblies
Where youth, and cost, and witless bravery keeps. 10
I have deliver'd to Lord Angelo—
A man of stricture and firm abstinence—
My absolute power and place here in Vienna,
And he supposes me travell'd to Poland;
For so I have strew'd it in the common ear, 15
And so it is receiv'd. Now, pious sir,
You will demand of me why I do this?
FRIAR T. Gladly, my lord.
DUKE. We have strict statutes and most biting laws,—
The needful bits and curbs to headstrong steeds,— 20
Which for this fourteen years we have let sleep;
Even like an o'ergrown lion in a cave,
That goes not out to prey. Now, as fond fathers,
Having bound up the threat'ning twigs of birch,
Only to stick it in their children's sight 25
For terror, not to use, in time the rod

159. **character too gross,** handwriting too large. 162. **fault and glimpse,** specious glamour. 167. **his place,** the office he holds. 168. **Or . . . up,** Or in the excellence (ironical) of him who occupies it. 169. **I stagger in,** I hesitate to say. 172. **zodiacs,** years. 173. **for a name,** to gain a reputation. 174-5. **Now . . . me,** Now applies anew a drowsy (from disuse) and neglected law to my situation. 176. **tickle,** precariously. 183. **receive her approbation,** begin her novitiate. 186. **assay him,** apply to him. 188. **prone . . . dialect,** ready wordless language. 189. **prosperous,** successful. 193. **the like,** i.e., lechery. 194. **imposition,** punishment. 196. **tick-tack,** a sort of backgammon played by fitting pegs into holes. Scene iii: 2. **dribbling,** weakly shot. 3. **complete,** completely protected. 8. **life remov'd,** life of retirement. 9. **in idle price,** futile. 10. **cost,** extravagance; **bravery,** ostentation; **keeps,** dwells. 12. **stricture,** strict morals. 13. **place,** office.

Becomes more mock'd than fear'd; so our decrees,
Dead to infliction, to themselves are dead,
And liberty plucks justice by the nose;
The baby beats the nurse, and quite athwart 30
Goes all decorum.

FRIAR T. It rested in your Grace
T' unloose this tied-up justice when you pleas'd;
And it in you more dreadful would have seem'd
Than in Lord Angelo.

DUKE. I do fear, too dreadful:
Sith 'twas my fault to give the people scope, 35
'Twould be my tyranny to strike and gall them
For what I bid them do: for we bid this be done,
When evil deeds have their permissive pass
And not the punishment. Therefore, indeed, my father,
I have on Angelo impos'd the office, 40
Who may, in the ambush of my name, strike home,
And yet my nature never in the sight
To do it slander. And to behold his sway,
I will, as 'twere a brother of your order,
Visit both prince and people: therefore, I prithee, 45
Supply me with the habit, and instruct me
How I may formally in person bear me
Like a true friar. Moe reasons for this action
At our more leisure shall I render you;
Only, this one: Lord Angelo is precise; 50
Stands at a guard with envy; scarce confesses
That his blood flows, or that his appetite
Is more to bread than stone: hence shall we see,
If power change purpose, what our seemers be. [*Exeunt.* 54

SCENE IV. *A Nunnery.*

[*Enter* ISABELLA *and* FRANCISCA.]

ISAB. And have you nuns no further privileges?

FRAN. Are not these large enough?

ISAB. Yes, truly; I speak not as desiring more,
But rather wishing a more strict restraint
Upon the sisterhood, the votarists of Saint Clare. 5

LUC. [*Within*] Ho! Peace be in this place!

ISAB. Who's that which calls?

FRAN. It is a man's voice. Gentle Isabella,
Turn you the key, and know his business of him:
You may, I may not; you are yet unsworn.
When you have vow'd, you must not speak with men 10
But in the presence of the prioress:
Then, if you speak, you must not show your face,
Or, if you show your face, you must not speak.
He calls again; I pray you, answer him. [*Exit.*

ISAB. Peace and prosperity! Who is 't that calls? 15

[*Enter* LUCIO.]

LUC. Hail, virgin, if you be, as those cheek-roses
Proclaim you are no less! Can you so stead me
As bring me to the sight of Isabella,
A novice of this place, and the fair sister
To her unhappy brother Claudio? 20

ISAB. Why "her unhappy brother"? let me ask;
The rather for I now must make you know
I am that Isabella and his sister.

LUC. Gentle and fair, your brother kindly greets you:
Not to be weary with you, he 's in prison. 25

ISAB. Woe me! for what?

LUC. For that which, if myself might be his judge,
He should receive his punishment in thanks:
He hath got his friend with child.

ISAB. Sir, make me not your story.

LUC. It is true. 30
I would not, though 'tis my familiar sin
With maids to seem the lapwing and to jest,

28. **infliction**, enforcement. 30. **athwart**, perversely. 31. **decorum**, social order. 35. **sith**, since; **scope**, license. 36. **gall**, harass. 38. **have . . . pass**, are allowed liberty. 41. **in the ambush**, under the cover. 42. **nature**, personality. 43. **To . . . slander**, to bring reproach upon itself; **sway**, methods of governing. 46. **habit**, garb. 48. **moe**, more. 50. **precise**, punctilious. 51. **stands . . . envy**, is on his guard against provoking malice. 52. **his blood flows**, he feels passion. 54. **If . . . be**, If power changes its aim, whether he is what he seems to be. **Scene iv:** 2. **large**, liberal. 5. **votarists . . . Clare**, nuns of the order of St. Clare of Assisi, who devoted their lives to meditation. 6. **which**, who. 8. **Turn . . . key**, unlock the door. 17. **stead**, help. 25. **weary**, tiresome. 29. **friend**, mistress. 30. **story**, laughing stock. 31. **familiar**, habitual. 32. **lapwing**, a bird which leads hunters away from her nest by fluttering with a pretended broken wing in the opposite direction. Hence, to seem the lapwing = to deceive.

Tongue far from heart, play with all virgins so:
I hold you as a thing enskied and sainted;
By your renouncement an immortal spirit, 35
And to be talk'd with in sincerity,
As with a saint.

ISAB. You do blaspheme the good in mocking me.

LUC. Do not believe it. Fewness and truth, 'tis thus:
Your brother and his lover have embrac'd: 40
As those that feed grow full, as blossoming time
That from the seedness the bare fallow brings
To teeming foison, even so her plenteous womb
Expresseth his full tilth and husbandry.

ISAB. Some one with child by him? My cousin Juliet? 45

LUC. Is she your cousin?

ISAB. Adoptedly; as school-maids change their names
By vain, though apt affection.

LUC. She it is.

ISAB. O! let him marry her.

LUC. This is the point.
The duke is very strangely gone from hence; 50
Bore many gentlemen, myself being one,
In hand and hope of action; but we do learn
By those that know the very nerves of state,
His givings out were of an infinite distance
From his true-meant design. Upon his place, 55
And with full line of his authority,
Governs Lord Angelo; a man whose blood
Is very snow-broth; one who never feels
The wanton stings and motions of the sense,
But doth rebate and blunt his natural edge 60
With profits of the mind, study and fast.
He,—to give fear to use and liberty,
Which have for long run by the hideous law,
As mice by lions, hath pick'd out an act,
Under whose heavy sense your brother's life 65
Falls into forfeit: he arrests him on it,
And follows close the rigour of the statute,
To make him an example. All hope is gone,
Unless you have the grace by your fair prayer
To soften Angelo; and that 's my pith of business 70
Twixt you and your poor brother.

ISAB. Doth he so seek his life?

LUC. He 's censur'd him
Already; and, as I hear, the provost hath
A warrant for his execution.

ISAB. Alas! what poor ability 's in me 75
To do him good?

LUC. Assay the power you have.

ISAB. My power? alas! I doubt—

LUC. Our doubts are traitors,
And make us lose the good we oft might win,
By fearing to attempt. Go to Lord Angelo,
And let him learn to know, when maidens sue, 80
Men give like gods; but when they weep and kneel,
All their petitions are as freely theirs
As they themselves would owe them.

ISAB. I'll see what I can do.

LUC. But speedily.

ISAB. I will about it straight; 85
No longer staying but to give the Mother
Notice of my affair. I humbly thank you:
Commend me to my brother; soon at night
I'll send him certain word of my success.

LUC. I take my leave of you.

ISAB. Good sir, adieu. [*Exeunt.* 90

ACT II

SCENE I. *A hall in* ANGELO'S *house.*

[*Enter* ANGELO, ESCALUS, *a* JUSTICE, *and* SERVANTS.]

ANG. We must not make a scarecrow of the law,
Setting it up to fear the birds of prey,

34. **enskied,** of celestial nature. 35. **renouncement,** renunciation of the world. 39. **Fewness,** In brief. 42. **seedness,** sowing; **fallow,** plowed land. 43. **teeming foison,** abundant harvest. 44. **tilth,** tillage. 48. **apt,** impressionable. 51-2. **Bore . . . action,** delude many gentlemen of whom I was one, into thinking we were going to war. 53. **nerves,** sinews. 54. **givings out,** announced plans. 55. **Upon,** in. 59. **motions,** impulses; **of the sense,** to sensuality. 60. **rebate,** dull; **natural edge,** sexual impulse. 62. **use and liberty,** widespread licentiousness. 63. **run by,** evaded. 65. **sense,** meaning. 70. **my . . . of,** the purpose of my. 72. **censur'd,** sentenced. 83. **As . . . them,** As if they themselves had the power to grant them. 85. **straight,** straightway. 86. **Mother,** abbess, mother superior. 88. **Soon at night,** this very night. 89. **my success,** the outcome (of my efforts). **Act II, Scene i:** 2. **fear,** frighten.

And let it keep one shape, till custom make it
Their perch and not their terror.
ESCAL. Ay, but yet
Let us be keen, and rather cut a little, 5
Than fall, and bruise to death. Alas, this gentleman
Whom I would save had a most noble father!
Let but your honour know,
Whom I believe to be most strait in virtue,
That, in the working of your own affections, 10
Had time coher'd with place or place with wishing,
Or that the resolute acting of your blood
Could have attain'd the effect of your own purpose,
Whether you had not sometime in your life
Err'd in this point which now you censure him,
And pull'd the law upon you. 16
ANG. 'Tis one thing to be tempted, Escalus,
Another thing to fall. I not deny,
The jury, passing on the prisoner's life,
May in the sworn twelve have a thief or two 20
Guiltier than him they try. What's open made to justice,
That justice seizes. What knows the laws
That thieves do pass on thieves? 'Tis very pregnant,
The jewel that we find, we stoop and take't
Because we see it; but what we do not see 25
We tread upon, and never think of it.
You may not so extenuate his offence
For I have had such faults; but rather tell me,
When I, that censure him, do so offend,
Let mine own judgement pattern out my death, 30
And nothing come in partial. Sir, he must die.

[*Enter* PROVOST.]

ESCAL. Be it as your wisdom will.
ANG. Where is the Provost?
PROV. Here, if it like your honour.
ANG. See that Claudio
Be executed by nine to-morrow morning
Bring him his confessor, let him be prepar'd; 35
For that's the utmost of his pilgrimage.
[*Exit* PROVOST.
ESCAL. [*Aside*] Well, Heaven forgive him! and forgive us all!
Some rise by sin, and some by virtue fall.
Some run from brakes of vice, and answer none;
And some condemnèd for a fault alone. 40

[*Enter* ELBOW, FROTH, POMPEY, *and* OFFICERS.]

ELB. Come, bring them away. If these be good people in a commonweal that do nothing but use their abuses in common houses, I know no law. Bring them away.
ANG. How now, sir! What's your name? 45 and what's the matter?
ELB. If it please your honour, I am the poor Duke's constable, and my name is Elbow. I do lean upon justice, sir, and do bring in here before your good honour two notorious 50 benefactors.
ANG. Benefactors? Well, what benefactors are they? Are they not malefactors?
ELB. If it please your honour, I know not well what they are; but precise villains they are, that I am sure of; and void of all prof- 55 anation in the world that good Christians ought to have.
ESCAL. This comes off well. Here's a wise officer.
ANG. Go to; what quality are they of? Elbow is your name? Why dost thou not speak, Elbow? 60
POM. He cannot, sir; he's out at elbow.
ANG. What are you, sir?
ELB. He, sir! A tapster, sir; parcel-bawd; one that serves a bad woman, whose house, sir, was, as they say, pluck'd down in the 65 suburbs; and now she professes a hot-house, which, I think, is a very ill house too.
ESCAL. How know you that?

6. **fall**, fell, i.e., rather prune than fell the tree. 8. **know**, consider. 11. **coher'd**, agreed. 12. **blood**, passion. 15. **which**, in which; **censure**, sentence. 21. **open**, evident. 22-3. **What . . . thieves**, how can the law take cognizance of the fact that one of the jurymen may be a thief? 23. **pregnant**, evident. 28. **For**, because. 29. **censure**, sentence. 30. **mine own judgement**, the judgment I pronounce. 31. **nothing . . . partial**, no partiality be shown. 36. **utmost . . . pilgrimage**, limit of his earthly life.

39. **brakes**, thickets, i.e., many vices; **answer**, pay the penalty for 43. **abuses**, wicked practices; **common houses**, brothels. 50. **benefactors**, the first of his many malapropisms. 54. **precise**, strict, Puritanical. 55. **profanation**, irreverence, blunder for reverence. 58. **This . . . well**, this is well told. 59. **Go to**, i.e., that's enough; **what . . . of**, what is their social status? 63. **parcel-bawd**, part-bawd (and part tapster). 66. **hothouse**, house for sweating and bathing, a bagnio or brothel.

ELB. My wife, sir, whom I detest before Heaven and your honour,— 70

ESCAL. How? Thy wife?

ELB. Ay, sir; whom, I thank Heaven, is an honest woman,—

ESCAL. Dost thou detest her therefore?

ELB. I say, sir, I will detest myself also, 75 as well as she, that this house, if it be not a bawd's house, it is a pity of her life, for it is a naughty house.

ESCAL. How dost thou know that, constable?

ELB. Marry, sir, by my wife; who, if she 80 had been a woman cardinally given, might have been accus'd in fornication, adultery, and all uncleanliness there.

ESCAL. By the woman's means?

ELB. Ay, sir, by Mistress Overdone's 85 means; but as she spit in his face, so she defi'd him.

POM. Sir, if it please your honour, this is not so.

ELB. Prove it before these varlets here, thou honourable man; prove it.

ESCAL. Do you hear how he misplaces? 90

POM. Sir, she came in great with child, and longing, saving your honour's reverence, for stew'd prunes. Sir, we had but two in the house, which at that very distant time stood, as it were, in a fruit-dish, a dish of some 95 three-pence. Your honours have seen such dishes; they are not china dishes, but very good dishes,—

ESCAL. Go to, go to; no matter for the dish, sir.

POM. No, indeed, sir, not of a pin; you are therein in the right. But to the point. As 100 I say, this Mistress Elbow, being, as I say, with child, and being great-bellied, and longing, as I said, for prunes; and having but two in the dish, as I said, Master Froth here, this very man, having eaten the rest, as I said, 105 and, as I say, paying for them very honestly; for, as you know, Master Froth, I could not give you three-pence again.

FROTH. No, indeed.

POM. Very well; you being then, if you be remem'red, cracking the stones of the 110 foresaid prunes,—

FROTH. Ay, so I did indeed.

POM. Why, very well. I telling you then, if you be rememb'red, that such a one and such a one were past cure of the thing 115 you wot of, unless they kept very good diet, as I told you,—

FROTH. All this is true.

POM. Why, very well, then,—

ESCAL. Come, you are a tedious fool. To the purpose. What was done to Elbow's wife, 120 that he hath cause to complain of? Come me to what was done to her.

POM. Sir, your honour cannot come to that yet.

ESCAL. No, sir, nor I mean it not.

POM. Sir, but you shall come to it, by 125 your honour's leave. And, I beseech you, look into Master Froth here, sir; a man of four-score pound a year; whose father died at Hallowmas. Was't not at Hallowmas, Master Froth?

FROTH. All-hallond eve. 130

POM. Why, very well; I hope here be truths. He, sir, sitting, as I say, in a lower chair, sir; 'twas in the Bunch of Grapes, where indeed you have a delight to sit, have you not?

FROTH. I have so; because it is an open 135 room and good for winter.

POM. Why, very well, then; I hope here be truths.

ANG. This will last out a night in Russia,
When nights are longest there. I'll take my leave, 140
And leave you to the hearing of the cause,
Hoping you'll find good cause to whip them all.

ESCAL. I think no less. Good morrow to your lordship. [*Exit* ANGELO.
Now, sir, come on. What was done to Elbow's wife, once more? 145

POM. Once, sir? There was nothing done to her once.

ELB. I beseech you, sir, ask him what this man did to my wife.

POM. I beseech your honour, ask me. 150

ESCAL. Well, sir; what did this gentleman to her?

69. **detest**, blunder for protest. 73. **honest**, chaste. 81. **cardinally**, for carnally. 83. **all uncleanliness**, all sorts of impurity. 89. **varlets**, knaves. 90. **misplaces**, mistakes the meaning. 92. **saving . . . reverence**, begging your honor's pardon [for using "stewed prunes," which was cant term for prostitutes from the "stews" or brothels]. 97. **china dishes**, a great luxury in Shakespeare's day. 99. **of a pin**, i.e., of the slightest consequence. 110. **be rememb'red**, recollect. 115. **wot of**, know about. 121. **come**, bring, "me" is an ethical dative. 130. **All . . . eve**, Hallowe'en, 132. **lower**, easy. 133. **Bunch of Grapes**, name of a room in the tavern. 135. **open room**, a public room (and so heated all the time), hence "good for winter."

POM. I beseech you, sir, look in this gentleman's face. Good Master Froth, look upon his honour; 'tis for a good purpose. Doth your honour mark his face? 155

ESCAL. Ay, sir, very well.

POM. Nay, I beseech you, mark it well.

ESCAL. Well, I do so.

POM. Doth your honour see any harm in his face? 160

ESCAL. Why, no.

POM. I'll be suppos'd upon a book, his face is the worst thing about him. Good, then: if his face be the worst thing about him, how could Master Froth do the constable's 165 wife any harm? I would know that of your honour.

ESCAL. He's in the right. Constable, what say you to it?

ELB. First, an it like you, the house is a respected house; next, this is a respected 170 fellow; and his mistress is a respected woman.

POM. By this hand, sir, his wife is a more respected person than any of us all.

ELB. Varlet, thou liest! Thou liest, wicked varlet! The time is yet to come that she 175 was ever respected with man, woman, or child.

POM. Sir, she was respected with him before he married with her.

ESCAL. Which is the wiser here, Justice or Iniquity? Is this true? 181

ELB. O thou caitiff! O thou varlet! O thou wicked Hannibal! I respected with her before I was married to her! If ever I was respected with her, or she with me, let not your worship think me the poor Duke's officer. Prove this, thou wicked Hannibal, or I'll have mine action of battery on thee.

ESCAL. If he took you a box o' the ear, you might have your action of slander too. 190

ELB. Marry, I thank your good worship for it. What is't your worship's pleasure I shall do with this wicked caitiff?

ESCAL. Truly, officer, because he hath some offences in him that thou wouldst dis- 195 cover if thou couldst, let him continue in his courses till thou know'st what they are.

ELB. Marry, I thank your worship for it. Thou seest, thou wicked varlet, now, what's come upon thee. Thou art to continue now, thou varlet; thou art to continue. 201

ESCAL. Where were you born, friend?

FROTH. Here in Vienna, sir.

ESCAL. Are you of fourscore pounds a year?

FROTH. Yes, an't please you, sir. 205

ESCAL. So. What trade are you of, sir?

POM. A tapster; a poor widow's tapster.

ESCAL. Your mistress' name?

POM. Mistress Overdone.

ESCAL. Hath she had any more than one husband? 211

POM. Nine, sir; Overdone by the last.

ESCAL. Nine! Come hither to me, Master Froth. Master Froth, I would not have you acquainted with tapsters; they will draw you, Master Froth, and you will hang them. Get you gone, and let me hear no more of you.

FROTH. I thank your worship. For mine own part, I never come into any room in a taphouse, but I am drawn in. 220

ESCAL. Well, no more of it, Master Froth. Farewell. [*Exit* FROTH.] Come you hither to me, Master tapster. What's your name, Master tapster?

POM. Pompey. 225

ESCAL. What else?

POM. Bum, sir.

ESCAL. Troth, and your bum is the greatest thing about you, so that in the beastliest sense you are Pompey the Great. Pompey, you 230 are partly a bawd, Pompey, howsoever you colour it in being a tapster, are you not? Come, tell me true; it shall be the better for you.

POM. Truly, sir, I am a poor fellow that would live. 235

ESCAL. How would you live, Pompey? By being a bawd? What do you think of the trade, Pompey? Is it a lawful trade?

POM. If the law would allow it, sir.

ESCAL. But the law will not allow it, Pompey; nor it shall not be allowed in Vienna. 241

POM. Does your worship mean to geld and splay all the youth of the city?

ESCAL. No, Pompey.

162. **suppos'd**, blunder for "deposed" = sworn. 169. **an it like**, if it please. 171. **respected**, blunder for "suspected." 174. **varlet**, scoundrel. 180. **Justice or Iniquity**, the constable or the clown. The Vice or Iniquity of morality plays. 182. **caitiff**, base wretch. 183. **Hannibal**, blunder for "cannibal." 200. **continue**, Elbow thinks the word describes some punishment. 215. **draw you**, (1) draw liquor for you, (2) drain you, i.e., swindle you, (3) draw to execution on a hurdle, (4) draw and quarter. 220. **drawn in**, taken in, cheated. 228. **Troth**, in truth. 231. **colour**, disguise. 242. **geld**, castrate; **splay**, remove the ovaries.

POM. Truly, sir, in my poor opinion, 245 they will to't then. If your worship will take order for the drabs and the knaves, you need not to fear the bawds.

ESCAL. There is pretty orders beginning, I can tell you. It is but heading and hanging. 250

POM. If you head and hang all that offend that way but for ten year together, you'll be glad to give out a commission for more heads. If this law hold in Vienna ten year, I'll rent the fairest house in it after three-pence a 255 bay. If you live to see this come to pass, say Pompey told you so.

ESCAL. Thank you, good Pompey; and, in requital of your prophecy, hark you: I advise you, let me not find you before me again 260 upon any complaint whatsoever; no, not for dwelling where you do. If I do, Pompey, I shall beat you to your tent, and prove a shrewd Cæsar to you; in plain dealing, Pompey, I shall have you whipt. So, for this time, Pompey, fare you well. 265

POM. I thank your worship for your good counsel; [*Aside*] but I shall follow it as the flesh and fortune shall better determine.
Whip me? No, no; let carman whip his jade;
The valiant heart's not whipt out of his
trade. [*Exit.* 270

ESCAL. Come hither to me, Master Elbow; come hither, Master constable. How long have you been in this place of constable?

ELB. Seven year and a half, sir.

ESCAL. I thought, by the readiness in 275 the office, you had continued in it some time. You say, seven years together?

ELB. And a half, sir.

ESCAL. Alas, it hath been great pains to you. They do you wrong to put you so oft 280 upon't. Are there not men in your ward sufficient to serve it?

ELB. Faith, sir, few of any wit in such matters. As they are chosen, they are glad to choose me for them. I do it for some piece of money, and go through with all. 285

ESCAL. Look you bring me in the names of some six or seven, the most sufficient of your parish.

ELB. To your worship's house, sir?

ESCAL. To my house. Fare you well.
[*Exit* ELBOW.]
What's o'clock, think you? 290

JUST. Eleven, sir.

ESCAL. I pray you home to dinner with me.

JUST. I humbly thank you.

ESCAL. It grieves me for the death of
Claudio;
But there's no remedy. 295

JUST. Lord Angelo is severe.

ESCAL. It is but needful.
Mercy is not itself, that oft looks so;
Pardon is still the nurse of second woe.
But yet,—poor Claudio! There is no remedy.
Come, sir. [*Exeunt.* 300

SCENE II. *Another room in the same.*

[*Enter* PROVOST *and a* SERVANT.]

SER. He's hearing of a cause; he will come straight. I'll tell him of you.

PROV. Pray you, do.
[*Exit* SERVANT.]
I'll know
His pleasure; may be he will relent. Alas,
He hath but as offended in a dream!
All sects, all ages smack of this vice; and he 5
To die for't!

[*Enter* ANGELO.]

ANG. Now, what's the matter, Provost?

PROV. Is it your will Claudio shall die to-
morrow?

ANG. Did not I tell thee yea? Hadst thou
not order?
Why dost thou ask again?

PROV. Lest I might be too rash.
Under your good correction, I have seen 10
When, after execution, judgement hath
Repented o'er his doom.

ANG. Go to; let that be mine.

246. take order for, attend to. 247. drabs, harlots. 249. There is, there are. 250. heading, beheading. 255. after . . . bay, at the rate of three pence a bay window. 258. in requital of, as a reward for. 263. beat . . . tent, as Cæsar did after the Battle of Pharsalia, 48 B.C.; shrewd, evil. 269. carman, teamster; jade, worn-out horse. 275. readiness in, familiarity with. 280. put . . . upon't, to impose it upon you so often. 281. sufficient . . . it, capable of assuming the burden. 283. choose . . . them, the constable, an elected officer, usually hired a deputy to perform his duties. 291. Eleven, the gentry and students dined at 11 A.M., the merchants about an hour later. Scene ii: 2. straight, straightway, at once. 4. but . . . dream, only, as it were, offended in a dream. 5. smack of, have a touch of. 12. o'er his doom, of its decree (to death); Go to, i.e., come, come; mine, i.e., my affair.

Do you your office, or give up your place,
And you shall well be spar'd.

PROV. I crave your honour's pardon.
What shall be done, sir, with the groaning Juliet? 15
She's very near her hour.

ANG. Dispose of her
To some more fitter place, and that with speed.

[*Re-enter* SERVANT.]

SERV. Here is the sister of the man condemn'd
Desires access to you.

ANG. Hath he a sister?

PROV. Ay, my good lord; a very virtuous maid, 20
And to be shortly of a sisterhood,
If not already.

ANG. Well, let her be admitted.
[*Exit* SERVANT.]
See you the fornicatress be remov'd.
Let her have needful, but not lavish, means;
There shall be order for't.

[*Enter* ISABELLA *and* LUCIO.]

PROV. God save your honour! 25

ANG. Stay a little while. [*To* ISAB.] You're welcome; what's your will?

ISAB. I am a woeful suitor to your honour,
Please but your honour hear me.

ANG. Well; what's your suit?

ISAB. There is a vice that most I do abhor,
And most desire should meet the blow of justice; 30
For which I would not plead, but that I must;
For which I must not plead, but that I am
At war 'twixt will and will not.

ANG. Well; the matter?

ISAB. I have a brother is condemn'd to die.
I do beseech you, let it be his fault, 35
And not my brother.

PROV. [*Aside*] Heaven give thee moving graces!

ANG. Condemn the fault, and not the actor of it?
Why, every fault's condemn'd ere it be done.
Mine were the very cipher of a function,
To fine the faults whose fine stands in record, 40
And let go by the actor.

ISAB. O just but severe law!
I had a brother, then. Heaven keep your honour!

LUC. [*Aside to* ISAB.] Give't not o'er so. To him again, entreat him,
Kneel down before him, hang upon his gown.
You are too cold. If you should need a pin, 45
You could not with more tame a tongue desire it.
To him, I say!

ISAB. Must he needs die?

ANG. Maiden, no remedy.

ISAB. Yes; I do think that you might pardon him,
And neither heaven nor man grieve at the mercy. 50

ANG. I will not do't.

ISAB. But can you, if you would?

ANG. Look, what I will not, that I cannot do.

ISAB. But might you do't, and do the world no wrong,
If so your heart were touch'd with that remorse
As mine is to him?

ANG. He's sentenc'd; 'tis too late.

LUC. [*Aside to* ISAB.] You are too cold. 56

ISAB. Too late? Why, no, I, that do speak a word,
May call it back again. Well believe this,
No ceremony that to great ones longs,
Not the king's crown, nor the deputed sword, 60
The marshal's truncheon, nor the judge's robe,
Become them with one half so good a grace
As mercy does.
If he had been as you and you as he,
You would have slipt like him; but he, like you, 65
Would not have been so stern.

ANG. Pray you, be gone.

ISAB. I would to heaven I had your potency,
And you were Isabel! Should it then be thus?

13. your office, the duties of your position. 14. And . . . spar'd, i.e., and we can get on well without you. 15. groaning, here = pregnant. 28. please but, if it but please. 33. 'twixt . . . not, between my affection which leads me to plead and my virtue which makes me detest the crime. 35. let . . . fault, i.e., let his faults be condemned to die, i.e., extirpated. 39. function, office. 40. fine, punishment; record, the statute. 41. go by, escape; actor, culprit. 43. o'er, up. 45. pin, i.e., trifle. 46. tame, spiritless; desire, ask. 54. remorse, pity. 58. Well . . . this, be completely assured of this. 59. ceremony, ritual; longs, belongs. 60. deputed sword, sword carried before a deputy, as the symbol of his authority. 61. truncheon, staff of office. 67. potency, power.

No; I would tell what 'twere to be a judge,
And what a prisoner.

LUC. [*Aside to* ISAB.] Ay, touch him; there's the vein.

ANG. Your brother is a forfeit of the law, 71
And you but waste your words.

ISAB. Alas, alas!
Why, all the souls that were were forfeit once;
And He that might the vantage best have took
Found out the remedy. How would you be, 75
If He, which is the top of judgement should
But judge you as you are? O, think on that;
And mercy then will breathe within your lips,
Like man new made.

ANG. Be you content, fair maid.
It is the law, not I condemn your brother. 80
Were he my kinsman, brother, or my son,
It should be thus with him. He must die tomorrow.

ISAB. To-morrow! O, that's sudden! Spare him, spare him!
He's not prepared for death. Even for our kitchens
We kill the fowl of season. Shall we serve Heaven 85
With less respect than we do minister
To our gross selves? Good, good my lord, bethink you:
Who is it that hath died for this offence?
There's many have committed it.

LUC. [*Aside to* ISAB.] Ay, well said.

ANG. The law hath not been dead, though it hath slept. 90
Those many had not dar'd to do that evil,
If [but] the first that did the edict infringe
Had answer'd for his deed. Now 'tis awake,
Takes note of what is done, and, like a prophet,
Looks in a glass that shows what future evils, 95
Either new, or by remissness new-conceiv'd,
And so in progress to be hatch'd and born,
Are now to have no successive degrees,
But, ere they live, to end.

ISAB. Yet show some pity.

ANG. I show it most of all when I show justice, 100
For then I pity those I do not know,
Which a dismiss'd offence would after gall;
And do him right that, answering one foul wrong,
Lives not to act another. Be satisfied.
Your brother dies to-morrow. Be content. 105

ISAB. So you must be the first that gives this sentence,
And he, that suffers. O, it is excellent
To have a giant's strength; but it is tyrannous
To use it like a giant.

LUC. [*Aside to* ISAB.] That's well said.

ISAB. Could great men thunder 110
As Jove himself does, Jove would ne'er be quiet;
For every pelting, petty officer
Would use his heaven for thunder,
Nothing but thunder! Merciful Heaven, 114
Thou rather with thy sharp and sulphurous bolt
Splits the unwedgeable and gnarlèd oak
Than the soft myrtle; but man, proud man,
Dress'd in a little brief authority,
Most ignorant of what he's most assur'd,
His glassy essence, like an angry ape, 120
Plays such fantastic tricks before high heaven
As makes the angels weep; who, with our spleens,
Would all themselves laugh mortal.

LUC. [*Aside to* ISAB.] O, to him, to him, wench! he will relent.
He's coming; I perceive't.

PROV. [*Aside*] Pray Heaven she win him! 125

ISAB. We cannot weigh our brother with ourself.
Great men may jest with saints; 'tis wit in them,
But in the less foul profanation.

LUC. Thou'rt i' the right, girl. More o' that.

ISAB. That in the captain's but a choleric word, 130

69. **tell**, show. 74. **the . . took**, i.e., punished mankind according to its deserts. 76. **top of judgement**, i.e., the Supreme Judge. 79. **new made**, regenerated. 85. **of season**, at the proper season, i.e., only when fattened. 87. **our gross selves**, the base side of our nature. 93. **answer'd**, paid the penalty. 95. **glass**, i.e., a beryl stone in which one reveals the future. 98. **successive degrees**, descendants. 103. **answering**, rendering account for. 107. **that suffers**, i.e., the first to suffer. 109. **like a giant**, i.e., a savage giant of the romances. 112. **pelting**, paltry. 116. **unwedgeable**, not to be split with wedges. 117. **soft**, delicate, because it cannot stand the cold. 119. **assur'd**, sure of. 120. **His . . . essence**, his spirit as destructible as glass and as incapable of lasting impressions. 122. **spleens**, uncontrollable fits of laughter. 123. **mortal**, i.e., to death. 126. **weigh**, compare, i.e., because "we have different names and different judgment for the same faults committed by persons of different condition." 130. **choleric**, hot tempered.

Which in the soldier is flat blasphemy.

LUC. [*Aside to* ISAB.] Art avis'd o' that? More on't.

ANG. Why do you put these sayings upon me?

ISAB. Because authority, though it err like others,
Hath yet a kind of medicine in itself, 135
That skins the vice o' the top. Go to your bosom;
Knock there, and ask your heart what it doth know
That's like my brother's fault. If it confess
A natural guiltiness such as is his,
Let it not sound a thought upon your tongue 140
Against my brother's life.

ANG. [*Aside*] She speaks, and 'tis
Such sense, that my sense breeds with it.—Fare you well.

ISAB. Gentle my lord, turn back.

ANG. I will bethink me. Come again to-morrow.

ISAB. Hark how I'll bribe you. Good my lord, turn back. 145

ANG. How! bribe me?

ISAB. Ay, with such gifts that Heaven shall share with you.

LUC. [*Aside to* ISAB.] You had marr'd all else.

ISAB. Not with fond shekels of the tested gold,
Or stones whose rates are either rich or poor 150
As fancy values them; but with true prayers
That shall be up at heaven and enter there
Ere sun-rise, prayers from preservèd souls,
From fasting maids whose minds are dedicate
To nothing temporal.

ANG. Well, come to me to-morrow.

LUC. [*Aside to* ISAB.] Go to; 'tis well. Away! 156

ISAB. Heaven keep your honour safe!

ANG. [*Aside*] Amen!
For I am that way going to temptation.
Where prayers cross.

ISAB. At what hour to-morrow
Shall I attend your lordship?

ANG. At any time 'fore noon. 160

ISAB. 'Save your honour!

[*Exeunt* ISABELLA, LUCIO, *and* PROVOST.

ANG. From thee, even from thy virtue.
What's this, what's this? Is this her fault or mine?
The tempter or the tempted, who sins most?
Ha!
Not she, nor doth she tempt; but it is I 165
That, lying by the violet in the sun,
Do as the carrion does, not as the flower,
Corrupt with virtuous season. Can it be
That modesty may more betray our sense
Than woman's lightness? Having waste ground enough, 170
Shall we desire to raze the sanctuary
And pitch our evils there? O, fie, fie, fie!
What dost thou, or what art thou, Angelo?
Dost thou desire her foully for those things
That make her good? O, let her brother live!
Thieves for their robbery have authority 176
When judges steal themselves. What, do I love her,
That I desire to hear her speak again
And feast upon her eyes? What is't I dream on?
O cunning enemy, that, to catch a saint, 180
With saints dost bait thy hook! Most dangerous
Is that temptation that doth goad us on
To sin in loving virtue. Never could the strumpet,
With all her double vigour, art and nature,
Once stir my temper; but this virtuous maid 185
Subdues me quite. Ever till now,
When men were fond, I smil'd and wond'red how. [*Exit.*

SCENE III. *A room in a prison.*

[*Enter, severally,* DUKE, *disguised as a friar, and* PROVOST.]

DUKE. Hail to you, Provost! so I think you are.

132. **avis'd,** aware. 136. **skins,** covers with skin. An unhealed sore, i.e., a vice. 142. **sense,** sensuality; **breeds,** is stimulated. 144. **bethink me,** think it over. 145. **turn back,** change sides (in the argument). 148. **you . . . else,** otherwise you would have spoiled everything. 149. **fond shekels,** shekels of trifling value. 150. **rates,** value. 153. **preserved souls,** souls preserved from the world's corruption. 159. **where . . . cross,** i.e., where his desire for Isabella conflicts with her desire that he act generously and honorably. 161. **'Save,** God Save. 168. **corrupt . . . the season,** decay in summer, when it comes to maturity. 169. **betray our sense,** (1) entrap our feelings, (2) sensuality. 170. **lightness,** lewdness. 172. **pitch our evils,** set our privies. 184. **art and nature,** natural ability and acquired skill. 185. **temper,** passion. 187. **fond,** foolishly doting.

PROV. I am the Provost. What's your will, good friar?
DUKE. Bound by my charity and my blest order,
I come to visit the afflicted spirits
Here in the prison. Do me the common right 5
To let me see them and to make me know
The nature of their crimes, that I may minister
To them accordingly.
PROV. I would do more than that, if more were needful.

[*Enter* JULIET.]

Look, here comes one; a gentlewoman of mine, 10
Who, falling in the flaws of her own youth,
Hath blister'd her report. She is with child;
And he that got it, sentenc'd; a young man
More fit to do another such offence
Than die for this. 15
DUKE. When must he die?
PROV. As I do think, to-morrow.
I have provided for you. Stay awhile,
[*To* JULIET]
And you shall be conducted.
DUKE. Repent you, fair one, of the sin you carry?
JUL. I do; and bear the shame most patiently. 20
DUKE. I'll teach you how you shall arraign your conscience,
And try your penitence, if it be sound
Or hollowly put on.
JUL. I'll gladly learn.
DUKE. Love you the man that wrong'd you?
JUL. Yes, as I love the woman that wrong'd him. 25
DUKE. So then it seems your most offenceful act
Was mutually committed?
JUL. Mutually.
DUKE. Then was your sin of heavier kind than his.
JUL. I do confess it, and repent it, father.
DUKE. 'Tis meet so, daughter; but lest you do repent, 30
As that the sin hath brought you to this shame,
Which sorrow is always towards ourselves, not heaven,
Showing we would not spare heaven as we love it,
But as we stand in fear,—
JUL. I do repent me, as it is an evil, 35
And take the shame with joy.
DUKE. There rest.
Your partner, as I hear, must die to-morrow,
And I am going with instruction to him.
Grace go with you, *Benedicite!* [*Exit.*
JUL. Must die to-morrow! O injurious law, 40
That respites me a life whose very comfort
Is still a dying horror!
PROV. 'Tis pity of him.
[*Exeunt.*

SCENE IV. *A room in* ANGELO'S *house.*

[*Enter* ANGELO.]

ANG. When I would pray and think, I think and pray
To several subjects. Heaven hath my empty words,
Whilst my invention, hearing not my tongue,
Anchors on Isabel; Heaven in my mouth,
As if I did but only chew his name, 5
And in my heart the strong and swelling evil
Of my conception. The state, whereon I studied,
Is like a good thing, being often read,
Grown sear'd and tedious; yea, my gravity,
Wherein—let no man hear me—I take pride, 10
Could I with boot change for an idle plume,
Which the air beats for vain. O place, O form,
How often dost thou with thy case, thy habit,

Scene iii: 4-5. **spirits . . . prison**, cf. I Peter III, 18, 19: "Christ . . . being put to death in the flesh, but quickened by the Spirit. By which also he went and preached unto the spirits in prison." 10. **of mine**, i.e., because she had been placed in his care. 11. **flaws**, gusty passions. 12. **blister'd**, blemished; **report**, reputation. 18. **conducted**, attended. 23. **hollowly**, insincerely. 31. **As**, because. 33. **Not . . . it**, Not keep from grieving God because we love him. 36. **There rest**, i.e., remain in this state of mind. 38. **instruction**, spiritual advice. 39. **Grace**, i.e., God (as the source of grace). 41. **respites**, reprieves, i.e., the law condemned the man to death and decreed that the woman should be "infamously noted" forever after. 42. **is still**, i.e., will always be. Scene iv: 2. **several subjects**, different objects. 3. **invention**, imagination. 5. **his**, its. 6. **swelling**, i.e., rapidly growing. 7. **state . . . studied**, the dignity of bearing which I studied (to attain). 9. **sear'd**, threadbare. 11. **with boot**, throwing in something to boot; **idle plume**, silly feather (on a gallant's hat). 12. **beats for vain**, flutters to no purpose with a play on vane = weathercock; **form**, external appearances. 13. **case**, covering, outergarment.

Wrench awe from fools and tie the wiser souls
To thy false seeming! Blood, thou art blood. 15
Let's write good angel on the devil's horn;
'Tis not the devil's crest.

[*Enter a* SERVANT.]

How now! who's there?

SERV. One Isabel, a sister, desires access to you.

ANG. Teach her the way. [*Exit* SERV.] O heavens!
Why does my blood thus muster to my heart, 20
Making both it unable for itself,
And dispossessing all my other parts
Of necessary fitness?
So play the foolish throngs with one that swoons;
Come all to help him, and so stop the air 25
By which he should revive; and even so
The general subject to a well-wish'd king
Quit their own part, and in obsequious fondness
Crowd to his presence, where their untaught love
Must needs appear offence.

[*Enter* ISABELLA.]

How now, fair maid?

ISAB. I am come to know your pleasure. 31

ANG. That you might know it, would much better please me
Than to demand what 'tis. Your brother cannot live.

ISAB. Even so. Heaven keep your honour!

ANG. Yet may he live a while; and, it may be, 35
As long as you or I. Yet he must die.

ISAB. Under your sentence?

ANG. Yea.

ISAB. When, I beseech you? that in his reprieve,
Longer or shorter, he may be so fitted 40
That his soul sicken not.

ANG. Ha! fie, these filthy vices! It were as good
To pardon him that hath from nature stolen
A man already made, as to remit
Their saucy sweetness that do coin Heaven's image 45
In stamps that are forbid. 'Tis all as easy
Falsely to take away a life true made
As to put metal in restrainèd means
To make a false one.

ISAB. 'Tis set down so in heaven, but not in earth. 50

ANG. Say you so? Then I shall pose you quickly.
Which had you rather, that the most just law
Now took your brother's life; or, to redeem him,
Give up your body to such sweet uncleanness
As she that he hath stain'd?

ISAB. Sir, believe this,
I had rather give my body than my soul. 56

ANG. I talk not of your soul; our compell'd sins
Stand more for number than for accompt.

ISAB. How say you?

ANG. Nay, I'll not warrant that; for I can speak
Against the thing I say. Answer to this: 60
I, now the voice of the recorded law,
Pronounce a sentence on your brother's life.
Might there not be a charity in sin
To save this brother's life?

ISAB. Please you to do't,
I'll take it as a peril to my soul, 65
It is no sin at all but charity.

ANG. Pleas'd you to do't at peril of your soul,
Were equal poise of sin and charity.

ISAB. That I do beg his life, if it be sin,
Heaven let me bear it! You granting of my suit, 70

15. **blood**, passion. 16-7. **Let's . . . crest**, let us call the devil a good angel then his badge ceases to be that of a devil. 19. **teach**, show. 20. **muster**, rush. 22. **parts**, organs. 25-30. **So . . . offence**, a flattering reference to King James' positive fear of crowds. 27. **general subject**, i.e., the populace. 28. **part**, duties; **fondness**, folly. 31. **pleasure**, Angelo puts a double entendre into the phrase. making it mean, "give you pleasure through sexual intercourse." 40 **fitted**, prepared for death (by a priest). 43. **hath . . . stolen**, i.e., murdered. 44. **remit**, forgive. 45. **saucy sweetness**, wanton pleasure. 46. **stamps**, dies (for making coins); **'Tis . . . easy**, it is no worse. 48. **metal**, the stuff of life; **put . . . means**, use a metal in a forbidden way, i.e., beget a bastard. 51. **pose**, put you in a quandary. 56. **give my body**, i.e., to death. 58. **stand . . . accompt**, however numerous are not laid up to our account as sins; **How say you?** What are you saying? 59. **warrant**, act as guarantor for. 67. **Pleas'd you**, if you should be pleased. 68. **were**, it would be; **poise**, weight

If that be sin, I'll make it my morn prayer
To have it added to the faults of mine,
And nothing of your answer.

ANG. Nay, but hear me;
Your sense pursues not mine. Either you are ignorant,
Or seem so craftily; and that's not good. 75

ISAB. Let me be ignorant, and in nothing good,
But graciously to know I am no better.

ANG. Thus wisdom wishes to appear most bright
When it doth tax itself; as these black masks
Proclaim an enshield beauty ten times louder 80
Than beauty could, displayed. But mark me:
To be receivèd plain, I'll speak more gross.
Your brother is to die.

ISAB. So.

ANG. And his offence is so, as it appears, 85
Accountant to the law upon that pain.

ISAB. True.

ANG. Admit no other way to save his life,—
As I subscribe not that, nor any other,
But in the loss of question,—that you, his sister, 90
Finding yourself desir'd of such a person
Whose credit with the judge, or own great place,
Could fetch your brother from the manacles
Of the all-building law; and that there were
No earthly mean to save him, but that either 95
You must lay down the treasures of your body
To this supposed, or else to let him suffer;
What would you do?

ISAB. As much for my poor brother as myself:
That is, were I under the terms of death, 100
The impression of keen whips I'd wear as rubies,
And strip myself to death, as to a bed
That, longing, have been sick for, ere I'd yield
My body up to shame.

ANG. Then must your brother die.

ISAB. And 'twere the cheaper way. 105
Better it were a brother died at once,
Than that a sister, by redeeming him,
Should die for ever.

ANG. Were not you then as cruel as the sentence
That you have slander'd so? 110

ISAB. Ignominy in ransom and free pardon
Are of two houses. Lawful mercy
Is nothing kin to foul redemption.

ANG. You seem'd of late to make the law a tyrant;
And rather prov'd the sliding of your brother
A merriment than a vice. 116

ISAB. O, pardon me, my lord. It oft falls out,
To have what we would have, we speak not what we mean.
I something do excuse the thing I hate,
For his advantage that I dearly love. 120

ANG. We are all frail.

ISAB. Else let my brother die,
If not a fedary, but only he
Owe and succeed this weakness.

ANG. Nay, women are frail too.

ISAB. Ay, as the glasses where they view themselves. 125
Which are as easy broke as they make forms.
Women! Help Heaven! men their creation mar
In profiting by them. Nay, call us ten times frail,
For we are soft as our complexions are,
And credulous to false prints.

ANG. I think it well. 130
And from this testimony of your own sex—
Since, I suppose, we are made to be no stronger
Than faults may shake our frames—let me be bold—
I do arrest your words. Be that you are,
That is, a woman. If you be more, you're none. 135
If you be one—as you are well expressed
By all external warrants—show it now,

73. **of your answer,** that you must answer for. 74. **are ignorant,** i.e., you do not get my meaning. 75. **craftily,** out of cunning. 79. **tax,** reproach; **these black masks,** i.e., the fashionable masks you women wear. 80. **enshield,** hidden. 82. **received plain,** clearly understood; **gross,** plainly. 86. **accountant,** accountable; **pain,** punishment. 88. **Admit,** suppose (there were). 89-90. **As . . . question,** As I admit that or anything else only for the sake of argument. 94. **all building,** probably a corruption of all-binding. 97. **supposed,** i.e., hypothetical person. 100. **were . . . death,** i.e., were I condemned to die. 111. **Ignominy in ransom,** an ignominious way of rescuing him. 112. **of two houses,** belong to two different families. 115. **sliding,** back sliding, offense. 121-3. **Else . . . weakness.** This passage is corrupt, but it means about as follows: Otherwise (i.e., if we are not all frail) let my brother die, since then no confederate but only he inherits and owns human weakness. 127. **creation,** i.e., woman's nature. 128. **profiting by,** taking advantage of. 130. **credulous . . . prints,** deceived by false impressions. 134. **I . . . words,** I take you at your word.

By putting on the destined livery.

ISAB. I have no tongue but one. Gentle my lord,
Let me entreat you speak the former language. 140

ANG. Plainly conceive, I love you.

ISAB. My brother did love Juliet
And you tell me he shall die for it.

ANG. He shall not, Isabel, if you give me love.

ISAB. I know your virtue hath a license in't, 145
Which seems a little fouler than it is,
To pluck on others.

ANG. Believe me, on mine honor,
My words express my purpose.

ISAB. Ha! Little honor to be much believed,
And most pernicious purpose! Seeming, seeming!— 150
I will proclaim thee, Angelo, look for't.
Sign me a present pardon for my brother,
Or with an outstretch'd throat I'll tell the world aloud
What man thou art.

ANG. Who will believe thee, Isabel?
My unsoil'd name, the austereness of my life,
My vouch against you, and my place i' the state, 156
Will so your accusation overweigh,
That you shall stifle in your own report
And smell of calumny. I have begun,
And now I give my sensual race the rein. 160
Fit thy consent to my sharp appetite;
Lay by all nicety and prolixious blushes
That banish what they sue for; redeem thy brother
By yielding up thy body to my will;
Or else he must not only die the death, 165
But thy unkindness shall his death draw out
To lingering sufferance. Answer me to-morrow,
Or, by the affection that now guides me most,
I'll prove a tyrant to him. As for you,
Say what you can, my false o'erweighs your true. [*Exit.* 170

ISAB. To whom should I complain? Did I tell this,
Who would believe me? O perilous mouths,
That bear in them one and the self-same tongue,
Either of condemnation or approof;
Bidding the law make curtsy to their will; 175
Hooking both right and wrong to the appetite,
To follow as it draws! I'll to my brother.
Though he hath fallen by prompture of the blood,
Yet hath he in him such a mind of honour
That, had he twenty heads to tender down 180
On twenty bloody blocks, he'd yield them up,
Before his sister should her body stoop
To such abhorr'd pollution.
Then, Isabel, live chaste, and, brother, die;
More than our brother is our chastity. 185
I'll tell him yet of Angelo's request,
And fit his mind to death, for his soul's rest. [*Exit.*

ACT III

SCENE I. *A room in the prison.*

[*Enter* DUKE, *disguised as before,* CLAUDIO, *and* PROVOST.]

DUKE. So then you hope of pardon from Lord Angelo?

CLAUD. The miserable have no other medicine
But only hope.
I've hope to live, and am prepar'd to die.

DUKE. Be absolute for death; either death or life 5
Shall thereby be the sweeter. Reason thus with life:
If I do lose thee, I do lose a thing
That none but fools would keep. A breath thou art,
Servile to all the skyey influences,
That dost this habitation where thou keep'st

138. destined livery, i.e., of submission to man. 140. former language, i.e., before you began to make indecent proposals. 152. sign . . . pardon, sign a pardon for me instantly. 156. vouch . . . you, denial of your charge. 160. race, natural disposition. 162. nicety, squeamishness; prolixious, superfluous; blushes, modesty. 167. sufferance, suffering. 168. affection, impulse, i.e., lust. 174. approof, approval. 178. prompture . . . blood, incitement of passion. 179. mind of honour, honorable mind. 180. tender down, offer to lay down. 182. stoop, yield. 186. yet, nevertheless. Act III, Scene i: 5. be absolute for death, fully make up your mind to die. 9. skyey influences, influences of the stars. 10. keep'st, dwell.

Hourly afflict. Merely, thou art Death's fool; 11
For him thou labour'st by thy flight to shun
And yet runn'st toward him still. Thou art not noble;
For all the accommodations that thou bear'st
Are nurs'd by baseness. Thou'rt by no means valiant; 15
For thou dost fear the soft and tender fork
Of a poor worm. Thy best of rest is sleep,
And that thou oft provok'st; yet grossly fear'st
Thy death, which is no more. Thou art not thyself;
For thou exist'st on many a thousand grains 20
That issue out of dust. Happy thou art not;
For what thou hast not, still thou striv'st to get,
And what thou hast, forget'st. Thou art not certain;
For thy complexion shifts to strange effects,
After the moon. If thou art rich, thou 'rt poor; 25
For, like an ass whose back with ingots bows,
Thou bear'st thy heavy riches but a journey,
And Death unloads thee. Friend hast thou none;
For thine own bowels, which do call thee sire,
The mere effusion of thy proper loins, 30
Do curse the gout, serpigo, and the rheum,
For ending thee no sooner. Thou hast nor youth nor age,
But, as it were, an after-dinner's sleep,
Dreaming on both; for all thy blessed youth
Becomes as aged, and doth beg the alms 35
Of palsied Eld; and when thou art old and rich,
Thou hast neither heat, affection, limb, nor beauty,
To make thy riches pleasant. What's yet in this
That bears the name of life? Yet in this life
Lie hid moe thousand deaths; yet death we fear,
That makes these odds all even. 41

CLAUD. I humbly thank you.
To sue to live, I find I seek to die;
And, seeking death, find life. Let it come on.

ISAB. [*Within.*] What, ho! Peace here; grace and good company!

PROV. Who's there? Come in; the wish deserves a welcome. 45

DUKE. Dear sir, ere long I'll visit you again.

CLAUD. Most holy sir, I thank you.

[*Enter* ISABELLA.]

ISAB. My business is a word or two with Claudio.

PROV. And very welcome. Look, signior, here's your sister. 50

DUKE. Provost, a word with you.

PROV. As many as you please.

DUKE. Bring me to hear them speak, where I may be conceal'd.

[*Exeunt* DUKE *and* PROVOST.

CLAUD. Now, sister, what's the comfort?

ISAB. Why,
As all comforts are; most good, most good indeed. 56
Lord Angelo, having affairs to heaven,
Intends you for his swift ambassador,
Where you shall be an everlasting leiger;
Therefore your best appointment make with speed, 60
To-morrow you set on.

CLAUD. Is there no remedy?

ISAB. None but such remedy as, to save a head,
To cleave a heart in twain.

CLAUD. But is there any?

ISAB. Yes, brother, you may live.
There is a devilish mercy in the judge, 65
If you'll implore it, that will free your life,
But fetter you till death.

CLAUD. Perpetual durance?

ISAB. Ay, just; perpetual durance, a restraint,
Though all the world's vastidity you had,
To a determin'd scope.

CLAUD. But in what nature? 70

ISAB. In such a one as, you consenting to't,

11. **Merely**, actually. The fool who vainly tried to escape Death was a favorite subject of dumb shows. 12. **labour'st**, make a strong effort. 13. **still**, always. 14. **accommodations**, comforts. 15. **nurs'd by baseness**, supplied by base services. 16. **fork**, forked tongue. 17. **poor worm**, insignificant snake. 18. **provok'st**, seek; **grossly**, out of all measure. 23. **certain**, stable. 24. **complexion**, constitution; **shifts . . . effects**, changes in strange ways. 25. **After**, like. 26. **ingots**, masses (of metal). 29. **bowels**, i.e., children. 30. **mere**, actual; **proper**, own. 31. **serpigo**, any skin disease; **rheum**, rheumatism. 31-41. None of Duke's arguments are based on Christian dogma; they are all Stoic commonplaces. 35-6. **beg . . . Eld**, charity for a paralyzed old man. 37. **heat**, ardor; **limb**, bodily vigor. 40. **moe thousand**, a thousand more. 56. **indeed**, essentially. 59. **leiger**, resident ambassador. 60. **appointment**, preparation. 69. **vastidity**, immensity. 70. **determin'd scope**, set confines (i.e., remorse for ignominy).

Would bark your honour from that trunk you bear,
And leave you naked.

CLAUD. Let me know the point.

ISAB. O, I do fear thee, Claudio; and I quake,
Lest thou a feverous life shouldst entertain, 75
And six or seven winters more respect
Than a perpetual honour. Dar'st thou die?
The sense of death is most in apprehension;
And the poor beetle, that we tread upon,
In corporal sufferance finds a pang as great 80
As when a giant dies.

CLAUD. Why give you me this shame?
Think you I can a resolution fetch
From flowery tenderness? If I must die,
I will encounter darkness as a bride,
And hug it in mine arms. 85

ISAB. There spake my brother; there my father's grave
Did utter forth a voice. Yes, thou must die.
Thou art too noble to conserve a life
In base appliances. This outward-sainted deputy,
Whose settled visage and deliberate word 90
Nips youth i' the head and follies doth emmew
As falcon doth the fowl, is yet a devil;
His filth within being cast, he would appear
A pond as deep as hell.

CLAUD. The prenzie Angelo!

ISAB. O, 'tis the cunning livery of hell, 95
The damned'st body to invest and cover
In prenzie guards! Dost thou think, Claudio?
If I would yield him my virginity,
Thou mightst be freed.

CLAUD. O heavens! it cannot be.

ISAB. Yes, he would give 't thee, from this rank offence, 100
So to offend him still. This night's the time
That I should do what I abhor to name,
Or else thou diest to-morrow.

CLAUD. Thou shalt not do't.

ISAB. O, were it but my life,
I'd throw it down for your deliverance 105
As frankly as a pin.

CLAUD. Thanks, dear Isabel.

ISAB. Be ready, Claudio, for your death to-morrow.

CLAUD. Yes. Has he affections in him,
That thus can make him bite the law by the nose,
When he would force it? Sure, it is no sin;
Or of the deadly seven it is the least. 111

ISAB. Which is the least?

CLAUD. If it were damnable, he being so wise,
Why would he for the momentary trick
Be perdurably fin'd? O Isabel! 115

ISAB. What says my brother?

CLAUD. Death is a fearful thing.

ISAB. And shamed life a hateful.

CLAUD. Ay, but to die, and go we know not where;
To lie in cold obstruction and to rot;
This sensible warm motion to become 120
A kneaded clod, and the delighted spirit
To bathe in fiery floods, or to reside
In thrilling region of thick-ribbed ice;
To be imprison'd in the viewless winds,
And blown with restless violence round about
The pendent world; or to be—worse than worst— 126
Of those that lawless and incertain thought
Imagine howling,—'tis too horrible!
The weariest and most loathed worldly life
That age, ache, penury, and imprisonment 130
Can lay on nature is a paradise
To what we fear of death.

ISAB. Alas, alas!

CLAUD. Sweet sister, let me live.
What sin you do to save a brother's life,
Nature dispenses with the deed so far 135
That it becomes a virtue.

ISAB. O you beast!
O faithless coward! O dishonest wretch!
Wilt thou be made a man out of my vice?
Is't not a kind of incest, to take life
From thine own sister's shame? What should I think? 140

72. bark, peel. 73. point, situation. 74. fear, fear for. 75. entertain, wish to maintain. 78. sense, physical pain; apprehension, imagination. 80. sufferance, suffering. 82. fetch, derive. 83. flowery tenderness, flowers of speech expressing compassion. 88. conserve, preserve. 89. in base appliances, through yielding to baseness. 90. settled, composed, grave. 91. emmew, coop up. 92. as . . . fowl, i.e., as sight of a falcon makes the chickens run for cover. 93. cast, cast up, vomited. 94. prenzie, an unknown word, probably a misreading; perhaps "prim" or "priestly." 96. invest, clothe. 97. guards, trimmings, embroidery; Dost . . . think, Can you believe it? 100. give't, allow; from, in consequence of. 101. so . . . still, to continue offending in this way forever. 106. frankly, freely. 108. affections, passions. 109. bite . . . nose, flout the law. 110. would force it, is enforcing it (against another). 115. perdurably fin'd, forever punished. 119. obstruction, rigidity. 120. sensible, feeling; motion, movement of the mind; hence, mind. 121. delighted, i.e., capable of delight. 123. thrilling, i.e., piercing (with cold). 124. viewless, invisible. 126. pendent, hanging (in the void). 135. dispenses with, excuses.

Heaven shield my mother play'd my father fair!
For such a warpèd slip of wilderness
Ne'er issu'd from his blood. Take my defiance!
Die, perish! Might but my bending down
Reprieve thee from thy fate, it should proceed.
I'll pray a thousand prayers for thy death, 146
No word to save thee.

CLAUD. Nay, hear me, Isabel.

ISAB. O, fie, fie, fie!
Thy sin's not accidental, but a trade.
Mercy to thee would prove itself a bawd; 150
'Tis best that thou diest quickly.

CLAUD. O hear me, Isabella!

[*Re-enter* DUKE.]

DUKE. Vouchsafe a word, young sister, but one word.

ISAB. What is your will?

DUKE. Might you dispense with your leisure, I would by and by have some speech 155 with you. The satisfaction I would require is likewise your own benefit.

ISAB. I have no superfluous leisure; my stay must be stolen out of other affairs; but I will attend you a while. [*Walks apart.* 160

DUKE. Son, I have overheard what hath pass'd between you and your sister. Angelo had never the purpose to corrupt her; only he hath made an assay of her virtue to practise his judgement with the disposition of 165 natures. She, having the truth of honour in her, hath made him that gracious denial which he is most glad to receive. I am confessor to Angelo, and I know this to be true; therefore prepare yourself to death. Do not satisfy 170 your resolution with hopes that are fallible; to-morrow you must die. Go to your knees and make ready.

CLAUD. Let me ask my sister pardon. I am so out of love with life that I will sue to 175 be rid of it.

DUKE. Hold you there! Farewell. [*Exit* CLAUDIO.] Provost, a word with you!

[*Re-enter* PROVOST.]

PROV. What's your will, father?

DUKE. That now you are come, you will be gone. Leave me a while with the maid. 180 My mind promises with my habit no loss shall touch her by my company.

PROV. In good time.

[*Exit* PROVOST. ISABELLA *comes forward.*

DUKE. The hand that hath made you fair hath made you good; the goodness that 185 is cheap in beauty makes beauty brief in goodness; but grace, being the soul of your complexion, shall keep the body of it ever fair. The assault that Angelo hath made to you, fortune hath convey'd to my understand- 190 ing; and, but that frailty hath examples for his falling, I should wonder at Angelo. How will you do to content this substitute, and to save your brother?

ISAB. I am now going to resolve him. I had rather my brother die by the law than 195 my son should be unlawfully born. But, O, how much is the good Duke deceiv'd in Angelo! If ever he return and I can speak to him, I will open my lips in vain, or discover his government.

DUKE. That shall not be much amiss: 200 yet, as the matter now stands, he will avoid your accusation; he made trial of you only. Therefore fasten your ear on my advisings. To the love I have in doing good a remedy presents itself. I do make myself believe 205 that you may most uprighteously do a poor wronged lady a merited benefit, redeem your brother from the angry law, do no stain to your own gracious person, and much please the absent Duke, if peradventure he shall ever return to have hearing of this business. 211

ISAB. Let me hear you speak farther. I have spirit to do anything that appears not foul in the truth of my spirit.

DUKE. Virtue is bold, and goodness 215

141. **shield**, forbid, i.e., God grant my mother deceived my father and that you are no son of his. 142. **wilderness**, wildness. 143. **defiance**, indignant rejection. 148. **fie**, in Shakespeare's day was an expression of deep disgust. 149. **accidental**, occasional. 155. **by and by**, at once. 156. **satisfaction**, payment. 160. **attend**, wait for. 164. **assay**, trial. 164-5. **practice . . . natures**, experiment with the constitution of human nature. 167. **gracious**, controlled by divine influence. 170-1. **satisfy . . . resolution**, sustain your courage. 171. **fallible**, false. 176. **Hold you there**, stick to that. 181. **habit**, i.e., priestly garments. 183. **In good time**, very well. 186. **in beauty**, when associated with beauty; **makes . . . goodness**, i.e., makes the association brief. 187. **soul . . . complexion**, the essence of your disposition. 188. **body of it**, external manifestations of your grace, i.e., your beauty. 193 **substitute**, deputy, i.e., Angelo. 194. **resolve**, set his mind at rest. 199. **discover his government**, expose his misgovernment. 201. **avoid**, refute. 202. **he . . . only**, i.e., this is what he will say. 206. **uprighteously**, uprightly, justly.

never fearful. Have you not heard speak of Mariana, the sister of Frederick, the great soldier who miscarried at sea?

ISAB. I have heard of the lady, and good words went with her name. 220

DUKE. She should this Angelo have married; was affianced to her by oath, and the nuptial appointed; between which time of the contract and limit of the solemnity, her brother Frederick was wreck'd at sea, having in 225 that perished vessel the dowry of his sister. But mark how heavily this befell to the poor gentlewoman. There she lost a noble and renowned brother, in his love toward her ever most kind and natural; with him, the portion and sinew of her fortune, her marriage-dowry; with both, her combinate husband, this well-seeming Angelo. 232

ISAB. Can this be so? Did Angelo so leave her?

DUKE. Left her in her tears, and dried not one of them with his comfort; swallowed 235 his vows whole, pretending in her discoveries of dishonour; in few, bestow'd her on her own lamentation, which she yet wears for his sake; and he, a marble to her tears, is washed with them, but relents not.

ISAB. What a merit were it in death to 240 take this poor maid from the world! What corruption in this life, that it will let this man live! But how out of this can she avail?

DUKE. It is a rupture that you may easily heal; and the cure of it not only saves 245 your brother, but keeps you from dishonour in doing it.

ISAB. Show me how, good father.

DUKE. This forenamed maid hath yet in her the continuance of her first affection; his unjust unkindness, that in all reason should 250 have quenched her love, hath, like an impediment in the current, made it more violent and unruly. Go you to Angelo; answer his requiring with a plausible obedience; agree with his demands to the point; only refer yourself to this advantage, first, that your stay 255 with him may not be long; that the time may have all shadow and silence in it; and the place answer to convenience. This being granted in course,—and now follows all,—we shall advise this wronged maid to stead 260 up your appointment, go in your place. If the encounter acknowledge itself hereafter, it may compel him to her recompense; and here, by this is your brother saved, your honour untainted, the poor Mariana ad- 265 vantaged, and the corrupt deputy scaled. The maid will I frame and make fit for his attempt. If you think well to carry this as you may, the doubleness of the benefit defends the deceit from reproof. What think you of it?

ISAB. The image of it gives me content 270 already; and I trust it will grow to a most prosperous perfection.

DUKE. It lies much in your holding up. Haste you speedily to Angelo. If for this night he entreat you to his bed, give him promise 275 of satisfaction. I will presently to Saint Luke's; there, at the moated grange, resides this dejected Mariana. At that place call upon me; and dispatch with Angelo, that it may be quickly.

ISAB. I thank you for this comfort. Fare you well, good father. 280

[*Exit* ISABELLA *and* DUKE.

SCENE II. *The street before the prison.*

[*Enter, on one side,* DUKE, *disguised as before; on the other,* ELBOW, *and* OFFICERS *with* POMPEY.]

ELB. Nay, if there be no remedy for it but that you will needs buy and sell men and women like beasts, we shall have all the world drink brown and white bastard.

DUKE. O heavens! what stuff is here? 5

POM. 'Twas never merry world since, of two usuries, the merriest was put down, and the worser allow'd by order of law a furr'd

218. miscarried, was lost. 222. affianced . . . oath, i.e., by the ceremony of troth-plight. 224. limit of, time appointed for; Solemnity, the wedding. 231. combinate, betrothed. 237. in few, in brief; bestow'd her on, left her to. 243. avail, profit. 255. to the point, to the minutest detail; refer yourself, have recourse to. 256. advantage, favorable condition. 258. shadow, darkness. 258-9. answer to convenience, be consistent with propriety. 260. stead . . . appointment, keep the appointment in your place. 262. If . . . itself, if the consequences of the meeting become evident.

266. scaled, weighed in the balance; frame, prepare. 268. carry, perform. 270. image, thought. 273. lies . . . up, it depends much upon you sustaining your part. 276. presently, at once. 277. moated grange, a farmhouse of enough importance to be protected by a moat. 279. dispatch, come to an agreement with. Scene ii: 4. bastard, a Spanish wine. 6-7. two usuries, (1) moneylending, (2) procuring.

gown to keep him warm; and furr'd with fox and lambskins too, to signify that craft, 10 being richer than innocency, stands for the facing.

ELB. Come your way, sir. 'Bless you, good father friar.

DUKE. And you, good brother father. What offence hath this man made you, sir? 15

ELB. Marry, sir, he hath offended the law; and, sir, we take him to be a thief too, sir, for we have found upon him, sir, a strange pick-lock, which we have sent to the deputy.

DUKE. Fie, sirrah! a bawd, a wicked bawd!
The evil that thou causest to be done, 21
That is thy means to live. Do thou but think
What 'tis to cram a maw or clothe a back
From such a filthy vice; say to thyself,
From their abominable and beastly touches 25
I drink, I eat, array myself, and live.
Canst thou believe thy living is a life,
So stinkingly depending? Go mend, go mend.

POM. Indeed, it does stink in some sort, sir; but yet, sir, I would prove— 30

DUKE. Nay, if the devil have given thee proofs for sin,
Thou wilt prove his. Take him to prison, officer.
Correction and instruction must both work
Ere this rude beast will profit.

ELB. He must before the deputy, sir; he 35 has given him warning. The deputy cannot abide a whoremaster. If he be a whoremonger, and comes before him, he were as good go a mile on his errand.

DUKE. That we were all, as some would seem to be, 40
Free from our faults, as faults from seeming, free!

[*Enter* LUCIO.]

ELB. His neck will come to your waist,—a cord, sir.

POM. I spy comfort; I cry bail. Here's a gentleman and a friend of mine.

LUC. How now, noble Pompey! What, 45 at the wheels of Cæsar? Art thou led in triumph? What, is there none of Pygmalion's images, newly made woman, to be had now, for putting the hand in the pocket and extracting it clutch'd? What reply, ha? 50 What say'st thou to this tune, matter, and method? Is't not drown'd i' the last rain, ha? What say'st thou, Trot? Is the world as it was, man? Which is the way? Is it sad, and few words? or how? The trick of it?

DUKE. Still thus, and thus; still worse! 55

LUC. How doth my dear morsel, thy mistress? Procures she still, ha?

POM. Troth, sir, she hath eaten up all her beef, and she is herself in the tub.

LUC. Why, 'tis good; it is the right of 60 it; it must be so. Ever your fresh whore and your powder'd bawd; an unshunn'd consequence; it must be so. Art going to prison, Pompey?

POM. Yes, faith, sir.

LUC. Why, 'tis not amiss, Pompey. Fare- 65 well. Go, say I sent thee thither. For debt, Pompey? or how?

ELB. For being a bawd, for being a bawd.

LUC. Well, then, imprison him. If imprisonment be the due of a bawd, why, 'tis his 70 right. Bawd he is doubtless, and of antiquity too; bawd-born. Farewell, good Pompey. Commend me to the prison, Pompey. You will turn good husband now, Pompey; you will keep the house.

POM. I hope, sir, your good worship 75 will be my bail.

LUC. No, indeed, will I not, Pompey; it is not the wear. I will pray, Pompey, to increase your bondage. If you take it not patiently, why, your mettle is the more. Adieu, trusty Pompey. 'Bless you, friar. 81

DUKE. And you.

LUC. Does Bridget paint still, Pompey, ha?

ELB. Come your ways, sir; come.

POM. You will not bail me, then, sir? 85

9-10. **fox and lambskins**, a usurer was often described as a fox clad in a lambskin. 11. **facing**, trimming, i.e., craft (foxskin) being stronger than innocence (lambskin) is used for the ornament. 12. **Come your way**, come on. 18-9. **pick-lock**, a skeleton key. 23. **maw**, belly. 28. **so . . . depended**, supported by such a disgusting trade. 39. **go . . . errand**, make a futile trip. 41. **as . . . free**, as faults are free from seeming, i.e., as from hypocrisy. 42. **His . . . waist**, i.e., his neck will come to have a cord around it as your waist has, i.e., his friar's frock.

46. **Are . . . triumph?** Pompey is led off captive by Elbow as the Roman Pompey was at Caesar's chariot wheels. 47-8. **Pygmalion's images**, Pygmalion's statue of a beautiful woman was brought to life by Aphrodite. Lucio asks "Have you no women as fresh and virginal for your customers as was Pygmalion's statue when it came to life"? 51. **tune**, humor. 53. **Trot**, contemptuous epithet for an old woman. 59. **tub**, (1) salting tub for curing beef, (2) sweating tub for treating syphilis. 62. **powder'd**, pickled in brine; **unshunn'd**, inevitable. 74. **husband**, house-bawd. 78. **wear**, fashion. 80. **mettle**, with a pun on "metal," i.e., irons. 84. **your ways**, along.

LUC. Then, Pompey, nor now. What news abroad, friar? what news?

ELB. Come your ways, sir; come.

LUC. Go to kennel, Pompey; go. [*Exeunt* ELBOW, POMPEY, *and* OFFICERS.] What news, friar, of the Duke? 91

DUKE. I know none. Can you tell me of any?

LUC. Some say he is with the Emperor of Russia; other some, he is in Rome; but where is he, think you? 95

DUKE. I know not where; but wheresoever, I wish him well.

LUC. It was a mad fantastical trick of him to steal from the state, and usurp the beggary he was never born to. Lord Angelo dukes it well in his absence; he puts transgression to't. 101

DUKE. He does well in't.

LUC. A little more lenity to lechery would do no harm in him. Something too crabbed that way, friar. 105

DUKE. It is too general a vice, and severity must cure it.

LUC. Yes, in good sooth, the vice is of a great kindred, it is will allied; but it is impossible to extirp it quite, friar, till eating 110 and drinking be put down. They say this Angelo was not made by man and woman after this downright way of creation. Is it true, think you?

DUKE. How should he be made, then?

LUC. Some report a sea-maid spawn'd 115 him; some, that he was begot between two stock-fishes. But it is certain that when he makes water his urine is congeal'd ice; that I know to be true; and he is a motion generative; that's infallible.

DUKE. You are pleasant, sir, and speak apace. 120

LUC. Why, what a ruthless thing is this in him, for the rebellion of a codpiece to take away the life of a man! Would the Duke that is absent have done this? Ere he would have hang'd a man for the getting a hundred 125 bastards, he would have paid for the nursing a thousand. He had some feeling of the sport; he knew the service, and that instructed him to mercy.

DUKE. I never heard the absent Duke much detected for women. He was not inclin'd that way. 130

LUC. O, sir, you are deceiv'd.

DUKE. 'Tis not possible.

LUC. Who, not the Duke? Yes, your beggar of fifty; and his use was to put a ducat in her clack-dish. The Duke had crotchets in 135 him. He would be drunk too; that let me inform you.

DUKE. You do him wrong, surely.

LUC. Sir, I was an inward of his. A shy fellow was the Duke; and I believe I know the cause of his withdrawing. 140

DUKE. What, I prithee, might be the cause?

LUC. No, pardon; 'tis a secret must be lock'd within the teeth and the lips. But this I can let you understand, the greater file of the subject held the Duke to be wise. 145

DUKE. Wise! Why, no question but he was.

LUC. A very superficial, ignorant, unweighing fellow.

DUKE. Either this is envy in you, folly, or mistaking. The very stream of his life 150 and the business he hath helmed must upon a warranted need give him a better proclamation. Let him be but testimonied in his own bringings-forth, and he shall appear to the envious a scholar, a statesman, and a sol- 155 dier. Therefore you speak unskilfully; or if your knowledge be more it is much dark'ned in your malice.

LUC. Sir, I know him, and I love him.

DUKE. Love talks with better knowledge, and knowledge with dearer love. 160

LUC. Come, sir, I know what I know.

DUKE. I can hardly believe that, since you know not what you speak. But, if ever the Duke return, as our prayers are he may, let me desire you to make your answer be- 165 fore him. If it be honest you have spoke, you have courage to maintain it. I am bound to call upon you; and, I pray you, your name?

LUC. Sir, my name is Lucio; well known to the Duke. 170

86. then . . . now, i.e., neither then nor now. 99. usurp, assume. 103. lenity to, mildness toward. 104. crabbed, harsh. 110. extirp, extirpate. 115. sea-maid, mermaid. 117. stockfishes, dried codfish. 119. motion generative, a puppet, yet able to procreate. 120. speak apace, talk nonsense. 122. codpiece, a covering for the opening in the front of a man's breeches. 129-130. detected for women, accused of intercourse with women. 133. your . . . fifty, i.e., he would take even old beggar women. 135. clack-dish, a wooden dish which beggars carried for the collection of alms. They clacked the cover to attract attention. 135. crotchets, strange whims. 138. inward, intimate friend; shy, demure. 144-5. greater . . . subject, larger number of his subjects. 147. unweighing, thoughtless. 149. envy, malice. 151. helmed, steered; upon . . . need, if warrant is needed. 152, proclamation, report. 153. testimonied, attested. 153-4, bringings-forth, deeds. 154. envious, malicious. 156. unskillfully, without knowledge.

DUKE. He shall know you better, sir, if I may live to report you.

LUC. I fear you not.

DUKE. O, you hope the Duke will return no more; or you imagine me too unhurtful 175 an opposite. But indeed I can do you little harm; you'll forswear this again.

LUC. I'll be hang'd first; thou art deceiv'd in me, friar. But no more of this. Canst thou tell if Claudio die to-morrow or no? 180

DUKE. Why should he die, sir?

LUC. Why? For filling a bottle with a tun-dish. I would the Duke we talk of were return'd again. This ungenitur'd agent will unpeople the province with continency. 185 Sparrows must not build in his house-eaves, because they are lecherous. The Duke yet would have dark deeds darkly answered; he would never bring them to light. Would he were return'd! Marry, this Claudio is 190 condemned for untrussing. Farewell, good friar; I prithee, pray for me. The Duke, I say to thee again, would eat mutton on Fridays. He's not past it; yet (and I say't to thee) he would mouth with a beggar, though she smelt brown bread and garlic. Say that I said so. Farewell. [*Exit.* 195

DUKE. No might nor greatness in mortality
Can censure scape; back-wounding calumny
The whitest virtue strikes. What king so strong
Can tie the gall up in the slanderous tongue?
But who comes here? 200

[*Enter* ESCALUS, PROVOST, *and* OFFICERS, *with* MISTRESS OVERDONE.]

ESCAL. Go; away with her to prison!

MRS. OV. Good my lord, be good to me; your honour is accounted a merciful man. Good my lord!

ESCAL. Double and treble admonition, 205 and still forfeit in the same kind! This would make mercy swear and play the tyrant.

PROV. A bawd of eleven years' continuance, may it please your honour. 209

MRS. OV. My lord, this is one Lucio's information against me. Mistress Kate Keepdown was with child by him in the Duke's time. He promis'd her marriage. His child is a year and a quarter old, come Philip and Jacob. I have kept it myself, and see how he goes about to abuse me! 215

ESCAL. That fellow is a fellow of much license; let him be call'd before us. Away with her to prison! Go to; no more words. [*Exeunt* OFFICERS *with* MISTRESS OV.] Provost, my brother Angelo will not be alter'd; Claudio must die to-morrow. Let him be fur- 220 nish'd with divines, and have all charitable preparation. If my brother wrought by my pity, it should not be so with him.

PROV. So please you, this friar hath been with him, and advis'd him for the entertainment of death. 226

ESCAL. Good even, good father.

DUKE. Bliss and goodness on you!

ESCAL. Of whence are you?

DUKE. Not of this country, though my chance is now 230
To use it for my time. I am a brother
Of gracious order, late come from the See
In special business from his Holiness.

ESCAL. What news abroad i' the world?

DUKE. None, but that there is so great 235 a fever on goodness that the dissolution of it must cure it. Novelty is only in request; and it is as dangerous to be aged in any kind of course, as it is virtuous to be constant in any undertaking. There is scarce truth 240 enough alive to make societies secure; but security enough to make fellowships accurst. Much upon this riddle runs the wisdom of the world. This news is old enough, yet it is every day's news. I pray you, sir, of what disposition was the Duke? 245

ESCAL. One that, above all other strifes, contended especially to know himself.

DUKE. What pleasure was he given to?

ESCAL. Rather rejoicing to see another merry, than merry at anything which 250 profess'd to make him rejoice; a gentleman of all temperance. But leave we him to his events,

176. **opposite**, opponent. 177. **forswear**, deny under oath. 182-3. **tun-dish**, funnel. 184. **ungenitur'd**, impotent. 190-1. **untrussing**, letting down his breeches. 193. **mutton**, (1) meat, (2) prostitute; **it**, i.e., fornication. 195. **mouth**, kiss. 196. **mortality**, human life. 199. **gall**, bitterness, spite. 206. **forfeit . . . kind**, liable to punishment for the same offence. 214. **come . . . Jacob**, at the next feast of St. Philip and St. James, i.e., May 1. 215. **goes about**, makes it his task. 222. **wrought by my pity**, was actuated as I am by pity. 225. **entertainment**, expectation. 231. **time**, present time. 232. **gracious**, religious; **the See**, i.e., Rome. 235-6. **there . . . goodness**, virtue has become so extreme (hectic). 236. **dissolution of it**, death of virtue. 237. **it**, the fever; **novelty. . . . request**, only innovation is desired. 241. **security**, i.e., requests for obtaining security (for a friend). 242. **fellowships**, friendships. 242-3. **Much . . . world**, the wisdom of the world is greatly concerned with this riddle. 252. **events**, affairs.

with a prayer they may prove prosperous; and let me desire to know how you find Claudio prepar'd. I am made to understand that you have lent him visitation. 256

DUKE. He professes to have received no sinister measure from his judge, but most willingly humbles himself to the determination of justice; yet had he framed to himself, 260 by the instruction of his frailty, many deceiving promises of life, which I by my good leisure have discredited to him, and now is he resolv'd to die.

ESCAL. You have paid the heavens your function, and the prisoner the very debt of 265 your calling. I have labour'd for the poor gentleman to the extremest shore of my modesty; but my brother justice have I found so severe, that he hath forc'd me to tell him he is indeed Justice.

DUKE. If his own life answer the strait- 270 ness of his proceeding, it shall become him well; wherein if he chance to fail, he hath sentenc'd himself.

ESCAL. I am going to visit the prisoner. Fare you well.

DUKE. Peace be with you!

[*Exeunt* ESCALUS *and* PROVOST.]

He who the sword of heaven will bear 275
Should be as holy as severe;
Pattern in himself to know,
Grace to stand, and virtue go,
More nor less to others paying
Than by self-offences weighing. 280
Shame to him whose cruel striking
Kills for faults of his own liking!
Twice treble shame on Angelo,
To weed my vice and let his grow!
O, what may man within him hide, 285
Though angel on the outward side!
How may likeness made in crimes,
Making practice on the times,
To draw with idle spiders' strings
Most ponderous and substantial things! 290
Craft against vice I must apply.
With Angelo to-night shall lie
His old betrothed but despised;
So disguise shall, by the disguised,
Pay with falsehood false exacting, 295
And perform an old contracting. [*Exit.*

ACT IV

SCENE I. *The moated grange at* ST. LUKE'S.

[*Enter* MARIANA, *and* BOY *singing.*]

SONG.

Take, O, take those lips away,
That so sweetly were forsworn;
And those eyes, the break of day,
Lights that do mislead the morn;
But my kisses bring again, bring again; 5
Seals of love, but seal'd in vain, seal'd in vain.

[*Enter* DUKE, *disguised as before.*]

MARI. Break off thy song, and haste thee quick away.
Here comes a man of comfort, whose advice
Hath often still'd my brawling discontent.

[*Exit* BOY.]

I cry you mercy, sir; and well could wish 10
You had not found me here so musical.
Let me excuse me, and believe me so,
My mirth it much displeas'd, but pleas'd my woe.

DUKE. 'Tis good; though music oft hath such a charm
To make bad good, and good provoke to harm. 15
I pray you, tell me, hath anybody inquir'd for me here to-day? Much upon this time have I promis'd here to meet.

MARI. You have not been inquir'd after. I have sat here all day. 20

257-8. **sinister measure**, unjust sentence. 260. **framed to himself**, planned for himself. 261. **instruction**, prompting. 262. **by . . . leisure**, by taking a propitious occasion. 262-3. **discredited**, deprived of credibility. 263, **is he resolved to die**, he has adjusted his mind to dying. 264. **function**, i.e., duties as a priest. 265. **very**, true. 267. **To . . . modesty**, i.e., just as far as I could without being offensively insistent. 269. **indeed Justice**, i.e., Justice untempered by Mercy. 270. **answer . . . proceeding**, is consistent with the severity of his course of action. 272. **wherein**, i.e., in the conduct of his life. 275-96. Few critics believe that these couplets were written by Shakespeare. 278. **to stand**, to stand firm; **to go**, to go forward. 284. **my vice**, i.e., everyone's vice. 287-90. A very obscure passage. Its meaning seems to be as follows: How often false appearance (deceit), assumed to hide crime, uses stratagems in order to effect important results by spinning a spider's web of cunning. Act IV, Scene i: 9. **brawling**, scolding, noisy. 10. **cry you mercy**, beg your pardon. 13. **My mirth . . . woe**, it did not give me enough pleasure to make me mirthful, but it did soothe my sorrow. 17. **Much upon**, at just about. 18. **meet**, i.e., meet someone.

[*Enter* ISABELLA.]

DUKE. I do constantly believe you. The time is come even now. I shall crave your forbearance a little. May be I will call upon you anon, for some advantage to yourself.

MARI. I am always bound to you. [*Exit.*

DUKE. Very well met, and well come. 26
What is the news from this good deputy?

ISAB. He hath a garden circummur'd with brick,
Whose western side is with a vineyard back'd,
And to that vineyard is a planchèd gate, 30
That makes his opening with this bigger key.
This other doth command a little door
Which from the vineyard to the garden leads;
There have I made my promise
Upon the heavy middle of the night 35
To call upon him.

DUKE. But shall you on your knowledge find this way?

ISAB. I have ta'en a due and wary note upon 't.
With whispering and most guilty diligence,
In action all of precept, he did show me 40
The way twice o'er.

DUKE. Are there no other tokens
Between you 'greed concerning her observance?

ISAB. No, none, but only a repair i' the dark;
And that I have possess'd him my most stay
Can be but brief; for I have made him know
I have a servant comes with me along, 46
That stays upon me, whose persuasion is
I come about my brother.

DUKE. 'Tis well borne up.
I have not made known to Mariana
A word of this. What, ho! within! come forth!

[*Re-enter* MARIANA.]

I pray you, be acquainted with this maid; 51
She comes to do you good.

ISAB. I do desire the like.

DUKE. Do you persuade yourself that I respect you?

MARI. Good friar, I know you do, and have found it.

DUKE. Take, then, this your companion by the hand, 55
Who hath a story ready for your ear.
I shall attend your leisure; but make haste;
The vaporous night approaches.

MARI. Will't please you walk aside?

[*Exeunt* MARIANA *and* ISABELLA.

DUKE. O place and greatness! millions of false eyes 60
Are stuck upon thee. Volumes of report
Run with these false and most contrarious quests
Upon thy doings; thousand escapes of wit
Make thee the father of their idle dream
And rack thee in their fancies.

[*Re-enter* MARIANA *and* ISABELLA.]

Welcome, how agreed? 65

ISAB. She'll take the enterprise upon her, father,
If you advise it.

DUKE. It is not my consent,
But my entreaty too.

ISAB. Little have you to say
When you depart from him, but, soft and low,
"Remember now my brother."

MARI. Fear me not. 70

DUKE. Nor, gentle daughter, fear you not at all.
He is your husband on a pre-contract:
To bring you thus together, 'tis no sin,
Sith that the justice of your title to him
Doth flourish the deceit. Come, let us go. 75
Our corn's to reap, for yet our tilth's to sow.
[*Exeunt.*

SCENE II. *A room in the prison.*

[*Enter* PROVOST *and* POMPEY.]

PROV. Come hither, sirrah. Can you cut off a man's head?

POM. If the man be a bachelor, sir, I can; but if he be a married man, he's his wife's head, and I can never cut off a woman's head. 5

21. **constantly**, firmly. 24. **anon**, in a little while. 28. **circummur'd**, walled round. 30. **planched**, made of planks. 31. **his**, its. 35. **heavy**, drowsy. 40. **in . . . precept**, i.e, as he illustrated his instructions with gestures. 41. **tokens**, signals. 42. **her observance**, what she must observe. 43. **repair**, resort, going. 44. **possess'd**, informed; **most**, utmost. 47. **stays upon**, waits for; **persuasion**, understanding of the matter. 48. **borne up**, arranged. 54. **it**, i.e., it to be true. 60. **place and greatness**, position of greatness; **false**, deceitful. 61. **stuck**, fixed. 62. **run with**, are spread by; **contrarious quests**, inconsistent inquiries; quests = pursuit of the hounds. 63. **escapes**, sallies. 64. **idle**, foolish. 65. **rack**, i.e., pull you to pieces. 75. **flourish**, justify. 76. **tilth**, plowed land.

PROV. Come, sir, leave me your snatches, and yield me a direct answer. To-morrow morning are to die Claudio and Barnardine. Here is in our prison a common executioner, who in his office lacks a helper. If you will take 10 it on you to assist him, it shall redeem you from your gyves; if not, you shall have your full time of imprisonment, and your deliverance with an unpitied whipping, for you have been a notorious bawd. 15

POM. Sir, I have been an unlawful bawd time out of mind; but yet I will be content to be a lawful hangman. I would be glad to receive some instruction from my fellow partner.

PROV. What, ho! Abhorson! Where's Abhorson, there? 21

[*Enter* ABHORSON.]

ABHOR. Do you call, sir?

PROV. Sirrah, here's a fellow will help you to-morrow in your execution. If you think it meet, compound with him by the year, 25 and let him abide here with you; if not, use him for the present and dismiss him. He cannot plead his estimation with you; he hath been a bawd.

ABHOR. A bawd, sir? Fie upon him! he will discredit our mystery. 30

PROV. Go to, sir; you weigh equally. A feather will turn the scale. [*Exit.*

POM. Pray, sir, by your good favour, for surely, sir, a good favour you have, but that you have a hanging look,—do you call, sir, your occupation a mystery? 36

ABHOR. Ay, sir; a mystery.

POM. Painting, sir, I have heard say, is a mystery; and your whores, sir, being members of my occupation, using painting, 40 do prove my occupation a mystery; but what mystery there should be in hanging, if I should be hang'd, I cannot imagine.

ABHOR. Sir, it is a mystery.

POM. Proof? 45

ABHOR. Every true man's apparel fits your thief. If it be too little for your thief, your true man thinks it big enough; if it be too big for your thief, your thief thinks it little enough; so every true man's apparel fits your thief. 50

[*Re-enter* PROVOST.]

PROV. Are you agreed?

POM. Sir, I will serve him, for I do find your hangman is a more penitent trade than your bawd; he doth oftener ask forgiveness.

PROV. You, sirrah, provide your block 55 and your axe to-morrow four o'clock.

ABHOR. Come on, bawd, I will instruct thee in my trade. Follow.

POM. I do desire to learn, sir; and I hope, if you have occasion to use me for your 60 own turn, you shall find me yare; for truly, sir, for your kindness I owe you a good turn. [*Exit.*

PROV. Call hither Barnardine and Claudio.
[*Exit* ABHORSON.
The one has my pity; not a jot the other,
Being a murderer, though he were my
brother. 65

[*Enter* CLAUDIO.]

Look, here's the warrant, Claudio, for thy
death.
'Tis now dead midnight, and by eight to-
morrow
Thou must be made immortal. Where's Barnardine?

CLAUD. As fast lock'd up in sleep as guiltless
labour
When it lies starkly in the traveller's bones. 70
He will not wake.

PROV. Who can do good on him?
Well, go, prepare yourself.
[*Knocking within.*]
But, hark, what noise?
Heaven give your spirits comfort!
[*Exit* CLAUDIO.]
By and by.
I hope it is some pardon or reprieve
For the most gentle Claudio.

[*Enter* DUKE, *disguised as before.*]

Welcome, father. 75

Scene ii: 6. leave . . . snatches, stop pulling wisecracks. 9. common, public. 12. gyves, fetters. 25. compound, come to terms. 27-8. plead . . . estimation, give as an excuse his reputation. 30. mystery, trade, calling. 31. you . . . equally, i.e., your callings are equally despised. 33. by . . . favour, I beg your pardon; "favour" also means "face." 35. occupation, trade. 46-7. Every . . . thief, a reference to the executioner's right to take possession of the clothes of the men he killed. 48. true, honest. 51. Are you agreed? Have you come to an agreement? 54. he . . . forgiveness, the executioner regularly asked the criminal to forgive him before he went about his business. 61. yare, ready in doing. 64. jot, little bit. 70. starkly, stiffly, as though dead. 73. By and by, right away. This is his answer to the knocking.

DUKE. The best and wholesomest spirits of the night
Envelop you, good Provost! Who call'd here of late?

PROV. None, since the curfew rung.

DUKE. Not Isabel?

PROV. No.

DUKE. They will, then, ere't be long.

PROV. What comfort is for Claudio? 80

DUKE. There's some in hope.

PROV. It is a bitter deputy.

DUKE. Not so, not so; his life is parallel'd
Even with the stroke and line of his great justice.
He doth with holy abstinence subdue
That in himself which he spurs on his power
To qualify in others. Were he meal'd with that 86
Which he corrects, then were he tyrannous;
But this being so, he's just.

[*Knocking within.*]

Now are they come.

[*Exit* PROVOST.]

This is a gentle Provost: seldom when
The steeled gaoler is the friend of men. 90

[*Knocking within.*]

How now! what noise? That spirit's possess'd with haste
That wounds the unsisting postern with these strokes.

[*Re-enter* PROVOST.]

PROV. There he must stay until the officer
Arise to let him in. He is call'd up.

DUKE. Have you no countermand for Claudio yet, 95
But he must die to-morrow?

PROV. None, sir, none.

DUKE. As near the dawning, Provost, as it is,
You shall hear more ere morning.

PROV. Happily
You something know, yet I believe there comes
No countermand; no such example have we.
Besides, upon the very siege of justice 101
Lord Angelo hath to the public ear
Profess'd the contrary.

[*Enter a* MESSENGER.]

This is his lordship's man.

DUKE. And here comes Claudio's pardon.

MES. [*Giving a paper*] My lord hath 105 sent you this note; and by me this further charge, that you swerve not from the smallest article of it, neither in time, matter, or other circumstance. Good morrow; for, as I take it, it is almost day.

PROV. I shall obey him. [*Exit* MESSENGER.

DUKE. [*Aside*] This is his pardon, purchas'd by such sin 111
For which the pardoner himself is in.
Hence hath offence his quick celerity,
When it is borne in high authority.
When vice makes mercy, mercy's so extended,
That for the fault's love is the offender friended. 116
Now, sir, what news?

PROV. I told you. Lord Angelo, belike thinking me remiss in mine office, awakens me with this unwonted putting-on; methinks strangely, for he hath not us'd it before. 121

DUKE. Pray you, let's hear.

PROV. [*Reads the letter*]
"Whatsoever you may hear to the contrary, let Claudio be executed by four of the clock; and in the afternoon Barnardine. For my 125 better satisfaction, let me have Claudio's head sent me by five. Let this be duly performed, with a thought that more depends on it than we must yet deliver. Thus fail not to do your office, as you will answer it at your peril." 130
What say you to this, sir?

DUKE. What is that Barnardine who is to be executed in the afternoon?

PROV. A Bohemian born, but here nurs'd up and bred; one that is a prisoner nine years old. 135

DUKE. How came it that the absent Duke had not either deliver'd him to his liberty or executed him? I have heard it was ever his manner to do so. 139

79. **They**, i.e., Isabel and the messenger with the pardon. 81. **It**, i.e., Angelo. 83. **stroke and line**, i.e., his justice and his virtue are like parallel lines and strokes in a musical score; "stroke" also = blow of the executioner's axe; and "line" = the hangman's rope. 86. **qualify**, moderate; **meal'd**, sprinkled, tainted. 89. **seldom when**, it is seldom that. 90. **steeled**, hardened. 92. **unsisting**, probably a slurred form for either "unassisting" or "unresisting"; **postern**, small private gate. 98. **Happily**, haply; perhaps. 100. **example**, precedent. 101. **siege**, seat. 113. **quick celerity**, swift speed. 115. **extended**, shown. 120. **putting on**, instigation. 129. **deliver**, communicate. 132. **What**, Who. 135. **nine years old**, for nine years.

PROV. His friends still wrought reprieves for him; and, indeed, his fact, till now in the government of Lord Angelo, came not to an undoubtful proof.

DUKE. It is now apparent?

PROV. Most manifest, and not denied by himself. 146

DUKE. Hath he borne himself penitently in prison? How seems he to be touch'd?

PROV. A man that apprehends death no more dreadfully but as a drunken sleep; care- 150 less, reckless, and fearless of what's past, present, or to come; insensible of mortality, and desperately mortal.

DUKE. He wants advice.

PROV. He will hear none. He hath ever- 155 more had the liberty of the prison; give him leave to escape hence, he would not; drunk many times a day, if not many days entirely drunk. We have very oft awak'd him, as if to carry him to execution, and show'd him a seeming warrant for it; it hath not moved him at all. 161

DUKE. More of him anon. There is written in your brow, Provost, honesty and constancy. If I read it not truly, my ancient skill beguiles me; but, in the boldness of my cunning, 165 I will lay myself in hazard. Claudio, whom here you have warrant to execute, is no greater forfeit to the law than Angelo who hath sentenc'd him. To make you understand this in a manifested effect, I crave but 170 four days' respite; for the which you are to do me both a present and a dangerous courtesy.

PROV. Pray, sir, in what?

DUKE. In the delaying death.

PROV. Alack, how may I do it, having 175 the hour limited, and an express command, under penalty, to deliver his head in the view of Angelo? I may make my case as Claudio's, to cross this in the smallest. 179

DUKE. By the vow of mine order I warrant you, if my instructions may be your guide. Let this Barnardine be this morning executed, and his head borne to Angelo.

PROV. Angelo hath seen them both, and will discover the favour. 185

DUKE. O, death's a great disguiser, and you may add to it. Shave the head, and tie the beard; and say it was the desire of the penitent to be so bar'd before his death. You know the course is common. If anything fall to 190 you upon this, more than thanks and good fortune, by the saint whom I profess, I will plead against it with my life.

PROV. Pardon me, good father; it is against my oath. 195

DUKE. Were you sworn to the Duke, or to the deputy?

PROV. To him, and to his substitutes.

DUKE. You will think you have made no offence, if the Duke avouch the justice of your dealing?

PROV. But what likelihood is in that? 201

DUKE. Not a resemblance, but a certainty. Yet since I see you fearful, that neither my coat, integrity, nor persuasion can with ease attempt you, I will go further than I 205 meant, to pluck all fears out of you. Look you, sir, here is the hand and seal of the Duke. You know the character, I doubt not; and the signet is not strange to you.

PROV. I know them both. 210

DUKE. The contents of this is the return of the Duke. You shall anon over-read it at your pleasure; where you shall find, within these two days he will be here. This is a thing that Angelo knows not; for he this very day 215 receives letters of strange tenour, perchance of the Duke's death, perchance entering into some monastery, but, by chance, nothing of what is here writ. Look, the unfolding star calls up the shepherd. Put not yourself 220 into amazement how these things should be. All difficulties are but easy when they are known. Call your executioner, and off with Barnardine's head. I will give him a present shrift and advise him for a better place. 225 Yet you are amaz'd, but this shall absolutely resolve you. Come away; it is almost clear dawn. [*Exeunt.*

140. still wrought, kept obtaining. 141. fact, deed, crime. 152-3. insensible . . . mortal, having no sense of death and destined to die without hope of salvation. 154. wants advice, i.e., needs spiritual instruction. 162. anon, in a moment. 164. My . . . me, my traditional skill leads me astray. 165. boldness . . . cunning, in the confidence of my wisdom. 166. hazard, danger. 169-70. in . . . effect, by means of manifest proof. 176. limited, fixed. 179, cross, hinder. 180. warrant you, will stand surety for you.

185. discover the favour, recognize the face. 187. tie, trim. 190-1. fall . . . this, befall you because of this. 205. attempt, win. 208. character, handwriting. 211 return, report, order. 212. over-read it, read it over. 219. unfolding, morning, i.e., the signal for letting the sheep out of the pen (fold). 220. calls up, awakens. 221. should, can. 224. present shrift, immediate confession and absolution. 226. absolutely resolve, completely convince. 227. clear, bright.

SCENE III. *Another room in the same.*

[*Enter* POMPEY.]

POM. I am as well acquainted here as I was in our house of profession. One would think it were Mistress Overdone's own house, for here be many of her old customers. First, here's young Master Rash. He's in for a com- 5 modity of brown paper and old ginger, nine-score and seventeen pounds; of which he made five marks, ready money. Marry, then ginger was not much in request, for the old women were all dead. Then is there here one 10 Master Caper, at the suit of Master Three-pile the mercer, for some four suits of peach-colour'd satin, which now peaches him a beggar. Then have we here young Dizzy, and young Master Deep-vow, and Master Copper-spur, and Master Starve-lackey the rapier 15 and dagger man, and young Drop-heir that killed lusty Pudding, and Master Forthlight the tilter, and brave Master Shooty the great traveller, and wild Half-can that stabb'd Pots, and, I think, forty more; all great doers in our trade, and are now "for the Lord's sake." 21

[*Enter* ABHORSON.]

ABHOR. Sirrah, bring Barnardine hither.
POM. Master Barnardine! You must rise and be hang'd, Master Barnardine!
ABHOR. What, ho, Barnardine! 25
BAR. [*Within*] A pox o' your throats! Who makes that noise there? What are you?
POM. Your friends, sir; the hangman. You must be so good, sir, to rise and be put to death.
BAR. [*Within*] Away, you rogue, away! I am sleepy. 31
ABHOR. Tell him he must awake, and that quickly too.
POM. Pray, Master Barnardine, awake till you are executed, and sleep afterwards. 35
ABHOR. Go in to him, and fetch him out.
POM. He is coming, sir, he is coming. I hear his straw rustle.

[*Enter* BARNARDINE.]

ABHOR. Is the axe upon the block, sirrah?
POM. Very ready, sir. 40
BAR. How now, Abhorson? What's the news with you?
ABHOR. Truly, sir, I would desire you to clap into your prayers; for, look you, the warrant's come. 45
BAR. You rogue, I have been drinking all night; I am not fitted for't.
POM. O, the better, sir; for he that drinks all night, and is hanged betimes in the morning, may sleep the sounder all the next day. 50

[*Enter* DUKE, *disguised as before.*]

ABHOR. Look you, sir; here comes your ghostly father. Do we jest now, think you?
DUKE. Sir, induced by my charity, and hearing how hastily you are to depart, I am come to advise you, comfort you, and pray with you. 55
BAR. Friar, not I. I have been drinking hard all night, and I will have more time to prepare me, or they shall beat out my brains with billets. I will not consent to die this day, that's certain.
DUKE. O, sir, you must; and therefore I beseech you 60
Look forward on the journey you shall go.
BAR. I swear I will not die to-day for any man's persuasion.
DUKE. But hear you.
BAR. Not a word. If you have anything 65 to say to me, come to my ward; for thence will not I to-day. [*Exit.*

[*Re-enter* PROVOST.]

DUKE. Unfit to live or die, O gravel heart!
After him, fellows; bring him to the block.
[*Exeunt* ABHORSON *and* POMPEY.
PROV. Now sir, how do you find the prisoner? 70
DUKE. A creature unprepar'd, unmeet for death;
And to transport him in the mind he is
Were damnable.
PROV. Here in the prison, father,
There died this morning of a cruel fever

Scene iii: 1. **well acquainted,** have as many acquaintances. 5. **commodity,** usurers, to avoid charging more than the legal 10 percent interest, gave the borrower, in addition a parcel (commodity) of valueless goods. Master Rash's commodity was brown paper and ginger (a popular medicine). 8. **marks,** 13s. 4c. 12. **mercer,** dry-goods merchant. 14. **peaches him,** denounces him as. 15. **rapier . . . man,** a hired ruffian. 17. **tilter,** fencer. 21. **"for . . . sake,"** the formula used by prisoners who were compelled to beg of passers-by for money to pay for their food. 44. **clap into,** rush hurriedly to. 49. **betimes,** early. 51. **ghostly,** spiritual. 58. **billets,** firewood, i.e., stout sticks. 66. **ward,** cell. 68. **gravel,** stony. 71. **unmeet,** unfitted. 72. **transport,** i.e., from this world to the next.

One Ragozine, a most notorious pirate, 75
A man of Claudio's years; his beard and head
Just of his colour. What if we do omit
This reprobate till he were well inclin'd,
And satisfy the deputy with the visage
Of Ragozine, more like to Claudio? 80

DUKE. O, 'tis an accident that Heaven provides!
Dispatch it presently. The hour draws on
Prefix'd by Angelo. See this be done,
And sent according to command, whiles I
Persuade this rude wretch willingly to die. 85

PROV. This shall be done, good father, presently.
But Barnardine must die this afternoon;
And how shall we continue Claudio,
To save me from the danger that might come
If he were known alive?

DUKE. Let this be done. 90
Put them in secret holds, both Barnardine
And Claudio.
Ere twice the sun hath made his journal greeting
To the under generation, you shall find
Your safety manifested.

PROV. I am your free dependant. 95

DUKE. Quick, dispatch, and send the head to Angelo. [*Exit* PROVOST.]
Now will I write letters to Angelo,—
The Provost, he shall bear them,—whose contents
Shall witness to him I am near at home,
And that, by great injunctions, I am bound 100
To enter publicly. Him I'll desire
To meet me at the consecrated fount
A league below the city; and from thence,
By cold gradation and well-balanc'd form,
We shall proceed with Angelo. 105

[*Re-enter* PROVOST.]

PROV. Here is the head; I'll carry it myself.

DUKE. Convenient is it. Make a swift return;
For I would commune with you of such things
That want no ear but yours.

PROV. I'll make all speed. [*Exit.*

ISAB. [*Within*] Peace, ho, be here! 110

DUKE. The tongue of Isabel. She's come to know
If yet her brother's pardon be come hither.
But I will keep her ignorant of her good,
To make her heavenly comforts of despair,
When it is least expected.

[*Enter* ISABELLA.]

ISAB. Ho, by your leave! 115

DUKE. Good morning to you, fair and gracious daughter.

ISAB. The better, given me by so holy a man.
Hath yet the deputy sent my brother's pardon?

DUKE. He hath releas'd him, Isabel, from the world.
His head is off and sent to Angelo. 120

ISAB. Nay, but it is not so.

DUKE. It is no other. Show your wisdom, daughter,
In your close patience.

ISAB. O, I will to him and pluck out his eyes!

DUKE. You shall not be admitted to his sight. 125

ISAB. Unhappy Claudio! Wretched Isabel!
Injurious world! Most damnèd Angelo!

DUKE. This nor hurts him nor profits you a jot,
Forbear it therefore; give your cause to heaven.
Mark what I say, which you shall find 130
By every syllable a faithful verity.
The Duke comes home to-morrow;—nay, dry your eyes;—
One of your covent, and his confessor,
Gives me this instance. Already he hath carried
Notice to Escalus and Angelo, 135
Who do prepare to meet him at the gates,
There to give up their power. If you can, pace your wisdom
In that good path that I would wish it go,
And you shall have your bosom on this wretch,

77. omit, leave unnoticed, pass on. 78. inclined, disposed. 81. accident, chance, opportunity. 82. dispatch it presently, carry it out at once. 86. presently, at once. 88. continue, keep. 91. holds, places of confinement. 92. journal, daily. 93. under generation, the Antipodes, people living "down under." 95. free dependent, willing slave. 100. great injunctions, urgent motives. 104. cold . . . form, coolly, methodically, and with due regard to form. 107. convenient, proper. 114. make her, make for her. 123. close, self-contained. 129. forbear it, desist from doing it. 133. covent, monastery. 134. this instance, intimation of this. 137. pace, guide. 139. bosom, heart's desire.

Grace of the Duke, revenges to your heart,
And general honour. 141

ISAB. I am directed by you.

DUKE. This letter, then, to Friar Peter give;
'Tis that he sent me of the Duke's return.
Say, by this token, I desire his company
At Mariana's house to-night. Her cause and yours 145
I'll perfect him withal, and he shall bring you
Before the Duke, and to the head of Angelo
Accuse him home and home. For my poor self,
I am combined by a sacred vow
And shall be absent. Wend you with this letter. 150
Command these fretting waters from your eyes
With a light heart. Trust not my holy order
If I pervert your course. Who's here?

[*Enter* LUCIO.]

LUC. Good even. Friar, where's the Provost?

DUKE. Not within, sir. 156

LUC. O pretty Isabella, I am pale at mine heart to see thine eyes so red. Thou must be patient. I am fain to dine and sup with water and bran; I dare not for my head fill my 160 belly; one fruitful meal would set me to't. But they say the Duke will be here to-morrow. By my troth, Isabel, I lov'd thy brother. If the old fantastical Duke of dark corners had been at home, he had lived. 165

[*Exit* ISABELLA.

DUKE. Sir, the Duke is marvellous little beholding to your reports; but the best is, he lives not in them.

LUC. Friar, thou knowest not the Duke so well as I do. He's a better woodman than thou tak'st him for. 171

DUKE. Well, you'll answer this one day. Fare ye well.

LUC. Nay, tarry; I'll go along with thee. I can tell thee pretty tales of the Duke. 175

DUKE. You have told me too many of him already, sir, if they be true; if not true, none were enough.

LUC. I was once before him for getting a wench with child. 180

DUKE. Did you such a thing?

LUC. Yes, marry, did I; but I was fain to forswear it. They would else have married me to the rotten medlar.

DUKE. Sir, your company is fairer than honest. Rest you well. 186

LUC. By my troth, I'll go with thee to the lane's end. If bawdy talk offend you, we'll have very little of it. Nay, friar, I am a kind of burr; I shall stick. [*Exeunt.* 190

SCENE IV. *A room in* ANGELO'S *house.*

[*Enter* ANGELO *and* ESCALUS.]

ESCAL. Every letter he hath writ hath disvouch'd other.

ANG. In most uneven and distracted manner. His actions show much like to madness; pray Heaven his wisdom be not tainted! And 5 why meet him at the gates, and redeliver our authorities there?

ESCAL. I guess not.

ANG. And why should we proclaim it in an hour before his entering, that if any crave 10 redress of injustice, they should exhibit their petitions in the street?

ESCAL. He shows his reason for that: to have a dispatch of complaints, and to deliver us from devices hereafter, which shall then have no power to stand against us. 16

ANG. Well, I beseech you, let it be proclaim'd betimes i' the morn. I'll call you at your house. Give notice to such men of sort and suit as are to meet him. 20

ESCAL. I shall, sir. Fare you well.

[*Exit* ESCALUS

ANG. Good night.
This deed unshapes me quite, makes me unpregnant
And dull to all proceedings. A deflow'red maid!
And by an eminent body that enforc'd 25

140. Grace, good will. 146. perfect, inform; withal, about. 147. head, face. 148. home and home, to the quick, sharply. 149. combined, bound, pledged. 151. fretting, corroding. 153. pervert . . . course, lead you astray. 159. fain, constrained. 164. fantastical, whimsical. 167. beholding, obliged. 167-8. he . . . them, his character does not correspond to them. 170. woodman, hunter (of women). 172. answer this, be called to account for this.

182-3. fain . . . it, forced to deny it. 184. medlar, a small pear edible only when it begins to rot. 185. fairer than honest, more amusing than decent. Scene iv: 1. hath . . . other, has contradicted all the others. 3. uneven, perplexing. 5. wisdom . . . tainted, mind be not touched. 11. exhibit, submit. 14. have . . . complaints, to dispose of complaints quickly. 15. devices, plots. 19. sort and suit, rank and following, i.e., men who hold their titles under the Duke, and who owe him "attendance" in the feudal sense. 23. unshapes, upsets; unpregnant, unfit for business.

The law against it! But that her tender shame
Will not proclaim against her maiden loss,
How might she tongue me! Yet reason dares her no;
For my authority bears a credent bulk,
That no particular scandal once can touch 30
But it confounds the breather. He should have liv'd,
Save that his riotous youth, with dangerous sense,
Might in the times to come have ta'en revenge,
By so receiving a dishonour'd life
With ransom of such shame. Would yet he had lived! 35
Alack, when once our grace we have forgot,
Nothing goes right; we would, and we would not. [*Exit.*

SCENE V. *Fields without the town.*

[*Enter* DUKE *in his own habit, and* FRIAR PETER.]

DUKE. These letters at fit time deliver me. [*Giving letters.*]
The Provost knows our purpose and our plot.
The matter being afoot, keep your instruction,
And hold you ever to our special drift,
Though sometimes you do blench from this to that, 5
As cause doth minister. Go call at Flavius' house,
And tell him where I stay. Give the like notice
To Valentinus, Rowland, and to Crassus,
And bid them bring the trumpets to the gate.
But send me Flavius first.
FRI. P. It shall be speeded well. 10
[*Exit.*

[*Enter* VARRIUS.]

DUKE. I thank thee, Varrius; thou hast made good haste:
Come, we will walk. There's other of our friends
Will greet us here anon, my gentle Varrius.
[*Exeunt.*

SCENE VI. *Street near the city gate.*

[*Enter* ISABELLA *and* MARIANA.]

ISAB. To speak so indirectly I am loath.
I would say the truth; but to accuse him so,
That is your part. Yet I am advis'd to do it;
He says, to veil full purpose.
MARI. Be rul'd by him.
ISAB. Besides, he tells me that, if peradventure 5
He speak against me on the adverse side,
I should not think it strange; for 'tis a physic
That's bitter to sweet end.

[*Enter* FRIAR PETER.]

MARI. I would Friar Peter—
ISAB. O, peace! the friar is come.
FRI. P. Come, I have found you out a stand most fit, 10
Where you may have such vantage on the Duke,
He shall not pass you. Twice have the trumpets sounded,
The generous and gravest citizens
Have hent the gates, and very near upon 14
The Duke is entering; therefore, hence, away!
[*Exeunt.*

ACT V

SCENE I. *The city gate.*

[*Enter* DUKE, VARRIUS, LORDS, ANGELO, ESCALUS, LUCIO, PROVOST, OFFICERS, *and* CITIZENS, *at several doors.*]

DUKE. My very worthy cousin, fairly met!
Our old and faithful friend, we are glad to see you.
ANG. / ESCAL. Happy return be to your royal Grace!

28. **tongue,** speak of; **dares her no,** taunts her with "no." 29. **credent bulk,** weight of credit (belief). 30. **particular,** personal. 31. **confounds,** shames; **He,** Claudio. 32. **dangerous sense,** feeling dangerous to me. 36. **grace,** virtue. **Scene v:** 1. **me,** for me. 4. **drift,** aim, scheme. 5. **blench,** start away. 6. **cause doth minister,** subject directs. 9. **trumpets,** trumpeters. **s.d. Varrius,** Though the name of this character appears also at the head of v, i, he is given nothing to say either here or there. **Scene vi:** 3. **advis'd,** i.e., well-advised. 4. **veil . . . purpose,** keep from revealing our full plan. 10. **stand,** place. 11. **vantage on,** such an advantageous position in relation to the Duke. 13. **generous:** of noble birth. 14. **hent the gates,** reached the gates [i.e., there to welcome the returning Duke].

DUKE. Many and hearty thankings to you both.
We have made inquiry of you, and we hear 5
Such goodness of your justice, that our soul
Cannot but yield you forth to public thanks,
Forerunning more requital.

ANG. You make my bonds still greater.

DUKE. O, your desert speaks loud; and I should wrong it,
To lock it in the wards of covert bosom, 10
When it deserves, with characters of brass,
A forted residence 'gainst the tooth of time
And razure of oblivion. Give me your hand,
And let the subject see, to make them know
That outward courtesies would fain proclaim 15
Favours that keep within. Come, Escalus,
You must walk by us on our other hand;
And good supporters are you.

[*Enter* FRIAR PETER *and* ISABELLA.]

FRI. P. Now is your time. Speak loud and kneel before him.

ISAB. Justice, O royal Duke! Vail your regard 20
Upon a wrong'd, I would fain have said, a maid!
O worthy Prince, dishonour not your eye
By throwing it on any other object
Till you have heard me in my true complaint
And given me justice, justice, justice, justice!

DUKE. Relate your wrongs. In what? By whom? Be brief. 26
Here is Lord Angelo shall give you justice:
Reveal yourself to him.

ISAB. O worthy Duke,
You bid me seek redemption of the devil.
Hear me yourself; for that which I must speak
Must either punish me, not being believ'd, 31
Or wring redress from you. Hear me, O hear me, here!

ANG. My lord, her wits, I fear me, are not firm.
She hath been a suitor to me for her brother,
Cut off by course of justice,—

ISAB. By course of justice!

ANG. And she will speak most bitterly and strange. 36

ISAB. Most strange, but yet most truly, will I speak.
That Angelo's forsworn, is it not strange?
That Angelo's a murderer, is't not strange?
That Angelo is an adulterous thief, 40
An hypocrite, a virgin-violator,
Is it not strange and strange?

DUKE. Nay, it is ten times strange.

ISAB. It is not truer he is Angelo
Than this is all as true as it is strange.
Nay, it is ten times true; for truth is truth 45
To the end of reckoning.

DUKE. Away with her! Poor soul,
She speaks this in the infirmity of sense.

ISAB. O Prince, I conjure thee, as thou believ'st
There is another comfort than this world,
That thou neglect me not, with that opinion
That I am touch'd with madness! Make not impossible 51
That which but seems unlike. 'Tis not impossible
But one, the wicked'st caitiff on the ground,
May seem as shy, as grave, as just, as absolute
As Angelo. Even so may Angelo, 55
In all his dressings, characts, titles, forms,
Be an arch-villain. Believe it, royal Prince!
If he be less, he's nothing; but he's more,
Had I more name for badness.

DUKE. By mine honesty,
If she be mad,—as I believe no other,— 60
Her madness hath the oddest frame of sense,
Such a dependency of thing on thing,
As e'er I heard in madness.

ISAB. O gracious Duke,
Harp not on that, nor do not banish reason
For inequality; but let your reason serve 65
To make the truth appear where it seems hid,
And hide the false seems true.

DUKE. Many that are not mad
Have, sure, more lack of reason. What would you say?

ISAB. I am the sister of one Claudio
Condemn'd upon the act of fornication 70
To lose his head: condemn'd by Angelo.

Act v, Scene i: 7. **yield you forth,** call you forth to give you. 8. **forerunning . . . requital,** in anticipation of more reward; **bonds,** obligations. 10. **wards,** prison-cells; **covert,** secret. 11. **characters,** letters. 12. **forted,** fortified. 13. **razure,** erasure. 14. **subject,** i.e., my subjects. 20. **vail your regard,** let your eyes fall. 38. **forsworn,** perjured. 47. **in . . . sense,** from an unsound mind. 51. **make,** consider. 52. **unlike,** unlikely. 53. **on the ground,** on the earth. 54. **shy,** staid; **absolute,** perfect. 56. **dressings,** robes of office; **characts,** distinctive characteristics. 59. **honesty,** honor. 60. **no other,** not otherwise. 61. **frame,** form. 63. **As . . . heard,** that I ever heard. 64. **banish reason,** become prejudiced. 65. **For inequality,** because it seems improbable. 67. **seems,** i.e., which seems. 70. **The . . . fornication,** i.e., the dead law against fornication which Angelo invoked against Claudio.

I, in probation of a sisterhood,
Was sent to by my brother; one Lucio
As then the messenger,—

LUC. That's I, an't like your Grace.
I came to her from Claudio, and desir'd her 75
To try her gracious fortune with Lord Angelo
For her poor brother's pardon.

ISAB. That's he indeed.

DUKE. You were not bid to speak.

LUC. No, my good lord;
Nor wish'd to hold my peace.

DUKE. I wish you now, then.
Pray you, take note of it; and when you have
A business for yourself, pray Heaven you then 81
Be perfect.

LUC. I warrant your honour.

DUKE. The warrant's for yourself; take heed to't.

ISAB. This gentleman told somewhat of my tale,—

LUC. Right. 85

DUKE. It may be right, but you are i' the wrong
To speak before your time. Proceed.

ISAB. I went
To this pernicious caitiff deputy,—

DUKE. That's somewhat madly spoken.

ISAB. Pardon it;
The phrase is to the matter. 90

DUKE. Mended again. The matter; proceed.

ISAB. In brief, to set the needless process by,
How I persuaded, how I pray'd, and kneel'd,
How he refell'd me, and how I repli'd,—
For this was of much length,—the vile conclusion 95
I now begin with grief and shame to utter.
He would not, but by gift of my chaste body
To his concupiscible intemperate lust,
Release my brother; and, after much debatement,
My sisterly remorse confutes mine honour, 100
And I did yield to him; but the next morn betimes,
His purpose surfeiting, he sends a warrant
For my poor brother's head.

DUKE. This is most likely!

ISAB. O, that it were as like as it is true!

DUKE. By heaven, fond wretch, thou know'st not what thou speak'st, 105
Or else thou art suborn'd against his honour
In hateful practice. First, his integrity
Stands without blemish. Next, it imports no reason
That with such vehemency he should pursue
Faults proper to himself. If he had so offended, 110
He would have weigh'd thy brother by himself,
And not have cut him off. Some one hath set you on.
Confess the truth, and say by whose advice
Thou cam'st here to complain.

ISAB. And is this all?
Then, O you blessed ministers above, 115
Keep me in patience, and with ripened time
Unfold the evil which is here wrapt up
In countenance! Heaven, shield your Grace from woe,
As I, thus wrong'd, hence unbelievèd go!

DUKE. I know you'd fain be gone. An officer! 120
To prison with her! Shall we thus permit
A blasting and a scandalous breath to fall
On him so near us? This needs must be a practice.
Who knew of your intent and coming hither?

ISAB. One that I would were here, Friar Lodowick. 125

DUKE. A ghostly father, belike. Who knows that Lodowick?

LUC. My lord, I know him; 'tis a meddling friar.
I do not like the man. Had he been lay, my lord,
For certain words he spake against your Grace
In your retirement, I had swing'd him soundly.

DUKE. Words against me! This's a good friar, belike! 131
And to set on this wretched woman here
Against our substitute! Let this friar be found.

72. probation, novitiate. 74. an't like, if it please. 82. I warrant, i.e., I assure you (I shall be). 83. warrant, surety. 90. to the matter, relevant to the case. 91. mended, set right. 92. set . . . by, pass over the unimportant order of events. 94. refell'd, refused. 98. concupiscible, lewd. 100. remorse, pity; confutes, prevails over. 101. betimes, early. 102. His purpose surfeiting, having indulged to satiety his desire. 104. like, i.e., likely to be believed. 105. fond, foolish. 106. suborn'd, bribed to bear false witness. 107. practice, plotting. 108. imports no reason, i.e., is thoroughly unreasonable. 110. proper, belonging. 118. countenance, reputation (of Angelo). 123. practice, plot. 124. intent . . . coming, intention to come. 126. ghostly, spiritual. 127. 'tis, this expresses contempt. 128. lay, i.e., a layman. 130. had swing'd, would have whipped.

LUC. But yesternight, my lord, she and that friar,
I saw them at the prison. A saucy friar, 135
A very scurvy fellow.

FRI. P. Blessed be your royal Grace!
I have stood by, my lord, and I have heard
Your royal ear abus'd. First, hath this woman
Most wrongfully accus'd your substitute, 140
Who is as free from touch or soil with her
As she from one ungot.

DUKE. We did believe no less.
Know you that Friar Lodowick that she speaks of?

FRI. P. I know him for a man divine and holy;
Not scurvy, nor a temporary meddler, 145
As he's reported by this gentleman;
And, on my trust, a man that never yet
Did, as he vouches, misreport your Grace.

LUC. My lord, most villanously; believe it.

FRI. P. Well, he in time may come to clear himself; 150
But at this instant he is sick, my lord,
Of a strange fever. Upon his mere request,
Being come to knowledge that there was complaint
Intended 'gainst Lord Angelo, came I hither,
To speak, as from his mouth, what he doth know 155
Is true and false; and what he with his oath
And all probation will make up full clear,
Whensoever he's convented. First, for this woman,
To justify this worthy nobleman,
So vulgarly and personally accus'd, 160
Her shall you hear disprovèd to her eyes,
Till she herself confess it.

DUKE. Good friar, let's hear it.

[ISABELLA *is carried off guarded.*]

Do you not smile at this, Lord Angelo?
O heaven, the vanity of wretched fools!
Give us some seats. Come, cousin Angelo; 165
In this I'll be impartial. Be you judge
Of your own cause. Is this the witness, friar?

[*Enter* MARIANA, *veiled.*]

First, let her show her face, and after speak.

MARI. Pardon, my lord; I will not show my face
Until my husband bid me. 170

DUKE. What, are you married?

MARI. No, my lord.

DUKE. Are you a maid?

MARI. No, my lord.

DUKE. A widow, then? 175

MARI. Neither, my lord.

DUKE. Why, you are nothing then: neither maid, widow, nor wife?

LUC. My lord, she may be a punk; for many of them are neither maid, widow, nor wife.

DUKE. Silence that fellow. I would he had some cause 181
To prattle for himself.

LUC. Well, my lord.

MARI. My lord, I do confess I ne'er was married;
And I confess besides I am no maid. 185
I have known my husband; yet my husband
Knows not that ever he knew me.

LUC. He was drunk then, my lord; it can be no better.

DUKE. For the benefit of silence, would thou wert so too! 191

LUC. Well, my lord.

DUKE. This is no witness for Lord Angelo.

MARI. Now I come to't, my lord.
She that accuses him of fornication, 195
In self-same manner doth accuse my husband,
And charges him, my lord, with such a time
When I'll depose I had him in mine arms
With all the effect of love.

ANG. Charges she moe than me?

MARI. Not that I know.

DUKE. No? You say your husband. 201

MARI. Why, just, my lord, and that is Angelo,
Who thinks he knows that he ne'er knew my body,
But knows he thinks that he knows Isabel's.

ANG. This is a strange abuse. Let's see thy face. 205

MARI. My husband bids me; now I will unmask. [*Unveiling.*]
This is that face, thou cruel Angelo.
Which once thou swor'st was worth the looking on;

135. saucy, grossly disrespectful. 139. abus'd, deceived. 141. soil, taint. 142. ungot, unbegotten, i.e., unborn. 145. temporary meddler, one that meddles in temporal affairs. 148. misreport, defame. 152. upon . . . request, only at his request. 157. probation, proof. 158. convented, summoned; for, as for. 160. vulgarly, publicly. 161. disproved . . . eyes, denied to his face. 166. be impartial, take no part. 179. punk, prostitute. 186. known, had sexual intercourse with. 190. it . . . better, i.e., it must have been as bad as that! 198. depose, swear. 200. moe than, other than. 205. abuse, deceptive nonsense.

This is the hand which, with a vow'd contract,
Was fast belock'd in thine; this is the body
That took away the match from Isabel, 211
And did supply thee at thy garden-house
In her imagin'd person.

DUKE. Know you this woman?

LUC. Carnally, she says.

DUKE. Sirrah, no more!

LUC. Enough, my lord. 215

ANG. My lord, I must confess I know this woman;
And five years since there was some speech of marriage
Betwixt myself and her; which was broke off,
Partly for that her promisèd proportions
Came short of composition, but in chief 220
For that her reputation was disvalued
In levity: since which time of five years
I never spake with her, saw her, nor heard from her,
Upon my faith and honour.

MARI. Noble Prince,
As there comes light from heaven and words from breath, 225
As there is sense in truth and truth in virtue,
I am affianc'd this man's wife as strongly
As words could make up vows; and, my good lord,
But Tuesday night last gone in 's garden-house
He knew me as a wife. As this is true, 230
Let me in safety raise me from my knees;
Or else for ever be confixèd here,
A marble monument!

ANG. I did but smile till now.
Now, good my lord, give me the scope of justice.
My patience here is touch'd. I do perceive 235
These poor informal women are no more
But instruments of some more mightier member
That sets them on. Let me have way, my lord,
To find this practice out.

DUKE. Ay, with my heart;
And punish them unto your height of pleasure. 240
Thou foolish friar, and thou pernicious woman,
Compact with her that's gone, think'st thou thy oaths,
Though they would swear down each particular saint,
Were testimonies against his worth and credit
That's seal'd in approbation? You, Lord Escalus, 245
Sit with my cousin. Lend him your kind pains
To find out this abuse, whence 'tis deriv'd.
There is another friar that set them on;
Let him be sent for.

FRI. P. Would he were here, my lord, for he indeed 250
Hath set the women on to this complaint.
Your provost knows the place where he abides,
And he may fetch him.

DUKE. Go, do it instantly.
[*Exit* PROVOST.]
And you, my noble and well-warranted cousin,
Whom it concerns to hear this matter forth,
Do with your injuries as seems you best, 256
In any chastisement. I for a while will leave you;
But stir not you till you have well determin'd
Upon these slanderers.

ESCAL. My lord, we'll do it throughly. 260
[*Exit* DUKE.]
Signior Lucio, did not you say you knew that Friar Lodowick to be a dishonest person?

LUC. "Cucullus non facit monachum:" honest in nothing but in his clothes; and one that hath spoke most villanous speeches of the Duke. 265

ESCAL. We shall entreat you to abide here till he come and enforce them against him. We shall find this friar a notable fellow.

LUC. As any in Vienna, on my word.

ESCAL. Call that same Isabel here once 270 again; I would speak with her. [*Exit an* ATTENDANT.] Pray you, my lord, give me leave to question; you shall see how I'll handle her.

211. match, appointment. 212. garden-house, summer house. 219. proportions, dowry. 220. composition, the agreed amount. 221-2. was disvalued in levity, was depreciated because of her loose behavior. 232. confixed, fastened. 234. give . . . justice, i.e., allow me to let justice have free sway. 236. informal, insane. 239. find . . . out, expose this plot. 242. compact, leagued. 244. credit, reputation. 245. seal'd in approbation, sealed and approved. 246. lend . . . pains, kindly take the trouble to help. 247. abuse, deception.

255. forth, out, to the end. 256. Do . . . injuries, treat the slander against you. 258-9. But . . . slanderers, But do not go away until you have definitely decided what punishment to inflict upon these slanderers. 263. Cucullus . . . monachum, a cowl does not make a monk. 267. enforce . . . him, bring them home to him. 268. notable, egregious, notorious.

LUC. Not better than he, by her own report.
ESCAL. Say you? 275
LUC. Marry, sir, I think, if you handled her privately, she would sooner confess. Perchance, publicly, she'll be asham'd.

[*Re-enter* OFFICERS *with* ISABELLA; *and* PROVOST *with the* DUKE *in his friar's habit.*]

ESCAL. I will go darkly to work with her.
LUC. That's the way, for women are light at midnight. 281
ESCAL. Come on, mistress. Here's a gentlewoman denies all that you have said.
LUC. My lord, here comes the rascal I spoke of; here with the Provost. 285
ESCAL. In very good time. Speak not you to him till we call upon you.
LUC. Mum.
ESCAL. Come, sir, did you set these women on to slander Lord Angelo? They have confess'd you did. 291
DUKE. 'Tis false.
ESCAL. How! know you where you are?
DUKE. Respect to your great place! and let the devil
Be sometimes honour'd for his burning throne!
Where is the Duke? 'Tis he should hear me speak. 296
ESCAL. The Duke's in us; and we will hear you speak.
Look you speak justly.
DUKE. Boldly, at least. But, O, poor souls,
Come you to seek the lamb here of the fox?
Good night to your redress! Is the Duke gone? 301
Then is your cause gone too. The Duke's unjust
Thus to retort your manifest appeal,
And put your trial in the villain's mouth
Which here you come to accuse. 305
LUC. This is the rascal; this is he I spoke of.
ESCAL. Why, thou unreverend and unhallowed friar,
Is't not enough thou hast suborn'd these women
To accuse this worthy man, but, in foul mouth
And in the witness of his proper ear, 310
To call him villain, and then to glance from him
To the Duke himself, to tax him with injustice?
Take him hence; to the rack with him! We'll touse you
Joint by joint, but we will know his purpose.
What, "unjust"!
DUKE. Be not so hot. The Duke 315
Dare no more stretch this finger of mine than he
Dare rack his own. His subject am I not,
Nor here provincial. My business in this state
Made me a looker on here in Vienna,
Where I have seen corruption boil and bubble
Till it o'er-run the stew; laws for all faults, 321
But faults so countenanc'd, that the strong statutes
Stand like the forfeits in a barber's shop,
As much in mock as mark.
ESCAL. Slander to the state! Away with him to prison! 325
ANG. What can you vouch against him, Signior Lucio?
Is this the man that you did tell us of?
LUC. 'Tis he, my lord. Come hither, goodman bald-pate. Do you know me? 329
DUKE. I remember you, sir, by the sound of your voice. I met you at the prison, in the absence of the Duke.
LUC. O, did you so? And do you remember what you said of the Duke?
DUKE. Most notedly, sir. 335
LUC. Do you so, sir? And was the Duke a fleshmonger, a fool, and a coward, as you then reported him to be?
DUKE. You must, sir, change persons with me, ere you make that my report. You, 340 indeed, spoke so of him, and much more, much worse.
LUC. O thou damnable fellow! Did not I pluck thee by the nose for thy speeches?
DUKE. I protest I love the Duke as I love myself. 345
ANG. Hark, how the villain would close now, after his treasonable abuses!
ESCAL. Such a fellow is not to be talk'd

280. darkly, secretly. **281. light**, wanton. **294. place**, office. **303. retort**, turn back (to the man from whom you appealed to the Duke). **308. suborn'd**, secretly incited. **310. proper**, own. **312. tax**, reproach. **313. touse**, tear. **318. provincial**, under the jurisdiction of an ecclesiastical province. **321. stew**, cauldron, with a possible reference to stews = brothel. **323. forfeits . . . shop**, barbers, the dentists of the time, hung up extracted teeth for advertisements in their shops. **324. As . . . mark**, as much to be laughed at as to be observed. **335. notedly**, exactly **337. fleshmonger**, fornicator. **346. close**, make his peace

withal. Away with him to prison! Where is the Provost? Away with him to prison! 350
Lay bolts enough upon him. Let him speak no more. Away with those giglots too, and with the other confederate companion!

[*The* PROVOST *lays hands on the* DUKE.

DUKE. Stay, sir; stay awhile.

ANG. What, resists he? Help him, Lucio. 355

LUC. Come, sir; come, sir; come, sir; foh, sir! Why, you bald-pated, lying rascal, you must be hooded, must you? Show your knave's visage, with a pox to you! Show your sheep-biting face, and be hang'd an hour! Will't not off? [*Pulls off the friar's hood.* 360

DUKE. Thou art the first knave that e'er mad'st a duke.
First Provost, let me bail these gentle three.
[*To* LUCIO] Sneak not away, sir; for the friar and you
Must have a word anon. Lay hold on him.

LUC. This may prove worse than hanging. 365

DUKE. [*To* ESCALUS] What you have spoke I pardon.
Sit you down;
We'll borrow place of him. Sir, [*taking* ANGELO's *seat*] by your leave.
Hast thou or word, or wit, or impudence,
That yet can do thee office? If thou hast,
Rely upon it till my tale be heard, 370
And hold no longer out.

ANG. O my dread lord,
I should be guiltier than my guiltiness,
To think I can be undiscernible,
When I perceive your Grace, like power divine,
Hath look'd upon my passes. Then, good Prince, 375
No longer session hold upon my shame,
But let my trial be mine own confession.
Immediate sentence, then, and sequent death
Is all the grace I beg.

DUKE. Come hither, Mariana.
Say, wast thou e'er contracted to this woman?

ANG. I was, my lord. 381

DUKE. Go take her hence, and marry her instantly.
Do you the office, friar; which consummate,
Return him here again. Go with him, Provost.

[*Exeunt* ANGELO, MARIANA, FRIAR PETER, *and* PROVOST.

ESCAL. My lord, I am more amaz'd at his dishonour
Than at the strangeness of it.

DUKE. Come hither, Isabel. 386
Your friar is now your prince. As I was then
Advertising and holy to your business,
Not changing heart with habit, I am still
Attorney'd at your service.

ISAB. O, give me pardon, 390
That I, your vassal, have employ'd and pain'd
Your unknown sovereignty!

DUKE. You are pardon'd, Isabel;
And now, dear maid, be you as free to us.
Your brother's death, I know, sits at your heart;
And you may marvel why I obscur'd myself, 395
Labouring to save his life, and would not rather
Make rash remonstrance of my hidden power
Than let him so be lost. O most kind maid,
It was the swift celerity of his death,
Which I did think with slower foot came on, 400
That brain'd my purpose. But, peace be with him!
That life is better life, past fearing death,
Than that which lives to fear. Make it your comfort,
So happy is your brother.

[*Re-enter* ANGELO, MARIANA, FRIAR PETER, *and* PROVOST.]

ISAB. I do, my lord.

DUKE. For this new-married man approaching here, 405
Whose salt imagination yet hath wrong'd
Your well defended honour, you must pardon
For Mariana's sake; but as he adjudg'd your brother,—
Being criminal, in double violation
Of sacred chastity and of promise-breach 410
Thereon dependent, for your brother's life,—
The very mercy of the law cries out
Most audible, even from his proper tongue,

352. giglots, wanton women. 353. other, i.e., Friar Peter. 359. sheep-biting, thieving; an hour, a whole hour. 369. do . . . office, do you a service. 371. hold . . . out, play your part no longer. 373. undiscernible, undetected. 375. passes, trespasses. 378. sequent, to follow. 383. consummate, having been performed. 388. advertising and holy, attentive and dedicated. 390. Attorney'd, acting as an attorney. 391. pain'd, made trouble for. 393. free, generous, i.e., in forgiving my part in your brother's death. 395. obscured, hid. 397. rash remonstrance, hasty demonstration. 401. brain'd, killed. 404. so . . . brother, i.e., that your brother is thus happy. 406. salt, lustful. 409. criminal, guilty. 413. proper, own.

"An Angelo for Claudio, death for death!" 414
Haste still pays haste, and leisure answers leisure;
Like doth quit like, and *Measure* still *for Measure*.
Then, Angelo, thy fault's thus manifested;
Which, though thou wouldst deny, denies thee vantage.
We do condemn thee to the very block
Where Claudio stoop'd to death, and with like haste. 420
Away with him!

MARI. O my most gracious lord,
I hope you will not mock me with a husband.

DUKE. It is your husband mock'd you with a husband.
Consenting to the safeguard of your honour,
I thought your marriage fit; else imputation, 425
For that he knew you, might reproach your life
And choke your good to come. For his possessions,
Although by confiscation they are ours,
We do instate and widow you withal,
To buy you a better husband.

MARI. O my dear lord,
I crave no other, nor no better man. 431

DUKE. Never crave him; we are definitive.

MARI. Gentle my liege,— [*Kneeling*.

DUKE. You do but lose your labour,
Away with him to death! [*To* LUCIO] Now, sir, to you.

MARI. O my good lord! Sweet Isabel, take my part! 435
Lend me your knees, and all my life to come
I'll lend you all my life to do you service.

DUKE. Against all sense you do importune her.
Should she kneel down in mercy of this fact,
Her brother's ghost his pavèd bed would break,
And take her hence in horror.

MARI. Isabel, 441
Sweet Isabel, do yet but kneel by me.
Hold up your hands, say nothing; I'll speak all.
They say, best men are moulded out of faults,
And, for the most, become much more the better
For being a little bad; so may my husband. 446
O Isabel, will you not lend a knee?

DUKE. He dies for Claudio's death.

ISAB. [*Kneeling*] Most bounteous sir,
Look, if it please you, on this man condemn'd,
As if my brother liv'd. I partly think 450
A due sincerity governed his deeds,
Till he did look on me. Since it is so,
Let him not die. My brother had but justice,
In that he did the thing for which he died;
For Angelo, 455
His act did not o'ertake his bad intent,
And must be buried but as an intent
That perish'd by the way. Thoughts are no subjects;
Intents, but merely thoughts.

MARI. Merely, my lord.

DUKE. Your suit's unprofitable; stand up, I say. 460
I have bethought me of another fault.
Provost, how came it Claudio was beheaded
At an unusual hour?

PROV. It was commanded so.

DUKE. Had you a special warrant for the deed?

PROV. No, my good lord; it was by private message.

DUKE. For which I do discharge you of your office: 466
Give up your keys.

PROV. Pardon me, noble lord.
I thought it was a fault, but knew it not;
Yet did repent me, after more advice.
For testimony whereof, one in the prison, 470
That should by private order else have died,
I have reserv'd alive.

DUKE. What's he?

PROV. His name is Barnardine.

DUKE. I would thou hadst done so by Claudio.
Go fetch him hither; let me look upon him.
[*Exit* PROVOST.

ESCAL. I am sorry, one so learned and so wise 475

416. **quit**, requite, pay for; **still**, always. 418. **wouldst**, shouldst; **denies thee vantage**, denies you advantage, i.e., would do you no good. 425. **imputation**, censure. 426. **reproach**, disgrace. 427. **For**, as for. 429. **instate . . . withal**, invest and dower you with them. 432. **definitive**, resolved. 439. **of this fact**, for this deed. 440. **paved**, i.e., under the pavement of the church. 442. **yet**, at least. 458. **that . . . way**, that died on a journey (and so was buried by the roadside in an obscure and forgotten grave); **subjects**, real things. 460. **unprofitable**, useless. 469. **after . . . advice**, on further consideration. 472. **What's he?** Who is he?

As you, Lord Angelo, have still appear'd,
Should slip so grossly, both in the heat of blood,
And lack of temper'd judgement afterward.

ANG. I am sorry that such sorrow I procure;
And so deep sticks it in my penitent heart 480
That I crave death more willingly than mercy.
'Tis my deserving, and I do entreat it.

[*Re-enter* PROVOST, *with* BARNARDINE, CLAUDIO *muffled, and* JULIET.]

DUKE. Which is that Barnardine?

PROV. This, my lord.

DUKE. There was a friar told me of this man.
Sirrah, thou art said to have a stubborn soul, 485
That apprehends no further than this world,
And squar'st thy life according. Thou'rt condemn'd;
But, for those earthly faults, I quit them all;
And pray thee take this mercy to provide
For better times to come. Friar, advise him; 490
I leave him to your hand. What muffl'd fellow's that?

PROV. This is another prisoner that I sav'd,
Who should have died when Claudio lost his head;
As like almost to Claudio as himself.
[*Unmuffles* CLAUDIO.

DUKE. [*To* ISABELLA] If he be like your brother, for his sake 495
Is he pardon'd; and, for your lovely sake—
Give me your hand and say you will be mine—
He is my brother too. But fitter time for that.
By this Lord Angelo perceives he's safe;
Methinks I see a quickening in his eye. 500
Well, Angelo, your evil quits you well.
Look that you love your wife; her worth worth yours.
I find an apt remission in myself;
And yet here's one in place I cannot pardon.
[*To* LUCIO] You, sirrah, that knew me for a fool, a coward, 505
One all of luxury, an ass, a madman,
Wherein have I so deserv'd of you,
That you extol me thus?

LUC. Faith, my lord, I spoke it but according to the trick. If you will hang me for 510 it, you may; but I had rather it would please you I might be whipp'd.

DUKE. Whipp'd first, sir, and hang'd after.
Proclaim it, Provost, round about the city;
Is any woman wrong'd by this lewd fellow, 515
As I have heard him swear himself there's one
Whom he begot with child, let her appear,
And he shall marry her. The nuptial finish'd,
Let him be whipp'd and hang'd.

LUC. I beseech your Highness do not 520 marry me to a whore. Your Highness said even now, I made you a duke; good my lord, do not recompense me in making me a cuckold.

DUKE. Upon mine honour, thou shalt marry her.
Thy slanders I forgive; and therewithal 525
Remit thy other forfeits. Take him to prison;
And see our pleasure herein executed.

LUC. Marrying a punk, my lord, is pressing to death, whipping, and hanging.

DUKE. Slandering a prince deserves it. 530
[*Exeunt* OFFICERS *with* LUCIO.]
She, Claudio, that you wrong'd, look you restore.
Joy to you, Mariana! Love her, Angelo!
I have confess'd her and I know her virtue.
Thanks, good friend Escalus, for thy much goodness;
There's more behind that is more gratulate. 535
Thanks, Provost, for thy care and secrecy;
We shall employ thee in a worthier place.
Forgive him, Angelo, that brought you home
The head of Ragozine for Claudio's;
The offence pardons itself. Dear Isabel, 540
I have a motion much imports your good;
Whereto if you'll a willing ear incline,
What's mine is yours and what is yours is mine.
So, bring us to our palace, where we'll show
What's yet behind, that's meet you all should know. [*Exeunt.*

476. still, always. 477. blood, passion. 479. procure, cause. s.d. muffled, his face covered with a muffler. 486. apprehends . . . world, recognizes the existence of nothing beyond this world. 487. squar'st, regulate; according, accordingly. 488. for, as for; quit, pardon. 490. advise, give him spiritual instruction. 497. Give, if you will give. 500. quickening, lightening. 501. quits you well, turns out well for you. 503. apt remission, readiness to forgive. 504. in place, present. 506. luxury, lust. 509-10. according . . . trick, according to my fashion of jesting. 518. nuptial, wedding ceremony. 526. forfeits, penalties (i.e., whipping and hanging). 528. punk, harlot; pressing to death, executing by crushing under heavy weights. 531. restores, make restitution. 535. behind, to come; gratulate, gratifying. 541. motion, proposal; much . . . good, of much importance to your welfare.

AFTERWORD

In the second act of *Measure for Measure,* Angelo, the hypocritical deputy, puts a distressing question to Isabella, the chaste sister of young Claudio, who has been condemned to death. Which had she rather, that her brother die, to satisfy the law or that her chastity be sacrificed to satisfy the deputy's pleasure? The question is, however, more than distressing. It is a preposterous question. That is the essential point to take hold of in approaching this ambiguous play.

Isabella, the type of the hard good woman, is horrified at the alternatives between which she is required to choose. But it does not occur to her, neither does it occur to Angelo, to query the propriety of these alternatives. Exactly like her adversary, she finds the extreme position congenial. She is by temperament a radical, who interprets moral and ethical problems in terms of either/or. In responding to her persecutor, she sees no need to pause or reflect. Her answer is assured, and is delivered, appropriately, in a glib and schematic couplet:

> Then, Isabel, live chaste, and, brother, die;
> More than our brother is our chastity.

An ear trained to poetry will find this utterance banal rather than convincing—like the little homilies of Friar Laurence, in *Romeo and Juliet.* Life is not so pat, or so amenable to easy generalization. Real answers to real questions demand an idiom less absolute and more circumstantial.

Isabella is unaware of the modification imposed by a total or circumstantial view. She pins her faith to abstractions dancing in air—like honor, like justice. Angelo, in the event, is a perverter of justice. But the virtuous young woman, who has already determined to live a life of virginity and iron restraint, and the lustful deputy who covets her body and seeks to persuade her to a life of "sweet uncleanness," are cut from the same cloth. In the language of the play, "there went but a pair of shears" between them. Each is supremely ready to judge and to pronounce. Each knows what he knows. Each inhabits a world of primary colors, where there are no shadows, or doubtful or difficult cases. The entire action of the play is intended to controvert or to explode the bigoted assurance they bring to bear, in addressing themselves to human behavior.

The extravagant dilemma with which Angelo confronts Isabella is a false dilemma, the staple of melodrama or two-penny romance. It hints, however, like a crude or counterfeit copy, at the thornier problem which we as auditors must confront in estimating the business of *Measure for Measure.* That is often Shakespeare's method. He brings us to the truth by way of specious approximations. To quote from the Chorus to *Henry V,* he makes us mind "true things by what their mockeries be." The more serious and more relevant problem with which we must grapple in *Measure for Measure* is the reconciling of legitimate but often contradictory claims: on the one hand, the claim of justice, as embodied in the law, and on the other, the claim of fellow-feeling or compassion, which we will wish to honor as we are human.

Vincentio, the Duke, who is in this play the positive pole about which our responses collect, puts the problem succinctly, in the opening scene. On Angelo who, in his absence, is to govern the state, a difficult function is enjoined:

> Mortality and mercy in Vienna
> Live in thy tongue and heart.

"Mortality" signifies the power of life and death, as invested in the governor. He is to be the dispenser of justice. As he fulfills his charge, he will not hesitate to punish the lawbreaker. The obligation is clear and, in Angelo's case, it is agreeable.

But Angelo is instructed to be merciful, not less than just. He will manifest the quality of mercy as he himself is "mortal" or human, which means as he himself is liable to err. This proneness or liability is the cardinal fact of human psychology, as Shakespeare construes it in *Measure for Measure.* The construction is not embittered or despairing; it is even indulgent. Shakespeare, unlike Angelo, unlike Isabella, does not require perfection of men. Mariana, who suffers grievously because Angelo is imperfect, is able nonetheless to observe:

> They say, best men are moulded out of faults,
> And, for the most, become much more the better
> For being a little bad.

Angelo disputes the proposition. He is unwilling to confess that blood flows in his body. When he falls from virtue—and, in this context, we understand that his fall is inevitable, the condition of "mortality"—he must pretend that he is virtuous still. And so he runs foul of the third part of the Duke's injunction. He has been adjured to reconcile the roles of justicer and merciful man, not only in his tongue or public demeanor but also in his heart. It is incumbent on him not merely to seem but to be. We go back in mind to the Latin tag on which Shakespeare in *Twelfth Night* has levied before, and which in this play he puts in the mouth of the slanderous Lucio: *Cucullus non facit monachum.* The cowl does not make the monk. In the person of Angelo, whose blood seems made of snow broth, the melancholy proverb is verified again.

The play, on this side, is an experiment or test, the enjoyment of which consists in discovering "what our seemers be." But more than the integrity of Angelo is at stake. What Shakespeare is attempting to get at or to define is nothing less than the nature of the well-conducted society. This ultimate intention, as conveyed by Vincentio in the first words he speaks, is "Of government the properties to unfold."

The Duke himself has faltered in the conduct of the state: in the precise articulation of the conflicting properties of mercy and justice. His bias—which we are willing, perhaps a shade too quickly, to pardon—is on the side of mercy.

He himself is not so complacent. He has been at fault, he thinks, in allowing the people too much "scope." The word recurs often, in the course of the play. "Your scope is as mine own," says the Duke, relinquishing his authority to Angelo,

> So to enforce or qualify the laws
> As to your soul seems good.

Angelo, who now possesses the full prerogative of the ruler, will, as he thinks fit, employ this prerogative to bear down hard or else to temper justice with mercy. In the exercise of power, how will he define proper "scope"?

We do not get very far before the answer is apparent. Angelo is a tyrant, who deals with the body public as with "A horse whereon the governor doth ride." His understanding is restricted to what he calls, in the final act, "the scope of justice." But that is also true of Isabella. Her appeal to the Duke on his resumption of power is, in keeping with her character, an exclusive appeal. What she craves is only "justice, justice, justice, justice!" The same narrowness is manifest when we meet her first, in the demand she makes of the sisterhood she has pledged herself to enter: not more liberal privileges but "a more strict restraint." The crying-up, by this man and this woman, of abstinence and a ruthless enforcing of the letter of the law and the life of cloistered virtue, is profoundly unattractive. So far, all our sympathies are given to mercy and permissiveness.

A lesser dramatist or psychologist than Shakespeare would be satisfied to leave us there. Shakespeare perceives, however, that the problem he is canvassing does not admit of so facile a resolution. (In this, he differs again from Angelo and Isabella.) In the second scene of the play, he acquaints us with a crew of unsavory libertines—a bawd, a pimp, and their scurrilous patrons—who are talking whimsically of venereal disease. To these disagreeable characters, young Claudio enters, under guard. He has got his betrothed with child, and so is on his way to prison. The impious Lucio, who thinks that fornication is only a game of tick-tack, the fitting of pegs into holes, wants to know the cause of Claudio's "restraint." He is answered: "From too much liberty." As Claudio continues, we begin to surmise that "the properties of government" are not exhausted in the qualifying or softening of the law. "Every scope," says the prisoner, "by the immoderate use Turns to restraint." Evidently, there is a kind of freedom, or license, which engenders the loss of freedom. Forbear to enforce the law, as Duke Vincentio has discovered, and the liberty which is license

> plucks justice by the nose;
> The baby beats the nurse, and quite athwart
> Goes all decorum.

The properties of government are summed in decorum: the rule of fitness and propriety, the establishing of "well-balanced form." Pompey, the comical and also beastly procurer, enacts the violating of decorum. The tendering of mercy to this incorrigible offender is merely a sentimental gesture. Even the kindly Escalus, whose voice is raised for leniency, understands that always to withhold punishment is to insure that fresh crimes will be committed tomorrow.

Mercy is not itself, that oft looks so;
Pardon is still the nurse of second woe.

Does it follow, in every case, that sentimentality and merciful behavior are the same?

Pompey, who crams his maw with the earnings of the brothel, whose life, as he concedes, "does stink in some sort," is sufficiently distasteful. But perhaps he is not so distasteful as Abhorson the hangman, who is the visible symbol of justice. Behind this grim figure stands the usurer, whose stealing is sanctioned and even honored by the law, and the wealthy burgher, who owns the whore house against which he inveighs in public, and the cruel and lecherous governor who, though he errs like others, has in his office a kind of medicine that skins or conceals his vicious conduct. In the bubbling stew of corruption which is Vienna, "craft, being richer than innocency," diverts the course of justice to its own improper ends. Do we conclude that justice, by definition, is a lie?

In fact, the conclusion to which the play moves us is that the explicit question, which must be answered dogmatically and once and for all, is not a question for human beings to raise. The properties of government, in man, in society, are not definable as capital-letter abstractions. Neither do they exist in a vacuum, but in a decorous equilibrium which is, literally, alive. Mercy and justice, rigor and leniency are good or bad, not in themselves, but good or bad as the context determines. Every human situation is an equivocal situation. Every human situation is concrete.

This is the discovery permitted to Isabella, who learns that the only unforgivable sin is to look on human beings with an impersonal or generalizing eye. On the transforming of this singleminded heroine, ultimate forgiveness depends. When, however, in the climactic moment of the play, Isabella implores mercy for Angelo, she is not asserting by her action that mercy is better than justice. That is the unambiguous conclusion at which the radical and the sentimentalist will arrive. The conclusion of *Measure for Measure* is more tentative, and so more nearly true.

SUGGESTED READING

BENNETT, JOSEPHINE W., "*Measure for Measure*" *as Royal Entertainment* (1966). Penguin.

CHAMBERS, R. W., *The Jacobean Shakespeare and "Measure for Measure"* (1937). Penguin.

DAICHES, DAVID, *Critical Approaches to Literature* (1956). Norton.

EMPSON, WILLIAM, "Sense in 'Measure for Measure,' " in *The Structure of Complex Words* (1951). Michigan.

FERGUSSON, FRANCIS, *The Human Image in Dramatic Literature* (1957). Anchor.

KNIGHT, G. WILSON, "'Measure for Measure' and the Gospels," in *The Wheel of Fire* (enlarged ed., 1954). Barnes and Noble.

LASCELLES, MARY, *Shakespeare's "Measure for Measure"* (1953).

LAWRENCE, W. W., *Shakespeare's Problem Comedies* (1931, 2nd ed. 1960). Penguin.

LEAVIS, F. R., *The Common Pursuit* (1952).

MURRAY, JOHN MIDDLETON, *Shakespeare* (1936). Hillary.

ORNSTEIN, ROBERT, *Discussions of Shakespeare's Problem Comedies* (1961). Heath.

PARROTT, THOMAS MARC, *Shakespearean Comedy* (1949).

SCHANZER, ERNEST, *The Problem Plays of Shakespeare* (1963). Schocken.

SEWELL, ARTHUR, *Character and Society in Shakespeare* (1951).

SISSON, C. J., *The Mythical Sorrows of Shakespeare* (1934).

STEVENSON, DAVID L., *The Achievement of Shakespeare's "Measure for Measure"* (1966). Penguin.

SYPHER, WYLIE, *Four Stages of Renaissance Style* (1956). Anchor.

TILLYARD, E. M. W., *Shakespeare's Problem Plays* (1949). Toronto.

King Lear

A NOTE ON THE TEXT

Internal evidence indicates that *King Lear* was written not later than 1606. Gloucester's superstitious ruminations, inspired by "these late eclipses in the sun and moon," perhaps refer to actual eclipses, recorded in the previous year. The almanac-writer Edward Gresham moralizes these untoward events in a tract dated February 11, 1606, and entitled, *Strange, fearful and true news which happened at Carlstadt in the kingdom of Croatia*. Shakespeare in his play is influenced perceptibly by Gresham's account.

An entry in the Register of the Stationers' Company, dated November 26, 1607, describes the play as having been acted before King James and the Court at Whitehall on St. Stephen's night "at Christmas Last" (December, 26, 1606). A first quarto appeared in 1608; it is known as the Pied Bull Quarto, after the sign which hung before the workshop of the printer. The second or N. Butter Quarto, named for the printer and issued in 1619, is dated erroneously in the year of Q1. Q2 depends on a corrected copy of Q1. The Folio text of 1623 draws also on a corrected copy of Q1, but omits a large number of lines occurring in that earlier printing, while including passages which Q1 omits. Evidently, the Folio text is based, not only on Q1, but on the prompt book, the shorter, acting version of the play, in the possession of the Folio editors.

Shakespeare's sources include, in addition to Gresham's sensational work on portents and prodigies, a rationalizing of diabolic activity by the Reverend Samuel Harsnett. It is Harsnett's *Declaration of egregious popish impostures*, written in 1602–03, which furnished Shakespeare with the names of the devils who trouble Edgar in his character of Poor Tom. Other details, for example, the hanging of Cordelia, derive from Edmund Spenser's epic narrative, *The Faerie Queene* (1590); from the *Essays* (translated 1603) of Shakespeare's great French contemporary, Montaigne; and from the *Mirror for Magistrates* (1574), a popular collection of cautionary tales on the overthrow of princes.

The tragic story of King Lear appears first in literature in a twelfth-century *History of the Kings of Britain* by Geoffrey of Monmouth. Holinshed, in the second edition of his *Chronicles of England, Scotland, and Ireland* (1587), retells the story, as does an anonymous playwright of the late 1580s, whose *Chronicle History of King Leir* was published and perhaps acted in 1605.

None of these source writers sees what Shakespeare sees—that the awful vision implicit in the account of Lear's destruction is not partial but plenary. Shakespeare alone insists that the story of Lear and his three daughters is not an aberrant or eccentric story. The introduction of the subplot, which tells of Gloucester and his good and evil sons, and which Shakespeare gathers from the *Arcadia,* a prose romance of the 1580s by Sir Philip Sidney, serves to recapitulate the horror of the major story. But this complementary or analogous action does more than magnify the horror. It seems almost to enforce the conviction that abnormal behavior is the norm.

KING LEAR

DRAMATIS PERSONÆ

LEAR, *king of Britain.*
KING OF FRANCE.
DUKE OF BURGUNDY.
DUKE OF CORNWALL.
DUKE OF ALBANY.
EARL OF KENT.
EARL OF GLOUCESTER.
EDGAR, *son to Gloucester.*
EDMUND, *bastard son to Gloucester.*
CURAN, *a courtier.*
OLD MAN, *tenant to Gloucester.*
DOCTOR.
FOOL.
OSWALD, *steward to Goneril.*
A CAPTAIN *employed by Edmund.*
GENTLEMAN *attendant on Cordelia.*
A HERALD.
SERVANTS *to Cornwall.*
GONERIL, REGAN, CORDELIA, *daughters to Lear.*
KNIGHTS *of Lear's train,* CAPTAINS, MESSENGERS, SOLDIERS, *and* ATTENDANTS.

SCENE: *Britain.*

ACT I

SCENE I. KING LEAR's *palace.*

[*Enter* KENT, GLOUCESTER, *and* EDMUND.]

KENT. I thought the king had more affected the Duke of Albany than Cornwall.

GLOU. It did always seem so to us: but now, in the division of the kingdom, it appears not which of the dukes he values most; for equalities are so weighed, that curiosity in neither can make choice of either's moiety. 7

KENT. Is not this your son, my lord?

GLOU. His breeding, sir, hath been at my charge: I have so often blushed to acknowledge him, that now I am brazed to it. 11

KENT. I cannot conceive you.

GLOU. Sir, this young fellow's mother could: whereupon she grew round-wombed, and had, indeed, sir, a son for her cradle ere she had a husband for her bed. Do you smell a fault?

KENT. I cannot wish the fault undone, the issue of it being so proper. 18

GLOU. But I have, sir, a son by order of law, some year elder than this, who yet is no dearer in my account: though this knave came something saucily into the world before he was sent for, yet was his mother fair; there was good sport at his making, and the whoreson must be acknowledged. Do you know this noble gentleman, Edmund? 25

EDM. No, my lord.

GLOU. My lord of Kent: remember him hereafter as my honourable friend.

EDM. My services to your lordship.

KENT. I must love you, and sue to know you better. 31

EDM. Sir, I shall study deserving.

GLOU. He hath been out nine years, and away he shall again. The king is coming.

[*Sennet. Enter* KING LEAR, CORNWALL, ALBANY, GONERIL, REGAN, CORDELIA, *and* ATTENDANTS.]

LEAR. Attend the lords of France and Burgundy, Gloucester. 35

Act I, Scene i: 1. affected, favored. 2. Albany, an old name for Scotland. 6. equalities . . . weighed, shares are so (evenly) balanced. 7. curiosity . . . moiety, careful examination, cannot decide which portion (moiety) is to be preferred. 10. charge, expense. 11. brazed, hardened.

12. conceive, understand. 18. proper, handsome. 19-20. by . . . law, legally. 20. some year, about a year. 22. something, somewhat. 24. whoreson, lit., son of a whore, hence bastard. 32. deserving, i.e., to deserve your favor. 33. out, i.e., of England, abroad. s.d. sennet, a series of notes sounded on a trumpet.

GLOU. I shall, my liege.
[*Exeunt* GLOUCESTER *and* EDMUND.
LEAR. Meantime we shall express our darker purpose.
Give me the map there. Know that we have divided
In three our kingdom: and 'tis our fast intent
To shake all cares and business from our age; 40
Conferring them on younger strengths, while we
Unburthen'd crawl toward death. Our son of Cornwall,
And you, our no less loving son of Albany,
We have this hour a constant will to publish
Our daughters' several dowers, that future strife 45
May be prevented now. The princes, France and Burgundy,
Great rivals in our youngest daughter's love,
Long in our court have made their amorous sojourn,
And here are to be answer'd. Tell me, my daughters,—
Since now we will divest us, both of rule, 50
Interest of territory, cares of state,—
Which of you shall we say doth love us most?
That we our largest bounty may extend
Where nature doth with merit challenge. Goneril,
Our eldest-born, speak first. 55
GON. Sir, I love you more than words can wield the matter;
Dearer than eye-sight, space, and liberty;
Beyond what can be valued, rich or rare;
No less than life, with grace, health, beauty, honour;
As much as child e'er loved, or father found;
A love that makes breath poor, and speech unable; 61
Beyond all manner of so much I love you.
COR. [*Aside*] What shall Cordelia do? Love, and be silent.
LEAR. Of all these bounds, even from this line to this,
With shadowy forests and with champains rich'd, 65
With plenteous rivers and wide-skirted meads,
We make thee lady: to thine and Albany's issue
Be this perpetual. What says our second daughter,
Our dearest Regan, wife to Cornwall? Speak.
REG. Sir, I am made 70
Of the self-same metal that my sister is,
And prize me at her worth. In my true heart
I find she names my very deed of love;
Only she comes too short: that I profess
Myself an enemy to all other joys, 75
Which the most precious square of sense possesses;
And find I am alone felicitate
In your dear highness' love.
COR. [*Aside*] Then poor Cordelia!
And yet not so; since, I am sure, my love's
More richer than my tongue. 80
LEAR. To thee and thine hereditary ever
Remain this ample third of our fair kingdom;
No less in space, validity, and pleasure,
Than that conferr'd on Goneril. Now, our joy,
Although the last, not least; to whose young love 85
The vines of France and milk of Burgundy
Strive to be interess'd; what can you say to draw
A third more opulent than your sisters? Speak.
COR. Nothing, my lord.
LEAR. Nothing! 90
COR. Nothing.
LEAR. Nothing will come of nothing: speak again.
COR. Unhappy that I am, I cannot heave
My heart into my mouth. I love your majesty
According to my bond; nor more nor less. 95
LEAR. How, how, Cordelia! mend your speech a little,

37. **darker**, more secret. 39. **fast intent**, firm purpose. 44. **constant**, firm; **publish**, make known. 46. **prevented**, forestalled; **France**, King of France; **Burgundy**, Duke of Burgundy. 51. **interest of**, claim to. 54. **Where . . . challenge**, where your merit and my natural affection lay equal claim (to my generosity). 56. **wield the matter**, serve to express the fact. 57. **space**, freedom from imprisonment; **liberty**, i.e., of action. 59. **grace**, favor. 60. **found**, i.e., in a child's love. 62. **all . . . much**, every sort of similar comparison. 65. **champains . . . rich'd**, enriched with fertile fields. 72. **And . . . worth**, and estimate my value to be the same as hers. 73. **very . . . love**, my love as it actually is. 74. that, in that. 76. **which . . . possesses**, which the most delicate test of feeling takes for joys. 77. **felicitate**, made happy. 78. **dear . . . love**, love of your dear highness. 80. **More . . . tongue**, i.e., greater than I can express in words. 83. **validity**, value. 86. **milk**, i.e., pastures. 87. **to be interess'd**, to have a right in. 95. **bond**, obligation (as a daughter).

Lest it may mar your fortunes.
COR. Good my lord,
You have begot me, bred me, loved me: I
Return those duties back as are right fit,
Obey you, love you, and most honour you. 100
Why have my sisters husbands, if they say
They love you all? Haply, when I shall wed,
That lord whose hand must take my plight shall carry
Half my love with him, half my care and duty:
Sure, I shall never marry like my sisters, 105
To love my father all.
LEAR. But goes thy heart with this?
COR. Ay, good my lord.
LEAR. So young, and so untender?
COR. So young, my lord, and true.
LEAR. Let it be so; thy truth, then, be thy dower. 110
For, by the sacred radiance of the sun,
The mysteries of Hecate, and the night;
By all the operation of the orbs
From whom we do exist, and cease to be;
Here I disclaim all my paternal care, 115
Propinquity and property of blood,
And as a stranger to my heart and me
Hold thee, from this, for ever. The barbarous Scythian,
Or he that makes his generation messes
To gorge his appetite, shall to my bosom 120
Be as well neighbour'd, pitied, and relieved,
As thou my sometime daughter.
KENT. Good my liege,—
LEAR. Peace, Kent!
Come not between the dragon and his wrath.
I loved her most, and thought to set my rest
On her kind nursery. Hence, and avoid my sight! 126
So be my grave my peace, as here I give
Her father's heart from her! Call France; who stirs?
Call Burgundy. Cornwall and Albany,
With my two daughters' dowers digest this third: 130
Let pride, which she calls plainness, marry her.
I do invest you jointly with my power,
Pre-eminence, and all the large effects
That troop with majesty. Ourself, by monthly course,
With reservation of an hundred knights, 135
By you to be sustain'd, shall our abode
Make with you by due turns. Only we still retain
The name, and all the additions to a king;
The sway, revenue, execution of the rest,
Belovèd sons, be yours: which to confirm, 140
This coronet part betwixt you.
[*Giving the crown.*
KENT. Royal Lear,
Whom I have ever honour'd as my king,
Loved as my father, as my master follow'd,
As my great patron thought on in my prayers,—
LEAR. The bow is bent and drawn, make from the shaft. 145
KENT. Let it fall rather, though the fork invade
The region of my heart: be Kent unmannerly,
When Lear is mad. What wilt thou do, old man?
Think'st thou that duty shall have dread to speak,
When power to flattery bows? To plainness honour's bound, 150
When majesty stoops to folly. Reverse thy doom;
And, in thy best consideration, check
This hideous rashness: answer my life my judgement,
Thy youngest daughter does not love thee least;
Nor are those empty-hearted whose low sound 155
Reverbs no hollowness.
LEAR. Kent, on thy life, no more.
KENT. My life I never held but as a pawn
To wage against thy enemies; nor fear to lose it,

99. as are right fit, which are most fitting (for a daughter). 102. love you all, i.e., give you all their love. 103. plight, pledge. 112. mysteries, secret religious rites; Hecate, goddess of the lower world, of witchcraft and of magic. 113. operation, influence; orbs, stars. 116. property, identity. 118. Scythian, inhabitant of Southern Russia, since classical times regarded as complete barbarians. 119. generation messes, food of his children. 124. dragon, i.e., his crest; his wrath, object of his wrath. 125. set my rest, rely entirely. 126. nursery, nursing; avoid, leave. 130. digest, assimilate, combine. 131. plainness, frankness. 133. large effects, lavish manifestations. 134. troop with, march in company with. 138. additions, titles. 139. rest, i.e., of my royal prerogatives. 145. make . . . shaft, avoid the arrow (of my anger). 146. fall, fly; fork, i.e., arrowhead. 151. doom, judgment (pronounced against Cordelia). 153. answer . . . judgement, i.e., I'll stake my life on the correctness of my opinion. 156. Reverbs, reverberates with. 158. wage, stake.

Thy safety being the motive.

LEAR. Out of my sight!

KENT. See better, Lear; and let me still remain 160
The true blank of thine eye.

LEAR. Now, by Apollo,—

KENT. Now, by Apollo, king,
Thou swear'st thy gods in vain.

LEAR. O, vassal! miscreant!
[*Laying his hand on his sword.*

ALB. / CORN. Dear sir, forbear.

KENT. Do; 165
Kill thy physician, and the fee bestow
Upon thy foul disease. Revoke thy doom;
Or, whilst I can vent clamour from my throat,
I'll tell thee thou dost evil.

LEAR. Hear me, recreant!
On thine allegiance, hear me! 170
Since thou hast sought to make us break our vow,
Which we durst never yet, and with strain'd pride
To come between our sentence and our power,
Which nor our nature nor our place can bear,
Our potency made good, take thy reward. 175
Five days we do allot thee, for provision
To shield thee from diseases of the world;
And on the sixth to turn thy hated back
Upon our kingdom: if, on the tenth day following,
Thy banish'd trunk be found in our dominions, 180
The moment is thy death. Away! by Jupiter,
This shall not be revoked.

KENT. Fare thee well, king: sith thus thou wilt appear,
Freedom lives hence, and banishment is here.
[*To* CORDELIA] The gods to their dear shelter take thee, maid, 185
That justly think'st, and hast most rightly said!
[*To* REGAN *and* GONERIL] And your large speeches may your deeds approve,
That good effects may spring from words of love.
Thus Kent, O princes, bids you all adieu;
He'll shape his old course in a country new.
[*Exit.*

[*Flourish. Re-enter* GLOUCESTER, *with* FRANCE, BURGUNDY, *and* ATTENDANTS.]

GLOU. Here's France and Burgundy, my noble lord. 191

LEAR. My lord of Burgundy,
We first address towards you, who with this king
Hath rivall'd for our daughter: what, in the least,
Will you require in present dower with her, 195
Or cease your quest of love?

BUR. Most royal majesty,
I crave no more than what your highness offer'd,
Nor will you tender less.

LEAR. Right noble Burgundy,
When she was dear to us, we did hold her so;
But now her price is fall'n. Sir, there she stands: 200
If aught within that little seeming substance,
Or all of it, with our displeasure pieced,
And nothing more, may fitly like your grace,
She's there, and she is yours.

BUR. I know no answer.

LEAR. Will you, with those infirmities she owes, 205
Unfriended, new-adopted to our hate,
Dower'd with our curse, and stranger'd with our oath,
Take her, or leave her?

BUR. Pardon me, royal sir;
Election makes not up on such conditions.

LEAR. Then leave her, sir; for, by the power that made me, 210
I tell you all her wealth. [*To* FRANCE] For you, great king,
I would not from your love make such a stray,
To match you where I hate; therefore beseech you
To avert your liking a more worthier way 214

161. blank, white center of a target. 163. miscreant, vile wretch. 169. recreant, breaker of your oath (of allegiance to me). 172. strain'd, excessive. 175. potency, authority; good, effective. 176. for provision, to provide means.

177. diseases, distresses, pains. 183. sith, since. 187. approve, justify. 190. course, conduct. 201. that . . . substance, that little person who only seems to be genuine. 203. like, please. 205. infirmities, defects; owes, owns. 209. Election . . . conditions, i.e., choice of wife is not made under such conditions. 211. For, as for. 214. avert . . . liking, turn your affection.

Than on a wretch whom nature is ashamed
Almost to acknowledge hers.

FRANCE. This is most strange,
That she, that even but now was your best object,
The argument of your praise, balm of your age,
Most best, most dearest, should in this trice of time 219
Commit a thing so monstrous, to dismantle
So many folds of favour. Sure, her offence
Must be of such unnatural degree,
That monsters it, or your fore-vouch'd affection
Fall'n into taint: which to believe of her, 224
Must be a faith that reason without miracle
Could never plant in me.

COR. I yet beseech your majesty,—
If for I want that glib and oily art,
To speak and purpose not; since what I well intend,
I'll do 't before I speak,—that you make known
It is no vicious blot, murder, or foulness, 230
No unchaste action, or dishonour'd step,
That hath deprived me of your grace and favour;
But even for want of that for which I am richer,
A still-soliciting eye, and such a tongue
As I am glad I have not, though not to have it 235
Hath lost me in your liking.

LEAR. Better thou
Hadst not been born than not to have pleased me better.

FRANCE. Is it but this,—a tardiness in nature
Which often leaves the history unspoke
That it intends to do? My lord of Burgundy, 240
What say you to the lady? Love's not love
When it is mingled with regards that stand
Aloof from the entire point. Will you have her?
She is herself a dowry.

BUR. Royal Lear,
Give but that portion which yourself proposed, 245
And here I take Cordelia by the hand,
Duchess of Burgundy.

LEAR. Nothing: I have sworn; I am firm.

BUR. I am sorry, then, you have so lost a father
That you must lose a husband.

COR. Peace be with Burgundy!
Since that respects of fortune are his love, 251
I shall not be his wife.

FRANCE. Fairest Cordelia, that art most rich, being poor;
Most choice, forsaken; and most loved, despised!
Thee and thy virtues here I seize upon: 255
Be it lawful I take up what's cast away.
Gods, gods! 'tis strange that from their cold'st neglect
My love should kindle to inflamed respect.
Thy dowerless daughter, king, thrown to my chance,
Is queen of us, of ours, and our fair France:
Not all the dukes of waterish Burgundy 261
Can buy this unprized precious maid of me.
Bid them farewell, Cordelia, though unkind:
Thou losest here, a better where to find.

LEAR. Thou hast her, France: let her be thine; for we 265
Have no such daughter, nor shall ever see
That face of hers again. Therefore be gone
Without our grace, our love, our benison.
Come, noble Burgundy.

[*Flourish. Exeunt all but* FRANCE, GONERIL, REGAN, *and* CORDELIA.]

FRANCE. Bid farewell to your sisters. 270

COR. The jewels of our father, with wash'd eyes
Cordelia leaves you: I know you what you are;
And like a sister am most loath to call
Your faults as they are named. Use well our father:
To your professèd bosoms I commit him: 275
But yet, alas, stood I within his grace,
I would prefer him to a better place.

217. **your best object**, the main object of your love. 218. **argument**, topic. 219. **Trice**, instant. 220. **To**, as to. 223. **monsters**, makes monstrous. 224. **taint**, decay. 227. **for**, because. 228. **purpose not**, i.e., not to mean what one says. 230. **vicious blot**, stain made by a vice; **foulness**, lack of chastity. 233. **for which**, for lack of which. 234. **still-soliciting**, ever-begging. 236. **lost . . . liking**, i.e., made me lose your affection. 238. **tardiness in nature**, natural reticence. 242-3. **regards . . . point**, considerations that have nothing to do with the essence of the matter. 251. **respects**, considerations. 258. **inflamed**, heightened. 261. **waterish**, marshy. 262. **unprized**, unappreciated. 268. **grace**, favor; **benison**, blessing. 274. **as . . . named**, by their proper names. 275. **professed**, full of professions (of love). 277. **prefer**, recommend.

So, farewell to you both.

REG. Prescribe not us our duties.

GON. Let your study
Be to content your lord, who hath received you 280
At fortune's alms. You have obedience scanted,
And well are worth the want that you have wanted.

COR. Time shall unfold what plaited cunning hides:
Who cover faults, at last shame them derides.
Well may you prosper!

FRANCE. Come, my fair Cordelia. 285

[*Exeunt* FRANCE *and* CORDELIA.

GON. Sister, it is not a little I have to say of what most nearly appertains to us both. I think our father will hence to-night.

REG. That's most certain, and with you; next month with us. 290

GON. You see how full of changes his age is; the observation we have made of it hath not been little: he always loved our sister most; and with what poor judgement he hath now cast her off appears too grossly.

REG. 'Tis the infirmity of his age: yet he hath ever but slenderly known himself. 297

GON. The best and soundest of his time hath been but rash; then must we look to receive from his age, not alone the imperfections of long-engraffed condition, but therewithal the unruly waywardness that infirm and choleric years bring with them. 303

REG. Such unconstant starts are we like to have from him as this of Kent's banishment.

GON. There is further compliment of leave-taking between France and him. Pray you, let's hit together: if our father carry authority with such dispositions as he bears, this last surrender of his will but offend us. 310

REG. We shall further think on't.

GON. We must do something, and i' the heat. [*Exeunt.*

281. **At . . . alms,** i.e., when Fortune was giving alms, i.e., petty gifts; **scanted,** grudged. 282. **And . . . wanted,** and well deserved that lack of affection (from your husband) in which you have been lacking. 283. **plaited,** folded. 295. **grossly,** obviously. 298. **the . . . time,** the best and soundest time of his life. 299. **rash,** headlong, hasty. 301. **long-engraffed condition,** temperament that has long been deeply imbedded in his nature. 302. **therewithal,** with it. 304. **unconstant starts,** freakish sudden impulses; **like,** likely. 306. **compliment,** ceremony. 308. **hit,** agree. 310. **offend,** injure. 312. **i' the heat,** i.e., while the iron is hot. Scene ii: 3. **Stand . . . custom,** occupy a position in which I suffer from disabilities dictated by mere custom.

SCENE II. *The* EARL OF GLOUCESTER'S *castle.*

[*Enter* EDMUND, *with a letter.*]

EDM. Thou, nature, art my goddess; to thy law
My services are bound. Wherefore should I
Stand in the plague of custom, and permit
The curiosity of nations to deprive me,
For that I am some twelve or fourteen moonshines 5
Lag of a brother? Why bastard? wherefore base?
When my dimensions are as well compact,
My mind as generous, and my shape as true,
As honest madam's issue? Why brand they us
With base? with baseness? bastardy? base, base? 10
Who, in the lusty stealth of nature, take
More composition and fierce quality
Than doth, within a dull, stale, tired bed,
Go to the creating a whole tribe of fops,
Got 'tween asleep and wake? Well, then, 15
Legitimate Edgar, I must have your land:
Our father's love is to the bastard Edmund
As to the legitimate: fine word,—legitimate!
Well, my legitimate, if this letter speed, 19
And my invention thrive, Edmund the base
Shall top the legitimate. I grow; I prosper:
Now, gods, stand up for bastards!

[*Enter* GLOUCESTER.]

GLOU. Kent banish'd thus! and France in choler parted!
And the king gone to-night! subscribed his power!
Confined to exhibition! All this done 25
Upon the gad! Edmund, how now! what news?

EDM. So please your lordship, none.

[*Putting up the letter.*

GLOU. Why so earnestly seek you to put up that letter?

4. **curiosity of nations,** nice distinction of universal law; **deprive me,** i.e., of my just inheritance. 6. **lag of,** behind. 7. **dimensions . . . compact,** structure of my body is as well built. 8. **generous,** noble; **true,** regular. 9. **honest,** chaste. 12. **more composition,** a stronger constitution. 19. **speed,** succeed. 20. **invention,** scheme. 23. **parted,** departed. 24. **subscribed his power,** his power signed away. 25. **exhibition,** an allowance. 26. **gad,** spur (of the moment).

EDM. I know no news, my lord.

GLOU. What paper were you reading? 30

EDM. Nothing, my lord.

GLOU. No? What needed, then, that terrible dispatch of it into your pocket? the quality of nothing hath not such need to hide itself. Let's see: come, if it be nothing, I shall not need spectacles. 36

EDM. I beseech you, sir, pardon me: it is a letter from my brother, that I have not all o'er-read; and for so much as I have perused, I find it not fit for your o'er-looking. 40

GLOU. Give me the letter, sir.

EDM. I shall offend, either to detain or give it. The contents, as in part I understand them, are to blame.

GLOU. Let's see, let's see. 45

EDM. I hope, for my brother's justification, he wrote this but as an essay or taste of my virtue.

GLOU. [*Reads*] "This policy and reverence of age makes the world bitter to the best of our times; keeps our fortunes from us till our oldness cannot relish them. I begin to find an idle and fond bondage in the oppression of aged tyranny; who sways, not as it hath power, but as it is suffered. Come to me, that of this I may speak more. If our father would sleep till I waked him, you should enjoy half his revenue for ever, and live the beloved of your brother, 57

"EDGAR."

Hum—conspiracy!—"Sleep till I waked him, —you should enjoy half his revenue,"—My son Edgar! Had he a hand to write this? a heart and brain to breed it in?—When came this to you? who brought it? 62

EDM. It was not brought me, my lord; there's the cunning of it; I found it thrown in at the casement of my closet.

GLOU. You know the character to be your brother's?

EDM. If the matter were good, my lord, I durst swear it were his; but, in respect of that, I would fain think it were not. 70

GLOU. It is his.

EDM. It is his hand, my lord; but I hope his heart is not in the contents.

GLOU. Hath he never heretofore sounded you in this business?

EDM. Never, my lord: but I have heard him oft maintain it to be fit, that, sons at perfect age, and fathers declining, the father should be as ward to the son, and the son manage his revenue. 79

GLOU. O villain, villain! His very opinion in the letter! Abhorred villain! Unnatural, detested, brutish villain! worse than brutish! Go, sirrah, seek him; I'll apprehend him: abominable villain! Where is he? 84

EDM. I do not well know, my lord. If it shall please you to suspend your indignation against my brother till you can derive from him better testimony of his intent, you shall run a certain course; where, if you violently proceed against him, mistaking his purpose, it would make a great gap in your own honour, and shake in pieces the heart of his obedience. I dare pawn down my life for him, that he hath wrote this to feel my affection to your honour, and to no further pretence of danger. 95

GLOU. Think you so?

EDM. If your honour judge it meet, I will place you where you shall hear us confer of this, and by an auricular assurance have your satisfaction; and that without any further delay than this very evening. 101

GLOU. He cannot be such a monster—

EDM. Nor is not, sure.

GLOU. To his father, that so tenderly and entirely loves him. Heaven and earth! Edmund, seek him out; wind me into him, I pray you: frame the business after your own wisdom. I would unstate myself, to be in a due resolution.

EDM. I will seek him, sir, presently; convey the business as I shall find means, and acquaint you withal. 111

GLOU. These late eclipses in the sun and moon portend no good to us: though the

33. terrible dispatch of it, frantic haste to put it. 34. quality, nature. 37. pardon me, excuse my not sharing it with you. 42. detain, withhold. 44. to blame, blameworthy. 47. essay, trial. 48. policy and reverence, established convention of revering the old. 48. best . . . times, best part of our life. 52. idle . . . bondage, a useless and foolish servitude. 53-4. who . . . suffered, which prevails not by virtue of its power, but as a result of our submission. 65. closet, private room. 66. character, handwriting. 68. matter, subject matter. 69. respect of, regard to. 78. perfect age, full maturity; declining, growing old. 89. where, whereas. 94-5. feel my affection, test my feeling. 95. pretence of danger, dangerous intention. 106. wind . . . him, worm your way into his confidence for my sake. 108. unstate myself, surrender the privileges of my rank. 109. due resolution, proper certainty. 109. presently, at once. 109-10. convey, manage secretly.

wisdom of nature can reason it thus and thus, yet nature finds itself scourged by the sequent effects: love cools, friendship falls off, brothers divide: in cities, mutinies; in 116 countries, discord; in palaces, treason; and the bond cracked 'twixt son and father. This villain of mine comes under the prediction; there's son against father: the king falls from bias of nature; there's father against child. We have seen the best of our time: machinations, hollowness, treachery, and all ruinous disorders, follow us disquietly to our graves. Find out this villain, Edmund; it shall lose thee nothing; do it carefully. And the noble and true-hearted Kent banished! his offence, honesty! 'Tis strange. 127

[*Exit.*

EDM. This is the excellent foppery of the world, that, when we are sick in fortune,—often the surfeit of our own behaviour,—we make guilty of our disasters the sun, the moon, and the stars: as if we were villains by necessity; fools by heavenly compulsion; knaves, thieves, and treachers, by spherical predominance; drunkards, liars, and adulterers, by an enforced obedience of plane- 135 tary influence; and all that we are evil in, by a divine thrusting on: an admirable evasion of whoremaster man, to lay his goatish disposition to the charge of a star! My father compounded with my mother under the dragon's tail; and my nativity was under Ursa major; so that it follows, I am rough and lecherous. Tut, I should have been that I am, had the maidenliest star in the firmament twinkled on my bastardizing. Edgar—145

[*Enter* EDGAR.]

and pat he comes like the catastrophe of the old comedy: my cue is villanous melancholy, with a sigh like Tom o' Bedlam. O, these eclipses do portend these divisions! fa, sol, la, mi.

EDG. How now, brother Edmund! what serious contemplation are you in? 151

EDM. I am thinking, brother, of a prediction I read this other day, what should follow these eclipses. 154

EDG. Do you busy yourself about that?

EDM. I promise you, the effects he writes of succeed unhappily; as of unnaturalness between the child and the parent; death, dearth, dissolutions of ancient amities; divisions in state, menaces and maledictions against king and nobles; needless diffidences, banishment of friends, dissipation of cohorts, nuptial breaches, and I know not what. 163

EDG. How long have you been a sectary astronomical?

EDM. Come, come; when saw you my father last?

EDG. Why, the night gone by.

EDM. Spake you with him?

EDG. Ay, two hours together. 170

EDM. Parted you in good terms? Found you no displeasure in him by word or countenance?

EDG. None at all.

EDM. Bethink yourself wherein you may have offended him: and at my entreaty forbear his presence till some little time hath qualified the heat of his displeasure; which at this instant so rageth in him, that with the mischief of your person it would scarcely allay. 179

EDG. Some villain hath done me wrong.

EDM. That's my fear. I pray you, have a continent forbearance till the speed of his rage goes slower; and, as I say, retire with me to my lodging, from whence I will fitly bring you to hear my lord speak: pray ye, go; there's my key: if you do stir abroad, go armed. 186

EDG. Armed, brother!

EDM. Brother, I advise you to the best; go armed: I am no honest man if there be any good meaning towards you: I have told you what I have seen and heard; but faintly, nothing like the image and horror of it: pray you, away. 192

EDG. Shall I hear from you anon?

114. **wisdom of nature**, scientific theory. 115-6. **sequent effects**, results which follow. 116. **mutinies**, tumults. 121. **bias**, the curve of a bowling ball, hence "tendency." 128. **foppery**, foolishness. 130. **surfeit**, overeating, indigestion. 133. **treachers**, traitors. 133-4. **spherical predominance**, because of the controlling influence of some planet. 138. **goatish**, licentious. 140. **compounded with**, came to terms with. 142-3. **that I am**, what I am. 146. **pat**, opportunely. 148. **Tom o' Bedlam**, common name of lunatics of Bethlehem Hospital (Bedlam), an insane asylum, who were sent out to beg. 157. **succeed**, follow. 159. **dearth**, famine. 161. **diffidences**, suspicions. 162. **dissipation of cohorts**, breaking up of military organizations. 164-5. **sectary astronomical**, believer in astrology. 175. **forbear**, avoid. 177. **qualified**, lessened. 179. **mischief . . . person**, harm to your body. 182. **continent**, restrained. 184. **fitly**, opportunely. 192. **image and horror**, the horrible truth. 193. **anon**, shortly.

EDM. I do serve you in this business.
[*Exit* EDGAR.]
A credulous father! and a brother noble, 195
Whose nature is so far from doing harms,
That he suspects none; on whose foolish honesty
My practices ride easy! I see the business.
Let me, if not by birth, have lands by wit:
All with me's meet that I can fashion fit. 200
[*Exit.*

SCENE III. *The* DUKE OF ALBANY'S *palace.*

[*Enter* GONERIL, *and* OSWALD, *her steward.*]

GON. Did my father strike my gentleman for chiding of his fool?
OSW. Yes, madam.
GON. By day and night he wrongs me; every hour
He flashes into one gross crime or other,
That sets us all at odds: I'll not endure it: 5
His knights grow riotous, and himself upbraids us
On every trifle. When he returns from hunting,
I will not speak with him; say I am sick:
If you come slack of former services,
You shall do well; the fault of it I'll answer. 10
OSW. He's coming, madam; I hear him.
[*Horns within.*
GON. Put on what weary negligence you please,
You and your fellows; I'ld have it come to question:
If he dislike it, let him to our sister,
Whose mind and mine, I know, in that are one, 15
Not to be over-ruled. Idle old man,
That still would manage those authorities
That he hath given away! Now, by my life,
Old fools are babes again; and must be used
With checks as flatteries,—when they are seen abused. 20
Remember what I tell you.
OSW. Well, madam.
GON. And let his knights have colder looks among you;
What grows of it, no matter; advise your fellows so:
I would breed from hence occasions, and I shall
That I may speak: I'll write straight to my sister, 25
To hold my very course. Prepare for dinner.
[*Exeunt.*

SCENE IV. *A hall in the same.*

[*Enter* KENT, *disguised.*]

KENT. If but as well I other accents borrow,
That can my speech defuse, my good intent
May carry through itself to that full issue
For which I razed my likeness. Now, banish'd Kent,
If thou canst serve where thou dost stand condemn'd, 5
So may it come, thy master, whom thou lovest,
Shall find thee full of labours.

[*Horns within. Enter* LEAR, KNIGHTS, *and* ATTENDANTS.]

LEAR. Let me not stay a jot for dinner; go get it ready. [*Exit an* ATTENDANT.] How now! what art thou? 10
KENT. A man, sir.
LEAR. What dost thou profess? what wouldst thou with us?
KENT. I do profess to be no less than I seem; to serve him truly that will put me in trust; to love him that is honest; to converse with him that is wise, and says little; to fear judgement; to fight when I cannot choose; and to eat no fish. 18
LEAR. What art thou?
KENT. A very honest-hearted fellow, and as poor as the king.
LEAR. If thou be as poor for a subject as he is for a king, thou art poor enough. What wouldst thou? 24
KENT. Service.
LEAR. Who wouldst thou serve?
KENT. You.

198. **practices**, plots. 200. **fashion fit**, make fitting by fraudulent management. Scene iii: 13. **to question**, i.e., to a showdown. 16. **Idle**, foolish. 19. **used**, managed. 20. **checks as**, rebukes as well as; **abused**, deceived. 23. **advise . . . so**, tell your servants to act the same way. 24. **occasions**, opportunities. Scene iv: 2. **defuse**, disguise. 4. **razed my likeness**, erased any likeness to myself.

5. **serve**, act as a servant. 12. **What . . . profess?** What is your profession? 16. **converse**, associate. 18. **choose**, i.e., help it; **eat no fish**, i.e., a Protestant and not disloyal like the fish-eating Catholics.

LEAR. Dost thou know me, fellow?

KENT. No, sir; but you have that in your countenance which I would fain call master.

LEAR. What's that? 31

KENT. Authority.

LEAR. What services canst thou do?

KENT. I can keep honest counsel, ride, run, mar a curious tale in telling it, and deliver a plain message bluntly: that which ordinary men are fit for, I am qualified in; and the best of me is diligence.

LEAR. How old art thou? 39

KENT. Not so young, sir, to love a woman for singing, nor so old to dote on her for any thing: I have years on my back forty eight.

LEAR. Follow me; thou shalt serve me: if I like thee no worse after dinner, I will not part from thee yet. Dinner, ho, dinner! Where's my knave? my fool? Go you, and call my fool hither. [*Exit an* ATTENDANT.] 47

[*Enter* OSWALD.]

You, you, sirrah, where's my daughter?

OSW. So please you,– [*Exit.*

LEAR. What says the fellow there? Call the clotpoll back. [*Exit a* KNIGHT.] Where's my fool, ho? I think the world's asleep. 52

[*Re-enter* KNIGHT.]

How now! where's that mongrel?

KNIGHT. He says, my lord, your daughter is not well. 55

LEAR. Why came not the slave back to me when I called him?

KNIGHT. Sir, he answered me in the roundest manner, he would not.

LEAR. He would not! 60

KNIGHT. My lord, I know not what the matter is; but, to my judgement, your highness is not entertained with that ceremonious affection as you were wont; there's a great abatement of kindness appears as well in the general dependants as in the duke himself also and your daughter. 67

LEAR. Ha! sayest thou so?

KNIGHT. I beseech you, pardon me, my lord, if I be mistaken; for my duty cannot be silent when I think your highness wronged. 71

LEAR. Thou but rememberest me of mine own conception: I have perceived a most faint neglect of late; which I have rather blamed as mine own jealous curiosity than as a very pretence and purpose of unkindness: I will look further into 't. But where's my fool? I have not seen him this two days.

KNIGHT. Since my young lady's going into France, sir, the fool hath much pined 80 away.

LEAR. No more of that; I have noted it well. Go you, and tell my daughter I would speak with her. [*Exit an* ATTENDANT.] Go you, call hither my fool. [*Exit an* ATTENDANT.]

[*Re-enter* OSWALD.]

O, you sir, you, come you hither, sir: who am I, sir?

OSW. My lady's father.

LEAR. "My lady's father!" my lord's knave: you whoreson dog! you slave! you cur!

OSW. I am none of these, my lord; I beseech your pardon. 91

LEAR. Do you bandy looks with me, you rascal? [*Striking him.*

OSW. I'll not be struck, my lord.

KENT. Nor tripped neither, you base football player. [*Tripping up his heels.*

LEAR. I thank thee, fellow; thou servest me, and I'll love thee. 98

KENT. Come, sir, arise, away! I'll teach you differences: away, away! If you will measure your lubber's length again, tarry: but away! go to; have you wisdom? so. 102 [*Pushes* OSWALD *out.*

LEAR. Now, my friendly knave, I thank thee: there's earnest of thy service. 104 [*Giving* KENT *money.*

[*Enter* FOOL.]

FOOL. Let me hire him too: here's my coxcomb. [*Offering* KENT *his cap.*

LEAR. How now, my pretty knave! how dost thou?

30. **countenance,** bearing. 34. **keep honest counsel,** keep an honorable secret. 35. **curious,** elaborate. 46. **knave,** boy. 51. **clotpoll,** blockhead. 59. **roundest,** plainest. 63. **entertained,** treated. 63-4. **ceremonious affection,** the affection which shows itself in formal respect. 66. **general dependants,** the house-servants. 72. **rememberest,** remind. 73. **conception,** idea. 74. **faint,** half-hearted. 75. **jealous curiosity,** overscrupulous watchfulness (for slights). 76. **very pretence,** deliberate intention. 92. **bandy,** strike a ball back and forth (as in tennis). 100. **differences,** proper distinctions in rank. 101. **lubber's,** awkward lout's. 104. **earnest of,** advance payment for.

FOOL. Sirrah, you were best take my coxcomb.

KENT. Why, fool? 110

FOOL. Why, for taking one's part that's out of favour: nay, an thou canst not smile as the wind sits, thou'lt catch cold shortly: there, take my coxcomb: why, this fellow has banished two on 's daughters, and did the third a blessing against his will; if thou follow him, thou must needs wear my coxcomb. How now, nuncle! Would I had two coxcombs and two daughters!

LEAR. Why, my boy? 119

FOOL. If I gave them all my living, I'ld keep my coxcombs myself. There's mine; beg another of thy daughters.

LEAR. Take heed, sirrah; the whip. 123

FOOL. Truth's a dog must to kennel; he must be whipped out, when Lady the brach may stand by the fire and stink.

LEAR. A pestilent gall to me!

FOOL. Sirrah, I'll teach thee a speech.

LEAR. Do.

FOOL. Mark it, nuncle: 130

Have more than thou showest,
Speak less than thou knowest,
Lend less than thou owest,
Ride more than thou goest,
Learn more than thou trowest, 135
Set less than thou throwest;
Leave thy drink and thy whore,
And keep in-a-door,
And thou shalt have more
Than two tens to a score. 140

KENT. This is nothing, fool.

FOOL. Then 'tis like the breath of an unfee'd lawyer; you gave me nothing for 't. Can you make no use of nothing, nuncle?

LEAR. Why, no, boy; nothing can be made out of nothing.

FOOL. [*To* KENT] Prithee, tell him, so much the rent of his land comes to: he will not believe a fool.

LEAR. A bitter fool! 150

FOOL. Dost thou know the difference, my boy, between a bitter fool and a sweet fool?

LEAR. No lad; teach me.

FOOL. That lord that counsell'd thee
To give away thy land, 155
Come place him here by me,
Do thou for him stand:
The sweet and bitter fool
Will presently appear;
The one in motley here, 160
The other found out there.

LEAR. Dost thou call me fool, boy?

FOOL. All thy other titles thou hast given away; that thou wast born with. 164

KENT. This is not altogether fool, my lord.

FOOL. No, faith, lords and great men will not let me; if I had a monopoly out, they would have part on't: and ladies too, they will not let me have all fool to myself; they'll be snatching. Give me an egg, nuncle, and I'll give thee two crowns. 171

LEAR. What two crowns shall they be?

FOOL. Why, after I have cut the egg i' the middle, and eat up the meat, the two crowns of the egg. When thou clovest thy crown i' the middle, and gavest away both parts, thou borest thy ass on thy back o'er the dirt: thou hadst little wit in thy bald crown, when thou gavest thy golden one away. If I speak like myself in this, let him be whipped that first finds it so. 180

[*Singing*] Fools had ne'er less wit in a year;
For wise men are grown foppish,
They know not how their wits to wear,
Their manners are so apish.

LEAR. When were you wont to be so full of songs, sirrah? 186

FOOL. I have used it, nuncle, ever since thou madest thy daughters thy mother: for when thou gavest them the rod, and put'st down thine own breeches, 190

[*Singing*] Then they for sudden joy did weep,
And I for sorrow sung,
That such a king should play bo-peep,
And go the fools among. 194

108. **were best**, had better; **coxcomb**, the hood crested with red like a cock's comb, worn by the professional fool. 112. **an**, if. 115. **on's**, of his. 118. **nuncle**, contraction for "mine uncle." 125. **brach**, bitch, personifying flattery. 127. **pestilent gall**, annoying irritation. 133. **owest**, ownest. 134. **goest**, walkest. 135. **trowest**, knowest. 136. **set**, stake; **throwest**, have a chance to throw, i.e., don't bet your all. 138. **in-a-door**, indoors, i.e., at home. 154. **That lord**, perhaps a reference to the Lord Skalligi in the old **King Lear** who suggests the love test. Nobody in this play gives Lear this stupid advice. 157. **for him stand**, impersonate him. 159. **presently**, immediately. 167. **monopoly**, a royal patent granting a monopoly on something; **out**, granted me. 167-8. **they . . . on't**, the lords who helped him get the monopoly would demand a share in it. 179-80. **like myself**, i.e., outspokenly. 182. **foppish**, foolish. 181-2. **Fools . . . foppish**, there is nothing left for fools to do, now that wise men have become fools. 187. **I . . . it**, it has been my custom. 193. **play bo-peep**, be so childish as play "Hide and Go Seek."

Prithee, nuncle, keep a schoolmaster that can teach thy fool to lie: I would fain learn to lie.

LEAR. An you lie, sirrah, we'll have you whipped. 198

FOOL. I marvel what kin thou and thy daughters are: they'll have me whipped for speaking true, thou'lt have me whipped for lying; and sometimes I am whipped for holding my peace. I had rather be any kind o' thing than a fool: and yet I would not be thee, nuncle; thou hast pared thy wit o' both sides, and left nothing i' the middle: here comes one o' the parings. 206

[*Enter* GONERIL.]

LEAR. How now, daughter! what makes that frontlet on? Methinks you are too much of late i' the frown. 209

FOOL. Thou wast a pretty fellow when thou hadst no need to care for her frowning; now thou art an O without a figure; I am better than thou art now; I am a fool, thou art nothing. [*To* GON.] Yes, forsooth, I will hold my tongue; so your face bids me, though you say nothing. Mum, mum, 216

He that keeps nor crust nor crum,
Weary of all, shall want some.

[*Pointing to* LEAR] That's a shealed peas-cod.

GON. Not only, sir, this your all-licensed fool,
But other of your insolent retinue 221
Do hourly carp and quarrel; breaking forth
In rank and not-to-be-endurèd riots. Sir,
I had thought, by making this well known unto you,
To have found a safe redress; but now grow fearful, 225
By what yourself too late have spoke and done,
That you protect this course, and put it on
By your allowance; which if you should, the fault
Would not 'scape censure, nor the redresses sleep, 229
Which, in the tender of a wholesome weal,
Might in their working do you that offence,
Which else were shame, that then necessity
Will call discreet proceeding.

FOOL. For, you know, nuncle,
The hedge-sparrow fed the cuckoo so long, 235
That it had it head bit off by it young.
So, out went the candle, and we were left darkling.

LEAR. Are you our daughter?

GON. Come, sir,
I would you would make use of that good wisdom, 240
Whereof I know you are fraught; and put away
These dispositions, that of late transform you
From what you rightly are.

FOOL. May not an ass know when the cart draws the horse? Whoop, Jug! I love thee.

LEAR. Doth any here know me? This is not Lear: 246
Doth Lear walk thus? speak thus? Where are his eyes?
Either his notion weakens, his discernings
Are lethargied—Ha! waking? 'tis not so.
Who is it that can tell me whom I am? 250

FOOL. Lear's shadow.

LEAR. I would learn that; for, by the marks of sovereignty, knowledge, and reason, I should be false persuaded I had daughters.

FOOL. Which they will make an obedient father. 256

LEAR. Your name, fair gentlewoman?

GON. This admiration, sir, is much o' the savour
Of other your new pranks. I do beseech you
To understand my purposes aright: 260
As you are old and reverend, you should be wise.
Here do you keep a hundred knights and squires;
Men so disorder'd, so debosh'd and bold,
That this our court, infected with their manners,
Shows like a riotous inn: epicurism and lust 265

208. **frontlet,** band worn on the forehead, here = frown. 211. **an O,** cipher. 219. **shealed peas-cod,** shelled pea pod. 222. **carp,** find fault. 227. **put it on,** encourage it. 228. **by your allowance,** with your approval. 229. **redresses,** acts of redress. 230. **in the tender . . . weal,** in our care to make the commonwealth sound. 232-3. **which . . . proceedings,** which would be shameful but which the demands (of the situation) would force one to call prudent action (discreet procedure). 235. **cuckoo,** the cuckoo lays its eggs in other birds' nests. 236. **it . . . it, it . . . its.** 237. **darkling,** in the dark. 241. **fraught,** stored. 245. **Whoop, Jug! . . . thee,** the tag of some song. The fool takes refuge in nonsense whenever he suspects that one of his sallies has been too impertinent. 248. **notion,** understanding. 249. **lethargied,** paralyzed; **waking?** Am I awake? 256. **which,** whom. 258. **admiration,** pretended astonishment. 263. **debosh'd,** debauched. 265. **epicurism,** unrestrained indulgence.

Make it more like a tavern or a brothel
Than a graced palace. The shame itself doth speak
For instant remedy: be then desired
By her, that else will take the thing she begs,
A little to disquantity your train; 270
And the remainder, that shall still depend,
To be such men as may besort your age,
And know themselves and you.

LEAR. Darkness and devils!
Saddle my horses; call my train together.
Degenerate bastard! I'll not trouble thee:
Yet have I left a daughter. 276

GON. You strike my people; and your disorder'd rabble
Make servants of their betters.

[*Enter* ALBANY.]

LEAR. Woe, that too late repents,–
[*To* ALB.]
O, sir, are you come?
Is it your will? Speak, sir. Prepare my horses.
Ingratitude, thou marble-hearted fiend, 281
More hideous when thou show'st thee in a child
Than the sea-monster!

ALB. Pray, sir, be patient.

LEAR. [*To* GON.] Detested kite! thou liest:
My train are men of choice and rarest parts,
That all particulars of duty know, 286
And in the most exact regard support
The worships of their name. O most small fault,
How ugly didst thou in Cordelia show!
That, like an engine, wrench'd my frame of nature 290
From the fix'd place; drew from my heart all love,
And added to the gall. O Lear, Lear, Lear!
Beat at this gate, that let thy folly in,
[*Striking his head.*]
And thy dear judgement out! Go, go, my people.

ALB. My lord, I am guiltless, as I am ignorant 295
Of what hath moved you.

LEAR. It may be so, my lord.
Hear, nature, hear; dear goddess, hear!
Suspend thy purpose, if thou didst intend
To make this creature fruitful!
Into her womb convey sterility! 300
Dry up in her the organs of increase;
And from her derogate body never spring
A babe to honour her! If she must teem,
Create her child of spleen; that it may live,
And be a thwart disnatured torment to her! 305
Let it stamp wrinkles in her brow of youth;
With cadent tears fret channels in her cheeks;
Turn all her mother's pains and benefits
To laughter and contempt; that she may feel
How sharper than a serpent's tooth it is 310
To have a thankless child! Away, away!
[*Exit.*

ALB. Now, gods that we adore, whereof comes this?

GON. Never afflict yourself to know the cause;
But let his disposition have that scope
That dotage gives it. 315

[*Re-enter* LEAR.]

LEAR. What, fifty of my followers at a clap!
Within a fortnight!

ALB. What's the matter, sir?

LEAR. I'll tell thee: [*To* GON.] Life and death! I am ashamed
That thou hast power to shame my manhood thus;
That these hot tears, which break from me perforce, 320
Should make thee worth them. Blasts and fogs upon thee!
The untented woundings of a father's curse
Pierce every sense about thee! Old fond eyes,
Beweep this cause again, I'll pluck ye out,
And cast you, with the waters that you lose,
To temper clay. Yea, is it come to this? 326
Let it be so: yet have I left a daughter,
Who, I am sure, is kind and comfortable:
When she shall hear this of thee, with her nails

267. **graced**, honored. 270. **disquantity**, reduce the numbers of. 271. **still depend**, remain as your dependents. 272. **besort**, befit. 283. **the sea-monster**, (1) perhaps the hippopotamus, which had a reputation for ingratitude, or (2) any sea monster of classical mythology; **be patient**, exercise self-control. 285. **parts**, accomplishments. 287-8. **And . . . name**, And in the smallest details uphold the honorable names they bear. 290. **like . . . nature**, like a powerful piece of mechanism, dislodged the whole structure of my nature.

301. **increase**, child-bearing. 302. **derogate**, deteriorated, blighted. 303. **teem**, be fruitful. 304. **her**, for her; **spleen**, malice. 305. **thwart**, perverse; **disnatured**, unnatural. 307. **cadent**, falling; **fret**, wear. 314. **disposition**, mood. 321. **fogs**, fogs and mists were supposed to be laden with the seeds of pestilence. 322. **untented**, too deep to be cleansed with a tent (a piece of lint). 323. **fond**, foolish. 326. **temper**, soften. 328. **comfortable**, bringing comfort.

She'll flay thy wolvish visage. Thou shalt find 330
That I'll resume the shape which thou dost think
I have cast off for ever: thou shalt, I warrant thee.
[*Exeunt* LEAR, KENT, *and* ATTENDANTS.
GON. Do you mark that, my lord?
ALB. I cannot be so partial, Goneril,
To the great love I bear you,— 335
GON. Pray you, content. What, Oswald, ho!
[*To the* FOOL] You, sir, more knave than fool, after your master.
FOOL. Nuncle Lear, nuncle Lear, tarry and take the fool with thee.

A fox, when one has caught her, 340
And such a daughter,
Should sure to the slaughter,
If my cap would buy a halter:
So the fool follows after. [*Exit.*

GON. This man hath had good counsel:—a hundred knights! 345
'Tis politic and safe to let him keep
At point a hundred knights: yes, that, on every dream,
Each buzz, each fancy, each complaint, dislike,
He may enguard his dotage with their powers, 349
And hold our lives in mercy. Oswald, I say!
ALB. Well, you may fear too far.
GON. Safer than trust too far:
Let me still take away the harms I fear,
Not fear still to be taken: I know his heart.
What he hath utter'd I have writ my sister:
If she sustain him and his hundred knights,
When I have show'd the unfitness,— 356

[*Re-enter* OSWALD.]

How now, Oswald!
What, have you writ that letter to my sister?
OSW. Yes, madam.
GON. Take you some company, and away to horse:
Inform her full of my particular fear; 360
And thereto add such reasons of your own
As may compact it more. Get you gone;
And hasten your return. [*Exit* OSWALD.] No, no, my lord,
This milky gentleness and course of yours
Though I condemn not, yet, under pardon,
You are much more attask'd for want of wisdom 366
Than praised for harmful mildness.
ALB. How far your eyes may pierce I cannot tell:
Striving to better, oft we mar what's well.
GON. Nay, then— 370
ALB. Well, well; the event. [*Exeunt.*

SCENE V. *Court before the same.*

[*Enter* LEAR, KENT, *and* FOOL.]

LEAR. Go you before to Gloucester with these letters. Acquaint my daughter no further with any thing you know than comes from her demand out of the letter. If your diligence be not speedy, I shall be there afore you. 5

KENT. I will not sleep, my lord, till I have delivered your letter. [*Exit.*

FOOL. If a man's brains were in 's heels, were't not in danger of kibes?

LEAR. Ay, boy. 10

FOOL. Then, I prithee, be merry; thy wit shall ne'er go slip-shod.

LEAR. Ha, ha, ha!

FOOL. Shalt see thy other daughter will use thee kindly; for though she's as like this as a crab's like an apple, yet I can tell what I can tell. 16

LEAR. Why, what canst thou tell, my boy?

FOOL. She will taste as like this as a crab does to a crab. Thou canst tell why one's nose stands i' the middle on 's face? 20

LEAR. No.

FOOL. Why, to keep one's eyes of either side's nose; that what a man cannot smell out, he may spy into.

LEAR. I did her wrong— 25

FOOL. Canst tell how an oyster makes his shell?

LEAR. No.

FOOL. Nor I neither; but I can tell why a snail has a house. 30

336. content, be satisfied. 346. politic, prudent. 347. At point, completely equipped. 348. buzz, rumor. 350. in mercy, at his mercy. 352-3. Let . . . taken, let me always remove what I fear will harm me, rather than always live in fear of being attacked by some harm. 353. still, always. 362. compact it more, give it more substance, i.e., make the argument more convincing. 364. milky . . . course, mild gentleness of this course. 366. attask'd, to be blamed. 371. the event, i.e., let's see what will be the outcome. Scene v: 9. kibes, chilblains. 11. slip-shod, in slippers (and so in danger of chilblains). 15. kindly, (1) according to her nature, (2) with kindness. 15. crab's, crab-apple's.

LEAR. Why?

FOOL. Why, to put his head in; not to give it away to his daughters, and leave his horns without a case. 34

LEAR. I will forget my nature. So kind a father! Be my horses ready?

FOOL. Thy asses are gone about 'em. The reason why the seven stars are no more than seven is a pretty reason.

LEAR. Because they are not eight? 40

FOOL. Yes, indeed: thou wouldst make a good fool.

LEAR. To take 't again perforce! Monster ingratitude!

FOOL. If thou wert my fool, nuncle, I'ld have thee beaten for being old before thy time. 46

LEAR. How's that?

FOOL. Thou shouldst not have been old till thou hadst been wise.

LEAR. O, let me not be mad, not mad, sweet heaven! 50
Keep me in temper: I would not be mad!

[*Enter* GENTLEMAN.]

How now! are the horses ready?

GENT. Ready, my lord.

LEAR. Come, boy.

FOOL. She that's a maid now, and laughs at my departure,
Shall not be a maid long, unless things be cut shorter. [*Exeunt.*

ACT II

SCENE I. *The* EARL OF GLOUCESTER'S *castle.*

[*Enter* EDMUND, *and* CURAN *meets him.*]

EDM. Save thee, Curan.

CUR. And you, sir. I have been with your father, and given him notice that the Duke of Cornwall and Regan his duchess will be here with him this night. 5

EDM. How comes that?

CUR. Nay, I know not. You have heard of the news abroad; I mean the whispered ones, for they are yet but ear-kissing arguments?

EDM. Not I: pray you, what are they? 10

CUR. Have you heard of no likely wars toward, 'twixt the Dukes of Cornwall and Albany?

EDM. Not a word.

CUR. You may do, then, in time. Fare you well, sir. [*Exit.* 15

EDM. The duke be here to-night? The better! best!
This weaves itself perforce into my business.
My father hath set guard to take my brother;
And I have one thing, of a queasy question,
Which I must act: briefness and fortune, work! 20
Brother, a word; descend: brother I say!

[*Enter* EDGAR.]

My father watches: O sir, fly this place;
Intelligence is given where you are hid;
You have now the good advantage of the night:
Have you not spoken 'gainst the Duke of Cornwall? 25
He's coming hither; now, i' the night, i' the haste,
And Regan with him: have you nothing said
Upon his party 'gainst the Duke of Albany?
Advise yourself.

EDG. I am sure on 't, not a word. 29

EDM. I hear my father coming: pardon me;
In cunning I must draw my sword upon you:
Draw; seem to defend yourself; now quit you well.
Yield: come before my father. Light, ho, here!
Fly, brother. Torches, torches! So, farewell.
[*Exit* EDGAR.]
Some blood drawn on me would beget opinion [*Wounds his arm.*]
Of my more fierce endeavour: I have seen drunkards 36
Do more than this in sport. Father, father!
Stop, stop! No help?

38. seven stars, Pleiades. 43. To . . . perforce, I will recover my kingdom by force. 51. temper, natural emotional equilibrium, i.e., sane. Act II, Scene i: 9. ear-kissing arguments, whispered remarks. 16. the better, so much the better. 19. of . . . question, of a ticklish nature. 21. descend, Edgar is in the balcony which represents Edmund's room. 31. In cunning, as a pretense. 32. quit you, acquit yourself. 35. beget opinion, give the impression. 36. drunkards, an Elizabethan gallant, when a little drunk, sometimes cut his arm to mix his blood with wine, to be drunk to his mistress's health.

[*Enter* GLOUCESTER, *and* SERVANTS *with torches.*]

GLOU. Now, Edmund, where's the villain?
EDM. Here stood he in the dark, his sharp sword out, 40
Mumbling of wicked charms, conjuring the moon
To stand auspicious mistress,—
GLOU. But where is he?
EDM. Look, sir, I bleed.
GLOU. Where is the villain, Edmund?
EDM. Fled this way, sir. When by no means he could—
GLOU. Pursue him, ho! Go after. [*Exeunt some* SERVANTS.] By no means what? 45
EDM. Persuade me to the murder of your lordship;
But that I told him, the revenging gods
'Gainst parricides did all their thunders bend;
Spoke, with how manifold and strong a bond
The child was bound to the father; sir, in fine, 50
Seeing how loathly opposite I stood
To his unnatural purpose, in fell motion,
With his preparèd sword, he charges home
My unprovided body, lanced mine arm:
But when he saw my best alarum'd spirits, 55
Bold in the quarrel's right, roused to the encounter,
Or whether gasted by the noise I made,
Full suddenly he fled.
GLOU. Let him fly far:
Not in this land shall he remain uncaught;
And found—dispatch. The noble duke my master, 60
My worthy arch and patron, comes to-night:
By his authority I will proclaim it,
That he which finds him shall deserve our thanks,
Bringing the murderous coward to the stake;
He that conceals him, death. 65
EDM. When I dissuaded him from his intent,
And found him pight to do it, with curst speech
I threaten'd to discover him: he replied,
"Thou unpossessing bastard! dost thou think,
If I would stand against thee, would the reposal 70
Of any trust, virtue, or worth in thee
Make thy words faith'd? No: what I should deny,—
As this I would; ay, though thou didst produce
My very character,—I'ld turn it all 74
To thy suggestion, plot, and damnèd practice:
And thou must make a dullard of the world,
If they not thought the profits of my death
Were very pregnant and potential spurs
To make thee seek it."
GLOU. Strong and fasten'd villain!
Would he deny his letter? I never got him. 80
[*Tucket within.*]
Hark, the duke's trumpets! I know not why he comes.
All ports I'll bar; the villain shall not 'scape;
The duke must grant me that: besides, his picture
I will send far and near, that all the kingdom
May have due note of him; and of my land,
Loyal and natural boy, I'll work the means 86
To make thee capable.

[*Enter* CORNWALL, REGAN, *and* ATTENDANTS.]

CORN. How now, my noble friend! since I came hither,
Which I can call but now, I have heard strange news.
REG. If it be true, all vengeance comes too short 90
Which can pursue the offender. How dost, my lord?
GLOU. O, madam! my old heart is crack'd, is crack'd!
REG. What, did my father's godson seek your life?
He whom my father named? your Edgar?
GLOU. O, lady, lady, shame would have it hid! 95
REG. Was he not companion with the riotous knights
That tend upon my father?
GLOU. I know not, madam: 'tis too bad, too bad.
EDM. Yes, madam, he was of that consort.

47. that, when. 48. bend, aim. 51. loathly opposite, loathingly opposed. 52. fell motion, fierce thrust. 53. prepared, drawn. 54. unprovided, undefended. 55. my . . . spirits, my best energies aroused (as by a call to arms). 57. gasted, terrified. 60. dispatch, finish him off. 61. arch and patron, chief patron. 67. pight, determined; curst, angry. 68. discover him, reveal his plan. 72. faith'd, believed. 74. character, handwriting. 75. practice, plotting.

78. pregnant and potential, cogent and powerful. 79. fasten'd, confirmed. 80. got, begot. s.d. tucket, a flourish on the trumpet, a fanfare. 82. ports, sea-ports; bar, guard. 87. capable, i.e., of inheriting, i.e., he promises to legitimize him. 99. consort, company.

REG. No marvel, then, though he were ill affected: 100
'Tis they have put him on the old man's death,
To have the expense and waste of his revenues.
I have this present evening from my sister
Been well inform'd of them; and with such cautions,
That if they come to sojourn at my house,
I'll not be there. 106

CORN. Nor I, assure thee, Regan.
Edmund, I hear that you have shown your father
A child-like office.

EDM. 'Twas my duty, sir.

GLOU. He did bewray his practice; and received
This hurt you see, striving to apprehend him. 110

CORN. Is he pursued?

GLOU. Ay, my good lord.

CORN. If he be taken, he shall never more
Be fear'd of doing harm: make your own purpose,
How in my strength you please. For you, Edmund, 114
Whose virtue and obedience doth this instant
So much commend itself, you shall be ours:
Natures of such deep trust we shall much need;
You we first seize on.

EDM. I shall serve you, sir,
Truly, however else.

GLOU. For him I thank your grace.

CORN. You know not why we came to visit you,— 120

REG. Thus out of season, threading dark-eyed night:
Occasions, noble Gloucester, of some poise,
Wherein we must have use of your advice:
Our father he hath writ, so hath our sister,
Of difference, which I least thought it fit 125
To answer from our home; the several messengers
From hence attend dispatch. Our good old friend,
Lay comforts to your bosom; and bestow
Your needful counsel to our business,
Which craves the instant use.

GLOU. I serve you, madam: 130
Your graces are right welcome. [*Exeunt.*

100. **though**, if; **ill affected**, evilly disposed. 101. **put him on**, incited him to. 102. **expense**, expenditure. 106. **assure thee**, be assured. 108. **child-like office**, filial service. 109. **bewray**, disclose; **practice**, plot. 113. **purpose**, plans. 114. **How . . . please**, using my authority however you please. 121. **threading**, passing through. 122. **poise**, weight. 125. **differences**, quarrels; **which**, i.e., letters. 126. **from**, away from. 127. **attend dispatch**, wait to be sent.

SCENE II. *Before* GLOUCESTER'S *castle.*

[*Enter* KENT *and* OSWALD, *severally.*]

OSW. Good dawning to thee, friend: art of this house?

KENT. Ay.

OSW. Where may we set our horses?

KENT. I' the mire. 5

OSW. Prithee, if thou lovest me, tell me.

KENT. I love thee not.

OSW. Why, then, I care not for thee.

KENT. If I had thee in Lipsbury pinfold, I would make thee care for me. 10

OSW. Why dost thou use me thus? I know thee not.

KENT. Fellow, I know thee.

OSW. What dost thou know me for?

KENT. A knave; a rascal; an eater of broken meats; a base, proud, shallow, beggarly, three-suited, hundred-pound, filthy, worsted-stocking knave; a lily-livered, action-taking knave, a whoreson, glass-gazing, super-serviceable, finical rogue; one-trunk-inheriting slave; 20 one that wouldst be a bawd, in way of good service, and art nothing but the composition of a knave, beggar, coward, pandar, and the son and heir of a mongrel bitch: one whom I will beat into clamorous whining, if thou deniest the least syllable of thy addition. 26

OSW. Why, what a monstrous fellow art thou, thus to rail on one that is neither known of thee nor knows thee! 29

KENT. What a brazen-faced varlet art thou, to deny thou knowest me! Is it two days ago since I tripped up thy heels, and beat thee before the king? Draw, you rogue: for, though it be night, yet the moon shines; I'll

130. **the instant use**, to be carried out instantly. **Scene ii:** 9. **Lipsbury pinfold**, pinfold is a pound for stray animals. Regarding Lipsbury pinfold, says Nares: "The enclosure adjacent to my teeth, in my jaws," so, in my clutches. 17. **three-suited**, alludes to the three suits a year regularly allowed to a man-servant. 18. **lily-livered**, a white liver was devoid of blood, i.e., of courage; **action-taking**, a man who settles his quarrels by going to the law. 19. **glass-gazing**, vain. 19-20. **super-serviceable**, one who serves in ways other than honorable, e.g., as a bawd. 20. **finical**, fussy; **one . . . inheriting**, whose possessions would fill only one trunk. 23. **composition**, mixture. 26. **addition**, descriptive titles.

make a sop o' the moonshine of you: draw, you whoreson cullionly barber-monger, draw. [*Drawing his sword.*

OSW. Away! I have nothing to do with thee. 37

KENT. Draw, you rascal: you come with letters against the king; and take Vanity the puppet's part against the royalty of her father: draw, you rogue, or I'll so carbonado your shanks: draw, you rascal; come your ways.

OSW. Help, ho! murder! help! 43

KENT. Strike, you slave; stand, rogue, stand; you neat slave, strike. [*Beating him.*

OSW. Help, ho! murder! murder! 46

[*Enter* EDMUND, *with his rapier drawn,* CORNWALL, REGAN, GLOUCESTER, *and* SERVANTS.]

EDM. How now! What's the matter?

KENT. With you, goodman boy, an you please: come, I'll flesh ye: come on, young master.

GLOU. Weapons! arms! What's the matter here? 51

CORN. Keep peace, upon your lives;
He dies that strikes again. What is the matter?

REG. The messengers from our sister and the king. 55

CORN. What is your difference? speak.

OSW. I am scarce in breath, my lord.

KENT. No marvel, you have so bestirred your valour. You cowardly rascal, nature disclaims in thee: a tailor made thee. 60

CORN. Thou art a strange fellow: a tailor make a man?

KENT. Ay, a tailor, sir: a stone-cutter or a painter could not have made him so ill, though he had been but two hours at the trade.

CORN. Speak yet, how grew your quarrel?

OSW. This ancient ruffian, sir, whose life I have spared at suit of his gray beard,— 68

KENT. Thou whoreson zed! thou unnecessary letter! My lord, if you will give me leave, I will tread this unbolted villain into mortar, and daub the walls of a jakes with him. Spare my gray beard, you wagtail?

CORN. Peace, sirrah! 74
You beastly knave, know you no reverence?

KENT. Yes, sir; but anger hath a privilege.

CORN. Why art thou angry?

KENT. That such a slave as this should wear a sword,
Who wears no honesty. Such smiling rogues as these,
Like rats, oft bite the holy cords a-twain 80
Which are too intrinse t' unloose; smooth every passion
That in the natures of their lords rebel;
Bring oil to fire, snow to their colder moods;
Renege, affirm, and turn their halcyon beaks
With every gale and vary of their masters, 85
Knowing nought, like dogs, but following.
A plague upon your epileptic visage!
Smile you my speeches, as I were a fool?
Goose, if I had you upon Sarum plain,
I'ld drive ye cackling home to Camelot. 90

CORN. What, art thou mad, old fellow?

GLOU. How fell you out? say that.

KENT. No contraries hold more antipathy
Than I and such a knave.

CORN. Why dost thou call him knave? What's his offence? 95

KENT. His countenance likes me not.

CORN. No more, perchance, does mine, nor his, nor hers.

KENT. Sir, 'tis my occupation to be plain:
I have seen better faces in my time
Than stands on any shoulder that I see 100
Before me at this instant.

CORN. This is some fellow,
Who, having been praised for bluntness, doth affect
A saucy roughness, and constrains the garb
Quite from his nature: he cannot flatter, he,

35. **make . . . of you,** steep you in moonshine, i.e., steep you in your own blood even if we fight by the uncertain light of the moon. 36. **cullionly . . . monger,** rascally haunter of barber shops (where he was beautified). 39-40. **Vanity . . . part,** Lady Vanity was a character in the morality-like puppet plays. 41. **carbonado,** slash. 42. **come your ways,** come on then. 45. **neat,** foppish. 49. **flesh,** feed with flesh for the first time, i.e., initiate you. 53. **the matter,** cause of the quarrel. 56. **difference,** dispute. 60. **disclaims,** disowns; **a . . . thee,** i.e., you are nothing but clothes. 69. **zed,** i.e., the letter "z"; **unnecessary,** because "s" can express its sound. 71. **unbolted,** unsifted, coarse. 72. **jakes,** privy. 73. **wagtail,** a ridiculously active bird. 79. **honesty,** sense of honor. 80. **holy cords,** sacred family bonds. 81. **intrinse,** intricately tied; **smooth,** flatter (into uncontrolled expression). 84. **Renege,** deny; **halcyon beaks,** it was believed that if a halcyon (Kingfisher) were hung by the neck, he would turn his beak into the wind. 85. **gale and vary,** varying gale. 87. **epileptic,** distorted by a (frightened) smile. 88. **fool,** professional jester. 89. **Sarum plain,** Salisbury plain where geese were bred. 90. **Camelot,** the site of King Arthur's Court. 96. **His . . . not,** I do not like his face. 98. **plain,** plain-spoken. 103. **constrains the garb,** forces himself to assume a bearing. 104. **Quite from,** completely foreign to.

An honest mind and plain, he must speak truth! 105
An they will take it, so; if not, he's plain.
These kind of knaves I know, which in this plainness
Harbour more craft and more corrupter ends
Than twenty silly ducking observants
That stretch their duties nicely. 110

KENT. Sir, in good sooth, in sincere verity,
Under the allowance of your great aspect,
Whose influence, like the wreath of radiant fire
On flickering Phœbus' front,—

CORN. What mean'st by this? 114

KENT. To go out of my dialect, which you discommend so much. I know, sir, I am no flatterer: he that beguiled you in a plain accent was a plain knave; which for my part I will not be, though I should win your displeasure to entreat me to 't. 120

CORN. What was the offence you gave him?

OSW. I never gave him any:
It pleased the king his master very late
To strike at me, upon his misconstruction;
When he, conjunct, and flattering his displeasure, 125
Tripp'd me behind; being down, insulted, rail'd,
And put upon him such a deal of man,
That worthied him, got praises of the king
For him attempting who was self-subdued;
And, in the fleshment of this dread exploit,
Drew on me here again. 131

KENT. None of these rogues and cowards
But Ajax is their fool.

CORN. Fetch forth the stocks!
You stubborn ancient knave, you reverend braggart,
We'll teach you—

KENT. Sir, I am too old to learn:
Call not your stocks for me: I serve the king;
On whose employment I was sent to you: 136
You shall do small respect, show too bold malice
Against the grace and person of my master,
Stocking his messenger.

CORN. Fetch forth the stocks! As I have life and honour, 140
There shall he sit till noon.

REG. Till noon! till night, my lord; and all night too.

KENT. Why, madam, if I were your father's dog,
You should not use me so.

REG. Sir, being his knave, I will.

CORN. This is a fellow of the self-same colour 145
Our sister speaks of. Come, bring away the stocks! [*Stocks brought out.*

GLOU. Let me beseech your grace not to do so:
His fault is much, and the good king his master
Will check him for 't: your purposed low correction 149
Is such as basest and contemned'st wretches
For pilferings and most common trespasses
Are punish'd with: the king must take it ill,
That he's so slightly valued in his messenger,
Should have him thus restrain'd.

CORN. I'll answer that.

REG. My sister may receive it much more worse, 155
To have her gentleman abused, assaulted,
For following her affairs. Put in his legs.
[KENT *is put in the stocks.*]
Come, my good lord, away.
[*Exeunt all but* GLOUCESTER *and* KENT.

GLOU. I am sorry for thee, friend; 'tis the duke's pleasure,
Whose disposition, all the world well knows,
Will not be rubb'd nor stopp'd: I'll entreat for thee. 161

KENT. Pray, do not, sir: I have watched and travell'd hard;
Some time I shall sleep out, the rest I'll whistle.
A good man's fortune may grow out at heels:
Give you good morrow! 165

GLOU. The duke's to blame in this; 'twill be ill taken. [*Exit.*

106. so, well and good; plain, frank. 109. ducking observants, obsequious (continually bowing) courtiers. 110. nicely, punctiliously. 111. Sir, etc., Kent parodies the speech of "ducking observants." 112. aspect, an astrological term. 114. front, forehead. 124. misconstruction, misapprehending [me]. 125. conjunct, joined with him (Lear). 127. deal of man, lot of manhood, i.e., he swaggered. 128. worthied him, as made him appear worthy. 129. For . . . self-subdued, for assailing one who makes no self-defence. 130. fleshment, ferocious excitement. 132. Ajax . . . fool, the cowardly swashbuckler Ajax is vastly inferior to them (in braggart talk). 144. should not, surely would not. 145. colour, sort. 146. away, along. 149. check, reprove. 154. answer, be responsible for. 161. rubb'd, obstructed; a "rub" in bowling was anything that deflected the course of the ball. 162. watched, stayed awake. 164. A good man's, Even a good man's. 165. Give you, God give you.

KENT. Good king, that must approve the
common saw,
Thou out of heaven's benediction comest
To the warm sun!
Approach, thou beacon to this under globe,
That by thy comfortable beams I may 171
Peruse this letter! Nothing almost sees miracles
But misery: I know 'tis from Cordelia,
Who hath most fortunately been inform'd
Of my obscurèd course; [*Reads*] "And shall
find time 175
From this enormous state, seeking to give
Losses their remedies." All weary and o'er-watch'd,
Take vantage, heavy eyes, not to behold
This shameful lodging.
Fortune, good night: smile once more; turn
thy wheel! [*Sleeps.* 180

SCENE III. *A wood.*

[*Enter* EDGAR.]

EDG. I heard myself proclaim'd;
And by the happy hollow of a tree
Escaped the hunt. No port is free; no place,
That guard, and most unusual vigilance,
Does not attend my taking. Whiles I may
'scape, 5
I will preserve myself: and am bethought
To take the basest and most poorest shape
That ever penury, in contempt of man,
Brought near to beast: my face I 'll grime with
filth;
Blanket my loins; elf all my hair in knots; 10
And with presented nakedness out-face
The winds and persecutions of the sky.
The country gives me proof and precedent
Of Bedlam beggars, who, with roaring voices,
Strike in their numb'd and mortified bare
arms 15
Pins, wooden pricks, nails, sprigs of rosemary;
And with this horrible object, from low
farms,
Poor pelting villages, sheep-cotes, and mills,
Sometime with lunatic bans, sometime with
prayers,
Enforce their charity. Poor Turlygod! poor
Tom! 20
That's something yet: Edgar I nothing am.
[*Exit.*

SCENE IV. *Before* GLOUCESTER'S *castle.* KENT *in the stocks.*

[*Enter* LEAR, FOOL, *and* GENTLEMAN.]

LEAR. 'Tis strange that they should so depart from home,
And not send back my messenger.

GENT. As I learn'd,
The night before there was no purpose in
them
Of this remove.

KENT. Hail to thee, noble master!

LEAR. Ha! 5
Makest thou this shame thy pastime?

KENT. No, my lord.

FOOL. Ha, ha! he wears cruel garters. Horses are tied by the heads, dogs and bears by the neck, monkeys by the loins, and men by the legs: when a man's over-lusty at legs, then he wears wooden nether-stocks. 11

LEAR. What's he that hath so much thy
place mistook
To set thee here?

KENT. It is both he and she;
Your son and daughter.

LEAR. No. 15

KENT. Yes.

LEAR. No, I say.

KENT. I say, yea.

LEAR. No, no, they would not.

KENT. Yes, they have. 20

LEAR. By Jupiter, I swear, no.

KENT. By Juno, I swear, ay.

LEAR. They durst not do 't;
They could not, would not do 't; 'tis worse
than murder,

167. saw, proverb, i.e., "To run out of God's blessing [of shade] into the sun" is "to go from bad to worse." 171. comfortable, comforting. 175. obscured course, career in disguise. 176. this enormous state, the present abnormal political situation. 177. o'er watch'd, exhausted from lack of sleep. 178. vantage, advantage (of feeling sleepy). 180. wheel, i.e., Fortune's wheel. Scene iii: 2. happy, helpful. 5. attend my taking, want to arrest me. 6. am bethought, it occurs to me. 10. elf, tangle; tangled hair was thought to be the work of mischievous elves. 11. out-face, defy. 14. Bedlam beggars, inhabitants of Bedlam (Bethlehem Hospital), an insane asylum, were sent out on the roads to beg. 15. mortified, insensible. 16. wooden pricks, skewers. 17. object, spectacle; low, humble. 18. pelting, paltry. 19. bans, curses. 20. Turlygod, a name beggars applied to themselves; its meaning is unknown. 21. That's . . . yet, i.e., in that character I have a future. Scene iv: 4. remove, change of residence. 7. cruel, pun on crewel = worsted. 9. monkeys . . . loins, the chain of pet-monkeys was so affixed. 11. nether-stocks, stockings. 12. place, position (as my messenger).

To do upon respect such violent outrage:
Resolve me, with all modest haste, which way
Thou mightst deserve, or they impose, this usage, 26
Coming from us.

KENT. My lord, when at their home
I did commend your highness' letters to them,
Ere I was risen from the place that show'd
My duty kneeling, came there a reeking post, 30
Stew'd in his haste, half breathless, panting forth
From Goneril his mistress salutations;
Deliver'd letters, spite of intermission,
Which presently they read: on whose contents,
They summon'd up their meiny, straight took horse; 35
Commanded me to follow, and attend
The leisure of their answer; gave me cold looks:
And meeting here the other messenger,
Whose welcome, I perceived, had poison'd mine,—
Being the very fellow that of late 40
Display'd so saucily against your highness,—
Having more man than wit about me, drew:
He raised the house with loud and coward cries.
Your son and daughter found this trespass worth
The shame which here it suffers. 45

FOOL. Winter's not gone yet, if the wild-geese fly that way.

Fathers that wear rags
Do make their children blind;
But fathers that bear bags 50
Shall see their children kind.
Fortune, that arrant whore,
Ne'er turns the key to the poor.

But, for all this, thou shalt have as many dolours for thy daughters as thou canst tell in a year. 55

LEAR. O, how this mother swells up toward my heart!
Hysterica passio, down, thou climbing sorrow,
Thy element's below! Where is this daughter?

KENT. With the earl, sir, here within.

LEAR. Follow me not;
Stay here. [*Exit.* 60

GENT. Made you no more offence but what you speak of?

KENT. None.
How chance the king comes with so small a train?

FOOL. An thou hadst been set i' the stocks for that question, thou hadst well deserved it.

KENT. Why, fool? 67

FOOL. We'll set thee to school to an ant, to teach thee there's no labouring i' the winter. All that follow their noses are led by their eyes but blind men; and there's not a nose among twenty but can smell him that's stinking. Let go thy hold when a great wheel runs down a hill, lest it break thy neck with following it; but the great one that goes up the hill, let him draw thee after. When a wise man gives thee better counsel give me mine again: I would have none but knaves follow it, since a fool gives it.

That sir which serves and seeks for gain,
And follows but for form, 80
Will pack when it begins to rain,
And leave thee in the storm.
But I will tarry; the fool will stay,
And let the wise man fly:
The knave turns fool that runs away; 85
The fool no knave, perdy.

KENT. Where learned you this, fool?

FOOL. Not i' the stocks, fool.

[*Re-enter* LEAR, *with* GLOUCESTER.]

LEAR. Deny to speak with me? They are sick? they are weary?
They have travell'd all the night? Mere fetches; 90
The images of revolt and flying off.

24. **upon respect**, contrary to the respect due me as their father and their King. 25. **Resolve me**, explain to me; modest, moderate. 30. **reeking post**, messenger stinking from sweat. 33. **spite of intermission**, in spite of interrupting me. 34. **presently**, immediately; **on**, as a result of. 35. **meiny**, household servants. 41. **Display'd so saucily**, behaved so impudently. 42. **man**, manhood. 50. **bear bags**, i.e., are rich. 53. **turns the key**, i.e., opens the door. 55. **dolours**, grief with a pun on "dollars"; **tell**, count. 56. **mother**, hysteria, supposed to be caused by wind rising from the stomach to cloud the brain and cause dizziness. 58. **element's**, proper sphere is. 66. **deserved it**, i.e., for asking a silly question. 68-78. The fool in stringing together these wise sayings describing Lear's situation is showing Kent how much wiser the fool is than he. 79. **sir**, great man. 81. **pack**, run away. 85-6. **The . . . no knave**, the fool that runs away from his master is a knave, but the fool who, like him, remains faithful is no knave. 86. **perdy**, "per dieu," literally: "by God," but is a mild oath about = "forsooth." 89. **deny**, refuse. 90. **fetches**, pretexts. 91. **images**, exact likenesses, i.e., clearest signs; **revolt**, gross departure from duty.

Fetch me a better answer.

GLOU. My dear lord,
You know the fiery quality of the duke;
How unremoveable and fix'd he is
In his own course. 95

LEAR. Vengeance! plague! death! confusion!
Fiery? what quality? Why, Gloucester, Gloucester,
I'ld speak with the Duke of Cornwall and his wife.

GLOU. Well, my good lord, I have inform'd them so.

LEAR. Inform'd them! Dost thou understand me, man? 100

GLOU. Ay, my good lord.

LEAR. The king would speak with Cornwall; the dear father
Would with his daughter speak, commands her service:
Are they inform'd of this? My breath and blood!
Fiery? the fiery duke? Tell the hot duke that— 105
No, but not yet: may be he is not well:
Infirmity doth still neglect all office
Whereto our health is bound; we are not ourselves
When nature, being oppress'd, commands the mind
To suffer with the body: I'll forbear; 110
And am fall'n out with my more headier will,
To take the indisposed and sickly fit
For the sound man. Death on my state! wherefore [*Looking on* KENT.]
Should he sit here? This act persuades me
That this remotion of the duke and her 115
Is practice only. Give me my servant forth.
Go tell the duke and 's wife I'ld speak with them,
Now, presently: bid them come forth and hear me,
Or at their chamber-door I'll beat the drum
Till it cry sleep to death. 120

GLOU. I would have all well betwixt you. [*Exit.*

LEAR. O me, my heart, my rising heart! but, down!

FOOL. Cry to it, nuncle, as the cockney did to the eels when she put 'em i' the paste alive; she knapped 'em o' the coxcombs with a stick, and cried "Down, wantons, down." 'Twas her brother that, in pure kindness to his horse, buttered his hay. 128

[*Enter* CORNWALL, REGAN, GLOUCESTER, *and* SERVANTS.]

LEAR. Good morrow to you both.

CORN. Hail to your grace!
[KENT *is set at liberty.*

REG. I am glad to see your highness. 130

LEAR. Regan, I think you are; I know what reason
I have to think so: if thou shouldst not be glad,
I would divorce me from thy mother's tomb,
Sepulchring an adultress. [*To* KENT] O, are you free?
Some other time for that. Belovèd Regan,
Thy sister's naught: O Regan, she hath tied 136
Sharp-tooth'd unkindness, like a vulture, here: [*Points to his heart.*]
I can scarce speak to thee; thou'lt not believe
With how depraved a quality—O Regan!

REG. I pray you, sir, take patience: I have hope 140
You less know how to value her desert
Than she to scant her duty.

LEAR. Say, how is that?

REG. I cannot think my sister in the least
Would fail her obligation: if, sir, perchance
She have restrain'd the riots of your followers, 145
'Tis on such ground, and to such wholesome end,
As clears her from all blame.

LEAR. My curses on her!

REG. O, sir, you are old;
Nature in you stands on the very verge
Of her confine: you should be ruled and led 150
By some discretion, that discerns your state
Better than you yourself. Therefore, I pray you,
That to our sister you do make return;
Say you have wrong'd her, sir.

107. office, duty. 11. headier, impulsive. 112. to take, for taking. 113. state, royal power. 115. remotion, removal. 116. practice, trickery. 118. presently, at once. 120. cry . . . death, murder sleep. 123. cockney, cook, perhaps a London cook who knows nothing about eels. 125. knapped, rapped; coxcombs, jocular for heads.

129. grace, i.e., Majesty. 134. sepulchring, i.e., as containing. 136. naught, wicked. 139. quality, character. 140. take patience, be calm. 150. confine, assigned boundary. 151. state, i.e., mental state.

LEAR. Ask her forgiveness?
Do you but mark how this becomes the house: 155
"Dear daughter, I confess that I am old; [*Kneeling.*]
Age is unnecessary: on my knees I beg
That you'll vouchsafe me raiment, bed, and food."

REG. Good sir, no more; these are unsightly tricks:
Return you to my sister.

LEAR. [*Rising*] Never, Regan: 160
She hath abated me of half my train;
Look'd black upon me; struck me with her tongue,
Most serpent-like, upon the very heart:
All the stored vengeances of heaven fall
On her ingrateful top! Strike her young bones, 165
You taking airs, with lameness!

CORN. Fie, sir, fie!

LEAR. You nimble lightnings, dart your blinding flames
Into her scornful eyes! Infect her beauty,
You fen-suck'd fogs, drawn by the powerful sun,
To fall and blast her pride! 170

REG. O the blest gods! so will you wish on me,
When the rash mood is on.

LEAR. No, Regan, thou shalt never have my curse:
Thy tender-hefted nature shall not give
Thee o'er to harshness: her eyes are fierce; but thine 175
Do comfort and not burn. 'Tis not in thee
To grudge my pleasures, to cut off my train,
To bandy hasty words, to scant my sizes,
And in conclusion to oppose the bolt
Against my coming in: thou better know'st
The offices of nature, bond of childhood, 181
Effects of courtesy, dues of gratitude;
Thy half o' the kingdom hast thou not forgot,
Wherein I thee endow'd.

REG. Good sir, to the purpose.

LEAR. Who put my man i' the stocks? [*Tucket within.*]

CORN. What trumpet's that?

REG. I know 't, my sister's: this approves her letter, 186
That she would soon be here.

[*Enter* OSWALD.]

Is your lady come?

LEAR. This is a slave, whose easy-borrow'd pride
Dwells in the fickle grace of her he follows.
Out, varlet, from my sight!

CORN. What means your grace?

LEAR. Who stock'd my servant? Regan, I have good hope 191
Thou didst not know on 't. Who comes here? O heavens,

[*Enter* GONERIL.]

If you do love old men, if your sweet sway
Allow obedience, if yourselves are old,
Make it your cause; send down, and take my part! 195
[*To* GON.] Art not ashamed to look upon this beard?
O Regan, wilt thou take her by the hand?

GON. Why not by the hand, sir? How have I offended?
All's not offence that indiscretion finds
And dotage terms so.

LEAR. O sides, you are too tough;
Will you yet hold? How came my man i' the stocks? 201

CORN. I set him there, sir: but his own disorders
Deserved much less advancement.

LEAR. You! did you?

REG. I pray you, father, being weak, seem so.
If, till the expiration of your month, 205
You will return and sojourn with my sister,
Dismissing half your train, come then to me:
I am now from home, and out of that provision
Which shall be needful for your entertainment.

LEAR. Return to her, and fifty men dismiss'd? 210
No, rather I abjure all roofs, and choose

155. becomes the house, is a fitting family relationship. 157. Age is unnecessary, old people are of no use. 161. abated . . . train, reduced my retinue by half. 165. young, bones, i.e., Goneril's youthful figure. 166. taking, infecting. 170. fall, fall upon. 174. tender-hefted, swayed by tender feelings. 178. sizes, allowances. 181. offices, duties; bond of childhood, the duties of a child to its parents. 182. Effects of courtesy, courteous action. 184. to the purpose, talk sense. 188. easy-borrow'd, easily assumed. 190. varlet, scoundrel. 194. allow, approve. 203. advancement, honor. 209. entertainment, maintenance.

To wage against the enmity o' the air;
To be a comrade with the wolf and owl,—
Necessity's sharp pinch! Return with her?
Why, the hot-blooded France, that dowerless took 215
Our youngest born, I could as well be brought
To knee his throne, and, squire-like, pension beg
To keep base life afoot. Return with her?
Persuade me rather to be slave and sumpter
To this detested groom. [*Pointing at* OSWALD.

GON. At your choice, sir.

LEAR. I prithee, daughter, do not make me mad: 221
I will not trouble thee, my child; farewell:
We'll no more meet, no more see one another:
But yet thou art my flesh, my blood, my daughter;
Or rather a disease that's in my flesh, 225
Which I must needs call mine: thou art a boil,
A plague-sore, an embossèd carbuncle,
In my corrupted blood. But I'll not chide thee;
Let shame come when it will, I do not call it:
I do not bid the thunder-bearer shoot, 230
Nor tell tales of thee to high-judging Jove:
Mend when thou canst; be better at thy leisure:
I can be patient; I can stay with Regan,
I and my hundred knights.

REG. Not altogether so:
I look'd not for you yet, nor am provided 235
For your fit welcome. Give ear, sir, to my sister;
For those that mingle reason with your passion
Must be content to think you old, and so—
But she knows what she does.

LEAR. Is this well spoken?

REG. I dare avouch it, sir: what, fifty followers? 240
Is it not well? What should you need of more?
Yea, or so many, sith that both charge and danger
Speak 'gainst so great a number? How, in one house,
Should many people, under two commands,
Hold amity? 'Tis hard; almost impossible.

GON. Why might not you, my lord, receive attendance 246
From those that she calls servants or from mine?

REG. Why not, my lord? If then they chanced to slack you,
We could control them. If you will come to me,—
For now I spy a danger,—I entreat you 250
To bring but five and twenty: to no more
Will I give place or notice.

LEAR. I gave you all—

REG. And in good time you gave it.

LEAR. Made you my guardians, my depositaries;
But kept a reservation to be follow'd 255
With such a number. What, must I come to you
With five and twenty, Regan? said you so?

REG. And speak 't again, my lord; no more with me.

LEAR. Those wicked creatures yet do look well-favour'd,
When others are more wicked; not being the worst 260
Stands in some rank of praise. [*To* GON.] I'll go with thee:
Thy fifty yet doth double five-and-twenty,
And thou art twice her love.

GON. Hear me, my lord:
What need you five and twenty, ten, or five,
To follow in a house where twice so many
Have a command to tend you? 266

REG. What need one?

LEAR. O, reason not the need: our basest beggars
Are in the poorest thing superfluous:
Allow not nature more than nature needs,
Man's life as cheap as beast's: thou art a lady;
If only to go warm were gorgeous, 271
Why, nature needs not what thou gorgeous wear'st,
Which scarcely keeps thee warm. But, for true need,—
You heavens, give me that patience, patience I need!

212. wage, wage war with. 217. knee, kneel before; squire-like, as if I were a servant. 219. sumpter, pack-horse, drudge. 220. groom, menial. 227. embossed, swollen. 237. mingle . . . passion, consider your violence in the light of reason. 240. avouch, affirm. 242. charge, expense. 248. slack, neglect. 252. notice, recognition. 254. depositaries, trustees. 259. well-favour'd, handsome. 267. reason, discuss. 268. Are . . . superfluous, have in their most meagre possessions more than the barest necessities. 274. patience, endurance.

You see me here, you gods, a poor old man,
As full of grief as age; wretched in both! 276
If it be you that stir these daughters' hearts
Against their father, fool me not so much
To bear it tamely; touch me with noble anger,
And let not women's weapons, water-drops,
Stain my man's cheeks! No, you unnatural hags, 281
I will have such revenges on you both,
That all the world shall—I will do such things,—
What they are, yet I know not; but they shall be
The terrors of the earth. You think I'll weep;
No, I'll not weep: 286
I have full cause of weeping; but this heart
Shall break into a hundred thousand flaws,
Or ere I'll weep. O fool, I shall go mad!

[*Exeunt* LEAR, GLOUCESTER, KENT, *and* FOOL. *Storm and tempest.*

CORN. Let us withdraw; 'twill be a storm.

REG. This house is little: the old man and his people 291
Cannot be well bestow'd.

GON. 'Tis his own blame; hath put himself from rest,
And must needs taste his folly.

REG. For his particular, I'll receive him gladly, 295
But not one follower.

GON. So am I purposed.
Where is my lord of Gloucester?

CORN. Follow'd the old man forth: he is return'd.

[*Re-enter* GLOUCESTER.]

GLOU. The king is in high rage.

CORN. Whither is he going?

GLOU. He calls to horse; but will I know not whither. 300

CORN. 'Tis best to give him way; he leads himself.

GON. My lord, entreat him by no means to stay.

GLOU. Alack, the night comes on, and the bleak winds
Do sorely ruffle; for many miles about
There's scarce a bush.

REG. O, sir, to wilful men, 305
The injuries that they themselves procure
Must be their schoolmasters. Shut up your doors:
He is attended with a desperate train;
And what they may incense him to, being apt 309
To have his ear abused, wisdom bids fear.

CORN. Shut up your doors, my lord; 'tis a wild night:
My Regan counsels well: come out o' the storm. [*Exeunt.*

ACT III

SCENE I. *A heath.*

[*Storm still. Enter* KENT *and a* GENTLEMAN, *meeting.*]

KENT. Who's there, besides foul weather?

GENT. One minded like the weather, most unquietly.

KENT. I know you. Where's the king?

GENT. Contending with the fretful element;
Bids the wind blow the earth into the sea, 5
Or swell the curlèd waters 'bove the main,
That things might change or cease; tears his white hair,
Which the impetuous blasts, with eyeless rage,
Catch in their fury, and make nothing of;
Strives in his little world of man to out-scorn 10
The to-and-fro-conflicting wind and rain.
This night, wherein the cub-drawn bear would couch,
The lion and the belly-pinchèd wolf
Keep their fur dry, unbonneted he runs,
And bids what will take all.

KENT. But who is with him?

GENT. None but the fool; who labours to out-jest 16

278-9. fool . . . tamely, do not make me so much of a weakling as to endure it tamely. 285. The . . . earth, deeds to terrify the whole world. 288. flaws, fragments. 292. bestow'd, lodged. 293. blame, fault. 294. taste, i.e., digest. 295. For his particular, as for him alone. 304. ruffle, bluster. 309. incense, incite; apt, ready.

310. abused, deceived. Act III, Scene i: 6. main, mainland. 7. things, world. 8. eyeless, hence undirected, indiscriminate. 9. make nothing of, show no respect for. 10. little . . . man, man was regarded as a universe (macrocosm) in miniature (microcosm). 12. cub-drawn, sucked dry by her cubs; couch, lie protected from the storm. 14. unbonneted, without a hat. 15. take all, the cry of a gambler when he stakes his last penny; so a gesture of desperation.

His heart-struck injuries.

KENT. Sir, I do know you;
And dare, upon the warrant of my note,
Commend a dear thing to you. There is division,
Although as yet the face of it be cover'd 20
With mutual cunning, 'twixt Albany and Cornwall;
Who have—as who have not, that their great stars
Throned and set high?—servants, who seem no less,
Which are to France the spies and speculations
Intelligent of our state; what hath been seen, 25
Either in snuffs and packings of the dukes,
Or the hard rein which both of them have borne
Against the old kind king; or something deeper,
Whereof perchance these are but furnishings;
But, true it is, from France there comes a power 30
Into this scatter'd kingdom; who already,
Wise in our negligence, have secret feet
In some of our best ports, and are at point
To show their open banner. Now to you:
If on my credit you dare build so far 35
To make your speed to Dover, you shall find
Some that will thank you, making just report
Of how unnatural and bemadding sorrow
The king hath cause to plain.
I am a gentleman of blood and breeding; 40
And, from some knowledge and assurance, offer
This office to you.

GENT. I will talk further with you.

KENT. No, do not.
For confirmation that I am much more
Than my out-wall, open this purse, and take 45
What it contains. If you shall see Cordelia,—
As fear not but you shall,—show her this ring;
And she will tell you who your fellow is
That yet you do not know. Fie on this storm!
I will go seek the king. 50

GENT. Give me your hand: have you no more to say?

KENT. Few words, but, to effect, more than all yet;
That, when we have found the king,—in which your pain
That way, I'll this,—he that first lights on him
Holla the other. [*Exeunt severally.* 55

SCENE II. *Another part of the heath. Storm still.*

[*Enter* LEAR *and* FOOL.]

LEAR. Blow, winds, and crack your cheeks! rage! blow!
You cataracts and hurricanoes, spout
Till you have drench'd our steeples, drown'd the cocks!
You sulphurous and thought-executing fires,
Vaunt-couriers to oak-cleaving thunderbolts,
Singe my white head! And thou, all-shaking thunder, 6
Smite flat the thick rotundity o' the world!
Crack nature's moulds, all germens spill at once,
That make ingrateful man! 9

FOOL. O nuncle, court holy-water in a dry house is better than this rain-water out o' door. Good nuncle, in, and ask thy daughters' blessing: here's a night pities neither wise man nor fool.

LEAR. Rumble thy bellyful! Spit, fire! spout, rain!
Nor rain, wind, thunder, fire, are my daughters: 15
I tax not you, you elements, with unkindness;
I never gave you kingdom, call'd you children,
You owe me no subscription: then let fall
Your horrible pleasure; here I stand, your slave,

18. **note**, knowledge (of the situation). 19. **Commend . . . thing**, entrust a momentous matter. 23. **no less**, not more nor less than servants. 24. **speculations**, observers. 25. **Intelligent . . . state**, giving information about our political situation. 26. **snuffs**, resentments; **packings**, plots. 29. **furnishings**, deceptive shows. 30. **power**, armed force. 31. **scatter'd**, divided. 32. **feet**, infantry. 33. **at point**, all ready. 35. **my credit**, your trust in me. 36. **To**, as to. 37. **making just**, if you make accurate. 39. **plain**, complain. 42. **office**, duty. 45. **out-wall**, exterior, i.e., the garb of a serving man. 48. **fellow**, companion. 52. **to effect**, in their importance. 53-4. **your . . . way**, i.e., your efforts to find him lie in that direction. **Scene ii**: 2. **hurricanoes**, water-spouts. 3. **cocks**, weathercocks. 4. **thought-executing**, having the speed of thought. 5. **Vaunt-couriers**, forerunners. 8. **nature's moulds**, i.e., molds in which nature fashions men; **germens**, seeds; **spill**, destroy. 10. **court holy-water**, i.e., flattery. 16. **tax**, reproach. 18. **subscription**, obedience.

A poor, infirm, weak, and despised old man:
But yet I call you servile ministers, 21
That have with two pernicious daughters join'd
Your high engender'd battles 'gainst a head
So old and white as this. O! O! 'tis foul!

FOOL. He that has a house to put 's head in has a good head-piece.

The cod-piece that will house
Before the head has any,
The head and he shall louse;
So beggars marry many. 30
The man that makes his toe
What he his heart should make
Shall of a corn cry woe,
And turn his sleep to wake.

For there was never yet fair woman but she made mouths in a glass. 36

LEAR. No, I will be the pattern of all patience;
I will say nothing.

[*Enter* KENT.]

KENT. Who's there?

FOOL. Marry, here's grace and a cod-piece; that's a wise man and a fool. 41

KENT. Alas, sir, are you here? things that love night
Love not such nights as these; the wrathful skies
Gallow the very wanderers of the dark,
And make them keep their caves: since I was man, 45
Such sheets of fire, such bursts of horrid thunder,
Such groans of roaring wind and rain, I never
Remember to have heard: man's nature cannot carry
The affliction nor the fear.

LEAR. Let the great gods,
That keep this dreadful pother o'er our heads, 50
Find out their enemies now. Tremble, thou wretch,
That hast within thee undivulgèd crimes,
Unwhipp'd of justice: hide thee, thou bloody hand;
Thou perjured, and thou simular man of virtue
That art incestuous: caitiff, to pieces shake, 55
That under covert and convenient seeming
Hast practised on man's life: close pent-up guilts,
Rive your concealing continents, and cry
These dreadful summoners grace. I am a man
More sinn'd against than sinning.

KENT. Alack, bare-headed! 60
Gracious my lord, hard by here is a hovel;
Some friendship will it lend you 'gainst the tempest:
Repose you there; while I to this hard house—
More harder than the stones whereof 'tis raised;
Which even but now, demanding after you, 65
Denied me to come in—return, and force
Their scanted courtesy.

LEAR. My wits begin to turn.
Come on, my boy: how dost, my boy? art cold?
I am cold myself. Where is this straw, my fellow?
The art of our necessities is strange, 70
That can make vile things precious. Come, your hovel.
Poor fool and knave, I have one part in my heart
That's sorry yet for thee.

FOOL. [*Singing*] He that has and a little tiny wit,— 74
With hey, ho, the wind and the rain,—
Must make content with his fortunes fit,
For the rain it raineth every day.

LEAR. True, my good boy. Come, bring us to this hovel. [*Exeunt* LEAR *and* KENT.

FOOL. This is a brave night to cool a courtezan.
I'll speak a prophecy ere I go: 80
When priests are more in word than matter;

21. ministers, agents. 23. high-engender'd, engendered on high; battles, battalions. 27-9. The cod-piece . . . louse, the man who begets children before he has a house will live a lousy existence; cod-piece, an appendage worn on the front of men's trousers. 31. The . . . makes, the man who puts his heart where his toe should be. 36. made . . . glass, grimaced before a looking-glass. 40. grace, an honorable gentleman. 44. gallow, terrify. 48. carry, bear. 49. affliction, the bodily pain. 50. pother, uproar. 54. simular man of, pretender to. 55. caitiff, despicable creature. 56. seeming, hypocrisy. 57. practised on, plotted against. 58. Rive . . . continents, rip open your coverings. 58-9. cry . . . grace, beg for mercy. 59. summoners, police of an ecclesiastical court. 62. lend, afford. 63. hard, cruel. 65. demanding after, asking for. 66. Denied, forbade. 70. art, a reference to alchemy. 79. brave, fine. 81. more . . . matter, better in their talk than in deeds.

When brewers mar their malt with water;
When nobles are their tailors' tutors;
No heretics burn'd, but wenches' suitors;
When every case in law is right; 85
No squire in debt, nor no poor knight;
When slanders do not live in tongues;
Nor cutpurses come not to throngs;
When usurers tell their gold i' the field;
And bawds and whores do churches build; 90
Then shall the realm of Albion
Come to great confusion:
Then comes the time, who lives to see 't,
That going shall be used with feet.
This prophecy Merlin shall make; for I live before his time. [*Exit.* 95

SCENE III. GLOUCESTER'S *castle.*

[*Enter* GLOUCESTER *and* EDMUND.]

GLOU. Alack, alack, Edmund, I like not this unnatural dealing. When I desired their leave that I might pity him, they took from me the use of mine own house; charged me, on pain of their perpetual displeasure, neither to speak of him, entreat for him, nor any way sustain him. 6

EDM. Most savage and unnatural!

GLOU. Go to; say you nothing. There's a division betwixt the dukes; and a worse matter than that: I have received a letter this night; 'tis dangerous to be spoken; I have locked the letter in my closet: these injuries the king now bears will be revenged home; there's part of a power already footed: we must incline to the king. I will seek him, and privily relieve him: go you and main- 15 tain talk with the duke, that my charity be not of him perceived: if he ask for me, I am ill, and gone to bed. Though I die for it, as no less is threatened me, the king my old master must be relieved. There is some strange thing toward, Edmund; pray you, be careful. [*Exit.* 21

EDM. This courtesy, forbid thee, shall the duke
Instantly know; and of that letter too:
This seems a fair deserving, and must draw me
That which my father loses; no less than all: 25
The younger rises when the old doth fall. [*Exit.*

SCENE IV. *The heath. Before a hovel.*

[*Enter* LEAR, KENT, *and* FOOL.]

KENT. Here is the place, my lord; good my lord, enter:
The tyranny of the open night's too rough
For nature to endure. [*Storm still.*

LEAR. Let me alone.

KENT. Good my lord, enter here.

LEAR. Wilt break my heart?

KENT. I had rather break mine own. Good my lord, enter.

LEAR. Thou think'st 'tis much that this contentious storm
Invades us to the skin: so 'tis to thee;
But where the greater malady is fix'd,
The lesser is scarce felt. Thou 'ldst shun a bear;
But if thy flight lay toward the raging sea, 10
Thou 'ldst meet the bear i' the mouth. When the mind's free,
The body's delicate: the tempest in my mind
Doth from my senses take all feeling else
Save what beats there. Filial ingratitude!
Is it not as this mouth should tear this hand 15
For lifting food to 't? But I will punish home:
No, I will weep no more. In such a night
To shut me out! Pour on; I will endure.
In such a night as this! O Regan, Goneril!
Your old kind father, whose frank heart gave all,— 20
O, that way madness lies; let me shun that;
No more of that.

KENT. Good my lord, enter here.

LEAR. Prithee, go in thyself; seek thine own ease:
This tempest will not give me leave to ponder
On things would hurt me more. But I'll go in. 25

89. **tell**, count. 91. **Albion**, Britain. 92. **confusion**, ruin. 94. **going**, walking. 95. **Merlin**, magician and prophet of King Arthur's Court. Scene iii: 6. **sustain**, relieve. 13. **home**, fully. 13. **power**, army; **footed**, landed. 14. **incline to the King**, take the King's part. 15. **privily**, secretly. 20. **toward**, in preparation. 22. **forbid thee**, forbidden to thee. 24. **This . . . deserving**, this will seem a meritorious action. Scene iv: 2. **open night**, night in the open. 11. **i' the mouth**, face to face; **free**, i.e., from trouble. 12. **delicate**, sensitive. 15. **as**, as if. 20. **frank**, generous.

[*To the* FOOL] In, boy; go first. You houseless poverty,—
Nay, get thee in. I'll pray, and then I'll sleep.
[FOOL *goes in.*]
Poor naked wretches, wheresoe'er you are,
That bide the pelting of this pitiless storm,
How shall your houseless heads and unfed sides, 30
Your loop'd and window'd raggedness, defend you
From seasons such as these? O, I have ta'en
Too little care of this! Take physic, pomp;
Expose thyself to feel what wretches feel,
That thou mayst shake the superflux to them, 35
And show the heavens more just.

EDG. [*Within*] Fathom and half, fathom and half! Poor Tom!
[*The* FOOL *runs out from the hovel.*

FOOL. Come not in here, nuncle, here's a spirit. Help me, help me! 40

KENT. Give me thy hand. Who's there?

FOOL. A spirit, a spirit: he says his name's poor Tom.

KENT. What art thou that dost grumble there i' the straw? Come forth.

[*Enter* EDGAR *disguised as a madman.*]

EDG. Away! the foul fiend follows me!
Through the sharp hawthorn blows the cold wind.
Hum! go to thy cold bed, and warm thee.

LEAR. Hast thou given all to thy two daughters?
And art thou come to this? 50

EDG. Who gives any thing to poor Tom? whom the foul fiend hath led through fire and through flame, through ford and whirlpool, o'er bog and quagmire; that hath laid knives under his pillow, and halters in his pew; set ratsbane by his porridge; made him proud of heart, to ride on a bay trotting-horse over four-inched bridges, to course his own shadow for a traitor. Bless thy five wits! 59 Tom's a-cold,—O, do de, do de, do de. Bless thee from whirlwinds, star-blasting, and taking! Do poor Tom some charity, whom the foul fiend vexes: there could I have him now,—and there,—and there again, and there.
[*Storm still.*

LEAR. What, have his daughters brought him to this pass? 65
Couldst thou save nothing? Didst thou give them all?

FOOL. Nay, he reserved a blanket, else we had been all shamed.

LEAR. Now, all the plagues that in the pendulous air
Hang faded o'er men's faults light on thy daughters! 70

KENT. He hath no daughters, sir.

LEAR. Death, traitor! nothing could have subdued nature
To such a lowness but his unkind daughters.
Is it the fashion, that discarded fathers 74
Should have thus little mercy on their flesh?
Judicious punishment! 'twas this flesh begot
Those pelican daughters.

EDG. Pillicock sat on Pillicock-hill:
Halloo, halloo, loo, loo!

FOOL. This cold night will turn us all to fools and madmen. 81

EDG. Take heed o' the foul fiend: obey thy parents; keep thy word justly; swear not; commit not with man's sworn spouse; set not thy sweet heart on proud array. Tom's a-cold.

LEAR. What hast thou been? 86

EDG. A serving-man, proud in heart and mind; that curled my hair; wore gloves in my cap; served the lust of my mistress' heart, and did the act of darkness with her; swore as many oaths as I spake words, and broke them in the sweet face of heaven: one that slept in the contriving of lust, and waked to do it: wine loved I deeply, dice dearly; and in woman out-paramoured the Turk: false of heart, light of ear, bloody of hand; hog in sloth, fox in stealth, wolf in greediness, dog in madness, lion in prey. Let not the creaking of shoes nor the rustling of silks betray thy poor heart to woman: keep thy foot out of

29. **bide,** endure. 31. **loop'd and window'd,** the two words are synonymous, meaning "full of holes." 35. **superflux,** superfluity (i.e., what pomp does not need). 37. **Fathom, etc.,** Tom pretends to be a sailor, taking soundings in a storm at sea. 54-5. **knives . . . pillow,** i.e., tempted him to commit suicide. 55. **pew,** a gallery of a house, not a church pew. 58. **course,** chase. 62. **taking,** infection. 63. **there . . . him,** i.e., he snatches at vermin.

69. **pendulous,** overhanging. 72. **subdued,** reduced; **nature,** i.e., man's nature. 75. **mercy . . . flesh,** Edgar has stuck thorns or skewers into his flesh. 77. **pelican daughters,** it was believed that young pelicans fed on their mother's blood. 78. **Pillicock,** suggested by pelican, meant darling. 84. **commit,** i.e., commit adultery. 88-9. **gloves . . . cap,** a gallant often wore his lady's glove in his hat. 94. **out-paramoured,** had more mistresses than; **the Turk,** the Sultan. 95. **light of ear,** foolishly credulous of evil gossip.

brothels, thy hand out of plackets, thy pen from lenders' books, and defy the foul fiend. 101

Still through the hawthorn blows the cold wind:
Says suum, mun, ha, no, nonny.
Dolphin my boy, my boy, sessa! let him trot by. [*Storm still.*

LEAR. Why, thou wert better in thy grave than to answer with thy uncovered body this extremity of the skies. Is man no more than this? Consider him well. Thou owest the worm no silk, the beast no hide, the sheep no wool, the cat no perfume. Ha! here's three 110 on's are sophisticated! Thou art the thing itself: unaccommodated man is no more but such a poor, bare, forked animal as thou art. Off, off, you lendings! come, unbutton 114 here. [*Tearing off his clothes.*

FOOL. Prithee, nuncle, be contented; 'tis a naughty night to swim in. Now a little fire in a wild field were like an old lecher's heart; a small spark, all the rest on 's body cold. Look, here comes a walking fire. 119

[*Enter* GLOUCESTER, *with a torch.*]

EDG. This is the foul fiend Flibbertigibbet: he begins at curfew, and walks till the first cock; he gives the web and the pin, squints the eye, and makes the hare-lip; mildews the white wheat, and hurts the poor creature of earth.

Saint Withold footed thrice the 'old; 125
He met the night-mare, and her nine-fold;
Bid her alight,
And her troth plight,
And, aroint thee, witch, aroint thee!

KENT. How fares your grace? 130

LEAR. What's he?

KENT. Who's there? What is 't you seek?

GLOU. What are you there? Your names?

EDG. Poor Tom; that eats the swimming frog, the toad, the tadpole, the wall-newt 135 and the water; that in the fury of his heart, when the foul fiend rages, eats cow-dung for sallets; swallows the old rat and the ditch-dog; drinks the green mantle of the standing pool; who is whipped from tithing to tithing, and stock-punished, and imprisoned; who hath had three suits to his back, six shirts to his body, horse to ride, and weapon to wear; 143
But mice and rats, and such small deer,
Have been Tom's food for seven long year.
Beware my follower. Peace, Smulkin; peace, thou fiend!

GLOU. What, hath your grace no better company?

EDG. The prince of darkness is a gentleman:
Modo he's call'd, and Mahu.

GLOU. Our flesh and blood is grown so vile, my lord, 150
That it doth hate what gets it.

EDG. Poor Tom's a-cold.

GLOU. Go in with me: my duty cannot suffer
To obey in all your daughters' hard commands:
Though their injunction be to bar my doors,
And let this tyrannous night take hold upon you, 156
Yet have I ventured to come seek you out,
And bring you where both fire and food is ready.

LEAR. First let me talk with this philosopher.
What is the cause of thunder? 160

KENT. Good my lord, take his offer; go into the house.

LEAR. I'll talk a word with this same learned Theban.
What is your study?

EDG. How to prevent the fiend, and to kill vermin. 164

LEAR. Let me ask you one word in private.

KENT. Importune him once more to go, my lord;
His wits begin to unsettle.

GLOU. Canst thou blame him? [*Storm still.*]

99. **plackets**, slits in petticoats. 103. **Dolphin, my boy**, reference to a ballad ridiculing the French Dauphin; **sessa**, hurry, go it. 106. **answer**, oppose. 107. **extremity . . . skies**, violence of the storm. 110. **cat**, civet cat. 112. **unaccommodated man**, man unprovided with clothes and other furnishings of civilization. 114. **lendings**, lent by art to the natural man. 116. **naughty**, very wicked. 122. **web and the pin**, old term for "cataract." 124. **white**, i.e., ripening. 125. **Withold**, i.e., St. Vitalis; **footed**, walked across; **old**, wold, an upland plain. 126. **night-mare**, a demon; **nine-fold**, nine offspring. 128. **her troth plight**, pledge her faith (to do no harm). 129. **aroint**, begone. 130. **grace**, majesty. 135-6. **wall . . . water**, the wall lizard and the water lizard. 137. **sallets**, salads. 139. **mantle**, scum; **standing**, stagnant. 140. **tithing to tithing**, parish to parish. 139-40. **stock-punished**, put in the stocks. 144. **deer**, animal. 146. **follower**, attendant friend. 151. **gets**, begets. 153. **suffer**, permit me. 159. **philosopher**, scientist. 162. **Theban**, i.e., Greek philosopher. 163. **study**, specialty. 164. **prevent**, forestall.

His daughters seek his death; ah, that good Kent!
He said it would be thus, poor banish'd man!
Thou say'st the king grows mad; I'll tell thee, friend, 170
I am almost mad myself: I had a son,
Now outlaw'd from my blood; he sought my life,
But lately, very late: I loved him, friend:
No father his son dearer: truth to tell thee,
The grief hath crazed my wits. What a night's this! 175
I do beseech your grace,—

LEAR. O, cry you mercy, sir.
Noble philosopher, your company.

EDG. Tom's a-cold.

GLOU. In, fellow, there, into the hovel: keep thee warm.

LEAR. Come, let's in all.

KENT. This way, my lord.

LEAR. With him;
I will keep still with my philosopher. 181

KENT. Good my lord, soothe him; let him take the fellow.

GLOU. Take him you on.

KENT. Sirrah, come on; go along with us.

LEAR. Come, good Athenian. 185

GLOU. No words, no words: hush.

EDG. Child Rowland to the dark tower came,
His word was still,—Fie, foh, and fum,
I smell the blood of a British man.
[*Exeunt.*

SCENE V. GLOUCESTER'S *castle.*

[*Enter* CORNWALL *and* EDMUND.]

CORN. I will have my revenge ere I depart his house.

EDM. How, my lord, I may be censured, that nature thus gives way to loyalty, something fears me to think of. 5

CORN. I now perceive, it was not altogether your brother's evil disposition made him seek his death; but a provoking merit, set a-work by a reproveable badness in himself. 9

EDM. How malicious is my fortune, that I must repent to be just! This is the letter he spoke of, which approves him an intelligent party to the advantages of France. O heavens! that this treason were not, or not I the detector! 14

CORN. Go with me to the duchess.

EDM. If the matter of this paper be certain, you have mighty business in hand.

CORN. True or false, it hath made thee earl of Gloucester. Seek out where thy father is, that he may be ready for our apprehension. 20

EDM. [*Aside*] If I find him comforting the king, it will stuff his suspicion more fully.—I will persevere in my course of loyalty, though the conflict be sore between that and my blood. 24

CORN. I will lay trust upon thee; and thou shalt find a dearer father in my love. [*Exeunt.*

SCENE VI. *A chamber in a farmhouse adjoining the castle.*

[*Enter* GLOUCESTER, LEAR, KENT, FOOL, *and* EDGAR.]

GLOU. Here is better than the open air; take it thankfully. I will piece out the comfort with what addition I can: I will not be long from you.

KENT. All the power of his wits have given way to his impatience: the gods reward your kindness! [*Exit* GLOUCESTER. 6

EDG. Frateretto calls me; and tells me Nero is an angler in the lake of darkness. Pray, innocent, and beware the foul fiend.

FOOL. Prithee, nuncle, tell me whether a madman be a gentleman or a yeoman? 11

LEAR. A king, a king!

FOOL. No, he's a yeoman that has a gentleman to his son; for he's a mad yeoman that sees his son a gentleman before him. 15

LEAR. To have a thousand with red burning spits
Come hissing in upon 'em,—

176. **cry you mercy,** beg your pardon (for not paying attention). 181. **still,** always. 182. **soothe,** humor. 187. **Child,** a candidate for knighthood; **Rowland,** Charlemagne's nephew and legendary hero. The line is probably a snatch from a lost ballad. **Scene v:** 3. **censured,** judged. 4-5. **something fears me,** I am somewhat frightened. 8. **provoking merit,** i.e., the fact that your father deserved to die also incited him. 9. **himself,** i.e., Gloucester. 11. **just,** righteous. 12. **approves,** proves. 12-3. **intelligent party,** a spy. 13. **France,** King of France. 20. **apprehension,** arrest. 21. **comforting,** giving aid and comfort. 24. **blood,** natural instincts. **Scene vi:** 7. **Frateretto,** the name of a fiend. 9. **innocent,** simpleton. 11. **yeoman,** a small landed proprietor, in rank lower than a gentleman. 15. **before him,** before he is one.

EDG. The foul fiend bites my back.

FOOL. He's mad that trusts in the tameness of a wolf, a horse's health, a boy's love, or a whore's oath. 21

LEAR. It shall be done; I will arraign them straight.
[*To* EDGAR] Come, sit thou here, most learned justicer;
[*To the* FOOL] Thou, sapient sir, sit here. Now, you she foxes!

EDG. Look, where he stands and glares! 25
Wantest thou eyes at trial, madam?
Come o'er the bourn, Bessy, to me,—

FOOL. Her boat hath a leak,
And she must not speak
Why she dares not come over to thee. 30

EDG. The foul fiend haunts poor Tom in the voice of a nightingale. Hopdance cries in Tom's belly for two white herring. Croak not, black angel; I have no food for thee.

KENT. How do you, sir? Stand you not so amazed: 35
Will you lie down and rest upon the cushions?

LEAR. I'll see their trial first. Bring in the evidence.
[*To* EDGAR] Thou robed man of justice, take thy place;
[*To the* FOOL] And thou, his yoke-fellow of equity,
Bench by his side: [*To* KENT] you are o' the commission, 40
Sit you too.

EDG. Let us deal justly.
Sleepest or wakest thou, jolly shepherd?
Thy sheep be in the corn;
And for one blast of thy minikin mouth,
Thy sheep shall take no harm. 46
Pur! the cat is gray.

LEAR. Arraign her first; 'tis Goneril. I here take my oath before this honourable assembly, she kicked the poor king her father. 50

FOOL. Come hither, mistress. Is your name Goneril?

LEAR. She cannot deny it.

FOOL. Cry you mercy, I took you for a joint-stool. 55

LEAR. And here's another, whose warp'd looks proclaim
What store her heart is made on. Stop her there!
Arms, arms, sword, fire! Corruption in the place!
False justicer, why hast thou let her 'scape?

EDG. Bless thy five wits! 60

KENT. O pity! Sir, where is the patience now,
That you so oft have boasted to retain?

EDG. [*Aside*] My tears begin to take his part so much,
They'll mar my counterfeiting.

LEAR. The little dogs and all, 65
Tray, Blanch, and Sweet-heart, see, they bark at me.

EDG. Tom will throw his head at them. Avaunt, you curs!
Be thy mouth or black or white,
Tooth that poisons if it bite; 70
Mastiff, greyhound, mongrel grim,
Hound or spaniel, brach or lym,
Or bobtail tike or trundle-tail,
Tom will make them weep and wail:
For, with throwing thus my head, 75
Dogs leap the hatch, and all are fled.
Do de, de, de. Sessa! Come, march to wakes and fairs and market-towns. Poor Tom, thy horn is dry. 79

LEAR. Then let them anatomize Regan; see what breeds about her heart. Is there any cause in nature that makes these hard hearts? [*To* EDGAR] You, sir, I entertain for one of my hundred; only I do not like the fashion of your garments: you will say they are Persian attire; but let them be changed.

KENT. Now, good my lord, lie here and rest awhile. 88

LEAR. Make no noise, make no noise; draw the curtains: so, so, so. We'll go to supper i' the morning. So, so, so. 91

FOOL. And I'll go to bed at noon.

23. **justicer**, judge. 26. **Wantest . . . trial?** Don't you see you have a spectator at your trial, i.e., the fiend? 27. **Come . . . me**, first line of an old ballad; **bourn**, brook. 32. **Hopdance**, a fiend. 33. **white**, fresh; **Croak not**, addressed to his rumbling belly. 35. **amazed**, in a daze. 37. **evidence**, witnesses. 40. **Bench**, sit on the judge's bench; **o' the commission**, a commissioned Justice of the Peace. 44. **corn**, wheat field. 45. **for one blast**, the time it takes to blow one blast; **minikin**, pretty little. 55. **joint-stool**, stool made by a joiner. 56. **warp'd**, distorted. 57. **store**, stuff.

58. **Corruption . . . place**, bribery in the court. 72. **brach or lym**, bitch or bloodhound. 73. **tike**, cur; **trundle-tail**, drooping-tail. 76. **hatch**, lower half of a divided [Dutch] door. 77. **Sessa**, about = "Let's go!" 79. **horn is dry**, a beggar's appeal for drink; horn was a bottle. 80. **anatomize**, dissect. 83. **entertain**, engage. 86. **Persian**, gorgeous. 90. **curtains**, i.e., imaginary bed curtains. 91. **So . . . so**, an indication that Lear goes through the motions of drawing curtains.

[*Re-enter* GLOUCESTER.]

GLOU. Come hither, friend: where is the king my master?

KENT. Here, sir; but trouble him not, his wits are gone.

GLOU. Good friend, I prithee, take him in thy arms; 95
I have o'erheard a plot of death upon him:
There is a litter ready; lay him in 't,
And drive towards Dover, friend, where thou shalt meet
Both welcome and protection. Take up thy master: 99
If thou shouldst dally half an hour, his life,
With thine, and all that offer to defend him,
Stand in assurèd loss: take up, take up;
And follow me, that will to some provision
Give thee quick conduct.

KENT. Oppressèd nature sleeps;
This rest might yet have balm'd thy broken sinews, 105
Which, if convenience will not allow,
Stand in hard cure. [*To the* FOOL] Come, help to bear thy master;
Thou must not stay behind.

GLOU. Come, come, away.
[*Exeunt all but* EDGAR.

EDG. When we our betters see bearing our woes,
We scarcely think our miseries our foes. 110
Who alone suffers suffers most i' the mind,
Leaving free things and happy shows behind:
But then the mind much sufferance doth o'erskip,
When grief hath mates, and bearing fellowship.
How light and portable my pain seems now, 115
When that which makes me bend makes the king bow,
He childed as I father'd! Tom, away!
Mark the high noises; and thyself bewray,
When false opinion, whose wrong thought defiles thee,
In thy just proof, repeals and reconciles thee.
What will hap more to-night, safe 'scape the king! 121
Lurk, lurk. [*Exit.*

SCENE VII. GLOUCESTER'S *castle.*

[*Enter* CORNWALL, REGAN, GONERIL, EDMUND, *and* SERVANTS.]

CORN. Post speedily to my lord your husband; show him this letter: the army of France is landed. Seek out the villain Gloucester. [*Exeunt some of the* SERVANTS.

REG. Hang him instantly.

GON. Pluck out his eyes.

CORN. Leave him to my displeasure. Edmund, keep you our sister company: the revenges we are bound to take upon your traitorous father are not fit for your beholding. Advise the duke, where you are going, to a most festinate preparation: we are 10 bound to the like. Our posts shall be swift and intelligent betwixt us. Farewell, dear sister: farewell, my lord of Gloucester.

[*Enter* OSWALD.]

How now! where's the king? 14

OSW. My lord of Gloucester hath convey'd him hence:
Some five or six and thirty of his knights,
Hot questrists after him, met him at gate;
Who, with some other of the lords dependants,
Are gone with him towards Dover; where they boast 19
To have well-armèd friends.

CORN. Get horses for your mistress.

GON. Farewell, sweet lord, and sister.

CORN. Edmund, farewell.
[*Exeunt* GONERIL, EDMUND, *and* OSWALD.]
Go seek the traitor Gloucester,
Pinion him like a thief, bring him before us.
[*Exeunt other* SERVANTS.]
Though well we may not pass upon his life
Without the form of justice, yet our power

96. upon, against. 100. dally, delay. 102. Stand . . . loss, are sure to be lost. 103. provision, i.e., for safety. 105. balm'd . . . sinews, healed your racked nerves. 107. Stand . . . cure, are hard to cure. 112. free, carefree; happy shows, appearances of happiness. 113. sufferance, suffering; o'erskip, escape. 114. bearing, i.e., of sorrow. 115. portable, endurable. 117. childed . . . father'd, having children like my father (in cruelty). 118. high noises, sounds of discord among the high and mighty; bewray, you reveal yourself, i.e., put off your disguise. 120. In . . . proof, on proof that you are guiltless; repeals, restores (i.e., to favor). 121. what, whatever. 122. Lurk, hide. Scene vii: 10. to . . . preparation, to make a most hasty preparation (for war). 11. bound to the like, getting ready for the like preparation; posts, messengers. 12. intelligent, carry information. 13. Lord of Gloucester, i.e., Edmund, who has been given the title as a reward for his treachery. 15. Lord of Gloucester, the old Earl. 17. questrists, searchers. 23. pinion, i.e., bind his elbows together. 24. pass, pass judgment.

Shall do a courtesy to our wrath, which men
May blame, but not control. Who's there? the traitor?

[*Enter* GLOUCESTER, *brought in by two or three.*]

REG. Ingrateful fox! 'tis he.
CORN. Bind fast his corky arms.
GLOU. What mean your graces? Good my friends, consider 30
You are my guests: do me no foul play, friends.
CORN. Bind him, I say.
[SERVANTS *bind him.*
REG. Hard, hard. O filthy traitor!
GLOU. Unmerciful lady as you are, I'm none.
CORN. To this chair bind him. Villain, thou shalt find— [REGAN *plucks his beard.*
GLOU. By the kind gods, 'tis most ignobly done 35
To pluck me by the beard.
REG. So white, and such a traitor!
GLOU. Naughty lady,
These hairs, which thou dost ravish from my chin,
Will quicken, and accuse thee: I am your host:
With robbers' hands my hospitable favours 40
You should not ruffle thus. What will you do?
CORN. Come, sir, what letters had you late from France?
REG. Be simple answerer, for we know the truth.
CORN. And what confederacy have you with the traitors
Late footed in the kingdom? 45
REG. To whose hands have you sent the lunatic king?
Speak.
GLOU. I have a letter guessingly set down,
Which came from one that's of a neutral heart,
And not from one opposed.
CORN. Cunning.
REG. And false.
CORN. Where hast thou sent the king? 50
GLOU. To Dover.
REG. Wherefore to Dover? Wast thou not charged at peril—
CORN. Wherefore to Dover? Let him first answer that.
GLOU. I am tied to the stake, and I must stand the course.
REG. Wherefore to Dover, sir? 55
GLOU. Because I would not see thy cruel nails
Pluck out his poor old eyes; nor thy fierce sister
In his anointed flesh stick boarish fangs.
The sea, with such a storm as his bare head
In hell-black night endured, would have buoy'd up, 60
And quench'd the stelled fires:
Yet, poor old heart, he holp the heavens to rain.
If wolves had at thy gate howl'd that stern time,
Thou shouldst have said "Good porter, turn the key,"
All cruels else subscribed: but I shall see 65
The wingèd vengeance overtake such children.
CORN. See 't shalt thou never. Fellows, hold the chair.
Upon these eyes of thine I'll set my foot.
GLOU. He that will think to live till he be old,
Give me some help! O cruel! O you gods! 70
REG. One side will mock another; the other too.
CORN. If you see vengeance,—
FIRST SERV. Hold your hand, my lord:
I have served you ever since I was a child;
But better service have I never done you
Than now to bid you hold.
REG. How now, you dog!
FIRST SERV. If you did wear a beard upon your chin, 76
I'd shake it on this quarrel. What do you mean?

26. **do a courtesy**, act in accordance with. 29. **corky**, withered. 37. **Naughty**, wicked. 39. **quicken**, come to life. 40. **hospitable favours**, the features of your host. 41. **ruffle**, treat with violence. 43. **simple**, straightforward. 45. **footed**, landed. 52. **at peril**, under peril (of death). 54. **course**, attack (of the dogs in bear-baiting). 58. **anointed**, i.e., with the consecrated oil at his coronation. 60. **buoy'd up**, heaved aloft. 61. **stelled fires**, the fires of the stars. 62. **holp**, helped. 63. **howl'd**, i.e., for shelter. 65. **All . . . subscribed**, all other cruel creatures except you gave way (to their need for shelter). 71. **one . . . another**, i.e., one good eye will mock the other blind one. 77. **quarrel**, this cause (over which I quarrel with you).

CORN. My villain! [*They draw and fight.*
FIRST SERV. Nay, then, come on, and take the chance of anger.
REG. Give me thy sword. A peasant stand up thus! 80
[*Takes a sword, and runs at him behind.*
FIRST SERV. O, I am slain! My lord, you have one eye left
To see some mischief on him. O!
[*Dies.*
CORN. Lest it see more, prevent it. Out, vile jelly!
Where is thy lustre now?
GLOU. All dark and comfortless. Where's my son Edmund? 85
Edmund, enkindle all the sparks of nature,
To quit this horrid act.
REG. Out, treacherous villain!
Thou call'st on him that hates thee: it was he
That made the overture of thy treasons to us;
Who is too good to pity thee. 90
GLOU. O my follies! then Edgar was abused.
Kind gods, forgive me that, and prosper him!
REG. Go thrust him out at gates, and let him smell
His way to Dover. [*Exit one with* GLOUCESTER.] How is 't, my lord? how look you?
CORN. I have received a hurt: follow me, lady. 95
Turn out that eyeless villain; throw this slave
Upon the dunghill. Regan, I bleed apace:
Untimely comes this hurt: give me your arm.
[*Exit* CORNWALL, *led by* REGAN.
SEC. SERV. I'll never care what wickedness I do,
If this man come to good.
THIRD SERV. If she live long, 100
And in the end meet the old course of death,
Women will all turn monsters.
SEC. SERV. Let's follow the old earl, and get the Bedlam
To lead him where he would: his roguish madness
Allows itself to any thing. 105
THIRD SERV. Go thou: I'll fetch some flax and whites of eggs
To apply to his bleeding face. Now, heaven help him! [*Exeunt severally.*

ACT IV

SCENE I. *The heath.*

[*Enter* EDGAR.]

EDG. Yet better thus, and known to be contemn'd,
Than still contemn'd and flatter'd. To be worst,
The lowest and most dejected thing of fortune,
Stands still in esperance, lives not in fear:
The lamentable change is from the best; 5
The worst returns to laughter. Welcome, then,
Thou unsubstantial air that I embrace!
The wretch that thou hast blown unto the worst
Owes nothing to thy blasts. But who comes here?

[*Enter* GLOUCESTER, *led by an* OLD MAN.]

My father, poorly led? World, world, O world! 10
But that thy strange mutations make us hate thee,
Life would not yield to age.
OLD MAN. O, my good lord, I have been your tenant, and your father's tenant, these fourscore years. 15
GLOU. Away, get thee away; good friend, be gone:
Thy comforts can do me no good at all;
Thee they may hurt.
OLD MAN. Alack, sir, you cannot see your way.
GLOU. I have no way, and therefore want no eyes; 20

78. **villain**, bondman, serf. 82. **mischief**, harm. 83. **prevent**, forestall. 87. **quit**, repay, revenge. 89. **overture**, disclosure. 91. **abused**, deceived (by Edmund). 92. **that**, i.e., my treatment of Edgar. 97. **apace**, fast. 98. **Untimely**, inopportunely. 102. **Women . . . monsters**, because they will know there is no divine justice. 103. **Bedlam**, lunatic, i.e., Edgar. 105. **Allows . . . thing**, permits him to do anything with impunity. **Act IV, Scene i**: 1. **contemn'd**, despised. 4. **esperance**, hope. 6. **returns to laughter**, changes to happiness. 10. **poorly led**, led by one poor old man, instead of his former attendants. 11. **mutations**, changes (of fortune). 20. **I . . . way**, i.e., no course in life is left me.

I stumbled when I saw: full oft 'tis seen,
Our means secure us, and our mere defects
Prove our commodities. O dear son Edgar,
The food of thy abusèd father's wrath!
Might I but live to see thee in my touch, 25
I'ld say I had eyes again!

OLD MAN. How now! Who's there?

EDG. [*Aside*] O gods! Who is 't can say "I am at the worst"?
I am worse than e'er I was.

OLD MAN. 'Tis poor mad Tom.

EDG. [*Aside*] And worse I may be yet: the worst is not
So long as we can say "This is the worst." 30

OLD MAN. Fellow, where goest?

GLOU. Is it a beggar-man?

OLD MAN. Madman and beggar too.

GLOU. He has some reason, else he could not beg.
I' the last night's storm I such a fellow saw;
Which made me think a man a worm: my son 35
Came then into my mind; and yet my mind
Was then scarce friends with him: I have heard more since.
As flies to wanton boys, are we to the gods,
They kill us for their sport.

EDG. [*Aside*] How should this be?
Bad is the trade that must play fool to sorrow, 40
Angering itself and others.—Bless thee, master!

GLOU. Is that the naked fellow?

OLD MAN. Ay, my lord.

GLOU. Then, prithee, get thee gone: if, for my sake,
Thou wilt o'ertake us, hence a mile or twain,
I' the way toward Dover, do it for ancient love; 45
And bring some covering for this naked soul,
Who I'll entreat to lead me.

OLD MAN. Alack, sir, he is mad.

GLOU. 'Tis the times' plague, when madmen lead the blind.
Do as I bid thee, or rather do thy pleasure;
Above the rest, be gone. 50

OLD MAN. I'll bring him the best 'parel that I have,
Come on 't what will. [*Exit.*

GLOU. Sirrah, naked fellow,—

EDG. Poor Tom's a-cold. [*Aside*] I cannot daub it further.

GLOU. Come hither, fellow. 55

EDG. [*Aside*] And yet I must.—Bless thy sweet eyes, they bleed.

GLOU. Knowst thou the way to Dover?

EDG. Both stile and gate, horse-way and foot-path. Poor Tom hath been scared out of his good wits: bless thee, good man's son, from the foul fiend! five fiends have been in poor Tom at once; of lust, as Obidicut; Hobbididance, prince of dumbness; Mahu, of stealing; Modo, of murder; Flibbertigibbet, of mopping and mowing, who since possesses chambermaids and waiting-women. So, bless thee, master! 66

GLOU. Here, take this purse, thou whom the heavens' plagues
Have humbled to all strokes: that I am wretched
Makes thee the happier: heavens, deal so still!
Let the superfluous and lust-dieted man, 70
That slaves your ordinance, that will not see
Because he doth not feel, feel your power quickly;
So distribution should undo excess,
And each man have enough. Dost thou know Dover?

EDG. Ay, master. 75

GLOU. There is a cliff, whose high and bending head
Looks fearfully in the confinèd deep
Bring me but to the very brim of it,
And I'll repair the misery thou dost bear
With something rich about me: from that place 80
I shall no leading need.

EDG. Give me thy arm:
Poor Tom shall lead thee. [*Exeunt.*

22. **Our . . . secure us,** prosperity makes us careless and overconfident. 22-3. **our mere . . . commodities,** our very deprivations prove to be benefits. 24. **food,** i.e., object; **abused,** deceived. 38. **wanton,** playful. 41. **Angering,** distressing. 48. **times' plague,** world's calamity. 49. **thy pleasure,** what you wish. 50. **above the rest,** above all. 54. **daub it,** dissemble. 65. **mopping and mowing,** grimacing and making faces; **since,** i.e., since a long time ago. 68. **Have . . . strokes,** have humbled you so that you accept every sort of adversity. 69. **deal so still,** i.e., continue to treat men overconfident in their prosperity as you have me. 70. **superfluous,** the man who has all that he needs, all that he lusts after. 71. **slaves your ordinance,** that makes heaven's will subservient to his own. 73. **distribution,** distributive justice; **undo,** correct. 77. **fearfully,** in a way to arouse terror in anyone who looks over it down to the sea; **confined deep,** i.e., the Straits of Dover; **confined,** shut in.

SCENE II. *Before the* DUKE OF ALBANY'S *palace.*

[*Enter* GONERIL *and* EDMUND.]

GON. Welcome, my lord: I marvel our mild husband
Not met us on the way.

[*Enter* OSWALD.]

Now, where's your master?
OSW. Madam, within; but never man so changed.
I told him of the army that was landed;
He smiled at it: I told him you were coming;
His answer was "The worse:" of Gloucester's treachery, 6
And of the loyal service of his son,
When I inform'd him, then he call'd me sot,
And told me I had turn'd the wrong side out:
What most he should dislike seems pleasant to him; 10
What like, offensive.
GON. [*To* EDM.] Then shall you go no further.
It is the cowish terror of his spirit,
That dares not undertake: he'll not feel wrongs
Which tie him to an answer. Our wishes on the way
May prove effects. Back, Edmund, to my brother; 15
Hasten his musters and conduct his powers:
I must change arms at home, and give the distaff
Into my husband's hands. This trusty servant
Shall pass between us: ere long you are like to hear,
If you dare venture in your own behalf, 20
A mistress's command. Wear this; spare speech; [*Giving a favor.*]
Decline your head: this kiss, if it durst speak,
Would stretch thy spirits up into the air:
Conceive, and fare thee well.
EDM. Yours in the ranks of death.
GON. My most dear Gloucester!
[*Exit* EDMUND.]

O, the difference of man and man! 26
To thee a woman's services are due:
My fool usurps my body.
OSW. Madam, here comes my lord.
[*Exit.*

[*Enter* ALBANY.]

GON. I have been worth the whistle.
ALB. O Goneril!
You are not worth the dust which the rude wind 30
Blows in your face. I fear your disposition:
That nature, which contemns it origin,
Cannot be border'd certain in itself;
She that herself will sliver and disbranch
From her material sap, perforce must wither
And come to deadly use. 36
GON. No more; the text is foolish.
ALB. Wisdom and goodness to the vile seem vile:
Filths savour but themselves. What have you done?
Tigers, not daughters, what have you perform'd? 40
A father, and a gracious agèd man,
Whose reverence even the head-lugg'd bear would lick,
Most barbarous, most degenerate! have you madded.
Could my good brother suffer you to do it?
A man, a prince, by him so benefited! 45
If that the heavens do not their visible spirits
Send quickly down to tame these vile offences,
It will come,
Humanity must perforce prey on itself,
Like monsters of the deep.
GON. Milk-liver'd man! 50
That bear'st a cheek for blows, a head for wrongs:
Who hast not in thy brows an eye discerning
Thine honour from thy suffering; that not know'st
Fools do those villains pity who are punish'd

Scene ii: 8. **sot**, fool. 9. **turn'd . . . out**, completely misinterpreted the situation. 12. **cowish**, cowardly. 13. **undertake**, take the initiative. 14. **on the way**, expressed on our way here. 15. **prove effects**, come to pass. 16. **powers**, forces. 17. **change**, exchange; **arms**, emblems of our professions. 24. **Conceive**, understand. 28. **fool**, i.e., fool of a husband; **usurps**, possesses without right. 29. **the whistle**, whistling for. 31. **disposition**, temperament. 33. **Cannot . . . itself**, can have no sure restraints in its own nature. 34. **sliver and disbranch**, both mean "break off." 35. **material sap**, its nourishing substance (i.e., the sap of the tree). 36. **deadly use**, i.e., to destruction. 39. **Filths . . . themselves**, everything tastes filthy to the filthy. 41. **gracious**, kindly. 42. **head-lugg'd**, pulled along by the head, showing he is surly. 43. **madded**, driven insane. 46. **visible**, in visible form. 48. **It will come**, this will be the result. 50. **milk-liver'd**, white-livered, cowardly. 52. **discerning**, able to distinguish. 53. **Thine honour**, things you can endure with honor. 54. **Fools**, i.e., only fools.

Ere they have done their mischief. Where's thy drum? 55
France spreads his banners in our noiseless land,
With plumèd helm thy state begins to threat;
Whiles thou, a moral fool, sit'st still, and criest
"Alack, why does he so?"

ALB. See thyself, devil!
Proper deformity seems not in the fiend 60
So horrid as in woman.

GON. O vain fool!

ALB. Thou changèd and self-cover'd thing, for shame,
Be-monster not thy feature. Were 't my fitness
To let these hands obey my blood,
They art apt enough to dislocate and tear 65
Thy flesh and bones: howe'er thou art a fiend,
A woman's shape doth shield thee.

GON. Marry, your manhood now—

[*Enter a* MESSENGER.]

ALB. What news?

MESS. O, my good lord, the Duke of Cornwall's dead; 70
Slain by his servant, going to put out
The other eye of Gloucester.

ALB. Gloucester's eyes!

MESS. A servant that he bred, thrill'd with remorse,
Opposed against the act, bending his sword
To his great master; who, thereat enraged, 75
Flew on him, and amongst them fell'd him dead;
But not without that harmful stroke, which since
Hath pluck'd him after.

ALB. This shows you are above,
You justicers, that these our nether crimes
So speedily can venge! But, O poor Gloucester! 80
Lost he his other eye?

MESS. Both, both, my lord.
This letter, madam, craves a speedy answer;
'Tis from your sister.

GON. [*Aside*] One way I like this well;
But being widow, and my Gloucester with her, 85
May all the building in my fancy pluck
Upon my hateful life: another way,
The news is not so tart.—I'll read, and answer.
[*Exit.*

ALB. Where was his son when they did take his eyes?

MESS. Come with my lady hither.

ALB. He is not here. 90

MESS. No, my good lord; I met him back again.

ALB. Knows he the wickedness?

MESS. Ay, my good lord; 'twas he inform'd against him;
And quit the house on purpose, that their punishment
Might have the freer course.

ALB. Gloucester, I live 95
To thank thee for the love thou show'dst the king,
And to revenge thine eyes. Come hither, friend:
Tell me what more thou know'st. [*Exeunt.*

SCENE III. *The French camp near Dover.*

[*Enter* KENT *and a* GENTLEMAN.]

KENT. Why the King of France is so suddenly gone back know you the reason?

GENT. Something he left imperfect in the state, which since his coming forth is thought of; which imports to the kingdom so much fear and danger that his personal return was most required and necessary. 7

KENT. Who hath he left behind him general?

GENT. The Marshal of France, Monsieur La Far. 10

KENT. Did your letters pierce the queen to any demonstration of grief?

GENT. Ay, sir; she took them, read them in my presence;

56. **France,** the King of France; **noiseless,** quiet, i.e., unprepared for warlike resistance. 57. **state,** realm. 58. **moral,** moralizing. 60. **Proper,** suitable to a fiend. 51. **vain,** silly, futile. 62. **changed,** transformed; **self-covered,** i.e., covering your real fiend's nature with a woman's form. 63. **Be-monster . . . feature,** don't allow your whole appearance to be changed to that of a monster; **were't my fitness,** if it were proper for me. 64. **blood,** passion. 65. **apt,** ready. 66. **howe'er,** however much. 68. **your . . . now,** what a fine specimen of manhood you are now! 73. **remorse,** pity. 74. **bending,** directing. 75. **To,** against. 76. **fell'd,** they felled. 78. **pluck'd him after,** i.e., pulled Cornwall down after him. 86-7. **May . . . hateful,** may pull down all my castles in the air (her plan to marry Edmund) and make my life a hated ruin. 88. **tart,** painful. 91. **back,** on his way back. **Scene iii: 5. imports,** portends.

And now and then an ample tear trill'd down
Her delicate cheek; it seem'd she was a queen
Over her passion; who, most rebel-like, 16
Sought to be king o'er her.

KENT. O, then it moved her.

GENT. Not to a rage: patience and sorrow strove
Who should express her goodliest. You have seen
Sunshine and rain at once: her smiles and tears 20
Were like a better way: those happy smilets,
That play'd on her ripe lip, seem'd not to know
What guests were in her eyes; which parted thence,
As pearls from diamonds dropp'd. In brief,
Sorrow would be a rarity most beloved, 25
If all could so become it.

KENT. Made she no verbal question?

GENT. 'Faith, once or twice she heaved the name of "father"
Pantingly forth, as if it press'd her heart;
Cried "Sisters! sisters! Shame of ladies! sisters!
Kent! father! sisters! What, i' the storm? i' the night? 30
Let pity not be believed!" There she shook
The holy water from her heavenly eyes,
And clamour moisten'd: then away she started
To deal with grief alone.

KENT. It is the stars,
The stars above us, govern our conditions; 35
Else one self mate and mate could not beget
Such different issues. You spoke not with her since?

GENT. No.

KENT. Was this before the king return'd?

GENT. No, since.

KENT. Well, sir, the poor distressèd Lear's i' the town; 40
Who sometime, in his better tune, remembers
What we are come about, and by no means
Will yield to see his daughter.

GENT. Why, good sir?

KENT. A sovereign shame so elbows him: his own unkindness,
That stripp'd her from his benediction, turn'd her 45
To foreign casualties, gave her dear rights
To his dog-hearted daughters, these things sting
His mind so venomously, that burning shame
Detains him from Cordelia.

GENT. Alack, poor gentleman!

KENT. Of Albany's and Cornwall's powers you heard not? 50

GENT. 'Tis so, they are afoot.

KENT. Well, sir, I'll bring you to our master Lear,
And leave you to attend him: some dear cause
Will in concealment wrap me up awhile;
When I am known aright, you shall not grieve
Lending me this acquaintance. I pray you, go 56
Along with me. [*Exeunt.*

SCENE IV. *The same. A tent.*

[*Enter, with drum and colours,* CORDELIA, DOCTOR, *and* SOLDIERS.]

COR. Alack, 'tis he: why, he was met even now
As mad as the vex'd sea; singing aloud;
Crown'd with rank fumiter and furrow-weeds,
With bur-docks, hemlock, nettles, cuckoo-flowers,
Darnel, and all the idle weeds that grow 5
In our sustaining corn. A century send forth;
Search every acre in the high-grown field,
And bring him to our eye. [*Exit an* OFFICER.]
What can man's wisdom
In the restoring his bereavèd sense?
He that helps him take all my outward worth.

DOCT. There is means, madam: 11
Our foster-nurse of nature is repose,
The which he lacks; that to provoke in him,

14. trill'd, trickled. 16. passion, emotion, i.e., grief. 18. rage, outburst (of grief). 19. express her goodliest, give her the most beautiful expression. 21. like . . . way, like mingled sunshine and rain, only more beautiful; smilets, little smiles. 23. which, i.e., the tears. 26. all . . . become it, it were so becoming to all (as to her); Made . . . question? Did she say nothing? question, speech. 31. believed, believed in. 33. clamour moisten'd, moistened her cries of grief (by weeping). 35. conditions, temperaments. 36. one self, one and the same. 41. sometime, sometimes; better tune, more lucid intervals. 43. yield, assent. 44. sovereign, overmastering; elbows, stands at his elbow. 45. benediction, parting blessing. 46. foreign casualties, hazards in a foreign land. 50. powers, troops. 53. dear, important. 56. Lending me, for having granted me. Scene iv: 3. rank . . . furrow-weeds, luxuriant fumitory (earth-smoke) and weeds growing in furrows of a plowed field. 4. cuckoo-flowers, flowers blooming when the cuckoo is abroad, i.e., in April and May—perhaps cowslips. 5. idle, useless. 6. sustaining corn, wheat that gives sustenance; century, detail of a hundred men. 8. What . . . wisdom, what can science do. 10. worth, property. 12. Our foster . . . of, the nurse that fosters our nature. 13. provoke, induce.

Are many simples operative, whose power
Will close the eye of anguish.

COR. All blest secrets, 15
All you unpublish'd virtues of the earth,
Spring with my tears! be aidant and remediate
In the good man's distress! Seek, seek for him;
Lest his ungovern'd rage dissolve the life
That wants the means to lead it.

[*Enter a* MESSENGER.]

MESS. News, madam; 20
The British powers are marching hitherward.

COR. 'Tis known before; our preparation stands
In expectation of them. O dear father,
It is thy business that I go about;
Therefore great France 25
My mourning and important tears hath pitied.
No blown ambition doth our arms incite,
But love, dear love, and our aged father's right:
Soon may I hear and see him! [*Exeunt.*

SCENE V. GLOUCESTER'S *castle.*

[*Enter* REGAN *and* OSWALD.]

REG. But are my brother's powers set forth?

OSW. Ay, madam.

REG. Himself in person there?

OSW. Madam, with much ado:
Your sister is the better soldier.

REG. Lord Edmund spake not with your lord at home?

OSW. No, madam. 5

REG. What might import my sister's letter to him?

OSW. I know not, lady.

REG. 'Faith, he is posted hence on serious matter.
It was great ignorance, Gloucester's eyes being out,
To let him live: where he arrives he moves 10
All hearts against us: Edmund, I think, is gone,
In pity of his misery, to dispatch
His nighted life; moreover, to descry
The strength o' the enemy.

OSW. I must needs after him, madam, with my letter. 15

REG. Our troops set forth to-morrow: stay with us;
The ways are dangerous.

OSW. I may not, madam:
My lady charged my duty in this business.

REG. Why should she write to Edmund? Might not you
Transport her purposes by word? Belike, 20
Something—I know not what: I'll love thee much,
Let me unseal the letter.

OSW. Madam, I had rather—

REG. I know your lady does not love her husband;
I am sure of that: and at her late being here
She gave strange œillades and most speaking looks 25
To noble Edmund. I know you are of her bosom.

OSW. I, madam?

REG. I speak in understanding; you are, I know 't:
Therefore I do advise you, take this note:
My lord is dead; Edmund and I have talk'd;
And more convenient is he for my hand 31
Than for your lady's: you may gather more.
If you do find him, pray you, give him this;
And when your mistress hears thus much from you,
I pray, desire her call her wisdom to her. 35
So, fare you well.
If you do chance to hear of that blind traitor,
Preferment falls on him that cuts him off.

OSW. Would I could meet him, madam! I should show
What party I do follow.

REG. Fare thee well. [*Exeunt.* 40

SCENE VI. *Fields near Dover.*

[*Enter* GLOUCESTER, *and* EDGAR *dressed like a peasant.*]

GLOU. When shall we come to the top of that same hill?

14. **simples operative**, effective medicinal herbs. 15. **secrets**, private remedies. 16. **unpublish'd virtues**, secret efficacious medicinal plants. 17. **be . . . remediate**, be helpful and remedial. 19. **rage**, delirium. 20. **the means**, i.e., his reason. 23. **In . . . of**, ready to meet. 26. **important**, importunate. 27. **blown**, swollen. **Scene v**: 2. **with much ado**, as a result of much effort. 6. **import**, mean. 8. **is posted**, has ridden fast; **matter**, business. 9. **ignorance**, stupidity. 20. **Belike**, probably. 25. **œillades**, amorous glances. 26. **of her bosom**, in her confidence. 30. **have talk'd**, have come to an understanding (about marrying). 31. **convenient**, suitable. 32. **gather more**, i.e., make further references. 34. **thus much**, as much as I have told you. 38. **Preferment**, advancement.

EDG. You do climb up it now: look, how we labour.

GLOU. Methinks the ground is even.

EDG. Horrible steep.

Hark, do you hear the sea?

GLOU. No, truly.

EDG. Why, then, your other senses grow imperfect 5

By your eyes' anguish.

GLOU. So may it be, indeed:

Methinks thy voice is alter'd; and thou speak'st

In better phrase and matter than thou didst.

EDG. You're much deceived: in nothing am I changed

But in my garments.

GLOU. Methinks you're better spoken. 10

EDG. Come on, sir; here's the place: stand still. How fearful

And dizzy 'tis, to cast one's eyes so low!

The crows and choughs that wing the mid-way air

Show scarce so gross as beetles: half way down

Hangs one that gathers samphire, dreadful trade! 15

Methinks he seems no bigger than his head:

The fishermen, that walk upon the beach,

Appear like mice; and yond tall anchoring bark,

Diminish'd to her cock; her cock, a buoy

Almost too small for sight: the murmuring surge, 20

That on the unnumber'd idle pebbles chafes,

Cannot be heard so high. I'll look no more;

Lest my brain turn, and the deficient sight

Topple down headlong.

GLOU. Set me where you stand.

EDG. Give me your hand: you are now within a foot 25

Of the extreme verge: for all beneath the moon

Would I not leap upright.

GLOU. Let go my hand.

Here, friend, 's another purse; in it a jewel

Well worth a poor man's taking: fairies and gods

Prosper it with thee! Go thou farther off; 30

Bid me farewell, and let me hear thee going.

EDG. Now fare you well, good sir.

GLOU. With all my heart.

EDG. Why I do trifle thus with his despair

Is done to cure it.

GLOU. [*Kneeling*] O you mighty gods!

This world I do renounce, and in your sights,

Shake patiently my great affliction off: 36

If I could bear it longer, and not fall

To quarrel with your great opposeless wills,

My snuff and loathèd part of nature should

Burn itself out. If Edgar live, O, bless him! 40

Now, fellow, fare thee well. [*He falls forward.*

EDG. Gone, sir: farewell.

And yet I know not how conceit may rob

The treasury of life, when life itself

Yields to the theft: had he been where he thought,

By this, had thought been past. Alive or dead?

Ho, you sir! friend! Hear you, sir! speak! 46

Thus might he pass indeed: yet he revives.

What are you, sir?

GLOU. Away, and let me die.

EDG. Hadst thou been aught but gossamer, feathers, air,

So many fathom down precipitating, 50

Thou 'dst shiver'd like an egg: but thou dost breathe;

Hast heavy substance; bleed'st not; speak'st; art sound.

Ten masts at each make not the altitude

Which thou hast perpendicularly fell:

Thy life's a miracle. Speak yet again. 55

GLOU. But have I fall'n, or no?

EDG. From the dread summit of this chalky bourn.

Look up a-height; the shrill-gorged lark so far

Cannot be seen or heard: do but look up.

GLOU. Alack, I have no eyes. 60

Is wretchedness deprived that benefit,

To end itself by death? 'Twas yet some comfort,

When misery could beguile the tyrant's rage,

And frustrate his proud will.

Scene vi: 10. **you're better spoken**, i.e., you speak with more propriety. 13. **choughs**, crow-like birds, something like grackles. 14. **gross**, large. 15. **samphire**, an aromatic herb, gathered from the face of cliffs by men lowered by a rope. 19. **cock**, cock-boat, tender. 21. **unnumber'd**, innumerable. 21. **idle**, useless, barren. 23. **the . . . sight**, my sight failing. 24. **Topple**, cause me to topple. 27. **upright**, i.e., even straight up. 29. **fairies**, because they were supposed to make it increase miraculously.

38. **quarrel . . . with**, rebel against; **opposeless**, irresistible. 39. **snuff**, burnt and smoking wick. 42. **conceit**, imagination. 43. **treasury of life**, life's treasury. 44. **yields . . . theft**, i.e., death's theft of the treasury of life. 47. **pass**, die. 49. **gossamer**, floating cobweb. 53. **at each**, end to end. 57. **bourn**, boundary. 58. **a-height**, on high; **shrill-gorged**, shrill-throated. 63. **beguile**, cheat.

EDG. Give me your arm:
Up: so. How is 't? Feel you your legs? You stand. 65

GLOU. Too well, too well.

EDG. This is above all strangeness.
Upon the crown o' the cliff, what thing was that
Which parted from you?

GLOU. A poor unfortunate beggar.

EDG. As I stood here below, methought his eyes
Were two full moons; he had a thousand noses, 70
Horns whelk'd and waved like the enridgèd sea:
It was some fiend; therefore, thou happy father,
Think that the clearest gods, who make them honours
Of men's impossibilities, have preserved thee.

GLOU. I do remember now: henceforth I'll bear 75
Affliction till it do cry out itself
"Enough, enough," and die. That thing you speak of,
I took it for a man; often 'twould say
"The fiend, the fiend:" he led me to that place.

EDG. Bear free and patient thoughts. But who comes here? 80

[*Enter* LEAR, *fantastically dressed with wild flowers.*]

The safer sense will ne'er accommodate
His master thus.

LEAR. No, they cannot touch me for coining;
I am the king himself.

EDG. O thou side-piercing sight! 85

LEAR. Nature's above art in that respect. There's your press-money. That fellow handles his bow like a crow-keeper: draw me a clothier's yard. Look, look, a mouse! Peace, peace; this piece of toasted cheese will 90 do 't. There's my gauntlet; I'll prove it on a giant. Bring up the brown bills. O, well flown, bird! i' the clout, i' the clout: hewgh! Give the word.

EDG. Sweet marjoram.

LEAR. Pass.

GLOU. I know that voice. 96

LEAR. Ha! Goneril, with a white beard! They flattered me like a dog; and told me I had white hairs in my beard ere the black ones were there. To say "ay" and "no" 100 to every thing that I said!—"Ay" and "no" too was no good divinity. When the rain came to wet me once, and the wind to make me chatter; when the thunder would not peace at my bidding; there I found 'em, there I smelt 'em out. Go to, they are not men o' their words: they told me I was every thing; 'tis a lie, I am not ague-proof. 107

GLOU. The trick of that voice I do well remember:
Is 't not the king?

LEAR. Ay, every inch a king:
When I do stare, see how the subject quakes.
I pardon that man's life. What was thy cause? 111
Adultery?
Thou shalt not die: die for adultery! No:
The wren goes to 't, and the small gilded fly
Does lecher in my sight. 115
Let copulation thrive; for Gloucester's bastard son
Was kinder to his father than my daughters
Got 'tween the lawful sheets.
To 't, luxury, pell-mell! for I lack soldiers.
Behold yond simpering dame, 120
Whose face between her forks presages snow;
That minces virtue, and does shake the head
To hear of pleasure's name;
The fitchew, nor the soilèd horse, goes to 't
With a more riotous appetite. 125
Down from the waist they are Centaurs,
Though women all above:
But to the girdle do the gods inherit,
Beneath is all the fiends';
There's hell, there's darkness, there's the sulphurous pit, 130
Burning, scalding, stench, consumption; fie, fie, fie! pah, pah! Give me an ounce of civet,

71. **whelk'd**, twisted. 73. **clearest**, most glorious. 74. **men's impossibilities**, things impossible to men. 80. **free**, i.e., from grief. 81. **safer**, saner; **accommodate**, equip. 83. **touch**, arrest; **coining**, making counterfeit money. 87. **press-money**, money to a recruit pressed into military service. 88. **crow-keeper**, a boy stationed to scare away crows. 89. **clothier's yard**, arrow a cloth-yard in length. 91. **prove**, defend it by combat. 92. **brown bills**, halberds, painted brown to prevent rust. 93. **bird**, i.e., arrow; **clout**, bulls-eye; **hewgh**, imitation of the whizzing of the arrow. 94. **word**, password. 104. **peace**, hold its peace. 108. **trick**, peculiarity. 119. **luxury**, lust. 121. **snow**, i.e., chastity. 122. **minces virtue**, makes a show of virtue by her mincing (affected) bearing. 124. **fitchew**, skunk, a supposedly oversexed animal; **soiled**, fed full with spring grass. 126. **Centaurs**, lustful fabulous monsters, half man, half horse. 128. **But**, only; **inherit**, rule. 132. **civet**, perfume.

good apothecary, to sweeten my imagination: there's money for thee.

GLOU. O, let me kiss that hand! 135

LEAR. Let me wipe it first; it smells of mortality.

GLOU. O ruin'd piece of nature! This great world
Shall so wear out to nought. Dost thou know me?

LEAR. I remember thine eyes well enough. Dost thou squiny at me? No, do thy worst, blind Cupid; I'll not love. Read thou this challenge; mark but the penning of it. 142

GLOU. Were all the letters suns, I could not see one.

EDG. I would not take this from report; it is,
And my heart breaks at it. 145

LEAR. Read.

GLOU. What, with the case of eyes?

LEAR. O, ho, are you there with me? No eyes in your head, nor no money in your purse? Your eyes are in a heavy case, your purse in a light: yet you see how this world goes.

GLOU. I see it feelingly. 152

LEAR. What, art mad? A man may see how this world goes with no eyes. Look with thine ears: see how yond justice rails upon yond simple thief. Hark, in thine ear: change places; and, handy-dandy, which is the justice, which is the thief? Thou hast seen a farmer's dog bark at a beggar?

GLOU. Ay, sir. 160

LEAR. And the creature run from the cur?
There thou mightst behold the great image of authority: a dog's obeyed in office.
Thou rascal beadle, hold thy bloody hand!
Why dost thou lash that whore? Strip thine own back; 165
Thou hotly lust'st to use her in that kind
For which thou whipp'st her. The usurer hangs the cozener.
Through tatter'd clothes small vices do appear;
Robes and furr'd gowns hide all. Plate sin with gold,
And the strong lance of justice hurtless breaks; 170
Arm it in rags, a pigmy's straw does pierce it.
None does offend, none I say, none; I'll able 'em:
Take that of me, my friend, who have the power
To seal the accuser's lips. Get thee glass eyes;
And, like a scurvy politician, seem 175
To see the things thou dost not. Now, now, now, now:
Pull off my boots: harder, harder: so.

EDG. O, matter and impertinency mix'd!
Reason in madness!

LEAR. If thou wilt weep my fortunes, take my eyes. 180
I know thee well enough; thy name is Gloucester:
Thou must be patient; we came crying hither:
Thou know'st, the first time that we smell the air,
We wawl and cry. I will preach to thee: mark.

GLOU. Alack, alack the day! 185

LEAR. When we are born, we cry that we are come
To this great stage of fools: this's a good block;
It were a delicate stratagem, to shoe
A troop of horse with felt: I'll put 't in proof;
And when I have stol'n upon these sons-in-law, 190
Then, kill, kill, kill, kill, kill, kill!

[*Enter a* GENTLEMAN, *with* ATTENDANTS.]

GENT. O, here he is: lay hand upon him. Sir,
Your most dear daughter—

LEAR. No rescue? What, a prisoner? I am even
The natural fool of fortune. Use me well; 195
You shall have ransom. Let me have surgeons;
I am cut to the brains.

GENT. You shall have any thing.

LEAR. No seconds? all myself?
Why, this would make a man a man of salt,

137. piece, masterpiece. 138. Shall . . . nought, shall likewise come to nothing. 140. squiny, squint. 141. blind Cupid, the sign usually hung over a brothel. 144. take, accept, believe. 147. case, sockets. 148. are . . . me? i.e., Is that what you are telling me? 150. heavy case, bad condition, with a pun on case-socket. 156. simple, mere. 157. handy-dandy, "Which hand will you have?" (a formula in a well-known child's game). 162. image, figure. 166. kind, way. 167. cozener, cheater, sharper. 169. Plate . . . with gold, clothe sin in golden armor-plates. 172. able, authorize. 173. that, i.e., an imaginary pardon. 174. glass eyes, spectacles. 175. scurvy politician, vile trickster. 178. matter and impertinency, sense and incoherence. 187. block, hat. 189. put 't in proof, make a trial of it. 195. The . . . fortune, man reduced by fortune to the con dition of a fool. 199. of salt, of salt tears.

To use his eyes for garden water-pots, 200
Ay, and laying autumn's dust.

GENT. Good sir,—

LEAR. I will die bravely, like a bridegroom. What!
I will be jovial: come, come; I am a king,
My masters, know you that.

GENT. You are a royal one, and we obey you. 205

LEAR. Then there's life in 't. Nay, if you get it, you shall get it with running. Sa, sa, sa, sa. [*Exit running;* ATTENDANTS *follow.*

GENT. A sight most pitiful in the meanest wretch,
Past speaking of in a king! Thou hast one daughter,
Who redeems nature from the general curse
Which twain have brought her to. 211

EDG. Hail, gentle sir.

GENT. Sir, speed you: what's your will?

EDG. Do you hear aught, sir, of a battle toward?

GENT. Most sure and vulgar: every one hears that,
Which can distinguish sound.

EDG. But, by your favour, 215
How near's the other army?

GENT. Near and on speedy foot; the main descry
Stands on the hourly thought.

EDG. I thank you, sir: that's all.

GENT. Though that the queen on special cause is here,
Her army is moved on.

EDG. I thank you, sir. 220
[*Exit* GENT.

GLOU. You ever- gentle gods, take my breath from me;
Let not my worser spirit tempt me again
To die before you please!

EDG. Well pray you, father.

GLOU. Now, good sir, what are you?

EDG. A most poor man, made tame to fortune's blows; 225
Who, by the art of known and feeling sorrows,
Am pregnant to good pity. Give me your hand,
I'll lead you to some biding.

GLOU. Hearty thanks:
The bounty and the benison of heaven
To boot, and boot!

[*Enter* OSWALD.]

OSW. A proclaim'd prize! Most happy! 230
That eyeless head of thine was first framed flesh
To raise my fortunes. Thou old unhappy traitor,
Briefly thyself remember: the sword is out
That must destroy thee.

GLOU. Now let thy friendly hand
Put strength enough to 't.
[EDGAR *interposes.*

OSW. Wherefore, bold peasant, 235
Darest thou support a publish'd traitor? Hence;
Lest that the infection of his fortune take
Like hold on thee. Let go his arm.

EDG. Chill not let go, zir, without vurther 'casion. 240

OSW. Let go, slave, or thou diest!

EDG. Good gentleman, go your gait, and let poor volk pass. An chud ha' bin zwaggered out of my life, 'twould not ha' bin zo long as 'tis by a vortnight. Nay, come not near th' old man; keep out, che vor ye, or ise try whether your costard or my ballow be the harder: chill be plain with you. 248

OSW. Out, dunghill!

EDG. Chill pick your teeth, zir: come; no matter vor your foins.
[*They fight, and* EDGAR *knocks him down.*

OSW. Slave, thou hast slain me: villain, take my purse:
If ever thou wilt thrive, bury my body;
And give the letters which thou find'st about me 254
To Edmund earl of Gloucester; seek him out
Upon the British party: O, untimely death!
[*Dies.*

EDG. I know thee well: a serviceable villain;

202. bravely, in fine clothes. **207. Sa . . . sa,** a hunter's cry to urge on the dogs. **210. general,** universal. **211. gentle,** noble. **213. toward,** at hand. **214. vulgar,** i.e., known to everyone. **215. which,** who. **217. the main descry,** the view of the main body of troops. **218. Stands . . . thought,** is expected any time. **222. worser spirit,** worse side of my nature. **226. feeling,** heartfelt. **227. pregnant to,** able to conceive. **228. biding,** abiding place. **229. bounty,** favor; **benison,** blessing. **230. To boot,** besides; **and boot,** and may it be your reward. **233. thyself remember,** repent your past sins. **236. published,** publicly proclaimed. **240. Chill,** I will. The following passage is in stage rustic dialect. **243. an chud,** if I could. **246. che vor ye,** I warn you. **247. ise,** I will; **costard,** apple, slang for head; **ballow,** cudgel. **251. foins,** sword thrusts. **256. British party,** side of the British.

As duteous to the vices of thy mistress
As badness would desire.

GLOU. What, is he dead?

EDG. Sit you down, father; rest you. 260
Let's see these pockets: the letters that he speaks of
May be my friends. He's dead; I am only sorry
He had no other death's-man. Let us see:
Leave, gentle wax; and, manners, blame us not:
To know our enemies' minds, we'ld rip their hearts; 265
Their papers, is more lawful.

[*Reads*] "Let our reciprocal vows be remembered. You have many opportunities to cut him off: if your will want not, time and place will be fruitfully offered. There is nothing done, if he return the conqueror: then am I the prisoner, and his bed my gaol; from the loathed warmth whereof deliver me, and supply the place for your labour.

"Your—wife, so I would say— 275
"Affectionate servant,
"GONERIL."

O undistinguish'd space of woman's will!
A plot upon her virtuous husband's life;
And the exchange my brother! Here, in the sands, 280
Thee I'll rake up, the post unsanctified
Of murderous lechers: and in the mature time
With this ungracious paper strike the sight
Of the death-practised duke: for him 'tis well
That of thy death and business I can tell.

GLOU. The king is mad: how stiff is my vile sense, 286
That I stand up, and have ingenious feeling
Of my huge sorrows! Better I were distract:
So should my thoughts be sever'd from my griefs,
And woes by wrong imaginations lose 290
The knowledge of themselves.

EDG. Give me your hand: [*Drum afar off.*]
Far off, methinks, I hear the beaten drum:
Come, father, I'll bestow you with a friend. [*Exeunt.*

SCENE VII. *A tent in the French camp.* LEAR *on a bed asleep, soft music playing;* GENTLEMAN, *and others attending.*

[*Enter* CORDELIA, KENT, *and* DOCTOR.]

COR. O thou good Kent, how shall I live and work,
To match thy goodness? My life will be too short,
And every measure fail me.

KENT. To be acknowledged, madam, is o'erpaid.
All my reports go with the modest truth; 5
Nor more nor clipp'd, but so.

COR. Be better suited:
These weeds are memories of those worser hours:
I prithee, put them off.

KENT. Pardon me, dear madam;
Yet to be known shortens my made intent: 9
My boon I make it, that you know me not
Till time and I think meet.

COR. Then be 't so, my good lord. [*To the* DOCTOR] How does the king?

DOCT. Madam, sleeps still.

COR. O you kind gods, 14
Cure this great breach in his abusèd nature!
The untuned and jarring senses, O, wind up
Of this child-changèd father!

DOCT. So please your Majesty
That we may wake the king: he hath slept long.

COR. Be govern'd by your knowledge, and proceed
I' the sway of your own will. Is he array'd? 20

GENT. Ay, madam; in the heaviness of his sleep
We put fresh garments on him.

DOCT. Be by, good madam, when we do awake him;
I doubt not of his temperance.

COR. Very well.

258. **duteous**, compliant. 263. **death's-man**, executioner. 264. **Leave**, allow me. 270. **fruitfully**, amply. 276. **servant**, lover. 278. **undistinguish'd space**, limitless range; **will**, lust. 281. **rake up**, bury hastily; **post**, messenger. 282. **in . . . time**, when the time is ripe. 283. **ungracious**, wicked. 284. **death . . . duke**, duke whose death is plotted. 286. **stiff . . . sense**, strong is my sanity. 287. **ingenious feeling**, keen consciousness. 288. **distract**, insane. Scene vii: 3. **measure**, i.e., measuring out (of benefits). 5. **modest truth**, moderate statement of the facts.

6. **clipp'd**, abridged; **suited**, clothed. 7. **weeds**, garments; **memories**, reminders. 9. **shortens . . . intent**, makes me fall short of my prearranged plan. 10. **my . . . it**, I ask it as a favor to me. 16. **wind up**, i.e., tighten the strings (as of a musical instrument) of his untuned senses. 17. **child-changed**, whose nature has become childish. 24. **temperance**, self-control, i.e., sanity.

DOCT. Please you, draw near. Louder the music there! 25

COR. O my dear father! Restoration hang
Thy medicine on my lips; and let this kiss
Repair those violent harms that my two sisters
Have in thy reverence made!

KENT. Kind and dear princess!

COR. Had you not been their father, these white flakes 30
Had challenged pity of them. Was this a face
To be opposed against the warring winds?
To stand against the deep dread-bolted thunder?
In the most terrible and nimble stroke
Of quick, cross lightning? to watch—poor perdu!— 35
With this thin helm? Mine enemy's dog,
Though he had bit me, should have stood that night
Against my fire; and wast thou fain, poor father,
To hovel thee with swine, and rogues forlorn,
In short and musty straw? Alack, alack! 40
'Tis wonder that thy life and wits at once
Had not concluded all. He wakes; speak to him.

DOCT. Madam, do you; 'tis fittest.

COR. How does my royal lord? How fares your majesty?

LEAR. You do me wrong to take me out o' the grave: 45
Thou art a soul in bliss; but I am bound
Upon a wheel of fire, that mine own tears
Do scald like molten lead.

COR. Sir, do you know me?

LEAR. You are a spirit, I know: when did you die?

COR. Still, still, far wide! 50

DOCT. He's scarce awake: let him alone awhile.

LEAR. Where have I been? Where am I? Fair daylight?
I am mightily abused. I should e'en die with pity,
To see another thus. I know not what to say.
I will not swear these are my hands: let's see; 55
I feel this pin prick. Would I were assured
Of my condition!

COR. O, look upon me, sir,
And hold your hands in benediction o'er me:
No, sir, you must not kneel.

LEAR. Pray, do not mock me:
I am a very foolish fond old man, 60
Fourscore and upward, not an hour more nor less;
And, to deal plainly,
I fear I am not in my perfect mind.
Methinks I should know you, and know this man; 64
Yet I am doubtful: for I am mainly ignorant
What place this is; and all the skill I have
Remembers not these garments; nor I know not
Where I did lodge last night. Do not laugh at me;
For, as I am a man, I think this lady
To be my child Cordelia.

COR. And so I am, I am. 70

LEAR. Be your tears wet? yes, 'faith. I pray, weep not:
If you have poison for me, I will drink it.
I know you do not love me; for your sisters
Have, as I do remember, done me wrong: 74
You have some cause, they have not.

COR. No cause, no cause.

LEAR. Am I in France?

KENT. In your own kingdom, sir.

LEAR. Do not abuse me.

DOCT. Be comforted, good madam: the great rage,
You see, is kill'd in him: and yet it is danger
To make him even o'er the time he has lost. 80
Desire him to go in; trouble him no more
Till further settling.

COR. Will 't please your highness walk?

LEAR. You must bear with me:
Pray you now, forget and forgive: I am old and foolish.

[*Exeunt all but* KENT *and* GENTLEMAN.

GENT. Holds it true, sir, that the Duke of
Cornwall was so slain? 86

KENT. Most certain, sir.

GENT. Who is conductor of his people?

29. **in thy reverence made**, done to you to whom they owe reverence. 33. **dread-bolted**, with its dreadful bolts. 35. **cross**, zigzag; **perdu**, a soldier on an isolated post of great danger. 36. **helm**, i.e., hair. 38. **fain**, glad. 39. **rogues**, tramps. 42. **concluded all**, altogether come to an end. 47. **that**, so that. 50. **wide**, i.e., of the mark. 53. **abused**, deluded. 57. **condition**, situation. 60. **fond**, doting. 65. **mainly**, completely. 66. **skill**, intelligence. 77. **abuse**, deceive. 78. **rage**, delirium. 80. **even o'er the time**, fill the interval by recalling what happened. 82. **Till . . . settling**, until he becomes calmer. 83. **walk**, i.e., come with me.

KENT. As 'tis said, the bastard son of Gloucester. 90

GENT. They say Edgar, his banished son, is with the Earl of Kent in Germany.

KENT. Report is changeable. 'Tis time to look about; the powers of the kingdom approach apace. 95

GENT. The arbitrement is like to be bloody. Fare you well, sir. [*Exit.*

KENT. My point and period will be throughly wrought,
Or well or ill, as this day's battle's fought. 99
[*Exit.*

ACT V

SCENE I. *The British camp, near Dover.*

[*Enter, with drum and colours,* EDMUND, REGAN, GENTLEMEN, *and* SOLDIERS.]

EDM. Know of the duke if his last purpose hold,
Or whether since he is advised by aught
To change the course: he's full of alteration
And self-reproving: bring his constant pleasure. [*To a* GENTLEMAN, *who goes out.*

REG. Our sister's man is certainly miscarried. 5

EDM. 'Tis to be doubted, madam.

REG. Now, sweet lord,
You know the goodness I intend upon you:
Tell me—but truly—but then speak the truth,
Do you not love my sister?

EDM. In honour'd love.

REG. But have you never found my brother's way 10
To the forfended place?

EDM. That thought abuses you.

REG. I am doubtful that you have been conjunct
And bosom'd with her, as far as we call hers.

EDM. No, by mine honour, madam.

REG. I never shall endure her: dear my lord, 15
Be not familiar with her.

EDM. Fear me not:
She and the duke her husband!

[*Enter, with drum and colours,* ALBANY, GONERIL, *and* SOLDIERS.]

GON. [*Aside*] I had rather lose the battle than that sister
Should loosen him and me.

ALB. Our very loving sister, well be-met. 20
Sir, this I hear; the king is come to his daughter,
With others whom the rigour of our state
Forced to cry out. Where I could not be honest,
I never yet was valiant: for this business,
It toucheth us, as France invades our land, 25
Not bolds the king, with others, whom, I fear,
Most just and heavy causes make oppose.

EDM. Sir, you speak nobly.

REG. Why is this reason'd?

GON. Combine together 'gainst the enemy;
For these domestic and particular broils 30
Are not the question here.

ALB. Let's then determine
With the ancient of war on our proceedings.

EDM. I shall attend you presently at your tent.

REG. Sister, you'll go with us?

GON. No. 35

REG. 'Tis most convenient; pray you, go with us.

GON. [*Aside*] O, ho, I know the riddle.—I will go.

[*As they are going out, enter* EDGAR *disguised.*]

94. **powers**, armed forces. 96. **arbitrement**, forcing of the decision. 98. **My point and period**, the final attainment of my ends; **wrought**, worked out. **Act V, Scene i**: 2. **advised**, induced. 4. **constant pleasure**, settled decision. 5. **miscarried**, come to grief. 11. **forfended**, forbidden; **abuses**, dishonors. 12. **am doubtful**, suspect; **conjunct**, joined. 13. **bosom'd**, intimate; **as . . . hers**, i.e., in all that she has. 16. **Fear me not**, don't worry about me. 20. **be-met**, met. 22. **state**, administration. 23. **cry out**, protest; **honest**, honorable. 24. **for**, as for. 25. **France**, the King of France. 26. **bolds**, emboldens. 27. **heavy causes**, weighty reasons; **make oppose**, force to oppose us. 28. **Why . . . reason'd**, Why do you search for reasons [for an action]? 30. **domestic and particular**, family and personal. 32. **ancient of war**, veteran soldiers. 36. **convenient**, fitting. 37. **riddle**, hidden reason (i.e., you want to be alone with Edmund).

EDG. If e'er your grace had speech with man so poor,
Hear me one word.

ALB. I'll overtake you. Speak.

[*Exeunt all but* ALBANY *and* EDGAR.

EDG. Before you fight the battle, ope this letter. 40
If you have victory, let the trumpet sound
For him that brought it: wretched though I seem,
I can produce a champion that will prove
What is avouchèd there. If you miscarry,
Your business of the world hath so an end, 45
And machination ceases. Fortune love you!

ALB. Stay till I have read the letter.

EDG. I was forbid it.
When time shall serve, let but the herald cry,
And I'll appear again.

ALB. Why, fare thee well: I will o'erlook thy paper. [*Exit* EDGAR. 50

[*Re-enter* EDMUND.]

EDM. The enemy's in view; draw up your powers.
Here is the guess of their true strength and forces
By diligent discovery; but your haste
Is now urged on you.

ALB. We will greet the time. [*Exit.*

EDM. To both these sisters have I sworn my love; 55
Each jealous of the other, as the stung
Are of the adder. Which of them shall I take?
Both? one? or neither? Neither can be enjoy'd,
If both remain alive: to take the widow
Exasperates, makes mad her sister Goneril; 60
And hardly shall I carry out my side,
Her husband being alive. Now then we'll use
His countenance for the battle; which being done,
Let her who would be rid of him devise
His speedy taking off. As for the mercy 65
Which he intends to Lear and to Cordelia,
The battle done, and they within our power,
Shall never see his pardon; for my state
Stands on me to defend, not to debate. 69
[*Exit.*

44. miscarry, i.e., are killed. 46. machination, intrigue (against you). 50. o'erlook, glance at. 53. discovery, scouting; your haste, prompt action on your part. 54. greet the time, meet the situation. 56. jealous, suspiciously afraid. 61. side, plans. 63. countenance, authority. 68-9. my state . . . debate, my situation requires defense by arms, not debate (as to the justification of my actions). Scene ii: s.d. Alarum, a call to arms. 4. Grace, the protection of the gods. 11. Ripeness, readiness (for death). Scene iii: 2. their greater pleasures, the wishes of those of higher rank. 3. censure, pass judgment upon.

SCENE II. *A field between the two camps.*

[*Alarum within. Enter, with drum and colours,* LEAR, CORDELIA, *and* SOLDIERS, *over the stage; and exeunt.*]

[*Enter* EDGAR *and* GLOUCESTER.]

EDG. Here, father, take the shadow of this tree
For your good host; pray that the right may thrive:
If ever I return to you again,
I'll bring you comfort.

GLOU. Grace go with you, sir!
[*Exit* EDGAR.

[*Alarum and retreat within. Re-enter* EDGAR.]

EDG. Away, old man; give me thy hand; away! 5
King Lear hath lost, he and his daughter ta'en:
Give me thy hand; come on.

GLOU. No farther, sir; a man may rot even here.

EDG. What, in ill thoughts again? Men must endure
Their going hence, even as their coming hither: 10
Ripeness is all: come on.

GLOU. And that's true too. [*Exeunt.*

SCENE III. *The British camp near Dover.*

[*Enter, in conquest, with drum and colours,* EDMUND; LEAR *and* CORDELIA, *prisoners;* CAPTAIN, SOLDIERS, &c.]

EDM. Some officers take them away: good guard,
Until their greater pleasures first be known
That are to censure them.

COR. We are not the first

Who, with best meaning, have incurr'd the worst.
For thee, oppressèd king, am I cast down; 5
Myself could else out-frown false fortune's frown.
Shall we not see these daughters and these sisters?

LEAR. No, no, no, no! Come, let's away to prison:
We two alone will sing like birds i' the cage:
When thou dost ask me blessing, I'll kneel down, 10
And ask of thee forgiveness: so we'll live,
And pray, and sing, and tell old tales, and laugh
At gilded butterflies, and hear poor rogues
Talk of court news; and we'll talk with them too,
Who loses and who wins; who's in, who's out; 15
And take upon 's the mystery of things,
As if we were God's spies: and we'll wear out,
In a wall'd prison, packs and sects of great ones,
That ebb and flow by the moon.

EDM. Take them away.

LEAR. Upon such sacrifices, my Cordelia, 20
The gods themselves throw incense. Have I caught thee?
He that parts us shall bring a brand from heaven,
And fire us hence like foxes. Wipe thine eyes;
The good-years shall devour them, flesh and fell,
Ere they shall make us weep: we'll see 'em starve first. 25
Come. [*Exeunt* LEAR *and* CORDELIA, *guarded.*

EDM. Come hither, captain; hark.
Take thou this note [*giving a paper*]; go follow them to prison:
One step I have advanced thee; if thou dost
As this instructs thee, thou dost make thy way
To noble fortunes: know thou this, that men
Are as the time is: to be tender-minded 31
Does not become a sword: thy great employment
Will not bear question; either say thou'lt do 't,
Or thrive by other means.

CAPT. I'll do 't, my lord.

EDM. About it; and write happy when thou hast done. 35
Mark, I say, instantly; and carry it so
As I have set it down.

CAPT. I cannot draw a cart, nor eat dried oats;
If it be man's work, I'll do it. [*Exit.*

[*Flourish. Enter* ALBANY, GONERIL, REGAN, *another* CAPTAIN, *and* SOLDIERS.]

ALB. Sir, you have shown to-day your valiant strain, 40
And fortune led you well: you have the captives
That were the opposites of this day's strife:
We do require them of you, so to use them
As we shall find their merits and our safety
May equally determine.

EDM. Sir, I thought it fit 45
To send the old and miserable king
To some retention and appointed guard;
Whose age has charms in it, whose title more,
To pluck the common bosom on his side,
And turn our impress'd lances in our eyes 50
Which do command them. With him I sent the queen;
My reason all the same; and they are ready
To-morrow, or at further space, to appear
Where you shall hold your session. At this time
We sweat and bleed: the friend hath lost his friend; 55
And the best quarrels, in the heat, are cursed
By those that feel their sharpness:
The question of Cordelia and her father
Requires a fitter place.

ALB. Sir, by your patience,

13. **gilded butterflies**, i.e., dandified courtiers; **rogues**, wretches. 16. **take . . . things**, assume that we can explain the mysteries of human life. 17. **wear out**, i.e., forget. 18. **packs**, parties. 23. **fire . . . foxes**, foxes can be driven from their holes by smoke and fire. 24. **good-years**, evils, perhaps "pestilence"; **fell**, skin. 27. **note**, i.e., an order for the execution of Lear and Cordelia. 31. **As . . . is**, as the situation demands. 33. **bear question**, permit discussion.

34. **other means**, i.e., than my favor. 35. **write happy**, write yourself down as fortunate. 36. **carry it**, carry it out. 40. **strain**, stock. 42. **the opposites of**, our opponents in. 47. **some retention . . . guard**, to the custody of some guards appointed for the purpose. 49. **pluck . . . bosom**, enlist the sympathies of the common soldiers. 50. **impress'd lances**, drafted troops. 51. **which**, who. 56. **quarrels**, causes. 59. **a fitter place**, i.e., than the battlefield; **by your patience**, i.e., if you will pardon my plain talk.

I hold you but a subject of this war, 60
Not as a brother.

REG. That's as we list to grace him.
Methinks our pleasure might have been demanded,
Ere you had spoke so far. He led our powers;
Bore the commission of my place and person;
The which immediacy may well stand up, 65
And call itself your brother.

GON. Not so hot:
In his own grace he doth exalt himself,
More than in your addition.

REG. In my rights,
By me invested, he compeers the best.

GON. That were the most, if he should husband you. 70

REG. Jesters do oft prove prophets.

GON. Holla, holla!
That eye that told you so look'd but a-squint.

REG. Lady, I am not well; else I should answer
From a full-flowing stomach. General,
Take thou my soldiers, prisoners, patrimony; 75
Dispose of them, of me; the walls are thine:
Witness the world, that I create thee here
My lord and master.

GON. Mean you to enjoy him?

ALB. The let-alone lies not in your good will.

EDM. Nor in thine, lord.

ALB. Half-blooded fellow, yes. 80

REG. [*To* EDMUND] Let the drum strike, and prove my title thine.

ALB. Stay yet; hear reason. Edmund, I arrest thee
On capital treason; and, in thine attaint,
This gilded serpent [*pointing to* GON.]. For your claim, fair sister,
I bar it in the interest of my wife; 85
'Tis she is sub-contracted to this lord,
And I, her husband, contradict your bans.
If you will marry, make your loves to me,
My lady is bespoke.

GON. An interlude!

ALB. Thou art arm'd, Gloucester: let the trumpet sound: 90
If none appear to prove upon thy head
Thy heinous, manifest, and many treasons,
There is my pledge [*throwing down a glove*]; I'll prove it on thy heart,
Ere I taste bread, thou art in nothing less
Than I have here proclaim'd thee.

REG. Sick, O, sick!

GON. [*Aside*] If not, I'll ne'er trust medicine. 96

EDM. There's my exchange [*throwing down a glove*]: what in the world he is
That names me traitor, villain-like he lies:
Call by thy trumpet: he that dares approach,
On him, on you, who not? I will maintain 100
My truth and honour firmly.

ALB. A herald, ho!

EDM. A herald, ho, a herald!

ALB. Trust to thy single virtue; for thy soldiers,
All levied in my name, have in my name 104
Took their discharge.

REG. My sickness grows upon me.

ALB. She is not well; convey her to my tent. [*Exit* REGAN, *led.*]

[*Enter a* HERALD.]

Come hither, herald,—Let the trumpet sound,—
And read out this. 108

CAPT. Sound, trumpet! [*A trumpet sounds.*

HER. [*Reads*] "If any man of quality or degree within the lists of the army will maintain upon Edmund, supposed Earl of Gloucester, that he is a manifold traitor, let him appear by the third sound of the trumpet: he is bold in his defence."

EDM. Sound! [*First trumpet.*

HER. Again! [*Second trumpet.*

HER. Again! [*Third trumpet.*

[*Trumpet answers within.*

[*Enter* EDGAR, *at the third sound, armed, with a trumpet before him.*]

61. **That's . . . him,** that depends on how far I wish to honor him. 62. **pleasure,** wishes in the matter. 64. **Bore . . . person,** exercised the authority of my rank and person. 65. **The which immediacy,** and this fact of immediate representation [of me]. 67. **own grace,** his personal deserts. 68. **your addition,** the title you gave him. 69. **compeers,** equals. 70. **the most,** most fully realized. 72. **that eye . . . asquint,** a reference to the proverb, "Love being jealous, makes a good eye look asquint." 74. **stomach,** anger. 76. **the walls are thine,** i.e., you have taken my outer defences by storm. 79. **let-alone . . . will,** the prohibition does not depend on what you wish. 80. **half-blooded,** bastard. 81. **prove,** i.e., by combat. 83. **in . . . attaint,** i.e., as a sharer in your corruption. 84. **claim,** i.e., to Edmund. 86. **is sub-contracted,** i.e., has made a contract depending on the abrogation of a previous one. 89. **interlude,** comedy (a reference to Albany's elaborate irony). 94. **nothing,** no respect. 97. **what,** whoever and whatever. 103. **virtue,** valor. 109. **trumpet,** trumpeter. 109-10. **quality or degree,** rank or high social position.

ALB. Ask him his purposes, why he appears
Upon this call o' the trumpet.
HER. What are you?
Your name, your quality? and why you answer 120
This present summons?
EDG. Know, my name is lost;
By treason's tooth bare-gnawn and canker-bit:
Yet am I noble as the adversary
I come to cope.
ALB. Which is that adversary?
EDG. What's he that speaks for Edmund Earl of Gloucester? 125
EDM. Himself: what say'st thou to him?
EDG. Draw thy sword,
That, if my speech offend a noble heart,
Thy arm may do thee justice: here is mine.
Behold, it is the privilege of mine honours,
My oath, and my profession: I protest, 130
Maugre thy strength, youth, place, and eminence,
Despite thy victor sword and fire-new fortune,
Thy valour and thy heart, thou art a traitor;
False to thy gods, thy brother, and thy father;
Conspirant 'gainst this high-illustrious prince; 135
And, from the extremest upward of thy head
To the descent and dust below thy foot,
A most toad-spotted traitor. Say thou "No,"
This sword, this arm, and my best spirits, are bent
To prove upon thy heart, whereto I speak, 140
Thou liest.
EDM. In wisdom I should ask thy name;
But, since thy outside looks so fair and warlike,
And that thy tongue some say of breeding breathes,
What safe and nicely I might well delay 144
By rule of knighthood, I disdain and spurn:
Back do I toss these treasons to thy head;
With the hell-hated lie o'erwhelm thy heart;
Which, for they yet glance by and scarcely bruise,
This sword of mine shall give them instant way,
Where they shall rest for ever. Trumpets, speak! 150
[*Alarums. They fight.* EDMUND *falls.*
ALB. Save him, save him!
GON. This is mere practice, Gloucester:
By the law of arms thou wast not bound to answer
An unknown opposite; thou art not vanquish'd,
But cozen'd and beguiled.
ALB. Shut your mouth, dame,
Or with this paper shall I stop it. Hold, sir;
Thou worse than any name, read thine own evil: 156
No tearing, lady; I perceive you know it.
[*Gives the letter to* EDMUND.
GON. Say, if I do, the laws are mine, not thine:
Who can arraign me for 't?
ALB. Most monstrous! oh!
Know'st thou this paper?
GON. Ask me not what I know. [*Exit.*
ALB. Go after her: she's desperate; govern her. 161
EDM. What you have charged me with, that have I done;
And more, much more; the time will bring it out:
'Tis past, and so am I. But what art thou
That hast this fortune on me? If thou'rt noble, 165
I do forgive thee.
EDG. Let's exchange charity.
I am no less in blood than thou art, Edmund;
If more, the more thou hast wrong'd me.
My name is Edgar, and thy father's son.
The gods are just, and of our pleasant vices
Make instruments to plague us: 171
The dark and vicious place where thee he got
Cost him his eyes.

122. **canker-bit**, eaten away by a canker-worm. 124. **cope**, cope with. 128. **arm**, weapon. 129. **mine honours**, my rank, i.e., as knight. 130. **oath**, i.e., which I swore when dubbed knight, i.e., to protect the honor of knighthood from such evils as treason. 131. **Maugre**, in spite of. 132. **fire-new**, brand-new. 133. **heart**, courage. 135. **Conspirant**, conspirator. 136. **upward**, top. 137. **descent**, lowest part [of you]. 138. **toad-spotted**, marked with poisonous spots. 141. **In wisdom**, i.e., a knight was not obliged to accept the challenge of an unknown opponent. 143. **say of breeding**, accent of a gentleman. 144. **safe and nicely**, safely and punctiliously. 146. **treasons**, accusations of treason. 147. **hell-hated**, hateful as hell. 148. **for**, because. 151. **mere practice**, out-and-out foul play. 152. **answer**, accept the challenge of. 153. **opposite**, opponent. 154. **cozen'd**, cheated. 155. **this paper**, i.e., her love letter which Edgar has found on Oswald's body. 158. **the laws . . . thine**, I, as ruler, make the laws, not you. 161. **govern**, restrain. 165. **fortune**, success. 172. **got**, begot.

EDM. Thou hast spoken right, 'tis true;
The wheel is come full circle; I am here.
ALB. Methought thy very gait did prophesy 175
A royal nobleness: I must embrace thee:
Let sorrow split my heart, if ever I
Did hate thee or thy father!
EDG. Worthy prince, I know't.
ALB. Where have you hid yourself?
How have you known the miseries of your father? 180
EDG. By nursing them, my lord. List a brief tale;
And when 'tis told, O, that my heart would burst!
The bloody proclamation to escape,
That follow'd me so near,—O, our lives' sweetness!
That we the pain of death would hourly die 185
Rather than die at once!—taught me to shift
Into a madman's rags; to assume a semblance
That very dogs disdain'd: and in this habit
Met I my father with his bleeding rings,
Their precious stones new lost; became his guide, 190
Led him, begg'd for him, saved him from despair;
Never,—O fault!—reveal'd myself unto him,
Until some half-hour past, when I was arm'd:
Not sure, though hoping, of this good success,
I ask'd his blessing, and from first to last 195
Told him my pilgrimage: but his flaw'd heart,
Alack, too weak the conflict to support!
'Twixt two extremes of passion, joy and grief,
Burst smilingly.
EDM. This speech of yours hath moved me,
And shall perchance do good: but speak you on; 200
You look as you had something more to say.
ALB. If there be more, more woeful, hold it in;
For I am almost ready to dissolve,
Hearing of this.
EDG. This would have seem'd a period
To such as love not sorrow; but another, 205
To amplify too much, would make much more,
And top extremity.
Whilst I was big in clamour came there in a man,
Who, having seen me in my worst estate,
Shunn'd my abhorr'd society; but then, finding 210
Who 'twas that so endured, with his strong arms
He fasten'd on my neck, and bellow'd out
As he'ld burst heaven; threw him on my father;
Told the most piteous tale of Lear and him
That ever ear received: which in recounting 215
His grief grew puissant, and the strings of life
Began to crack: twice then the trumpets sounded,
And there I left him tranced.
ALB. But who was this?
EDG. Kent, sir, the banish'd Kent; who in disguise
Follow'd his enemy king, and did him service 220
Improper for a slave.

[*Enter a* GENTLEMAN, *with a bloody knife.*]

GENT. Help, help, O, help!
EDG. What kind of help?
ALB. Speak, man.
EDG. What means that bloody knife?
GENT. 'Tis hot, it smokes;
It came even from the heart of—O, she's dead!
ALB. Who dead? speak, man. 225
GENT. Your lady, sir, your lady: and her sister
By her is poisoned; she hath confess'd it.
EDM. I was contracted to them both: all three
Now marry in an instant.
EDG. Here comes Kent.
ALB. Produce their bodies, be they alive or dead: 230
This judgement of the heavens, that makes us tremble,
Touches us not with pity. [*Exit* GENTLEMAN.]

174. **wheel**, i.e., of Fortune. 175. **gait**, bearing. 178. **Worthy**, honorable. 183. **The . . . escape**, in order to escape from the proclamation for my arrest. 185-6. **That . . . once**, that we prefer to suffer the pain of death hour by hour than to die at once. 192. **fault**, mistake.

196. **flaw'd**, cracked. 203. **dissolve**, i.e., in tears. 204. **period**, end (of sorrow). 207. **top extremity**, exceed the extreme limit. 208. **big in clamour**, loud in lament. 209. **estate**, condition. 216. **puissant**, overpowering; **strings of life**, heart-strings. 218. **tranced**, in a swoon. 221. **for**, even for.

[*Enter* KENT.]

O, is this he?
The time will not allow the compliment
Which very manners urges.

KENT. I am come
To bid my king and master aye good night: 235
Is he not here?

ALB. Great thing of us forgot!
Speak, Edmund, where's the king? and where's Cordelia?
See'st thou this object, Kent?

[*The bodies of* GONERIL *and* REGAN *are brought in.*

KENT. Alack, why thus?

EDM. Yet Edmund was beloved:
The one the other poison'd for my sake, 240
And after slew herself.

ALB. Even so. Cover their faces.

EDM. I pant for life: some good I mean to do,
Despite of mine own nature. Quickly send,
Be brief in it, to the castle; for my writ 245
Is on the life of Lear and on Cordelia:
Nay, send in time.

ALB. Run, run, O, run!

EDG. To who, my lord! Who hath the office? send
Thy token of reprieve.

EDM. Well thought on: take my sword, 250
Give it the captain.

ALB. Haste thee, for thy life. [*Exit* EDGAR.

EDM. He hath commission from thy wife and me
To hang Cordelia in the prison, and
To lay the blame upon her own despair,
That she fordid herself. 255

ALB. The gods defend her! Bear him hence awhile. [EDMUND *is borne off.*

[*Re-enter* LEAR, *with* CORDELIA *dead in his arms;* EDGAR, CAPTAIN, *and others following.*]

LEAR. Howl, howl, howl, howl! O, you are men of stones:
Had I your tongues and eyes, I'ld use them so
That heaven's vault should crack. She's gone for ever!
I know when one is dead, and when one lives; 260
She's dead as earth. Lend me a looking-glass;
If that her breath will mist or stain the stone,
Why, then she lives.

KENT. Is this the promised end?

EDG. Or image of that horror?

ALB. Fall, and cease!

LEAR. This feather stirs; she lives! if it be so, 265
It is a chance which does redeem all sorrows
That ever I have felt.

KENT. [*Kneeling*] O my good master!

LEAR. Prithee, away.

EDG. 'Tis noble Kent, your friend.

LEAR. A plague upon you, murderers, traitors all!
I might have saved her; now she's gone for ever! 270
Cordelia, Cordelia! stay a little. Ha!
What is 't thou say'st? Her voice was ever soft,
Gentle, and low, an excellent thing in woman.
I kill'd the slave that was a-hanging thee.

CAPT. 'Tis true, my lords, he did.

LEAR. Did I not, fellow?
I have seen the day, with my good biting falchion 276
I would have made them skip: I am old now,
And these same crosses spoil me. Who are you?
Mine eyes are not o' the best: I'll tell you straight.

KENT. If fortune brag of two she loved and hated, 280
One of them we behold.

LEAR. This is a dull sight. Are you not Kent?

KENT. The same,
Your servant Kent. Where is your servant Caius?

LEAR. He's a good fellow, I can tell you that;
He'll strike, and quickly too: he's dead and rotten. 285

KENT. No, my good lord; I am the very man,—

LEAR. I'll see that straight.

233. compliment, ceremony. 235. aye, forever. 236. of, by. 255. fordid, destroyed. 262. stone, crystal mirror. 263. promised end, i.e., of the world, the Last Judgment. 264. image, exact likeness; Fall, and cease, i.e., let Doomsday come and all things cease to be. 266. redeem, repay. 276. falchion, a curved, broad-bladed sword. 278. crosses, troubles. 279. straight, straightway. 281. one . . . behold, certainly no more than two men in all human history have experienced such violent ups and downs of Fortune as Lear. 287. see that, see to that.

KENT. That, from your first of difference and decay,
Have follow'd your sad steps.

LEAR. You are welcome hither.

KENT. Nor no man else: all's cheerless, dark, and deadly. 290
Your eldest daughters have fordone themselves,
And desperately are dead.

LEAR. Ay, so I think.

ALB. He knows not what he says: and vain it is
That we present us to him.

EDG. Very bootless.

[*Enter a* CAPTAIN.]

CAP. Edmund is dead, my lord.

ALB. That's but a trifle here. 295
You lords and noble friends, know our intent.
What comfort to this great decay may come
Shall be applied: for us, we will resign
During the life of this old majesty,
To him our absolute power: [*To* EDGAR *and* KENT] you, to your rights; 300
With boot, and such addition as your honours
Have more than merited. All friends shall taste
The wages of their virtue, and all foes
The cup of their deservings. O, see, see!

LEAR. And my poor fool is hang'd! No, no, no life! 305
Why should a dog, a horse, a rat, have life,
And thou no breath at all? Thou'lt come no more,
Never, never, never, never, never!
Pray you, undo this button: thank you, sir.
Do you see this? Look on her, look, her lips, 310
Look there, look there! [*Dies.*

EDG. He faints! My lord, my lord!

KENT. Break, heart; I prithee, break!

EDG. Look up, my lord.

KENT. Vex not his ghost: O, let him pass! he hates him much
That would upon the rack of this tough world
Stretch him out longer.

EDG. He is gone, indeed. 315

KENT. The wonder is, he hath endured so long:
He but usurp'd his life.

ALB. Bear them from hence. Our present business
Is general woe. [*To* KENT *and* EDGAR] Friends of my soul, you twain
Rule in this realm, and the gored state sustain. 320

KENT. I have a journey, sir, shortly to go;
My master calls me, I must not say no.

ALB. The weight of this sad time we must obey;
Speak what we feel, not what we ought to say.
The oldest hath borne most: we that are young 325
Shall never see so much, nor live so long.

[*Exeunt, with a dead march.*

288. **from . . . decay,** from the beginning of the decline and decay of your fortunes. 290. **No . . . else,** not I nor any one else. 291. **foredone,** killed. 292. **desperately,** in despair. 297. **great decay,** great man fallen into decay. 300. **our absolute power,** the sovereign power I now exercise. 301. **boot,** something given in the bargain. 305. **poor fool,** i.e., Cordelia; "fool" was used as a term of endearment. 313. **ghost,** departing spirit. 317. **usurp'd his life,** i.e., lived longer than the usual term of life. 322. **calls me,** i.e., to follow him through Death. 325. **oldest,** i.e., Lear and Gloucester. 326. **Shall . . . long,** i.e., even if we shall live as long as Lear has, we should never experience so much misery.

AFTERWORD

As the fourth act of *King Lear* opens, Edgar, the just man whom injustice has victimized, is discovered alone in a desolate place. Edgar, to disguise himself from his pursuers, has put on the filthy rags and witless behavior of a madman or Bedlam beggar. But though he is, as he himself acknowledges, the "lowest and most dejected thing of fortune," he remains to this point the optimistic man. He has plumbed the depths; now, he thinks, better days are in prospect. "The worst returns to laughter."

This hopeful observation is, however, premature. Edgar, having spoken, is confronted at once by the horrifying presence of his father, whose eyes have been torn from their sockets. And so Edgar is lessoned. The ferocious cruelty with which this play abounds instructs him that no man is at liberty to say, "I am at the worst." Merely to live is to be endlessly vulnerable. "The worst is not So long as we can say 'This is the worst.'" In the pitiless world of *King Lear*, the easy optimism is rejected, to which all of us are naturally prone.

Mostly, we are inclined to assume that, as we are good, in any case as we are circumspect, our passage through life to death will be made a more comfortable passage. That is the principle of poetic justice. Albany who, like Edgar, is essentially the good man and is willing to suppose that things go on as he would wish, enunciates this principle. In the dreadful scene with which the play concludes, he announces smoothly,

All friends shall taste
The wages of their virtue, and all foes
The cup of their deservings.

In fact, it does not happen like that. Albany's little speech, which is more appropriate to fiction than to life as it is actually lived, is preceded by the death of Cordelia, the embodiment of virtue and desert. It is followed by the death of King Lear, a man infinitely more sinned against than sinning.

Poetic justice is a lie. Evil conduct is accompanied often by material satisfaction. Virtuous conduct may be rewarded in Heaven. But Shakespeare, as he knows nothing of Heaven, does not presume to say. What he does say, or show, is that no certain correlation is evident, between moral integrity or intellectual acumen, and the rewards or penalities fortune dispenses. It rains on the just and the unjust alike, as also on the wise man and fool. The goodness of Cordelia is approved, as she goes about her father's business. Nonetheless, she is destroyed, not in consequence but capriciously, as the wheel of fortune revolves. Cordelia is not the first "Who, with best meaning . . . [has] incurr'd the worst."

In this deeply troubling discovery, she is preceded by Kent, the honest and loyal retainer who, for his fidelity to the King, is punished like a vulgar criminal. But Kent, as he is wise in the way of the world, does not expect the operation of poetic justice. In the stocks, reflecting on the miserable condition to which unlucky fortune has brought him, he speaks inferentially to the predicament which is common to us all. "A good man's fortune may grow out at heels." Goodness is no stay against the turning of the wheel.

Kent, who has "more man than wit" about him, forbears to expostulate or to bewail his unfortunate condition. Acceptance in the face of ill fortune, equanimity in confronting the event that's coming on—this, we are led to conclude, is the right posture or psychology for human beings to manifest, given the uncertain nature of their portion. The storm on the heath which assaults the aged Lear is too rough, Kent supposes, "For nature to endure." But Lear, who stands against it, is able to cry: "Pour on; I will endure." Lear elects to be the pattern of all patience. That is not as he is hopeful of an upward turning of the wheel. Good hope, like constancy, like kindness, is its own reward. The gods are indifferent to what we require. Entreaty is gratuitous, except as it eases the heart. The man whom suffering has lessoned "will say nothing."

Evidently, no alternative offers.

> Men must endure
> Their going hence, even as their coming hither.

The night of our existence is such a night as "pities neither wise man nor fool." The wisest man is insufficiently wise to prevent the onset of the wind and the rain. And so he must content himself with a fortune as diminished as his own capacity or stature, "For the rain it raineth every day." That is the saying of Lear's Fool who, in this topsy-turvy world in which our normal expectations are inverted, takes the role of philosopher or knowledgeable man.

The Fool, presenting knowledge, is threatened with the whip. That is another comment on the way of the world. "Truth's a dog must to kennel; he must be whipped out, when Lady the brach"—or bitch—"may stand by the fire and stink." The tragedy of *King Lear* may be described, on one side, as a remorseless dramatizing, in scene after scene, of this inequitable sequence. The play, on this side, reaches its appropriate climax in the monstrous death of Cordelia. As equity governs, the restoration of Cordelia should follow. It is a chance which, if conceded, would redeem all sorrows. But this chance is not conceded. Lear's agonized question, which is also a plea for just proportion, goes unanswered:

> Why should a dog, a horse, a rat, have life,
> And thou no breath at all?

In the winding up of Shakespeare's story, "all's cheerless, dark, and deadly."

Modern persons who believe that Shakespeare is, to a degree, obsolete or inadequately schooled because he lacks acquaintance with the terrifying history of our own times, would do well to consult the unrelieved gloom of the conclusion to *King Lear*. Shakespeare in this conclusion looks steadfastly on the overthrow of the just, and records, without flinching or softening, what he sees. It is not that he is revelling in bleakness for its own sake. Nor is his vision, although it is indubitably bleak, to be characterized as despairing or pessimistic. The right characterization will employ such terms as catholic—in the sense of total—and unreservedly honest.

The horror of *King Lear* is not denied but it is qualified, as representation of character is total. Evil is overmastering; still, goodness lodges its claim. Cordelia, the virtuous daughter, who is said to shake the holy water from her eyes —to offer grace, like the Deity—mitigates the unnatural conduct of the wicked sisters. Oswald, the bad servant, has his fellow in Kent or Caius, who serves where he stands condemned. Against the Duke of Cornwall, who indulges his blood or passion, is placed the Duke of Albany, who understands that it is not fitting to let his hands obey his blood. As Cordelia is stripped of her dowry, love in Burgundy grows cold; in France, love is kindled "to inflamed respect." The Captain, in his role as unthinking subordinate to Edmund, undertakes without demur the murder of Lear and Cordelia. Cornwall's servant, who opposes his sword against the cruelty of his master, cannot help, as he is human, but demur. Gloucester determines to relieve the banished king though he dies for it; and the Old Man to succor the blinded Gloucester, "Come on't what will." Edmund, who looks without pity on the afflictions of his father, is brother to Edgar, who is "pregnant to good pity."

The prime truth of the play is the snuffing out of the virtuous man. Shakespeare the faithful reporter declines to interpose. But the good man in his agony grows and changes. He comes to know himself: the case of Gloucester, preeminently the case of King Lear. Shakespeare, who is alert to the presence of goodness, who records in his tragedy the renascence of fellow feeling, is not prey to despair.

Neither is he especially optimistic. Catholicity demands that the representation of goodness, in a notable phrase of Thomas Hardy's, "exacts a full look at the Worst." In *King Lear*, this full or total look is vouchsafed us. The great stage on which Shakespeare's protagonists act out their tragic play is a stage of fools, on which the unwinking stars in their influence comment. Across this stage, madmen lead the blind. Humanity preys on itself, "Like monsters of the deep." Bestiality, as of the Centaur, describes the human condition. Unaccommodated man, " a poor, bare, forked animal" stripped of his civilizing accouterments, is the thing itself. This thing smells of mortality. Edgar, begrimed with filth and "Brought near to beast," is the emblem of man; or Lear, in whose flesh his daughters stick boarish fangs; or Gloucester, who is tied to the stake like a bear in the bear pit, torn and baited by savage dogs.

Society is a mirror of this bear pit, where right goes down and only power is of consequence.

> Through tatter'd clothes small vices do appear;
> Robes and furr'd gowns hide all. Plate sin with gold,
> And the strong lance of justice hurtless breaks.

Justice is a mockery. The Trial Scene in the farmhouse (III. vi), a ghastly parody presided over by a madman whose colleagues in equity are the Bedlam and Fool, is its faithful enactment. Cornwall, whose disposition "Will not be rubbed nor stopped," is the type of the magistrate. In theory, "the form of justice"—at which he glances in the scene that follows at once—should dissuade him from consulting his unruly disposition or impulse. In practice, his power, "which men May blame, but not control," gives sanction to his wrath. Unspeakable cruelty follows.

Out, vile jelly!
Where is thy lustre now?

Barbarism is supportable as it is understood to be eccentric, the peculiar or isolated case. *King Lear* denies us this comfort or support. Nature seems dowered with a "general curse." Or else Nature disclaims her role in the constituting of human beings—for example, in the person of Oswald, the opportunist and sycophant who estimates people as things. Woman's will to evil is marked by "undistinguished space": it is apparently limitless. Lear's wicked daughters are "pelican daughters" who, for their own sustenance, suck their parent's blood.

Filial ingratitude is raised to the ultimate power in these daughters, but it is not peculiar to them. Edmund, the natural son of Gloucester, who shows his father what is called ironically a "childlike office," is their perfect complement. Spinning the web in which Gloucester is ensnared, Edmund communicates to us, in a single line, his egoistic philosophy: "All with me's meet that I can fashion fit." Nothing is inappropriate, nothing is forbidden, so long as the egoist is able to bring it off. Debate as of the right and wrong of a question is to no purpose. "For my state," says the spokesman of naked power and self-aggrandizement, "Stands on me to defend, not to debate."

The achieving and maintaining of this state requires, at first, the dispossessing of Edgar, the innocent brother. It requires, at last, the strangling of Cordelia. Neither event is the occasion of remorse or reflection. To be tenderhearted or reflective does not become the man on his way. Gloucester, holding the forged letter he believes his legitimate son to have written, asks incredulously: "Had he a hand to write this? A heart and brain to breed it in?" The question is rich with implication. It is essentially a question directed to the nature of human beings—or, more precisely, to what is latent and potential in human beings. Edmund, as the action instructs us, is the possessor of just such a hand and heart and brain. And not only Edmund.

Such character or conduct we would not take from report, at second hand. Shakespeare, in this unsparing and encyclopedic representation of the "images of revolt and flying off," compels us to bear witness to it. *King Lear* is the most nearly comprehensive of tragedies in its delineating of all sorrows and its anatomizing of the endless evil that breeds about the human heart.

Suggested Reading

Bickerseth, Geoffrey L., *The Golden World of "King Lear"* (1947).
Bodkin, Maud, *Studies of Type-Images in Poetry, Religion, and Philosophy* (1951).
Bonheim, Helmut, *The Lear Perplex* (1960). Wadsworth Guides.
Bradley, A. C., *Shakespearean Tragedy* (1904). Papermac. Premier.
Bransom, James S. H., *The Tragedy of King Lear* (1934).
Campbell, Lily B., *Shakespeare's Tragic Heroes* (1930). Barnes and Noble.
Charlton, H. B., *Shakespearian Tragedy* (1948).
Coe, Charles N., *Shakespeare's Villains* (1957).
Cunningham, J. V., *Woe or Wonder* (1951). Swallow.
Danby, John F., *Poets on Fortune's Hill* (1952).
———, *Shakespeare's Doctrine of Nature* (1949). Humanities.
Dowden, Edward, *Shakespeare: A Critical Study* (1962). Capricorn.
Elton, William R., *King Lear and the Gods* (1966).
Empson, William, *The Structure of Complex Words* (1951). Michigan.
Fairchild, Arthur H. R., *Shakespeare and the Tragic Theme* (1944).
Farnham, Willard, *The Medieval Heritage of Elizabethan Tragedy* (1936).
Fraser, Russell A., *Shakespeare's Poetics in Relation to "King Lear"* (1962).
Gardner, Helen, *King Lear* (1967).
Goldsmith, Robert H., *Wise Fools in Shakespeare* (1955).
Hayden, Hiram, *The Counter-Renaissance* (1950). Harbinger.
Heilman, Robert B., *This Great Stage: Image and Structure in "King Lear"* (1948). Penguin. University of Washington.
Holloway, John, *The Story of the Night* (1961). Bison.
James, David G., *The Dream of Learning: An Essay on "The Advancement of Learning," "Hamlet," and "King Lear"* (1951).
Jorgensen, Paul, A., *Lear's Self-Discovery* (1967).
Knight, G. Wilson, *The Shakespearian Tempest* (1932).
———, *The Wheel of Fire* (enlarged ed. 1954). Barnes and Noble.
Knights, L. C., *Shakespeare's Politics* (1957).
———, *Some Shakespearean Themes* (1959). Stanford.
Leech, Clifford, *Shakespeare's Tragedies* (1950). Phoenix.
Lothian, John M., *"King Lear": A Tragic Reading of Life* (1949).
Mack, Maynard, *"King Lear" in Our Time* (1965). Penguin.
Michel, L., and R. Sewell, eds., *Tragedy: Modern Essays in Criticism* (1963).
Muir, Edwin, *The Politics of "King Lear"* (1947).
Muller, Herbert J., *The Spirit of Tragedy* (1956). Washington Square.
Ornstein, Robert, *The Ethics of Jacobean Tragedy* (1954).
Perrett, Wilfrid, *The Story of King Lear from Geoffrey of Monmouth to Shakespeare* (1904).
Ribner, Irving, *Patterns in Shakespearian Tragedy* (1960).
Sewall, Richard B., *The Vision of Tragedy* (1959). Penguin. Yale.

Shakespeare Survey, XIII (1960; reprinted 1966). Volume devoted to *King Lear.*
SIEGEL, PAUL N., *Shakespearean Tragedy and the Elizabethan Compromise* (1957).
SPENCER, HAZELTON, *Shakespeare Improved* (1927).
SPIVACK, BERNARD, *Shakespeare and the Allegory of Evil* (1958). Penguin.
TANNENBAUM, SAMUEL A., *Shakespeare's "Lear": A Concise Bibliography* (1940).
WATKINS, WALTER B. C., *Shakespeare and Spenser* (1950). Princeton.
WELSFORD, ENID, *The Fool* (1935).
WILSON, HAROLD S., *On the Design of Shakespearian Tragedy* (1957). Toronto.

The Tempest

A NOTE ON THE TEXT

An entry in the Revels Accounts records a performance of *The Tempest* before King James at Whitehall Palace on Hallowmas Night (November 1) in 1611. Presumably the play was written in that year. A subsequent performance, in honor of the marriage of the King's daughter Elizabeth with Frederick, Count Palatine, a German prince, took place in February 1613. The masque-like character of the play, its emphasis, as in Act IV, on dancing and gorgeous costume, conceivably reflect this nuptial celebration.

The Tempest did not appear in quarto, but was published for the first time in the Folio of 1623. The text is unconventional, in that it is divided into acts and scenes. (No edition of a play of Shakespeare's published in his lifetime is fully divided in this way. Some of the plays, *Romeo and Juliet* for example, were published without any division into acts and scenes.)

For the story of the shipwreck and the miraculous island, Shakespeare was indebted to contemporary pamphlets on the *Discovery of the Bermudas* (1610), and the *Wreck and Redemption of Sir Thomas Gates*, a servant of the Virginia Company, whose perilous exploits, as recounted by William Strachey, and perhaps familiar to Shakespeare in manuscript form, were not published until 1625. Other possible sources include William Parry's *New and Large Discourse of the Travels of Sir Anthony Shirley* (1601), a narrative of adventures in Persia and Russia; and John Florio's translation of the *Essays* of Montaigne (1603), whence Shakespeare drew Gonzalo's account of the ideal commonwealth.

The plot of *The Tempest,* and the vision which informs it, are, however, Shakespeare's own. Man in the state of nature excites the sentimental admiration of Montaigne. Shakespeare, though he believes in Ferdinand and Miranda, stops this side of sentimental belief. In Caliban, a monstrous creature whom "stripes may move, not kindness," he offers his version of the noble savage. Goodness is contingent on civilization. The natural life, in *The Tempest* not less than *King Lear*, is "solitary, poor, nasty, brutish, and short."

THE TEMPEST

DRAMATIS PERSONÆ

ALONSO, *King of Naples.*
SEBASTIAN, *his brother.*
PROSPERO, *the right Duke of Milan.*
ANTONIO, *his brother, the usurping Duke of Milan.*
FERDINAND, *son to the King of Naples.*
GONZALO, *an honest old Counsellor.*
ADRIAN, FRANCISCO, } *Lords.*
CALIBAN, *a savage and deformed Slave.*
TRINCULO, *a Jester.*
STEPHANO, *a drunken Butler.*
MASTER *of a Ship.*
BOATSWAIN.
MARINERS.
MIRANDA, *daughter to Prospero.*
ARIEL, *an airy Spirit.*
IRIS, CERES, JUNO, NYMPHS, REAPERS, } *presented by* SPIRITS.
Other SPIRITS *attending on Prospero.*
SCENE—*A ship at Sea: an island.*

ACT I

SCENE I. *On a ship at sea: a tempestuous noise of thunder and lightning heard.*

[*Enter a* SHIP-MASTER *and a* BOATSWAIN.]

MAST. Boatswain!
BOATS. Here, master: what cheer?
MAST. Good, speak to the mariners: fall to 't, yarely, or we run ourselves aground: bestir, bestir. [*Exit.* 5

[*Enter* MARINERS.]

BOATS. Heigh, my hearts! cheerly, cheerly, my hearts! yare, yare! Take in the topsail. Tend to the master's whistle. Blow, till thou burst thy wind, if room enough!

[*Enter* ALONSO, SEBASTIAN, ANTONIO, FERDINAND, GONZALO, *and others.*]

ALON. Good boatswain, have care. Where's the master? Play the men. 11
BOATS. I pray now, keep below.
ANT. Where is the master, boatswain?
BOATS. Do you not hear him? You mar our labour: keep your cabins: you do assist the storm.
GON. Nay, good, be patient. 16
BOATS. When the sea is. Hence! What cares these roarers for the name of king? To cabin: silence! trouble us not.
GON. Good, yet remember whom thou hast aboard. 21
BOATS. None that I more love than myself. You are a counsellor; if you can command these elements to silence, and work the peace of the present, we will not hand a rope more; use your authority: if you cannot, give thanks you have lived so long, and make yourself ready in your cabin for the mischance of the hour, if it so hap. Cheerly, good hearts! Out of our way, I say. 29
[*Exit.*
GON. I have great comfort from this fellow: methinks he hath no drowning mark upon him; his complexion is perfect gallows. Stand fast, good Fate, to his hanging: make the rope of his destiny our cable, for our own

Act I, Scene i: 2. master, captain; what cheer? How do we fare? 4. yarely, promptly. 8. Tend, attend. 9. if room, if there is open sea. 11. Play the, play the part of. 16. good, i.e., good fellow. 18. roarers, i.e., the winds and waves. 24-5. work . . . present, i.e., calm the present storm. 25. hand, handle. 32. his . . . gallows, an allusion to the proverb, "He who is born to be hanged, will never be drowned"; complexion, face.

doth little advantage. If he be not born to be hanged, our case is miserable. [*Exeunt.* 36

[*Re-enter* BOATSWAIN.]

BOATS. Down with the topmast! yare! lower, lower! Bring her to try with maincourse. [*A cry within.*] A plague upon this howling! they are louder than the weather or our office. 40

[*Re-enter* SEBASTIAN, ANTONIO, *and* GONZALO.]

Yet again! what do you here? Shall we give o'er and drown? Have you a mind to sink?

SEB. A pox o' your throat, you bawling, blasphemous, incharitable dog!

BOATS. Work you then.

ANT. Hang, cur! hang, you whoreson, insolent noisemaker! We are less afraid to be drowned than thou art.

GON. I'll warrant him for drowning; though the ship were no stronger than a nutshell and as leaky as an unstanched wench. 51

BOATS. Lay her a-hold, a-hold! set her two courses off to sea again; lay her off.

[*Enter* MARINERS *wet.*]

MARINERS. All lost! to prayers, to prayers! all lost! 55

BOATS. What, must our mouths be cold?

GON. The king and prince at prayers! let's assist them,
For our case is as theirs.

SEB. I'm out of patience.

ANT. We are merely cheated of our lives by drunkards:
This wide-chapp'd rascal—would thou mightst lie drowning 60
The washing of ten tides!

GON. He'll be hang'd yet,
Though every drop of water swear against it
And gape at widest to glut him.

[*A confused noise within:* "Mercy on us!"—"We split, we split!"—"Farewell my wife and children!"—
"Farewell, brother!"—"We split, we split, we split!"] 65

ANT. Let's all sink with the king.

SEB. Let's take leave of him.

[*Exeunt* ANT. *and* SEB.

GON. Now would I give a thousand furlongs of sea for an acre of barren ground, long heath, brown furze, any thing. The wills above be done! but I would fain die a dry death. [*Exeunt.* 72

SCENE II. *The island. Before* PROSPERO'S *cell.*

[*Enter* PROSPERO *and* MIRANDA.]

MIR. If by your art, my dearest father, you have
Put the wild waters in this roar, allay them.
The sky, it seems, would pour down stinking pitch,
But that the sea, mounting to the welkin's cheek,
Dashes the fire out. O, I have suffer'd 5
With those that I saw suffer: a brave vessel,
Who had, no doubt, some noble creature in her,
Dash'd all to pieces. O, the cry did knock
Against my very heart. Poor souls, they perish'd.
Had I been any god of power, I would 10
Have sunk the sea within the earth or ere
It should the good ship so have swallow'd and
The fraughting souls within her.

PROS. Be collected:
No more amazement: tell your piteous heart
There's no harm done.

MIR. O, woe the day!

PROS. No harm. 15
I have done nothing but in care of thee,
Of thee, my dear one, thee, my daughter, who
Art ignorant of what thou art, nought knowing
Of whence I am, nor that I am more better
Than Prospero, master of a full poor cell, 20
And thy no greater father.

38. Bring . . . maincourse, bring her close to the wind under mainsail. 40. our office, the noise of our orders. 41-2. give o'er, give up. 43. A pox o', a plague on. 49. warrant him, guarantee him; for, against. 52. a-hold, close to the wind. 53. two courses, two sails, i.e., foresail and mainsail. 53. off, i.e., away from shore. 56. What . . . cold, the boatswain here takes to drink. 59. merely, completely. 60. wide-chapp'd, wide-mouthed and so "insolent." 61. ten tides, the punishment for a pirate was to be hanged on the shore and left till three tides flowed over him. 63. glut, swallow. 71. long heath, brown furze, the phrase means, "no matter how worthless"; heath, heather; furze, evergreen shrub. Scene ii: 2. allay, calm. 4. welkin's, sky's. 6. brave, gallant. 13. fraughting, forming her cargo; collected, calm. 14. amazement, alarm. 20. full, thoroughly.

MIR. More to know
Did never meddle with my thoughts.
PROS. 'Tis time
I should inform thee farther. Lend thy hand,
And pluck my magic garment from me. So:
[*Lays down his mantle.*]
Lie there, my art. Wipe thou thine eyes; have comfort. 25
The direful spectacle of the wreck, which touch'd
The very virtue of compassion in thee,
I have with such provision in mine art
So safely ordered that there is no soul—
No, not so much perdition as an hair 30
Betid to any creature in the vessel
Which thou heard'st cry, which thou saw'st sink. Sit down;
For thou must now know farther.
MIR. You have often
Begun to tell me what I am, but stopp'd
And left me to a bootless inquisition, 35
Concluding "Stay: not yet."
PROS. The hour 's now come;
The very minute bids thee ope thine ear;
Obey and be attentive. Canst thou remember
A time before we came unto this cell?
I do not think thou canst, for then thou wast not 40
Out three years old.
MIR. Certainly, sir, I can.
PROS. By what? by any other house or person?
Of any thing the image tell me that
Hath kept with thy remembrance.
MIR. 'Tis far off
And rather like a dream than an assurance 45
That my remembrance warrants. Had I not
Four or five women once that tended me?
PROS. Thou hadst, and more, Miranda. But how is it
That this lives in thy mind? What seest thou else
In the dark backward and abysm of time? 50
If thou remember'st aught ere thou camest here,
How thou camest here thou mayst.
MIR. But that I do not.
PROS. Twelve year since, Miranda, twelve year since,
Thy father was the Duke of Milan and
A prince of power.
MIR. Sir, are not you my father? 55
PROS. Thy mother was a piece of virtue, and
She said thou wast my daughter; and thy father
Was Duke of Milan; and thou his only heir
And princess no worse issued.
MIR. O the heavens!
What foul play had we, that we came from thence? 60
Or blessed was 't we did?
PROS. Both, both, my girl:
By foul play, as thou say'st, were we heaved thence,
But blessedly holp hither.
MIR. O, my heart bleeds
To think o' the teen that I have turn'd you to,
Which is from my remembrance! Please you, farther. 65
PROS. My brother and thy uncle, call'd Antonio—
I pray thee, mark me—that a brother should
Be so perfidious!—he whom next thyself
Of all the world I loved and to him put
The manage of my state; as at that time 70
Through all the signories it was the first
And Prospero the prime duke, being so reputed
In dignity, and for the liberal arts
Without a parallel; those being all my study,
The government I cast upon my brother 75
And to my state grew stranger, being transported
And rapt in secret studies. Thy false uncle—
Dost thou attend me?
MIR. Sir, most heedfully.
PROS. Being once perfected how to grant suits,
How to deny them, who to advance and who 80
To trash for over-topping, new created

22. **meddle**, mingle. 27. **very virtue**, essential nature. 28. **provision**, foresight. 29. **ordered**, managed. 30. **perdition**, loss. 31. **Betid**, happened. 35. **bootless inquisition**, profitless inquiry. 41. **Out**, fully. 46. **remembrance warrants**, memory guarantees. 50. **dark backward**, dim past. 56. **piece**, masterpiece. 59. **no worse issued**, descended from no lower stock. 64. **teen . . . to**, sorrow I have forced you to recall. 65. **from**, out of. 69. **put**, entrusted. 71. **signories**, dukedoms. 72. **prime**, first in importance. 73. **liberal arts**, learning. 76. **state**, duties of government. 77. **secret**, occult, i.e., magic. 79. **Being . . . perfected**, having learned perfectly. 81. **trash for over-topping**, to clip to keep from growing too high, i.e., to restrain from becoming too ambitious; **new created**, made over (so that they were no longer loyal to me).

The creatures that were mine, I say, or changed 'em,
Or else new form'd 'em; having both the key
Of officer and office, set all hearts i' the state
To what tune pleased his ear; that now he was 85
The ivy which had hid my princely trunk,
And suck'd my verdure out on 't. Thou attend'st not.

MIR. O, good sir, I do.

PROS. I pray thee, mark me.
I, thus neglecting worldly ends, all dedicated
To closeness and the bettering of my mind 90
With that which, but by being so retired,
O'er-prized all popular rate, in my false brother
Awaked an evil nature; and my trust,
Like a good parent, did beget of him
A falsehood in its contrary as great 95
As my trust was; which had indeed no limit,
A confidence sans bound. He being thus lorded,
Not only with what my revénue yielded,
But what my power might else exact, like one
Who having into truth, by telling of it, 100
Made such a sinner of his memory,
To credit his own lie, he did believe
He was indeed the duke; out o' the substitution,
And executing the outward face of royalty,
With all prerogative: hence his ambition growing— 105
Dost thou hear?

MIR. Your tale, sir, would cure deafness.

PROS. To have no screen between this part he play'd
And him he play'd it for, he needs will be
Absolute Milan. Me, poor man, my library
Was dukedom large enough: of temporal royalties 110
He thinks me now incapable; confederates—
So dry he was for sway—wi' the King of Naples
To give him annual tribute, do him homage,
Subject his coronet to his crown and bend
The dukedom yet unbow'd—alas, poor Milan!— 115
To most ignoble stooping.

MIR. O the heavens!

PROS. Mark his condition and the event; then tell me
If this might be a brother.

MIR. I should sin
To think but nobly of my grandmother:
Good wombs have borne bad sons.

PROS. Now the condition. 120
This King of Naples, being an enemy
To me inveterate, hearkens my brother's suit;
Which was, that he, in lieu o' the premises
Of homage and I know not how much tribute,
Should presently extirpate me and mine 125
Out of the dukedom and confer fair Milan
With all the honours on my brother: whereon,
A treacherous army levied, one midnight
Fated to the purpose did Antonio open
The gates of Milan, and, i' the dead of darkness, 130
The ministers for the purpose hurried thence
Me and thy crying self.

MIR. Alack, for pity!
I, not remembering how I cried out then,
Will cry it o'er again: it is a hint
That wrings mine eyes to 't.

PROS. Hear a little further 135
And then I'll bring thee to the present business
Which now 's upon 's; without the which this story
Were most impertinent.

MIR. Wherefore did they not
That hour destroy us?

PROS. Well demanded, wench:
My tale provokes that question. Dear, they durst not, 140
So dear the love my people bore me, nor set
A mark so bloody on the business, but

83. **key,** the tuning key. 84. **state,** government. 85. **that,** so that. 87. **on 't,** of it. 90. **closeness,** privacy. 91. **but . . . retired,** but for the fact it kept me out of touch with the duties of my office. 92. **o'er-prized . . . rate,** (would have) surpassed in value all popular estimate. 95. **falsehood,** treachery; **contrary,** opposite kind. 97. **lorded,** made lord (i.e., supreme ruler) of the state. 99. **power,** i.e., tyrannical power. 100. **it,** i.e., his lie. 100-02. **Who . . . lie,** who by telling a lie often has so corrupted his memory as to mistake his lie for the truth. 103. **out . . . substitution,** by reason of acting as my substitute. 104. **executing . . . face,** performing the obvious duties. 109. **Absolute Milan,** actual Duke of Milan. 110. **temporal,** i.e., as contrasted with "spiritual"; **royalties,** royal prerogatives. 111. **confederates,** conspires. 112. **dry,** thirsty. 117. **condition,** the terms of his agreement; **event,** result. 123. **in . . . premises,** in return for the stipulations. 125. **presently,** at once. 127. **whereon,** i.e., in carrying out this agreement. 131. **ministers,** agents. 134. **hint,** occasion. 138. **impertinent,** irrelevant. 139. **wench,** here used affectionately. 141. **set,** i.e., dare set.

With colours fairer painted their foul ends.
In few, they hurried us aboard a bark,
Bore us some leagues to sea; where they prepared 145
A rotten carcass of a boat, not rigg'd,
Nor tackle, sail, nor mast; the very rats
Instinctively have quit it: there they hoist us,
To cry to the sea that roar'd to us, to sigh
To the winds whose pity, sighing back again,
Did us but loving wrong.

MIR. Alack, what trouble 151
Was I then to you!

PROS. O, a cherubin
Thou wast that did preserve me. Thou didst smile,
Infusèd with a fortitude from heaven,
When I have deck'd the sea with drops full salt, 155
Under my burthen groan'd; which raised in me
An undergoing stomach, to bear up
Against what should ensue.

MIR. How came we ashore?

PROS. By Providence divine.
Some food we had and some fresh water that
A noble Neapolitan, Gonzalo, 161
Out of his charity, who being then appointed
Master of this design, did give us, with
Rich garments, linens, stuffs and necessaries,
Which since have steaded much; so, of his gentleness, 165
Knowing I loved my books, he furnish'd me
From mine own library with volumes that
I prize above my dukedom.

MIR. Would I might
But ever see that man!

PROS. Now I arise: [*Resumes his mantle.*]
Sit still, and hear the last of our sea-sorrow.
Here in this island we arrived; and here 171
Have I, thy schoolmaster, made thee more profit
Than other princesses can that have more time
For vainer hours and tutors not so careful.

MIR. Heavens thank you for 't! And now, I pray you, sir, 175
For still 'tis beating in my mind, your reason
For raising this sea-storm?

PROS. Know thus far forth.
By accident most strange, bountiful Fortune,
Now my dear lady, hath mine enemies
Brought to this shore; and by my prescience 180
I find my zenith doth depend upon
A most auspicious star, whose influence
If now I court not but omit, my fortunes
Will ever after droop. Here cease more questions:
Thou art inclined to sleep; 'tis a good dulness, 185
And give it way: I know thou canst not choose. [MIRANDA *sleeps.*]
Come away, servant, come. I am ready now.
Approach, my Ariel, come.

[*Enter* ARIEL.]

ARI. All hail, great master! grave sir, hail! I come
To answer thy best pleasure; be 't to fly, 190
To swim, to dive into the fire, to ride
On the curl'd clouds, to thy strong bidding task
Ariel and all his quality.

PROS. Hast thou, spirit,
Perform'd to point the tempest that I bade thee?

ARI. To every article. 195
I boarded the king's ship; now on the beak,
Now in the waist, the deck, in every cabin,
I flamed amazement: sometime I 'ld divide,
And burn in many places; on the topmast,
The yards and bowsprit, would I flame distinctly, 200
Then meet and join. Jove's lightnings, the precursors
O' the dreadful thunder-claps, more momentary
And sight-outrunning were not; the fire and cracks
Of sulphurous roaring the most mighty Neptune
Seem to besiege and make his bold waves tremble, 205
Yea, his dread trident shake.

143. **colours**, i.e., pretexts; **fairer**, more specious. 144. **few**, short. 155. **deck'd**, covered. 157. **undergoing stomach**, courage to endure. 165. **steaded**, helped; **gentleness**, nobility of nature. 179. **dear lady**, kind patroness. 181. **my zenith**, rising to the top of my fortune. 183. **omit**, ignore. 185. **dulness**, drowsiness. 187. **away**, hither. 192. **task**, put to the test. 193. **quality**, skill. 194. **to point**, to the most exact detail. 196. **beak**, prow. 198. **flamed amazement**, caused terror by becoming flame (i.e., he became St. Elmo's fire). 200. **distinctly**, in several places at once. 202. **momentary**, instantaneous. 203. **cracks**, sharp, loud noises.

PROS. My brave spirit!
Who was so firm, so constant, that this coil
Would not infect his reason?

ARI. Not a soul
But felt a fever of the mad and play'd
Some tricks of desperation. All but mariners 210
Plunged in the foaming brine and quit the vessel,
Then all afire with me: the king's son, Ferdinand,
With hair up-staring,—then like reeds, not hair,—
Was the first man that leap'd; cried, "Hell is empty, 214
And all the devils are here."

PROS. Why, that's my spirit!
But was not this nigh shore?

ARI. Close by, my master.

PROS. But are they, Ariel, safe?

ARI. Not a hair perish'd;
On their sustaining garments not a blemish,
But fresher than before: and, as thou badest me,
In troops I have dispersed them 'bout the isle. 220
The king's son have I landed by himself;
Whom I left cooling of the air with sighs
In an odd angle of the isle and sitting,
His arms in this sad knot.

PROS. Of the king's ship
The mariners say how thou hast disposed 225
And all the rest o' the fleet.

ARI. Safely in harbour
Is the king's ship; in the deep nook, where once
Thou call'dst me up at midnight to fetch dew
From the still-vex'd Bermoothes, there she's hid:
The mariners all under hatches stow'd; 230
Who, with a charm join'd to their suffer'd labour,
I have left asleep: and for the rest o' the fleet
Which I dispersed, they all have met again
And are upon the Mediterranean flote,
Bound sadly home for Naples, 235
Supposing that they saw the king's ship wreck'd
And his great person perish.

PROS. Ariel, thy charge
Exactly is performed: but there's more work.
What is the time o' the day?

ARI. Past the mid season.

PROS. At least two glasses. The time 'twixt six and now 240
Must by us both be spent most preciously.

ARI. Is there more toil? Since thou dost give me pains,
Let me remember thee what thou hast promised,
Which is not yet perform'd me.

PROS. How now? moody?
What is 't thou canst demand?

ARI. My liberty. 245

PROS. Before the time be out? no more!

ARI. I prithee,
Remember I have done thee worthy service;
Told thee no lies, made thee no mistakings, served
Without or grudge or grumblings: thou didst promise
To bate me a full year.

PROS. Dost thou forget 250
From what a torment I did free thee?

ARI. No.

PROS. Thou dost, and think'st it much to tread the ooze
Of the salt deep,
To run upon the sharp wind of the north,
To do me business in the veins o' the earth 255
When it is baked with frost.

ARI. I do not, sir.

PROS. Thou liest, malignant thing! Hast thou forgot
The foul witch Sycorax, who with age and envy
Was grown into a hoop? hast thou forgot her?

ARI. No, sir.

PROS. Thou hast. Where was she born? speak; tell me. 260

ARI. Sir, in Argier.

PROS. O, was she so? I must

206. brave, fine. 207. coil, turmoil. 209. fever . . . mad, such fever as madmen feel. 213. up-staring, standing on end. 218. sustaining, holding them up. 223. odd angle, out-of-the-way spot. 224. this sad knot, folded sadly, in this way. 229. still-vex'd Bermoothes, ever storm-beaten Bermuda. 232. for, as for. 234. flote, sea. 240. glasses, hourglasses, hours. 241. preciously, i.e., as though each moment were precious. 242. pains, hard tasks. 250. bate me, reduce my term of service by. 258. envy, malice. 261. Argier, Algiers.

Once in a month recount what thou hast been,
Which thou forget'st. This damn'd witch Sycorax,
For mischiefs manifold and sorceries terrible
To enter human hearing, from Argier, 265
Thou know'st, was banish'd: for one thing she did
They would not take her life. Is not this true?

ARI. Ay, sir.

PROS. This blue-eyed hag was hither brought with child
And here was left by the sailors. Thou, my slave, 270
As thou report'st thyself, wast then her servant;
And, for thou wast a spirit too delicate
To act her earthy and abhorr'd commands,
Refusing her grand hests, she did confine thee,
By help of her more potent ministers 275
And in her most unmitigable rage,
Into a cloven pine; within which rift
Imprison'd thou didst painfully remain
A dozen years; within which space she died
And left thee there; where thou did'st vent thy groans 280
As fast as mill-wheels strike. Then was this island—
Save for the son that she did litter here,
A freckled whelp hag-born—not honour'd with
A human shape.

ARI. Yes, Caliban her son.

PROS. Dull thing, I say so; he, that Caliban 285
Whom now I keep in service. Thou best know'st
What torment I did find thee in; thy groans
Did make wolves howl and penetrate the breasts
Of ever angry bears: it was a torment
To lay upon the damn'd, which Sycorax 290
Could not again undo: it was mine art,
When I arrived and heard thee, that made gape
The pine and let thee out.

ARI. I thank thee, master.

PROS. If thou more murmur'st, I will rend an oak
And peg thee in his knotty entrails till 295
Thou hast howl'd away twelve winters.

ARI. Pardon, master;
I will be correspondent to command
And do my spiriting gently.

PROS. Do so, and after two days
I will discharge thee.

ARI. That's my noble master!
What shall I do? say what; what shall I do? 300

PROS. Go make thyself like a nymph o' the sea: be subject
To no sight but thine and mine, invisible
To every eyeball else. Go take this shape
And hither come in 't: go, hence with diligence! [*Exit* ARIEL.]
Awake, dear heart, awake! thou hast slept well; 305
Awake!

MIR. The strangeness of your story put
Heaviness in me.

PROS. Shake it off. Come on;
We'll visit Caliban my slave, who never
Yields us kind answer.

MIR. 'Tis a villain, sir,
I do not love to look on.

PROS. But, as 'tis, 310
We cannot miss him: he does make our fire,
Fetch in our wood and serves in offices
That profit us. What, ho! slave! Caliban!
Thou earth, thou! speak.

CAL. [*Within*] There's wood enough within.

PROS. Come forth, I say! there's other business for thee: 315
Come, thou tortoise! when?

[*Re-enter* ARIEL *like a water-nymph.*]

Fine apparition! My quaint Ariel,
Hark in thine ear.

ARI. My lord, it shall be done. [*Exit.*

PROS. Thou poisonous slave, got by the devil himself
Upon thy wicked dam, come forth! 320

[*Enter* CALIBAN.]

266. **for one thing**, because of one good deed. 269. **blue-eyed**, with dark circles under her eyes. 274. **grand hests**, important commands. 275. **ministers**, agents. 281. **As . . . strike**, as fast as the clacks of water mills. 283. **hag-born**, born of a witch. 297. **correspondent**, submissive.

298. **gently**, quietly, i.e., without complaint. 307. **Heaviness**, drowsiness. 311. **miss**, do without. 312. **offices**, duties. 316. **when?** an exclamation of impatience. 317. **quaint**, ingenious.

CAL. As wicked dew as e'er my mother brush'd
With raven's feather from unwholesome fen
Drop on you both! a south-west blow on ye
And blister you all o'er!

PROS. For this, be sure, to-night thou shalt have cramps, 325
Side-stitches that shall pen thy breath up; urchins
Shall, for that vast of night that they may work,
All exercise on thee; thou shalt be pinch'd
As thick as honeycomb, each pinch more stinging
Than bees that made 'em.

CAL. I must eat my dinner. 330
This island's mine, by Sycorax my mother,
Which thou takest from me. When thou camest first,
Thou strokedst me and madest much of me, wouldst give me
Water with berries in 't, and teach me how
To name the bigger light, and how the less,
That burn by day and night: and then I loved thee 336
And show'd thee all the qualities o' the isle,
The fresh springs, brine-pits, barren place and fertile:
Cursed be I that did so! All the charms
Of Sycorax, toads, beetles, bats, light on you!
For I am all the subjects that you have, 341
Which first was mine own king: and here you sty me
In this hard rock, whiles you do keep from me
The rest o' the island.

PROS. Thou most lying slave,
Whom stripes may move, not kindness! I have used thee, 345
Filth as thou art, with human care, and lodged thee
In mine own cell, till thou didst seek to violate
The honour of my child.

CAL. O ho, O ho! would 't had been done!
Thou didst prevent me; I had peopled else 350
This isle with Calibans.

PROS. Abhorrèd slave,
Which any print of goodness wilt not take,
Being capable of all ill! I pitied thee,
Took pains to make thee speak, taught thee each hour
One thing or other: when thou didst not, savage, 355
Know thine own meaning, but wouldst gabble like
A thing most brutish, I endow'd thy purposes
With words that made them known. But thy vile race,
Though thou didst learn, had that in 't which good natures
Could not abide to be with; therefore wast thou 360
Deservedly confined into this rock,
Who hadst deserved more than a prison.

CAL. You taught me language; and my profit on 't
Is, I know how to curse. The red plague rid you
For learning me your language!

PROS. Hag-seed, hence! 365
Fetch us in fuel; and be quick, thou'rt best,
To answer other business. Shrug'st thou, malice?
If thou neglect'st or dost unwillingly
What I command, I'll rack thee with old cramps,
Fill all thy bones with aches, make thee roar 370
That beasts shall tremble at thy din.

CAL. No, pray thee.
[*Aside*] I must obey: his art is of such power,
It would control my dam's god, Setebos,
And make a vassal of him.

PROS. So, slave; hence! [*Exit* CALIBAN. 375

[*Re-enter* ARIEL, *invisible, playing and singing;* FERDINAND *following.*]

ARIEL'S SONG.

Come unto these yellow sands,
And then take hands:
Courtesied when you have and kiss'd
The wild waves whist,
Foot it featly here and there; 380
And, sweet sprites, the burthen bear.

323. **south-west**, southwest wind in England was supposed to bring infection with its fog. 326. **urchins**, imps in the shape of hedgehogs. 327. **vast**, abyss. 328. **exercise**, practice. 337. **qualities**, properties. 342. **Which**, who.

364. **red plague rid you**, i.e., the bubonic plague destroy you. 365. **Hag-seed**, son of a witch. 366. **thou'rt best**, it will be best for you. 367. **answer**, attend to; **malice**, malignant creature. 369. **old**, a lot of. 373. **Setebos**, a god or devil thought to be worshiped by American savages. 379. **whist**, being hushed. 380. **featly**, gracefully. 381. **burthen**, refrain.

BURTHEN [*dispersedly*]. Hark, hark!
Bow-wow.
The watch-dogs bark:
Bow-wow.
ARI. Hark, hark! I hear
The strain of strutting chanticleer
Cry, Cock-a-diddle-dow.
FER. Where should this music be? i' the air or the earth?
It sounds no more: and, sure, it waits upon
Some god o' the island. Sitting on a bank,
Weeping again the king my father's wreck,
This music crept by me upon the waters, 391
Allaying both their fury and my passion
With its sweet air: thence I have follow'd it,
Or it hath drawn me rather. But 'tis gone.
No, it begins again.

ARIEL SINGS.

Full fathom five thy father lies;
Of his bones are coral made;
Those are pearls that were his eyes:
Nothing of him that doth fade
But doth suffer a sea-change 400
Into something rich and strange.
Sea-nymphs hourly ring his knell:
BURTHEN. Ding-dong.
ARI. Hark! now I hear them,—Ding-dong, bell.
FER. The ditty does remember my drown'd father. 405
This is no mortal business, nor no sound
That the earth owes. I hear it now above me.
PROS. The fringèd curtains of thine eye advance
And say what thou seest yond.
MIR. What is 't? a spirit?
Lord, how it looks about! Believe me, sir 410
It carries a brave form. But 'tis a spirit.
PROS. No, wench; it eats and sleeps and hath such senses
As we have, such. This gallant which thou seest
Was in the wreck; and, but he's something stain'd
With grief that's beauty's canker, thou mightst call him 415
A goodly person: he hath lost his fellows
And strays about to find 'em.
MIR. I might call him
A thing divine, for nothing natural
I ever saw so noble.
PROS. [*Aside*] It goes on, I see,
As my soul prompts it. Spirit, fine spirit! I'll free thee 420
Within two days for this.
FER. Most sure, the goddess
On whom these airs attend! Vouchsafe my prayer
May know if you remain upon this island;
And that you will some good instruction give
How I may bear me here: my prime request, 425
Which I do last pronounce, is, O you wonder!
If you be maid or no?
MIR. No wonder, sir;
But certainly a maid.
FER. My language! heavens!
I am the best of them that speak this speech,
Were I but where 'tis spoken.
PROS. How? the best? 430
What wert thou, if the King of Naples heard thee?
FER. A single thing, as I am now, that wonders
To hear thee speak of Naples. He does hear me;
And that he does I weep: myself am Naples,
Who with mine eyes, never since at ebb, beheld 435
The king my father wreck'd.
MIR. Alack, for mercy!
FER. Yes, faith, and all his lords; the Duke of Milan
And his brave son being twain.
PROS. [*Aside*] The Duke of Milan
And his more braver daughter could control thee,
If now 'twere fit to do 't. At the first sight 440
They have changed eyes. Delicate Ariel,
I'll set thee free for this. [*To* FER.] A word, good sir;
I fear you have done yourself some wrong: a word.

382. s.d. **dispersedly**, coming from different directions. 405. **ditty**, words to the song; **remember**, commemorate. 407. **owes**, possesses. 408. **advance**, lift up. 411. **brave**, handsome, gallant. 414. **something**, somewhat; **stain'd**, spoiled. 415. **canker**, canker-worm or caterpillar that eats the rosebuds. 416. **goodly**, handsome. 422. **attend**, accompany. 423. **May know**, may gain the knowledge from you; **remain**, dwell. 425. **prime**, first. 427. **or no**, i.e., or a goddess. 432. **single**, solitary and so "helpless." 434. **Naples**, king of Naples. 439. **control**, confute. 441. **changed eyes**, i.e., have eyes for each other only. 443. **done . . . wrong**, have not been true to your better nature.

MIR. Why speaks my father so ungently? This
Is the third man that e'er I saw, the first 445
That e'er I sigh'd for: pity move my father
To be inclined my way!
FER. O, if a virgin,
And your affection not gone forth, I'll make you
The queen of Naples.
PROS. Soft, sir! one word more.
[*Aside*] They are both in either's powers; but this swift business 450
I must uneasy make, lest too light winning
Make the prize light. [*To* FER.] One word more; I charge thee
That thou attend me: thou dost here usurp
The name thou owest not; and hast put thyself
Upon this island as a spy, to win it 455
From me, the lord on 't.
FER. No, as I am a man.
MIR. There's nothing ill can dwell in such a temple:
If the ill spirit have so fair a house,
Good things will strive to dwell with 't.
PROS. Follow me.
Speak not you for him; he's a traitor. Come;
I'll manacle thy neck and feet together: 461
Sea-water shalt thou drink; thy food shall be
The fresh-brook muscles, wither'd roots and husks
Wherein the acorn cradled. Follow.
FER. No;
I will resist such entertainment till 465
Mine enemy has more power.
[*Draws, and is charmed from moving.*
MIR. O dear father,
Make not too rash a trial of him, for
He's gentle and not fearful.
PROS. What? I say,
My foot my tutor? Put thy sword up, traitor;
Who makest a show but darest not strike, thy conscience 470
Is so possess'd with guilt: come from thy ward,
For I can here disarm thee with this stick
And make thy weapon drop.
MIR. Beseech you, father.
PROS. Hence! hang not on my garments.
MIR. Sir, have pity;
I'll be his surety.
PROS. Silence! one word more 475
Shall make me chide thee, if not hate thee. What!
An advocate for an imposter! hush!
Thou think'st there is no more such shapes as he,
Having seen but him and Caliban: foolish wench!
To the most of men this is a Caliban 480
And they to him are angels.
MIR. My affections
Are then most humble; I have no ambition
To see a goodlier man.
PROS. Come on; obey:
Thy nerves are in their infancy again
And have no vigour in them.
FER. So they are; 485
My spirits, as in a dream, are all bound up.
My father's loss, the weakness which I feel,
The wreck of all my friends, nor this man's threats,
To whom I am subdued, are but light to me,
Might I but through my prison once a day 490
Behold this maid: all corners else o' the earth
Let liberty make use of; space enough
Have I in such a prison.
PROS. [*Aside*] It works. [*To* FER.] Come on.
Thou hast done well, fine Ariel! [*To* FER.] Follow me.
[*To* ARI.] Hark what thou else shalt do me.
MIR. Be of comfort;
My father's of a better nature, sir, 496
Than he appears by speech: this is unwonted
Which now came from him.
PROS. Thou shalt be as free
As mountain winds: but then exactly do
All points of my command.
ARI. To the syllable. 500
PROS. Come, follow. Speak not for him.
[*Exeunt.*

449. Soft, wait a moment. 451. uneasy, difficult; light, easy. 452. light, lightly valued. 454. owest, ownest. 459. strive . . . 't, strive to occupy the same house (in order to drive out the evil spirit). 465. entertainment, treatment. 468. gentle, well-born; not fearful, no coward. 469. foot, an inferior part of the body, i.e., Miranda. 471. come . . . ward, abandon your posture of defence. 472. stick, his magic wand. 473. Beseech you, i.e., I beseech you. 480. To, in comparison with. 483. goodlier, handsomer. 484. nerves, sinews. 486. spirits, energies. 491-2. all . . . use of, let those who are free have all the rest of the world.

ACT II

SCENE I. *Another part of the island.*

[*Enter* ALONSO, SEBASTIAN, ANTONIO, GONZALO, ADRIAN, FRANCISCO, *and others.*]

GON. Beseech you, sir, be merry; you have cause,
So have we all, of joy; for our escape
Is much beyond our loss. Our hint of woe
Is common; every day some sailor's wife,
The masters of some merchant and the merchant 5
Have just our theme of woe; but for the miracle,
I mean our preservation, few in millions
Can speak like us: then wisely, good sir, weigh
Our sorrow with our comfort.

ALON. Prithee, peace.

SEB. He receives comfort like cold porridge. 10

ANT. The visitor will not give him o'er so.

SEB. Look, he's winding up the watch of his wit; by and by it will strike.

GON. Sir,—

SEB. One: tell. 15

GON. When every grief is entertain'd that 's offer'd,
Comes to the entertainer—

SEB. A dollar.

GON. Dolour comes to him, indeed: you have spoken truer than you purposed. 20

SEB. You have taken it wiselier than I meant you should.

GON. Therefore, my lord,—

ANT. Fie, what a spendthrift is he of his tongue!

ALON. I prithee, spare. 25

GON. Well, I have done: but yet,—

SEB. He will be talking.

ANT. Which, of he or Adrian, for a good wager, first begins to crow?

SEB. The old cock. 30

ANT. The cockerel.

SEB. Done. The wager?

ANT. A laughter.

SEB. A match!

ADR. Though this island seem to be desert,— 35

SEB. Ha, ha, ha! So, you're paid.

ADR. Uninhabitable and almost inaccessible,—

SEB. Yet,—

ADR. Yet,—

ANT. He could not miss 't. 40

ADR. It must needs be of subtle, tender and delicate temperance.

ANT. Temperance was a delicate wench.

SEB. Ay, and a subtle; as he most learnedly delivered. 45

ADR. The air breathes upon us here most sweetly.

SEB. As if it had lungs and rotten ones.

ANT. Or as 'twere perfumed by a fen.

GON. Here is every thing advantageous to life.

ANT. True; save means to live. 50

SEB. Of that there's none, or little.

GON. How lush and lusty the grass looks! how green!

ANT. The ground indeed is tawny.

SEB. With an eye of green in 't. 55

ANT. He misses not much.

SEB. No; he doth but mistake the truth totally.

GON. But the rarity of it is,—which is indeed almost beyond credit,—

SEB. As many vouched rarities are. 60

GON. That our garments, being, as they were, drenched in the sea, hold notwithstanding their freshness and glosses, being rather new-dyed than stained with salt water.

ANT. If but one of his pockets could speak, would it not say he lies? 66

SEB. Ay, or very falsely pocket up his report.

Act II, Scene i: 3. **hint of**, occasion for. 5. **merchant**, merchantman; **merchant**, i.e., the owner. 6. **for**, as for. 11. **visitor**, spiritual counsellor; **give . . . so**, give him up with so little preaching. 15. **tell**, count. 16. **entertain'd**, accepted (without resistance). 18. **dollar**, pun on "dolour" = grief. 21. **taken it wiselier**, understood my remark more subtly. 25. **spare**, i.e., your words. 30. **The old cock**, Gonzalo. 31. **The cockerel**, Adrian. 33. **laughter**, i.e., the winner has a laugh on the loser; **laughter** also = a nest of eggs. 36. **you're paid**, i.e., you've had your laugh. 42. **temperance**, temperature. 43. **Temperance**, a character in a morality play or in Chapman's **May Day** (1611). 45. **delivered**, reported. 55. **eye**, touch. 58. **rarity of it**, strange thing about it. 60. **vouched rarities**, strange tales vouched for by their narrators. 65. **pockets . . . speak**, and say they were wet. 67. **pocket up**, accept without examining.

GON. Methinks our garments are now as fresh as when we put them on first in Afric, at the marriage of the king's fair daughter Claribel to the King of Tunis. 71

SEB. 'Twas a sweet marriage, and we prosper well in our return.

ADR. Tunis was never graced before with such a paragon to their queen. 75

GON. Not since widow Dido's time.

ANT. Widow! a pox o' that! How came that widow in? widow Dido!

SEB. What if he had said "widower Æneas" too? Good Lord, how you take it! 80

ADR. "Widow Dido" said you? you make me study of that: she was of Carthage, not of Tunis.

GON. This Tunis, sir, was Carthage.

ADR. Carthage?

GON. I assure you, Carthage. 85

SEB. His word is more than the miraculous harp; he hath raised the wall and houses too.

ANT. What impossible matter will he make easy next?

SEB. I think he will carry this island home in his pocket and give it his son for an apple. 91

ANT. And, sowing the kernels of it in the sea, bring forth more islands.

GON. Ay.

ANT. Why, in good time. 95

GON. Sir, we were talking that our garments seem now as fresh as when we were at Tunis at the marriage of your daughter, who is now queen.

ANT. And the rarest that e'er came there.

SEB. Bate, I beseech you, widow Dido. 100

ANT. O, widow Dido! ay, widow Dido.

GON. Is not, sir, my doublet as fresh as the first day I wore it? I mean, in a sort.

ANT. That sort was well fished for.

GON. When I wore it at your daughter's marriage? 105

ALON. You cram these words into mine ears against
The stomach of my sense. Would I had never
Married my daughter there! for, coming thence,
My son is lost and, in my rate, she too,
Who is so far from Italy removed 110
I ne'er again shall see her. O thou mine heir
Of Naples and of Milan, what strange fish
Hath made his meal on thee?

FRAN. Sir, he may live:
I saw him beat the surges under him,
And ride upon their backs; he trod the water, 115
Whose enmity he flung aside, and breasted
The surge most swoln that met him; his bold head
'Bove the contentious waves he kept, and oar'd
Himself with his good arms in lusty stroke
To the shore, that o'er his wave-worn basis bow'd, 120
As stooping to relieve him: I not doubt
He came alive to land.

ALON. No, no, he's gone.

SEB. Sir, you may thank yourself for this great loss,
That would not bless our Europe with your daughter,
But rather lose her to an African; 125
Where she at least is banish'd from your eye,
Who hath cause to wet the grief on 't.

ALON. Prithee, peace.

SEB. You were kneel'd to and importunèd otherwise
By all of us, and the fair soul herself
Weigh'd between loathness and obedience, at
Which end o' the beam should bow. We have lost your son, 131
I fear, for ever: Milan and Naples have
Moe widows in them of this business' making
Than we bring men to comfort them:
The fault's your own.

ALON. So is the dear'st o' the loss.

GON. My lord Sebastian, 136
The truth you speak doth lack some gentleness
And time to speak it in: you rub the sore,
When you should bring the plaster.

SEB. Very well.

82. of that, about that. 86-7. miraculous harp, Amphion is said to have made the walls of Thebes rise by playing on his harp. 87. the . . . too, i.e., of Carthage (by identifying it with Tunis). 95. in good time, that's a good idea. 100. bate, subtract, except. 104. That . . . for, the word "sort" was a lucky catch. 107. stomach . . . sense, inclination of my feelings. 109. rate, estimation. 120. his, its; basis, base. 121. As, as if. 127. Who, i.e., the eye. 128. importuned otherwise, begged him to do otherwise, i.e., not to marry his daughter to the King of Tunis. 130. Weigh'd, balanced. 131. beam, the bar at the ends of which the two balances hung; should, i.e., she should. 133. Moe, more. 135. dear'st, worst. 138. time, fitting time.

ANT. And most chirurgeonly. 140
GON. It is foul weather in us all, good sir,
When you are cloudy.
SEB. Foul weather?
ANT. Very foul.
GON. Had I plantation of this isle, my lord,—
ANT. He 'ld sow 't with nettle-seed.
SEB. Or docks, or mallows.
GON. And were the king on 't, what would I do? 145
SEB. 'Scape being drunk for want of wine.
GON. I' the commonwealth I would by contraries
Execute all things; for no kind of traffic
Would I admit; no name of magistrate;
Letters should not be known; riches, poverty, 150
And use of service, none; contract, succession,
Bourn, bound of land, tilth, vineyard, none;
No use of metal, corn, or wine, or oil;
No occupation; all men idle, all;
And women too, but innocent and pure; 155
No sovereignty;—
SEB. Yet he would be king on 't.
ANT. The latter end of his commonwealth forgets the beginning.
GON. All things in common nature should produce 159
Without sweat or endeavour: treason, felony,
Sword, pike, knife, gun, or need of any engine,
Would I not have; but nature should bring forth,
Of it own kind, all foison, all abundance,
To feed my innocent people.
SEB. No marrying 'mong his subjects? 165
ANT. None, man; all idle: whores and knaves.
GON. I would with such perfection govern, sir,
To excel the golden age.
SEB. God save his majesty!
ANT. Long live Gonzalo!
GON. And,—do you mark me, sir?
ALON. Prithee, no more: thou dost talk nothing to me. 171
GON. I do well believe your highness; and did it to minister occasion to these gentlemen, who are of such sensible and nimble lungs that they always use to laugh at nothing. 175
ANT. 'Twas you we laughed at.
GON. Who in this kind of merry fooling am nothing to you: so you may continue and laugh at nothing still.
ANT. What a blow was there given! 180
SEB. An it had not fallen flat-long.
GON. You are gentlemen of brave mettle; you would lift the moon out of her sphere, if she would continue in it five weeks without changing.

[*Enter* ARIEL, *invisible, playing solemn music.*]

SEB. We would so, and then go a bat-fowling. 185
ANT. Nay, good my lord, be not angry.
GON. No, I warrant you; I will not adventure my discretion so weakly. Will you laugh me asleep, for I am very heavy?
ANT. Go sleep, and hear us. 190
[*All sleep except* ALON., SEB., *and* ANT.
ALON. What, all so soon asleep! I wish mine eyes
Would, with themselves, shut up my thoughts: I find
They are inclined to do so.
SEB. Please you, sir,
Do not omit the heavy offer of it:
It seldom visits sorrow; when it doth, 195
It is a comforter.
ANT. We two, my lord,
Will guard your person while you take your rest,
And watch your safety.
ALON. Thank you. Wondrous heavy.
[ALONSO *sleeps. Exit* ARIEL.
SEB. What a strange drowsiness possesses them!
ANT. It is the quality o' the climate.
SEB. Why 200
Doth it not then our eyelids sink? I find not
Myself disposed to sleep.

140. **chirurgeonly**, like a surgeon. 143. **plantation of**, the charter to colonize. 147. **by contraries**, by methods the direct opposite of the usual ones. 150. **Letters**, learning. 151. **service**, ceremony. 152. **Bourn**, boundary; **tilth**, tillage. 161. **engine**, military machines. 163. **it**, its; **foison**, plenty. 166. **idle**, worthless. 168. **To**, as to. 173. **minister occasion**, furnish opportunity (for laughter). 174. **sensible**, sensitive. 181. **An**, if; **flat-long**, with the flat of the sword. 182. **brave mettle**, fine spirit. 185. **bat-fowling**, hunting birds at night with a light and a stick with which to beat the bushes. 187. **adventure**, risk. 189. **heavy**, drowsy. 190. **hear us**, i.e., let our laughter put you to sleep. 194. **omit**, fail to accept; **heavy offer**, the invitation which your drowsiness extends.

ANT. Nor I; my spirits are nimble.
They fell together all, as by consent;
They dropp'd, as by a thunder-stroke. What might,
Worthy Sebastian? O, what might?—No more:— 205
And yet methinks I see it in thy face,
What thou shouldst be: the occasion speaks thee, and
My strong imagination sees a crown
Dropping upon thy head.

SEB. What, art thou waking?

ANT. Do you not hear me speak?

SEB. I do; and surely
It is a sleepy language and thou speak'st 211
Out of thy sleep. What is it thou didst say?
This is a strange repose, to be asleep
With eyes wide open; standing, speaking, moving,
And yet so fast asleep.

ANT. Noble Sebastian, 215
Thou let'st thy fortune sleep—die, rather; wink'st
Whiles thou art waking.

SEB. Thou dost snore distinctly;
There's meaning in thy snores.

ANT. I am more serious than my custom: you
Must be so too, if heed me; which to do 220
Trebles thee o'er.

SEB. Well, I am standing water.

ANT. I'll teach you how to flow.

SEB. Do so: to ebb
Hereditary sloth instructs me.

ANT. O,
If you but knew how you the purpose cherish
Whiles thus you mock it! how, in stripping it, 225
You more invest it! Ebbing men, indeed,
Most often do so near the bottom run
By their own fear or sloth.

SEB. Prithee, say on:
The setting of thine eye and cheek proclaim
A matter from thee, and a birth indeed 230
Which throes thee much to yield.

ANT. Thus, sir:
Although this lord of weak remembrance, this,
Who shall be of as little memory
When he is earth'd, hath here almost persuaded,—
For he's a spirit of persuasion, only 235
Professes to persuade,—the king his son's alive,
'Tis as impossible that he's undrown'd
As he that sleeps here swims.

SEB. I have no hope
That he's undrown'd.

ANT. O, out of that "no hope"
What great hope have you! no hope that way is 240
Another way so high a hope that even
Ambition cannot pierce a wink beyond,
But doubt discovery there. Will you grant with me
That Ferdinand is drown'd?

SEB. He's gone.

ANT. Then, tell me,
Who's the next heir of Naples?

SEB. Claribel. 245

ANT. She that is queen of Tunis; she that dwells
Ten leagues beyond man's life; she that from Naples
Can have no note, unless the sun were post—
The man i' the moon's too slow—till new-born chins
Be rough and razorable; she that—from whom? 250
We all were sea-swallow'd, though some cast again,
And by that destiny to perform an act
Whereof what's past is prologue, what to come
In yours and my discharge.

SEB. What stuff is this! how say you?
'Tis true, my brother's daughter's queen of Tunis; 255
So is she heir of Naples; 'twixt which regions
There is some space.

ANT. A space whose every cubit

202. **nimble**, alert. 203. **consent**, agreement. 207. **speaks thee**, proclaims thee [king]. 216. **wink'st**, Do you close your eyes [to this chance]? 217. **waking**, awake. 220. **if heed me**, if you pay attention to me. 221. **Trebles . . . o'er**, makes you three times as great; **standing water**, i.e., when the tide neither ebbs nor flows. 224. **purpose**, i.e., to be king. 225. **stripping**, i.e., of pretense. 226. **invest it**, clothe it with reality; **Ebbing men**, men who are stranded when their fortune ebbs. 228. **By**, because of. 229. **setting**, fixed expression. 230 **matter, i.e., of importance.**

231. **throes**, pains; **yield**, utter. 232. **remembrance**, memory. 234. **earth'd**, buried, i.e., the memory of him after he is dead will be as short as his own. 235-6. **only Professes**, his sole profession is. 238. **hope**, expectation. 242. **wink**, the least bit; **beyond**, i.e., hope of the crown. 243. **But . . . there**, but must doubt the truth of what it sees there. 248. **note**, information. 250. **from whom**, returning from whom. 251. **cast**, (1) vomited up, (2) cast for a rôle in a play. 254. **discharge**, performance, i.e., yours and mine to perform.

Seems to cry out, "How shall that Claribel
Measure us back to Naples? Keep in Tunis,
And let Sebastian wake." Say, this were
death 260
That now hath seized them; why, they were
no worse
Than now they are. There be that can rule
Naples
As well as he that sleeps; lords that can prate
As amply and unnecessarily
As this Gonzalo; I myself could make 265
A chough of as deep chat. O, that you bore
The mind that I do! what a sleep were this
For your advancement! Do you understand
me?

SEB. Methinks I do.

ANT. And how does your content
Tender your own good fortune?

SEB. I remember
You did supplant your brother Prospero.

ANT. True: 271
And look how well my garments sit upon
me;
Much feater than before: my brother's
servants
Were then my fellows; now they are my men.

SEB. But, for your conscience? 275

ANT. Ay, sir; where lies that? if 'twere a
kibe,
'Twould put me to my slipper: but I feel not
This deity in my bosom: twenty consciences,
That stand 'twixt me and Milan, candied be
they
And melt ere they molest! Here lies your
brother, 280
No better than the earth he lies upon,
If he were that which now he's like, that's
dead;
Whom I, with this obedient steel, three inches
of it,
Can lay to bed for ever; whiles you, doing
thus,
To the perpetual wink for aye might put 285
This ancient morsel, this Sir Prudence, who
Should not upbraid our course. For all the
rest,
They'll take suggestion as a cat laps milk;
They'll tell the clock to any business that
We say befits the hour.

SEB. Thy case, dear friend, 290
Shall be my precedent; as thou got'st Milan,
I'll come by Naples. Draw thy sword: one
stroke
Shall free thee from the tribute which thou
payest;
And I the king shall love thee.

ANT. Draw together;
And when I rear my hand, do you the
like, 295
To fall it on Gonzalo.

SEB. O, but one word. [*They talk apart.*

[*Re-enter* ARIEL, *invisible.*]

ARI. My master through his art foresees the
danger
That you, his friend, are in; and sends me
forth—
For else his project dies—to keep them living.
[*Sings in* GONZALO'*s ear.*]

While you here do snoring lie, 300
Open-eyed conspiracy
His time doth take.
If of life you keep a care,
Shake off slumber, and beware:
Awake, awake! 305

ANT. Then let us both be sudden.

GON. Now, good angels
Preserve the king. [*They wake.*

ALON. Why, how now? ho, awake! Why
are you drawn?
Wherefore this ghastly looking?

GON. What's the matter?

SEB. Whiles we stood here securing your
repose, 310
Even now, we heard a hollow burst of bellow-
ing
Like bulls, or rather lions: did 't not wake
you?
It struck mine ear most terribly.

ALON. I heard nothing.

259. **Measure us back,** find her way back to us; **Keep,** stay. 261. **them,** i.e., all the sleepers; **were,** would be. 262. **that,** those who. 266. **chough . . . chat,** a crow talk as deep stuff; **bore,** had. 269. **content,** pleasure. 270. **Tender,** regard, i.e., With how much pleasure do you regard? 273. **feater,** more becomingly. 275. **for,** as to. 276. **kibe,** sore heel. 277. **put me to,** force me to wear. 278-80. **twenty . . . molest,** let the twenty consciences that stand between me and the duchy of Milan be frozen stiff and then melt like candy rather than disturb me. 285. **perpetual wink,** everlasting sleep. 286. **morsel,** piece of a man. 287. **For,** as for. 288. **take suggestion,** act on our suggestion. 289. **tell . . . business,** count the strokes and say when it is the proper time for. 296. **fall it,** let it fall. 298. **his friend,** Gonzalo. 299. **project dies,** plan miscarries. 308. **Why . . . drawn?** Why have you drawn your swords?

ANT. O, 'twas a din to fright a monster's ear,
To make an earthquake! sure, it was the roar 315
Of a whole herd of lions.

ALON. Heard you this, Gonzalo?

GON. Upon mine honour, sir, I heard a humming,
And that a strange one too, which did awake me:
I shaked you, sir, and cried: as mine eyes open'd, 319
I saw their weapons drawn: there was a noise,
That's verily. 'Tis best we stand upon our guard,
Or that we quit this place: let's draw our weapons.

ALON. Lead off this ground; and let's make further search
For my poor son.

GON. Heavens keep him from these beasts!
For he is, sure, i' the island.

ALON. Lead away.

ARI. Prospero my lord shall know what I have done:
So, king, go safely on to seek thy son.
[*Exeunt.*

SCENE II. *Another part of the island.*

[*Enter* CALIBAN *with a burden of wood. A noise of thunder heard.*]

CAL. All the infections that the sun sucks up
From bogs, fens, flats, on Prosper fall and make him
By inch-meal a disease! His spirits hear me
And yet I needs must curse. But they'll nor pinch,
Fright me with urchin-shows, pitch me i' the mire, 5
Nor lead me, like a firebrand, in the dark
Out of my way, unless he bid 'em; but
For every trifle are they set upon me;
Sometime like apes that mow and chatter at me 9
And after bite me, then like hedgehogs which
Lie tumbling in my barefoot way and mount
Their pricks at my footfall; sometime am I
All wound with adders who with cloven tongues
Do hiss me into madness.

[*Enter* TRINCULO.]

Lo, now, lo!
Here comes a spirit of his, and to torment me 15
For bringing wood in slowly. I'll fall flat;
Perchance he will not mind me.

TRIN. Here's neither bush nor shrub, to bear off any weather at all, and another storm brewing; I hear it sing i' the wind: yond same black cloud, yond huge one, looks like a foul bombard that would shed his liquor. If it should thunder as it did before, I know not where to hide my head: yond same cloud cannot choose but fall by pailfuls. What have we here? a man or a fish? dead or alive? A fish: he smells like a fish; a very ancient and fish-like smell; a kind of not of the newest Poor-John. A strange fish! Were I in 29 England now, as once I was, and had but this fish painted, not a holiday fool there but would give a piece of silver: there would this monster make a man; any strange beast there makes a man: when they will not give a doit to relieve a lame beggar, they will lay out ten to see a dead Indian. Legged like a man! and his fins like arms! Warm o' my troth! I do now let loose my opinion; hold it no longer: this is no fish, but an islander, that hath lately suffered by a thunderbolt. [*Thunder.*] Alas, the storm is come again! my best way is to creep under his gaberdine; there is no other shelter hereabout: misery acquaints a man with strange bed-fellows. I will here shroud till the dregs of the storm be past. 43

[*Enter* STEPHANO, *singing: a bottle in his hand.*]

STE. I shall no more to sea, to sea,
Here shall I die ashore—
This is a very scurvy tune to sing at a man's funeral: well, here's my comfort. [*Drinks.*] [*Sings.*]

317. humming, i.e., Ariel's song. 321. verily, the truth. Scene ii: 3. By inch-meal, inch by inch. 5. urchin-shows, apparition of goblins. 6. firebrand, will-o'-the-wisp. 9. mow, make faces. 17. mind, notice. 19. bear off, keep off.

21. bombard, a wine jug made of black leather, so called because of its fancied resemblance to a cannon. 25. cannot . . . fall, cannot help falling. 29. Poor-John, salted hake (a kind of codfish). 34. makes a man, makes a man's fortune. 34. doit, the smallest coin = half a farthing. 39. gaberdine, a long cloak. 43. shroud, cover myself. 46. scurvy, mean, "lousy."

The master, the swabber, the boatswain and I,
The gunner and his mate
Loved Mall, Meg and Marian and Margery, 50
But none of us cared for Kate;
For she had a tongue with a tang,
Would cry to a sailor, Go hang!
She loved not the savour of tar nor of pitch,
Yet a tailor might scratch her where'er she did itch: 55
Then to sea, boys, and let her go hang!

This is a scurvy tune too: but here's my comfort. [*Drinks.*

CAL. Do not torment me: Oh! 58

STE. What's the matter? Have we devils here? Do you put tricks upon 's with savages and men of Ind, ha? I have not 'scaped drowning to be afeard now of your four legs; for it hath been said, As proper a man as ever went on four legs cannot make him give ground; and it shall be said so again while Stephano breathes at nostrils.

CAL. The spirit torments me; Oh! 66

STE. This is some monster of the isle with four legs, who hath got, as I take it, an ague. Where the devil should he learn our language? I will give him some relief, if it be but for that. If I can recover him and keep him tame and get to Naples with him, he's a present for any emperor that ever trod on neat's-leather. 73

CAL. Do not torment me, prithee; I'll bring my wood home faster.

STE. He's in his fit now and does not talk after the wisest. He shall taste of my bottle: if he have never drunk wine afore, it will go near to remove his fit. If I can recover him and keep him tame, I will not take too much for him; he shall pay for him that hath him, and that soundly.

CAL. Thou dost me yet but little hurt; thou wilt anon, I know it by thy trembling: now Prosper works upon thee. 84

STE. Come on your ways; open your mouth; here is that which will give language to you, cat: open your mouth; this will shake your shaking, I can tell you, and that soundly: you cannot tell who's your friend: open your chaps again. 89

TRIN. I should know that voice: it should be—but he is drowned; and these are devils: O defend me!

STE. Four legs and two voices: a most delicate monster! His forward voice now is to speak well of his friend; his backward voice is to utter foul speeches and to detract. If all the wine in my bottle will recover him, I will help his ague. Come. Amen! I will pour some in thy other mouth.

TRIN. Stephano! 100

STE. Doth thy other mouth call me? Mercy, mercy! This is a devil, and no monster: I will leave him; I have no long spoon.

TRIN. Stephano! If thou beest Stephano, touch me and speak to me; for I am Trinculo —be not afeard—thy good friend Trinculo.

STE. If thou beest Trinculo, come forth: I'll pull thee by the lesser legs: if any be Trinculo's legs, these are they. Thou art very Trinculo indeed! How camest thou to be the siege of this moon-calf? can he vent Trinculos? 111

TRIN. I took him to be killed with a thunder-stroke. But art thou not drowned, Stephano? I hope now thou art not drowned. Is the storm overblown? I hid me under the dead moon-calf's gaberdine for fear of the storm. And art thou living, Stephano? O Stephano, two Neapolitans 'scaped!

STE. Prithee, do not turn me about; my stomach is not constant.

CAL. [*Aside*] These be fine things, an if they be not sprites. 120
That's a brave god and bears celestial liquor.
I will kneel to him.

STE. How didst thou 'scape? How camest thou hither? swear by this bottle how thou camest hither. I escaped upon a butt

60. **Ind,** the Indies (East or West). 61. **your four legs,** any four-legged creature. 62. **proper,** handsome. 71. **recover,** cure. 73. **neat's-leather,** a shoe made out of cowhide. 76. **fit,** fit of fever. 77. **after the wisest,** in the most intelligent way. 80-1. **I will . . . for him,** i.e., no price will be too high for him. 83. **trembling,** a sign of being possessed of a devil. 85. **Come . . . ways,** an expression of encouragement. 87. **cat,** an allusion to the proverb, "Good liquor will make a cat speak." 89. **chaps,** jaws.

92. **defend,** God defend. 96. **detract,** slander. 103. **long spoon,** an allusion to the proverb: "He that sups with the Devil has need of a long spoon." 111. **siege,** excrement; **moon-calf,** monster, congenital idiot. 119. **constant,** settled. 121. **brave,** fine. 134. **kiss the book,** he gives him the bottle instead of the Bible on which to take an oath. 142. **when time was,** once upon a time. 114. **thy dog and thy bush,** there was a folk tradition that a peasant was banished to the moon for gathering brush on Sunday. His dog went along, so did the last bush he had cut. 118. **constant,** settled.

of sack which the sailors heaved o'erboard, by this bottle! which I made of the bark of a tree with mine own hands since I was cast ashore.

CAL. I'll swear upon that bottle to be thy true subject; for the liquor is not earthy. 130

STE. Here; swear then how thou escapedst.

TRIN. Swum ashore, man, like a duck: I can swim like a duck, I'll be sworn.

STE. Here, kiss the book. Though thou canst swim like a duck, thou art made like a goose.

TRIN. O Stephano, hast any more of this?

STE. The whole butt, man: my cellar is in a rock by the sea-side where my wine is hid. How now, moon-calf! how does thine ague? 139

CAL. Hast thou not dropp'd from heaven?

STE. Out o' the moon, I do assure thee: I was the man i' the moon when time was.

CAL. I have seen thee in her and I do adore thee:
My mistress show'd me thee and thy dog and thy bush.

STE. Come, swear to that; kiss the book: I will furnish it anon with new contents: swear.

TRIN. By this good light, this is a very shallow monster! I afeard of him! A very weak monster! The man i' the moon! A most poor credulous monster! Well drawn, monster, in good sooth! 150

CAL. I'll show thee every fertile inch o' th' island;
And I will kiss thy foot: I prithee, be my god.

TRIN. By this light, a most perfidious and drunken monster! when 's god's asleep, he'll rob his bottle. 155

CAL. I'll kiss thy foot; I'll swear myself thy subject.

STE. Come on then; down, and swear.

TRIN. I shall laugh myself to death at this puppy-headed monster. A most scurvy monster! I could find in my heart to beat him,—

STE. Come, kiss. 161

TRIN. But that the poor monster's in drink: an abominable monster!

CAL. I'll show thee the best springs; I'll pluck thee berries;
I'll fish for thee and get thee wood enough. 165
A plague upon the tyrant that I serve!
I'll bear him no more sticks, but follow thee,
Thou wondrous man.

TRIN. A most ridiculous monster, to make a wonder of a poor drunkard! 170

CAL. I prithee, let me bring thee where crabs grow;
And I with my long nails will dig thee pig-nuts;
Show thee a jay's nest and instruct thee how
To snare the nimble marmoset; I'll bring thee
To clustering filberts and sometimes I'll get thee 175
Young scamels from the rock. Wilt thou go with me?

STE. I prithee now, lead the way without any more talking. Trinculo, the king and all our company else being drowned, we will inherit here: here; bear my bottle: fellow Trinculo, we'll fill him by and by again. 181

CAL. [*Sings drunkenly*]
Farewell, master; farewell, farewell!

TRIN. A howling monster; a drunken monster!

CAL. No more dams I'll make for fish;
Nor fetch in firing 185
At requiring;
Nor scrape trencher, nor wash dish:
'Ban, 'Ban, Ca-Caliban
Has a new master: get a new man.
Freedom, hey-day! hey-day, freedom! freedom, hey-day, freedom! 191

STE. O brave monster! Lead the way.
[*Exeunt.*

ACT III

SCENE I. *Before* PROSPERO'S *cell.*

[*Enter* FERDINAND, *bearing a log.*]

FER. There be some sports are painful, and their labour

150. **Well drawn,** i.e., that was a good swig; **drawn,** swigged. 171. **crabs,** crab-apples. 174. **marmoset,** a small monkey. 176. **scamels,** probably sea gulls. 179-80. **inherit,** take possession. 181. **by and by,** right away. 187. **trencher,** wooden plate. **Act III, Scene i:** 1. **labour,** fatigue.

Delight in them sets off: some kinds of baseness
Are nobly undergone and most poor matters
Point to rich ends. This my mean task
Would be as heavy to me as odious, but 5
The mistress which I serve quickens what's dead
And makes my labours pleasures: O, she is
Ten times more gentle than her father's crabbed,
And he's composed of harshness. I must remove
Some thousands of these logs and pile them up, 10
Upon a sore injunction: my sweet mistress
Weeps when she sees me work, and says, such baseness
Had never like executor. I forget:
But these sweet thoughts do even refresh my labours,
Most busy lest, when I do it.

[*Enter* MIRANDA; *and* PROSPERO *at a distance, unseen.*]

MIR. Alas, now, pray you, 15
Work not so hard: I would the lightning had
Burnt up those logs that you are enjoin'd to pile!
Pray, set it down and rest you: when this burns,
'Twill weep for having wearied you. My father
Is hard at study; pray now, rest yourself; 20
He's safe for these three hours.

FER. O most dear mistress,
The sun will set before I shall discharge
What I must strive to do.

MIR. If you'll sit down,
I'll bear your logs the while: pray, give me that;
I'll carry it to the pile.

FER. No, precious creature;
I had rather crack my sinews, break my back, 26
Than you should such dishonour undergo,
While I sit lazy by.

MIR. It would become me
As well as it does you: and I should do it
With much more ease; for my good will is to it, 30
And yours it is against.

PROS. Poor worm, thou art infected!
This visitation shows it.

MIR. You look wearily,

FER. No, noble mistress: 'tis fresh morning with me
When you are by at night. I do beseech you—
Chiefly that I might set it in my prayers— 35
What is your name?

MIR. Miranda.—O my father,
I have broke your hest to say so!

FER. Admired Miranda!
Indeed the top of admiration! worth
What's dearest to the world! Full many a lady
I have eyed with best regard and many a time 40
The harmony of their tongues hath into bondage
Brought my too diligent ear: for several virtues
Have I liked several women; never any
With so full soul, but some defect in her
Did quarrel with the noblest grace she owed
And put it to the foil: but you, O you, 46
So perfect and so peerless, are created
Of every creature's best!

MIR. I do not know
One of my sex; no woman's face remember,
Save, from my glass, mine own; nor have I seen 50
More that I may call men than you, good friend,
And my dear father: how features are abroad,
I am skilless of; but, by my modesty,
The jewel in my dower, I would not wish
Any companion in the world but you, 55
Nor can imagination form a shape,
Besides yourself, to like of. But I prattle
Something too wildly and my father's precepts
I therein do forget.

2. **sets off**, cancels. 3. **Are**, which are; **most poor**, the poorest. 11. **sore injunction**, an order under severe penalties. 12. **baseness**, menial toil. 13. **I forget**, i.e., to work (in thinking about my sweet mistress). 15. **lest**, least, i.e., when I seem least busy; **do it**, i.e., forget it (my work, and merely think of her). This is Furness' explanation of this crux. 19. **weep**, i.e., exude sap. 32. **visitation**, visit (upon Ferdinand). 37. **hest**, command; **Admired**, admirable. 39. **What's dearest**, whatever is most valuable. 40. **regard**, gaze. 42. **several virtues**, particular excellencies. 45. **owed**, owned. 46. **put . . . foil**, made it ineffective. 52. **how . . . abroad**, what beauty is like out in the world. 53. **skilless**, ignorant. 57. **like of**, be pleased with.

FER. I am in my condition
A prince, Miranda; I do think, a king; 60
I would, not so!—and would no more endure
This wooden slavery than to suffer
The flesh-fly blow my mouth. Hear my soul speak:
The very instant that I saw you, did
My heart fly to your service; there resides, 65
To make me slave to it; and for your sake
Am I this patient log-man.

MIR. Do you love me?

FER. O heaven, O earth, bear witness to this sound
And crown what I profess with kind event
If I speak true! if hollowly, invert 70
What best is boded me to mischief! I
Beyond all limit of what else i' the world
Do love, prize, honour you.

MIR. I am a fool
To weep at what I am glad of.

PROS. Fair encounter
Of two most rare affections! Heavens rain grace 75
On that which breeds between 'em!

FER. Wherefore weep you?

MIR. At mine unworthiness that dare not offer
What I desire to give, and much less take
What I shall die to want. But this is trifling;
And all the more it seeks to hide itself, 80
The bigger bulk it shows. Hence, bashful cunning!
And prompt me, plain and holy innocence!
I am your wife, if you will marry me;
If not, I'll die your maid: to be your fellow
You may deny me; but I'll be your servant,
Whether you will or no. 86

FER. My mistress, dearest;
And I thus humble ever.

MIR. My husband, then?

FER. Ay, with a heart as willing
As bondage e'er of freedom: here's my hand.

MIR. And mine, with my heart in 't: and now farewell 90
Till half an hour hence.

FER. A thousand thousand!
[*Exeunt* FER. *and* MIR. *severally*.

PROS. So glad of this as they I cannot be,
Who are surprised withal; but my rejoicing
At nothing can be more. I'll to my book,
For yet ere supper-time must I perform 95
Much business appertaining. [*Exit*.

SCENE II. *Another part of the island.*

[*Enter* CALIBAN, STEPHANO, *and* TRINCULO.]

STE. Tell not me; when the butt is out, we will drink water; not a drop before: therefore bear up, and board 'em. Servant-monster, drink to me.

TRIN. Servant-monster! the folly of this island! They say there's but five upon this isle: we are three of them; if th' other two be brained like us, the state totters.

STE. Drink, servant-monster, when I bid thee: thy eyes are almost set in thy head. 10

TRIN. Where should they be set else? he were a brave monster indeed, if they were set in his tail.

STE. My man-monster hath drown'd his tongue in sack: for my part, the sea cannot drown me; I swam, ere I could recover the shore, five and thirty leagues off and on. By this light, thou shalt be my lieutenant, monster, or my standard.

TRIN. Your lieutenant, if you list; he's no standard. 20

STE. We'll not run, Monsieur Monster.

TRIN. Nor go neither; but you'll lie like dogs and yet say nothing neither.

STE. Moon-calf, speak once in thy life, if thou beest a good moon-calf.

CAL. How does thy honour? Let me lick thy shoe.
I'll not serve him; he is not valiant. 27

TRIN. Thou liest, most ignorant monster: I am in case to justle a constable. Why, thou deboshed fish, thou, was there ever man a coward that hath drunk so much sack as I to-day? Wilt thou tell a monstrous lie, being but half a fish and half a monster?

59. condition, rank. 63. blow, deposit eggs on. 69. event, outcome. 70. hollowly, insincerely; invert, convert. 71. boded, destined (by Fate); mischief, ill fortune. 72. limit, bounds; what else, everything else, whatever it may be. 74. Fair, fortunate. 75. affections, dispositions. 79. want, be without. 84. maid, maid-servant; fellow, wife. 86. mistress, lady-love. 93. withal, at it. 96. appertaining, i.e., to the marriage. Scene ii: 1. Tell me not, don't talk to me (about drinking more slowly). 3. bear, sail. 5-6. the . . . island, what a place for fools this island must be! 10. set, fixed (in a drunken stare). 16. recover, reach. 19. standard, standard-bearer. 22. go, walk. 29. in case, in a condition; justle, wrestle with. 30. deboshed, debauched.

CAL. Lo, how he mocks me! wilt thou let him, my lord?

TRIN. "Lord" quoth he. That a monster should be such a natural! 37

CAL. Lo, lo, again! bite him to death, I prithee.

STE. Trinculo, keep a good tongue in your head: if you prove a mutineer,—the next tree! The poor monster's my subject and he shall not suffer indignity.

CAL. I thank my noble lord. Wilt thou be pleased to hearken once again to the suit I made to thee?

STE. Marry, will I: kneel and repeat it; I will stand, and so shall Trinculo.

[*Enter* ARIEL, *invisible.*]

CAL. As I told thee before, I am subject to a tyrant, a sorcerer, that by his cunning hath cheated me of the island. 50

ARI. Thou liest.

CAL. Thou liest, thou jesting monkey, thou: I would my valiant master would destroy thee! I do not lie. 54

STE. Trinculo, if you trouble him any more in 's tale, by this hand, I will supplant some of your teeth.

TRIN. Why, I said nothing.

STE. Mum, then, and no more. Proceed.

CAL. I say, by sorcery he got this isle; 60
From me he got it. If thy greatness will
Revenge it on him,—for I know thou darest,
But this thing dare not,—

STE. That's most certain.

CAL. Thou shalt be lord of it and I'll serve thee. 65

STE. How now shall this be compassed?
Canst thou bring me to the party?

CAL. Yea, yea, my lord: I'll yield him thee asleep,
Where thou mayst knock a nail into his head.

ARI. Thou liest; thou canst not. 70

CAL. What a pied ninny's this! Thou scurvy patch!
I do beseech thy greatness, give him blows
And take his bottle from him: when that's gone
He shall drink nought but brine; for I'll not show him
Where the quick freshes are. 75

STE. Trinculo, run into no further danger: interrupt the monster one word further, and, by this hand, I'll turn my mercy out o' doors and make a stock-fish of thee.

TRIN. Why, what did I? I did nothing. I'll go farther off. 81

STE. Didst thou not say he lied?

ARI. Thou liest.

STE. Do I so? take thou that. [*Beats* TRIN.]
As you like this, give me the lie another time.

TRIN. I did not give the lie. Out o' your wits and hearing too? A pox o' your bottle! this can sack and drinking do. A murrain on your monster, and the devil take your fingers!

CAL. Ha, ha, ha! 90

STE. Now, forward with your tale. Prithee, stand farther off.

CAL. Beat him enough: after a little time
I'll beat him too.

STE. Stand farther. Come, proceed.

CAL. Why, as I told thee, 'tis a custom with him, 95
I' th' afternoon to sleep: there thou mayst brain him,
Having first seized his books, or with a log
Batter his skull, or paunch him with a stake,
Or cut his wezand with thy knife. Remember
First to possess his books; for without them 100
He's but a sot, as I am, nor hath not
One spirit to command: they all do hate him
As rootedly as I. Burn but his books.
He has brave utensils,—for so he calls them,—
Which, when he has a house, he'll deck withal. 105
And that most deeply to consider is
The beauty of his daughter; he himself
Calls her a nonpareil: I never saw a woman,
But only Sycorax my dam and she;
But she as far surpasseth Sycorax 110
As great'st does least.

STE. Is it so brave a lass?

CAL. Ay, lord; she will become thy bed, I warrant.
And bring thee forth brave brood.

STE. Monster, I will kill this man: his

37. **natural,** idiot. 49. **tyrant,** usurper. 66. **compassed,** brought to pass. 71. **pied,** parti-colored, i.e., clad in a jester's motley; **patch,** fool. 75. **quick freshes,** springs of running fresh water. 79. **stock-fish,** cod, because it was beaten to make it soft enough for cooking. 88. **murrain,** a pestilence attacking cattle. 98. **paunch,** disembowel. 99. **wezand,** windpipe. 101. **sot,** simpleton. 104. **brave utensils,** fine ornaments. 108. **nonpareil,** paragon.

daughter and I will be king and queen,—save our graces!—and Trinculo and thyself shall be viceroys. Dost thou like the plot, Trinculo?

TRIN. Excellent.

STE. Give me thy hand: I am sorry I beat thee; but, while thou livest, keep a good tongue in thy head. 121

CAL. Within this half hour will he be asleep:
Wilt thou destroy him then?

STE. Ay, on mine honour.

ARI. This will I tell my master.

CAL. Thou makest me merry; I am full of pleasure:
Let us be jocund: will you troll the catch
You taught me but while-ere?

STE. At thy request, monster, I will do reason, any reason. Come on, Trinculo, let us sing. [*Sings.*]

Flout 'em and scout 'em 130
And scout 'em and flout 'em;
Thought is free.

CAL. That's not the tune.

[ARIEL *plays the tune on a tabor and pipe.*

STE. What is this same?

TRIN. This is the tune of our catch, played by the picture of Nobody. 136

STE. If thou beest a man, show thyself in thy likeness: if thou beest a devil, take 't as thou list.

TRIN. O, forgive me my sins!

STE. He that dies pays all debts: I defy thee.
Mercy upon us! 141

CAL. Art thou afeard?

STE. No, monster, not I.

CAL. Be not afeard; the isle is full of noises,
Sounds and sweet airs, that give delight and hurt not. 145
Sometimes a thousand twangling instruments
Will hum about mine ears, and sometime voices
That, if I then had waked after long sleep,
Will make me sleep again: and then, in dreaming,
The clouds methought would open and show riches 150
Ready to drop upon me, that, when I waked,
I cried to dream again.

STE. This will prove a brave kingdom to me, where I shall have my music for nothing.

CAL. When Prospero is destroyed. 155

STE. That shall be by and by: I remember the story.

TRIN. The sound is going away; let's follow it, and after do our work.

STE. Lead, monster; we'll follow. I would I could see this taborer; he lays it on. 160

TRIN. Wilt come? I'll follow, Stephano.

[*Exeunt.*

SCENE III. *Another part of the island.*

[*Enter* ALONSO, SEBASTIAN, ANTONIO, GONZALO, ADRIAN, FRANCISCO, *and others.*]

GON. By 'r lakin, I can go no further, sir;
My old bones ache: here's a maze trod indeed
Through forth-rights and meanders! By your patience,
I needs must rest me.

ALON. Old lord, I cannot blame thee,
Who am myself attach'd with weariness, 5
To the dulling of my spirits: sit down, and rest.
Even here I will put off my hope and keep it
No longer for my flatterer: he is drown'd
Whom thus we stray to find, and the sea mocks
Our frustrate search on land. Well, let him go. 10

ANT. [*Aside to* SEB.] I am right glad that he's so out of hope.
Do not, for one repulse, forego the purpose
That you resolved to effect.

SEB. [*Aside to* ANT.] The next advantage
Will we take throughly.

ANT. [*Aside to* SEB.] Let it be to-night;
For, now they are oppress'd with travel, they 5

126. **troll the catch**, sing the round (for three voices). 127. **but while-ere**, only a little while ago. 129. **any reason**, anything reasonable. 130. **Flout**, mock; **scout**, jeer at. 133. **tabor**, a small drum. 136. **picture of Nobody**, refers to a picture on the title page of a play **No-body and Some-body** (1606). The figure is all head, neck, arms, legs, and particularly nose, and so has no body. 140. **He . . . debts**, i.e., you cannot collect debts from a dead man. 144. **noises**, musical sounds. 146. **twangling**, loud. 151. **that**, so that. 153. **brave**, fine. 156. **by and by**, at once; **the story**, i.e., what you have said. **Scene iii:** 1. **By 'r lakin**, by our Lady, the Blessed Virgin. 3. **forth-rights and meanders**, straight paths and winding paths; **By . . . patience**, if you will be patient enough to allow me. 5. **attach'd**, seized. 6. **spirits**, vital spirits, vitality. 13. **advantage**, advantageous opportunity.

Will not, nor cannot, use such vigilance
As when they are fresh.

SEB. [*Aside to* ANT.] I say, to-night: no more. [*Solemn and strange music.*

ALON. What harmony is this? My good friends, hark!

GON. Marvellous sweet music!

[*Enter* PROSPERO *above, invisible. Enter several strange* SHAPES, *bringing in a banquet; they dance about it with gentle actions of salutation; and, inviting the* KING, &C. *to eat, they depart.*]

ALON. Give us kind keepers, heavens! What were these? 20

SEB. A living drollery. Now I will believe
That there are unicorns, that in Arabia
There is one tree, the phœnix' throne, one phœnix
At this hour reigning there.

ANT. I'll believe both;
And what does else want credit, come to me, 25
And I'll be sworn 'tis true: travellers ne'er did lie,
Though fools at home condemn 'em.

GON. If in Naples
I should report this now, would they believe me?
If I should say, I saw such islanders—
For, certes, these are people of the island— 30
Who, though they are of monstrous shape, yet, note,
Their manners are more gentle-kind than of
Our human generation you shall find
Many, nay, almost any.

PROS. [*Aside*] Honest lord,
Thou hast said well; for some of you there present 35
Are worse than devils.

ALON. I cannot too much muse
Such shapes, such gesture and such sound, expressing,
Although they want the use of tongue, a kind
Of excellent dumb discourse.

PROS [*Aside*] Praise in departing.

FRAN. They vanish'd strangely.

SEB. No matter, since 40
They have left their viands behind; for we have stomachs.
Will 't please you taste of what is here?

ALON. Not I.

GON. Faith, sir, you need not fear. When we were boys,
Who would believe that there were mountaineers
Dew-lapp'd like bulls, whose throats had hanging at 'em 45
Wallets of flesh? or that there were such men
Whose heads stood in their breasts? which now we find
Each putter-out of five for one will bring us
Good warrant of.

ALON. I will stand to and feed,
Although my last: no matter, since I feel 50
The best is past. Brother, my lord the duke,
Stand to and do as we.

[*Thunder and lightning. Enter* ARIEL, *like a harpy; claps his wings upon the table; and, with a quaint device, the banquet vanishes.*]

ARI. You are three men of sin, whom Destiny,
That hath to instrument this lower world
And what is in 't, the never-surfeited sea 55
Hath caused to belch up you; and on this island
Where man doth not inhabit; you 'mongst men
Being most unfit to live. I have made you mad;
And even with such-like valour men hang and drown
Their proper selves.

[ALON., SEB. &C. *draw their swords.*]

You fools! I and my fellows 60
Are ministers of Fate: the elements,
Of whom your swords are temper'd, may as well
Wound the loud winds, or with bemock'd-at stabs
Kill the still-closing waters, as diminish
One dowle that's in my plume: my fellow-ministers 65

s.d. **banquet**, light refreshments, usually sweets, fruit and wine. 20. **keepers**, guardian angels. 21. **drollery**, puppet show. 25. **does . . . credit**, is incredible. 34. **Honest**, honorable. 36. **muse**, wonder at. 37. **gesture**, demeanor. 39. **Praise in departing**, the proverb was "Praise at the parting." 41. **stomachs**, appetites. 45. **Dew-lapp'd**, i.e., having a fold of skin or goiter under the neck. 48. **Each . . . one**, each traveler who insures his safe return home at a premium of 1 to 5 or 20 per cent. 49. **stand to**, take the risk. 51. **best**, i.e., the best part of life. s.d. **harpy**, foul creature, half bird, half woman; **quaint device**, ingenious stage machine. 54. **to instrument**, as its instrument. 59. **such-like valour**, i.e., the courage of madness. 60. **proper**, own. 65. **dowle**, a tiny downy feather.

Are like invulnerable. If you could hurt,
Your swords are now too massy for your strengths
And will not be uplifted. But remember—
For that's my business to you—that you three
From Milan did supplant good Prospero; 70
Exposed unto the sea, which hath requit it,
Him and his innocent child: for which foul deed
The powers, delaying, not forgetting, have
Incensed the seas and shores, yea, all the creatures,
Against your peace. Thee of thy son, Alonso, 75
They have bereft; and do pronounce by me
Lingering perdition, worse than any death
Can be at once, shall step by step attend
You and your ways; whose wraths to guard you from—
Which here, in this most desolate isle, else falls 80
Upon your heads—is nothing but heart-sorrow
And a clear life ensuing.

[*He vanishes in thunder; then, to soft music, enter the* SHAPES *again, and dance, with mocks and mows, and carrying out the table.*]

PROS. Bravely the figure of this harpy hast thou
Perform'd, my Ariel; a grace it had, devouring:
Of my instruction hast thou nothing bated 85
In what thou hadst to say: so, with good life
And observation strange, my meaner ministers
Their several kinds have done. My high charms work
And these mine enemies are all knit up
In their distractions; they now are in my power; 90
And in these fits I leave them, while I visit
Young Ferdinand, whom they suppose is drown'd,
And his and mine loved darling. [*Exit above.*

GON. I' the name of something holy, sir, why stand you
In this strange stare?

ALON. O, it is monstrous, monstrous! 95
Methought the billows spoke and told me of it;
The winds did sing it to me, and the thunder,
That deep and dreadful organ-pipe, pronounced
The name of Prosper: it did bass my trespass.
Therefore my son i' the ooze is bedded, and 100
I'll seek him deeper than e'er plummet sounded
And with him there lie mudded. [*Exit.*

SEB. But one fiend at a time,
I'll fight their legions o'er.

ANT. I'll be thy second.
[*Exeunt* SEB. *and* ANT.

GON. All three of them are desperate: their great guilt,
Like poison given to work a great time after,
Now 'gins to bite the spirits. I do beseech you 106
That are of suppler joints, follow them swiftly
And hinder them from what this ecstasy
May now provoke them to.

ADR. Follow, I pray you. [*Exeunt.*

ACT IV

SCENE I. *Before* PROSPERO'S *cell.*

[*Enter* PROSPERO, FERDINAND, *and* MIRANDA.]

PROS. If I have too austerely punish'd you,
Your compensation makes amends, for I
Have given you here a third of mine own life,
Or that for which I live; who once again
I tender to thy hand: all thy vexations 5
Were but my trials of thy love, and thou

66. **like,** likewise. 67. **massy,** heavy. 71. **requit,** requited it (i.e., the crime). 74. **Incensed,** aroused; **all the creatures,** all creation. 77. **perdition,** destruction. 82. **clear,** guiltless. s.d. **mocks and mows,** mocking gestures and grimaces. 84. **devouring,** i.e., even while you were devouring the banquet. 85. **bated,** left undone. 86. **with good life,** in a lifelike manner. 87. **observation strange,** careful attention (to my commands); **meaner ministers,** inferior [to Ariel] agents. 88. **several kinds,** particular tasks. 90. **In . . . distractions,** each in his special form of madness. 99. **did . . . trespass,** publish my trespass in a bass voice. 103. **o'er,** one after another. 108. **ecstasy,** frenzy.
Act IV, Scene i: 3. **third,** Miranda; the other thirds are himself and his kingdom. Kittredge suggests Miranda = Prospero's future; the other thirds are then his past and his present. 4. **Or,** in other words.

Hast strangely stood the test: here, afore Heaven,
I ratify this my rich gift. O Ferdinand,
Do not smile at me that I boast her off,
For thou shalt find she will outstrip all praise 10
And make it halt behind her.

FER. I do believe it
Against an oracle.

PROS. Then, as my gift and thine own acquisition
Worthily purchased, take my daughter: but
If thou dost break her virgin-knot before 15
All sanctimonious ceremonies may
With full and holy rite be minister'd,
No sweet aspersion shall the heavens let fall
To make this contract grow; but barren hate,
Sour-eyed disdain and discord shall bestrew 20
The union of your bed with weeds so loathly
That you shall hate it both: therefore take heed,
As Hymen's lamps shall light you.

FER. As I hope
For quiet days, fair issue and long life,
With such love as 'tis now, the murkiest den,
The most oppórtune place, the strong'st suggestion 26
Our worser genius can, shall never melt
Mine honour into lust, to take away
The edge of that day's celebration
When I shall think, or Phœbus' steeds are founder'd, 30
Or Night kept chain'd below.

PROS. Fairly spoke.
Sit then and talk with her; she is thine own.
What, Ariel! my industrious servant, Ariel!

[*Enter* ARIEL.]

ARI. What would my potent master? here I am.

PROS. Thou and thy meaner fellows your last service 35
Did worthily perform; and I must use you
In such another trick. Go bring the rabble,
O'er whom I give thee power, here to this place:
Incite them to quick motion; for I must
Bestow upon the eyes of this young couple 40
Some vanity of mine art: it is my promise,
And they expect it from me.

ARI. Presently?

PROS. Ay, with a twink.

ARI. Before you can say "come" and "go,"
And breathe twice and cry "so, so," 45
Each one, tripping on his toe,
Will be here with mop and mow.
Do you love me, master? no?

PROS. Dearly, my delicate Ariel. Do not approach
Till thou dost hear me call.

ARI. Well, I conceive. [*Exit.* 50

PROS. Look thou be true; do not give dalliance
Too much the rein: the strongest oaths are straw
To the fire i' the blood: be more abstemious,
Or else, good night your vow!

FER. I warrant you, sir;
The white cold virgin snow upon my heart 55
Abates the ardour of my liver.

PROS. Well.
Now come, my Ariel! bring a corollary,
Rather than want a spirit: appear, and pertly!
No tongue! all eyes! be silent. [*Soft music.*

[*Enter* IRIS.]

IRIS. Ceres, most bounteous lady, thy rich leas 60
Of wheat, rye, barley, vetches, oats and pease;
Thy turfy mountains, where live nibbling sheep,
And flat meads thatch'd with stover, them to keep;
Thy banks with pionèd and twillèd brims,
Which spongy April at thy hest betrims, 65
To make cold nymphs chaste crowns; and thy broom-groves,
Whose shadow the dismissed bachelor loves,

7. **strangely**, unusually well. 9. **boast her off**, exhibit her virtues by boasting. 11. **halt**, limp. 12. **Against an oracle**, i.e., even though an oracle should declare the opposite to be true. 14. **purchased**, won. 16. **sanctimonious**, sacred. 18. **aspersion**, sprinkling (of dew as holy water). 23. **Hymen's**, Hymen was the Greek and Roman god of marriage; **light you**, i.e., that the marriage torch not burn smokily, for that was a bad omen. 26. **suggestion**, temptation. 27. **worser genius**, evil attendant spirit. 28. **to**, so as to. 30. **or**, either. 37. **rabble**, i.e., the lesser spirits. 41. **vanity**, slight example; **art**, magic. 42. **Presently**, immediately. 43. **twink**, twinkle (of an eye). 47. **mop and mow**, grin and grimace. 50. **conceive**, understand (what you want). 51. **dalliance**, fondling. 56. **liver**, the supposed seat of the passions. 57. **corollary**, surplus (of spirits). 58. **pertly**, quickly. 60. **leas**, fields. 61. **vetches**, grass for fodder. 63. **stover**, another sort of fodder grass. 64. **pioned . . . brims**, furrowed and ridged edges. 65. **hest**, command. 66. **cold**, passionless; **broom-groves**, thickets of broom. 67. **dismissed**, rejected.

Being lass-lorn; thy pole-clipt vineyard;
And thy sea-marge, sterile and rocky-hard,
Where thou thyself dost air;—the queen o' the sky, 70
Whose watery arch and messenger am I,
Bids thee leave these, and with her sovereign grace,
Here on this grass-plot, in this very place,
To come and sport: her peacocks fly amain:
Approach, rich Ceres, her to entertain. 75

[*Enter* CERES.]

CER. Hail, many-colour'd messenger, that ne'er
Dost disobey the wife of Jupiter;
Who with thy saffron wings upon my flowers
Diffusest honey-drops, refreshing showers,
And with each end of thy blue bow dost crown 80
My bosky acres and my unshrubb'd down,
Rich scarf to my proud earth; why hath thy queen
Summon'd me hither, to this short-grass'd green?

IRIS. A contract of true love to celebrate;
And some donation freely to estate 85
On the blest lovers.

CER. Tell me, heavenly bow,
If Venus or her son, as thou dost know,
Do now attend the queen? Since they did plot
The means that dusky Dis my daughter got,
Her and her blind boy's scandal'd company 90
I have forsworn.

IRIS. Of her society
Be not afraid: I met her deity
Cutting the clouds towards Paphos and her son
Dove-drawn with her. Here thought they to have done
Some wanton charm upon this man and maid, 95
Whose vows are, that no bed-right shall be paid
Till Hymen's torch be lighted: but in vain;
Mars's hot minion is return'd again;
Her waspish-headed son has broke his arrows,
Swears he will shoot no more but play with sparrows 100
And be a boy right out.

CER. High'st queen of state,
Great Juno, comes; I know her by her gait.

[*Enter* JUNO.]

JUNO. How does my bounteous sister? Go with me
To bless this twain, that they may prosperous be
And honour'd in their issue. [*They sing:*

JUNO. Honour, riches, marriage-blessing,
Long continuance, and increasing,
Hourly joys be still upon you!
Juno sings her blessings on you.

CER. Earth's increase, foison plenty, 110
Barns and garners never empty,
Vines with clustering bunches growing,
Plants with goodly burthen bowing;

Spring come to you at the farthest
In the very end of harvest! 115
Scarcity and want shall shun you;
Ceres' blessing so is on you.

FER. This is a most majestic vision, and
Harmonious charmingly. May I be bold
To think these spirits?

PROS. Spirits, which by mine art 120
I have from their confines call'd to enact
My present fancies.

FER. Let me live here ever;
So rare a wonder'd father and a wife
Makes this place Paradise.

[JUNO *and* CERES *whisper, and send* IRIS *on employment.*

PROS. Sweet, now, silence!
Juno and Ceres whisper seriously; 125
There's something else to do: hush, and be mute,
Or else our spell is marr'd.

IRIS. You nymphs, call'd Naiads, of the windring brooks,
With your sedged crowns and ever-harmless looks,

68. **pole-clipt**, with vines clinging to poles. 70. **air**, take the air. 71. **watery arch**, rainbow. 72. **these** i.e., the places just enumerated. 74. **amain**, swiftly. 81. **bosky**, covered with shrubs and bushes; **down**, open upland. 85. **donation**, i..e, that expressed in the song of blessing; **estate**, bestow. 89. **means**, scheme by which; **Dis**, Pluto, who carried Proserpine, Ceres' daughter, off to make her Queen of the Lower World. 90. **scandal'd**, scandalous. 93. **Paphos**, a town in Cyprus, sacred to Venus. 98. **hot minion**, lustful darling (Venus). 99. **waspish-headed**, irritable. 101. **right out**, outright; **state**, majesty. 108. **still**, always. 110. **foison plenty**, plentiful harvest. 129. **sedged crowns**, garlands of sedge (sweet-flag).

Leave your crisp channels and on this green
land 130
Answer your summons; Juno does command:
Come, temperate nymphs, and help to celebrate
A contract of true love; be not too late.

[*Enter certain* NYMPHS.]

You sunburnt sicklemen, of August weary,
Come hither from the furrow and be merry:
Make holiday; your rye-straw hats put on 136
And these fresh nymphs encounter every one
In country footing.

[*Enter certain* REAPERS, *properly habited: they join with the* NYMPHS *in a graceful dance; towards the end whereof* PROSPERO *starts suddenly, and speaks; after which, to a strange, hollow, and confused noise, they heavily vanish.*]

PROS. [*Aside*] I had forgot that foul conspiracy
Of the beast Caliban and his confederates 140
Against my life: the minute of their plot
Is almost come. [*To the* SPIRITS] Well done! avoid; no more!

FER. This is strange: your father's in some passion
That works him strongly.

MIR. Never till this day
Saw I him touch'd with anger so distemper'd. 145

PROS. You do look, my son, in a movèd sort,
As if you were dismay'd: be cheerful, sir.
Our revels now are ended. These our actors,
As I foretold you, were all spirits and
Are melted into air, into thin air: 150
And, like the baseless fabric of this vision,
The cloud-capp'd towers, the gorgeous palaces,
The solemn temples, the great globe itself,
Yea, all which it inherit, shall dissolve
And, like this insubstantial pageant faded, 155
Leave not a rack behind. We are such stuff
As dreams are made on, and our little life
Is rounded with a sleep. Sir, I am vex'd;
Bear with my weakness; my old brain is troubled:
Be not disturb'd with my infirmity: 160
If you be pleased, retire into my cell
And there repose: a turn or two I'll walk,
To still my beating mind.

FER. MIR. We wish your peace. [*Exeunt.*

PROS. Come with a thought. I thank thee, Ariel: come.

[*Enter* ARIEL.]

ARI. Thy thoughts I cleave to. What's thy pleasure?

PROS. Spirit, 165
We must prepare to meet with Caliban.

ARI. Aye, my commander: when I presented Ceres,
I thought to have told thee of it, but I fear'd
Lest I might anger thee.

PROS. Say again, where didst thou leave these varlets? 170

ARI. I told you, sir, they were red-hot with drinking;
So full of valour that they smote the air
For breathing in their faces; beat the ground
For kissing of their feet; yet always bending
Towards their project. Then I beat my tabor; 175
At which, like unback'd colts, they prick'd their ears,
Advanced their eyelids, lifted up their noses
As they smelt music: so I charm'd their ears
That calf-like they my lowing follow'd through
Tooth'd briers, sharp furzes, pricking goss and thorns, 180
Which enter'd their frail shins: at last I left them
I' the filthy-mantled pool beyond your cell,
There dancing up to the chins, that the foul lake
O'erstunk their feet.

PROS. This was well done, my bird.
Thy shape invisible retain thou still: 185
The trumpery in my house, go bring it hither,
For stale to catch these thieves.

130. **crisp**, curled, rippling. 132. **temperate**, chaste. 137. **fresh**, young and pretty; **encounter**, join (as partners). 138. **footing**, dances. s.d. **heavily vanish**, vanish slowly and reluctantly. 142. **avoid**, begone. 145. **distemper'd**, violent. 151. **baseless fabric**, structure lacking a foundation. 156. **rack**, vestige. 158. **rounded**, surrounded. 163. **beating**, excited. 164. **with a thought**, on the instant.

165. **thy . . . to**, I am at hand whenever you think of me. 167. **presented**, acted the part of. 170. **varlets**, scoundrels. 174. **bending**, directing their course. 175. **project**, i.e., the murder of Prospero. 176. **unback'd**, unbroken. 177. **Advanced**, lifted. 180. **goss**, gorse (spiny evergreen shrub). 182. **filthy-mantled**, covered with scum. 186. **trumpery**, showy stuff. 187. **stale**, decoy.

ARI. I go, I go. [*Exit.*

PROS. A devil, a born devil, on whose nature
Nurture can never stick; on whom my pains,
Humanely taken, all, all lost, quite lost; 190
And as with age his body uglier grows,
So his mind cankers. I will plague them all,
Even to roaring.

[*Re-enter* ARIEL, *loaden with glistering apparel, &c.*]

Come, hang them on this line.

[PROSPERO *and* ARIEL *remain, invisible. Enter* CALIBAN, STEPHANO, *and* TRINCULO, *all wet.*]

CAL. Pray you, tread softly, that the blind mole may not
Hear a foot fall: we now are near his cell.

STE. Monster, your fairy, which you say is a harmless fairy, has done little better than played the Jack with us.

TRIN. Monster, I do smell all horse-piss; at which my nose is in great indignation. 200

STE. So is mine. Do you hear, monster? If I should take a displeasure against you, look you,–

TRIN. Thou wert but a lost monster.

CAL. Good my lord, give me thy favour still.
Be patient, for the prize I'll bring thee to 205
Shall hoodwink this mischance: therefore speak softly.
All's hush'd as midnight yet.

TRIN. Ay, but to lose our bottles in the pool,–

STE. There is not only disgrace and dishonour in that, monster, but an infinite loss. 210

TRIN. That's more to me than my wetting: yet this is your harmless fairy, monster.

STE. I will fetch off my bottle, though I be o'er ears for my labour.

CAL. Prithee, my king, be quiet. See'st thou here, 215
This is the mouth o' the cell: no noise, and enter.
Do that good mischief which may make this island
Thine own for ever, and I, thy Caliban,
For aye thy foot-licker.

STE. Give me thy hand. I do begin to have bloody thoughts. 220

TRIN. O king Stephano! O peer! O worthy Stephano! look what a wardrobe here is for thee!

CAL. Let it alone, thou fool; it is but trash.

TRIN. O, ho, monster! we know what belongs to a frippery. O king Stephano! 226

STE. Put off that gown, Trinculo; by this hand, I'll have that gown.

TRIN. Thy grace shall have it.

CAL. The dropsy drown this fool! what do you mean 230
To dote thus on such luggage? Let's alone
And do the murder first: if he awake,
From toe to crown he'll fill our skins with pinches,
Make us strange stuff. 234

STE. Be you quiet, monster. Mistress line, is not this my jerkin? Now is the jerkin under the line: now, jerkin, you are like to lose your hair and prove a bald jerkin.

TRIN. Do, do: we steal by line and level, an't like your grace. 240

STE. I thank thee for that jest; here's a garment for 't: wit shall not go unrewarded while I am king of this country. "Steal by line and level" is an excellent pass of pate; there's another garment for 't. 245

TRIN. Monster, come, put some lime upon your fingers, and away with the rest.

CAL. I will have none on 't: we shall lose our time,
And all be turn'd to barnacles, or to apes
With foreheads villanous low. 250

STE. Monster, lay to your fingers: help to bear this away where my hogshead of wine is, or I'll turn you out of my kingdom: go to, carry this.

TRIN. And this.

STE. Ay, and this. 255

189. **Nurture**, education. 192. **cankers**, corrodes. s.d. **glistering**, glittering. 193. **line**, linden tree. 198. **Jack**, knave. 206. **hoodwink**, blind yourself to. 213. **fetch off**, rescue. 217. **good**, profitable (to us). 221. **O . . . peer**, Trinculo refers to an old ballad the first lines of which were,

King Stephen was a worthy peer,
His breches cost him but a crown.

226. **frippery**, a second-hand clothing shop. 229. **Thy grace**, your Majesty. 231. **Let's alone**, let it alone. 234. **Make . . . stuff**, transform us into some strange substance. 236. **jerkin**, short jacket. 237. **under the line**, a pun on line = (1) linden, (2) equator. 238. **lose your hair**, i.e., as a result of a tropical fever. 239. **Do, do**, keep on, you are doing fine; **line**, plumb line; **level**, carpenter's level. 240. **an't . . . grace**, if your majesty approve (the pun). 244. **pass of pate**, sally of wit. 246. **lime**, bird-lime. 249. **barnacles**, geese, that were strangely thought to develop from barnacles.

[*A noise of hunters heard. Enter divers* SPIRITS, *in shape of dogs and hounds and hunt them about,* PROSPERO *and* ARIEL *setting them on.*]

PROS. Hey, Mountain, hey!

ARI. Silver! there it goes, Silver!

PROS. Fury, Fury! there, Tyrant, there! hark! hark!

[CAL., STE., *and* TRIN. *are driven out.*

Go charge my goblins that they grind their joints
With dry convulsions, shorten up their sinews 260
With agèd cramps, and more pinch-spotted make them
Than pard or cat o' mountain.

ARI. Hark, they roar!

PROS. Let them be hunted soundly. At this hour
Lie at my mercy all mine enemies:
Shortly shall all my labours end, and thou 265
Shalt have the air at freedom: for a little
Follow, and do me service. [*Exeunt.*

ACT V

SCENE I. *Before* PROSPERO'S *cell.*

[*Enter* PROSPERO *in his magic robes, and* ARIEL.]

PROS. Now does my project gather to a head:
My charms crack not; my spirits obey; and time
Goes upright with his carriage. How's the day?

ARI. On the sixth hour; at which time, my lord,
You said our work should cease.

PROS. I did say so, 5
When first I raised the tempest. Say, my spirit,
How fares the king and 's followers?

ARI. Confined together
In the same fashion as you gave in charge,
Just as you left them; all prisoners, sir,
In the line-grove which weather-fends your cell; 10
They cannot budge till your release. The king,
His brother and yours, abide all three distracted
And the remainder mourning over them,
Brimful of sorrow and dismay; but chiefly
Him that you term'd, sir, "The good old lord, Gonzalo;" 15
His tears run down his beard, like winter's drops
From eaves of reeds. Your charm so strongly works 'em
That if you now beheld them, your affections
Would become tender.

PROS. Dost thou think so, spirit?

ARI. Mine would, sir, were I human.

PROS. And mine shall. 20
Hast thou, which art but air, a touch, a feeling
Of their afflictions, and shall not myself
One of their kind, that relish all as sharply,
Passion as they, be kindlier moved than thou art?
Though with their high wrongs I am struck to the quick, 25
Yet with my nobler reason 'gainst my fury
Do I take part: the rarer action is
In virtue than in vengeance: they being penitent,
The sole drift of my purpose doth extend
Not a frown further. Go release them, Ariel:
My charms I'll break, their senses I'll restore, 31
And they shall be themselves.

ARI. I'll fetch them, sir. [*Exit.*

PROS. Ye elves of hills, brooks, standing lakes and groves,
And ye that on the sands with printless foot
Do chase the ebbing Neptune and do fly him
When he comes back; you demi-puppets that 36

258. hark, equivalent to "sick 'em." 260. **dry convulsions,** cramps which come when the joints seem to be dry from age. 262. pard, leopard; **cat o' mountain,** catamount or mountain lion. **Act V, Scene i: 2. crack not,** show no flaw. 3. **Goes upright,** i.e., does not stoop, his burden is so light; **carriage,** burden. 10. **line,** linden; **weather-fends,** protects from wind and rain. 17. **reeds,** thatched roofs. 18. **affections,** feelings. 23. **relish all,** feel quite. 24. **Passion,** suffer. 26. **nobler,** i.e., than fury. 27-8. **the . . . vengeance,** it is a finer action to be controlled by reason than to take vengeance. 29. **drift,** intention. 33. **standing,** tideless. 34. **printless,** leaving no foot-print. 35. **ebbing Neptune,** the out-going tide. 36. **demi-puppets,** half as big as figures of a puppet show.

By moonshine do the green sour ringlets make,
Whereof the ewe not bites, and you whose pastime
Is to make midnight mushrooms, that rejoice
To hear the solemn curfew; by whose aid,
Weak masters though ye be, I have be-dimm'd 41
The noontide sun, call'd forth the mutinous winds,
And 'twixt the green sea and the azured vault
Set roaring war: to the dread rattling thunder
Have I given fire and rifted Jove's stout oak
With his own bolt; the strong-based promontory 46
Have I made shake and by the spurs pluck'd up
The pine and cedar: graves at my command
Have waked their sleepers, oped, and let 'em forth
By my so potent art. But this rough magic
I here abjure, and, when I have required 51
Some heavenly music, which even now I do,
To work mine end upon their senses that
This airy charm is for, I'll break my staff,
Bury it certain fathoms in the earth, 55
And deeper than did ever plummet sound
I'll drown my book. [*Solemn music.*]

[*Re-enter* ARIEL *before: then* ALONSO, *with a frantic gesture, attended by* GONZALO; SEBASTIAN *and* ANTONIO *in like manner, attended by* ADRIAN *and* FRANCISCO: *they all enter the circle which* PROSPERO *had made, and there stand charmed; which* PROSPERO *observing, speaks:*]

A solemn air and the best comforter
To an unsettled fancy cure thy brains,
Now useless, boil'd within thy skull! There stand, 60
For you are spell-stopp'd.
Holy Gonzalo, honourable man,
Mine eyes, even sociable to the show of thine,
Fall fellowly drops. The charm dissolves apace,
And as the morning steals upon the night, 65
Melting the darkness, so their rising senses
Begin to chase the ignorant fumes that mantle
Their clearer reason. O good Gonzalo,
My true preserver, and a loyal sir
To him thou follow'st! I will pay thy graces 70
Home both in word and deed. Most cruelly
Didst thou, Alonso, use me and my daughter:
Thy brother was a furtherer in the act.
Thou art pinch'd for 't now, Sebastian. Flesh and blood,
You, brother mine, that entertain'd ambition, 75
Expell'd remorse and nature; who, with Sebastian,
Whose inward pinches therefore are most strong,
Would here have kill'd your king; I do forgive thee,
Unnatural though thou art. Their understanding
Begins to swell, and the approaching tide 80
Will shortly fill the reasonable shore
That now lies foul and muddy. Not one of them
That yet looks on me, or would know me: Ariel,
Fetch me the hat and rapier in my cell:
I will discase me, and myself present 85
As I was sometime Milan: quickly, spirit;
Thou shalt ere long be free.

[ARIEL *sings and helps to attire him.*]

Where the bee sucks, there suck I:
In a cowslip's bell I lie;
There I couch when owls do cry. 90
On the bat's back I do fly
After summer merrily.
Merrily, merrily shall I live now
Under the blossom that hangs on the bough.

PROS. Why, that's my dainty Ariel! I shall miss thee; 95
But yet thou shalt have freedom: so, so, so.

37. **green . . . ringlets,** circles of dark green grass, supposed to be made by fairies dancing in a ring. 39. **midnight,** produced by fairy art at midnight. 40. **curfew,** because after it has sounded at 9 p.m. fairy creatures may wander where they wish. 42. **mutinous,** turbulent. 43. **azured vault,** the blue sky. 45. **given fire,** set off. 47. **spurs,** roots. 53. **that,** whom. 54. **staff,** magic wand. 57. **book,** i.e., one containing magic formulas for controlling spirits. **s.d. gestures,** mien. 61. **spell-stopp'd,** rendered motionless by the spell. 63. **sociable,** sympathetic; **show,** appearance. 64. **Fall . . . drops,** shed sympathetic tears. 67. **ignorant fumes,** fumes which rose and covered the brain, thus causing unconsciousness. 69. **sir,** gentleman. 70-1. **pay . . . Home,** fully repay your favors. 75. **entertain'd,** welcomed. 81. **reasonable shore,** shore of reason. 85. **discase me,** remove my magician's robe. 86. **sometime Milan,** formerly Duke of Milan. 95. **that's . . . Ariel,** referring to Ariel's deftness in helping him to change his clothes.

To the king's ship, invisible as thou art:
There shalt thou find the mariners asleep
Under the hatches; the master and the boatswain
Being awake, enforce them to this place, 100
And presently, I prithee.

ARI. I drink the air before me, and return
Or ere your pulse twice beat. [*Exit.*

GON. All torment, trouble, wonder and amazement
Inhabits here: some heavenly power guide us
Out of this fearful country!

PROS. Behold, sir king, 106
The wrongèd Duke of Milan, Prospero:
For more assurance that a living prince
Does now speak to thee, I embrace thy body;
And to thee and thy company I bid 110
A hearty welcome.

ALON. Whether thou be'st he or no,
Or some enchanted trifle to abuse me,
As late I have been, I not know: thy pulse
Beats as of flesh and blood; and, since I saw thee,
The affliction of my mind amends, with which, 115
I fear, a madness held me: this must crave,
An if this be at all, a most strange story.
Thy dukedom I resign and do entreat
Thou pardon me my wrongs. But how should Prospero
Be living and be here?

PROS. First, noble friend, 120
Let me embrace thine age, whose honour cannot
Be measured or confined.

GON. Whether this be
Or be not, I'll not swear.

PROS. You do yet taste
Some subtilties o' the isle, that will not let you
Believe things certain. Welcome, my friends all! 125
[*Aside to* SEB. *and* ANT.] But you, my brace of lords, were I so minded,
I here could pluck his highness' frown upon you
And justify you traitors: at this time
I will tell no tales.

SEB. [*Aside*] The devil speaks in him.

PROS. No.
For you, most wicked sir, whom to call brother 130
Would even infect my mouth, I do forgive
Thy rankest fault; all of them; and require
My dukedom of thee, which perforce, I know,
Thou must restore.

ALON. If thou be'st Prospero,
Give us particulars of thy preservation; 135
How thou hast met us here, who three hours since
Were wreck'd upon this shore; where I have lost—
How sharp the point of this remembrance is!—
My dear son Ferdinand.

PROS. I am woe for 't, sir.

ALON. Irreparable is the loss, and patience
Says it is past her cure.

PROS. I rather think 141
You have not sought her help, of whose soft grace
For the like loss I have her sovereign aid
And rest myself content.

ALON. You the like loss!

PROS. As great to me as late; and, supportable 145
To make the dear loss, have I means much weaker
Than you may call to comfort you, for I
Have lost my daughter.

ALON. A daughter?
O heavens, that they were living both in Naples,
The king and queen there! that they were, I wish 150
Myself were mudded in that oozy bed
Where my son lies. When did you lose your daughter?

PROS. In this last tempest. I perceive, these lords
At this encounter do so much admire
That they devour their reason and scarce think 155
Their eyes do offices of truth, their words

101. **presently,** at once. 112. **trifle,** apparition caused by enchantment; **abuse,** deceive. 119. **my wrongs,** wrongs I have done you. 121. **age,** i.e., aged body. 123. **taste,** are under the influence of. 124. **subtilties,** illusions. 125. **things certain,** the reality of things. 127. **pluck,** bring down. 128. **justify you,** prove you to be. 139. **woe,** sorry. 142. **soft grace,** comforting favor. 144. **rest,** remain. 145. **as late,** and as recently happened. 146. **dear,** deeply felt. 150. **that,** provided that. 154. **admire,** wonder. 155. **devour,** swallow, destroy. 156. **do offices of truth,** perform their functions properly.

Are natural breath: but, howsoe'er you have
Been justled from your senses, know for certain
That I am Prospero and that very duke
Which was thrust forth of Milan, who most strangely 160
Upon this shore, where you were wreck'd, was landed,
To be the lord on 't. No more yet of this;
For 'tis a chronicle of day by day,
Not a relation for a breakfast nor
Befitting this first meeting. Welcome, sir;
This cell's my court: here have I few attendants 166
And subjects none abroad: pray you, look in.
My dukedom since you have given me again,
I will requite you with as good a thing;
At least bring forth a wonder, to content ye
As much as me my dukedom. 171

[*Here* PROSPERO *discovers* FERDINAND *and* MIRANDA, *playing at chess.*]

MIR. Sweet lord, you play me false.
FER. No, my dear'st love,
I would not for the world.
MIR. Yes, for a score of kingdoms you should wrangle,
And I would call it fair play.
ALON. If this prove 175
A vision of the island, one dear son
Shall I twice lose.
SEB. A most high miracle!
FER. Though the seas threaten, they are merciful;
I have cursed them without cause. [*Kneels.*
ALON. Now all the blessings
Of a glad father compass thee about! 180
Arise, and say how thou camest here.
MIR. O, wonder!
How many goodly creatures are there here!
How beauteous mankind is! O brave new world,
That has such people in 't!
PROS. 'Tis new to thee.
ALON. What is this maid with whom thou wast at play? 185
Your eld'st acquaintance cannot be three hours:
Is she the goddess that hath sever'd us,
And brought us thus together?
FER. Sir, she is mortal;
But by immortal Providence she's mine:
I chose her when I could not ask my father 190
For his advice, nor thought I had one. She
Is daughter to this famous Duke of Milan,
Of whom so often I have heard renown,
But never saw before; of whom I have
Received a second life; and second father 195
This lady makes him to me.
ALON. I am hers:
But, O, how oddly will it sound that I
Must ask my child forgiveness!
PROS. There, sir, stop:
Let us not burthen our remembrance with
A heaviness that's gone.
GON. I have inly wept 200
Or should have spoke ere this. Look down, you gods,
And on this couple drop a blessed crown!
For it is you that have chalk'd forth the way
Which brought us hither.
ALON. I say, Amen, Gonzalo!
GON. Was Milan thrust from Milan, that his issue 205
Should become kings of Naples? O, rejoice
Beyond a common joy, and set it down
With gold on lasting pillars: In one voyage
Did Claribel her husband find at Tunis
And Ferdinand, her brother, found a wife 210
Where he himself was lost, Prospero his dukedom
In a poor isle and all of us ourselves
When no man was his own.
ALON. [*To* FER. *and* MIR.] Give me your hands:
Let grief and sorrow still embrace his heart
That doth not wish you joy!
GON. Be it so! Amen! 215

[*Re-enter* ARIEL, *with the* MASTER *and* BOATSWAIN *amazedly following.*]

O, look, sir, look, sir! here is more of us:
I prophesied, if a gallows were on land,

157. howsoe'er, however much. 167. abroad, i.e., elsewhere on the island. 169. requite, pay back. 170. wonder, marvel; content, please. s.d. discovers, reveals (by drawing the curtain of the inner stage). 174. score, (1) wager, (2) twenty. 174-5. you . . . fair play, I should allow you to argue that you had played fair. 182. goodly, comely. 183. brave, splendid. 186. eld'st, longest possible. 196. hers, her father's, i.e., I accept her as a daughter. 200. heaviness, grief. 203. chalk'd forth, marked out. 213. When . . . own, when no man was in his right wits (because of the enchantment). s.d. amazedly, distractedly.

This fellow could not drown. Now, blasphemy,
That swear'st grace o'erboard, not an oath on shore?
Hast thou no mouth by land? What is the news? 220

BOATS. The best news is, that we have safely found
Our king and company; the next, our ship—
Which, but three glasses since, we gave out split—
Is tight and yare and bravely rigg'd as when
We first put out to sea.

ARI. [*Aside to* PROS.] Sir, all this service 225
Have I done since I went.

PROS. [*Aside to* ARI.] My tricksy spirit!

ALON. These are not natural events; they strengthen
From strange to stranger. Say, how came you hither?

BOATS. If I did think, sir, I were well awake,
I 'ld strive to tell you. We were dead of sleep, 230
And—how we know not—all clapp'd under hatches;
Where but even now with strange and several noises
Of roaring, shrieking, howling, jingling chains,
And moe diversity of sounds, all horrible,
We were awaked; straightway, at liberty; 235
Where we, in all her trim, freshly beheld
Our royal, good and gallant ship, our master
Capering to eye her: on a trice, so please you,
Even in a dream, were we divided from them
And were brought moping hither.

ARI. [*Aside to* PROS.] Was 't well done? 240

PROS. [*Aside to* ARI.] Bravely, my diligence. Thou shalt be free.

ALON. This is as strange a maze as e'er men trod;
And there is in this business more than nature
Was ever conduct of: some oracle
Must rectify our knowledge.

PROS. Sir, my liege, 245
Do not infest your mind with beating on
The strangeness of this business; at pick'd leisure
Which shall be shortly, single I'll resolve you,
Which to you shall seem probable, of every
These happen'd accidents; till when, be cheerful 250
And think of each thing well. [*Aside to* ARI.] Come hither, spirit:
Set Caliban and his companions free;
Untie the spell. [*Exit* ARIEL.] How fares my gracious sir?
There are yet missing of your company
Some few odd lads that you remember not. 255

[*Re-enter* ARIEL, *driving in* CALIBAN, STEPHANO *and* TRINCULO, *in their stolen apparel.*]

STE. Every man shift for all the rest, and let no man take care for himself; for all is but fortune. Coragio, bully-monster, coragio!

TRIN. If these be true spies which I wear in my head, here's a goodly sight. 260

CAL. O Setebos, these be brave spirits indeed!
How fine my master is! I am afraid
He will chastise me.

SEB. Ha, ha!
What things are these, my lord Antonio?
Will money buy 'em?

ANT. Very like; one of them 265
Is a plain fish, and, no doubt, marketable.

PROS. Mark but the badges of these men, my lords,
Then say if they be true. This mis-shapen knave,
His mother was a witch, and one so strong
That could control the moon, make flows and ebbs, 270
And deal in her command without her power.
These three have robb'd me; and this demi-devil—

218. blasphemy, blasphemous fellow. **219. swear'st . . . o'erboard,** drives God's protection away from the ship by swearing. **221. safely,** safe and sound. **223. glasses,** hours. **224. yare,** ready, seaworthy. **226. tricksy,** roguish. **230. of sleep,** asleep. **232. several,** particular. **234. moe,** more. **235. at liberty,** released from our confinement (under the hatches). **236. trim,** rigging; **freshly,** as good as new. **237. master,** captain. **238. capering,** i.e., dancing for joy; **on a trice,** in an instant. **240. moping,** bewildered. **241. Bravely,** splendidly; **diligence,** diligent fellow. **242. maze,** confusion. **244. conduct,** guide; **oracle,** i.e., message from Heaven. **245. rectify,** proclaim correct. **246. infest,** harass; **beating on,** dwelling upon. **247. pick'd,** chosen. **248. single,** i.e., when I am alone with you; **resolve you,** clear up your doubts. **249. Which,** i.e., my explanation; **probable,** reasonable. **249-50. every . . . accidents,** all the events that have happened. **253. gracious sir,** Alonzo. **258. bully,** fine. **262. fine,** splendidly dressed. **267. badges,** emblems worn on the arms of retainers to show to what family they belonged. The stolen garments are the badges of these men. **268. true,** honest. **271. deal . . . power,** act in the area of her (the moon's) authority with power greater than hers.

For he's a bastard one—had plotted with them 273
To take my life. Two of these fellows you
Must know and own; this thing of darkness I
Acknowledge mine.

CAL. I shall be pinch'd to death.

ALON. Is not this Stephano, my drunken butler?

SEB. He is drunk now: where had he wine?

ALON. And Trinculo is reeling ripe: where should they 279
Find this grand liquor that hath gilded 'em?
How camest thou in this pickle?

TRIN. I have been in such a pickle since I saw you last that, I fear me, will never out of my bones: I shall not fear fly-blowing.

SEB. Why, how now, Stephano! 285

STE. O, touch me not; I am not Stephano, but a cramp.

PROS. You'll be king o' the isle, sirrah?

STE. I should have been a sore one then.

ALON. This is a strange thing as e'er I look'd on. [*Pointing to* CALIBAN.

PROS. He is as disproportion'd in his manners 290
As in his shape. Go, sirrah, to my cell;
Take with you your companions; as you look
To have my pardon, trim it handsomely.

CAL. Ay, that I will; and I'll be wise hereafter
And seek for grace. What a thrice-double ass 295
Was I, to take this drunkard for a god
And worship this dull fool!

PROS. Go to; away!

ALON. Hence, and bestow your luggage where you found it.

SEB. Or stole it, rather.

[*Exeunt* CAL., STE., *and* TRIN.

PROS. Sir, I invite your highness and your train 300
To my poor cell, where you shall take your rest
For this one night; which, part of it, I'll waste
With such discourse as, I not doubt, shall make it
Go quick away; the story of my life
And the particular accidents gone by 305
Since I came to this isle: and in the morn
I'll bring you to your ship and so to Naples,
Where I have hope to see the nuptial
Of these our dear-belovèd solémnizèd;
And thence retire me to my Milan, where 310
Every third thought shall be my grave.

ALON. I long
To hear the story of your life, which must
Take the ear strangely.

PROS. I'll deliver all;
And promise you calm seas, auspicious gales
And sail so expeditious that shall catch 315
Your royal fleet far off. [*Aside to* ARI.] My Ariel, chick,
That is thy charge: then to the elements
Be free, and fare thou well! Please you, draw near. [*Exeunt.*

EPILOGUE

SPOKEN BY PROSPERO.

Now my charms are all o'erthrown,
And what strength I have 's mine own,
Which is most faint: now, 'tis true,
I must be here confined by you,
Or sent to Naples. Let me not, 5
Since I have my dukedom got
And pardon'd the deceiver, dwell
In this bare island by your spell;
But release me from my bands
With the help of your good hands: 10
Gentle breath of yours my sails
Must fill, or else my project fails,
Which was to please. Now I want
Spirits to enforce, art to enchant,
And my ending is despair, 15
Unless I be relieved by prayer,
Which pierces so that it assaults
Mercy itself and frees all faults.
As you from crimes would pardon'd be,
Let your indulgence set me free. 20
[*Exit.*

275. own, i.e., admit to be your servants. 279. **reeling ripe**, ripe for reeling, so drunk he can't walk straight. 280. **gilded**, flushed, intoxicated. 281. **in this pickle**, to be pickled in this way. 284. **fly-blowing**, i.e., because pickled meat is never fly-blown. 295. **grace**, forgiveness. 302. **waste**, spend. 305. **accidents**, events. 313. **Take**, charm; **deliver all**, tell everything. 315. **sail**, trip. 318. **draw near**, i.e., enter my cave. **Epilogue**: 9. **bands**, bonds. 10. **hands**, i.e., applause. 11. **Gentle breath**, favorable comment. 13. **want**, lack. 16. **prayer**, i.e., the one he is now making to the audience. 18. **Mercy**, God's mercy; **frees**, gains forgiveness for. 19. **crimes**, sins. 20. **indulgence**, lack of censure.

AFTERWORD

At the end of his career, Shakespeare, forsaking tragedy, turns to the writing of romance. His last plays, *Pericles* and *Cymbeline, The Winter's Tale* and *The Tempest,* are of a piece, in that the action each dramatizes is fantastic, often perilous, and happily resolved. That is a way of defining romance. The definition holds for *The Two Noble Kinsmen,* in the making of which Shakespeare collaborated with his young associate in the King's Men, John Fletcher. Standing a little apart from this group of plays, but connected in general attitude or feeling, is the historical pageant called *Henry VIII.* Six plays, then, manifesting strong affinities to one another, and seeming to confess, by their common insistence on harmony at the end, that Shakespeare in his declining years had come out of darkness to the light. This version of the tragic poet enjoying a last measure of serenity is a commonplace of Shakespearean criticism. As often, however, with the commonplace saying, it is only a half truth at best.

The horrendous evil dramatized in *King Lear* is potential in the romances, sometimes it is actualized or incarnate. The train of events leading up to the story of *The Tempest,* which is the most successful of these plays, begins with the casting out of a lawful ruler and his innocent child—it is essentially the story of King Lear and Cordelia, and not least in the ultimate intention, which is to compass the death of Prospero and Miranda. As the action builds, this wicked intention is recapitulated many times. The murder of Alonso, King of Naples, whose treachery in the past engenders new treachery in the present, is attempted by Sebastian, his brother. Evidently, "What's past is prologue." Caliban, who is understood to be the type of all evil, seeks to batter the skull of his master, or cut his wind-pipe, or drive a stake through his belly. In this dubious undertaking, Caliban is assisted by Trinculo, a cowardly jester, and Stephano, a drunken butler, who prosecute in comic ways the vicious design which their betters have begun. So far, the mirror which the playwright is holding up to nature reflects the same unhallowed conduct, in tragedy as in romance.

The vicious design is, however, not brought to completion in *The Tempest.* Against tragedy, the door is barred, and the wages of virtue are paid. This pleasing conclusion to much unhappy business is owing partly to the geniality of the playwright, partly to the resoluteness and intelligence of his characters, who give of their best and see the best rewarded. It is as if Shakespeare, who has witnessed the implacable turning of the wheel of fire on which Lear and Hamlet and Othello are borne, is inquiring now, of himself, how the revolution of the wheel may be stayed. The question arises from considerations of humanity, and is also technically inspired. Given, the same initial situation in the story of *The Tempest* as in that of *King Lear,* how can the tragic conclusion be averted? That is the question Shakespeare is asking.

Tragedy begins at the beginning, as with Lear's renunciation of power. The action of *The Tempest* is more compressed, and begins just before the moment of crisis, when the heavenly powers "Put on their instruments" and take order with the wicked man. The initial complication which precedes this final ordering is reported, not enacted, in *The Tempest.* Nonetheless, it is crucial, and absolutely reminiscent of the complication which moves the action of *King Lear*. Prospero, like Lear, is self-indulgent. He grows a stranger to his proper state, which is the governing of Milan. "Neglecting worldly ends," he awakes an evil nature in his brother, Antonio. Punishment follows. As Lear, abdicating responsibility, is driven out on the heath, so Prospero must put to sea in the "rotten carcass of a butt" or leaky vessel, which even the rats have abandoned. Lear from this point goes down to death. Prospero's fortune turns upward. But that is not because he is better or wiser than Lear, or not at first. It is because he is luckier.

Here Shakespeare confronts his first important decision in averting and making good the tragic close. Extrahuman intercession, which men may crave but which they cannot command, is required. Shakespeare, in his magnanimity or perhaps in his fatigue, is willing to afford this intercession. In the romance, swords are drawn, the protagonist is in danger of his life. But no home thrust is permitted. "How came we ashore?" Miranda inquires. And Prospero answers: "By Providence divine." The operation of this kindly Providence—or "bountiful Fortune," or "accident most strange"—is mandatory. It is also gratuitous: it comes into play without logic or desert. Lear, who dies brokenhearted, deserves a better fate. In *The Tempest,* the more gracious gods, at the instigation of the playwright, chalk forth the way that brings the hero to safety.

This fortunate chance, or magnanimous decision, is not, however, the whole story. The hero whose life is spared today must make himself over tomorrow. Partly, the struggle belongs to him. In Shakespeare's early comedies—for example, in *A Midsummer-Night's Dream*—the characters remain puppets to the end. The conclusion is happy, but not for necessary reasons. It depends entirely on the whim or good nature of the playwright.

In the romances, and notably in *The Tempest*, the hero must collaborate in the achieving of this final happiness. The subsequent conduct of Prospero illustrates the way in which he collaborates in the forging of his destiny. Banishment is not the occasion of despair but the cultivating of self-knowledge and self-control. Caliban's injunction to his vulgar accomplices, as they prepare the murder of Prospero, is instructive:

> Remember
> First to possess his books; for without them
> He's but a sot, as I am, nor hath not
> One spirit to command.

These esoteric books, like the spirits that attend on the magician as he grows proficient in his craft, function metaphorically. Prospero's power derives from, it is expressed by, unremitting study and restraint. Real proficiency means awareness, and action on awareness. Prospero, having been tendered a second chance, works his own salvation as he perceives that we are menaced always by a "fire i' the blood," or solicited to evil by a "worser genius," which is part and parcel of ourselves.

The acquiring of this perception and, consequent on it, the remaking of the enlightened man, is the primary business of the plot. At first Prospero, like Lear, is myopic; at last, as his eyes are opened, he puts on the new man. The critical point of the action coincides with the final accomplishing of the hero's transformation. As Act V begins, his hand is stretched forth to smite his enemies. And then abruptly, while the action stands still and the future trembles in the instant, the vengeful hand is withheld.

> Though with their high wrongs I am struck to the quick,
> Yet with my nobler reason 'gainst my fury
> Do I take part: the rarer action is
> In virtue than in vengeance.

But not only Prospero undergoes this transformation or sea change. The wicked brothers, the foolish and aspiring servants, even Caliban, who has been represented as incorrigible, are blessed with a degree of understanding.

> As the morning steals upon the night,
> Melting the darkness, so their rising senses
> Begin to chase the ignorant fumes that mantle
> Their clearer reason.

Understanding accrues as the sinful man is penitent. In sorrow of heart, he determines on "a clear life ensuing." What ensues is proper to comedy. But though this hopeful sequence is verified, the description of it remains inadequate or partial. In the ending as in the beginning, the agency of beneficent chance is imperative, that good may bring forth good.

The pardon conferred on the principal conspirators is absolutely gratuitous, unearned. Antonio and Sebastian, though perhaps their eyes are opened, do not repent. What happens to them in the course of the action does not invade them to the heart, and so they are not regenerated, not really changed. Prospero, in his grudging and very human forgiveness of Antonio, appears to emphasize the persistent quality of evil, which is not so easily sloughed.

> For you, most wicked sir, whom to call brother
> Would even infect my mouth, I do forgive
> Thy rankest fault.

In the conclusion of the play, the rankness is still there, not purged but circumscribed by the discretional benignity of the playwright.

The action concludes with the imminent restoration of Prospero to his Dukedom of Milan. But as Prospero acknowledges in his final words, his ending is despair, unless the heavenly powers sustain him. The capacity of human beings—what we can do of ourselves—is not sufficient to bring us through the vale of mischance. Relief or succor is necessary, as when our prayers are answered which might as easily be ignored. The willingness to concede this necessary relief, while understanding that it is in the last analysis arbitrary, and independent of wishing and willing, is the great difference between the tragic playwright and the author of the late romances. Shakespeare in *The Tempest* displays a weary generosity. His manner is by turns rueful and amusèd. He is agreeable to accommodating our hopeful and quite preposterous expectations of good success. Only he lets us see that the comic denouement is not so much deserved or self-engendered as capricious.

Gonzalo, the benevolent old courtier who lends a helping hand to the banished Prospero, has no inkling that our condition is so desperate as this. Gonzalo supposes that human beings are naturally good and in their goodness, effective. Were we to be left to ourselves, unhampered or uncorrupted by the artificial clogs of law and society, we would do well enough. Succor is not required, but the absence of restraint. That is the point implicit in the ideal commonwealth or Utopian society elaborated by Gonzalo in the second act of the play. We want no magistrate, no commitment to letters or learning, no line of demarcation between mine and thine,

> No occupation; all men idle, all;
> And women too, but innocent and pure;
> No sovereignty.

This touching and generous faith in native virtue is the faith which most of us instinctively avow. The plot of the play suggests how unfounded it is.

Miranda, the ingenuous daughter of Prospero, who for most of her years has been shut away from human kind, is our spokesman here. It is a brave new world she hypothesizes, peopled with goodly creatures in whom nothing ill can dwell. To accept this hypothesis is to run a risk that is potentially mortal. Humanity flowers sometimes in Ferdinand and Miranda, and is nonetheless, as the plot discovers, "capable of all ill!" Shakespeare is unique in representing the high pitch of human goodness attained to by his young hero and heroine. He is also unique in his estimating of human depravity. Miranda, as she is uninstructed or naïve, sees too little. The world is new to her.

But the villains, in their reading of what is proper and possible to human kind, are still more imperceptive. In logic, in propriety, they ought to get their just deserts. Antonio and Sebastian, Alonso, Caliban and his drunken colleagues, are, however, more favored than Gloucester in *King Lear*, who stumbled when he saw, and who, in consequence, loses his eyes.

Shakespeare in the tragedies requites promptly and in fatal ways the imperfect seeing of the villainous man. The cause proceeds irresistibly to the dreadful effect. The romances, of which *The Tempest* is the supreme exemplification, modify or enlarge this iron sequence. A disaster-ridden voyage by sea figures the indispensable passage of time, which heals and also lessons, and brings to birth a new and more hopeful generation. This younger generation, presented in *The Tempest* by Ferdinand and Miranda, cancels the wickedness and sorrows of the old.

Macbeth, the type of the tragic protagonist, has no children. This means that no second chance is afforded him. In comedy, it is different. The virtuous child, vouchsafed to Prospero and Alonso, is the remiss or evil parent reborn.

Sebastian, who disbelieves in the story of the phoenix, the miraculous bird which rises from its ashes, is reproved. In the conclusion of *The Tempest,* this miracle is attested. But there is in it, says Alonso, "more than nature Was ever conduct of." After all, we have the playwright to thank.

Suggested Reading

Brower, Reuben, *The Fields of Light* (1951).
Chambers, E. K., *Shakespearean Gleanings* (1944).
Curry, Walter Clyde, *Shakespeare's Philosophical Patterns* (1937).
Danby, John, *Poets on Fortune's Hill* (1952).
Dowden, Edward, *Shakspere: A Critical Study* (1875).
Gordon, George, *Shakespearian Comedy* (1944).
Kermode, Frank, ed., *The Tempest* (New Arden) (1954).
Knight, G. Wilson, *The Crown of Life: Interpretation of Shakespeare's Final Plays* (1947). Barnes and Noble.
Leavis, F. R., *The Common Pursuit* (1952).
Leech, Clifford, *Shakespeare's Tragedies* (1950). Phoenix.
Moulton, R. G., *Shakespeare As a Dramatic Artist* (1893; reprinted 1966). Dover.
Muir, Kenneth, *Last Plays of Shakespeare, Racine, Ibsen* (1961).
Murry, John Middleton, *Shakespeare* (1936). Hillary.
Neilson, Frances, *Shakespeare and "The Tempest."* (1956).
Northam, John R., *Dividing Worlds: Shakespeare's "The Tempest" and Ibsen's "Rosmersholm"* (1966). Humanities.
Pettet, E. C., *Shakespeare and the Romance Tradition* (1949).
Quiller-Couch, Sir Arthur, *Shakespeare's Workmanship* (1918).
Speaight, Robert, *Nature in Shakespearean Tragedy* (1955).
Spencer, Theodore, *Shakespeare and the Nature of Man* (1942). Macmillan.
Stauffer, Donald A., *Shakespeare's World of Images* (1949). Midland.
Still, Colin, *Shakespeare's Mystery Play* (1921).
———, *The Timeless Theme* (1936).
Stoll, Elmer Edgar, *Shakespeare and Other Masters* (1940).
Tillyard, E. M. W., *Shakespeare's Last Plays* (1938).
Traversi, Derek A., *Shakespeare: The Last Phase* (1954).
Wilson, J. Dover, *The Meaning of "The Tempest"* (1936).

The Sonnets

A NOTE ON THE TEXT

The first and rather careless printing of Shakespeare's Sonnets, by Thomas Thorpe, is a piratical or unauthorized quarto, appearing in 1609. There is no likelihood that Shakespeare saw his poems through the press and little reason to suppose that he is responsible for the order in which they appear. In 1640, John Benson, pilfering from Thorpe, brought out a second quarto, in which many of the sonnets are run together to form compound poems, and in which the young man Shakespeare addresses is transformed (by altering pronouns) to a woman. A number of the sonnets were in print before the end of the sixteenth century. They are mentioned first by Francis Meres, a clergyman with a taste for plays and poems, in a miscellaneous notebook of 1598. Probably composition belongs to the early 1590s, though Shakespeare may have continued to work at his Sonnets up to the date of the printed book.

The book itself includes the 154 poems given in this edition. Most of the poems —numbers 1 through 126—celebrate the fair youth. A second group—127 through 152—is devoted to the poet's mistress. The two poems which conclude the cycle are conventional exercises on Cupid.

Since the later eighteenth century, commentators have expended much effort to little purpose in seeking to identify real persons behind the fictive characters of the Sonnets. The chief candidates for the role of the fair youth are Henry Wriothesley, Earl of Southampton, and William Herbert, Earl of Pembroke. Oscar Wilde enjoyed himself in hypothesizing a boy actor named Willie Hughes, for whom Shakespeare is made to conceive a romantic attachment.

The notion of the Great Poet involved in an "unnatural" affair has given considerable trouble to many. "Good Heavens!" exclaimed a nineteenth-century critic, re-reading the earlier sonnets. "What do I notice. . . ? He instead of she. . . ? Can I be mistaken? Can these sonnets be addressed to a man? Shakespeare! Great Shakespeare!" Then comes the pietistic deferring to the classics: "Did you feel yourself authorized by Virgil's example?" Coleridge, on the other hand, seeking to clear his hero of the charge of homosexuality, is at least as far off the mark. In all Shakespeare's work, says this misguided apologist, there is "not even an allusion to that very worst of all possible vices."

Somewhere between the jars of these two agonized opinions, the truth resides. To define the precise nature of this truth is not easy, and perhaps it is not especially important. The powerful attachment of masculine friends, expressed sometimes in the language of erotic endearment, is suspect in our time but was a literary convention in Shakespeare's. Compare the case of Antonio, in *Twelfth*

Night, who is said to "adore" Sebastian. Some of the sonnets which declare the poet's love for his friend seem, to a modern reader, sexually equivocal. Others—like Sonnet 20, "A woman's face with Nature's own hand painted"—assert the maleness and heterosexuality of the poet. Shakespeare has no equal in his knowledge of the heart, or in his willingness to dilate on the varying emotions that find welcome there. But the heart he is revealing is not necessarily his own. The poet John Donne, who is Shakespeare's near contemporary, once wrote: "I did best when I had least truth for my subjects."

The Rival Poet has been identified with various contemporaries of Shakespeare, among them Christopher Marlowe and the playwright George Chapman; and the Dark Lady with various ladies of easy virtue, not excluding Queen Elizabeth. A modern commentator wants us to see her as Shakespeare's mother. That is an amusing and apposite suggestion, in the Age of Freud.

THE SONNETS

1

From fairest creatures we desire increase,
That thereby beauty's rose might never die,
But as the riper should by time decrease,
His tender heir might bear his memory:
But thou, contracted to thine own bright eyes, 5
Feed'st thy light's flame with self-substantial fuel,
Making a famine where abundance lies,
Thyself thy foe, to thy sweet self too cruel.
Thou that art now the world's fresh ornament
And only herald to the gaudy spring, 10
Within thine own bud buriest thy content
And, tender churl, makest waste in niggarding.
Pity the world, or else this glutton be,
To eat the world's due, by the grave and thee.

2

When forty winters shall besiege thy brow
And dig deep trenches in thy beauty's field,
Thy youth's proud livery, so gazed on now,
Will be a tatter'd weed, of small worth held:
Then being ask'd where all thy beauty lies, 5
Where all the treasure of thy lusty days,
To say, within thine own deep-sunken eyes,
Were an all-eating shame, and thriftless praise.
How much more praise deserved thy beauty's use,
If thou couldst answer "This fair child of mine 10
Shall sum my count and make my old excuse,"
Proving his beauty by succession thine!
This were to be new made when thou art old,
And see thy blood warm when thou feel'st it cold.

3

Look in thy glass, and tell the face thou viewest
Now is the time that face should form another;
Whose fresh repair if now thou not renewest,
Thou dost beguile the world, unbless some mother.
For where is she so fair whose unear'd womb 5
Disdains the tillage of thy husbandry?
Or who is he so fond will be the tomb
Of his self-love, to stop posterity?
Thou art thy mother's glass, and she in thee
Calls back the lovely April of her prime: 10
So thou through windows of thine age shalt see,
Despite of wrinkles, this thy golden time.
But if thou live, remember'd not to be,
Die single, and thine image dies with thee.

4

Unthrifty loveliness, why dost thou spend
Upon thyself thy beauty's legacy?
Nature's bequest gives nothing, but doth lend,
And being frank, she lends to those are free.
Then, beauteous niggard, why dost thou abuse 5
The bounteous largess given thee to give?
Profitless usurer, why dost thou use
So great a sum of sums, yet canst not live?
For having traffic with thyself alone,

Sonnet 1: 5. contracted, betrothed. 6. self-substantial, of the same substance as the flame. 10. only, chief. 11. thy content, i.e., your potential child. 14. To . . . thee, to consume what is due the world (i.e., children) by death and your refusal to beget heirs.

Sonnet 2: 4. weed, garment. 8. all-eating shame, shame that consumes the man and his descendants; thriftless, unprofitable. 11. sum, compute; old excuse, excuse of being old. 12. succession, i.e., right of succession.

Sonnet 3: 4. unbless, refuse to make happy. 5. unear'd, unplowed. 7. fond, foolish. 10. prime, spring. 13. remember'd . . . be, only to be forgotten.

Sonnet 4: 2. beauty's legacy, inherited beauty. 4. frank, liberal; free, generous. 6. largess, liberality. 7. use, put out to interest. 8. live, survive. 9. thyself alone, i.e., with no woman.

Thou of thyself thy sweet self dost deceive. 10
Then how, when nature calls thee to be gone,
What acceptable audit canst thou leave?
Thy unused beauty must be tomb'd with thee,
Which, used, lives th' executor to be.

5

Those hours that with gentle work did frame
The lovely gaze where every eye doth dwell,
Will play the tyrants to the very same
And that unfair which fairly doth excel:
For never-resting time leads summer on 5
To hideous winter and confounds him there;
Sap check'd with frost and lusty leaves quite gone,
Beauty o'ersnow'd and bareness every where:
Then, were not summer's distillation left,
A liquid prisoner pent in walls of glass, 10
Beauty's effect with beauty were bereft,
Nor it, nor no remembrance what it was:
But flowers distill'd, though they with winter meet,
Leese but their show; their substance still lives sweet.

6

Then let not winter's ragged hand deface
In thee thy summer, ere thou be distill'd:
Make sweet some vial; treasure thou some place
With beauty's treasure, ere it be self-kill'd.
That use is not forbidden usury, 5
Which happies those that pay the willing loan;
That 's for thyself to breed another thee,
Or ten times happier, be it ten for one;
Ten times thyself were happier than thou art,
If ten of thine ten times refigured thee: 10
Then what could death do, if thou shouldst depart,
Leaving thee living in posterity?
Be not self-will'd, for thou art much too fair
To be death's conquest and make worms thine heir.

7

Lo, in the orient when the gracious light
Lifts up his burning head, each under eye
Doth homage to his new-appearing sight,
Serving with looks his sacred majesty;
And having climb'd the steep-up heavenly hill, 5
Resembling strong youth in his middle age,
Yet mortal looks adore his beauty still,
Attending on his golden pilgrimage;
But when from highmost pitch, with weary car,
Like feeble age, he reeleth from the day, 10
The eyes, 'fore duteous, now converted are
From his low tract and look another way:
So thou, thyself out-going in thy noon,
Unlook'd on diest, unless thou get a son.

8

Music to hear, why hear'st thou music sadly?
Sweets with sweets war not, joy delights in joy.
Why lovest thou that which thou receivest not gladly,
Or else receivest with pleasure thine annoy?
If the true concord of well tunèd sounds, 5
By unions marrièd, do offend thine ear,
They do but sweetly chide thee, who confounds
In singleness the parts that thou shouldst bear.
Mark how one string, sweet husband to another,
Strikes each in each by mutual ordering; 10
Resembling sire and child and happy mother,
Who, all in one, one pleasing note do sing:
Whose speechless song, being many, seeming one,
Sings this to thee: "Thou single wilt prove none."

12. **acceptable audit**, praiseworthy account. 13. **unused beauty**, beauty not put out at interest. 14. **which . . . lives**, which, if put out at interest, survives.

Sonnet 5: 2. **gaze**, object gazed at. 4. **that unfair**, deprive that of beauty. 6. **confounds**, destroys. 9. **summer's distillation**, perfume. 14. **Leese**, Lose.

Sonnet 6: 1. **ragged**, rough. 3. **treasure**, enrich. 5. **use**, interest. 6. **happies**, makes happy. 10. **refigured**, reproduced.

Sonnet 7: 9. **highmost pitch**, i.e., at noon, when having reached the height of attainment, he begins to descend. 12. **tract**, track. 13. **out-going**, declining. 14. **get**, beget.

Sonnet 8: 1. **Music to hear**, you who are like music. 7. **confounds**, destroys. 8. **bear**, i.e., sing. 9. **string**, strain. 14. **Thou . . . none**, you by yourself can produce no harmony (and so you will cease to sing at all).

9

Is it for fear to wet a widow's eye
That thou consumest thyself in single life?
Ah! if thou issueless shalt hap to die,
The world will wail thee, like a makeless wife;
The world will be thy widow, and still weep 5
That thou no form of thee hast left behind,
When every private widow well may keep
By children's eyes her husband's shape in mind.
Look, what an unthrift in the world doth spend
Shifts but his place, for still the world enjoys it; 10
But beauty's waste hath in the world an end,
And kept unused, the user so destroys it.
No love toward others in that bosom sits
That on himself such murderous shame commits.

10

For shame deny that thou bear'st love to any,
Who for thyself art so unprovident.
Grant, if thou wilt, thou art beloved of many,
But that thou none lovest is most evident;
For thou art so possess'd with murderous hate 5
That 'gainst thyself thou stick'st not to conspire,
Seeking that beauteous roof to ruinate
Which to repair should be thy chief desire.
O, change thy thought, that I may change my mind!
Shall hate be fairer lodged than gentle love? 10
Be, as thy presence is, gracious and kind,
Or to thyself at least kind-hearted prove:
Make thee another self, for love of me,
That beauty still may live in thine or thee.

11

As fast as thou shalt wane, so fast thou grow'st
In one of thine, from that which thou departest;
And that fresh blood which youngly thou bestow'st
Thou mayst call thine when thou from youth convertest.
Herein lives wisdom, beauty and increase; 5
Without this, folly, age and cold decay:
If all were minded so, the times should cease
And threescore year would make the world away.
Let those whom Nature hath not made for store,
Harsh, featureless and rude, barrenly perish: 10
Look, whom she best endow'd she gave the more;
Which bounteous gift thou shouldst in bounty cherish:
She carved thee for her seal, and meant thereby
Thou shouldst print more, not let that copy die.

12

When I do count the clock that tells the time,
And see the brave day sunk in hideous night;
When I behold the violet past prime,
And sable curls all silver'd o'er with white;
When lofty trees I see barren of leaves, 5
Which erst from heat did canopy the herd,
And summer's green all girded up in sheaves,
Borne on the bier with white and bristly beard,
Then of thy beauty do I question make,
That thou among the wastes of time must go, 10
Since sweets and beauties do themselves forsake
And die as fast as they see others grow;
And nothing 'gainst Time's scythe can make defense
Save breed, to brave him when he takes thee hence.

Sonnet 9: 4. makeless, mateless. 9. unthrift, prodigal. 10. his, its. 14. murderous shame, shameful murder.
Sonnet 10: 1. For shame, i.e., for shame's sake. 6. Stick'st not, do not scruple. 7. that . . . roof, i.e., your body; roof = house, i.e., family; ruinate, destroy.

Sonnet 11: 3. youngly, in youth. 4. convertest, turn. 7. times, i.e., generations (of men). 9. for store, for breeding. 11. more, i.e., power of reproducing your kind.
Sonnet 12: 1. count, take account of. 2. brave, fine. 6. erst, formerly. 9. do . . . make, feel doubt about. 14. breed, children; brave, defy.

13

O, that you were yourself! but, love, you are
No longer yours than you yourself here live:
Against this coming end you should prepare,
And your sweet semblance to some other give.
So should that beauty which you hold in lease 5
Find no determination; then you were
Yourself again, after yourself's decease,
When your sweet issue your sweet form should bear.
Who lets so fair a house fall to decay,
Which husbandry in honor might uphold 10
Against the stormy gusts of winter's day
And barren rage of death's eternal cold?
O, none but unthrifts: dear my love, you know
You had a father; let your son say so.

14

Not from the stars do I my judgment pluck;
And yet methinks I have astronomy,
But not to tell of good or evil luck,
Of plagues, of dearths, or season's quality;
Nor can I fortune to brief minutes tell, 5
Pointing to each his thunder, rain and wind,
Or say with princes if it shall go well,
By oft predict that I in heaven find:
But from thine eyes my knowledge I derive,
And, constant stars, in them I read such art, 10
As truth and beauty shall together thrive,
If from thyself to store thou wouldst convert;
Or else of thee this I prognosticate:
Thy end is truth's and beauty's doom and date.

15

When I consider every thing that grows
Holds in perfection but a little moment,
That this huge stage presenteth nought but shows
Whereon the stars in secret influence comment;
When I perceive that men as plants increase, 5
Cheered and check'd even by the self-same sky,
Vaunt in their youthful sap, at height decrease,
And wear their brave state out of memory;
Then the conceit of this inconstant stay
Sets you most rich in youth before my sight, 10
Where wasteful Time debateth with Decay,
To change your day of youth to sullied night;
And all in war with Time for love of you,
As he takes from you, I engraft you new.

16

But wherefore do not you a mightier way
Make war upon this bloody tyrant, Time?
And fortify yourself in your decay
With means more blessed than my barren rhyme?
Now stand you on the top of happy hours, 5
And many maiden gardens, yet unset,
With virtuous wish would bear your living flowers
Much liker than your painted counterfeit:
So should the lines of life that life repair,
Which this, Time's pencil, or my pupil pen, 10
Neither in inward worth nor outward fair,
Can make you live yourself in eyes of men.
To give away yourself keeps yourself still;
And you must live, drawn by your own sweet skill.

17

Who will believe my verse in time to come,
If it were fill'd with your most high deserts?
Though yet, heaven knows, it is but as a tomb
Which hides your life and shows not half your parts.
If I could write the beauty of your eyes 5

Sonnet 13: 6. **Find no determination**, have no end. 13. **unthrifts**, prodigals.

Sonnet 14: 2. **have astronomy**, know astrology. 6. **Pointing**, appointing. 8. **oft predict**, frequent prognostication. 10. **art**, learning. 12. **store**, a large number (of offspring); **convert**, turn. 14. **doom**, Doomsday.

Sonnet 15: 6. **check'd**, repressed. 7. **vaunt**, exult. 9. **conceit**, fanciful notion. 14. **engraft you**, i.e., into my verse.

Sonnet 16: 6. **unset**, unplanted. 8. **counterfeit**, portrait. 9. **lines of life**, (1) children, (2) a portrait, (3) lines of verse. 10-12. Man is a portrait drawn by Time. Neither this likeness, nor any description can successfully give an idea of your character or your beauty. 13. **To . . . still**, to beget children will give you immortality.

And in fresh numbers number all your graces,
The age to come would say "This poet lies;
Such heavenly touches ne'er touch'd earthly faces."
So should my papers, yellowed with their age,
Be scorn'd, like old men of less truth than tongue, 10
And your true rights be term'd a poet's rage
And stretchèd meter of an antique song:
But were some child of yours alive that time,
You should live twice, in it and in my rhyme.

18

Shall I compare thee to a summer's day?
Thou art more lovely and more temperate:
Rough winds do shake the darling buds of May,
And summer's lease hath all too short a date:
Sometime too hot the eye of heaven shines, 5
And often is his gold complexion dimm'd;
And every fair from fair sometime declines,
By chance or nature's changing course untrimm'd;
But thy eternal summer shall not fade,
Nor lose possession of that fair thou owest; 10
Nor shall Death brag thou wander'st in his shade,
When in eternal lines to time thou grow'st:
So long as men can breathe, or eyes can see,
So long lives this, and this gives life to thee.

19

Devouring Time, blunt thou the lion's paws,
And make the earth devour her own sweet brood;
Pluck the keen teeth from the fierce tiger's jaws,
And burn the long-lived phœnix in her blood;
Make glad and sorry seasons as thou fleet'st, 5
And do whate'er thou wilt, swift-footed Time,
To the wide world and all her fading sweets;
But I forbid thee one most heinous crime:
O, carve not with thy hours my love's fair brow,
Nor draw no lines there with thine antique pen; 10
Him in thy course untainted do allow
For beauty's pattern to succeeding men.
Yet do thy worst, old Time: despite thy wrong,
My love shall in my verse ever live young.

20

A woman's face with Nature's own hand painted
Hast thou, the master-mistress of my passion;
A woman's gentle heart, but not acquainted
With shifting change, as is false women's fashion;
An eye more bright than theirs, less false in rolling, 5
Gilding the object whereupon it gazeth;
A man in hue, all "hues" in his controlling,
Which steals men's eyes and women's souls amazeth.
And for a woman wert thou first created;
Till Nature, as she wrought thee, fell a-doting, 10
And by addition me of thee defeated,
By adding one thing to my purpose nothing.
But since she prick'd thee out for women's pleasure,
Mine be thy love, and thy love's use their treasure.

21

So is it not with me as with that Muse
Stirr'd by a painted beauty to his verse,
Who heaven itself for ornament doth use
And every fair with his fair doth rehearse,
Making a couplement of proud compare, 5

Sonnet 17: 6. **fresh numbers,** lively verses. 8. **touches,** traits. 11. **poet's rage,** poetical inspiration. 12. **stretched meter,** exaggerated verse.

Sonnet 18: 7. **fair from fair,** fair one from beauty. 8. **untrimm'd,** shorn of ornaments. 10. **owest,** own, possess.

Sonnet 19: 4. **phoenix,** fabled Arabian bird, supposed to live 500 years, then to be consumed in a self-induced fire, and finally to rise in youthful vigor from its own ashes. 5. **fleet'st,** pass rapidly by.

Sonnet 20: 2. **master-mistress,** both master and mistress; **passion,** love poem. 7. **hue,** form; **controlling,** overpowering. 8. **which,** i.e., hues. 11. **defeated,** deprived. 12. **one thing,** i.e., a phallus. 13. **pricked . . . out,** selected.

Sonnet 21: 4. **And . . . rehearse,** And mention every sort of beautiful object in connection with this beautiful person (probably a woman). 5. **couplement,** combination.

With sun and moon, with earth and sea's rich gems,
With April's first-born flowers, and all things rare
That heaven's air in this huge rondure hems.
O, let me, true in love, but truly write,
And then believe me, my love is as fair 10
As any mother's child, though not so bright
As those gold candles fix'd in heaven's air:
Let them say more that like of hearsay well;
I will not praise that purpose not to sell.

22

My glass shall not persuade me I am old,
So long as youth and thou are of one date;
But when in thee time's furrows I behold,
Then look I death my days should expiate.
For all that beauty that doth cover thee 5
Is but the seemly raiment of my heart,
Which in thy breast doth live, as thine in me:
How can I then be elder than thou art?
O, therefore, love, be of thyself so wary
As I, not for myself, but for thee will; 10
Bearing thy heart, which I will keep so chary
As tender nurse her babe from faring ill.
Presume not on thy heart when mine is slain;
Thou gavest me thine, not to give back again.

23

As an unperfect actor on the stage,
Who with his fear is put besides his part,
Or some fierce thing replete with too much rage,
Whose strength's abundance weakens his own heart;
So I, for fear of trust, forget to say 5
The perfect ceremony of love's rite,
And in mine own love's strength seem to decay,
O'ercharged with burthen of mine own love's might.
O, let my books be then the eloquence
And dumb presagers of my speaking breast;
Who plead for love, and look for recompense, 11
More than that tongue that more hath more express'd.
O, learn to read what silent love hath writ:
To hear with eyes belongs to love's fine wit.

24

Mine eye hath play'd the painter and hath stell'd
Thy beauty's form in table of my heart;
My body is the frame wherein 'tis held,
And perspective it is best painter's art.
For through the painter must you see his skill, 5
To find where your true image pictured lies;
Which in my bosom's shop is hanging still,
That hath his windows glazèd with thine eyes.
Now see what good turns eyes for eyes have done:
Mine eyes have drawn thy shape, and thine for me 10
Are windows to my breast, where-through the sun
Delights to peep, to gaze therein on thee;
Yet eyes this cunning want to grace their art,
They draw but what they see, know not the heart.

25

Let those who are in favor with their stars
Of public honor and proud titles boast,
Whilst I, whom fortune of such triumph bars,
Unlook'd for joy in that I honor most.
Great princes' favorites their fair leaves spread 5
But as the marigold at the sun's eye,
And in themselves their pride lies burièd,
For at a frown they in their glory die.
The painful warrior famousèd for fight,
After a thousand victories once foil'd, 10

8. rondure, circle, i.e., of the horizon. 13. like . . . well, are pleased with extravagant rhetoric. 14. that . . . sell, who does not intend to sell (the thing he is praising).
Sonnet 22: 4. expiate, bring to a close. 11. chary, carefully. 13. Presume . . . heart, Do not lay claim to your own heart.
Sonnet 23: 2. besides, out of. 5. fear of trust, want of self-confidence. 10. dumb presagers, preliminary dumb shows. 12. that tongue, i.e., any tongue more eloquent than mine. 14. wit, intelligence, insight.
Sonnet 24: 1. stell'd, fixed, engraved. 2. table, tablet. 5. painter, i.e., my eye and so myself. 7. still, forever.
Sonnet 25: 4. Unlook'd for joy, rejoice inconspicuously. 6. marigold . . . eye, because it closes when the sun sets. 10. foil'd, defeated.

Is from the book of honor razèd quite,
And all the rest forgot for which he toil'd;
Then happy I, that love and am beloved
Where I may not remove nor be removed.

26

Lord of my love, to whom in vassalage
Thy merit hath my duty strongly knit,
To thee I send this written ambassage,
To witness duty, not to show my wit:
Duty so great, which wit so poor as mine 5
May make seem bare, in wanting words to show it,
But that I hope some good conceit of thine
In thy soul's thought, all naked, will bestow it;
Till whatsoever star that guides my moving,
Points on me graciously with fair aspéct, 10
And puts apparel on my tatter'd loving,
To show me worthy of thy sweet respect:
Then may I dare to boast how I do love thee;
Till then not show my head where thou mayst prove me.

27

Weary with toil, I haste me to my bed,
The dear repose for limbs with travel tired;
But then begins a journey in my head
To work my mind, when body's work 's expired:
For then my thoughts, from far where I abide
Intend a zealous pilgrimage to thee, 6
And keep my drooping eyelids open wide,
Looking on darkness which the blind do see:
Save that my soul's imaginary sight
Presents thy shadow to my sightless view, 10
Which, like a jewel hung in ghastly night,
Makes black night beauteous and her old face new.
Lo, thus, by day my limbs, by night my mind,
For thee and for myself no quiet find.

14. Where . . . remove, by a person I cannot leave and by whom I cannot be left.

Sonnet 26: This sonnet is an envoy, perhaps sent to his patron with the preceding sonnets. 4. witness duty, be a witness to my respect; wit, poetic invention. 7. conceit, concept. 8. bestow, lodge. 9. moving, i.e., living. 10. fair aspect, favorable influence.

Sonnet 27: 6. Intend, direct. 9. imaginary, imaginative. 10. shadow, image. 11. ghastly, death-like.

28

How can I then return in happy plight,
That am debarr'd the benefit of rest?
When day's oppression is not eased by night,
But day by night, and night by day, oppress'd?
And each, though enemies to either's reign, 5
Do in consent shake hands to torture me;
The one by toil, the other to complain
How far I toil, still farther off from thee.
I tell the day, to please him thou art bright,
And dost him grace when clouds do blot the heaven: 10
So flatter I the swart-complexion'd night;
When sparkling stars twire not, thou gild'st the even.
But day doth daily draw my sorrows longer,
And night doth nightly make grief's strength seem stronger.

29

When, in disgrace with fortune and men's eyes,
I all alone beweep my outcast state,
And trouble deaf heaven with my bootless cries,
And look upon myself, and curse my fate,
Wishing me like to one more rich in hope, 5
Featured like him, like him with friends possess'd,
Desiring this man's art and that man's scope,
With what I most enjoy contented least;
Yet in these thoughts myself almost despising,
Haply I think on thee, and then my state, 10
Like to the lark at break of day arising
From sullen earth, sings hymns at heaven's gate;
For thy sweet love remember'd such wealth brings
That then I scorn to change my state with kings.

30

When to the sessions of sweet silent thought
I summon up remembrance of things past,

Sonnet 28: 6. consent, agreement. 12. twire not, do not twinkle.

Sonnet 29: 3. bootless, useless. 6. featured, formed. 7. art, skill; scope, range of accomplishment.

I sigh the lack of many a thing I sought,
And with old woes' new wail my dear time's waste:
Then can I drown an eye, unused to flow, 5
For precious friends hid in death's dateless night,
And weep afresh love's long since cancel'd woe,
And moan the expense of many a vanish'd sight:
Then can I grieve at grievances foregone,
And heavily from woe to woe tell o'er 10
The sad account of fore-bemoanèd moan,
Which I new pay as if not paid before.
But if the while I think on thee, dear friend,
All losses are restored and sorrows end.

31

Thy bosom is endearèd with all hearts,
Which I by lacking have supposèd dead;
And there reigns love, and all love's loving parts,
And all those friends which I thought burièd.
How many a holy and obsequious tear 5
Hath dear religious love stol'n from mine eye,
As interest of the dead, which now appear
But things removed that hidden in thee lie!
Thou art the grave where buried love doth live,
Hung with the trophies of my lovers gone, 10
Who all their parts of me to thee did give:
That due of many now is thine alone:
Their images I loved I view in thee,
And thou, all they, hast all the all of me.

32

If thou survive my well-contented day,
When that churl Death my bones with dust shall cover,
And shalt by fortune once more re-survey
These poor rude lines of thy deceasèd lover
Compare them with the bettering of the time,
And though they be outstripp'd by every pen, 6
Reserve them for my love, not for their rhyme,
Exceeded by the height of happier men.
O, then vouchsafe me but this loving thought:
"Had my friend's Muse grown with this growing age, 10
A dearer birth than this his love had brought,
To march in ranks of better equipage:
But since he died, and poets better prove,
Theirs for their style I 'll read, his for his love."

33

Full many a glorious morning have I seen
Flatter the mountain-tops with sovereign eye,
Kissing with golden face the meadows green,
Gilding pale streams with heavenly alchemy;
Anon permit the basest clouds to ride 5
With ugly rack on his celestial face,
And from the forlorn world his visage hide,
Stealing unseen to west with this disgrace:
Even so my sun one early morn did shine
With all-triumphant splendor on my brow; 10
But, out, alack! he was but one hour mine,
The region cloud hath mask'd him from me now.
Yet him for this my love no whit disdaineth;
Suns of the world may stain when heaven's sun staineth.

34

Why didst thou promise such a beauteous day,
And make me travel forth without my cloak,
To let base clouds o'ertake me in my way,
Hiding thy bravery in their rotten smoke?
'Tis not enough that through the cloud thou break,
To dry the rain on my storm-beaten face, 6
For no man well of such a salve can speak
That heals the wound and cures not the disgrace:
Nor can thy shame give physic to my grief;

Sonnet 30: 4. **And . . . waste,** And I waste my precious time bewailing anew old woes. 6. **dateless,** eternal. 8. **expense,** loss. 9. **foregone,** past. 10. **tell o'er,** count up.
Sonnet 31: 5. **obsequious,** funereal. 6. **religious,** devoted. 7. **interest,** claim. 10. **lovers,** friends. 11. **parts of me,** shares in me.
Sonnet 32: 1. **my . . . day,** i.e., day of the poet's burial. 5. **bettering,** improvement (in poetic art). 7. **Reserve,** preserve; **for,** for the sake of. 8. **height,** i.e., excellence.
Sonnet 33: 6. **rack,** mass of clouds. 12. **region,** the upper air. 14. **stain,** grow dim.
Sonnet 34: 4. **bravery,** splendor; **smoke,** mist. 8. **disgrace,** disfigurement.

Though thou repent, yet I have still the loss:
The offender's sorrow lends but weak relief 11
To him that bears the strong offense's cross.
Ah, but those tears are pearl which thy love sheds,
And they are rich and ransom all ill deeds.

35

No more be grieved at that which thou hast done:
Roses have thorns, and silver fountains mud;
Clouds and eclipses stain both moon and sun,
And loathsome canker lives in sweetest bud.
All men make faults, and even I in this, 5
Authorizing thy trespass with compare,
Myself corrupting, salving thy amiss,
Excusing thy sins more than thy sins are;
For to thy sensual fault I bring in sense–
Thy adverse party is thy advocate– 10
And 'gainst myself a lawful plea commence:
Such civil war is in my love and hate,
That I an accessary needs must be
To that sweet thief which sourly robs from me.

36

Let me confess that we two must be twain,
Although our undivided loves are one:
So shall those blots that do with me remain,
Without thy help, by me be borne alone.
In our two loves there is but one respect, 5
Though in our lives a separable spite,
Which though it alter not love's sole effect,
Yet doth it steal sweet hours from love's delight.
I may not evermore acknowledge thee,
Lest my bewailèd guilt should do thee shame,
Nor thou with public kindness honor me, 11
Unless thou take that honor from thy name:
But do not so; I love thee in such sort,
As thou being mine, mine is thy good report.

37

As a decrepit father takes delight
To see his active child do deeds of youth,
So I, made lame by fortune's dearest spite,
Take all my comfort of thy worth and truth;
For whether beauty, birth, or wealth, or wit, 5
Or any of these all, or all, or more,
Entitled in thy parts do crownèd sit,
I make my love engrafted to this store:
So then I am not lame, poor, nor despised,
Whilst that this shadow doth such substance give 10
That I in thy abundance am sufficed
And by a part of all thy glory live.
Look, what is best, that best I wish in thee:
This wish I have; then ten times happy me!

38

How can my Muse want subject to invent,
While thou dost breathe, that pour'st into my verse
Thine own sweet argument, too excellent
For every vulgar paper to rehearse?
O, give thyself the thanks, if aught in me 5
Worthy perusal stand against thy sight;
For who 's so dumb that cannot write to thee
When thou thyself dost give invention light?
Be thou the tenth Muse, ten times more in worth
Than those old nine which rhymers invocate;
And he that calls on thee, let him bring forth 11
Eternal numbers to outlive long date.
If my slight Muse do please these curious days
The pain be mine, but thine shall be the praise.

12. cross, burden.

Sonnet 35: 4. canker, cankerworm. 6. Authorizing . . . compare, justifying your offense with my similes. 7. corrupting, i.e., by his too great love for his friend; amiss, offence. 9. sense, reason. 10. adverse party, i.e., "sense" or sensuality.

Sonnet 36: 3. those blots, probably the poet's inferior social position rather than any immorality. 5. respect, regard, point of view. 6. separable, separating. 10. Lest . . . shame, i.e., lest my relation to the "dark lady," which I lament, should convict you of being a faithless friend.

Sonnet 37: 3. dearest, bitterest. 7. Entitled . . . sit (these excellent qualities) sit crowned in your endowments (to which they have a valid title). 10. shadow, a copy of the substance (i.e., the eternal pattern of Beauty).

Sonnet 38: 3. argument, theme. 4. rehearse, touch upon. 8. invention, the imaginative faculty. 10. old nine, the nine Muses who were the patron goddesses of the different forms of art. 12. numbers, verses. 13. curious, difficult to please.

39

O, how thy worth with manners may I sing,
When thou art all the better part of me?
What can mine own praise to mine own self bring
And what is 't but mine own when I praise thee?
Even for this let us divided live, 5
And our dear love lose name of single one,
That by this separation I may give
That due to thee which thou deservest alone.
O absence, what a torment wouldst thou prove,
Were it not thy sour leisure gave sweet leave
To entertain the time with thoughts of love,
Which time and thoughts so sweetly doth deceive, 12
And that thou teachest how to make one twain,
By praising him here who doth hence remain!

40

Take all my loves, my love, yea, take them all;
What hast thou then more than thou hadst before?
No love, my love, that thou mayst true love call;
All mine was thine before thou hadst this more.
Then, if for my love thou my love receivest, 5
I cannot blame thee for my love thou usest;
But yet be blamed, if thou thyself deceivest
By willful taste of what thyself refusest.
I do forgive thy robbery, gentle thief,
Although thou steal thee all my poverty: 10
And yet, love knows, it is a greater grief
To bear love's wrong than hate's known injury.
Lascivious grace, in whom all ill well shows,
Kill me with spites; yet we must not be foes.

Sonnet 39: 2. better . . . me, i.e., my soul. 13. one twain, i.e., the actual absent person and the one present in the imagination.
Sonnet 40: 5. my love, love of me; my love, the one I love. 6. for . . . usest, for taking my loved one for your mistress. 8. taste, enjoyment; By . . . refusest, By wilfully indulging the lust which you must despise.
Sonnet 41: 1. liberty, licentiousness. 6. assailed, tempted. 9. my seat forbear, refrain from taking my place with the dark lady. 11. riot, debauchery. 12. truth, loyalty.

41

Those pretty wrongs that liberty commits,
When I am sometime absent from thy heart,
Thy beauty and thy years full well befits,
For still temptation follows where thou art.
Gentle thou art, and therefore to be won, 5
Beauteous thou art, therefore to be assailed;
And when a woman woos, what woman's son
Will sourly leave her till she have prevailed?
Aye me! but yet thou mightst my seat forbear,
And chide thy beauty and thy straying youth, 10
Who lead thee in their riot even there
Where thou art forced to break a twofold truth,
Hers, by thy beauty tempting her to thee,
Thine, by thy beauty being false to me.

42

That thou hast her, it is not all my grief,
And yet it may be said I loved her dearly;
That she hath thee, is of my wailing chief,
A loss in love that touches me more nearly.
Loving offenders, thus I will excuse ye: 5
Thou dost love her, because thou know'st I love her;
And for my sake even so doth she abuse me,
Suffering my friend for my sake to approve her.
If I lose thee, my loss is my love's gain,
And losing her, my friend hath found that loss; 10
Both find each other, and I lose both twain,
And both for my sake lay on me this cross:
But here 's the joy: my friend and I are one;
Sweet flattery! then she loves but me alone.

43

When most I wink, then do mine eyes best see,
For all the day they view things unrespected;
But when I sleep, in dreams they look on thee,

Sonnet 42: 7. abuse, deceive. 8. approve, make trial of. 9. love's, mistress'.
Sonnet 43: 1. wink, close my eyes. 2. unrespected, unnoticed.

And, darkly bright, are bright in dark directed.
Then thou, whose shadow shadows doth make bright, 5
How would thy shadow's form form happy show
To the clear day with thy much clearer light,
When to unseeing eyes thy shade shines so!
How would, I say, mine eyes be blessèd made
By looking on thee in the living day, 10
When in dead night thy fair imperfect shade
Through heavy sleep on sightless eyes doth stay!
All days are nights to see till I see thee,
And nights bright days when dreams do show thee me.

44

If the dull substance of my flesh were thought,
Injurious distance should not stop my way;
For then, despite of space, I would be brought,
From limits far remote, where thou dost stay.
No matter then although my foot did stand 5
Upon the farthest earth removed from thee;
For nimble thought can jump both sea and land,
As soon as think the place where he would be.
But, ah, thought kills me, that I am not thought,
To leap large lengths of miles when thou art gone,
But that, so much of earth and water wrought, 11
I must attend time's leisure with my moan;
Receiving nought by elements so slow
But heavy tears, badges of either's woe.

45

The other two, slight air and purging fire,
Are both with thee, wherever I abide;
The first my thought, the other my desire,
These present-absent with swift motion slide.
For when these quicker elements are gone 5
In tender embassy of love to thee,
My life, being made of four, with two alone
Sinks down to death, oppress'd with melancholy;
Until life's composition be recured
By those swift messengers return'd from thee, 10
Who even but now come back again, assured
Of thy fair health, recounting it to me:
This told, I joy; but then no longer glad,
I send them back again, and straight grow sad.

46

Mine eye and heart are at a mortal war,
How to divide the conquest of thy sight;
Mine eye my heart thy picture's sight would bar,
My heart mine eye the freedom of that right.
My heart doth plead that thou in him dost lie, 5
A closet never pierced with crystal eyes,
But the defendant doth that plea deny,
And says in him thy fair appearance lies.
To 'cide this title is impanelèd
A quest of thoughts, all tenants to the heart; 10
And by their verdict is determinèd
The clear eye's moiety and the dear heart's part:
As thus; mine eye's due is thine outward part,
And my heart's right thine inward love of heart.

47

Betwixt mine eye and heart a league is took,
And each doth good turns now unto the other:
When that mine eye is famish'd for a look,
Or heart in love with sighs himself doth smother,
With my love's picture then my eye doth feast 5

4. **darkly bright,** though in the dark, they see; **are . . . directed,** and in the darkness are clearly directed. 5. **whose . . . bright,** "whose image makes bright the shades of night" (Dowden). 11. **shade,** dream image; **imperfect,** i.e., because only an image.

Sonnet 44: 4. **where,** to the place where. 11. **So . . . wrought,** so much composed of these two heavy elements, i.e., earth and water.

Sonnet 45: 7. **four,** the four elements of which man was supposed to be composed: earth, water, air, fire. 9. **recured,** restored to the proper balance. 12. **fair,** fine.

Sonnet 46: 1. **Mine . . . war,** i.e., my eye would bar the sight of his portrait from my heart. 9. **'cide,** decide. 10. **quest,** jury. 12. **moiety,** share.

Sonnet 47: 1. **is took,** has been established.

And to the painted banquet bids my heart;
Another time mine eye is my heart's guest
And in his thoughts of love doth share a part:
So, either by thy picture or my love,
Thyself away art present still with me; 10
For thou not farther than my thoughts canst move,
And I am still with them and they with thee;
Or, if they sleep, thy picture in my sight
Awakes my heart to heart's and eye's delight.

48

How careful was I, when I took my way,
Each trifle under truest bars to thrust,
That to my use it might unusèd stay
From hands of falsehood, in sure wards of trust!
But thou, to whom my jewels trifles are, 5
Most worthy comfort, now my greatest grief,
Thou, best of dearest and mine only care,
Art left the prey of every vulgar thief.
Thee have I not lock'd up in any chest,
Save where thou art not, though I feel thou art, 10
Within the gentle closure of my breast,
From whence at pleasure thou mayst come and part;
And even thence thou wilt be stol'n, I fear.
For truth proves thievish for a prize so dear.

49

Against that time, if ever that time come,
When I shall see thee frown on my defects,
When as thy love hath cast his utmost sum,
Call'd to that audit by advised respects;
Against that time when thou shalt strangely pass, 5
And scarcely greet me with that sun, thine eye,
When love, converted from the thing it was,
Shall reasons find of settled gravity;
Against that time do I ensconce me here
Within the knowledge of mine own desert, 10
And this my hand against myself uprear,
To guard the lawful reasons on thy part:
To leave poor me thou hast the strength of laws,
Since why to love I can allege no cause.

50

How heavy do I journey on the way,
When what I seek, my weary travel's end,
Doth teach that ease and that repose to say,
"Thus far the miles are measured from thy friend!"
The beast that bears me, tired with my woe, 5
Plods dully on, to bear that weight in me,
As if by some instinct the wretch did know
His rider loved not speed, being made from thee:
The bloody spur cannot provoke him on
That sometimes anger thrusts into his hide; 10
Which heavily he answers with a groan,
More sharp to me than spurring to his side;
For that same groan doth put this in my mind;
My grief lies onward, and my joy behind.

51

Thus can my love excuse the slow offense
Of my dull bearer when from thee I speed:
From where thou art why should I haste me thence?
Till I return, of posting is no need.
O, what excuse will my poor beast then find, 5
When swift extremity can seem but slow?
Then should I spur, though mounted on the wind,
In winged speed no motion shall I know:
Then can no horse with my desire keep pace;
Therefore desire, of perfect'st love being made, 10
Shall neigh—no dull flesh—in his fiery race;
But love, for love, thus shall excuse my jade;

6. painted banquet, i.e., the picture. 10. still, always.

Sonnet 48: 1. took my way, went away, i.e., left home. 4. wards of trust, trustworthy bolts. 5. to, in comparison with. 6. comfort, pleasure, enjoyment. This sonnet was surely addressed to a woman.

Sonnet 49: 1. Against, in anticipation of. 3. cast . . . sum, closed his accounts and determined the total sum. 4. advised respects, careful considerations. 5. strangely, as a stranger. 8. of settled gravity, i.e., weighty.

Sonnet 50: 1. heavy, sorrowfully. 8. made . . . thee, directed away from thee.

Sonnet 51: 1. slow offense, offense of slowness. 4. posting, hurrying. 6. swift extremity, extreme speed. 8. In . . . know, i.e., the speed of the wind will seem no motion at all. 12. for love, out of love of the horse.

Since from thee going he went willful-slow,
Towards thee I'll run and give him leave to go.

52

So am I as the rich, whose blessèd key
Can bring him to his sweet up-lockèd treasure,
The which he will not every hour survey,
For blunting the fine point of seldom pleasure.
Therefore are feasts so solemn and so rare, 5
Since, seldom coming, in the long year set,
Like stones of worth they thinly placèd are,
Or captain jewels in the carcanet.
So is the time that keeps you as my chest,
Or as the wardrobe which the robe doth hide,
To make some special instant special blest,
By new unfolding his imprison'd pride.
Blessèd are you, whose worthiness gives scope,
Being had, to triumph, being lack'd, to hope.

53

What is your substance, whereof are you made,
That millions of strange shadows on you tend?
Since every one hath, every one, one shade,
And you, but one, can every shadow lend.
Describe Adonis, and the counterfeit 5
Is poorly imitated after you;
On Helen's cheek all art of beauty set,
And you in Grecian tires are painted new:
Speak of the spring and foison of the year,
The one doth shadow of your beauty show,
The other as your bounty doth appear; 11
And you in every blessèd shape we know.
In all external grace you have some part,
But you like none, none you, for constant heart.

14. go, walk.
Sonnet 52: 4. For, for fear of. 8. captain, principal; carcanet, collar of jewels.
Sonnet 53: 2. strange, belonging to another; tend, attend. 3. Since . . . shade, since everyone has but one shadow. 4. every . . . lend, make every object reflect your beauty. 5. counterfeit, portrait. 8. tires, attires. 9. foison, harvest. 10. shadow . . . show, appears to be the image of your beauty. 14. None you, i.e., none like you.
Sonnet 54: 2. truth, constancy. 5. canker-blooms, dog-rose or wild briar. 6. tincture, color. 9. for, because. 10. unrespected, unregarded.

54

O, how much more doth beauty beauteous seem
By that sweet ornament which truth doth give!
The rose looks fair, but fairer we it deem
For that sweet odor which doth in it live.
The canker-blooms have full as deep a dye 5
As the perfumèd tincture of the roses,
Hang on such thorns, and play as wantonly
When summer's breath their maskèd buds discloses:
But, for their virtue only is their show,
They live unwoo'd and unrespected fade; 10
Die to themselves. Sweet roses do not so;
Of their sweet deaths are sweetest odors made:
And so of you, beauteous and lovely youth,
When that shall fade, by verse distills your truth.

55

Not marble, nor the gilded monuments
Of princes, shall outlive this powerful rhyme;
But you shall shine more bright in these contents
Than unswept stone, besmear'd with sluttish time.
When wasteful war shall statues overturn, 5
And broils root out the work of masonry,
Nor Mars his sword nor war's quick fire shall burn
The living record of your memory.
'Gainst death and all-oblivious enmity
Shall you pace forth; your praise shall still find room 10
Even in the eyes of all posterity
That wear this world out to the ending doom.
So, till the judgment that yourself arise,
You live in this, and dwell in lovers' eyes.

56

Sweet love, renew thy force; be it not said
Thy edge should blunter be than appetite,

Sonnet 55: 4. unswept, i.e., dusty; stone, a horizontal grave; stone in the floor of a church. 10. pace forth, endure. 13. judgment that, Judgment Day when.

Which but to-day by feeding is allay'd,
To-morrow sharpen'd in his former might:
So, love, be thou; although to-day thou fill 5
Thy hungry eyes even till they wink with fullness,
To-morrow see again, and do not kill
The spirit of love with a perpetual dullness.
Let this sad interim like the ocean be
Which parts the shore, where two contracted new 10
Come daily to the banks, that, when they see
Return of love, more blest may be the view;
Or call it winter, which, being full of care,
Makes summer's welcome thrice more wish'd, more rare.

57

Being your slave, what should I do but tend
Upon the hours and times of your desire?
I have no precious time at all to spend,
Nor services to do, till you require.
Nor dare I chide the world-without-end hour 5
Whilst I, my sovereign, watch the clock for you,
Nor think the bitterness of absence sour
When you have bid your servant once adieu;
Nor dare I question with my jealous thought
Where you may be, or your affairs suppose, 10
But, like a sad slave, stay and think of nought
Save, where you are how happy you make those.
So true a fool is love that in your will,
Though you do any thing, he thinks no ill.

58

What god forbid that made me first your slave,
I should in thought control your times of pleasure,
Or at your hand the account of hours to crave,
Being your vassal, bound to stay your leisure!
O, let me suffer, being at your beck, 5
The imprison'd absence of your liberty;
And patience, tame to sufferance, bide each check,
Without accusing you of injury.
Be where you list, your charter is so strong
That you yourself may privilege your time 10
To what you will; to you it doth belong
Yourself to pardon of self-doing crime.
I am to wait, though waiting so be hell,
Not blame your pleasure, be it ill or well.

59

If there be nothing new, but that which is
Hath been before, how are our brains beguiled
Which, laboring for invention, bear amiss
The second burthen of a former child!
O, that recórd could with a backward look, 5
Even of five hundred courses of the sun,
Show me your image in some antique book,
Since mind at first in character was done.
That I might see what the old world could say
To this composèd wonder of your frame; 10
Whether we are mended, or whether better they,
Or whether revolution be the same.
O, sure I am, the wits of former days
To subjects worse have given admiring praise.

60

Like as the waves make towards the pebbled shore,
So do our minutes hasten to their end;
Each changing place with that which goes before,
In sequent toil all forwards do contend.
Nativity, once in the main of light, 5
Crawls to maturity, wherewith being crown'd,
Crookèd eclipses 'gainst his glory fight,

Sonnet 56: 6. **wink,** close. 8. **dullness,** drowsiness. 10. **contracted,** betrothed. 13. **care,** sorrow.

Sonnet 57: 5. **world-without-end,** i.e., everlasting. 8. **servant,** lover: The word suggests that the sonnet was addressed to a woman. 10. **suppose,** imagine. 13. **will,** with a possible pun on the poet's name—Will.

Sonnet 58: 6. **The . . . liberty,** your absence, freedom to you, is to me imprisonment. 7. **patience, tame to sufferance,** bearing tamely even suffering. 10. **privilege,** license. 12. **self-doing,** done by yourself.

Sonnet 59: 3. **invention,** originality of imagination. 5. **record,** memory. 8. **since . . . done,** written since thought was first put into writing. 10. **composed wonder,** wonderful composition. 12. **whether . . . same,** whether time brings back the same situation, i.e., whether history takes a cyclic course.

Sonnet 60: 5. **main,** broad expanse. The phrase means "the firmament." 7. **crooked,** malignant.

And Time that gave doth now his gift confound.
Time doth transfix the flourish set on youth
And delves the parallels in beauty's brow 10
Feeds on the rarities of nature's truth
And nothing stands but for his scythe to mow:
And yet to times in hope my verse shall stand
Praising thy worth despite his cruel hand.

61

Is it thy will thy image should keep open
My heavy eyelids to the weary night?
Dost thou desire my slumbers should be broken,
While shadows like to thee do mock my sight?
Is it thy spirit that thou send'st from thee 5
So far from home into my deeds to pry,
To find out shames and idle hours in me,
The scope and tenor of thy jealousy?
O, no! thy love, though much, is not so great:
It is my love that keeps mine eye awake; 10
Mine own true love that doth my rest defeat,
To play the watchman ever for thy sake:
For thee watch I whilst thou doth wake elsewhere,
From me far off, with others all too near.

62

Sin of self-love possesseth all mine eye
And all my soul and all my every part;
And for this sin there is no remedy,
It is so grounded inward in my heart.
Methinks no face so gracious is as mine, 5
No shape so true, no truth of such account;
And for myself mine own worth do define,
As I all other in all worths surmount.
But when my glass shows me myself indeed,
Beated and chopp'd with tann'd antiquity, 10
Mine own self-love quite contrary I read;
Self so self-loving were iniquity.
'Tis thee, myself, that for myself I praise
Painting my age with beauty of thy days.

8. confound, destroy. 9. flourish, gloss. 13. times in hope, i.e., the future.
Sonnet 61: 11. defeat, destroy. 13. watch, keep awake.
Sonnet 62: 10. Beated and chopp'd, battered and wrinkled; antiquity, old age. 13. thee, myself, you who are my other self.

63

Against my love shall be, as I am now,
With Time's injurious hand crush'd and o'erworn;
When hours have drain'd his blood and fill'd his brow
With lines and wrinkles; when his youthful morn
Hath travel'd on to age's steepy night, 5
And all those beauties whereof now he 's king
Are vanishing or vanish'd out of sight,
Stealing away the treasure of his spring;
For such a time do I now fortify
Against confounding age's cruel knife, 10
That he shall never cut from memory
My sweet love's beauty, though my lover's life:
His beauty shall in these black lines be seen,
And they shall live, and he in them still green.

64

When I have seen by Time's fell hand defaced
The rich-proud cost of outworn buried age;
When sometime lofty towers I see down-razed,
And brass eternal slave to mortal rage;
When I have seen the hungry ocean gain 5
Advantage on the kingdom of the shore,
And the firm soil win of the watery main,
Increasing store with loss and loss with store;
When I have seen such interchange of state,
Or state itself confounded to decay; 10
Ruin hath taught me thus to ruminate,
That Time will come and take my love away.
This thought is as a death, which cannot choose
But weep to have that which it fears to lose.

65

Since brass, nor stone, nor earth, nor boundless sea,
But sad mortality o'er-sways their power,

Sonnet 63: 1. Against, in anticipation of the time when. 5. steepy, i.e., steep decline to. 9. fortify, i.e., myself. 10. confounding, destroying.
Sonnet 64: 2. cost, expenditure. 8. store, abundance. 9. state, condition. 10. state, pomp; confounded, wasted. 13. which, modifies "thought."
Sonnet 65: 2. o'er-sways, surpasses.

How with this rage shall beauty hold a plea
Whose action is no stronger than a flower?
O, how shall summer's honey breath hold out 5
Against the wreckful siege of battering days,
When rocks impregnable are not so stout,
Nor gates of steel so strong, but Time decays?
O fearful meditation! where, alack,
Shall Time's best jewel from Time's chest lie hid? 10
Or what strong hand can hold his swift foot back?
Or who his spoil of beauty can forbid?
O, none, unless this miracle have might,
That in black ink my love may still shine bright.

66

Tired with all these, for restful death I cry,
As, to behold desert a beggar born,
And needy nothing trimm'd in jollity,
And purest faith unhappily forsworn,
And gilded honor shamefully misplaced, 5
And maiden virtue rudely strumpeted,
And right perfection wrongfully disgraced,
And strength by limping sway disablèd,
And art made tongue-tied by authority,
And folly, doctor-like, controlling skill, 10
And simple truth miscall'd simplicity,
And captive good attending captain ill:
Tired with all these, from these would I be gone,
Save that, to die, I leave my love alone.

67

Ah, wherefore with infection should he live
And with his presence grace impiety,
That sin by him advantage should achieve
And lace itself with his society?
Why should false painting imitate his cheek, 5
And steal dead seeing of his living hue?
Why should poor beauty indirectly seek
Roses of shadow, since his rose is true?
Why should he live, now Nature bankrupt is,
Beggar'd of blood to blush through lively veins? 10
For she hath no exchequer now but his,
And, proud of many, lives upon his gains.
O, him she stores, to show what wealth she had
In days long since, before these last so bad.

68

Thus is his cheek the map of days outworn,
When beauty lived and died as flowers do now,
Before these bastard signs of fair were born,
Or durst inhabit on a living brow;
Before the golden tresses of the dead, 5
The right of sepulchers, were shorn away,
To live a second life on second head;
Ere beauty's dead fleece made another gay:
In him those holy antique hours are seen,
Without all ornament itself and true, 10
Making no summer of another's green,
Robbing no old to dress his beauty new;
And him as for a map doth Nature store,
To show false Art what beauty was of yore.

69

Those parts of thee that the world's eye doth view
Want nothing that the thought of hearts can mend;
All tongues, the voice of souls, give thee that due,
Uttering bare truth, even so as foes commend.
Thy outward thus with outward praise is crown'd; 5
But those same tongues, that give thee so thine own,
In other accents do this praise confound
By seeing farther than the eye hath shown.
They look into the beauty of thy mind,
And that, in guess, they measure by thy deeds; 10
Then, churls, their thoughts, although their eyes were kind,

4. **action**, i.e., legal action. 6. **wreckful**, destructive. 12. **spoil**, plundering.

Sonnet 66: This sonnet, written in Hamlet's mood, is usually thought to express the poet's own personal feeling. 4. **unhappily**, mischievously. 5. **misplaced**, i.e., placed above desert. 6. **strumpeted**, debauched. 10. **doctor-like**, with learned airs. 11. **simplicity**, folly.

Sonnet 67: 1. **with infection**, i.e., in this tainted world. 4. **lace**, adorn. 5. **false painting**, i.e., use of cosmetics. 8. **roses of shadow**, imaginary roses, i.e., painted cheeks. 13. **stores**, preserves.

Sonnet 68: 1. **map**, picture; **outworn**, passed. 3. **signs of fair**, deceptive semblances of beauty, here = cosmetics.

Sonnet 69: 4. **even . . . commend**, which even an enemy would admit. 7. **confound**, destroy. 10. **in guess**, by guess-work.

To thy fair flower add the rank smell of weeds:
But why thy odor matcheth not thy show,
The soil is this, that thou dost common grow.

70

That thou art blamed shall not be thy defect,
For slander's mark was ever yet the fair;
The ornament of beauty is suspect,
A crow that flies in heaven's sweetest air.
So thou be good, slander doth but approve 5
Thy worth the greater, being woo'd of time;
For canker vice the sweetest buds doth love,
And thou present'st a pure unstainèd prime.
Thou hast pass'd by the ambush of young days,
Either not assail'd, or victor being charged; 10
Yet this thy praise cannot be so thy praise,
To tie up envy evermore enlarged:
If some suspect of ill mask'd not thy show,
Then thou alone kingdoms of hearts shouldst owe.

71

No longer mourn for me when I am dead
Than you shall hear the surly sullen bell
Give warning to the world that I am fled
From this vile world, with vilest worms to dwell:
Nay, if you read this line, remember not 5
The hand that writ it; for I love you so,
That I in your sweet thoughts would be forgot,
If thinking on me then should make you woe.
O, if, I say, you look upon this verse
When I perhaps compounded am with clay, 10
Do not so much as my poor name rehearse,
But let your love even with my life decay;
Lest the wise world should look into your moan,
And mock you with me after I am gone.

14. soil, blemish.
Sonnet 70: 3. suspect, suspicion. 5. approve, prove. 6. woo'd of time, courted by the temptations of the present age (which is evidence of your charm). 8. prime, spring time. 10. charged, attacked. 12. enlarged, set at liberty. 14. owe, own, possess.
Sonnet 72: 4. prove, find. 10. untrue, untruly. 13. that . . . forth, i.e., my poems and plays.

72

O, lest the world should task you to recite
What merit lived in me, that you should love
After my death, dear love, forget me quite,
For you in me can nothing worthy prove;
Unless you would devise some virtuous lie, 5
To do more for me than mine own desert,
And hang more praise upon deceasèd I
Than niggard truth would willingly impart:
O, lest your true love may seem false in this,
That you for love speak well of me untrue, 10
My name be buried where my body is,
And live no more to shame nor me nor you.
For I am shamed by that which I bring forth,
And so should you, to love things nothing worth.

73

That time of year thou mayst in me behold
When yellow leaves, or none, or few, do hang
Upon those boughs which shake against the cold,
Bare ruin'd choirs, where late the sweet birds sang.
In me thou see'st the twilight of such day 5
As after sunset fadeth in the west;
Which by and by black night doth take away,
Death's second self, that seals up all in rest.
In me thou see'st the glowing of such fire,
That on the ashes of his youth doth lie, 10
As the death-bed whereon it must expire,
Consumed with that which it was nourish'd by.
This thou perceivest, which makes thy love more strong,
To love that well which thou must leave ere long.

74

But be contented: when that fell arrest
Without all bail shall carry me away,

Sonnet 73: 4. Bare . . . choirs, i.e., leafless boughs are compared to the Gothic tracery of ruined abbeys. 7. by and by, at once. 8. seals up all, concludes everything. 12. consumed with that, i.e., choked with the ashes.
Sonnet 74: 1. fell, cruel; arrest, i.e., by Death's officer.

My life hath in this line some interest,
Which for memorial still with thee shall stay.
When thou reviewest this, thou dost review 5
The very part was consecrate to thee:
The earth can have but earth, which is his due;
My spirit is thine, the better part of me:
So then thou hast but lost the dregs of life,
The prey of worms, my body being dead; 10
The coward conquest of a wretch's knife,
Too base of thee to be rememberèd.
The worth of that is that which it contains,
And that is this, and this with thee remains.

75

So are you to my thoughts as food to life,
Or as sweet-season'd showers are to the ground;
And for the peace of you I hold such strife
As 'twixt a miser and his wealth is found;
Now proud as an enjoyer, and anon 5
Doubting the filching age will steal his treasure;
Now counting best to be with you alone,
Then better'd that the world may see my pleasure:
Sometime all full with feasting on your sight,
And by and by clean starvèd for a look; 10
Possessing or pursuing no delight,
Save what is had or must from you be took.
Thus do I pine and surfeit day by day,
Or gluttoning on all, or all away.

76

Why is my verse so barren of new pride,
So far from variation or quick change?
Why with the time do I not glance aside
To new-found methods and to compounds strange?
Why write I still all one, ever the same, 5
And keep invention in a noted weed,
That every word doth almost tell my name,
Showing their birth and where they did proceed?
O, know, sweet love, I always write of you,
And you and love are still my argument; 10
So all my best is dressing old words new,
Spending again what is already spent:
For as the sun is daily new and old,
So is my love still telling what is told.

77

Thy glass will show thee how thy beauties wear,
Thy dial how thy precious minutes waste;
The vacant leaves thy mind's imprint will bear,
And of this book this learning mayst thou taste.
The wrinkles which thy glass will truly show 5
Of mouthèd graves will give thee memory;
Thou by thy dial's shady stealth mayst know
Time's thievish progress to eternity.
Look, what thy memory cannot contain
Commit to these waste blanks, and thou shalt find 10
Those children nursed, deliver'd from thy brain
To take a new acquaintance of thy mind.
These offices, so oft as thou wilt look,
Shall profit thee and much enrich thy book.

78

So oft have I invoked thee for my Muse
And found such fair assistance in my verse
As every alien pen hath got my use
And under thee their poesy disperse.
Thine eyes, that taught the dumb on high to sing 5
And heavy ignorance aloft to fly,
Have added feathers to the learnèd's wing
And given grace a double majesty.
Yet be most proud of that which I compile,
Whose influence is thine and born of thee: 10
In others' works thou dost but mend the style,

3. **interest,** claim. 9. **dregs of life,** the body. 14. **that is this,** i.e., my spirit is this [poem of mine].

Sonnet 75: 2. **sweet-season'd,** well tempered. 3. **peace of you,** contentment in you. 6. **Doubting,** suspecting. 8. **better'd,** made happier. 10. **by and by,** immediately. 14. **Or,** either; **or all away,** or all pleasure being absent.

Sonnet 76: 1. **new pride,** novelty. 2. **quick,** lively. 3. **time,** age. 4. **compounds,** i.e., compound epithets, made by joining two words in one, e.g., "giant-rude." 6. **invention,** poetic fancy; **noted weed,** familiar dress. 10. **argument,** theme.

Sonnet 77: This poem was sent with three gifts: a mirror, a sun dial, and a notebook. 1. **glass,** looking glass. 6. **mouthed,** gaping. 7. **shady stealths,** stealthy shadow. 13. **offices,** functions of the three objects.

Sonnet 78: 3. **As,** that; **got my use,** adopted my practice. 4. **thee,** i.e., your patronage. 5. **on high,** in an elevated style. 9. **compile,** compose. 10. **influence,** inspiration.

And arts with thy sweet graces graced be;
But thou art all my art, and dost advance
As high as learning my rude ignorance.

79

Whilst I alone did call upon thy aid,
My verse alone had all thy gentle grace;
But now my gracious numbers are decay'd,
And my sick Muse doth give another place.
I grant, sweet love, thy lovely argument 5
Deserves the travail of a worthier pen;
Yet what of thee thy poet doth invent
He robs thee of, and pays it thee again.
He lends thee virtue, and he stole that word
For thy behavior; beauty doth he give, 10
And found it in thy cheek: he can afford
No praise to thee but what in thee doth live.
Then thank him not for that which he doth say,
Since what he owes thee thou thyself dost pay.

80

O, how I faint when I of you do write,
Knowing a better spirit doth use your name,
And in the praise thereof spends all his might,
To make me tongue-tied, speaking of your fame!
But since your worth, wide as the ocean is, 5
The humble as the proudest sail doth bear,
My saucy bark, inferior far to his,
On your broad main doth wilfully appear.
Your shallowest help will hold me up afloat,
Whilst he upon your soundless deep doth ride; 10
Or, being wreck'd, I am a worthless boat,
He of tall building and of goodly pride:
Then if he thrive and I be cast away,
The worst was this; my love was my decay.

81

Or I shall live your epitaph to make,
Or you survive when I in earth am rotten;
From hence your memory death cannot take,
Although in me each part will be forgotten.
Your name from hence immortal life shall have, 5
Though I, once gone, to all the world must die:
The earth can yield me but a common grave,
When you entombèd in men's eyes shall lie.
Your monument shall be my gentle verse,
Which eyes not yet created shall o'er-read; 10
And tongues to be your being shall rehearse,
When all the breathers of this world are dead;
You still shall live—such virtue hath my pen—
Where breath most breathes, even in the mouths of men.

82

I grant thou wert not married to my Muse,
And therefore mayst without attaint o'erlook
The dedicated words which writers use
Of their fair subject, blessing every book.
Thou art as fair in knowledge as in hue, 5
Finding thy worth a limit past my praise;
And therefore art enforced to seek anew
Some fresher stamp of the time-bettering days,
And do so, love; yet when they have devised
What strainèd touches rhetoric can lend, 10
Thou truly fair wert truly sympathized
In true plain words by thy true-telling friend;
And their gross painting might be better used
Where cheeks need blood; in thee it is abused.

83

I never saw that you did painting need,
And therefore to your fair no painting set;
I found, or thought I found, you did exceed
The barren tender of a poet's debt:
And therefore have I slept in your report, 5

12. **arts**, learning. 13. **advance**, raise in worth. In this poem Shakespeare begins to write of "the rival poet."
Sonnet 79: 4. **give . . . place**, give place to another. 5. **thy . . . argument**, the theme of your loveliness.
Sonnet 80: 2. **better spirit**, generally thought to be George Chapman. 7. **saucy**, presumptuous. 8. **wilfully**, boldly. 10. **soundless**, unfathomable. 12. **tall**, fine. 14. **decay**, ruin.
Sonnet 81: 4. **in . . . part**, each of my characteristics. 7. **common**, lowly. 12. **world**, age.
Sonnet 82: 2. **attaint**, disgrace; **o'erlook**, peruse. 3. **dedicated words**, eulogistic words used in dedications to patrons. 5. **hue**, beauty. 6. **limit**, reach; **past**, beyond. 11. **sympathized**, expressed with sympathy. 13. **gross painting**, i.e., exaggeration. 14. **abused**, misused, i.e., your beauty needs no exaggeration.
Sonnet 83: 1. **painting**, rhetorical decoration. 4. **tender**, offering. 5. **slept . . . report**, been inactive in describing you.

That you yourself, being extant, well might show
How far a modern quill doth come too short,
Speaking of worth, what worth in you doth grow.
This silence for my sin you did impute,
Which shall be most my glory, being dumb;
For I impair not beauty being mute, 11
When others would give life and bring a tomb.
Their lives more life in one of your fair eyes
Than both your poets can in praise devise.

84

Who is it that says most? which can say more
Than this rich praise, that you alone are you?
In whose confine immurèd is the store
Which should example where your equal grew.
Lean penury within that pen doth dwell 5
That to his subject lends not some small glory;
But he that writes of you, if he can tell
That you are you, so dignifies his story.
Let him but copy what in you is writ,
Not making worse what nature made so clear, 10
And such a counterpart shall fame his wit,
Making his style admirèd every where.
You to your beauteous blessings add a curse,
Being fond on praise, which makes your praises worse.

85

My tongue-tied Muse in manners holds her still,
While comments of your praise, richly compiled,
Reserve their character with golden quill,
And precious phrase by all the Muses filed.
I think good thoughts, whilst other write good words, 5
And, like unletter'd clerk, still cry "Amen"
To every hymn that able spirit affords,
In polish'd form of well refinèd pen.
Hearing you praised, I say " 'Tis so, 'tis true,"
And to the most of praise add something more; 10
But that is in my thought, whose love to you,
Though words come hindmost, holds his rank before.
Then others for the breath of words respect,
Me for my dumb thoughts, speaking in effect.

86

Was it the proud full sail of his great verse,
Bound for the prize of all too precious you,
That did my ripe thoughts in my brain inhearse,
Making their tomb the womb wherein they grew?
Was it his spirit, by spirits taught to write 5
Above a mortal pitch, that struck me dead?
No, neither he, nor his compeers by night
Giving him aid, my verse astonishèd.
He, nor that affable familiar ghost
Which nightly gulls him with intelligence, 10
As victors, of my silence cannot boast;
I was not sick of any fear from thence:
But when your countenance fill'd up his line,
Then lack'd I matter; that enfeebled mine.

87

Farewell! thou art too dear for my possessing,
And like enough thou know'st thy estimate:
The charter of thy worth gives thee releasing;
My bonds in thee are all determinate.

7. **modern**, ordinary. 9. **for . . . impute**, you rated as a sin in me. 14. **both your poets**, i.e., Shakespeare and his rival.

Sonnet 84: 1. **Who . . . more**, Who is it, even he who says most, that can say more. 3-4. **In . . . grew**, who possesses a store of beauty that can furnish examples of beauty equal to yours. 10. **clear**, glorious. 11. **fame his wit**, make famous the product of his wit, i.e., his poems. 14. **fond on**, doting on; **which . . . worse**, which debases you.

Sonnet 85: 1. **in manners**, modestly. 2. **compiled**, composed. 3. **Reserve**, preserve; **character**, handwriting. 4. **filed**, polished. 6. **unletter'd**, illiterate. 7. **that . . . spirit**, i.e., the rival poet. 13-4. **Then . . . effect**, Then let others be highly regarded for spoken words, me for silent thoughts which are of real importance.

Sonnet 86: 3. **inhearse**, bury. 7. **compeers by night**, thought to refer to Chapman's associates in the study of the new astronomy, called by Shakespeare in Love's Labour's Lost, "the school of night." 8. **astonished**, dismayed. 10. **gulls**, cheats; **intelligence**, news.

Sonnet 87: 2. **estimate**, value. 4. **determinate**, ended.

For how do I hold thee but by thy granting? 5
And for that riches where is my deserving?
The cause of this fair gift in me is wanting,
And so my patent back again is swerving.
Thyself thou gavest, thy own worth then not knowing,
Or me, to whom thou gavest it, else mistaking; 10
So thy great gift, upon misprision growing,
Comes home again, on better judgment making.
Thus have I had thee, as a dream doth flatter,
In sleep a king, but waking no such matter.

88

When thou shalt be disposed to set me light,
And place my merit in the eye of scorn,
Upon thy side against myself I'll fight,
And prove thee virtuous, though thou art forsworn.
With mine own weakness being best acquainted, 5
Upon thy part I can set down a story
Of faults conceal'd, wherein I am attainted;
That thou in losing me shalt win much glory:
And I by this will be a gainer too;
For bending all my loving thoughts on thee,
The injuries that to myself I do, 11
Doing thee vantage, double-vantage me.
Such is my love, to thee I so belong,
That for thy right myself will bear all wrong.

89

Say that thou didst forsake me for some fault,
And I will comment upon that offense:
Speak of my lameness, and I straight will halt,
Against thy reasons making no defense.
Thou canst not, love, disgrace me half so ill, 5
To set a form upon desirèd change,
As I'll myself disgrace; knowing thy will,
I will acquaintance strangle and look strange;
Be absent from thy walks; and in my tongue
Thy sweet belovèd name no more shall dwell, 10
Lest I, too much profane, should do it wrong,
And haply of our old acquaintance tell.
For thee, against myself I'll vow debate,
For I must ne'er love him whom thou dost hate.

90

Then hate me when thou wilt; if ever, now;
Now, while the world is bent my deeds to cross,
Join with the spite of fortune, make me bow,
And do not drop in for an after-loss:
Ah, do not, when my heart hath 'scaped this sorrow, 5
Come in the rearward of a conquer'd woe;
Give not a windy night a rainy morrow,
To linger out a purposed overthrow.
If thou wilt leave me, do not leave me last,
When other petty griefs have done their spite, 10
But in the onset come: so shall I taste
At first the very worst of fortune's might;
And other strains of woe, which now seem woe,
Compared with loss of thee will not seem so.

91

Some glory in their birth, some in their skill,
Some in their wealth, some in their body's force;
Some in their garments, though new-fangled ill;
Some in their hawks and hounds, some in their horse;
And every humor hath his adjunct pleasure, 5
Wherein it finds a joy above the rest:
But these particulars are not my measure;
All these I better in one general best.
Thy love is better than high birth to me,

8. patent, privilege. 11. upon . . . growing, being founded upon a misunderstanding.
Sonnet 88: 1. set me light, esteem me of little worth. 4. thou . . . forsworn, you are perjured. 6. Upon . . . part, in your behalf. 7. attainted, dishonored.
Sonnet 89: 2. comment, expatiate. 3. halt, limp. 6. to . . . change, to give a good appearance to the change you desire. 13. debate, contest. 8. look strange, appear to be a stranger to you.
Sonnet 90: 2. cross, thwart. 4. And . . . after-loss, and do not come in for grief at a later time. 11. in the onset, in the beginning. 13. strains, feelings.
Sonnet 91: 3. though . . . ill, though fashionable, yet unbecoming. 5. humor, disposition; adjunct, associated. 7. measure, i.e., of joy.

Richer than wealth, prouder than garments' cost, 10
Of more delight than hawks or horses be;
And having thee, of all men's pride I boast:
Wretched in this alone, that thou mayst take
All this away and me most wretched make.

92

But do thy worst to steal thyself away,
For term of life thou art assurèd mine;
And life no longer than thy love will stay,
For it depends upon that love of thine.
Then need I not to fear the worst of wrongs, 5
When in the least of them my life hath end.
I see a better state to me belongs.
Than that which on thy humor doth depend:
Thou canst not vex me with inconstant mind,
Since that my life on thy revolt doth lie. 10
O, what a happy title do I find,
Happy to have thy love, happy to die!
But what's so blessed-fair that fears no blot?
Thou mayst be false, and yet I know it not.

93

So shall I live, supposing thou art true,
Like a deceivèd husband; so love's face
May still seem love to me, though alter'd new;
Thy looks with me, thy heart in other place:
For there can live no hatred in thine eye, 5
Therefore in that I cannot know thy change.
In many's looks the false heart's history
Is writ in moods and frowns and wrinkles strange,
But heaven in thy creation did decree
That in thy face sweet love should ever dwell; 10
Whate'er thy thoughts or thy heart's workings be,
Thy looks should nothing thence but sweetness tell.
How like Eve's apple doth thy beauty grow,
If thy sweet virtue answer not thy show.

94

They that have power to hurt and will do none,
That do not do the thing they most do show,
Who, moving others, are themselves as stone,
Unmovèd, cold and to temptation slow;
They rightly do inherit heaven's graces 5
And husband nature's riches from expense;
They are the lords and owners of their faces,
Others but stewards of their excellence.
The summer's flower is to the summer sweet,
Though to itself it only live and die, 10
But if that flower with base infection meet,
The basest weed outbraves his dignity:
For sweetest things turn sourest by their deeds;
Lilies that fester smell far worse than weeds.

95

How sweet and lovely dost thou make the shame
Which, like a canker in the fragrant rose,
Doth spot the beauty of thy budding name!
O, in what sweets dost thou thy sins inclose!
That tongue that tells the story of thy days, 5
Making lascivious comments on thy sport,
Cannot dispraise but in a kind of praise;
Naming thy name blesses an ill report.
O, what a mansion have those vices got
Which for their habitation chose out thee, 10
Where beauty's veil doth cover every blot
And all things turn to fair that eyes can see!
Take heed, dear heart, of this large privilege;
The hardest knife ill used doth lose his edge.

96

Some say, thy fault is youth, some wantonness;
Some say, thy grace is youth and gentle sport;

Sonnet 92: 5-6. **Then . . . end,** Then I do not need to fear continuing to live without your love, when the initial loss of it would bring death. 10. **on . . . lie,** depends on whether or not you desert me.

Sonnet 93: 13. **Eve's apple,** good to look at, but disastrous to taste; **answer not,** does not correspond with.

Sonnet 94: 2. **That . . . show,** i.e., whose beauty most awakens love they will not return. 6. **husband,** hoard; **expense,** waste. 12. **outbraves his dignity,** surpasses its worth.

Sonnet 95: 2. **canker,** cankerworm. 6. **sport,** sensuality. 8. **blesses an ill report,** removes, like a priest's blessing, the sting from the evil said of you. 13. **privilege,** license. This and the following sonnet are probably addressed to the dark lady.

Both grace and faults are loved of more and less:
Thou makest faults graces that to thee resort.
As on the finger of a thronèd queen 5
The basest jewel will be well esteem'd,
So are those errors that in thee are seen
To truths translated and for true things deem'd.
How many lambs might the stern wolf betray,
If like a lamb he could his looks translate! 10
How many gazers mightst thou lead away,
If thou wouldst use the strength of all thy state!
But do not so; I love thee in such sort,
As thou being mine, mine is thy good report.

97

How like a winter hath my absence been
From thee, the pleasure of the fleeting year:
What freezings have I felt, what dark days seen!
What old December's bareness every where!
And yet this time removed was summer's time; 5
The teeming autumn, big with rich increase,
Bearing the wanton burthen of the prime,
Like widowed wombs after their lord's decease:
Yet this abundant issue seem'd to me
But hope of orphans and unfather'd fruit; 10
For summer and his pleasures wait on thee,
And, thou away, the very birds are mute;
Or, if they sing, 'tis with so dull a cheer
That leaves look pale, dreading the winter's near.

98

From you have I been absent in the spring,
When proud-pied April, dress'd in all his trim,
Hath put a spirit of youth in every thing,
That heavy Saturn laugh'd and leap'd with him.
Yet nor the lays of birds, nor the sweet smell 5
Of different flowers in odor and in hue,
Could make me any summer's story tell,
Or from their proud lap pluck them where they grew:
Nor did I wonder at the lily's white,
Nor praise the deep vermilion in the rose; 10
They were but sweet, but figures of delight,
Drawn after you, you pattern of all those.
Yet seem'd it winter still, and, you away,
As with your shadow I with these did play.

99

The forward violet thus did I chide:
Sweet thief, whence didst thou steal thy sweet that smells,
If not from my love's breath? The purple pride
Which on thy soft cheek for complexion dwells
In my love's veins thou hast too grossly dyed. 5
The lily I condemnèd for thy hand,
And buds of marjoram had stol'n thy hair;
The roses fearfully on thorns did stand,
One blushing shame, another white despair;
A third, nor red nor white, had stol'n of both, 10
And to his robbery had annex'd thy breath;
But, for his theft, in pride of all his growth
A vengeful canker eat him up to death.
More flowers I noted, yet I none could see
But sweet or color it had stol'n from thee. 15

100

Where art thou, Muse, that thou forget'st so long
To speak of that which gives thee all thy might?
Spend'st thou thy fury on some worthless song,

Sonnet 96: 3. **more and less**, persons of all ranks. 7. **errors**, vices. 8. **truths translated**, transformed to virtues. 12. **strength . . . state**, the full measure of your strength.

Sonnet 97: 5. **time removed**, time of absence. 7. **prime**, spring. 10. **of orphans**, of leaving posthumous children. 13. **so dull a cheer**, spirits so low.

Sonnet 98. 2. **proud-pied**, proudly decked in many colors; **trim**, finery. 4. **heavy Saturn**, Saturn was supposed to be cold and melancholy. 11. **figures**, phantoms. 14. **shadow**, figment of memory or the imagination.

Sonnet 99: This is the only one of Shakespeare's sonnets of 15 lines. 1. **forward**, early. 6. **for thy hand**, for stealing the whiteness of your hand. 7. **buds of marjoram**, are of a reddish brown color.

Sonnet 100: 1. **so long**, three years as in 104, 3. 3. **fury**, inspiration.

Darkening thy power to lend base subjects light?
Return, forgetful Muse, and straight redeem 5
In gentle numbers time so idly spent;
Sing to the ear that doth thy lays esteem
And gives thy pen both skill and argument.
Rise, resty Muse, my love's sweet face survey,
If Time have any wrinkle graven there; 10
If any, be a satire to decay,
And make Time's spoils despisèd every where.
Give my love fame faster than Time wastes life;
So thou prevent'st his scythe and crooked knife.

101

O truant Muse, what shall be thy amends
For thy neglect of truth in beauty dyed?
Both truth and beauty on my love depends;
So dost thou too, and therein dignified.
Make answer, Muse: wilt thou not haply say, 5
"Truth needs no color, with his color fix'd;
Beauty no pencil, beauty's truth to lay;
But best is best, if never intermix'd"?
Because he needs no praise, wilt thou be dumb?
Excuse not silence so, for 't lies in thee 10
To make him much outlive a gilded tomb
And to be praised of ages yet to be.
Then do thy office, Muse; I teach thee how
To make him seem long hence as he shows now.

102

My love is strengthen'd, though more weak in seeming;
I love not less, though less the show appear:
That love is merchandized whose rich esteeming
The owner's tongue doth publish every where.
Our love was new, and then but in the spring, 5
When I was wont to greet it with my lays;
As Philomel in summer's front doth sing,
And stops her pipe in growth of riper days:
Not that the summer is less pleasant now
Than when her mournful hymns did hush the night, 10
But that wild music burthens every bough,
And sweets grown common lose their dear delight.
Therefore, like her, I sometime hold my tongue,
Because I would not dull you with my song.

103

Alack, what poverty my Muse brings forth,
That having such a scope to show her pride,
The argument, all bare, is of more worth
Than when it hath my added praise beside!
O, blame me not, if I no more can write! 5
Look in your glass, and there appears a face
That over-goes my blunt invention quite,
Dulling my lines and doing me disgrace.
Were it not sinful then, striving to mend,
To mar the subject that before was well? 10
For to no other pass my verses tend
Than of your graces and your gifts to tell;
And more, much more, than in my verse can sit,
Your own glass shows you when you look in it.

104

To me, fair friend, you never can be old,
For as you were when first your eye I eyed,
Such seems your beauty still. Three winters' cold
Have from the forests shook three summers' pride,
Three beauteous springs to yellow autumn turn'd 5
In process of the seasons have I seen,
Three April perfumes in three hot Junes burn'd,
Since first I saw you fresh, which yet are green.
Ah, yet doth beauty, like a dial-hand,

9. resty, torpid. 11. be . . . decay, satirize Time's power to destroy. 12. spoils, loot. 14. prevent'st, forestall.
Sonnet 101: 4. dignified, i.e., art dignified. 6. color, artificial appearance, i.e., extenuation; fix'd, unchangeable. 7. lay, apply as color. 13. do thy office, perform your function.
Sonnet 102: 3. esteeming, worth. 7. Philomel, the nightingale; front, forehead, i.e., early days.

Sonnet 103: 3. argument, theme; all bare, i.e., in itself, without embellishment. 7. blunt, clumsy; invention, imaginative faculty. 11. pass, end. 13. sit, be contained.
Sonnet 104: 6. process, course. 8. fresh, not previously known, i.e., for the first time. 9. dial-hand, shadow on the sun dial.

Steal from his figure, and no pace perceived; 10
So your sweet hue, which methinks still doth stand,
Hath motion, and mine eye may be deceived:
For fear of which, hear this, thou age unbred;
Ere you were born was beauty's summer dead.

105

Let not my love be call'd idolatry,
Nor my belovèd as an idol show,
Since all alike my songs and praises be
To one, of one, still such, and ever so.
Kind is my love to-day, to-morrow kind, 5
Still constant in a wondrous excellence;
Therefore my verse to constancy confined,
One thing expressing, leaves out difference.
"Fair, kind, and true," is all my argument,
"Fair, kind, and true," varying to other words; 10
And in this change is my invention spent,
Three themes in one, which wondrous scope affords.
"Fair, kind, and true," have often lived alone,
Which three till now never kept seat in one.

106

When in the chronicle of wasted time
I see descriptions of the fairest wights,
And beauty making beautiful old rhyme
In praise of ladies dead and lovely knights,
Then, in the blazon of sweet beauty's best, 5
Of hand, of foot, of lip, of eye, of brow,
I see their antique pen would have express'd
Even such a beauty as you master now.
So all their praises are but prophecies
Of this our time, all you prefiguring; 10
And, for they look'd but with divining eyes,
They had not skill enough your worth to sing:
For we, which now behold these present days,
Have eyes to wonder, but lack tongues to praise.

107

Not mine own fears, nor the prophetic soul
Of the wide world dreaming on things to come,
Can yet the lease of my true love control,
Supposed as forfeit to a cónfined doom.
The mortal moon hath her eclipse endured, 5
And the sad augurs mock their own presage;
Incertainties now crown themselves assured,
And peace proclaims olives of endless age.
Now with the drops of this most balmy time
My love looks fresh, and Death to me subscribes, 10
Since, spite of him, I'll live in this poor rhyme,
While he insults o'er dull and speechless tribes:
And thou in this shalt find thy monument,
When tyrants' crests and tombs of brass are spent.

108

What's in the brain, that ink may character,
Which hath not figured to thee my true spirit?
What's new to speak, what new to register,
That may express my love, or thy dear merit?
Nothing, sweet boy; but yet, like prayers divine, 5
I must each day say o'er the very same;
Counting no old thing old, thou mine, I thine,
Even as when first I hallowed thy fair name.
So that eternal love in love's fresh case
Weighs not the dust and injury of age, 10
Nor gives to necessary wrinkles place,
But makes antiquity for aye his page;
Finding the first conceit of love there bred,
Where time and outward form would show it dead.

Sonnet 105: 2. slow, appear. 8. difference, variety.
Sonnet 106: 1. chronicle . . . time, history of past time. 2. wights, men. 5. blazon, description of a coat of arms. 8. master, possess. 11. for, because; divining, foreseeing.
Sonnet 107: This sonnet is thought to have been written in 1603, the year of the Queen's death and Southampton's release from prison by King James. 3. lease, duration. 4. confined doom, i.e., Southampton's imprisonment. 5. mortal . . . endured, the Queen's death or possibly the safe passing of her "climacteric" or sixty-third year, Sept. 6, 1596. 10. subscribes, submits. 12. insults, triumphs.
Sonnet 108: 1. character, write. 9. case, condition, i.e., of being always fresh. 12. antiquity, old age; page, servant. 13. first . . . love, i.e., passion; conceit, conception.

109

O, never say that I was false of heart,
Though absence seem'd my flame to qualify.
As easy might I from myself depart
As from my soul, which in thy breast doth lie:
That is my home of love: if I have ranged, 5
Like him that travels, I return again;
Just to the time, not with the time exchanged,
So that myself bring water for my stain.
Never believe, though in my nature reign'd
All frailties that besiege all kinds of blood, 10
That it could so preposterously be stain'd,
To leave for nothing all thy sum of good;
For nothing this wide universe I call,
Save thou, my rose; in it thou art my all.

110

Alas, 'tis true I have gone here and there,
And made myself a motley to the view,
Gored mine own thoughts, sold cheap what is most dear,
Made old offenses of affections new;
Most true it is that I have look'd on truth 5
Askance and strangely: but, by all above,
These blenches gave my heart another youth,
And worse essays proved thee my best of love.
Now all is done, have what shall have no end:
Mine appetite I never more will grind 10
On newer proof, to try an older friend,
A god in love, to whom I am confined.
Then give me welcome, next my heaven the best,
Even to thy pure and most most loving breast.

111

O, for my sake do you with Fortune chide,
The guilty goddess of my harmful deeds,
That did not better for my life provide
Than public means which public manners breeds.
Thence comes it that my name receives a brand, 5
And almost thence my nature is subdued
To what it works in, like the dyer's hand:
Pity me then and wish I were renew'd;
Whilst, like a willing patient, I will drink
Potions of eisel 'gainst my strong infection; 10
No bitterness that I will bitter think,
Nor double penance, to correct correction.
Pity me then, dear friend, and I assure ye
Even that your pity is enough to cure me.

112

Your love and pity doth the impression fill
Which vulgar scandal stamp'd upon my brow;
For what care I who calls me well or ill,
So you o'er-green my bad, my good allow?
You are my all the world, and I must strive 5
To know my shames and praises from your tongue;
None else to me, nor I to none alive,
That my steel'd sense or changes right or wrong.
In so profound abysm I throw all care
Of others' voices, that my adder's sense 10
To critic and to flatterer stoppèd are.
Mark how with my neglect I do dispense:
You are so strongly in my purpose bred
That all the world besides methinks are dead.

113

Since I left you mine eye is in my mind,
And that which governs me to go about
Doth part his function and is partly blind,
Seems seeing, but effectually is out;
For it no form delivers to the heart 5

Sonnet 109: 2. **qualify**, moderate. 7. **just to the time**, punctual to the time, i.e., not altered by time; **exchanged**, changed. 8. **stain**, i.e., his absence. This and the following sonnet were probably addressed to a woman.

Sonnet 110: 2. **motley to the view**, i.e., a public jester, a reference to his profession as an actor. 3. **Gored**, wounded. 4. **made . . . new**, made new friends who were offenses to my old ones. 5. **truth**, fidelity. 6. **strangely**, in a mistrustful manner. 7. **blenches**, side glances. 10. **grind**, whet. 11. **try**, test.

Sonnet 111: 4. **public means**, gaining my livelihood from public favor; **public**, vulgar. 6. **subdued**, subjugated. 8. **renew'd**, restored. 10. **eisel**, vinegar. 12. **correct correction**, perfect the correction (of my conduct).

Sonnet 112: 4. **o'er-green**, cover with grass. 7-8. **None . . . wrong**, no one but you and me exist for me, and only you can endow my hardened sensibility or my vacillating temper with a sense of right and wrong. 10. **adder's sense**, i.e., deafness. 12. **Mark . . . dispense**, notice how little I care for the neglect of others.

Sonnet 113: 1. **mine . . . mind**, I keep your image in my mind. 3. **part his function**, partly perform its office.

Of bird, of flower, or shape, which it doth latch:
Of his quick object hath the mind no part,
Nor his own vision holds what it doth catch;
For if it see the rudest or gentlest sight,
The most sweet favor or deformed'st creature, 10
The mountain or the sea, the day or night,
The crow or dove, it shapes them to your feature:
Incapable of more, replete with you,
My most true mind thus maketh mine untrue.

114

Or whether doth my mind, being crown'd with you,
Drink up the monarch's plague, this flattery?
Or whether shall I say, mine eye saith true,
And that your love taught it this alchemy,
To make of monsters and things indigest 5
Such cherubins as your sweet self resemble,
Creating every bad a perfect best,
As fast as objects to his beams assemble?
O, 'tis the first; 'tis flattery in my seeing,
And my great mind most kingly drinks it up: 10
Mine eye well knows what with his gust is 'greeing,
And to his palate doth prepare the cup:
If it be poison'd, 'tis the lesser sin
That mine eye loves it and doth first begin.

115

Those lines that I before have writ do lie,
Even those that said I could not love you dearer:
Yet then my judgment knew no reason why
My most full flame should afterwards burn clearer.
But reckoning Time, whose million'd accidents 5
Creep in 'twixt vows, and change decrees of kings,
Tan sacred beauty, blunt the sharp'st intents,
Divert strong minds to the course of altering things;
Alas, why, fearing of Time's tyranny,
Might I not then say "Now I love you best," 10
When I was certain o'er incertainty,
Crowning the present, doubting of the rest?
Love is a babe; then might I not say so,
To give full growth to that which still doth grow?

116

Let me not to the marriage of true minds
Admit impediments. Love is not love
Which alters when it alteration finds,
Or bends with the remover to remove:
O, no; it is an ever-fixèd mark, 5
That looks on tempests and is never shaken;
It is the star to every wandering bark,
Whose worth 's unknown, although his height be taken.
Love 's not Time's fool, though rosy lips and cheeks
Within his bending sickle's compass come; 10
Love alters not with his brief hours and weeks,
But bears it out even to the edge of doom.
If this be error and upon me proved,
I never writ, nor no man ever loved.

117

Accuse me thus: that I have scanted all
Wherein I should your great deserts repay,
Forgot upon your dearest love to call,
Whereto all bonds do tie me day by day;
That I have frequent been with unknown minds, 5
And given to time your own dear-purchased right;
That I have hoisted sail to all the winds

6. latch, lay hold of. 7. quick object, objects passing rapidly before the eye. 10. favor, countenance. 14. mine, i.e., my eye.

Sonnet 114: 1. Or whether doth, is it true that; crown'd with, brimful with. 5. indigest, formless. 11. gust, taste (of my mind).

Sonnet 115: 5. reckoning Time, taking Time's power into consideration; million'd, millionfold.

Sonnet 116: 4. remover, inconstant person; to remove, to change his place of abode. 5. mark, prominent object by which sailors guided their course. 8. whose . . . taken, whose occult influence is unknown, although his altitude be ascertained. 9. Love's . . . fool, Love is not mocked by Time. 12. doom, Doomsday.

Sonnet 117: 1. scanted all, furnished an inadequate supply of everything. 5. frequent, familiar; unknown minds, persons of little importance. 6. time, the age.

Which should transport me farthest from your sight.
Book both my willfulness and errors down,
And on just proof surmise accumulate; 10
Bring me within the level of your frown,
But shoot not at me in your waken'd hate;
Since my appeal says I did strive to prove
The constancy and virtue of your love.

118

Like as, to make our appetites more keen,
With eager compounds we our palate urge;
As, to prevent our maladies unseen,
We sicken to shun sickness when we purge;
Even so, being full of your ne'er-cloying sweetness, 5
To bitter sauces did I frame my feeding;
And sick of welfare found a kind of meetness
To be diseased, ere that there was true needing.
Thus policy in love, to anticipate
The ills that were not, grew to faults assured, 10
And brought to medicine a healthful state,
Which, rank of goodness, would by ill be cured:
But thence I learn, and find the lesson true,
Drugs poison him that so fell sick of you.

119

What potions have I drunk of Siren tears,
Distill'd from limbecks foul as hell within,
Applying fears to hopes and hopes to fears,
Still losing when I saw myself to win!
What wretched errors hath my heart committed, 5
Whilst it hath thought itself so blessèd never!
How have mine eyes out of their spheres been fitted,
In the distraction of this madding fever!
O benefit of ill! now I find true
That better is by evil still made better; 10
And ruin'd love, when it is built anew,
Grows fairer than at first, more strong, far greater.
So I return rebuked to my content,
And gain by ill thrice more than I have spent.

120

That you were once unkind befriends me now,
And for that sorrow which I then did feel
Needs must I under my transgressions bow,
Unless my nerves were brass or hammer'd steel.
For if you were by my unkindness shaken, 5
As I by yours, you've pass'd a hell of time;
And I, a tyrant, have no leisure taken
To weigh how once I suffer'd in your crime.
O, that our night of woe might have remember'd
My deepest sense, how hard true sorrow hits, 10
And soon to you, as you to me, then tender'd
The humble salve which wounded bosoms fits!
But that your trespass now becomes a fee;
Mine ransoms yours, and yours must ransom me.

121

'Tis better to be vile than vile esteemed,
When not to be receives reproach of being;
And the just pleasure lost, which is so deemed
Not by our feeling, but by others' seeing:
For why should others' false adulterate eyes 5
Give salutation to my sportive blood?
Or on my frailties why are frailer spies,
Which in their wills count bad what I think good?
No, I am that I am, and they that level
At my abuses reckon up their own: 10
I may be straight, though they themselves be bevel;
By their rank thoughts my deeds must not be shown;

10. **on . . . accumulate**, add to what you know what you suspect. 11. **level**, aim.
Sonnet 118: 2. **eager**, pungent. 7. **sick of welfare**, sated with happiness. 7-8. **meetness to be**, fitness in being. 9. **policy**, prudence. 10. **assured**, positive. 11. **brought to medicine**, prescribed medicine for. 12. **rank of**, overfed with.
Sonnet 119: 2. **limbecks**, alembics, stills. 4. **still . . . win**, gaining victories over new loves which were really losses. 7. **fitted**, convulsed. 8. **madding fever**, i.e., his passion for the dark lady.
Sonnet 120: 4. **nerves**, sinews. 8. **weigh**, consider; **your crime**, i.e., your offense against me. 9. **remember'd**, reminded. 13. **fee**, recompense.
Sonnet 121: 5. **adulterate**, vicious. 6. **sportive**, amorous, wanton. 8. **in their wills**, according to their pleasure. 9. **level**, aim. 10. **my abuses**, wrongs I do. 11. **bevel**, crooked.

Unless this general evil they maintain,
All men are bad and in their badness reign.

122

Thy gift, thy tables, are within my brain
Full character'd with lasting memory,
Which shall above that idle rank remain,
Beyond all date, even to eternity:
Or, at the least, so long as brain and heart 5
Have faculty by nature to subsist;
Till each to razed oblivion yield his part
Of thee, thy record never can be miss'd.
That poor retention could not so much hold,
Nor need I tallies thy dear love to score; 10
Therefore to give them from me was I bold,
To trust those tables that receive thee more:
To keep an adjunct to remember thee
Were to import forgetfulness in me.

123

No, Time, thou shalt not boast that I do change:
Thy pyramids built up with newer might
To me are nothing novel, nothing strange;
They are but dressings of a former sight.
Our dates are brief, and therefore we admire 5
What thou dost foist upon us that is old;
And rather make them born to our desire
Than think that we before have heard them told.
Thy registers and thee I both defy,
Not wondering at the present nor the past, 10
For thy records and what we see doth lie,
Made more or less by thy continual haste.
This I do vow, and this shall ever be,
I will be true, despite thy scythe and thee.

124

If my dear love were but the child of state,
It might for Fortune's bastard be unfather'd,
As subject to Time's love or to Time's hate,
Weeds among weeds, or flowers with flowers gather'd.
No, it was builded far from accident; 5
It suffers not in smiling pomp, nor falls
Under the blow of thrallèd discontent,
Whereto the inviting time our fashion calls:
It fears not policy, that heretic,
Which works on leases of short-number'd hours. 10
But all alone stands hugely politic,
That it nor grows with heat nor drowns with showers
To this I witness call the fools of time,
Which die for goodness, who have lived for crime.

125

Were 't aught to me I bore the canopy,
With my extern the outward honoring,
Or laid great bases for eternity,
Which prove more short than waste or ruining?
Have I not seen dwellers on form and favor 5
Lose all, and more, by paying too much rent,
For compound sweet forgoing simple savor,
Pitiful thrivers, in their gazing spent?
No, let me be obsequious in thy heart,
And take thou my oblation, poor but free, 10
Which is not mix'd with seconds, knows no art
But mutual render, only me for thee.
Hence, thou suborn'd informer! a true soul
When most impeach'd stands least in thy control.

126

O thou, my lovely boy, who in thy power
Dost hold Time's fickle glass, his sickle, hour;

14. **reign**, exult.

Sonnet 122: 1. **tables**, notebook. 2. **character'd**, written. 3. **idle rank**, empty series of leaves. 7. **razed oblivion**, the oblivion of obliteration. 9. **poor retention**, the notebook poor in retention as compared to the brain. 10. **tallies**, sticks on which notches were cut, by which accounts were kept. 13. **adjunct**, object.

Sonnet 123: 2. **pyramids**, any massive structures; **newer**, more recent. 4. **dressings**, refurbishings; **former sight**, what we have seen before. 5. **dates**, years. 12. **Made . . . less**, made to wax and wane.

Sonnet 124: 1. **state**, accident. 2. **unfather'd**, without an acknowledged father. 5. **accident**, chance. 7. **thralled discontent**, discontent held in subjection. 8. **our fashion calls**, makes fashionable. 9. **policy**, self-interest; **heretic**, i.e., faithless in love. 11. **hugely politic**, vastly wise. 13. **fools**, play things. 14. **which . . . goodness**, who die in the odor of piety.

Sonnet 125: 1. **Were't**, would it be; **bore the canopy**, rendered public homage. 2. **extern**, outward appearance. 3. **eternity**, i.e., loving forever. 5. **favor**, features. 6. **and more**, i.e., even liking. 8. **Pitiful thrivers**, i.e., bad business men, because they expended all without any return. 9. **obsequious**, devoted. 11. **seconds**, inferior matter. 12. **mutual render**, equal exchange. 13. **suborn'd**, perjured; **informer**, i.e., jealousy.

Sonnet 126: This poem in six rhymed couplets marks the close of one series. 2. **hold**, hold in check (all the changes wrought by Time).

Who hast by waning grown, and therein show'st
Thy lovers withering as thy sweet self grow'st;
If Nature, sovereign mistress over wrack, 5
As thou goest onwards, still will pluck thee back,
She keeps thee to this purpose, that her skill
May time disgrace and wretched minutes kill.
Yet fear her, O thou minion of her pleasure!
She may detain, but not still keep, her treasure: 10
Her audit, though delay'd, answer'd must be
And her quietus is to render thee.

127

In the old age black was not counted fair,
Or if it were, it bore not beauty's name;
But now is black beauty's successive heir,
And beauty slander'd with a bastard shame:
For since each hand hath put on nature's power, 5
Fairing the foul with art's false borrow'd face,
Sweet beauty hath no name, no holy bower,
But is profaned, if not lives in disgrace.
Therefore my mistress' eyes are raven black,
Her eyes so suited, and they mourners seem 10
At such who, not born fair, no beauty lack,
Slandering creation with a false esteem:
Yet so they mourn, becoming of their woe,
That every tongue says beauty should look so.

128

How oft, when thou, my music, music play'st,
Upon that blessed wood whose motion sounds
With thy sweet fingers, when thou gently sway'st
The wiry concord that mine ear confounds,
Do I envy those jacks that nimble leap 5
To kiss the tender inward of thy hand,
Whilst my poor lips, which should that harvest reap,
At the wood's boldness by thee blushing stand
To be so tickled, they would change their state
And situation with those dancing chips, 10
O'er whom thy fingers walk with gentle gait,
Making dead wood more blest than living lips.
Since saucy jacks so happy are in this,
Give them thy fingers, me thy lips to kiss.

129

The expense of spirit in a waste of shame
Is lust in action; and till action, lust
Is perjured, murderous, bloody, full of blame,
Savage, extreme, rude, cruel, not to trust;
Enjoy'd no sooner but despisèd straight; 5
Past reason hunted; and no sooner had,
Past reason hated, as a swallowed bait,
On purpose laid to make the taker mad:
Mad in pursuit, and in possession so;
Had, having, and in quest to have, extreme; 10
A bliss in proof, and proved, a very woe;
Before, a joy proposed; behind, a dream.
All this the world well knows; yet none knows well
To shun the heaven that leads men to this hell.

130

My mistress' eyes are nothing like the sun;
Coral is far more red than her lips' red:
If snow be white, why then her breasts are dun;
If hairs be wires, black wires grow on her head.
I have seen roses damask'd, red and white, 5
But no such roses see I in her cheeks;
And in some perfumes is there more delight
Than in the breath that from my mistress reeks.

3. **Who . . . grown**, who has grown more beautiful as he has grown older. 5. **wrack**, destruction. 6. **pluck thee back**, i.e., keep you young. 12. **quietus**, settling of the account; **render**, surrender.

Sonnet 127: 1. **black**, dark complexion. 3. **successive**, legitimate. 4. **And . . . shame**, i.e., because blonde beauty was supposed to be produced by bleaches. 10. **suited**, clothed. 11. **No beauty lack**, because the result of artificial aid. 12. **creation**, nature. 13. **becoming of**, gracing.

Sonnet 128: 2. **wood**, i.e., keys of the virginal. 5. **jacks**, Shakespeare means "keys," really = the quill that plucked the strings of a virginal. The only mistake made anywhere by Shakespeare in musical terminology.

Sonnet 129: 1. **expense**, expenditure; **spirit**, vital power. 2. **till action**, until expressed in deeds. 11. **in proof**, in the act of testing; **proved**, experienced. 12. **dream**, i.e., distortion.

Sonnet 130: This sonnet ridicules the extravagant comparisons of the imitators of Petrarch. 5. **damask'd**, of mingled white and red.

I love to hear her speak, yet well I know
That music hath a far more pleasing sound: 10
I grant I never saw a goddess go,
My mistress, when she walks, treads on the ground:
And yet, by heaven, I think my love as rare
As any she belied with false compare.

131

Thou art as tyrannous, so as thou art,
As those whose beauties proudly make them cruel;
For well thou know'st to my dear doting heart
Thou art the fairest and most precious jewel.
Yet, in good faith, some say that thee behold, 5
Thy face hath not the power to make love groan:
To say they err I dare not be so bold,
Although I swear it to myself alone.
And to be sure that is not false I swear,
A thousand groans, but thinking on thy face, 10
One on another's neck, do witness bear
Thy black is fairest in my judgment's place.
In nothing art thou black save in thy deeds,
And thence this slander, as I think, proceeds.

132

Thine eyes I love, and they, as pitying me,
Knowing thy heart torments me with disdain,
Have put on black and loving mourners be,
Looking with pretty ruth upon my pain.
And truly not the morning sun of heaven 5
Better becomes the gray cheeks of the east,
Nor that full star that ushers in the even
Doth half that glory to the sober west,
As those two mourning eyes become thy face:
O, let it then as well beseem thy heart 10
To mourn for me, since mourning doth thee grace,
And suit thy pity like in every part.
Then will I swear beauty herself is black,
And all they foul that thy complexion lack.

133

Beshrew that heart that makes my heart to groan
For that deep wound it gives my friend and me!
Is 't not enough to torture me alone,
But slave to slavery my sweet'st friend must be?
Me from myself thy cruel eye hath taken, 5
And my next self thou harder hast engrossed:
Of him, myself, and thee, I am forsaken;
A torment thrice threefold thus to be crossed.
Prison my heart in thy steel bosom's ward,
But then my friend's heart let my poor heart bail; 10
Whoe'er keeps me, let my heart be his guard;
Thou canst not then use rigor in my jail:
And yet thou wilt; for I, being pent in thee,
Perforce am thine, and all that is in me.

134

So, now I have confess'd that he is thine
And I myself am mortgaged to thy will,
Myself I'll forfeit, so that other mine
Thou wilt restore, to be my comfort still:
But thou wilt not, nor he will not be free, 5
For thou art covetous and he is kind;
He learn'd but surety-like to write for me,
Under that bond that him as fast doth bind.
The statute of thy beauty thou wilt take,
Thou usurer, that put'st forth all to use, 10
And sue a friend came debtor for my sake;
So him I lose through my unkind abuse.
Him have I lost; thou hast both him and me:
He pays the whole, and yet am I not free.

135

Whoever hath her wish, thou hast thy "Will,"
And "Will" to boot, and "Will" in overplus;
More than enough am I that vex thee still,

11. go, walk.
Sonnet 131: 11. One . . . neck, in rapid succession.
Sonnet 132: 4. ruth, pity. 12. suit, clothe; like, alike. 14. foul, ugly.
Sonnet 133: 6. next self, other self, i.e., my friend; engrossed, obtained a monopoly of. 9. ward, protection. 10. bail, secure the freedom of.
Sonnet 134: 3. other mine, my alter ego. 7. surety-like, like one who endorses a note or bond. 10. put'st . . . use, lends it all at interest. 11. came, who became. 12. abuse, i.e., in exposing him to danger.
Sonnet 135: This and the following sonnet pun on four significations of "will": (1) the poet's name, (2) the friend's name, (3) volition, (4) physical desire.

To thy sweet will making addition thus.
Wilt thou, whose will is large and spacious, 5
Not once vouchsafe to hide my will in thine?
Shall will in others seem right gracious,
And in my will no fair acceptance shine?
The sea, all water, yet receives rain still,
And in abundance addeth to his store; 10
So thou, being rich in "Will," add to thy "Will"
One will of mine, to make thy large "Will" more.
Let no unkind, no fair beseechers kill;
Think all but one, and me in that one "Will."

136

If thy soul check thee that I come so near,
Swear to thy blind soul that I was thy "Will,"
And will, thy soul knows, is admitted there;
Thus far for love, my love-suit, sweet, fulfill.
"Will" will fulfill the treasure of thy love, 5
Aye, fill it full with wills, and my will one.
In things of great receipt with ease we prove
Among a number one is reckon'd none:
Then in the number let me pass untold,
Though in thy store's account I one must be; 10
For nothing hold me, so it please thee hold
That nothing me, a something sweet to thee:
Make but my name thy love, and love that still,
And then thou lovest me, for my name is "Will."

137

Thou blind fool, Love, what dost thou to mine eyes,
That they behold, and see not what they see?
They know what beauty is, see where it lies,
Yet what the best is take the worst to be.
If eyes, corrupt by over-partial looks, 5
Be anchor'd in the bay where all men ride,
Why of eyes' falsehood hast thou forgèd hooks
Whereto the judgment of my heart is tied?
Why should my heart think that a several plot
Which my heart knows the wide world's common place? 10
Or mine eyes seeing this, say this is not,
To put fair truth upon so foul a face?
In things right true my heart and eyes have erred,
And to this false plague are they now transferred.

138

When my love swears that she is made of truth,
I do believe her, though I know she lies,
That she might think me some untutor'd youth,
Unlearnèd in the world's false subtleties.
Thus vainly thinking that she thinks me young, 5
Although she knows my days are past the best,
Simply I credit her false-speaking tongue:
On both sides thus is simple truth suppress'd.
But wherefore says she not she is unjust?
And wherefore say not I that I am old? 10
O, love's best habit is in seeming trust,
And age in love loves not to have years told:
Therefore I lie with her and she with me,
And in our faults by lies we flatter'd be.

139

O call not me to justify the wrong
That thy unkindness lays upon my heart;
Wound me not with thine eye, but with thy tongue;
Use power with power, and slay me not by art.
Tell me thou lovest elsewhere; but in my sight, 5
Dear heart, forbear to glance thine eye aside:
What need'st thou wound with cunning, when thy might
Is more than my o'er-pressed defense can bide?

14. **Think . . . Will**, imagine all your lovers incorporated in me, whose name is a synonym of all your desires.
Sonnet 136: 1. **check**, chide. 3. **will**, desire. 7. **things . . . receipt**, large capacity; **prove**, ascertain. 9. **untold**, uncounted. 10. **thy store's account**, value of your possessions.

Sonnet 137: 6. **bay . . . ride**, the harbor where any man's ship may ride. 9. **several**, enclosed, private.
Sonnet 138: 7. **Simply I credit**, I believe absolutely. 9. **unjust**, faithless. 11. **habit**, garment. 12. **told**, counted.
Sonnet 139: 4. **art**, i.e., magic. 8. **bide**, endure.

Let me excuse thee: ah, my love well knows
Her pretty looks have been mine enemies; 10
And therefore from my face she turns my foes,
That they elsewhere might dart their injuries:
Yet do not so; but since I am near slain,
Kill me outright with looks, and rid my pain.

140

Be wise as thou art cruel; do not press
My tongue-tied patience with too much disdain;
Lest sorrow lend me words, and words express
The manner of my pity-wanting pain.
If I might teach thee wit, better it were, 5
Though not to love, yet, love, to tell me so;
As testy sick men, when their deaths be near,
No news but health from their physicians know;
For, if I should despair, I should grow mad,
And in my madness might speak ill of thee: 10
Now this ill-wresting world is grown so bad,
Mad slanderers by mad ears believed be.
That I may not be so, nor thou belied,
Bear thine eyes straight, though thy proud heart go wide.

141

In faith, I do not love thee with mine eyes,
For they in thee a thousand errors note;
But 'tis my heart that loves what they despise,
Who, in despite of view, is pleased to dote;
Nor are mine ears with thy tongue's tune delighted; 5
Nor tender feeling, to base touches prone,
Nor taste, nor smell, desire to be invited
To any sensual feast with thee alone:
But my five wits nor my five senses can
Dissuade one foolish heart from serving thee, 10
Who leaves unsway'd the likeness of a man,
Thy proud heart's slave and vassal wretch to be:
Only my plague thus far I count my gain,
That she that makes me sin awards me pain.

142

Love is my sin, and thy dear virtue hate,
Hate of my sin, grounded on sinful loving:
O, but with mine compare thou thine own state,
And thou shalt find it merits not reproving;
Or, if it do, not from those lips of thine, 5
That have profaned their scarlet ornaments
And seal'd false bonds of love as oft as mine,
Robb'd others' beds' revénues of their rents.
Be it lawful I love thee, as thou lovest those
Whom thine eyes woo as mine importune thee: 10
Root pity in thy heart, that, when it grows,
Thy pity may deserve to pitied be.
If thou dost seek to have what thou dost hide,
By self-example mayst thou be denied!

143

Lo, as a careful housewife runs to catch
One of her feather'd creatures broke away,
Sets down her babe, and makes all swift dispatch
In pursuit of the thing she would have stay;
Whilst her neglected child holds her in chase, 5
Cries to catch her whose busy care is bent
To follow that which flies before her face,
Not prizing her poor infant's discontent:
So runn'st thou after that which flies from thee,
Whilst I thy babe chase thee afar behind; 10
But if thou catch thy hope, turn back to me,
And play the mother's part, kiss me, be kind:
So will I pray that thou mayst have thy "Will,"
If thou turn back and my loud crying still.

11. foes, i.e., "her pretty looks" of l. 10.
Sonnet 140: 6. Though . . . love, though you do not love me. 7. testy, fretful. 11. ill-wrestling, interpreting everything in the worst way.
Sonnet 141: 9. five wits, i.e., common wit, imagination, fantasy, estimation, and memory. 11. Who, i.e., the heart; unsway'd, i.e., by either the heart or the senses; likeness of a man, mere husk of a man.
Sonnet 142: 1. dear, cherished. 12. Thy pity, the object of your pity. 13. hide, suppress. 14. By self-example, following the precedent of your own example.

144

Two loves I have of comfort and despair,
Which like two spirits do suggest me still:
The better angel is a man right fair,
The worser spirit a woman color'd ill.
To win me soon to hell, my female evil 5
Tempteth my better angel from my side,
And would corrupt my saint to be a devil,
Wooing his purity with her foul pride.
And whether that my angel be turn'd fiend
Suspect I may, yet not directly tell; 10
But being both from me, both to each friend,
I guess one angel in another's hell:
Yet this shall I ne'er know, but live in doubt,
Till my bad angel fire my good one out.

145

Those lips that Love's own hand did make
Breathed forth the sound that said "I hate,"
To me that languish'd for her sake:
But when she saw my woeful state,
Straight in her heart did mercy come, 5
Chiding that tongue that ever sweet
Was used in giving gentle doom;
And taught it thus anew to greet;
"I hate" she alter'd with an end,
That follow'd it as gentle day 10
Doth follow night, who, like a fiend,
From heaven to hell is flown away;
"I hate" from hate away she threw,
And saved my life, saying "not you."

146

Poor soul, the center of my sinful earth,
Thrall to these rebel powers that thee array,
Why dost thou pine within and suffer dearth,
Painting thy outward walls so costly gay?
Why so large cost, having so short a lease, 5
Dost thou upon thy fading mansion spend?
Shall worms, inheritors of this excess,
Eat up thy charge? is this thy body's end?
Then, soul, live thou upon thy servant's loss,
And let that pine to aggravate thy store; 10
Buy terms divine in selling hours of dross;
Within be fed, without be rich no more:
So shalt thou feed on Death, that feeds on men,
And Death once dead, there's no more dying then.

147

My love is as a fever, longing still
For that which longer nurseth the disease;
Feeding on that which doth preserve the ill,
The uncertain sickly appetite to please.
My reason, the physician to my love, 5
Angry that his prescriptions are not kept,
Hath left me, and I desperate now approve
Desire is death, which physic did except.
Past cure I am, now reason is past care,
And frantic-mad with evermore unrest; 10
My thoughts and my discourse as madmen's are,
At random from the truth vainly express'd;
For I have sworn thee fair, and thought thee bright,
Who art as black as hell, as dark as night.

148

O me, what eyes hath Love put in my head,
Which have no correspondence with true sight!
Or, if they have, where is my judgment fled,
That censures falsely what they see aright?
If that be fair whereon my false eyes dote, 5
What means the world to say it is not so?
If it be not, then love doth well denote
Love's eye is not so true as all men's: no,
How can it? O, how can Love's eye be true,
That is so vex'd with watching and with tears? 10
No marvel then, though I mistake my view;
The sun itself sees not till heaven clears.

Sonnet 144: 2. **suggest me still**, continue to tempt me. 4. **color'd ill**, i.e., of dark complexion. 11. **from**, away from; **both to each friend**, each friendly to the other.

Sonnet 145: This sonnet is written in tetrameter lines. 7. **doom**, censure.

Sonnet 146: 2. **array**, afflict. 8. **charge**, i.e., what has cost you so much. 10. **aggravate**, increase. 11. **terms divine**, eternity; **terms** = conditions.

Sonnet 147: 6. **kept**, followed. 7. **approve**, i.e., find by experience that. 8. **Desire . . . except**, desire which refuses the physic of reason is death. 12. **vainly**, foolishly.

Sonnet 148: 4. **censures**, judges. 7. **denote**, indicate. 8. **true as all men's**, i.e., more inaccurate than any other man's. 10. **watching**, lying awake. 11. **my view**, what I see.

O cunning Love! with tears thou keep'st me blind,
Lest eyes well-seeing thy foul faults should find.

149

Canst thou, O cruel! say I love thee not,
When I against myself with thee partake?
Do I not think on thee, when I forgot
Am of myself, all tyrant, for thy sake?
Who hateth thee that I do call my friend? 5
On whom frown'st thou that I do fawn upon?
Nay, if thou lour'st on me, do I not spend
Revenge upon myself with present moan?
What merit do I in myself respect,
That is so proud thy service to despise, 10
When all my best doth worship thy defect,
Commanded by the motion of thine eyes?
But, love, hate on, for now I know thy mind;
Those that can see thou lovest, and I am blind.

150

O, from what power hast thou this powerful might
With insufficiency my heart to sway?
To make me give the lie to my true sight,
And swear that brightness doth not grace the day?
Whence hast thou this becoming of things ill, 5
That in the very refuse of thy deeds
There is such strength and warrantise of skill,
That, in my mind, thy worst all best exceeds?
Who taught thee how to make me love thee more,
The more I hear and see just cause of hate? 10
O, though I love what others do abhor,
With others thou shouldst not abhor my state:
If thy unworthiness raised love in me,
More worthy I to be beloved of thee.

151

Love is too young to know what conscience is;
Yet who knows not conscience is born of love?
Then, gentle cheater, urge not my amiss,
Lest guilty of my faults thy sweet self prove:
For, thou betraying me, I do betray 5
My nobler part to my gross body's treason;
My soul doth tell my body that he may
Triumph in love; flesh stays no farther reason,
But rising at thy name doth point out thee
As his triumphant prize. Proud of this pride, 10
He is contented thy poor drudge to be,
To stand in thy affairs, fall by thy side.
No want of conscience hold it that I call
Her "love" for whose dear love I rise and fall.

152

In loving thee thou know'st I am forsworn,
But thou art twice forsworn, to me love swearing;
In act thy bed-vow broke, and new faith torn,
In vowing new hate after new love bearing.
But why of two oaths' breach do I accuse thee, 5
When I break twenty! I am perjured most;
For all my vows are oaths but to misuse thee,
And all my honest faith in thee is lost:
For I have sworn deep oaths of thy deep kindness,
Oaths of thy love, thy truth, thy constancy; 10
And, to enlighten thee, gave eyes to blindness,
Or made them swear against the thing they see;
For I have sworn thee fair; more perjured I,
To swear against the truth so foul a lie!

Sonnet 149: 2. partake, take part. 4. all tyrant, a complete tyrant.

Sonnet 150: 2. insufficiency, defects. 5. becoming, grace. 7. warrantise, guarantee.

Sonnet 151: 3. cheater, rogue; urge, insist upon; amiss, offences. 10. triumphant prize, prize of his triumph or victory; pride, i.e., proud conquest. This sonnet frankly treats of the physical aspects of love.

Sonnet 152: 1. am forsworn, have broken my oath, i.e., marriage vows. 3. In . . . torn, broken your marriage vows and her new faith with the poet's friend. 7. oaths . . . thee, oaths designed to deceive. 8. honest faith, sincerity. 9. kindness, affection. 11. enlighten, shed light upon.

153

Cupid laid by his brand and fell asleep:
A maid of Dian's this advantage found,
And his love-kindling fire did quickly steep
In a cold valley-fountain of that ground;
Which borrow'd from this holy fire of Love 5
A dateless lively heat, still to endure,
And grew a seething bath, which yet men prove
Against strange maladies a sovereign cure.
But at my mistress' eye Love's brand new-fired,
The boy for trial needs would touch my breast; 10
I, sick withal, the help of bath desired,
And thither hied, a sad distemper'd guest,
But found no cure: the bath for my help lies
Where Cupid got new fire, my mistress' eyes.

Sonnet 153: This and the following poem are versions of the same epigram in The Greek Anthology. Shakespeare found it translated in Giles Fletcher's Licia (1593).

154

The little Love-god lying once asleep
Laid by his side his heart-inflaming brand,
Whilst many nymphs that vow'd chaste life to keep
Came tripping by; but in her maiden hand
The fairest votary took up that fire 5
Which many legions of true hearts had warm'd;
And so the general of hot desire
Was sleeping by a virgin hand disarm'd.
This brand she quenchèd in a cool well by,
Which from Love's fire took heat perpetual, 10
Growing a bath and healthful remedy
For men diseased; but I, my mistress' thrall,
Came there for cure, and this by that I prove.
Love's fire heats water, water cools not love.

6. dateless, eternal. 7. seething, boiling. 8. sovereign, efficacious. 12. distemper'd, diseased.

Sonnet 154: 7. general, chief inciter. 4. by, near by. 13. this, i.e., the statement in the following line.

AFTERWORD

Shakespeare's sonnet sequence was especially valued by the poet Wordsworth as a personal document. "With this key," Wordsworth thought, "Shakespeare unlocked his heart." The identifying of art with fictionalized autobiography seems reasonable to most of us. We tend to assume that, as a poet is sincere, writing with conviction and power, he is writing necessarily about himself. But this assumption is fallacious, and sometimes it is actively harmful. As we busy ourselves with biographical matters, our attention is diverted from the poem to the writer of the poem. That is to misplace the emphasis. In fact, the writer himself is ideally of little consequence to us. We may gather that he was a scoundrel, like François Villon, or a drunkard, like Poe, or, in our own time, an insurance executive, like the American poet Wallace Stevens. How he lived his life is, however, of interest mostly to himself. We want to distinguish this kind of interest from our proper and more rewarding concern, which is not with the man on his personal side but with the man in his role as artist or maker.

Shakespeare early in his career was evidently involved with a young nobleman named Henry Wriothesley, Earl of Southampton. It is too late now to characterize this involvement, or to say how deep it ran, or whether the record of it is embedded in the sonnets. These are questions for which no answers are available. But more than this—as Falstaff, in another context, reminds us—they are questions not to be asked. That is because they are impertinent, in the root sense. They do not signify. Shakespeare was also a competent man of business, who made money in the theatre and invested his money shrewdly in land. This practical side of his nature is admirable, and was no doubt of much value to him. But it is not why we remember Shakespeare.

Many of the sonnets describe the unhappy relationship of a young man and his false friend, and the dark and promiscuous lady who moves from one friend to the other. We can, if we like, give a name to the anguished young man. We can agree to present him as Shakespeare. But we should put the name in quotation marks, as signalizing the mask or "persona" which the poet has elected to wear, for this particular occasion. What Shakespeare is dramatizing for us in the sonnets is the old familiar story, which may be no part of our personal experience—or of his—but which we recognize instantly as the eternal triangle. There are vivid and explosive possibilities in this story, and that is one reason why Shakespeare finds it congenial. He is after all a professional story teller and intent in that capacity on putting his best foot forward.

Perhaps at the same time Shakespeare wrote his sonnets, or some of the sonnets, he was occupied with the writing of an early comedy called *The Two Gentlemen of Verona*. In this comedy, the treacherous Proteus betrays his friend Valentine by attempting to seduce the young woman with whom Valentine is in love. The parallel to the sonnets is striking, and gives rise naturally to the supposition that Shakespeare the man had suffered a similar betrayal. Why else, we might ask, is this particular situation so important to him? But the supposition cannot be verified, and is not relevant finally to our estimate of the play or the poems. Shakespeare is not Proteus; he is not Valentine either. Nor is he to be identified absolutely with his tormented sonneteer. The right way to characterize Shakespeare is as a dramatic poet, in the poems not less than in the plays. This means, by definition, he is the connoisseur and exploiter of human emotions, whatever their nature, whatever their source. At one and the same time, he is able to identify with his hero and his villain—and also with his heroine. He is not Proteus, but he is protean: endlessly mutable, like the mythological figure who could change his shape at will. This Shakespeare the artist has no personality, or rather he contains all personalities in himself and expresses them all in his art. On this various and impersonal side, he is more interesting to us, and far more important, than the merely personal or singular man who is supposed to be opening his heart.

Shakespeare's sonnets are perceived, rightly as works of art, wrongly as exercises in autobiography. But to characterize the sonnets as insincere or lacking in conviction because they are artful is to be guilty of an even graver misunderstanding. The misunderstanding arises from this, that we are generally too narrow or too little imaginative, in defining sincerity and conviction. Shakespeare the man was not, like King Lear, cast off by his daughters, or driven to murder, like the insanely jealous Othello. The problem of succession to the Danish throne was obviously remote from his experience. Nevertheless, he is powerfully engrossed by the plight of Lear and Othello and Hamlet. As he approaches each play, each different situation, he puts a question to himself: Given, this agreed-on fact or point of departure, what follows from it? His plays, in other words, are so many experiments. Or they are like dependent or interrogative clauses, which demand, in grammatical propriety, their resolution. Shakespeare's concern with the resolution is fascinated and intense. In the process of creation, he becomes for a little while his tragic hero. He suffers with Hamlet, and even with King Claudius. In the face of so total a commitment as this, it is hard to describe him as insincere.

So with the writing of the sonnets. Always a question, which may or may not be explicit, is posed. This question requires an answer. "Shall I compare thee to a summer's day?" That is the informing question, with which Shakespeare begins Sonnet 18. He has an eye for the complexity of things, and so he does not answer flatly or at once. He works out his answer, in the thirteen lines remaining to him, by convention. Superficially, the comparison makes for the credit of the young man the poet is addressing. But sincerity is the enemy of superficiality. And so Shakespeare, as he is seeking to be truthful or sincere, looks deeper. Summer days, he discovers, are often turbulent or imperfect—shaken by storms, overcast by haze or cloud. Summer itself is not forever, but goes down at last to fall. These facts, which the poet ascertains as he puts his mind to the problem before him, indicate that the comparison on which he has ventured is not really satisfactory or just.

The exploding of the comparison, the revelation that it will not do, is the business of the first eight lines of the sonnet. These lines make up two quatrains or four-line units. In each of these units, a nugget of fact, bearing on the point at issue, is scrutinized or assayed. This assaying, this testing suggests certain conclusions. The poet, as he is honest, does not evade the conclusion. He follows where the facts lead. Precisely where they lead is disclosed in a third quatrain, which represents, in this particular poem, a sharp departure or turn from the eight lines that have gone before. It is true that summer fades and changes, and therefore the initial comparison is invalid.

> But thy eternal summer shall not fade,
> Not lose possession of that fair thou owest.

With this bold assertion, the poem might conceivably finish. But were it to finish here, we would not be entirely persuaded of the poet's conviction or, more crucially, of his intelligence. We would feel uneasily that he has sought to put us off, and possibly himself, with a good ringing affirmation that does not hold up, when tested. For how can changeless beauty, and the power to overcome death, be attributed to the young man? Clearly, as we are mortal, all of us are subject to decay. So far, then, the poem remains unfinished, in logic, in honesty.

The answer to the question posed, or the complement required by the subordinate clause, is given in the final two lines which, as they are rhyming lines, combine to form a couplet. The sense of the couplet is anticipated in the line just before, and that is to the good. We do not want to be tricked or excessively surprised, when matter of truth is before us. We want to feel that the truth is proceeding organically or naturally from close and patient observation, not that it is being produced abruptly, as from a hat. This ultimate truth at which Shakespeare arrives is audacious and, for the moment, heartfelt, cogent, and convincing. It is that the essence of the young man, whose physical body is doomed, will live forever in the verse of the poet.

> So long as men can breathe, or eyes can see,
> So long lives this, and this gives life to thee.

The poem, in Hamlet's phrase, has gone a progress. Beginning with a question that most of us would answer affirmatively, as we are unthinking and merely polite, it subjects this question to the rigors of an empirical investigation and discovers that the easy answer will not suffice. The discovery is more convincing because of the laborious and exacting method by which it is pursued. The poet cannot be endlessly expansive or indulgent of irrelevant fancies, however pleasing. He must sift and interpret his facts in no more and no less than fourteen lines, which rhyme according to a predetermined pattern, and which are made up of a given number of feet or combinations of syllables. And when he is done, he must make his readers believe—and must believe himself—that his conclusion is a real *Q.E.D.*, that no other conclusion would in honesty be possible, given the facts he has deployed.

This poetic journey to a believable or tenable close deserves further comment. The poem, as it leaves the poet's hand, is right and true, to him as also to us who read him. Our own experience will instruct us, however, that we might return tomorrow to the same set of facts and find a quite different conclusion potential in them. To work through to that different conclusion does not lessen the integrity or sincerity of what we have felt and discovered today. Shakespeare's practice in the plays should help us here. In *Romeo and Juliet,* he celebrates romantic love; in *A Midsummer-Night's Dream,* romantic love excites in him sardonic amusement. The governing facts in the tragedy and in the comedy are essentially the same; the conclusions differ as day from night. We are not inclined, thereby, to disparage the truth or sincerity of either play. Sometimes in the sonnets, as often in the plays, honest perusal of the data or the given leads the writer to reverse himself. These reversals or contradictions do not impair his credibility, but enhance it. As he is human and scrupulous, he returns again and again to the problems that beset him and considers them from a fresh point of view.

In Sonnet 18, the poet puts forward his verse as a stay against mortality and time. In other sonnets, for example numbers 60 and 63, the high claim that the verse will endure and preserve the man it commemorates, is reiterated. But Shakespeare continues to worry the problem. Though, in Sonnet 63, he vanquishes the "steepy night" and "cruel knife" of age, in the very next sonnet the taste of victory is as dust and ashes to him. Now his eye and mind are riveted on last things—the descent into the grave, the annihilating power of time against which no man, and not even a poet, can contend. Time's "fell hand" defaces the hardiest monuments and destroys at last the great globe itself. The consciousness of universal wreck is, in this poem, not redeemed or offset by the exultation of the poet in his poetry. Instead, his mind is seized with images of ruining. And so, as he is faithful to his mordant vision, he concludes, as he must conclude:

> This thought is as a death, which cannot choose
> But weep to have that which it fears to lose.

The conclusion is earned. It emanates from what has gone before. It is tenable and, for the moment, it is true.

The "wreckful siege of battering days" is hateful to the poet, as in Sonnet 65, since it threatens with oblivion "Time's best jewel," the fair youth who is depicted in these poems. But this youth is not always fair, or not beneath the skin. In Sonnet 18, the poet makes no question of his beauty, which is intrinsic as well as superficial. The youth is "more lovely and more temperate" than a summer's day. Shakespeare, reflecting, is, however, not so sure. In Sonnets 33 and 34, the same image recurs to his mind, but the application of it is startlingly different. The "beauteous day" or "glorious morning" is a lie, not because the youth is superior to it but because he falls short of its promise. Like the sun which "rotten" clouds are about to obscure, he "flatters" or "gilds" and then withdraws his warmth. The friend, evidently, is a bundle of contradictions.

And so is the poet. Each is protean. Each plays many parts in one person. The rendering of so much variety and complexity in the Sonnets, the willingness to brave contradiction, these bespeak the artist, who is more nearly perfect in his role as he understands that each man is an amalgam of possibilities and psychological states, and that every considerable situation is open to more than one reading. In this limited sense, art and life are not so much different as the same. The poem is biography, but the subject is not the poet but man in his manifold guises.

Suggested Reading

Baldwin, Thomas W., *On the Literary Genetics of Shakespeare's Poems and Sonnets* (1950).

Bentley, Gerald E., *Shakespeare and Jonson: Their Reputations in the 17th Century Compared* (1945).

Chambers, E. K., *Shakespearean Gleanings* (1944).

Cruttwell, Patrick, *The Shakespearean Moment* (1953). Vintage.

Empson, William, *English Pastoral Poetry* (1938).

Hubler, Edward, ed., *Shakespeare's Songs and Poems* (1959).

———, et al., *The Riddle of Shakespeare's Sonnets* (1962).

———, *The Sense of Shakespeare's Sonnets* (1952). Hill and Wang Drama Book.

Knight, G. Wilson, *The Mutual Flame: An Interpretation of Shakespeare's Sonnets* (1955).

Knights, L. C., *Explorations* (1946). New York University.

Krieger, Murray, *A Window to Criticism: Shakespeare's Sonnets and Modern Poetics* (1964).

Landry, Hilton, *Interpretations in Shakespeare's Sonnets* (1964).

Leishman, J. B., *Themes and Variations in Shakespeare's Sonnets* (1961).

Lever, J. W., *The Elizabethan Love Sonnet* (1956). Barnes and Noble.

Muir, Kenneth, and Sean O'Laughlin, *The Voyage to Illyria* (1937).

Ransom, John Crowe, *The World's Body* (1938). Louisiana State University.

Schaar, Claes, *Elizabethan Sonnet Themes and the Dating of Shakespeare's Sonnets* (1962).

Shakespeare Survey, XV (1962), ed. Allardyce Nicoll.

Sitwell, Edith, *A Notebook on William Shakespeare* (1948). Beacon.

Stirling, Brents, *The Shakespeare Sonnet Order: Poems and Groups* (1968).

Tannenbaum, Samuel A., *Shakespeare's Sonnets: A Concise Bibliography* (1940).

Willen, Gerald, and Victor B. Reed, *A Casebook on Shakespeare's Sonnets* (1964). Crowell.

Wilson, J. Dover, *Shakespeare's Sonnets: An Introduction for Historians and Others* (1963).

Appendixes

A GENERAL READING LIST

Criticism

ARMSTRONG, EDWARD A., *Shakespeare's Imagination* (1946).
ARTHOS, JOHN, *The Art of Shakespeare* (1964).
BARBER, C. L., *Shakespeare's Festive Comedy* (1959). Meridian.
BRADBROOK, MURIEL C., *Shakespeare and Elizabethan Poetry* (1951).
BRADLEY, A. C., *Shakespearean Tragedy* (1904). Premier. Papermac.
BROWN, JOHN R., *Shakespeare and His Comedies* (1957). Methuen.
CAMPBELL, LILY B., *Shakespeare's Tragic Heroes* (1930). Barnes and Noble.
CAMPBELL, OSCAR J., *Shakespeare's Satire* (1943).
CHAMBERS, E. K., *Shakespeare: A Survey* (1925). Hill and Wang Drama Book.
CHARLTON, H. B., *Shakespearean Comedy* (1938). Barnes and Noble.
———, *Shakespearean Tragedy* (1948).
CLEMEN, WOLFGANG, *The Development of Shakespeare's Imagery* (1951). Hill and Wang Drama Book.
COLERIDGE, SAMUEL T., *Shakespearean Criticism*, ed. T. M. Raysor (1930).
CRAIG, HARDIN, *An Interpretation of Shakespeare* (1948).
CRANE, MILTON, *Shakespeare's Prose* (1951). Phoenix.
CUNNINGHAM, J. V., *Woe or Wonder* (1951). Swallow.
CURRY, WALTER CLYDE, *Shakespeare's Philosophical Patterns* (1937).
DANBY, JOHN F., *Shakespeare's Doctrine of Nature* (1949). Humanities.
DEAN, LEONARD F., ed., *Shakespeare, Modern Essays in Criticism* (rev. ed., 1967). Oxford.
DOWDEN, EDWARD, *Shakspeare: A Critical Study* (1872). Capricorn.
EASTMAN, ARTHUR M., *A Short History of Shakespearean Criticism* (1968). Random House.
ELLIS-FERMOR, UNA M., *Shakespeare the Dramatist* (1961).
EVANS, BERTRAND, *Shakespeare's Comedies* (1960). Oxford.
FRYE, NORTHRUP, *A Natural Perspective: The Development of Shakespearean Comedy and Romance* (1965). Harbinger.
———, *Fools of Time* (1967).
FRYE, ROLAND M., *Shakespeare and Christian Doctrine* (1963). Princeton.
GOLDSMITH, ROBERT H., *Wise Fools in Shakespeare* (1958).
GRANVILLE-BARKER, HARLEY, *Prefaces to Shakespeare*, ed. M. St. Clare Byrne, 4 vols. (1948). Princeton.
HARBAGE, ALFRED, *Conceptions of Shakespeare* (1966). Schocken.
———, *Shakespeare. The Tragedies: A Collection of Critical Essays* (1964).

HARRISON, G. B., *Shakespeare's Tragedies* (1951). Oxford.
HAWKES, TERENCE, *Shakespeare and the Reason* (1964).
HAZLITT, WILLIAM, *Characters of Shakespeare's Plays* (1917).
HOLLOWAY, JOHN, *The Story of the Night* (1961). Bison.
JOHNSON, SAMUEL, *On Shakespeare*, ed. W. K. Wimsatt, Jr. (1960).
KNIGHT, G. WILSON, *The Imperial Theme* (1931). Barnes and Noble.
———, *The Shakespearian Tempest* (1932).
———, *The Wheel of Fire* (enlarged ed., 1954). Barnes and Noble.
KNIGHTS, L. C., *Some Shakespearean Themes* (1959). Stanford.
LAMB, CHARLES, *On the Tragedies of Shakespeare* (1811).
LAWLOR, JOHN, *The Tragic Sense in Shakespeare* (1960).
LAWRENCE, W. W., *Shakespeare's Problem Comedies* (1931; 2nd ed., 1960). Penguin.
LEECH, CLIFFORD, *Shakespeare's Tragedies* (1950). Phoenix.
LERNER, LAWRENCE D., ed., *Shakespeare's Comedies: An Anthology of Modern Criticism* (1957). Pelican.
———, ed., *Shakespeare's Tragedies: An Anthology of Modern Criticism* (1964). Pelican.
LEWIS, WYNDHAM, *The Lion and the Fox* (1966). University.
MACKAIL, J. W., *The Approach to Shakespeare* (1930).
MAHOOD, M. M., *Shakespeare's Wordplay* (1957).
MOULTON, R. G., *Shakespeare As a Dramatic Artist* (1893, reprinted 1966). Dover.
MUIR, KENNETH, ed., *Shakespeare. The Comedies: A Collection of Critical Essays* (1965). Spectrum.
MURRY, JOHN MIDDLETON, *Shakespeare* (1936). Hillary.
ORNSTEIN, ROBERT, ed., *Discussions of Shakespeare's Problem Comedies* (1961). Heath.
PALMER, JOHN, *Comic Characters of Shakespeare* (1946). Papermac.
———, *Political Characters of Shakespeare* (1945). Papermac.
PARROTT, THOMAS MARC, *Shakespearean Comedy* (1962).
QUILLER-COUCH, SIR ARTHUR, *Shakespeare's Workmanship* (1931).
RABKIN, NORMAN, ed., *Approaches to Shakespeare* (1964). McGraw-Hill.
———, *Shakespeare and the Common Understanding* (1967). Free Press.
RALEIGH, WALTER, *Shakespeare* (1907). Macmillan.
RALLI, AUGUSTUS, *A History of Shakespearian Criticism*, 2 vols. (1932).
REESE, MAX M., *The Cease of Majesty* (1961).
RIBNER, IRVING, *The English History Play in the Age of Shakespeare* (revised ed., 1965).
RIDLER, ANNE BRADBY, *Shakespeare Criticism 1919–1935* (1936).
RIGHTER, ANNE, *Shakespeare and the Idea of the Play* (1962). Penguin.
ROSEN, WILLIAM, *Shakespeare and the Craft of Tragedy* (1960).
VON SCHLEGEL, AUGUST WILHELM, *Lectures on Dramatic Art and Literature* (1809–11; trans. 1880; ed. A. J. W. Morrison, 1965).
SCHÜCKING, LEVIN L., *Character Problems in Shakespeare's Plays* (1927).
SEWELL, ARTHUR, *Character and Society in Shakespeare* (1951).

SMITH, D. NICHOL, ed., *Shakespeare Criticism 1623–1840* (1923).
SMITH, LOGAN PEARSALL, *On Reading Shakespeare* (1933).
SPURGEON, CAROLINE, *Shakespeare's Imagery and What It Tells Us* (1935). Beacon.
STAUFFER, DONALD A., *Shakespeare's World of Images* (1949). Midland.
STEWART, J. I. M., *Character and Motive in Shakespeare* (1949).
STIRLING, BRENTS, *Unity in Shakespearian Tragedy* (1956).
STOLL, ELMER EDGAR, *Art and Artifice in Shakespeare* (1933). University.
———, *Shakespeare Studies* (2nd ed., with corrections, 1960).
THALER, ALWIN, *Shakespeare and Our World* (1966).
TILLYARD, E. M. W., *Shakespeare's History Plays* (1944). Macmillan.
TRAVERSI, DEREK A., *An Approach to Shakespeare* (enlarged ed., 2 vols., 1968). Anchor.
VAN DOREN, MARK, *Shakespeare* (1939). Anchor.
WAITH, EUGENE M., ed., *Shakespeare. The Histories: A Collection of Critical Essays* (1965). Spectrum.
WEBSTER, MARGARET, *Shakespeare Without Tears* (rev. ed., 1955). Premier.
WEST, REBECCA, *The Court and the Castle* (1957).
WHITAKER, VIRGIL K., *The Mirror up to Nature* (1965).
WILSON, HAROLD S., *On the Design of Shakespearian Tragedy* (1957). Toronto.

BACKGROUND AND BIOGRAPHY

ADAMS, JOHN C., *The Globe Playhouse* (rev. ed. 1961).
ADAMS, JOSEPH Q., *Shakespearean Playhouses* (1917).
ALEXANDER, PETER, *Shakespeare* (1964).
———, *Shakespeare's Life and Art* (1939). Gotham Library.
ALLEN, DON CAMERON, *The Star-Crossed Renaissance* (1941).
ALLEN, JOHN W., *A History of Political Thought in the Sixteenth Century* (1928, reprinted 1951). Barnes and Noble.
———, *English Political Thought 1603–1660* (1938).
BAKER, HERSCHEL, *The Dignity of Man* (1947).
BALDWIN, THOMAS W., *William Shakespeare's Petty School* (1943).
———, *William Shakespeare's Small Latine and Less Greeke*, 2 vols. (1944).
BECKERMAN, BERNARD, *Shakespeare at the Globe* (1962). Macmillan.
BENNETT, H. S., *English Books and Readers 1558 to 1603* (1965).
BENTLEY, GERALD E., *Shakespeare: A Biographical Handbook* (1961). Yale.
BETHELL, SAMUEL L., *Shakespeare and the Popular Dramatic Tradition* (1944).
BEVINGTON, DAVID M., *Tudor Drama and Politics* (1968).
BINDOFF, STANLEY T., *Tudor England* (1951). Pelican, Penguin.
BLACK, JOHN B., *The Reign of Elizabeth 1558–1603* (2nd ed., 1959).
BOAS, F. S., *An Introduction to Tudor Drama* (1933).
BRADBROOK, MURIEL C., *The Rise of the Common Player* (1962).
———, *Themes and Conventions of Elizabethan Tragedy* (rev. ed., 1960). Cambridge.
BROOKE, C. F. TUCKER, *Shakespeare of Stratford, A Handbook for Students* (1926).

BROWN, IVOR, *How Shakespeare Spent the Day* (1963). Hill and Wang Drama Book.

BULLOUGH, GEOFFREY, ed., *Narrative and Dramatic Sources of Shakespeare*, 7 vols. (1957–68).

BUSH, GEOFFREY, *Shakespeare and the Natural Condition* (1956).

BUXTON, JOHN, *Elizabethan Taste* (1963).

BYRNE, MURIEL ST. CLARE, *Elizabethan Life in Town and Country* (7th ed., 1954). Barnes and Noble.

CAMPBELL, LILY B., *Scenes and Machines on the English Stage during the Renaissance* (1923).

CHUTE, MARCHETTE, *Shakespeare of London* (1949). Everyman.

CRAIG, HARDIN, *The Enchanted Glass* (1936).

DAVIES, GODFREY, *The Early Stuarts, 1603–1660* (2nd ed., 1959).

FARNHAM, WILLARD, *The Medieval Heritage of Elizabethan Tragedy* (1936).

FRIPP, EDGAR I., *Shakespeare's Stratford* (1928).

GRANVILLE-BARKER, HARLEY, and G. B. HARRISON, eds., *A Companion to the Shakespeare Studies* (1935). Anchor.

GREEN, JOHN RICHARD, *A Short History of the English People* (rev. ed., 1921). Everyman.

HALLIDAY, FRANK E., *Shakespeare: A Pictorial Biography* (1964).

HARBAGE, ALFRED, *As They Liked It* (1947).

———, *Shakespeare's Audience* (1941). Columbia.

HARRISON, G. B., *Shakespeare at Work* (1958). Michigan.

HAYDEN, HIRAM, *The Counter-Renaissance* (1950). Harbinger.

HODGES, WALTER C., *The Globe Restored* (1956).

HOLLAND, NORMAN N., *Psychoanalysis and Shakespeare* (1966).

JOHNSON, FRANCIS R., *Astronomical Thought in Renaissance England* (1937).

JORGENSEN, PAUL A., *Shakespeare's Military World* (1956).

JOSEPH, BERTRAM, *Acting Shakespeare* (1960).

JOSEPH, SISTER MIRIAM, *Shakespeare's Use of the Arts of Language* (1947). Hafner.

KOCHER, PAUL, *Science and Religion in Elizabethan England* (1953).

KOKERITZ, HELGE, *Shakespeare's Pronunciation* (1953).

LEWINTER, OSWALD, *Shakespeare in Europe* (1963).

LINTHICUM, MARIE CHANNING, *Costume in the Drama of Shakespeare and His Contemporaries* (1936).

LUCAS, F. L., *Seneca and Elizabethan Tragedy* (1922).

MILLER, EDWIN H., *The Professional Writer in Elizabethan England* (1959).

NAGLER, ALOIS M., *Shakespeare's Stage* (1958). Yale.

NEALE, J. E., *Queen Elizabeth* (1934). Anchor.

NEILSON, WILLIAM ALLEN, and A. H. THORNDIKE, *The Facts About Shakespeare* (rev. ed., 1959). Macmillan.

NICOLL, ALLARDYCE, ed., "Shakespeare in His Own Age," *Shakespeare Survey*, XVII (1964).

ODELL, G. C. D., *Shakespeare from Betterton to Irving*, 2 vols (1963). Dover.

PARROTT, THOMAS MARC, and ROBERT H. BALL, *A Short View of Elizabethan Drama* (1943). Scribner.

SCHELLING, FELIX E., *Elizabethan Drama 1558–1642*, 2 vols. (1908).

SMITH, IRWIN, and JAMES G. MCMANAWAY, *Shakespeare's Globe Playhouse* (1956).

SPENCER, HAZELTON, *The Art and Life of William Shakespeare* (1940).

SPENCER, THEODORE, *Shakespeare and the Nature of Man* (2nd. ed., 1949). Macmillan.

SPRAGUE, ARTHUR COLBY, *Shakespeare and the Audience* (1935).

STERNFELD, FREDERICK W., *Music in Shakespearean Tragedy* (1963).

STIRLING, BRENTS, *The Populace in Shakespeare* (1949).

STYAN, J. L., *Shakespeare's Stagecraft* (1967). Cambridge.

THORNDIKE, ASHLEY H., *Shakespeare's Theatre* (1916). Macmillan.

TILLYARD, E. M. W., *The Elizabethan World Picture* (1944). Modern Library.

WADSWORTH, FRANK W., *The Poacher from Stratford* (1958).

WATKINS, RONALD, *On Producing Shakespeare* (2nd. ed., 1964).

WHITAKER, VIRGIL K., *Shakespeare's Use of Learning* (1953).

WILSON, J. DOVER, *Life in Shakespeare's England* (1911). Penguin.

WRIGHT, LOUIS B., *Middle-Class Culture in Elizabethan England* (1935).

REFERENCE WORKS

ABBOT, EDWIN A., *A Shakespearian Grammar* (1896). Dover.

BARTLETT, JOHN, *Complete Concordance to Shakespeare's Dramatic Works and Poems* (1894).

BERMAN, RONALD S., *A Reader's Guide to Shakespeare's Plays: A Discursive Bibliography* (1965). Scott, Foresman.

CHAMBERS, E. K., *Elizabethan Stage*, 4 vols. (reprinted, with corrections, 1951).

———, *William Shakespeare: A Study of Facts and Problems*, 2 vols. (1930).

EBISCH, WALTHER, and LEVIN S. SCHÜCKING, *A Shakespeare Bibliography* (1931).

FURNESS, HORACE HOWARD, ed., *A New Variorum Edition of Shakespeare*, 15 vols. (1871–1903).

GREG, SIR W. W., *A Bibliography of the English Printed Drama to the Restoration*, 4 vols. (1939–59).

———, *Dramatic Documents from the Elizabethan Playhouse*, 2 vols. (1931).

———, ed., *Henslowe's Diary*, 2 vols. (1904–1908). Re-edited R. A. FOAKES and R. T. RICKERT (1961).

HARBAGE, ALFRED, *Annals of English Drama 975–1700* (1940). Rev. by SAMUEL SCHOENBAUM (1964).

———, *William Shakespeare: A Reader's Guide* (1963). Noonday.

KOKERITZ, HELGE, *Shakespeare's Names* (1959).

MUIR, KENNETH, *Shakespeare's Sources*, 2 vols. (1957–).

New Arden Shakespeare, ed. H. F. BROOKS and HAROLD JENKINS, et al. (1950–).

New Cambridge Shakespeare, ed. J. DOVER WILSON, et al. (1921–66).

ONIONS, CHARLES T., *A Shakespeare Glossary* (2nd ed., 1953).

PARTRIDGE, ERIC, *Shakespeare's Bawdy* (2nd ed., 1955). Dutton.
READ, CONYERS, *Bibliography of British History: Tudor Period 1485–1603* (2nd ed., 1959).
SCHMIDT, ALEXANDER, *Shakespeare-Lexicon*, 2 vols. (3rd ed., revised and enlarged by GREGOR SARRAZIN, 1968).
Shakespeare Association of America Bulletin (1924–49).
Shakespeare Quarterly (1950—).
Shakespeare Studies (1965—).
Shakespeare Survey (1948—).
Signet Classic Shakespeare (1963—), ed. SYLVAN BARNET, et al. New American Library.
SMITH, G. R., *A Classified Shakespeare Bibliography 1936–1958* (1963).
Studies in Philology (1922—). Records work published since 1938.
Year's Work in English Studies, The (1919—).

SHAKESPEARE ON FILM

Romeo and Juliet (1936). Adapted by Talbot Jennings. Directed by George Cukor. Produced by Irving Thalberg for Metro-Goldwyn-Mayer. Starring Norma Shearer and Leslie Howard, with John Barrymore, Edna Mae Oliver, Basil Rathbone, C. Aubrey Smith, Andy Devine, Ralph Forbes, Reginald Denny, Henry Kolker.

Romeo and Juliet (1944). Mexican, with English subtitles. A parody, adapted by Jaime Salvador. Directed by Miguel Delgado. Produced by Posa Films, S.A. Released by Azteca Films. Starring Cantinflas and Elena Marques.

Romeo and Juliet (1954). Anglo-Italian. Adapted and directed by Renato Castellani. Produced by Sandro Ghenzi in association with Joseph Janni. A J. Arthur Rank Organization Presentation. Released by United Artists. Starring Laurence Harvey, Susan Shentall, Flora Robson, Mervyn Johns.

Romeo and Juliet (1955). Mosfilm. Scenario (from Ballet by Sergei Prokofiev) and Direction by Leo Arnstam and L. Lavrovsky. Music by Prokofiev. Starring Galina Ulanova, Yuri Fhdanov, A. Yermolayev, Sergei Koren.

Romeo and Juliet (1966). The Royal Ballet Company. Produced and directed by Paul Czinner. Released by Embassy Pictures. Starring Margot Fonteyn and Rudolf Nureyev.

Romeo and Juliet (1968). Screenplay by Franco Brusati, Masolino D'Amico, and Franco Zefirelli, based on Shakespeare's play. Produced by Anthony Havelock-Allen and John Brabourne for Cerona Produzione and Dino di Laurentiis. A BHE film sponsored by Paramount Pictures. Directed by Franco Zefirelli. Starring Leonard Whiting and Olivia Hussey.

Midsummer-Night's Dream (1935). Produced by Max Reinhardt. Directed by William Dieterle. Presented by Warner Brothers. Music by Felix Mendelssohn. Starring Dick Powell, Olivia DeHaviland, Anita Louise, Mickey Rooney, James Cagney, Ian Hunter, Joe E. Brown, Jean Muir, Victor Jory.

A Midsummer-Night's Dream (1961). Show Corporation of America. A photo-play, directed and adapted by Howard Sachler. Created and designed by Jiri Trnka. (Production features animated puppets with voice-overs done by members of the Old Vic.) Narrator: Richard Burton and with Hugh Manning, Alec McCowan, Barbara Jefford.

A Midsummer-Night's Dream (1967). A feature-length, color film version of George Ballanchine's ballet, with music by Felix Mendelssohn. Directed by Don Eriksen, produced by Richard Davis and released through Oberon Productions, Ltd. Presented by Columbia Pictures in association with the City Center of Music and Drama, Inc. Starring Suzanne Farrell, Edward Villella, Arthur Mitchell, Mimi Paul, Nicholas Magallanes, Patricia McBride, Roland Vazquez,

Francisco Moncion, Gloria Govin, Richard Rapp, and the New York City Ballet and the children of The School of American Ballet.

The Chimes at Midnight (1967). Retitled as *Falstaff*. Adapted by Orson Welles from Shakespeare's *Henry IV: Parts I and II.* Produced by Emiliano Piedra and Angel Escolano. Directed by Orson Welles. Presented by Harry Saltzman and released by Peppercorn-Wormser, Inc. Starring Orson Welles, Jeanne Moreau, Margaret Rutherford, John Gielgud. Narration by Ralph Richardson.

Twelfth Night (1956). Russian. Screenplay and direction by Y. Fried. A Lenfilm Studio Production, presented by Artkino. English subtitles. Starring Katya Luchko, Anna Larionova, V. Medevdiev, M. Yanchin, G. Vipin, V. Mercuriev, S. Lukianov.

Hamlet (1947). Produced and directed by Laurence Olivier. A Two Cities Film, released by the J. Arthur Rank Organization. Starring Laurence Olivier, Jean Simmons, Basil Sidney, Eileen Herlie, Norman Woodland, Felix Aylmer, Terence Morgan.

Hamlet (1964). Produced by Hans Gottshalk. Directed and adapted by Franz Peter Wirth. Starring Maximilian Schell in the title role, supported by a German Cast. The film is in English.

Hamlet (1964). The Broadway play, filmed under the combined auspices of Electronovision Inc., A. H. Cohen, and Warner Brothers. Starring Richard Burton, Hume Cronin, Eileen Herlie.

Hamlet (1966). Screenplay and direction by Grigori Kozintzev, from the Russian translation by Boris Pasternak. Music by Dmitri Shostakovich. A Lenfilm Production, released through United Artists. Starring Innokenti Smoktunovsky, Mikhail Nazvanov, Elsa Radzin, Yuri Tolubeyev, Anastasia Vertinskaya.

Othello (1955). Produced and directed by Orson Welles. A Mercury Production, released by United Artists. Starring Orson Welles, Michael MacLiammoir, Suzanne Cloutier, Robert Coote, Michael Lawrence, Fay Compton.

Othello (1960). A Mosfilm Studio Production. Directed by Sergei Youtkevitch. Starring Sergei Bondarchuk, Irma Shobtseva, and Andrei Popov. This film is spoken in English by a company of British actors.

Othello (1966). Produced by Anthony Havelock-Allen and John Brabourne. Directed by Stuart Bourge. A film version of the National Theater of Great Britain production of Shakespeare's play. Starring Laurence Olivier, Frank Finlay, Maggie Smith, Robert Lane, Derek Jacobi, Joyce Redman.

Measure for Measure (1951). Italian, with English subtitles. Adapted by Guglielmo Usellini and Enrico Ribulsi. Directed by Marco Elter. A production of the F.E.N.T. Studios, Turino, Italy. Released by Hoffberg Productions. Starring Alfredo Varelli, Aldo Silvani, Nella Corradi, Carol Tamberiani, Caterina Borrato.

SHAKESPEARE ON RECORDS

Works. Performed by the Marlowe Society and Professional Players; George Rylands, director. London Records. A 4335.

Ages of Man. Read by John Gielgud. Based on George Rylands' Shakespeare anthology. Columbia Records OL 5390 and OL 5550.

John Barrymore Reads Shakespeare, vol. II. Containing scenes from *Hamlet, Twelfth Night, Richard III*, and *Macbeth*. Audio Rarities LPA 2281.

Scenes from Shakespeare. With Paul Rogers of the Old Vic Company. Spoken Arts (Great Artists Series) 723.

Romeo and Juliet. Scenes from the J. Arthur Rank film, starring Laurence Harvey and Susan Shentall, with prologue by John Gielgud. Epic LC 3126.

Romeo and Juliet. With Claire Bloom, Albert Finney, and Edith Evans; directed by Howard Sackler. Shakespeare Recording Society SRS-M 228.

Romeo and Juliet. Movie soundtrack of the Paramount production, directed by Franco Zeffirelli. With Olivia Hussey and Leonard Whiting. Capitol Stereo ST-400.

Scenes from "Romeo and Juliet." With John Gielgud and Pamela Brown. Decca DL 9504.

Scenes from "Romeo and Juliet." With Blanche Yurka, Geraldine Brooks, and Hurd Hatfield. Victor LM 6028.

A Midsummer-Night's Dream. With Paul Scofield and Joy Parker; directed by Howard Sackler. Shakespeare Recording Society SRS-M-208.

A Midsummer-Night's Dream. With the Old Vic Company, starring Moira Shearer, Robert Helpmann, and Stanley Holloway; directed by Michael Benthall. Victor LM 6115.

Henry IV: Part I. With Michael Redgrave, Anthony Quayle, Edith Evans, and Pamela Brown; directed by Peter Wood. Shakespeare Recording Society SRS-M-217.

Twelfth Night. With Siobhan McKenna, Paul Scofield, and John Neville; directed by Howard Sackler. Shakespeare Recording Society SRS-M-213.

Twelfth Night. An Eamonn Andrews Studio Presentation, performed by the Dublin Gate Theatre Group. Spoken Word SW 116–118.

John Barrymore in "Twelfth Night." Excerpts from the play, recorded from a radio broadcast made in 1937. Audio Rarities LPA 2204.

Hamlet. With Paul Scofield in the title role, with Diana Wynyard and Wilfrid Lawson; Howard Sackler, director. Shakespeare Recording Society SRS M 232.

Hamlet. A Theatre Guild of the Air production, recorded from the broadcast of the National Broadcasting Company, March 4, 1951. Starring John Gielgud, Dorothy McGuire, and Pamela Brown. Adapted by John Gielgud. Music composed and conducted by Harold Levey. RCA Victor LM 6007.

Hamlet. Performed by the Marlowe Society; George Rylands, director. London Records A 4507.

Hamlet. Starring Richard Burton in the title role; with notes on the play by John Gielgud and others. Columbia Records DOS 702.

Soliloquies from "Hamlet," and Five Sonnets. Read by John Gielgud. Decca DL 9504.

Sir Laurence Olivier in Scenes from "Hamlet" and "Henry V." Music by William Walton. RCA Victor LM 1924.

Othello. With Laurence Olivier and the National Theatre of Great Britain. Victor VDM 100.

Othello. With Frank Silvera, Cyril Cusack, Celia Johnson, and Anna Massey; directed by Howard Sackler. Shakespeare Recording Society SRS 225.

Othello. With Paul Robeson, José Ferrer, Uta Hagen, and Edith King. (Minor deletions from the text of the play were made on this recording.) Columbia SL 153.

Measure for Measure. With John Gielgud, Margaret Leighton, and Ralph Richardson. Directed by Peter Wood. The Shakespeare Recording Society. A Caedmon Production SRS-M 204 (1961).

King Lear. An Eamonn Andrews Studio Presentation, performed by the Dublin Gate Theatre Group. Spoken Word SW 134-136X.

King Lear. With Paul Scofield, Rachel Roberts, Pamela Brown, Cyril Cusack, Robert Stephens, and John Stride; directed by Howard Sackler. Shakespeare Recording Society SRS-M 233.

The Tempest. With Michael Redgrave, Hugh Griffith, and Anna Massey. Directed by Peter Wood. The Shakespeare Recording Society, Inc. SRS-201 (1964).

Sixteen Sonnets. Read by David Allen, accompanied by Margaret Ross on the harp. Poetry Records PR 201.

Sonnets. Read by Robert Speaight. Spoken Arts SA 947–949.

Sonnets. Read by John Gielgud. Shakespeare Recording Society SRS-M 241.

Sonnets. Selections, read by Edith Evans. Angel ANG 35220.

Twenty-three Sonnets. Read by Anthony Quayle. Includes other Elizabethan sonnets and lyrics. Spoken Arts 729.